THE
OXFORD-DUDEN
PICTORIAL
SPANISH AND ENGLISH
DICTIONARY

THE
OXFORD-DUDEN
PICTORIAL
SPANISH AND
ENGLISH
DICTIONARY

SECOND EDITION

CLARENDON PRESS · OXFORD

AUG 0 9 2005

ABC
L63,2
098
1995

OXFORD

UNIVERSITY PRESS

Great Clarendon Street, Oxford OX2 6DP

Oxford University Press is a department of the University of Oxford.
It furthers the University's objective of excellence in research, scholarship,
and education by publishing worldwide in

Oxford New York

Auckland Bangkok Buenos Aires Cape Town Chennai
Dar es Salaam Delhi Hong Kong Istanbul Karachi Kolkata
Kuala Lumpur Madrid Melbourne Mexico City Mumbai
Nairobi São Paulo Shanghai Taipei Tokyo Toronto

Oxford is a registered trade mark of Oxford University Press
in the UK and in certain other countries

Published in the United States
by Oxford University Press Inc., New York

Second Edition frist published 1995

British Library Cataloguing in Publication Data
Data available

Library of Congress Cataloging in Publication Data
Data available

ISBN 0-19-864515-5

Spanish text of the second edition edited by Manuel Alvar Ezquerra;
English text edited by Michael Clark and Bernadette Mohan.
Illustrations by Jochen Schmidt, Mannheim.

15 17 19 20 18 16 14

Printed in Hong Kong

PREFACE

The *Oxford-Duden Pictorial Spanish and English Dictionary* has a firmly established reputation as a uniquely useful learning aid and reference tool. Based on the German *Bildwörterbuch*, published as Volume 3 of the twelve-volume *Duden* series of authoritative monolingual German dictionaries, the *Oxford-Duden Pictorial* has been produced with the assistance of numerous Spanish and British companies, institutions, and technical experts.

A picture is worth a thousand words, and this is never more true than when learning a foreign language. A visual clue can guide the user quickly to the appropriate translation and remove the uncertainty of deciding between alternatives offered by traditional bilingual dictionaries. In particular, information about objects and their names can be conveyed more readily and clearly by pictures than by explanations or definitions, however precise and unambiguous, and an illustration will support a bare translation by helping the user to visualize the object referred to by a given word.

The *Oxford-Duden Pictorial Spanish and English Dictionary* identifies over 28,000 numbered objects, ranging from the familiar to the highly specialized, and offers at a glance their names in both languages. Each double page contains a plate illustrating the vocabulary of a whole subject, together with the exact Spanish names and their correct English translations. Detailed and comprehensive alphabetical indexes in Spanish and in English allow the dictionary to be used either way—as a Spanish–English or an English–Spanish dictionary.

For this new edition the *Oxford-Duden Pictorial* has been revised to reflect recent developments in technical and everyday vocabulary and contains over 1,500 new items in fast-changing fields such as computing, audio and video, photography, typesetting, communications, and transport. Its wide range of vocabulary, accuracy of translation, and ease of use make it an indispensable supplement to any Spanish–English or English–Spanish dictionary.

PRÓLOGO

El diccionario en imágenes inglés y español se ha preparado a partir de la nueva versión del *Bildwörterbuch*, volumen tercero del diccionario Duden en diez tomos. La versión español es equivalente del original alemán, a pesar de las dificultades surgidas en más de una ocasión, pues el mundo que se nos presenta en las ilustraciones no es el español o hispanoamericano, sino el centroeuropeo: algunos objetos no existen en nuestro ámbito, o no hay otro semejante. Sin embargo, estos casos son los menos, y por ello mismo los diferenciadores; el resto es propio de nuestra cultura, de nuestra industria, de nuestras técnicas, esto es, común a todos nosotros, alemanes, ingleses e hispanohablantes. Por otra parte, hemos intentado dar cabida al mundo americano a través de la única vía posible, el léxico peculiar utilizado en ámbitos más o menos extensos de aquel continente y que se pudiera aplicar a imágenes surgidas en Alemania -ni siquiera en España.

La traducción se ha realizado bajo mi dirección por licenciados en filología hispánica y por especialistas con conocimientos sobrados para efectuar la tarea encomendada. El peso mayor del trabajo lo han soportado D. Antonio Ruiz Noguera (professor agregado de Lengua Española de INB), Da. María José Blanco Rodríguez (becaria de investigación del Departamento de Lengua Española de la Universidad de Málaga), Da. María Aurora Miró Domínguez (profesora ayudante del Departamento de Historia del Arte de la Universidad de Málaga) y Da. Inmaculada Anaya Revuelta (becaria de investigación del Departmento de Geografía Lingüística del CSIC). Hemos tenido numerosos colaboradores e informantes ocasionales, comerciantes, artesanos, profesionales diversos que nos han facilitado valiosos datos, muchas veces sin saberlo ellos mismos; quienes más ayuda nos han prestado han sido D. Carlos Alvar (catedrático de Literaturas Románicas de la Universidad de Murcia), D. Conrado Salmerón Rodriguez (tecnólogo de automoción del Instituto de Formación Profesional de Tarifa, Cádiz), Da. María del Pilar Nuño Álvarez (profesora ayudante del Departamento de Lengua Española de la Universidad Complutense), Da. María del Pilar Palanco Aguado (profesora agregada de Lengua Española de INB), Da. Marta C. Ayla Castro (profesora ayudante del Departmento de Lengua Española de la Universidad de Málaga), y D. Jorge Denis Zambrana (librero). He de dejar constancia, también, de la generosa ayuda prestada en todo momento por el Departamento de Geografía Lingüística del Consejo Superior de Investigaciones Científicas, y por la Oficina de Información y Observación del Español del Instituto de Cooperación Iberoamericana.

Las imágenes proporcionan cierta información con mayor facilidad y rapidez que las explicaciones y descripciones. Una imagen permite a menudo identificar antes el objeto designado por una palabra que la definición de esa palabra; es bien sabido aquello de ,,una imagen vale más que mil palabras".

Cada doble página del diccionario tiene una lámina que ilustra el vocabulario de un dominio completo con los términos ingleses y sus correspondientes españoles. La organización temática evita la enojosa búsqueda de las distintas voces proporcionando en dos páginas enfrentadas toda la información concerniente a un dominio completo. La presentación del texto y el índice final permiten utilizar esta obra como si se tratara de un diccionario bilingüe de doble entrada. Pero que nadie se llame a engaño éste no es un diccionario ideológico, sino temático, y por tanto más restringido, al serle imposible dar cuenta de aquellas palabras cuyo contenido no su puede expresar en forma de imágenes. La temática es, tal vez, la manera más antigua de organizar los saberes del hombre; arranca de los enciclopedistas medievales y llega hasta nuestros días, habiendo tenido entre nosotros cultivadores tan insignes como San Isidoro, Lorenzo Palmireno, Francisco Sobrino o el P. Esteban de Terreros.

La forma de presentar los materiales, y la modernidad de la obra, hacen que el vocabulario esté constituido en gran medida por términos especiales y técnicos, de modo que este diccionario se convierte, así, en el complemento indispensable de cualquier diccionario bilingüe español-inglés e inglés-español. Al mismo tiempo, la presencia del vocabulario científico y técnico impide la aparición de voces de ámbitos geográficos restringidos; es el precio que tiene que pagar la riqueza de la lengua en aras de la comprensión general.

Por último, si un diccionario debe ser un instrumento, una herramienta para conocer el mundo que nos rodea, éste lo es sobradamente. Y cumple con generosidad con la misión didáctica, que encierra todo diccionario: no sólo nos presenta el mundo de una manera organizada, sino que nos enseña a nombrarlo en varias lenguas. Es una obra que no sólo aprovechará a los adultos, sino que, utilizada adecuadamenta, servirá a los más jóvenes para conocer la realidad y para aprender idiomas, esto es, les permitirá entender y ser entendidos por los demás, en su lengua y en otra. ¿Cabe esperar nada mejor de un diccionario?

Manuel Alvar Ezquerra

PRÓLOGO DE LA SEGUNDA EDICIÓN

En esta nueva edición del Oxford-Duden Pictorial Spanish–English Dictionary la editorial ha introducio cambios (correcciones en unas láminas, otras son nuevas) que han hecho necesario modificar el contenido léxico de la obra tanto en las series de palabras de la parte ilustrada como en el índice final. Se ha aprovechado la ocasión para corregir el texto anterior, para eliminar las inexactitudes detectadas, y para actualizarlo. En esta nueva tarea he contado con la ayuda del Dr. D. Juan Crespo Hidalgo y de Da. Mercedes Martin Cinto (ambos profesores de los Estudios de Traducción e Interpretación de la Facultad de Filosofía y Letras de la Universidad de Málaga), y de D. Miguel Ángel Jiménez Cuenca y Da. María Rosa Carrasco Escobar (colaboradores del grupo de investigación Lexicología y Lexicografía de la misma Universidad) para el establecimiento de los nuevos índices, así como la de especialistas en distintas materias para problemas muy concretos. Esperamos, de esta manera, haber contribuido a la corrección y modernización de un diccionario que debe ser útil no sólo a quienes empiezan a aprender una nueva lengua, sino también a los que necesitan de un instrumento así para realizar sus traducciones.

Manuel Alvar Ezquerra

Abbreviations used in the English text

Am.	*American usage*
c.	*castrated (animal)*
coll.	*colloquial*
f.	*female (animal)*
form.	*formerly*
joc.	*jocular*
m.	*male (animal)*
poet.	*poetic*
sg.	*singular*
sim.	*similar*
y.	*young (animal)*

Abreviaturas empleadas en el texto español

amb.	*ambivalente*	Hond.	*Honduras*
Amér.	*América*	m	*masculino*
Amér. Merid.	*América Meridional*	Mé.	*Méjico*
anál.	*análogo*	Nicar.	*Nicaragua*
angl.	*anglicismo*	Pan.	*Panamá*
ant.	*anticuado*	Par.	*Paraguay*
Arg.	*Argentina*	p. e.	*por ejemplo*
Bol.	*Bolivia*	pop.	*lenguaje popular*
col.	*lenguaje coloquial*	P. Rico	*Puerto Rico*
Col.	*Colombia*	Salv.	*El Salvador*
C. Rica	*Costa Rica*	S. Dgo.	*República Dominicana*
Ec.	*Ecuador*	sin.	*sinónimo*
f	*femenino*	Urug.	*Uruguay*
fam.	*lenguaje familiar*	var.	*variedades*
Filip.	*Filipinas*	Venez.	*Venezuela*
Guat.	*Guatemala*		

Índice

Los números arábigos son los de la lámina

Contents

The arabic numerals are the numbers of the pictures

Índice

Contents

Índice

Contents

Índice

Contents

Índice

Contents

13

Índice

Contents

Índice

Contents

1 Átomo I   *Atom I*

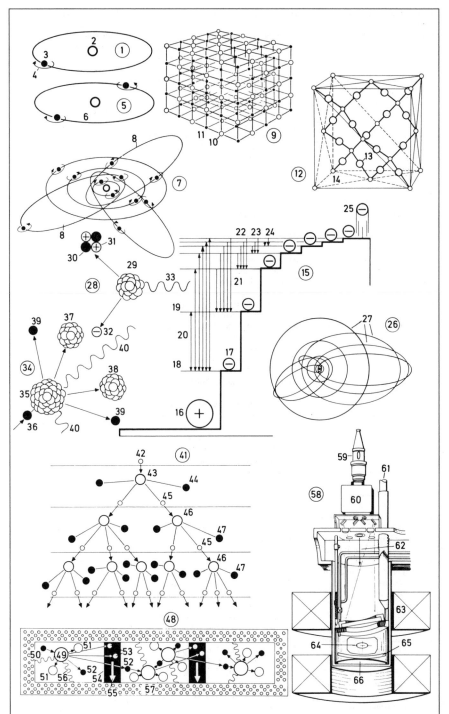

1-23 los detectores de irradiación *f*
(los contadores de irradiación)
– *radiation detectors (radiation
meters)*
1 el monitor de irradiación *f*
– *radiation monitor*
2 la cámara de ionización *f*
– *ionization chamber (ion chamber)*
3 el electrodo central
– *central electrode*
4 el selector de alcance *m* regulable
– *measurement range selector*
5 el alojamiento (la caja) de los
instrumentos
– *instrument housing*
6 el medidor
– *meter*
7 el ajuste en cero *m* (el botón de
puesta en cero *m*)
– *zero adjustment*
8-23 los dosímetros
– *dosimeter (dosemeter)*
8 el dosímetro de película *f*
– *film dosimeter*
9 el filtro
– *filter*
10 la película
– *film*
11 el dosímetro anular de película *f*
– *film-ring dosimeter*
12 el filtro
– *filter*
13 la película
– *film*
14 la cubierta con filtro *m*
– *cover with filter*
15 el medidor de bolsillo *m* (el medidor de pluma *f*, la cámara de bolsillo *m*)
– *pocket meter (pen meter, pocket
chamber)*
16 el visor
– *window*
17 la cámara de ionización *f*
– *ionization chamber (ion chamber)*
18 el sujetador (el clip de la pluma)
– *clip (pen clip)*
19 el contador Geiger
– *Geiger counter (Geiger-Müller
counter)*
20 la cubierta del tubo contador *m*
– *counter tube casing*
21 el tubo contador *m*
– *counter tube*
22 la caja de los instrumentos
– *instrument housing*
23 el selector de alcance *m* regulable
– *measurement range selector*
24 la cámara de niebla *f* de Wilson
(la cámara de condensación *f*)
– *Wilson cloud chamber (Wilson
chamber)*
25 la plancha de compresión *f*
– *compression plate*

26 la fotografía de la cámara de
Wilson
– *cloud chamber photograph*
27 la estela en la cámara de Wilson
(estela *f* de ionización *f*) de una
partícula alfa
– *cloud chamber track of an alpha
particle*
28 el aparato de telerradiación *f* **de
cobalto** *m* (col. la bomba de
cobalto *m*)
– *telecobalt unit (coll. cobalt bomb)*
29 la columna de soporte *m*
– *pillar stand*
30 los cables de apoyo *m*
– *support cables*
31 el escudo protector de la
radiación
– *radiation shield (radiation shielding)*
32 el escudo de corredera *f*
– *sliding shield*
33 el diafragma laminar
– *bladed diaphragm*
34 el visor luminoso
– *light-beam positioning device*
35 el dispositivo pendular (el péndulo)
– *pendulum device (pendulum)*
36 la mesa de irradiación *f* (la mesa
de radioterapia *f*)
– *irradiation table*
37 la corredera
– *rail (track)*
38 el manipulador de bolas *f* (el
manipulador)
– *manipulator with sphere unit*
39 el mango
– *handle*
40 el pestillo de seguridad *f*
– *safety catch (locking lever)*
41 la articulación de bolas *f* (la rótula)
– *wrist joint*
42 la barra de dirección *f*
– *master arm*
43 el dispositivo de sujeción *f* (la
abrazadera)
– *clamping device (clamp)*
44 las tenazas
– *tongs*
45 el tablero de ranuras *f*
– *slotted board*
46 el escudo protector de la irradiación, una pared protectora de
plomo *m* [sección]
– *radiation shield (protective shield,
protective shielding), a lead shielding wall [section]*
47 el brazo de sujeción *f* de un
manipulador gemelo (de un
manipulador master-slave)
– *grasping arm of a pair of manipu-
lators (of a master/slave manipulator)*

48 el protector del polvo
– *dust shield*
49 el sincrotrón
– *synchrotron*
50 la zona de peligro *m*
– *danger zone*
51 el imán
– *magnet*
52 las bombas para hacer el vacío en
la cámara de vacío *m*
– *pumps for emptying the vacuum
chamber*

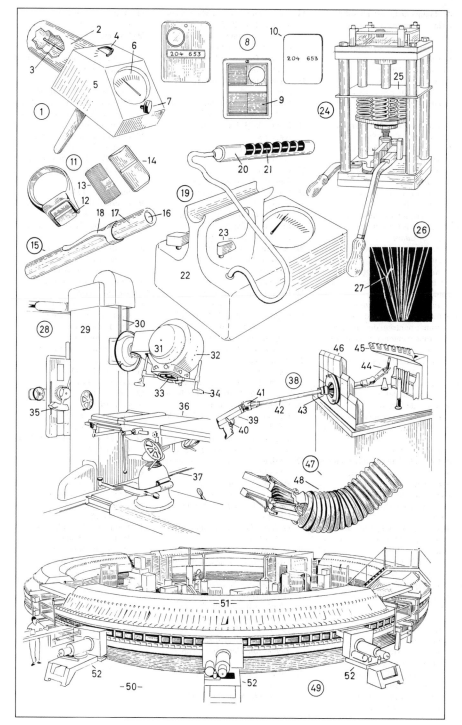

1-35 el mapa de las estrellas del cielo septentrional (el hemisferio norte)
– *star map of the northern sky (northern hemisphere)*
1-8 la división del cielo
– *divisions of the sky*
1 el polo celeste con la Estrella Polar (la Polar, la Estrella del Norte)
– *celestial pole with the Pole Star (Polaris, the North Star)*
2 la eclíptica (órbita *f* aparente anual del sol)
– *ecliptic (apparent annual path of the sun)*
3 el ecuador celeste (la línea equinoccial)
– *celestial equator (equinoctial line)*
4 el trópico de Cáncer
– *tropic of Cancer*
5 el círculo límite de las estrellas circumpolares
– *circle enclosing circumpolar stars*
6 *u.* **7** los puntos equinocciales (los equinoccios)
– *equinoctial points (equinoxes)*
6 el punto equinoccial de primavera *f* (primer punto *m* de Aries, punto *m* vernal, comienzo *m* de la primavera)
– *vernal equinoctial point (first point of Aries)*
7 el punto equinoccial de otoño *m* (comienzo *m* del otoño, primer punto *m* de Libra)
– *autumnal equinoctial point*
8 el solsticio de verano *m* (el solsticio)
– *summer solstice*
9-48 Constelaciones *f* (agrupaciones *f* de las estrellas fijas en figuras *f*) **y nombres** *m* de estrellas *f*
– *constellations (grouping of fixed stars into figures) and names of stars*
9 Aquila (el Águila *f*) con la estrella principal Altaír (la estrella brillante)
– *Aquila (the Eagle) with Altair the principal star (the brightest star)*
10 Pegaso (el Caballo Alado)
– *Pegasus (the Winged Horse)*
11 Cetus (la Ballena) con Mira *f*, una estrella variable
– *Cetus (the Whale) with Mira, a variable star*
12 Erídano (el Río Celeste)
– *Eridamus (the Celestial River)*
13 Orión (el Cazador) con Rigel, Betelgeuse y Bellatrix
– *Orion (the Hunter) with Rigel, Betelgeuse and Bellatrix*

14 Canis Maior (el Can Mayor) con Sirio (la Estrella Perro), una estrella de primera magnitud *f*
– *Canis Major (the Great Dog, the Greater Dog) with Sirius (the Dog Star), a star of the first magnitude*
15 Canis Minor (el Can Menor) con Porción
– *Canis Minor (the Little Dog, the Lesser Dog) with Procyon*
16 Hydra (la Hidra, la Culebra de Agua *f*)
– *Hydra (the Water Snake, the Sea Serpent)*
17 Leo (el León)
– *Leo (the Lion) with Regulus*
18 Virgo (la Virgen) con Spica (Espiga)
– *Virgo (the Virgin) with Spica*
19 Libra (la Balanza)
– *Libra (the Balance, the Scales)*
20 Serpens (la Serpiente)
– *Serpens (the Serpent)*
21 Hércules
– *Hercules*
22 Lyra (la Lira) con Vega
– *Lyra (the Lyre) with Vega*
23 Cygnus (el Cisne, la Cruz del Norte) con Deneb
– *Cygnus (the Swan, the Northern Cross) with Deneb*
24 Andrómeda
– *Andromeda*
25 Taurus (el Toro) con Aldebarán
– *Taurus (the Bull) with Aldebaran*
26 las Pléyades (las Siete Hermanas), un grupo abierto de estrellas *f*
– *The Pleiades (Pleiads, the Seven Sisters), an open cluster of stars*
27 Auriga (el Cochero) con Capella (la Cabra)
– *Auriga (the Wagoner, the Charioteer) with Capella*
28 Gemini (los Gemelos) con Cástor y Pólux
– *Gemini (the Twins) with Castor and Pollux*
29 Ursa Maior (la Osa Mayor, el Gran Carro) con la estrella doble Mizar y Alcor
– *Ursa Major (the Great Bear, the Greater Bear, the Plough, Charles's Wain, Am. the Big Dipper) with the double star (binary star) Mizar and Alcor*
30 Bootes (el Boyero) con Arturo
– *Boötes (the Herdsman) with Arcturus*
31 Corona Boreal (la Corona del Norte)
– *Corona Borealis (the Northern Crown)*

32 Draco (el Dragón)
– *Draco (the Dragon)*
33 Casiopea
– *Cassiopeia*
34 Ursa Minor (la Osa Menor, el Pequeño Carro) con la Estrella Polar
– *Ursa Minor (the Little Bear, Lesser Bear, Am. Little Dipper) with the Pole Star (Polaris, the North Star)*
35 la Vía Láctea (la Galaxia, el Camino de Santiago)
– *the Milky Way (the Galaxy)*
36-48 el cielo meridional (el hemisferio sur *m*)
– *the southern sky*
36 Capricornus (el Capricornio, la Cabra de Mar)
– *Capricorn (the Goat, the Sea Goat)*
37 Sagittarius (el Sagitario, el Arquero)
– *Sagittarius (the Archer)*
38 Scorpius (el Escorpión)
– *Scorpio (the Scorpion)*
39 Centaurus (el Centauro)
– *Centaurus (the Centaur)*
40 Triangulum Australe (el Triángulo Austral)
– *Triangulum Australe (the Southern Triangle)*
41 Pavo (el Pavo Real)
– *Pavo (the Peacock)*
42 Grus (la Grulla)
– *Grus (the Crane)*
43 Octans (el Octante)
– *Octans (the Octant)*
44 Crux (la Cruz del Sur, la Cruz)
– *Crux (the Southern Cross, the Cross)*
45 Argo (el Navío Argos, el Navío Celeste)
– *Argo (the Celestial Ship)*
46 Carina (la Quilla)
– *Carina (the Keel)*
47 Pictor, Machina Pictoris (el Pintor, el Caballete)
– *Pictor (the Painter)*
48 Reticulum (la Red)
– *Reticulum (the Net)*

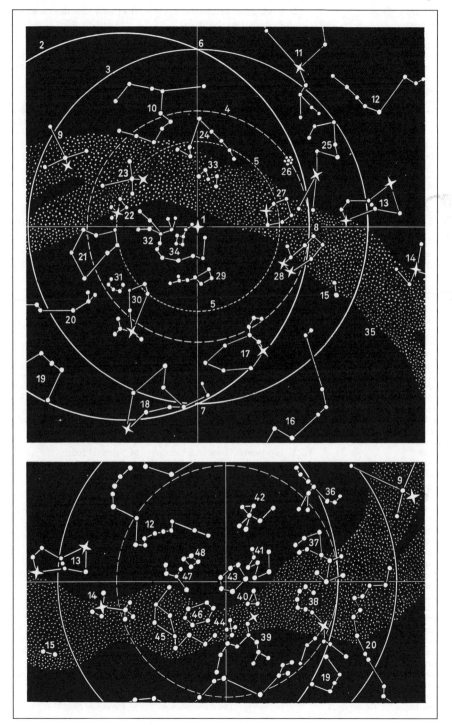

4 Astronomía II   *Astronomy II*

1-9 la Luna
– *the moon*
1 la trayectoria de la Luna (la órbita de la Luna alrededor de la Tierra)
– *moon's path (moon's orbit round the earth)*
2-7 las fases lunares (las fases de la Luna, lunación *f*)
– *lunar phases (moon's phases) (lunation)*
2 la Luna nueva
– *new moon*
3 la creciente de la Luna (la Luna creciente)
– *crescent (crescent moon, waxing moon)*
4 el primer cuarto (cuarto *m* creciente)
– *half-moon (first quarter)*
5 la Luna llena
– *full moon*
6 el último cuarto (cuarto *m* menguante)
– *half-moon (last quarter, third quarter)*
7 la menguante de la Luna (la Luna menguante)
– *crescent (crescent moon, waning moon)*
8 la Tierra (el globo terráqueo)
– *the earth (terrestrial globe)*
9 la dirección de los rayos del Sol
– *direction of the sun's rays*
10-21 el curso aparente del Sol al comienzo de las estaciones
– *apparent path of the sun at the beginning of the seasons*
10 el eje celeste
– *celestial axis*
11 el cenit
– *zenith*
12 el plano horizontal
– *horizontal plane*
13 el nadir
– *nadir*
14 el este
– *east point*
15 el oeste
– *west point*
16 el norte
– *north point*
17 el sur
– *south point*
18 el curso aparente del Sol el 21 de diciembre
– *apparent path of the sun on 21 December*
19 el curso aparente del Sol el 21 de marzo y el 23 de septiembre *m*
– *apparent path of the sun on 21 March and 23 September*
20 el curso aparente del Sol el 21 de junio *m*
– *apparent path of the sun on 21 June*

21 la orla del área *f* crepuscular (la zona límite del crepúsculo)
– *border of the twilight area*
22-28 los movimientos de rotación *f* del eje de la Tierra
– *rotary motions of the earth's axis*
22 el eje de la eclíptica
– *axis of the ecliptic*
23 la esfera celeste
– *celestial sphere*
24 el curso del polo celeste (precesión *f* y nutación *f*)
– *path of the celestial pole [precession and nutation]*
25 el eje instantáneo de rotación *f*
– *instantaneous axis of rotation*
26 el polo celeste
– *celestial pole*
27 el eje medio de rotación *f*
– *mean axis of rotation*
28 la polodía
– *polhode*
29-35 el eclipse solar y lunar [no precisado a escala]
– *solar and lunar eclipse [not to scale]*
29 el Sol
– *the sun*
30 la Tierra
– *the earth*
31 la Luna
– *the moon*
32 el eclipse solar
– *solar eclipse*
33 el área *f* de la Tierra en que el eclipse aparece total
– *area of the earth in which the eclipse appears total*
34 *u.* **35** el eclipse lunar
– *lunar eclipse*
34 la penumbra (la oscuridad parcial)
– *penumbra (partial shadow)*
35 la sombra (la oscuridad total)
– *umbra (total shadow)*
36-41 el Sol
– *the sun*
36 el disco solar (la esfera solar)
– *solar disc (disk) (solar globe, solar sphere)*
37 las manchas solares
– *sunspots*
38 los torbellinos del área *f* de las manchas solares
– *cyclones in the area of sunspots*
39 la corona (la corona solar) observable durante un eclipse total de Sol o por medio de instrumentos *m* especiales
– *corona (solar corona), observable during total solar eclipse or by means of special instruments*
40 las protuberancias (protuberancias *f* solares)
– *prominences (solar prominences)*

41 el borde lunar durante un eclipse total de Sol *m*
– *moon's limb during a total solar eclipse*
42-52 los planetas (el sistema planetario, el sistema solar) [no precisado a escala] y los signos de los planetas (los símbolos de los planetas)
– *planets (planetary system, solar system) [not to scale] and planet symbols*
42 el Sol
– *the sun*
43 Mercurio
– *Mercury*
44 Venus
– *Venus*
45 la Tierra, con la Luna, un satélite
– *Earth, with the moon, a satellite*
46 Marte con dos satélites *m*
– *Mars, with two moons*
47 los asteroides (planetas *m* menores)
– *asteroids (minor planets)*
48 Júpiter
– *Jupiter*
49 Saturno
– *Saturn*
50 Urano
– *Uranus*
51 Neptuno
– *Neptune*
52 Plutón con el satélite Carón
– *Pluto, with the moon Charon*
53-64 los signos del Zodiaco (los símbolos del Zodiaco)
– *signs of the zodiac (zodiacal signs)*
53 Aries (el Carnero)
– *Aries (the Ram)*
54 Tauro (el Toro)
– *Taurus (the Bull)*
55 Gemini (los Gemelos)
– *Gemini (the Twins)*
56 Cancer (el Cangrejo)
– *Cancer (the Crab)*
57 Leo (el León)
– *Leo (the Lion)*
58 Virgo (la Virgen)
– *Virgo (the Virgin)*
59 Libra (la Balanza)
– *Libra (the Balance, the Scales)*
60 Scorpio (el Escorpión)
– *Scorpio (the Scorpion)*
61 Sagitario (el Arquero)
– *Sagittarius (the Archer)*
62 Capricornio (la Cabra, la Cabra de Mar)
– *Capricorn (the Goat, the Sea Goat)*
63 Acuario (el Aguador)
– *Aquarius (the Water Carrier, the Water Bearer)*
64 Piscis (los Peces)
– *Pisces (the Fish)*

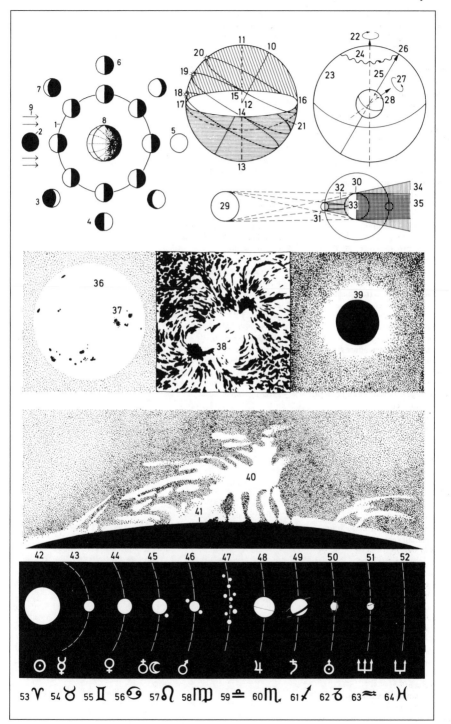

1-16 el observatorio meridional europeo (ESO) de La Silla (Chile), un observatorio [sección]
– *the European Southern Observatory (ESO) on Cerro la Silla, Chile, an observatory [section]*
1 el espejo principal con un diámetro de 3,6 m
– *primary mirror (main mirror) with a diameter of 3.6 m (144 inches)*
2 el objetivo primario con montaje *m* para los espejos secundarios
– *prime focus cage with mounting for secondary mirrors*
3 el espejo plano para la observación de la trayectoria de los rayos coudé
– *flat mirror for the coudé ray path*
4 la cabina Cassegrain
– *Cassegrain cage*
5 el espectrógrafo de rejilla *f*
– *grating spectrograph*
6 la cámara espectrográfica
– *spectrographic camera*
7 el mecanismo de transmisión *f* del eje horario
– *hour axis drive*
8 el eje horario
– *hour axis*
9 el montaje de herradura *f*
– *horseshoe mounting*
10 el soporte hidráulico
– *hydrostatic bearing*
11 los dispositivos de enfoque *m* primario y secundario
– *primary and secondary focusing devices*
12 la cúpula del observatorio (la cúpula giratoria)
– *observatory dome, a revolving dome*
13 la abertura de observación *f*
– *observation opening*
14 la contraventana vertical de la cúpula movible
– *vertically movable dome shutter*
15 la pantalla enrollada (el biombo)
– *wind screen*
16 el sideroestato
– *siderostat*
17-28 el planetario de Stuttgart [sección]
– *the Stuttgart Planetarium [section]*
17 la administración, los talleres y los almacenes
– *administration, workshop, and store area*
18 el andamio de acero *m*
– *steel scaffold*
19 la pirámide de vidrio *m*
– *glass pyramid*
20 la escalera giratoria abovedada
– *revolving arched ladder*

21 la cúpula de proyección *f*
– *projection dome*
22 el obturador de la luz (el diafragma)
– *light stop*
23 el proyector planetario
– *planetarium projector*
24 el pozo
– *well*
25 el vestíbulo
– *foyer*
26 la sala de proyección *f*
– *theatre (Am. theater)*
27 la cabina de proyección *f*
– *projection booth*
28 el pilar del cimiento
– *foundation pile*
29-33 el observatorio solar Kitt Peack de Tucson (Arizona) [sección]
– *the Kitt Peak solar observatory near Tucson, Ariz. [section]*
29 el helioestato
– *heliostat*
30 el pozo de observación *f* semisubterráneo
– *sunken observation shaft*
31 el escudo protector refrigerado por agua *f*
– *water-cooled windshield*
32 el espejo cóncavo
– *concave mirror*
33 la sala de observación *f*, alojamiento *m* del espectrógrafo
– *observation room housing the spectrograph*

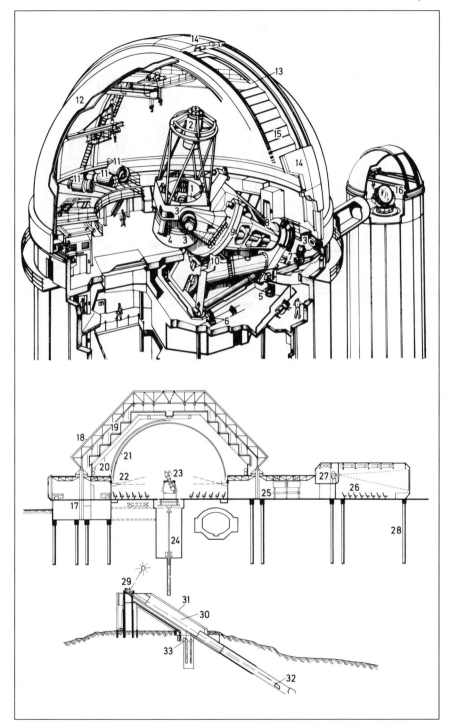

1 la nave espacial Apolo
- *Apollo spacecraft*
2 el módulo de servicio *m* (Service Module SM)
- *service module (SM)*
3 la tobera del propulsor principal
- *nozzle of the main rocket engine*
4 la antena direccional
- *directional antenna*
5 los cohetes de maniobra *f* (de pilotaje *m*)
- *manoeuvring (Am. maneuvering) rockets*
6 los tanques de oxígeno *m* e hidrógeno *m* para el sistema de energía *f* de la nave espacial
- *oxygen and hydrogen tanks for the spacecraft's energy system*
7 el depósito de combustible *m*
- *fuel tank*
8 los radiadores del sistema de energía *f* de la nave espacial
- *radiators of the spacecraft's energy system*
9 el módulo de mando *m* (la cápsula espacial Apolo)
- *command module (Apollo space capsule)*
10 la escotilla de entrada *f* a la cápsula espacial
- *entry hatch of the space capsule*
11 el astronauta
- *astronaut*
12 el módulo lunar
- *lunar module (LM)*
13 la superficie lunar, una superficie de polvo *m*
- *moon's surface (lunar surface), a dust-covered surface*
14 el polvo lunar
- *lunar dust*
15 el trozo de roca *f* (la roca lunar)
- *piece of rock*
16 el cráter de un meteorito
- *meteorite crater*
17 la Tierra
- *the earth*

18-27 el traje espacial
- *space suit (extra-vehicular suit)*
18 el aparato con el oxígeno de emergencia *f* (la reserva de oxígeno *m*)
- *emergency oxygen apparatus*
19 el bolsillo de las gafas de sol *m* de a bordo *m*
- *sunglass pocket [with sunglasses for use on board]*
20 el equipamiento autónomo de supervivencia *f*, un aparato portátil
- *life support system (life support pack), a backpack unit*
21 la válvula de acceso *m*
- *access flap*
22 el casco del traje espacial con filtros *m* solares
- *space suit helmet with sun filters*
23 la caja de control *m* del equipo de supervivencia *f*
- *control box of the life support pack*
24 el bolsillo para la linterna
- *penlight pocket*
25 la trampilla de acceso *m* a la válvula de limpieza *f*
- *access flap for the purge valve*
26 las conexiones de los cables para la radio *y* de los tubos de los sistemas de ventilación *f* y refrigeración *f*
- *tube and cable connections for the radio, ventilation, and water-cooling systems*
27 el bolsillo para los lápices, los utensilios, etc.
- *pocket for pens, tools, etc.*
28-36 el piso de bajada *f*
- *descent stage*
28 el conectador
- *connector*
29 el depósito de combustible *m*
- *fuel tank*
30 el motor (el propulsor)
- *engine*

31 el mecanismo de despliegue *m* del sistema de alunizaje *m*
- *mechanism for unfolding the legs*
32 el amortiguador principal
- *main shock absorber*
33 la almohadilla de alunizaje *m*
- *landing pad*
34 la plataforma de acceso *m* y de salida *f*
- *ingress/egress platform (hatch platform)*
35 la escalera de la plataforma y de la escotilla (la escalera de acceso *m*)
- *ladder to platform and hatch*
36 el cardan del propulsor
- *cardan mount for engine*
37-47 el piso de subida *f*
- *ascent stage*
37 el depósito de combustible *m*
- *fuel tank*
38 la escotilla de entrada *f* y de salida *f* (la escotilla de acceso *m*)
- *ingress/egress hatch (entry/exit hatch)*
39 los cohetes de maniobra *f* del módulo lunar
- *LM manoeuvring (Am. maneuvering) rockets*
40 la ventanilla
- *window*
41 la cabina de la tripulación
- *crew compartment*
42 la antena del radar de acoplamiento *m*
- *rendezvous radar antenna*
43 la unidad de medición *f* de la inercia (la central de la inercia)
- *inertial measurement unit*
44 la antena direccional para el control con la estación de tierra *f*
- *directional antenna for ground control*
45 la escotilla superior
- *upper hatch (docking hatch)*
46 la antena de aproximación *f*
- *inflight antenna*
47 el sistema activo de anclaje *m*
- *docking target recess*

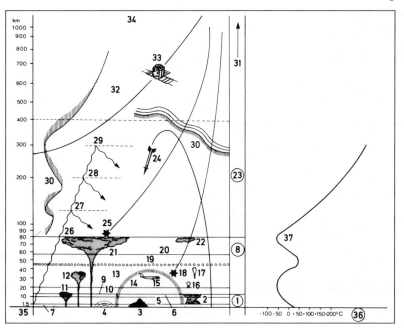

1 **la troposfera**
 – *the troposphere*
2 los nubarrones
 – *thunderclouds*
3 la montaña más alta del mundo, el monte Everest [8 882 m.] *f*
 – *the highest mountain,* Mount Everest *[8,882 m]*
4 el arco iris
 – *rainbow*
5 la capa de las corrientes chorro (jet-stream *m*)
 – *jet stream level*
6 el nivel cero (la inversión de los movimientos verticales del aire)
 – *zero level [inversion of vertical air movement]*
7 la capa del suelo (la capa límite de la superficie exterior)
 – *ground layer (surface boundary layer)*
8 **la estratosfera**
 – *the stratosphere*
9 la tropopausa
 – *tropopause*
10 la capa de separación *f* (la capa de movimientos *m* débiles del aire)
 – *separating layer (layer of weaker air movement)*
11 la explosión atómica
 – *atomic explosion*
12 la explosión de la bomba de hidrógeno *m*
 – *hydrogen bomb explosion*
13 la capa de ozono *m*
 – *ozone layer*

14 el radio de propagación *f* de las ondas sonoras
 – *range of sound wave propagation*
15 el avión estratosférico
 – *stratosphere aircraft*
16 el globo pilotado
 – *manned balloon*
17 el globo sonda
 – *sounding balloon*
18 el meteorito
 – *meteor*
19 el límite superior de la capa de ozono *m*
 – *upper limit of ozone layer*
20 el nivel cero
 – *zero level*
21 la explosión del Krakatoa
 – *eruption of Krakatoa*
22 las nubes luminosas (nubes *f* nocturnas luminosas)
 – *luminous clouds (noctilucent clouds)*
23 **la ionosfera**
 – *the ionosphere*
24 el radio de exploración *f* de los cohetes
 – *range of research rockets*
25 la estrella fugaz
 – *shooting star*
26 la onda corta (alta frecuencia *f*)
 – *short wave (high frequency)*
27 la capa E
 – *E-layer (Heaviside-Kennelly Layer)*
28 la capa F₁
 – *F₁-layer*
29 la capa F₂
 – *F₂-layer*

30 la aurora boreal (la luz polar)
 – *aurora (polar light)*
31 **la exosfera**
 – *the exosphere*
32 la capa atómica
 – *atom layer*
33 el radio de exploración de los satélites
 – *range of satellite sounding*
34 el margen de la zona (el paso hacia la zona interestelar)
 – *fringe region*
35 la escala de altitud *f*
 – *altitude scale*
36 la escala de las temperaturas
 – *temperature scale (thermometric scale)*
37 la gráfica de las temperaturas (curva *f* de las temperaturas)
 – *temperature graph*

1-19 las nubes y el tiempo
– *clouds and weather*
**1-4 las nubes de masas *f* de aire *m*
homogéneas**
– *clouds found in homogeneous air
masses*
1 el cúmulo (cumulus, cumulus
humilis), una nube fluida (conjunto *m* de nubes *f* bajas, nubes *f* de
buen tiempo *m*)
– *cumulus (woolpack cloud), a heap
cloud; here: cumulus humilis (fair-
weather cumulus), a flat-based
heap cloud*
2 el cumulus congestus, un conjunto
de nubes *f* muy fluidas
– *cumulus congestus, a heap cloud
with more marked vertical development*
3 el estratocúmulo, una serie de
nubes *f* bajas y en capas *f*
– *stratocumulus, a layer cloud (sheet
cloud) arranged in heavy masses*
4 el estrato (la niebla alta), una
capa de nubes *f* espesas y
homogéneas
– *stratus (high fog), a thick, uniform
layer cloud (sheet cloud)*
5-12 las nubes de los frentes cálidos
– *clouds found at warm fronts*
5 el frente cálido
– *warm front*
6 el cirro (cirrus), una nube alta o
muy alta de cristales *f* de hielo *m*
delgados, con formas *f* muy diversas
– *cirrus, a high to very high ice-crystal cloud, thin and assuming a
wide variety of forms*
7 el cirroestrato, una nube de
cristales *f* de hielo *m* en forma *f*
de velo *m*
– *cirrostratus, an ice-crystal cloud
veil*
8 el altoestrato, una capa de nubes *f*
de altura *f* media
– *altostratus, a layer cloud (sheet
cloud) of medium height*
9 el altoestrato precipitante, una
nube en capas *f* con precipitaciones *f* en la parte superior
– *altostratus praecipitans, a layer
cloud (sheet cloud) with precipitation in its upper parts*
10 el nimboestrato, una nube de lluvia *f*, nube *f* de formación *f* vertical
muy marcada de la que caen precipitaciones *f* (lluvia *f* o nieve *f*)
– *nimbostratus, a rain cloud, a layer
cloud (sheet cloud) of very large
vertical extent which produces precipitation (rain or snow)*

11 el fractoestrato, jirones *m* de
nubes *f* que se encuentran debajo
del nimboestrato
– *fractostratus, a ragged cloud
occurring beneath nimbostratus*
12 el fractocúmulo, unos jirones de
nubes *f* como el 11, pero con formas *f* onduladas
– *fractocumulus, a ragged cloud like
11 but with billowing shapes*
13-17 las nubes de los frentes fríos
– *clouds at cold fronts*
13 el frente frío
– *cold front*
14 el cirrocúmulo, una nube ligeramente aborregada (enladrillada)
– *cirrocumulus, thin fleecy cloud in
the form of globular masses; covering the sky: mackerel sky*
15 el altocúmulo, una nube volumi-
nosamente aborregada
– *altocumulus, a cloud in the form
of large globular masses*
16 el altocúmulo castellano y el altocúmulo floccus, variantes *f* del 15
– *altocumulus castellanus and
altocumulus floccus, species of 15*
17 el cúmulonimbo, una nube fluida
vertical muy marcada, asociada
con las nubes de tormenta *f*
pertenecientes al grupo *m* 1-4
– *cumulonimbus, a heap cloud of
very large vertical extent, to be
classified under 1-4 in the case of
tropical storms*
18-19 los tipos de precipitaciones *f*
– *types of precipitation*
18 la lluvia constante o la nevada
cubierta, unas precipitaciones de
intensidad *f* uniforme (*Col., Guat.
y Venez.:* la llovedera)
– *steady rain or snow covering a
large area, precipitation of uniform intensity*
19 el chubasco (aguacero *m*, chaparrón *m*), una precipitación irregular (precipitaciones *f* locales)
(*Col. y P. Rico:* el aguaceral;
Amer. Central, Cuba y Ec.: el
aguaje)
– *shower, scattered precipitation*

flecha *f* negra = aire *m* frio
black arrow = cold air
flecha *f* blanca = aire *m* caliente
white arrow = warm air

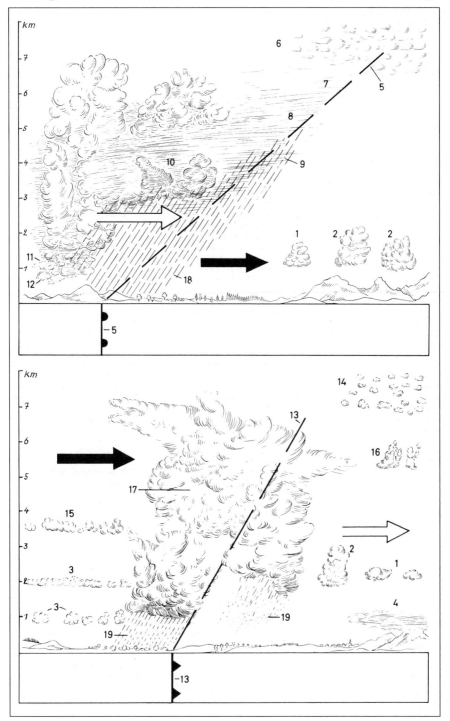

9 Meteorología II y climatología

Meteorology II and Climatology

1-39 el mapa meteorológico
- *weather chart (weather map, surface chart, surface synoptic chart)*
1 la isobara (línea *f* de igual presión *f* atmosférica al nivel del mar)
- *isobar (line of equal or constant atmospheric or barometric pressure at sea level)*
2 la pliobara (isobara *f* por encima de 1 000 mb)
- *pleiobar (isobar of over 1,000 mb)*
3 la miobara (isobara *f* de menos de 1 000 mb)
- *meiobar (isobar of under 1,000 mb)*
4 la presión atmosférica indicada en milibares *m*
- *atmospheric (barometric) pressure given in millibars*
5 el área *f* de (baja) presión *f* (el ciclón, la depresión)
- *low-pressure area (low, cyclone, depression)*
6 el área *f* de (alta) presión *f* (el anticiclón)
- *high-pressure area (high, anticyclone)*
7 una estación para la observación del tiempo (la estación meteorológica) o un barco meteorológico
- *observatory (meteorological watch office, weather station) or ocean station vessel (weather ship)*
8 la temperatura
- *temperature*
9-19 la representación de la dirección y de la velocidad del viento (los símbolos que representan el viento)
- *means of representing wind direction (wind-direction symbols)*
9 la flecha que indica la dirección del viento
- *wind-direction shaft (wind arrow)*
10 el trazo que indica la velocidad (la fuerza) del viento
- *wind-speed barb (wind-speed feather) indicating wind speed*
11 la calma
- *calm*
12 1-2 nudos *m*
- *1-2 knots (1 knot = 1.852 kph)*
13 3-7 nudos *m*
- *3-7 knots*
14 8-12 nudos *m*
- *8-12 knots*
15 13-17 nudos *m*
- *13-17 knots*
16 18-22 nudos *m*
- *18-22 knots*
17 23-27 nudos *m*
- *23-27 knots*
18 28-32 nudos *m*
- *28-32 knots*
19 58-62 nudos *m*
- *58-62 knots*
20-24 el estado del cielo (grado *m* de nubosidad *f*)
- *state of the sky (distribution of the cloud cover)*

20 despejado (sin nubes *f*)
- *clear (cloudless)*
21 casi despejado
- *fair*
22 poco nuboso (semicubierto)
- *partly cloudy*
23 nuboso
- *cloudy*
24 cubierto
- *overcast (sky mostly or completely covered)*
25-29 frentes *m* y corrientes *f* de aire *m*
- ***fronts and air currents***
25 la oclusión
- *occlusion (occluded front)*
26 el frente cálido
- *warm front*
27 el frente frío
- *cold front*
28 la corriente de aire *m* cálido
- *warm airstream (warm current)*
29 la corriente de aire *m* frío
- *cold airstream (cold current)*
30-39 fenómenos *m* meteorológicos
- ***meteorological phenomena***
30 el área *f* de precipitaciones *f*
- *precipitation area*
31 la niebla (el nublado; *Mé., Perú, Guat. y P. Rico:* el nublazón; *Ec.:* la lancha)
- *fog*
32 la lluvia
- *rain*
33 la llovizna (el calabobos, la garúa, el mojabobos)
- *drizzle*
34 la nieve (nevada *f; Arg., Chile y Ec.:* la nevazón)
- *snow*
35 la nieve granulada (nevisca *f,* cellisca *f*)
- *ice pellets (graupel, soft hail)*
36 el granizo (el pedrisco, la granizada; *Col., Chile, Guat. y Mé.:* el granizal)
- *hail*
37 el chubasco
- *shower*
38 la tormenta (la tempestad)
- *thunderstorm*
39 relámpago (*Arg. y Urug.:* el refocilo)
- *lightning*
40-58 el mapa climático
- ***climatic map***
40 la isoterma (línea *f* que une los puntos que tienen igual temperatura *f* media)
- *isotherm (line connecting points having equal mean temperature)*
41 la isoterma cero (línea *f* que une los puntos que tienen una temperatura media anual de 0 ° C)
- *0 ° C (zero) isotherm (line connecting points having a mean annual temperature of 0 ° C)*

42 la isoquímena (línea *f* que une los puntos de igual temperatura *f* invernal)
- *isocheim (line connecting points having equal mean winter temperature)*
43 la isótera (línea *f* que une los puntos de igual temperatura *f* estival)
- *isothere (line connecting points having equal mean summer temperature)*
44 la isohelia (línea *f* que une los puntos de igual insolación *f*)
- *isohel (line connecting points having equal duration of sunshine)*
45 la isoyeta (línea *f* que une los puntos de igual cantidad *f* de lluvia *f*)
- *isohyet (line connecting points having equal amounts of precipitation)*
46-47 las zonas de calmas *f*
- *calm belts*
46-52 los sistemas de vientos *m*
- *atmospheric circulation (wind systems)*
46 las zonas de calmas *f* ecuatoriales
- *equatorial trough (equatorial calms, doldrums)*
47 las zonas de calmas *f* subtropicales
- *subtropical high-pressure belts (horse latitudes)*
48 el alisio del Nordeste
- *north-east trade winds (north-east trades, tropical easterlies)*
49 el alisio del Sudeste
- *south-east trade winds (south-east trades, tropical easterlies)*
50 las zonas de los vientos variables del Oeste
- *zones of the variable westerlies*
51 las zonas de los vientos polares
- *polar wind zones*
52 el monzón de verano *m*
- *summer monsoon*
53-58 los climas de la Tierra
- ***earth's climates***
53 el clima ecuatorial: la zona de lluvias *f* tropicales
- *equatorial climate: tropical zone (tropical rain zone)*
54 las zonas secas: las zonas desérticas y esteparias
- *the two arid zones (equatorial dry zones): desert and steppe zones*
55 las dos zonas lluviosas templadas
- *the two temperate rain zones*
56 el clima boreal (clima *m* de nieve y bosque *m*)
- *boreal climate (snow forest climate)*
57 *u.* 58 los climas polares
- *polar climates*
57 el clima de la tundra
- *tundra climate*
58 el clima del hielo eterno
- *perpetual frost climate*

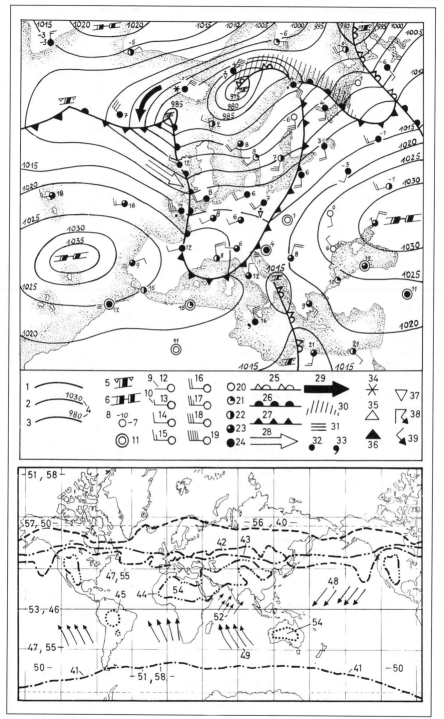

10 Los instrumentos meteorológicos

1 el barómetro de mercurio *m*, un barómetro de sifón *m*, un barómetro de columna *f* líquida
- *mercury barometer, a siphon barometer, a liquid-column barometer*

2 la columna de mercurio *m*
- *mercury column*

3 la escala en milibares *m* (escala *f* en milímetros *m*)
- *millibar scale, a millimetre (Am. millimeter) scale*

4 el barógrafo, un barómetro aneroide registrador
- *barograph, a self-registering aneroid barometer*

5 el tambor (el cilindro)
- *drum (recording drum)*

6 la serie de cápsulas *f* aneroides (las cajas aneroides)
- *bank of aneroid capsules (aneroid boxes)*

7 el brazo (la palanca, la varilla) registrador(a)
- *recording arm*

8 el higrógrafo
- *hygrograph*

9 el hilo higrométrico (el haz de cabellos *m*)
- *hygrometer element (hair element)*

10 el reglaje de lectura *f* (el tornillo de reglaje *m* de lectura *f*)
- *reading adjustment*

11 el reglaje de amplitud *f* del registro
- *amplitude adjustment*

12 el brazo (la palanca, la varilla) registrador(a)
- *recording arm*

13 la pluma registradora
- *recording pen*

14 las ruedas intercambiables del mecanismo de relojería *f*
- *change gears for the clockwork drive*

15 la palanca de desbloqueo *m* de la varilla registradora
- *off switch for the recording arm*

16 el tambor (el cilindro)
- *drum (recording drum)*

17 la escala de tiempos *m*
- *time scale*

18 la caja
- *case (housing)*

19 el termógrafo
- *thermograph*

20 el tambor (el cilindro)
- *drum (recording drum)*

21 el brazo (la palanca, la varilla) registrador(a)
- *recording arm*

22 el elemento de percepción *f* (el elemento sensitivo)
- *sensing element*

23 el pirheliómetro de disco *m* de plata *f*, un instrumento para medir la energía de los rayos del Sol
- *silver-disc (silver-disk) pyrheliometer, an instrument for measuring the sun's radiant energy*

24 el disco de plata *f*
- *silver disc (disk)*

25 el termómetro
- *thermometer*

26 el revestimiento aislante de madera *f*
- *wooden insulating casing*

27 el tubo con diafragma *m*
- *tube with diaphragm (diaphragmed tube)*

28 el aparato medidor del viento (el anemómetro)
- *wind gauge (Am. gage) (anemometer)*

29 el indicador de la velocidad del viento
- *wind-speed indicator (wind-speed meter)*

30 la cruz de paletillas *f* semiesféricas
- *cross arms with hemispherical cups*

31 el indicador de la dirección del viento
- *wind-direction indicator*

32 la veleta
- *wind vane*

33 el psicrómetro de aspiración *f*
- *aspiration psychrometer*

34 el termómetro "seco"
- *dry bulb thermometer*

35 el termómetro "húmedo"
- *wet bulb thermometer*

36 el protector de los rayos solares
- *solar radiation shielding*

37 el tubo de succión *f* (el tubo de aspiración *f*)
- *suction tube*

38 el pluviógrafo (pluviómetro *m* registrador)
- *recording rain gauge (Am. gage)*

39 la caja protectora
- *protective housing (protective casing)*

40 el recipiente colector (el colector de lluvia *f*)
- *collecting vessel*

41 la cubierta de protección *f* (el sombrerete para la lluvia)
- *rain cover*

42 el mecanismo registrador
- *recording mechanism*

43 el tubo sifón *m*
- *siphon tube*

44 el medidor de las precipitaciones (el medidor de la lluvia: el pluviómetro)
- *precipitation gauge (Am. gage) (rain gauge)*

45 el recipiente colector (el colector de lluvia *f*)
- *collecting vessel*

46 la cuba
- *storage vessel*

47 la probeta graduada
- *measuring glass*

48 el instrumento para medir la nevada
- *insert for measuring snowfall*

49 la garita (la estación) meteorológica
- *thermometer screen (thermometer shelter)*

50 el higrógrafo
- *hygrograph*

51 el termógrafo
- *thermograph*

52 el psicrómetro
- *psychrometer (wet and dry bulb thermometer)*

53 u. 54 los termómetros para medir las temperaturas extremas
- *thermometers for measuring extremes of temperature*

53 el termómetro de máxima *f*
- *maximum thermometer*

54 el termómetro de mínima *f*
- *minimum thermometer*

55 la radiosonda
- *radiosonde assembly*

56 el globo de hidrógeno *m*
- *hydrogen balloon*

57 el paracaídas
- *parachute*

58 el reflector radar *m* con líneas *f* de espaciamiento *m*
- *radar reflector with spacing lines*

59 la caja de instrumentos *m* con radiosonda *f* (un transmisor de onda *f* corta) y antena *f*
- *instrument housing with radiosonde [a short-wave transmitter] and antenna*

60 el transmisómetro, un instrumento para medir la visibilidad
- *transmissometer, an instrument for measuring visibility*

61 el instrumento registrador
- *recording instrument (recorder)*

62 el transmisor
- *transmitter*

63 el receptor
- *receiver*

64 el satélite meteorológico (ITOS)
- *weather satellite (ITOS satellite)*

65 las trampillas de regulación *f* de la temperatura
- *temperature regulation flaps*

66 el panel solar
- *solar panel*

67 la cámara de televisión *f*
- *television camera*

68 la antena
- *antenna*

69 el sensor solar
- *solar sensor (sun sensor)*

70 la antena telemétrica
- *telemetry antenna*

71 el radiómetro
- *radiometer*

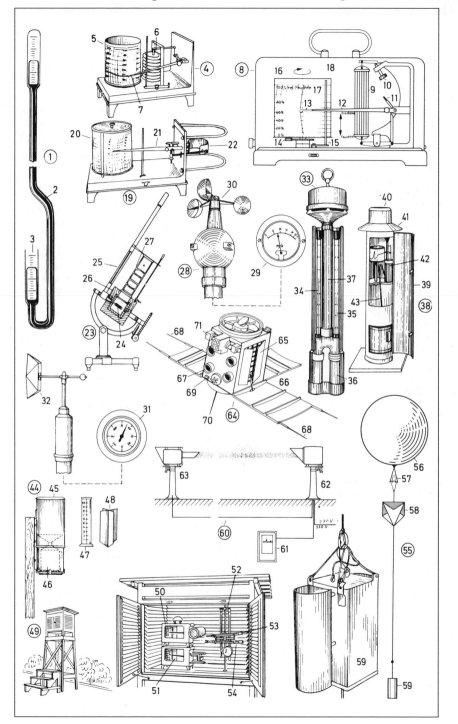

11 Geografía general I

Physical Geography I

1-5 la estructura en estratos *m* de la Tierra
- *layered structure of the earth*

1 la corteza terrestre (litosfera *f*)
- *earth's crust (outer crust of the earth, lithosphere, oxysphere)*

2 la hidrosfera (la zona fluida)
- *hydrosphere*

3 el manto (la capa inferior)
- *mantle*

4 el sima (la capa intermedia)
- *sima (intermediate layer)*

5 el núcleo (el núcleo terrestre)
- *core (earth core, centrosphere, barysphere)*

6-12 la curva hipsométrica de la superficie terrestre
- *hypsographic curve of the earth's surface*

6 la cima (lo más alto)
- *peak*

7 la plataforma continental
- *continental mass*

8 la plataforma submarina superior (el "schelf")
- *continental shelf (continental platform, shelf)*

9 la vertiente continental
- *continental slope*

10 el fondo oceánico (la plataforma submarina inferior)
- *deep-sea floor (abyssal plane)*

11 el nivel del mar
- *sea level*

12 la fosa submarina
- *deep-sea trench*

13-28 el volcanismo
- *volcanism (vulcanicity)*

13 el volcán en escudo *m*
- *shield volcano*

14 la meseta de lava *f*
- *lava plateau*

15 el volcán activo, un estrato de volcán *m*, un volcán compuesto
- *active volcano, a stratovolcano (composite volcano)*

16 el cráter volcánico (el cráter)
- *volcanic crater (crater)*

17 la chimenea volcánica
- *volcanic vent*

18 el río de lava *f*
- *lava stream*

19 la toba (la masa de materia *f* volcánica)
- *tuff (fragmented volcanic material)*

20 el volcán subterráneo
- *subterranean volcano*

21 el géiser (el surtidor termal)
- *geyser*

22 el surtidor de agua *f* caliente y de vapor *m*
- *jet of hot water and steam*

23 las terrazas de geiserita *f*
- *sinter terraces (siliceous sinter terraces, fiorite terraces, pearl sinter terraces)*

24 el cono
- *cone*

25 el "maar" (el volcán apagado)
- *maar (extinct volcano)*

26 el depósito de toba *f*
- *tuff deposit*

27 la escoria (brecha *f*) de la chimenea
- *breccia*

28 la chimenea de un volcán apagado
- *vent of extinct volcano*

29-31 el magmatismo plutónico (el magma de las profundidades, el hipomagma)
- *plutonic magmatism*

29 el batolito (la roca de profundidad *f*)
- *batholite (massive protrusion)*

30 el lacolito, una intrusión
- *lacolith, an intrusion*

31 el yacimiento, un yacimiento de mena *f*
- *sill, an ore deposit*

32-38 el terremoto (el seísmo; *S. Dgo.*: el turrumote; *clases:* el terremoto tectónico, el terremoto volcánico, el terremoto por hundimiento; *Amér.*: el remezón) y la sismología
- *earthquake (kinds: tectonic quake, volcanic quake) and seismology*

32 el hipocentro
- *earthquake focus (seismic focus, hypocentre, Am. hypocenter)*

33 el epicentro (el punto de la superficie de la tierra situado encima del hipocentro)
- *epicentre (Am. epicenter), point on the earth's surface directly above the focus*

34 la profundidad del foco
- *depth of focus*

35 la propagación de la onda
- *shock wave*

36 las ondas superficiales (las ondas sísmicas)
- *surface waves (seismic waves)*

37 la isosísmica (la línea que une los puntos de igual intensidad *f* sísmica)
- *isoseismal (line connecting points of equal intensity of earthquake shock)*

38 el área *f* epicentral (el área *f* de mayor vibración *f* sísmica)
- *epicentral area, an area of macroseismic vibration*

39 el sismógrafo horizontal (el sismómetro)
- *horizontal seismograph (seismometer)*

40 el amortiguador magnético
- *electromagnetic damper*

41 el botón de ajuste *m* para el periodo de oscilación *f* libre del péndulo
- *adjustment knob for the period of free oscillation of the pendulum*

42 el dispositivo del resorte para la suspensión del péndulo
- *spring attachment for the suspension of the pendulum*

43 la masa pendular (la masa estacionaria)
- *mass*

44 los carretes de inducción *f* para el voltaje del galvanómetro registrador
- *induction coils for recording the voltage of the galvanometer*

45-54 los efectos de los terremotos
- *effects of earthquakes*

45 la cascada (la catarata)
- *waterfall (cataract, falls)*

46 el desprendimiento de tierras *f* (el deslizamiento de tierras)
- *landslide (rockslide, landslip, Am. rock slip)*

47 el talud (cascotes *m*, cantos *m* rodados)
- *talus (rubble, scree)*

48 la concavidad
- *scar (scaur, scaw)*

49 el hundimiento en forma *f* de embudo *m* (el cráter de hundimiento *m*)
- *sink (sinkhole, swallowhole)*

50 la dislocación (el corrimiento de tierras *f*, el desplazamiento de tierras *f*)
- *dislocation (displacement)*

51 el desbordamiento de fango *m* (el cono de fango *m*)
- *solifluction lobe (solifluction tongue)*

52 la fisura
- *fissure*

53 la ola sísmica producida por un maremoto (el "tsunami")
- *tsunami (seismic sea wave) produced by seaquake (submarine earthquake)*

54 la playa en realce *m* (terraza *f* de la playa)
- *raised beach*

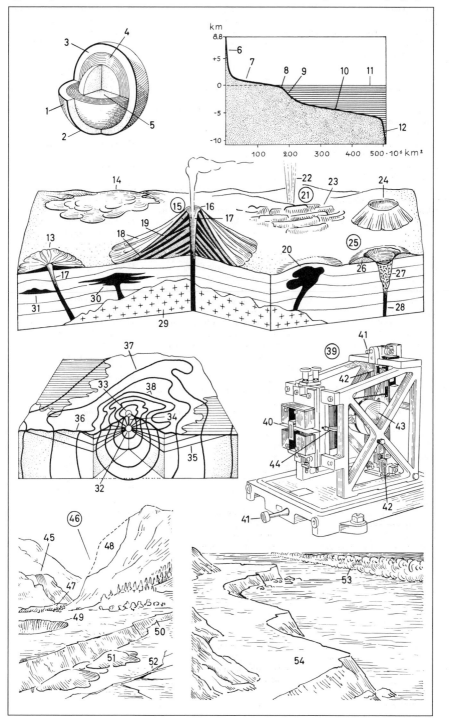

12 Geografía general II

1-33 la geología
- *geology*
1 la estratificación de las rocas sedimentarias
- *stratification of sedimentary rock*
2 la orientación
- *strike*
3 el buzamiento (el ángulo de inclinación *f*)
- *dip (angle of dip, true dip)*
4-20 los movimientos orogénicos (orogénesis *f*, tectogénesis *f*, deformación *f* de las rocas por pliegues *m* y fallas *f*)
- *orogeny (orogenis, tectogenis, deformation of rocks by folding and faulting)*
4-11 las montañas de bloques *m* de fallas *f*
- *fault-block mountain (block mountain)*
4 la falla
- *fault*
5 el plano de falla *f*
- *fault line (fault trace)*
6 el salto de falla *f*
- *fault throw*
7 la falla normal (la falla de dislocación *f* normal: la falla oblicua inversa)
- *normal fault (gravity fault, normal slip fault, slump fault)*
8-11 las fallas complejas
- *complex faults*
8 la falla en escalera *f* (falla *f* distributiva, falla *f* múltiple)
- *step fault (distributive fault, multiple fault)*
9 el bloque de inclinación *f*
- *tilt block*
10 el horst
- *horst*
11 la fosa tectónica
- *graben*
12-20 los pliegues orogénicos (la montaña de pliegues *m*)
- *range of fold mountains (folded mountains)*
12 el pliegue simétrico (el pliegue derecho –vertical–)
- *symmetrical fold (normal fold)*
13 el pliegue asimétrico (el pliegue oblicuo)
- *asymmetrical fold*
14 el pliegue inclinado
- *overfold*
15 el pliegue recostado (el pliegue tendido)
- *recumbent fold (reclined fold)*
16 la cresta (el anticlinal)
- *saddle (anticline)*
17 el eje del anticlinal
- *anticlinal axis*

18 la hoya (el sinclinal)
- *trough (syncline)*
19 el eje del sinclinal
- *trough surface (trough plane, synclinal axis)*
20 la montaña plegada de fallas *f*
- *anticlinorium*
21 **el agua *f* subterránea a presión *f*** (el agua *f* artesiana)
- **groundwater under pressure (artesian water)**
22 la capa portadora de agua *f* (capa *f* freática)
- *water-bearing stratum (aquifer, aquafer)*
23 la roca impermeable
- *impervious rock (impermeable rock)*
24 la cuenca de drenaje *m* (la zona de captación *f*)
- *drainage basin (catchment area)*
25 el tubo del pozo
- *artesian well*
26 el surtidor de agua *f*, un pozo artesiano (*Amér.*: la casimba)
- *rising water, an artesian spring*
27 el depósito de petróleo *m* en un anticlinal
- **petroleum reservoir in an anticline**
28 el estrato impermeable
- *impervious stratum (impermeable stratum)*
29 la capa porosa como roca *f* depósito *m*
- *porous stratum acting as reservoir rock*
30 el gas natural, un casquete de gas *m*
- *natural gas, a gas cap*
31 el petróleo (aceite *m* mineral, el crudo)
- *petroleum (crude oil)*
32 el agua *f* subyacente
- *underlying water*
33 la torre de perforación *f*
- *derrick*
34 **el área *f* montañosa** (la montaña secundaria)
- **mountainous area**
35 la cima de la montaña
- *rounded mountain top*
36 la cresta de la montaña (*Amér. Merid.*: la cuchilla)
- *mountain ridge (ridge)*
37 la pendiente de la montaña (*Chile, Ec., Guat. y Perú:* la gradiente)
- *mountain slope*
38 la fuente de la ladera
- *hillside spring*
39-47 la alta montaña
- **high-mountain region**

Physical Geography II

39 la cordillera, un macizo (*Amér. Merid.:* la cerrillada)
- *mountain range, a massif*
40 la cima (la cumbre, el pico de la montaña)
- *summit (peak, top of the mountain)*
41 la espalda (la antecumbre) de la montaña (*Chile:* la placeta)
- *shoulder*
42 el collado
- *saddle*
43 la pendiente escarpada (el tajo)
- *rock face (steep face)*
44 el barranco (la quebrada)
- *gully*
45 el talud (cantos *m* rodados, talud *m* detrítico)
- *talus (scree, detritus)*
46 el camino de herradura *f* (*Amér. Central, Arg., Bol., Cuba, Urug.:* la picada)
- *bridle path*
47 el paso (paso *m* de montaña *f*, el puerto)
- *pass (col)*
48-56 el glaciar
- **glacial ice**
48 el circo de alimentación *f* (el banco de nieve *f*, el "névé")
- *firn field (firn basin, nevé)*
49 el glaciar del valle
- *valley glacier*
50 la grieta del glaciar
- *crevasse*
51 la boca del glaciar
- *glacier snout*
52 el arroyo del glaciar
- *subglacial stream*
53 la morena (morrena *f*) lateral
- *lateral moraine*
54 la morena (morrena *f*) media
- *medial moraine*
55 la morena (morrena *f*) final
- *end moraine*
56 la mesa del glaciar
- *glacier table*

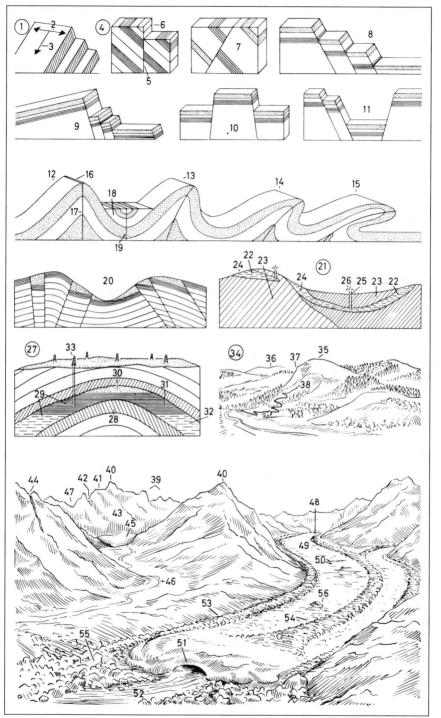

13 Geografía general III

Physical Geography III

1-13 la topografía fluvial
- *fluvial topography*
1 la desembocadura de un río, un delta
- (*Amér.:* la bocana)
- *river mouth, a delta*
2 el brazo de la desembocadura, un brazo de río *m* (un brazo fluvial)
- *distributary (distributary channel), a river branch (river arm)*
3 el lago
- *lake*
4 la orilla (*Chile:* el ribo)
- *bank*
5 la península
- *peninsula (spit)*
6 la isla
- *island*
7 la bahía (la ensenada, el golfo)
- *bay (cove)*
8 el arroyo (*Amér. Merid.:* la acequia; *Amér. Central, Bol., Pan., Perú, P. Rico y Venez.:* la quebrada)
- *stream (brook, rivulet, creek)*
9 el cono de aluvión *m*
- *levee*
10 la zona aluvial (la zona de sedimentación *f*)
- *alluvial plain*
11 el meandro (un recodo del río)
- *meander (river bend)*
12 el monte contorneado (el monte causante del meandro)
- *meander core (rock island)*
13 la vega (*Chile, Guat., Mé. y Venez.:* el plan)
- *meadow*
14-24 el pantano (*Col.:* el pantanero)
- *bog (marsh)*
14 el páramo bajo del pantano (el pantano superficial)
- *low-moor bog*
15 las capas de material *m* vegetal podrido (las capas de fango *m*)
- *layers of decayed vegetable matter*
16 la bolsa de agua *f*
- *entrapped water*
17 la turba del pantano (la turba de juncos *m* y cañas *f*)
- *fen peat [consisting of rush and sedge]*
18 la turba de aliso *m*
- *alder-swamp peat*
19 el páramo alto del pantano (el pantano alto)
- *high-moor bog*
20 la bolsa reciente de turba *f* de musgo *m*
- *layer of recent sphagnum mosses*
21 el límite entre capas *f*
- *boundary between layers (horizons)*
22 la bolsa antigua de turba *f* de musgo *m*
- *layer of older sphagnum mosses*
23 la charca del pantano (*Col. y Ec.:* la chamba)
- *bog pool*
24 la ciénaga (la zona cubierta de agua *f*)
- *swamp*
25-31 los acantilados
- *cliffline (cliffs)*
25 la roca (el peñasco, el escollo; *Cuba:* el molejón)
- *rock*
26 el mar
- *sea (ocean)*

27 las olas (rompientes)
- *surf*
28 el acantilado (el farallón)
- *cliff (cliff face, steep rock face)*
29 los guijarros (la rocalla)
- *scree*
30 el hueco producido por la erosión del oleaje (el socavón)
- *[wave-cut] notch*
31 la planicie de erosión *f* (el llano del rompiente)
- *abrasion platform (wave-cut platform)*
32 el atolón (arrecife *m* coralino en forma *f* circular), un arrecife coralino
- *atoll, a ring-shaped coral reef*
33 la laguna (*Amér.:* el aguaje; *Bol., Ec. y Perú:* la cocha; *Cuba:* el itabo)
- *lagoon*
34 la brecha (el canal de la laguna)
- *breach (hole)*
35-44 la playa
- *beach*
35 la línea de la marea (el límite de la pleamar)
- *high-water line (high-water mark, tide-mark)*
36 las olas rompiéndose en la orilla
- *waves breaking on the shore*
37 el malecón (la escollera)
- *groyne (Am. groin)*
38 la cabeza del malecón
- *groyne (Am. groin) head*
39 la duna movediza, una duna
- *wandering dune (migratory dune, travelling, Am. traveling, dune), a dune*
40 la duna en forma *f* de media luna *f*
- *barchan (barchane, barkhan, crescentic dune)*
41 las marcas rizadas (las marcas del viento)
- *ripple marks*
42 el morón (forma *f* de erosión *f* eólica)
- *hummock*
43 el árbol azotado por el viento
- *wind cripple*
44 el lago costero (la laguna de la playa)
- *coastal lake*
45 **el cañón** (*Amér.:* el cajón; *Arg., Cuba y Urug.:* el cañadón)
- *canyon (cañon, coulee)*
46 la meseta (*Amér.:* la sabana)
- *plateau (tableland)*
47 la terraza de roca *f*
- *rock terrace*
48 la roca sedimentaria (la roca estratificada)
- *sedimentary rock (stratified rock)*
49 el escalón estratificado (la terraza estratificada)
- *river terrace (bed)*
50 la grieta
- *joint*
51 el río del cañón
- *canyon river*
52-56 formas *f* de valles *m* [corte transversal]
- *types of valley [cross section]*
52 la garganta (el barranco)
- *gorge (ravine)*
53 el valle en forma *f* de V
- *V-shaped valley (V-valley)*
54 el valle en forma *f* de V abierta
- *widened V-shaped valley*

55 el valle en forma *f* de U (el valle de depresión *f*)
- *U-shaped valley (U-valley, trough valley)*
56 el valle sinclinal (el valle viejo)
- *synclinal valley*
57-70 el valle fluvial
- *river valley*
57 la pendiente escarpada (el acantilado)
- *scarp (escarpment)*
58 la pendiente suave (*Arg. y Chile:* el faldeo)
- *slip-off slope*
59 la meseta
- *mesa*
60 la sierra (la cordillera)
- *ridge*
61 el río
- *river*
62 la vega (la avenida)
- *flood plain*
63 la terraza de roca *f*
- *river terrace*
64 la terraza de grava *f*
- *terracette*
65 la pendiente (*Chile, Ec., Guat. y Perú:* la gradiente)
- *pediment*
66 la colina
- *hill*
67 el fondo del valle
- *valley floor (valley bottom)*
68 el lecho del río (*Chile:* la caja)
- *riverbed*
69 los depósitos sedimentarios
- *sediment*
70 el lecho de roca *f* (la roca sólida)
- *bedrock*
71-83 las formaciones kársticas en las rocas calcáreas
- *karst formation in limestone*
71 la dolina, un hundimiento en forma *f* de embudo *m*
- *dolina, a sink (sinkhole, swallowhole)*
72 el poljé (las depresiones)
- *polje*
73 la infiltración de un río
- *percolation of a river*
74 el manantial del karst
- *karst spring*
75 el valle seco
- *dry valley*
76 el sistema de grutas *f*
- *system of caverns (system of caves)*
77 el nivel del agua *f* del karst
- *water level (water table) in a karst formation*
78 la capa rocosa impermeable
- *impervious rock (impermeable rock)*
79 la cueva de estalactitas *f* (la cueva de karst *m*)
- *limestone cave (dripstone cave)*
80 *u.* 81 concreciones *f* calcáreas
- *speleothems (cave formations)*
80 la estalactita (*Chile y Mé.:* el achichicle)
- *stalactite (dripstone)*
81 la estalagmita
- *stalagmite*
82 la columna de concreciones *f* calcáreas
- *linked-up stalagmite and stalactite*
83 el río subterráneo
- *subterranean river*

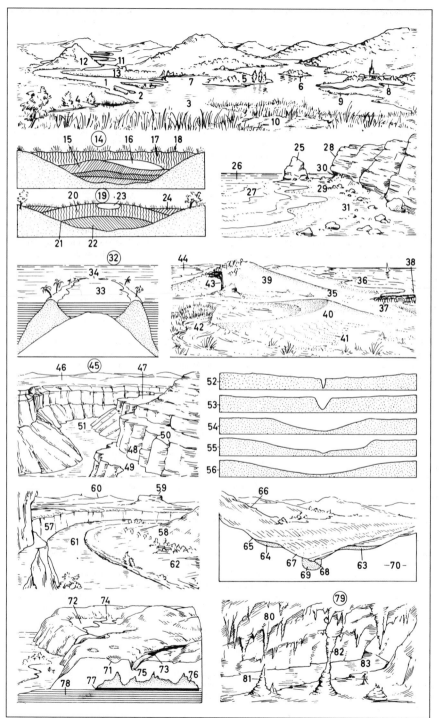

14 Mapa I

Map I

1-7 **las coordenadas geográficas** (la red de meridianos *m* y paralelos *m* de la superficie terrestre)
- *graticule of the earth (network of meridians and parallels on the earth's surface)*
1 el ecuador
- *equator*
2 un paralelo
- *line of latitude (parallel of latitude, parallel)*
3 el polo (el polo norte o el polo sur), un polo terrestre
- *pole (North Pole or South Pole), a terrestrial pole (geographical pole)*
4 el meridiano
- *line of longitude (meridian of longitude, meridian, terrestrial meridian)*
5 el meridiano cero (el meridiano de origen *m*, el meridiano de Greenwich)
- *Standard meridian (Prime meridian, Greenwich meridian, meridian of Greenwich)*
6 la latitud (latitud *f* geográfica)
- *latitude*
7 la longitud (longitud *f* geográfica)
- *longitude*
8 *u.* 9 proyecciones *f* cartográficas
- *map projections*
8 la proyección cónica
- *conical (conic) projection*
9 la proyección cilíndrica
- *cylindrical projection (Mercator projection, Mercator's projection)*
10-45 **el mapamundi** (el mapa de la Tierra)
- *map of the world*
10 los trópicos
- *tropics*
11 los círculos polares
- *polar circles*
12 *u.* 13 América *f*
- *America*
12-18 **los continentes**
- *continents*
12 América del Norte (Norteamérica *f*)
- *North America*
13 América del Sur (Sudamérica *f*)
- *South America*
14 África *f*
- *Africa*
15 *u.* 16 Eurasia *f*
- *Europe and Asia*
15 Europa *f*
- *Europe*
16 Asia *f*
- *Asia*
17 Australia *f*
- *Australia*
18 la Antártida (el continente antártico)
- *Antarctica (Antarctic Continent)*
19-26 **el océano**
- *ocean (sea)*
19 el océano Pacífico
- *Pacific Ocean*

20 el océano Atlántico
- *Atlantic Ocean*
21 el océano Glacial Ártico
- *Arctic Ocean*
22 el océano Glacial Antártico
- *Antarctic Ocean (Southern Ocean)*
23 el océano Índico
- *Indian Ocean*
24 el estrecho de Gibraltar, un estrecho de mar *m*
- *Strait of Gibraltar, a sea strait*
25 el mar Mediterráneo (el Mediterráneo)
- *Mediterranean (Mediterranean Sea, European Mediterranean)*
26 el mar del Norte, un mar marginal
- *North Sea, a marginal sea (epeiric sea, epicontinental sea)*
27-29 **la leyenda (la explicación de los símbolos)**
- *key (explanation of map symbols)*
27 la corriente marina fría
- *cold ocean current*
28 la corriente marina cálida
- *warm ocean current*
29 la escala
- *scale*
30-45 **las corrientes marinas**
- *ocean (oceanic) currents (ocean drifts)*
30 la corriente del Golfo (el Gulf Stream)
- *Gulf Stream (North Atlantic Drift)*
31 el Kuro-Sivo
- *Kuroshio (Kuro Siwo, Japan Current)*
32 la corriente ecuatorial del Norte
- *North Equatorial Current*
33 la contracorriente ecuatorial
- *Equatorial Countercurrent*
34 la corriente ecuatorial del Sur
- *South Equatorial Current*
35 la corriente del Brasil
- *Brazil Current*
36 la corriente de Somalia
- *Somali Current*
37 la corriente de las Agulhas
- *Agulhas Current*
38 la corriente australiana oriental
- *East Australian Current*
39 la corriente de California
- *California Current*
40 la corriente del Labrador
- *Labrador Current*
41 la corriente de las Canarias
- *Canary Current*
42 la corriente de Humboldt (la corriente del Perú)
- *Peru Current*
43 la corriente de Benguela
- *Benguela (Benguella) Current*
44 la corriente de viento del Oeste
- *West Wind Drift (Antarctic Circumpolar Drift)*
45 la corriente australiana occidental
- *West Australian Current*

46-62 **la agrimensura** (topografía *f*, geodesia *f*)
- *surveying (land surveying, geodetic surveying, geodesy)*
46 la nivelación (medición *f* geométrica de la altura)
- *levelling (Am. leveling) (geometrical measurement of height)*
47 la mira (regla *f* de nivelación)
- *graduated measuring rod (levelling, Am. leveling, staff)*
48 el nivel, un anteojo de nivelación *f*
- *level (surveying level, surveyor's level), a surveyor's telescope*
49 el punto trigonométrico
- *triangulation station (triangulation point)*
50 la armazón
- *supporting scaffold*
51 la torre de señalización *f*
- *signal tower (signal mast)*
52-62 **el teodolito, un aparato para medir ángulos *m***
- *theodolite, an instrument for measuring angles*
52 el botón micrométrico
- *micrometer head*
53 el ocular del microscopio
- *micrometer eyepiece*
54 el tornillo del nonio de inclinación *f*
- *vertical tangent screw*
55 la tuerca de inclinación *f*
- *vertical clamp*
56 el tornillo del nonio de rotación *f*
- *tangent screw*
57 la tuerca de rotación *f*
- *horizontal clamp*
58 el botón de ajuste *m* para el espejo de iluminación *f*
- *adjustment for the illuminating mirror*
59 el espejo de iluminación *f*
- *illuminating mirror*
60 el telescopio
- *telescope*
61 el nivel de burbuja *f* transversal
- *spirit level*
62 el ajuste circular
- *circular adjustment*
63-66 **la fotogrametría** (la fototopografía)
- *photogrammetry (phototopography)*
63 la cámara topográfica para la producción de series *f* coincidentes de imágenes *f*
- *air survey camera for producing overlapping series of pictures*
64 el estereotopo
- *stereoscope*
65 el pantógrafo
- *pantograph*
66 el estereoplanígrafo
- *stereoplanigraph*

15 Mapa II   *Map II*

1-114 los signos convencionales de un mapa a escala 1 : 25 000
- *map signs (map symbols, conventional signs) on a 1:25 000 map*

1 el bosque de coníferas f
- *coniferous wood (coniferous trees)*

2 el claro
- *clearing*

3 la oficina forestal
- *forestry office*

4 el bosque de árboles m de hojas f caducas
- *deciduous wood (non-coniferous trees)*

5 el erial
- *heath (rough grassland, rough pasture, heath and moor, bracken)*

6 la arena
- *sand or sand hills*

7 el elimo arenario
- *beach grass*

8 el faro
- *lighthouse*

9 el límite de los bajos
- *mean low water*

10 la boya
- *beacon*

11 las curvas de nivel m submarinas (las líneas isobáticas)
- *submarine contours*

12 el transbordador de trenes m (*Amér.:* el ferryboat)
- *train ferry*

13 el buque faro
- *lightship*

14 el bosque mixto
- *mixed wood (mixed trees)*

15 la maleza (el monte bajo)
- *brushwood*

16 la autopista con rampa f de acceso m
- *motorway with slip road (Am. freeway with on-ramp, freeway with acceleration lane)*

17 la carretera principal
- *trunk road*

18 la pradera
- *grassland*

19 la pradera pantanosa
- *marshy grassland*

20 la marisma
- *marsh*

21 la línea principal de ferrocarril m
- *main line railway (Am. trunk line) [no symbol]*

22 el paso bajo la carretera
- *road over railway*

23 el ramal (la línea secundaria de ferrocarril m)
- *branch line*

24 la estación de enclavamiento m (la casilla del guardavía)
- *signal box (Am. switch tower)*

25 la línea local de ferrocarril m (la vía estrecha)
- *local line*

26 el paso a nivel m
- *level crossing*

27 la estación (la parada)
- *halt*

28 el área f residencial
- *residential area*

29 el fluviómetro
- *water gauge (Am. gage)*

30 la carretera de tercer orden m
- *good, metalled road*

31 el molino de viento m
- *windmill*

32 la salina
- *thorn house (graduation house, salina, salt-works)*

33 la torre emisora de radio f
- *broadcasting station (wireless or television mast)*

34 la mina
- *mine*

35 la mina abandonada
- *disused mine*

36 la carretera secundaria
- *secondary road (B road)*

37 la fábrica
- *works*

38 la chimenea
- *chimney*

39 la cerca de alambre (la alambrada)
- *wire fence*

40 el paso elevado de la carretera
- *bridge over railway*

41 la estación de ferrocarril m
- *railway station (Am. railroad station)*

42 el paso elevado de la vía férrea
- *bridge under railway*

43 la senda
- *footpath*

44 el paso inferior de la senda
- *bridge for footpath under railway*

45 el río navegable
- *navigable river*

46 el puente de barcas f (el pontón de barcas f)
- *pontoon bridge*

47 el transbordador de vehículos m
- *vehicle ferry*

48 el espigón de piedra f (el malecón)
- *mole*

49 el fanal
- *beacon*

50 el puente de piedra f
- *stone bridge*

51 la ciudad
- *town or city*

52 la plaza del mercado
- *market place (market square)*

53 la iglesia mayor con dos torres f
- *large church with two towers*

54 el edificio público
- *public building*

55 el puente de la carretera
- *road bridge*

56 el puente de hierro m
- *iron bridge*

57 el canal
- *canal*

58 el dique de esclusas f
- *lock*

59 el embarcadero
- *jetty*

60 el transbordador de pasajeros m
- *foot ferry (foot passenger ferry)*

61 la capilla (la ermita)
- *chapel (church) without tower or spire*

62 las curvas de nivel m (las isohipsas)
- *contours*

63 el monasterio (el convento)
- *monastery or convent*

64 la iglesia visible a larga distancia f
- *church landmark*

65 la viña
- *vineyard*

66 la presa
- *weir*

67 el funicular aéreo (el teleférico)
- *aerial ropeway*

68 la torre de observación f
- *view point [tower]*

69 la esclusa de retención f
- *dam*

70 el túnel
- *tunnel*

71 el punto trigonométrico (el punto geodésico)
- *triangulation station (triangulation point)*

72 la ruina
- *remains of a building*

73 el molinillo de viento m
- *wind pump*

74 el fuerte
- *fortress*

75 el meandro aislado
- *ox-bow lake*

76 el río
- *river*

77 el molino de agua f
- *watermill*

78 la pasadera
- *footbridge*

79 el estanque
- *pond*

80 el arroyo
- *stream (brook, rivulet, creek)*

81 la alcubilla (el arca f de agua f)
- *water tower*

82 la fuente (el manantial)
- *spring*

83 la carretera principal
- *main road (A road)*

84 el desmonte
- *cutting*

85 la cueva
- *cave*

86 el horno de cal f
- *lime kiln*

87 la cantera
- *quarry*

88 el hoyo de arcilla f (el gredal)
- *clay pit*

89 el tejar (*Col.:* el chircal)
- *brickworks*

90 el ferrocarril ligero de explotación f
- *narrow-gauge (Am. narrow gage) railway*

91 el cargadero
- *goods depot (freight depot)*

92 el monumento
- *monument*

93 el campo de batalla f
- *site of battle*

94 la hacienda, una finca rústica
- *country estate, a demesne*

95 el muro
- *wall*

96 el castillo
- *stately home*

97 el parque
- *park*

98 el seto
- *hedge*

99 el camino transitable regularmente cuidado (la carretera local)
- *poor or unmetalled road*

100 el pozo
- *well*

101 el caserío (el cortijo)
- *farm*

102 el camino forestal
- *unfenced path (unfenced track)*

103 el límite del término municipal
- *district boundary*

104 el terraplén
- *embankment*

105 el pueblo
- *village*

106 el cementerio
- *cemetery*

107 la iglesia del pueblo
- *church or chapel with spire*

108 el huerto (el vergel)
- *orchard*

109 el mojón kilométrico (el hito kilométrico)
- *milestone*

110 el poste indicador
- *guide post*

111 el plantel
- *tree nursery*

112 la vereda
- *ride (aisle, lane, section line)*

113 la línea de conducción f eléctrica (la línea de alta tensión f)
- *electricity transmission line*

114 la plantación de lúpulo m
- *hop garden*

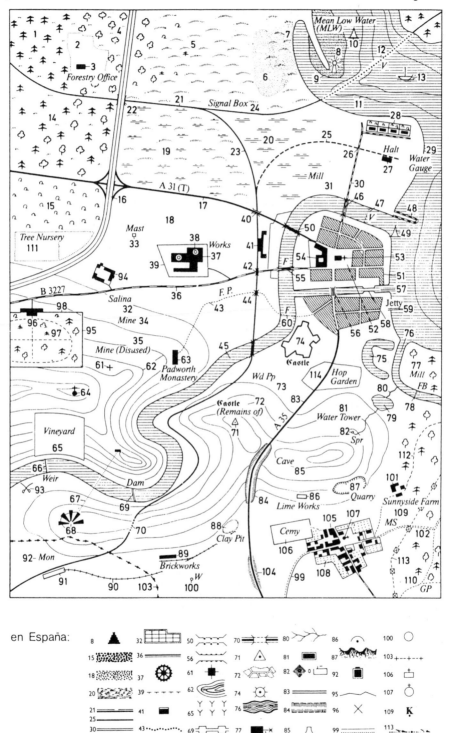

en España:

43

1-54 el cuerpo humano
- *the human body*
1-18 la cabeza (*Chile y Río de la Plata:* el mate)
- *head*
1 la coronilla (el vértice)
- *vertex (crown of the head, top of the head)*
2 el occipucio (la parte posterior de la cabeza)
- *occiput (back of the head)*
3 el cabello (el pelo)
- *hair*
4-5 la frente
- *forehead*
4-17 la cara
- *face*
4 la eminencia frontal
- *frontal eminence (frontal protuberance)*
5 la protuberancia frontal
- *superciliary arch*
6 la sien (*Amér.:* el sentido)
- *temple*
7 el ojo
- *eye*
8 el pómulo
- *zygomatic bone (malar bone, jugal bone, cheekbone)*
9 la mejilla (el carrillo)
- *cheek*
10 la nariz (las narices; *Amér.:* las ñatas)
- *nose*
11 el surco nasolabial (el surco desde la nariz hasta la comisura de la boca)
- *nasolabial fold*
12 el philtrum (el surco subnasal)
- *philtrum*
13 la boca (*Chile:* la borotera)
- *mouth*
14 la comisura labial (el ángulo de la boca; *C. Rica:* el camanance)
- *angle of the mouth (labial commissure)*
15 la barbilla
- *chin*
16 el hoyuelo de la barbilla
- *dimple (fossette) in the chin*
17 la mandíbula
- *jaw*
18 la oreja
- *ear*
19-21 el cuello
- *neck*
19 la garganta
- *throat*
20 la fosa yugular (el hueco de la garganta, la hoyuela)
- *hollow of the throat*
21 la nuca
- *nape of the neck*

22-25 la espalda
- *back*
22-41 el tronco
- *trunk*
22 el hombro
- *shoulder*
23 el omóplato
- *shoulderblade (scapula)*
24 la región lumbar
- *loins*
25 la región del sacro
- *small of the back*
26 el hombro (el sobaco, la axila)
- *armpit*
27 el vello de la axila
- *armpit hair*
28-30 el tórax (el pecho)
- *thorax (chest)*
28-29 los pechos (*Amér.:* los chiches)
- *breasts (breast, mamma)*
28 el pezón
- *nipple*
29 la aréola
- *areola*
30 el pecho
- *bosom*
31 la cintura
- *waist*
32 el flanco (el costado)
- *flank (side)*
33 la cadera
- *hip*
34 el ombligo (*Amér.:* el pupo)
- *navel*
35-37 el abdomen (el vientre, *fam.:* la barriga)
- *abdomen (stomach)*
35 la parte superior del abdomen (el epigastrio)
- *upper abdomen*
36 el abdomen medio (el mesogastrio)
- *abdomen*
37 el bajo vientre (el hipogastrio)
- *lower abdomen*
38 la ingle
- *groin*
39 el pubis
- *pudenda (vulva)*
40 el trasero (las posaderas, las nalgas, los glúteos, *fam.:* el culo; *Arg., Bol., Chile y Perú:* el poto)
- *seat (backside,* coll. *bottom)*
41 el pliegue anal (*fam.:* la raja del culo)
- *anal groove (anal cleft)*
42 el pliegue glúteo (la arruga glútea)
- *gluteal fold (gluteal furrow)*
43-54 las extremidades
- *limbs*
43-48 el brazo (la extremidad superior)
- *arm*

43 el brazo
- *upper arm*
44 el pliegue del codo
- *crook of the arm*
45 el codo
- *elbow*
46 el antebrazo
- *forearm*
47 la mano
- *hand*
48 el puño (los puños; *Ecuad.:* los ñeques)
- *fist (clenched fist, clenched hand)*
49-54 la pierna (la extremidad inferior)
- *leg*
49 el muslo
- *thigh*
50 la rodilla
- *knee*
51 la corva (el hueco poplíteo; *Arg., Col., Guat. y Venez.:* el garrete)
- *popliteal space*
52 la caña (la pierna)
- *shank*
53 la pantorrilla (*Mé.:* el chamorro)
- *calf*
54 el pie
- *foot*

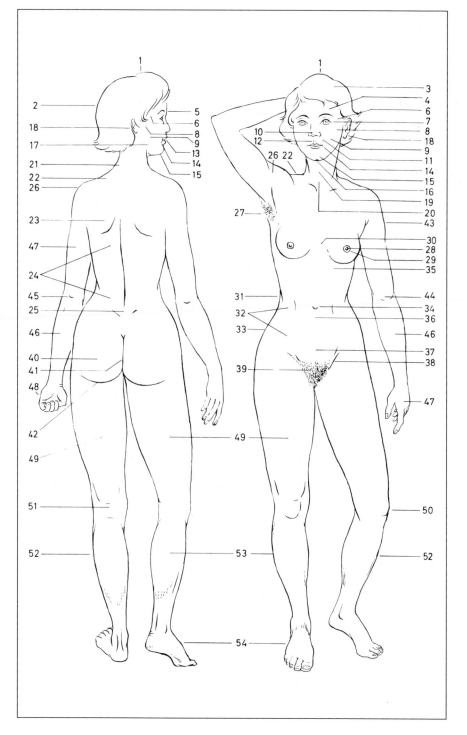

1-29 el esqueleto (la armazón ósea, la osamenta, los huesos)
– *skeleton (bones)*
1 el cráneo
– *skull*
2-5 la columna vertebral
– *vertebral column (spinal column, spine, backbone)*
2 las vértebras cervicales
– *cervical vertebra*
3 las vértebras dorsales
– *dorsal vertebra (thoracic vertebra)*
4 las vértebras lumbares
– *lumbar vertebra*
5 el cóccix (las vértebras coccígeas)
– *coccyx (coccygeal vertebra)*
6 *u.* **7** los huesos del hombro (la cintura escapular)
– *shoulder girdle*
6 la clavícula
– *collarbone (clavicle)*
7 el omóplato (la escápula)
– *shoulderblade (scapula)*
8-11 el tórax (la caja torácica)
– *thorax (chest)*
8 el esternón
– *breastbone (sternum)*
9 las costillas verdaderas
– *true ribs*
10 las costillas falsas
– *false ribs*
11 el cartílago costal
– *costal cartilage*
12-14 el brazo (la extremidad superior)
– *arm*
12 el húmero
– *humerus*
13 el radio
– *radius*
14 el cúbito
– *ulna*
15-17 la mano
– *hand*
15 los huesos del carpo (el carpo)
– *carpus*
16 los huesos del metacarpo (el metacarpo)
– *metacarpal bone (metacarpal)*
17 las falanges del dedo
– *phalanx (phalange)*
18-21 la pelvis
– *pelvis*
18 el ilion
– *ilium (hip bone)*
19 el isquion
– *ischium*
20 el pubis
– *pubis*
21 el sacro
– *sacrum*
22-25 la pierna (la extremidad inferior)
– *leg*
22 el fémur
– *femur (thigh bone, thigh)*

23 la rótula
– *patella (kneecap)*
24 el peroné
– *fibula (splint bone)*
25 la tibia
– *tibia (shinbone)*
26-29 el pie
– *foot*
26 los huesos del tarso (el tarso)
– *tarsal bones (tarsus)*
27 el calcáneo
– *calcaneum (heelbone)*
28 los huesos del metatarso (el metatarso)
– *metatarsus*
29 las falanges
– *phalanges*
30-41 el cráneo
– *skull*
30 el frontal
– *frontal bone*
31 el parietal izquierdo
– *left parietal bone*
32 el occipital
– *occipital bone*
33 el temporal
– *temporal bone*
34 el conducto auditivo
– *external auditory canal*
35 el maxilar inferior
– *lower jawbone (lower jaw, mandible)*
36 el maxilar superior
– *upper jawbone (upper jaw, maxilla)*
37 el hueso pómulo
– *zygomatic bone (cheekbone)*
38 el esfenoides
– *sphenoid bone (sphenoid)*
39 el etmoides
– *ethmoid bone (ethmoid)*
40 el unguis (el lacrimal)
– *lachrimal (lacrimal) bone*
41 el nasal
– *nasal bone*
42-55 la cabeza [corte]
– *head [section]*
42 el cerebro
– *cerebrum (great brain)*
43 la glándula pituitaria (la hipófisis cerebral)
– *pituitary gland (pituitary body, hypophysis cerebri)*
44 el cuerpo calloso
– *corpus callosum*
45 el cerebelo
– *cerebellum (little brain)*
46 el puente de Varolio
– *pons (pons cerebri, pons cerebelli)*
47 la médula oblonga
– *medulla oblongata (brain stem)*
48 la médula espinal
– *spinal cord*
49 el esófago
– *oesophagus (esophagus, gullet)*

50 la tráquea
– *trachea (windpipe)*
51 la epiglotis
– *epiglottis*
52 la lengua
– *tongue*
53 la cavidad nasal
– *nasal cavity*
54 el seno esfenoidal
– *sphenoidal sinus*
55 el seno frontal
– *frontal sinus*
56-65 el órgano del equilibrio y del oído
– *organ of equilibrium and hearing*
56-58 el oído externo
– *external ear*
56 el pabellón auditivo (la oreja)
– *auricle*
57 el lóbulo de la oreja
– *ear lobe*
58 el conducto auditivo
– *external auditory canal*
59-61 el oído medio
– *middle ear*
59 la membrana del tímpano
– *tympanic membrane*
60 la caja del tímpano
– *tympanic cavity*
61 los huesecillos: el martillo, el yunque, el estribo
– *auditory ossicles: hammer, anvil, and stirrup (malleus, incus, and stapes)*
62-64 el oído interno
– *inner ear (internal ear)*
62 el laberinto
– *labyrinth*
63 el caracol
– *cochlea*
64 el nervio auditivo
– *auditory nerve*
65 la trompa de Eustaquio
– *eustachian tube*

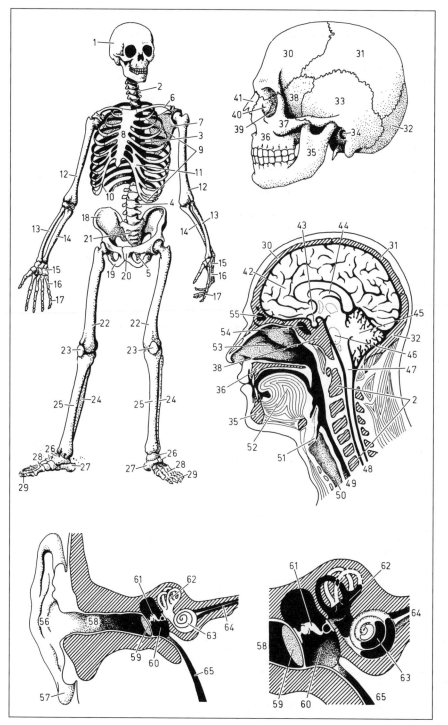

18 Hombre III

Man III

1-21 la circulación sanguínea (el sistema circulatorio)
– **blood circulation** (circulatory system)
1 la carótida, una arteria
– common carotid artery, an artery
2 la yugular, una vena
– jugular vein, a vein
3 la arteria temporal
– temporal artery
4 la vena temporal
– temporal vein
5 la arteria frontal
– frontal artery
6 la vena frontal
– frontal vein
7 la arteria subclavia
– subclavian artery
8 la vena subclavia
– subclavian vein
9 la vena cava superior
– superior vena cava
10 el cayado de la aorta (la aorta)
– arch of the aorta (aorta)
11 la arteria pulmonar [con sangre f venosa]
– pulmonary artery [with venous blood]
12 la vena pulmonar [con sangre f arterial]
– pulmonary vein [with arterial blood]
13 los pulmones
– lungs
14 el corazón
– heart
15 la vena cava inferior
– inferior vena cava
16 la aorta abdominal (rama f descendente de la aorta)
– abdominal aorta (descending portion of the aorta)
17 la arteria ilíaca
– iliac artery
18 la vena ilíaca
– iliac vein
19 la arteria femoral
– femoral artery
20 la arteria tibial
– tibial artery
21 la arteria radial
– radial artery
22-33 el sistema nervioso
– **nervous system**
22 el cerebro
– cerebrum (great brain)
23 el cerebelo
– cerebellum (little brain)
24 la médula oblonga
– medulla oblongata (brain stem)
25 la médula espinal
– spinal cord
26 los nervios torácicos
– thoracic nerves

27 el plexo branquial
– brachial plexus
28 el nervio radical
– radial nerve
29 el nervio cubital
– ulnar nerve
30 el nervio ciático mayor [en la parte posterior]
– great sciatic nerve [lying posteriorly]
31 el nervio femoral
– femoral nerve (anterior crural nerve)
32 el nervio tibial
– tibial nerve
33 el nervio peroneo
– peroneal nerve
34-64 la musculatura (el sistema muscular)
– **musculature** (muscular system)
34 el esternocleidomastoideo
– sternocleidomastoid muscle (sternomastoid muscle)
35 el músculo deltoide
– deltoid muscle
36 el pectoral mayor
– pectoralis major (greater pectoralis muscle, greater pectoralis)
37 el bíceps
– biceps brachii (biceps of the arm)
38 el tríceps
– triceps brachii (triceps of the arm)
39 el supinador largo
– brachioradialis
40 el radical anterior
– flexor carpi radialis (radial flexor of the wrist)
41 el flexor corto del pulgar
– thenar muscle
42 el serrato mayor
– serratus anterior
43 el oblicuo mayor
– obliquus externus abdominis (external oblique)
44 el recto del abdomen
– rectus abdominis
45 el sartorio
– sartorius
46 el vasto externo y el vasto interno
– vastus lateralis and vastus medialis
47 el tibial anterior
– tibialis anterior
48 el tendón de Aquiles
– tendo calcaneus (Achilles' tendon)
49 el abductor del pie, un músculo del pie
– abductor hallucis (abductor of the hallux), a foot muscle
50 el músculo occipital
– occipitalis
51 el esplenio
– splenius of the neck
52 el trapecio
– trapezius

53 el infraespinoso
– infraspinatus
54 el redondo menor
– teres minor (lesser teres)
55 el redondo mayor
– teres major (greater teres)
56 el extensor largo del pulgar (el supinador largo)
– extensor carpi radialis longus (long radial extensor of the wrist)
57 el extensor común de los dedos de la mano
– extensor communis digitorum (common extensor of the digits)
58 el cubital posterior
– flexor carpi ulnaris (ulnar flexor of the wrist)
59 el dorsal ancho
– latissimus dorsi
60 el glúteo mayor
– gluteus maximus
61 el bíceps crural
– biceps femoris (biceps of the thigh)
62 los gemelos
– gastrocnemius, medial and lateral heads
63 el extensor común de los dedos del pie
– extensor communis digitorum (common extensor of the digits)
64 el peroneo largo
– peroneus longus (long peroneus)

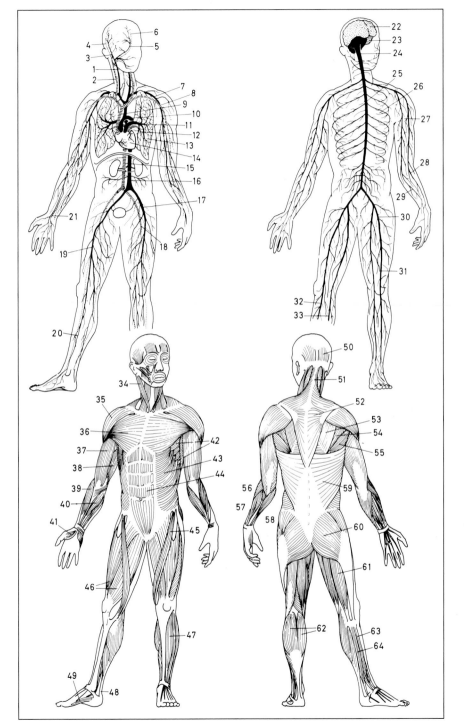

19 Hombre IV   *Man IV*

1-13 la cabeza y el cuello
- *head and neck*
1 el esternocleidomastoideo
- *sternocleidomastoid muscle (sternomastoid muscle)*
2 el músculo occipital
- *occipitalis*
3 el músculo temporal
- *temporalis (temporal, temporal muscle)*
4 el músculo frontal
- *occipito frontalis (frontalis)*
5 el músculo orbicular de los párpados
- *orbicularis oculi*
6 los músculos de la expresión facial (músculos *m* faciales)
- *muscles of facial expression*
7 el masetero
- *masseter*
8 el músculo orbicular de los labios
- *orbicularis oris*
9 la glándula parótida
- *parotid gland*
10 el ganglio linfático; *mal llamado:* la glándula linfática
- *lymph node (submandibular lymph gland)*
11 la glándula submaxilar
- *submandibular gland (submaxillary gland)*
12 los músculos de cuello
- *muscles of the neck*
13 el bocado de Adán (la nuez) [más apreciable en los hombres]
- *Adam's apple (laryngeal prominence) [in men only]*
14-37 la boca y la faringe
- *mouth and pharynx*
14 el labio superior
- *upper lip*
15 la encía
- *gum*
16-18 la dentadura
- *teeth (set of teeth)*
16 los incisivos
- *incisors*
17 el colmillo
- *canine tooth (canine)*
18 los molares (las muelas)
- *premolar (bicuspid) and molar teeth (premolars and molars)*
19 la comisura de los labios
- *angle of the mouth (labial commissure)*
20 el paladar duro
- *hard palate*
21 el paladar blando (el velo del paladar)
- *soft palate (velum palati, velum)*
22 la úvula (la campanilla)
- *uvula*
23 la amígdala
- *palatine tonsil (tonsil)*
24 la cavidad faríngea (la faringe)
- *pharyngeal opening (pharynx)*
25 la lengua
- *tongue*
26 el labio inferior
- *lower lip*

27 la mandíbula superior
- *upper jaw (maxilla)*
28-37 el diente (*Salv.:* el tuco)
- *tooth*
28 el periostio dental
- *periodontal membrane (periodontium, pericementum)*
29 el cemento
- *cement (dental cementum, crusta petrosa)*
30 el esmalte
- *enamel*
31 la dentina (el marfil)
- *dentine (dentin)*
32 la pulpa dental
- *dental pulp (tooth pulp, pulp)*
33 los nervios y los vasos sanguíneos
- *nerves and blood vessels*
34 el incisivo
- *incisor*
35 la muela (el molar)
- *molar tooth (molar)*
36 la raíz
- *root (fang)*
37 la corona
- *crown*
38-51 el ojo
- *eye*
38 la ceja
- *eyebrow (supercilium)*
39 el párpado superior
- *upper eyelid (upper palpebra)*
40 el párpado inferior
- *lower eyelid (lower palpebra)*
41 la pestaña
- *eyelash (cilium)*
42 el iris
- *iris*
43 la pupila
- *pupil*
44 los músculos del ojo
- *eye muscles (ocular muscles)*
45 el globo ocular
- *eyeball*
46 el humor (cuerpo *m*) vítreo
- *vitreous body*
47 la córnea
- *cornea*
48 el cristalino
- *lens*
49 la retina
- *retina*
50 el punto ciego (la mácula)
- *blind spot*
51 el nervio óptico
- *optic nerve*
52-63 el pie
- *foot*
52 el dedo gordo
- *big toe (great toe, first toe, hallux, digitus I)*
53 el segundo dedo
- *second toe (digitus II)*
54 el tercer dedo
- *third toe (digitus III)*
55 el cuarto dedo
- *fourth toe (digitus IV)*
56 el dedo chico
- *little toe (digitus minimus, digitus V)*

57 la uña del pie
- *toenail*
58 la parte lateral del pie (la región tenar, el pulpejo)
- *ball of the foot*
59 el maléolo externo
- *lateral malleolus (external malleolus, outer malleolus, malleolus fibulae)*
60 el maléolo interno
- *medial malleolus (internal malleolus, inner malleolus, malleolus tibulae, malleolus medialis)*
61 el empeine (el dorso del pie)
- *instep (medial longitudinal arch, dorsum of the foot, dorsum pedis)*
62 la planta del pie
- *sole of the foot*
63 el talón (el calcaño)
- *heel*
64-83 la mano
- *hand*
64 el pulgar
- *thumb (pollex, digitus I)*
65 el dedo índice
- *index finger (forefinger, second finger, digitus II)*
66 el dedo corazón (el cordial)
- *middle finger (third finger, digitus medius, digitus III)*
67 el dedo anular
- *ring finger (fourth finger, digitus anularis, digitus IV)*
68 el dedo meñique (el auricular)
- *little finger (fifth finger, digitus minimus, digitus V)*
69 el lado radial de la mano
- *radial side of the hand*
70 el lado cubital de la mano
- *ulnar side of the hand*
71 la palma de la mano
- *palm of the hand (palma manus)*
72-74 las líneas de la mano
- *lines of the hand*
72 la línea de la vida
- *life line (line of life)*
73 la línea de la cabeza
- *head line (line of the head)*
74 la línea del corazón
- *heart line (line of the heart)*
75 la región tenar (el pulpejo)
- *ball of the thumb (thenar eminence)*
76 la muñeca
- *wrist (carpus)*
77 la falange
- *phalanx (phalange)*
78 la yema del dedo
- *finger pad*
79 la punta del dedo
- *fingertip*
80 la uña del dedo
- *fingernail (nail)*
81 la lúnula
- *lunule (lunula) of the nail*
82 el nudillo
- *knuckle*
83 el dorso de la mano
- *back of the hand (dorsum of the hand, dorsum manus)*

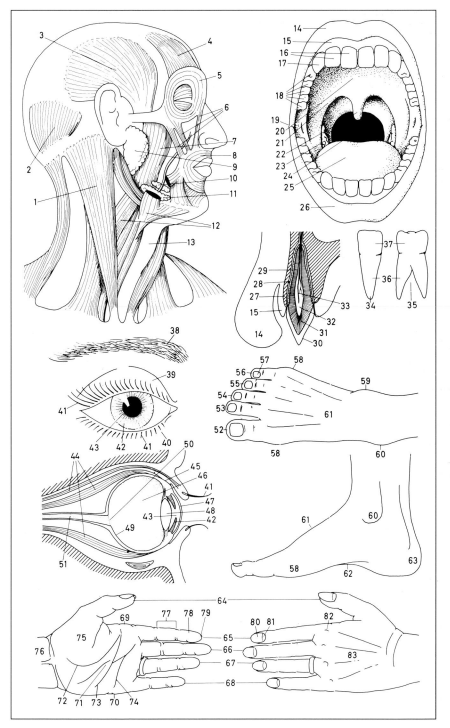

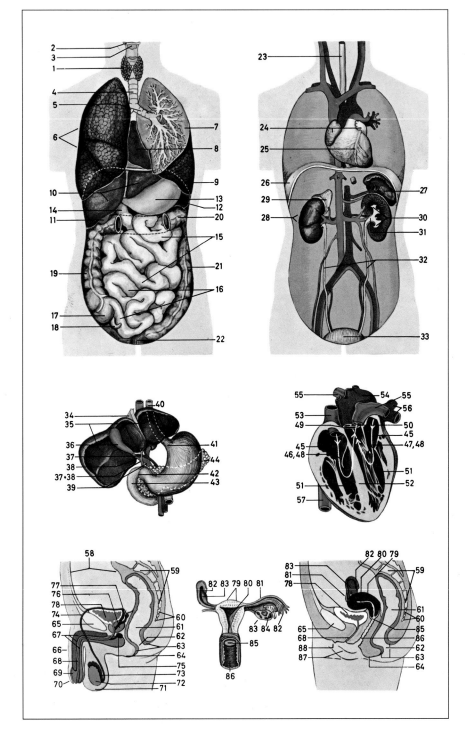

1-57 los órganos internos [vistos de frente]
- *internal organs [front view]*
1 la glándula tiroides
- *thyroid gland*
2 *u.* 3 la laringe
- *larynx*
2 el hueso hioides
- *hyoid bone (hyoid)*
3 el cartílago tiroides
- *thyroid cartilage*
4 la tráquea
- *trachea (windpipe)*
5 los bronquios
- *bronchus*
6 *u.* 7 los pulmones
- *lung*
6 el pulmón derecho
- *right lung*
7 el lóbulo pulmonar superior [corte]
- *upper pulmonary lobe (upper lobe of the lung) [section]*
8 el corazón
- *heart*
9 el diafragma
- *diaphragm*
10 el hígado
- *liver*
11 la vesícula biliar
- *gall bladder*
12 el bazo
- *spleen*
13 el estómago
- *stomach*
14-22 los intestinos
- *intestines (bowel)*
14-16 el intestino delgado
- *small intestine (intestinum tenue)*
14 el duodeno
- *duodenum*
15 el yeyuno
- *jejunum*
16 el íleon
- *ileum*
17-22 el intestino grueso
- *large intestine (intestinum crassum)*
17 el ciego
- *caecum (cecum)*
18 el apéndice
- *appendix (vermiform appendix)*
19 el colon ascendente
- *ascending colon*
20 el colon transverso
- *transverse colon*
21 el colon descendente
- *descending colon*
22 el recto
- *rectum*
23 el esófago
- *oesophagus (esophagus, gullet)*
24 *u.* 25 el corazón
- *heart*
24 la aurícula
- *auricle*
25 el surco longitudinal anterior (el surco interventricular anterior)
- *anterior longitudinal cardiac sulcus*
26 el diafragma
- *diaphragm*
27 el bazo
- *spleen*
28 el riñón derecho
- *right kidney*
29 las glándulas suprarrenales
- *suprarenal gland*
30 *u.* 31 el riñón izquierdo [corte longitudi-

nal]
- *left kidney [longitudinal section]*
30 el cáliz renal
- *calyx (renal calyx)*
31 la pelvis renal
- *renal pelvis*
32 el uréter
- *ureter*
33 la vejiga
- *bladder*
34 *u.* 35 el hígado [visto desde atrás]
- *liver [from behind]*
34 el ligamento suspensor del hígado
- *falciform ligament of the liver*
35 el lóbulo del hígado
- *lobe of the liver*
36 la vesícula biliar
- *gall bladder*
37 *u.* 38 el conducto común de la bilis
- *common bile duct*
37 el conducto hepático
- *hepatic duct (common hepatic duct)*
38 el conducto cístico
- *cystic duct*
39 la vena porta
- *portal vein (hepatic portal vein)*
40 el esófago
- *oesophagus (esophagus, gullet)*
41 *u.* 42 el estómago
- *stomach*
41 el cardias
- *cardiac orifice*
42 el píloro
- *pylorus*
43 el duodeno
- *duodenum*
44 el páncreas
- *pancreas*
45-57 el corazón [corte longitudinal]
- *heart [longitudinal section]*
45 la aurícula
- *atrium*
46 *u.* 47 las válvulas del corazón
- *valves of the heart*
46 la válvula tricúspide
- *tricuspid valve (right atrioventricular valve)*
47 la válvula mitral
- *bicuspid valve (mitral valve, left atrioventricular valve)*
48 la válvula semilunar (válvula *f* de Eustaquio)
- *cusp*
49 la válvula aórtica
- *aortic valve*
50 la válvula pulmonar
- *pulmonary valve*
51 el ventrículo
- *ventricle*
52 el tabique interventricular
- *ventricular septum (interventricular septum)*
53 la vena cava superior
- *superior vena cava*
54 la aorta
- *aorta*
55 la arteria pulmonar
- *pulmonary artery*
56 la vena pulmonar
- *pulmonary vein*
57 la vena cava inferior
- *inferior vena cava*
58 el peritoneo
- *peritoneum*
59 el sacro

- *sacrum*
60 el cóccix
- *coccyx (coccygeal vertebra)*
61 el recto
- *rectum*
62 el ano
- *anus*
63 el esfínter anal
- *anal sphincter*
64 el perineo
- *perineum*
65 el sínfisis del pubis
- *pubic symphisis (symphisis pubis)*
66-77 los órganos sexuales masculinos
[corte longitudinal]
- *male sex organs [longitudinal section]*
66 el pene (*Cuba*: la virtud)
- *penis*
67 el cuerpo cavernoso
- *corpus cavernosum and spongiosum of the penis (erectile tissue of the penis)*
68 la uretra
- *urethra*
69 el glande (bálano *m*)
- *glans penis*
70 el prepucio
- *prepuce (foreskin)*
71 el escroto
- *scrotum*
72 el testículo derecho (*Mé.*: el tompeate)
- *right testicle (testis)*
73 el epidídimo
- *epididymis*
74 el conducto espermático
- *spermatic duct (vas deferens)*
75 la glándula de Cowper
- *Cowper's gland (bulbourethral gland)*
76 la próstata
- *prostate (prostate gland)*
77 la vesícula seminal
- *seminal vesicle*
78 la vejiga
- *bladder*
79-88 los órganos sexuales femeninos
[corte longitudinal]
- *female sex organs [longitudinal section]*
79 el útero
- *uterus (matrix, womb)*
80 la cavidad uterina
- *cavity of the uterus*
81 la trompa de Falopio
- *fallopian tube (uterine tube, oviduct)*
82 la fimbria
- *fimbria (fimbriated extremity)*
83 el ovario
- *ovary*
84 el folículo con el óvulo
- *follicle with ovum (egg)*
85 el orificio uterino externo (el cuello del útero)
- *os uteri externum*
86 la vagina
- *vagina*
87 los labios de la vulva
- *lip of the pudendum (lip of the vulva)*
88 el clítoris
- *clitoris*

21 Primeros auxilios

First Aid

1-13 vendajes *m* **de urgencia** *f*
– *emergency bandages*
1 el vendaje de brazo *m*
– *arm bandage*
2 el pañuelo triangular usado como cabestrillo *m* (un brazo en cabestrillo *m*)
– *triangular cloth used as a sling (an arm sling)*
3 el vendaje de cabeza *f* (la capellina)
– *head bandage (capeline)*
4 el paquete de vendajes *m*
– *first aid kit*
5 el vendaje adhesivo (el vendaje plástico; una tirita)
– *first aid dressing*
6 la gasa esterilizada
– *sterile gauze dressing*
7 el esparadrapo
– *adhesive plaster (sticking plaster)*
8 la herida (*Amér. Central y Mé.*: el tajarrazo)
– *wound*
9 la venda de gasa *f*
– *bandage*
10 el entablillado de urgencia *f* para la fractura de un miembro
– *emergency splint for a broken limb (fractured limb)*
11 la pierna fracturada
– *fractured leg (broken leg)*
12 la tablilla
– *splint*
13 la almohadilla
– *headrest*
14-17 medidas *f* **para restañar la sangre (cuidados** *m* **en caso** *m* **de hemorragia** *f* **)** (la ligadura de un vaso sanguíneo)
– *measures for stanching the blood flow (tying up (ligature) of a blood vessel)*
14 los puntos de presión *f* de las arterias
– *pressure points of the arteries*
15 el torniquete de emergencia *f* en el muslo
– *emergency tourniquet on the thigh*
16 el bastón utilizado para apretar el torniquete
– *walking stick used as a screw*
17 el vendaje de compresión *f*
– *compression bandage*
18-23 el rescate y el transporte de una persona herida
– *rescue and transport of an injured person*
18 el asimiento Rautek (para el rescate de la víctima de un accidente de tráfico *m*)
– *Rautek grip (for rescue of a car accident victim)*
19 el asistente (el auxiliador)
– *helper*
20 el herido sin conocimiento *m* (la víctima de un accidente)
– *injured person (casualty)*

21 el agarre de silla *f* (la silla de la reina)
– *chair grip*
22 la silla de anilla *f* improvisada
– *carrying grip*
23 la camilla de emergencia *f* hecha con bastones *m* y una chaqueta
– *emergency stretcher of sticks and a jacket*
24-27 la posición de una persona inconsciente y la respiración artificial
– *positioning of an unconscious person and artificial respiration (resuscitation)*
24 la posición lateral de seguridad *f*
– *coma position*
25 la persona inconsciente
– *unconscious person*
26 la respiración boca *f* a boca *f* (*variable*: la respiración boca *f* a nariz *f*)
– *mouth-to-mouth resuscitation (variation: mouth-to-nose resuscitation)*
27 el reanimador eléctrico, un aparato de reanimación *f*, un aparato de respiración *f* artificial
– *resuscitator (respiratory apparatus, resuscitation apparatus), a respirator (artificial breathing device)*
28-33 métodos *m* **de rescate** *m* **en los accidentes sobre hielo** *m*
– *methods of rescue in ice accidents*
28 la persona hundida en el hielo
– *person who has fallen through the ice*
29 el socorrista
– *rescuer*
30 la cuerda (*Amér. Central y Merid.*: el peal)
– *rope*
31 la mesa (u otro medio de socorro *m*)
– *table (or similar device)*
32 la escalera
– *ladder*
33 el salvamento por uno mismo (el autosalvamento)
– *self-rescue*
34-38 el rescate de los ahogados
– *rescue of a drowning person*
34 la liberación del apretón
– *method of release (release grip, release) to free rescuer from the clutch of a drowning person*
35 el ahogado (la persona que se está ahogando)
– *drowning person*
36 el socorrista
– *lifesaver*
37 *u.* **38 el remolque** (presas *f* de transporte *m*)
– *towing (tows)*
37 la presa axilar
– *double shoulder tow*
38 la presa por la cabeza
– *head tow*

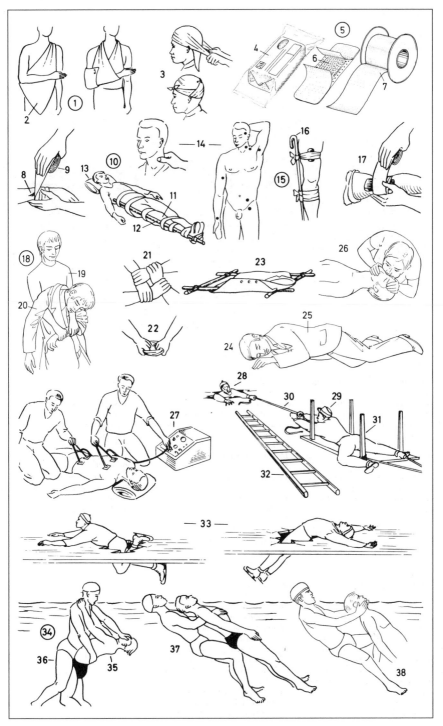

1-74 el consultorio de medicina *f* **general**
- *general practice* (Am. *physician's office)*

1 la sala de espera *f*
- *waiting room*

2 el paciente
- *patient*

3 los pacientes citados (para un reconocimiento de rutina *f* o para la renovación de recetas *f*)
- *patients with appointments (for a routine check-up or renewal of prescription)*

4 las revistas de la sala de espera *f*
- *magazines [for waiting patients]*

5 la consulta (el despacho de la consulta)
- *reception*

6 el fichero de pacientes *m*
- *patients file*

7 las fichas médicas caducadas
- *eliminated index cards*

8 la ficha médica
- *medical record (medical card)*

9 el volante de asistencia *f* médica
- *health insurance certificate*

10 el almanaque de propaganda *f*
- *advertising calendar (publicity calendar)*

11 el libro de citas *f*
- *appointments book*

12 el archivador de correspondencia *f*
- *correspondence file*

13 el teléfono con contestador *m* y grabador *m* automáticos
- *automatic telephone answering and recording set (telephone answering device)*

14 el radioteléfono
- *radiophone*

15 el micrófono
- *microphone*

16 el panel de exhibición *f*
- *illustrated chart*

17 el almanaque de pared *f*
- *wall calendar*

18 el teléfono
- *telephone*

19 la enfermera
- *[doctor's] assistant*

20 la receta
- *prescription*

21 el listín telefónico
- *telephone index*

22 el diccionario médico
- *medical dictionary*

23 la farmacopea (el vademécum de los medicamentos registrados)
- *pharmacopoeia (list of registered medicines)*

24 la máquina de franquear (*Amér.:* el contador de franqueo)
- *franking machine (Am. postage meter)*

25 la grapadora (la cosegrapas)
- *stapler*

26 el fichero de diabéticos *m*
- *diabetics file*

27 el dictáfono
- *dictating machine*

28 la taladradora de papeles *m*
- *paper punch*

29 el sello (la estampilla) del médico
- *doctor's stamp*

30 el tampón (la almohadilla) de tinta *f*
- *ink pad*

31 el portalápices
- *pencil holder*

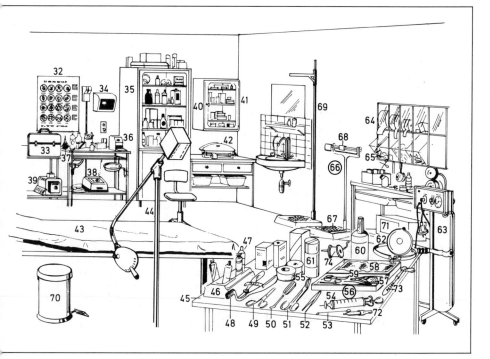

32-74 la sala de curas *f*
- *surgery*
32 el cuadro de agudeza *f* visual
- *chart of eyegrounds*
33 el maletín del médico
- *doctor's bag (doctor's case)*
34 el interfono
- *intercom*
35 el armario de las medicinas
- *medicine cupboard*
36 el dispensador de algodón *m*
- *swab dispenser*
37 el inhalador (el globo de Politzer)
- *inflator (Politzer bag)*
38 el electrotomo
- *electrotome*
39 el esterilizador de vapor *m*
- *steam sterilizer*
40 el armario de pared *f*
- *cabinet*
41 las muestras de medicamentos *m*
- *medicine samples (from the phar-
maceutical industry)*
42 el pesabebés
- *baby scales*
43 la mesa de reconocimiento *m*
- *examination couch*
44 la lámpara con el haz de luz *f* dirigible
- *directional lamp*
45 la mesa de instrumentos *m*
- *instrument table*
46 el portatubos
- *tube holder*
47 el tubo de pomada *f*
- *tube of ointment*

48-50 los instrumentos de cirugía *f*
menor
- *instruments for minor surgery*
48 el abreboca
- *mouth gag*
49 las pinzas Kocher
- *Kocher's forceps*
50 el raspador
- *scoop (curette)*
51 las tijeras curvas
- *angled scissors*
52 las pinzas
- *forceps*
53 la sonda de botón *m*
- *olive-pointed (bulb-headed) probe*
54 la jeringa para irrigación *f* del oído
o de la vejiga (*Hond., Mé., P. Rico,
S. Dgo.:* la visitadora)
- *syringe for irrigations of the ear or
bladder*
55 el esparadrapo
- *adhesive plaster (sticking plaster)*
56 el material quirúrgico de sutura *f*
- *surgical suture material*
57 una aguja curva para suturas *f*
- *curved surgical needle*
58 la gasa esterilizada
- *sterile gauze*
59 el portaagujas
- *needle holder*
60 el pulverizador para desinfectar la
piel
- *spray for disinfecting the skin*
61 el portahílos
- *thread container*

62 el oftalmoscopio
- *ophthalmoscope*
63 el aparato de congelación *f* para
intervención *f* crioquirúrgica
- *freezer for cryosurgery*
64 el dispensador de esparadrapo *m* y
de elementos *m* pequeños
- *dispenser for plasters and small
pieces of equipment*
65 las agujas y las jeringas de un solo uso
- *disposable hypodermic needles and
syringes*
66 el peso, un peso de corredera *f*
- *scales, sliding-weight scales*
67 la plataforma (el platillo) del peso
- *weighing platform*
68 la corredera del peso
- *sliding weight (jockey)*
69 la talla (el listón para tallar)
- *height gauge (Am. gage)*
70 el cubo de la basura
- *waste bin (Am. trash bin)*
71 el esterilizador caliente
- *hot-air sterilizer*
72 la pipeta
- *pipette*
73 el martillo de reflejos *m* (el martillo
percusor)
- *percussor*
74 el otoscopio (el espéculo auricular)
- *aural speculum (auriscope, aural
syringe)*

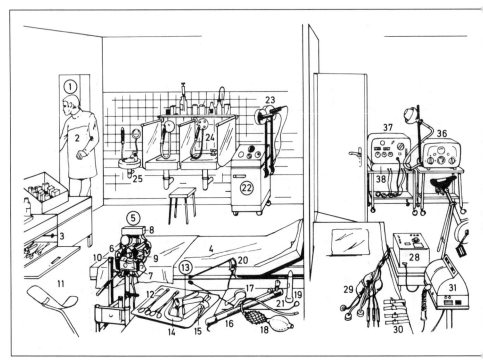

1 la consulta
– *consulting room*
2 el médico de medicina *f* general
– *general practitioner*
**3-21 los instrumentos de
reconocimiento *m* ginecológico y
proctológico**
– *instruments for gynaecological and
proctological examinations*
3 el calentador de los instrumentos a
la temperatura del cuerpo
– *warming the instruments up to body
temperature*
4 la mesa de reconocimiento *m*
– *examination couch*
5 el colposcopio
– *colposcope*
6 el binocular
– *binocular eyepiece*
7 la cámara miniatura (la cámara para
fotos *m* de pequeño formato *m*)
– *miniature camera*
8 la fuente de luz *f* fría
– *cold light source*
9 el disparador
– *cable release*
10 el tubo para la fijación del pie
– *bracket for the leg support*
11 el soporte para la pierna
– *leg support (leg holder)*
12 las pinzas de asidero *m* (para coger
los apósitos de algodón *m*)
– *holding forceps (sponge holder)*
13 el espéculo vaginal
– *vaginal speculum*

14 la paleta inferior del espéculo
– *lower blade of the vaginal speculum*
15 la corcheta de platino *m* (para los
frotis)
– *platinum loop (for smears)*
16 el rectoscopio
– *rectoscope*
17 las pinzas de biopsia *f* para el rectoscopio
– *biopsy forceps used with the rectoscope (proctoscope)*
18 el insuflador de aire *m* para el rectoscopio
– *insufflator for proctoscopy (rec-
toscopy)*
19 el proctoscopio (el espéculo rectal)
– *proctoscope (rectal speculum)*
20 el fibroscopio urinario (el uretro-
scopio)
– *urethroscope*
21 la sonda guía para el proctoscopio
– *guide for inserting the proctoscope*
22 la unidad diatérmica (el aparato de
ondas *f* cortas)
– *diathermy unit (short-wave therapy
apparatus)*
23 el radiador
– *radiator*
24 el inhalador
– *inhaling apparatus (inhalator)*
25 la escupidera (el lavabo para los
esputos; *Arg., Chile y Urug.:* la sali-
vadera)
– *basin [for sputum]*

26-31 la ergometría
– *ergometry*
26 el cicloergómetro (el ergómetro de
bicicleta *f*)
– *bicycle ergometer*
27 el monitor (la pantalla de visualización *f* del ECG y de la frecuencia
cardíaca y respiratoria durante el
esfuerzo)
– *monitor (for visual display of the
ECG and of pulse and respiratory
rates when performing work)*
28 el ECG (el electrocardiógrafo)
– *ECG (electrocardiograph)*
29 los electrodos de ventosa *f*
– *suction electrodes*
30 los electrodos de correa *f* para las
extremidades
– *strap-on electrodes for the limbs*
31 el espirómetro (para medir las funciones respiratorias)
– *spirometer (for measuring respiratory functions)*
32 la toma de la presión sanguínea (de
la tensión)
– *measuring blood pressure*
33 el tensiómetro (el esfigmómetro)
– *sphygmomanometer*
34 la abrazadera hinchable
– *inflatable cuff*
35 el estetoscopio
– *stethoscope*
36 la unidad de tratamiento *f* por
microondas *f*
– *microwave treatment unit*

37 el aparato de faradización *f* (aplicación *f* de las corrientes de baja frecuencia *f* con diferentes formas *f* de impulsos *m*)
– *faradization unit (for applying low-frequency currents with different pulse shapes)*
38 el aparato de sintonización *f* automática
– *automatic tuner*
39 el aparato de terapia *f* con ondas *f* cortas
– *short-wave therapy apparatus*
40 el microcronómetro
– *timer*
41-59 el laboratorio
– *laboratory*
41 la ayudante técnica del laboratorio (la laborante)
– *medical laboratory technician*
42 el soporte de los tubos capilares para la sedimentación de la sangre
– *capillary tube stand for blood sedimentation*
43 la probeta para medir
– *measuring cylinder*
44 la pipeta automática
– *automatic pipette*
45 la cubeta de forma *f* arriñonada
– *kidney dish*
46 el electrocardiógrafo portátil para urgencias *f*
– *portable ECG machine for emergency use*

47 el aparato de pipeta *f* automático (el titrímetro automático)
– *automatic pipetting device*
48 el baño de agua a temperatura *f* constante
– *constant temperature water bath*
49 el grifo con trompa *f* de agua *f*
– *tap with water jet pump*
50 la cubeta de coloración *f* (para la coloración de los frotis sanguíneos, los sedimentos y otros frotis *m*)
– *staining dish (for staining blood smears, sediments, and other smears)*
51 el microscopio binocular de investigación *f*
– *binocular research microscope*
52 el soporte de pipetas *f* para la fotometría
– *pipette stand for photometry*
53 el calculador y analizador *m* de fotometría *f*
– *computer and analyser for photometry*
54 el fotómetro
– *photometer*
55 el contador potenciométrico
– *potentiometric recorder*
56 la sección de transformación *f*
– *transforming section*
57 el material de laboratorio *m*
– *laboratory apparatus (laboratory equipment)*

58 el cuadro de sedimentos *m* de la orina
– *urine sediment chart*
59 la centrifugadora
– *centrifuge*

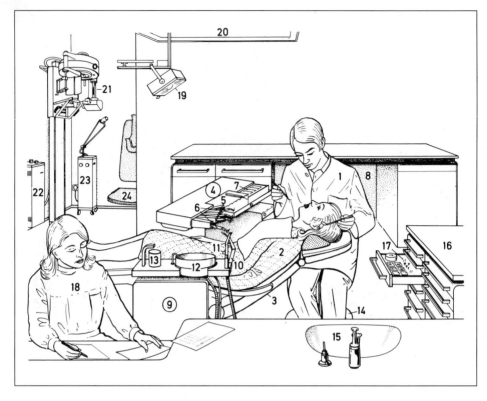

1 el dentista (el odontólogo)	**12** la escudilla para escupir (la escupidera)	**23** el aparato de microondas *f*, un aparato de irradiación *f*
– *dentist (dental surgeon)*	– *basin*	– *microwave treatment unit, a radiation unit*
2 el paciente	**13** el vaso de agua con relleno automático	**24** el asiento
– *patient*	– *water glass, filled automatically*	– *seat*
3 el sillón de dentista *m*	**14** el taburete del dentista	
– *dentist's chair*	– *stool*	
4 los instrumentos dentales	**15** el lavamanos (*sin.:* la palangana. *Amér.:* el platón; *Chile:* la taza)	
– *dental instruments*	– *washbasin*	
5 la bandeja de los instrumentos	**16** el mueble de los instrumentos	
– *instrument tray*	– *instrument cabinet*	
6 las fresas con diferentes piezas *f* de mano *f*	**17** el cajón de las fresas	
– *drills with different handpieces*	– *drawer for drills*	
7 la caja de las medicinas	**18** la ayudante del dentista (la enfermera)	
– *medicine case*	– *dentist's assistant*	
8 la unidad (el armario) de almacenaje (para los instrumentos dentales)	**19** la lámpara de dentista *m*	
– *storage unit (for dental instruments)*	– *dentist's lamp*	
9 la unidad de asistencia *f*	**20** la luz del techo	
– *assistant's unit*	– *ceiling light*	
10 la jeringa multifuncional (para agua *f* fría y caliente, spray *m* o aire *m*)	**21** el aparato de rayos *m* X para radiografías *f* panorámicas	
– *multi-purpose syringe (for cold and warm water, spray, or air)*	– *X-ray apparatus for panoramic pictures*	
11 el aparato de succión *f* de la saliva	**22** el generador de rayos *m* X	
– *suction apparatus*	– *X-ray generator*	

25 la prótesis dental (la dentadura postiza)
– denture (set of false teeth)
26 el puente dental
– bridge (dental bridge)
27 el raigón debidamente preparado
– prepared stump of the tooth
28 la corona (clases: la corona de oro m, la corona de pasta f)
– crown (kinds: gold crown, jacket crown)
29 el diente de porcelana f
– porcelain tooth (porcelain pontic)
30 el empaste
– filling
31 el diente de pivote m
– post crown
32 el revestimiento
– facing
33 el anillo
– diaphragm
34 el pivote
– post
35 el disco de carborundo m
– carborundum disc (disk)
36 el disco de esmeril m
– grinding wheel
37 fresas f para cavidades f
– burs
38 la fresa en forma f de llama f
– flame-shaped finishing bur
39 fresas f de fisuras f
– fissure burs
40 la fresa diamantada
– diamond point
41 el espejo de boca f
– mouth mirror
42 la lámpara de boca f
– mouth lamp
43 el termocauterio (el cauterio)
– cautery
44 el electrodo de platino m iridiado
– platinum-iridium electrode
45 instrumentos m para limpiar los dientes
– tooth scalers
46 la sonda
– probe
47 las tenazas de extracción f
– extraction forceps
48 el elevador (el botador de pie m de cabra f)
– tooth-root elevator
49 el cincel de huesos m
– bone chisel
50 la espátula
– spatula
51 el mezclador del material de empaste m
– mixer for filling material
52 el sincronizador
– synchronous timer

53 la jeringa hipodérmica para la anestesia local (anestesia f del nervio)
– hypodermic syringe for injection of local anaesthetic
54 la aguja hipodérmica
– hypodermic needle
55 el portamatrices
– matrix holder
56 la cubeta para la impresión
– impression tray
57 la lamparilla de alcohol m
– spirit lamp

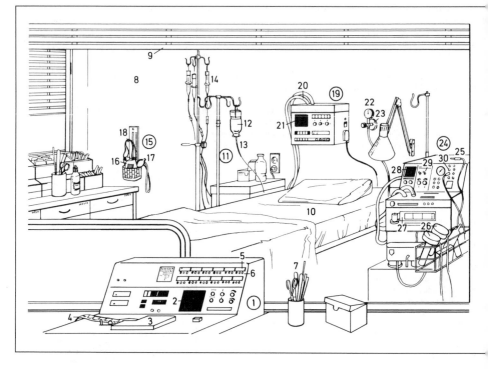

1-30 la sala de cuidados *m* intensivos
(la unidad de vigilancia *f* intensiva,
UVI)
– *intensive care unit*
1-9 la sala de control *m*
– *control room*
1 el pupitre (la consola) para vigilar
el ritmo *m* cardíaco y la presión
sanguínea
– *central control unit for monitoring
heart rhythm (cardiac rhythm) and
blood pressure*
2 el monitor del electrocardiograma
(ECG)
– *electrocardiogram monitor (ECG
monitor)*
3 el aparato registrador
– *recorder*
4 el papel de registro *m*
– *recording paper*
5 la ficha del paciente
– *patient's card*
6 la lámpara indicadora (con una
tecla de selección para cada enfermo *m*)
– *indicator lights (with call buttons
for each patient)*
7 la espátula
– *spatula*
8 la pared transparente
– *window (observation window, glass
partition)*
9 la persiana de separación
– *blind*

10 la cama del paciente
– *bed (hospital bed)*
11 el soporte para los dispositivos de
infusión *f*
– *stand for infusion apparatus*
12 el frasco de infusión *f*
– *infusion bottle*
13 el tubo para el goteo intravenoso
(el gotero)
– *tube for intravenous drips*
14 el dispositivo de infusión *f* para los
medicamentos hidrosolubles
– *infusion device for water-soluble
medicaments*
15 el esfigmómetro (el tensiómetro)
– *sphygmomanometer*
16 la abrazadera hinchable
– *cuff*
17 la pera para inflar
– *inflating bulb*
18 el manómetro de mercurio *m*
– *mercury manometer*
19 el monitor de cama *f*
– *bed monitor*
20 los cables de conexión *f* con la
unidad de control *m* central
– *connecting lead to the central control unit*
21 el monitor del electrocardiograma
(ECG)
– *electrocardiogram monitor (ECG
monitor)*

22 el manómetro de distribución *f* de
oxígeno *m*
– *manometer for the oxygen supply*
23 la conexión de pared *f* para el
tratamiento con oxígeno *m*
– *wall connection for oxygen treatment*
24 la unidad móvil de vigilancia *f* del
paciente
– *mobile monitoring unit*
25 el cable del electrodo del estimulador cardíaco temporal
– *electrode lead to the short-term
pacemaker*
26 los electrodos para el tratamiento
de un shock
– *electrodes for shock treatment*
27 el electrocardiógrafo
– *ECG recording unit*
28 el monitor del electrocardiograma
(ECG)
– *electrocardiogram monitor (ECG
monitor)*
29 los botones para regular el monitor
– *control switches and knobs (controls) for adjusting the monitor*
30 los botones de control *m* del estimulador cardíaco
– *control buttons for the pacemaker
unit*

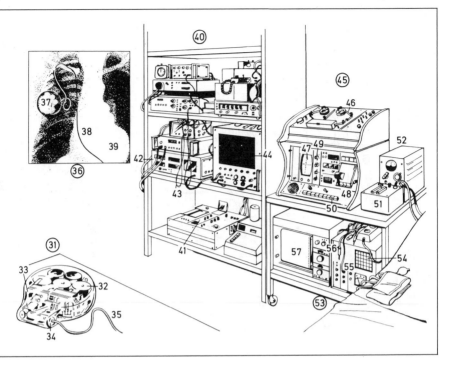

31 **el estimulador cardíaco (el marca-**
   pasos)
   – *pacemaker (cardiac pacemaker)*
32 la pila de mercurio *m*
   – *mercury battery*
33 el generador de impulsos *m* programable
   – *programmed impulse generator*
34 la salida del electrodo
   – *electrode exit point*
35 el electrodo
   – *electrode*
36 la implantación del marcapasos
   – *implantation of the pacemaker*
37 el marcapasos interno
   – *internal cardiac pacemaker (internal
   pacemaker, pacemaker)*
38 el electrodo introducido a través de
   la vena
   – *electrode inserted through the vein*
39 la silueta cardíaca en rayos *m* X
   – *cardiac silhouette on the X-ray*
40 **la unidad de control del marcapasos**
   – *pacemaker control unit*
41 el electrocardiógrafo
   – *electrocardiograph (ECG recorder)*
42 el contador automático de impulsos *m*
   – *automatic impulse meter*
43 el cable de conexión *f* con el
   paciente (cable *m* ECG)

– *ECG lead to the patient*
44 el monitor para el control visual de
   los impulsos del marcapasos
   – *monitor unit for visual monitoring
   of the pacemaker impulses*
45 el analizador del ECG de larga
   duración *f*
   – *long-term ECG analyser*
46 la cinta magnética para la
   grabación de los impulsos del ECG
   durante el análisis
   – *magnetic tape for recording the
   ECG impulses during analysis*
47 el monitor de control del ECG
   – *ECG monitor*
48 el análisis automático del ritmo del
   ECG sobre papel *m*
   – *automatic analysis on paper of the
   ECG rhythm*
49 el botón de ajuste *m* de amplitud *f*
   del ECG
   – *control knob for the ECG amplitude*
50 el teclado de selección *f* del programa de análisis *m* del ECG
   – *program selector switches for the
   ECG analysis*
51 el cargador de las pilas del marcapasos del paciente
   – *charger for the pacemaker batteries*

52 el comprobador de las pilas
   – *battery tester*
53 el manómetro del catéter cardíaco
   derecho
   – *pressure gauge* (Am. *gage*) *for the
   right cardiac catheter*
54 el monitor de control *m* de curvas *f*
   – *trace monitor*
55 el indicador de presión *f*
   – *pressure indicator*
56 el cable de conexión *f* con la impresora de papel *m*
   – *connecting lead to the paper
   recorder*
57 la impresora de papel *m* para las
   curvas de presión *f*
   – *paper recorder for pressure traces*

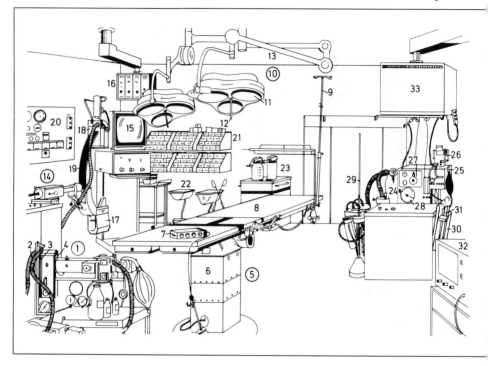

1-54 la sección quirúrgica (la clínica
quirúrgica)
– *surgical unit*
1-33 el quirófano (la sala de operaciones *f*)
– *operating theatre* (Am. *theater)*
1 el aparato de anestesia *f* y de respiración *f*
– *anaesthesia and breathing apparatus (respiratory machine)*
2 los tubos de inhalación *f*
– *inhalers (inhaling tubes)*
3 el indicador volumétrico del
óxido nitroso (protóxido *m* de
nitrógeno *m*)
– *flowmeter for nitrous oxide*
4 el indicador volumétrico del
oxígeno
– *oxygen flow meter*
5 la mesa de operaciones *f* sobre
pedestal *m*
– *pedestal operating table*
6 el pedestal de la mesa de operaciones *f*
– *table pedestal*
7 el aparato de control *m*
– *control device (control unit)*
8 la superficie (el tablero) regulable
de la mesa de operaciones *f*
– *adjustable top of the operating
table*

9 el soporte para el goteo intravenoso
– *stand for intravenous drips*
10 la lámpara de operaciones *f* giratoria sin sombras *f*
– *swivel-mounted shadow-free operating lamp*
11 la lámpara
– *individual lamp*
12 la agarradera
– *handle*
13 el brazo orientable
– *swivel arm*
14 el aparato móvil de radiología *f*
– *mobile fluoroscope*
15 el monitor transformador de la
imagen
– *monitor of the image converter*
16 el monitor [parte trasera]
– *monitor [back]*
17 el tubo
– *tube*
18 el transformador de la imagen
– *image converter*
19 la armazón en forma *f* de C
– *C-shaped frame*
20 el panel de control *m* del aire
acondicionado
– *control panel for the air-conditioning*
21 el material quirúrgico de sutura *f*
– *surgical suture material*

22 la batea para apósitos *m*
– *mobile waste tray*
23 el bote de compresas *f* no esteril-
izadas
– *containers for unsterile (unsteril-
ized) pads*
24 la anestesia y el respirador artificial
– *anaesthesia and respiratory apparatus*
25 la bolsa de control *m* de la respiración (el respirador)
– *respirator*
26 el recipiente de fluotano *m*
(halotano *m*)
– *fluothane container (halothane
container)*
27 el botón de regulación *f* de la ventilación
– *ventilation control knob*
28 el panel de registro *m* con indicador *m* del volumen respiratorio
– *indicator with pointer for respiratory volume*
29 el soporte con los tubos inhal-
adores y el manómetro
– *stand with inhalers (inhaling
tubes) and pressure gauges* (Am.
gages)

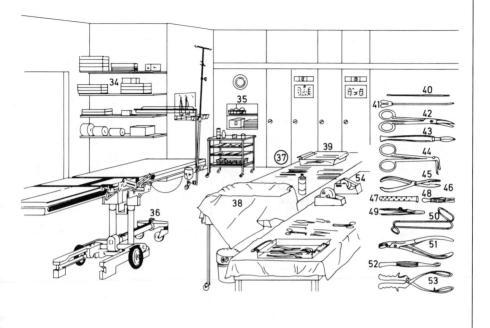

30 el portacatéter
 – catheter holder
31 el catéter en el envase estéril
 – catheter in sterile packing
32 el esfigmógrafo (el registrador de
   las pulsaciones arteriales)
 – sphygmograph
33 el monitor
 – monitor
34-54 la sala de preparación f y de
   esterilización f
 – preparation and sterilization
   room
34 el material de vendaje m
 – dressing material
35 el esterilizador pequeño
 – small sterilizer
36 el carro de la mesa de operaciones f
 – carriage of the operating table
37 la mesa de instrumentos m móvil
 – mobile instrument table
38 el paño estéril
 – sterile cloth
39 la cubeta de los instrumentos
 – instrument tray
40-53 los instrumentos quirúrgicos
 – surgical instruments
40 la sonda de botón m
 – olive-pointed (bulb-headed) probe
41 la sonda acanalada
 – hollow probe

42 las tijeras curvadas
 – curved scissors
43 el bisturí
 – scalpel (surgical knife)
44 las pinzas para ligaduras f
 – ligature-holding forceps
45 las pinzas de secuestro m
 – sequestrum forceps
46 la mandíbula de las pinzas
 – jaw
47 el tubo de drenaje m
 – drainage tube
48 el torniquete (el clamp arterial)
 – surgeon's tourniquet
49 las pinzas para arterias f
 – artery forceps
50 el separador de alambre m
 – blunt hook
51 las cizallas para huesos m
 – bone nippers (bone-cutting forceps)
52 la cucharilla (la cureta) para el
   raspado m (para el curetaje)
 – scoop (curette) for erasion (curet-
   tage)
53 los fórceps
 – obstetrical forceps
54 el rollo de esparadrapo m
 – roll of plaster

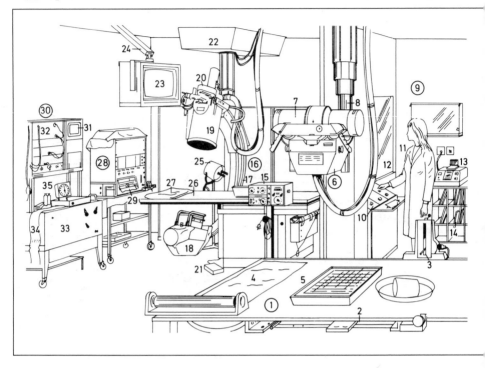

1-35 el servicio de radiología (la unidad de rayos *m* X)
– *X-ray unit*
1 la mesa de reconocimiento *m* de rayos *m* X
– *X-ray examination table*
2 el soporte para las placas de rayos *m* X
– *support for X-ray cassettes*
3 el ajuste vertical del haz central para los clichés laterales
– *height adjustment of the central beam for lateral views*
4 la compresa para la radiografía de los riñones y de las vías biliares (urografía *f* y colecistografía *f*)
– *compress for pyelography and cholecystography*
5 la cubeta de los instrumentos
– *instrument basin*
6 el equipo de rayos *m* X para la urétero-pielografía
– *X-ray apparatus for pyelograms*
7 el tubo de rayos *m* X
– *X-ray tube*
8 el soporte telescópico del tubo de rayos *m* X
– *telescopic X-ray support*
9 la sala de control *m* central de rayos *m* X
– *central X-ray control unit*

10 el pupitre de control *m*
– *control panel (control desk)*
11 la enfermera radiógrafa
– *radiographer (X-ray technician)*
12 la ventana que da a la sala de angiografía *f*
– *window to the angiography room*
13 el oxímetro
– *oxymeter*
14 las placas para urografía *f*
– *pyelogram cassettes*
15 el aparato para inyección *f* de productos *m* de contraste *m*
– *contrast medium injector*
16 el amplificador de imagen *f* de rayos *m* X
– *X-ray image intensifier*
17 la armazón en forma *f* de C
– *C-shaped frame*
18 la cabeza de radiografía *f* con el tubo de rayos *m* X
– *X-ray head with X-ray tube*
19 el transformador de imagen *f* con el tubo transformador
– *image converter with converter tube*
20 la cámara de película *f*
– *film camera*
21 el interruptor de pedal *m*
– *foot switch*

22 el soporte móvil
– *mobile mounting*
23 el monitor
– *monitor*
24 el brazo giratorio del monitor
– *swivel-mounted monitor support*
25 la lámpara sin sombras *f*
– *operating lamp*
26 la mesa de reconocimientos *m* angiográficos
– *angiographic examination table*
27 la almohada
– *pillow*
28 el registrador de ocho canales *m*
– *eight-channel recorder*
29 el papel de registro *m*
– *recording paper*
30 la unidad de control *m* del catéter para la cateterización del corazón
– *catheter gauge* (Am. *gage) unit for catheterization of the heart*

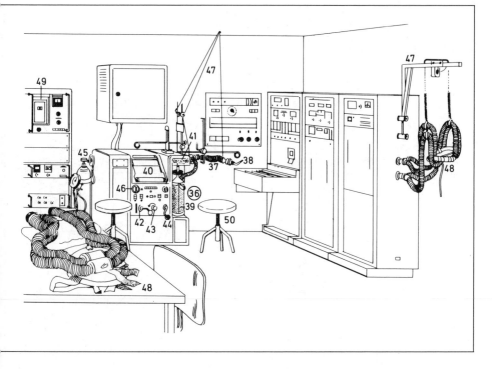

31 el monitor de seis canales *m* para
las curvas de tensión *f* y ECG *m*
– *six-channel monitor for pressure
graphs and ECG*
32 las cajas transductoras de presión *f*
– *slide-in units of the pressure trans-
ducer*
33 la unidad del papel de registro *m*
con revelador *m* para la reproducción fotográfica
– *paper recorder unit with developer
for photographic recording*
34 el papel de registro *m* (de
grabación *f*)
– *recording paper*
35 el cronómetro (el reloj)
– *timer*
36-50 espirometría *f*
– *spirometry*
36 el espirógrafo para la exploración
del funcionamiento respiratorio
– *spirograph for pulmonary function tests*
37 el tubo respiratorio
– *breathing tube*
38 la boquilla
– *mouthpiece*
39 el absorbedor de cal *f* sosa
– *soda-lime absorber*
40 el papel de registro *m*
– *recording paper*

41 la regulación para el suministro
de gas *m*
– *control knobs for gas supply*
42 el estabilizador de O_2
– *O_2 stabilizer*
43 la válvula reguladora
– *throttle valve*
44 la conexión del absorbedor
– *absorber attachment*
45 la botella de oxígeno *m*
– *oxygen cylinder*
46 el suministro de agua *f*
– *water supply*
47 el soporte del tubo flexible
– *tube support*
48 la mascarilla
– *mask*
49 el contador del consumo de CO_2
– *CO_2 consumption meter*
50 el taburete del paciente
– *stool for the patient*

1 la cuna con ruedecillas *f*
– *collapsible cot*
2 el balancín de bebé *m*
– *bouncing cradle*
3 la bañera
– *baby bath*
4 el soporte para poner los pañales (el vestidor, el envolvedero)
– *changing top*
5 el recién nacido (el bebé; *Amér.:* la guagua; *Perú:* el ñaño)
– *baby (new-born baby)*
6 la madre
– *mother*
7 el cepillo del pelo
– *hairbrush*
8 el peine
– *comb*
9 la toalla de mano *m*
– *hand towel*
10 el juguete flotante
– *toy duck*
11 la cómoda de la ropita del niño
– *changing unit*
12 el anillo de dentición *f*
– *teething ring*
13 la caja de crema *f*
– *cream jar*

14 el bote de polvos *m* de talco *m*
– *box of baby powder*
15 el chupete (*Amér.:* el chupón)
– *dummy*
16 la pelota
– *ball*
17 el saco de dormir del bebé (*Guat.:* el jatico)
– *sleeping bag*
18 la caja de aseo *m*
– *layette box*
19 el biberón (*Amér.:* la mamadera; *Col. y Venez.:* el tetero; *Guat. y Hond.:* el pepe; *Col.:* el chupo)
– *feeding bottle*
20 la tetilla (la tetina)
– *teat*
21 el calientabiberones
– *bottle warmer*
22 las braguitas de plástico *m* para los pañales de usar y tirar (de un solo uso)
– *rubber baby pants for disposable nappies* (Am. *diapers*)
23 la camisita de niño *m*
– *vest*
24 las polainas
– *leggings*

25 la chaquetita del bebé
– *baby's jacket*
26 el gorro
– *hood*
27 la taza para niño *m*
– *baby's cup*
28 el plato para niño *m* (el plato para papillas *f*), un plato calentador
– *baby's plate, a stay-warm plate*
29 el termómetro
– *thermometer*
30 el moisés, un cochecito de niño *m*
– *bassinet, a wicker pram*
31 el juego de ropa de cama *f* del moisés
– *set of bassinet covers*
32 el baldaquín (el dosel)
– *canopy*
33 la silla alta de niño *m*, una silla plegable
– *baby's high chair, a folding chair*
34 el landó (cochecito *m* de niño *m*) con visión *f* panorámica
– *pram (baby-carriage) [with windows]*
35 la capota plegable
– *folding hood*

36 la ventana
 – *window*
37 la silla con ruedas *f*
 – *pushchair* (Am. *stroller*)
38 el folgo (bolsa *f* para abrigar los
 pies)
 – *foot-muff* (Am. *foot-bag*)
39 el parque plegable (el corral plegable)
 – *play pen*
40 el suelo del parque
 – *floor of the play pen*
41 el juego de construcción *f*
 – *building blocks (building bricks)*
42 el niño pequeño (*Amér.:* el pibe;
 Arg. y Urug.: el pabete)
 – *small child*
43 el babero
 – *bib*
44 el sonajero (*Chile:* la sonajera)
 – *rattle (baby's rattle)*
45 las botitas de bebé *m*
 – *bootees*
46 el osito de peluche *m*
 – *teddy bear*

47 el orinal (*Chile:* la pava; *Cuba:* el
 tibor; *Mé.:* la cotorra)
 – *potty (baby's pot)*
48 el capacho (el capazo) portabebés
 – *carrycot*
49 la ventana
 – *window*
50 las asas
 – *handles*

29 Ropa de niños

1-12 la ropa de niños *m* **pequeños**
- *baby clothes*
1 el conjunto de calle *f*
- *pram suit*
2 el gorro (la capucha; *Antillas:* la escofieta)
- *hood*
3 la chaqueta
- *pram jacket (matinée coat)*
4 el pompón (la borla)
- *pompon (bobble)*
5 los patucos (los patines)
- *bootees*
6 la camiseta
- *sleeveless vest*
7 la camiseta de mangas *f* cortas
- *envelope-neck vest*
8 la camisita de bebé *m*
- *wrapover vest*
9 el jersey de bebé *m*
- *baby's jacket*
10 el bragapañal de plástico *m*
- *rubber baby pants*
11 el pelele entero (el pelele con pies *m*)
- *playsuit*
12 el traje de dos piezas *f* para el bebé
- *two-piece suit*
13-30 los trajes de niños *m*
- *infants' wear*
13 el vestido de verano *m*, un vestido con tirantes *m*
- *child's sundress, a pinafore dress*
14 el tirante con volantes *m*
- *frilled shoulder strap*
15 el peto de pliegues *m* fruncidos y bordados
- *shirred top*
16 el sombrero de sol *m*
- *sun hat*
17 el traje de punto *m* de una pieza
- *one-piece jersey suit*
18 la cremallera delantera
- *front zip* (Am. *zipper*)
19 el mono
- *catsuit (playsuit)*
20 la aplicación (el bordado sobre-puesto)
- *motif (appliqué)*
21 el pantaloncito de jugar (el pelele)
- *romper*
22 el jubón (la ranita)
- *playsuit (romper suit)*
23 el pijama entero (el pijama de una pieza)
- *coverall (sleeper and strampler)*
24 el albornoz
- *dressing gown (bath robe)*
25 los pantalones cortos
- *children's shorts*
26 los tirantes
- *braces* (Am. *suspenders*)

27 la camiseta (el tee-shirt)
- *children's T-shirt*
28 el vestido de punto *m*
- *jersey dress (knitted dress)*
29 el bordado
- *embroidery*
30 los calcetines de niño *m* (*Chile:* los botines)
- *children's ankle socks*
31-47 los trajes del escolar
- *school children's wear*
31 el impermeable
- *raincoat*
32 los pantalones de piel *f* (los pan-talones de cuero *m*)
- *leather shorts (lederhosen)*
33 el botón de asta *f*
- *staghorn button*
34 el tirante de cuero *m*
- *braces* (Am. *suspenders*)
35 la braguela
- *flap*
36 el vestido tirolés infantil
- *girl's dirndl*
37 el cordón cruzado
- *cross lacing*
38 el traje entero de nieve *f* (el traje guateado)
- *snow suit (quilted suit)*
39 el pespunte (el enguatado)
- *quilt stitching (quilting)*
40 el pantalón con peto *m* (el mono)
- *dungarees (bib and brace)*
41 la falda con peto *m*
- *bib skirt (bib top pinafore)*
42 los leotardos, los pantis (*ant.:* las calzas)
- *tights*
43 el suéter (el jersey)
- *sweater (jumper)*
44 la chaqueta de símil piel *f*
- *pile jacket*
45 los pantalones de trabillas *f*
- *leggings*
46 la falda (*Amér.:* la pollera)
- *girl's skirt*
47 el jersey (el niqui)
- *child's jumper*
48-68 la ropa de jóvenes *m*
- *teenagers' clothes*
48 la marinera (el blusón de muchacha)
- *girl's overblouse (overtop)*
49 los pantalones de chica *f*
- *slacks*
50 el conjunto de dos piezas *f* (falda *f* y chaqueta *f*) de chica *f*
- *girl's skirt suit*
51 la chaqueta (*Amér.:* el saco)
- *jacket*
52 la falda (*Amér.:* la pollera)
- *skirt*
53 las medias-calcetín
- *knee-length socks*

54 el abrigo de chica *f*
- *girl's coat*
55 el cinturón
- *tie belt*
56 el bolso de chica *f*
- *girl's bag*
57 el sombrero de lana *f*
- *woollen* (Am. *woolen*) *hat*
58 la blusa de chica *f*
- *girl's blouse*
59 la falda-pantalón
- *culottes*
60 los pantalones
- *boy's trousers*
61 la camisa
- *boy's shirt*
62 el anorak
- *anorak*
63 los bolsillos sesgados
- *inset pockets*
64 el cordón de la capucha
- *hood drawstring (drawstring)*
65 los puños de punto *m*
- *knitted welt*
66 la cazadora
- *parka coat (parka)*
67 el cordón para atar
- *drawstring (draw cord)*
68 los bolsillos pegados (los bolsillos de parche *m*)
- *patch pockets*

1 la chaqueta de visón *m*
– *mink jacket*
2 el jersey de cuello *m* enrollado
– *cowl neck jumper*
3 el cuello enrollado (*variedades:*
cuello vuelto, cuello de cisne)
– *cowl collar*
4 el gabán de punto *m*
– *knitted overtop*
5 el cuello marinero
– *turndown collar*
6 la manga vuelta
– *turn-up (turnover) sleeve*
7 el polo de cuello *m* alto
– *polo neck jumper*
8 la saya de vestir (*Cuba:* la
sayuela)
– *pinafore dress*
9 la blusa (con el cuello de solapa *f*)
– *blouse (with revers collar)*
10 el vestido de blusa *f*, un vestido
enteramente abotonado
– *shirt-waister dress, a button-
through dress*
11 el cinturón (*Antillas y Perú:* la
correa)
– *belt*
12 el vestido de invierno *m*
– *winter dress*
13 el ribete
– *piping*
14 el puño
– *cuff*
15 la manga larga
– *long sleeve*
16 el chaleco acolchado (enguatado)
– *quilted waistcoat*
17 el punto de colcha *f* (el pespunte)
– *quilt stitching (quilting)*
18 el adorno de cuero *m*
– *leather trimming*
19 el pantalón largo de invierno *m*
– *winter slacks*
20 el jersey a rayas *f*
– *striped polo jumper*
21 el mono
– *boiler suit (dungarees, bib and
brace)*
22 el bolsillo de parche *m*
– *patch pocket*
23 el bolsillo del pecho
– *front pocket*
24 el peto
– *bib*
25 el vestido de cubrir por encima (el
guardapolvo)
– *wrapover dress (wrap-around
dress)*
26 la blusa de polo *m*
– *shirt*
27 el vestido de folklore *m*
– *peasant-style dress*
28 el ribete de flores *f*
– *floral braid*

29 la túnica (el vestido de túnica *f*)
– *tunic (tunic top)*
30 el puño
– *ribbed cuff*
31 los pespuntes decorativos
– *quilted design*
32 la falda plisada
– *pleated skirt*
33 el vestido de dos piezas *f* de punto *m*
– *two-piece knitted dress*
34 el escotado de barco *m*
– *boat neck, a neckline*
35 la vuelta de manga *f*
– *turn-up*
36 la manga de quimono *m*
– *kimono sleeve*
37 el dibujo de punto *m*
– *knitted design*
38 la cazadora (*Arg.:* la campera)
– *lumber-jacket*
39 el dibujo de trenza *f*
– *cable pattern*
40 la blusa (*Mé.:* el caracol; *Perú:* el
polquín)
– *shirt-blouse*
41 la presilla
– *loop fastening*
42 el bordado
– *embroidery*
43 el cuello alto
– *stand-up collar*
44 el pantalón bombacho
– *cossack trousers*
45 el combinado de dos piezas *f* (el
vestido de casaca *f*)
– *two-piece combination (shirt top
and long skirt)*
46 el lazo
– *tie (bow)*
47 el canesú
– *decorative facing*
48 la raja de la manga
– *cuff slit*
49 la raja del costado
– *side slit*
50 la casulla
– *tabard*
51 la falda abierta por el costado
– *inverted pleat skirt*
52 el pliegue invertido
– *godet*
53 el vestido de noche *f*
– *evening gown*
54 la manga de campana *f* plisada
– *pleated bell sleeve*
55 la blusa de gala *f*
– *party blouse*
56 la falda de gala *f*
– *party skirt*
57 el traje pantalón *m*
– *trouser suit (slack suit)*
58 la chaqueta (*Amér.:* el saco) de
ante *m*
– *suede jacket*

59 el adorno de piel *f*
– *fur trimming*
60 el abrigo de piel *f* (*variedades:*
astracán, breitschwanz *m*, visón
m, marta *f* cebellina)
– *fur coat* (kinds: *Persian lamb,
broadtail, mink, sable*)
61 el abrigo de invierno *m* (el abrigo
de paño *m*) (*Arg., Chile y Salv.:* el
tapado)
– *winter coat (cloth coat)*
62 el puño de piel *f*
– *fur cuff (fur-trimmed cuff)*
63 el cuello de piel *f*
– *fur collar (fur-trimmed collar)*
64 el abrigo de loden *m*
– *loden coat*
65 la esclavina (*Chile y Arg.:* el
capingo)
– *cape*
66 los botones de palillo *m*
– *toggle fastenings*
67 la falda de loden *m*
– *loden skirt*
68 la capa-poncho
– *poncho-style coat*
69 la capucha
– *hood*

31 Ropa de señora II (ropa de verano)   *Ladies' Wear II (Summer Wear)*

1 el traje sastre
 – *skirt suit*
2 la chaqueta (*Amér.*: el saco) del traje
 – *jacket*
3 la falda del traje
 – *skirt*
4 el bolsillo sesgado
 – *inset pocket*
5 el pespunte
 – *decorative stitching*
6 el traje chaqueta *f*
 – *dress and jacket combination*
7 el ribete
 – *piping*
8 el vestido de tirantes *m*
 – *pinafore dress*
9 el vestido de verano *m*
 – *summer dress*
10 el cinturón (*Antillas y Perú:* la correa)
 – *belt*
11 el vestido de dos piezas *f*
 – *two-piece dress*
12 la hebilla de cinturón *m*
 – *belt buckle*
13 la falda cruzada
 – *wrapover (wrap-around) skirt*
14 la línea tubo *m*
 – *pencil silhouette*
15 los botones de la hombrera *f*
 – *shoulder buttons*
16 la manga de murciélago *m*
 – *batwing sleeve*
17 el sobrevestido
 – *overdress*
18 el canesú quimono *m*
 – *kimono yoke*
19 el cinturón anudado
 – *tie belt*
20 el abrigo de verano *m*
 – *summer coat*
21 la capucha fija
 – *detachable hood*
22 la blusa de verano *m*
 – *summer blouse*
23 la solapa
 – *lapel*
24 la falda
 – *skirt*
25 el pliegue delantero
 – *front pleat*
26 el vestido tirolés (el vestido dirndl)
 – *dirndl (dirndl dress)*
27 la manga fofa (la manga abombada)
 – *puffed sleeve*
28 el collar tirolés (el collar de folklore *m*)
 – *dirndl necklace*
29 la blusa tirolesa
 – *dirndl blouse*

30 el corpiño
 – *bodice*
31 el delantal tirolés
 – *dirndl apron*
32 el adorno de encaje *m* (el encaje), un encaje de algodón *m*
 – *lace trimming (lace), cotton lace*
33 el delantal de volantes *m*
 – *frilled apron*
34 el volante (*Arg. y Venez.*: el colado)
 – *frill*
35 la casaca (*Col., C. Rica y Chile:* el palto)
 – *smock overall*
36 el vestido de casa *f*
 – *house frock (house dress)*
37 la chaqueta (*Amér.*: el saco) de popelina *f*
 – *poplin jacket*
38 la camiseta (el tee-shirt)
 – *T-shirt*
39 el pantalón corto de señora *f* (el short)
 – *ladies' shorts*
40 la vuelta del pantalón
 – *trouser turn-up*
41 el cinturón
 – *waistband*
42 la cazadora
 – *bomber jacket*
43 la cinturilla elástica
 – *stretch welt*
44 las bermudas
 – *Bermuda shorts*
45 el pespunte
 – *saddle stitching*
46 el cuello de volantes *m*
 – *frill collar*
47 el nudo
 – *knot*
48 la falda-pantalón
 – *culotte*
49 el conjunto
 – *twin set*
50 la chaqueta (*Amér.*: el saco) de punto *m*
 – *cardigan*
51 el suéter
 – *sweater*
52 el pantalón de verano *m*
 – *summer (lightweight) slacks*
53 el mono
 – *jumpsuit*
54 la vuelta de manga *f* (el puño vuelto)
 – *turn-up*
55 la cremallera
 – *zip* (Am. *zipper*)
56 el bolsillo de parche *m* (*Amér. Central, Mé., y Perú:* la bolsa)
 – *patch pocket*

57 el pañuelo de cuello *m*
 – *scarf (neckerchief)*
58 el conjunto de dos piezas *f* vaqueras
 – *denim suit*
59 la chaqueta vaquera
 – *denim waistcoat*
60 el pantalón vaquero (los jeans, blue jeans)
 – *jeans (denims)*
61 la sobreblusa (la túnica; *Ec. y Perú:* la polca)
 – *overblouse*
62 la manga remangada
 – *turned-up sleeve*
63 el cinturón elástico
 – *stretch belt*
64 la camiseta de espaldas *f* desnudas (el tee-shirt de espaldas *f* desnudas)
 – *halter top*
65 el jersey casaca *f*
 – *knitted overtop*
66 el cinturón de jareta *f*
 – *drawstring waist*
67 el suéter de verano *m*
 – *short-sleeved jumper*
68 el escote en forma *f* de V
 – *V-neck (vee-neck)*
69 el cuello camisero
 – *turndown collar*
70 la elástico de punto *m*
 – *knitted welt*
71 el chal (el chal triangular; *Mé.:* el tápalo)
 – *shawl*

1-15 la ropa interior de señora *f* (la lencería)
- *ladies' underwear (ladies' underclothes, lingerie)*
1 el sostén (el sujetador)
- *brassière (bra)*
2 la faja de braga *f*
- *pantie-girdle*
3 la faja corsé *m*
- *pantie-corselette*
4 el sostén de cuerpo *m* (el sostén largo)
- *longline brassière (longline bra)*
5 la faja elástica
- *stretch girdle*
6 la liga
- *suspender*
7 la camiseta de señora *f*
- *vest*
8 las bragas
- *pantie briefs*
9 la media corta (la calceta) de señora *f*
- *ladies' knee-high stocking*
10 la braga pantalón *m*
- *long-legged (long leg) panties*
11 los calzoncillos largos (los leotardos sin pie *m*)
- *long pants*
12 los leotardos (*ant.*: las calzas)
- *tights (pantie-hose)*
13 la combinación (*Amér.*: el fustán)
- *slip*
14 la media combinación (la enagua)
- *waist slip*
15 las bragas slip *m*
- *bikini briefs*
16-21 la ropa de noche *f* de señora *f*
- *ladies' nightwear*
16 el camisón (*Col.* y *P. Rico:* la camisola)
- *nightdress (nightgown, nightie)*
17 el pijama
- *pyjamas* (Am. *pajamas*)
18 la camiseta del pijama
- *pyjama top*
19 el pantalón del pijama
- *pyjama trousers*
20 la bata de casa *f* y de baño *m* (*Col.*: el chingue)
- *housecoat*
21 el juego de camiseta *f* y pantalón *m* corto (utilizado como pijama *m* o para los ratos de ocio *m*)
- *vest and shorts set [for leisure wear and as nightwear]*
22-29 la ropa interior de caballero *m*
- *men's underwear (men's underclothes)*
22 la camiseta de red *f* (de malla *f*)
- *string vest*

23 los calzoncillos de red *f*
- *string briefs*
24 la bragueta
- *front panel*
25 la camiseta sin mangas *f* (*P. Rico y Río de Plata:* la camisilla; *Cuba, P. Rico y Venez.:* la franela; *Col.:* el capisayo; *Cuba y Chile:* la paloma)
- *sleeveless vest*
26 los calzoncillos (el slip; *P. Rico:* los pantaloncillos)
- *briefs*
27 los calzoncillos largos
- *trunks*
28 la camiseta de mangas *f* cortas
- *short-sleeved vest*
29 los calzones
- *long johns*
30 los tirantes (*Arg., Bol.* y *Urug.:* los tiradores; *Col.* y *Mé.:* las tirantas; *Arg.:* los tiros; *Chile:* los suspensores; *Col.:* las cargaderas)
- *braces* (Am. *suspenders*)
31 el clip de los tirantes
- *braces clip*
32-34 los calcetines de caballero *m*
- *men's socks*
32 el calcetín de caña *f* larga
- *knee-length sock*
33 el elástico del calcetín
- *elasticated top*
34 el calcetín bajo (*Chile:* el botín)
- *long sock*
35-37 la ropa de noche *f* de caballero *m*
- *men's nightwear*
35 el batín (la bata)
- *dressing gown*
36 el pijama
- *pyjamas* (Am. *pajamas*)
37 la camisa de cama *f* (de caballero *m*)
- *nightshirt*
38-47 las camisas de caballero *m*
- *men's shirts*
38 la camisa de sport *m*
- *casual shirt*
39 el cinturón (la correa; *Amér.:* el fajo)
- *belt*
40 el pañuelo de cuello *m* (el fular)
- *cravat*
41 la corbata
- *tie*
42 el nudo de corbata
- *knot*
43 la camisa de smoking *m*
- *dress shirt*
44 la pechera plisada (el plastrón plisado)
- *frill (frill front)*
45 el puño
- *cuff*

46 los gemelos (*P. Rico, Urug.* y *Venez.:* las yuntas)
- *cuff link*
47 la pajarita (el lazo de smoking *m*, la palomita)
- *bow-tie*

1-67 la moda masculina
- *men's fashion*
1 el traje de chaqueta *f*, un traje de caballero *m* (*Antillas, Arg. y Col.:* el flus)
- *single-breasted suit, a man's suit*
2 la chaqueta (la americana; *Amér.:* el saco)
- *jacket*
3 el pantalón
- *suit trousers*
4 el chaleco
- *waistcoat (vest)*
5 la solapa
- *lapel*
6 la pernera del pantalón con raya *f*
- *trouser leg with crease*
7 el smoking, un traje de noche *f* (un traje de fiesta *f*)
- *dinner dress, an evening suit*
8 la solapa de seda *f*
- *silk lapel*
9 el bolsillo de pecho *m*
- *breast pocket*
10 el pañuelo del traje (el pañuelo que se coloca en el bolsillo superior de la chaqueta)
- *dress handkerchief*
11 la pajarita (el lazo de smoking *m*, la palomita)
- *bow-tie*
12 el bolsillo exterior
- *side pocket*
13 el frac, un traje de etiqueta *f*
- *tailcoat (tails), evening dress*
14 el faldón
- *coat-tail*
15 el chaleco blanco del frac
- *white waistcoat (vest)*
16 la pajarita blanca
- *white bow-tie*
17 el traje de sport *m*
- *casual suit*
18 la solapa del bolsillo
- *pocket flap*
19 el canesú delantero
- *front yoke*
20 el traje vaquero
- *denim suit*
21 la chaqueta (*Amér.:* el saco) vaquera
- *denim jacket*
22 el pantalón vaquero (los jeans, blue jeans)
- *jeans (denims)*
23 el cinturón (la correa; *Amér.:* el fajo)
- *waistband*
24 el traje playero
- *beach suit*
25 el pantalón corto (los shorts)
- *shorts*
26 la chaqueta de mangas *f* cortas
- *short-sleeved jacket*

27 el traje de deporte *m* (el chandal)
- *tracksuit*
28 la chaqueta del chandal con cremallera *f*
- *tracksuit top with zip*
29 el pantalón del chandal
- *tracksuit bottoms*
30 la chaqueta de punto *m*
- *cardigan*
31 el cuello de punto *m*
- *knitted collar*
32 el jersey de verano *m* para hombres *m*
- *men's short-sleeved pullover (men's short-sleeved sweater)*
33 la camisa de mangas *f* cortas
- *short-sleeved shirt*
34 el botón de la camisa
- *shirt button*
35 la vuelta de la manga
- *turn-up*
36 la camisa de punto *m* (el polo)
- *knitted shirt*
37 la camisa de sport *m* (*Amér.:* la guayabera; *S. Dgo.:* la guerrillera)
- *casual shirt*
38 el bolsillo de parche *m*
- *patch pocket*
39 la chaqueta de sport *m* (la cazadora; *Arg.:* la campera)
- *casual jacket*
40 el pantalón de cinturilla en la rodilla (el pantalón de media pierna *f*)
- *knee-breeches*
41 la cinturilla de la rodilla *f*
- *knee strap*
42 el calcetín largo (la calceta)
- *knee-length sock*
43 la chaqueta de cuero *m*
- *leather jacket*
44 el mono de peto *m* y tirantes *m*
- *bib and brace overalls*
45 los tirantes regulables
- *adjustable braces* (Am. suspenders)
46 el bolsillo de pecho *m*
- *front pocket*
47 el bolsillo del pantalón
- *trouser pocket*
48 la bragueta
- *fly*
49 el bolsillo para el metro
- *rule pocket*
50 la camisa a cuadros *m*
- *check shirt*
51 el jersey de hombre *m*
- *men's pullover*
52 el jersey de esquí *m*
- *heavy pullover*
53 el chaleco de punto *m*
- *knitted waistcoat (vest)*
54 el blazer (la chaqueta ligera)
- *blazer*

55 el botón de la chaqueta
- *jacket button*
56 el guardapolvo de trabajo *m* (el guardapolvo blanco; la bata blanca)
- *overall*
57 la trinchera de lluvia *f*, una trinchera
- *trenchcoat*
58 el cuello de la trinchera
- *coat collar*
59 el cinturón de la trinchera
- *coat belt*
60 el abrigo (de entretiempo *m*) de popelina *f*
- *poplin coat*
61 el bolsillo del abrigo
- *coat pocket*
62 la hilera oculta de botones *m*
- *fly front*
63 el chaquetón de paño *m* (el gabán, el sobretodo)
- *car coat*
64 el botón del abrigo
- *coat button*
65 el pañuelo de cuello *m* (el fular)
- *scarf*
66 el abrigo de paño *m*
- *cloth coat*
67 el guante
- *glove*

1-25 cortes *m* **de barba** *f* **y peinados** *m* **de caballero** *m*
– *men's beards and hairstyles (haircuts)*
1 el cabello largo y suelto
– *long hair worn loose*
2 la peluca larga (la peluca de Estado *m*, peluca *f* de circunstancias *f*), una peluca; *más corta y lisa:* la media peluca (el bisoñé)
– *allonge periwig (full-bottomed wig), a wig;* shorter and smoother: *bob wig, toupet*
3 los rizos (*Amér.:* los churos; *Bol.:* los quimachis; *Chile:* los lulos; *Ec.:* los enganchabobos; *Mé.:* los compromisos)
– *curls*
4 la peluca de bolsa *f* (la peluca a lo Mozart)
– *bag wig (purse wig)*
5 la peluca de coleta *f*
– *pigtail wig*
6 la coleta
– *queue (pigtail)*
7 el lazo de la coleta (*Bol.:* el jarichi)
– *bow (ribbon)*
8 el bigote
– *handlebars (handlebar moustache, Am. mustache)*
9 la raya en medio *m*
– *centre (Am. center) parting*
10 la barba en punta *f* (la perilla)
– *goatee (goatee beard), chintuft*
11 el corte de pelo *m* al cepillo *m* (cabellos *m* al cepillo *m*)
– *closely-cropped head of hair (crew cut)*
12 las patillas (*Col. y Ec.:* las balcarrotas)
– *whiskers*
13 la barba a lo Enrique IV, una barba puntiaguda y bigote *m* (la barba de chivo *m*)
– *Vandyke beard (stiletto beard, bodkin beard), with waxed moustache (Am. mustache)*
14 la raya al lado *m*
– *side parting*
15 la barba cerrada (la barba corrida)
– *full beard (circular beard, round beard)*
16 la barba cuadrada
– *tile beard*
17 la mosca [bajo el labio inferior] (*Mé.:* la piocha; *Col.:* el candado)
– *shadow*
18 el cabello ensortijado (la cabeza de artista *m*)
– *head of curly hair*
19 el bigote estilo *m* inglés (el bigote de cepillo *m*)
– *military moustache (Am. mustache) (English-style moustache)*

20 la cabeza calva (el calvo)
– *partly bald head*
21 la calva (la calvicie)
– *bald patch*
22 la calva total (el calvo; *Arg., Ec. y Perú:* el mate)
– *bald head*
23 la barba de tres días *m* (la barba hirsuta; los cañones de la barba)
– *stubble beard (stubble, short beard bristles)*
24 las patillas (*Col. y Ec.:* las balcarrotas)
– *side-whiskers (sideboards, sideburns)*
25 el afeitado completo (la cara afeitada)
– *clean shave*
26 el peinado afro (para hombres *m* y mujeres *f*)
– *Afro look (for men and women)*
27-38 peinados *m* **de mujer** *f* (peinados *m* de señoras *f* y señoritas *f*)
– *ladies' hairstyles (coiffures, women's and girls' hairstyles)*
27 la cola de caballo *m*
– *ponytail*
28 el cabello tirante hacia atrás
– *swept-back hair (swept-up hair, pinned-up hair)*
29 el moño (el rodete; *Amér.:* el molote; *S. Dgo. y Venez.:* la clineja)
– *bun (chignon)*
30 las trenzas (*Col. y Chile:* los chapes; *Venez.:* las crinejas; *Bol.:* las chanecas; *Col. y Ec.:* las chimbas; *Ec.:* las jimbas; *Bol.:* las pichicas; *Guat. y Mé.:* las chongas)
– *plaits (bunches)*
31 el peinado estilo *m* guirnalda (peinado *m* estilo *m* griego)
– *chaplet hairstyle (Gretchen style)*
32 la guirnalda (la corona) de cabello
– *chaplet (coiled plaits)*
33 el pelo rizado
– *curled hair*
34 el corte a lo garçon (el pelo a lo garçon)
– *shingle (shingled hair, bobbed hair)*
35 el pelo a lo Colón (el peinado a la romana; el peinado estilo *m* paje)
– *pageboy style*
36 el flequillo (*Mé.:* el burrito)
– *fringe (Am. bangs)*
37 el peinado de caracoles *m* (de rodetes *m; Col.:* la llovizna)
– *earphones*
38 el caracol (el rodete) de pelo *m*
– *earphone (coiled plait)*

1-21 los sombreros y las gorras de señora *f*
- *ladies' hats and caps*
1 la sombrerera haciendo un sombrero
- *milliner making a hat*
2 la capucha (la forma)
- *hood*
3 la horma
- *block*
4 los diferentes adornos (un adorno; *Arg., Mé., Perú y Urug.:* el cabuchón)
- *decorative pieces*
5 el sombrero (*Col.:* la coterna)
- *sombrero*
6 el sombrero de moer *m* con plumas *f*
- *mohair hat with feathers*
7 el sombrero con encajes *m* de adorno *m*
- *model hat with fancy appliqué*
8 la gorra de lino *m*
- *linen cap (jockey cap)*
9 el gorro hecho con lana *f* gruesa
- *hat made of thick candlewick yarn*
10 el gorro de punto *m*
- *woollen (Am. woolen) hat (knitted hat)*
11 el gorro de tejido *m* de moer *m*
- *mohair hat*

12 el sombrero con plumas *f*
- *cloche with feathers*
13 el sombrero grande de hombre *m* hecho de fibra *f* de pita *f* con cinta *f* encordelada
- *large men's hat made of sisal with corded ribbon*
14 el sombrero de hombre *m* con cinta *f* de adorno *m*
- *trilby-style hat with fancy ribbon*
15 el sombrero blando de fieltro *m* (*Venez.:* el garrotín)
- *soft felt hat*
16 el panamá (el sombrero de jipijapa *f*)
- *Panama hat with scarf*
17 la gorra de visón *m*
- *peaked mink cap*
18 el sombrero de visón *m*
- *mink hat*
19 el gorro de zorro *m* con la parte alta de cuero *m*
- *fox hat with leather top*
20 el gorro de visón *m*
- *mink cap*
21 el sombrero florentino (una pamela)
- *slouch hat trimmed with flowers*
22-40 sombreros *m* **y gorras** *f* **de caballero** *m*
- *men's hats and caps*

22 el sombrero de fieltro *m*
- *trilby hat (trilby)*
23 el sombrero de loden *m*
- *loden hat (Alpine hat)*
24 el sombrero de fieltro *m* con borlas *f*
- *felt hat with tassels (Tyrolean hat, Tyrolese hat)*
25 la gorra de terciopelo *m* (gorra *f* de pana *f*)
- *corduroy cap*
26 el gorro de lana *f*
- *woollen (Am. woolen) hat*
27 la boina
- *beret*
28 la gorra príncipe *m* Enrique, una gorra de marino *m*
- *German sailor's cap (Prinz Heinrich' cap)*
29 la gorra de visera *f* (la gorra de velero *m*)
- *peaked cap (yachting cap)*
30 el sueste
- *sou'wester (southwester)*
31 el gorro de piel *f* de zorro *m* con solapas *f* para las orejas
- *fox cap with earflaps*
32 la gorra de cuero *m* con solapas *f* de piel *f*
- *leather cap with fur flaps*
33 la gorra de piel *f* de almizclero *m*
- *musquash cap*

34 el gorro de piel *f*, un gorro de
astracán *m*, un gorro de cosaco *m*
– *astrakhan cap, a real or imitation
astrakhan cap*
35 el sombrero de paja *f* (el canotié;
Mé.: el chilapeño; *Chile y Mé.:* la
chupalla; *Col., Ec., P. Rico y
Venez.:* la pava; *Arg.:* el rancho;
Perú: la sarita)
– *boater*
36 el sombrero de copa *f* hecho de
tafetán *m* de seda *f* (la chistera;
*Amér. Central, Col., Pan. y
Venez.:* el cubilete; *Amér. Central
y Mé.:* el bolero; *Mé.:* la cubeta, el
sorbete); *plegable:* el bicornio (el
clac)
– *(grey,* Am. *gray, or black) top hat
made of silk taffeta;* collapsible:
crush hat (opera hat, claque)
37 el sombrero de verano *m* de tela *f*
con bolsillito *m*
– *sun hat (lightweight hat) made of
cloth with small patch pocket*
38 el sombrero flexible de alas *f*
anchas (el sombrero de artista *m;*
Bol., Chile y Perú: el guarapón)
– *wide-brimmed hat*

39 el gorro con borla *f* (el gorro de
esquí *m*)
– *toboggan cap (skiing cap, ski cap)*
40 la gorra
– *workman's cap (for farmers,
foresters, craftsmen)*

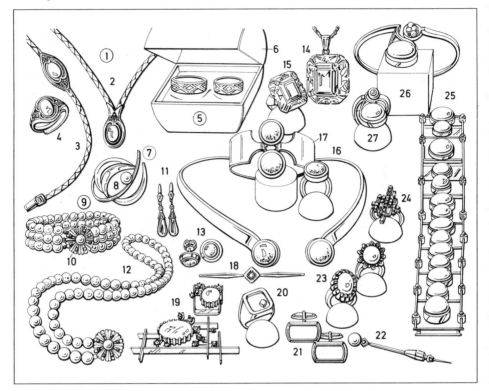

1 los adornos de joyas *f* (la joya; *Col.:* la finca)
– *set of jewellery (Am. jewelry)*
2 el collar
– *necklace*
3 el brazalete (la pulsera; *Col. y Cuba:* el pulso)
– *bracelet*
4 el anillo (la sortija)
– *ring*
5 las alianzas (los anillos de boda *f*)
– *wedding rings*
6 el estuche de las alianzas
– *wedding ring box*
7 el broche, un broche de perlas *f* (*Amér. Central:* la gacilla)
– *brooch, a pearl brooch*
8 la perla
– *pearl*
9 el brazalete de perlas *f* cultivadas
– *cultured pearl bracelet*
10 el cierre (el broche), un cierre de oro *m* blanco
– *clasp, a white gold clasp*
11 los pendientes (los aretes, los zarcillos; *Arg., Bol., Hond., Perú, Urug.:* las caravanas, los colgantes)
– *pendant earrings (drop earrings)*
12 el collar de perlas *f* cultivadas
– *cultured pearl necklace*
13 los zarcillos (los aretes, los pendientes; *Col., Ec.:* las candongas; *Col.:* las aretas; *Col., Guat. y S. Dgo.:* los aritos; *Arg., Chile, P. Rico y Urug.:* los aros)
– *earrings*

14 el dije de piedras *f* finas (piedras *f* preciosas)
– *gemstone pendant*
15 el anillo de piedras *f* finas (piedras *f* preciosas)
– *gemstone ring*
16 el aro del cuello
– *choker (collar, neckband)*
17 el brazalete
– *bangle*
18 el broche alargado con brillante *m*
– *diamond pin*
19 el broche moderno
– *modern-style brooches*
20 el anillo de caballero *m*
– *man's ring*
21 los gemelos (*P. Rico, Urug. y Venez.:* las yuntas)
– *cuff links*
22 el alfiler de corbata *f* (*Mé.:* el fistol)
– *tiepin*
23 el anillo de brillantes *m* con perla *f*
– *diamond ring with pearl*
24 el anillo de brillantes *m* moderno
– *modern-style diamond ring*
25 el brazalete de piedras *f* finas (piedras *f* preciosas)
– *gemstone bracelet*
26 el brazalete rígido asimétrico
– *asymmetrical bangle*
27 el anillo asimétrico
– *asymmetrical ring*
28 el collar de marfil *m*
– *ivory necklace*

29 la rosa de marfil *m* tallado
– *ivory rose*
30 el broche de marfil *m*
– *ivory brooch*
31 el estuche de joyas *f* (el joyero; *Arg., Chile, Guat., Urug.:* la alhajera; *Col. y P. Rico:* el cofre)
– *jewel box (jewel case)*
32 el collar de perlas *f*
– *pearl necklace*
33 el reloj joya *f*
– *bracelet watch*
34 el collar de coral *m* puro
– *coral necklace*
35 los dijes
– *charms*
36 la cadena con monedas *f*
– *coin bracelet*
37 la moneda de oro *m*
– *gold coin*
38 el engaste de la moneda
– *coin setting*
39 el eslabón de la cadena
– *link*
40 el anillo de sello *m* (el sello)
– *signet ring*
41 el grabado (el monograma)
– *engraving (monogram)*
42-86 las diferentes tallas *f* (cortes *m*) de piedras *f*
– *cuts and forms*
42-71 las piedras talladas con facetas *f* (caras *f*)
– *faceted stones*

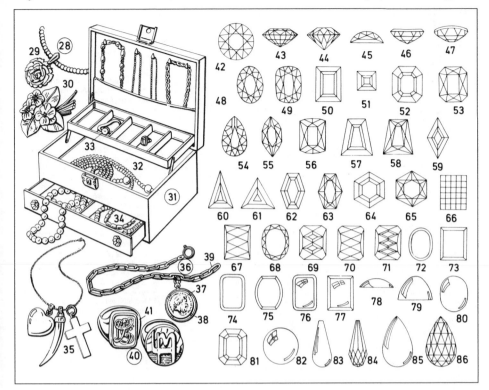

42 u. 43 la talla redonda normal con facetas
f (caras f)
– *standard round cut*
44 la talla brillante m
– *brilliant cut*
45 la talla rosa f
– *rose cut*
46 la tabla llana
– *flat table*
47 la tabla en cabujón m
– *table en cabochon*
48 la talla ovalada normal
– *standard cut*
49 la talla antigua (la talla inglesa)
– *standard antique cut*
50 la talla escalonada rectangular
– *rectangular step-cut*
51 la talla escalonada cuadrada
– *square step-cut*
52 la talla escalonada octogonal
– *octagonal step-cut*
53 la talla octogonal con caras f cruzadas
– *octagonal cross-cut*
54 la talla en forma f de pera f
– *standard pear-shape (pendeloque)*
55 la naveta (la navette)
– *marquise (navette)*
56 la talla en forma f de barril m normal
– *standard barrel-shape*
57 la talla escalonada de trapecio m
– *trapezium step-cut*
58 la talla de trapecio m con caras f
cruzadas
– *trapezium cross-cut*

59 la talla escalonada de rombo m (el
rombo en talla f escalonada)
– *rhombus step-cut*
60 u. 61 el triángulo en talla f escalonada
– *triangular step-cut*
62 la talla escalonada hexagonal
– *hexagonal step-cut*
63 la talla hexagonal ovalada con caras f
cruzadas
– *oval hexagonal cross-cut*
64 la talla escalonada hexagonal redonda
– *round hexagonal step-cut*
65 la talla hexagonal con caras f cruzadas
– *round hexagonal cross-cut*
66 la talla a cuadros m
– *chequer-board cut*
67 la talla a triángulos m
– *triangle cut*
68-71 tallas f de fantasía f
– *fancy cuts*
72-77 piedras f preciosas para anillos m
– *ring gemstones*
72 la tabla llana ovalada
– *oval flat table*
73 la tabla llana rectangular
– *rectangular flat table*
74 la tabla llana rectangular con ángulos m
redondos
– *octagonal flat table*
75 la forma de tonel m
– *barrel-shape*
76 la tabla abombada antigua (con ángulos
m redondos)
– *antique table en cabochon*

77 la tabla abombada rectangular con
ángulos m agudos
– *rectangular table en cabochon*
78-81 los cabujones
– *cabochons*
78 el cabujón redondo
– *round cabochon (simple cabochon)*
79 el cono redondo
– *high dome (high cabochon)*
80 el cabujón ovalado
– *oval cabochon*
81 el cabujón octogonal
– *octagonal cabochon*
82-86 esferas f y formas f de peras f
– *spheres and pear-shapes*
82 la esfera lisa
– *plain sphere*
83 la forma de pera f lisa
– *plain pear-shape*
84 la forma de pera f con caras f
– *faceted pear-shape*
85 la gota lisa
– *plain drop*
86 el briolet con caras f
– *faceted briolette*

1-53 la vivienda unifamiliar
- *detached house*
1 el sótano
- *basement*
2 la planta baja
- *ground floor (Am. first floor)*
3 el primer piso
- *upper floor (first floor, Am. second floor)*
4 el desván (el sobrado; *Col.:* el zarzo)
- *loft*
5 el tejado, un tejado a dos aguas *f*
- *roof, a gable roof (saddle roof, saddleback roof)*
6 el canalón (el canelón, el canal del tejado)
- *gutter*
7 el caballete
- *ridge*
8 el cordón y el guardacabio
- *verge with bargeboards*
9 el ristrel, un cornisamento de cabrio *m*
- *eaves, rafter-supported eaves*
10 la chimenea (*Venez.:* el torreón; *Mé.:* la tronera)
- *chimney*
11 la bajada de aguas *f*
- *gutter*
12 el codo de la bajada de aguas *f*
- *swan's neck (swan-neck)*
13 el tubo de la bajada de aguas *f*
- *rainwater pipe (downpipe, Am. downspout, leader)*
14 el tubo de hierro *m* fundido
- *vertical pipe, a cast-iron pipe*
15 la fachada lateral
- *gable (gable end)*
16 la pared de cristal *m* (la mampara)
- *glass wall*
17 el zócalo
- *base course (plinth)*
18 la galería
- *balcony*
19 la barandilla
- *parapet*
20 la jardinera
- *flower box*
21 la puerta de dos hojas *f* en la galería
- *French window (French windows) opening on to the balcony*
22 la ventana de dos batientes *m* (*Col.:* la ventana de dos abras *f*)
- *double casement window*
23 la ventana de un batiente
- *single casement window*
24 el alféizar con antepecho *m*
- *window breast with window sill*
25 el dintel de la ventana
- *lintel (window head)*
26 la jamba de la ventana
- *reveal*
27 el respiradero del sótano (el tragaluz)
- *cellar window*
28 la persiana enrollable
- *rolling shutter*
29 la guía de la persiana enrollable
- *rolling shutter frame*
30 la contraventana (el postigo)
- *window shutter (folding shutter)*
31 el pestillo de la contraventana
- *shutter catch*
32 el garaje, con cuarto *m* de herramientas *f*
- *garage with tool shed*
33 el espaldar
- *espalier*
34 la puerta de tablas *f* de madera *f*
- *batten door (ledged door)*

35 el montante con travesaños *m* en cruz *f*
- *fanlight with mullion and transom*
36 la terraza
- *terrace*
37 el muro del jardín con albardilla *f*
- *garden wall with coping stones*
38 la lámpara del jardín
- *garden light*
39 la escalera del jardín
- *steps*
40 la rocalla (el jardín de rocas *f*)
- *rockery (rock garden)*
41 el grifo de la manguera
- *outside tap (Am. faucet) for the hose*
42 la manguera para regar
- *garden hose*
43 la rociadera del césped (*Amér.:* de la grama)
- *lawn sprinkler*
44 el estanque para chapotear
- *paddling pool*
45 el camino de losas *f*
- *stepping stones*
46 el césped (*Amér.:* la grama) para los baños de sol *m* (para tenderse al sol)
- *sunbathing area (lawn)*
47 la tumbona
- *deck-chair*
48 la sombrilla de jardín *m*
- *sunshade (garden parasol)*
49 la silla de jardín *m*
- *garden chair*
50 la mesa de jardín *m*
- *garden table*
51 el colgadero (el bastidor) para sacudir alfombras *f*
- *frame for beating carpets*
52 la entrada al garaje *m*
- *garage driveway*
53 la cerca, una valla de madera *f*
- *fence, a wooden fence*

54-57 la urbanización residencial
- *housing estate (housing development)*
54 la casa de la urbanización
- *house on a housing estate (on a housing development)*
55 el tejado caedizo (*Amér.:* el caedizo)
- *pent roof (penthouse roof)*
56 la buhardilla (*Col.:* el ventolín)
- *dormer (dormer window)*
57 el jardín particular
- *garden*

58-63 la serie de casas *f* escalonadas
- *terraced house [one of a row of terraced houses], stepped*
58 el jardín delantero
- *front garden*
59 el seto
- *hedge*
60 la acera (*Guat., Mé.:* la banqueta)
- *pavement (Am. sidewalk, walkway)*
61 la calle
- *street (road)*
62 la farola de la calle
- *street lamp (street light)*
63 la papelera
- *litter bin (Am. litter basket)*

64-68 la vivienda para dos familias *f*
- *house divided into two flats (Am. house divided into two apartments, duplex house)*
64 el tejado a cuatro aguas *f*
- *hip (hipped) roof*
65 la puerta de la casa (la puerta de entrada; *Col.:* la umbralada)
- *front door*

66 la escalera de entrada *f*
- *front steps*
67 la marquesina (el colgadizo)
- *canopy*
68 la ventana para plantas *f* o para flores *f*
- *flower window (window for house plants)*
69-71 la vivienda doble para cuatro familias *f*
- *pair of semi-detached houses divided into four flats (Am. apartments)*
69 el balcón
- *balcony*
70 la vidriera (la solana)
- *sun lounge (Am. sun parlor)*
71 el toldo (la marquesina)
- *awning (sun blind, sunshade)*
72-76 el bloque de galerías *f* cubiertas
- *block of flats (Am. apartment building, apartment house) with access balconies*
72 el cubo de la escalera
- *staircase*
73 la galería cubierta
- *balcony*
74 el estudio de artista *m* (taller *m* de artista *m*)
- *studio flat (Am. studio apartment)*
75 la terraza, un solario
- *sun roof, a sun terrace*
76 la superficie verde
- *open space*
77-81 el bloque de pisos *m*
- *multi-storey block of flats (Am. multistory apartment building, multistory apartment house)*
77 el tejado plano
- *flat roof*
78 el tejado de pendiente *f*
- *pent roof (shed roof, lean-to roof)*
79 el garaje
- *garage*
80 la pérgola
- *pergola*
81 la ventana de la caja de la escalera
- *staircase window*
82 la torre de pisos *m*
- *high-rise block of flats (Am. high-rise apartment building, high-rise apartment house)*
83 el ático (la vivienda de la azotea *f*)
- *penthouse*
84-86 la residencia secundaria (la segunda vivienda *f*), una casa de madera *f*
- *weekend house, a timber house*
84 el encofrado de tablas *f* horizontal (la tablazón horizontal)
- *horizontal boarding*
85 el zócalo de piedra *f* natural (el basamento de piedra *f*)
- *natural stone base course (natural stone plinth)*
86 el ventanal
- *strip windows (ribbon windows)*

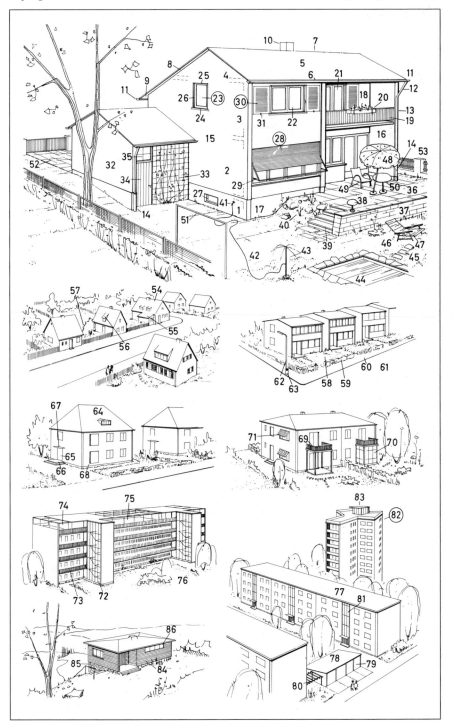

38 Tejado y sótano para la caldera de calefacción   *Roof and Boiler Room*

1-29 el desván, (el sobrado; *Col.:* el zarzo)
– *attic*
1 el tejado
– *roof cladding (roof covering)*
2 el tragaluz
– *skylight*
3 la pasarela
– *gangway*
4 la escalera (la escala del tejado)
– *cat ladder (roof ladder)*
5 la chimenea (*Mé.:* la tronera; *Venez.:* el torreón)
– *chimney*
6 el gancho del tejado
– *roof hook*
7 el tragaluz (la lumbrera)
– *dormer window (dormer)*
8 el enrejado paranieves *m* (el guardanieves)
– *snow guard (roof guard)*
9 el canalón (el canelón, el canal del tejado)
– *gutter*
10 el tubo de bajada de aguas *f*
– *rainwater pipe (downpipe,* Am. *downspout, leader)*
11 la cornisa
– *eaves*
12 el desván superior
– *pitched roof*
13 la trampilla
– *trapdoor*
14 el hueco de la trampilla
– *hatch*
15 la escalera de mano *m* (la escala; *Cuba, Mé. y P. Rico:* el burro)
– *ladder*
16 el larguero
– *stile*
17 el peldaño
– *rung*
18 el desván (el sobrado; *Col.:* el zarzo)
– *loft (attic)*
19 el tabique de madera *f*
– *wooden partition*
20 la puerta de la buhardilla
– *lumber room door (boxroom door)*
21 el candado
– *padlock*
22 el gancho de la cuerda para tender la ropa
– *hook [for washing line]*
23 la cuerda para tender la ropa
– *clothes line (washing line)*
24 el depósito de expansión *f* de la calefacción
– *expansion tank for boiler*
25 la escalera de madera *f* y la barandilla
– *wooden steps and balustrade*
26 la zanca
– *string (*Am. *stringer)*

27 el peldaño
– *step*
28 el pasamano
– *handrail (guard rail)*
29 el pilar de la barandilla
– *baluster*
30 el pararrayos
– *lightning conductor (lightning rod)*
31 el deshollinador
– *chimney sweep (*Am. *chimney sweeper)*
32 el cepillo con el peso esférico para golpear
– *brush with weight*
33 el raspador
– *shoulder iron*
34 el saco para el hollín
– *sack for soot*
35 la escoba de deshollinar
– *flue brush*
36 la escoba
– *broom (besom)*
37 el palo de escoba
– *broomstick (broom handle)*
38-43 el cuarto de la caldera
– *boiler room*
38-81 la calefacción por agua *f* caliente, una calefacción central
– *hot-water heating system, full central heating*
38 el sistema de calefacción *f* de coque *m* (el quemador de coque *m*)
– *coke-fired central heating system*
39 la portezuela de la ceniza
– *ash box door (*Am. *cleanout door)*
40 el humero
– *flueblock*
41 el atizador
– *poker*
42 el hurgón
– *rake*
43 la pala de carbón *m*
– *coal shovel*
44-60 la calefacción de fuel-oil *m*
– *oil-fired central heating system*
44 el depósito de fuel-oil *m*
– *oil tank*
45 el registro
– *manhole*
46 la tapa del registro
– *manhole cover*
47 el tubo de carga *f*
– *tank inlet*
48 la tapa abovedada
– *dome cover*
49 la válvula de fondo *m* del depósito
– *tank bottom valve*
50 el fuel-oil (el gasóleo)
– *fuel oil (heating oil)*
51 el conducto de evacuación *f* de aire *m*
– *air-bleed duct*
52 el casquete de ventilación *f*
– *air vent cap*

53 la tubería del nivel del fuel-oil
– *oil level pipe*
54 el indicador del fuel-oil
– *oil gauge (*Am. *gage)*
55 la tubería de succión *f*
– *suction pipe*
56 la tubería de retorno *m*
– *return pipe*
57 la caldera de la calefacción de fuel-oil *m*
– *central heating furnace (oil heating furnace)*
58-60 el quemador de fuel-oil *m*
– *oil burner*
58 el inyector de aire *m* (el ventilador)
– *fan*
59 el motor eléctrico
– *electric motor*
60 el fuego piloto (el quemador) revestido
– *covered pilot light*
61 la portezuela para cargar
– *charging door*
62 la mirilla de inspección *f*
– *inspection window*
63 el indicador del nivel del agua *f*
– *water gauge (*Am. *gage)*
64 el termómetro de la caldera
– *furnace thermometer*
65 el grifo de carga *f* y vaciado *m*
– *bleeder*
66 el asiento de la caldera
– *furnace bed*
67 el tablero de control *m*
– *control panel*
68 el calentador de agua *f* (el termosifón)
– *hot water tank (boiler)*
69 el rebosadero
– *overflow pipe (overflow)*
70 la válvula de seguridad *f*
– *safety valve*
71 el conducto principal de distribución *f*
– *main distribution pipe*
72 el aislamiento
– *lagging*
73 la válvula
– *valve*
74 el tubo de alimentación *f*
– *flow pipe*
75 la válvula de regulación *f*
– *regulating valve*
76 el radiador
– *radiator*
77 el elemento del radiador
– *radiator rib*
78 el termostato de la habitación
– *room thermostat*
79 el tubo de retorno *m*
– *return pipe (return)*
80 el conducto principal de retorno *m* (la línea colectora de retorno *m*)
– *return pipe (in two-pipe system)*
81 la salida de humo *m*
– *smoke outlet (smoke extract)*

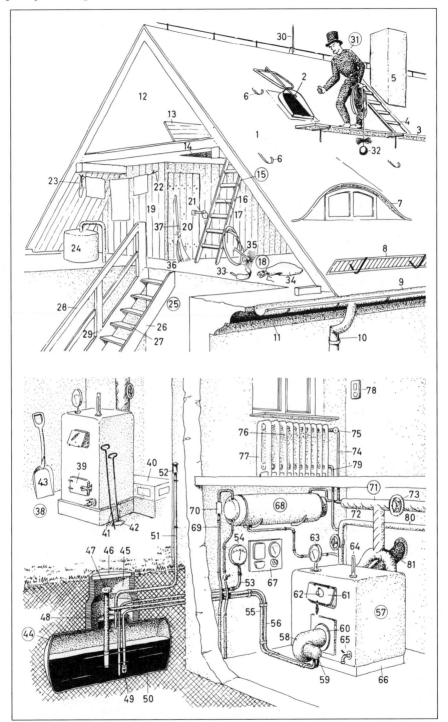

1 el microondas
 – *microwave oven (microwave)*
2 el frigorífico (la nevera, el refrigerador; *Argent.:* la heladera)
 – *refrigerator (fridge, Am. icebox)*
3 la parrilla del frigorífico
 – *refrigerator shelf*
4 la cubeta de la verdura
 – *salad drawer*
5 el compartimiento congelador
 – *freezing compartment*
6 el botellero de la puerta del frigorífico
 – *bottle rack (in storage door)*
7 el congelador
 – *upright freezer*
8 el armario de pared *f*, un armario para la vajilla
 – *wall cupboard, a kitchen cupboard*
9 el módulo (el mueble) base
 – *base unit*
10 el cajón de los cubiertos
 – *cutlery drawer*
11 la encimera (el poyo)
 – *work surface (worktop)*
12-17 el mueble de cocina *f*
 – **cooker unit**
12 la cocina eléctrica (*también:* la cocina de gas *m*)
 – *electric cooker (also: gas cooker)*
13 el horno
 – *oven*
14 la ventanilla del horno
 – *oven window*
15 la placa de cocina *f* (la placa calentadora rápida automática)
 – *hotplate, an automatic high-speed plate*

16 el hervidor (el hervidor de silbato *m*; *Amér.:* la pava)
 – *kettle (whistling kettle)*
17 la campana
 – *cooker hood*
18 la manopla (el agarrador)
 – *pot holder*
19 el cuelgamanoplas
 – *pot holder rack*
20 el reloj de cocina *f*
 – *kitchen clock*
21 el avisador
 – *timer*
22 la batidora
 – *hand mixer*
23 la varilla de batir
 – *whisk*
24 el molinillo de café *m* eléctrico
 – *electric coffee grinder (with rotating blades)*
25 el cordón eléctrico (el cable de la corriente)
 – *lead*
26 el enchufe de pared *f*
 – *wall socket*
27 el módulo (el mueble) de ángulo *m*
 – *corner unit*
28 el anaquel giratorio
 – *revolving shelf*
29 la olla (*Mé. y Guat.:* el apaste; *Bol.:* la manca; *Arg. y Col.:* la cayana; *Hond.:* el platón)
 – *pot (cooking pot)*
30 la jarra (la cafetera)
 – *jug*
31 el estante de las especias (el especiero)
 – *spice rack*

32 el tarro de especia *f*
 – *spice jar*
33-36 el fregadero (*Chile:* el lavaplatos)
 – **sink unit**
33 el escurridor de platos *m* (escurreplatos *m*)
 – *dish drainer*
34 el plato de desayuno *m*
 – *tea plate*
35 el fregadero (la pila)
 – *sink*
36 el grifo de agua *f*, el grifo mezclador (*Col., P. Rico y Urug.:* la pluma; *Amér. Central:* el chorro; *Col., Guat. y Nicar.:* la paja; *Mé. y Río de la Plata:* el bitoque)
 – *water tap (Am. faucet); here: mixer tap (Am. mixing faucet)*
37 la planta de maceta *f*, una planta de follaje *m*
 – *pot plant, a foliage plant*
38 la cafetera eléctrica (una cafetera de filtro *m*; *Antillas, Col. y Venez.:* la freca)
 – *coffee maker*
39 la lámpara de la cocina
 – *kitchen lamp*
40 el lavavajillas
 – *dishwasher (dishwashing machine)*
41 la rejilla de los platos
 – *dish rack*
42 el plato
 – *dinner plate*
43 la silla de cocina *f*
 – *kitchen chair*
44 la mesa de cocina *f*
 – *kitchen table*
45 el tostador de pan
 – *toaster*

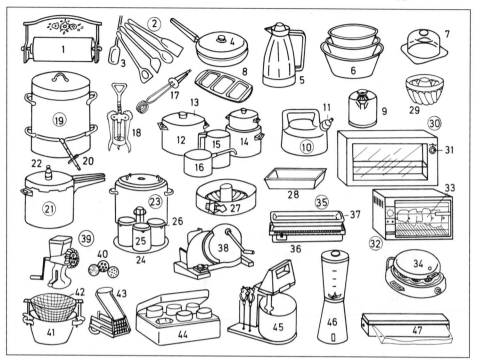

1 el distribuidor de papel *m* de cocina *f*
– *general-purpose roll holder with kitchen roll (paper towels)*
2 el juego de utensilios *m* de madera *f*
– *set of wooden spoons*
3 la cuchara de madera *f* (*Mé.*: la jumaca; *Col.*: la panadora)
– *mixing spoon*
4 la sartén (*Cuba y Mé.*: la freidera)
– *frying pan*
5 el termo (la jarra termo *m*)
– *Thermos jug*
6 las fuentes de cocina *f*
– *set of bowls*
7 la quesera
– *cheese dish with glass cover*
8 el plato de entremeses *m* (el plato de compartimientos *m*)
– *three-compartment dish*
9 el exprimidor
– *lemon squeezer*
10 el hervidor de silbato *m* (el hervidor; *Amér.*: la pava)
– *whistling kettle*
11 el silbato de vapor *m*
– *whistle*
12-16 **el juego de cacerolas** *f* (la batería de cocina *f*)
– ***pan set***
12 la olla (*Arg. y Col.*: la cayana; *Hond.*: el platón; *Mé. y Guat.*: el apaste; *Bol.*: la manca)
– *pot (cooking pot)*
13 la tapadera
– *lid*

14 la marmita
– *casserole dish*
15 el jarro de la leche
– *milk pot*
16 el cacillo (*Col. y Venez.*: la gacha; *Col. y Cuba*: el pailón)
– *saucepan*
17 el calentador de inmersión *f*
– *immersion heater*
18 el sacacorchos con brazos *m*
– *corkscrew [with levers]*
19 el extractor de jugos *m*
– *juice extractor*
20 la pinza del tubo
– *tube clamp (tube clip)*
21 la olla a presión *f* (la olla exprés)
– *pressure cooker*
22 la válvula de seguridad *f*
– *pressure valve*
23 el esterilizador
– *fruit preserver*
24 el portabotes
– *removable rack*
25 el bote de conserva *f*
– *preserving jar*
26 el aro de goma *f*
– *rubber ring*
27 el molde redondo con muelles *m*
– *spring form*
28 el molde rectangular
– *cake tin*
29 el molde de escudilla *f* (el molde alto)
– *cake tin*
30 el microondas
– *microwave oven (microwave)*

31 el programador
– *timer*
32 el asador
– *rotisserie*
33 el espetón del asador
– *spit*
34 el barquillero eléctrico
– *electric waffle iron*
35 el peso de cocina *f* con pesa *f* corredera
– *sliding-weight scales*
36 la pesa corredera
– *sliding weight*
37 el platillo del peso
– *scale pan*
38 la máquina para cortar (para rebanar)
– *food slicer*
39 la máquina para picar carne
– *mincer* (*Am. meat chopper*)
40 las cuchillas
– *blades*
41 la freidora de patatas *f*
– *chip pan*
42 la canastilla (el escurridor del aceite)
– *basket*
43 la máquina de cortar patatas *f*
– *potato chipper*
44 la yogurtera
– *yoghurt maker*
45 el robot de cocina *f* (la máquina batidora y amasadora)
– *mixer*
46 la batidora
– *blender*
47 la soldadora de bolsas
– *bag sealer*

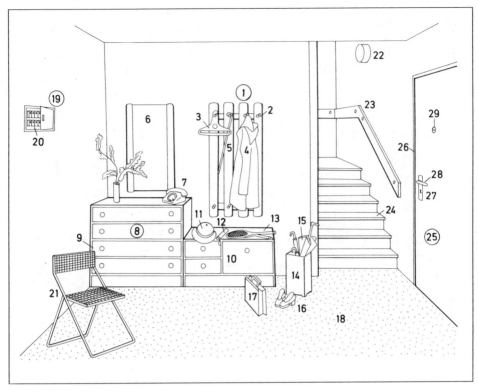

1-29 el vestíbulo (el recibidor, la entrada)
– *hall (entrance hall)*
1 el perchero (*Chile, Guat. y Hond.*: la capotera)
– *coat rack*
2 el colgadero (el gancho)
– *coat hook*
3 la percha
– *coat hanger*
4 el impermeable (el chubasquero)
– *rain cape*
5 el bastón
– *walking stick*
6 el espejo
– *hall mirror*
7 el teléfono
– *telephone*
8 la cómoda para los zapatos, el maletín *m*, etc.
– *chest of drawers for shoes, etc.*
9 el cajón
– *drawer*
10 el banco
– *seat*
11 el sombrero de señora *f*
– *ladies' hat*
12 el paraguas plegable
– *telescopic umbrella*

13 las raquetas de tenis *m*
– *tennis rackets (tennis racquets)*
14 el paragüero (*Col., Chile y P. Rico:* la paragüera)
– *umbrella stand*
15 el paraguas
– *umbrella*
16 los zapatos
– *shoes*
17 la cartera (el maletín)
– *briefcase*
18 la moqueta
– *fitted carpet*
19 la caja de fusibles *m*
– *fuse box*
20 los fusibles automáticos
– *miniature circuit breaker*
21 la silla metálica de tubo *m*
– *tubular steel chair*
22 el aplique de luz *f* de la escalera
– *stair light*
23 el pasamano
– *handrail*
24 el escalón
– *step*
25 la puerta de entrada *f* (la puerta principal)
– *front door*

26 el marco de la puerta
– *door frame*
27 la cerradura de la puerta
– *door lock*
28 la manivela de la puerta
– *door handle*
29 la mirilla
– *spyhole*

1-20 el mueble combinado (la estantería por módulos *m*, por elementos *m*)
- **wall units** *(shelf units)*
2 el panel lateral
- *side wall*
3 el estante (la balda, el anaquel)
- *bookshelf*
4 la hilera de libros *m*
- *row of books*
5 la vitrina
- *display cabinet unit*
6 el módulo de base *f*
- *cupboard base unit*
7 el módulo armario *m*
- *cupboard unit*
8 el televisor
- *television set (TV set)*
9 la cadena estereofónica
- *stereo system (stereo equipment)*
10 el altavoz (la pantalla)
- *speaker (loudspeaker)*
11 el portapipas (el pipario)
- *pipe rack*
12 la pipa (*Amér.:* la churumbela)
- *pipe*
13 el globo terráqueo
- *globe*

14 la tetera de cobre *m* (*Amér.:* la pava)
- *brass kettle*
15 el telescopio
- *telescope*
16 el reloj de mesa *f*
- *mantle clock*
17 el busto
- *bust*
18 la enciclopedia en varios volúmenes *m*
- *encyclopaedia [in several volumes]*
19 el separador de ambientes *m*
- *room divider*
20 el mueble bar *m*
- *drinks cupboard*
21-26 el tresillo por módulos *m*
- **upholstered suite** *(seating group)*
21 el sillón (la butaca)
- *armchair*
22 el brazo
- *arm*
23 el cojín del asiento
- *seat cushion (cushion)*
24 el sofá
- *settee*

25 el respaldo
- *back cushion*
26 la rinconera (la esquinera)
- *[round] corner section*
27 el cojín
- *scatter cushion*
28 la mesa de centro *m*
- *coffee table*
29 el cenicero
- *ashtray*
30 la bandeja
- *tray*
31 la botella de güisqui *m* (de whisky *m*)
- *whisky (whiskey) bottle*
32 la botella de soda *f*
- *soda water bottle (soda bottle)*
33-34 el comedor
- *dining set*
33 la mesa de comedor *m*
- *dining table*
34 la silla (*Col., Chile, Perú y Venez.:* la silleta)
- *chair*
35 el visillo (la cortina)
- *net curtain*
36 las plantas de interior *m*
- *indoor plants (houseplants)*

1 el armario del dormitorio (el ropero; *Col., Cuba, Chile, Pan. y Venez.:* el escaparate)
– *wardrobe* (Am. *clothes closet*)
2 el anaquel (el estante) de ropa *f* blanca
– *linen shelf*
3 el sillón de mimbre *m*
– *cane chair*
4-6 **la cuja** (la armazón de la cama)
– *bedstead*
4-13 **la cama de matrimonio** *m*
– *double bed (*sim.: *double divan)*
4 los pies de la cama
– *foot of the bed*
5 el larguero de la cama
– *bed frame*
6 la cabecera
– *headboard*
7 la colcha (*Amér. Central y Venez.:* la chamarra)
– *bedspread*
8 la manta, una manta edredón *m* (*Ec.:* el cobijo; *Col.:* la coriana; *Amér. Central, Mé. y Chile:* el chamarro)
– *duvet, a quilted duvet*
9 la sábana, una sábana de lino *m*
– *sheet, a linen sheet*

10 el colchón, un colchón de espuma *f* con funda *f* de cutí *m*
– *mattress, a foam mattress with drill tick*
11 el travesaño
– *[wedge-shaped] bolster*
12 *u.* **13** la almohada
– *pillow*
12 la funda de la almohada
– *pillowcase (pillowslip)*
13 la funda interior de la almohada
– *tick*
14 el estante para libros *m*
– *bookshelf [attached to the headboard]*
15 la lámpara de cabecera *f*
– *reading lamp*
16 el despertador eléctrico
– *electric alarm clock*
17 la consola de la cama (*Arg., Perú y Venez.:* el velador)
– *bedside cabinet*
18 el cajón
– *drawer*
19 el aplique de iluminación *f* del dormitorio
– *bedroom lamp*
20 el cuadro
– *picture*

21 el marco del cuadro
– *picture frame*
22 la alfombra de cama *f* (*Chile y Perú:* el piso)
– *bedside rug*
23 la moqueta
– *fitted carpet*
24 el taburete del tocador
– *dressing stool*
25 el tocador (*Arg., Bol., Cuba y Chile:* el peinador; *Col.:* la peinadora)
– *dressing table*
26 el pulverizador de perfume *m*
– *perfume spray*
27 el frasco de perfume *m*
– *perfume bottle*
28 la polvera (*Cuba:* la motera; *Ec. y Perú:* la polvorera; *P. Rico:* la polveta)
– *powder box*
29 el espejo del tocador
– *dressing-table mirror (mirror)*

1-11 la sección (el rincón) de comer
- *dining set*
1 la mesa
- *dining table*
2 la pata de la mesa
- *table leg*
3 el tablero de la mesa
- *table top*
4 el salvamantel (el posaplatos)
- *place mat*
5 el cubierto
- *place (place setting, cover)*
6 el plato sopero (el plato hondo)
- *soup plate (deep plate)*
7 el plato llano
- *dinner plate*
8 la sopera
- *soup tureen*
9 el vaso de vino *m*
- *wineglass*
10 la silla del comedor
- *dining chair*
11 el asiento
- *seat*
12 la lámpara, una lámpara colgante
- *lamp (pendant lamp)*
13 la cortina
- *curtains*

14 el visillo
- *net curtain*
15 el riel de la cortina
- *curtain rail*
16 la alfombra (*Arg., Perú y Urug.*: el camino; *Perú*: la pisadera)
- *carpet*
17 el mueble de pared *f* (*Mé.*: el trinchador)
- *wall unit*
18 la puerta de cristal *m*
- *glass door*
19 el estante
- *shelf*
20 el aparador (*Col., P. Rico, S. Dgo. y Venez.*: el seibo)
- *sideboard*
21 el cajón de los cubiertos
- *cutlery drawer*
22 el cajón de la mantelería
- *linen drawer*
23 la base (el zócalo)
- *base*
24 la bandeja redonda
- *round tray*
25 la planta de maceta *f*
- *pot plant*
26 el armario de la vajilla (la vitrina)
- *china cabinet (display cabinet)*

27 el juego de café *m* (el servicio de café *m*)
- *coffee set (coffee service)*
28 la cafetera
- *coffee pot*
29 la taza de café *m*
- *coffee cup*
30 el platillo de la taza (*Guat.*: la porcelana)
- *saucer*
31 el jarrito de la leche
- *milk jug*
32 el azucarero
- *sugar bowl*
33 el servicio de mesa *f*
- *dinner set (dinner service)*

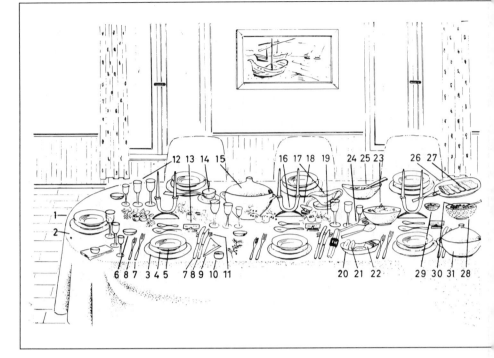

1 la mesa de comedor *m*
- *dining table*
2 el mantel, un mantel adamascado
- *tablecloth, a damask cloth*
3-12 el servicio de mesa *f* (el cubierto)
- *place (place setting, cover)*
3 el posaplatos (el salvamantel)
- *bottom plate*
4 el plato llano
- *dinner plate*
5 el plato sopero (el plato hondo)
- *deep plate (soup plate)*
6 el plato de postre *m*
- *dessert plate (dessert bowl)*
7 el cubierto
- *knife and fork*
8 el cubierto de pescado *m*
- *fish knife and fork*
9 la servilleta
- *serviette (napkin, table napkin)*
10 el servilletero
- *serviette ring (napkin ring)*
11 el portacuchillo (el soporte de los cuchillos)
- *knife rest*
12 las copas de vino *m*
- *wineglasses*
13 la tarjeta de mesa *f*
- *place card*
14 el cucharón (el cazo) de la sopa
- *soup ladle*
15 la sopera
- *soup tureen (tureen)*

16 el candelabro de mesa *f* (*Mé.:* el candil)
- *candelabra*
17 la salsera
- *sauceboat (gravy boat)*
18 la cuchara para la salsa
- *sauce ladle (gravy ladle)*
19 el adorno de la mesa
- *table decoration*
20 la canastilla del pan (la panera)
- *bread basket*
21 el panecillo
- *roll*
22 la rebanada de pan *m*
- *slice of bread*
23 la ensaladera
- *salad bowl*
24 el cubierto de la ensalada
- *salad servers*
25 el plato (la fuente) de legumbres *f*
- *vegetable dish*
26 el plato del asado
- *meat plate (Am. meat platter)*
27 el asado
- *roast meat (roast)*
28 el plato de compota *f* (la compotera)
- *fruit dish*
29 la escudilla de compota *f* (el cuenco de compota *f*)
- *fruit bowl*
30 la compota
- *fruit (stewed fruit)*
31 la fuente de las patatas
- *potato dish*

32 el carrito de servicio *m*
- *serving trolley*
33 la fuente de verdura *f*
- *vegetable plate* (Am. *vegetable platter*)
34 la tostada
- *toast*
35 el plato de quesos *m*
- *cheeseboard*
36 la mantequera
- *butter dish*
37 la rebanada de pan *m*
- *open sandwich*
38 la guarnición de la rebanada
- *filling*
39 el sándwich (emparedado *m*)
- *sandwich*
40 el frutero
- *fruit bowl*
41 las almendras (*también:* las patatas crujientes, los cacahuetes)
- *almonds (also: potato crisps, peanuts)*
42 las vinagreras (el convoy)
- *oil and vinegar bottle*
43 la salsa de tomate *m* picante (el catchup)
- *ketchup (catchup, catsup)*
44 el aparador
- *sideboard*
45 el calientaplatos eléctrico
- *electric hotplate*
46 el sacacorchos
- *corkscrew*

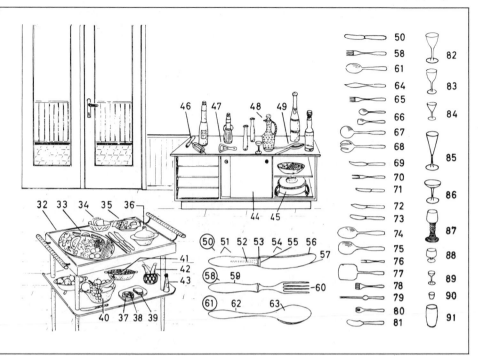

47 el abridor de tapones *m* de corona *f*
(un abrebotellas)
– *crown cork bottle opener (crown
cork opener), a bottle opener*
48 la garrafita para el licor
– *liqueur decanter*
49 el cascanueces
– *nutcrackers (nutcracker)*
50 el cuchillo (*Arg., Bol. y Urug.*: el
alfajor)
– *knife*
51 el mango
– *handle*
52 la espiga
– *tang (tongue)*
53 la virola
– *ferrule*
54 la hoja
– *blade*
55 el cabezal (el tope)
– *bolster*
56 el lomo (el canto)
– *back*
57 el filo (el filo cortante)
– *edge (cutting edge)*
58 el tenedor (*Col., Chile, Ec., Mé.*: el
trinche)
– *fork*
59 el mango
– *handle*
60 el diente (la púa)
– *prong (tang, tine)*
61 la cuchara sopera
– *spoon (dessert spoon, soup spoon)*

62 el mango
– *handle*
63 el cuenco (la pala) de la cuchara
– *bowl*
64 el cuchillo de pescado *m*
– *fish knife*
65 la pala de pescado *m*
– *fish fork*
66 la cucharilla de postre *m*
– *dessert spoon (fruit spoon)*
67 la cuchara para servir la ensalada
– *salad spoon*
68 el tenedor para servir la ensalada
– *salad fork*
69 *u.* 70 el juego de trinchantes *m* (el
cubierto de trinchar)
– *carving set (serving cutlery)*
69 el cuchillo de trinchar
– *carving knife*
70 el tenedor de trinchar (el trinchante;
Col: el trinchete)
– *serving fork*
71 el cuchillo para la fruta
– *fruit knife*
72 el cuchillo para el queso
– *cheese knife*
73 el cuchillo para la mantequilla
– *butter knife*
74 la cuchara para servir la verdura
– *vegetable spoon, a serving spoon*
75 la cuchara para servir patatas *f*
– *potato server (serving spoon for
potatoes)*
76 el tenedor para sándwich *m*
– *cocktail fork*

77 la pala para espárragos *m*
– *asparagus server (asparagus slice)*
78 el tenedor para sardinas *f*
– *sardine server*
79 el tenedor para las langostas
– *lobster fork*
80 el tenedor para las ostras
– *oyster fork*
81 el cuchillo para el caviar
– *caviare knife*
82 la copa de vino *m* blanco
– *white wine glass*
83 la copa de vino *m* tinto
– *red wine glass*
84 la copa de vino *m* dulce (la copa de
madeira)
– *sherry glass (madeira glass)*
85 *u.* 86 las copas de champaña *m*
– *champagne glasses*
85 la copa alta
– *tapered glass*
86 la copa llana
– *champagne glass, a crystal glass*
87 la copa para vinos *m* del Rin
– *rummer*
88 la copa de coñac *m*
– *brandy glass*
89 la copa de licor *m*
– *liqueur glass*
90 el vasito de aguardiente *m*
– *spirit glass*
91 el vaso de cerveza *f*
– *beer glass*

1 la pared del apartamento (los
muebles de pared *f*, la estantería)
– *wall units (shelf units)*
2 el frente del armario (la puerta
del armario)
– *wardrobe door (Am. clothes closet
door)*
3 el cuerpo
– *body*
4 el panel lateral
– *side wall*
5 la cornisa
– *trim*
6 el módulo de dos puertas *f*
– *two-door cupboard unit*
7 el estante de los libros (el estante
de vitrina *f; Mé.*: el librero)
– *bookshelf unit (bookcase unit)
[with glass door]*
8 los libros
– *books*
9 la vitrina
– *display cabinet*
10 el tocadiscos
– *record player*
11 el cajón
– *drawer*
12 la bombonera
– *decorative biscuit tin*

13 el animal de tela *f*
– *soft toy animal*
14 el televisor
– *television set (TV set)*
15 los discos
– *records (discs)*
16 la cama empotrable (la cama-
mueble)
– *bed unit*
17 el cojín (el almohadón) del sofá
– *scatter cushion*
18 el cajón de la cama-mueble
– *bed unit drawer*
19 el estante de la cama-mueble
– *bed unit shelf*
20 las revistas
– *magazines*
21 el emplazamiento del escritorio
– *desk unit (writing unit)*
22 el escritorio (la mesa escritorio *m*)
– *desk*
23 la carpeta
– *desk mat (blotter)*
24 la lámpara de mesa *f*
– *table lamp*
25 el cesto de los papeles (la papelera)
– *wastepaper basket*

26 el cajón del escritorio
– *desk drawer*
27 el sillón del escritorio
– *desk chair*
28 el brazo del sillón
– *arm*
29 el mueble de la cocina (el módulo
de la cocina)
– *kitchen unit*
30 el armario alto
– *wall cupboard*
31 la campana extractora de humos *m*
– *cooker hood*
32 la cocina eléctrica
– *electric cooker*
33 el frigorífico (la nevera, el refrigerador)
– *refrigerator (fridge, Am. icebox)*
34 la mesa de comedor *m*
– *dining table*
35 el tapete de la mesa
– *table runner*
36 la alfombra oriental
– *oriental carpet*
37 la lámpara de pie *m*
– *standard lamp*

1 la cama de los niños, una litera
– *children's bed, a bunk bed*
2 el cajón de la cama
– *storage box*
3 el colchón
– *mattress*
4 la almohada
– *pillow*
5 la escala
– *ladder*
6 un elefante de tela *f* (de trapo *m*)
– *soft toy elephant, a cuddly toy animal*
7 el perro de tela *f* (de trapo *m*)
– *soft toy dog*
8 el puf
– *cushion*
9 la muñeca-maniquí (la muñeca para vestir; *Hond.:* la pichinga)
– *fashion doll*
10 el cochecito de la muñeca
– *doll's pram*
11 la muñeca acostada
– *sleeping doll*
12 el baldaquín (el dosel)
– *canopy*
13 la pizarra
– *blackboard*
14 las bolas para contar (una bolita; *Chile, Mé. y Perú:* el tiro)
– *counting beads*

15 el caballo de peluche *m* con balancín y ruedecillas *f*
– *toy horse for rocking and pulling*
16 los patines-balancín
– *rockers*
17 el libro infantil
– *children's book*
18 la caja de juegos *m*
– *compendium of games*
19 el juego de los caballitos
– *ludo*
20 el tablero de ajedrez *m* (el damero)
– *chessboard*
21 el armario de la habitación de los niños
– *children's cupboard*
22 el cajón de la ropa blanca
– *linen drawer*
23 el escritorio
– *drop-flap writing surface*
24 el cuaderno (la libreta)
– *notebook (exercise book)*
25 los libros de clase *f* (de la escuela)
– *school books*
26 el lápiz (*también:* el lápiz de color *m*, el rotulador, el bolígrafo)
– *pencil (also: crayon, felt tip pen, ballpoint pen)*
27 la tienda de ultramarinos *m*
– *toy shop*

28 el mostrador
– *counter*
29 el estante de especias *f*
– *spice rack*
30 el escaparate (*Amér.:* la vidriera)
– *display*
31 los caramelos surtidos
– *assortment of sweets* (Am. *candy*)
32 el cartucho para los caramelos
– *bag of sweets* (Am. *candies*)
33 la balanza (el peso)
– *scales*
34 la caja registradora
– *cash register*
35 el teléfono de juguete *m*
– *toy telephone*
36 la estantería de las mercancías (*Amér.:* de las mercaderías)
– *shop shelves (goods shelves)*
37 el tren de madera *f*
– *wooden train set*
38 el volquete, un camión de juguete *m*
– *dump truck, a toy lorry (toy truck)*
39 la grúa
– *tower crane*
40 la hormigonera
– *concrete mixer*
41 el perro de peluche *m* grande
– *large soft toy dog*
42 el cubilete de los dados
– *dice cup*

1-20 la educación preescolar
- *pre-school education (nursery education)*
1 la maestra del parvulario (la profesora)
- *nursery teacher*
2 el niño del parvulario (el párvulo)
- *nursery child*
3 los trabajos manuales
- *handicraft*
4 el pegamento
- *glue*
5 la acuarela
- *watercolour (Am. watercolor) painting*
6 la caja de pinturas *f*
- *paintbox*
7 el pincel
- *paintbrush*
8 el vaso de agua *f*
- *glass of water*
9 el rompecabezas (el puzzle)
- *jigsaw puzzle (puzzle)*
10 la pieza del rompecabezas (del puzzle)
- *jigsaw puzzle piece*
11 los lápices de colores *m* (lápices *m* de cera *f*)
- *coloured (Am. colored) pencils (wax crayons)*

12 la pasta de modelar (la plastilina)
- *modelling (Am. modeling) clay (Plasticine)*
13 las figuras modeladas (las figuras de plastilina *f*)
- *clay figures (Plasticine figures)*
14 el tablero para modelar
- *modelling (Am. modeling) board*
15 la tiza (la barra de tiza *f*)
- *chalk (blackboard chalk)*
16 la pizarra
- *blackboard*
17 los cubos de contar
- *counting blocks*
18 el rotulador
- *felt pen (felt tip pen)*
19 el juego de las formas
- *shapes game*
20 el grupo de jugadores *m*
- *group of players*
21-32 los juguetes
- *toys*
21 el juego de los cubos
- *building and filling cubes*
22 la caja de construcciones *f*
- *construction set*
23 los libros infantiles
- *children's books*
24 el cochecito de la muñeca, un cochecito de mimbre *m*
- *doll's pram, a wicker pram*

25 la muñeca bebé *m*
- *baby doll*
26 el baldaquín (el dosel)
- *canopy*
27 los bloques de construcción *f*
- *building bricks (building blocks)*
28 la construcción de madera *f*
- *wooden model building*
29 el tren de madera *f*
- *wooden train set*
30 el oso de peluche *m* con balancín *m*
- *rocking teddy bear*
31 el cochecito de la muñeca
- *doll's pushchair*
32 la muñeca-maniquí (la muñeca para vestir)
- *fashion doll*
33 el niño en edad *f* preescolar
- *child of nursery school age*
34 el guardarropa (el vestuario)
- *cloakroom*

1 la bañera (*Amér.:* la bañadera)
– *bath*
2 el grifo mezclador del agua *f* caliente y fría (*Col., P. Rico y Urug.:* la pluma; *Amér. Central:* el chorro; *Col., Guat. y Nicar.:* la paja; *Mé. y Río de la Plata:* el bitoque)
– *mixer tap* (Am. *mixing faucet) for hot and cold water*
3 el baño de espuma *f*
– *foam bath (bubble bath)*
4 el patito de caucho *m* (de goma *f*)
– *toy duck*
5 las sales de baño *m*
– *bath salts*
6 la esponja de baño *m*
– *bath sponge (sponge)*
7 el bidé (*Antillas, Col., Perú, Mé., Urug. y Venez.:* el bidel)
– *bidet*
8 el toallero
– *towel rail*
9 la toalla de felpa *f*
– *terry towel*
10 el portarrollo de papel *m* higiénico
– *toilet roll holder* (Am. *bathroom tissue holder)*
11 el papel higiénico, un rollo de papel *m* crepé
– *toilet paper* (coll. *loo paper,* Am. *bathroom tissue)*
12 el retrete (el excusado, el wáter, el inodoro)
– *toilet (lavatory, W.C.,* coll. *loo)*
13 la taza del retrete
– *toilet pan (toilet bowl)*
14 la tapa del retrete con una cubierta de felpa *f*
– *toilet lid with terry cover*

15 el asiento del retrete
– *toilet seat*
16 la cisterna
– *cistern*
17 la palanca de la cisterna
– *flushing lever*
18 la esterilla de los pies
– *pedestal mat*
19 el azulejo
– *tile*
20 la ventilación (el respiradero)
– *ventilator (extraction vent)*
21 la jabonera
– *soap dish*
22 el jabón
– *soap*
23 la toalla de mano *f* (*Guat. y Hond.:* los limpiamanos)
– *hand towel*
24 el lavabo (*Arg., Chile, Ec., Perú, Urug. y Venez.:* el lavatorio; *Guat.:* el lavador)
– *washbasin*
25 el rebosadero
– *overflow*
26 el grifo de agua *f* fría y caliente
– *hot and cold water tap*
27 el pedestal del lavabo con sifón *m*
– *washbasin pedestal with trap (anti-syphon trap)*
28 el vaso para los dientes
– *tooth glass (tooth mug)*
29 el cepillo de dientes *m* eléctrico
– *electric toothbrush*
30 los cepillos de recambio *m*
– *detachable brush heads*
31 el armario de tocador *m* con espejos *m*
– *mirrored bathroom cabinet*
32 el tubo fluorescente
– *fluorescent lamp*

33 el espejo
– *mirror*
34 el cajón
– *drawer*
35 la polvera (*Cuba:* la motera; *Ec. y Perú:* la polvorera; *P. Rico:* la polveta)
– *powder box*
36 el elixir dentífrico
– *mouthwash*
37 la máquina de afeitar eléctrica
– *electric shaver*
38 la loción para después del afeitado (el after-shave)
– *aftershave lotion*
39 el cuartito de la ducha
– *shower cubicle*
40 la cortina de la ducha
– *shower curtain*
41 la ducha regulable (la ducha de mano)
– *adjustable shower head*
42 el pulverizador (la roseta) de la ducha
– *shower nozzle*
43 el riel de regulación *f* de la altura
– *shower adjustment rail*
44 el plato de ducha *f*
– *shower base*
45 el rebosadero
– *waste pipe*
46 las zapatillas de baño *m*
– *bathroom mule*
47 la báscula de baño *m*
– *bathroom scales*
48 la alfombra del baño
– *bath mat*
49 el botiquín
– *medicine cabinet*

1-20 los aparatos para la plancha
- *irons*
1 la plancha automática eléctrica
- *electric ironing machine*
2 el interruptor de pie *m* eléctrico
- *electric foot switch*
3 el rodillo con envoltura *f* de muletón *m*
- *roller covering*
4 la cabeza de planchado *m*
- *ironing head*
5 la sábana de cama *f*
- *sheet*
6 la plancha eléctrica (la plancha de viaje *m*)
- *electric iron (lightweight iron)*
7 la planta (el pie) de la plancha
- *sole-plate*
8 el selector de temperatura *f*
- *temperature selector*
9 el mango de la plancha
- *handle (iron handle)*
10 la luz piloto *m*
- *pilot light*
11 la plancha de vapor *m*, la plancha con pulverizador *m* y secado *m*
- *steam, spray, and dry iron*
12 el orificio de relleno *m*
- *filling inlet*
13 el pulverizador para humedecer la ropa
- *spray nozzle for damping the washing*
14 el agujero del vapor (el canal de vaporización *f*)
- *steam hole (steam slit)*
15 la mesa de planchar
- *ironing table*
16 la tabla de planchar
- *ironing board (ironing surface)*
17 la cubierta de la tabla de planchar
- *ironing-board cover*
18 el reposaplancha
- *iron well*
19 la armazón de aluminio *m*
- *aluminium* (Am. *aluminum) frame*
20 la tabla para (planchar) las mangas
- *sleeve board*
21 el cubo de la ropa blanca
- *linen bin*
22 la ropa blanca sucia
- *dirty linen*

23-34 los aparatos de lavado *m* y secado *m*
- *washing machines and driers*
23 la lavadora (la lavadora automática, la automática)
- *automatic washing machine*
24 el tambor de lavado *m*
- *washing drum*
25 el pestillo de seguridad *f* (el dispositivo de seguridad *f*)
- *safety latch (safety catch)*
26 el selector de programas *m*
- *program selector control*
27 la cubeta delantera del detergente (con varios compartimientos *m*)
- *front soap dispenser [with several compartments]*
28 la secadora eléctrica con aire *m* de salida *f*
- *tumble drier*
29 el tambor de secado *m*
- *drum*
30 la puerta delantera con rajas *f* para la ventilación
- *front door with ventilation slits*

31 la encimera
- *worktop*
32 el tendedero
- *airer*
33 la cuerda de la ropa (*Cuba y Guat.:* la tendedera; *Amér. Central, Chile y S. Dgo.:* el cáñamo)
- *clothes line (washing line)*
34 el tendedero de tijeras *f*
- *extending airer*
35 la escalera de tijeras *f*, una escalera metálica
- *stepladder (steps), an aluminium (Am. aluminum) ladder*
36 el montante
- *stile*
37 el apoyo
- *prop*
38 el peldaño
- *tread (rung)*

39-43 los utensilios para el cuidado de (para limpiar) los zapatos
- *shoe care utensils*
39 la lata de betún *m* (crema *f*)
- *tin of shoe polish*
40 el pulverizador de zapatos *m*, un pulverizador para impregnar
- *shoe spray, an impregnating spray*
41 el cepillo para zapatos *m*
- *shoe brush*
42 el cepillo para aplicar el betún (la crema)
- *brush for applying polish*
43 el tubo de betún *m* (crema *f*)
- *tube of shoe polish*
44 el cepillo de la ropa
- *clothes brush*
45 el cepillo de la alfombra
- *carpet brush*
46 el cepillo de barrer (*Col.:* la pichanga)
- *broom*
47 las cerdas del cepillo (la pelambre)
- *bristles*
48 la armazón del cepillo
- *broom head*
49 el palo del cepillo
- *broomstick (broom handle)*
50 la rosca
- *screw thread*
51 el cepillo para la vajilla
- *washing-up brush*
52 el recogedor
- *pan (dustpan)*

53-86 la limpieza del suelo
- *floor and carpet cleaning*
53 el escobillón (la escoba de mano *f*)
- *brush*
54 el cubo (*Venez.:* el tobo)
- *bucket (pail)*
55 el trapo del suelo (el trapo de limpieza *f*, la bayeta; *Mé.:* el chapalolo)
- *floor cloth (cleaning rag)*
56 la bruza (la estregadera, un cepillo de cerdas *f* fuertes para fregar)
- *scrubbing brush*
57 el cepillo mecánico
- *carpet sweeper*
58 la aspiradora de mano *f*
- *upright vacuum cleaner*
59 el interruptor de cambio *m* (el selector de posición *f*)
- *changeover switch*

60 la cabeza de articulación *f*
- *swivel head*
61 el indicador del saco del polvo
- *bag-full indicator*
62 el depósito del saco del polvo
- *dust bag container*
63 el mango
- *handle*
64 el tubo
- *tubular handle*
65 el gancho del cordón
- *flex hook*
66 el cordón de la corriente enrollado
- *wound-up flex*
67 la boquilla chupadora para todo uso *m*
- *all-purpose nozzle*
68 la aspiradora rodante
- *cylinder vacuum cleaner*
69 la articulación giratoria
- *swivel coupling*
70 el tubo de prolongación *f*
- *extension tube*
71 la boquilla chupadora para el suelo (*sin.:* la boquilla para la alfombra)
- *floor nozzle* (sim.: *carpet beater nozzle)*
72 el mando de succión *f*
- *suction control*
73 el indicador del saco del polvo
- *bag-full indicator*
74 el mando regulador de succión *f*
- *sliding fingertip suction control*
75 el tubo de succión *f* (la manguera)
- *hose (suction hose)*
76 el aparato para el cuidado (la limpieza) de la alfombra combinado
- *combined carpet sweeper and shampooer*
77 el cordón eléctrico
- *electric lead (flex)*
78 la toma de corriente *f*
- *plug socket*
79 la cabeza para sacudir la alfombra (*sin.:* la cabeza para limpiar en seco la alfombra, la cabeza para cepillar la alfombra)
- *carpet beater head* (sim.: *shampooing head, brush head)*
80 la aspiradora para todo uso *m*
- *all-purpose vacuum cleaner (wet and dry vacuum cleaner)*
81 la ruedecilla
- *castor*
82 el motor (el bloque del motor)
- *motor unit*
83 el cierre de la tapa
- *lid clip*
84 la manguera para la succión de la suciedad (basura *f*) gruesa
- *coarse dirt hose*
85 el accesorio especial para la suciedad gruesa
- *special accessory (special attachment) for coarse dirt*
86 el depósito del polvo
- *dust container*
87 el carrito de la compra
- *shopper (shopping trolley)*

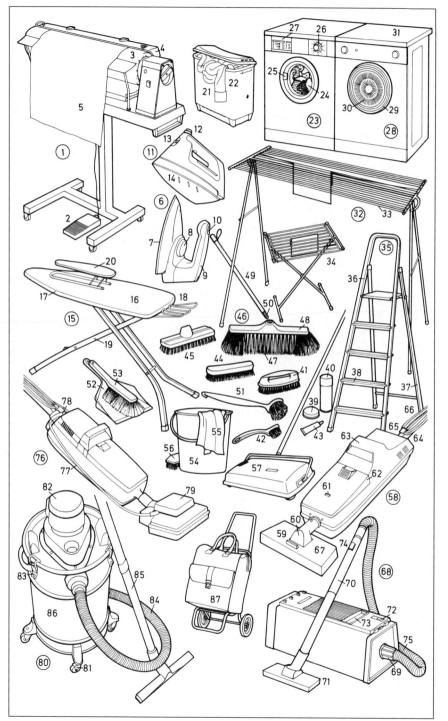

1-35 el jardín
– *flower garden*
1 la pérgola
– *pergola*
2 la hamaca (la tumbona)
– *deck-chair*
3 la escoba de césped *m* (la escoba de hojas *f*)
– *lawn rake (wire-tooth rake)*
4 el rastrillo del césped
– *garden rake*
5 la vid silvestre, una planta trepadora
– *Virginia creeper (American ivy, woodbine), a climbing plant (climber, creeper)*
6 el jardín adornado con piedras *f* (la rocalla)
– *rockery (rock garden)*
7 las plantas de rocalla *f* (las plantas alpestres); *variedades:* el telefio, la uña de gato *m* (la siempreviva menor), la dríada, la aubrietia
– *rock plants; varieties: stonecrop (wall pepper), houseleek, dryas, aubretia*
8 la hierba de las pampas
– *pampas grass*
9 el seto del jardín
– *garden hedge*

10 el abeto azul (la epícea)
– *blue spruce*
11 las hortensias
– *hydrangeas*
12 el roble
– *oak (oak tree)*
13 el abedul
– *birch (birch tree)*
14 la senda (la vereda, el camino; *Amér.:* la picada) del jardín
– *garden path*
15 el bordillo de la senda
– *edging*
16 el estanque del jardín
– *garden pond*
17 la rosa (la baldosa)
– *flagstone (stone slab)*
18 el nenúfar (el lirio de agua *f*)
– *water lily*
19 las begonias de tubérculos *m*
– *tuberous begonias*
20 las dalias
– *dahlias*
21 la regadera
– *watering can* (Am. *sprinkling can*)
22 la azada de desherbar (escabuche *m*)
– *weeding hoe*
23 el lupino noble
– *lupin*

24 las margaritas
– *marguerites (oxeye daisies, white oxeye daisies)*
25 la rosa de tallo *m* alto
– *standard rose*
26 la gerbera
– *gerbera*
27 el lirio
– *iris*
28 los gladiolos
– *gladioli*
29 los crisantemos
– *chrysanthemums*
30 la amapola
– *poppy*
31 la serrátula
– *blazing star*
32 la boca de dragón *m*
– *snapdragon (antirrhinum)*
33 el césped (*Amér.:* la grama)
– *lawn*
34 el diente de león *m*
– *dandelion*
35 el girasol
– *sunflower*

1-32 el huerto familiar (la plantación de hortalizas *f* y árboles *m* frutales; *P. Rico:* la tala)
– **allotment** *(fruit and vegetable garden)*
1, 2, 16, 17, 29 árboles *m* frutales enanos (árboles *m* frutales de espaldera *f,* árboles frutales de forma *f* plana)
– *dwarf fruit trees (espaliers, espalier fruit trees)*
1 la palmeta Verrier, un árbol de espaldera *f*
– *quadruple cordon, a wall espalier*
2 el cordón vertical
– *vertical cordon*
3 el cobertizo de las herramientas
– *tool shed (garden shed)*
4 el bidón (barril *m*) para el agua *f* de lluvia *f* (*Arg., Cuba, Perú y Venez.:* la casimba)
– *water butt (water barrel)*
5 la planta trepadora (la enredadera)
– *climbing plant (climber, creeper, rambler)*
6 el montón de abono *m* compuesto
– *compost heap*
7 el girasol
– *sunflower*
8 la escala de huerto *m*
– *garden ladder (ladder)*
9 la planta vivaz
– *perennial (flowering perennial)*

10 la valla del huerto (la valla de madera *f,* la empalizada, la cerca; *Amér. Central, Arg., Col., Chile, P. Rico y Urug.:* el cerco)
– *garden fence (paling fence, paling)*
11 las bayas de tronco *m* alto
– *standard berry tree*
12 el rosal trepador, en la espaldera de arco *m*
– *climbing rose (rambling rose) on the trellis arch*
13 el rosal arbusto (el rosal común)
– *bush rose (standard rose tree)*
14 el cenador (la glorieta)
– *summerhouse (garden house)*
15 el farolillo (farolillo *m* a la veneciana, el farol de papel *m*)
– *Chinese lantern (paper lantern)*
16 el árbol piramidal, la pirámide, un árbol de espaldera *f* sin apoyo *m*
– *pyramid tree (pyramidal tree, pyramid), a free-standing espalier*
17 el cordón horizontal de dos brazos *m*
– *double horizontal cordon*
18 el arriate de flores *f,* un arriate
– *flower bed, a border*
19 el arbusto de baya *f* (el arbusto de uva *f* espina, el grosellero negro)
– *berry bush (gooseberry bush, currant bush)*
20 el bordillo de losetas *f* de cemento *m*
– *concrete edging*

21 el rosal de tallo *m* alto (rosal *m,* la rosa de tallo alto)
– *standard rose (standard rose tree)*
22 el arriate con plantas *f* vivaces
– *border with perennials*
23 el sendero (*Amér.:* la picada) del huerto
– *garden path*
24 el hortelano aficionado
– *allotment holder*
25 el arriate de espárragos *m*
– *asparagus patch (asparagus bed)*
26 el arriate de verduras *f*
– *vegetable patch (vegetable plot)*
27 el espantapájaros (el espantajo; *Chile y Perú:* el dominguejo)
– *scarecrow*
28 las judías (rodrigadas con estacas *f*), una planta de judías *f* (*Amér.:* fríjoles *m*) con estaca (caña *f*) (las estacas de judías *f*)
– *runner bean (Am. scarlet runner), a bean plant on poles (bean poles)*
29 el cordón horizontal simple, de un brazo
– *horizontal cordon*
30 el árbol frutal de tronco *m* alto
– *standard fruit tree*
31 el rodrigón
– *tree stake*
32 el seto
– *hedge*

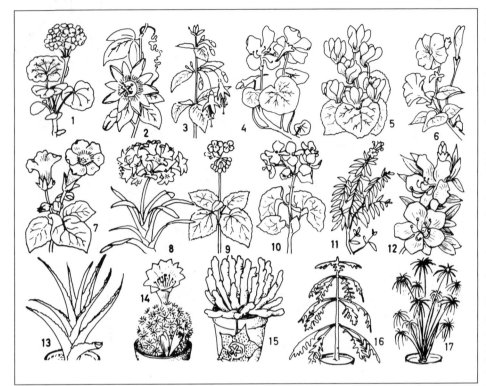

1 el geranio (el pelargonio), una
geraniácea (*Chile:* el cardenal)
– *pelargonium (crane's bill), a gera-
nium*
2 la pasionaria, una pasiflora, una
de las parietales (*Ec., Perú:* el
tumbo)
– *passion flower (Passiflora), a
climbing plant (climber, creeper)*
3 la fucsia, una onagrácea
– *fuchsia, an anagraceous plant*
4 la capuchina (espuela *f* de galán
m), un tropaeolum
– *nasturtium (Indian cress, tropaeolum)*
5 el ciclamen, una primulácea
– *cyclamen, a primulaceous herb*
6 la petunia, una solanácea
– *petunia, a solanaceous herb*
7 la gloxínea (siningia *f*), una gesneriácea
– *gloxinia (Sinningia), a gesneria-
ceous plant*
8 la clivia, una amarilidácea, una
narcisácea
– *Clivia minata, an amaryllis (narcissus)*

9 el cáñamo africano, una sparmannia, una tiliea
– *African hemp (Sparmannia), a
tiliaceous plant, a linden plant*
10 la begonia (*Mé.:* la tronadora)
– *begonia*
11 el mirto (el arrayán)
– *myrtle (common myrtle, Myrtus)*
12 la azalea, una ericácea
– *azalea, an ericaceous plant*
13 el áloe, una liliácea
– *aloe, a liliaceous plant*
14 el equinocacto (el asiento de la
suegra)
– *globe thistle (Echinops)*
15 la estapelia (la flor de la carroña),
una asclepiadácea
– *stapelia (carrion flower), an ascle-
piadaceous plant*
16 la araucaria excelsa
– *Norfolk Island Pine (an araucaria
grown as an ornamental)*
17 la juncia, una ciperácea
– *galingale, a cyperacious plant of
the sedge family*

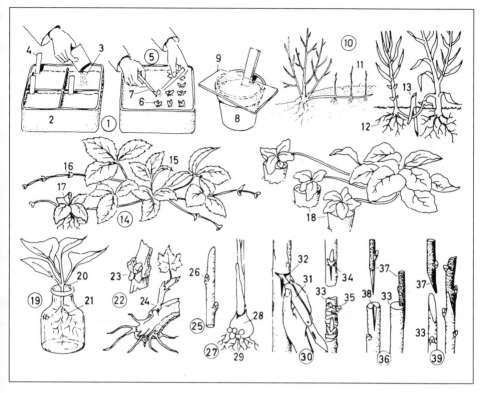

1 la siembra
- *seed sowing (sowing)*
2 la cubeta de la semilla (el semillero, la almáciga)
- *seed pan*
3 la semilla
- *seed*
4 la etiqueta con el nombre
- *label*
5 el trasplante
- *pricking out (pricking off, transplanting)*
6 la planta (el plantón)
- *seedling (seedling plant)*
7 el plantador
- *dibber (dibble)*
8 la maceta, el tiesto
- *flower pot (pot)*
9 la hoja de vidrio *m*
- *sheet of glass*
10 la propagación por acodo *m*
- *propagation by layering*
11 el acodo
- *layer*
12 el acodo enraizado (*Cuba y Venez.*: el margullo)
- *layer with roots*
13 la rama horquillada para la fijación
- *forked stick used for fastening*

14 la propagación por estolones *m*
- *propagation by runners*
15 la planta madre *f*
- *parent (parent plant)*
16 el estolón (el tallo rastrero, el vástago)
- *runner*
17 la plántula (el retoño) enraizada(-o)
- *small rooted leaf cluster*
18 la acodadura en macetas *f*
- *setting in pots*
19 el desqueje en agua *f*
- *cutting in water*
20 el esqueje
- *cutting (slip, set)*
21 la raíz
- *root*
22 el desqueje de la viña por esquejes *m* de yema *f*
- *bud cutting on vine tendril*
23 la yema, un botón
- *scion bud, a bud*
24 la planta de esqueje *m* (el vástago)
- *sprouting (shooting) cutting*
25 el esqueje leñoso (la estaca de rama *f*)
- *stem cutting (hardwood cutting)*
26 el botón (la yema, el brote)
- *bud*

27 la propagación por bulbos *m*
- *propagation by bulbils (brood bud bulblets)*
28 el bulbo
- *old bulb*
29 el bulbo reproductor
- *bulbil (brood bud bulblet)*
30-39 **el injerto**
- ***grafting** (graftage)*
30 el injerto en escudete *m*
- *budding; here: shield budding*
31 la navaja
- *budding knife*
32 la incisión en forma *f* de T
- *T-cut*
33 el patrón (el masto)
- *support (stock, rootstock)*
34 la yema injertada
- *inserted scion bud*
35 la ligadura de rafia *f*
- *raffia layer (bast layer)*
36 el injerto de púa *f*
- *side grafting*
37 la púa con yema *f*
- *scion (shoot)*
38 el corte en forma de cuña *f*
- *wedge-shaped notch*
39 el injerto de cúpula *f* (el injerto de empalme *m*)
- *splice grafting*

55 Horticultura y cultivo de hortalizas

1-51 la explotación hortícola (la horticultura, los trabajos hortícolas)
– **market garden** (Am. *truck garden, truck farm*)
1 el cobertizo de los útiles
– *tool shed*
2 el depósito elevado de agua *f*
– *water tower (water tank)*
3 el vivero
– *market garden (Am. truck garden, truck farm), a tree nursery*
4 el invernáculo (la estufa, el invernadero)
– *hothouse (forcing house, warm house)*
5 el tejado de cristal *m*
– *glass roof*
6 la estera de cañizo *m* (estera *f* de paja *f*, el sombrajo)
– *[roll of] matting (straw matting, reed matting, shading)*
7 el cuarto de la calefacción
– *boiler room (boiler house)*
8 el tubo de la calefacción (la cañería de alta presión *f*)
– *heating pipe (pressure pipe)*
9 la cubierta de tablas *f* (la cubierta de madera *f*, las tablas para dar sombra *f*)
– *shading panel (shutter)*

10 *u.* **11** la ventilación
– *ventilators (vents)*
10 la ventana de ventilación *f* (el panel de la lumbrera)
– *ventilation window (window vent, hinged ventilator)*
11 la ventana de corredera *f* para la ventilación
– *ridge vent*
12 el tablero para plantar en macetas *f*
– *potting table (potting bench)*
13 la criba de apoyo *m* (la zaranda)
– *riddle (sieve, garden sieve, upright sieve)*
14 la pala para el mantillo
– *garden shovel (shovel)*
15 el montón de tierra *f* (el abono compuesto, la tierra vegetal, el mantillo, el compost)
– *heap of earth (composted earth, prepared earth, garden mould, Am. mold)*
16 la cama caliente (la almajara)
– *hotbed (forcing bed, heated frame)*
17 la cajonera del semillero
– *hotbed vent (frame vent)*
18 la cala de ventilación *f* (el puntal con muescas *f* para la ventilación)
– *vent prop*

19 el regador giratorio (la rociadera)
– *sprinkler (sprinkling device)*
20 el jardinero (el horticultor, el hortelano)
– *gardener (nursery gardener, grower, commercial grower)*
21 el cultivador de mano *f* (la grada de mano *f*)
– *cultivator (hand cultivator, grubber)*
22 la pasarela
– *plank*
23 las plantas jóvenes trasplantadas
– *pricked-out seedlings (pricked-off seedlings)*
24 las flores precoces (las flores tempranas)
– *forced flowers [forcing]*
25 las plantas de macetas *f*
– *potted plants (plants in pots, pot plants)*
26 la regadera con asa *f*
– *watering can (Am. sprinkling can)*
27 el asa *f*
– *handle*
28 la alcachofa de la regadera (la roseta)
– *rose*
29 el estanque de agua *f* (la pileta de agua *f*)
– *water tank*

108

30 el tubo del agua *f*
– *water pipe*
31 la bala de turba *f* (la paca de
turba *f*)
– *bale of peat*
32 el invernadero templado
– *warm house (heated greenhouse)*
33 el invernadero frío
– *cold house (unheated greenhouse)*
34 el generador eólico (el molino de
viento *m*)
– *wind generator*
35 la rueda de paletas *f* (de aletas *f*)
– *wind wheel*
36 la paleta (la aleta)
– *wind vane*
37 el arriate, un macizo de flores *f*
– *shrub bed, a flower bed*
38 el reborde de anillos *m*
– *hoop edging*
39 el arriate de verduras *f*
– *vegetable plot*
40 el invernadero de abrigo *m* (el
túnel de plástico *m*)
– *plastic tunnel (polythene greenhouse)*
41 el tragaluz
– *ventilation flap*
42 la calle central
– *central path*
43 las cajas de verduras *f*
– *vegetable crate*

44 la planta de tomates *m* (la tomat-
era)
– *tomato plant*
45 el ayudante del hortelano (*Mé.*: el
tecolero)
– *nursery hand*
46 la ayudante del hortelano
– *nursery hand*
47 la planta en tina *f*
– *tub plant*
48 la tina
– *tub*
49 el plantón de naranjo *m* (un
naranjo pequeño)
– *orange tree*
50 el cesto de alambre *m*
– *wire basket*
51 la caja de las plantas de semilla *f*
– *seedling box*

56 Útiles de jardinería   *Garden Tools*

1 el plantador
– *dibber (dibble)*
2 la laya (pala *f* para remover la tierra)
– *spade*
3 la escoba para el césped
– *lawn rake (wire-tooth rake)*
4 el rastrillo
– *rake*
5 el aporcador
– *ridging hoe*
6 el desplantador
– *trowel*
7 el escardillo de mano *f* (el combinado de azada *f* y horquilla *f*; *Amér.*: el carpidor)
– *combined hoe and fork*
8 la hoz (*Arg. y Chile:* la echona)
– *sickle*
9 la navaja jardinera
– *gardener's knife (pruning knife, billhook)*
10 el cuchillo esparraguero (el cortaespárragos)
– *asparagus cutter (asparagus knife)*
11 las tijeras de podar (la podadera de mango *m* largo, podadera de varilla *f*)
– *tree pruner (long-handled pruner)*
12 la laya semiautomática
– *semi-automatic spade*
13 el cultivador de tres dientes *m*
– *three-pronged cultivator*
14 el raspador de árboles *m* (el raspador de corteza *f*)
– *tree scraper (bark scraper)*
15 el aireador del césped
– *lawn aerator (aerator)*
16 la sierra de poda *f* (la sierra para cortar ramas *f*)
– *pruning saw (saw for cutting branches)*
17 el cortasetos impulsado por batería *f*
– *battery-operated hedge trimmer*
18 el cultivador de motor *m*
– *motor cultivator*
19 la taladradora de mano *f*
– *electric drill*
20 la transmisión
– *gear*
21 los dos juegos de fresas *f*
– *cultivator attachment*
22 el cogedor de frutas *f*
– *fruit picker*
23 el cepillo de árboles *m* (el cepillo para la corteza)
– *tree brush (bark brush)*
24 el pulverizador para el insecticida
– *sprayer for pest control*
25 la varilla (la boquilla) de aspersión *f*
– *lance*

26 el enrollador móvil
– *hose reel (reel and carrying cart)*
27 la manguera de riego *m*
– *garden hose*
28 el cortacésped de motor *m*
– *motor lawn mower (motor mower)*
29 el recipiente para la hierba
– *grassbox*
30 el motor de dos tiempos *m*
– *two-stroke motor*
31 el cortacésped eléctrico
– *electric lawn mower (electric mower)*
32 el cable de la corriente
– *electric lead (electric cable)*
33 la superficie de corte *m*
– *cutting unit*
34 el cortacésped mecánico
– *hand mower*
35 el cilindro de corte *m*
– *cutting cylinder*
36 la cuchilla
– *blade*
37 el cortacésped autoportado
– *riding mower*
38 la palanca del freno (el freno de mano *f*)
– *brake lock*
39 el arranque eléctrico
– *electric starter*
40 el pedal del freno (el freno de pie *m*)
– *brake pedal*
41 el mecanismo de cortar
– *cutting unit*
42 el remolque volquete *m*
– *tip-up trailer*
43 el regador giratorio, un regador (la rociadera)
– *revolving sprinkler, a lawn sprinkler*
44 el torniquete
– *revolving nozzle*
45 el manguito de unión *f* del tubo
– *hose connector*
46 la regadora fija
– *oscillating sprinkler*
47 la carretilla
– *wheelbarrow*
48 la cizalla para el césped
– *grass shears*
49 la cizalla para los setos
– *hedge shears*
50 las tijeras de podar
– *secateurs (pruning shears)*

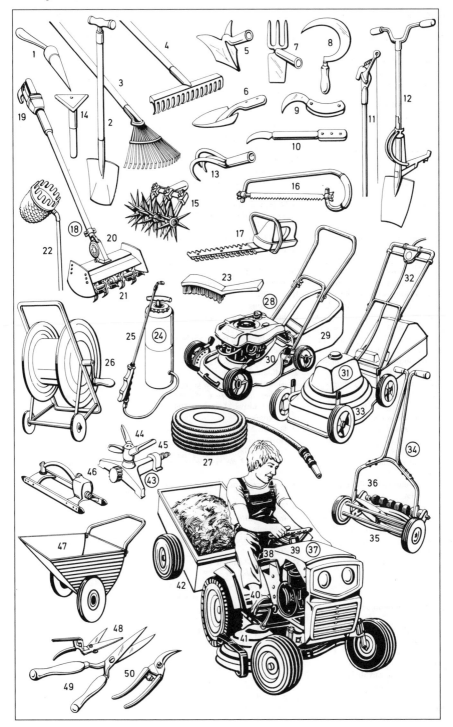

1-11 plantas *f* leguminosas (legumbres *f*)
– *leguminous plants (Leguminosae)*
1 el guisante (la arveja), una planta papilionácea
– *pea, a plant with a papilionaceous corola*
2 la flor del guisante
– *pea flower*
3 la hoja pinada
– *pinnate leaf*
4 el zarcillo del guisante, un zarcillo foliáceo
– *pea tendril, a leaf tendril*
5 la estípula
– *stipule*
6 la vaina, la cápsula de la semilla
– *legume (pod), a seed vessel (pericarp, legume)*
7 el guisante [la semilla]
– *pea [seed]*
8 la judía (la alubia, la habichuela; *Amér.:* el poroto, el frijol, el fríjol, el fréjol), una planta trepadora; *clases:* la judía verde (*Amér. Central:* el ejote; *Amér. Merid.:* la chaucha), la judía de enrame *m,* la judía de España; más pequeña: la judía enana; *otras clases:* la judía de careta *f,* la judía de panoja *f,* la judía de grande estandarte *m,* la judía lunada, la judía purpúrea
– *bean plant (bean), a climbing plant (climber, creeper); varieties: broad bean (runner bean, Am. scarlet runner), climbing bean (climber, pole bean), scarlet runner bean; smaller: dwarf French bean (bush bean)*
9 la flor de la judía
– *bean flower*
10 el tallo voluble (el tallo trepador) de la judía
– *twining beanstalk*
11 la judía [la vaina con las semillas]
– *bean [pod with seeds]*
12 el tomate
– *tomato*
13 el pepino (el cohombro)
– *cucumber*
14 el espárrago
– *asparagus*
15 el rábano redondo
– *radish*
16 el rábano largo (el rábano negro)
– *white radish*
17 la zanahoria larga
– *carrot*
18 la zanahoria de cascabel *m*
– *stump-rooted carrot*
19 el perejil
– *parsley*

20 el rábano blanco
– *horse-radish*
21 el puerro
– *leeks*
22 la cebolleta
– *chives*
23 la calabaza; *anal.:* el melón
– *pumpkin (Am. squash); sim.: melon*
24 la cebolla
– *onion*
25 la binza (la cáscara de la cebolla)
– *onion skin*
26 el nabo
– *kohlrabi*
27 el apio (*Chile:* el panul)
– *celeriac*
28-34 las verduras
– *brassicas (leaf vegetables)*
28 la acelga
– *chard (Swiss chard, seakale beet)*
29 la espinaca
– *spinach*
30 la col de Bruselas
– *Brussels sprouts (sprouts)*
31 la coliflor
– *cauliflower*
32 la col, una berza; *clases:* el repollo, la lombarda; *otras clases:* la col arbórea, el brécol (el brócoli), la col de san Dionisio, la col de Estrasburgo, la col de York, el colinabo
– *cabbage (round cabbage, head of cabbage), a brassica; cultivated races (cultivars): green cabbage, red cabbage*
33 la col de Milán (la lombarda blanca)
– *savoy (savoy cabbage)*
34 la col rizada
– *kale (curly kale, kail), a winter green*
35 la escorzonera (el salsifí negro)
– *scorzonera (black salsify)*
36-40 verduras *f* para ensalada *f*
– *salad plants*
36 la lechuga
– *lettuce (cabbage lettuce, head of lettuce)*
37 la hoja de lechuga
– *lettuce leaf*
38 la lechuga silvestre (la hierba de los canónigos, la valeriana de huerta *f,* el rapónchigo, el ruiponce)
– *corn salad (lamb's lettuce)*
39 la escarola (la endibia)
– *endive (endive leaves)*
40 la achicoria amarga (la achicoria silvestre)
– *chicory (succory, salad chicory)*
41 la alcachofa
– *globe artichoke*

42 el pimiento picante (la guindilla; *Amér.:* el ají, el chile)
– *sweet pepper (Spanish paprika)*

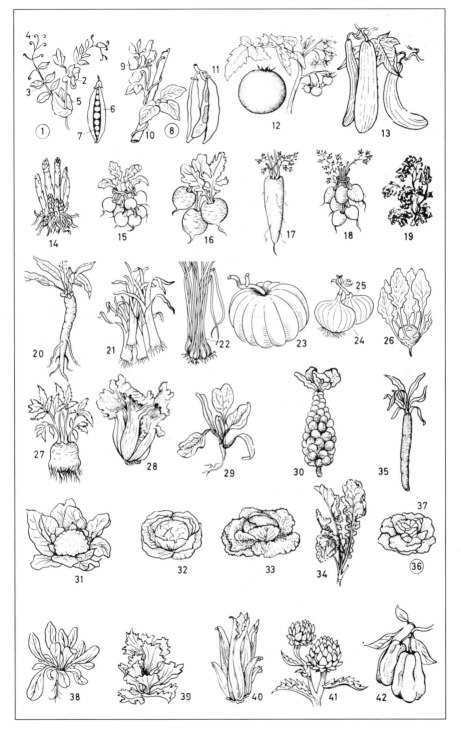

1-30 frutas *f* **de bayas** *f* (arbustos *m* de baya *f*)
- *soft fruit (berry bushes)*

1-15 plantas *f* **grosulariáceas**
- *Ribes*

1 la grosella espinosa (la uva espina)
- *gooseberry bush*

2 la rama florecida de la grosella espinosa
- *flowering gooseberry cane*

3 la hoja
- *leaf*

4 la flor
- *flower*

5 la oruga geómetra de la grosella espinosa
- *magpie moth larva*

6 la flor de la grosella espinosa
- *gooseberry flower*

7 el ovario inferior
- *epigynous ovary*

8 el cáliz (los sépalos)
- *calyx (sepals)*

9 la grosella espinosa, una baya
- *gooseberry, a berry*

10 el grosellero de racimo *m*
- *currant bush*

11 el racimo de frutas *f*
- *cluster of berries*

12 la grosella
- *currant*

13 el pedúnculo
- *stalk*

14 la rama en flor *f* del grosellero
- *flowering cane of the currant*

15 el racimo de flores *f*
- *raceme*

16 la fresa; *clases:* la fresa silvestre, el fresón, la fresa alpina
- *strawberry plant;* varieties: *wild strawberry (woodland strawberry), garden strawberry, alpine strawberry*

17 la planta con flores *f* y frutos *m*
- *flowering and fruit-bearing plant*

18 el rizoma
- *rhizome*

19 la hoja trifoliada
- *ternate leaf (trifoliate leaf)*

20 el estolón (el tallo rastrero, el brote rastrero)
- *runner (prostrate stem)*

21 la fresa, una fruta compuesta
- *strawberry, a pseudocarp*

22 el calículo
- *epicalyx*

23 el aquenio (la semilla, la pepita)
- *achene (seed)*

24 la carne (la pulpa)
- *flesh (pulp)*

25 el frambueso
- *raspberry bush*

26 la flor del frambueso
- *raspberry flower*

27 el capullo floral (el botón)
- *flower bud (bud)*

28 el fruto (la frambuesa), un fruto compuesto
- *fruit (raspberry), an aggregate fruit (compound fruit)*

29 la mora (la zarzamora)
- *blackberry*

30 la espina (la púa)
- *thorny tendril*

31-61 frutos *m* **de pepitas** *f*
- *pomiferous plants*

31 el peral (*Arg., Bol.:* el pero); *var.:* el peral silvestre
- *pear tree;* wild: *wild pear tree*

32 la rama en flor *f* del peral
- *flowering branch of the pear tree*

33 la pera [corte longitudinal]
- *pear [longitudinal section]*

34 el pedúnculo (el rabillo de la pera)
- *pear stalk (stalk)*

35 la carne (la pulpa)
- *flesh (pulp)*

36 el corazón, el lóculo (la cápsula de las pepitas)
- *core (carpels)*

37 la pepita (la semilla)
- *pear pip (seed), a fruit pip*

38 la flor del peral
- *pear blossom*

39 el óvulo
- *ovules*

40 el ovario
- *ovary*

41 el estigma
- *stigma*

42 el estilo
- *style*

43 el pétalo
- *petal*

44 el sépalo
- *sepal*

45 el estambre (la antera)
- *stamen*

46 el membrillero (el membrillo)
- *quince tree*

47 la hoja del membrillo
- *quince leaf*

48 la estípula
- *stipule*

49 el membrillo en forma *f* de manzana *f* [corte longitudinal]
- *apple-shaped quince [longitudinal section]*

50 el membrillo en forma *f* de pera *f* [corte longitudinal]
- *pear-shaped quince [longitudinal section]*

51 el manzano; *var.:* el manzano silvestre (el maguillo)
- *apple tree;* wild: *crab apple tree*

52 la rama en flor *f* del manzano
- *flowering branch of the apple tree*

53 la hoja
- *leaf*

54 la flor del manzano
- *apple blossom*

55 la flor marchita
- *withered flower*

56 la manzana [corte longitudinal]
- *apple [longitudinal section]*

57 la piel de la manzana
- *apple skin*

58 la carne (la pulpa)
- *flesh (pulp)*

59 el corazón, el lóculo (la cápsula con las semillas)
- *core (apple core, carpels)*

60 la pepita (la semilla)
- *apple pip, a fruit pip*

61 el pedúnculo (el rabillo de la manzana)
- *apple stalk (stalk)*

62 la mariposa de la manzana, un lepidóptero
- *codling moth (codlin moth), a small moth*

63 la galería del gusano
- *burrow (tunnel)*

64 la larva (el gusano, la oruga de la mariposa)
- *larva (grub, caterpillar) of a small moth*

65 el agujero del gusano
- *wormhole*

59 Frutas de hue

1-36 plantas f de
(drupas f
— drupes (
— 1-18 el
— ch
1

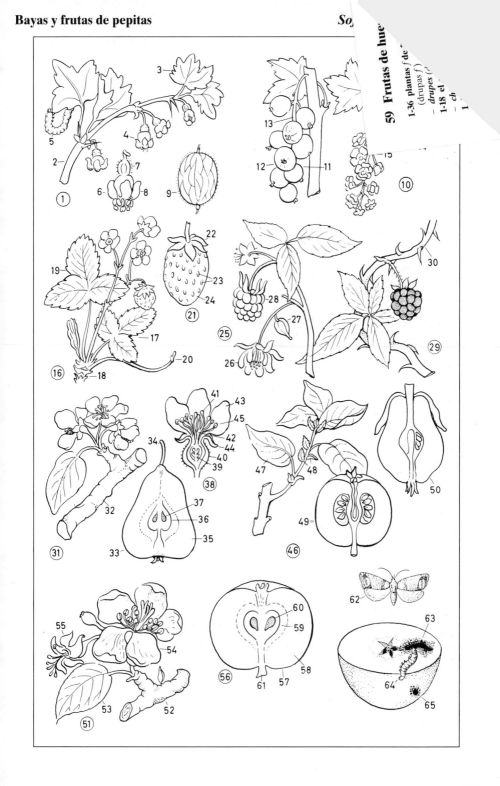

...utas *f* de hueso *m*
  ...*upaceous plants*)
  ...erezo
  ...*rry tree*
  la rama en flor *f* del cerezo
– *flowering branch of the cherry tree (branch of the cherry tree in blossom)*
2 la hoja del cerezo
– *cherry leaf*
3 la flor del cerezo
– *cherry flower (cherry blossom)*
4 el tallo floral (el pedúnculo)
– *peduncle (pedicel, flower stalk)*
5 la cereza; *clases:* la cereza de corazón *m* negro, la cereza dulce, la cereza silvestre, la picota
– *cherry;* varieties: *sweet cherry (heart cherry), wild cherry (bird cherry), sour cherry, morello cherry (morello)*
6-8 **la cereza** [corte longitudinal]
– **cherry** *(cherry fruit) [cross section]*
6 la carne (la pulpa)
– *flesh (pulp)*
7 el hueso (*Amér.:* el carozo) de la cereza
– *cherry stone*
8 la almendra (la semilla)
– *seed*
9 la flor [corte longitudinal]
– *flower (blossom) [cross section]*
10 el estambre (la antera)
– *stamen*
11 el pétalo
– *petal*
12 el sépalo
– *sepal*
13 el carpelo
– *pistil*
14 el óvulo en el ovario central
– *ovule enclosed in perigynous ovary*
15 el estilo
– *style*
16 el estigma
– *stigma*
17 la hoja
– *leaf*
18 el nectario peciolar
– *nectary (honey gland)*
19-23 **el ciruelo**
– **plum tree**
19 la rama con frutos *m* del ciruelo
– *fruit-bearing branch*
20 la ciruela damascena, una ciruela
– *oval, black-skinned plum*
21 la hoja del ciruelo
– *plum leaf*
22 la yema (el botón)
– *bud*

23 el hueso (*Amér.:* el carozo) de la ciruela
– *plum stone*
24 la ciruela claudia
– *greengage*
25 la mirabel (una ciruela pequeña y amarilla)
– *mirabelle (transparent gage), a plum*
26-32 **el melocotonero**
– **peach tree**
26 la rama florida
– *flowering branch (branch in blossom)*
27 la flor del melocotonero
– *peach flower (peach blossom)*
28 la inserción de la flor (el pimpollo de la flor)
– *flower shoot*
29 la hoja joven (la hoja naciente)
– *young leaf (sprouting leaf)*
30 la rama con frutos *m*
– *fruiting branch*
31 el melocotón
– *peach*
32 la hoja del melocotonero
– *peach leaf*
33-36 **el albaricoquero**
– **apricot tree**
33 la rama en flor *f* del albaricoquero
– *flowering apricot branch (apricot branch in blossom)*
34 la flor del albaricoquero
– *apricot flower (apricot blossom)*
35 el albaricoque (*Perú:* el aurimelo)
– *apricot*
36 la hoja del albaricoquero
– *apricot leaf*
37-51 **nueces** *f*
– **nuts**
37-43 **el nogal**
– **walnut tree**
37 la rama en flor *f* del nogal
– *flowering branch of the walnut tree*
38 el amento femenino (flores *f* femeninas)
– *female flower*
39 el amento masculino (flores *f* masculinas con los estambres)
– *male inflorescence (male flowers, catkins with stamens)*
40 la hoja imparipinada plumada
– *alternate pinnate leaf*
41 la nuez, una drupa dehiscente
– *walnut, a drupe (stone fruit)*
42 el pericarpio (la cáscara, la cubierta exterior blanda)
– *soft shell (cupule)*
43 la nuez, una drupa dehiscente (un fruto de hueso *m*)
– *walnut, a drupe (stone fruit)*

44-51 **el avellano,** una planta anemófila
– **hazel tree** *(hazel bush), an anemophilous shrub (a wind-pollinating shrub)*
44 la rama en flor *f* del avellano
– *flowering hazel branch*
45 el amento masculino
– *male catkin*
46 el amento femenino
– *female inflorescence*
47 el brote de la hoja (la yema)
– *leaf bud*
48 la rama con frutos *m*
– *fruit-bearing branch*
49 la avellana, un fruto de hueso *m* (*Amér.:* de carozo *m*)
– *hazelnut (hazel, cobnut, cob), a drupe (stone fruit)*
50 la cúpula (el cáliz)
– *involucre (husk)*
51 la hoja del avellano
– *hazel leaf*

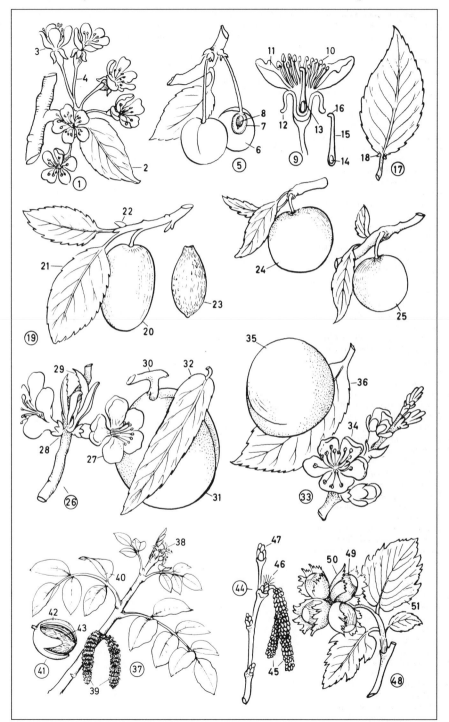

1 el narciso de las nieves (la campanilla de invierno *m,* el galanto
de las nieves)
– *snowdrop (spring snowflake)*
2 el pensamiento, una violácea
– *garden pansy (heartsease pansy), a*
pansy
3 el narciso atrompetado, un narciso
– *trumpet narcissus (trumpet daf-*
fodil, Lent lily), a narcissus
4 el narciso de los poetas (el narciso
blanco); *otros:* el narciso junquillo, el narciso oloroso
– *poet's narcissus (pheasant's eye,*
poet's daffodil); sim.: polyanthus
narcissus
5 la flor de corazón *m,* una dicentra,
una fumariácea
– *bleeding heart (lyre flower), a*
fumariaceous flower
6 la minutisa (el clavel de ramillete
m, el clavel de los poetas), un
clavel (una cariofilácea)
– *sweet william (bunch pink), a car-*
nation
7 el clavel de jardín *m*
– *gillyflower (gilliflower, clove pink,*
clove carnation)
8 el lirio, el lirio de jardín *m* (lirio *m*
de agua *f*), una iridácea (un iris)
– *yellow flag (yellow water flag, yel-*
low iris), an iris
9 el nardo
– *tuberose*
10 la aguileña común (pajarilla *f,* los
pelícanos, el manto real, las campanillas)
– *columbine (aquilegia)*
11 el gladíolo (la espadaña, la hierba
estoque *m,* la cresta de gallo *m*)
– *gladiolus (sword lily)*
12 el lirio blanco (la azucena), un
lirio
– *Madonna lily (Annunciation lily,*
Lent lily), a lily
13 la espuela de caballero *m* (la consuelda real), una consólida
– *larkspur (delphinium), a ranuncu-*
laceous plant
14 el polemonio, un flox
– *moss pink (moss phlox), a phlox*
15 la rosa india (rosa *f* china)
– *garden rose (China rose)*
16 el capullo de la rosa
– *rosebud, a bud*
17 la rosa doble
– *double rose*
18 la espina de la rosa
– *rose thorn, a thorn*
19 la gallardía
– *gaillardia*
20 el tagetes (el clavelón, la maravi-
lla, la flamenquilla)
– *African marigold (tagetes)*

21 la carricera (la cola de zorra *f*),
un amaranto *m*
– *love-lies-bleeding, an amaranthine*
flower
22 la zinnia (el rascamoño)
– *zinnia*
23 la dalia borla, una dalia
– *pompon dahlia, a dahlia*

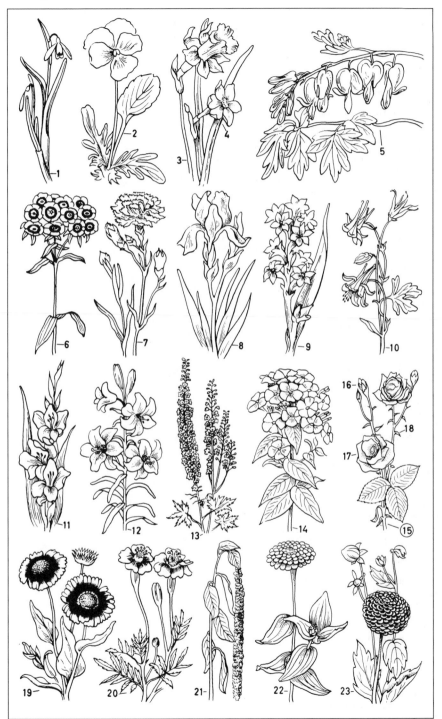

1 el azulejo (el aciano), una centáurea
– *corn flower (bluebottle), a centaury*
2 la amapola, una papaverácea
– *corn poppy (field poppy), a poppy*
3 el capullo
– *bud*
4 la flor de la amapola
– *poppy flower*
5 la cápsula de la amapola con las
semillas
– *seed capsule containing poppy
seeds*
6 la neguilla (la arañuela)
– *corn cockle (corn campion,
crown-of-the-field)*
7 los ojos de los sembrados (la margarita del trigo), un crisantemo
– *corn marigold (field marigold), a
chrysanthemum*
8 la manzanilla bastarda (la manzanilla hedionda)
– *corn camomile (field camomile,
camomile, chamomile)*
9 la bolsa de pastor *m*
– *shepherd's purse*
10 la flor
– *flower*
11 el fruto (la vaina) en forma *f* de
bolsa *f*
– *fruit (pouch-shaped pod)*
12 la hierba cana (el zuzón, el
senecio, la hierba de las que-
maduras, el lechocino)
– *common groundsel*
13 el diente de león *m*
– *dandelion*
14 la cabezuela
– *flower head (capitulum)*
15 la fructificación
– *infructescence*
16 el erísimo
– *hedge mustard, a mustard*
17 el aliso [una crucífera]
– *stonecrop*
18 la mostaza silvestre
– *wild mustard (charlock, runch)*
19 la flor
– *flower*
20 el fruto, una vaina
– *fruit, a siliqua (pod)*
21 el rabanillo
– *wild radish (jointed charlock)*
22 la flor
– *flower*
23 el fruto (la vaina)
– *fruit (siliqua, pod)*
24 el armuelle silvestre
– *common orache (common orach)*
25 el cenizo
– *goosefoot*
26 la correhuela
– *field bindweed (wild morning
glory), a bindweed*

27 los murajes
– *scarlet pimpernel (shepherd's
weatherglass, poor man's weatherglass, eye-bright)*
28 la cebada de las ratas (la cebadilla)
– *wild barley (wall barley)*
29 la cizaña (el joyo)
– *wild oat*
30 la grama (la grama de olor *m*, la
grama canina, la grama de playa *f*,
el rabo de zorra *f*); *anál.:* la
agróstide (el carrizo)
– *common couch grass (couch,
quack grass, quick grass, quitch
grass, scutch grass, twitch grass,
witchgrass);* sim.: *bearded couch
grass, sea couch grass*
31 la galinsoga parviflora
– *gallant soldier*
32 el cardo borriquero (el cardo de
los campos, el cardo corredor, el
erigio; *Amér.:* el caraguatá), un
cardo
– *field eryngo (Watling Street thistle), a thistle*
33 la ortiga
– *stinging nettle, a nettle*

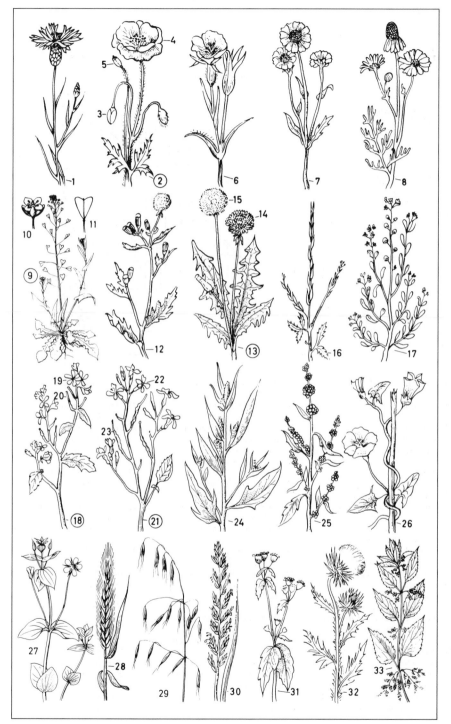

1 la casa (la vivienda)
– *house*
2 la cuadra
– *stable*
3 el gato doméstico
– *house cat (cat)*
4 la granjera
– *farmer's wife*
5 la escoba
– *broom*
6 el granjero (el cultivador, el campesino) (*Amér.:* el paisano; *Arg.:* el afincado)
– *farmer*
7 el establo (la vaquería)
– *cowshed*
8 la pocilga (la corte)
– *pigsty (sty, Am. pigpen, hogpen)*
9 el comedero exterior (el pesebre)
– *outdoor trough*
10 el cerdo (el puerco, el marrano, el cochino, el guarro, el gorrino) (*Amér.:* el chancho)
– *pig*
11 el silo-torre o silo elevado (el silo para el forraje)
– *above-ground silo (fodder silo)*
12 la columna montante de abastecimiento *m* (de carga *f*) del silo
– *silo pipe (standpipe for filling the silo)*

13 el silo de abono *m* líquido
– *liquid manure silo*
14 el edificio colateral
– *outhouse*
15 el cobertizo de las máquinas (el garaje; *Amér.:* el galpón)
– *machinery shed*
16 la puerta corredera
– *sliding door*
17 la puerta de acceso *m* al taller
– *door to the workshop*
18 el volquete de tres bandas, un vehículo de transporte *m*
– *three-way tip-cart, a transport vehicle*
19 el cilindro basculante
– *tipping cylinder*
20 la lanza (el brazo de tiro *m*, la barra de tracción *f*)
– *shafts*
21 la esparcidora de estiércol *m* (el distribuidor de estiércol *m*)
– *manure spreader (fertilizer spreader, manure distributor)*
22 el grupo (el dispositivo) de esparcimiento *m* (de distribución *f*)
– *spreader unit (distributor unit)*
23 el cilindro distribuidor
– *spreader cylinder (distributor cylinder)*

24 la batea rascadora fija
– *movable scraper floor*
25 el panel lateral (el adral)
– *side planking (side board)*
26 el adral de reja *f*
– *wire mesh front*
27 el vehículo de riego *m*
– *sprinkler cart*
28 el soporte (el chasis, el armazón) de riego *m*
– *sprinkler stand*
29 el regador (el regador-devanadera de caudal *m* pequeño), un regador giratorio
– *sprinkler, a revolving sprinkler*
30 la goma flexible de riego *m* enrollada en la devanadera
– *sprinkler hoses*
31 el patio de la granja
– *farmyard*
32 el perro de la granja
– *watchdog*
33 el ternero
– *calf*
34 la vaca lechera
– *dairy cow (milch-cow, milker)*
35 el seto de la granja
– *farmyard hedge*
36 la gallina
– *chicken*

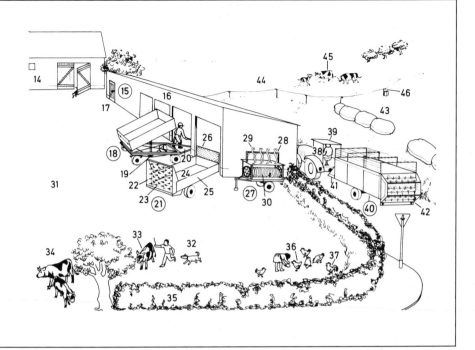

37 el gallo
– *cock (Am. rooster)*
38 el tractor
– *tractor*
39 el conductor del tractor
– *tractor driver*
40 el remolque de carga *f* universal
– *all-purpose trailer*
41 el dispositivo de recogida *f* (de carga) replegado (levantado)
– *[folded] pick-up attachment*
42 el dispositivo de descarga *f* (el distribuidor)
– *unloading unit*
43 el silo de polietileno *m*, un silo para el forraje
– *polythene silo, a fodder silo*
44 el pasto
– *meadow*
45 el ganado de pasto *m*
– *grazing cattle*
46 la cerca electrificada
– *electrified fence*

1-41 labores *f* del campo (las labores agrícolas)
– **work in the fields**
1 el barbecho (*Col. y Cuba:* el placer)
– *fallow (fallow field, fallow ground)*
2 el mojón
– *boundary stone*
3 la linde (lindero *m*, límite *m*)
– *boundary ridge, a balk (baulk)*
4 el campo (la tierra de labor *f*)
– *field*
5 la volea
– *swingletree (Am. whiffletree, whippletree)*
6 el arado
– *plough (Am. plow)*
7 el terrón
– *clod*
8 el surco
– *furrow*
9 la piedra
– *stone*
10-12 la siembra (la sementera)
– *sowing*
10 el sembrador (*Amér. Central:* el tayacán)
– *sower*
11 el sementero
– *seedlip*
12 la simiente (la semilla)
– *seed corn (seed)*
13 el guarda de campo *m* (el meseguero)
– *field guard*
14 el abono artificial (el abono químico); *clases:* el abono potásico, el abono fosfático, el abono cálcico, el abono nitrogenado
– *chemical fertilizer (artificial fertilizer);* kinds: *potash fertilizer, phosphoric acid fertilizer, lime fertilizer, nitrogen fertilizer*
15 la carretada de estiércol *m*
– *cartload of manure (farmyard manure, dung)*
16 la yunta de bueyes *m*
– *oxteam (team of oxen, Am. span of oxen)*
17 la campiña
– *fields (farmland)*
18 el camino vecinal (*Col. y S. Dgo.:* la trilla; *Amér. Central, Antillas, Ec., Pan., Urug.:* el trillo)
– *farm track (farm road)*
19-30 **la siega del heno** (de la hierba)
– **hay harvest** *(haymaking)*
19 la segadora agavilladora
– *rotary mower with swather (swath reaper)*
20 la barra de enganche *m*
– *connecting shaft (connecting rod)*
21 la toma de fuerza *f*
– *power take-off (power take-off shaft)*
22 el prado
– *meadow*
23 el tajo de heno *m* (la ringlera de heno *m* segado)
– *swath (swathe)*
24 la henificadora giratoria
– *tedder (rotary tedder)*
25 el heno esparcido (la hierba esparcida)
– *tedded hay*
26 la agavilladora giratoria
– *rotary swather*
27 la recogedora-cargadora
– *trailer with pick-up attachment*
28 el caballete sueco para el secado del heno, un secador de heno *m*
– *fence rack (rickstand), a drying rack for hay*
29 el colgadero de heno *m*
– *rickstand, a drying rack for hay*
30 el trípode para el secado del heno *m*
– *hay tripod*
31-41 la cosecha (la recolección) y la preparación de la tierra (*Col. y Venez.:* la cogienda)
– *grain harvest and seedbed preparation*
31 la segadora-trilladora (la cosechadora)
– *combine harvester*
32 la mies
– *cornfield*
33 la rastrojera
– *stubble field*
34 la bala (la paca) de paja *f* (una bala de paja *f* prensada)
– *bale of straw*
35 la empacadora de paja *f*, una empacadora de alta presión *f*
– *straw baler (straw press), a high-pressure baler*
36 el rastrojo
– *swath (swathe) of straw (windrow of straw)*
37 el cargador hidráulico de balas *f*
– *hydraulic bale loader*
38 el remolque de carga *f*
– *trailer*
39 el distribuidor de estiércol *m* (la esparcidora de estiércol *m*)
– *manure spreader*
40 el arado de cuatro rejas *f*
– *four-furro plough (Am. plow)*
41 la sembradora a chorrillo *m*
– *combination seed-harrow*

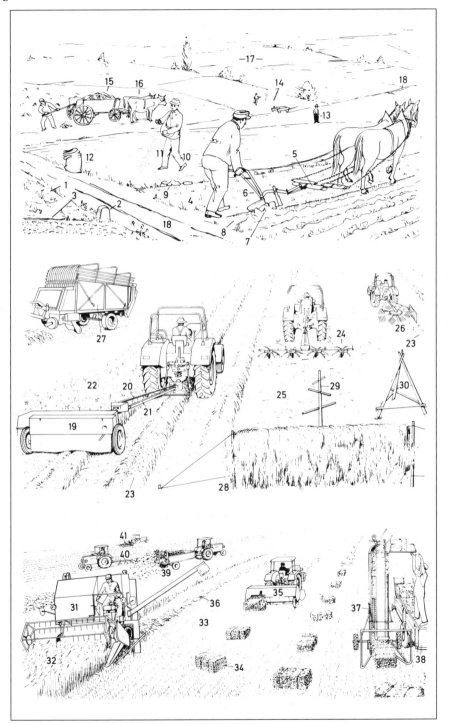

64 Máquinas agrícolas I

Agricultural Machinery I

1-33 **la cosechadora**
- **combine harvester** *(combine)*
1 el separador de cañas *f*
- *divider*
2 el elevador de espigas *f*
- *grain lifter*
3 la barra de cuchillas *f* (la barra de corte *m*)
- *cutter bar*
4 el tambor (el rodillo) de recolección *f* (el tambor con púas *f* de muelle *m*)
- *pick-up reel, a spring-tine reel*
5 el mecanismo de regulación *f* del tambor
- *reel gearing*
6 el rodillo de entrada *f*
- *auger*
7 la cinta transportadora con cadenas *f*
- *chain and slat elevator*
8 el cilindro hidráulico para la regulación del sistema de energía *f*
- *hydraulic cylinder for adjusting the cutting unit*
9 el dispositivo de eliminación *f* de piedras *f*
- *stone catcher (stone trap)*
10 la desbarbadora (la desgranadora)
- *awner*
11 el cóncavo del tambor desgranador (la reja trilladora)
- *concave*
12 el tambor desgranador
- *threshing drum (drum)*
13 el tambor de conducción *f* de la paja
- *revolving beater [for freeing straw from the drum and preparing it for the shakers]*
14 el tamiz (la criba) de la paja
- *straw shaker (strawwalker)*
15 el aventador para la limpieza con aire *m* a presión *f*
- *fan for compressed-air winnowing*
16 la cinta de preparación *f*
- *preparation level*
17 el tamiz (la criba) de la paja corta
- *louvred-type sieve*
18 el alargamiento del tamiz
- *sieve extension*
19 la vuelta del tamiz
- *shoe sieve (reciprocating sieve)*
20 el tornillo sin fin *m* [para introducir el grano en la tolva]
- *grain auger*
21 el tornillo sin fin *m* hacia el desgranador
- *tailings auger*
22 la salida de la parte trasera (la salida de la rosca)
- *tailings outlet*
23 el depósito del grano
- *grain tank*
24 el tornillo sin fin *m* de alimentación *f* del depósito del grano
- *grain tank auger*
25 el tornillo sin fin *m* para el vaciado del depósito del grano
- *augers feeding to the grain tank unloader*
26 el conducto de vaciado *m* del depósito del grano
- *grain unloader spout*
27 la abertura para controlar el relleno del depósito
- *observation ports for checking tank contents*
28 el motor Diesel de seis cilindros *m*
- *six-cylinder diesel engine*
29 la bomba hidráulica con reserva *f* de aceite *m*
- *hydraulic pump with oil reservoir*
30 el árbol de transmisión *f*
- *driving axle gearing*
31 el neumático de una rueda motriz
- *driving wheel tyre* (Am. *tire*)
32 el neumático de una rueda direccional
- *rubber-tyred* (Am. *rubber-tired*) *wheel on the steering axle*
33 el puesto del conductor
- *driver's position*

34-39 **la recogedora picadora automotriz**
- **self-propelled forage harvester** *(self-propelled field chopper)*
34 el tambor de corte *m*
- *cutting drum (chopper drum)*
35 el pico (la dentadura) para el maíz
- *corn head*
36 la cabina del conductor
- *cab (driver's cab)*
37 el tubo de eyección *f*
- *swivel-mounted spout (discharge pipe)*
38 el escape
- *exhaust*
39 una rueda direccional trasera
- *rear-wheel steering system*
40-45 **la gavilladora de torbellino *m***
- **rotary swather**
40 el árbol de articulación *f*
- *cardan shaft*
41 la rueda
- *running wheel*
42 las púas de muelle *m*
- *double spring tine*
43 la manivela
- *crank*
44 el rastrillo
- *swath rake*
45 el acoplamiento (el soporte) de tres puntos *m*
- *three-point linkage*
46-58 **la henificadora giratoria**
- **rotary tedder**
46 el tractor
- *tractor*
47 la lanza de remolque *m*
- *draw bar*
48 el árbol de articulación *f*
- *cardan shaft*
49 la toma de fuerza *f*
- *power take-off (power take-off shaft)*
50 el mecanismo
- *gearing (gears)*
51 el tubo de soporte *m* (el chasis)
- *frame bar*
52 el platillo giratorio
- *rotating head*
53 el tubo de soporte *m* de las púas
- *tine bar*
54 las púas de muelle *m*
- *double spring tine*
55 la brida de protección *f*
- *guard rail*
56 la rueda
- *running wheel*
57 la manivela de regulación *f* de la altura
- *height adjustment crank*
58 la regulación de las ruedas
- *wheel adjustment*
59-84 **la arrancadora-recogedora de patatas *f***
- **potato harvester**
59 las palancas de mando *m*
- *control levers for the lifters of the digger and the hopper and for adjusting the shaft*
60 el gancho de tiro *m* para regular la altura
- *adjustable hitch*
61 la lanza de tiro *m* (de tracción *f*)
- *drawbar*
62 el soporte de la lanza
- *drawbar support*
63 el empalme de la toma de fuerza *f*
- *cardan shaft connection*
64 el cilindro compresor
- *press roller*
65 el mecanismo del motor hidráulico
- *gearing (gears) for the hydraulic system*
66 la cuchilla de disco *m* (la cuchilla circular)
- *disc (disk) coulter* (Am. *colter*) *(rolling coulter)*
67 la reja de tres láminas *f*
- *three-bladed share*
68 el mecanismo de mando *m* de la cuchilla de disco *m*
- *disc (disk) coulter* (Am. *colter*) *drive*

69 la cinta transportadora
- *open-web elevator*
70 el mecanismo de sacudida *f* de la cinta transportadora
- *agitator*
71 el desmultiplicador de varias velocidades *f*
- *multi-step reduction gearing*
72 el cargador
- *feeder*
73 el arrancador de hierbas *f* (el rotor de aletas *f*)
- *haulm stripper (flail rotor)*
74 la rueda elevadora
- *rotary elevating drum*
75 el separador oscilante
- *mechanical tumbling separator*
76 la cinta transportadora de hierbas *f* con arrancadores *m* flexibles
- *haulm conveyor with flexible haulm strippers*
77 el dispositivo de sacudida *f* de la cinta transportadora de hierbas *f*
- *haulm conveyor agitator*
78 el mecanismo de mando *m* con correa *f* trapezoidal
- *haulm conveyor drive with V-belt*
79 la correa de caucho *m* claveteada para la separación de los tallos, de los terrones de tierra *f* y de las piedras
- *studded rubber belt for sorting vines, clods and stones*
80 la cinta transportadora de las impurezas
- *trash conveyor*
81 la cinta de inspección *f* y clasificación *f*
- *sorting table*
82 los rodillos de discos *m* de caucho *m* para asegurar la primera selección *f*
- *rubber-disc (rubber-disk) rollers for presorting*
83 la cinta de descarga *f*
- *discharge conveyor*
84 la tolva con fondo *m* móvil
- *endless-floor hopper*
85-96 **la extractora de remolachas *f* (una arrancadora-cortadora-cargadora de remolachas *f*)**
- **beet harvester**
85 la cortadora
- *topper*
86 la rueda direccional
- *feeler*
87 la cuchilla de extracción *f*
- *topping knife*
88 la rueda de apoyo *m* con regulación *f* de profundidad *f*
- *feeler support wheel with depth adjustment*
89 el limpiador de remolachas *f*
- *beet cleaner*
90 el elevador de las hojas
- *haulm elevator*
91 la bomba hidráulica
- *hydraulic pump*
92 el depósito de aire *m* comprimido
- *compressed-air reservoir*
93 el depósito de aceite *m*
- *oil tank (oil reservoir)*
94 el dispositivo de regulación *f* de la tensión del elevador de remolachas *f*
- *tensioning device for the beet elevator*
95 la cinta elevadora de remolachas *f*
- *beet elevator belt*
96 la tolva de las remolachas
- *beet hopper*

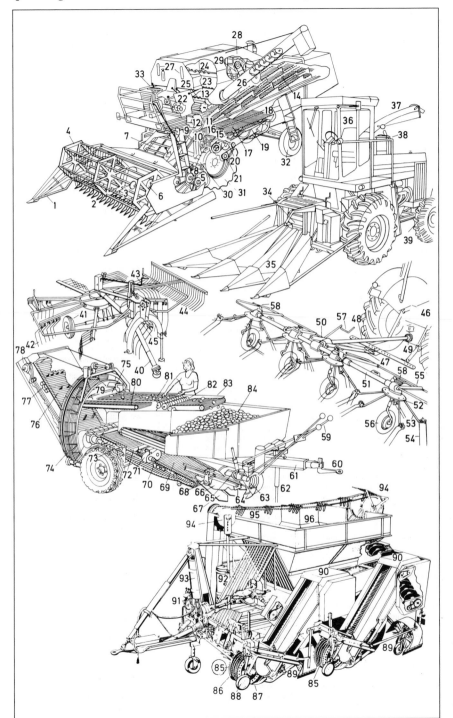

1 el arado de vertedera f
– *wheel plough* (Am. *plow*), *a single-bottom plough* [form.]
2 la empuñadura
– *handle*
3 la esteva (la mancera)
– *plough* (Am. *plow*) *stilt (plough handle)*
4-8 el cuerpo del arado
– *plough* (Am. *plow*) *bottom*
4 la vertedera
– *mouldboard* (Am. *moldboard*)
5 el montante vertical
– *landside*
6 la cabeza
– *sole (slade)*
7 la reja
– *ploughshare (share,* Am. *plowshare)*
8 el montante (el puntal)
– *frog (frame)*
9 la cama del arado
– *beam (plough beam,* Am. *plowbeam)*
10 la cuchilla (el punzón)
– *knife coulter* (Am. *colter), a coulter*
11 la reja anterior
– *skim coulter* (Am. *colter)*
12 el regulador para la dirección f automática por cadena f
– *guide-chain crossbar*
13 la cadena para la guía automática
– *guide chain*
14-19 el carro del arado (el carro, el antetrén; *Cuba:* el trinqueval)
– *forecarriage*
14 el yugo (el estribo)
– *adjustable yoke*
15 la rueda del caballón
– *land wheel*
16 la rueda del surco
– *furrow wheel*
17 la cadena de suspensión f
– *hake chain*
18 la lanza de tiro m
– *draught beam (drawbar)*
19 el gancho de tiro m
– *hake*
20 el tractor agrícola
– *tractor (general-purpose tractor)*
21 el bastidor de la cabina (el arco de seguridad f)
– *cab frame (roll bar)*
22 el asiento
– *seat*
23 el cambio de velocidad f de la toma de fuerza f
– *power take-off gear-change (gearshift)*
24-29 el sistema hidráulico de elevación f
– *power lift*
24 el pistón hidráulico
– *ram piston*
25 el regulador del puntal de elevación f
– *lifting rod adjustment*
26 el marco de unión f
– *drawbar frame*
27 la barra conductora superior
– *top link*
28 la barra conductora inferior
– *lower link*
29 el puntal (la varilla) de elevación f
– *lifting rod*
30 el engache (el acoplamiento de remolque m)
– *drawbar coupling*

31 la toma de fuerza f del motor (la toma de fuerza f independiente)
– *live power take-off (live power take-off shaft, take-off shaft)*
32 el engranaje diferencial (el diferencial)
– *differential gear (differential)*
33 el eje fijo
– *floating axle*
34 la palanca de cambio m del par motor
– *torque converter lever*
35 la palanca de velocidad f
– *gear-change (gearshift)*
36 la transmisión de velocidades f múltiples
– *multi-speed transmission*
37 el embrague hidráulico
– *fluid clutch (fluid drive)*
38 la transmisión de toma de fuerza f
– *power take-off gear*
39 el embrague principal (el embrague)
– *main clutch*
40 el cambio de velocidad f de la toma de fuerza f, con embrague m de toma f de fuerza f
– *power take-off gear-change (gearshift) with power take-off clutch*
41 la dirección hidráulica con transmisión f reversible
– *hydraulic power steering and reversing gears*
42 el depósito de combustible m
– *fuel tank*
43 la palanca flotante
– *float lever*
44 el motor Diesel de cuatro cilindros m
– *four-cylinder diesel engine*
45 el cárter de aceite m con bomba f para la lubrificación por circulación f forzada
– *oil sump and pump for the pressure-feed lubrication system*
46 el depósito de aceite m fresco
– *fresh oil tank*
47 la barra de acoplamiento m
– *track rod* (Am. *tie rod)*
48 el soporte del eje delantero
– *front axle pivot pin*
49 la suspensión del eje delantero
– *front axle suspension*
50 el dispositivo de remolque m de la delantera
– *front coupling (front hitch)*
51 el radiador
– *radiator*
52 el ventilador
– *fan*
53 la batería
– *battery*
54 el filtro de aire m con baño m de aceite m
– *oil bath air cleaner (oil bath air filter)*
55 el cultivador
– *cultivator (grubber)*
56 el bastidor
– *sectional frame*
57 la púa de muelle m
– *spring tine*
58 la reja de arado m
– *share, a diamond-shaped share* (sim.: *chisel-shaped share)*
59 la rueda de apoyo m
– *depth wheel*
60 el regulador de profundidad f
– *depth adjustment*

61 el dispositivo de remolque m
– *coupling (hitch)*
62 el arado reversible, un arado de cultivo m
– *reversible plough* (Am. *plow), a mounted plough*
63 la rueda de apoyo m
– *depth wheel*
64-67 el cuerpo del arado, un cuerpo de arado m universal
– *plough* (Am. *plow) bottom, a general-purpose plough bottom*
64 la vertedera
– *mouldboard* (Am. *moldboard)*
65 la reja del arado
– *ploughshare (share,* Am. *plowshare), a pointed share*
66 la cabeza
– *sole (slade)*
67 el montante vertical
– *landside*
68 la cuchilla (el punzón)
– *skim coulter* (Am. *colter)*
69 la cuchilla de disco m (la cuchilla circular)
– *disc (disk) coulter* (Am. *colter) (rolling coulter)*
70 el bastidor del arado
– *plough* (Am. *plow) frame*
71 la cama del arado
– *beam (plough beam,* Am. *plowbeam)*
72 el enganche de tres puntos m
– *three-point linkage*
73 el mecanismo basculante (el mecanismo de báscula f)
– *swivel mechanism*
74 la sembradora a chorrillo m
– *drill*
75 la caja de la semilla
– *seed hopper*
76 la cuchilla de hacer surcos m
– *drill coulter* (Am. *colter)*
77 el tubo de llegada f, un tubo telescópico
– *delivery tube, a telescopic tube*
78 el aparato distribuidor
– *feed mechanism*
79 la caja de engranajes m
– *gearbox*
80 la rueda motriz
– *drive wheel*
81 el indicador del surco
– *track indicator*
82 el pulverizador de discos m
– *disc (disk) harrow, a semimounted implement*
83 la disposición de los discos en forma f de X
– *discs (disks) in X-configuration*
84 el disco redondo
– *plain disc (disk)*
85 el disco dentado
– *serrated-edge disc (disk)*
86 el enganche rápido
– *quick hitch*
87 la combinación grada-desterronador
– *combination seed-harrow*
88 la grada con dientes m de tres secciones f
– *three-section spike-tooth harrow*
89 el desterronador de tres secciones f
– *three-section rotary harrow*
90 el bastidor (la armazón) fijo (-a)
– *frame*

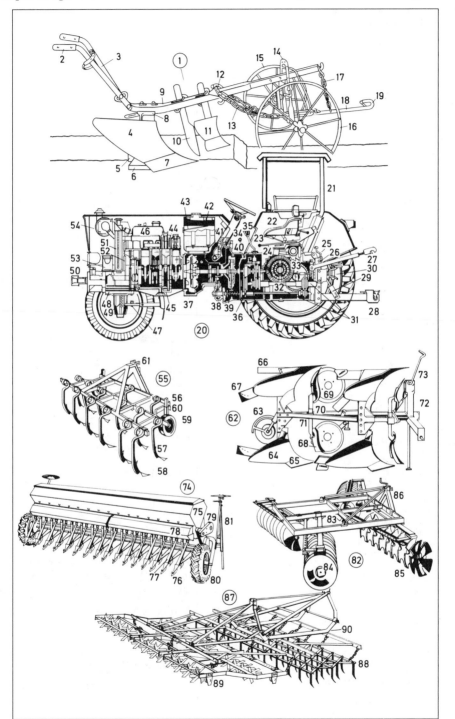

66 Herramientas agrícolas

1 la azada de arrastre *m* (*Arg., Bol., Ec.
  y Perú:* la lampa; *Col.:* la palendra)
– *draw hoe (garden hoe)*
2 el mango de la azada
– *hoe handle*
3 la horca de tres puntas *f* para el heno
  (la horca del heno, la horca)
– *three-pronged (three-tined) hay fork
  (fork)*
4 la púa (la punta, el pincho, el gajo)
– *prong (tine)*
5 la horca para las patatas (la bielda
  para las patatas, el trente, la pala de
  las patatas; *Col.:* la garlancha)
– *potato fork*
6 la azada para las patatas (*Ec.:* el
  palancón)
– *potato hook*
7 la horca de cuatro puntas *f* para el
  estiércol (la horca del estiércol, la
  horca)
– *four-pronged (four-tined) manure
  fork (fork)*
8 la azada para el estiércol (*Perú, P.
  Rico, Guat., S. Dgo. y Venez.:* el
  desyerbo)
– *manure hoe*
9 el martillo de la guadaña
– *whetting hammer [for scythes]*
10 el corte del martillo
– *peen (pane)*
11 el yunque de la guadaña
– *whetting anvil [for scythes]*
12 la guadaña (el dalle, la dalla)
– *scythe*
13 la hoja de la guadaña
– *scythe blade*
14 el filo de la guadaña (el corte de la
  guadaña)
– *cutting edge*
15 el talón de la guadaña (la culata de la
  guadaña)
– *heel*
16 el mango de la guadaña (el asta *f* de
  la guadaña)
– *snath (snathe, snead, sneath)*
17 la manija de la guadaña
– *handle*
18 la guarda (el protector del filo de la
  guadaña)
– *scythe sheath*
19 la piedra de afilar (la afiladera) [*se
  lleva en* la aliara]
– *whetstone (scythestone)*
20 el rastro para las patatas
– *potato rake*
21 el cesto (la sera) para patatas *f* de
  siembra *f* (*Mé.:* el quiligua)
– *potato planter*
22 la laya
– *digging fork (fork)*
23 el rastrillo para el heno (el rastrillo,
  el rastro para el heno)
– *wooden rake (rake, hayrake)*
24 el azadón de rozar (el azadón de
  patatas *f; Chile:* el gualato)
– *hoe (potato hoe)*
25 el cesto de las patatas, un cesto de
  alambre *m*
– *potato basket, a wire basket*
26 la carretilla del trébol, una máquina
  sembradora de trébol *m*
– *clover broadcaster*

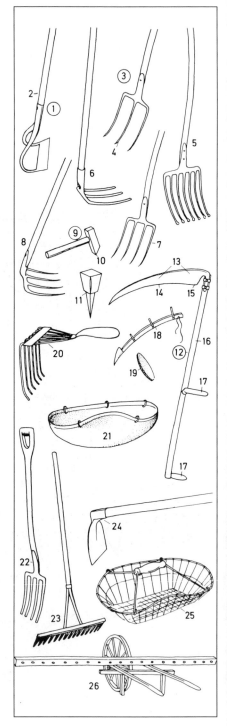

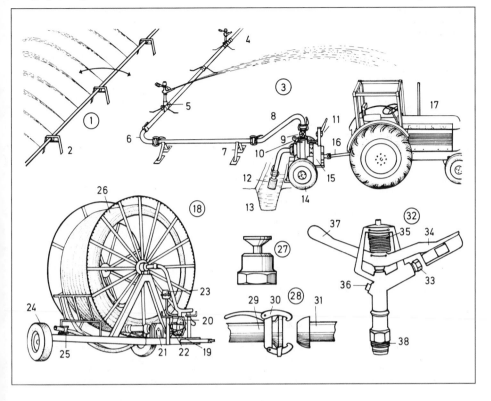

1 el tubo oscilante con surtidores *m*
– *oscillating spray line*
2 el caballete de soporte *m*
– *stand (steel chair)*
3 el dispositivo móvil de riego *m*
– *portable irrigation system*
4 el regador giratorio
– *revolving sprinkler*
5 el empalme de tubo *m*
– *standpipe coupler*
6 el codo de cardán *m*
– *elbow with cardan joint (cardan coupling)*
7 el caballete de soporte *m*
– *pipe support (trestle)*
8 el codo de empalme *m* de la bomba
– *pump connection*
9 el empalme a presión *f*
– *delivery valve*
10 el manómetro
– *pressure gauge* (Am. *gage*) *(manometer)*
11 la bomba de evacuación *f*
– *centrifugal evacuating pump*
12 la alcachofa de aspiración *f*
– *basket strainer*
13 la zanja (el canal)
– *channel*

14 el chasis de la bomba accionada por la toma de fuerza *f* del tractor
– *chassis of the p.t.o.-driven pump (power take-off-driven pump)*
15 la bomba de tractor *m* (la bomba accionada por la toma de fuerza *f* del tractor)
– *p.t.o.-driven (power take-off-driven) pump*
16 el árbol de articulación *f*
– *cardan shaft*
17 el tractor
– *tractor*
18 el regador para grandes superficies *f*
– *long-range irrigation unit*
19 la tubuladura de propulsión *f*
– *drive connection*
20 la turbina
– *turbine*
21 el cambio de velocidades *f* (el reductor)
– *gearing (gears)*
22 el apoyo ajustable
– *adjustable support*
23 la bomba de evacuación *f*
– *centrifugal evacuating pump*
24 la rueda
– *wheel*
25 la guía del tubo
– *pipe support*

26 el tubo de poliéster *m*
– *polyester pipe*
27 la boquilla (la tobera) del regador
– *sprinkler nozzle*
28 el tubo de empalme *m* instantáneo con junta *f* de articulación *f* cardán *m*
– *quick-fitting pipe connection with cardan joint*
29 la pieza macho del cardán
– *M-cardan*
30 el acoplamiento
– *clamp*
31 la pieza hembra del cardán
– *V-cardan*
32 el regador giratorio
– *revolving sprinkler, a field sprinkler*
33 la boquilla
– *nozzle*
34 la palanca oscilante
– *breaker*
35 el muelle de la palanca oscilante
– *breaker spring*
36 el tapón
– *stopper*
37 el contrapeso
– *counterweight*
38 la rosca
– *thread*

1-47 frutos *m* del campo (productos *m* agrícolas)
– **arable crops** *(agricultural produce, farm produce)*
1-37 clases *f* de cereales *m* (granos *m* panificables)
– *varieties of grain (grain, cereals, farinaceous plants, bread-corn)*
1 el centeno (*también:* el grano; "grano" significa a menudo el principal grano panificable, en España: el trigo, en el norte de Alemania: el centeno, en el sur de Alemania e Italia: el trigo, en Suecia y Noruega: la cebada, en Escocia: la avena, en Norteamérica: el maíz, en China: el arroz)
– *rye (also: corn, 'corn' often meaning the main cereal of a country or region; in Northern Germany: rye; in Southern Germany and Italy: wheat; in Sweden: barley; in Scotland: oats; in North America: maize; in China: rice)*
2 la espiga de centeno *m*, una espiga
– *ear of rye, a spike (head)*
3 la espiguilla
– *spikelet*
4 el cornezuelo, un grano deformado por un hongo
– *ergot, a grain deformed by fungus [shown with mycelium]*
5 la macolla de un cereal
– *corn stem after tillering*
6 la caña
– *culm (stalk)*
7 el nudo
– *node of the culm*
8 la hoja
– *leaf (grain leaf)*
9 la vaina de la hoja
– *leaf sheath (sheath)*
10 la espiguilla
– *spikelet*
11 el cascabillo
– *glume*
12 la arista (la barba)
– *awn (beard, arista)*
13 la semilla (el grano, la cariópside)
– *seed (grain, kernel, farinaceous grain)*
14 el germen de la planta (el grano germinado)
– *embryo plant*
15 la semilla
– *seed*
16 el brote
– *embryo*
17 la raíz
– *root*

18 los pelos absorbentes de la raíz
– *root hair*
19 la hoja del cereal
– *grain leaf*
20 el limbo
– *leaf blade (blade, lamina)*
21 la vaina de la hoja
– *leaf sheath*
22 la lígula
– *ligule (ligula)*
23 el trigo
– *wheat*
24 la espelta (la escanda común, escaña *f* mayor)
– *spelt*
25 la semilla; *no madurada:* la espelta verde, un grano verde para guisos *m*
– *seed; unripe: green spelt, a soup vegetable*
26 la cebada
– *barley*
27 la avena, una panícula
– *oat panicle, a panicle*
28 el mijo
– *millet*
29 el arroz
– *rice*
30 el grano de arroz *m*
– *rice grain*
31 el maíz; *variedades:* maíz perlado, maíz de diente *m* de caballo *m*, maíz duro, maíz de vainas, maíz tierno, maíz dulce, maíz tostado (*Arg. y Chile:* el ancua), maíz morocho, maíz dental, maíz amarillo, maíz híbrido
– *maize (Indian corn, Am. corn); varieties: popcorn, dent corn, flint corn (flint maize, Am. Yankee corn), pod corn (Am. cow corn, husk corn), soft corn (Am. flour corn, squaw corn), sweet corn*
32 la inflorescencia femenina
– *female inflorescence*
33 la perfolla (la farfolla; *Arg., Bol., Chile, Mé., Perú y Urug.:* la chala)
– *husk (shuck)*
34 el pistilo
– *style*
35 la inflorescencia masculina en panícula *f*
– *male inflorescence (tassel)*
36 la mazorca (la panoja, la panocha; *Mé.:* el cenancle; *Arg. y Par.:* el abatí)
– *maize cob (Am. corn cob)*
37 el grano de maíz *m* (*Arg. y Par.:* el grano de abatí *m*)
– *maize kernel (grain of maize)*

38-45 tubérculos *m*
– **root crops**
38 la patata (*Amér.:* la papa), un tubérculo; *clases:* redonda, ovalada, alargada, arriñonada; *según el color:* blanca, amarilla, roja, rosa; *según la precocidad:* muy precoz, precoz, semitardía, tardía; *según la utilidad:* industrial, forrajera, de huerta
– *potato plant (potato), a tuberous plant;* varieties: *round, round-oval (pear-shaped), flat-oval, long, kidney-shaped potato;* according to colour: *white (Am. Irish), yellow, red, purple potato*
39 la patata de siembra *f* (el tubérculo madre *f*)
– *seed potato (seed tuber)*
40 la patata (el tubérculo) (*Amér.:* la papa, el bulbo)
– *potato tuber (potato, tuber)*
41 la hoja de la patata
– *potato top (potato haulm)*
42 la flor
– *flower*
43 la baya no comestible (la baya de la patata)
– *poisonous potato berry (potato apple)*
44 la remolacha azucarera, una remolacha
– *sugar beet, a beet*
45 la raíz (la remolacha)
– *root (beet)*
46 el cuello de la remolacha
– *beet top*
47 la hoja de la remolacha
– *beet leaf*

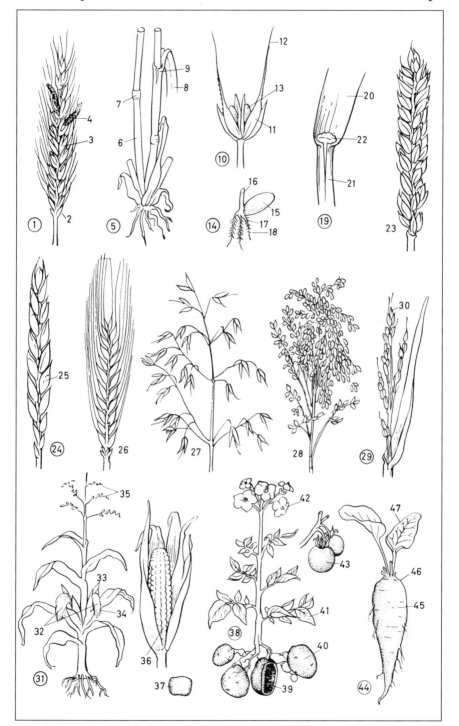

69 Plantas forrajeras

1-28 plantas *f* forrajeras cultivadas
– *fodder plants (forage plants) for tillage*
1 el trébol del prado *m* (*Col.*: el carretonero)
– *red clover (purple clover)*
2 el trébol blanco
– *white clover (Dutch clover)*
3 el trébol híbrido
– *alsike clover (alsike)*
4 el trébol encarnado
– *crimson clover*
5 el trébol de cuatro hojas *f* (*pop.*: el trébol de la suerte)
– *four-leaf (four-leaved) clover*
6 la vulneraria
– *kidney vetch (lady's finger, ladyfinger)*
7 la flor del trébol
– *flower*
8 la vaina
– *pod*
9 la alfalfa
– *lucerne (lucern, purple medick)*
10 la esparceta (el pipirigallo, la gallocresta)
– *sainfoin (cock's head, cockshead)*
11 el trébol de pie de pájaro *m* (la serradella)
– *bird's foot (bird-foot, bird's foot trefoil)*
12 la arenaria, una cariofilácea
– *corn spurrey (spurrey, spurry), a spurrey (spurry)*
13 la consuelda (el sínfito mayor)
– *common comfrey, one of the borage family (Boraginaceae)*
14 la flor
– *flower (blossom)*
15 el haba *f* gruesa (el haba *f* panosa; *anál.*: el haba *f* común, la judía escarlata, el haba *f* del ganado, el haba *f* de los caballos)
– *field bean (broad bean, tick bean, horse bean)*
16 la vaina
– *pod*
17 el lupino amarillo (el altramuz amarillo)
– *yellow lupin*
18 la arveja (la veza)
– *common vetch*
19 la almorta (el garbanzo forrajero, la muela, la guija)
– *chick-pea*
20 el girasol
– *sunflower*
21 la remolacha forrajera
– *mangold (mangelwurzel, mangoldwurzel, field mangel)*
22 la espiguilla
– *false oat (oat-grass)*
23 la espiguilla
– *spikelet*
24 la cañuela (la festuca de los prados), una festuca
– *meadow fescue grass, a fescue*
25 la grama en jopillos *m*, un dáctilo
– *cock's foot (cocksfoot)*
26 el ballico (el césped inglés, el raigrás italiano)
– *Italian ryegrass; sim.: perennial ryegrass (English ryegrass)*
27 la cola de zorra *f* (el alopecuro), una graminácea
– *meadow foxtail, a paniculate grass*
28 la pimpinela mayor (la sanguisorba)
– *greater burnet saxifrage*

1-14 dogos *m*
- *mastiffs*
1 el bulldog
- *bulldog*
2 la oreja colgante
- *ear, a rose-ear*
3 el hocico (la boca)
- *muzzle*
4 las narices
- *nose*
5 la pata delantera (el brazo)
- *foreleg*
6 la mano
- *forepaw*
7 la pata trasera
- *hind leg*
8 el pie
- *hind paw*
9 el doguino (el doguillo)
- *pug (pug dog)*
10 el bóxer
- *boxer*
11 la cruz
- *withers*
12 la cola, una cola cortada
- *tail, a docked tail*
13 el collar de perro *m*
- *collar*

14 el gran danés (el dogo alemán)
- *Great Dane*
15-18 terrier *m*
- *terriers*
15 el foxterrier
- *wire-haired fox terrier*
16 el bullterrier
- *bull terrier*
17 el terrier escocés
- *Scotch terrier (Scottish terrier)*
18 el terrier bedlington
- *Bedlington terrier*
19 el perrito pequinés
- *Pekinese (Pekingese, Pekinese dog, Pekingese dog)*
20-22 spitz *m*
- *spitzes*
20 el lulú (el perro de Pomerania)
- *spitz (Pomeranian)*
21 el chow-chow
- *chow (chow-chow)*
22 el perro esquimal
- *husky*
23 *u.* **24 galgos** *m* (lebreles *m*)
- *greyhounds* (Am. *grayhounds*)
23 el afgano (el galgo afgano)
- *Afghan (Afghan hound)*

24 el galgo
- *greyhound* (Am. *grayhound*)*, a courser*
25 el pastor alemán (un perro lobo *m*), un perro de ayuda *f*, un perro guardián y de compañía *f*
- *Alsatian (German sheepdog,* Am. *German shepherd), a police dog, watch dog, and guide dog*
26 los belfos
- *flews (chaps)*
27 el doberman
- *Dobermann terrier*

28-31 el equipo del perro
– *dog's outfit*
28 el cepillo para perros *m*
– *dog brush*
29 el peine para perros *m*
– *dog comb*
30 la correa; *en cacerías:* la traílla
– *lead (dog lead, leash);* for hunting: *leash*
31 el bozal (*Cuba y Perú:* la hociquera)
– *muzzle*
32 la escudilla de la comida (el comedero)
– *feeding bowl (dog bowl)*
33 el hueso
– *bone*
34 el perro de Terranova (el terranova)
– *Newfoundland dog*
35 el grifón
– *schnauzer*
36 el perro de lanas (el caniche); *más pequeño:* el perro de lanas *f* enano (el caniche enano; *Amér. Merid.:* el choco)
– *poodle;* sim. and smaller: *pygmy (pigmy) poodle*

37 el perro de san Bernardo (el san Bernardo)
– *St. Bernard (St. Bernard dog)*
38-43 perros *m* de caza *f*
– *hunting dogs*
38 el cócker
– *cocker spaniel*
39 el teckel de pelo *m* corto (el perro zarcero, el teckel, el basset, el perro tejonero)
– *dachshund, a terrier*
40 el perro de muestra *f* alemán
– *German pointer*
41 el setter (un perro de muestra *f* inglés)
– *English setter*
42 el perro perdiguero, un perro de muestra *f*
– *trackhound*
43 el pointer, un perro rastrero
– *pointer, a trackhound*

1-6 equitación *f* (el arte de montar a caballo *m*, la equitación de alta escuela *f*)
– *equitation (high school riding, haute école)*
1 el piafe
– *piaffe*
2 el paso (el paso corto, el paso de escuela *f*)
– *walk*
3 el passage (el paso español)
– *passage*
4 la levade (la pirueta)
– *levade (pesade)*
5 la cabriola
– *capriole*
6 la corveta
– *courbette (curvet)*
7-25 los arreos (los arneses; *Antillas, Chile, Guat.* y *Perú:* el aparejo; *Col.* y *Cuba:* los arretrancos; *P. Rico:* los ensillos)
– *harness*
7-13 *u.* **25 los arreos** (los arneses; *Antillas, Chile, Guat.* y *Perú:* el aparejo; *Col.* y *Cuba:* los arretrancos; *P. Rico:* los ensillos)
– *bridle*
7-11 la cabezada (*Amér. Central:* el gamarrón; *Ec., Mí.* y *Perú:* el bozalillo; *Mé.* y *Chile:* el cabeceador; *Col.:* la martingala; *Col.* y *Ec.:* la tapanca)
– *headstall (headpiece, halter)*
7 la muserola
– *noseband*
8 la quijera
– *cheek piece (cheek strap)*
9 la frontalera
– *browband (front band)*
10 la testera
– *crownpiece*
11 el ahogadero
– *throatlatch (throatlash)*
12 la cadenilla de barbada *f*
– *curb chain*
13 el bocado con la barbada
– *curb bit*
14 el gancho del tirante
– *hasp (hook) of the hame* (Am. *drag hook)*
15 la collera (*Mé.:* el gargantón)
– *pointed collar, a collar*
16 el adorno de la collera
– *trappings (side trappings)*
17 el sillín
– *saddle-pad*
18 la cincha (la barriguera; *Arg., Col., Chile, Urug.* y *Venez.:* el cinchón)
– *girth*
19 la sufra (*Cuba:* la tiradera)
– *backband*
20 la cadena de la vara
– *shaft chain (pole chain)*

21 la vara (la lanza, la flecha)
– *pole*
22 el tirante
– *trace*
23 la cincha (la barriguera) auxiliar
– *second girth (emergency girth)*
24 el tiro
– *trace*
25 las riendas (las bridas)
– *reins* (Am. *lines)*
26-36 los arreos de pecho *m*
– *breast harness*
26 las anteojeras (*Cuba* y *P. Rico:* la visera)
– *blinker* (Am. *blinder, winker)*
27 la anilla del petral
– *breast collar ring*
28 el petral
– *breast collar (Dutch collar)*
29 la horquilla del sobrecuello
– *fork*
30 el sobrecuello
– *neck strap*
31 el sillín
– *saddle-pad*
32 la correa del lomo
– *loin strap*
33 las riendas (las bridas)
– *reins (rein,* Am. *line)*
34 la baticola (la correa de la cola, el ataharre)
– *crupper (crupper-strap)*
35 el tirante
– *trace*
36 la cincha (la barriguera)
– *girth (belly-band)*
37-49 sillas *f* **de montar** [*la silla para mujer en Guat., Hond., S. Dgo.* y *Venez.:* el galápago; *en Ec.* y *Cuba:* el gancho]
– *saddles*
37-44 la silla de paseo *m*
– *stock saddle* (Am. *western saddle)*
37 el sillín (el asiento)
– *saddle seat*
38 el borrén delantero
– *pommel horn (horn)*
39 el borrén trasero
– *cantle*
40 la hoja (el faldón) lateral (*Arg.* y *Chile:* el mandil; *Arg.* y *Urug.:* el sobrepelo)
– *flap* (Am. *fender)*
41 los refuerzos
– *bar*
42 la ación (*Amér.:* la estribera)
– *stirrup leather*
43 el estribo
– *stirrup (stirrup iron)*
44 la manta de la silla (el sudadero; *Arg.* y. *Urug.:* el sobrepelo; *Col.* y *Venez.:* el sufridor; *S. Dgo.:* el panó; *Amér. Central* y *Chile:* el pelero; *Mé.:* el cuascle)
– *blanket*

45-49 la silla inglesa
– *English saddle (cavalry saddle)*
45 el sillín (el asiento)
– *seat*
46 el pomo
– *cantle*
47 la hoja (el faldón) lateral
– *flap*
48 la hoja falsa
– *roll (knee roll)*
49 el baste
– *pad*
50 *u.* **51 las espuelas** (*Col.* y *Venez.:* las orejonas)
– *spurs*
50 el espolín (la espuela fija, la espuela clavada)
– *box spur (screwed jack spur)*
51 la espuela de correílla *f*
– *strapped jack spur*
52 el bocado (*Antillas, C. Rica, Ec.* y *Mé.:* el basbiquejo)
– *curb bit*
53 el freno de boca *f*
– *gag bit (gag)*
54 la almohaza (*Amér. Merid.:* la rasqueta)
– *currycomb*
55 la bruza
– *horse brush (body brush, dandy brush)*

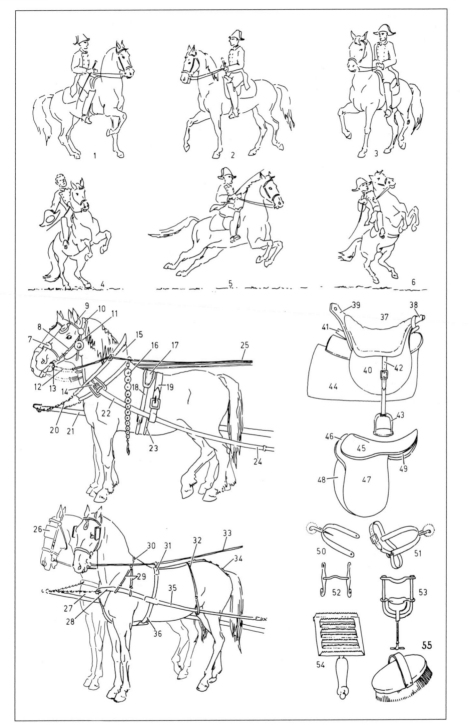

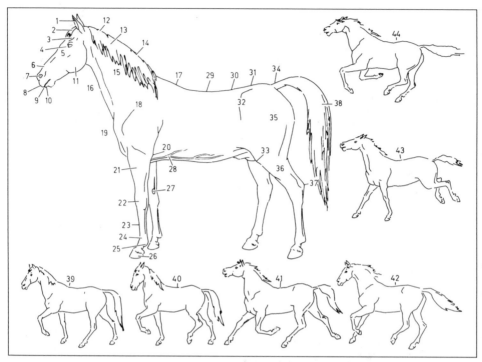

1-38 la forma exterior del caballo
- *points of the horse*
1-11 la cabeza (la cabeza del caballo)
- *head (horse's head)*
1 la oreja
- *ear*
2 el copete (*Chile:* el moño; *Venez.:* la guaya)
- *forelock*
3 la frente
- *forehead*
4 el ojo
- *eye*
5 la cara (la mejilla)
- *face*
6 el testuz
- *nose*
7 el ollar
- *nostril*
8 el labio (belfo *m*) superior
- *upper lip*
9 la boca
- *mouth*
10 el labio (belfo *m*) inferior
- *underlip (lower lip)*
11 la quijada inferior
- *lower jaw*
12 la nuca
- *crest (neck)*
13 la crin
- *mane (horse's mane)*
14 la cerviz (las crines; *Chile:* la tusa)
- *crest (horse's crest)*
15 el cuello
- *neck*
16 la garganta
- *throat (Am. throatlatch, throatlash)*

17 la cruz
- *withers*
18-27 la mano delantera
- *forehand*
18 la espaldilla (la paletilla)
- *shoulder*
19 el pecho
- *breast*
20 el codillo
- *elbow*
21 el brazuelo
- *forearm*
22-26 la pata delantera
- *forefoot*
22 la rodilla delantera
- *knee (carpus, wrist)*
23 la caña
- *cannon*
24 el menudillo
- *fetlock*
25 el espolón
- *pastern*
26 el casco
- *hoof*
27 el espejuelo (la castaña), una callosidad
- *chestnut (castor), a callosity*
28 la vena torácica larga (la vena de la espuela)
- *spur vein*
29 el lomo
- *back*
30 los riñones
- *loins (lumbar region)*
31 la grupa (*Venez.:* la tarraza; *Guat.:* la tenedora)
- *croup (rump, crupper)*
32 el anca *f*
- *hip*

33-37 el cuarto trasero
- *hind leg*
33 la babilla (el gordetillo)
- *stifle (stifle joint)*
34 el maslo de la cola
- *root (dock) of the tail*
35 el muslo
- *haunch*
36 la pierna
- *gaskin*
37 el corvejón
- *hock*
38 la cola
- *tail*
39-44 los pasos de los caballos (los aires del caballo)
- *gaits of the horse*
39 el paso (*Urug.:* el tranco)
- *walk*
40 el paso de andadura *f*
- *pace*
41 el trote (*Col. y Venez.:* la trocha; *Col.:* el troche)
- *trot*
42 el galope a la izquierda
- *canter (hand gallop)*
43 u. 44 el galope tendido (el galope de carrera *f*)
- *full gallop*
43 el galope en el momento de la caída sobre los remos anteriores
- *full gallop at the moment of descent on to the two forefeet*
44 el galope en el momento en que los cuatro pies están en el aire
- *full gallop at the moment when all four feet are off the ground*

Abreviaturas:
m. = macho; *c.* = castrado;
h. = hembra; *j.* = joven
Abbreviations:
m. = *male;* c. = *castrated;*
f. = *female;* y. = *young*

1 *u.* **2** ganado *m* mayor
– *cattle and horses*
1 el ganado vacuno, un animal con cuernos *m*, un rumiante; *m.* el toro; *c.* el
buey; *h.* la vaca; *j. m.* el ternero; *j. h.* la
ternera
– *cow, a bovine animal, a horned animal,
a ruminant;* m. *bull;* c. *ox;* f. *cow;* y. *calf*
2 el caballo; *m.* el caballo padre (el caballo semental; *Amér.:* el garañón); *c.* el
caballo castrado; *h.* la yegua; *j.* el potro
– *horse;* m. *stallion;* c. *gelding;* f. *mare;* y.
foal
3 el asno (burro *m*, borrico m); *m.* el
garañón; *j.* el pollino
– *donkey*
4 la albarda
– *pack saddle (carrying saddle)*
5 la carga
– *pack (load)*
6 la cola empenachada
– *tufted tail*
7 la borla
– *tuft*
8 el mulo, un cruce de asno *m* y yegua *f*
(el muleto; el burdégano, un cruce de
caballo *m* y burro *f*)
– *mule, a cross between a male donkey
and a mare*

9 el cerdo (el puerco, el cochino, el marrano, el guarro, el gorrino; *Amér.:* el
chancho; *Perú:* el cuchí), un animal con
cerdas *f*, un animal con pezuñas *f* hendidas (artiodáctilo *m*); *m.* el cerdo
padre (el verraco); *h.* la perca; *j.* el
lechón, el cochinillo
– *pig, a cloven-hoofed animal;* m. *boar;* f.
sow; y. *piglet*
10 el hocico
– *pig's snout (snout)*
11 la oreja
– *pig's ear*
12 la cola ensortijada
– *curly tail*
13 la oveja; *m.* el morueco; *c.* el carnero; *h.*
la oveja; *j.* el cordero (el borrego)
– *sheep;* m. *ram;* c. *wether;* f. *ewe;* y. *lamb*
14 la cabra; *m.* el cabrón; *j.* el chivo
– *goat*
15 la barba de la cabra (*también tiene:* las
mamellas)
– *goat's beard*
16 el perro, un perro Leonberg; *h.* la perra;
j. el cachorro
– *dog, a Leonberger;* m. *dog;* f. *bitch;* y.
pup (puppy, whelp)
17 el gato, un gato de angora; *h.* la gata
– *cat, an Angora cat (Persian cat);* m. *tom
(tom cat)*
18-36 animales *m* **de corral** *f*
– *small domestic animals*
18 el conejo; *m.* el conejo macho; *h.* la
coneja; *j.* el gazapo
– *rabbit;* m. *buck;* f. *doe*
19-36 aves *f* **de corral** *m*
– *poultry (domestic fowl)*
19-26 la gallina y el gallo
– *chicken*

19 la gallina
– *hen*
20 el buche
– *crop (craw)*
21 el gallo; *c.* el capón; *j.* el pollo
– *cock* (Am. *rooster);* c. *capon*
22 la cresta (*Bol.:* la corota; *Pan.:* la sierra)
– *cockscomb (comb, crest)*
23 la carúncula (el lóbulo de la oreja)
– *lap*
24 la barba
– *wattle (gill, dewlap)*
25 la cola en forma *f* de hoz *f*
– *falcate (falcated) tail*
26 el espolón (*Amér.:* la espuela)
– *spur*
27 la gallina de Guinea (la pintada)
– *guinea fowl*
28 el pavo; *h.* la pava
– *turkey;* m. *turkey cock (gobbler);* f.
turkey hen
29 la cola en abanico *m* (la rueda)
– *fan tail*
30 el pavo real
– *peacock*
31 la pluma del pavo real
– *peacock's feather*
32 el ocelo
– *eye (ocellus)*
33 la paloma; *m.* el palomo; *j.* el pichón
– *pigeon;* m. *cock pigeon*
34 el ganso; *h.* la gansa; *j.* el ansarino
– *goose;* m. *gander;* y. *gosling*
35 el pato; *h.* la pata; *j.* el patito
– *duck;* m. *drake;* y. *duckling*
36 la membrana interdigital [de las aves
palmípedas]
– *web (palmations) of webbed foot
(palmate foot)*

74 Postura de las gallinas, la producción de huevos

1-27 la avicultura (la cría intensiva)
- *poultry farming (intensive poultry management)*
1-17 la cría en el suelo
- *straw yard (strawed yard) system*
1 la pollera
- *fold unit for growing stock (chick unit)*
2 el pollito
- *chick*
3 la incubadora (la pollera) artificial
- *brooder (hover)*
4 el reguero móvil del alimento (el comedero móvil)
- *adjustable feeding trough*
5 el gallinero de los pollos
- *pullet fold unit*
6 el abrevadero, el bebedero
- *drinking trough*
7 el tubo del agua *f*
- *water pipe*
8 la pajaza
- *litter*
9 el pollo
- *pullet*
10 el ventilador
- *ventilator*
11-17 la cría de pollos *m*
- *broiler rearing (rearing of broiler chickens)*
11 el gallinero
- *chicken run (Am. fowl run)*
12 el pollo
- *broiler chicken (broiler)*
13 el comedero automático
- *mechanical feeder (self-feeder, feed dispenser)*
14 la cadena de apoyo *m*
- *chain*
15 la reguera de alimentación *f*
- *feed supply pipe*
16 el abrevadero automático (el bebedero automático)
- *mechanical drinking bowl (mechanical drinker)*
17 el ventilador
- *ventilator*
18 la postura en batería *f*
- *battery system (cage system)*
19 la jaula superior
- *battery (laying battery)*
20 la jaula inferior (la jaula de escalones *m*, la jaula en batería *f*)
- *tiered cage (battery cage, stepped cage)*
21 el comedero
- *feeding trough*
22 la cinta recolectora de huevos *m*
- *egg collection by conveyor*
23-27 el sistema automático de alimentación *f* y recogida *f*
- *mechanical feeding and dunging (manure removal, droppings removal)*

23 el sistema rápido de alimentación *f* para la batería (la máquina de alimentación *f*)
- *rapid feeding system for battery feeding (mechanical feeder)*
24 el silo (la tolva)
- *feed hopper*
25 la cinta transportadora del alimento
- *endless-chain feed conveyor (chain feeder)*
26 la conducción del agua *f*
- *water pipe (liquid feed pipe)*
27 la cinta transportadora de excrementos *m*
- *dunging chain (dunging conveyor)*
28 el armario de incubación *f* y de nacimiento *m* (de salida del huevo)
- *setting and hatching machine*
29 el ventilador de la cámara de incubación *f*
- *ventilation drum [for the setting compartment]*
30 el departamento de la incubación
- *hatching compartment (hatcher)*
31 la carretilla metálica con los casilleros de huevos *m*
- *metal trolley for hatching trays*
32 el casillero de los huevos
- *hatching tray*
33 el motor del ventilador
- *ventilation drum motor*
34-53 la producción de huevos *m*
- *egg productions*
34 el sistema de recogida *f* de los huevos
- *egg collection system (egg collection)*
35 la cinta transportadora
- *multi-tier transport*
36 la mesa de clasificación *f*
- *collection by pivoted fingers*
37 el motor de impulsión *f*
- *drive motor*
38 la clasificadora de huevos *m*
- *sorting machine*
39 el carrito de transporte *m*
- *conveyor trolley*
40 la pantalla para mirar los huevos al trasluz
- *fluorescent screen*
41 el mecanismo de succión *f* para el transporte de los huevos
- *suction apparatus (suction box) for transporting eggs*
42 el estante para las bandejas de los huevos llenos o vacíos
- *shelf for empty and full egg boxes*
43 el peso de los huevos
- *egg weighers*
44 la clasificación
- *grading*
45 la bandeja de los huevos
- *egg box*

46 la empaquetadora automática de huevos *m*
- *fully automatic egg-packing machine*
47 la cabina para mirar los huevos al trasluz
- *radioscope box*
48 la mesa de mirado *m*
- *radioscope table*
49-51 el sistema de alimentación *f*
- *feeder*
49 el transportador de depresión *f*
- *suction transporter*
50 el tubo flexible de vacío *m*
- *vacuum line*
51 la mesa de alimentación *f*
- *supply table*
52 la escogedora-clasificadora automática
- *automatic counting and grading*
53 el distribuidor de cajas *f*
- *packing box dispenser*
54 la anilla de la pata de la gallina
- *leg ring*
55 la placa de identificación *f* de las aves
- *wing tally (identification tally)*
56 la gallina americana (la gallina enana, la gallina bantam)
- *bantam*
57 la gallina ponedora
- *laying hen*
58 el huevo de gallina *f* (Cuba: el blanquín de gallina; Mé.: el blanquillo)
- *hen's egg (egg)*
59 la cáscara caliza, un integumento del huevo
- *eggshell, an egg integument*
60 la membrana de la cáscara
- *shell membrane*
61 la cámara de aire *m*
- *air space*
62 la clara del huevo
- *white [of the egg] (albumen)*
63 la chalaza
- *chalaza (Am. treadle)*
64 la membrana de la yema (la membrana vitelina)
- *vitelline membrane (yolk sac)*
65 el blastodisco (la marca del gallo; Chile: el migajón)
- *blastodisc (germinal disc, cock's tread, cock's treadle)*
66 la vesícula germinativa (la cicatrícula)
- *germinal vesicle*
67 la yema blanca
- *white*
68 la yema amarilla
- *yolk*

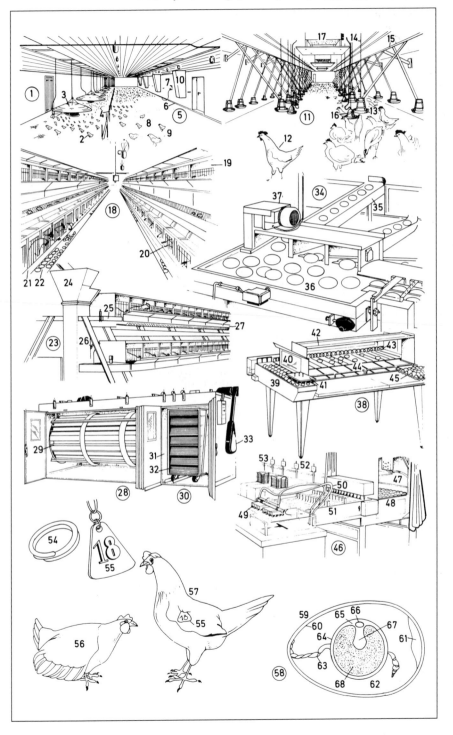

1 **la caballeriza** (la cuadra)
– *stable*
2 el compartimiento de los caballos (el box)
– *horse stall (stall, horse box, box)*
3 el pasillo de circulación *f*
– *feeding passage*
4 el poney
– *pony*
5 las barras
– *bars*
6 la cama de paja *f* (la pajaza)
– *litter*
7 la bala de paja *f*
– *bale of straw*
8 la claraboya (la lumbrera)
– *ceiling light*
9 **el aprisco** (la majada, la tenada)
– *sheep pen*
10 la oveja
– *mother sheep (ewe)*
11 el cordero
– *lamb*
12 el pesebre (el comedero) de heno *m*
– *double hay rack*
13 el heno
– *hay*
14 **el establo de las vacas lecheras** (la vaqueriza)
– *dairy cow shed (cow shed) in which cows require tying*
15 *u.* 16 el amarre
– *tether*
15 la cadena
– *chain*
16 la barra de fijación
– *rail*
17 la vaca lechera
– *dairy cow (milch-cow, milker)*
18 la ubre
– *udder*
19 el pezón
– *teat*
20 la reguera de los excrementos
– *manure gutter*
21 las barras de evacuación *f* del estiércol
– *manure removal by sliding bars*
22 el compartimiento pequeño
– *short standing*
23 **la sala de ordeñar**
– *milking parlour* (Am. *parlor), a herringbone parlour*
24 el pasillo de servicio *m*
– *working passage*
25 el ordeñador
– *milker* (Am. *milkman)*
26 el racimo de ventosas *f* de goma *f* de la ordeñadora
– *teat cup cluster*
27 el tubo de la leche
– *milk pipe*
28 el tubo del aire
– *air line*
29 el tubo de vacío *m* (el tubo de pulsación *f*)
– *vacuum line*
30 el cubilete del ordeñador
– *teat cup*
31 el cristal de visión *f* (el visor, la mirilla)
– *window*
32 el colector-pulsador de la leche
– *pulsator*
33 la fase de reposo *m*
– *release phase*
34 la fase de aspiración (la fase de succión *f*)
– *squeeze phase*
35 **la porqueriza** (la pocilga)
– *pigsty* (Am. *pigpen, hogpen)*
36 el compartimiento de los cochinillos
– *pen for young pigs*
37 el comedero
– *feeding trough*
38 el tabique de separación *f*
– *partition*
39 el cochinillo
– *pig, a young pig*
40 el compartimiento de parto *m* (el paridero)
– *farrowing and store pen*
41 la cerda madre (*Amér.:* la verraca)
– *sow*
42 el lechón (el lechoncillo, el cerdo de leche [hasta 8 semanas])
– *piglets* (Am. *shoats, shotes) (sucking pigs [for first 8 weeks])*
43 la reja de cierre *m*
– *farrowing rails*
44 la reguera del estiércol
– *liquid manure channel*

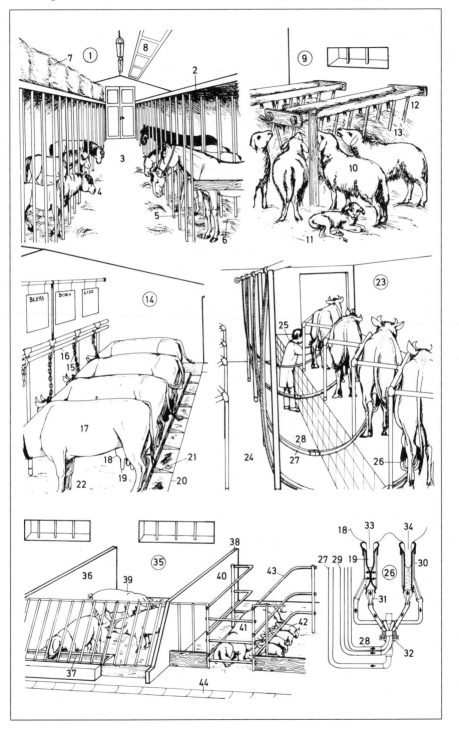

1-48 la central lechera
- *dairy (dairy plant)*
1 **la recepción de la leche**
- *milk reception*
2 el camión cisterna *f* de leche *f*
- *milk tanker*
3 la bomba de la leche cruda
- *raw milk pump*
4 el indicador volumétrico (el contador de reloj *m*, el caudalímetro), un contador de rueda ovalada
- *flowmeter, an oval (elliptical) gear meter*
5 el tanque de la leche cruda
- *raw milk storage tank*
6 el indicador del nivel
- *gauge (Am. gage)*
7 **la sala de mandos** *m*
- *central control room*
8 el diagrama de la fábrica (el panel sinóptico)
- *chart of the dairy*
9 el esquema funcional de la fábrica
- *flow chart (flow diagram)*
10 los indicadores del nivel de los tanques
- *storage tank gauges (Am. gages)*
11 el pupitre de mando *m* (la consola de mando *m*)
- *control panel*
12-48 la instalación de tratamiento *m*
de la leche
- *milk processing area*
12 el centrifugador (el homogeneizador)
- *sterilizer (homogenizer)*
13 el pasteurizador
- *milk heater;* sim.: *cream heater*
14 la descremadora
- *cream separator*
15 los tanques de leche *f* fresca
- *fresh milk tanks*
16 el tanque de la leche esterilizada
- *tank for sterilized milk*
17 el tanque de la leche descremada
- *skim milk (skimmed milk) tank*
18 el tanque de suero *m* (para la mantequilla)
- *buttermilk tank*
19 el tanque de nata *f* (de crema *f*)
- *cream tank*
20 la instalación de acondicionamiento *m* y envase *m* de la leche fresca
- *fresh milk filling and packing plant*
21 la máquina de llenado *m* de los cartones de leche *f*
- *filling machine for milk cartons;* sim.: *milk tub filler*

22 el cartón de leche *f* (el tetrabrik)
- *milk carton*
23 la cinta transportadora
- *conveyor belt (conveyor)*
24 la máquina para empaquetar con hojas *f* de plástico *m* retractables
- *shrink-sealing machine*
25 el paquete de doce cartones *m* hecho con la hoja de plástico *m* retractable
- *pack of twelve in shrink foil*
26 la instalación de envase *m* en bolsas *f* de diez litros *m*
- *ten-litre filling machine*
27 la máquina de cierre *m* por calor *m* (Amér.: la tapadora)
- *heat-sealing machine*
28 la hoja de plástico *m*
- *plastic sheets*
29 la bolsa cerrada herméticamente
- *heat-sealed bag*
30 la caja de transporte *m*
- *crate*
31 el tanque de afinado *m* de la nata
- *cream maturing vat*
32 la instalación de moldeado *m* y envase *m* de la mantequilla
- *butter shaping and packing machine*
33 la mantequera, una máquina de hacer mantequilla *f* de funcionamiento *m* continuo
- *butter churn, a creamery butter machine for continuous butter making*
34 el tubo transporte *m* de la mantequilla
- *butter supply pipe*
35 la moldeadora (la máquina de dar forma *f* a la mantequilla)
- *shaping machine*
36 la máquina de embalaje *m*
- *packing machine*
37 la mantequilla de marca *f* en paquetes *m* de 250 gramos *m*
- *branded butter in 250 g packets*
38 la instalación de producción *f* de la cuajada
- *plant for producing curd cheese (curd cheese machine)*
39 la bomba de la cuajada
- *curd cheese pump*
40 la bomba dosificadora de la crema
- *cream supply pump*
41 el separador de la cuajada
- *curds separator*
42 el tanque de la leche agria (de la cuajada)
- *sour milk vat*

43 el batidor
- *stirrer*
44 la máquina de envase *m* de la cuajada
- *curd cheese packing machine*
45 el tarro de cuajada *f*
- *curd cheese packet (curd cheese;* sim.: *cottage cheese)*
46 la capsuladora de botellas *f*
- *bottle-capping machine (capper)*
47 la máquina de hacer queso *m* en lonchas *f*
- *cheese machine*
48 el tanque del cuajo
- *rennet vat*

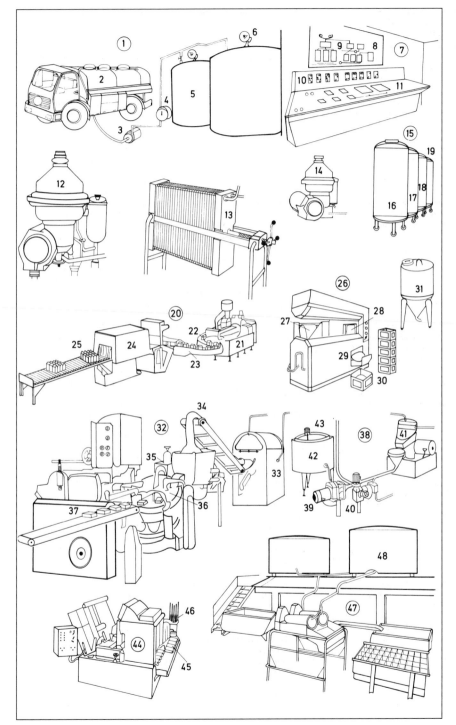

1-25 la abeja (abeja melífica, abeja de colmena *f*)
– *bee (honey-bee, hive-bee)*
1 *u.* **4-5 las castas** de las abejas
– *castes (social classes) of bees*
1 la obrera (la abeja neutra)
– *worker (worker bee)*
2 los tres ojos sencillos (tres ocelos *m*)
– *three simple eyes (ocelli)*
3 la carga de polen *m* en la pata trasera
– *load of pollen on the hind leg*
4 la abeja machiega (maesa, maestra, la reina)
– *queen (queen bee)*
5 el zángano (la abeja macho)
– *drone (male bee)*
6-9 la pata trasera izquierda de una obrera
– *left hind leg of a worker*
6 el cestillo de polen *m*
– *pollen basket*
7 el cepillo
– *pollen comb (brush)*
8 el gancho bífido
– *double claw*
9 la pinza suctoria
– *suctorial pad*
10-19 el abdomen de la obrera
– *abdomen of the worker*
10-14 el órgano de defensa *f*
– *stinging organs*
10 el gancho
– *barb*
11 el aguijón (el rejo; *Chile, Guat., Mé. y Perú:* la lanceta)
– *sting*
12 la vaina del aguijón
– *sting sheath*
13 la vejiga del veneno
– *poison sac*
14 la glándula del veneno
– *poison gland*
15-19 el tubo digestivo
– *stomachic-intestinal canal*
15 el intestino
– *intestine*
16 el estómago
– *stomach*
17 el esfínter (el tejido contráctil)
– *contractile muscle*
18 la bolsa de la miel
– *honey bag (honey sac)*
19 el esófago
– *oesophagus (esophagus, gullet)*
20-24 el ojo afacetado (ojo compuesto, ojo de insecto *m*)
– *compound eye*
20 la faceta
– *facet*
21 el cono cristalino
– *crystal cone*
22 la parte sensitiva
– *light-sensitive section*

23 la fibra del nervio óptico
– *fibre (*Am. *fiber) of the optic nerve*
24 el nervio óptico
– *optic nerve*
25 las laminillas (las escamas) de cera *f*
– *wax scale*
26-30 la celda
– *cell*
26 el huevo
– *egg*
27 la celda con el huevo en su interior *m*
– *cell with the egg in it*
28 la cresa
– *young larva*
29 la larva
– *larva (grub)*
30 la ninfa (la crisálida)
– *chrysalis (pupa)*
31-43 el panal de miel *f*
– *honeycomb*
31 la celda de incubación *f*
– *brood cell*
32 la celda tapada con la ninfa
– *sealed (capped) cell with chrysalis (pupa)*
33 la celda operculada llena de miel *f*
– *sealed (capped) cell with honey (honey cell)*
34 las celdas de las obreras
– *worker cells*
35 las celdas depósito de polen *m*
– *storage cells, with pollen*
36 las celdas de los zánganos
– *drone cells*
37 la celda real
– *queen cell*
38 la reina (machiega, maesa, maestra) saliendo
– *queen emerging from her cell*
39 el opérculo
– *cap (capping)*
40 el bastidor (el marco)
– *frame*
41 el asa *f* separadora
– *distance piece*
42 el panal artificial
– *[artificial] honeycomb*
43 la base de cera *f* prensada troquelada
– *septum (foundation, comb foundation)*
44 la caja para transportar la reina
– *queen's travelling (*Am. *traveling) box*
45-50 la colmena de madera *f* (*Col.:* la pegadilla)
– *frame hive (movable-frame hive, movable-comb hive [into which frames are inserted from the rear], a beehive (hive))*

45 la colmena movilista (colmena *f* múltiple) con los panales
– *super (honey super) with honey-combs*
46 la cámara de incubación *f* con los panales para la cresa
– *brood chamber with breeding combs*
47 el separador (la rejilla que impide el paso de la reina)
– *queen-excluder*
48 la piquera
– *entrance*
49 la tablilla para el vuelo
– *flight board (alighting board)*
50 la ventana
– *window*
51 el colmenar antiguo
– *old-fashioned bee shed*
52 la colmena
– *straw hive (skep), a hive*
53 el enjambre de abejas *f*
– *swarm (swarm cluster) of bees*
54 la red del enjambre
– *swarming net (bag net)*
55 el gancho candente
– *hooked pole*
56 el colmenar moderno
– *apiary (bee house)*
57 el apicultor (el colmenero)
– *beekeeper (apiarist, *Am. *beeman)*
58 el velo contra las abejas
– *bee veil*
59 la pipa del apicultor (la pipa ahumadora)
– *bee smoker*
60 el panal natural
– *natural honeycomb*
61 el meloextractor
– *honey extractor (honey separator)*
62 *u.* 63 la miel colada
– *strained honey (honey)*
62 la vasija para la miel
– *honey pail*
63 el tarro de miel *f*
– *honey jar*
64 la miel en panales *m*
– *honey in the comb*
65 el torzal de cera *f* (la cerilla)
– *wax taper*
66 la candela de cera *f* (el cirio)
– *wax candle*
67 la cera de abejas *f*
– *beeswax*
68 la pomada contra las picaduras de abejas *f*
– *bee sting ointment*

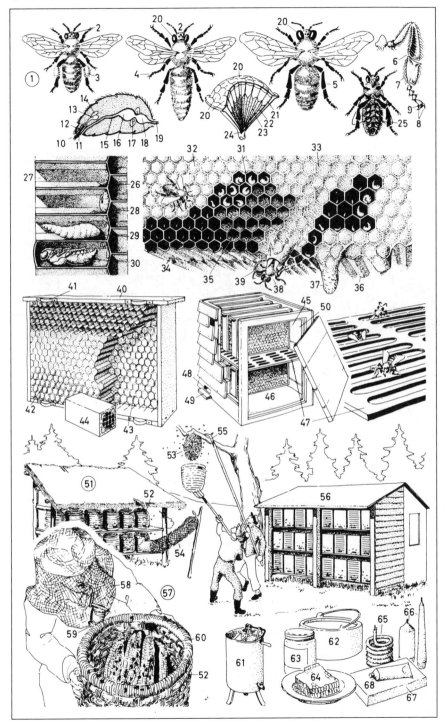

1-21 **la región vitícola** (la región
vinícola)
– *vineyard area*
1 el viñedo (la viña) con enrejado *m*
de alambre *m* para cultivo *m* de la vid
– *vineyard using wire trellises for
training vines*
2-9 **la vid**
– *vine (*Am. *grapevine)*
2 el sarmiento (el pámpano)
– *vine shoot*
3 el brote largo (el retoño, el zarcillo, la tijereta)
– *long shoot*
4 la pámpana (la hoja de la vid)
– *vine leaf*
5 el racimo de uvas *f*
– *bunch of grapes (cluster of grapes)*
6 la cepa
– *vine stem*
7 el rodrigón
– *post (stake)*
8 el amarre del enrejado de alambre *m*
– *guy (guy wire)*
9 el enrejado de alambre *m*
– *wire trellis*
10 el recipiente de recolección *f*
– *tub for grape gathering*

11 la vendimiadora
– *grape gatherer*
12 las tijeras de la vid (unas tijeras
de podar)
– *secateurs for pruning vines*
13 el viñador (el viticultor)
– *wine grower (viniculturist, viticul-
turist)*
14 el portador de cuévanos *m*
– *dosser carrier*
15 el cuévano
– *dosser (pannier)*
16 el tanque cisterna *f* del mosto
– *crushed grape transporter*
17 la prensa de uva *f*
– *grape crusher*
18 la tolva
– *hopper*
19 la pared de quita y pon de tres
lados *m*
– *three-sided flap extension*
20 la tarima
– *platform*
21 el tractor de viña *f,* un tractor de
vía *f* estrecha
– *vineyard tractor, a narrow-track
tractor*

1-22 la bodega (la cava)
– *wine cellar (wine vault)*
1 la bóveda
– *vault*
2 el tonel (el barril) de bodega *f*
– *wine cask*
3 el depósito del vino, un depósito de hormigón *m*
– *wine vat, a concrete vat*
4 el depósito de acero *m* fino (*también:* el tanque de materia *f* plástica)
– *stainless steel vat (also: vat made of synthetic material)*
5 el agitador de hélice *f*
– *propeller-type high-speed mixer*
6 la hélice
– *propeller mixer*
7 la bomba centrífuga
– *centrifugal pump*
8 el filtro de capas *f* de acero *m* fino
– *stainless steel sediment filter*
9 el embotellador circular semiautomático
– *semi-automatic circular bottling machine*
10 la máquina semiautomática para taponar (las botellas) con corchos *m* naturales
– *semi-automatic corking machine*

11 la estantería de las botellas (el botellero)
– *bottle rack*
12 el ayudante de bodega *f*
– *cellarer's assistant*
13 la canastilla de las botellas
– *bottle basket*
14 la botella de vino *m*
– *wine bottle*
15 la jarra del vino
– *wine jug*
16 la cata del vino
– *wine tasting*
17 el maestro tonelero (el bodeguero)
– *head cellarman*
18 el tonelero (el catador de vino *m*)
– *cellarman*
19 el vaso de vino *m* (un catavinos)
– *wineglass*
20 el aparato de examen *m* rápido
– *inspection apparatus [for spot-checking samples]*
21 la prensa para uvas *f* horizontal
– *horizontal wine press*
22 el humectador
– *humidifier*

80 Parásitos del jardín y del campo

Garden and Field Pests

1-19 parásitos de los frutos
- *fruit pests*
1 la lagarta, un lepidóptero
- *gipsy (gypsy) moth*
2 la bolsa de huevos *m*
- *batch (cluster) of eggs*
3 la oruga
- *caterpillar*
4 la crisálida (el capullo)
- *chrysalis (pupa)*
5 la polilla del ciruelo, un hiponomeuta
- *small ermine moth, an ermine moth*
6 la larva
- *larva (grub)*
7 la red hilada
- *tent*
8 la oruga comiendo las partes blandas de la hoja
- *caterpillar skeletonizing a leaf*
9 la polilla del manzano, un tortrícido
- *fruit surface eating tortrix moth (summer fruit tortrix moth)*
10 el gorgojo de la flor del manzano (el gorgojo del manzano)
- *appleblossom weevil, a weevil*
11 la flor destruida
- *punctured, withered flower (blossom)*
12 la picadura
- *hole for laying eggs*
13 la mariposa de la oruga de librea *f*, la falsa lagarta
- *lackey moth*
14 la oruga
- *caterpillar*
15 los huevos
- *eggs*
16 la mariposa de la escarcha (la defoliadora invernal, el azote de los frutales)
- *winter moth, a geometrid*
17 la oruga
- *caterpillar*
18 la mosca del cerezo (la mosca del fruto del cerezo), una mosca taladradora
- *cherry fruit fly, a borer*
19 la larva (el gusano blanco; la cresa)
- *larva (grub, maggot)*
20-27 parásitos *m* de la vid
- *vine pests*
20 **el mildiu, una enfermedad que causa la caida de las hojas**
- *downy mildew, a mildew, a disease causing leaf drop*
21 la uva dañada
- *grape affected with downy mildew*
22 el piral de la vid
- *grape-berry moth*

23 la oruga de la 1ª generación
- *first-generation larva of the grape-berry moth (Am. grape worm)*
24 la oruga de la 2ª generación
- *second-generation larva of the grape-berry moth (Am. grape worm)*
25 la ninfa (la crisálida)
- *chrysalis (pupa)*
26 la filoxera
- *root louse, a grape phylloxera*
27 la excrecencia vesicular de la raíz (la agalla de la raíz)
- *root gall (knotty swelling of the root, nodosity, tuberosity)*
28 la mariposa de cola *f* dorada
- *brown-tail moth*
29 la oruga
- *caterpillar*
30 la bolsa de huevos *m*
- *batch (cluster) of eggs*
31 el nido de invernación *f*
- *hibernation cocoon*
32 el pulgón lanígero
- *woolly apple aphid (American blight), an aphid*
33 la agalla del pulgón, una excrecencia
- *gall caused by the woolly apple aphid*
34 la colonia de pulgones *m*
- *woolly apple aphid colony*
35 la cochinilla de San José, un cocoideo
- *San-José scale, a scale insect (scale louse)*
36 las larvas [las masculinas, alargadas; las femeninas, redondas]
- *larvae (grubs) [male elongated, female round]*
37-55 parásitos *m* del campo
- *field pests*
37 el escarabajo elástico (el escarabajo de resorte, de muelle), un elaténido
- *click beetle, a snapping beetle (Am. snapping bug)*
38 el gusano de alambre *m*, una larva de elaténido
- *wireworm, larva of the click beetle*
39 el escarabajo pulga *f*
- *flea beetle*
40 la mosca de Hessen (el mosquito de Hessen), un mosquito de agalla *f*
- *Hessian fly, a gall midge (gall gnat)*
41 la larva
- *larva (grub)*
42 el agrotis de los sembrados, un noctuido
- *turnip moth, an earth moth*

43 la crisálida (la ninfa)
- *chrysalis (pupa)*
44 una larva de agrótido *m*, una oruga
- *cutworm, a caterpillar*
45 el escarabajo de la remolacha
- *beet carrion beetle*
46 la larva
- *larva (grub)*
47 la gran mariposa blanca de la col
- *large cabbage white butterfly*
48 la oruga de la pequeña mariposa blanca de la col
- *caterpillar of the small cabbage white butterfly*
49 el gorgojo, un curculiónido
- *brown leaf-eating weevil, a weevil*
50 la parte comida
- *feeding site*
51 la anguílula de la remolacha, un nematodo
- *sugar beet eelworm, a nematode (a threadworm, hairworm)*
52 el escarabajo de la patata (el escarabajo de Colorado)
- *Colorado beetle (potato beetle)*
53 la larva adulta
- *mature larva (grub)*
54 la larva joven
- *young larva (grub)*
55 los huevos
- *eggs*

152

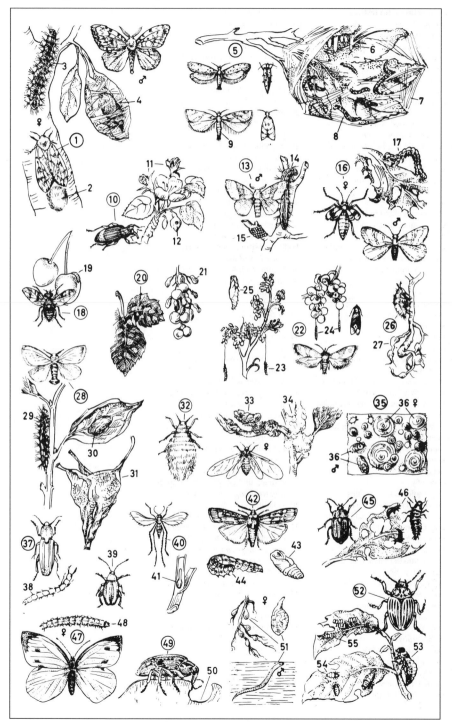

81 Insectos domésticos, dañinos y parásitos

1-14 insectos *m* domésticos
- *house insects*
1 la mosquita doméstica
- *lesser housefly*
2 la mosca doméstica común
- *common housefly*
3 la crisálida (la ninfa)
- *chrysalis (pupa, coarctate pupa)*
4 el tábano
- *stable fly (biting housefly)*
5 la antena tricótoma
- *trichotomous antenna*
6 la cochinilla de humedad *f*, un crustáceo segmentado
- *wood louse (slater,* Am. *sow bug)*
7 el grillo doméstico (*Bol.:* la siripita; *Arg.:* el chilicote)
- *house cricket*
8 el ala *f* con élitro *m* (órgano *m* que produce un sonido estridente)
- *wing with stridulating apparatus (stridulating mechanism)*
9 la araña doméstica
- *house spider*
10 la telaraña
- *spider's web*
11 la tijereta (el cortapicos)
- *earwig*
12 la pinza abdominal
- *caudal pincers*
13 la polilla de la ropa, una polilla
- *clothes moth, a moth*
14 el pececillo de plata (el lepisma saccharina), un tisanuro
- *silverfish* (Am. *slicker), a bristletail*

15-30 insectos *m* dañinos para los alimentos
- *food pests (pests to stores)*
15 la mosca del queso (del gusanillo del queso)
- *cheesefly*
16 el gorgojo de los cereales
- *grain weevil (granary weevil)*
17 la cucaracha doméstica (la curiana; *Chile:* la barata)
- *cockroach (black beetle)*
18 el escarabajo molinero (el escarabajo del gusano de la harina), un tenebriónido
- *meal beetle (meal worm beetle, flour beetle)*
19 el gorgojo de las judías
- *spotted bruchus*
20 la larva
- *larva (grub)*
21 la crisálida (la ninfa)
- *chrysalis (pupa)*
22 el escarabajo del tocino (el dermesto), un derméstido
- *leather beetle (hide beetle)*

23 la carcoma del pan
- *yellow meal beetle*
24 la crisálida (la ninfa)
- *chrysalis (pupa)*
25 el cascarudo cigarrero (la lasioderma serricorne)
- *cigarette beetle (tobacco beetle)*
26 el gorgojo del maíz
- *maize billbug (corn weevil)*
27 un parásito de los cereales
- *one of the Cryptolestes, a grain pest*
28 la polilla de los frutos secos
- *Indian meal moth*
29 la polilla de los cereales
- *Angoumois grain moth (Angoumois moth)*
30 la oruga de la polilla de los cereales en el grano de trigo *m*
- *Angoumois grain moth caterpillar inside a grain kernel*

31-42 parásitos *m* del hombre
- *parasites of man*
31 la lombriz intestinal (la ascáride)
- *round worm (maw worm)*
32 la hembra
- *female*
33 la cabeza
- *head*
34 el macho
- *male*
35 la tenia (la solitaria), un platelminto
- *tapeworm, a flatworm*
36 la cabeza (el escólex), un órgano de adherencia *f*
- *head, a suctorial organ*
37 la ventosa
- *sucker*
38 la corona de ganchos *m*
- *crown of hooks*
39 la chinche (la chinche de las camas), un hemíptero heteróptero
- *bug (bed bug,* Am. *chinch)*
40 la ladilla
- *crab louse (a human louse)*
41 el piojo de las ropas (el piojo del cuerpo; un piojo humano)
- *clothes louse (body louse, a human louse)*
42 la pulga del hombre
- *flea (human flea, common flea)*
43 la mosca tsetsé (la mosca del sueño)
- *tsetse fly*
44 el mosquito del paludismo (de la malaria), el anofeles
- *malaria mosquito*

154

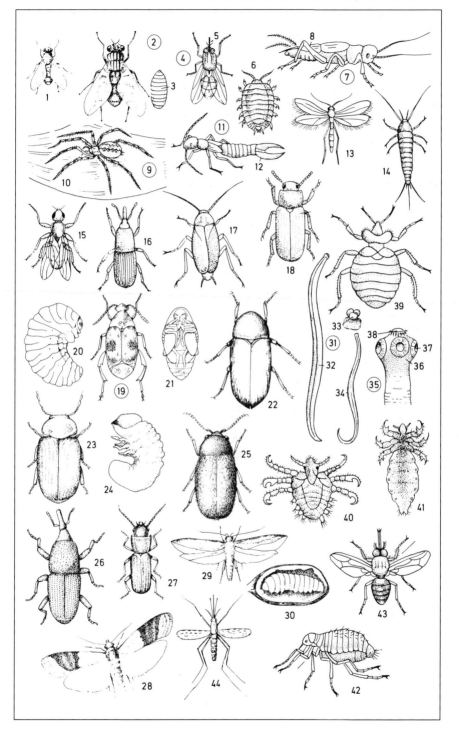

1 el escarabajo sanjuanero (el cochorro, el abejorro de San Juan), un coleóptero
– *cockchafer (May bug), a lamellicorn*
2 la cabeza
– *head*
3 la antena
– *antenna (feeler)*
4 el protórax
– *thoracic shield (prothorax)*
5 el escudete
– *scutellum*
6-8 las patas
– *legs*
6 la pata anterior
– *front leg*
7 la pata media
– *middle leg*
8 la pata trasera
– *back leg*
9 el abdomen
– *abdomen*
10 el élitro
– *elytron (wing case)*
11 el ala *f* membranosa
– *membranous wing*
12 la larva del abejorro sanjuanero (el gusano blanco), una larva
– *cockchafer grub, a larva*
13 la crisálida (la ninfa)
– *chrysalis (pupa)*
14 la procesionaria, una mariposa nocturna
– *processionary moth, a nocturnal moth (night-flying moth)*
15 la mariposa
– *moth*
16 las orugas marchando en procesión *f*
– *caterpillars in procession*
17 la monja
– *nun moth (black arches moth)*
18 la mariposa
– *moth*
19 los huevos
– *eggs*
20 la oruga
– *caterpillar*
21 la crisálida (la ninfa)
– *chrysalis (pupa) in its cocoon*
22 el escarabajo tipógrafo, un escarabajo de las cortezas (un barrenillo)
– *typographer beetle, a bark beetle*
23 *u.* 24 las galerías bajo la corteza
– *galleries under the bark*
23 la galería de la madre
– *egg gallery*
24 la galería de la larva
– *gallery made by larva*
25 la larva
– *larva (grub)*

26 el escarabajo
– *beetle*
27 la esfinge del pino, un esfíngido
– *pine hawkmoth, a hawkmoth*
28 la mariposa blanca orlada, un geómetra
– *pine moth, a geometrid*
29 la mariposa macho
– *male moth*
30 la mariposa hembra
– *female moth*
31 la oruga
– *caterpillar*
32 la crisálida (la ninfa)
– *chrysalis (pupa)*
33 la avispa de las agallas del roble, un cinípedo
– *oak-gall wasp, a gall wasp*
34 la agalla
– *oak gall (oak apple), a gall*
35 la avispa
– *wasp*
36 la larva en la cámara larval
– *larva (grub) in its chamber*
37 la agalla de la hoja de roble *m*
– *beech gall*
38 el pulgón de la agalla del abeto, un adélgido
– *spruce-gall aphid*
39 el pulgón en la forma alada
– *winged aphid*
40 la agalla de la piña
– *pineapple gall*
41 el gorgojo del pino
– *pine weevil*
42 el gorgojo (el escarabajo)
– *beetle (weevil)*
43 la piral del roble, un tortrícido
– *green oak roller moth (green oak tortrix), a leaf roller*
44 la oruga
– *caterpillar*
45 la mariposa
– *moth*
46 la esfinge del pino
– *pine beauty*
47 la oruga
– *caterpillar*
48 la mariposa
– *moth*

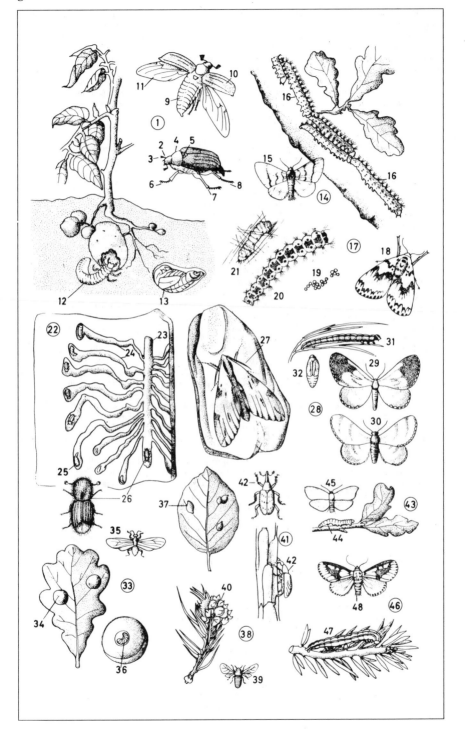

83 Lucha antiparasitaria · *Pest Control*

1 la pulverización de superficie *f*
 – *area spraying*
2 la armazón del pulverizador
 – *tractor-mounted sprayer*
3 el bastidor de aspersión *f*
 – *spray boom*
4 el surtidor de chorro *m* plano
 – *fan nozzle*
5 el depósito del caldo de pulverización *f*
 – *spray fluid tank*
6 el depósito de espuma *f* de plástico para hacer marcas *f* de espuma *f*
 – *foam canister for blob marking*
7 la suspensión
 – *spring suspension*
8 la pulverización de niebla *f*
 – *spray*
9 el dispositivo de hacer marcas *f* con la espuma
 – *blob marker*
10 la tubería de alimentación de espuma *f*
 – *foam feed pipe*
11 la instalación de desinfección *f* por vacío *m* en una fábrica de tabaco *m*
 – *vacuum fumigator (vacuum fumigation plant) of a tobacco factory*
12 la cámara de vacío *m*
 – *vacuum chamber*
13 las balas de tabaco *m* en rama *f*
 – *bales of raw tobacco*
14 el tubo del gas
 – *gas pipe*
15 la cámara móvil de fumigación *f* para tratar con fumigación *m* los planteles, los viñedos jóvenes, los depósitos de semillas *f* y los sacos vacíos
 – *mobile fumigation chamber for fumigating nursery saplings, vine layers, seeds, and empty sacks with hydrocyanic (prussic) acid*
16 el dispositivo de circulación *f* del gas
 – *gas circulation unit*
17 la batea
 – *tray*
18 la pistola pulverizadora
 – *spray gun*
19 la empuñadura giratoria para la regulación del chorro
 – *twist grip (control grip, handle) for regulating the jet*
20 el asa *f* de protección *f*
 – *finger guard*
21 la palanca de accionamiento *m*
 – *control lever (operating lever)*
22 el tubo (la lanza) del chorro
 – *spray tube*
23 el pulverizador circular
 – *cone nozzle*

24 el pulverizador de mano *m*
 – *hand spray*
25 el depósito de plástico *m*
 – *plastic container*
26 el gatillo (la bomba de mano *m*)
 – *hand pump*
27 el varillaje de pulverización *f* de péndulo *m* para el cultivo del lúpulo
 – *pendulum spray for hop growing on slopes*
28 la boquilla de aspersión *f*
 – *pistol-type nozzle*
29 el tubo (la lanza) de aspersión *f*
 – *spraying tube*
30 el manguito de tubo *m* flexible
 – *hose connection*
31 el tubo para la diseminación de cebo *m* envenenado
 – *tube for laying poisoned bait*
32 la pala matamoscas
 – *fly swat*
33 el inyector de suelo *m* (el inyector de bisulfuro *m* de carbono *m*) para matar la filoxera
 – *soil injector (carbon disulphide, Am. carbon disulfide, injector) for killing the vine root louse*
34 la válvula inyectora
 – *foot lever (foot pedal, foot treadle)*
35 el tubo del gas (el tubo de inyección *f*, la boquilla)
 – *gas tube*
36 la ratonera (*Perú:* la pericotera)
 – *mousetrap*
37 la trampa para topos *m* y campañoles *m*
 – *vole and mole trap*
38 el pulverizador móvil para los árboles frutales
 – *mobile orchard sprayer, a wheelbarrow sprayer (carriage sprayer)*
39 el depósito de insecticida *m*
 – *spray tank*
40 la tapa de rosca *f*
 – *screw-on cover*
41 la motobomba con motor de gasolina *f*
 – *direct-connected motor-driven pump with petrol motor*
42 el manómetro
 – *pressure gauge (Am. gage) (manometer)*
43 el pulverizador portátil de pistón *m*
 – *plunger-type knapsack sprayer*
44 el depósito del pulverizador con cámara *f* de aire *m* a presión
 – *spray canister with pressure chamber*
45 la palanca de la bomba de pistón *m*
 – *piston pump lever*
46 la lanza de pulverización *f* con boquilla *f*
 – *hand lance with nozzle*

47 el pulverizador semitransportado
 – *semi-mounted sprayer*
48 el tractor de viñedos *m*
 – *vineyard tractor*
49 el ventilador
 – *fan*
50 el depósito del insecticida
 – *spray fluid tank*
51 la hilera (el liño) de cepas *f*
 – *row of vines*
52 el aparato de desinfección *f* de semillas *f* secas
 – *dressing machine (seed-dressing machine) for dry-seed dressing (seed dusting)*
53 el ventilador de desinfección *f* con motor *m* eléctrico
 – *dedusting fan (dust removal fan) with electric motor*
54 el filtro tubular
 – *bag filter*
55 la tubuladura de ensacado *m*
 – *bagging nozzle*
56 el saco de desinfección *f*
 – *dedusting screen (dust removal screen)*
57 el depósito de agua *f* de pulverización *f*
 – *water canister [containing water for spraying]*
58 el dispositivo de pulverización *f*
 – *spray unit*
59 el grupo de transporte *m* con tornillo *m* sin fin *m* mezclador
 – *conveyor unit with mixing screw*
60 el depósito de polvos *m* desinfectantes con dispositivo *m* para dosificar
 – *container for disinfectant powder with dosing mechanism*
61 la ruedecilla
 – *castor*
62 la cámara de mezcla *f*
 – *mixing chamber*

Lucha antiparasitaria

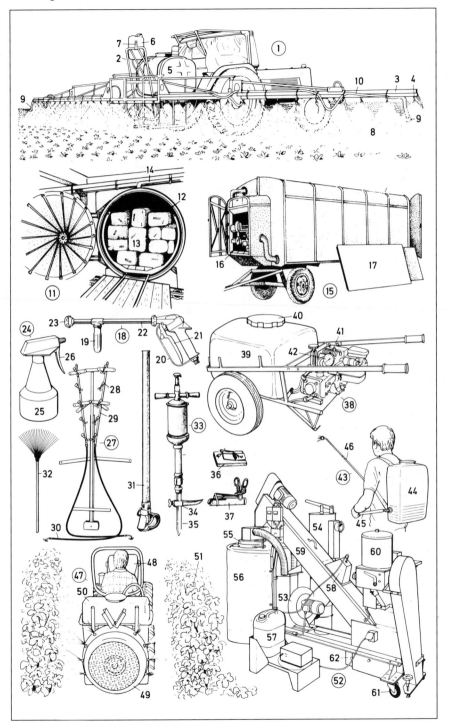

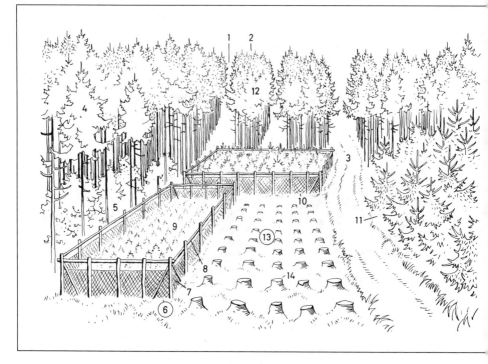

1-34 el bosque
- *forest, a wood*
1 la vereda del bosque (el camino abierto en el monte)
- *ride (aisle, lane, section line)*
2 la sección forestal
- *compartment (section)*
3 el arrastradero, un camino forestal (*Hond.:* el tiro)
- *wood haulage way, a forest track*
4-14 el sistema de tala *f* (de desmonte *m; Cuba y P. Rico:* la tumba)
- *clear-felling system*
4 el bosque viejo (el monte alto), un oquedal
- *standing timber*
5 el monte bajo
- *underwood (underbrush, undergrowth, brushwood,* Am. *brush)*
6 la almáciga, un semillero de árboles *m*
- *seedling nursery, a tree nursery*
7 el enrejado contra los animales monteses, un enrejado de alambre *m*
- *deer fence (fence), a wire netting fence (protective fence for seedlings); sim.: rabbit fence*

8 el listón de protección *f* (la barrera)
- *guard rail*
9 los plantones
- *seedlings*
10 *u.* **11** la plantación joven
- *young trees*
10 el plantel (el criadero, el cultivo después del trasplante, la plantación nueva)
- *tree nursery after transplanting*
11 la espesura de la plantación joven
- *young plantation*
12 la plantación joven (después de la poda)
- *young plantation after brashing*
13 el claro (el espacio talado)
- *clearing*
14 el tocón
- *tree stump (stump, stub)*

15-37 la tala y recogida ƒ de madera ƒ
– *wood cutting (timber cutting, tree felling, Am. lumbering)*
15 los troncos apilados
– *timber skidded to the stack (stacked timber, Am. yarded timber)*
16 el estéreo, un metro cúbico de madera ƒ
– *stack of logs, one cubic metre (Am. meter) of wood*
17 el poste (la estaca)
– *post (stake)*
18 el obrero forestal dando la vuelta a un madero
– *forest labourer (woodsman, Am. logger, lumberer, lumberjack, lumberman, timberjack) turning (Am. canting) timber*
19 el tronco (el madero)
– *bole (tree trunk, trunk, stem)*
20 el capataz numerando
– *feller numbering the logs*
21 el gran pie m de rey m (la terraja de medir) de acero m
– *steel tree calliper (caliper)*
22 la motosierra (cortando un tronco)
– *power saw (motor saw) cutting a bole*

23 el casco de protección ƒ con visera ƒ y protección ƒ acústica
– *safety helmet with visor and ear pieces*
24 los cercos (anillos m) anuales
– *annual rings*
25 el gato hidráulico
– *hydraulic felling wedge*
26 la vestimenta protectora [camisa ƒ naranja, pantalón m verde]
– *protective clothing [orange top, green trousers]*
27 el corte (el derribo, la tala) con motosierra ƒ
– *felling with a power saw (motor saw)*
28 el corte (la muesca, la entalladura)
– *undercut (notch, throat, gullet, mouth, sink, kerf, birdsmouth)*
29 el corte de sierra ƒ
– *back cut*
30 el bolsillo con la cuña de tala ƒ
– *sheath holding felling wedge*
31 el trozo
– *log*
32 la sierra para cortar los troncos bajos y las malas hierbas
– *free-cutting saw for removing underwood and weeds*

33 la sierra circular (o cuchilla ƒ circular) adaptable
– *circular saw (or activated blade) attachment*
34 el motor
– *power unit (motor)*
35 el bidón de aceite m adherente para las cadenas de la sierra
– *canister of viscous oil for the saw chain*
36 el bidón de gasolina ƒ
– *petrol canister (Am. gasoline canister)*
37 el derribo (la tala) del tronco menudo (el aclarado)
– *felling of small timber (of small-sized thinnings) (thinning)*

1 el hacha *f*
– *axe (Am. ax)*
2 el filo (el corte)
– *edge (cutting edge)*
3 el mango (el astil)
– *handle (helve)*
4 la cuña de tala *f* con inserción *f* de
madera *f* y anilla *f*
– *felling wedge (falling wedge) with
wood insert and ring*
5 el martillo de hender (el hacha *f*
de rajar)
– *riving hammer (cleaving hammer,
splitting hammer)*
6 el gancho de palanca *f* (el pico
para dar la vuelta a los troncos)
– *lifting hook*
7 el gancho para dar la vuelta a los
troncos
– *cant hook*
8 el descortezador (el escoplo de
descortezar)
– *barking iron (bark spud)*
9 la cuña de fijación *f* con gancho *m*
para los troncos
– *peavy*
10 el calibrador
– *slide calliper (caliper) (calliper
square)*
11 el podón (el bodollo), un machete
– *billhook, a knife for lopping*
12 el martillo numerador giratorio
– *revolving die hammer (marking
hammer, marking iron, Am.
marker)*
13 la motosierra
– *power saw (motor saw)*
14 la cadena de la sierra
– *saw chain*
15 el freno de seguridad *f* (para la
cadena de la sierra) con protector
m de manos *f*
– *safety brake for the saw chain,
with finger guard*
16 la guía (el raíl, la llanta) de la
cadena
– *saw guide*
17 el bloqueo del acelerador
– *accelerator lock*
18 la máquina de mondar (de desra-
mar)
– *snedding machine (trimming
machine, Am. knotting machine,
limbing machine)*
19 los cilindros de avance *m*
– *feed rolls*
20 la cuchilla articulada
– *flexible blade*
21 el gato hidráulico
– *hydraulic arm*
22 la herramienta para cortar las
puntas
– *trimming blade*

23 el descortezamiento de los troncos
– *debarking (barking, bark stripping) of boles*
24 el cilindro de avance *m*
– *feed roller*
25 el rotor de cuchillas *f*
– *cylinder trimmer*
26 la cuchilla rotativa
– *rotary cutter*
27 el tractor forestal (para el transporte de la madera en el bosque)
– *short-haul skidder*
28 la grúa de carga *f*
– *loading crane*
29 el gancho para la madera
– *log grips*
30 el telero de la caja
– *post*
31 la dirección de acodamiento *m* (la
dirección pivotante)
– *Ackermann steering system*
32 la pila de troncos *m*
– *log dump*
33 la numeración
– *number (identification number)*
34 el tractor de troncos *m* (el skidder)
– *skidder*
35 la placa frontal
– *front blade (front plate)*
36 la cabina con arco *m* de seguridad *f*
– *crush-proof safety bonnet (Am.
safety hood)*
37 la dirección de acodamiento *m* (la
dirección pivotante)
– *Ackermann steering system*
38 el torno de cable *m*
– *cable winch*
39 el rodillo guía del cable
– *cable drum*
40 la placa trasera
– *rear blade (rear plate)*
41 los troncos levantados
– *boles with butt ends held off the
ground*
42 el transporte por carretera *f* de los
troncos
– *haulage of timber by road*
43 el tractor
– *tractor (tractor unit)*
44 la grúa de carga *f*
– *loading crane*
45 el apoyo hidráulico
– *hydraulic jack*
46 el torno de cable *m*
– *cable winch*
47 el telero
– *post*
48 el banquillo de acoplamiento *m*
articulado
– *bolster plate*
49 el remolque (la base) trasero (-a)
– *rear bed (rear bunk)*

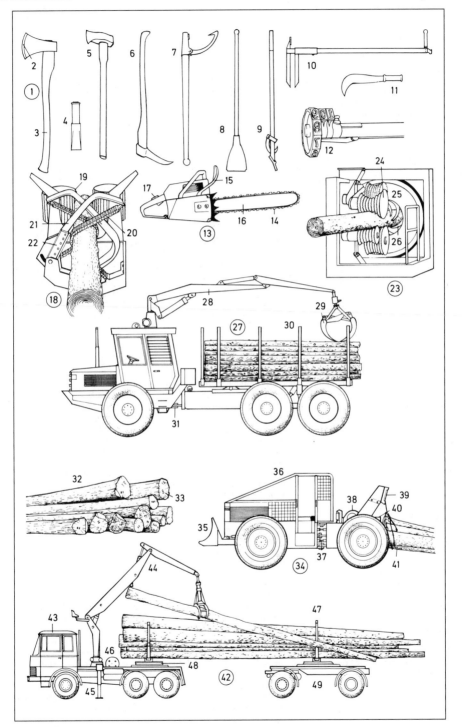

1-52 la caza (las diferentes clases de cacería *f*)
– *kinds of hunting*
1-8 la caza con perro *m* (la caza en cotos *m* o vedados *m*)
– *stalking (deer stalking, Am. still-hunting) in the game preserve*
1 el cazador (el tirador, el montero)
– *huntsman (hunter)*
2 el traje de caza *f*
– *hunting clothes*
3 el morral (la mochila)
– *knapsack*
4 la escopeta de caza *f*
– *sporting gun (sporting rifle, hunting rifle)*
5 el sombrero de caza *f* (el sombrero de cazador *m*)
– *huntsman's hat*
6 los gemelos de campo *m*
– *field glasses, binoculars*
7 el perro de caza *f*
– *gun dog*
8 el rastro (la huella de pisadas *f*)
– *track (trail, hoofprints)*
9-12 la caza en época *f* **de brama** *f* **y celo** *m*
– *hunting in the rutting season and the pairing season*
9 la paranza
– *hunting screen (screen, Am. blind)*

10 el bastón-taburete (el asiento de caza *f*)
– *shooting stick (shooting seat, seat stick)*
11 el urogallo (el gallo silvestre) haciendo la rueda
– *blackcock, displaying*
12 el ciervo en brama *f* (bramando)
– *rutting stag*
13 la cierva pastando (paciendo)
– *hind, grazing*
14-17 el puesto (el aguardo, el tiradero)
– *hunting from a raised hide (raised stand)*
14 el puesto en alto *m* (el mirador)
– *raised hide (raised stand, high seat)*
15 la manada a tiro *m*
– *herd within range*
16 el paso (el paso de los animales montaraces)
– *game path (Am. runway)*
17 el corzo, herido en una paletilla y rematado por un disparo final
– *roebuck, hit in the shoulder and killed by a finishing shot*
18 el coche de caza *f*
– *phaeton*
19-27 la caza con trampas *f*
– *types of trapping*

19 la caza de animales *m* de presa *f* con trampas *f*
– *trapping of small predators*
20 la trampa de caja *f* (*Hond.:* la tapegua)
– *box trap (trap for small predators)*
21 el cebo
– *bait*
22 la marta, un animal carnicero (un depredador)
– *marten, a small predator*
23 la caza con hurón *m* (la caza de conejos *m* sacados de sus madrigueras *f*)
– *ferreting (hunting rabbits out of their warrens)*
24 el hurón (el bicho)
– *ferret*
25 el huronero
– *ferreter*
26 la madriguera (la conejera)
– *burrow (rabbit burrow, rabbit hole)*
27 la bolsa de red *f* en la boca de la madriguera
– *net (rabbit net) over the burrow opening*
28 el comedero de invierno *m*
– *feeding place for game (winter feeding place)*

29 Waidmann, Waidsack
el cazador furtivo
- *poacher*
30 la carabina, un rifle corto
- *carbine, a short rifle*
31 la caza del jabalí
- *boar hunt*
32 el jabalí
- *wild sow (sow, wild boar)*
33 el perro de jabalí *m* (el mastín, el
perro jabalinero; *varios:* la jauría,
la muta)
- *boarhound (hound, hunting dog;*
collectively: *pack, pack of*
hounds)
34-39 la batida (la caza de la liebre)
- **beating** *(driving, hare hunting)*
34 la puntería (el encaro)
- *aiming position*
35 la liebre, un animal de pelo *m*
- *hare, furred game (ground game)*
36 la cobranza
- *retrieving*
37 el batidor
- *beater*
38 la caza (las piezas cobradas)
- *bag (kill)*
39 la carreta para la caza
- *cart for carrying game*
40 la caza acuática (la caza de patos *m*)
- *waterfowling (wildfowling, duck*
shooting, Am. duck hunting)

41 la bandada de patos *m* silvestres,
la caza de pluma *f*
- *flight of wild ducks, winged game*
42-46 la cetrería (la halconería, la
caza con halcones *m*, la caza con
gerifaltes *m*)
- *falconry (hawking)*
42 el halconero (el cetrero)
- *falconer*
43 la gorga (la cortesía), un trozo de
carne *f* (*C. Rica:* la tureca)
- *reward, a piece of meat*
44 el capirote del halcón
- *falcon's hood*
45 la pihuela
- *jess*
46 un halcón macho (terzuelo *m*)
abatiéndose sobre una garza real
- *falcon, a hawk, a male hawk (tier-*
cel) swooping (stooping) on a
heron
**47-52 la caza con reclamo *m* desde un
tollo**
- *shooting from a butt*
47 el árbol al que acuden las aves
- *tree to which birds are lured*
48 el búho, un pájaro reclamo (cim-
bel *m*)
- *eagle owl, a decoy bird (decoy)*
49 la percha
- *perch*

50 el ave *f* atraída, una corneja
- *decoyed bird, a crow*
51 el tollo (el tiradero)
- *butt for shooting crows or eagle*
owls
52 la aspillera
- *gun slit*

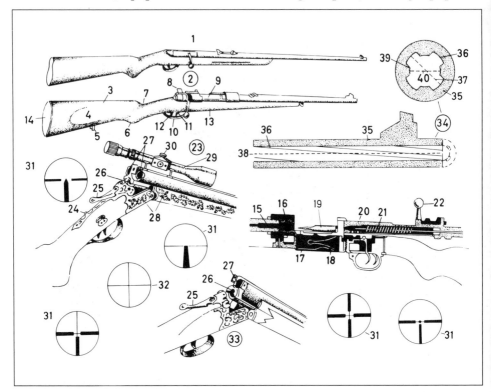

1-40 armas *f* deportivas (escopetas *f* de caza *f*)
– ***sporting guns*** *(sporting rifles, hunting rifles)*
1 la carabina
– *single-loader (single-loading rifle)*
2 el rifle de repetición *f*, una arma de fuego *m* portátil, un rifle de caza *f* de repetición *f* automático (un rifle con depósito *m*)
– *repeating rifle, a small-arm (firearm), a repeater (magazine rifle, magazine repeater)*
3, 4, 6, 13 la caja del rifle
– *stock*
3 la culata
– *butt*
4 la carrillera
– *cheek [on the left side]*
5 la anilla de la correa
– *sling ring*
6 el puño de pistola *f*
– *pistol grip*
7 la garganta de la culata
– *small of the butt*
8 la aleta del seguro (del fiador)
– *safety catch*
9 el cierre
– *lock*
10 el guardamonte
– *trigger guard*

11 el punto del disparador
– *second set trigger (firing trigger)*
12 el disparador (el gatillo)
– *hair trigger (set trigger)*
13 la caña
– *foregrip*
14 la cantonera
– *butt plate*
15 la recámara
– *cartridge chamber*
16 el cajón de los mecanismos
– *receiver*
17 el cargador
– *magazine*
18 el elevador
– *magazine spring*
19 la munición
– *ammunition (cartridge)*
20 el cerrojo
– *chamber*
21 el percutor
– *firing pin (striker)*
22 la bola del cerrojo
– *bolt handle (bolt lever)*
23 la escopeta de tres cañones *m*, una escopeta que se monta automáticamente
– *triple-barrelled (triple-barreled) rifle, a self-cocking gun*

24 el pasador de cambio *m*
– *reversing catch; in various guns: safety catch*
25 la palanca (la llave) de cierre *m*
– *sliding safety catch*
26 el cañón de rifle *m* (de bala *f*)
– *rifle barrel (rifled barrel)*
27 el cañón de perdigones *m*
– *smooth-bore barrel*
28 los grabados (las incrustaciones)
– *chasing*
29 la mira telescópica
– *telescopic sight (riflescope, telescope sight)*
30 el tornillo para el ajuste del retículo
– *graticule adjuster screws*
31 *u.* **32** el retículo visual
– *graticule (sight graticule)*
31 diversos sistemas *m* de retículo *m*
– *various graticule systems*
32 los hilos cruzados (la cruz reticular)
– *cross wires (Am. cross hairs)*
33 el rifle de dos cañones *m* superpuestos (una escopeta de cañón *m* doble)
– *over-and-under shotgun*
34 el cañón rayado (el cañón de ánima *f* rayada)
– *rifled gun barrel*

35 la pared del cañón
– *barrel casing*
36 la estría (la raya)
– *rifling*
37 el calibre de estría *f*
– *rifling calibre (Am. caliber)*
38 el eje del ánima *f*
– *bore axis*
39 la pared del ánima *f*
– *land*
40 el calibre del fusil
– *calibre (bore diameter, Am. caliber)*
41-48 útiles *m* de caza *f*
– *hunting equipment*
41 el cuchillo de caza *f* de doble filo *m*
– *double-edged hunting knife*
42 el puñal, el cuchillo de monte *m*
– *[single-edged] hunting knife*
43-47 reclamos *m* para atraer la caza
– *calls for luring game (for calling game)*
43 el reclamo del corzo
– *roe call*
44 el reclamo de la liebre
– *hare call*
45 el reclamo de la codorniz
– *quail call*
46 el reclamo del ciervo
– *stag call*
47 el reclamo de la perdiz
– *partridge call*
48 la trampa "cuello *m* de cisne *m*", una trampa de arco *m*
– *bow trap (bow gin), a jaw trap*
49 el cartucho de perdigones *m*
– *small-shot cartridge*
50 la vaina de cartón *m*
– *cardboard case*
51 la carga de perdigones *m*
– *small-shot charge*
52 el taco de fieltro
– *felt wad*
53 la pólvora sin humo *m* (la pólvora negra)
– *smokeless powder (different kind: black powder)*
54 el cartucho de bala *f*
– *cartridge*
55 el proyectil (la bala con su envuelta *f*; Arg. y Urug.: el chumbo)
– *full-jacketed cartridge*
56 el núcleo de plomo *m* blando
– *soft-lead core*
57 la carga de pólvora *f*
– *powder charge*
58 el culote
– *detonator cap*
59 la cápsula fulminante (el pistón con el fulminante)
– *percussion cap*
60 la trompa de caza *f* (el cuerno de caza *f*)
– *hunting horn*

61-64 los avíos para la limpieza de las armas
– *rifle cleaning kit*
61 el lavador (la baqueta)
– *cleaning rod*
62 la escobilla para la limpieza de los cañones
– *cleaning brush*
63 la estopa de limpieza *f*
– *cleaning tow*
64 el cordel para la limpieza
– *pull-through (Am. pull-thru)*
65 el alza *f* de mira *f*
– *sights*
66 la muesca
– *notch (sighting notch)*
67 el alza del alza *f*
– *back sight leaf*
68 la escala del pie del alza *f*
– *sight scale division*
69 la corredera
– *back sight slide*
70 la muesca para la fijación del muelle
– *notch [to hold the spring]*
71 el punto de mira *f*
– *front sight (foresight)*
72 la cúspide del punto de mira *f*
– *bead*
73 balística *f*
– *ballistics*
74 el horizonte
– *azimuth*
75 el ángulo de proyección *f*
– *angle of departure*
76 el ángulo de elevación *f*
– *angle of elevation*
77 la sagita (la flecha)
– *apex (zenith)*
78 el ángulo de caída *f*
– *angle of descent*
79 la curva balística (la trayectoria)
– *ballistic curve*

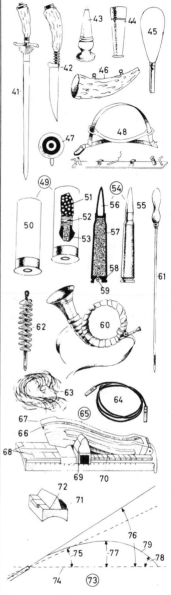

1-27 la caza de montería (la caza mayor)
– *red deer*
1 el animal (la cierva, la hembra del ciervo), una madre o una hembra sin cubrir; *varias:* la manada; *el joven:* el cervatillo, el gabato
– *hind (red deer), a young hind or a dam;* collectively: *antlerless deer,* (y.) *calf*
2 la lengua
– *tongue*
3 el cuello
– *neck*
4 el ciervo en celo *m*
– *rutting stag*
5-11 los cuernos (la cornamenta, la cuerna)
– *antlers*
5 la roseta
– *burr (rose)*
6 el candil de ojo *m* (el candil basilar, la luchadera, la garceta)
– *brow antler (brow tine, brow point, brow snag)*
7 el candil de hierro *m*
– *bez antler (bay antler, bay, bez tine)*
8 el candil medio
– *royal antler (royal, tray)*
9 la paleta (la corona, la palma)
– *surroyal antlers (surroyals)*
10 las puntas (las hitas)
– *point (tine)*
11 el asta *f*
– *beam (main trunk)*
12 la cabeza
– *head*
13 la boca (el hocico)
– *mouth*
14 la fosa lacrimal
– *larmier (tear bag)*
15 el ojo
– *eye*
16 la oreja
– *ear*
17 el codillo
– *shoulder*
18 el lomo
– *loin*
19 la cola
– *scut (tail)*
20 el espejo (la mancha blanca)
– *rump*
21 el pernil
– *leg (haunch)*
22 la pata trasera (el cuarto trasero)
– *hind leg*
23 el espolón
– *dew claw*
24 la pezuña
– *hoof*
25 la pata delantera (el cuarto delantero)
– *foreleg*
26 el flanco
– *flank*
27 la melena de la brama
– *collar (rutting mane)*
28-39 el corzo
– *roe (roe deer)*

28 el corzo macho
– *roebuck (buck)*
29-31 los cuernos (la cornamenta, la cuerna)
– *antlers (horns)*
29 la roseta
– *burr (rose)*
30 el asta *f* con las perlas
– *beam with pearls*
31 la punta
– *point (tine)*
32 la oreja
– *ear*
33 el ojo
– *eye*
34 la corza, una hembra joven o una madre
– *doe (female roe), a female fawn or a barren doe*
35 el lomo
– *loin*
36 el espejo (la mancha blanca)
– *rump*
37 el pernil
– *leg (haunch)*
38 el codillo
– *shoulder*
39 el corcino, un corzo joven o una corza joven
– *fawn, (m.) young buck, (f.) young doe*
40-41 el gamo
– *fallow deer*
40 el gamo (el paleto); *hembra:* la gama
– *fallow buck, a buck with palmate (palmated) antlers,* (f.) *doe*
41 la palma
– *palm*
42 el zorro común (el zorro rojo); *hembra:* la zorra
– *red fox,* (m.) *dog,* (f.) *vixen,* (y.) *cub*
43 los ojos
– *eyes*
44 la oreja
– *ear*
45 el hocico
– *muzzle (mouth)*
46 las patas
– *pads (paws)*
47 el rabo (la cola, el hopo)
– *brush (tail)*
48 el tejón
– *badger,* (f.) *sow*
49 el rabo (la cola)
– *tail*
50 las garras
– *paws*
51 el jabalí; *hembra:* la jabalina; *joven:* el rayón, el jabato, el bermejo
– *wild boar,* (m.) *boar,* (f.) *wild sow (sow),* (y.) *young boar*
52 las cerdas
– *bristles*
53 el hocico (la jeta)
– *snout*
54 el colmillo (la navaja)
– *tusk*

55 el escudo (la cota, la piel especialmente dura en la espaldilla)
– *shield*
56 la corteza del tocino (la piel)
– *hide*
57 el espolón
– *dew claw*
58 la cola del jabalí (el rabo)
– *tail*
59 la liebre; *macho:* lebrón, el matacán; *joven:* el lebrato
– *hare,* (m.) *buck,* (f.) *doe*
60 el ojo
– *eye*
61 la oreja
– *ear*
62 el rabo (la cola)
– *scut (tail)*
63 la pata trasera
– *hind leg*
64 la pata delantera
– *foreleg*
65 el conejo; *hembra:* la coneja; *joven:* el gazapo
– *rabbit*
66 el grigallo (el gallo silvestre, el faisán de montaña *f*)
– *blackcock*
67 la cola (la lira)
– *tail*
68 las plumas de hoz *f*
– *falcate (falcated) feathers*
69 la ortega (la corteza)
– *hazel grouse (hazel hen)*
70 la perdiz
– *partridge*
71 la mancha del pecho
– *horseshoe (horseshoe marking)*
72 el urogallo (el gallo de bosque *m;* el faisán de bosque *m*)
– *wood grouse (capercaillie)*
73 la barba de plumas *f*
– *beard*
74 el espejo (la mancha blanca)
– *axillary marking*
75 la cola (el abanico)
– *tail (fan)*
76 el ala *f*
– *wing (pinion)*
77 el faisán común, un faisán; *macho:* el faisán; *hembra:* la faisana
– *common pheasant, a pheasant,* (m.) *cock pheasant (pheasant cock),* (f.) *hen pheasant (pheasant hen)*
78 el moñito (el copete)
– *plumicorn (feathered ear, ear tuft, ear, horn)*
79 el ala *f*
– *wing*
80 la cola
– *tail*
81 la pata
– *leg*
82 el espolón
– *spur*
83 la chocha (la becada, la ardea sorda)
– *snipe*
84 el pico
– *bill (beak)*

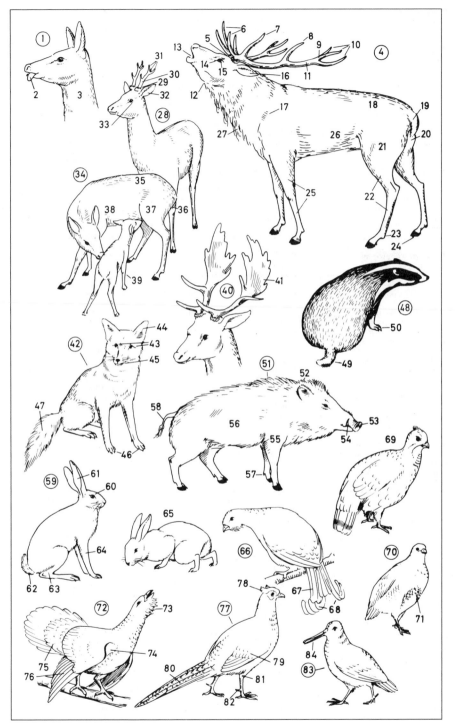

89 Piscicultura y el deporte de la pesca con anzuelo

1-19 la piscicultura
- *fish farming (fish culture, pisciculture)*
1 la jaula en agua *f* corriente
- *cage in running water*
2 la sacadera (el salabre, la manga, la cuchara)
- *hand net (landing net)*
3 el tonelete de transporte *m* de los pescados
- *semi-oval barrel for transporting fish*
4 la tina
- *vat*
5 el enrejado del rebosadero
- *trellis in the overflow*
6 el vivero (la cría de truchas *f*); *también:* el estanque para carpas *f*, el estanque de cría *f*
- *trout pond; sim.: carp pond, a fry pond, fattening pond, or cleansing pond*
7 la llegada de agua *f*
- *water inlet (water supply pipe)*
8 el desagüe (la salida de agua *f*)
- *water outlet (outlet pipe)*
9 el dispositivo de vaciado *m*
- *monk*
10 la rejilla de retención *f* (el filtro)
- *screen*
11-19 el criadero de peces *m*
- *hatchery*
11 la recolección de huevos *m* de lucio *m*
- *stripping the spawning pike (seed pike)*
12 los huevos del pez (la hueva, la desova, la freza)
- *fish spawn (spawn, roe, fish eggs)*
13 el pez hembra (el pez que tiene huevas *f*)
- *female fish (spawner, seed fish)*
14 la cría de truchas *f*
- *trout breeding (trout rearing)*
15 la incubadora californiana
- *Californian incubator*
16 los huevos de trucha *f*
- *trout fry*
17 la botella de cría *f* del esturión
- *hatching jar for pike*
18 la artesa de incubación *f* en la corriente de agua *f* continua
- *long incubation tank*
19 la rejilla para contar los huevos
- *Brandstetter egg-counting board*
20-94 la pesca (la pesca con caña *f*)
- *angling*
20-31 la pesca de fondo *m*
- *bottom fishing (coarse fishing)*
20 la caña de lanzar
- *line shooting*
21 el rollo de hilo *m*
- *coils*
22 el trozo de trapo *m* o de papel *m*
- *cloth (rag) or paper*
23 el soporte de cañas *f*
- *rod rest*
24 la lata (caja *f*) del cebo (de los gusanos)
- *bait tin*
25 la cestilla de los pescadores (*Venez.:* el humare)
- *fish basket (creel)*
26 la pesca de la carpa en bote *m*
- *fishing for carp from a boat*
27 el bote de remos *m* (el bote de pesca *f*)
- *rowing boat (fishing boat)*
28 la nasa (el butrón; *Arg.:* el tilbe)
- *keep net*
29 la red cuadrada (la red de fondo *m; Col.:* el congolo, la charqueza)
- *drop net*
30 la pértiga (la vara)
- *pole (punt pole, quant pole)*
31 la red de lanzamiento *m*
- *casting net*

32 el lanzamiento de dos manos *m* con carrete *m* de instalación *f* fija
- *two-handed side cast with fixed-spool reel*
33 la posición inicial (la posición de partida)
- *initial position*
34 el punto de lanzamiento *m*
- *point of release*
35 la trayectoria del extremo de la caña
- *path of the rod tip*
36 la trayectoria de vuelo *m* de la plomada del cebo
- *trajectory of the baited weight*
37-94 los útiles de pesca *f*
- *fishing tackle*
37 las tenazas de pescador *m*
- *fishing pliers*
38 el cuchillo de descuartizar
- *filleting knife*
39 el cuchillo de pescado *m* (el cuchillo para quitar las escamas; *Col.:* la pacora)
- *fish knife*
40 el desembuchador de gancho *m*
- *disgorger (hook disgorger)*
41 la aguja del cebo
- *bait needle*
42 la mordaza para lucios *m*
- *gag*
43-48 flotadores *m* (corchos *m*)
- *floats*
43 el corcho de caña *f* fusiforme
- *sliding cork float*
44 el flotador de materia *f* plástica
- *plastic float*
45 el flotador con pluma *f* (la pluma)
- *quill float*
46 el flotador de espuma *f* de plástico *m*
- *polystyrene float*
47 la bola de agua *f* ovalada
- *oval bubble float*
48 el flotador cargado de plomo *m*
- *lead-weighted sliding float*
49-58 las cañas de pescar
- *rods*
49 la caña de fibra *f* de vidrio *m*
- *solid glass rod*
50 la empuñadura de corcho *m* aglomerado
- *cork handle (cork butt)*
51 la anilla de acero para resortes *m*
- *spring-steel ring*
52 la anilla del extremo
- *top ring (end ring)*
53 la caña telescópica
- *telescopic rod*
54 la varilla
- *rod section*
55 la parte de la empuñadura enfundada
- *bound handle (bound butt)*
56 la anilla de rodadura *f*
- *ring*
57 la caña de fibra *f* de carbono *m; también:* la caña de vidrio *m* hueco (vidrio *m* soplado)
- *carbon-fibre rod; sim.: hollow glass rod*
58 la anilla para un lanzamiento largo, una anilla de puente *m* metálico
- *all-round ring (butt ring for long cast), a steel bridge ring*
59-64 los carretes (*Amér. Central, Mé. y Venez.:* las carruchas)
- *reels*
59 el carrete multiplicador
- *multiplying reel (multiplier reel)*
60 la guía del hilo
- *line guide*
61 el carrete de instalación *f* fija
- *fixed-spool reel (stationary-drum reel)*

62 el asa *f* de recogida del hilo
- *bale arm*
63 el hilo de pescar
- *fishing line*
64 el control del lanzamiento con el dedo índice
- *controlling the cast with the index finger*
65-76 cebos *m*
- *baits*
65 la mosca
- *fly*
66 el cebo de ninfas *f* (la ninfa)
- *artificial nymph*
67 el cebo de lombriz *f* de tierra *f*
- *artificial earthworm*
68 el cebo de saltamontes *m*
- *artificial grasshopper*
69 el pez artificial de metal *m* de una sola parte
- *single-jointed plug (single-jointed wobbler)*
70 el pez artificial de metal *m* de dos partes *f*
- *double-jointed plug (double-jointed wobbler)*
71 el pez artificial de metal *m* esférico
- *round wobbler*
72 el pez cuchara *f* imitando a uno vivo
- *wiggler*
73 la cucharilla
- *spoon bait (spoon)*
74 la cucharilla moteada
- *spinner*
75 la cucharilla con anzuelo *m* oculto
- *spinner with concealed hook*
76 la guadañeta
- *long spinner*
77 el gancho
- *swivel*
78 la hijuela (la sotileza, el reinal)
- *cast (leader)*
79-87 anzuelos *m*
- *hooks*
79 el anzuelo
- *fish hook*
80 la punta del anzuelo con púa *f*
- *point of the hook with barb*
81 la curva del anzuelo
- *bend of the hook*
82 la laminilla (el ojete)
- *spade (eye)*
83 el anzuelo doble
- *open double hook*
84 el anzuelo inglés derecho
- *limerick*
85 el anzuelo triple
- *closed treble hook (triangle)*
86 el anzuelo de carpa *f*
- *carp hook*
87 el anzuelo de anguila *f*
- *eel hook*
88-92 pesas *f* de plomo *m*
- *leads (lead weights)*
88 la aceituna de plomo *m*
- *oval lead (oval sinker)*
89 las bolas de plomo *m*
- *lead shot*
90 el plomo piriforme
- *pear-shaped lead*
91 la plomada (la sonda)
- *plummet*
92 el plomo (para la pesca) de mar
- *sea lead*
93 el paso de los peces
- *fish ladder (fish pass, fish way)*
94 la red de estaca *f*
- *stake net*

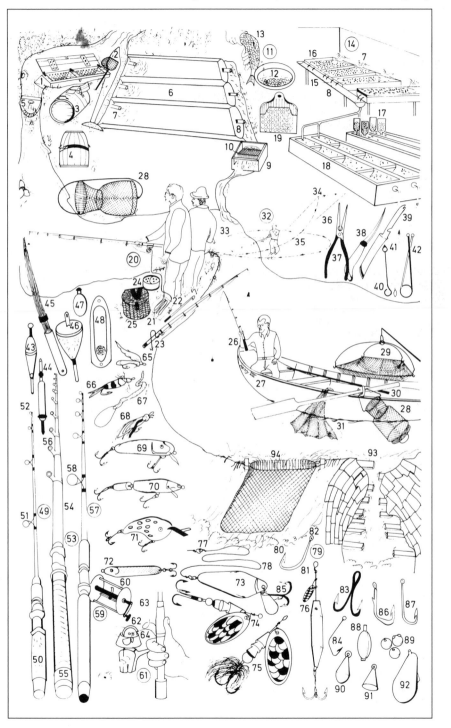

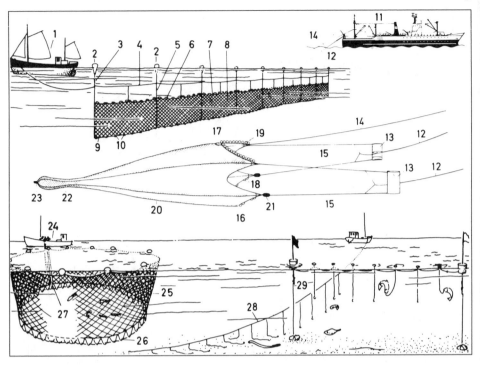

1-23 la pesca de altura
- *deep-sea fishing*

1-10 la pesca con red *f* de arrastre
- *drift net fishing*

1 el lugre para la pesca de arenques *m*
- *herring lugger (fishing lugger, lugger)*

2-10 la red de arrastre para la pesca de arenques *m*
- *herring drift net*

2 el boyarín
- *buoy*

3 la cuerda del boyarín
- *buoy rope*

4 la cuerda flotante (la guindaleza)
- *float line*

5 la atadura
- *seizing*

6 los flotadores de corcho *m*
- *wooden float*

7 la cuerda superior
- *headline*

8 la red (la red vertical)
- *net*

9 la cuerda de fondo *m* (la relinga)
- *footrope*

10 los pesos de fondo *m*
- *sinkers (weights)*

11-23 la pesca con red *f* barredera
- *trawl fishing (trawling)*

11 un buque factoría *f*
- *factory ship, a trawler*

12 la sirga (la malleta)
- *warp (trawl warp)*

13 el panel divergente
- *otter boards*

14 el cable de las sondas de la red
- *net sonar cable*

15 el calabrote de alambre *m*
- *wire warp*

16 la banda
- *wing*

17 la sonda de la red
- *net sonar device*

18 la relinga de fondo *m*
- *footrope*

19 las esferas de corcho *m*
- *spherical floats*

20 el vientre (la panza) de la red
- *belly*

21 el peso de hierro *m* de 1 800 kgs.
- *1,800 kg iron weight*

22 el copo
- *cod end (cod)*

23 la cuerda para cerrar el copo
- *cod line for closing the cod end*

24-29 la pesca costera (la pesca de bajura *f*)
- *inshore fishing*

24 el barco de pesca *f* (la trainera)
- *fishing boat*

25 la traíña, una red circular flotante (*Guat., Hond. y Mé.:* la billarda)
- *ring net cast in a circle*

26 el cable para cerrar la red, la jareta
- *cable for closing the ring net*

27 el dispositivo de cierre *m*
- *closing gear*

28 *u.* 29 la pesca con palangre *m*
- *long-line fishing (long-lining)*

28 el palangre (el cordel largo)
- *long line*

29 la pernada (el reinal, el pipio, la brazolada), un sedal de algodón *m*
- *suspended fishing tackle*

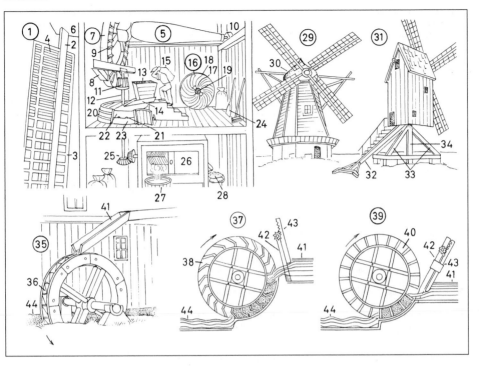

1-34 el molino de viento *m*
– **windmill**
1 el aspa *f* del molino de viento *m*
– *windmill vane (windmill sail, windmill arm)*
2 el alma *f* central del aspa *f*
– *stock (middling, back, radius)*
3 el listón del borde
– *frame*
4 la persiana (la compuerta del viento)
– *shutter*
5 el árbol (el eje de giro *m*)
– *wind shaft (sail axle)*
6 la cabeza del aspa *f*
– *sail top*
7 la rueda dentada
– *brake wheel*
8 el freno de la rueda
– *brake*
9 el diente de madera *f* (el álabe)
– *wooden cog*
10 el cojinete de soporte *m*
– *pivot bearing (step bearing)*
11 el engranaje del molino de viento *m*
– *wallower*
12 el eje del molino
– *mill spindle*
13 la tolva
– *hopper*
14 el vibrador (la caja oscilante)
– *shoe (trough, spout)*
15 el molinero
– *miller*
16 la muela
– *millstone*

17 la estría de refrigeración *f* por aire *m*
– *furrow (flute)*
18 la estría de molienda *f*
– *master furrow*
19 el ojo de la muela (el foramen)
– *eye*
20 la caja de las muelas
– *hurst (millstone casing)*
21 el juego de muelas *f*
– *set of stones (millstones)*
22 la volandera (la corredera, la voladora)
– *runner (upper millstone)*
23 la solera (la muela fija)
– *bed stone (lower stone, bedder)*
24 la pala de madera *f*
– *wooden shovel*
25 el engranaje cónico
– *bevel gear (bevel gearing)*
26 el cilindro cernedor
– *bolter (sifter)*
27 el cubo de madera *f*
– *wooden tub (wooden tun)*
28 la harina
– *flour*
29 el molino de viento *m* holandés
– *smock windmill (Dutch windmill)*
30 el casquete giratorio del molino de viento *m*
– *rotating (revolving) windmill cap*
31 el molino de caja *f* giratoria
– *post windmill (German windmill)*
32 el timón (la cola, el gobierno)
– *tailpole (pole)*

33 la armazón de soporte *m*
– *base*
34 el árbol real (el poste de giro *m*)
– *post*
35-44 el molino de agua *f* (la aceña)
– **watermill**
35 la rueda hidráulica de corriente *f* alta, una rueda de molino *m* de agua *f*, un rodezno
– *overshot mill wheel (high-breast mill wheel), a mill wheel (waterwheel)*
36 el cangilón (el arcaduz)
– *bucket (cavity)*
37 la rueda hidráulica de corriente *f* media
– *middleshot mill wheel (breast mill wheel)*
38 la paleta curva
– *curved vane*
39 la rueda hidráulica de corriente *f* baja
– *undershot mill wheel*
40 la paleta recta
– *flat vane*
41 el caz de traída *f*
– *headrace (discharge flume)*
42 la presa del molino (el azud)
– *mill weir*
43 la compuerta
– *overfall (water overfall)*
44 el caz de salida *f* (el riachuelo) del molino
– *millstream (millrace, Am. raceway)*

1-41 la preparación de la malta
- *preparation of malt (malting)*
1 la torre de maltaje *m* (la instalación de producción *f* de malta *f*)
- *malting tower (maltings)*
2 la entrada de la cebada
- *barley hopper*
3 la planta de lavado *m* con aire *m* comprimido
- *washing floor with compressed-air washing unit*
4 el condensador de desagüe *m*
- *outflow condenser*
5 el depósito colector *m* de agua *f*
- *water-collecting tank*
6 el condensador para el agua *f* de remojo *m*
- *condenser for the steep liquor*
7 el recolector medio de refrigeración *f*
- *coolant collecting plant*
8 la planta de remojo *m* y de germinación *f*
- *steeping floor (steeping tank, dressing floor)*
9 el depósito de agua *f* fría
- *cold water tank*
10 el depósito de agua *f* caliente
- *hot water tank*
11 la sala de las bombas de agua *f*
- *pump room*
12 la instalación neumática
- *pneumatic plant*
13 la instalación hidráulica
- *hydraulic plant*
14 la chimenea de ventilación *f*
- *ventilation shaft (air inlet and outlet)*
15 el ventilador
- *exhaust fan*

16-18 el secadero de la malta
- *kilning floors*
16 la planta de secado *m*
- *drying floor*
17 el ventilador del quemador
- *burner ventilator*
18 la planta de desecación *f*
- *curing floor*
19 el conducto de evacuación *f* del secador
- *outlet duct from the kiln*
20 la tolva de la malta preparada
- *finished malt collecting hopper*
21 la instalación de los transformadores
- *transformer station*
22 los compresores frigoríficos
- *cooling compressors*
23 la malta verde (la cebada en germinación *f*)
- *green malt (germinated barley)*
24 la rejilla rotativa
- *turner (plough)*

25 la central de conexión *f* con diagrama sinóptico
- *central control room with flow diagram*
26 el tornillo sin fin *m* de alimentación *f*
- *screw conveyor*
27 la planta de lavado *m*
- *washing floor*
28 la planta de remojo *m* y de germinación *f*
- *steeping floor*
29 la planta de secado *m*
- *drying kiln*
30 la planta de desecación *f*
- *curing kiln*
31 el silo de cebada *f*
- *barley silo*
32 la balanza
- *weighing apparatus*
33 el elevador de cebada *f*
- *barley elevator*
34 el distribuidor de tres vías *f*
- *three-way chute (three-way tippler)*
35 el elevador de malta *f*
- *malt elevator*
36 el dispositivo de limpieza *f*
- *cleaning machine*
37 el silo de malta *f*
- *malt silo*
38 el dispositivo de aspiración *f* de los gérmenes
- *corn removal by suction*
39 la máquina de ensacado *m*
- *sacker*
40 el aspirador del polvo
- *dust extractor*
41 la recepción de cebada *f*
- *barley reception*

42-53 el proceso de cocción *f* en la cámara de cocción *f*
- *mashing process in the mash-house*
42 el macerador para la mezcla de harina *f* de malta y de agua *f*
- *premasher (converter) for mixing grist and water*
43 la tina de mezcla *f* (la cuba de maceración *f*) para la maceración de la malta
- *mash tub (mash tun) for mashing the malt*
44 la caldera de sacarificación *f* (la caldera de la mezcla)
- *mash copper (mash tun, Am. mash kettle) for boiling the mash*
45 la tapadera (la cúpula) de la caldera
- *dome of the tun*
46 la batidora (el girador)
- *propeller (paddle)*
47 la puerta de corredera *f*
- *sliding door*

48 la tubería para la entrada de agua *f*
- *water (liquor) supply pipe*
49 el cervecero (el maestro cervecero)
- *brewer (master brewer, masher)*
50 la tina de clarificación *f* para asentar los residuos y filtrar el mosto
- *lauter tun for settling the draff (grains) and filtering off the wort*
51 la batería de clarificación *f* para la comprobación de la finura del mosto
- *lauter battery for testing the wort for quality*
52 la caldera para la cocción del mosto con el lúpulo (la tina de mosto *m*)
- *hop boiler (wort boiler) for boiling the wort*
53 el termómetro en forma *f* de cucharón *m*
- *ladle-type thermometer (scoop thermometer)*

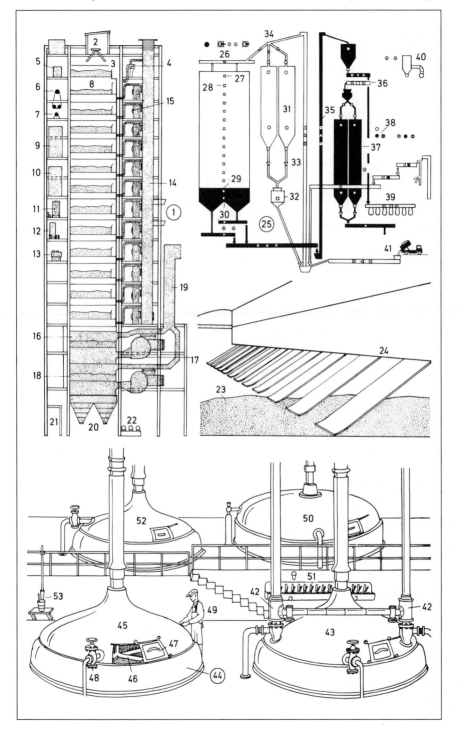

1-31 la cervecería (la fábrica de cerveza *f*)
- *brewery (brewhouse)*
1-5 la refrigeración del mosto y la separación de los residuos
- *wort cooling and break removal (trub removal)*
1 el pupitre de mando *m*
- *control desk (control panel)*
2 el separador de torbellino *m* para la eliminación por calor *m* de los residuos
- *whirlpool separator for removing the hot break (hot trub)*
3 el recipiente dosificador del kieselgur
- *measuring vessel for the kieselguhr*
4 el filtro para kieselgur *f*
- *kieselguhr filter*
5 el refrigerador del mosto lupulado
- *wort cooler*
6 el aparato de preparación *f* de la levadura biológicamente pura
- *pure culture plant for yeast (yeast propagation plant)*
7 la bodega de fermentación *f*
- *fermenting cellar*
8 la cuba de fermentación *f*
- *fermentation vessel (fermenter)*
9 el termómetro de fermentación *f* (el termómetro de maceración *f*)
- *fermentation thermometer (mash thermometer)*
10 el mosto
- *mash*
11 el sistema de serpentín *m* refrigerador
- *refrigeration system*
12 la bodega (el depósito subterráneo de conservación *f*)
- *lager cellar*
13 el orificio de acceso *m* al depósito *m* de almacenamiento *m*
- *manhole to the storage tank*
14 el grifo para sacar la cerveza
- *broaching tap*
15 el filtro de la cerveza
- *beer filter*
16 el almacenamiento en toneles *m*
- *barrel store*
17 el tonel (el barril) de cerveza *f* de aluminio *m*
- *beer barrel, an aluminium (Am. aluminum) barrel*
18 la instalación de lavado *m* de las botellas
- *bottle-washing plant*
19 la máquina de lavar botellas *f*
- *bottle-washing machine (bottle washer)*
20 la instalación de mando *m*
- *control panel*
21 las botellas limpias
- *cleaned bottles*

22 el llenado de las botellas (el embotellado)
- *bottling*
23 la carretilla elevadora de horquilla *f*
- *forklift truck (fork truck, forklift)*
24 la pila de cajas *f* de cerveza *f*
- *stack of beer crates*
25 la lata de cerveza *f*
- *beer can*
26 la botella de cerveza *f*, una botella conforme a las normas europeas; *clases de cerveza:* cerveza dorada, cerveza negra, cerveza estilo Pilsen, cerveza de Munich, cerveza sin alcohol *m*, cerveza malteada, cerveza fuerte (cerveza bock), porter, ale, stout, salvator, cerveza de Goslar, cerveza de trigo *m*, cerveza suave, cerveza floja
- *beer bottle, a Eurobottle with bottled beer; kinds of beer: light beer (lager, light ale, pale ale or bitter), dark beer (brown ale, mild), Pilsener beer, Munich beer, malt beer, strong beer (bock beer), porter, ale, stout, Salvator beer, wheat beer, small beer*
27 la cápsula de la botella (la chapa de la botella, el tapón de la botella)
- *crown cork (crown cork closure)*
28 el paquete de un solo uso (el envase perdido)
- *disposable pack (carry-home pack)*
29 la botella de un solo uso (la botella desechable, la botella no retornable)
- *non-returnable bottle (single-trip bottle)*
30 el vaso de cerveza *f*
- *beer glass*
31 la espuma
- *head*

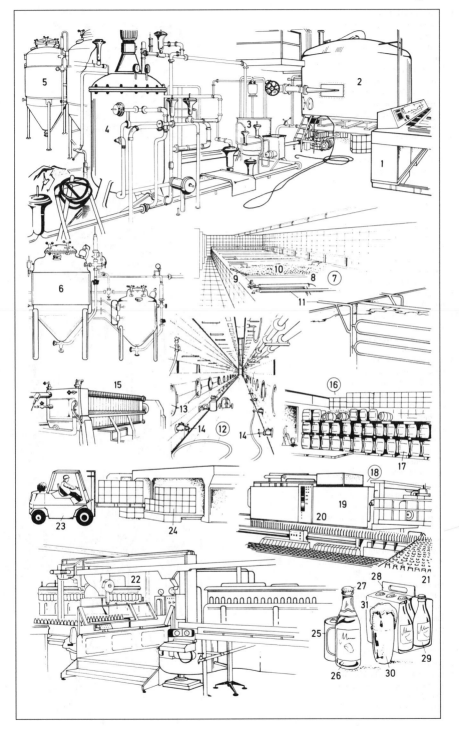

1 el matarife (el carnicero, el jifero)
- *slaughterman* (Am. *slaughterer, killer)*
2 la res de matanza *f,* una vaca
- *animal for slaughter, an ox*
3 la pistola de perno *m* percutor, un aparato para atronar
- *captive-bolt pistol (pneumatic gun), a stunning device*
4 el perno percutor (el percutor)
- *bolt*
5 los cartuchos
- *cartridges*
6 el disparador (el gatillo)
- *release lever (trigger)*
7 el aparato de atronamiento *m* eléctrico
- *electric stunner*
8 el electrodo
- *electrode*
9 el cable de alimentación *f*
- *lead*
10 la protección de la mano (el aislamíento de protección *f*)
- *hand guard (insulation)*
11 el cerdo de matanza *f*
- *pig* (Am. *hog) for slaughter*
12 la vaina de cuchillos *m*
- *knife case*
13 el cuchillo de desollar
- *flaying knife*
14 el cuchillo de matar
- *sticking knife (sticker)*
15 el cuchillo de carnicero *m*
- *butcher's knife (butcher knife)*
16 el afilador de acero *m* (el afilón, la chaira)
- *steel*
17 el cuchillo-rajadera
- *splitter*
18 la cuchilla
- *cleaver (butcher's cleaver, meat axe* (Am. *meat ax))*
19 la sierra para cortar los huesos
- *bone saw (butcher's saw)*
20 la sierra para cortar la carne en trozos *m* (en porciones *f,* la sierra para despiezar)
- *meat saw for sawing meat into cuts*
21-24 el frigorífico (la cámara frigorífica)
- **cold store** *(cold room)*
21 la percha (el colgadero, el gancho)
- *gambrel (gambrel stick)*
22 el cuarto de vaca *f*
- *quarter of beef*
23 la mitad del cerdo (medio cerdo)
- *side of pork*
24 el sello de sanidad (de control) puesto por la inspección del matadero
- *meat inspector's stamp*

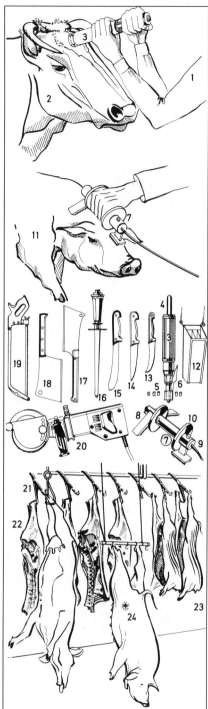

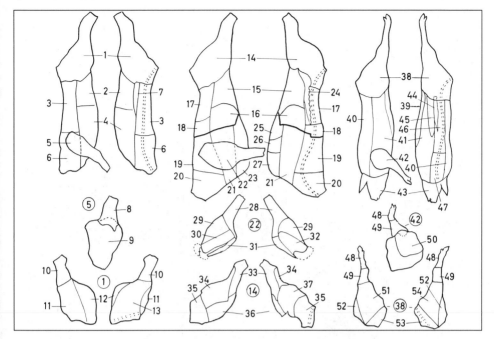

a la izquierda: parte de la carne
a la derecha: parte del hueso
left: meat side;
right: bone side

1-13 la ternera
– animal: *calf;* meat: *veal*
1 la pierna con la culata
– *leg with hind knuckle*
2 la falda
– *flank*
3 la costilla (la costilla de ternera, la mediana)
– *loin and rib*
4 el pecho (el pecho de ternera, la aleta)
– *breast (breast of veal)*
5 la espalda con la pierna delantera (con el garrón)
– *shoulder with fore knuckle*
6 el cuello
– *neck with scrag (scrag end)*
7 la riñonada (*Mé.:* el diezmillo)
– *best end of loin (of loin of veal)*
8 el brazuelo (el morcillo) de la espalda
– *fore knuckle*
9 la espalda
– *shoulder*
10 el garrón (el jarrete de la pierna)
– *hind knuckle*
11 la babilla y la cadera
– *roasting round (oyster round)*
12 el fricandó (el tajo redondo)
– *cutlet for frying or braising*
13 la tapa y la contra
– *undercut (fillet)*
14-37 la vaca
– animal: *ox;* meat: *beef*
14 la pierna con el jarrete
–· *round with rump and shank*
15 *u.* **16** las faldas
– *flank*
15 la falda trasera
– *thick flank*

16 la punta de costillas *f* (ternillas *f*)
– *thin flank*
17 el lomo bajo
– *sirloin*
18 el lomo alto
– *prime rib (fore ribs, prime fore rib)*
19 la espaldilla
– *middle rib and chuck*
20 el cuello
– *neck*
21 el antepecho
– *flat rib*
22 la espalda con el jarrete delantero
– *leg of mutton piece (bladebone) with shin*
23 el pecho de la vaca
– *brisket (brisket of beef)*
24 el solomillo de vaca *f*
– *fillet (fillet of beef)*
25 la parte trasera del pecho
– *hind brisket*
26 la parte central del pecho
– *middle brisket*
27 el esternón
– *breastbone*
28 el morcillo delantero
– *shin*
29 la carne de la espaldilla
– *leg of mutton piece*
30 la carne de la paletilla
– *part of bladebone*
31 el tajo redondo de la espalda
– *part of top rib*
32 el revés de la paletilla
– *part of bladebone*
33 el morcillo trasero
– *shank*
34 la contra
– *silverside*
35 la cadera
– *rump*
36 la babilla
– *thick flank*

37 la tapa y el tajo redondo
– *top side*
38-54 el cerdo
– animal: *pig;* meat: *pork*
38 el jamón con la mano y el codillo
– *leg with knuckle and trotter*
39 la panza (el cuadro)
– *ventral part of the belly*
40 el tocino del lomo (la canal)
– *back fat*
41 la falda
– *belly*
42 la paletilla con la mano
– *bladebone with knuckle and trotter*
43 la cabeza de cerdo *m*
– *head (pig's head)*
44 el solomillo de cerdo *m*
– *fillet (fillet of pork)*
45 la grasa de riñón *m* de cerdo *m* (la manteca de cerdo *m*)
– *leaf fat (pork flare)*
46 la chuleta de cerdo *m* (la cinta)
– *loin (pork loin)*
47 la aguja de cerdo *m*
– *spare rib*
48 la mano de cerdo *m*
– *trotter*
49 el codillo (el brazuelo)
– *knuckle*
50 la carne magra de la espalda
– *butt*
51 la carne del jamón
– *fore end (ham)*
52 la nuez
– *round end for boiling*
53 el tocino del jamón (la culata, la cadera)
– *fat end*
54 el codillo trasero
– *gammon steak*

1-30 la carnicería (la tablajería; *Amér.*: la chanchería; *Col., C. Rica y Venez.*: la pesa; *Ec.*: la tercena)
– *butcher's shop*
1-4 los productos cárnicos
– *meat*
1 el jamón
– *ham on the bone*
2 la hoja de tocino *m* (la panceta, el bacon)
– *flitch of bacon*
3 la carne seca (la carne ahumada; la cecina)
– *smoked meat*
4 el lomo (el solomillo)
– *piece of loin (piece of sirloin)*
5 la manteca de cerdo *m*
– *lard*
6-11 los embutidos (la salchichería)
– *sausages*
6 la etiqueta del precio
– *price label*
7 la mortadela
– *mortadella*
8 las salchichas cocidas; *clases:* la salchicha de Viena, de Francfort
– *scalded sausage; kinds: Vienna sausage (Wiener), Frankfurter sausage (Frankfurter)*

9 el queso de cerdo *m*
– *collared pork* (Am. *headcheese)*
10 la longaniza
– *ring of [Lyoner] sausage*
11 la salchicha (el chorizo; la salchicha para asar)
– *bratwurst (sausage for frying or grilling)*
12 la vitrina frigorífica (el mostrador frigorífico)
– *cold shelves*
13 la ensalada de fiambres *m*
– *meat salad (diced meat salad)*
14 las lonjas de carne *f*
– *cold meats* (Am. *cold cuts)*
15 el pâté
– *pâté*
16 la carne picada
– *mince (mincemeat, minced meat)*
17 el jamón cocido
– *knuckle of pork*
18 el cesto con las ofertas especiales
– *basket for special offers*
19 el letrero con el precio especial
– *price list for special offers*
20 el producto en oferta *f*
– *special offer*
21 el congelador
– *freezer*

22 el asado preempaquetado
– *pre-packed joints*
23 el plato preparado congelado
– *deep-frozen ready-to-eat meal*
24 el pollo
– *chicken*
25 las conservas (las conservas de larga duración *f; con fecha límite de venta:* semiconservas *f*)
– *canned food*
26 la caja de conserva *f*
– *can*
27 las legumbres en conserva *f* (las conservas vegetales)
– *canned vegetables*
28 el pescado en conserva *f* (la conserva de pescado *m)*
– *canned fish*
29 la salsa mayonesa con mostaza *f*
– *salad cream*
30 los refrescos
– *soft drinks*

31-59 la cocina de la charcutería (la sala de adobo *m*)
- *kitchen for making sausages*

31-37 cuchillos *m* de carnicero *m*
- *butcher's knives*

31 el cuchillo de corte *m*
- *slicer*

32 la hoja del cuchillo
- *knife blade*

33 el filo de sierra *f* (la sierra del cuchillo)
- *saw teeth*

34 el mango del cuchillo
- *knife handle*

35 el cuchillo para la carne (la rajadera)
- *carver (carving knife)*

36 el cuchillo de desosar
- *boning knife*

37 el cuchillo de carnicero *m*
- *butcher's knife (butcher knife)*

38 el maestro carnicero (el carnicero; *Cuba:* el mataronero; *Col. y Venez.:* el pesador)
- *butcher (master butcher)*

39 el delantal del carnicero
- *butcher's apron*

40 la artesa de la carne (la cuba de amasar)
- *meat-mixing trough*

41 el relleno de las salchichas (la masa de las salchichas)
- *sausage meat*

42 el rascador
- *scraper*

43 la espumadera (la rasera)
- *skimmer*

44 el tenedor de las salchichas
- *sausage fork*

45 el colador del caldo
- *scalding colander*

46 el cubo de la basura
- *waste bin (Am. trash bin)*

47 el armario de cocinar (el horno) con dispositivo *m* de producción *f* de vapor *m* o aire *m* caliente para estofar
- *cooker, for cooking with steam or hot air*

48 el ahumadero (la cámara de ahumar)
- *smoke house*

49 el embutidor de mano *m* (el embutidor de mesa *f*)
- *sausage filler (sausage stuffer)*

50 el tubo de rellenar
- *feed pipe (supply pipe)*

51 el recipiente de las verduras
- *containers for vegetables*

52 la máquina para preparar la carne de las salchichas
- *mincing machine for sausage meat*

53 la máquina de picar carne *f*
- *mincing machine (meat mincer, mincer, Am. meat grinder)*

54 las rejillas con cuchilla *f* para picar
- *plates (steel plates)*

55 el garabato (de cocinero *m*)
- *meathook (butcher's hook)*

56 la sierra para huesos *m*
- *bone saw*

57 la tabla de carnicero *m*
- *chopping board*

58 el mozo de carnicero *m* cortando la carne
- *butcher, cutting meat*

59 el trozo de carne *f*
- *piece of meat*

1-54 el local de venta *f* de la panadería (la panadería, la confitería)
- *baker's shop*
1 la vendedora
- *shop assistant* (Am. *salesgirl, saleslady*)
2 el pan
- *bread (loaf of bread, loaf)*
3 la miga
- *crumb*
4 la corteza
- *crust (bread crust)*
5 el cantero
- *crust* (Am. *heel*)
6-12 clases *f* **de pan** *m*
- *kinds of bread (breads)*
6 el pan redondo (el pan cateto, la hogaza, un pan moreno)
- *round loaf, a wheat and rye bread*
7 el pan redondo pequeño
- *small round loaf*
8 el pan alargado, un pan de mezcla *f* (un pan de trigo *m* y centeno *m*)
- *long loaf (bloomer), a wheat and rye bread*
9 el pan blanco (el pan de Viena)
- *white loaf*
10 el pan inglés, un pan integral
- *pan loaf, a wholemeal rye bread*
11 el pan trenzado (el bollo de Nochebuena, el bollo de Navidad)
- *yeast bread* (Am. *stollen*)
12 el pan blanco francés (la barra de pan *m*)
- *French loaf (baguette, French stick)*
13-16 panecillos *m*
- *rolls*

13 el panecillo (blanco o de canela; *Amér.:* el pancito)
- *roll*
14 el panecillo de canela *f* o trigo *m* (panecillo blanco, el bollo de pan *m;* también: panecillo salado, panecillo con adormidera, panecillo con comino *m; Amér.:* el besito)
- *[white] roll*
15 el panecillo doble
- *double roll*
16 el panecillo de centeno *m*
- *rye-bread roll*
17-47 dulces *m* (confites *m*, pasteles *m*)
- *cakes (confectionery)*
17 el rollito de nata *f*
- *cream roll*
18 el hojaldre
- *vol-au-vent, a puff pastry* (Am. *puff paste)*
19 el bizcocho enrollado
- *Swiss roll* (Am. *jelly roll)*
20 la tartita (*Amér.:* las masitas)
- *tartlet*
21 el merengue
- *cream slice*
22-24 tartas *f*
- *flans* (Am. *pies*) *and gateaux (torten)*
22 la tarta de frutas *f* (*var.:* tarta de fresas *f,* tarta de cerezas *f,* tarta de grosellas *f,* tarta de melocotón *m,* tarta de ruibarbo *m)*
- *fruit flan* (kinds: *strawberry flan, cherry flan, gooseberry flan, peach flan, rhubarb flan)*

23 la tarta de queso *m*
- *cheesecake*
24 la tarta de crema *f* (*también:* la tarta de nata *f; var.:* la tarta de crema *f* de mantequilla *f,* la tarta de cerezas *f* de la Selva Negra)
- *cream cake* (Am. *cream pie*) (kinds: *butter-cream cake, Black Forest gateau)*
25 la bandeja de tarta *f*
- *cake plate*
26 el merengue
- *meringue*
27 la col de crema *f* (el suspiro de monja *f*)
- *cream puff*
28 la nata batida (la crema chantillí)
- *whipped cream*
29 el bollo de Berlín (*Chile:* el queque)
- *doughnut* (Am. *bismarck)*
30 la palmera
- *Danish pastry*
31 la barrita salada (*también:* la barrita con comino *m)*
- *saltstick (Salzstange)* (also: *caraway roll, caraway stick)*
32 el cuernecito (el croissant; *Amér.:* la media luna)
- *croissant (crescent roll,* Am. *crescent)*

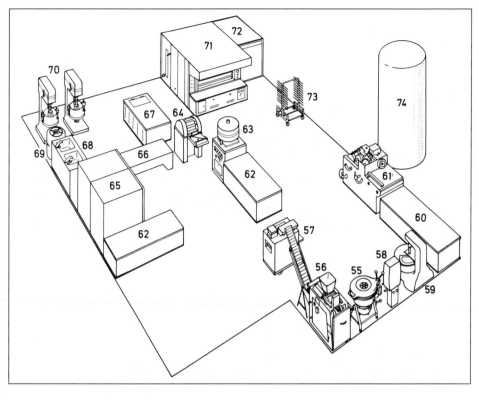

33 el pastel de molde *m* (la torta alemana; *también:* el bizcocho de Saboya)
- *ring cake (gugelhupf)*
34 el dulce de molde *m* cubierto con una capa de chocolate *m*
- *slab cake with chocolate icing*
35 la tortita espolvoreada
- *streusel cakes*
36 la cabeza de moro *m*
- *marshmallow*
37 el macarrón (el mostachón, el almendrado)
- *coconut macaroon*
38 la rosca (la ensaimada)
- *schnecke*
39 el dulce americano
- *[kind of] iced bun*
40 el bizcocho tostado blando
- *sweet bread*
41 la trenza
- *plaited bun (plait)*
42 la corona de Francfort
- *Frankfurter garland cake*
43 el dulce en trozos (*var.:* el dulce espolvoreado con recortes *m* de pasta *f*, el dulce cubierto de azúcar *f* el dulce de ciruelas *f*)
- *slices (kinds: streusel slices, sugared slices, plum slices)*
44 la rosquilla
- *pretzel*
45 el barquillo
- *wafer* (Am. *waffle)*
46 el dulce de pisos *m*
- *tree cake (baumkuchen)*
47 el suelo de masa *f* para las tartas
- *flan case*

48-50 clases *f* de pan *m* empaquetado
- *wrapped bread*
48 el pan integral (*también:* el pan de germen *m* de trigo *m*)
- *wholemeal bread (also: wheatgerm bread)*
49 el pan negro de Westfalia
- *pumpernickel (wholemeal rye bread)*
50 el biscote
- *crispbread*
51 el pan de especias *f* (el alajú)
- *gingerbread* (Am. *lebkuchen)*
52 la harina (*var.:* la harina de trigo *m*, la harina de centeno *m*)
- *flour (kinds: wheat flour, rye flour)*
53 la levadura
- *yeast (baker's yeast)*
54 los bizcochos (los bizcochos tostados para los niños; *C. Rica:* los tosteles)
- *rusks (French toast)*
55-74 la tahona
- *bakery (bakehouse)*
55 la amasadora
- *kneading machine (dough mixer)*
56-57 la unidad de fabricación *f* del pan
- *bread unit*
56 la máquina de cortar la masa
- *divider*
57 la unidad para dar la forma al pan
- *moulder* (Am. *molder)*
58 el aparato para medir y mezclar el agua *f*
- *premixer*
59 el mezclador (la amasadera)
- *dough mixer*
60 la mesa de trabajo *m*
- *workbench*

61 la unidad de fabricación *f* de los panecillos
- *roll unit*
62 la mesa de trabajo *m*
- *workbench*
63 la máquina de cortar y redondear la masa
- *divider and rounder (rounding machine)*
64 la máquina para dar la forma a los croissants
- *crescent-forming machine*
65 el congelador
- *freezers*
66 la freidora
- *oven [for baking with fat]*
67-70 la confitería
- *confectionery unit*
67 la mesa de enfriamiento *m*
- *cooling table*
68 el fregadero
- *sink*
69 el hornillo
- *boiler*
70 la batidora-mezcladora
- *whipping unit [with beater]*
71 el horno de pisos *m* (el horno de panificación *f*)
- *reel oven (oven)*
72 la cámara de fermentación *f*
- *fermentation room*
73 la carretilla de la cámara de fermentación *f*
- *fermentation trolley*
74 el silo de harina *f*
- *flour silo*

1-87 la tienda de comestibles *m* (el almacén de ultramarinos *m*, el colmado; *Amér.*: la fiambrería, la pulpería), una tienda de venta *f* al por menor
– **grocer's shop** *(grocer's, delicatessen shop,* Am. *grocery store, delicatessen store), a retail shop (Am. retail store)*
1 el escaparate
– *window display*
2 el cartel de propaganda (el anuncio)
– *poster (advertisement)*
3 la vitrina frigorífica
– *cold shelves*
4 los embutidos (los fiambres)
– *sausages*
5 el queso
– *cheese*
6 el pollo para asar
– *roasting chicken (broiler)*
7 la pularda, una gallina cebada
– *poulard, a fattened hen*
8-11 los ingredientes de pastelería *f*
– *baking ingredients*
8 las pasas; *anál.*: las pasas gorronas
– *raisins;* sim.: *sultanas*
9 las pasas de Corinto
– *currants*
10 la cidra confitada
– *candied lemon peel*
11 la naranja confitada
– *candied orange peel*
12 la balanza automática (el peso)
– *computing scale, a rapid scale*
13 el vendedor
– *shop assistant (Am. salesclerk)*
14 la estantería (el anaquel de los artículos)
– *goods shelves (shelves)*

15-20 las conservas
– *canned food*
15 la leche condensada (la leche en lata *f*)
– *canned milk*
16 las frutas en conserva *f*
– *canned fruit (cans of fruit)*
17 las verduras en conserva *f*
– *canned vegetables*
18 el zumo (el jugo de frutas *f*)
– *fruit juice*
19 las sardinas en aceite *m*, una conserva de pescado *m*
– *sardines in oil, a can of fish*
20 la carne en conserva *f*
– *canned meat (cans of meat)*
21 la margarina
– *margarine*
22 la mantequilla
– *butter*
23 la manteca de coco *m*, una grasa vegetal
– *coconut oil, a vegetable oil*
24 el aceite; *clases:* el aceite de mesa, el aceite de oliva *f*, el aceite de girasol *m*, el aceite de germen *m* de trigo *m*, el aceite de cacahuetes *m*, el aceite de maíz
– *oil; kinds: salad oil, olive oil, sunflower oil, wheatgerm oil, ground-nut oil*
25 el vinagre
– *vinegar*
26 el cubito (la pastilla) de sopa *f*
– *stock cube*
27 el cubito (la pastilla) de caldo *m*
– *bouillon cube*
28 la mostaza
– *mustard*

29 el pepinillo en vinagre *m*
– *pickled gherkin*
30 el condimento para sopas *f*
– *soup seasoning*
31 la vendedora
– *shop assistant (Am. salesgirl, saleslady)*
32-34 las pastas alimenticias
– *pastas*
32 los spaghetti
– *spaghetti*
33 los macarrones
– *macaroni*
34 los tallarines
– *noodles*
35-39 productos *m* **alimenticios** (los cereales)
– *cereal products*
35 la cebada perlada
– *pearl barley*
36 la sémola
– *semolina*
37 los copos de avena *f*
– *rolled oats (porridge oats, oats)*
38 el arroz
– *rice*
39 la fécula de sagú *m* (la tapioca)
– *sago*
40 la sal
– *salt*
41 el comerciante, un comerciante al por menor
– *grocer (Am. groceryman), a shopkeeper (tradesman, retailer,* Am. *storekeeper)*
42 las alcaparras
– *capers*
43 la clienta
– *customer*

44 el vale
– *receipt (sales check)*
45 la bolsa para las compras
– *shopping bag*
46-49 el material para envolver
– *wrapping material*
46 el papel de envolver
– *wrapping paper*
47 la cinta adhesiva
– *adhesive tape*
48 la bolsa de papel *m* (el cartucho)
– *paper bag*
49 el cucurucho
– *cone-shaped paper bag*
50 los polvos para budines *m*
– *blancmange powder*
51 la confitura
– *whole-fruit jam (preserve)*
52 la mermelada
– *jam*
53-55 azúcar *m* y *f*
– *sugar*
53 el azúcar en terrones *m*
– *cube sugar*
54 el azúcar en polvo *m*
– *icing sugar (Am. confectioner's sugar)*
55 el azúcar cristalizado (el azúcar refinado)
– *refined sugar in crystals*
56-59 las bebidas alcohólicas (los licores)
– *spirits*
56 el aguardiente (*P. Rico, S. Dgo. y Venez.:* el romo; *Arg., Bol., S. Dgo. y Urug.:* la tafia; *Perú:* el trinque)
– *schnapps distilled from grain [usually wheat]*
57 el ron
– *rum*

58 el licor
– *liqueur*
59 el coñac
– *brandy (cognac)*
60-64 vino embotellado *m*
– *wine in bottles (bottled wine)*
60 el vino blanco
– *white wine*
61 el chianti
– *Chianti*
62 el vermut
– *vermouth*
63 el champaña (el vino espumoso)
– *sparkling wine*
64 el vino tinto
– *red wine*
65-68 los estimulantes
– *tea, coffee, etc.*
65 el café (el café en grano *m*)
– *coffee (pure coffee)*
66 el cacao
– *cocoa*
67 la variedad de café *m*
– *coffee*
68 el té en bolsitas *f*
– *tea bag*
69 el molinillo eléctrico de café *m*
– *electric coffee grinder*
70 la tostadora de café *m*
– *coffee roaster*
71 el bombo para tostar el café
– *roasting drum*
72 la paleta para probar el café
– *sample scoop*
73 la lista de precios *m*
– *price list*
74 el mostrador frigorífico
– *freezer*

75-86 los dulces (las golosinas)
– *confectionery* (Am. *candies*)
75 el caramelo
– *sweet* (Am. *candy*)
76 los drops (los caramelos ácidos)
– *drops*
77 el caramelo
– *toffees*
78 la tableta de chocolate *m*
– *bar of chocolate*
79 la caja de bombones *m*
– *chocolate box*
80 el bombón, un artículo de confitería *f*
– *chocolate, a sweet*
81 el nuégado [un turrón de nueces *f*]
– *nougat*
82 el mazapán
– *marzipan*
83 el bombón de licor *m*
– *chocolate liqueur*
84 la lengua de gato *m*
– *cat's tongue*
85 el crocante (el guirlache)
– *croquant*
86 las trufas de chocolate *m*
– *truffle*
87 el agua *f* de mesa *f* (agua *f* de Seltz, agua *f* carbónica, agua mineral)
– *soda water*

1-96 el supermercado, una tienda de alimentación *f* de autoservicio *m*
- *supermarket, a self-service food store*
1 el carro para las compras
- *shopping trolley*
2 el cliente (el comprador)
- *customer*
3 la bolsa de la compra
- *shopping bag*
4 la entrada al local de venta *f*
- *entrance to the sales area*
5 la barrera
- *barrier*
6 la señal prohibiendo la entrada a los perros
- *sign (notice) banning dogs*
7 los perros atados
- *dogs tied by their leads*
8 el cesto de ventas *f*
- *basket*
9 **la sección de los productos de panadería *f* y confitería *f***
- *bread and cake counter (bread counter, cake counter)*
10 el expositor
- *display counter for bread and cakes*
11 las variedades de pan *m*
- *kinds of bread (breads)*
12 los panecillos (los bollos de pan *m*)
- *rolls*
13 los cuernos (las medias lunas, los croissants)
- *croissants (crescent rolls, Am. crescents)*
14 el pan casero (el pan cateto, la hogaza)
- *round loaf (strong rye bread)*
15 la tarta
- *gateau*

16 la rosquilla grande [desconocida en España]
- *pretzel [made with yeast dough]*
17 la vendedora
- *shop assistant (Am. salesgirl, saleslady)*
18 la clienta (la compradora)
- *customer*
19 el cartel de las ofertas
- *sign listing goods*
20 la tarta de frutas *f*
- *fruit flan*
21 el bizcocho
- *slab cake*
22 el pastel de molde *m*
- *ring cake*
23 **la góndola de los cosméticos,** una góndola (una estantería)
- *cosmetics gondola, a gondola (sales shelves)*
24 el baldaquín
- *canopy*
25 el estante de las medias
- *hosiery shelf*
26 la bolsa de medias *f*
- *pack of stockings (nylons)*
27-35 los productos para el aseo personal (los cosméticos)
- *toiletries (cosmetics)*
27 el tarro de crema *f* (la crema; *clases:* crema *f* hidratante, crema *f* de día *m*, crema *f* de noche *f*, crema *f* para las manos)
- *jar of cream (cream; kinds: moisturising cream, day cream, night-care cream, hand cream)*
28 el paquete de algodón *m* en rama *f*
- *packet of cotton wool*
29 la caja de polvos *m*
- *tin of powder*

30 el paquete de tapones *m* de algodón *m*
- *packet of cotton wool balls*
31 el tubo de pasta *f* dentífrica
- *tube of toothpaste*
32 el esmalte para las uñas
- *nail varnish (nail polish)*
33 el tubo de crema *f*
- *tube of cream*
34 las sales de baño *m*
- *bath salts*
35 artículos *m* de higiene *f*
- *sanitary articles*
36 u. 37 la comida para animales *m*
- *pet foods*
36 la comida completa para perros *m*
- *complete dog food*
37 el paquete de bizcochos *m* para perros *m*
- *packet of dog biscuits*
38 el paquete de serrín *m* para gatos *m*
- *bag of cat litter*
39 la sección del queso (la quesería)
- *cheese counter*
40 el pan (la rueda) de queso *m*
- *whole cheese*
41 el queso suizo (el queso emmental) con agujeros *m*
- *Swiss cheese (Emmental cheese) with holes*
42 el queso de bola *f* (el queso holandés), un queso redondo
- *Edam cheese, a round cheese*
43 la góndola (la estantería) de productos *m* lecheros
- *gondola for dairy products*
44 la leche (la leche de larga duración *f*, leche pasteurizada y homogeneizada)
- *long-life milk (milk with good keeping properties, pasteurized and homogenized milk)*

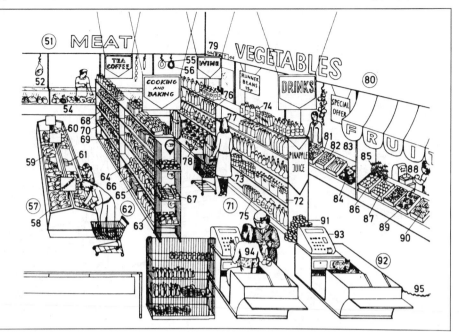

45 el cartón de leche *f* (el brik de leche *f*)
– *carton of milk*
46 la crema (la nata)
– *cream*
47 la mantequilla
– *butter*
48 la margarina
– *margarine*
49 la cajita de queso *m*
– *box of cheeses*
50 el paquete (el cartón) de huevos *m*
– *box of eggs*
51 **la sección de la carne fresca**
– *fresh meat counter (meat counter)*
52 el jamón
– *ham on the bone*
53 los productos cárnicos (la carne)
– *meat (meat products)*
54 los embutidos
– *sausages*
55 la salchicha (la longaniza)
– *ring of [pork] sausage*
56 la morcilla (*Col. y Mé.:* la rellena)
– *ring of blood sausage*
57 el congelador
– *freezer*
58-61 **los productos congelados**
– *frozen food*
58 la pularda (la gallina cebada)
– *poulard*
59 el muslo de pavo *m*
– *turkey leg (drumstick)*
60 la gallina para caldo *m*
– *boiling fowl*
61 las verduras congeladas
– *frozen vegetables*
62 **la góndola de productos *m* de pastelería *f* y de alimentos *m***
– *gondola for baking ingredients and cereal products*

63 la harina de trigo *m*
– *wheat flour*
64 el pilón de azúcar *m* y *f*
– *sugar loaf*
65 el paquete de pastas para sopas *f*
– *packet of noodles [for soup]*
66 el aceite de mesa *f*
– *salad oil*
67 el paquete de especias *f*
– *packet of spices*
68-70 **los estimulantes**
– *tea, coffee, etc.*
68 el café
– *coffee*
69 el paquete de té *m*
– *packet of tea*
70 el café soluble (el café instantáneo)
– *instant coffee*
71 **la góndola (la estantería) de las bebidas**
– *drinks gondola*
72 la caja de cerveza *f*
– *crate of beer*
73 la lata de cerveza *f* (la cerveza en lata *f*)
– *beer can (canned beer)*
74 la botella de zumo *m* de frutas *f*
– *bottle of fruit juice*
75 la lata de zumo *m* de frutas *f*
– *can of fruit juice*
76 la botella de vino *m*
– *bottle of wine*
77 la botella de chianti *m*
– *bottle of Chianti*
78 la botella de vino *m* espumoso
– *bottle of champagne*
79 la salida de urgencia *f*
– *emergency exit*
80 **la sección de verduras *f* y frutas *f***
– *fruit and vegetable counter*

81 la caja de las verduras
– *vegetable basket*
82 los tomates
– *tomatoes*
83 los pepinos
– *cucumbers*
84 la coliflor
– *cauliflower*
85 la piña tropical
– *pineapple*
86 las manzanas
– *apples*
87 las peras
– *pears*
88 la balanza (el peso)
– *scales for weighing fruit*
89 las uvas
– *grapes (bunches of grapes)*
90 los plátanos (las bananas)
– *bananas*
91 las latas de conservas *f*
– *can*
92 **la caja**
– *checkout*
93 la caja registradora
– *cash register*
94 la cajera
– *cashier*
95 la cadena
– *chain*
96 el mozo reponedor
– *assistant departmental manager*

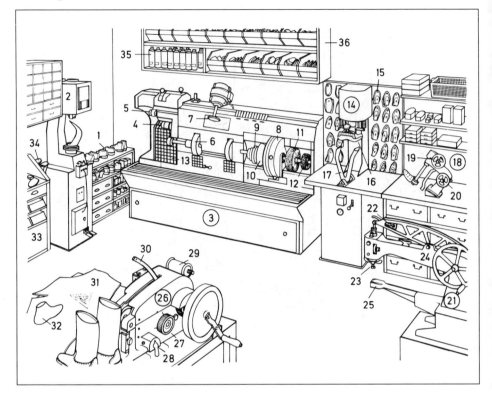

1-68 el taller de zapatero *m* (la zapatería)
– *shoemaker's workshop (bootmaker's workshop)*
1 los zapatos arreglados
– *finished (repaired) shoes*
2 la máquina de pespuntear
– *auto-soling machine*
3 la máquina pulidora
– *finishing machine*
4 la fresa para el tacón
– *heel trimmer*
5 las fresas de recambio *m*
– *sole trimmer*
6 la muela
– *scouring wheel*
7 el disco de pulimentar
– *naum keag*
8 la propulsión
– *drive unit (drive wheel)*
9 el pulsador de corte *m*
– *iron*
10 el disco de paño *m*
– *buffing wheel*
11 el cepillo para pulir
– *polishing brush*
12 el cepillo de cerdas *f*
– *horsehair brush*
13 la rejilla de aspiración *f*
– *extractor grid*

14 la prensa automática para las suelas
– *automatic sole press*
15 la horma
– *press attachment*
16 la almohadilla de prensa *f*
– *pad*
17 el arco de prueba *f*
– *press bar*
18 el aparato para ensanchar (la máquina de ahormar, la horma)
– *stretching machine*
19 el dispositivo para regular la anchura
– *width adjustment*
20 el dispositivo para regular el largo
– *length adjustment*
21 la máquina de coser
– *stitching machine*
22 el dispositivo para regular la tensión del hilo
– *power regulator (power control)*
23 la barra para la aguja
– *foot*
24 el volante
– *handwheel*
25 el pie prensatelas
– *arm*
26 la máquina para montar las suelas
– *sole stitcher (sole-stitching machine)*

27 la palanca del pie
– *foot bar lever*
28 el reglaje de avance *m*
– *feed adjustment (feed setting)*
29 la bobina de hilo *m*
– *bobbin (cotton bobbin)*
30 el guiahílos
– *thread guide (yarn guide)*
31 el cuero para las suelas
– *sole leather*
32 la horma
– *[wooden] last*
33 la mesa de trabajo *m*
– *workbench*
34 la horma de hierro *m*
– *last*
35 el pulverizador de tinte *m*
– *dye spray*
36 el estante del material
– *shelves for materials*

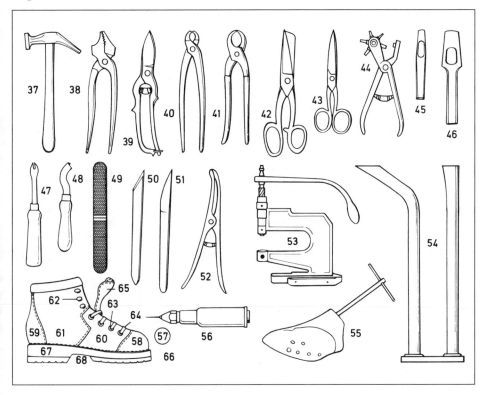

37 el martillo de zapatero *m*
 – *shoemaker's hammer*
38 las tenazas para el cuero
 – *shoemaker's pliers (welt pincers)*
39 las cizallas para el cuero de las suelas
 – *sole-leather shears*
40 las tenazas pequeñas
 – *small pincers (nippers)*
41 las tenazas gruesas
 – *large pincers (nippers)*
42 las tijeras para cortar el cuero superior
 – *upper-leather shears*
43 las tijeras para el hilo
 – *scissors*
44 los alicates sacabocados
 – *revolving punch (rotary punch)*
45 el sacabocados
 – *punch*
46 el sacabocados de asa *f*
 – *punch [with a handle]*
47 el sacaclavos
 – *nail puller*
48 el desvirador
 – *welt cutter*
49 la lima de zapatero *m*
 – *shoemaker's rasp*

50 el cuchillo de zapatero *m* (el tranchete de zapatero *m*)
 – *cobbler's knife (shoemaker's knife)*
51 el tranchete cortante
 – *skiving knife (skife knife, paring knife)*
52 las pinzas desmochadas (las pinzas con las puntas cortadas)
 – *toecap remover*
53 la máquina para colocar a presión *f* ojetes *m*, corchetes *m* y botones *m*
 – *eyelet, hook, and press-stud setter*
54 la horma de trabajo *m*
 – *stand (with iron lasts)*
55 la horma tensora
 – *width-setting tree*
56 el puño con punzón *m*
 – *nail grip*
57 la bota
 – *boot*
58 la puntera
 – *toecap*
59 el contrafuerte
 – *counter*
60 la pala (la empella)
 – *vamp*

61 la parte lateral (la caña)
 – *quarter*
62 el corchete
 – *hook*
63 el ojete
 – *eyelet*
64 el cordón
 – *lace (shoelace, bootlace)*
65 la lengüeta; *anál.:* la oreja del zapato
 – *tongue*
66 la suela (la planta)
 – *sole*
67 el tacón
 – *heel*
68 el arqueo (el enfranque)
 – *shank (waist)*

1 la bota de invierno *m*
– *winter boot*
2 la suela de PVC (la suela de materia
   f plástica)
– *PVC sole (plastic sole)*
3 el forro de peluche *m* (de felpa *f*)
– *high-pile lining*
4 el nylon
– *nylon*
5 el botín de caballero *m*
– *men's boot*
6 el cierre de cremallera *f* en el interior
– *inside zip (Am. zipper)*
7 la bota alta para caballeros *m*
– *men's high leg boot*
8 la suela de plataforma *f*
– *platform sole (platform)*
9 las botas vaqueras
– *Western boot (cowboy boot)*
10 la bota de piel *f* de potro *m*
– *pony-skin boot*
11 la suela moldeada sobre la piel
– *cemented sole*
12 la bota de señora *f*
– *ladies' boot*
13 la bota de calle *f* de caballero *m*
– *men's high leg boot*
14 la bota de PVC inyectado sin cos-
   turas *f* para la lluvia
– *seamless PVC waterproof wellington
   boot*
15 la suela translúcida
– *natural-colour (Am. natural-color)
   sole*
16 la puntera de la bota
– *toecap*
17 el forro de tejido *m* de punto *m*
– *tricot lining (knitwear lining)*
18 la bota de marcha *f* (para excur-
   siones *f*)
– *hiking boot*
19 la suela perfilada
– *grip sole*
20 el alto de la caña relleno
– *padded collar*
21 los cordones
– *tie fastening (lace fastening)*
22 las zapatillas de baño *m*
– *open-toe mule*
23 la parte superior (la pala) de tejido
   m de rizo *m*
– *terry upper*
24 la suela corrida
– *polo outsole*
25 las babuchas (las pantuflas)
– *mule*
26 la pala de pana *f* de canutillo *m*
– *corduroy upper*
27 el zapato de tacón *m* alto con hebi-
   llas *f*
– *evening sandal (sandal court shoe)*
28 el tacón alto (el tacón aguja)
– *high heel (stiletto heel)*
29 el zapato de tacón *m*
– *court shoe (Am. pump)*
30 el mocasín
– *moccasin*

31 el zapato bajo (el zapato de
   cordones *m*)
– *shoe, a tie shoe (laced shoe,
   Oxford shoe, Am. Oxford)*
32 la lengüeta
– *tongue*
33 el zapato bajo con tacón *m* alto
– *high-heeled shoe (shoe with
   raised heel)*
34 el mocasín
– *casual*
35 la zapatilla de deporte *m*
– *trainer (training shoe)*
36 la zapatilla de tenis *m*
– *tennis shoe*
37 el contrafuerte
– *counter (stiffening)*
38 la suela de caucho *m* translúcido
– *natural-colour (Am. natural-
   color) rubber sole*
39 el calzado de trabajo *m*
– *heavy-duty boot (Am. stogy,
   stogie)*
40 la puntera reforzada
– *toecap*
41 la zapatilla de casa *f* (la pantu-
   fla)
– *slipper*
42 el patín de lana *f*
– *woollen (Am. woolen) slip sock*
43 el modelo de punto *m*
– *knit stitch (knit)*
44 el zueco
– *clog*
45 la suela de madera *f*
– *wooden sole*
46 la pala de cuero *m* flexible
– *soft-leather upper*
47 la suela de materia *f* plástica
– *sabot*
48 la sandalia de tirilla *f* (un calzado de playa *f*)
– *toe post sandal*
49 la sandalia
– *ladies' sandal*
50 la plantilla ortopédica
– *surgical footbed (sock)*
51 la sandalia frailuna
– *sandal*
52 la hebilla
– *shoe buckle (buckle)*
53 el zapato de tacón *m* alto con
   presilla *f*
– *sling-back court shoe (Am.
   sling pump)*
54 el zapato de tela *f* con tacón *m*
   alto
– *fabric court shoe*
55 el tacón de cuña *f*
– *wedge heel*
56 la bota de marcha *f* para niños *m*
– *baby's first walking boot*

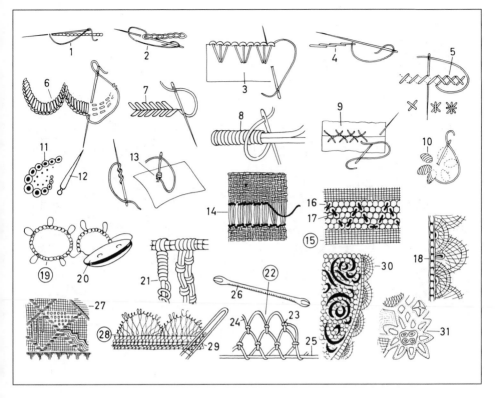

1 el pespunte
– backstitch seam
2 el punto de cadeneta f
– chain stitch
3 el punto de adorno m (el punto de fantasía f)
– ornamental stitch
4 el punto de tallo m
– stem stitch
5 el punto de cruz f
– cross stitch
6 el punto de festón m (el festón de uña f)
– buttonhole stitch (button stitch)
7 el punto de espiga f
– fishbone stitch
8 el punto de cordón m
– overcast stitch
9 el punto de escapulario m (el punto de arista f)
– herringbone stitch (Russian stitch, Russian cross stitch)
10 el bordado plano
– satin stitch (flat stitch)
11 el bordado inglés
– eyelet embroidery (broderie anglaise)
12 el punzón para bordado m inglés
– stiletto

13 el punto de nudos m
– French knot (French dot, knotted stitch, twisted knot stitch)
14 la vainica (el calado)
– hem stitch work
15 el bordado de tul m (la puntilla de tul m)
– tulle work (tulle lace)
16 el fondo de tul m
– tulle background (net background)
17 el punto de zurcidura f
– darning stitch
18 el encaje de bolillos m; especialidades: puntillas f de Valenciennes y de Bruselas
– pillow lace (bobbin lace, bone lace); kinds: Valenciennes, Brussels lace
19 el trabajo con lanzadera f (el encaje con lanzadera f)
– tatting
20 la lanzadera
– tatting shuttle (shuttle)
21 el macramé
– knotted work (macramé)
22 la malla (la red)
– filet (netting)
23 el nudo de la malla
– netting loop

24 el hilo de la malla
– netting thread
25 la varilla de la malla
– mesh pin (mesh gauge)
26 la lanzadera para malla f
– netting needle
27 el deshilado (el calado)
– open work
28 el trabajo con horquillas f
– gimping (hairpin work)
29 la horquilla
– gimping needle (hairpin)
30 los encajes (las puntillas); especialidades: encajes m de Reticella, de Venecia, de Alençon; anál.: la filigrana (con hilo m de metal m)
– needlepoint lace (point lace, needlepoint); kinds: reticella lace, Venetian lace, Alençon lace; sim. with metal thread: filigree work
31 el bordado con cintas f
– braid embroidery (braid work)

1-27 el taller del modisto
- ***dressmaker's workroom***
1 el modisto
- *dressmaker*
2 la cinta métrica, un metro
- *tape measure (measuring tape), a metre* (Am. *meter*) *tape measure*
3 las tijeras de corte *m*
- *cutting shears*
4 la mesa de corte *m*
- *cutting table*
5 el vestido modelo
- *model dress*
6 el maniquí
- *dressmaker's model (dressmaker's dummy, dress form)*
7 el abrigo modelo
- *model coat*
8 la máquina de coser de modista *f*
- *sewing machine*
9 el motor de impulsión *f*
- *drive motor*
10 la correa de transmisión *f*
- *drive belt*
11 el pedal
- *treadle*
12 el hilo de la máquina de coser (una bobina de hilo *m*)
- *sewing machine cotton (sewing machine thread) (bobbin)*

13 el patrón de corte *m*
- *cutting template*
14 la cinta de costura *f* (la cinta para los extremos)
- *seam binding*
15 la caja de los botones
- *button box*
16 el resto (el retal) de tela *f*
- *remnant*
17 el perchero de pie *m* móvil
- *movable clothes rack*
18 la mesa (la superficie) de planchado *m*
- *hand-iron press*
19 la planchadora
- *presser (ironer)*
20 la plancha de vapor *m*
- *steam iron*
21 el tubo de alimentación *f* del agua *f*
- *water feed pipe*
22 el depósito del agua *f*
- *water container*
23 la superficie de planchado *m* inclinable
- *adjustable-tilt ironing surface*
24 el mecanismo de suspensión *f* de la plancha
- *lift device for the iron*
25 el recipiente de aspiración *f* para el vapor

- *steam extractor*
26 el pedal de aspiración *f*
- *foot switch controlling steam extraction*
27 el tejido de lana *f* planchado
- *pressed non-woven woollen* (Am. *woolen*) *fabric*

1-32 el taller del sastre
- *tailor's workroom*
1 el espejo triple
- *triple mirror*
2 los cortes de tejido *m*
- *lengths of material*
3 el tejido para trajes *m*
- *suiting*
4 la revista de moda *f*
- *fashion journal (fashion magazine)*
5 el cenicero
- *ashtray*
6 el catálogo de moda *f*
- *fashion catalogue*
7 la mesa de trabajo *m*
- *workbench*
8 la estantería de pared *f*
- *wall shelves (wall shelf unit)*
9 la bobina (el carrete) de hilo *m* para coser
- *cotton reel*
10 la bobina de seda *f* para coser
- *small reels of sewing silk*
11 las tijeras de mano *m*
- *hand shears*
12 la máquina de coser combinada, eléctrica y de pedal *m*
- *combined electric and treadle sewing machine*

13 el pedal
- *treadle*
14 el guardafaldas (la pieza de protección *f*)
- *dress guard*
15 la rueda volante (el volante)
- *band wheel*
16 el rebobinador del hilo (el dispositivo para encanillar)
- *bobbin thread*
17 la mesa de la máquina de coser
- *sewing machine table*
18 el cajón de la máquina de coser
- *sewing machine drawer*
19 la cinta para los extremos (la cinta de extrafort *m*)
- *seam binding*
20 la almohadilla para clavar los alfileres (el alfiletero, el acerico)
- *pincushion*
21 la acción de marcar
- *marking out*
22 el sastre
- *tailor*
23 el cojín de molde *m*
- *shaping pad*
24 la tiza de sastre *m* (el jaboncillo de sastre *m*)
- *tailor's chalk (French chalk)*

25 la pieza
- *workpiece*
26 la mesa de planchar al vapor
- *steam press (steam pressing unit)*
27 el brazo orientable
- *swivel arm*
28 la tabla para planchar las mangas
- *pressing cushion (pressing pad)*
29 la plancha
- *iron*
30 la manopla para planchar
- *hand-ironing pad*
31 el cepillo de la ropa
- *clothes brush*
32 el paño de planchar
- *pressing cloth*

1-39 el salón de peluquería f de señoras f
(el instituto de belleza f), un salón de
cosmética f
– *ladies' hairdressing salon and beauty
salon* (Am. *beauty parlor, beauty shop*)
1-16 los utensilios de peluquería f
– *hairdresser's tools*
1 la escudilla para el agente (el producto)
de decoloración f
– *bowl containing bleach*
2 el cepillo para desenredar los cabellos
– *detangling brush*
3 el tubo del producto de decoloración f
(el producto para teñir los cabellos)
– *bleach tube*
4 el rizador (el bigudí) del tinte
– *curler [used in dyeing]*
5 las tenacillas de rizar
– *curling tongs (curling iron)*
6 la peineta
– *comb (back comb, side comb)*
7 las tijeras para cortar el cabello
– *haircutting scissors*
8 las tijeras de aclarar el cabello
– *thinning scissors* (Am. *thinning shears*)
9 la cuchilla para aclarar (entresacar) el
cabello
– *thinning razor*
10 el cepillo para el cabello
– *hairbrush*
11 la pinza para el cabello
– *hair clip*
12 el rulo (el rizador, el bigudí)
– *roller*

13 el cepillo para ondular los cabellos
– *curl brush*
14 la pinza para rizar el cabello
– *curl clip*
15 el peine de tocador m
– *dressing comb*
16 el cepillo de púas f
– *stiff-bristle brush*
17 el sillón de peluquería f regulable
– *adjustable hairdresser's chair*
18 el reposapiés
– *footrest*
19 el tocador
– *dressing table*
20 el espejo de peluquería f (la luna)
– *salon mirror (mirror)*
21 la máquina eléctrica para cortar el pelo
– *electric clippers*
22 el peine secapelos eléctrico (el secador
eléctrico)
– *warm-air comb*
23 el espejo de mano m
– *hand mirror (hand glass)*
24 el fijador para el cabello (la laca para el
cabello)
– *hairspray (hair-fixing spray)*
25 el casco secador, un casco de brazo m
orientable
– *drier, a swivel-mounted drier*
26 el brazo orientable del casco
– *swivel arm of the drier*
27 el pie (el pedestal) de disco m
– *round base*

28 la instalación de lavado m
– *shampoo unit*
29 el lavabo para los cabellos
– *shampoo basin*
30 la ducha de mano m
– *hand spray (shampoo spray)*
31 la mesita de servicio m
– *service tray*
32 la botella de champú m
– *shampoo bottle*
33 el secador
– *hair drier (hand hair drier, hand-held
hair drier)*
34 el peinador
– *cape (gown)*
35 la peluquera
– *hairdresser*
36 el frasco de perfume m
– *perfume bottle*
37 el frasco con agua f de olor m
– *bottle of toilet water*
38 la peluca
– *wig*
39 la cabeza para la peluca (el portapelucas)
– *wig block*

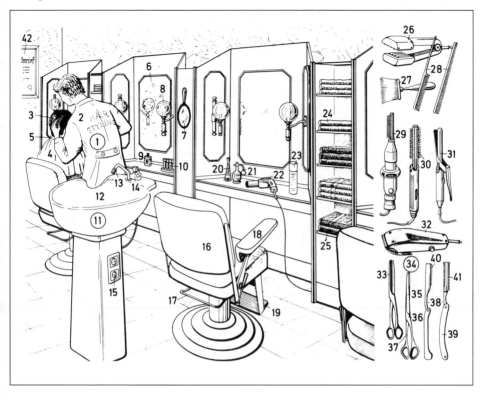

1-42 el salón de peluquería *f* de caballeros *m*
- **men's salon** *(men's hairdressing salon, barber's shop,* Am. *barbershop)*
1 el peluquero (el maestro peluquero)
- *hairdresser (barber)*
2 la bata (la blusa) de trabajo *m* (la blusa de peluquero *m*)
- *overalls (hairdresser's overalls)*
3 el peinado (el corte del cabello)
- *hairstyle (haircut)*
4 el peinador
- *cape (gown)*
5 el cuello de papel *m*
- *paper towel*
6 el espejo de peluquería *f* (la luna)
- *salon mirror (mirror)*
7 el espejo de mano *f*
- *hand mirror (hand glass)*
8 la lámpara de peluquería *f*
- *light*
9 el agua *f* de olor *m* (agua *f* de Colonia)
- *toilet water*
10 la loción capilar (el tónico capilar)
- *hair tonic*
11 la instalación para lavar el cabello (el lavabo)
- *shampoo unit*
12 el lavamanos
- *shampoo basin*
13 la ducha de mano *f*
- *hand spray (shampoo spray)*
14 la grifería mezcladora
- *mixer tap* (Am. *mixing faucet)*
15 la toma de corriente *f* para el enchufe del secador
- *sockets, e.g. for hair drier*

16 el sillón de peluquería *f* regulable
- *adjustable hairdresser's chair (barber's chair)*
17 la barra de regulación *f* (la barra de ajuste *m*)
- *height-adjuster bar (height adjuster)*
18 el brazo del sillón
- *armrest*
19 el descansapiés
- *footrest*
20 el champú
- *shampoo*
21 el pulverizador de perfume *m*
- *perfume spray*
22 el secador del pelo
- *hair drier (hand hair drier, hand-held hair drier)*
23 el fijador para el pelo (la laca) en un bote pulverizador
- *setting lotion in a spray can*
24 las toallas para secar el pelo
- *hand towels for drying hair*
25 las toallas pequeñas para compresas *f* faciales
- *towels for face compresses*
26 el rizador para el pelo (la plancha para cardar el pelo)
- *crimping iron*
27 el cepillo para el cuello
- *neck brush*
28 el peine de peluquero *m*
- *dressing comb*
29 el peine de aire *m* caliente
- *warm-air comb*
30 el cepillo de aire *m* caliente
- *warm-air brush*

31 el rizador para el pelo (el moldeador)
- *curling tongs (hair curler, curling iron)*
32 la maquinilla eléctrica para cortar el pelo
- *electric clippers*
33 las tijeras de aclarar (entresacar) el pelo
- *thinning scissors* (Am. *thinning shears)*
34 las tijeras para cortar el pelo; *anál:* las tijeras de esculpir
- *haircutting scissors;* sim.: *styling scissors*
35 la hoja de las tijeras
- *scissor-blade*
36 el eje (el clavillo)
- *pivot*
37 el mango
- *handle*
38 la navaja de afeitar (la navaja barbera; *P. Rico y S. Dgo.:* la jusilla)
- *open razor (straight razor)*
39 el mango de la navaja
- *razor handle*
40 la hoja de afeitar (el filo de la navaja de afeitar)
- *edge (cutting edge, razor's edge, razor's cutting edge)*
41 la navaja de aclarar (entresacar) el pelo
- *thinning razor*
42 el diploma de maestría (el diploma de mastero *m* peluquero)
- *diploma*

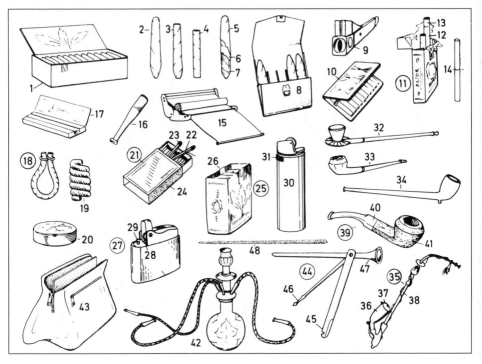

1 la caja de puros *m* (de cigarros *m* puros)
– *cigar box*
2 el puro (el cigarro puro); *clases:* el habano, el puro canario, el puro de Brasil, el puro de Sumatra
– *cigar;* kinds: *Havana cigar (Havana), Brazilian cigar, Sumatra cigar*
3 el entreacto (el bocadito)
– *cigarillo*
4 la señorita (un purito)
– *cheroot*
5 la capa
– *wrapper*
6 la sobretripa (el capillo)
– *binder*
7 la tripa
– *filler*
8 la cigarrera (la petaca de puros *m*)
– *cigar case*
9 el cortapuros (el cortacigarros)
– *cigar cutter*
10 la pitillera (*Amér.:* la petaca)
– *cigarette case*
11 el paquete (la cajetilla) de cigarros *m* (de cigarrillos *m*)
– *cigarette packet* (Am. *pack*)
12 el cigarro (el cigarrillo, el pitillo; *P. Rico y S. Dgo.:* el túbano), un cigarro con filtro *m* (un cigarro emboquillado)
– *cigarette, a filter-tipped cigarette*
13 el filtro (la boquilla); *clases:* dorado, de corcho *m*, blanco
– *cigarette tip;* kinds: *cork tip, gold tip*
14 el cigarrillo ruso
– *Russian cigarette*
15 la maquinilla para liar cigarros *m*
– *cigarette roller*
16 la boquilla
– *cigarette holder*

17 el librillo (el cuaderno) de papel *m* de fumar
– *packet of cigarette papers*
18 el andullo (la hoja larga de tabaco *m* arrollada)
– *pigtail (twist of tobacco)*
19 el tabaco para mascar; un pedazo de tabaco *m* para mascar, una mascada (una mascadura de tabaco *m*)
– *chewing tobacco;* a piece: *plug (quid, chew)*
20 la cajita (la tabaquera) con rapé (con tabaco *m* en polvo *m*)
– *snuff box, containing snuff*
21 la caja de cerillas *f* (de mixtos *m*, de fósforos *m*)
– *matchbox*
22 la cerilla (el mixto, el fósforo; *Bol.:* la pajuela)
– *match*
23 la cabeza de la cerilla
– *head (match head)*
24 el raspador (el frotador)
– *striking surface*
25 el paquete de tabaco *m; clases:* picadura *f* fina, picadura *f* entrefina
– *packet of tobacco;* kinds: *fine cut, shag, navy plug*
26 el sello (la precinta) de impuestos (el timbre fiscal) [*en España:* el sello (el timbre) de la Tabacalera]
– *revenue stamp*
27 el encendedor (el mechero) de gasolina *f* (*Amér.:* el quemador)
– *petrol cigarette lighter (petrol lighter)*
28 la piedra
– *flint*
29 la mecha
– *wick*
30 el encendedor (el mechero) de gas *m*, un encendedor no recargable
– *gas cigarette lighter (gas lighter), a disposable lighter*

31 el regulador de la llama
– *flame regulator*
32 el chibuquí
– *chibonk (chibonque)*
33 la pipa (la cachimba) corta (*Amér.:* la churumbela; *Hond.:* la faifa; *Arg., Bol., Chile y Urug.:* el pito)
– *short pipe*
34 la pipa de barro *m*
– *clay pipe (Dutch pipe)*
35 la pipa larga
– *long pipe*
36 la cazoleta
– *pipe bowl (bowl)*
37 la tapa de la cazoleta (la tapadera de la pipa)
– *bowl lid*
38 el tubo de la pipa
– *pipe stem (stem)*
39 la pipa de madera *f* de brezo *m*
– *briar pipe*
40 la boquilla de la pipa
– *mouthpiece*
41 el brezo veteado (abrillantado con arena *f* o pulido)
– *sand-blast finished or polished briar grain*
42 el narguile, una pipa de agua *f*
– *hookah (narghile, narghileh), a water pipe*
43 la bolsa tabaquera (la petaca)
– *tobacco pouch*
44 el equipo de fumador *m*
– *smoker's companion*
45 el raspador
– *pipe scraper*
46 el limpiador de la pipa (el mondapipas)
– *pipe cleaner*
47 el prensador
– *tobacco presser*
48 la escobilla para limpiar la pipa
– *pipe cleaner*

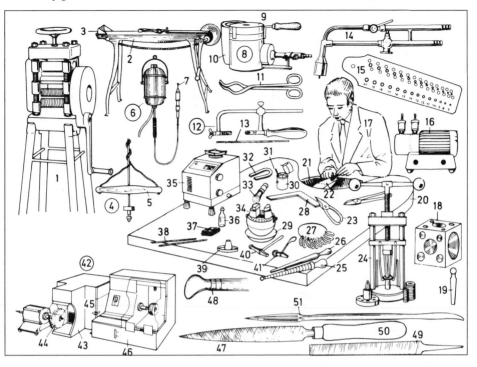

1 el laminador para alambre *m* y chapa *f*
– *wire and sheet roller*
2 el banco de estirar
– *drawbench (drawing bench)*
3 el alambre (alambre *m* de oro *m* o de plata *f*)
– *wire (gold or silver wire)*
4 el berbiquí de vaivén *m*
– *archimedes drill (drill)*
5 la traviesa (la empuñadura)
– *crossbar*
6 la taladradora eléctrica suspendida
– *suspended (pendant) electric drilling machine*
7 la fresa esférica
– *spherical cutter (cherry)*
8 el hornillo de fusión *f*
– *melting pot*
9 la tapadera (el crisol)
– *fireclay top*
10 el crisol de grafito *m*
– *graphite crucible*
11 las tenazas para el crisol
– *crucible tongs*
12 la sierra de arco *m*
– *piercing saw (jig saw)*
13 la hoja de sierra *f* de marquetería *f*
– *piercing saw blade*
14 el soplete
– *soldering gun*
15 la terraja
– *thread tapper*
16 el soplete de cilindro *m*
– *blast burner (blast lamp) for soldering*
17 el orfebre
– *goldsmith*
18 el dado de embutir
– *swage block*

19 el punzón
– *punch*
20 el tablero de trabajo *m* (el obrador)
– *workbench (bench)*
21 el tapete de piel *m*
– *bench apron*
22 la astillera [un soporte de madera *f* para limar]
– *needle file*
23 las tijeras para chapa *f*
– *metal shears*
24 la máquina de alianzas *f*
– *wedding ring sizing machine*
25 la lastra de medidas *f*
– *ring gauge (Am. gage)*
26 la lastra de ajuste *m*
– *ring-rounding tool*
27 el sortijero (la anillera)
– *ring gauge (Am. gage)*
28 la escuadra de acero *m*
– *steel set-square*
29 la almohadilla de cuero *m*
– *(circular) leather pad*
30 la caja de punzones *m*
– *box of punches*
31 el punzón
– *punch*
32 el imán
– *magnet*
33 la escobilla de mesa *f*
– *bench brush*
34 la bola para grabar
– *engraving ball (joint vice, clamp)*
35 la balanza para el oro y la plata, una balanza de precisión *f*
– *gold and silver balance (assay balance), a precision balance*

36 el líquido para soldar
– *soldering flux (flux)*
37 la placa incandescente, de carbón *m* vegetal
– *charcoal block*
38 la varilla de soldar
– *stick of solder*
39 el bórax
– *soldering borax*
40 el martillo de modelar
– *shaping hammer*
41 el martillo para cincelar
– *chasing (enchasing) hammer*
42 la pulidora (la alisadora)
– *polishing and burnishing machine*
43 el ventilador de mesa *f* (el aspirador de polvo *m* de mesa *f*)
– *dust exhauster (vacuum cleaner)*
44 la brocha de pulir
– *polishing wheel*
45 la caja colectora del polvo
– *dust collector (dust catcher)*
46 la máquina para pulir en líquido *m*
– *buffing machine*
47 la lima redonda
– *round file*
48 la hematites roja (el bruñidor)
– *bloodstone (haematite, hematite)*
49 la lima plana
– *flat file*
50 el mango de la lima
– *file handle*
51 el pulidor
– *polishing iron (burnisher)*

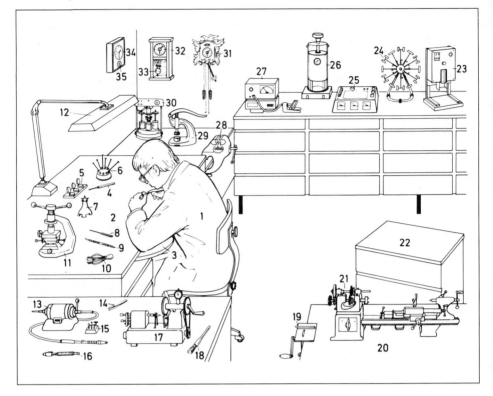

1 el relojero
- *watchmaker; also: clockmaker*
2 la mesa de trabajo *m*
- *workbench*
3 el reposabrazo
- *armrest*
4 el distribuidor de aceite *m*
- *oiler*
5 la aceitera para relojes *m* pequeños
- *oil stand*
6 el juego de destornilladores *m*
- *set of screwdrivers*
7 el yunque para las agujas
- *clockmaker's anvil*
8 la lezna plana, un escariador
- *broach, a reamer*
9 el instrumento para colocar y quitar los resortes
- *spring pin tool*
10 la manecilla para el reloj de pulsera *m*
- *hand-removing tool*
11 el instrumento para abrir y cerrar la caja del reloj
- *watchglass-fitting tool [for armoured, Am. armored, glass]*
12 la lámpara de trabajo *m*, una lámpara de varios usos *m*
- *workbench lamp, a multi-purpose lamp*
13 el motor de varios usos *m*
- *multi-purpose motor*

14 las pinzas
- *tweezers*
15 los accesorios de la máquina de pulir
- *polishing machine attachments*
16 el mandril de mano *m*
- *pin vice (pin holder)*
17 la máquina para enrollar, pulir, redondear y acortar los ejes
- *burnisher, for burnishing, polishing, and shortening of spindles*
18 el pincel para el polvo
- *dust brush*
19 el cortador para los brazaletes metálicos
- *cutter for metal watch straps*
20 el torno de relojero *m* (el torno para mecánica *f* de precisión *f*)
- *precision bench lathe (watchmaker's lathe)*
21 la contramarcha de la correa trapezoidal
- *drive-belt gear*
22 la mesita de taller *m* para las piezas de repuesto *m*
- *workshop trolley for spare parts*
23 la máquina de limpiar mediante vibraciones *f*
- *ultrasonic cleaner*
24 el aparato giratorio para comprobar los relojes automáticos
- *rotating watch-testing machine for automatic watches*

25 el pupitre de medida para comprobar los componentes electrónicos
- *watch-timing machine for electronic components*
26 el aparato para comprobar la impermeabilidad de los relojes
- *testing device for waterproof watches*
27 el cronocomparador
- *electronic timing machine*
28 el torno de banco *m*
- *vice* (Am. *vise*)
29 el dispositivo de ajuste *m* para armar (colocar) los cristales de los relojes
- *watchglass-fitting tool for armoured (Am. armored) glasses*
30 la máquina automática para la limpieza convencional
- *[automatic] cleaning machine for conventional cleaning*
31 el reloj de cuco *m* (reloj *m* de la Selva Negra)
- *cuckoo clock (Black Forest clock)*
32 el reloj de pared *f* (el regulador)
- *wall clock (regulator)*
33 el péndulo compensador
- *compensation pendulum*
34 el reloj de cocina *f*
- *kitchen clock*
35 el cuentaminutos (el avisador)
- *timer*

Relojes

1 el reloj de pulsera *f* electrónico
– *electronic wristwatch*
2 el registro digital (numérico) (un registro con diodos *m* luminosos; *también:* el registro de cristal líquido)
– *digital display (a light-emitting diode (LED) display; also: a liquid crystal display, LCD)*
3 el pulsador para las horas y los minutos
– *hour and minute button (on 6, also for setting the analogue) (Am. analog) display*
4 el pulsador para la fecha y los segundos
– *date and second button*
5 la pulsera (el brazalete)
– *strap (watch strap)*
6 el reloj electrónico multifuncional de muñeca *f*
– *multifunction electronic watch*
7 el indicador analógico
– *analogue (Am. analog) display*
8 el pulsador de la alarma-despertador
– *alarm button*
9 el pulsador anulador del programa
– *stopwatch button*
10 el anillo móvil indicador del tiempo
– *rotating bezel (time-lapse indicator ring)*
11 el despertador (el reloj despertador)
– *calendar clock (alarm clock)*
12 el registro (la lectura) digital (numérico, -a) con cifras *f* giratorias
– *digital display with flip-over numerals*
13 el registro de las horas del despertador
– *alarm indicator*
14 el pulsador de parada *f*
– *stop button*
15 la rueda de ajuste *m*
– *forward and backward wind knob*
16 el reloj de antesala *f*
– *grandfather clock*
17 el cuadrante (la esfera; *Mé. y Guat.:* la carátula)
– *face*
18 la caja del reloj
– *clock case*
19 el péndulo
– *pendulum*
20 la pesa de los toques (de las campanadas)
– *striking weight*
21 la pesa de la marcha
– *time weight*
22 el reloj de sol *m*
– *sundial*
23 el reloj de arena *f* (la ampolleta)
– *hourglass (egg timer)*
24-35 los componentes de salto *m* de un reloj de pulsera *f* automático (el reloj con un mecanismo de cuerda *f* automático)
– *components of an automatic watch (automatic wristwatch, self-winding watch)*

24 la masa oscilante (el rotor)
– *weight (rotor)*
25 la piedra (la piedra de cojinete *m*), un rubí sintético
– *stone (jewel, jewelled bearing) a synthetic ruby*
26 el trinquete de ajuste *m* (de sujeción *f*)
– *click*
27 la rueda de sujeción *f*
– *click wheel*
28 el mecanismo del reloj
– *clockwork (clockwork mechanism)*
29 la platina
– *bottom train plate*
30 el barrilete
– *spring barrel*
31 el volante
– *balance wheel*
32 la rueda de áncora *f*
– *escape wheel*
33 la rueda de la cuerda (la rueda de corona *f*)
– *crown wheel*
34 la corona (la corona de la cuerda)
– *winding crown*
35 el mecanismo de impulsión *f*
– *drive mechanism*
36 el principio del reloj de cuarzo *m* electrónico
– *principle of the electronic quartz watch*
37 el cuarzo (el cuarzo oscilante)
– *quartz*
38 la fuente de impulsión *f* (una pila de botón *m*)
– *power source (a button cell)*
39 la aguja pequeña (la aguja de las horas; *Bol. Ec. y Mé.:* el horero)
– *hour hand*
40 la aguja grande (la aguja de los minutos, el minutero)
– *minute hand*
41 el engranaje
– *wheels*
42 el motor paso a paso *m*
– *stepping motor (stepper motor)*
43 la subdivisión de frecuencia *f* (circuitos *m* integrados)
– *frequency divider (integrated circuit)*
44 el descodificador
– *decoder*

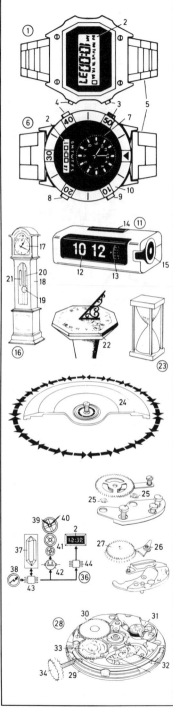

1-19 **el local de venta** *f*
- *sales premises*
1-4 **la prueba de las gafas**
- *spectacle fitting*
1 el óptico
- *optician*
2 el cliente
- *customer*
3 la montura de prueba *f*
- *trial frame*
4 el espejo
- *mirror*
5 el estante de las monturas (la
elección de montura *f*, la elección
de gafas *f*)
- *stand with spectacle frames (display of frames, range of spectacles)*
6 las gafas de sol *m*
- *sunglasses (sun spectacles)*
7 la montura metálica
- *metal frame*
8 la montura de carey *m* (la montura de pasta *f*)
- *tortoiseshell frame (shell frame)*
9 las gafas (*Amér.:* los anteojos)
- *spectacles (glasses)*
10-14 **la montura de las gafas**
- *spectacle frame*

10 la montura
- *fitting (mount) of the frame*
11 el puente
- *bridge*
12 la placa del puente
- *pad bridge*
13 la patilla
- *side*
14 la bisagra de la patilla
- *side joint*
15 el cristal de las gafas, un cristal
bifocal (un cristal de doble foco *m*)
- *spectacle lens, a bifocal lens*
16 el espejo de mano *f*
- *hand mirror (hand glass)*
17 los gemelos (los prismáticos)
- *binoculars*
18 el tubo monocular (el anteojo, el
catalejo)
- *monocular telescope (tube)*
19 el microscopio
- *microscope*

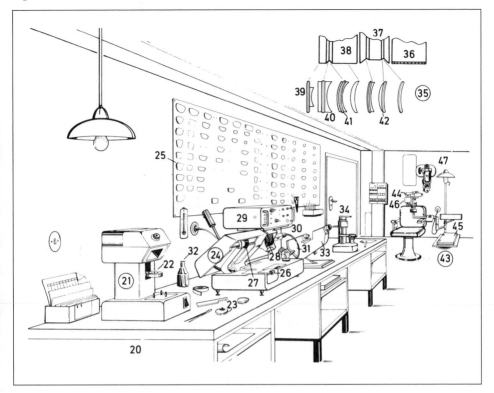

20-47 el taller de óptico *m*
- *optician's workshop*
20 la mesa de trabajo *m*
- *workbench*
21 el aparato para centrar universal (el focómetro universal)
- *universal centring (centering) apparatus*
22 el soporte de la ventosa de centrado *m*
- *centring (centering) suction holder*
23 la ventosa de centrado *m*
- *sucker*
24 el aparato automático para modelar los bordes de los cristales de las gafas
- *edging machine*
25 los cristales de molde *m* para la modelación automática de los bordes (los cristales que se utilizan como modelos *m*)
- *formers for the lens edging machine*
26 el cristal modelo *m* colocado en el aparato
- *inserted former*
27 la copia de cristal a cristal *m*
- *rotating printer*
28 el juego de piedras *f* de afilar (el conjunto de muelas *f*)
- *abrasive wheel combination*

29 el aparato de mando *m*
- *control unit*
30 la maquinaria (el mecanismo)
- *machine part*
31 la llegada del agua *f* refrigerante
- *cooling water pipe*
32 el líquido de limpieza *f*
- *cleaning fluid*
33 el focómetro de vértice *m*
- *focimeter (vertex refractionometer)*
34 el aparato de bloque *m* de metal *m* para centrar y poner ventosas *f*
- *metal-blocking device*
35 el juego de muelas *f* para dar forma *f* a los cristales
- *abrasive wheel combination and forms of edging*
36 la muela de desbaste *m*
- *roughing wheel for preliminary surfacing*
37 la muela de acabado *m* para el biselado de los cristales positivos y negativos
- *fining lap for positive and negative lens surfaces*
38 la muela de acabado *m* para el biselado de los cristales especiales y llanos
- *fining lap for special and flat lenses*

39 el cristal plano-cóncavo con cara *f* plana
- *plano-concave lens with a flat surface*
40 el cristal plano-cóncavo con cara *f* especial
- *plano-concave lens with a special surface*
41 el cristal cóncavo-convexo con cara *f* especial
- *concave and convex lens with a special surface*
42 el cristal cóncavo-convexo con cara *f* negativa
- *convex and concave lens with a special surface*
43 el sillón para el reconocimiento oftalmológico
- *ophthalmic test stand*
44 el foropter con el oftalmómetro y el refractómetro
- *phoropter with ophthalmometer and optometer (refractometer)*
45 la caja de los cristales de prueba *f*
- *trial lens case*
46 el soporte de proyección *f* de las letras
- *collimator*
47 el proyector de la señal óptica
- *acuity projector*

1 el microscopio de laboratorio *m* e investigación *f*, sistema *m* Leitz [corte parcial]
– *laboratory and research microscope, Leitz system*
2 el soporte (la montura)
– *stand*
3 el pie
– *base*
4 el ajuste (el botón) grueso
– *coarse adjustment*
5 el ajuste (el botón) fino
– *fine adjustment*
6 la trayectoria de los rayos luminosos
– *illumination beam path (illumination path)*
7 la óptica de iluminación *f*
– *illumination optics*
8 el condensador
– *condenser*
9 el portaobjetos
– *microscope (microscopic, object) stage*
10 el portaobjetos cruzado
– *mechanical stage*
11 el revólver de objetivos *m* (el portaobjetivos)
– *objective turret (revolving nosepiece)*
12 el tubo binocular
– *binocular head*
13 los prismas de desviación *f*
– *beam-splitting prisms*
14 el microscopio de luz *f* transmitida con cámara *f* fotográfica y polarizador, sistema *m* Zeiss
– *transmitted-light microscope with camera and polarizer, Zeiss system*
15 la base del portaobjetos
– *stage base*
16 el cursor del diafragma de abertura *f*
– *aperture-stop slide*
17 el portaobjetos giratorio universal
– *universal stage*
18 el módulo portaobjetivos
– *lens panel*
19 el módulo de observación *f*
– *polarizing filter*
20 la parte de la cámara fotográfica
– *camera*
21 la pantalla de ajuste *m*
– *focusing screen*
22 la pieza de fijación *f* de los tubos de discusión *f*
– *discussion tube arrangement*
23 el microscopio de metalografía *f* de gran campo *m* visual, un microscopio de luz *f* reflejada
– *wide-field metallurgical microscope, a reflected-light microscope (microscope for reflected light)*
24 el cristal esmerilado de proyección *f*
– *matt screen (ground glass screen, projection screen)*
25 la cámara fotográfica de gran formato *m*
– *large-format camera*

26 la cámara fotográfica de pequeño formato *m*
– *miniature camera*
27 la plataforma de base *f* (el zócalo)
– *base plate*
28 la caja de la lámpara
– *lamphouse*
29 el portaobjetivos cruzado giratorio
– *mechanical stage*
30 el revólver de objetivos *m*
– *objective turret (revolving nosepiece)*
31 el microscopio quirúrgico
– *surgical microscope*
32 el soporte de columna *f*
– *pillar stand*
33 la iluminación del campo del objeto
– *field illumination*
34 el microscopio de microfotografía *f*
– *photomicroscope*
35 el chasis de pequeño formato *m*
– *miniature film cassette*
36 la toma de foto *m* adicional para la cámara de gran formato *m* o de televisión *f*
– *photomicrographic camera attachment for large-format or television camera*
37 el comprobador de superficies *f*
– *surface-finish microscope*
38 el tubo de cortes *m* ópticos
– *light section tube*
39 el piñón (la rueda motriz)
– *rack and pinion*
40 el estereomicroscopio de gran campo *m* equipado con un zoom
– *zoom stereomicroscope*
41 el zoom
– *zoom lens*
42 el aparato para medir el polvo óptico
– *dust counter*
43 la cámara de medida *f*
– *measurement chamber*
44 la salida de los datos
– *data output*
45 la salida analógica
– *analogue* (Am. *analog*) *output*
46 el selector de la zona de medida *f*
– *measurement range selector*
47 el indicador de los datos numéricos (el indicador numérico)
– *digital display (digital readout)*
48 el refractómetro de inmersión *f*, para examen *m* de alimentos *m*
– *dipping refractometer for examining food*
49 el microscopio fotómetro
– *microscopic photometer*
50 la fuente de luz *f* del fotómetro
– *photometric light source*
51 el dispositivo de medida *f* (el fotomultiplicador)
– *measuring device (photomultiplier, multiplier phototube)*
52 la fuente de luz *f* para la iluminación panorámica
– *light source for survey illumination*

53 el bloque electrónico
– *remote electronics*
54 el microscopio universal de gran campo *m*
– *universal wide-field microscope*
55 el adaptador para la cámara o para el accesorio de proyección *f*
– *adapter for camera or projector attachment*
56 el botón de ajuste *m* del ocular
– *eyepiece focusing knob*
57 el alojamiento del filtro
– *filter pick-up*
58 el soporte de apoyo *m*
– *handrest*
59 la lámpara para la luz reflejada
– *lamphouse for incident (vertical) illumination*
60 el enchufe de la lámpara para la luz transmitida
– *lamphouse connector for transillumination*
61 el estereomicroscopio de gran campo *m*
– *wide-field stereomicroscope*
62 los objetivos intercambiables
– *interchangeable lenses (objectives)*
63 la iluminación reflejada
– *incident (vertical) illumination (incident top lighting)*
64 la cámara de microscopio *m* completamente automática, una cámara fotográfica con adaptador *m*
– *fully automatic microscope camera, a camera with photomicro mount adapter*
65 la cajita de la película (del film) fotográfica (-o)
– *film cassette*
66 el condensador universal del microscopio de investigación *f*
– *universal condenser for research microscope 1*
67 la cámara métrica universal para fotogrametría *f* (el fototeodolito)
– *universal-type measuring machine for photogrammetry (phototheodolite)*
68 la cámara de fotogrametría *f*
– *photogrammetric camera*
69 el nivelador de motor *m*, un nivelador compensador
– *motor-driven level, a compensator level*
70 el aparato electro-óptico para medir las distancias
– *electro-optical distance-measuring instrument*
71 la cámara de estereometría *f*
– *stereometric camera*
72 la base horizontal
– *horizontal base*
73 el teodolito universal
– *one-second theodolite*

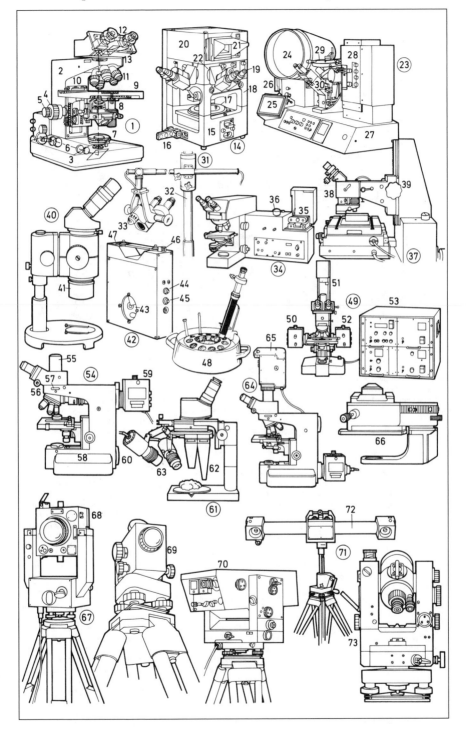

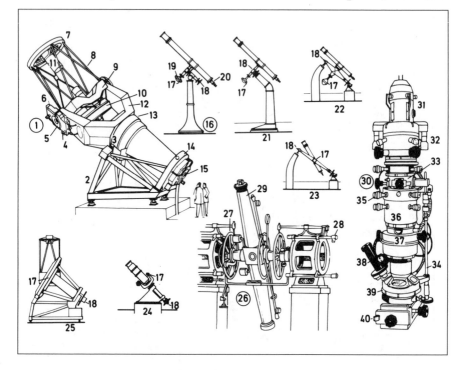

1 **el telescopio de espejo** *m* **de 2,2 m**
– *2.2 m reflecting telescope (reflector)*
2 la estructura de soporte *m* (la armazón inferior)
– *pedestal (base)*
3 el soporte axial y radial
– *axial-radial bearing*
4 el mecanismo de declinación *f*
– *declination gear*
5 el eje de declinación *f*
– *declination axis*
6 el soporte de declinación *f*
– *declination bearing*
7 el anillo de frente *m* (el anillo superior)
– *front ring*
8 el tubo del telescopio
– *tube (body tube)*
9 la parte central del tubo
– *tube centre* (Am. *center*) *section*
10 el espejo principal
– *primary mirror (main mirror)*
11 el espejo de desviación *f* (el espejo secundario)
– *secondary mirror (deviation mirror, corrector plate)*
12 la horquilla (la montura en forma *f* de horquilla *f*)
– *fork mounting (fork)*
13 el recubrimiento
– *cover*
14 el cojinete guía *f*
– *guide bearing*
15 el mando principal del eje horario
– *main drive unit of the polar axis*

16-25 **monturas** *f* **de telescopio** *m*
– *telescope mountings (telescope mounts)*
16 el telescopio de lentes *f* (el refractor) sobre montura *f* alemana
– *refractor (refracting telescope) on a German-type mounting*
17 el eje de declinación *f*
– *declination axis*
18 el eje horario (el eje polar)
– *polar axis*
19 el contrapeso
– *counterweight (counterpoise)*
20 el ocular
– *eyepiece*
21 la montura con columna *f* de acodamiento *m*
– *knee mounting with a bent column*
22 la montura inglesa de eje *m*
– *English-type axis mounting (axis mount)*
23 la montura inglesa con soporte *m*
– *English-type yoke mounting (yoke mount)*
24 la montura de horquilla *f*
– *fork mounting (fork mount)*
25 la montura de herradura *f*
– *horseshoe mounting (horseshoe mount)*
26 el círculo meridiano
– *meridian circle*
27 el círculo graduado
– *divided circle (graduated circle)*
28 el microscopio de lectura *f*
– *reading microscope*

29 el telescopio meridiano
– *meridian telescope*
30 el microscopio electrónico
– *electron microscope*
31-39 el tubo del microscopio
– *microscope tube (microscope body, body tube)*
31 el sistema de producción de la radiación *f* (la cabeza de radiación *f*)
– *electron gun*
32 las lentes del condensador
– *condensers*
33 el orificio de introducción *f* del objeto
– *specimen insertion air lock*
34 el ajuste del portaobjetos del objetivo (el desplazamiento del objeto)
– *control for the specimen stage adjustment*
35 el botón de apertura *f* del diafragma
– *control for the objective apertures*
36 la lente del objetivo
– *objective lens*
37 el visor de la imagen intermedia
– *intermediate image screen*
38 el visor de observación *f* (la lente de aumento *m*)
– *telescope magnifier*
39 el visor de la imagen final (la pantalla fluorescente de la imagen final)
– *final image tube*
40 la cámara fotográfica para película *f* y para placas *f*
– *photographic chamber for film and plate magazines*

1 la cámara fotográfica de pequeño formato *m* (de paso *m* universal)
– *miniature camera (35 mm camera)*
2 la ventana del visor
– *viewfinder eyepiece*
3 el fotómetro (la ventanilla del
fotómetro)
– *meter cell*
4 la guía de accesorios *m*
– *accessory shoe*
5 el objetivo escamoteable
– *flush lens*
6 la palanca de rebobinado *m*
– *rewind handle (rewind, rewind crank)*
7 el carrete de pequeño formato *m* 135
(de paso *m* universal)
– *miniature film cassette (135 film cassette,
35 mm cassette)*
8 la canilla del carrete (el eje del carrete)
– *film spool*
9 la lengüeta de la película (la película
con la lengüeta de carga *f*) y la perforación
– *film with leader and perforations*
10 la ranura del chasis
– *cassette slit (cassette exit slot)*
11 la cámara fotográfica de cartuchos *m*
(una cámara instamatic)
– *cartridge-loading camera*
12 el disparador
– *shutter release (shutter release button)*
13 el contacto de cuboflash *m*
– *flash cube contact*
14 el visor cuadrangular
– *rectangular viewfinder*
15 el cartucho de película *f* 126 (el cartucho instamatic)
– *126 cartridge (instamatic cartridge)*
16 la cámara fotográfica pocket
– *pocket camera (subminiature camera)*
17 el cartucho de pequeño formato *m* 110
– *110 cartridge (subminiature cartridge)*
18 la ventanilla de numeración *f* del carrete
– *film window*
19 el rollo de película *f* de 120
– *120 rollfilm*
20 la bobina del rollo de película *f*
– *rollfilm spool*
21 el papel de protección *f*
– *backing paper*
22 la cámara fotográfica réflex de doble
lente *f*
– *twin-lens reflex camera*
23 la tapa de la pantalla de enfoque *m*
– *folding viewfinder hood (focusing
hood)*
24 la ventanilla del fotómetro
– *meter cell*
25 el objetivo de enfoque *m*
– *viewing lens*
26 el objetivo de toma *f* de vista *f*
– *object lens*
27 el botón de la bobina
– *spool knob*
28 el botón para ajustar la distancia
– *distance setting (focus setting)*
29 el mando del fotómetro acoplado
– *exposure meter using needle-matching
system*
30 el contacto de flash *m*
– *flash contact*
31 el disparador
– *shutter release*
32 la manivela de arrastre *m* de la película
– *film transport (film advance, film wind)*
33 el conmutador del flash
– *flash switch*
34 la rueda de graduación del diafragma
– *aperture-setting control*

35 la rueda del tiempo de exposición *f*
– *shutter speed control*
36 la cámara fotográfica de mano *m* de
gran formato *m* (la cámara de prensa *f*)
– *large-format hand camera (press camera)*
37 la empuñadura
– *grip (handgrip)*
38 el cable disparador
– *cable release*
39 el anillo grafilado para el enfoque de la
distancia
– *distance-setting ring (focusing ring)*
40 la ventana del telémetro
– *rangefinder window*
41 el visor multiformato
– *multiple-frame viewfinder (universal
viewfinder)*
42 el pie tubular (el trípode)
– *tripod*
43 la pata del trípode
– *tripod leg*
44 el brazo de tubo *m*
– *tubular leg*
45 el pie de caucho *m*
– *rubber foot*
46 la columna central
– *central column*
47 la cabeza de articulación *f* esférica
– *ball and socket head*
48 la cabeza niveladora de cine *m*
– *cine camera pan and tilt head*
49 la cámara de fuelle *m* de gran formato *m*
– *large-format folding camera*
50 el banco óptico
– *optical bench*
51 el piñón de regulación *f* frontal
– *standard adjustment*
52 la chapa del objetivo *m*
– *lens standard*
53 el fuelle
– *bellows*
54 el respaldo de la cámara
– *camera back*
55 el piñón de regulación *f* trasera
– *back standard adjustment*
56 el fotómetro
– *hand-held exposure meter (exposure
meter)*
57 el disco de cálculo *m*
– *calculator dial*

58 la escala con aguja *f* indicadora
– *scales (indicator scales) with indicator
needle (pointer)*
59 el selector de escala *f* (el selector de
banda *f* alta y baja)
– *range switch (high/low range selector)*
60 el difusor para medir la luz incidente
– *diffuser for incident light measurement*
61 el fotómetro para cámaras *f* de gran
formato *m*
– *probe exposure meter for large-format
cameras*
62 el aparato de medida *f*
– *meter*
63 la sonda
– *probe*
64 la corredera del chasis
– *dark slide*
65 el flash electrónico portátil de batería *f*
– *battery-portable electronic flash (battery-portable electronic flash unit)*
66 el acumulador (la batería)
– *power pack unit (battery)*
67 la lámpara del flash (la antorcha del
flash)
– *flash head*
68 el flash electrónico de una sola pieza
– *single-unit electronic flash (flashgun)*
69 el reflector orientable
– *swivel-mounted reflector*
70 el fotodiodo
– *photodiode*
71 la zapata
– *foot*
72 el contacto central
– *hot-shoe contact*
73 el cuboflash
– *flash cube unit*
74 la lámpara del cuboflash
– *flash cube*
75 la barra de flash *m* (AGFA)
– *flash bar (AGFA)*
76 el proyector de diapositivas *f*
– *slide projector*
77 el carro de diapositivas *f*
– *rotary magazine*

1-24 la cámara fotográfica con objetivos
m **intercambiables** (la cámara fotográfica réflex de pequeño formato *m* con un solo objetivo)
– *system camera (fully automatic miniature single-lens reflex camera)*
1   el interruptor principal
– *main switch*
2   el botón de enfoque *m* funcional (para correcciones *f* de luz *f*, motor *m* y de la amplitud del autofoco)
– *function adjustment button (to set exposure adjustment value, drive mode, and focus area)*
3   el botón para las funciones de iluminación *f*
– *exposure mode button*
4   la uña (la zapata) de los accesorios
– *accessory shoe*
5   el botón de vuelta atrás del programa
– *program reset button*
6   el monitor de la fecha (el visualizador de la fecha)
– *data panel (data monitor, data display)*
7   el botón encendido/apagado (on/off) para la tarjeta del chip
– *card on/off key*
8   el selector de función *f*
– *function selector key*
9   la tarjeta del chip con programas *m* especiales de fotos *f*
– *chip program card*
10 la ranura del compartimiento para las tarjetas
– *card door*
11 la ventanilla para ver la tarjeta
– *card window*
12 el compartimiento de la pila
– *battery chamber*
13 la conexión del mando a distancia *f*
– *remote control terminal*
14 el disparador
– *shutter release (shutter release button)*
15 la ventanilla para el flash graduable de enfoque *m* automático y para la señal del disparador automático
– *autofocus (AF) illuminator and self-timer light*
16 la palanca para bajar o subir los valores programados manualmente
– *manual shutter control [up/down control]*
17 el espejo retrooscilante
– *reflex mirror*
18 el sensor del enfoque automático, un transformador de imagen *f* CCD
– *autofocus sensor, a CCD image converter (image sensor)*
19 el anillo mecánico de bayoneta *f*
– *bayonet mounting ring*
20 el botón de graduación *f* del diafragma
– *aperture setting button*
21 el botón de cierre de la bayoneta
– *lens release*
22 el conmutador de enfoque *m* automático (para conmutar a enfoque *m* manual)
– *focus-mode switch (to switch to manual focusing)*
23 el objetivo de zoom *m* con enfoque *m* automático, el objetivo de zoom *m* triple (30–105 mm)
– *autofocus zoom lens, a ×3 zoom lens (35-105 mm)*

24 las conexiones de los mandos para el diafragma y el enfoque automático
– *aperture and autofocus contacts*
25-35 la pantalla del visor (pantalla de ajuste *m*, pop. pantalla mate), la pantalla de microcélulas *f*
– *viewfinder screen (focusing screen, matt screen), a micro-honeycombed focusing screen*
25 la señal de conexión *f* del flash *m*
– *flash-on signal*
26 la señal de flash *m* preparado
– *flash-ready signal*
27 los indicadores de la nitidez
– *focus signals*
28 la amplitud total del enfoque automático
– *wide focus area*
29 el indicador del tiempo del cierre *m*
– *shutter speed display*
30 el indicador de la sintonización para la regulación manual de la exposición
– *manual-exposure compensation-value indicator*
31 el indicador del ajuste de la solarización o del diafragma
– *aperture or exposure adjustment indicator*
32 la señal del punto de medición *f*
– *spot metering indicator*
33 el círculo métrico para el punto de medición *f*
– *spot metering area*
34 la amplitud del enfoque automático
– *centre focus area*
35 el indicador de la amplitud del enfoque elegido
– *focus area indicator*
36-42 el monitor LCD de la fecha
– *LCD data panel (data monitor)*
36 el indicador del programa
– *program exposure-mode indicator*
37 el indicador del número de foto *f*
– *frame counter*
38 los indicadores funcionales
– *function indicators*
39 el indicador del ajuste de la solarización o del diafragma
– *aperture or exposure adjustment indicator*
40 el indicador de la sensibilidad de la película o del tiempo de cierre *m*
– *shutter speed or film speed (film sensitivity) indicator*
41 el indicador del arrastre de la película
– *film transport indicator*
42 la flecha de función *f*
– *function pointer*
43 los objetivos intercambiables (objectivos de enfoque *m* automático, objetivos A F)
– *interchangeable lenses (autofocus lenses, AF lenses)*
44 el objetivo ojo *m* de pez *m*
– *fisheye lens (fisheye)*
45 el objetivo gran angular (de distancia *f* focal corta)
– *wide-angle lens (short focal-length lens)*
46 el objetivo normal
– *standard lens*
47 el objetivo de distancia *f* focal media
– *medium focal-length lens*

48 el teleobjetivo (el objetivo de distancia *f* focal larga), un objectivo con zoom *m*
– *telephoto lens (long focal-length lens), a zoom lens (variable focus lens, varifocal lens)*
49 el objetivo para gran distancia *f* (la lente para imágenes *f* lejanas)
– *long-focus lens*
50 el objetivo de espejo *m*
– *mirror lens*
51 el teleconvertidor
– *tele converter*
52 la tapa posterior para los datos (los Data-Back)
– *data back*
53 la carga de película *f* de diez metros *m*
– *ten-metre (Am. ten-meter) film back (magazine back)*
54-74 los accesorios para macrofotografías *f* y fotografías *f* de cerca
– *accessories for close-up and macro shots*
54 el tubo alargador
– *extension tube*
55 el anillo adaptador
– *adapter ring*
56 el anillo de inversión *f*
– *reversing ring*
57 el objetivo en posición *f* invertida
– *lens in retrofocus position*
58 el fuelle
– *bellows unit (extension bellows, close-up bellows attachment)*
59 el carro de regulación *f*
– *focusing stage*
60 el adaptador para reproducción *f* de diapositivas *f*
– *slide-copying attachment*
61 el portadiapositivas
– *slide-copying adapter*
62 el disparador de cable *m*
– *cable release*
63 el pie de reproducción *f*
– *copying stand (copy stand)*
64 el brazo de reproducción *f*
– *arm of the copying stand (copy stand)*
65 el soporte de hombro *m*
– *rifle grip*
66 el pie de mesa *f* (el trípode de mesa *f*)
– *table(-top) tripod (mini tripod)*
67 la bolsa (la funda) de la cámara
– *ever-ready case*
68 el estuche del objetivo
– *lens case*
69 la bolsa de cuero *m* flexible del objetivo
– *soft-leather lens pouch*
70 la bolsa de la cámara
– *camera bag, of metallic construction: aluminium (Am. aluminum) case*
71 los estuches de películas *f*
– *film container*
72 el sujetafiltros
– *filter case*
73 el estuche supletorio
– *second body*
74 el aparato de flash para macrofotografías *f*
– *ring flash for macro shots*

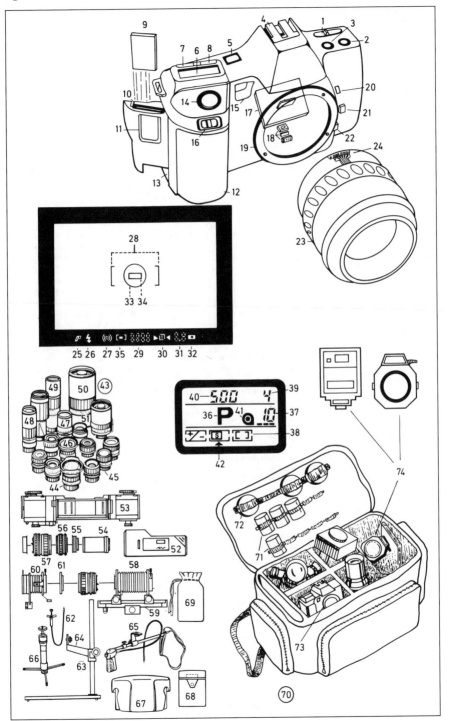

1-60 equipo *m* de laboratorio *m*
- *darkroom equipment*
1 la caja de revelado *m*
- *developing tank*
2 la espiral portapelícula
- *spiral (developing spiral, tank reel)*
3 la caja de revelado *m* de varias unidades *f*
- *multi-unit developing tank*
4 la espiral de película *f* de varias unidades *f*
- *multi-unit tank spiral*
5 la caja de carga *f* a plena luz *f*
- *daylight-loading tank*
6 el receptor de la película
- *loading chamber*
7 el botón de arrastre *m* de la película
- *film transport handle*
8 el termómetro de revelado *m*
- *developing tank thermometer*
9 la botella plisada para el líquido revelador
- *collapsible bottle for developing solution*
10 las botellas con productos *m* químicos para primer revelador *m*, baño *m* de parada *f*, revelador *m* de color, baño *m* de blanqueo *m*, estabilizador *m*
- *chemical bottles for first developer, stop bath, colour developer, bleach-hardener, stabilizer*
11 las probetas graduadas
- *measuring cylinders*
12 el embudo
- *funnel*
13 el termómetro de baño *m* (el termómetro de cubeta *f*)
- *tray thermometer (dish thermometer)*
14 la pinza para película *f* (el sujetapelículas)
- *film clip*
15 la bañera (la cubeta) de lavado *m*
- *wash tank (washer)*
16 la llegada de agua *f*
- *water supply pipe*
17 el desagüe
- *water outlet pipe*
18 el reloj de laboratorio *m* (el reloj de corta duración *f*)
- *laboratory timer (timer)*
19 el agitador de película *f*
- *automatic film agitator*
20 el tambor de revelado *m*
- *developing tank*
21 la lámpara de laboratorio *m* (también: cuarto *m* oscuro)
- *darkroom lamp (safelight)*
22 el cristal de filtro *m*
- *filter screen*
23 el secador de películas *f*
- *film drier (drying cabinet)*

24 el interruptor horario de exposición *f*
- *exposure timer*
25 la cubeta de revelado *m*
- *developing dish (developing tray)*
26 la ampliadora
- *enlarger*
27 la placa base (la platina)
- *baseboard*
28 la columna inclinada
- *angled column*
29 la cabeza de la lámpara (la caja de la lámpara)
- *lamphouse (lamp housing)*
30 el portanegativo
- *negative carrier*
31 el fuelle
- *bellows*
32 el objetivo
- *lens*
33 la transmisión fina por fricción *f*
- *friction drive for fine adjustment*
34 la regulación de la altura (regulación *f* en escala *f*)
- *height adjustment (scale adjustment)*
35 el bastidor de ampliación *f*
- *masking frame (easel)*
36 el analizador del color
- *colour (Am. color) analyser*
37 la lámpara de control *m* del color
- *colour (Am. color) analyser lamp*
38 el cable de medida *f*
- *probe lead*
39 el botón de corrección *f* del tiempo
- *exposure time balancing knob*
40 la ampliadora de color *m*
- *colour (Am. color) enlarger*
41 la cabeza del aparato
- *enlarger head*
42 la columna perfilada
- *column*
43-45 la cabeza mezcladora del color
- *colour-mixing (Am. color-mixing) knob*
43 el regulador del filtro púrpura
- *magenta filter adjustment (minus green filter adjustment)*
44 el regulador del filtro amarillo
- *yellow filter adjustment (minus blue filter adjustment)*
45 el regulador del filtro gris azulado
- *cyan filter adjustment (minus red filter adjustment)*
46 el filtro regulable
- *red swing filter*
47 las pinzas de revelado *m*
- *print tongs*
48 el tambor de revelado *m* de papel *m*
- *processing drum*
49 el rodillo de secado *m*
- *squeegee*
50 el surtido de papel *m*
- *range (assortment) of papers*

51 el papel de ampliación *f* en color *m*, un paquete de papel *m* fotográfico
- *colour (Am. color) printing paper, a packet of photographic printing paper*
52 los productos químicos para el revelado en color *m*
- *colour (Am. color) chemicals (colour processing chemicals)*
53 el exposímetro del papel (el exposímetro de ampliación *f*)
- *enlarging meter (enlarging photometer)*
54 el botón de ajuste *m* con la sensibilidad del papel
- *adjusting knob with paper speed scale*
55 la célula (la sonda) de medida *f*
- *probe*
56 la cubeta semiautomática de revelado *m* con termostato *m*
- *semi-automatic thermostatically controlled developing dish*
57 la prensa de secado *m* rápido
- *rapid print drier (heated print drier)*
58 la hoja (la lámina) de brillo *m* intenso
- *glazing sheet*
59 la tela de tensión *f* (de presión *f*)
- *pressure cloth*
60 la máquina de revelado *m* de rodillos *m*
- *automatic processor (machine processor)*

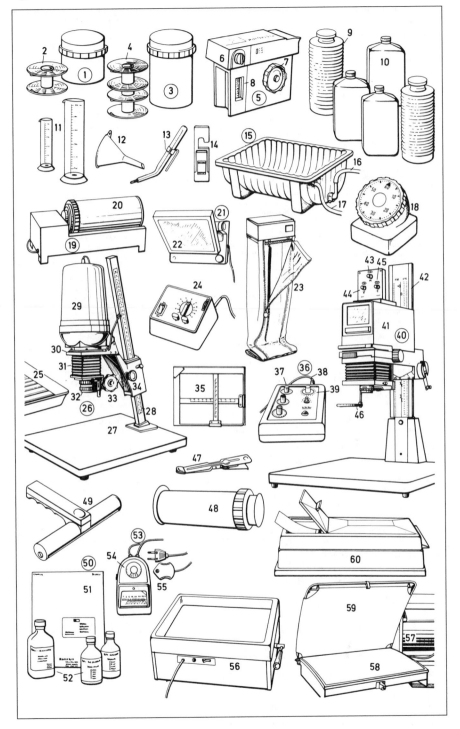

1 **la cámara de película** *f* **estrecha,** una cámara sonora de súper 8
- *cine camera, a Super-8 sound camera*
2 el objetivo zoom *m* intercambiable
- *interchangeable zoom lens (variable focus lens, varifocal lens)*
3 el enfoque de la distancia y la regulación manual de la distancia focal
- *distance setting (focus setting) and manual focal length setting*
4 el anillo de los diafragmas para regular manualmente la abertura
- *aperture ring (aperture-setting ring, aperture control ring) for manual aperture setting*
5 la empuñadura de batería *f*
- *handgrip with battery chamber*
6 el disparador con empalme *m* para el disparador de cable *m*
- *shutter release with cable release socket*
7 la toma de señal *f* de sincronización *f* o del generador de impulsos *m* para el registro sonoro (para el procedimiento de doble banda *f*)
- *pilot tone or pulse generator socket for the sound recording equipment (with the dual film-tape system)*
8 el cable de conexión *f* del sonido para el micrófono o para la fuente sonora (para el procedimiento de banda *f* única)
- *sound connecting cord for microphone or external sound source (in single-system recording)*
9 la conexión del disparador a distancia *f*
- *remote control socket (remote control jack)*
10 la conexión de los auriculares
- *headphone socket (sim.: earphone socket)*
11 el conmutador del sistema de regulación *f*
- *autofocus override switch*
12 el conmutador de la velocidad de la película
- *filming speed selector*
13 el selector de toma *f* de sonido *m* para el funcionamiento automático o manual
- *sound recording selector switch for automatic or manual operation*
14 el ocular con reborde *m* para el ojo
- *eyepiece with eyecup*
15 el regulador de las dioptrías
- *diopter control ring (dioptric adjustment ring)*
16 el regulador del nivel de la toma de sonido *m*
- *recording level control (audio level control, recording sensitivity selector)*
17 el fotómetro-selector
- *manual/automatic exposure control switch*
18 el selector de sensibilidad *f* de la película
- *film speed setting*
19 el mando del zoom automático
- *power zooming arrangement*
20 el sistema automático del diafragma
- *automatic aperture control*
21 **el sistema para la grabación sobre pista** *f* **sonora**
- *sound track system*
22 la cámara sonora
- *sound camera*
23 el brazo del micrófono telescópico
- *telescopic microphone boom*
24 el micrófono
- *microphone*
25 el cable del micrófono
- *microphone connecting lead (microphone connecting cord)*
26 **el estuche (la caja) de mezcla** *f* (el mezclador)
- *mixing console (mixing desk, mixer)*
27 las entradas para las diferentes fuentes sonoras
- *inputs from various sound sources*
28 la salida hacia la cámara
- *output to camera*
29 **el cartucho** (la cassette) **de película** *f* **sonora de súper 8**
- *Super-8 sound film cartridge*

30 la ventana del cartucho
- *film gate of the cartridge*
31 la bobina de alimentación *f*
- *feed spool*
32 la bobina receptora
- *take-up spool*
33 la cabeza de grabación *f* del sonido
- *recording head (sound head)*
34 el rodillo de transporte *m* (el cabrestante)
- *transport roller (capstan)*
35 el contrarrodillo de goma *f*
- *rubber pinch roller (capstan idler)*
36 la ranura guía
- *guide step (guide notch)*
37 la ranura de sensibilidad *f* de la película *f*
- *exposure meter control step*
38 la ranura de inserción *f* de filtros *m*
- *conversion filter step (colour, Am. color, conversion filter step)*
39 **el cartucho** (la cassette) **de película** *f* **8 mm**
- *single-8 cassette*
40 la ventana de exposición *f*
- *film gate opening*
41 la película sin impresionar
- *unexposed film*
42 la película impresionada
- *exposed film*
43 **la cámara de 16 mm**
- *16 mm camera*
44 el visor réflex
- *reflex finder (through-the-lens reflex finder)*
45 la carga
- *magazine*
46-49 **la cabeza del objetivo**
- *lens head*
46 el revólver del objetivo
- *lens turret (turret head)*
47 el teleobjetivo
- *telephoto lens*
48 el objetivo gran angular
- *wide-angle lens*
49 el objetivo normal
- *normal lens (standard lens)*
50 la manivela
- *winding handle*
51 **la cámara de súper 8 compacta**
- *compact Super-8 camera*
52 el contador de la película
- *footage counter*
53 el objetivo macrozoom *m*
- *macro zoom lens*
54 la palanca del zoom
- *zooming lever*
55 la macrolente adicional (la lente suplementaria)
- *macro lens attachment (close-up lens)*
56 el macrorraíl (el dispositivo fijador para las muestras pequeñas)
- *macro frame (mount for small originals)*
57 **la caja** (la cámara) **submarina**
- *underwater housing (underwater case)*
58 la dioptra
- *direct-vision frame finder*
59 el distanciador (el espaciador)
- *measuring rod*
60 la superficie de estabilización *f*
- *stabilizing wing*
61 la empuñadura
- *grip (handgrip)*
62 el cierre (el bloqueo)
- *locking bolt*
63 la palanca de mando *m*
- *control lever (operating lever)*
64 el cristal frontal
- *porthole*
65 **la sincronización**
- *synchronization start (sync start)*
66 la cámara de reportaje *m* cinematográfico
- *professional press-type camera*
67 el operador (el cameraman)
- *cameraman*
68 el ayudante del operador (el ayudante del sonido)
- *camera assistant (sound assistant)*
69 la palmada de sincronización *f*
- *handclap marking sync start*

70 **la toma de imagen** *f* **y la grabación de sonido** *m* **a doble pista** *f*
- *dual film-tape recording using a tape recorder*
71 la cámara generadora de impulsos *m*
- *pulse-generating camera*
72 el cable de impulsos *m*
- *pulse cable*
73 la grabadora de cassettes *f*
- *cassette recorder*
74 el micrófono
- *microphone*
75 **la proyección sonora de doble cinta** *f*
- *dual film-tape reproduction*
76 el cassette de la cinta del sonido
- *tape cassette*
77 el dispositivo de sincronización *f*
- *synchronization unit*
78 el proyector de película *f* estrecha
- *cine projector*
79 la bobina de la película original
- *film feed spool*
80 la bobina receptora, una bobina para enrollado *m* automático
- *take-up reel (take-up spool), an automatic take-up reel (take-up spool)*
81 el proyector sonoro
- *sound projector*
82 la película sonora con banda *f* lateral magnética
- *sound film with magnetic stripe (sound track, track)*
83 el botón de grabación *f*
- *automatic-threading button*
84 el botón de trucaje *m*
- *trick button*
85 el regulador del nivel del sonido
- *volume control*
86 el botón de borrado *m*
- *reset button*
87 el conmutador de programa *m* de trucaje *m*
- *fast and slow motion switch*
88 el selector del modo de funcionamiento *m*
- *forward, reverse, and still projection switch*
89 el pegacintas
- *splicer for wet splices*
90 el sujetador de cinta *f* articulado
- *hinged clamping plate*
91 **el visor de películas** *f* (el visor de película *f* cinematográfica)
- *film viewer (animated viewer editor)*
92 el brazo portabobinas giratorio
- *foldaway reel arm*
93 la manivela de rebobinaje *m*
- *rewind handle (rewinder)*
94 el cristal opaco (el cristal esmerilado)
- *viewing screen*
95 la punzadora de la película
- *film perforator (film marker)*
96 **la mesa de montaje** *m* **sonoro de seis platos** *m*
- *six-turntable film and sound cutting table (editing table, cutting bench, animated sound editor)*
97 el monitor
- *monitor*
98 las teclas de mando *m*
- *control buttons (control well)*
99 el plato de la película
- *film turntable*
100 el primer plato del sonido, para el sonido live (sonido *m* original)
- *first sound turntable, e.g. for live sound*
101 el segundo plato del sonido, para el sonido procurado (sonido *m* secundario)
- *second sound turntable for post-sync sound*
102 la cabeza unificadora del sonido y de la imagen
- *film and tape synchronizing head*

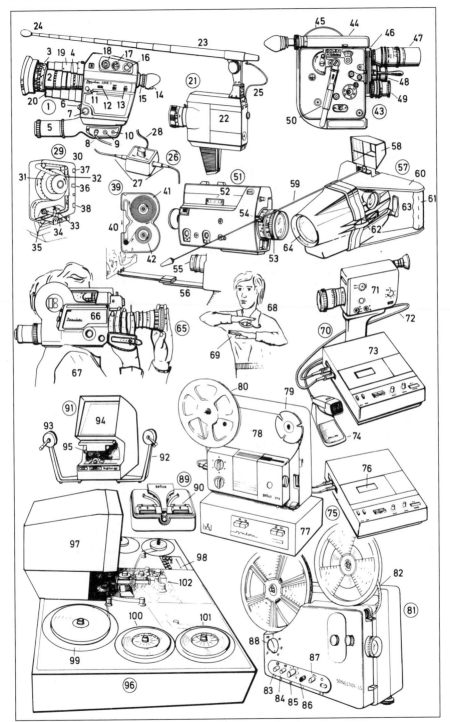

118 Construcción I

Building Site (Construction Site) I

1-49 la obra [la construcción de una casa]
- *carcase (carcass, fabric) [house construction, carcassing]*
1 el sótano de hormigón *m* apisonado
- *basement of tamped (rammed) concrete*
2 el zócalo de hormigón *m* (*Amér.:* de concreto *m*)
- *concrete base course*
3 la ventana del sótano (el respiradero)
- *cellar window (basement window)*
4 la escalera de acceso *m* al sótano por la parte exterior
- *outside cellar steps*
5 la ventana del lavadero
- *utility room window*
6 la puerta del lavadero
- *utility room door*
7 la planta baja
- *ground floor (Am. first floor)*
8 la pared de ladrillos *m*
- *brick wall*
9 el dintel de la ventana
- *lintel (window head)*
10 el marco exterior lateral de la ventana (el intradós de la ventana)
- *reveal*
11 el marco interior lateral de la ventana (el intradós interior de la ventana)
- *jamb*
12 el antepecho (*Bol.:* la patilla)
- *window ledge (window sill)*
13 el dintel de cemento *m* armado
- *reinforced concrete lintel*
14 la primera planta
- *upper floor (first floor, Am. second floor)*
15 la pared de ladrillos *m* huecos
- *hollow-block wall*
16 el suelo macizo
- *concrete floor*
17 el andamio de trabajo *m* (el andamio de caballete *m*)
- *work platform (working platform)*
18 el albañil
- *bricklayer (Am. brickmason)*
19 el peón
- *bricklayer's labourer (Am. laborer);* also: *builder's labourer*
20 el cuezo de argamasa *f*
- *mortar trough*
21 la chimenea
- *chimney*
22 la cubierta provisional de la caja de la escalera
- *cover (boards) for the staircase*
23 el pie del andamio (el arbotante del andamio)
- *scaffold pole (scaffold standard)*
24 la baranda de protección *f*
- *platform railing*
25 el puntal en diagonal *f* (la riostra)
- *angle brace (angle tie) in the scaffold*
26 la carrera
- *ledger*
27 la almojaya del andamio
- *putlog (putlock)*
28 la plataforma de tablones *m*
- *plank platform (board platform)*
29 la pasarela
- *guard board*
30 la ligadura del andamio, con cables *m* o cuerdas *f* de seguridad *f*
- *scaffolding joint with chain or lashing or whip or bond*
31 el montacargas
- *builder's hoist*

32 el operador de máquinas *f* (el maquinista)
- *mixer operator*
33 la mezcladora de hormigón *m*, una hormigonera
- *concrete mixer, a gravity mixer*
34 el tambor mezclador
- *mixing drum*
35 el cargador (la cuchara para llenar la hormigonera)
- *feeder skip*
36 los áridos [arena *f* y gravilla *f*]
- *concrete aggregate [sand and gravel]*
37 la carretilla
- *wheelbarrow*
38 la manguera del agua *f*
- *hose (hosepipe)*
39 la amasadora del mortero (la balsa del mortero)
- *mortar pan (mortar trough, mortar tub)*
40 el montón de los bloques (la pila de ladrillos *m*)
- *stack of bricks*
41 la pila de madera *f* para encofrar
- *stacked shutter boards (lining boards)*
42 la escalera de mano *f* (las escalas)
- *ladder*
43 el saco de cemento *m* (*Chile y Ec.:* la concagua)
- *bag of cement*
44 la valla de protección *f*, una valla de madera *f*
- *site fence, a timber fence*
45 la superficie para la publicidad
- *signboard (billboard)*
46 la puerta de quita y pon (la puerta desmontable)
- *removable gate*
47 los letreros (los rótulos) de empresas *f* y técnicos *m* constructores
- *contractors' name plates*
48 la barraca de la obra
- *site hut (site office)*
49 el retrete de la obra
- *building site latrine*
50-57 las herramientas del albañil
- *bricklayer's (Am. brickmason's) tools*
50 la plomada
- *plumb bob (plummet)*
51 el lápiz de albañil *m*
- *thick lead pencil*
52 la paleta de albañil *m* (el palustre; *Bol., Mé., Perú y S. Dgo.:* la barreta)
- *trowel*
53 la piqueta (el martillo de albañil *m*, la alcotana)
- *bricklayer's (Am. brickmason's) hammer (brick hammer)*
54 la maceta (*Ec. y Perú:* la comba)
- *mallet*
55 el nivel de aire *m* (el nivel de burbuja *f*)
- *spirit level*
56 la llana (la trulla; *Amér.:* la cuchara; *Col.:* el babilejo)
- *laying-on trowel*
57 el fratás
- *float*
58-68 aparejos *m* de construcción *f*
- *masonry bonds*
58 el ladrillo de dimensiones *f* normales (de forma *f* normal; *Mé.:* la solera)
- *brick (standard brick)*
59 las hiladas
- *stretching bond*
60 los aparejos de ladrillo *m*
- *heading bond*

61 el aparejo escalonado
- *racking (raking) back*
62 el aparejo de bloque *m*
- *English bond*
63 el ladrillo colocado a soga *f*
- *stretching course*
64 el ladrillo colocado a tizón *m*
- *heading course*
65 el aparejo en cruz *f*
- *English cross bond (Saint Andrew's cross bond)*
66 los aparejos de chimenea *f*
- *chimney bond*
67 la primera hilada
- *first course*
68 la segunda hilada
- *second course*
69-82 la excavación de la obra
- *excavation*
69 las camillas de replanteo *m*
- *profile (Am. batterboard) [fixed on edge at the corner]*
70 el punto de intersección *f* de las cuerdas
- *intersection of strings*
71 la plomada
- *plumb bob (plummet)*
72 el talud
- *excavation side*
73 la pasarela superior
- *upper edge board*
74 la pasarela inferior
- *lower edge board*
75 la zanja de cimentación *f*
- *foundation trench*
76 el peón zapador
- *navvy (Am. excavator)*
77 la cinta transportadora (de tierra *f*)
- *conveyor belt (conveyor)*
78 los escombros (la tierra excavada)
- *excavated earth*
79 la pasarela (el camino) de tablones *m*
- *plank roadway*
80 la jaula protectora del árbol
- *tree guard*
81 la pala excavadora
- *mechanical shovel (excavator)*
82 la cuchara de la excavadora
- *shovel bucket (bucket)*
83-91 los trabajos de enlucimiento *m*
- *plastering*
83 el yesero (el estuquista)
- *plasterer*
84 el cuezo para el mortero
- *mortar trough*
85 la criba (*Chile:* el chayo)
- *screen*
86-89 el andamio de escalera *f*
- *ladder scaffold*
86 la escalera (los montantes)
- *standard ladder*
87 la pasarela
- *boards (planks, platform)*
88 la riostra en forma *f* de cruz *f*
- *diagonal strut (diagonal brace)*
89 la baranda
- *railing*
90 la reja de protección *f*
- *guard netting*
91 la cuerda de la polea
- *rope-pulley hoist*

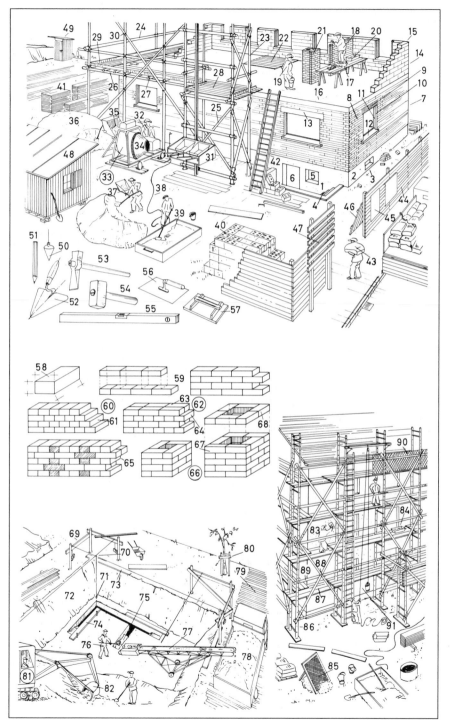

1-89 la construcción de hormigón *m* armado
– *reinforced concrete (ferroconcrete) construction*
1 la estructura de hormigón *m* armado
– *reinforced concrete (ferroconcrete) skeleton construction*
2 el bastidor de hormigón *m* armado
– *reinforced concrete (ferroconcrete) frame*
3 la viga maestra
– *inferior purlin*
4 el cabio de hormigón *m*
– *concrete purlin*
5 la jácena
– *ceiling joist*
6 la cartela
– *arch (flank)*
7 la pared de hormigón *m* colado
– *rubble concrete wall*
8 el techo de hormigón *m* armado
– *reinforced concrete (ferroconcrete) floor*
9 el especialista en hormigón *m* aplanando
– *concreter (concretor), flattening out*
10 el hierro (la varilla) de empalme *m*
– *projecting reinforcement (Am. connection rebars)*
11 el encofrado
– *column box*
12 el encofrado de las jácenas
– *joist shuttering*
13 los puntales del encofrado (los rollizos)
– *shuttering strut*
14 el puntal de arriostramiento *m*
– *diagonal bracing*
15 la cuña
– *wedge*
16 el madero (el tablón)
– *board*
17 la hilera de estacas (el tablestacado)
– *sheet pile wall (sheet pile, sheet piling)*
18 las tablas para encofrar
– *shutter boards (lining boards)*
19 la sierra circular
– *circular saw (buzz saw)*
20 el banco para el doblado (de varillas *f* de hierro *m*)
– *bending table*
21 el ferrallista
– *bar bender (steel bender)*
22 la cizalla de mano *f*
– *hand steel shears*
23 el hierro de armadura *f* (de refuerzo *m*)
– *reinforcing steel (reinforcement rods)*
24 el bloque hueco de piedra *f* pómez
– *pumice concrete hollow block*
25 la mampara para separación *f*, una mampara de madera *f*
– *partition wall, a timber wall*
26 las materias primas para el hormigón [arena *f* y gravilla *f* de distinto grueso *m*]
– *concrete aggregate [gravel and sand of various grades]*
27 el carril de la grúa
– *crane track*
28 la vagoneta basculante
– *tipping wagon (tipping truck)*

29 la hormigonera
– *concrete mixer*
30 el silo para el cemento
– *cement silo*
31 la grúa de torre *f* giratoria (la pluma)
– *tower crane (tower slewing crane)*
32 la plataforma (el carro de grúa *f*)
– *bogie (Am. truck)*
33 el contrapeso
– *counterweight*
34 la torre
– *tower*
35 la cabina del conductor de la grúa
– *crane driver's cabin (crane driver's cage)*
36 el aguilón (el pescante)
– *jib (boom)*
37 el cable portador
– *bearer cable*
38 el cubilote para el hormigón
– *concrete bucket*
39 las traviesas de madera *f*
– *sleepers (Am. ties)*
40 la zapata de freno *m*
– *chock*
41 la rampa
– *ramp*
42 la carretilla
– *wheelbarrow*
43 el pasamano (la barandilla)
– *safety rail*
44 la barraca de la obra
– *site hut*
45 la cantina
– *canteen*
46 el andamio hecho con tubos *m* de acero *m*
– *tubular steel scaffold (scaffolding)*
47 el pie derecho (el pilar)
– *standard*
48 el crucero (el tubo horizontal)
– *ledger tube*
49 la almojaya (el tubo perpendicular a la pared)
– *tie tube*
50 el plinto (la base)
– *shoe*
51 el puntal en diagonal *f* (la riostra)
– *diagonal brace*
52 la plataforma
– *planking (platform)*
53 la abrazadera de unión *f*
– *coupling (coupler)*
54-76 los encofrados de hormigón *m* y el montaje del hierro
– *formwork (shuttering) and reinforcement*
54 el suelo encofrado (el encofrado)
– *bottom shuttering (lining)*
55 el encofrado lateral de la jácena
– *side shutter of a purlin*
56 el encofrado inferior de la jácena
– *cut-in bottom*
57 el travesaño
– *cross beam*
58 la grapa de obra *f*
– *cramp iron (cramp, dog)*
59 el puntal del extremo, el puntal de encabezamiento *m*
– *upright member, a standard*

60 la pieza de unión *f*
– *strap*
61 el travesaño de apoyo *m*
– *cross piece*
62 el tablón de presión *f*
– *stop fillet*
63 la tabla de sujeción *f*
– *strut (brace, angle brace)*
64 el travesaño de refuerzo *m*
– *frame timber (yoke)*
65 el cubrejunta
– *strap*
66 la riostra de alambre *m*
– *reinforcement binding*
67 el tirante de tope *m*
– *cross strut (strut)*
68 la armadura
– *reinforcement*
69 las barras de repartición *f*
– *distribution steel*
70 el estribo
– *stirrup*
71 el hierro de empalme *m*
– *projecting reinforcement (Am. connection rebars)*
72 el hormigón (el hormigón seco; Amér.: el concreto; Col.: el gorgón)
– *concrete (heavy concrete)*
73 el encofrado de puntales *m*
– *column box*
74 el marco de madera *f* atornillado
– *bolted frame timber (bolted yoke)*
75 el tornillo (el perno)
– *nut (thumb nut)*
76 el tablón para encofrados *m*
– *shutter board (shuttering board)*
77-89 herramientas *f*
– *tools*
77 la barra para doblar los hierros
– *bending iron*
78 el transportador móvil de encofrados *m*
– *adjustable service girder*
79 el tornillo de ajuste *m*
– *adjusting screw*
80 la barra de acero *m* (el redondo)
– *round bar reinforcement*
81 el distanciador (el fiel para cortar los hierros)
– *distance piece (separator, spacer)*
82 la barra de acero *m* grabado
– *Torsteel*
83 el pisón del hormigón
– *concrete tamper*
84 el molde para cubos *m* de muestra *f*
– *mould (Am. mold) for concrete test cubes*
85 las tenazas
– *concreter's tongs*
86 el puntal para encofrados *m*
– *sheeting support*
87 la cizalla de mano *f* (para cortar hierros *m*)
– *hand shears*
88 el vibrador para hormigón *m* armado
– *immersion vibrator (concrete vibrator)*
89 la aguja de vibrar
– *vibrating cylinder (vibrating head, vibrating poker)*

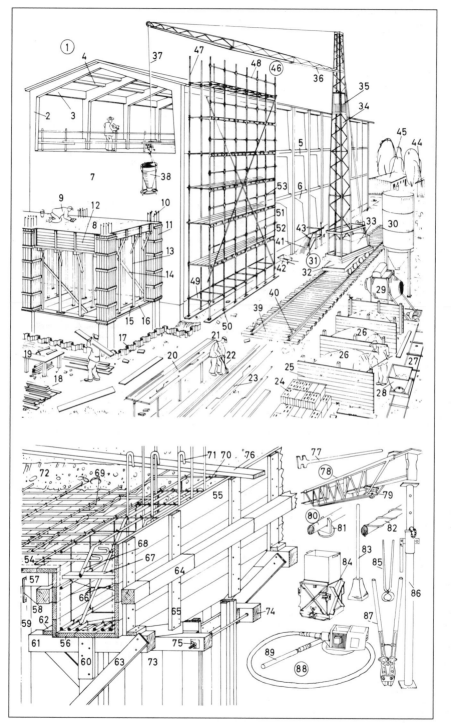

1-59 la carpintería de armar
– *carpenter's yard*
1 el acopio de tablones *m*
– *stack of boards (planks)*
2 los troncos largos (rollizos *m*, la madera de construcción *f*)
– *long timber (Am. lumber)*
3 el cobertizo de aserrado *m*
– *sawing shed*
4 el taller de carpintería *f*
– *carpenter's workshop*
5 la puerta del taller
– *workshop door*
6 el carro de mano *f*
– *handcart*
7 el entramado del tejado (la armazón para techar)
– *roof truss*
8 el árbol con la corona puesta (*en España:* la bandera al cubrir de aguas *f*)
– *tree [used for topping out ceremony], with wreath*
9 el entablado
– *timber wall*
10 los cuartones (la madera para construcciones *f*, la madera escuadrada)
– *squared timber (building timber, scantlings)*
11 el plano de montea *f*
– *drawing floor*
12 el carpintero
– *carpenter*
13 el sombrero del carpintero
– *carpenter's hat*
14 la sierra tronzadora, una sierra de cadena *f*
– *cross-cut saw, a chain saw*
15 el portacadena guía
– *chain guide*
16 la cadena de la sierra
– *saw chain*
17 la escopleadora (la fresadora de cadena *f* cortante)
– *mortiser (chain cutter)*
18 el caballete de soporte *m* (la asnilla)
– *trestle (horse)*
19 la viga en el caballete
– *beam mounted on a trestle*
20 la caja de las herramientas
– *set of carpenter's tools*
21 el taladrador eléctrico
– *electric drill*
22 el agujero para la espiga
– *dowel hole*
23 la señal para el agujero de la espiga
– *mark for the dowel hole*
24 el material listo para ensamblar
– *beams*
25 la columna (el pilar)
– *post (stile, stud, quarter)*
26 el pasador
– *corner brace*
27 el travesaño (el puntal)
– *brace (strut)*
28 el zócalo de la casa
– *base course (plinth)*
29 la pared de la casa
– *house wall (wall)*
30 el hueco de la ventana
– *window opening*
31 el intradós exterior (el marco exterior, el cerco exterior)
– *reveal*
32 el intradós interior (el marco interior, el cerco interior)
– *jamb*

33 la solera (el alféizar)
– *window ledge (window sill)*
34 el zuncho perimetral
– *cornice*
35 el rollizo
– *roundwood (round timber)*
36 la pasarela (el entablado, el entarimado)
– *floorboards*
37 la cuerda del montacargas
– *hoisting rope*
38 la viga del techo (la viga maestra)
– *ceiling joist (ceiling beam, main beam)*
39 la viga de la pared
– *wall joist*
40 la viga de retallo *m*
– *wall plate*
41 la traviesa (el brochal, la viga secundaria)
– *trimmer (trimmer joist, Am. header, header joist)*
42 el cabestrillo
– *dragon beam (dragon piece)*
43 el entrevigado (las piezas de relleno *m*)
– *false floor (inserted floor)*
44 el relleno entre vigas *f*, de bloques *m*, de coque *m*, o de arcilla *f*
– *floor filling of breeze, loam, etc.*
45 el listón
– *fillet (cleat)*
46 el hueco de la escalera
– *stair well (well)*
47 la chimenea
– *chimney*
48 el maderaje de la fachada (la pared entramada)
– *framed partition (framed wall)*
49 la viga solera (el durmiente)
– *wall plate*
50 el travesaño de solera *f*
– *girt*
51 la jamba de la ventana, el bastidor
– *window jamb, a jamb*
52 el pie derecho de esquina *f* (el cornijal)
– *corner stile (corner strut, corner stud)*
53 el pie derecho de unión *f*
– *principal post*
54 la riostra
– *brace (strut) with skew notch*
55 el travesaño intermedio (el contrapuente)
– *nogging piece*
56 la barra de apoyo *m*
– *sill rail*
57 el dintel de la ventana (el cargadero)
– *window lintel (window head)*
58 el cabezal (la carrera)
– *head (head rail)*
59 el forjado del entramado
– *filled-in panel (bay, pan)*
60-82 las herramientas de carpintero *m*
– **carpenter's tools**
60 el serrucho
– *hand saw*
61 la sierra de mano *f*
– *bucksaw*
62 la hoja de la sierra
– *saw blade*
63 el serrucho de calar (la sierra de punta *f*)
– *compass saw (keyhole saw)*
64 el cepillo de carpintero *m* (la garlopa)
– *plane*
65 la barrena de cola *f* (la broca)
– *auger (gimlet)*
66 el gato (la cárcel)
– *screw clamp (cramp, holdfast)*

67 el mazo
– *mallet*
68 el tronzador
– *two-handed saw*
69 el gramil
– *try square*
70 el hacha *f* de carpintero *m*
– *broad axe (Am. broadax)*
71 el formón
– *chisel*
72 el escoplo
– *mortise axe (mortice axe, Am. mortise ax)*
73 la azuela (el hacha *f*)
– *axe (Am. ax)*
74 el martillo de carpintero *m*
– *carpenter's hammer*
75 la boca sacaclavos
– *claw head (nail claw)*
76 el metro plegable
– *folding rule*
77 el lápiz de carpintero *m*
– *carpenter's pencil*
78 la escuadra de hierro *m*
– *iron square*
79 el rascador (el cuchillo de desbastar)
– *drawknife (drawshave, drawing knife)*
80 la viruta
– *shaving*
81 la falsa escuadra
– *bevel*
82 la escuadra a inglete *m*
– *mitre square (Am. miter square, miter angle)*
83-96 maderas *f* de construcción *f*
– **building timber**
83 la troza (el trunco)
– *round trunk (undressed timber, Am. rough lumber)*
84 el núcleo (el corazón) del tronco (el duramen)
– *heartwood (duramen)*
85 el sámago (la albura)
– *sapwood (sap, alburnum)*
86 la corteza
– *bark (rind)*
87 el corte para una sola pieza de sección *f* cuadrangular (el tronco de sección *f* entera)
– *baulk (balk)*
88 el corte para dos piezas en aristas *f* vivas (el tronco de sección *f* media)
– *halved timber*
89 el corte en aristas *f* truncadas (el tronco de media sección *f*)
– *wane (waney edge)*
90 el madero cortado en cruz *f* (el tronco de cuarto de sección *f*)
– *quarter baulk (balk)*
91 el tablón
– *plank (board)*
92 la madera de testa *f*
– *end-grained timber*
93 el tablón del núcleo (del corazón, del duramen)
– *heartwood plank (heart plank)*
94 la tabla no escuadrada
– *unsquared (untrimmed) plank (board)*
95 la tabla escuadrada
– *squared (trimmed) board*
96 el costero
– *slab (offcut)*

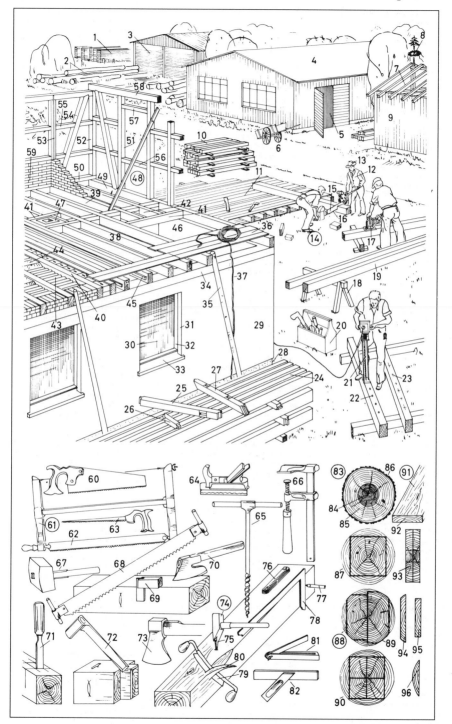

1-26 estilos *m* y partes *f* del tejado
- *styles and parts of roofs*
1 el tejado a dos vertientes *m*
- *gable roof (saddle roof, saddleback roof)*
2 el caballete del tejado
- *ridge*
3 el borde (el saliente del tejado)
- *verge*
4 el alero del tejado
- *eaves*
5 el frontón (la fachada)
- *gable*
6 la buhardilla rampante (*Arg., Chile y Urug.:* el entretecho)
- *dormer window (dormer)*
7 el tejado a una sola vertiente
- *pent roof (shed roof, lean-to roof)*
8 la claraboya (el tragaluz, la lumbrera; *Col:* la aojada)
- *skylight*
9 la pared cortafuegos *m*
- *fire gable*
10 el tejado de faldón *m* (el tejado a cuatro aguas *f*)
- *hip (hipped) roof*
11 la terminación *f* del tejado de copete *m* (el chaflán)
- *hip end*
12 la cresta del copete (la lima tesa)
- *hip (arris)*
13 la buhardilla de copete *m* (*Arg., Chile y Urug.:* el entretecho)
- *hip (hipped) dormer window*
14 el linternón
- *ridge turret*
15 la lima hoya
- *valley (roof valley)*
16 el tejado de semicopete *m*
- *hipped-gable roof (jerkin head roof)*
17 el chaflán (el faldoncillo)
- *partial-hip (partial-hipped) end*
18 el tejado a la Mansard (la cubierta quebrantada)
- *mansard roof (Am. gambrel roof)*
19 la ventana de mansarda *f*
- *mansard dormer window*
20 el tejado en diente *m* de sierra *f*
- *sawtooth roof*
21 el lucernario
- *north light*
22 el tejado de pabellón *m*
- *broach roof*
23 la buhardilla redondeada (*Arg., Chile y Urug.:* el entretecho)
- *eyebrow*
24 el tejado cónico
- *conical broach roof*
25 el tejado imperial (la cúpula en forma *f* de bulbo *m*)
- *imperial dome (imperial roof)*
26 la veleta
- *weather vane*

27-83 la construcción de tejados *m* de madera *f*
- *roof structures of timber*
27 el tejado de cabrios *m*
- *rafter roof*
28 el cabrio
- *rafter*
29 la viga del tejado
- *roof beam*
30 la riostra
- *diagonal tie (cross tie, sprocket piece, cocking piece)*
31 el ristrel (el cabrio de quiebra *f*)
- *arris fillet (tilting fillet)*

32 la pared exterior
- *outer wall*
33 la cabeza de la viga
- *beam head*
34 el tejado con viga *f* de lima *f*
- *collar beam roof (trussed rafter roof)*
35 la viga de lima *f* (el puente, el falso tirante)
- *collar beam (collar)*
36 el cabrio
- *rafter*
37 la cubierta de puentes *m* con doble apoyo *m* vertical (el tejado con buhardilla *f*)
- *strutted collar beam roof structure*
38 la viga de lima *f* (el falso tirante *m*)
- *collar beams*
39 el cabio lateral
- *purlin*
40 el poste (el pilar)
- *post (stile, stud)*
41 el codillo
- *brace*
42 la cubierta de una sola cámara
- *unstrutted (king pin) roof structure*
43 el cabio del caballete
- *ridge purlin*
44 el cabio inferior
- *inferior purlin*
45 la cabeza del cabrio
- *rafter head (rafter end)*
46 la armadura con buhardilla *f* y cámara *f* de aire *m*
- *purlin roof with queen post and pointing sill*
47 el jabalcón (la jamba)
- *pointing sill*
48 la viga del caballete (la viga cumbrera)
- *ridge beam (ridge board)*
49 la pinza sencilla
- *simple tie*
50 la pinza doble
- *double tie*
51 el cabio central
- *purlin*
52 la armadura de dos pisos *m* con cabios *m* (correas *f*) horizontales
- *purlin roof structure with queen post*
53 la viga de unión *f*
- *tie beam*
54 la viga del techo
- *joist (ceiling joist)*
55 el cabrio principal (el cabrio de unión *f*)
- *principal rafter*
56 el cabrio central
- *common rafter*
57 el codillo de ángulo *m*
- *angle brace (angle tie)*
58 el tornapunta
- *brace (strut)*
59 las pinzas
- *ties*
60 la cubierta holandesa con armadura *f* de copete *m*
- *hip (hipped) roof with purlin roof structure*
61 el cabrio de unión *f* (de copete *m*)
- *jack rafter*
62 el cabio de lima tesa *f* (de la cresta)
- *hip rafter*
63 el cabrio del copete
- *jack rafter*
64 el cabrio de la lima hoya
- *valley rafter*

65 el techo de doble suspensión *f* (la armadura de doble espolón *m*)
- *queen truss*
66 la viga suspendida (la viga principal)
- *main beam*
67 la viga maestra (la jácena)
- *summer (summer beam)*
68 el pendolón
- *queen post (truss post)*
69 la tornapunta
- *brace (strut)*
70 la viga de trabazón *f*
- *collar beam (collar)*
71 el brochal
- *trimmer (Am. header)*
72 la armadura de cubierta *f* con huecos *m* macizados (la viga de alma *f* llena)
- *solid-web girder*
73 el tirante (la cabeza inferior)
- *lower chord*
74 el par (la cabeza superior)
- *upper chord*
75 el entablado
- *boarding*
76 el cabio (la correa)
- *purlin*
77 la pared exterior de soporte *m*
- *supporting outer wall*
78 la armadura de celosía *f*
- *roof truss*
79 el tirante (la cabeza inferior)
- *lower chord*
80 el par (la cabeza superior)
- *upper chord*
81 el poste (el pilar)
- *post*
82 la tornapunta
- *brace (strut)*
83 el soporte
- *support*

84-98 las uniones de madera *f*
- *timber joints*
84 la mecha sencilla (unión *f* de caja *f* y espiga *f*)
- *mortise (mortice) and tenon joint*
85 la unión de espiga *f* de doble mecha *f*
- *forked mortise (mortice) and tenon joint*
86 la unión recta a media madera *f*
- *halving (halved) joint*
87 el ensamble con resalte *m*
- *simple scarf joint*
88 la unión oblicua con resalte *m* (ensamble oblicuo con resalte *m*)
- *oblique scarf joint*
89 el ensamble a media madera *f* en cola *f* de milano *m*
- *dovetail halving*
90 el bisel con muesca *f* de encaje *m*
- *single skew notch*
91 el doble bisel de encaje *m*
- *double skew notch*
92 el clavo de madera *f*
- *wooden nail*
93 la clavija
- *pin*
94 el clavo de hierro *m* forjado
- *clout nail (clout)*
95 la punta de París (el clavo de cabeza *f* redonda)
- *wire nail*
96 la cuña de madera *f* dura
- *hardwood wedges*
97 la grapa
- *cramp iron (timber dog, dog)*
98 el perno roscado
- *bolt*

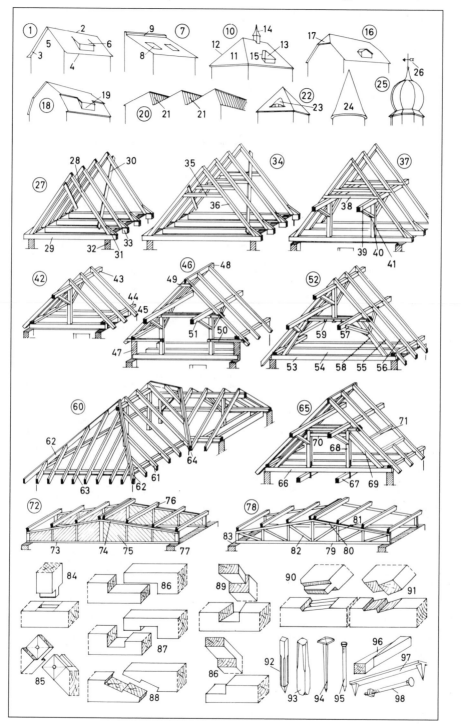

1 el tejado (la cubierta) de tejas *f*
– *tiled roof*
2 la teja plana de doble falda *f*
– *plain-tile double-lap roofing*
3 la teja de caballete *m*
– *ridge tile*
4 la media teja terminal, junto al caballete
– *ridge course tile*
5 la teja de alero *m* (la bocateja)
– *under-ridge tile*
6 la teja plana
– *plain (plane) tile*
7 la teja de ventilación *f*
– *ventilating tile*
8 la teja de cresta *f* (de copete *m*)
– *ridge tile*
9 la teja de casquete *m* para tejado *m* holandés
– *hip tile*
10 el chaflán del tejado
– *hipped end*
11 la lima hoya
– *valley (roof valley)*
12 la claraboya (el tragaluz; *Col.:* la aojada)
– *skylight*
13 la chimenea
– *chimney*
14 el cerco metálico de la chimenea, de zinc *m*
– *chimney flashing, made of sheet zinc*
15 el gancho para las escalas
– *ladder hook*
16 el soporte del enrejado paranieve
– *snow guard bracket*
17 el listón
– *battens (slating and tiling battens)*
18 el medidor de distancia *f* entre listones *m*
– *batten gauge* (Am. *gage*)
19 el cabrio
– *rafter*
20 el martillo de tejador *m*
– *tile hammer*
21 el hacha *f* de enlistonar
– *lath axe* (Am. *ax*)
22 el cubo de tejador *m* (el cuezo)
– *hod*
23 el gancho del cubo
– *hod hook*
24 la salida
– *opening (hatch)*
25 la fachada (el frontispicio)
– *gable (gable end)*
26 el listón dentado
– *toothed lath*
27 el sofito
– *soffit*
28 el canalón del tejado
– *gutter*
29 el bajante (el tubo de desagüe *m*)
– *rainwater pipe (downpipe)*
30 el tubo de entrada *f* (la embocadura)
– *swan's neck (swan-neck)*
31 la abrazadera (la brida)
– *pipe clip*
32 el soporte del canalón
– *gutter bracket*
33 la máquina para agujerear tejas *f*
– *tile cutter*
34 el andamio de trabajo *m*
– *scaffold*
35 la pared de protección *f*
– *safety wall*
36 la cornisa del tejado
– *eaves*
37 la pared exterior
– *outer wall*

38 el revestimiento exterior
– *exterior rendering*
39 el ramate de obra *f*
– *frost-resistant brickwork*
40 el cabio inferior
– *inferior purlin*
41 la cabeza del cabrio
– *rafter head (rafter end)*
42 el encofrado de la cornisa
– *eaves fascia*
43 el doble listón
– *double lath (tilting lath)*
44 las placas de aislamiento *m*
– *insulating boards*
45-60 las tejas y las cubiertas (los tejados) de tejas *f*
– *tiles and tile roofings*
45 el tejado con eclisas *f*
– *split-tiled roof*
46 la teja plana
– *plain (plane) tile*
47 la teja de remate *m*
– *ridge course*
48 la eclisa
– *slip*
49 el remate del alero
– *eaves course*
50 el tejado real
– *plain-tiled roof*
51 la nariz
– *nib*
52 la teja de caballete *m*
– *ridge tile*
53 el tejado acanalado (el tejado italiano)
– *pantiled roof*
54 la teja acanalada
– *pantile*
55 el relleno con mortero *m*
– *pointing*
56 el tejado árabe (el tejado de teja *f* cóncava y teja *f* convexa)
– *Spanish-tiled roof* (Am. *mission-tiled roof*)
57 la teja de canal *m*
– *under tile*
58 la teja superior (la cobija)
– *over tile*
59 la teja de encaje *m*
– *interlocking tile*
60 la teja de tejado *m* plano
– *flat interlocking tile*
61-89 el tejado de pizarra *f*
– *slate roof*
61 el entarimado del tejado
– *roof boards (roof boarding, roof sheathing)*
62 la tela asfáltica (el cartón asfaltado)
– *roofing paper (sheathing paper);* also: *roofing felt* (Am. *rag felt*)
63 la escalera de tejado *m*
– *cat ladder (roof ladder)*
64 el gancho de conexión *f*
– *coupling hook*
65 el gancho de cumbrera *f*
– *ridge hook*
66 el caballete
– *roof trestle*
67 la cuerda de sujeción *f* del caballete
– *trestle rope*
68 el nudo
– *knot*
69 el gancho de la escalera
– *ladder hook*
70 el tablón del andamio (el tablón puente)
– *scaffold board*
71 el pizarrero
– *slater*

72 la cajita para los clavos
– *nail bag*
73 el martillo del pizarrero
– *slate hammer*
74 el clavo para colocar pizarra *f*, un clavo de alambre *m* galvanizado
– *slate nail, a galvanized wire nail*
75 el zapato de pizarrero *m*, una alpargata de cáñamo *m* o esparto *m*
– *slater's shoe, a bast or hemp shoe*
76 la pizarra del alero
– *eaves course (eaves joint)*
77 la pieza en ángulo *m*
– *corner bottom slate*
78 la pieza corriente (la pizarra de tejado *m*)
– *roof course*
79 la pizarra de caballete *m*
– *ridge course (ridge joint)*
80 la pizarra del copete (la pieza del faldón)
– *gable slate*
81 la línea límite (la línea a cubrir)
– *tail line*
82 la lima hoya
– *valley (roof valley)*
83 el canalón rectangular
– *box gutter (trough gutter, parallel gutter)*
84 las tijeras (la cizalla) para pizarra *f*
– *slater's iron*
85 la pizarra
– *slate*
86 la espalda
– *back*
87 la cabeza
– *head*
88 el borde frontal
– *front edge*
89 la cola
– *tail*
90-103 la cubierta de tela *f* asfáltica y la cubierta de fibrocemento *m* ondulado (la cubierta de uralita® *f*)
– *asphalt-impregnated paper roofing and corrugated asbestos cement roofing*
90 la cubierta de cartón *m* asfáltico (de tela *f* asfáltica)
– *asphalt-impregnated paper roof*
91 la tira [paralela al canalón]
– *width [parallel to the gutter]*
92 el canalón
– *gutter*
93 el caballete (la cumbrera)
– *ridge*
94 la unión
– *join*
95 la tira [perpendicular al canalón]
– *width [at right angles to the gutter]*
96 el clavo para el cartón
– *felt nail (clout nail)*
97 la cubierta (el techo) de fibrocemento *m* ondulado
– *corrugated asbestos cement roof*
98 la chapa ondulada (la uralita®)
– *corrugated sheet*
99 la cubierta del caballete (de la cumbrera)
– *ridge capping piece*
100 el recubrimiento (la pieza sobrepuesta, la solapa)
– *lap*
101 el tornillo para madera *f*
– *wood screw*
102 el sombrerete de zinc *m* para la lluvia
– *rust-proof zinc cup*
103 la arandela de plomo *m*
– *lead washer*

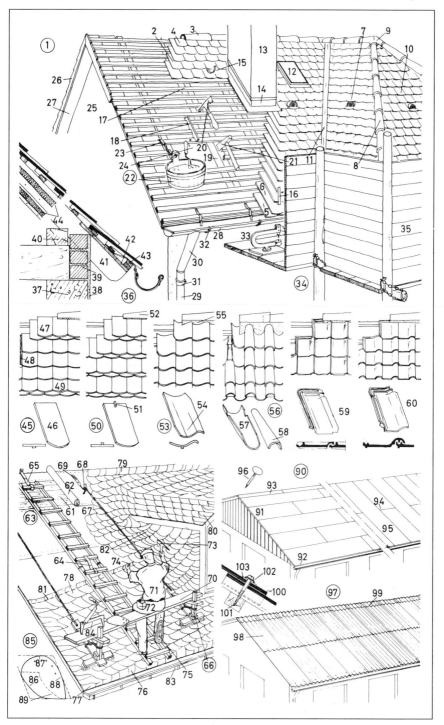

123 Construcción de suelos, techos, escaleras

1 la pared del sótano, una pared de
   hormigón *m*
 – *basement wall, a concrete wall*
2 la fundación (la faja del cimiento)
 – *footing (foundation)*
3 el arranque del cimiento
 – *foundation base*
4 la capa aislante horizontal
 – *damp course (damp-proof course)*
5 la capa protectora (la capa impermeable)
 – *waterproofing*
6 la primera capa de revoque *m*
 – *rendering coat*
7 la solería de ladrillos *m*
 – *brick paving*
8 el lecho de arena *f*
 – *sand bed*
9 la tierra
 – *ground*
10 el tablón lateral
 – *shuttering*
11 la estaquilla
 – *peg*
12 el firme del suelo
 – *hardcore*
13 el lecho de hormigón *m*
 – *oversite concrete*
14 el pavimento de cemento *m*
 – *cement screed*
15 el muro de ladrillos *m*
 – *brickwork base*
16 la escalera del sótano, una
   escalera maciza
 – *basement stairs, solid concrete
   stairs*
17 el peldaño macizo (el peldaño en
   bloque *m* enterizo)
 – *block step*
18 el primer peldaño (el peldaño de
   arranque *m*)
 – *curtail step (bottom step)*
19 el peldaño del descansillo
 – *top step*
20 la protección del canto (la moldura de protección *f*)
 – *nosing*
21 el embaldosado del zócalo
 – *skirting (skirting board, Am. mopboard, washboard, scrub board,
   base)*
22 el pasamano, la balaustrada
   metálica
 – *balustrade of metal bars*
23 el descansillo (la meseta)
 – *ground-floor (Am. first-floor)
   landing*
24 la puerta de entrada *f* de la casa
 – *front door*
25 el limpiabarros de los pies
 – *foot scraper*
26 el pavimento de losetas *f*
 – *flagstone paving*
27 la capa de mortero *m*
 – *mortar bed*
28 el techo macizo, un techo de
   hormigón *m* armado
 – *concrete ceiling, a reinforced concrete slab*

29 la pared de ladrillos *m* de la planta baja
 – *ground-floor (Am. first-floor)
   brick wall*
30 la rampa
 – *ramp*
31 el escalón de cuña *f*
 – *wedge-shaped step*
32 el escalón (la huella)
 – *tread*
33 la contrahuella (la altura)
 – *riser*
34-41 el descansillo (la meseta)
 – *landing*
34 la viga del descansillo
 – *landing beam*
35 el techo nervado de hormigón *m*
   armado
 – *ribbed reinforced concrete floor*
36 la nervadura (la viga)
 – *rib*
37 la armadura de acero *m*
 – *steel-bar reinforcement*
38 la placa prensada
 – *subfloor (blind floor)*
39 la capa de nivel *m*
 – *level layer*
40 la capa de acabado *m*
 – *finishing layer*
41 el revestimiento del suelo (el
   piso)
 – *top layer (screed)*
**42-44 la escalera truncada, una
   escalera con descansillo** *m*
 – *dog-legged staircase, a staircase
   without a well*
42 el primer peldaño (el peldaño de
   arranque *m*)
 – *curtail step (bottom step)*
43 el pilar (el poste) de arranque *m*
 – *newel post (newel)*
44 la zanca libre
 – *outer string (Am. outer stringer)*
45 la zanca (el alma *f*) de la pared
 – *wall string (Am. wall stringer)*
46 el tornillo de escalera *f*
 – *staircase bolt*
47 el escalón (la huella)
 – *tread*
48 la contrahuella
 – *riser*
49 la pieza de ángulo *m*
 – *wreath piece (wreathed string)*
50 la barandilla de la escalera
 – *balustrade*
51 el balaustre
 – *baluster*
52-62 el descansillo intermedio
 – *intermediate landing*
52 la curvadura de la barandilla
 – *wreath*
53 el pasamano (el barandal)
 – *handrail (guard rail)*
54 el pilar (el poste) de llegada *f*
 – *head post*
55 la viga del descansillo
 – *landing beam*
56 la tabla de revestimiento *m*
 – *lining board*

57 la varilla de recubrimiento *m*
 – *fillet*
58 la plancha aislante ligera
 – *lightweight building board*
59 el enlucido del techo
 – *ceiling plaster*
60 el enlucido de la pared
 – *wall plaster*
61 el techo intermedio (el forjado
   del techo)
 – *false ceiling*
62 el suelo de tiras *f* (el suelo de
   tabletas *f*)
 – *strip flooring (overlay flooring,
   parquet strip)*
63 el listón del zócalo
 – *skirting board (Am. mopboard,
   washboard, scrub board, base)*
64 la varilla de recubrimiento *m* (el
   junquillo, el tapajuntas)
 – *beading*
65 la ventana de la caja de la
   escalera
 – *staircase window*
66 la viga principal (la viga maestra)
   del descansillo
 – *main landing beam*
67 el listón de soporte *m*
 – *fillet (cleat)*
68 u. 69 el techo intermedio
 – *false ceiling*
68 el suelo intermedio
 – *false floor (inserted floor)*
69 el relleno del suelo intermedio
 – *floor filling (plugging, pug)*
70 los listones
 – *laths*
71 el soporte del enlucido (el cañizo)
 – *lathing*
72 el enlucido del techo
 – *ceiling plaster*
73 el suelo falso
 – *subfloor (blind floor)*
74 el entarimado (el machiembrado)
   de ranuras *f* y lengüetas *f*
 – *parquet floor with tongued-and-
   grooved blocks*
75 la escalera de cuarto de conver-
   sión *f*
 – *quarter-newelled (Am. quarter-
   neweled) staircase*
76 la escalera circular de abanico *m*
   (la escalera de caracol *m*), con eje
   m (con árbol *m*) abierto
 – *winding staircase (spiral staircase)
   with open newels (open-newel
   staircase)*
77 la escalera de caracol *m* de eje *m*
   cerrado
 – *winding staircase (spiral staircase)
   with solid newels (solid-newel
   staircase)*
78 el eje (el árbol)
 – *newel (solid newel)*
79 el pasamano (el barandal)
 – *handrail*

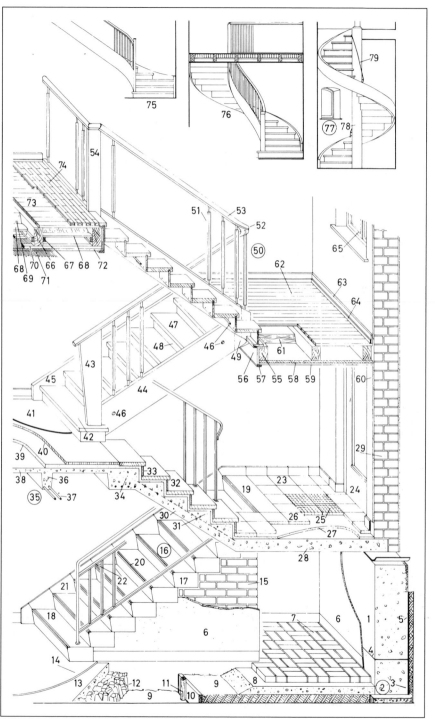

1 la vidriería (la cristalería)
– *glazier's workshop*
2 las muestras de molduras *f* (las muestras de marcos *m*)
– *frame wood samples (frame samples)*
3 la moldura (el marco)
– *frame wood*
4 el inglete (la ensambladura)
– *mitre joint (mitre,* Am. *miter joint, miter)*
5 el vidrio plano; *clases:* vidrio de ventana *f,* vidrio mate (vidrio esmerilado), vidrio muselina, vidrio luna, vidrio grueso, vidrio opalino, vidrio compuesto, vidrio inastillable (cristal *m* de seguridad *f*)
– *sheet glass; kinds: window glass, frosted glass, patterned glass, crystal plate glass, thick plate glass, milk glass, laminated glass (safety glass, shatterproof glass)*
6 el vidrio de fundición *f; clases:* vidrio de catedral (vidrio de colores *m*), vidrio ornamental, vidrio basto, vidrio de ojo *m* de buey *m,* vidrio armado, cristal hilado
– *cast glass; kinds: stained glass, ornamental glass, raw glass, bull's-eye glass, wired glass, line glass (lined glass)*

7 el montador de ingletes *m*
– *mitring (Am. mitering) machine*
8 el vidriero; *categorías:* vidriero de construcción *f,* vidriero de marcos *m,* vidriero artístico
– *glassworker (e.g. building glazier, glazier, decorative glass worker)*
9 el portacristales
– *glass holder*
10 los pedazos de cristal *m* (los añicos de vidrio *m*)
– *piece of broken glass*
11 el martillo de plomo *m*
– *lead hammer*
12 el cuchillo de plomo *m* (el tingle)
– *lead knife*
13 la varilla de plomo *m*
– *came (lead came)*
14 la ventana de cristal *m* emplomado
– *leaded light*
15 la mesa de trabajo *m*
– *workbench*
16 la hoja de vidrio *m*
– *pane of glass*
17 la masilla
– *putty*
18 el martillo de pico *m* (el martillo de vidriero *m*)
– *glazier's hammer*
19 las tenazas de vidriero *m*
– *glass pliers*

20 la escuadra de vidriero *m* para cortar
– *glazier's square*
21 la regla para cortar
– *glazier's rule*
22 el cortador del vidrio en círculo *m* (el compás cortador)
– *glazier's beam compass*
23 la corcheta
– *eyelet*
24 la punta (el ángulo) de vidrio *m*
– *glazing sprig*
25 *u.* **26** cortadores *m* de cristal *m*
– *glass cutters*
25 el diamante de cristalero *m,* un cortador de diamante *m*
– *diamond glass cutter*
26 el cortavidrios de disco *m* de acero *m*
– *steel-wheel (steel) glass cutter*
27 la espátula para la masilla
– *putty knife*
28 el alambre de espiga *f*
– *pin wire*
29 el alfiler de espiga *f*
– *panel pin*
30 la sierra para cortar en ingletes *m*
– *mitre (Am. miter) block (mitre box) [with saw]*
31 el ensamblador de ingletes *m*
– *mitre (Am. miter) shoot (mitre board)*

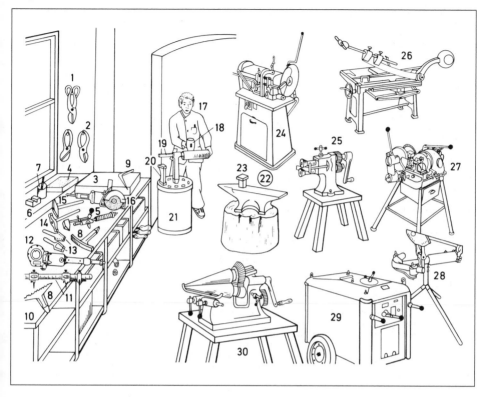

1 las tijeras para chapa *f*
– *metal shears (tinner's snips,* Am. *tinner's shears)*
2 las tijeras angulares
– *elbow snips (angle shears)*
3 la placa para enderezar
– *gib*
4 la placa para alisar
– *lapping plate*
5-7 los aparatos para soldar de gas *m* propano
– *propane soldering apparatus*
5 el soldador (el soplete de gas *m* propano, un soldador tipo martillo *m*)
– *propane soldering iron, a hatchet iron*
6 la piedra para soldar, una piedra de amoníaco *m*
– *soldering stone, a sal-ammoniac block*
7 el ácido para soldar
– *soldering fluid (flux)*
8 la bigornia, para formar bordes *m*
– *beading iron for forming reinforcement beading*
9 el escariador de ángulo *m*, un rayador
– *angled reamer*

10 el banco de trabajo *m*
– *workbench (bench)*
11 el compás de varas *f*
– *beam compass (trammel,* Am. *beam trammel)*
12 la terraja eléctrica de cojinetes *m*
– *electric hand die*
13 el sacabocados
– *hollow punch*
14 el martillo de embutir (de rebordear)
– *chamfering hammer*
15 el martillo de orlar
– *beading swage (beading hammer)*
16 la máquina para afilar y cortar
– *abrasive-wheel cutting-off machine*
17 el hojalatero (el lampista; *Venez.:* el perolero)
– *plumber*
18 el mazo
– *mallet*
19 el cuerno
– *mandrel*
20 la trancha
– *socket (tinner's socket)*
21 el tronco (el cepo)
– *block*

22 el yunque
– *anvil*
23 el tas
– *stake*
24 la sierra mecánica circular
– *circular saw (buzz saw)*
25 la máquina para enchapar, acanalar y rebordear
– *flanging, swaging, and wiring machine*
26 la cizalla para plancha *f*
– *sheet shears (guillotine)*
27 la máquina de filetear (aterrajar)
– *screw-cutting machine (thread-cutting machine, die stocks)*
28 la máquina para doblar los tubos
– *pipe-bending machine (bending machine, pipe bender)*
29 el transformador de soldadura *f*
– *welding transformer*
30 la máquina para doblar dándole a la chapa la forma de embudo *m*
– *bending machine (rounding machine) for shaping funnels*

1 el instalador del agua *f* y del gas
(el fontanero; *Venez.:* el perolero)
– *gas fitter and plumber*
2 la escalera de tijeras *f* (*Cuba, Mé.
y P. Rico:* el burro)
– *stepladder*
3 la cadena de seguridad *f*
– *safety chain*
4 la llave de paso *m*
– *stop valve*
5 el contador de gas *m*
– *gas meter*
6 el soporte (la repisa)
– *bracket*
7 la tubería de subida *f*
– *service riser*
8 la tubería de ramificación *f* (el
ramal)
– *distributing pipe*
9 la tubería de distribución *f*
– *supply pipe*
10 la sierra mecánica para tubos *m*
– *pipe-cutting machine*
11 el burro para sujetar el tubo
– *pipe repair stand*
12 *u.* 13 el calentador continuo de
agua *f*, un calentador de agua *f*
– *geyser, an instantaneous water
heater*
12-25 aparatos *m* de gas *m* y de agua *f*
– *gas and water appliances*
12 el calentador de gas *m*
– *gas water heater*
13 el calentador eléctrico
– *electric water heater*
14 el depósito del retrete (WC) (la
cisterna)
– *toilet cistern*
15 el flotador (el nivel)
– *float*
16 la válvula de desagüe *m*
– *bell*
17 el tubo de vaciado *m*
– *flush pipe*
18 la entrada de agua *f*
– *water inlet*
19 la palanca de servicio *m* (la
manivela)
– *flushing lever (lever)*
20 el radiador
– *radiator*
21 la nervadura del radiador
– *radiator rib*
22 el sistema de dos tuberías *f*
– *two-pipe system*
23 la tubería de salida *f*
– *flow pipe*
24 la tubería de vuelta *f*
– *return pipe*
25 la estufa (el radiador) de gas *m*
– *gas heater*
26-37 grifería *f*
– *plumbing fixtures*
26 el sifón inodoro
– *trap (anti-syphon trap)*
27 la batería mezcladora para el
lavamanos
– *mixer tap* (Am. *mixing faucet*) *for
washbasins*
28 el grifo de agua *f* caliente
– *hot tap*

29 el grifo de agua *f* fría
– *cold tap*
30 la ducha de tubo *m* flexible
– *extendible shower attachment*
31 el grifo de lavabo *m*
– *water tap (pillar tap) for washbasins*
32 el huso
– *spindle top*
33 la capa protectora
– *shield*
34 el grifo de agua *f* (el grifo, el grifo
codillo, la canilla; *Mé.:* el bitoque)
– *draw-off tap* (Am. *faucet*)
35 el grifo de doble cierre *m*, con
junta *f* especial
– *supatap*
36 el grifo giratorio
– *swivel tap*
37 el pulsador a presión *f*
– *flushing valve*
38-52 accesorios *m* de tubo *m*
– *fittings*
38 la juntura con rosca *f* macho *m*
– *joint with male thread*
39 la reducción macho-hembra
– *reducing socket (reducing coupler)*
40 la atornilladura de ángulo *m*
– *elbow screw joint (elbow coupling)*
41 la reducción macho-hembra con
rosca *f* interior
– *reducing socket (reducing coupler) with female thread*
42 la atornilladura
– *screw joint*
43 el manguito
– *coupler (socket)*
44 la pieza en forma *f* de T (la te)
– *T-joint (T-junction joint, tee)*
45 la atornilladura de ángulo *m* con
rosca *f* interior
– *elbow screw joint with female
thread*
46 el recodo
– *bend*
47 la pieza en forma *f* de T con rosca
f interior hembra *f*
– *T-joint (T-junction joint, tee) with
female taper thread*
48 la juntura de techo *m*
– *ceiling joint*
49 el codo reductor
– *reducing elbow*
50 la cruz
– *cross*
51 la juntura de codo *m* con rosca *f*
macho
– *elbow joint with male thread*
52 el codo
– *elbow joint*
53-57 fijación *f* de tubos *m*
– *pipe supports*
53 la abrazadera de tubo *m*
– *saddle clip*
54 la abrazadera de espaciamiento *m*
– *spacing bracket*
55 la espiga
– *plug*
56 las abrazaderas de tubo *m* simples
– *pipe clips*

57 la abrazaderas de distanciamiento
m de dos piezas *f* (el puente)
– *two-piece spacing clip*
58-86 herramientas *f* de instalación *f*
(herramientas *f* de fontanero *m*)
– *plumber's tools, gas fitter's tools*
58 las tenazas de gasista *m*
– *gas pliers*
59 la llave para tubos *m*
– *footprints*
60 los alicates universales
– *combination cutting pliers*
61 la llave corrediza (el cocodrilo, el
sargento)
– *water pump pliers*
62 los alicates de boca *f* plana
– *flat-nose pliers*
63 la chaveta de boquilla *f* roscada
– *nipple key*
64 las tenazas de puntas *f* redondas
– *round-nose pliers*
65 las tenazas
– *pincers*
66 la llave ajustable [forma sueca]
– *adjustable S-wrench*
67 la llave francesa, una llave de
tuercas *f*
– *screw wrench*
68 la llave inglesa
– *shifting spanner*
69 el destornillador
– *screwdriver*
70 el serrucho de calar o de punta *f*
– *compass saw (keyhole saw)*
71 el arco de sierra *f* de metal *m*
– *hacksaw frame*
72 el serrucho
– *hand saw*
73 el soldador
– *soldering iron*
74 la lámpara de soldar (el soplete;
Amér.: la antorcha)
– *blowlamp (blowtorch) [for soldering]*
75 la cinta aislante
– *sealing tape*
76 el estaño para soldar
– *tin-lead solder*
77 el martillo de porra *f* (la maza)
– *club hammer*
78 el martillo de mano *f*
– *hammer*
79 el nivel de agua *f* (el nivel de burbuja *f*)
– *spirit level*
80 el tornillo de banco *m* de cerrajero *m*
– *steel-leg vice* (Am. *vise*)
81 el tornillo de banco *m* para tubos *m*
(el sujetatubos)
– *pipe vice* (Am. *vise*)
82 la curvadora de tubos *m*
– *pipe-bending machine*
83 la forma curvada (la cimbra)
– *former (template)*
84 el cortatubos
– *pipe cutter*
85 la terraja de cojinetes *m*
– *hand die*
86 la máquina de terrajar
– *screw-cutting machine (thread-cutting machine)*

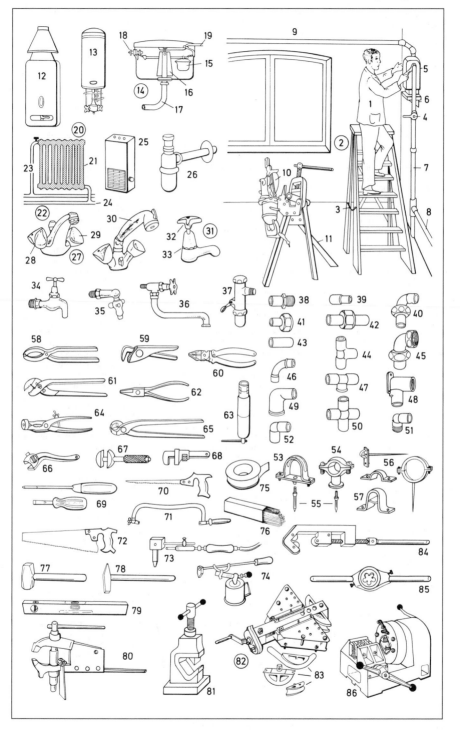

1 el instalador-electricista (el electricista)
- *electrician (electrical fitter, wireman)*
2 el pulsador del timbre para bajo voltaje *m*
- *bell push (doorbell) for low-voltage safety current*
3 el interfono con botón *m* de llamada *f*
- *house telephone with call button*
4 el interruptor con mando *m* basculante empotrable
- *[flush-mounted] rocker switch*
5 la caja de enchufe *m* empotrable
- *[flush-mounted] earthed socket (wall socket, plug point,* Am. *wall outlet, convenience outlet, outlet)*
6 la caja de enchufe *m* doble empotrable
- *[surface-mounted] earthed double socket (double wall socket, double plug point,* Am. *double wall outlet, double convenience outlet, double outlet)*
7 la caja combinada (un interruptor y un enchufe)
- *switched socket (switch and socket)*
8 la caja (el adaptador) de cuatro enchufes *m*
- *four-socket (four-way) adapter (socket)*
9 la clavija macho (la clavija de contacto *m; Amér.:* la ficha)
- *earthed plug*
10 la alargadera (el cordón prolongador)
- *extension lead (Am. extension cord)*
11 la clavija macho (*Amér.:* la ficha) de la alargadera
- *extension plug*
12 la clavija hembra (el enchufe) de la alargadera
- *extension socket*
13 el enchufe de superficie *f* tripolar [para circuito *m* trifásico] con toma *f* de tierra *f*
- *surface-mounted three-pole earthed socket [for three-phase circuit] with neutral conductor*
14 la clavija trifásica
- *three-phase plug*
15 el timbre eléctrico
- *electric bell (electric buzzer)*
16 el interruptor con cordón *m*
- *pull-switch (cord-operated wall switch)*
17 el interruptor con regulador *m* de voltaje *m* [para ajustar con progresión *f* continua la intensidad de luz *f* de una lámpara]
- *dimmer switch [for smooth adjustment of lamp brightness]*
18 el interruptor giratorio con caja *f* de hierro *m* fundido
- *drill-cast rotary switch*
19 el automático de seguridad *f* de tornillo *m*
- *miniature circuit breaker (screw-in circuit breaker, fuse)*

20 el pulsador automático (el chivato)
- *resetting button*
21 el tornillo calibrado [para fusibles *m* e interruptores *m* automáticos]
- *set screw [for fuses and miniature circuit breakers]*
22 la caja de enchufe *m* empotrable en el suelo
- *underfloor mounting (underfloor sockets)*
23 el enchufe de bisagra *f* de suelo *m* para corriente *f* y líneas *f* de comunicación *f*
- *hinged floor socket for power lines and communication lines*
24 el enchufe empotrable en el suelo con tapadera *f* de bisagra *f*
- *sunken floor socket with hinged lid (snap lid)*
25 el enchufe de superficie *f* con caja *f* de toma *f*
- *surface-mounted socket outlet (plug point) box*
26 la lámpara de bosillo *m,* una lámpara de pilas *f* (la linterna)
- *pocket torch, a torch (Am. flashlight)*
27 la pila seca (la pila de linterna *f*)
- *dry cell battery*
28 el muelle de contacto *m*
- *contact spring*
29 la regleta (la clema)
- *strip of thermoplastic connectors*
30 el alambre de acero *m* para pasar el conductor
- *steel draw-in wire (draw wire) with threading key, and ring attached*
31 el cajetín del contador
- *electricity meter cupboard*
32 el contador de la electricidad
- *electricity meter*
33 el interruptor automático
- *miniature circuit breakers (miniature circuit breaker consumer unit)*
34 la cinta aislante
- *insulating tape (Am. friction tape)*
35 el portafusibles
- *fuse holder*
36 el fusible, un cartucho con pieza *f* fusible
- *circuit breaker (fuse), a fuse cartridge with fusible element*
37 el indicador de color *m* (que señala el paso de corriente *f*)
- *colour (Am. color) indicator [showing current rating]*
38 u. 39 el contacto
- *contact maker*
40 la grapa de plástico *m*
- *cable clip*
41 el voltímetro
- *universal test meter (multiple meter for measuring current and voltage)*
42 el cable termoplástico resistente a la humedad
- *thermoplastic moisture-proof cable*
43 el conductor de cobre *m*
- *copper conductor*

44 el cable de tres polos *m*
- *three-core cable*
45 el soldador eléctrico
- *electric soldering iron*
46 el destornillador
- *screwdriver*
47 la llave corrediza (el cocodrilo, el sargento)
- *water pump pliers*
48 el casco de seguridad *f* de plástico *m* antigolpes
- *shock-resisting safety helmet*
49 el maletín (la caja) de herramientas *f*
- *tool case*
50 los alicates redondos (los alicates de puntas *f* redondas)
- *round-nose pliers*
51 los alicates para cortar
- *cutting pliers*
52 la sierra pequeña
- *junior hacksaw*
53 los alicates universales
- *combination cutting pliers*
54 la funda protectora
- *insulated handle*
55 el comprobador (el detector) de electricidad *f* (de tensión *f*)
- *continuity tester*
56 la bombilla incandescente (la bombilla; *Amér. Central, Col., Pan., P. Rico y S. Dgo.:* el bombillo)
- *electric light bulb (general service lamp, filament lamp)*
57 la ampolla de vidrio *m*
- *glass bulb (bulb)*
58 el filamento luminoso incandescente
- *coiled-coil filament*
59 la rosca de la bombilla
- *screw base*
60 el casquillo portabombillas (portalámparas *m*)
- *lampholder*
61 el tubo fluorescente
- *fluorescent tube*
62 el portatubos fluorescentes
- *bracket for fluorescent tubes*
63 la navaja de electricista *m*
- *electrician's knife*
64 los alicates pelacables
- *wire strippers*
65 el portalámparas de bayoneta *f*
- *bayonet fitting*
66 el enchufe tripolar con interruptor *m*
- *three-pin socket with switch*
67 la clavija tripolar
- *three-pin plug*
68 el portafusibles con fusible *m* de cable *m*
- *fuse carrier with fuse wire*
69 la bombilla de bayoneta *f*
- *light bulb with bayonet fitting*

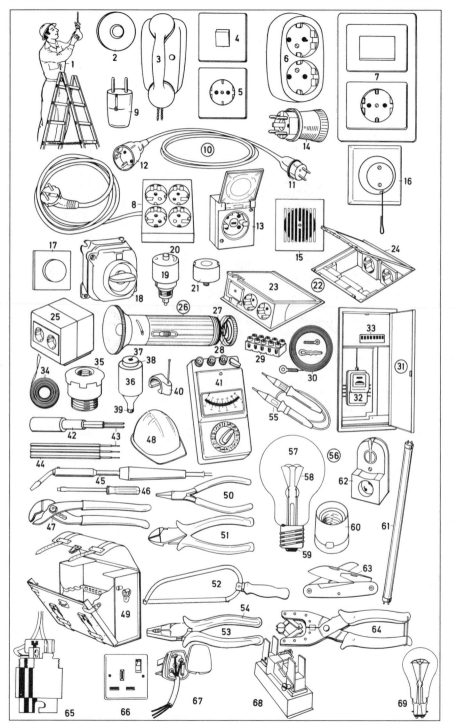

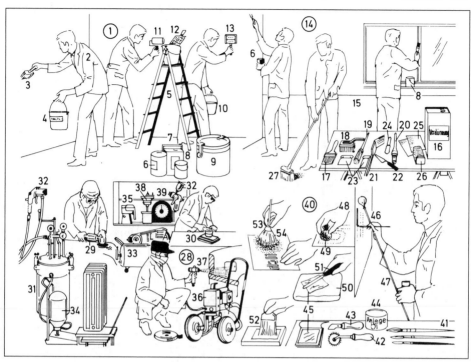

1 la pintura
– *painting*
2 el pintor
– *painter*
3 la brocha de recubrir
– *paintbrush*
4 la pintura de dispersión *f*
– *emulsion paint (emulsion)*
5 la escalera plegable (la escalera doble)
– *stepladder*
6 el bote de pintura *f*
– *can (tin) of paint*
7 *u.* **8** las latas de pintura *f*
– *cans (tins) of paint*
7 la lata con mango *m* (con empuñadura *f*)
– *can (tin) with fixed handle*
8 la lata con asa *f*
– *paint kettle*
9 el barril de pintura *f*
– *drum of paint*
10 el cubo de pintura *f*
– *paint bucket*
11 el rodillo de pintar
– *paint roller*
12 la rejilla raspadora
– *grill [for removing excess paint from the roller]*
13 el rodillo para granear
– *stippling roller*
14 **el barnizado**
– *varnishing*
15 el zócalo pintado con óleo *m*
– *oil-painted dado*
16 el bidón de disolvente *m*
– *canister for thinner*
17 la brocha plana (para superficies *f*)
– *flat brush for larger surfaces (flat wall brush)*
18 la brocha de motear
– *stippler*

19 el pincel redondo
– *fitch*
20 el pincel para resaltar los contornos
– *cutting-in brush*
21 el pincel para los radiadores
– *radiator brush (flay brush)*
22 la espátula de pintor *m*
– *paint scraper*
23 la espátula japonesa (el raspador)
– *scraper*
24 el cuchillo para la masilla
– *putty knife*
25 el papel de lija *f*
– *sandpaper*
26 el bloque para lijar
– *sandpaper block*
27 el cepillo para el suelo
– *floor brush*
28 **el pulimento y la pintura con pistola *f*** (el pulverizado)
– ***sanding and spraying***
29 la lijadora
– *grinder*
30 la lijadora orbital
– *sander*
31 el depósito del aire
– *pressure pot*
32 la pistola de pulverización *f*
– *spray gun*
33 el compresor
– *compressor (air compressor)*
34 el aparato para rellenar de agua *f* los radiadores
– *flow coating machine for flow coating radiators, etc.*
35 la pistola pulverizadora de mano *f*
– *hand spray*
36 el equipo de pulverizar sin aire *m*
– *airless spray unit*

37 la pistola pulverizadora sin aire *m*
– *airless spray gun*
38 el cubilete de salida *f* para medir la viscosidad
– *efflux viscometer*
39 el cuentasegundos
– *seconds timer*
40 **la inscripción y el dorado**
– ***lettering and gilding***
41 el pincel para las letras
– *lettering brush (signwriting brush, pencil)*
42 la ruleta para calcar
– *tracing wheel*
43 el cuchillo para plantillas *f*
– *stencil knife*
44 el aceite de aplique *m*
– *oil gold size*
45 el oro de aplique *m* (el oro en hojas *f,* la hoja de oro *m*)
– *gold leaf*
46 el trazado de los contornos
– *outline drawing*
47 el bastón de pintura *f*
– *mahlstick*
48 el pulimento del dibujo
– *pouncing*
49 la bolsa de calco *m*
– *pounce bag*
50 la almohadilla para el oro
– *gilder's cushion*
51 el cuchillo para el oro
– *gilder's knife*
52 el cepillo para coger las hojas de oro *m*
– *sizing gold leaf*
53 el relleno de las letras con pintura *f* granulada
– *filling in the letters with stipple paint*
54 el pincel de dorador (el pincel de motear)
– *gilder's mop*

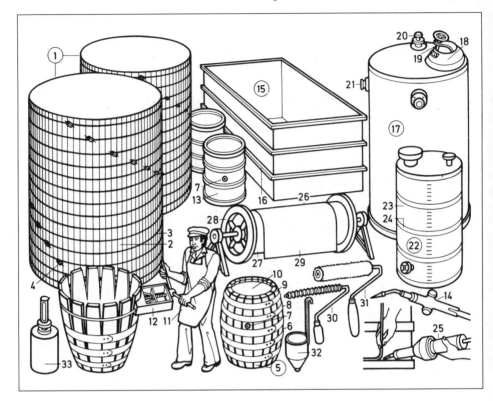

1-33 la tonelería y la construcción de depósitos *m*
- *cooper's and tank construction engineer's workshops*
1 la cuba
- *tank*
2 la circunferencia hecha de duelas *f*
- *circumference made of staves (staved circumference)*
3 el aro metálico (el cincho)
- *iron rod*
4 el tensor
- *turnbuckle*
5 el tonel (el barril)
- *barrel (cask)*
6 el cuerpo del barril
- *body of barrel (of cask)*
7 el agujero del barril (el canillero)
- *bunghole*
8 el aro del barril (el cincho)
- *band (hoop) of barrel*
9 la duela
- *barrel stave*
10 el témpano
- *barrelhead (heading)*
11 el tonelero
- *cooper*

12 el gato de armar
- *trusser*
13 el bidón metálico
- *drum*
14 el soplete de soldar autógeno
- *gas welding torch*
15 la cuba de pintura *f* de materia *f* termoplástica
- *staining vat, made of thermoplastics*
16 el cerco de refuerzo *m* perfilado
- *iron reinforcing bands*
17 el depósito de bodega *f*, hecho de resina *f* de poliéster *m* reforzada con fibra *f* de vidrio *m*
- *storage container, made of glass fibre (Am. glass fiber) reinforced polyester resin*
18 el agujero de entrada *f*
- *manhole*
19 la tapadera del agujero de entrada *f* con *f* rueda de rosca *f*
- *manhole cover with handwheel*
20 el soporte para brida *f*
- *flange mount*
21 el obturador
- *flange-type stopcock*

22 el depósito graduado
- *measuring tank*
23 la envoltura (la pared)
- *shell (circumference)*
24 la virola
- *shrink ring*
25 la pistola de aire *m* caliente
- *hot-air gun*
26 el tubo de resina *f* sintética reforzada con fibra *f* de vidrio *m*
- *roller made of glass fibre (Am. glass fiber) reinforced synthetic resin*
27 el cilindro
- *cylinder*
28 el disco de soporte *m* del cilindro
- *flange*
29 el tejido de fibra *f* de vidrio *m*
- *glass cloth*
30 el cilindro acanalado
- *grooved roller*
31 el rodillo de piel *f* de cordero *m*
- *lambskin roller*
32 el cazo para medir la viscosidad
- *ladle for testing viscosity*
33 el dosificador del endurecedor
- *measuring vessel for hardener*

1-25 el taller de peletero *m*
- *furrier's workroom*
1 el peletero
- *furrier*
2 la pistola pulverizadora de vapor *m*
- *steam spray gun*
3 la plancha de vapor *m*
- *steam iron*
4 la máquina de sacudir
- *beating machine*
5 la máquina de cortar para alargar las pieles
- *cutting machine for letting out furskins*
6 la piel no cortada
- *uncut furskin*
7 la piel cortada en tiras *f*
- *let-out strips (let-out sections)*
8 la trabajadora de la piel (la peletera; la costurera de piel *f*)
- *fur worker*
9 la máquina de coser las pieles
- *fur-sewing machine*
10 el ventilador
- *blower for letting out*
11-21 pieles *m*
- *furskins*
11 la piel de visón *m*
- *mink skin*

12 la flor del cuero (la cara del pelo, el lado del pelo)
- *fur side*
13 el lado del cuero
- *leather side*
14 la piel cortada
- *cut furskin*
15 la piel de lince *m* antes de ser alargada
- *lynx skin before letting out*
16 la piel de lince *m* alargada
- *let-out lynx skin*
17 la flor del cuero (la cara del pelo, el lado del pelo)
- *fur side*
18 el lado del cuero
- *leather side*
19 la piel de visón *m* alargada
- *let-out mink skin*
20 la piel de lince *m* empalmada
- *lynx fur, sewn together (sewn)*
21 la piel de astracán *m* (de breitschwanz *m*)
- *broadtail*
22 la puntilla para la piel
- *fur marker*
23 la trabajadora de la piel (la cortadora de la piel; la peletera)
- *fur worker*

24 el abrigo de visón *m*
- *mink coat*
25 el abrigo de ocelote *m*
- *ocelot coat*

1-73 el taller de carpintero *m* (la carpintería)
– *joiner's workshop*
1-28 las herramientas de carpintero *m*
– *joiner's tools*
1 la escofina de madera *f*
– *wood rasp*
2 la escofina de media caña *f*
– *wood file*
3 el serrucho de calar (el serrucho de punta *f*)
– *compass saw (keyhole saw)*
4 la manija del serrucho
– *saw handle*
5 el mazo de madera *f* cuadrado
– *[square-headed] mallet*
6 la escuadra de carpintero *m*
– *try square*
7-11 formón *m* **de carpintero** *m*
– *chisels*
7 el escoplo de alfajía *f*
– *bevelled-edge chisel (chisel)*
8 el escoplo para agujeros *m* (el escoplo de fijas *f*)
– *mortise (mortice) chisel*
9 la gubia
– *gouge*
10 el mango
– *handle*
11 el escoplo en bisel *m*
– *framing chisel (cant chisel)*
12 el pote para hacer la cola al baño de María
– *glue pot in water bath*
13 el bote con cola *f*, un bote con cola *f* de carpintero *m* (*Col. y Mé.:* un bote con aguacola *f*)
– *glue pot (glue well), an insert for joiner's glue*
14 la prensa de tornillo *m* (el sargento)
– *handscrew*
15-28 cepillos *m* **de carpintero** *m*
– *planes*
15 el cepillo de alisar (*Chile:* el rodón)
– *smoothing plane*
16 el cepillo de desbastar
– *jack plane*
17 el cepillo dentado
– *toothing plane*
18 la empuñadura
– *handle (toat)*
19 la cuña
– *wedge*
20 el hierro (la cuchilla del cepillo)
– *plane iron (cutter)*
21 el hueco de la cuña
– *mouth*
22 la suela (el talón)
– *sole*
23 la parte lateral
– *side*

24 el zoquete (la caja)
– *stock (body)*
25 el cepillo de molduras *f* (el cepillo bocel)
– *rebate (rabbet) plane*
26 la guimbarda
– *router plane (old woman's tooth)*
27 la raedera
– *spokeshave*
28 el cepillo combado (el cepillo en forma *f* de barco *m*)
– *compass plane*
29-37 el banco de carpintero *m*
– *woodworker's bench*
29 el pie
– *foot*
30 el torno frontal
– *front vice (Am. vise)*
31 el tornillo del torno con mango *m*
– *vice (Am. vise) handle*
32 el husillo
– *vice (Am. vise) screw*
33 la mandíbula del torno
– *jaw*
34 la plataforma del banco
– *bench top*
35 el herramental
– *well*
36 el gancho (la uña) del banco (el hierro del banco)
– *bench stop (bench holdfast)*
37 el torno trasero
– *tail vice (Am. vise)*
38 el carpintero
– *cabinet maker (joiner)*
39 la garlopa
– *trying plane*
40 las virutas (*Amér. Central:* los colochos)
– *shavings*
41 el tornillo para madera *f*
– *wood screw*
42 el triscador
– *saw set*
43 la caja para cortar en inglete *m*
– *mitre (Am. miter) box*
44 el serrucho, un serrucho de costilla *f*
– *tenon saw*
45 la cepilladora de regrosar (de poner a grueso *m*) las maderas
– *thicknesser (thicknessing machine)*
46 la mesa de cepillado *m*, la mesa con los rodillos
– *thicknessing table with rollers*
47 la defensa contra el retroceso
– *kick-back guard*
48 el colector de virutas *f* con aspirador *m*
– *chip-extractor opening*
49 la fresadora de cadena *f*
– *chain mortising machine (chain mortiser)*

50 la cadena fresadora sin fin *m*
– *endless mortising chain*
51 el dispositivo de fijación *f* de la madera (la abrazadera)
– *clamp (work clamp)*
52 la máquina fresadora de nudo *m*
– *knot hole moulding (Am. molding) machine*
53 la fresa de nudo *m*
– *knot hole cutter*
54 el mandril de sujeción *f* rápido
– *quick-action chuck*
55 la palanca de mano *f*
– *hand lever*
56 la palanca de cambio *m*
– *change-gear handle*
57 la sierra circular para cantear y dar la forma
– *sizing and edging machine*
58 el interruptor principal (el botón de mando *m*)
– *main switch*
59 la hoja de la sierra circular
– *circular-saw (buzz saw) blade*
60 el volante de regulación *f* de la altura
– *height (rise and fall) adjustment wheel*
61 la guía prismática
– *V-way*
62 la mesa para encuadrar la madera
– *framing table*
63 el brazo de extensión *f*
– *extension arm (arm)*
64 la mesa de cantear
– *trimming table*
65 la guía de ingletes *m*
– *fence*
66 el volante para regular la guía
– *fence adjustment handle*
67 la palanca de sujeción *f*
– *clamp lever*
68 la sierra circular para tableros *m*
– *board-sawing machine*
69 el motor móvil (el motor basculante)
– *swivel motor*
70 el dispositivo fijador de los tableros
– *board support*
71 el carro de la sierra
– *saw carriage*
72 el pedal para levantar los rodillos transportadores
– *pedal for raising the transport rollers*
73 el tablero de carpintería *f*
– *blockboard*

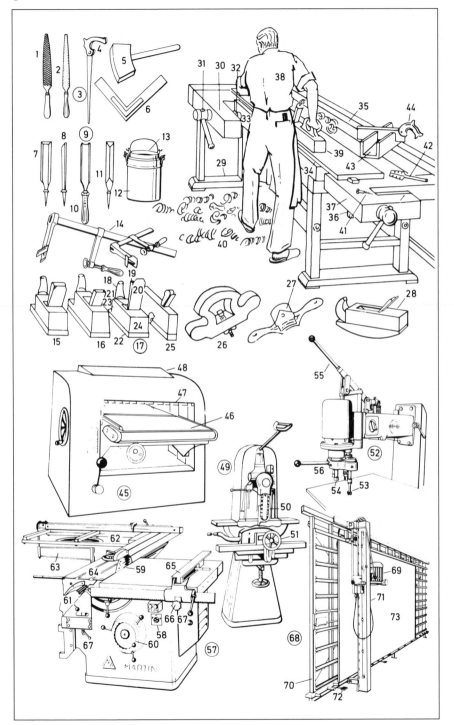

1 la máquina para desenrollar chapas *f* de madera *f*
– *veneer-peeling machine (peeling
machine, peeler)*
2 la chapa de madera *f*
– *veneer*
3 la máquina para pegar (con cola *f*)
la chapa de madera *f*
– *veneer-splicing machine*
4 la canilla de hilo *m* de nylon *m*
– *nylon-thread cop*
5 el dispositivo de costura *f*
– *sewing mechanism*
6 la taladradora de espiga *f*
– *dowel hole boring machine (dowel
hole borer)*
7 el motor de taladrar con broca *f*
de eje *m* hueco
– *boring motor with hollow-shaft
boring bit*
8 el volante de sujeción *f*
– *clamp handle*
9 el estribo de sujeción *f*
– *clamp*
10 la uña de sujeción *f*
– *clamping shoe*
11 el tope (el riel de tope *m*)
– *stop bar*
12 la máquina afiladora de los cantos
– *edge sander (edge-sanding
machine)*
13 el rodillo tensor con brazo *m* de
extensión *f*
– *tension roller with extension arm*
14 el tornillo para regular la cinta
abrasiva
– *sanding belt regulator (regulating
handle)*
15 la cinta abrasiva sin fin *m*
– *endless sanding belt (sand belt)*
16 la palanca de sujeción de la cinta
– *belt-tensioning lever*
17 la mesa de apoyo *m* inclinable
– *canting table (tilting table)*
18 el rodillo de la cinta
– *belt roller*
19 la regla de ángulo *m* para ingletes
m (la guía para ingletes *m*)
– *angling fence for mitres (*Am.
miters)*
20 el colector del polvo articulado
– *opening dust hood*
21 el dispositivo para regular la profundidad de la mesa de apoyo *m*
– *rise adjustment of the table*
22 el volante para regular la altura
de la mesa
– *rise adjustment wheel for the table*
23 el tornillo prisionero para regular
la altura de la mesa
– *clamping screw for the table rise
adjustment*

24 la repisa de la mesa
– *console*
25 el pie de la máquina
– *foot of the machine*
26 la máquina para pegar los cantos
– *edge-veneering machine*
27 el disco abrasivo
– *sanding wheel*
28 el dispositivo de aspiración *f* del
polvo de esmerilado *m*
– *sanding dust extractor*
29 el dispositivo de pegar
– *splicing head*
30 la máquina lijadora de cinta *f* simple (de una sola cinta)
– *single-belt sanding machine (single-belt sander)*
31 el recubrimiento de la cinta
– *belt guard*
32 el recubrimiento circular de la
cinta
– *band wheel cover*
33 el extractor
– *extractor fan (exhaust fan)*
34 el patín lijador del bastidor
– *frame-sanding pad*
35 la mesa de lijar
– *sanding table*
36 el ajuste de precisión *f*
– *fine adjustment*
37 la máquina de precisión *f* para
cortar y ensamblar
– *fine cutter and jointer*
38 el carro de la sierra (la combinación de sierra *f* y cepillo *m*) con
transmisión *f* por cadena *f*
– *saw carriage with chain drive*
39 el soporte del cable colgado
– *trailing cable hanger (trailing
cable support)*
40 el tubo extractor del aire
– *air extractor pipe*
41 el riel (la guía) transportador(a)
– *rail*
42 la prensa de bastidor *m* (la prensa
de encuadrar)
– *frame-cramping (frame-clamping)
machine*
43 el soporte del bastidor
– *frame stand*
44 la pieza de trabajo *m*, un bastidor
de ventana *f*
– *workpiece, a window frame*
45 el conducto de llegada *f* del aire
comprimido
– *compressed-air line*
46 el cilindro de presión *f*
– *pressure cylinder*
47 el émbolo (el patín de presión *f*)
– *pressure foot*
48 la sujeción del bastidor
– *frame-mounting device*

49 la máquina para chapear rápida-
mente
– *rapid-veneer press*
50 el suelo (el lecho) de la prensa
– *bed*
51 el techo de la prensa (la prensa)
– *press*
52 el pistón de la prensa
– *pressure piston*

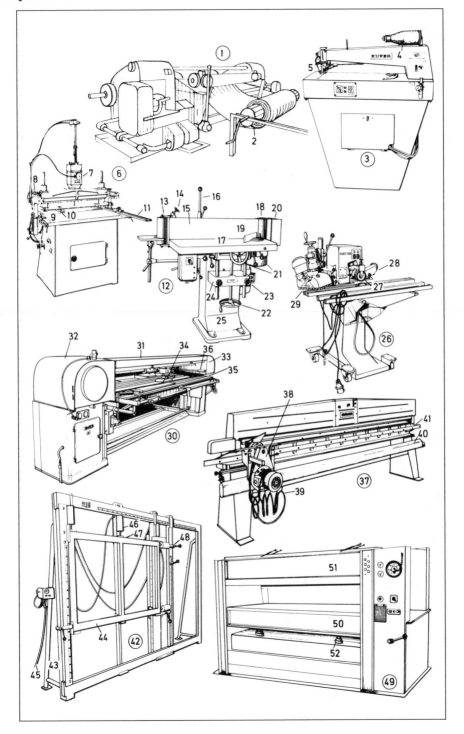

1-34 el armario de herramientas *f* para bricolaje *m* (para chapuzas *f*)
– *tool cupboard (tool cabinet) for do-it-yourself work*
1 el cepillo de alisar
– *smoothing plane*
2 el juego de llaves *f* de boca *f*
– *set of fork spanners (fork wrenches, open-end wrenches)*
3 la sierra de arco *m*
– *hacksaw*
4 el destornillador
– *screwdriver*
5 el destornillador de estrella *f* (americano)
– *cross-point screwdriver*
6 el raspador de sierra *f* (la escofina)
– *saw rasp*
7 el martillo (*Chile y Perú:* el combo)
– *hammer*
8 la escofina de madera *f*
– *wood rasp*
9 la lima gruesa
– *roughing file*
10 el tornillo (el torno) de banco *m* pequeño (*C. Rica, Chile y Ec.:* la taquilla)
– *small vice (Am. vise)*
11 la llave para apretar los tubos *m*
– *corner pipe wrench*
12 la llave de tubo *m* (la llave corrediza, el sargento, el cocodrilo)
– *water pump pliers*
13 las tenazas
– *pincers*
14 los alicates universales
– *all-purpose wrench*
15 los alicates pelacables
– *wire stripper and cutter*
16 la taladradora eléctrica
– *electric drill*
17 la sierra para metales *m*
– *hacksaw*
18 el cubo para el yeso (el cuezo)
– *plaster cup*
19 el soldador
– *soldering iron*
20 el hilo de estaño *m* para soldar
– *tin-lead solder wire*
21 el disco de piel *f* de cordero *m* (el bonete de pulir)
– *lamb's wool polishing bonnet*
22 el disco de pulir (el disco de goma *f*) para la taladradora
– *rubber backing disc (disk)*
23 la muela abrasiva (el disco abrasivo)
– *grinding wheel*
24 el cepillo metálico (con forma *f* de disco *m*)
– *wire wheel brush*
25 el papel de lija *f* (con forma *f*) de disco *m* (el disco lija *f*)
– *sanding discs (disks)*

26 la escuadra con espaldón *m*
– *try square*
27 el serrucho
– *hand saw*
28 el cortador universal
– *universal cutter*
29 el nivel de agua *f* (el nivel de burbuja *f*)
– *spirit level*
30 el formón de carpintero *m*
– *firmer chisel*
31 el punzón (el granete)
– *centre* (Am. *center*) *punch*
32 el punzón de mano *f* (el sacaclavos)
– *nail punch*
33 el metro plegable
– *folding rule (rule)*
34 la caja para las piezas pequeñas
– *storage box for small parts*
35 la caja de las herramientas
– *tool box*
36 la cola blanca (la cola de carpintero; *Col. y Mé.:* la aguacola)
– *woodworking adhesive*
37 la espátula
– *stripping knife*
38 la cinta adhesiva
– *adhesive tape*
39 la caja con compartimientos para clavos *m*, tornillos *m* y espigas *f*
– *storage box with compartments for nails, screws, and plugs*
40 el martillo de cerrajero *m*
– *machinist's hammer*
41 el banco de trabajo *m* plegable
– *collapsible workbench (collapsible bench)*
42 el dispositivo de sujeción *f*
– *jig*
43 la taladradora *f* eléctrica con percutor *m*
– *electric percussion drill (electric hammer drill)*
44 la empuñadura de pistola *f* (la empuñadura de revólver *m*)
– *pistol grip*
45 la empuñadura adicional
– *side grip*
46 el pulsador para el cambio de velocidad *f*
– *gearshift switch*
47 la empuñadura con distanciador *m*
– *handle with depth gauge* (Am. *gage*)
48 el cabezal portabrocas
– *chuck*
49 la broca espiral
– *twist bit (twist drill)*
50-55 accesorios *m* y suplementos *m* para taladradora *f* eléctrica
– *attachments for an electric drill*

50 la sierra mixta (circular y de vaivén *m*)
– *combined circular saw (buzz saw) and bandsaw*
51 el torno para madera *f*
– *wood-turning lathe*
52 el protector de la sierra circular
– *circular saw attachment*
53 la lijadora orbital
– *orbital sanding attachment (orbital sander)*
54 el soporte para la taladradora
– *drill stand*
55 el recortasetos
– *hedge-trimming attachment (hedge trimmer)*
56 la pistola de soldar
– *soldering gun*
57 el soldador
– *soldering iron*
58 el soldador instantáneo
– *high-speed soldering iron*
59 la tapicería, el tapizado de un sillón
– *upholstery, upholstering an armchair*
60 la tela del forro
– *fabric (material) for upholstery*
61 el chapucero (el trabajador que hace toda clase de oficios, el manitas)
– *do-it-yourself enthusiast*

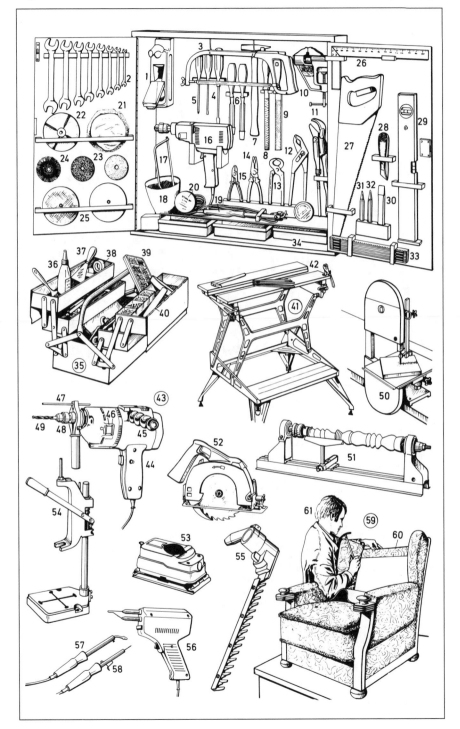

1-26 la tornería (el taller de tornero *m*)
– **turnery** (*turner's workshop*)
1 el torno al aire (el torno para madera *f*)
– *wood-turning lathe (lathe)*
2 el banco del torno de punta *f*
– *lathe bed*
3 el reóstato de puesta *f* en marcha *f*
– *starting resistance (starting resistor)*
4 la caja de engranajes *m*
– *gearbox*
5 el soporte de la herramienta de mano *f*
– *tool rest*
6 el mandril de agujero *m* simple
– *chuck*
7 el cabezal móvil
– *tailstock*
8 la punta fija
– *centre* (Am. *center*)
9 la polea, una garrucha con perno *m* de arrastre *m*
– *driving plate with pin*
10 el mandril de dos mordazas *f*
– *two-jaw chuck*
11 la broca de centrar de tres puntas *f* (la broca de madera *f*)
– *live centre* (Am. *center*)

12 la sierra de calar (la sierra de contornear)
– *fretsaw*
13 la hoja de la sierra de contornear
– *fretsaw blade*
14, 15, 24 herramientas *f* de tornero *m*
– *turning tools*
14 el peine para roscado *m* interior de madera *f*
– *thread chaser, for cutting threads in wood*
15 el punzón, para practicar el agujero preparatorio del centrado
– *gouge, for rough turning*
16 la broca de cuchara *f*
– *spoon bit (shell bit)*
17 el gancho circular
– *hollowing tool*
18 el calibrador exterior
– *outside calliper (caliper)*
19 la pieza de madera *f* torneada
– *turned work (turned wood)*
20 el maestro tornero (el tornero)
– *master turner (turner)*
21 la madera en bruto *m*
– *[piece of] rough wood*

22 el berbiquí de carrete *m* (*Amér. Central, Ec. y Perú:* el biriquí)
– *drill*
23 el calibrador interior
– *inside calliper (caliper)*
24 el escoplo de acanalar
– *parting tool*
25 el papel de lija *f*
– *glass paper (sandpaper, emery paper)*
26 las virutas
– *shavings*

1-40 la cestería
- *basket making (basketry, basketwork)*

1-4 clases *f* de trenzado *m*
- *weaves (strokes)*

1 el enrejado
- *randing*

2 el cruzadillo
- *rib randing*

3 el trenzado en series *f* diagonales
- *oblique randing*

4 el trenzado simple, un enrejado de mimbre *m*
- *randing, a piece of wickerwork (screen work)*

5 la trama horizontal
- *weaver*

6 la armazón (el montante)
- *stake*

7 el tablero de trabajo *m*
- *workboard; also: lapboard*

8 el listón transversal
- *screw block*

9 el agujero para fijar el listón
- *hole for holding the block*

10 el caballete
- *stand*

11 el cesto hecho con virutas *f*
- *chip basket (spale basket)*

12 la viruta
- *chip (spale)*

13 la tina de remojo *m*
- *soaking tub*

14 las varillas de mimbre *m*
- *willow stakes (osier stakes)*

15 los palos de mimbre *m*
- *willow rods (osier rods)*

16 el cesto (*Bol., Col., Cuba, Chile y Perú:* el balay), un trabajo trenzado
- *basket, a piece of wickerwork (basketwork)*

17 el ribete
- *border*

18 el trenzado lateral
- *woven side*

19 el fondo
- *round base*

20 el trenzado del fondo
- *woven base*

21 la cruz del fondo
- *slath*

22-24 el trabajo de bastidor *m* (de armazón *f*)
- *covering a frame*

22 la armazón (el bastidor)
- *frame*

23 el cabo
- *end*

24 la varilla guía
- *rib*

25 el varillaje
- *upsett*

26 las gramíneas; *clases:* esparto *m*, alfalfa *f*
- *grass; kinds: esparto grass, alfalfa grass*

27 la caña
- *rush (bulrush, reed mace)*

28 el junco (cordón *m* de junco *m* de la China)
- *reed (China reed, string)*

29 la rafia
- *raffia (bast)*

30 la paja
- *straw*

31 la caña de bambú *m*
- *bamboo cane*

32 la rota (el bejuco)
- *rattan (ratan) chair cane*

33 el cestero
- *basket maker*

34 el curvador
- *bending tool*

35 el rajador
- *cutting point (bodkin)*

36 el batidor
- *rapping iron*

37 las tenazas
- *pincers*

38 la raedera
- *picking knife*

39 el cepillo para las varillas guías
- *shave*

40 la sierra de arco *m*
- *hacksaw*

1-8 la fragua con el fuego de fragua *f*
– *hearth (forge) with blacksmith's fire*
1 la fragua
– *hearth (forge)*
2 el badil (la pala para mover el fuego)
– *shovel (slice)*
3 el escobillón para la extinción
– *swab*
4 el hurgón
– *rake*
5 el atizador
– *poker*
6 la llegada del aire
– *blast pipe (tue iron)*
7 la campana de la chimenea
– *chimney (cowl, hood)*
8 la pila para el remojo
– *water trough (quenching trough, bosh)*
9 el martillo neumático (el martillo pilón) de herrería *f*
– *power hammer*
10 la maza
– *ram (tup)*
11-16 el yunque
– *anvil*
11 el yunque
– *anvil*
12 el cuerno cuadrado
– *flat beak (beck, bick)*

13 el cuerno redondo
– *round beak (beck, bick)*
14 la tabla auxiliar del yunque
– *auxiliary table*
15 el pie del yunque
– *foot*
16 el tronco para golpear (el bloque para remachar)
– *upsetting block*
17 la placa matriz de agujeros *m*
– *swage block*
18 la máquina para afilar las herramientas (la afiladora)
– *tool-grinding machine (tool grinder)*
19 la muela abrasiva
– *grinding wheel*
20 el aparejo (el polipasto)
– *block and tackle*
21 el banco de trabajo *m*
– *workbench (bench)*
22-39 herramientas *f* **de herrería** *f*
– *blacksmith's tools*
22 el martillo a dos manos *f* (el macho de fragua *f*; *Amér.:* el marrón)
– *sledge hammer*
23 el martillo de mano *f*
– *blacksmith's hand hammer*
24 las tenazas de boca *f* plana
– *flat tongs*

25 las tenazas de pico *m* redondo
– *round tongs*
26 las partes de los martillos
– *parts of the hammer*
27 el corte (la pala, la peña)
– *peen (pane, pein)*
28 el plano (el cotillo)
– *face*
29 el ojo
– *eye*
30 el mango (el astil)
– *haft*
31 la cuña
– *cotter punch*
32 la tajadera
– *hardy (hardie)*
33 el martillo plano
– *set hammer*
34 el martillo de calderero *m*
– *sett (set, sate)*
35 la aplanadora de forja (el martillo de allanar)
– *flat-face hammer (flatter)*
36 el martillo para agujerear
– *round punch*
37 las tenazas angulares
– *angle tongs*
38 el cincel tajador (el cortafrío)
– *blacksmith's chisel (scaling hammer, chipping hammer)*
39 el hierro para curvar
– *moving iron (bending iron)*

1 la instalación de aire *m* comprimido
– *compressed-air system*
2 el motor eléctrico
– *electric motor*
3 el compresor
– *compressor*
4 el depósito de aire *m* comprimido
– *compressed-air tank*
5 la canalización (la tubería) del aire comprimido
– *compressed-air line*
6 el destornillador de percusión *f* de aire *m* comprimido
– *percussion screwdriver*
7 el aparato para afilar (la máquina afiladora de taller *m*)
– *pedestal grinding machine (floor grinding machine)*
8 la muela
– *grinding wheel*
9 la cubierta de protección *f*
– *guard*
10 el remolque
– *trailer*
11 el tambor del freno
– *brake drum*
12 las zapatas del freno
– *brake shoe*
13 el forro del freno
– *brake lining*

14 la caja de prueba *f*
– *testing kit*
15 el aparato para medir el aire comprimido (el manómetro)
– *pressure gauge* (Am. *gage*)
16 el banco de prueba *f* de los frenos, un banco de prueba *f* de los frenos de rodillos *m*
– *brake-testing equipment, a rolling road*
17 el foso
– *pit*
18 el rodillo de frenada *f*
– *braking roller*
19 el aparato de registro *m* (el registrador)
– *meter (recording meter)*
20 el torno de precisión *f* para el tambor del freno
– *precision lathe for brake drums*
21 la rueda de camión *m*
– *lorry wheel*
22 el mecanismo de perforación *f*
– *boring mill*
23 la sierra rápida, una sierra de arco *m*
– *power saw, a hacksaw (power hacksaw)*
24 el tornillo de banco *m*
– *vice* (Am. *vise*)
25 el arco de la sierra *f*
– *saw frame*

26 la canalización de refrigerante *m*
– *coolant supply pipe*
27 la remachadora
– *riveting machine*
28 el chasis de remolque *m* en construcción *f*
– *trailer frame (chassis) under construction*
29 el aparato para soldar en atmósfera *f* controlada (con gas *m* inerte)
– *inert-gas welding equipment*
30 el rectificador de corriente *f*
– *rectifier*
31 la unidad de control (el aparato de mando *m*)
– *control unit*
32 la botella de CO$_2$
– *CO$_2$ cylinder*
33 el yunque
– *anvil*
34 la fragua con el fuego de fragua *f*
– *hearth (forge) with blacksmith's fire*
35 el carrito de soldadura *f* autógena
– *trolley for gas cylinders*
36 el vehículo en reparación *f*, un tractor
– *vehicle under repair, a tractor*

139 Taller de forja libre y en estampa (Forja industrial)

1 el horno de empuje *m* (impulsión
f) continuo(a) con solera *f* de
rejilla *f* para calentar los materiales redondos (redondeles *m*)
– *continuous furnace with grid
hearth for annealing of round
stock*
2 la puerta (la boca) de descarga *f*
– *discharge opening (discharge
door)*
3 el quemador de gas *m*
– *gas burners*
4 la puerta de carga *f*
– *charging door*
5 el martillo pilón de contragolpe *m*
– *counterblow hammer*
6 la maza superior
– *upper ram*
7 la maza inferior
– *lower ram*
8 la guía de la masa
– *ram guide*
9 la impulsión hidráulica (el empuje
hidráulico)
– *hydraulic drive*
10 el pilar (el montante)
– *column*
11 el martillo estampador de corta
elevación *f*
– *short-stroke drop hammer*
12 la maza del martillo pilón (la
maza, el martillo pilón)
– *ram (tup)*
13 la matriz superior (de forjar en
estampa *f*)
– *upper die block*
14 la matriz inferior (de forjar en
estampa *f*)
– *lower die block*
15 la impulsión hidráulica (el empuje
hidráulico)
– *hydraulic drive*
16 el montante (la armazón) del
martillo pilón
– *frame*
17 el yunque
– *anvil*
18 la prensa de forjar en estampa *f* y
de calibrar
– *forging and sizing press*
19 el pilar (el montante) de la
máquina
– *standard*
20 el tablero de la mesa
– *table*
21 el embrague de fricción *f* de láminas *f*
– *disc (disk) clutch*
22 la tubería del aire comprimido
– *compressed-air pipe*
23 la válvula magnética
– *solenoid valve*

24 el martillo pilón neumático
– *air-lift gravity hammer (air-lift
drop hammer)*
25 el motor de impulsión *f*
– *drive motor*
26 la maza
– *hammer (tup)*
27 el pedal
– *foot control (foot pedal)*
28 la pieza forjada en estampa *f*
– *preshaped (blocked) workpiece*
29 la cabeza guía de la maza
– *hammer guide*
30 el cilindro de la maza
– *hammer cylinder*
31 el yunque (el macho de estampa *f*)
– *anvil*
32 el manipulador para mover la
pieza en la forja libre
– *mechanical manipulator to move
the workpiece in hammer forging*
33 las tenazas (la quijada)
– *dogs*
34 el contrapeso
– *counterweight*
35 la prensa de forja *f* hidráulica
– *hydraulic forging press*
36 el sistema hidráulico
– *crown*
37 la cruceta de cabeza *f*
– *cross head*
38 la matriz superior (de forjar en
estampa *f*)
– *upper die block*
39 la matriz inferior (de forjar en
estampa *f*)
– *lower die block*
40 el tajo del yunque (la chabota)
– *anvil*
41 el pistón hidráulico
– *hydraulic piston*
42 la columna guía
– *pillar guide*
43 el mecanismo de vuelta *f*
– *rollover device*
44 la cadena grúa
– *burden chain (chain sling)*
45 el gancho de la grúa
– *crane hook*
46 la pieza de forja *f*
– *workpiece*
47 el horno de forja *f* de gas *m*
– *gas furnace (gas-fired furnace)*
48 el quemador (el mechero) de gas *m*
– *gas burner*
49 la boca de carga *f*
– *charging opening*
50 la cortina de cadenas *f*
– *chain curtain*
51 la puerta levadiza
– *vertical-lift door*

52 la tubería de aire *m* caliente
– *hot-air duct*
53 el precalentador de aire *m*
– *air preheater*
54 la tubería de conducción *f* del gas
– *gas pipe*
55 el dispositivo de elevación *f* de la
puerta
– *electric door-lifting mechanism*
56 la cortina de aire *m*
– *air blast*

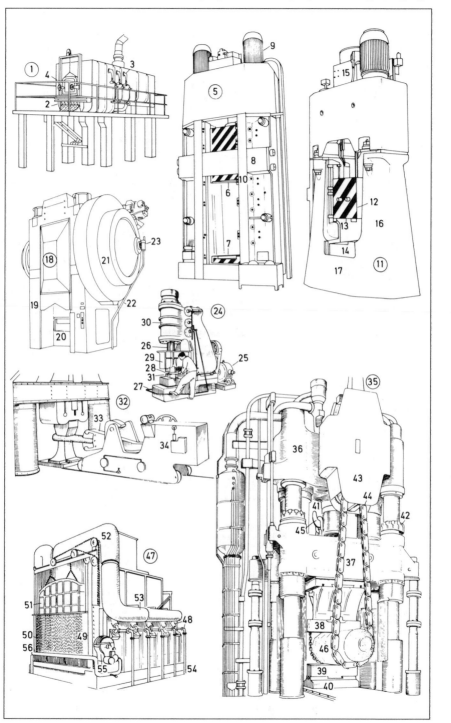

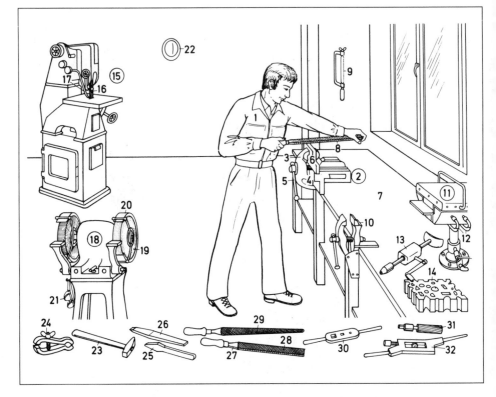

1-22 el taller de cerrajero *m* (la cerrajería)
- **metalwork shop** *(mechanic's workshop, fitter's workshop, locksmith's workshop)*
1 el cerrajero *(ejemplos:* el cerrajero mecánico, el cerrajero de taller *m,* el cerrajero de taller *m* de acero *m)*
- *metalworker (e.g. mechanic, fitter, locksmith; form. also: wrought-iron craftsman)*
2 el tornillo paralelo
- *parallel-jaw vice (Am. vise)*
3 la mandíbula
- *jaw*
4 la barra de rosca *f*
- *screw*
5 la palanca
- *handle*
6 la pieza de trabajo *m*
- *workpiece*
7 el banco de trabajo *m*
- *workbench (bench)*
8 la lima *(clases:* lima *f* bastarda, lima *f* dulce, lima *f* de precisión *f*)
- *files (kinds: rough file, smooth file, precision file)*
9 la sierra de arco *m*
- *hacksaw*
10 el tornillo de banco *m* plano, el tornillo de mordaza *f*
- *leg vice (Am. vise), a spring vice*
11 la mufla, un horno de banco *m* (horno *m* de forja *f* de gas *m,* horno *m* para templar)
- *muffle furnace, a gas-fired furnace*

12 la entrada del gas
- *gas pipe*
13 la taladradora de mano *f*
- *hand brace (hand drill)*
14 el tas (la estampa) de banco *m,* para curvar, enderezar y estampar
- *swage block*
15 la máquina de limar (la limadora)
- *filing machine*
16 la lima de cinta *f*
- *file*
17 el tubo quitalimaduras
- *compressed-air pipe*
18 la máquina de afilar (la afiladora)
- *grinding machine (grinder)*
19 la muela
- *grinding wheel*
20 la cubierta protectora
- *guard*
21 las gafas de protección *f*
- *goggles (safety glasses)*
22 el casco de protección *f*
- *safety helmet*
23 el martillo de cerrajero *m* (el martillo de remachar)
- *machinist's hammer*
24 el tornillo de mano *f* (las entenallas)
- *hand vice (Am. vise)*
25 el cincel cruciforme (el cincel puntiagudo)
- *cape chisel (cross-cut chisel)*
26 el cincel plano
- *flat chisel*
27 la lima plana
- *flat file*

28 la picadura de la lima
- *file cut (cut)*
29 la lima redonda (la lima de media caña *f*)
- *round file (also: half-round file)*
30 el giramachos
- *tap wrench*
31 el escariador
- *reamer*
32 la terraja de cojinetes *m*
- *die (die and stock)*
33-35 la llave
- *key*
33 la tija
- *stem (shank)*
34 el ojo (el anillo)
- *bow*
35 el paletón
- *bit*
36-43 la cerradura de puerta *f,* **una cerradura empotrable**
- *door lock, a mortise (mortice) lock*
36 el palastro
- *back plate*
37 el pestillo
- *spring bolt (latch bolt)*
38 el fiador (la gacheta)
- *tumbler*
39 el cerrojo (el pestillo)
- *bolt*
40 el ojo de la cerradura (la bocallave)
- *keyhole*
41 la espiga guía del pestillo
- *bolt guide pin*
42 el muelle *m* de la gacheta (del fiador)
- *tumbler spring*

43 la nuez, con agujero *m* cuadrangular
- *follower, with square hole*
44 la cerradura cilíndrica (cerradura *f* de seguridad *f*)
- *cylinder lock (safety lock)*
45 el cilindro
- *cylinder (plug)*
46 el muelle
- *spring*
47 la clavija de tope *m*
- *pin*
48 la llave de seguridad *f*, una llave plana
- *safety key, a flat key*
49 el gozne
- *lift-off hinge*
50 la bisagra acodada
- *hook-and-ride band*
51 la bisagra de ramal *m* (el pernio)
- *strap hinge*
52 el calibre para medir gruesos *m* (el pie de rey *m*)
- *vernier calliper (caliper) gauge* (Am. *gage)*
53 la galga de espesores *m*
- *feeler gauge* (Am. *gage)*
54 el calibre para huecos *m* (para alturas *f*, para profundidades *f*)
- *vernier depth gauge* (Am. *gage)*
55 el nonio
- *vernier*
56 la regla de filo *m*
- *straightedge*
57 la escuadra de medida *f*
- *square*
58 el taladro de pecho *m*
- *breast drill*
59 la broca espiral
- *twist bit (twist drill)*
60 el macho de roscar
- *screw tap (tap)*
61 los cojinetes de rosca *f*
- *halves of a screw die*
62 el destornillador
- *screwdriver*
63 el rascador (*igual:* el rascador triangular)
- *scraper (also: pointed triangle scraper)*
64 el granete (el punzón) de marcar
- *centre* (Am. *center) punch*
65 el taladro
- *round punch*
66 los alicates planos
- *flat-nose pliers*
67 las tenazas articuladas de corte *m*
- *detachable-jaw cut nippers*
68 las mordazas para tubos *m* (mordazas *f* de gas *m*)
- *gas pliers*
69 las tenazas
- *pincers*

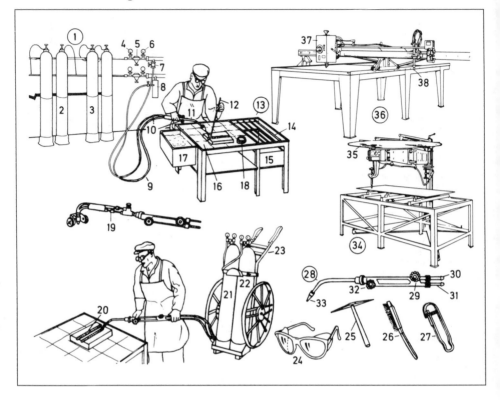

1 la batería de botellas *f*	**13** la mesa de soldar	**26** el cepillo de alambre *m*
– *gas cylinder manifold*	– *welding bench*	– *wire brush*
2 la botella de acetileno *m*	**14** el enrejado de corte *m*	**27** el encendedor del soplete
– *acetylene cylinder*	– *grating*	– *torch lighter (blowpipe lighter)*
3 la botella de oxígeno *m*	**15** la caja de hierro *m* de desecho *m*	**28** el soplete de soldar (*Amér.*: la
– *oxygen cylinder*	– *scrap box*	antorcha)
4 el manómetro de alta presión *f*	**16** la cubierta de la mesa, de ladrillo	– *welding torch (blowpipe)*
– *high-pressure manometer*	*m* refractario	**29** la válvula del oxígeno
5 la válvula reductora de la presión	– *bench covering of chamotte slabs*	– *oxygen control*
– *pressure-reducing valve (reducing*	**17** el depósito de agua *f*	**30** la conexión del oxígeno
valve, pressure regulator)	– *water tank*	– *oxygen connection*
6 el manómetro de baja presión *f*	**18** la pasta de soldar	**31** la conexión del gas combustible
– *low-pressure manometer*	– *welding paste (flux)*	– *gas connection (acetylene connec-*
7 la válvula de cierre *m*	**19** el soplete de soldar, equipado con	*tion)*
– *stop valve*	boquilla *f* de corte *m* y carrito *m*	**32** la válvula del gas combustible
8 la válvula hidráulica de baja pre-	guía de la llama	– *gas control (acetylene control)*
sión *f*	– *welding torch (blowpipe) with cut-*	**33** la boquilla de soldar
– *hydraulic back-pressure valve for*	*ting attachment and guide tractor*	– *welding nozzle*
low-pressure installations	**20** la pieza de trabajo (la pieza para	**34** la máquina de corte *m* autógeno
9 el tubo (de goma *f*) del gas	soldar)	(la máquina de oxicorte *m*)
– *gas hose*	– *workpiece*	– *cutting machine*
10 el tubo (de goma *f*) del oxígeno	**21** la botella de oxígeno *m*	**35** la plantilla (el modelo) circular
– *oxygen hose*	– *oxygen cylinder*	– *circular template*
11 el soplete de soldar (*Amér.*: la	**22** la botella de acetileno *m*	**36** la máquina de corte *m* autógeno
antorcha)	– *acetylene cylinder*	universal
– *welding torch (blowpipe)*	**23** la carretilla de las botellas	– *universal cutting machine*
12 la varilla de aportación *f* (la vari-	– *cylinder trolley*	**37** la cabeza de mando *m*
lla de fusión *f*)	**24** las gafas de soldador *m*	– *tracing head*
– *welding rod (filler rod)*	– *welding goggles*	**38** la boquilla del soplete
	25 el martillo de desbastar	– *cutting nozzle*
	– *chipping hammer*	

1 el transformador de soldadura *f*
- *welding transformer*
2 el soldador eléctrico
- *arc welder*
3 la capucha de soldar
- *arc welding helmet*
4 el vidrio protector abatible
- *flip-up window*
5 la protección de los hombros
- *shoulder guard*
6 la manga de protección *f*
- *protective sleeve*
7 el carcaj de los electrodos
- *electrode case*
8 el guante de soldador de tres dedos *m*
- *three-fingered welding glove*
9 el portaelectrodos
- *electrode holder*
10 el electrodo
- *electrode*
11 el mandil (el delantal de cuero *m*)
- *leather apron*
12 la protección de las espinillas (las polainas de protección *f*, la espinillera)
- *shin guard*
13 la mesa de soldar por aspiración *f*
- **welding table with fume extraction equipment**
14 el tablero (la superficie) de la mesa de aspiración *f*
- *table top*

15 la trompa (el tubo) de aspiración *f* orientable
- *movable extractor duct*
16 la tubuladura del aire de escape *m*
- *extractor support*
17 el martillo de desbastar
- *chipping hammer*
18 el cepillo de alambre *m* de acero *m*
- *wire brush*
19 el cable de soldar
- *welding lead*
20 el portaelectrodos
- *electrode holder*
21 la mesa de soldar
- *welding bench*
22 la soldadura por puntos *m*
- **spot welding**
23 las pinzas para soldar por puntos *m*
- *spot welding electrode holder*
24 el brazo portaelectrodos
- *electrode arm*
25 la llegada de corriente *f* (el cable de conexión *f*)
- *power supply (lead)*
26 el cilindro de presión *f* del electrodo
- *electrode-pressure cylinder*
27 el transformador de soldadura *f*
- *welding transformer*
28 la pieza de trabajo *m* (la pieza para soldar)
- *workpiece*
29 la máquina de soldar por puntos *m* accionada por pedal *m*
- *foot-operated spot welder*

30 los brazos de soldar
- *welder electrode arms*
31 el pedal para regular la presión *f* del electrodo
- *foot pedal for welding pressure adjustment*
32 el guante de soldador *m* de cinco dedos *m*
- *five-fingered welding glove*
33 el soplete (*Amér.:* la antorcha) de soldadura *f* en atmósfera *f* controlada (la soldadura con gas *m* inerte)
- *inert-gas torch for inert-gas welding (gas-shielded arc welding)*
34 la llegada del gas inerte
- *inert-gas (shielding-gas) supply*
35 el borne de tierra *f* (la pinza de masa *f*)
- *work clamp (earthing clamp)*
36 el calibre de soldadura *f* de ángulo *m*
- *fillet gauge* (Am. *gage*) (*weld gauge*) *[for measuring throat thickness]*
37 el tornillo micrométrico
- *micrometer*
38 el brazo de medida *f*
- *measuring arm*
39 el escudo (el casco) de protección *f* para soldar
- *arc welding helmet*
40 el cristal del casco de soldar
- *filter lens*
41 la mesa giratoria pequeña
- *small turntable*

143 Perfiles, tornillos y piezas de máquinas

1 el ángulo (el hierro de ángulo, la rinconera)
– *angle iron (angle)*
2 el ala f (el lado)
– *leg (flange)*
3-7 **viguetas f de hierro** m (vigas f de acero m de construcción f)
– **steel girders**
3 el hierro en T (la T)
– *T-iron (tee-iron)*
4 el alma f
– *vertical leg*
5 el ala f
– *flange*
6 el hierro en doble T
– *H-girder (H-beam)*
7 el hierro en U (la U)
– *E-channel (channel iron)*
8 el hierro cilíndrico (el hierro redondo)
– *round bar*
9 el hierro cuadrado
– *square iron* (Am. *square stock)*
10 el hierro plano
– *flat bar*
11 el fleje de hierro m
– *strip steel*
12 el alambre
– *iron wire*
13-50 **tornillos** m
– **screws and bolts**
13 el tornillo de cabeza f hexagonal
– *hexagonal-head bolt*
14 la cabeza
– *head*
15 el vástago (el tallo, la varilla)
– *shank*
16 el filete (la rosca)
– *thread*
17 la arandela
– *washer*
18 la tuerca hexagonal
– *hexagonal nut*
19 la chaveta (el pasador)
– *split pin*
20 el extremo redondo
– *rounded end*
21 la abertura de la llave
– *width of head (of flats)*
22 el espárrago
– *stud*
23 la punta (el extremo)
– *point (end)*
24 la tuerca hexagonal con entalladuras f (la tuerca corona)
– *castle nut (castellated nut)*
25 el orificio para la chaveta
– *hole for the split pin*
26 el tornillo de cabeza f cruciforme (un tornillo para chapa f)
– *cross-head screw, a sheet-metal screw (self-tapping screw)*
27 el tornillo de cabeza f cilíndrica con seis lados m en el interior
– *hexagonal socket head screw*
28 el tornillo de cabeza f avellanada (el tornillo embutido)
– *countersunk-head bolt*
29 el fiador (la uña)
– *catch*
30 la contratuerca
– *locknut (locking nut)*
31 la espiga
– *bolt (pin)*
32 el tornillo con collar m
– *collar-head bolt*
33 el collar
– *set collar (integral collar)*
34 la arandela de muelle m
– *spring washer (washer)*
35 la tuerca redonda con agujero m, una tuerca de ajuste m
– *round nut, an adjusting nut*
36 el tornillo de cabeza f cilíndrica, un tornillo de cabeza f ranurada
– *cheese-head screw, a slotted screw*
37 el pasador cónico
– *tapered pin*

38 la ranura (la muesca) del tornillo
– *screw slot (screw slit, screw groove)*
39 el tornillo de cabeza f cuadrada
– *square-head bolt*
40 el pasador con muesca f, un pasador cilíndrico
– *grooved pin, a cylindrical pin*
41 el tornillo de cabeza f de martillo m (de cabeza f en T)
– *T-head bolt*
42 la tuerca de orejas f
– *wing nut (fly nut, butterfly nut)*
43 el tornillo para piedra f (el perno de anclaje m)
– *rag bolt*
44 el garfio
– *barb*
45 el tornillo para madera f
– *wood screw*
46 la cabeza avellanada
– *countersunk head*
47 la rosca de madera f (la rosca golosa)
– *wood screw thread*
48 el tornillo prisionero (la punta con filete m)
– *grub screw*
49 la ranura (la muesca)
– *pin slot (pin slit, pin groove)*
50 la punta esférica
– *round end*
51 el clavo (la punta de París)
– *nail (wire nail)*
52 la cabeza
– *head*
53 la espiga
– *shank*
54 la punta
– *point*
55 la punta para cartón m asfaltado (el clavo de techar, la tachuela)
– *roofing nail*
56 el remachado (la roblonadura)
– *riveting (lap riveting)*
57-60 **el remache** (el roblón)
– **rivet**
57 la cabeza de la matriz, una cabeza de roblón m
– *set head (swage head, die head), a rivet head*
58 la espiga del remache
– *rivet shank*
59 la cabeza de cierre m
– *closing head*
60 la distancia entre los remaches
– *pitch of rivets*
61 el eje (el árbol)
– *shaft*
62 el chaflán (el bisel)
– *chamfer (bevel)*
63 el gorrón (el muñón)
– *journal*
64 el cuello
– *neck*
65 el asiento
– *seat*
66 el encaje del pasador (la ranura para la chaveta)
– *keyway*
67 el asiento cónico (el cono)
– *conical seat (cone)*
68 la rosca
– *thread*
69 el rodamiento de bolas f, un rodamiento (cojinete m de bolas f)
– **ball bearing**, *an antifriction bearing*
70 la bola de acero m
– *steel ball (ball)*
71 el anillo exterior
– *outer race*
72 el anillo interior
– *inner race*
73 u. 74 **las chavetas**
– **keys**
73 la chaveta embutida (la chaveta de resorte m)
– *sunk key (feather)*
74 la chaveta con talón m (la contraclavija)
– *gib (gib-headed key)*

75 u. 76 **el rodamiento de agujas** f
– **needle roller bearing**
75 la jaula de las agujas f
– *needle cage*
76 la aguja
– *needle*
77 la tuerca hexagonal con entalladuras f
– *castle nut (castellated nut)*
78 la chaveta (el pasador)
– *split pin*
79 la caja
– *casing*
80 la cubierta de la caja
– *casing cover*
81 la boquilla roscada para el engrase a presión f
– *grease nipple (lubricating nipple)*
82-96 **ruedas** f **dentadas** (engranajes m)
– **gear wheels, cog wheels**
82 el engranaje escalonado
– *stepped gear wheel*
83 el diente
– *cog (tooth)*
84 el fondo del diente
– *space between teeth*
85 la ranura para la chaveta
– *keyway (key seat, key slot)*
86 el calibre
– *bore*
87 la rueda dentada cilíndrica doble helicoidal (rueda f de dientes m en ángulo m)
– *herringbone gear wheel*
88 el rayo (de rueda f)
– *spoke (arm)*
89 el engranaje helicoidal
– *helical gearing (helical spur wheel)*
90 la corona dentada
– *sprocket*
91 la rueda dentada cónica
– *bevel gear wheel (bevel wheel)*
92 u. 93 **el engranaje en espiral** f
– **spiral toothing**
92 el piñón
– *pinion*
93 la corona dentada
– *crown wheel*
94-96 **el engranaje (el tren) planetario**
– **epicyclic gear (planetary gear)**
94 el engranaje (el tren) planetario
– *planet wheels*
95 el engranaje interior
– *internal gear*
96 el engranaje exterior
– *sun wheel (sun gear)*
97-107 **frenos** m **dinamométricos**
– **absorption dynamometer**
97 el freno de zapatas f
– *shoe brake (check brake, block brake)*
98 el disco de freno m
– *brake pulley*
99 el árbol del freno
– *brake shaft (brake axle)*
100 la zapata (almohadilla f) de freno m
– *brake block (brake shoe)*
101 el tirante
– *pull rod*
102 la magneto del freno
– *brake magnet*
103 el contrapeso del freno
– *brake weight*
104 el freno de cinta f
– *band brake*
105 la cinta de freno m
– *brake band*
106 la cubierta del freno
– *brake lining*
107 el tornillo de ajuste m, para asegurar una aplicación uniforme del freno
– *adjusting screw, for even application of the brake*

[material de fabricación: acero, latón m, aluminio m, plástico m etc.; en los siguientes ha sido escogido como ejemplo el acero]
[material: steel, brass, aluminium (Am. *aluminum), plastics, etc: in the following, steel was chosen as an example]*

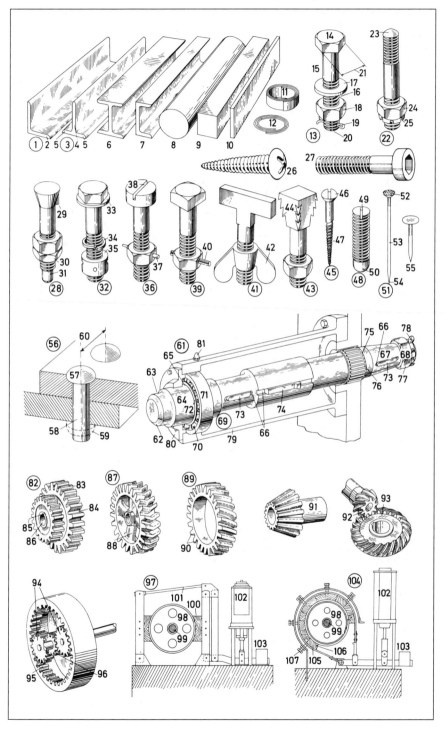

1-51 la mina de carbón *m* **de piedra**
f (la mina de hulla *f*, la mina)
– **coal mine** *(colliery, pit)*
1 el castillete de extracción *f*
– *pithead gear (headgear)*
2 la sala de máquinas *f*
– *winding engine house*
3 la torre de extracción *f*
– *pithead frame (head frame)*
4 el edificio del pozo (de la mina)
– *pithead building*
5 la planta de preparación *f*
– *processing plant*
6 el aserradero
– *sawmill*
7-11 la coquería
– **coking plant**
7 la batería de horno *m* de coque *m*
– *battery of coke ovens*
8 el vagón de carga *f*
– *larry car (larry, charging car)*
9 la torre de carbón *m* de coque *m*
– *coking coal tower*
10 la torre de extinción *f* del coque
– *coke-quenching tower*
11 el vagón de extinción *f* del coque
– *coke-quenching car*
12 el gasómetro
– *gasometer*
13 la central eléctrica
– *power plant (power station)*
14 la torre de agua *f*
– *water tower*
15 la torre de refrigeración *f*
– *cooling tower*
16 el ventilador de la mina
– *mine fan*
17 el emplazamiento (*Amér.:* la ubicación) del almacén de material *m*
– *depot*
18 el edificio de la administración
– *administration building (office building, offices)*
19 el escorial
– *tip heap (spoil heap)*
20 la estación de depuración *f* (de aguas *f* residuales)
– *cleaning plant*
21-51 la explotación subterránea
– **underground workings** *(underground mining)*
21 el pozo de ventilación *f*
– *ventilation shaft*
22 el canal de tiro *m* del ventilador
– *fan drift*
23 el montacargas con jaulas de extracción *f* [transporte de productos]
– *cage-winding system with cages*
24 el pozo principal
– *main shaft*

25 la instalación de extracción *f* por montacargas *m*
– *skip-winding system*
26 el cargadero
– *winding inset*
27 el pozo interior (el pozo ciego)
– *staple shaft*
28 el resbaladero en espiral *f*
– *spiral chute*
29 la galería del yacimiento
– *gallery along seam*
30 la galería recta
– *lateral*
31 la galería (el corte) transversal
– *cross-cut*
32 la máquina de propulsión *f* para los trazados (la máquina para hacer túneles *m*)
– *tunnelling* (Am. *tunneling*) *machine*
33-37 cortes *m*
– **longwall faces**
33 el corte horizontal a cepillo *m*
– *horizontal ploughed longwall face*
34 el corte horizontal por capas *f* paralelas a la estratificación
– *horizontal cut longwall face*
35 el corte vertical a martillo *m* neumático
– *vertical pneumatic pick longwall face*
36 el corte vertical a martillo *m* pilón
– *diagonal ram longwall face*
37 los desechos (*Bol., Chile, Hond. y Perú:* el desmonte)
– *goaf (gob, waste)*
38 la esclusa de aire *m* (la esclusa de ventilación *f*)
– *air lock*
39 el traslado del personal en vagonetas *f*
– *transportation of men by cars*
40 la cinta transportadora
– *belt conveying*
41 la carbonera de hulla *f* en bruto *m*
– *raw coal bunker*
42 la cinta de carga *f*
– *charging conveyor*
43 el transporte de las mercancías en monocarril *m* aéreo
– *transportation of supplies by monorail car*
44 el traslado del personal en monocarril *m* aéreo
– *transportation of men by monorail car*
45 el transporte de materiales *m* en vagonetas *f*
– *transportation of supplies by mine car*

46 el drenaje de agua *f*
– *drainage*
47 el sumidero del pozo
– *sump (sink)*
48 el terreno de recubrimiento *m*
– *capping*
49 el terreno de carbón *m* de piedra *f* (de hulla *f*)
– *[layer of] coal-bearing rock*
50 el filón de hulla *f*
– *coal seam*
51 la falla
– *fault*

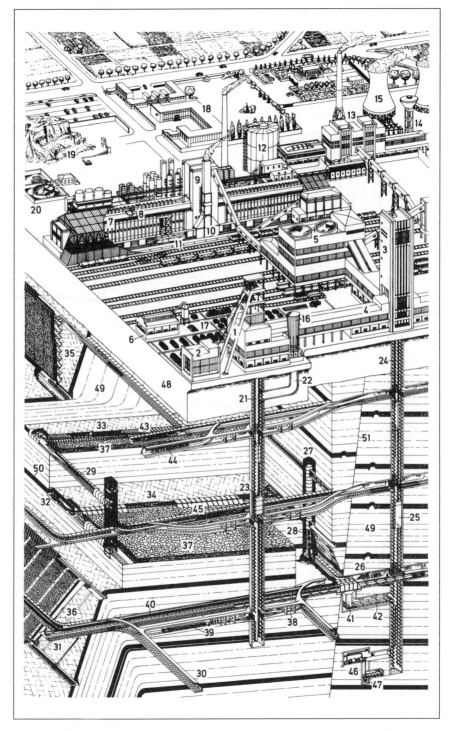

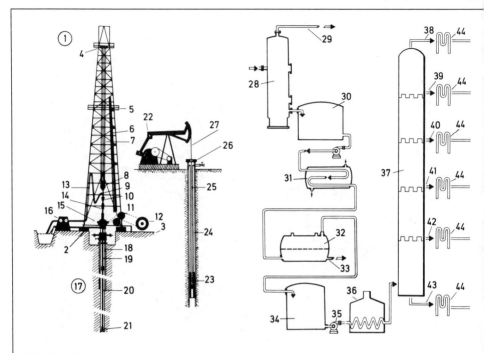

1-21 el sondeo petrolífero
- *oil drilling*
1 la torre de perforación *f*
- *drilling rig*
2 la subestructura (el cimiento)
- *substructure*
3 la plataforma de trabajo *m*
- *crown safety platform*
4 las poleas de la torre
- *crown blocks*
5 la plataforma de celosías *f*, una plataforma intermedia
- *working platform, an intermediate platform*
6 los tubos de perforación *f*
- *drill pipes*
7 el cable de perforación *f*
- *drilling cable (drilling line)*
8 el polipasto (el grupo móvil de poleas *f*)
- *travelling* (Am. *traveling*) *block*
9 el gancho de tracción *f*
- *hook*
10 el eslabón giratorio (la unión giratoria)
- *[rotary] swivel*
11 el mecanismo elevador, un torno (*Amér. Merid.*: el guinche)
- *draw works, a hoist*
12 la máquina motriz (el motor)
- *engine*
13 el tubo de extracción *f* del fango
- *standpipe and rotary hose*
14 la varilla de arrastre *m*
- *kelly*
15 el platillo giratorio
- *rotary table*
16 la bomba de extracción *f* del fango
- *slush pump (mud pump)*
17 el pozo de sondeo *m* (el taladro)
- *well*
18 el tubo vertical de revestimiento *m*
- *casing*
19 la varilla de perforación *f*
- *drilling pipe*
20 el entubado
- *tubing*
21 el punzón (el taladro, la broca, la barrena); *clases:* barrena *f* de cola *f* de pescado *m*, taladro *m* de ballesta *f*, barrena *f* sacamuestras
- *drilling bit;* kinds: *fishtail (blade) bit, rock* (Am. *roller*) *bit, core bit*

22-27 la extracción de petróleo *m*
- *oil (crude oil) production*
22 el grupo impulsor de bombeo *m*
- *pumping unit (pump)*
23 el émbolo buzo
- *plunger*
24 los tubos elevadores
- *tubing*
25 la varilla de la bomba
- *sucker rods (pumping rods)*
26 el prensaestopas
- *stuffing box*
27 la varilla pulimentada
- *polish (polished) rod*

28-35 el refino del petróleo crudo
[esquema]
- *treatment of crude oil [diagram]*
28 el separador de gas *m*
- *gas separator*
29 la tubería (la conducción) de gas *m*
- *gas pipe (gas outlet)*
30 el depósito del petróleo líquido
- *wet oil tank (wash tank)*
31 el precalentador
- *water heater*
32 la unidad de drenaje *m* y de desmineralización *f*
- *water and brine separator*
33 la canalización del agua *f* salada
- *salt water pipe (salt water outlet)*
34 el depósito del petróleo refinado
- *oil tank*
35 la canalización de transporte *m* del petróleo refinado [para la refinería o para transporte *m* por camión *m* cisterna *f*, petrolero *m*, oleoducto *m*]
- *trunk pipeline for oil [to the refinery or transport by tanker lorry (Am. tank truck), oil tanker, or pipeline]*

36-64 la transformación del petróleo crudo [esquema]
- *processing of crude oil [diagram]*
36 el calentador del petróleo (el horno tubular)
- *oil furnace (pipe still)*

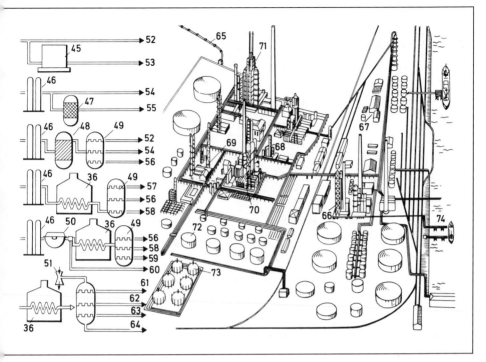

37 la columna de destilación *f* (la torre fraccionadora) con plataformas *f* superpuestas
– *fractionating column (distillation column) with trays*
38 los gases ligeros (acumulados en la cima de la columna)
– *top gases (tops)*
39 la fracción de bencina *f* ligera
– *light distillation products*
40 la fracción de bencina *f* pesada
– *heavy distillation products*
41 el petróleo lampante
– *petroleum*
42 la fracción de gasoil *m*
– *gas oil component*
43 los residuos
– *residue*
44 el refrigerador
– *condenser (cooler)*
45 el compresor
– *compressor*
46 la unidad de desulfuración *f*
– *desulphurizing (desulphurization, Am. desulfurizing, desulfurization) plant*
47 la unidad de reforma *f*
– *reformer (hydroformer, platformer)*
48 la instalación de craqueo *m* catalítico
– *catalytic cracker (cat cracker)*
49 la columna de destilación *f*
– *distillation column*

50 la separación de la parafina
– *de-waxing (wax separation)*
51 la instalación de vacío *m* (el canal de aspiración *f*)
– *vacuum equipment*
52-64 los productos derivados del petróleo
– *oil products*
52 el gas de combustión *f*
– *fuel gas*
53 el gas líquido
– *liquefied petroleum gas (liquid gas)*
54 la gasolina normal (la gasolina para automóvil; *Amér.:* la nafta)
– *regular grade petrol (Am. gasoline)*
55 la gasolina súper
– *super grade petrol (Am. gasoline)*
56 el carburante diesel (el combustible para motores *m* diesel)
– *diesel oil*
57 la gasolina de aviación *f* (el carburante para reactores *m*)
– *aviation fuel*
58 el fuel-oil ligero (el aceite combustible ligero)
– *light fuel oil*
59 el fuel-oil pesado
– *heavy fuel oil*
60 la parafina
– *paraffin (paraffin oil, kerosene)*
61 el lubricante para ejes *m*
– *spindle oil*

62 el aceite lubrificante
– *lubricating oil*
63 el lubrificante para cilindros *m*
– *cylinder oil*
64 el betún
– *bitumen*
65-74 la refinería de petróleo *m*
– *oil refinery*
65 el oleoducto
– *pipeline (oil pipeline)*
66 las instalaciones de destilación *f*
– *distillation plants*
67 la refinería del aceite lubrificante
– *lubricating oil refinery*
68 la recuperación del azufre
– *desulphurizing (desulphurization, Am. desulfurizing, desulfurization) plant*
69 la instalación de separación *f* del gas
– *gas-separating plant*
70 el fraccionador (craqueador *m*) catalítico
– *catalytic cracking plant*
71 el reformador catalítico (el hidroformador)
– *catalytic reformer*
72 el tanque de almacenamiento *m*
– *storage tank*
73 el tanque esférico
– *spherical tank*
74 el puerto petrolero
– *tanker terminal*

146 Perforación a poca distancia de la costa (Perforación off-shore)

1-39 la plataforma de perforación f
(la plataforma de extracción f)
– *drilling rig (oil rig)*
**1-37 la plataforma del castillete de
perforación** f
– *drilling platform*
1 la instalación de abastecimiento
m de energía f
– *power station*
2 las chimeneas para los gases quemados (los tubos de escape m) de
los generadores
– *generator exhausts*
3 la grúa giratoria
– *revolving crane (pedestal crane)*
4 el almacén de los tubos
– *piperack*
5 los tubos de escape m de las
turbinas
– *turbine exhausts*
6 el almacén de los materiales
– *materials store*
7 la cubierta (el puente) para
helicópteros m
– *helicopter deck (heliport deck,
heliport)*
8 el montacargas
– *elevator*
9 el dispositivo para separar el gas y
el petróleo
– *production oil and gas separator*
10 el separador de muestras f
– *test oil and gas separators (test
separators)*
11 la antorcha de emergencia f
– *emergency flare stack*
12 la torre de perforación f
– *derrick*
13 el tanque de gasóleo m
– *diesel tank*
14 las oficinas
– *office building*
15 los tanques para el almacenamiento de cemento m
– *cement storage tanks*
16 el tanque para el agua f potable
– *drinking water tank*
17 el tanque de reserva para el agua
f salada
– *salt water tank*
18 los tanques de carburante m para
helicópteros m
– *jet fuel tanks*
19 los botes salvavidas
– *lifeboats*
20 la caja del ascensor
– *elevator shaft*
21 el depósito del aire comprimido
– *compressed-air reservoir*
22 la estación de bombeo m
– *pumping station*

23 el compresor del aire
– *air compressor*
24 la instalación de climatización f
– *air lock*
25 la instalación de desmineralización f del agua f del mar
– *seawater desalination plant*
26 la instalación para filtrar el
gasóleo
– *inlet filters for diesel fuel*
27 el refrigerador de gas m
– *gas cooler*
28 el pupitre de mando m (el panel
de control m) para los separadores
– *control panel for the separators*
29 los servicios (los aseos, los lavabos)
– *toilets (lavatories)*
30 el taller
– *workshop*
31 la esclusa del tritón [el "tritón" se
utiliza para limpiar el oleoducto]
– *pig trap [the 'pig' is used to clean
the oil pipeline]*
32 la sala de control m
– *control room*
33 las habitaciones
– *accommodation modules (accommodation)*
34 las bombas de cimentación f a alta
presión f
– *high-pressure cementing pumps*
35 la cubierta inferior
– *lower deck*
36 la cubierta intermedia
– *middle deck*
37 la cubierta superior
– *top deck (main deck)*
38 la construcción de soporte m (la
infraestructura)
– *substructure*
39 el nivel del mar
– *mean sea level*

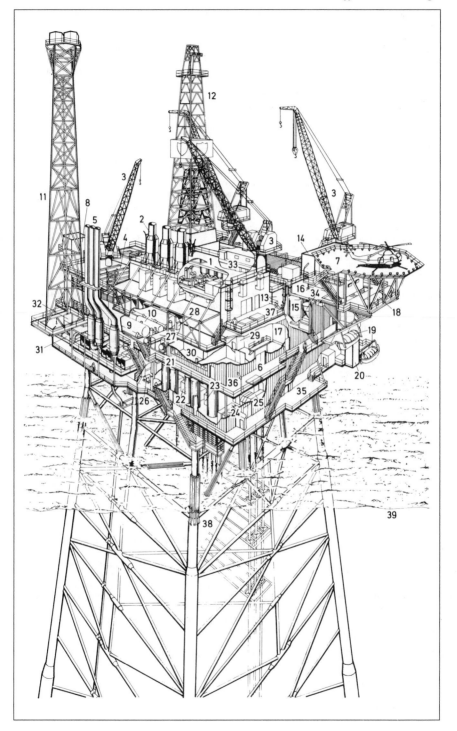

1-20 la instalación de los altos hornos
- *blast furnace plant*
1 el alto horno, un horno de cubilote *m*
- *blast furnace, a shaft furnace*
2 el montacargas inclinado, para el mineral y fundentes *m* o coque *m*
- *furnace incline (lift) for ore and flux or coke*
3 el carro corredizo
- *skip hoist*
4 la plataforma del tragante (de carga *f*)
- *charging platform*
5 la cuba de la tolva
- *receiving hopper*
6 el cono de cierre *m* (la campana del tragante)
- *bell*
7 la cuba del alto horno
- *blast furnace shaft*
8 la zona de reducción *f*
- *smelting section*
9 el caño de la escoria
- *slag escape*
10 la cuba de la escoria
- *slag ladle*
11 el caño del hierro crudo
- *pig iron (crude iron, iron) runout*
12 el caldero del hierro crudo
- *pig iron (crude iron, iron) ladle*
13 el tubo de salida *f* del gas del tragante
- *downtake*
14 el colector de polvo *m*
- *dust catcher, a dust-collecting machine*
15 el calentador del aire
- *hot-blast stove*
16 el pozo externo de combustión *f*
- *external combustion chamber*
17 la entrada de aire *m* frío
- *blast main*
18 el conducto del gas
- *gas pipe*
19 el conducto del aire caliente
- *hot-blast pipe*
20 la tobera
- *tuyère*
21-69 la fábrica de acero *m*
- *steelworks*
21-30 el horno Martin-Siemens
- *Siemens-Martin open-hearth furnace*
21 el caldero (el crisol) del hierro crudo
- *pig iron (crude iron, iron) ladle*
22 la reguera del bebedero (el canal de alimentación *f*)
- *feed runner*
23 el horno fijo
- *stationary furnace*

24 el hogar
- *hearth*
25 la máquina de carga *f*
- *charging machine*
26 el molde (la lingotera) para chatarra *f*
- *scrap iron charging box*
27 el conducto del gas
- *gas pipe*
28 la cámara para calentar el gas
- *gas regenerator chamber*
29 la tubería de alimentación *f* de aire *m*
- *air feed pipe*
30 la cámara para calentar el aire
- *air regenerator chamber*
31 el caldero del acero fundido, con cierre *m* tapón *m* [descarga por el fondo]
- *[bottom-pouring] steel-casting ladle with stopper*
32 la lingotera
- *ingot mould* (Am. *mold*)
33 el lingote de acero *m* (el tocho)
- *steel ingot*
34-44 la máquina de colar lingotes *m*
- *pig-casting machine*
34 el recogedor de colada *f*
- *pouring end*
35 el canal del hierro
- *metal runner*
36 la cinta de lingoteras *f* [la serie de moldes *m* de tochos *m*]
- *series (strand) of moulds* (Am. *molds)*
37 la lingotera
- *mould* (Am. *mold*)
38 la pasarela
- *catwalk*
39 el dispositivo de caída *f*
- *discharging chute*
40 el lingote (el hierro crudo)
- *pig*
41 la grúa de corredera *f*
- *travelling* (Am. *traveling*) *crane*
42 el caldero de hierro *m* crudo con descarga *f* por arriba
- *top-pouring pig iron (crude iron, iron) ladle*
43 el pico del caldero de colada *f*
- *pouring ladle lip*
44 el dispositivo basculante
- *tilting device (tipping device,* Am. *dumping device)*
45-50 el convertidor soplado por oxígeno *m* (el convertidor L-D, el convertidor Linz-Donawitz)
- *oxygen-blowing converter (L-D converter, Linz-Donawitz converter)*
45 el sombrerete del convertidor
- *conical converter top*

46 el anillo portador
- *mantle*
47 el fondo del convertidor
- *solid converter bottom*
48 la mampostería refractaria
- *fireproof lining (refractory lining)*
49 la lanza para oxígeno *m*
- *oxygen lance*
50 la piquera de colada *f*
- *tapping hole (tap hole)*
51-54 el horno eléctrico de arco *m* Siemens, un horno de cubilote *m* bajo
- *Siemens electric low-shaft furnace*
51 la boca de carga *f*
- *feed*
52 los electrodos [dispuestos en círculo]
- *electrodes [arranged in a circle]*
53 la tubería circular, para expulsar los gases del horno
- *bustle pipe*
54 la colada
- *runout*
55-69 el convertidor Thomas
- *Thomas converter (basic Bessemer converter)*
55 la posición de carga *f* para el hierro crudo líquido
- *charging position for molten pig iron*
56 la posición de carga *f* para la cal
- *charging position for lime*
57 la posición para el soplado
- *blow position*
58 la posición de descarga *f*
- *discharging position*
59 el dispositivo volcador
- *tilting device (tipping device,* Am. *dumping device)*
60 el caldero movido por grúa *f*
- *crane-operated ladle*
61 la cabria auxiliar de la grúa
- *auxiliary crane hoist*
62 la tolva de la cal
- *lime bunker*
63 el tubo de caída *f*
- *downpipe*
64 la vagoneta con chatarra *f* ligera de hierro *m*
- *tipping car* (Am. *dump truck)*
65 la alimentación de chatarra *f* de hierro *m*
- *scrap iron feed*
66 la mesa de control *m*
- *control desk*
67 la chimenea del convertidor
- *converter chimney*
68 el tubo de inyección *f* de aire *m*
- *blast main*
69 el fondo de convertidor *m*
- *wind box*

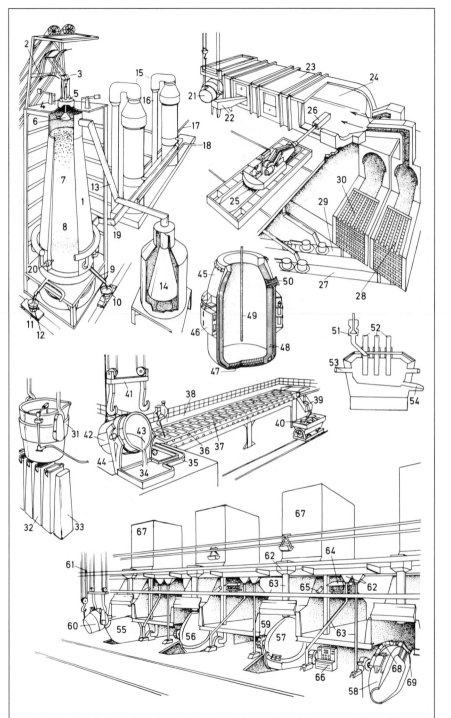

1-45 el taller de fundición (*Ec. y Perú:* la factoría)
– *iron foundry*
1-12 la fusión
– *melting plant*
1 el cubilote, un horno de fusión *f*
– *cupola furnace (cupola), a melting furnace*
2 el conducto de aire *m* (la tubería de aire *m*)
– *blast main (blast inlet, blast pipe)*
3 el canal de la colada
– *tapping spout*
4 el agujero de observación *f* (la mirilla)
– *spyhole*
5 el antecrisol basculante
– *tilting-type [hot-metal] receiver*
6 el caldero de tambor *m* móvil
– *mobile drum-type ladle*
7 el fundidor
– *melter*
8 el vaciador
– *founder (caster)*
9 la varilla de colada *f*
– *tap bar (tapping bar)*
10 la varilla tapón *m*
– *bott stick* (Am. *bot stick*)
11 el hierro líquido
– *molten iron*
12 el canal de la escoria
– *slag spout*
13 la cuadrilla de vaciadores *m*
– *casting team*

14 el caldero para horquilla *f* (el caldero portátil)
– *hand shank*
15 la horquilla portacaldero
– *double handle (crutch)*
16 la barra de transporte *m*
– *carrying bar*
17 la varilla de la escoria
– *skimmer rod*
18 la caja cerrada de moldeo *m*
– *closed moulding* (Am. *molding*) *box*
19 la caja superior
– *upper frame (cope)*
20 la caja inferior
– *lower frame (drag)*
21 el bebedero (la piquera)
– *runner (runner gate, down-gate)*
22 el respiradero
– *riser (riser gate)*
23 el caldero de mano *f* (la cuchara de colada *f*)
– *hand ladle*
24-29 la colada continua
– *continuous casting*
24 la mesa de colada descendente
– *sinking pouring floor*
25 el lingote de metal *m* solidificándose
– *solidifying pig*
26 la fase sólida
– *solid stage*
27 la fase líquida
– *liquid stage*

28 la refrigeración por agua *f*
– *water-cooling system*
29 la pared de la lingotera
– *mould* (Am. *mold*) *wall*
30-37 el moldeo
– *moulding* (Am. *molding*) *department* (*moulding shop*)
30 el moldeador
– *moulder* (Am. *molder*)
31 el atacador de aire *m* comprimido
– *pneumatic rammer*
32 el atacador de mano *f*
– *hand rammer*
33 la caja abierta de moldeado *m*
– *open moulding* (Am. *molding*) *box*
34 el molde (la impresión del molde)
– *pattern*
35 la arena de moldear
– *moulding* (Am. *molding*) *sand*
36 el macho
– *core*
37 la portada de macho *m*
– *core print*
38-45 el taller de rebarbado *m*
– *cleaning shop (fettling shop)*
38 el tubo de alimentación *f* de gravilla *f* de acero *m* o de arena *f*
– *steel grit or sand delivery pipe*
39 el soplete automático de mesa *m* giratoria
– *rotary-table shot-blasting machine*
40 la defensa de la piedra arenisca
– *grit guard*

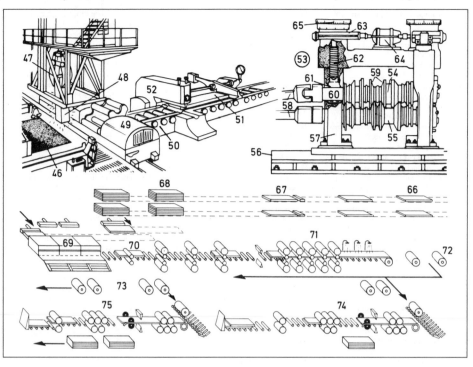

41 la mesa giratoria
– *revolving table*
42 la pieza de fundición *f*
– *casting*
43 el rebarbador
– *fettler*
44 la máquina afiladora de aire *m* comprimido
– *pneumatic grinder*
45 el cincel de aire *m* comprimido
– *pneumatic chisel*
46-75 el laminador
– *rolling mill*
46 el horno de foso *m*
– *soaking pit*
47 la grúa para el horno de foso *m*, una grúa de tenazas *f*
– *soaking pit crane*
48 el lingote en bruto (el lingote de acero *m* bruto moldeado)
– *ingot*
49 la vagoneta volquete *m* para los lingotes
– *ingot tipper*
50 el tren blooming
– *roller table*
51 el material laminado
– *workpiece*
52 las tijeras para lingotes *m*
– *bloom shears*
53 el laminador dúo
– *two-high mill*
54-55 el juego de cilindros *m*
– *set of rolls (set of rollers)*

54 el cilindro superior
– *upper roll (upper roller)*
55 el cilindro inferior
– *lower roll (lower roller)*
56-60 la caja de laminado *m*
– *roll stand*
56 la plataforma base
– *base plate*
57 el montante de cilindros *m*
– *housing (frame)*
58 el árbol de acoplamiento *m*
– *coupling spindle*
59 el calibre
– *groove*
60 el cojinete del cilindro
– *roll bearing*
61-65 el dispositivo de ajuste *m*
– *adjusting equipment*
61 la guarnición del bastidor
– *chock*
62 el tornillo de presión *f*
– *main screw*
63 el engranaje
– *gear*
64 el motor
– *motor*
65 el indicador, para el ajuste grueso o fino
– *indicator for rough and fine adjustment*

66-75 el tren de laminado *m* continuo para manufacturar flejes *m* de acero *m* (el tren de bandas *f*) [esquema]
– *continuous rolling mill train for the manufacture of strip [diagram]*
66-68 el acabado del producto semi-manufacturado
– *processing of semi-finished product*
66 el producto semimanufacturado
– *semi-finished product*
67 la instalación de corte *m* autógeno
– *gas cutting installation*
68 la pila de láminas *f* acabadas
– *stack of finished steel sheets*
69 el horno de empuje *m*
– *continuous reheating furnaces*
70 el tren desbastador
– *blooming train*
71 el tren de acabado
– *finishing train*
72 el rodillo (la bobina para enro-llar)
– *coiler*
73 el almacén de flejes (coronas *f*) para la venta
– *collar bearing for marketing*
74 el tren de corte *m* de 5 mm
– *5 mm shearing train*
75 el tren de corte *m* de 10 mm
– *10 mm shearing train*

1 **el torno para cilindrar y roscar** (filetear)
– *centre* (Am. *center*) *lathe*
2 el cabezal fijo con el cambio de velocidades *f*
– *headstock with gear control (geared headstock)*
3 la palanca de mando *m* del reductor
– *reduction drive lever*
4 la palanca para roscas *f* normales y de paso *m* empinado
– *lever for normal and coarse threads*
5 el reglaje de la velocidad
– *speed change lever*
6 la palanca para el mecanismo de viraje *m* del husillo patrón
– *leadscrew reverse-gear lever*
7 la caja de engranajes *m* para cambiar
– *change-gear box*
8 la caja de avances *m* (el dispositivo Norton, la caja Norton)
– *feed gearbox (Norton tumbler gear)*
9 las palancas para los cambios de avance *m* y de pasos *m* de rosca *f*
– *levers for changing the feed and thread pitch*
10 la palanca del mecanismo de avance *m*
– *feed gear lever (tumbler lever)*
11 la palanca de maniobra *f* para la marcha a la derecha o a la izquierda del husillo principal
– *switch lever for right or left hand action of main spindle*
12 el pie (la base) del torno
– *lathe foot (footpiece)*
13 el volante para el movimiento longitudinal del carro
– *leadscrew handwheel for traversing of saddle (longitudinal movement of saddle)*
14 la palanca para el mecanismo inversor del sentido del avance
– *tumbler reverse lever*
15 el husillo de regulación *f*
– *feed screw*
16 el tablero del carro
– *apron (saddle apron, carriage apron)*
17 la palanca para el movimiento longitudinal y transversal
– *lever for longitudinal and transverse motion*
18 el tornillo sin fin *m* de caída *f* para embragar los avances
– *drop (dropping) worm (feed trip, feed tripping device) for engaging feed mechanisms*
19 la palanca para la tuerca partida del husillo principal
– *lever for engaging half nut of leadscrew (lever for clasp nut engagement)*
20 el husillo giratorio (el husillo de trabajo *m*, el portabrocas)
– *lathe spindle*
21 el portaherramientas
– *tool post*
22 el carro superior (el carrito longitudinal)
– *top slide (tool slide, tool rest)*
23 el carrito transversal
– *cross slide*

24 el carro de la bancada
– *bed slide*
25 el tubo para el refrigerante
– *coolant supply pipe*
26 la contrapunta del cabezal móvil
– *tailstock centre* (Am. *center*)
27 el casquillo (el cañón)
– *barrel (tailstock barrel)*
28 la palanca para el bloqueo del casquillo
– *tailstock barrel clamp lever*
29 el cabezal móvil
– *tailstock*
30 el volante para el ajuste del casquillo
– *tailstock barrel adjusting handwheel*
31 la bancada del torno
– *lathe bed*
32 el husillo principal (la barra de roscar)
– *leadscrew*
33 el husillo de tracción *f* (la barra de cilindrar, el árbol de guía *f*)
– *feed shaft*
34 el árbol de cambio *m* de marcha *f* para movimiento *m* a la derecha e izquierda *f*
– *reverse shaft for right and left hand motion and engaging and disengaging*
35 el mandril (el plato) de cuatro mordazas *f* (garras *f*)
– *four-jaw chuck (four-jaw independent chuck)*
36 la mordaza de sujeción *f*
– *gripping jaw*
37 el mandril (el plato) de tres mordazas *f* (garras *f*)
– *three-jaw chuck (three-jaw self-centring, Am. self-centering, chuck)*
38 **el torno (de) revólver** *m*
– **turret lathe**
39 el carrito transversal
– *cross slide*
40 el cabezal revólver
– *turret*
41 el portapunteros (el portacuchillas) múltiple
– *combination toolholder (multiple turning head)*
42 el carrito longitudinal
– *top slide*
43 la palanca cruciforme
– *star wheel*
44 la cubeta para las virutas y para refrigerar la sustancia (el aceite) lubricante
– *coolant tray for collecting coolant and swarf*
45-53 **herramientas (cuchillas** *f* **) de torno** *m*
– **lathe tools**
45 la herramienta con placas *f* giratorias para cortar
– *tool bit holder (clamp tip tool) for adjustable cutting tips*
46 la placa cortante de metal *m* duro o de cerámica *f* de óxidos *m*
– *adjustable cutting tip (clamp tip) of cemented carbide or oxide ceramic*
47 las formas de las placas ajustables de cerámica *f* de óxidos *m*
– *shapes of adjustable oxide ceramic tips*

48 la cuchilla de torno con corte *m* de metal *m* duro
– *lathe tool with cemented carbide cutting edge*
49 el mango de la cuchilla
– *tool shank*
50 la placa de metal *m* duro (la cuchilla de metal *m* duro) soldada
– *brazed cemented carbide cutting tip (cutting edge)*
51 la herramienta para los ángulos interiores
– *internal facing tool (boring tool) for corner work*
52 la cuchilla de torno *m* encorvada
– *general-purpose lathe tool*
53 la cuchilla de torno *m* para punzar
– *parting (parting-off) tool*
54 el perro de arrastre *m*
– *lathe carrier*
55 el tope de arrastre *m*
– *driving (driver) plate*
56-72 **instrumental** *m* **de medida** *f*
– *measuring instruments*
56 el calibre de interiores *m* para agujeros *m* (calibre *m* macho)
– *plug gauge* (Am. *gage*)
57 el tapón "bueno" (o de aceptación *f*)
– *'GO' gauging* (Am. *gaging*) *member (end)*
58 el tapón "malo" (o de rechazo *m*)
– *'NOT GO' gauging* (Am. *gaging*) *member (end)*
59 el calibrador de exteriores *m* (calibrador *m* de mordazas *f*)
– *calliper (caliper, snap) gauge* (Am. *gage*)
60 el lado pasa (la abertura máxima)
– *'GO' side*
61 el lado no pasa (la abertura mínima)
– *'NOT GO' side*
62 el tornillo micrométrico (el pálmer)
– *micrometer calliper (caliper) (micrometer)*
63 la escala graduada
– *measuring scale*
64 el tambor graduado
– *graduated thimble*
65 el arco de medida *f*
– *frame*
66 el husillo de medida *f* (la punta de contacto *m*)
– *spindle (screwed spindle)*
67 el pie de rey *m*
– *vernier calliper (caliper) gauge* (Am. *gage*)
68 la medida de profundidad *f*
– *depth gauge* (Am. *gage*) *attachment rule*
69 la escala de nonio *m*
– *vernier scale*
70 los picos de medida *f* exterior
– *outside jaws*
71 los picos de medida *f* interior
– *inside jaws*
72 el calibrador de profundidades *f*
– *vernier depth gauge* (Am. *gage*)

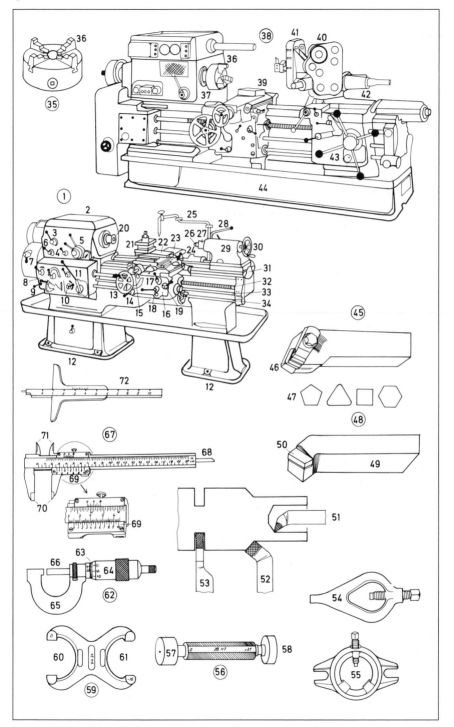

1 la máquina rectificadora cilíndrica universal
– **universal grinding machine**
2 el cabezal fijo
– *headstock*
3 el carrito de rectificación *f*
– *wheelhead slide*
4 la muela
– *grinding wheel*
5 el cabezal móvil
– *tailstock*
6 el banco de la rectificadora
– *grinding machine bed*
7 la mesa de la rectificadora
– *grinding machine table*
8 la cepilladora de dos montantes *m*
– **two-column planing machine** (two-column planer)
9 el motor de accionamiento *m*, un motor de corriente *f* continua con velocidad *f* regulable
– *drive motor, a direct current motor*
10 el montante
– *column*
11 la mesa de cepillado *m*
– *planer table*
12 el travesaño
– *cross slide (rail)*
13 el carrito portaherramientas
– *tool box*
14 la sierra de arco *m*
– **hacksaw**
15 el dispositivo de fijación *f*
– *clamping device*
16 la hoja de sierra *f*
– *saw blade*
17 el arco de sierra *f*
– *saw frame*
18 la taladradora giratoria o (taladradora) radial
– **radial** (radial-arm) **drilling machine**
19 el plinto (*sin.:* el pie, la base, el zócalo)
– *bed (base plate)*
20 la mesa para guardar las piezas de trabajo *m*
– *block for workpiece*
21 la columna
– *pillar*
22 el motor elevador
– *lifting motor*
23 el husillo portabrocas
– *drill spindle*
24 el brazo radial
– *arm*
25 la fresadora universal
– **universal milling machine**
26 la mesa de fresar
– *milling machine table*
27 el accionamiento del avance de la mesa
– *table feed drive*

28 la palanca de cambio *m* de velocidad *f* de rotación *f* de la broca de fresado *m*
– *switch lever for spindle rotation speed*
29 la caja de velocidades *f*
– *control box (control unit)*
30 la broca de fresado *m* vertical
– *vertical milling spindle*
31 la cabeza de accionamiento *m* vertical
– *vertical drive head*
32 la broca de fresado *m* horizontal
– *horizontal milling spindle*
33 el cojinete delantero para estabilizar la broca horizontal
– *end support for steadying horizontal spindle*
34 el macho de roscar a máquina *f*
– *machine tap*
35 el robot articulado
– **articulated robot,** an industrial robot
36 la placa de la base
– *base plate*
37 el mecanismo giratorio (el eje principal giratorio)
– *rotating column (base rotating axis)*
38 la articulación del brazo
– *shoulder joint*
39 el antebrazo
– *upper arm*
40 el codo
– *elbow joint*
41 el brazo en forma *f* de tubo *m*
– *tubular forearm*
42 la muñeca
– *wrist joint*
43 la arandela de conexión *f* de las piezas
– *gripper mounting flange*
44 la pinza
– *gripper*
45 los dedos
– *fingers*
46 la base del robot
– *upright robot (linear-axis robot, rectilinear robot)*
47 el robot de pórtico *m*
– *portal robot (gantry robot)*

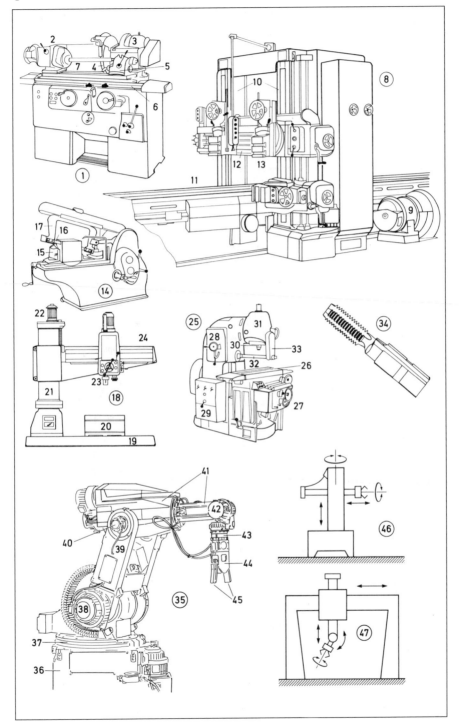

1 el tablero de dibujo *m*
- *drawing board*
2 la máquina de dibujar con guía *f*
- *drafting machine with parallel motion*
3 la cabeza de dibujar regulable
- *adjustable knob*
4 la regla de escuadra *f*
- *drawing head (adjustable set square)*
5 la regulación del tablero de dibujo *m*
- *drawing board adjustment*
6 la mesa de dibujar
- *drawing table*
7 la escuadra de dibujar (la escuadra de delineante *m*)
- *set square (triangle)*
8 la escuadra equilátera
- *triangle*
9 la regla en forma *f* de T
- *T-square (tee-square)*
10 el rollo de plano *m*
- *rolled drawing*
11 la representación gráfica (el diagrama)
- *diagram*
12 el panel para el plano terminado (el planning mural)
- *time schedule*
13 el soporte para el papel
- *paper stand*
14 el rollo de papel *m*
- *roll of paper*
15 el dispositivo de corte *m* (la cuchilla)
- *cutter*
16 el plano industrial
- *technical drawing (drawing, design)*
17 la vista de frente *m* (la vista frontal)
- *front view (front elevation)*
18 la vista lateral (la vista de lado *m*)
- *side view (side elevation)*
19 la vista superior
- *plan*
20 la superficie no trabajada
- *surface not to be machined*
21 la superficie pulida, una superficie trabajada
- *surface to be machined*
22 la superficie alisada en fino
- *surface to be superfinished*
23 el borde visible
- *visible edge*
24 el borde no visible
- *hidden edge*
25 la línea de cota *f*
- *dimension line*
26 la flecha de cota *f*
- *arrow head*
27 la indicación (la dirección) de corte *m*
- *section line*

28 el corte A-B
- *section A-B*
29 la superficie rayada
- *hatched surface*
30 la mediana (el eje)
- *centre* (Am. *center*) *line*
31 el cuadrito de los caracteres
- *title panel (title block)*
32 la nomenclatura (los datos técnicos)
- *technical data*
33 la regla plana graduada
- *ruler (rule)*
34 la escala de reducción *f* triangular
- *triangular scale*
35 la plantilla para grabar
- *erasing shield*
36 el tintero de tinta *f* china
- *drawing ink cartridge*
37 el soporte para las plumas de tinta *f* china
- *holders for tubular drawing pens*
38 el juego de plumas *f* de tinta *f* china
- *set of tubular drawing pens*
39 el higrómetro
- *hygrometer*
40 el capuchón con indicación *f* del espesor del trazo (del punto)
- *cap with indication of nib size*
41 el lápiz de borrar
- *pencil-type eraser*
42 la goma de borrar (*Amér.:* el borrador)
- *eraser*
43 el (cuchillo) raspador
- *erasing knife*
44 la cuchilla de raspar
- *erasing knife blade*
45 el lapicero de presión *f* (el portaminas)
- *clutch-type pencil*
46 la mina de grafito *m*
- *pencil lead (refill lead, refill, spare lead)*
47 el pincel de borrar (el borrador de fibra *f* de vidrio *m*)
- *glass eraser*
48 las fibras de vidrio *m*
- *glass fibres* (Am. *fibers*)
49 el tiralíneas
- *ruling pen*
50 la bisagra de cruz *f*
- *cross joint*
51 el disco graduado
- *index plate*
52 el compás de puntas *f* recambiables
- *compass with interchangeable attachments*
53 la guía (la corredera)
- *compass head*
54 la unión de las puntas
- *needle point attachment*

55 la mina de plomo *m*
- *pencil point attachment*
56 la aguja (la punta)
- *needle*
57 la alargadera
- *lengthening arm (extension bar)*
58 el recambio del tiralíneas
- *ruling pen attachment*
59 la bigotera de bomba *f*
- *pump compass (drop compass)*
60 la punta corrediza
- *piston*
61 el tiralíneas del compás
- *ruling pen attachment*
62 el suplemento de mina *f* de plomo *m*
- *pencil attachment*
63 el frasco de tinta *f* china
- *drawing ink container*
64 el compás de ajuste *m* rápido (el compás de precisión *f*)
- *spring bow (rapid adjustment, ratchet-type) compass*
65 la arandela de muelle
- *spring ring hinge*
66 el arco de ajuste *m* micrométrico con muelle *m*
- *spring-loaded fine adjustment for arcs*
67 la aguja desviada
- *right-angle needle*
68 el suplemento tubular de tinta *f* china
- *tubular ink unit*
69 la plantilla de letras *f*
- *stencil lettering guide (lettering stencil)*
70 la plantilla de círculos *m* (el trazacírculos)
- *circle template*
71 la plantilla de elipses *f* (el trazaelipses)
- *ellipse template*

Oficina de proyectos (oficina de dibujo)

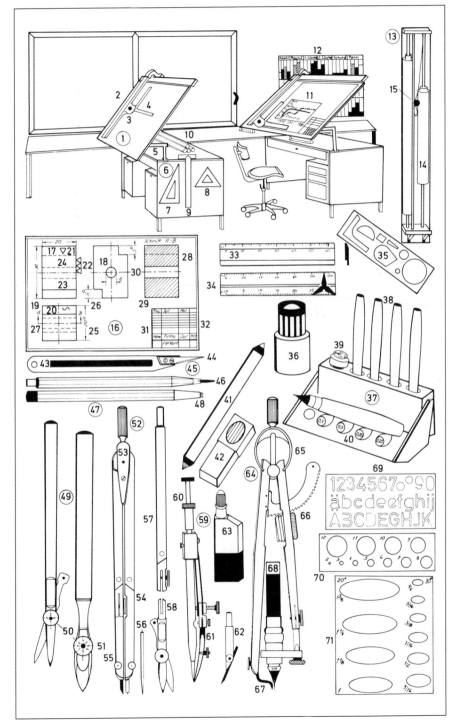

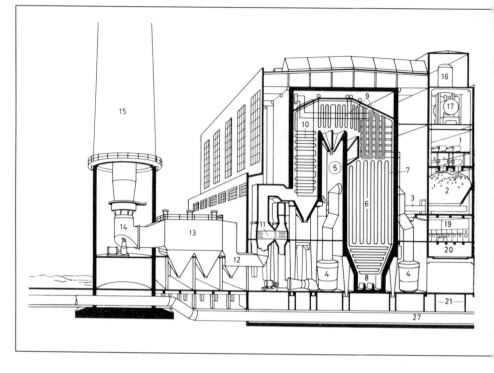

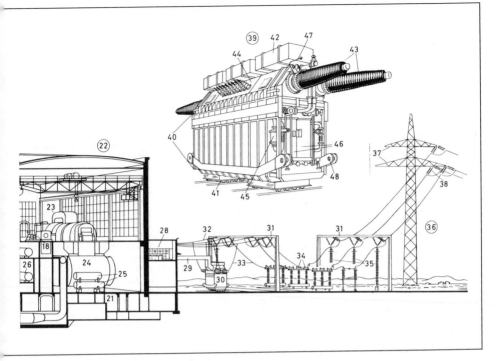

35 el desviador de sobretensión *f*
  – *surge diverter* (Am. *lightning arrester, arrester*)
36 el poste de alta tensión *f*, una torre reticular (poste *m* de celosía *f*)
  – *overhead line support, a lattice steel tower*
37 la traviesa (el travesaño)
  – *cross arm (traverse)*
38 el aislador de amarre *m* (el aislador de suspensión *f*)
  – *strain insulator*
39 **el transformador transportable** (el transformador de energía *f*, el transformador)
  – *mobile (transportable) transformer (power transformer, transformer)*
40 la caja (la caldera) del transformador
  – *transformer tank*
41 el bastidor de ruedas *f*
  – *bogie (Am. truck)*
42 el conservador del aceite
  – *oil conservator*
43 el terminal de alta tensión *f*
  – *primary voltage terminal (primary voltage bushing)*
44 los terminales de baja tensión *f*
  – *low-voltage terminals (low-voltage bushings)*

45 la bomba de circulación *f* del aceite
  – *oil-circulating pump*
46 el refrigerador de agua *f* para el aceite
  – *oil cooler*
47 el brazo para el arco voltaico (para las chispas)
  – *arcing horn*
48 la corcheta para el transporte
  – *transport lug*

1-8 la sala de control *m*
– *control room*
1-6 el pupitre de control *m*
– *control console (control desk)*
1 los controles para los generadores trifásicos
– *control board (control panel) for the alternators*
2 el interruptor de control *m*
– *master switch*
3 el avisador luminoso (la lámpara de señalización *f*)
– *signal light*
4 el tablero de control *m* de los circuitos de alta tensión *f*
– *feeder panel*
5 el aparato supervisor, para el control de los conmutadores
– *monitoring controls for the switching systems*
6 los botones de control *m*
– *controls*
7 el panel, con los instrumentos de medición *f* del control de ejecución *f*
– *revertive signal panel*
8 el diagrama luminoso, para indicar el estado de la red
– *matrix mimic board*
9-18 el transformador
– *transformer*
9 el depósito de dilatación *f* del aceite
– *oil conservator*
10 la ventilación (el respiradero)
– *breather*
11 el indicador del nivel del aceite
– *oil gauge* (Am. *gage)*
12 el aislador de verificación *f* (terminal)
– *feed-through terminal (feed-through insulator)*
13 el interruptor de toma *f* de alta tensión *f*
– *on-load tap changer*
14 la culata
– *yoke*
15 el enrollamiento primario (enrollamiento *m* de alta tensión *f*)
– *primary winding (primary)*
16 el enrollamiento secundario (enrollamiento *m* de baja tensión *f*)
– *secondary winding (secondary, low-voltage winding)*
17 el núcleo
– *core*
18 el conductor de toma *f*
– *tap (tapping)*
19 la conexión del transformador
– *transformer connection*
20 la conexión en estrella *f*
– *star connection (star network, Y-connection)*

21 la conexión en triángulo *m* (la conexión delta)
– *delta connection (mesh connection)*
22 el punto neutro
– *neutral point*
23-30 la turbina de vapor *m*, un grupo turboalternador a vapor *m*
– *steam turbine, a turbogenerator unit*
23 el cilindro de alta presión *f*
– *high-pressure cylinder*
24 el cilindro de presión *f* media
– *medium-pressure cylinder*
25 el cilindro de baja presión *f*
– *low-pressure cylinder*
26 el alternador (el generador) trifásico
– *three-phase generator (generator)*
27 el enfriador de hidrógeno *m*
– *hydrogen cooler*
28 el codo conductor de vapor *m*
– *leakage steam path*
29 la válvula reguladora
– *jet nozzle*
30 la mesa de control *m* de la turbina con los instrumentos de medición *f*
– *turbine monitoring panel with measuring instruments*
31 el regulador de la tensión
– *[automatic] voltage regulator*
32 el dispositivo de sincronización *f* (el sincronizador)
– *synchro*
33 la caja terminal de cables *m*
– *cable box*
34 el conductor
– *conductor*
35 el aislador (terminal)
– *feed-through terminal (feed-through insulator)*
36 el cono de refuerzo *m*
– *core*
37 la caja
– *casing*
38 la pasta de relleno *m*
– *filling compound (filler)*
39 la envoltura de plomo *m*
– *lead sheath*
40 la cápsula de entrada *f*
– *lead-in tube*
41 el cable
– *cable*
42 el cable de alta tensión *f*, para corriente trifásica *f*
– *high voltage cable, for three-phase current*
43 el conductor
– *conductor*
44 el papel metálico
– *metallic paper (metallized paper)*
45 el aislamiento del conductor
– *tracer (tracer element)*

46 la cinta de batista *f*
– *varnished-cambric tape*
47 la envoltura de plomo *m*
– *lead sheath*
48 el papel asfáltico
– *asphalted paper*
49 la envoltura de yute *m*
– *jute serving*
50 la armadura de cinta *f* de acero *m* o de alambre *m* de acero *m*
– *steel tape or steel wire armour (Am. armor)*
51-62 el conmutador rápido de aire *m* **comprimido,** un disyuntor
– *air-blast circuit breaker, a circuit breaker*
51 el depósito de aire *m* comprimido
– *compressed-air tank*
52 la válvula de control *m*
– *control valve (main operating valve)*
53 la conexión del aire comprimido
– *compressed-air inlet*
54 el aislador de aguja *f* hueca, un aislador en cadena *f*, un aislador tipo casquete *m*
– *support insulator, a hollow porcelain supporting insulator*
55 la cámara de conexión *f* (la cámara de extinción *f*)
– *interrupter*
56 la resistencia
– *resistor*
57 los contactos auxiliares
– *auxiliary contacts*
58 el transformador de corriente *f*
– *current transformer*
59 el transformador de la tensión
– *voltage transformer (potential transformer)*
60 la caja de bornes *m* (de terminales *m*)
– *operating mechanism housing*
61 el cuerno de chispas *f*
– *arcing horn*
62 el descargador de chispas *f*
– *spark gap*

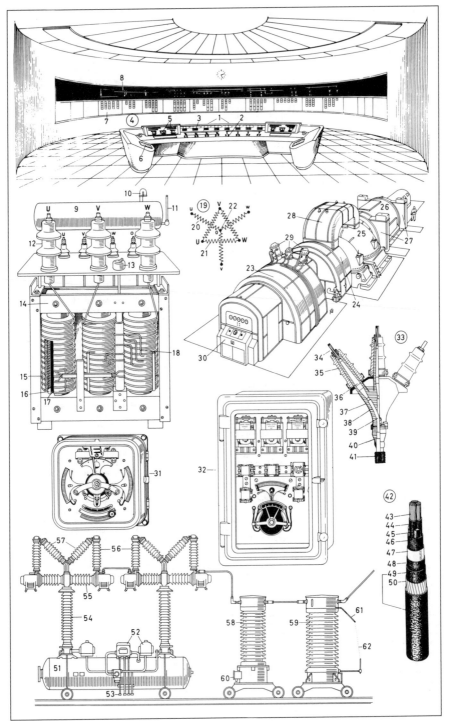

1 **el reactor superregenerador rápido** [esquema]
– *fast-breeder reactor (fast breeder) [diagram]*
2 el circuito primario de enfriamiento m (el circuito primario de sodio m)
– *primary circuit (primary loop, primary sodium system)*
3 el reactor
– *reactor*
4 los ensamblajes de elementos m combustibles (el combustible nuclear)
– *fuel rods (fuel pins)*
5 la bomba de circulación f primaria
– *primary sodium pump*
6 el intercambiador de calor m
– *heat exchanger*
7 el circuito secundario de enfriamiento m (el circuito secundario de sodio m)
– *secondary circuit (secondary loop, secondary sodium system)*
8 la bomba de circulación f secundaria
– *secondary sodium pump*
9 el generador de vapor m
– *steam generator*
10 el circuito terciario (el circuito de agua f de refrigeración f)
– *cooling water flow circuit*
11 la tubería de vapor m
– *steam line*
12 la tubería del agua f de alimentación f
– *feedwater line*
13 la bomba del agua f de alimentación f
– *feed pump*
14 la turbina de vapor m
– *steam turbine*
15 el generador
– *generator*
16 la alimentación de la red (eléctrica) (la línea de transmisión f)
– *transmission line*
17 el condensador
– *condenser*
18 el agua f de refrigeración f
– *cooling water*
19 **el reactor nuclear,** un reactor de agua f a presión f (la central nuclear; *fam.:* la central atómica)
– *nuclear reactor, a pressurized-water reactor (nuclear power plant, atomic power plant)*
20 la cubierta de hormigón m (el edificio del reactor)
– *concrete shield (reactor building)*
21 el recinto de seguridad f de acero m con hendidura f para la aspiración de aire m
– *steel containment (steel shell) with air extraction vent*
22 el recipiente a presión f del reactor
– *reactor pressure vessel*
23 el mecanismo de impulsión f de los reactores
– *control rod drive*
24 las barras absorbentes (las barras de mando)
– *control rods*
25 la bomba del refrigerante principal
– *primary coolant pump*
26 el generador de vapor m
– *steam generator*
27 la máquina de carga f para los elementos combustibles
– *fuel-handling hoists*
28 el depósito para los elementos combustibles
– *fuel storage*

29 la tubería del refrigerante del reactor
– *coolant flow passage*
30 la tubería del agua f de alimentación f
– *feedwater line*
31 la tubería del vapor vivo
– *prime steam line*
32 la esclusa personal
– *manway*
33 el juego de turbinas f
– *turbogenerator set*
34 el generador trifásico
– *turbogenerator*
35 el condensador
– *condenser*
36 el edificio contiguo
– *service building*
37 la chimenea de evacuación f
– *exhaust gas stack*
38 el puente grúa f circular
– *polar crane*
39 la torre refrigerante, una torre refrigerante seca
– *cooling tower, a dry cooling tower*
40 el sistema (el principio) de agua f a presión f
– *pressurized-water system*
41 el reactor
– *reactor*
42 el circuito primario
– *primary circuit (primary loop)*
43 la bomba de circulación f
– *circulation pump (recirculation pump)*
44 el intercambiador de calor m (el generador de vapor m)
– *heat exchanger (steam generator)*
45 el circuito secundario (el circuito de vapor m y del agua f de alimentación f)
– *secondary circuit (secondary loop, feedwater steam circuit)*
46 la turbina de vapor m
– *steam turbine*
47 el generador
– *generator*
48 el sistema de refrigeración f
– *cooling system*
49 el sistema (el principio) de agua f en ebullición f [esquema]
– *boiling water system [diagram]*
50 el reactor
– *reactor*
51 el circuito de vapor m condensado (de vapor m de agua f)
– *steam and recirculation water flow paths*
52 la turbina de vapor m
– *steam turbine*
53 el generador
– *generator*
54 la bomba de circulación f
– *circulation pump (recirculation pump)*
55 el sistema de agua f de refrigeración f (la refrigeración con agua f corriente)
– *coolant system (cooling with water from river)*
56 **el almacenamiento de desechos m atómicos** en una mina de sal f
– *radioactive waste storage in salt mine*
57-68 las condiciones geológicas de una mina de sal f acondicionada para el almacenamiento de residuos m radiactivos (desechos m atómicos)
– *geological structure of abandoned salt mine converted for disposal of radioactive waste (nuclear waste)*
57 el keuper inferior (el triásico inferior, las margas abigarradas)
– *Lower Keuper*

58 la caliza de conchas f superior
– *Upper Muschelkalk*
59 la caliza de conchas f media
– *Middle Muschelkalk*
60 la caliza de conchas f inferior
– *Lower Muschelkalk*
61 el zócalo de arenisca f roja
– *Bunter downthrow*
62 los residuos de lixiviación f de la piedra calcárea
– *residue of leached (lixiviated) Zechstein (Upper Permian)*
63 la sal gema de Aller
– *Aller rock salt*
64 la sal gema de Leine
– *Leine rock salt*
65 la vena de Stassfurt (la vena – el filón – de sal f potásica)
– *Stassfurt seam (potash salt seam, potash salt bed)*
66 la sal gema de Stassfurt
– *Stassfurt salt*
67 la anhidrita límite
– *grenzanhydrite*
68 la arcilla de piedra f calcárea
– *Zechstein shale*
69 el pozo
– *shaft*
70 la explotación a cielo m abierto
– *minehead buildings*
71 la cámara de almacenamiento m
– *storage chamber*
72 el almacenamiento de desechos m de actividad f media en una mina de sal f
– *storage of medium-active waste in salt mine*
73 la planta (el fondo) a 511 m
– *511 m level*
74 la pared de protección f contra las radiaciones
– *protective screen (anti-radiation screen)*
75 la ventanilla de cristal m de plomo m
– *lead glass window*
76 la cámara de almacenamiento m
– *storage chamber*
77 el barril encarado con desechos m radiactivos
– *drum containing radioactive waste*
78 la cámara de televisión f
– *television camera*
79 la cámara de alimentación f
– *charging chamber*
80 el pupitre de control m
– *control desk (control panel)*
81 la instalación para evacuar el aire
– *upward ventilator*
82 el depósito blindado
– *shielded container*
83 la planta (el fondo) a 490 m
– *490 m level*

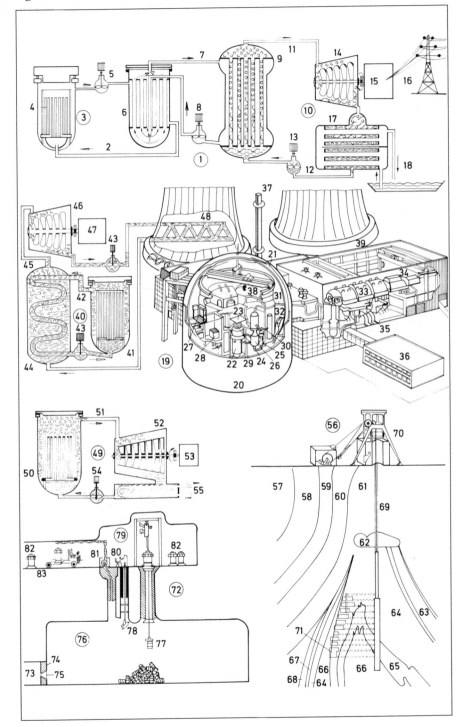

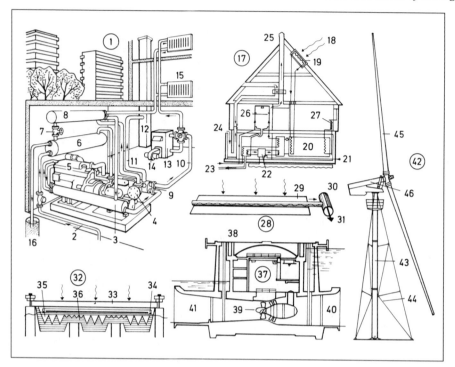

1 el sistema de bomba *f* de calor *m*
– *heat pump system*
2 la entrada de agua *f* subterránea
– *source water inlet*
3 el intercambiador de calor *m* del agua *f* de refrigeración *f*
– *cooling water heat exchanger*
4 el compresor
– *compressor*
5 el motor Diesel o de gas *m* natural
– *natural-gas or diesel engine*
6 el evaporizador
– *evaporator*
7 la válvula reductora
– *pressure release valve*
8 el condensador
– *condenser*
9 el intercambiador de calor *m* para gas *m* de escape *m*
– *waste-gas heat exchanger*
10 el tubo de alimentación *f*
– *flow pipe*
11 la tubería del aire de escape *m*
– *vent pipe*
12 la chimenea
– *chimney*
13 la caldera de la calefacción
– *boiler*
14 el soplante (el fuelle)
– *fan*
15 el aparato de calefacción *f* (el radiador)
– *radiator*
16 el pozo de filtración *f* (el sumidero)
– *sink*
17-36 el aprovechamiento de la energía solar
– *utilization of solar energy*

17 la casa calentada por la energía solar
– *solar (solar-heated) house*
18 la admisión del calor irradiado por el sol
– *solar radiation (sunlight, insolation)*
19 el colector (la placa solar)
– *collector*
20 el acumulador de calor *m*
– *hot reservoir (heat reservoir)*
21 la alimentación eléctrica
– *power supply*
22 la bomba de calor *m*
– *heat pump*
23 la tubería de evacuación *f* del agua *f*
– *water outlet*
24 la entrada de aire *m*
– *air supply*
25 la chimenea del aire de escapa *m*
– *flue*
26 el aprovisionamiento de agua *f* caliente
– *hot water supply*
27 la calefacción por radiador *m*
– *radiator heating*
28 el elemento (el colector) de central *f* (*Amér.*: usina *f*) solar
– *flat plate solar collector*
29 el colector negro (con lámina *f* de aluminio *m* recubierta de asfalto *m*)
– *blackened receiver surface with asphalted aluminium (Am. aluminium) foil*
30 el tubo de acero *m*
– *steel tube*
31 el medio de transporte *m* del calor
– *heat transfer fluid*
32 el colector solar (la placa solar, el ladrillo solar, la teja solar)
– *flat plate solar collector, containing solar cell*

33 el recubrimiento de cristal *m*
– *glass cover*
34 la célula solar
– *solar cell*
35 los canales de aire *m*
– *air ducts*
36 el aislamiento
– *insulation*
37 **la central** (*Amér.*: la usina) **maremotriz**
– *tidal power plant [section]*
38 el dique de contención *f*
– *dam*
39 la turbina reversible
– *reversible turbine*
40 el canal de la turbina al lado del mar (el canal de traída *f* del agua *f*)
– *turbine inlet for water from the sea*
41 el canal de la turbina al lado de la cuenca (el canal de evacuación *f* del agua *f*)
– *turbine inlet for water from the basin*
42 **la central eólica**
– *wind power plant (wind generator aerogenerator)*
43 la torre de tubos *m*
– *truss tower*
44 la retención (el soporte) de cable *m* metálico
– *guy wire*
45 el rotor
– *rotor*
46 el generador y el servomotor de orientación *f* (mecanismo *m* de auto-orientación *f*)
– *generator with variable pitch for power regulation*

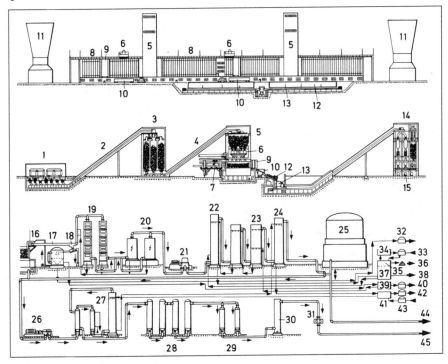

1-15 **la coquería**
- *coking plant*
1 la descarga del carbón de coque *m*
- *dumping of coking coal*
2 la cinta transportadora
- *belt conveyor*
3 el silo de los componentes de carbón *m* de coque *m*
- *blending bunker*
4 la cinta transportadora de la torre de carbón *m*
- *service bunker conveyor*
5 la torre de carbón *m*
- *service bunker*
6 el vagón (el carrito) de carga *f*
- *larry car (larry, charging car)*
7 la (máquina) deshornadora de coque *m*
- *pusher ram*
8 la batería del horno de coque *m*
- *battery of coke ovens*
9 el carro guía de la torta de coque *m*
- *coke guide*
10 el carro de extinción *f* con locomotora *f*
- *quenching car, with engine*
11 la torre de extinción *f*
- *quenching tower*
12 la rampa del coque
- *coke loading bay (coke wharf)*
13 la cinta de la rampa del coque
- *coke wharf conveyor*
14 la instalación de cribado *m* del coque fino y grueso
- *screening of coke and breeze*
15 el cargamento de coque *m*
- *coke loading*
16-45 **el tratamiento del gas de coquería** *f*
- *coke-oven gas processing*

16 la salida del gas de los hornos de coque *m*
- *discharge (release) of gas from the coke ovens*
17 la canalización principal del gas
- *gas-collecting main*
18 la extracción del alquitrán mineral
- *coal tar extraction*
19 el refrigerador de gas *m*
- *gas cooler*
20 el electrofiltro
- *electrostatic precipitator*
21 el extractor de gas *m*
- *gas extractor*
22 el lavador de ácido *m* sulfhídrico
- *hydrogen sulphide (Am. hydrogen sulfide) scrubber (hydrogen sulphide wet collector)*
23 el lavador de amoníaco *m*
- *ammonia scrubber (ammonia wet collector)*
24 el lavador de benceno *m*
- *benzene (benzol) scrubber*
25 el depósito colector de gas *m*
- *gas holder*
26 el compresor de gas *m*
- *gas compressor*
27 el desbenzolaje por refrigerador *m* e intercambiador *m* de calor *m*
- *debenzoling by cooler and heat exchanger*
28 la desulfuración del gas a presión *f*
- *desulphurization (Am. desulfurization) of pressure gas*
29 la refrigeración del gas
- *gas cooling*
30 el secado del gas
- *gas drying*

31 el contador de gas *m*
- *gas meter*
32 el depósito de alquitrán *m* bruto
- *crude tar tank*
33 la entrada de ácido *m* sulfúrico
- *sulphuric acid (Am. sulfuric acid) supply*
34 la producción de ácido *m* sulfúrico
- *production of sulphuric acid (Am. sulfuric acid)*
35 la producción de sulfato *m* de amonio *m*
- *production of ammonium sulphate (Am. ammonium sulfate)*
36 el sulfato de amonio *m*
- *ammonium sulphate (Am. ammonium sulfate)*
37 la instalación de regeneración *f* de los productos de lavado *m*
- *recovery plant for recovering the scrubbing agents*
38 la evacuación de las aguas residuales
- *waste water discharge*
39 la extracción del fenol de las aguas gaseosas
- *phenol extraction from the gas water*
40 el depósito de fenol *m* crudo
- *crude phenol tank*
41 la producción de benceno *m* crudo
- *production of crude benzol (crude benzene)*
42 el depósito de benceno *m* crudo
- *crude benzol (crude benzene) tank*
43 el depósito de aceite *m* de lavado *m*
- *scrubbing oil tank*
44 la tubería de gas *m* de baja presión *f*
- *low-pressure gas main*
45 la tubería de gas *m* de alta presión *f*
- *high-pressure gas main*

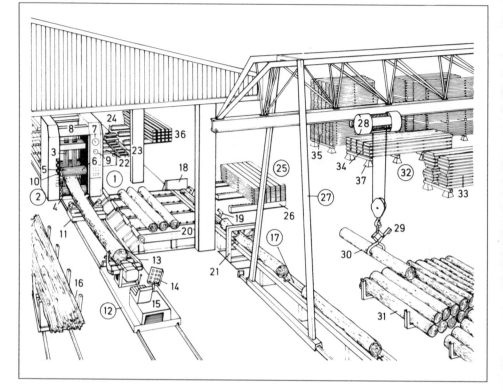

1 el aserradero (la serrería; *Col. y Ec.:* el aserrío)	13 las pinzas de sujeción *f*	25 la pila
– *sawmill*	– *log grips*	– *piling*
2 la sierra alternativa de hojas *f* múltiples	14 el mando a distancia *f* (el telemando)	26 los soportes de rodillo *m*
– *vertical frame saw (Am. gang mill)*	– *remote control panel*	– *roller trestles*
3 las hojas de sierra *f*	15 (el sistema) de accionamiento *m* del carro de presa *f*	27 la grúa de pórtico *m*
– *saw blades*	– *carriage motor*	– *gantry crane*
4 el cilindro de entrada *f*	16 el carro para las astillas (las tablillas)	28 el motor de la grúa
– *feed roller*	– *truck for splinters (splints)*	– *crane motor*
5 el cilindro trepador (el rodillo guía)	17 el transportador de trozas *f* (la cadena sin fin *m* para troncos *m*)	29 las pinzas (la garra) orientables
– *guide roller*	– *endless log chain (Am. jack chain)*	– *pivoted log grips*
6 la acanaladura	18 el tablero de tope *m*	30 el rollo (de madera *f*) (el rollizo)
– *fluting (grooving, grooves)*	– *stop plate*	– *roundwood (round timber)*
7 el manómetro de presión *f* del aceite (el indicador de la presión del aceite)	19 el eyector de troncos *m*	31 el montón de rollizos *m* (el montón de rollizos *m* seleccionados)
– *oil pressure gauge (Am. gage)*	– *log-kicker arms*	– *log dump*
8 el bastidor de la sierra	20 el transportador transversal	32 el emplazamiento (*Amér.:* la ubicación) de la madera cortada
– *saw frame*	– *cross conveyor*	– *squared timber store*
9 el indicador de avance *m*	21 la instalación de lavado *m*	33 la troza serrada
– *feed indicator*	– *washer (washing machine)*	– *sawn logs*
10 la escala para la altura del corte	22 el transportador de cadenas *f* para la madera cortada	34 los maderos
– *log capacity scale*	– *cross chain conveyor for sawn timber*	– *planks*
11 el carrito auxiliar	23 la mesa de rodillos *m*	35 las planchas (de madera *f*)
– *auxiliary carriage*	– *roller table*	– *boards (planks)*
12 el carro de presa *f*	24 la sierra oscilante bajo la mesa	36 la madera escuadrada
– *carriage*	– *undercut swing saw*	– *squared timber*
		37 la cuña (de hormigón *m*) de la pila
		– *stack bearer*

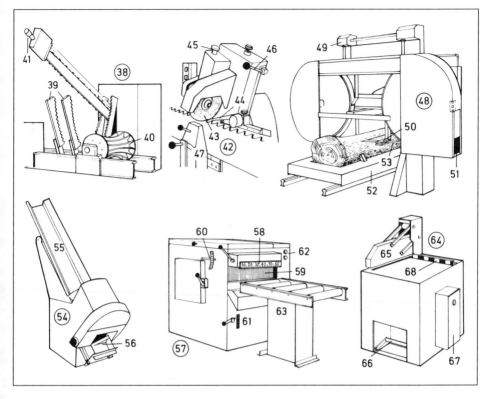

38 la tronzadora de cadenas *f* automática
– *automatic cross-cut chain saw*
39 la sujeción del tronco de madera *f*
– *log grips*
40 el cilindro de avance *m*
– *feed roller*
41 el dispositivo de sujeción *f* de cadenas *f*
– *chain-tensioning device*
42 la máquina de afilar y aserrar automática
– *saw-sharpening machine*
43 la muela
– *grinding wheel (teeth grinder)*
44 el trinquete de avance *m*
– *feed pawl*
45 el regulador de profundidad *f* para la muela
– *depth adjustment for the teeth grinder*
46 la palanca para la cabeza de afilado *m*
– *lifter (lever) for the grinder chuck*
47 el dispositivo fijador de la hoja de la sierra
– *holding device for the saw blade*
48 la sierra de cinta *f* horizontal
– *horizontal bandsaw for sawing logs*

49 la regulación de la altura
– *height adjustment*
50 el frotador de virutas *f*
– *chip remover*
51 el aspirador de virutas *f*
– *chip extractor*
52 el carro transportador
– *carriage*
53 la hoja de la sierra de cinta *f*
– *bandsaw blade*
54 la sierra automática para la leña
– *automatic blocking saw*
55 el canal de alimentación *f* (de entrada)
– *feed channel*
56 la abertura de eyección *f*
– *discharge opening*
57 la sierra de cantear doble
– *twin edger (double edger)*
58 la escala de la anchura
– *breadth scale (width scale)*
59 la pantalla de protección *f* (el dispositivo de seguridad *f*, las láminas de protección *f*)
– *kick-back guard (plates)*
60 la escala de la altura
– *height scale*
61 la escala de avance *m*
– *in-feed scale*

62 los indicadores luminosos
– *indicator lamps*
63 la mesa de carga *f*
– *feed table*
64 la sierra oscilante (la sierra con movimiento *m* de vaivén *m*)
– *undercut swing saw*
65 el prensador automático (con cubierta *f* protectora)
– *automatic hold-down with protective hood*
66 el interruptor de pie *m* (el conmutador de pedal *m*)
– *foot switch*
67 la instalación de distribución *f*
– *distribution board (panelboard)*
68 el tope longitudinal
– *length stop*

1 la cantera, una explotación a cielo *m* abierto	**13** la excavadora universal	**26** el jalón
– *quarry, an open-cast working*	– *universal excavator*	– *measuring rod*
2 la tierra de recubrimiento *m* (los escombros)	**14** la vagoneta de gran capacidad *f*	**27** el cartucho explosivo
– *overburden*	– *large-capacity truck*	– *blasting cartridge*
3 el frente de arranque *m*	**15** la pared de roca *f*	**28** la mecha
– *working face*	– *rock face*	– *fuse (blasting fuse)*
4 el montón de piedras *f* sueltas (de piedras *f* arrancadas)	**16** el montacargas inclinado	**29** el cubo con arena *f* de relleno *m*
– *loose rock pile (blasted rock)*	– *inclined hoist*	– *plugging sand (stemming sand) bucket*
5 el picapedrero, un trabajador de la cantera	**17** la trituradora previa	**30** el sillar (la piedra de sillería *f*)
– *quarryman (quarrier), a quarry worker*	– *primary crusher*	– *dressed stone*
6 el mazo (la almádena, el martillo de cuña *f*)	**18** la instalación productora de grava *f*	**31** el pico
– *sledge hammer*	– *stone-crushing plant*	– *pick*
7 la cuña	**19** la trituradora giratoria en grueso (*anál.:* la trituradora giratoria en fino; *Chile:* la chancadora)	**32** la palanca
– *wedge*	– *coarse rotary (gyratory) crusher; sim.: fine rotary (gyratory) crusher (rotary or gyratory crusher)*	– *crowbar (pinch bar)*
8 el bloque de roca *f*	**20** la machacadora (la trituradora de mordazas *f*)	**33** la horca de rocas *f*
– *block of stone*	– *hammer crusher (impact crusher)*	– *fork*
9 el barrenero	**21** la criba vibradora	**34** el picapedrero (el cantero)
– *driller*	– *vibrating screen*	– *stonemason*
10 el casco protector	**22** la piedra pulverizada	**35-38 las herramientas de cantero** *m*
– *safety helmet*	– *screenings (fine dust)*	– ***stonemason's tools***
11 la perforadora de percusión *f* (el martillo perforador, la perforadora de roca *f*)	**23** la gravilla	**35** el martillo de mano *f*
– *hammer drill (hard-rock drill)*	– *stone chippings*	– *stonemason's hammer*
12 el taladro	**24** la grava	**36** el mazo
– *borehole*	– *crushed stone*	– *mallet*
	25 el maestro en explosivos *m* (el artificiero)	**37** el cincel de raspar
	– *shot firer*	– *drove chisel (drove, boaster, broad chisel)*
		38 la trincheta (la escoda)
		– *dressing axe* (Am. *ax*)

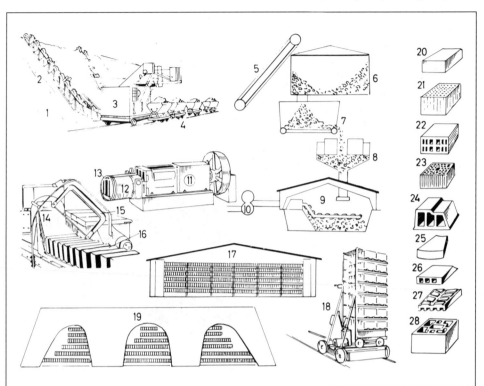

1 la barrera (el pozo de barro *m*)
– *clay pit*
2 el barro, una arcilla impura (arcilla *f* bruta)
– *loam, an impure clay (raw clay)*
3 la excavadora del terreno de cobertura *f*, una excavadora de gran capacidad *f*
– *overburden excavator, a large-scale excavator*
4 el ferrocarril de vía *f* estrecha
– *narrow-gauge* (Am. *narrow-gage) track system*
5 el montacargas inclinado
– *inclined hoist*
6 el pudridero del barro
– *souring chambers*
7 el alimentador
– *box feeder (feeder)*
8 el triturador de muelas *f* verticales
– *edge runner mill (edge mill, pan grinding mill)*
9 la laminadora
– *rolling plant*
10 la mezcladora de árbol *m* doble
– *double-shaft trough mixer (mixer)*

11 la prensa de extrusión *f* (una prensa de ladrillos *m*)
– *extrusion press (brick-pressing machine)*
12 la cámara de vacío *m*
– *vacuum chamber*
13 la boca de salida *f*
– *die*
14 la columna de arcilla *f*
– *clay column*
15 la cortadora (la cortadora de ladrillos *m*)
– *cutter (brick cutter)*
16 el ladrillo crudo (el ladrillo sin cocer)
– *unfired brick (green brick)*
17 el secadero (la cámara secadora)
– *drying shed*
18 la carretilla elevadora de horquilla *f* (la carretilla apiladora)
– *mechanical finger car (stacker truck)*
19 el horno circular (horno *m* para ladrillos *m*)
– *circular kiln (brick kiln)*
20 el ladrillo macizo (ladrillo *m*)
– *solid brick (building brick)*

21 *u.* 22 los ladrillos perforados
– *perforated bricks and hollow blocks*
21 el ladrillo con perforaciones *f* verticales
– *perforated brick with vertical perforations*
22 el ladrillo hueco con canales *m* horizontales
– *hollow clay block with horizontal perforations*
23 el ladrillo de rejilla *f*
– *hollow clay block with vertical perforations*
24 el ladrillo de techar (la bovedilla)
– *floor brick*
25 el ladrillo de chimenea *f* (ladrillo *m* radial)
– *compass brick (radial brick, radiating brick)*
26 el ladrillo hueco plano (el ladrillo hueco para bóvedas *f*)
– *hollow flooring block*
27 el ladrillo aplanillado de establo *m*
– *paving brick*
28 el ladrillo perfilado de chimenea *f*
– *cellular brick [for fireplaces] (chimney brick)*

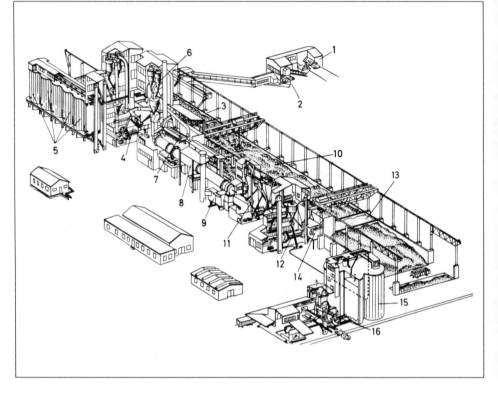

1 las materias primas (caliza *f*, arcilla *f* y marga *f* arcillosa)
– *raw materials (limestone, clay and
marl)*
2 la trituradora de martillos *m*
– *hammer crusher (hammer mill)*
3 el almacén de las materias primas
– *raw material store*
4 el molino para la molienda y el
secado simultáneos de las materias primas mediante el gas de
escape *m* de la instalación intercambiadora de calor *m*
– *raw mill for simultaneously grinding and drying the raw materials
with exhaust gas from the heat
exchanger*
5 los silos para las materias primas
pulverizadas (los silos de homogeneización *f*)
– *raw meal silos*
6 la instalación intercambiadora de
calor *m* (el intercambiador de
calor *m* de ciclón *m*)
– *heat exchanger (cyclone heat
exchanger)*

7 la instalación de desem-
polvamiento (un electrofiltro)
para el gas de escape *m* del intercambiador de calor *m* del molino
de materia *f* cruda
– *dust collector (an electrostatic precipitator) for the heat exchanger
exhaust from the raw mill*
8 el horno rotatorio (horno *m* giratorio)
– *rotary kiln*
9 el refrigerador de clinker *m*
– *clinker cooler*
10 el almacén de clinker *m*
– *clinker store*
11 el soplante (el fuelle) de aire *m*
primario
– *primary air blower*
12 la instalación trituradora de
cemento *m*
– *cement-grinding mill*
13 el almacén (el depósito) de yeso *m*
– *gypsum store*
14 la trituradora (*sin.:* la quebranta-
dora, la machacadora) de yeso *m*
– *gypsum crusher*

15 el silo para el cemento
– *cement silo*
16 las máquinas envasadoras de
cemento *m* en sacos *m* de papel *m*
– *cement-packing plant for paper
sacks*

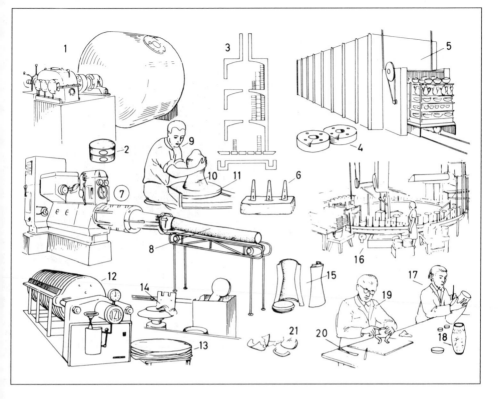

1 el molino de tambor *m* (molino *m* de bolas *f*), para la preparación por vía *f* húmeda de la mezcla de materias *f* primas
 – *grinding cylinder (ball mill) for the preparation of the raw material in water*
2 la cápsula refractaria, con abertura *f* para la observación del proceso de cocción *f*
 – *sample sagger (saggar, seggar), with aperture for observing the firing process*
3 el horno redondo (horno *m* discontinuo) [esquema]
 – *bottle kiln (beehive kiln) [diagram]*
4 el molde de cocción *f*
 – *firing mould (Am. mold)*
5 el horno de túnel *m*
 – *tunnel kiln*
6 el cono Seger, para medir altas temperaturas *f*
 – *Seger cone (pyrometric cone, Am. Orton cone) for measuring high temperatures*
7 la prensa de vacío *m*, una prensa de extrusión *f*
 – *de-airing pug mill (de-airing pug press), an extrusion press*

8 la barra de material *m* (de masa *f*)
 – *clay column*
9 el tornero, torneando una pieza en bruto
 – *thrower throwing a ball (bat) of clay*
10 la masa de arcilla *f* (la pieza en bruto)
 – *slug of clay*
11 el plato giratorio; *anál.:* el torno de alfarero *m*
 – *turntable; sim.: potter's wheel*
12 el filtro-prensa
 – *filter press*
13 la torta de masa *f* (la torta del filtro-prensa)
 – *filter cake*
14 el torneado, con la plantilla de tornear
 – *jiggering, with a profiling tool; sim.: jollying*
15 el molde, para echar barro *m* (para el colado)
 – *plaster mould (Am. mold) for slip casting*
16 la máquina de vidriar de mesa *f* circular
 – *turntable glazing machine*

17 el pintor (el esmaltador) de porcelana *f*
 – *porcelain painter (china painter)*
18 el jarrón pintado a mano *f*
 – *hand-painted vase*
19 el modelador (retocador *m*)
 – *repairer*
20 la varilla (la espátula) de modelar
 – *pallet (modelling, Am. modeling, tool)*
21 los añicos de porcelana *f* (los trozos)
 – *shards (sherds, potsherds)*

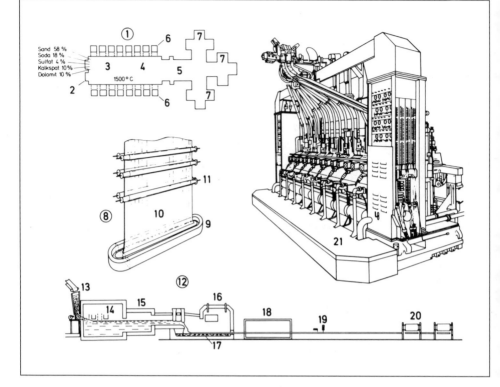

Sand 58 %
Soda 18 %
Sulfat 4 %
Kalkspat 10 %
Dolomit 10 %

1500° C

1-20 la producción de vidrio *m* plano
– *sheet glass production (flat glass production)*
1 el horno de fundir vidrio *m* por el procedimiento Fourcault [esquema]
– *glass furnace (tank furnace) for the Fourcault process [diagram]*
2 el alimentador frontal, para la introducción de la mezcla
– *filling end, for feeding in the batch (frit)*
3 la cubeta de fusión *f*
– *melting bath*
4 la cubeta de clarificación *f*
– *refining bath (fining bath)*
5 las cubetas de trabajo *m*
– *working baths (working area)*
6 el quemador
– *burners*
7 las máquinas de estirar
– *drawing machines*
8 la máquina de estirar vidrio *m* Fourcault
– *Fourcault glass-drawing machine*
9 la boquilla de estirar
– *slot*
10 la hoja de vidrio *m* ascendente
– *glass ribbon (ribbon of glass, sheet of glass) being drawn upwards*

11 los rodillos transportadores
– *rollers (drawing rolls)*
12 el procedimiento de vidrio *m* flotado [esquema]
– *float glass process*
13 la tolva de mezcla *f*
– *batch (frit) feeder (funnel)*
14 la cubeta de fusión *f*
– *melting bath*
15 el depósito (la cubeta) refrigerante
– *cooling tank*
16 el baño de flotado *m* bajo gas *m* de protección *f*
– *float bath in a protective inert-gas atmosphere*
17 el estaño fundido
– *molten tin*
18 el horno para la segunda cochura
– *annealing lehr*
19 el dispositivo de corte *m*
– *automatic cutter*
20 la apiladora
– *stacking machines*
21 la máquina SI (la máquina de sección *f* individual), una máquina para soplar botellas *f* (una máquina para la fabricación de botellas *f*)
– *IS (individual-section) machine, a bottle-making machine*

22-37 los procedimientos de soplado m
– *blowing processes*
22 el procedimiento de soplado *m* doble
– *blow-and-blow process*
23 la introducción de la masa de vidrio *m*
– *introduction of the gob of molten glass*
24 el primer soplado
– *first blowing*
25 el contrasoplado
– *suction*
26 el traslado del molde de prensa *f* al molde de soplado *m*
– *transfer from the parison mould (Am. mold) to the blow mould (Am. mold)*
27 el recalentamiento
– *reheating*
28 el soplado (la formación del vacío)
– *blowing (suction, final shaping)*
29 la salida del vidrio hueco acabado
– *delivery of the completed vessel*
30 el procedimiento de prensado *m* y soplado *m*
– *press-and-blow process*

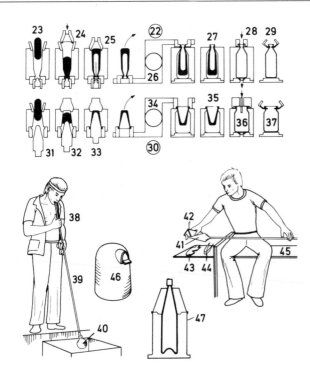

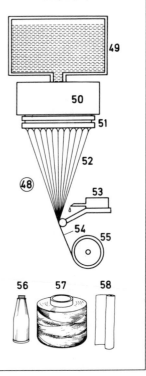

31 la introducción de la masa de vidrio *m*
– *introduction of the gob of molten glass*
32 el macho (el punzón) de prensa *f*
– *plunger*
33 el prensado
– *pressing*
34 el traslado del molde de prensa *f* al molde de soplado *m*
– *transfer from the press mould (Am. mold) to the blow mould (Am. mold)*
35 el recalentamiento
– *reheating*
36 el soplado (la formación del vacío)
– *blowing (suction, final shaping)*
37 la salida del vidrio hueco acabado
– *delivery of the completed vessel*
38-47 la fabricación de vidrio *m* (soplado *m* con la boca, el trabajo de dar forma *f*)
– *glassmaking (glassblowing, glass-blowing by hand, glass forming)*
38 el vidriero (el soplador de vidrio *m*)
– *glassmaker (glassblower)*
39 el tubo de vidriero *m* (la caña de soplador *m*)
– *blowing iron*

40 la masa de vidrio *m*
– *gob*
41 la copa (en forma *f* de cáliz *m*) soplada con la boca
– *hand-blown goblet*
42 la tablilla, para dar forma *f* al pie de la copa
– *clappers for shaping the base (foot) of the goblet*
43 el calibre de forma *f*
– *trimming tool*
44 las tenazas de soplador *m* (las pinzas cortantes)
– *tongs*
45 el banco de vidriero *m*
– *glassmaker's chair (gaffer's chair)*
46 el crisol de vidriería *f* cubierto
– *covered glasshouse pot*
47 el molde, para acabar de soplar la masa soplada previamente
– *mould (Am. mold), into which the parison is blown*
48-55 la producción de vidrio *m* textil
– *production of glass fibre (Am. glass fiber)*
48 el procedimiento de filamento *m* continuo
– *continuous filament process*
49 el horno de fusión *f* del vidrio
– *glass furnace*

50 la cuba con la fusión de vidrio *m* (la cubeta con vidrio *m* fundido)
– *bushing containing molten glass*
51 la boquilla agujereada
– *bushing tips*
52 los hilos elementales del vidrio textil
– *glass filaments*
53 el encolado (el ensimaje)
– *sizing*
54 el hilado
– *strand (thread)*
55 la cabeza de la bobina
– *spool*
56-58 los productos de vidrio *m* textil
– *glass fibre (Am. glass fiber) products*
56 el hilo de vidrio *m* textil
– *glass yarn (glass thread)*
57 el hilo de vidrio *m* en bobina *f*
– *sleeved glass yarn (glass thread)*
58 el fieltro de vidrio *m*
– *glass wool*

**1-13 el aprovisionamiento de algo-
dón** *m*
– *supply of cotton*
1 el copo de algodón *m* maduro
– *ripe cotton boll*
2 la husada de hilo *m* (la husada, la
bobina)
– *full cop (cop wound with weft
yarn)*
3 la bala de algodón *m* prensado
– *compressed cotton bale*
4 el embalaje (la arpillera) de yute *m*
– *jute wrapping*
5 el fleje de hierro *m*
– *steel band*
6 los números de la partida de la
bala
– *identification mark of the bale*
7 la abridora abrebalas (el
limpiador de algodón *m*)
– *bale opener (bale breaker)*
8 la telera sin fin *m* de alimentación *f*
– *cotton-feeding brattice*
9 el depósito de alimentación *f*
– *cotton feed*
10 la tolva aspiradora del polvo
– *dust extraction fan*
11 el conducto de la cámara de polvo *m*
– *duct to the dust-collecting chamber*
12 el motor impulsor
– *drive motor*
13 la telera sin fin *m* reunidora
– *conveyor brattice*
14 el batán doble
– *double scutcher (machine with
two scutchers)*
15 el dispositivo de enrollamiento *m*
(el soporte para las telas)
– *lap cradle*
16 la guía de compresión *f* (el
corchete compresor)
– *rack head*
17 la palanca de puesta *f* en marcha *f*
– *starting handle*
18 el volante, para subir o bajar la
guía de presión *f*
– *handwheel, for raising and lowering the rack head*
19 la tabla móvil de la tela de batán *m*
– *movable lap-turner*
20 los cilindros de presión *f*
– *calender rollers*
21 la cubierta, para el par de cilindros *m* de aspiración *f*
– *cover for the perforated cylinders*
22 el canal de polvo *m*
– *dust escape flue (dust discharge
flue)*
23 los motores impulsores
– *drive motors (beater drive motors)*
24 el eje, para el movimiento de las
alas batidoras
– *beater driving shaft*

25 la devanadera triple cardante
– *three-blade beater (Kirschner
beater)*
26 la rejilla
– *grid [for impurities to drop]*
27 el cilindro de alimentación *f*
– *pedal roller (pedal cylinder)*
28 la palanca reguladora de alimentación *f*, una palanca de pedal *m*
– *control lever for the pedal roller, a
pedal lever*
29 el variador de velocidad *f*
– *variable change-speed gear*
30 la caja de conos *m*
– *cone drum box*
31 el sistema de palancas *f*, para la
regulación de la alimentación
– *stop and start levers for the hopper*
32 el cilindro de presión *f* de madera *f*
– *wooden hopper delivery roller*
33 la cargadora automática
– *hopper feeder*
34 la carda de chapones *m* (carda *f*,
percha *f*)
– *carding machine (card, carding
engine)*
35 el bote de la carda, para el depósito de la mecha de carda *f*
– *card can (carding can), for receiving the coiled sliver*
36 el soporte giratorio del bote
– *can holder*
37 los cilindros de calandria *f* (los
cilindros compresores)
– *calender rollers*
38 la cinta de carda *f*
– *carded sliver (card sliver)*
39 el peine descargador
– *vibrating doffer comb*
40 la palanca para parar
– *start-stop lever*
41 el soporte del esmerilador
– *grinding-roller bearing*
42 el cardador (el rastrillador)
– *doffer*
43 la bota (el gran tambor)
– *cylinder*
44 el mecanismo para limpiar los
chapones
– *flat clearer*
45 la cadena de los chapones
– *flats*
46 las poleas tensoras, para la cadena
de los chapones
– *supporting pulleys for the flats*
47 el rollo de tela *f* del batán
– *scutcher lap (carded lap)*
48 el soporte del rollo
– *scutcher lap holder*
49 el motor impulsor, con correa *f*
plana
– *drive motor with flat belt*

50 la polea principal de accionamiento *m*
– *main drive pulley (fast-and-loose
drive pulley)*
51 el esquema de la carda
– *principle of the card (of the carding engine)*
52 el cilindro de alimentación *f*
– *fluted feed roller*
53 el cilindro tomador (el cilindro
abridor)
– *licker-in (taker-in, licker-in roller)*
54 la rejilla del tomador
– *licker-in undercasing*
55 la rejilla del gran tambor
– *cylinder undercasing*
56 la peinadora
– *combing machine (comber)*
57 la caja de engranajes *m*
– *drive gearbox (driving gear)*
58 la napa
– *laps ready for combing*
59 el condensador de la mecha
– *calender rollers*
60 el cabezal (el banco) de estiraje *m*
– *comber draw box*
61 el contador
– *counter*
62 el dispositivo de plegado *m* de la
cinta
– *coiler top*
63 el esquema de la peinadora
– *principle of the comber*
64 la cinta de carda *f*
– *lap*
65 la mordaza inferior
– *bottom nipper*
66 la mordaza superior
– *top nipper*
67 el peine fijo
– *top comb*
68 el peine circular
– *combing cylinder*
69 el segmento de cuero *m*
– *plain part of the cylinder*
70 el segmento de agujas *f*
– *needled part of the cylinder*
71 los cilindros de arranque *m* (los
cilindros condensadores)
– *detaching rollers*
72 el peinado (la cinta peinada)
– *carded and combed sliver*

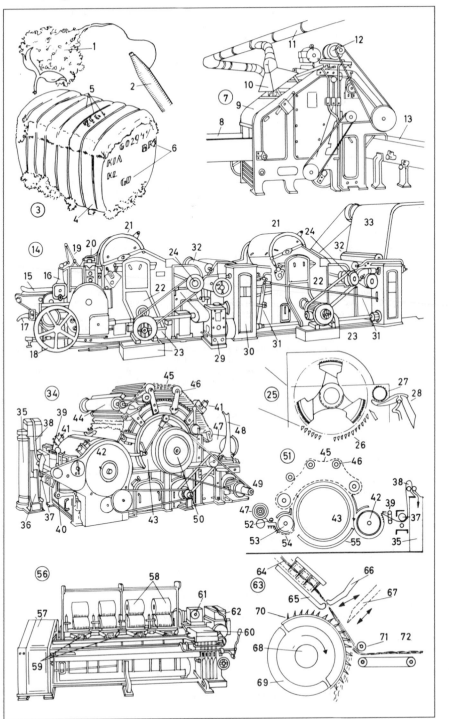

1 **el estirado** (el manuar)
– *draw frame*
2 la caja de engranajes *m*, con motor *m* incorporado
– *gearbox with built-in motor*
3 los botes de la carda
– *sliver cans*
4 el cilindro de contacto *m*, para el paro automático de la máquina en caso de rotura *f* de la mecha
– *broken thread detector roller*
5 el doblado de las mechas de carda *f*
– *doubling of the slivers*
6 la palanca de paro *m* de la máquina
– *stopping handle*
7 el recubrimiento de los cilindros (del banco) de estiraje *m*
– *draw frame cover*
8 las lámparas de control *m*
– *indicator lamps (signal lights)*
9 el banco de estiraje *m* sencillo de cuatro cilindros *m* [esquema]
– *simple four-roller draw frame [diagram]*
10 los cilindros inferiores (los cilindros de acero *m* ranurado)
– *bottom rollers (lower rollers), fluted steel rollers*
11 los cilindros superiores con recubrimiento *m* de plástico *m*
– *top rollers (upper rollers) covered with synthetic rubber*
12 la cinta gruesa (la napa), antes del estiraje
– *doubled slivers before drafting*
13 la cinta adelgazada mediante los cilindros de estiraje *m*
– *thin sliver after drafting*
14 el tren de gran estiraje *m* [esquema]
– *high-draft system (high-draft draw frame) [diagram]*
15 el embudo de entrada (el embudo guía *f*) de las mechas
– *feeding-in of the sliver*
16 la correa de cuero *m* (*Antillas y Amér. Merid.*: la guasca)
– *leather apron (composition apron)*
17 el raíl de viraje *m*
– *guide bar*
18 el cilindro de presión *f* (el cilindro de retención *f*)
– *light top roller (guide roller)*
19 la mechera en grueso
– *high-draft speed frame (fly frame, slubbing frame)*
20 los botes de estiraje *m* (los botes del manuar)
– *sliver cans*
21 la entrada de las cintas en el banco de estiraje *m*
– *feeding of the slivers to the drafting rollers*

22 el estiraje de la mechera, con chapón *m* de limpieza *f* (limpiador *m*)
– *drafting rollers with top clearers*
23 las bobinas de la mechera
– *roving bobbins*
24 la operaria mechera
– *fly frame operator (operative)*
25 la aleta de la mechera
– *flyer*
26 la bancada extrema de la máquina
– *frame end plate*
27 la mechera intermedia
– *intermediate yarn-forming frame*
28 la fileta de las bobinas
– *bobbin creel (creel)*
29 la mecha saliendo del banco de estiraje *m*
– *roving emerging from the drafting rollers*
30 la bancada portabobinas
– *lifter rail (separating rail)*
31 el mando de los husos
– *spindle drive*
32 la palanca de paro *m* de la máquina
– *stopping handle*
33 la caja de engranajes *m*, con motor incorporado
– *gearbox, with built-on motor*
34 **la continua de hilar** (continua de aros *m*, continua de anillos *m*)
– **ring frame** (*ring spinning frame*)
35 el motor colector trifásico
– *three-phase motor*
36 la placa-base del motor
– *motor base plate (bedplate)*
37 la anilla para el transporte del motor
– *lifting bolt [for motor removal]*
38 el regulador de hilado *m*
– *control gear for spindle speed*
39 la caja de engranajes *m*
– *gearbox*
40 el piñón de cambio *m*, para la variación del número de finura *f* del hilo
– *change wheels for varying the spindle speed [to change the yarn count]*
41 la fileta llena de bobinas *f*
– *full creel*
42 los ejes y los soportes para impulsar el banco de anillas *f*
– *shafts and levers for raising and lowering the ring rail*
43 los husos, con los separadores de hilo *m*
– *spindles with separators*
44 la caja colectora de los hilos aspirados
– *suction box connected to the front roller underclearers*

45 **el huso modelo** de la continua de aros *m*
– **standard ring spindle**
46 la caña del huso
– *spindle shaft*
47 el cojinete de rodillos *m*
– *roller bearing*
48 el piñón (la poleíta de accionamiento *m*)
– *wharve (pulley)*
49 el gancho del huso
– *spindle catch*
50 el portahúsos (la regla portahúsos)
– *spindle rail*
51 el órgano hilador
– *ring and traveller (Am. traveler)*
52 el huso desnudo (vacío)
– *top of the ring tube (of the bobbin)*
53 el hilado (el hilo)
– *yarn (thread)*
54 el aro fijo del banco portaaros
– *ring fitted into the ring rail*
55 el corredor
– *traveller (Am. traveler)*
56 el hilado (el hilo) enrollado
– *yarn wound onto the bobbin*
57 **la máquina retorcedora**
– **doubling frame**
58 la fileta, con bobinas *f* cruzadas
– *creel, with cross-wound cheeses*
59 el dispositivo alimentador
– *delivery rollers*
60 la husada de hilo *m* retorcido
– *bobbins of doubled yarn*

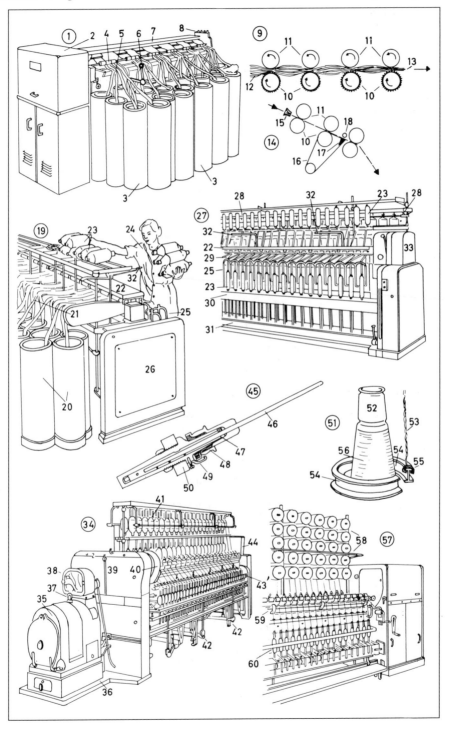

1-57 la preparación del tejido
- *processes preparatory to weaving*
1 la bobinadora (la encarretadora) de cruzado *m*
- *cone-winding frame*
2 el soplante móvil
- *travelling (Am. traveling) blower*
3 el carril guía *f*, para el soplante móvil
- *guide rail, for the travelling (Am. traveling) blower*
4 el soplante (el fuelle) del ventilador
- *blowing assembly*
5 la boquilla de soplado *m*
- *blower aperture*
6 las barras soporte del carril del ventilador
- *superstructure for the blower rail*
7 el indicador del diámetro de la bobina cruzada
- *full-cone indicator*
8 la bobina cónica (la bobina cruzada) de plegado cruzado
- *cross-wound cone*
9 el portabobinas
- *cone creel*
10 el cilindro ranurado (tambor *m* con muescas *f*)
- *grooved cylinder*
11 la ranura en zigzag *m*, para el cruzado del hilo
- *guiding slot for cross-winding the threads*
12 la testera enrolladora, con motor *m*
- *side frame, housing the motor*
13 la palanca reguladora, para retirar la bobina cruzada
- *tension and slub-catching device*
14 la bancada extrema, con filtro *m*
- *off-end framing with filter*
15 la husada
- *yarn package, a ring tube or mule cop*
16 el depósito de husadas *f*
- *yarn package container*
17 el mando de embrague *m* y desembrague *m*
- *starting and stopping lever*
18 el arco, para enhilar automáticamente
- *self-threading guide*
19 el mecanismo de paro *m* automático en caso *m* de rotura *f* de hilo *m*
- *broken thread stop motion*
20 la rendija purgadora para el hilo
- *thread clearer*
21 el disco frotador, para tensar el hilo
- *weighting disc (disk) for tensioning the thread*
22 el urdidor mecánico
- *warping machine*

23 el ventilador
- *fan*
24 la bobina cruzada
- *cross-wound cone*
25 la fileta
- *creel*
26 el peine ajustable (el peine de expansión *f*)
- *adjustable comb*
27 el bastidor (la bancada) del urdidor
- *warping machine frame*
28 el contador métrico de hilado *m* (de urdimbre *f*)
- *yarn length recorder*
29 el plegador de urdimbre *f*
- *warp beam*
30 el disco (la arandela) del plegador
- *beam flange*
31 el listón de protección *f*
- *guard rail*
32 el cilindro de contacto *m* (el tambor impulsor)
- *driving drum (driving cylinder)*
33 la transmisión por correa *f*
- *belt drive*
34 el motor
- *motor*
35 el pedal de puesta *f* en marcha *f*
- *release for starting the driving drum*
36 el tornillo, para regular (ajustar) la anchura del peine
- *screw for adjusting the comb setting*
37 las agujas, para parar en caso *m* de rotura *f* del hilo
- *drop pins, for stopping the machine when a thread breaks*
38 la barra guía *f*
- *guide bar*
39 el par de cilindros *m* de sujeción *f*
- *drop pin rollers*
40 la máquina de encolado *m* y de teñir con índigo *m*
- *indigo dying and sizing machine*
41 el bastidor de desenrollar
- *take-off stand*
42 el plegador de urdimbre *f*
- *warp beam*
43 la urdimbre (el hilado)
- *warp*
44 el depósito reticular (el depósito de mojado *m*)
- *wetting trough*
45 el cilindro de inmersión *f*
- *immersion roller*
46 el cilindro escurridor
- *squeeze roller (mangle)*
47 el depósito (la cuba) de la pintura
- *dye liquor padding trough*
48 la cámara de aire *m*
- *air oxidation passage*

49 la cuba de aclarado *m*
- *washing trough*
50 el secador de cilindros *m* para el presecado
- *drying cylinders for pre-drying*
51 el compensador acumulador
- *tension compensator (tension equalizer)*
52 la máquina encoladora
- *sizing machine*
53 el secador de cilindros *m*
- *drying cylinders*
54 el trozo seco
- *for cotton: stenter; for wool: tenter*
55 la máquina plegadora
- *beaming machine*
56 el plegador de urdimbre *f* encolado
- *sized warp beam*
57 los cilindros prensadores
- *rollers*

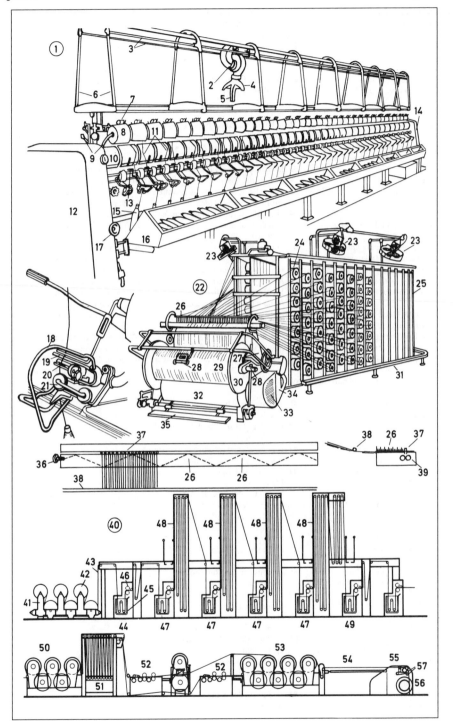

1 el telar automático
– **weaving machine** (automatic loom)
2 el contador de vueltas f (de pasadas f)
– pick counter (tachometer)
3 el carril guía f de los lizos
– shaft (heald shaft, heald frame) guide
4 los lizos
– shafts (heald shafts, heald frames)
5 el tambor de revólver m, para el cambio automático de las canillas
– rotary battery for weft replenishment
6 la tapa del batán
– sley (slay) cap
7 la canilla
– weft pirn
8 la palanca de embrague m y desembrague m
– starting and stopping handle
9 la caja de las lanzaderas, con lanzaderas f de tejer
– shuttle box, with shuttles
10 el peine de telar m
– reed
11 el orillo del tejido
– selvedge (selvage)
12 el tejido (la tela terminada)
– cloth (woven fabric)
13 el templazo (templén m)
– temple (cloth temple)
14 el pulsador eléctrico del hilo (de la trama)
– electric weft feeler
15 el volante
– flywheel
16 la tabla del antepecho
– breast beam board
17 la espada (el brazo) de batir
– picking stick (pick stick)
18 el motor eléctrico
– electric motor
19 los piñones de cambio m
– cloth take-up motion
20 el plegador del tejido
– cloth roller (fabric roller)
21 la caja de las bobinas, para las canillas vacías
– can for empty pirns
22 la correa, para la impulsión de la espada
– lug strap, for moving the picking stick
23 la caja de fusibles m
– fuse box
24 el bastidor (la bancada) del telar
– loom framing
25 la punta metálica
– metal shuttle tip
26 la lanzadera
– shuttle

27 el lizo (el lizo de alambre m)
– heald (heddle, wire heald, wire heddle)
28 el ojal para el hilo (el ojal del lizo)
– eye (eyelet, heald eyelet, heddle eyelet)
29 el ojal de la lanzadera
– eye (shuttle eye)
30 la canilla
– pirn
31 la banda metálica, para el contacto del pulsador
– metal contact sleeve for the weft feeler
32 la ranura para el pulsador
– slot for the feeler
33 el muelle de sujeción f de la canilla
– spring-clip pirn holder
34 el caballero (la laminilla) para el hilo de urdimbre f
– drop wire
35 el telar [corte transversal esquemático]
– weaving machine (automatic loom) [side elevation]
36 las poleas de los lizos
– heald shaft guiding wheels
37 el guiahílos móvil
– backrest
38 la cruz
– lease rods
39 la urdimbre (el hilo de urdimbre m)
– warp (warp thread)
40 la calada
– shed
41 el peine en el batán
– sley (slay)
42 las tablas (el zócalo) del batán
– race board
43 la uña para el dispositivo de paro m
– stop rod blade for the stop motion
44 el encaje del tope
– bumper steel
45 el vástago del tope del paro
– bumper steel stop rod
46 el antepecho (el plegador delantero)
– breast beam
47 el cilindro estriado
– cloth take-up roller
48 el plegador de urdimbre f
– warp beam
49 el disco (la arandela) del plegador
– beam flange
50 el árbol (el eje) principal
– crankshaft
51 el piñón (la rueda dentada) del eje cigüeñal
– crankshaft wheel
52 la biela ajustable
– connector
53 el soporte del batán
– sley (slay)

54 el tensor de los lizos
– lam rods
55 el piñón del árbol de excéntrica f
– camshaft wheel
56 el árbol de excéntrica f
– camshaft (tappet shaft)
57 la excéntrica
– tappet (shedding tappet)
58 la palanca de accionamiento m de la excéntrica
– treadle lever
59 el freno del plegador de urdimbre f
– let-off motion
60 el disco del freno
– beam motion control
61 el cable del freno
– rope of the warp let-off motion
62 la palanca del freno
– let-off weight lever
63 el contrapeso del freno
– control weight [for the treadle]
64 el taco con almohadilla f de cuero m o de resina f sintética
– picker with leather or bakelite pad
65 el amortiguador de la espada
– picking stick buffer
66 la excéntrica de gatillo m de la espada (la excéntrica de golpeo m)
– picking cam
67 el rodillo de excéntrica f
– picking bowl
68 el muelle recuperador de la espada
– picking stick return spring

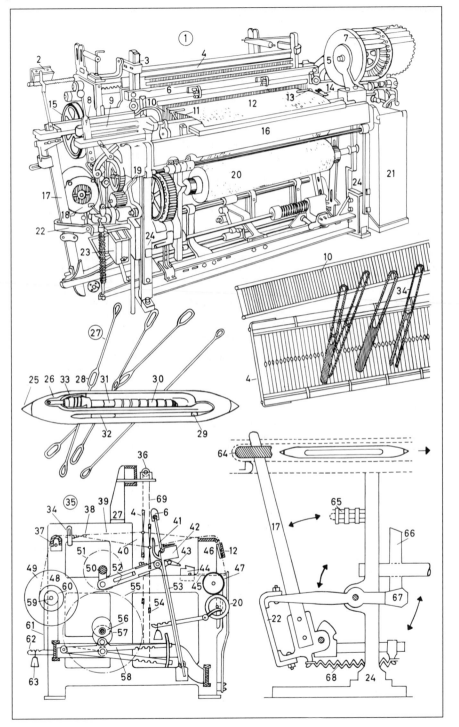

1-66 la fábrica de medias *f*
- *hosiery mill*

1 el telar (la tricotosa) circular, para la elaboración de tejido *m* de punto *m* tubular
- *circular knitting machine for the manufacture of tubular fabric*

2 la pértiga soporte *m* del guiahílos
- *yarn guide support post (thread guide support post)*

3 el guiahílos
- *yarn guide (thread guide)*

4 la bobina botella *f*
- *bottle bobbin*

5 el tensor del hilo
- *yarn-tensioning device*

6 el cerrojo
- *yarn feeder*

7 el volante, para la colocación del hilo detrás de las agujas
- *handwheel for rotating the machine by hand*

8 el cilindro de agujas *f*
- *needle cylinder (cylindrical needle holder)*

9 el tejido tubular
- *tubular fabric*

10 el depósito del tejido
- *fabric drum (fabric box, fabric container)*

11 el cilindro de agujas *f* [sección]
- *needle cylinder (cylindrical needle holder) [section]*

12 las agujas de lengüeta *f* dispuestas radialmente
- *latch needles arranged in a circle*

13 la cubierta de la leva
- *cam housing*

14 la leva de aguja *f*
- *needle cams*

15 la ranura (el canal) de la aguja
- *needle trick*

16 el diámetro del cilindro; *al mismo tiempo:* anchura *f* del tejido tubular
- *cylinder diameter (also: diameter of tubular fabric)*

17 el hilo
- *thread (yarn)*

18 la máquina Cotton, para la fabricación de medias *f* de señora *f*
- *Cotton's patent flat knitting machine for ladies' fully-fashioned hose*

19 la cadena patrón *m* (la cadena modelo *m*)
- *pattern control chain*

20 la bancada lateral
- *side frame*

21 la fontura (la zona de trabajo *m*); *varias fonturas:* producción *f* simultánea de varias medias *f*
- *knitting head; with several knitting heads: simultaneous production of several stockings*

22 la barra de puesta *f* en marcha *f* y paro *m*
- *starting rod*

23 la máquina Raschel (un telar de urdimbre *f* de dos fonturas *f*)
- *Raschel warp-knitting machine*

24 la urdimbre (el plegador de urdimbre *f*)
- *warp (warp beam)*

25 el plegador de distribución *f*
- *yarn-distributing (yarn-dividing) beam*

26 la arandela del plegador de distribución *f*
- *beam flange*

27 la fontura de agujas *f* (la serie de agujas *f* de lengüeta *f*)
- *row of needles*

28 la barra de agujas *f*
- *needle bar*

29 el tejido (el tejido de Raschel) [cortinas *f* y géneros *m* de malla *f*] en el plegador del tejido
- *fabric (Raschel fabric) [curtain lace and net fabrics] on the fabric roll*

30 el volante para la impulsión a mano *f*
- *handwheel*

31 las ruedas impulsoras y el motor
- *motor drive gear*

32 el dispositivo tensor (el peso)
- *take-down weight*

33 el bastidor
- *frame*

34 la placa de base *f*
- *base plate*

35 la tricotosa rectilínea (máquina *f* manual de hacer punto *m*)
- *hand flat (flat-bed) knitting machine*

36 el hilo
- *thread (yarn)*

37 el resorte de retorno *m* (el muelle recuperador)
- *return spring*

38 el soporte, para los resortes
- *support for springs*

39 el carro deslizante
- *carriage*

40 el cerrojo (las levas)
- *feeder-selecting device*

41 la empuñadura para el deslizamiento del carro
- *carriage handles*

42 la escala para regular el tamaño de los puntos
- *scale for regulating size of stitches*

43 el contador de pasadas *f*
- *course counter (tachometer)*

44 la palanca conmutadora
- *machine control lever*

45 el riel guía *f*
- *carriage rail*

46 la hilera superior de agujas *f*
- *back row of needles*

47 la hilera inferior de agujas *f*
- *front row of needles*

48 el tejido de punto *m*
- *knitted fabric*

49 la barra tensora
- *tension bar*

50 el peso tensor
- *tension weight*

51 la fontura dispuesta para hacer punto *m*
- *needle bed showing knitting action*

52 los dientes del peine de desprendimiento *m*
- *teeth of knock-over bit*

53 las agujas dispuestas en orden *m* paralelo
- *needles in parallel rows*

54 el guiahílos
- *yarn guide (thread guide)*

55 el lecho de agujas *f*
- *needle bed*

56 el raíl de recubrimiento *m*, sobre las agujas *f* de lengüeta *f*
- *retaining plate for latch needles*

57 la leva de acoplamiento *m* de las agujas
- *guard cam*

58 la leva de descenso *m* de las agujas
- *sinker*

59 la leva de ascenso *m* de las agujas
- *needle-raising cam*

60 el talón de aguja *f*
- *needle butt*

61 la aguja de lengüeta *f*
- *latch needle*

62 la malla
- *loop*

63 el empuje de la aguja a través de la malla
- *pushing the needle through the fabric*

64 la colocación del hilo sobre el gancho de la aguja mediante el guiahílos
- *yarn guide (thread guide) placing yarn in the needle hook*

65 la confección (la formación) de la malla
- *loop formation*

66 la retención de la malla
- *casting off of loop*

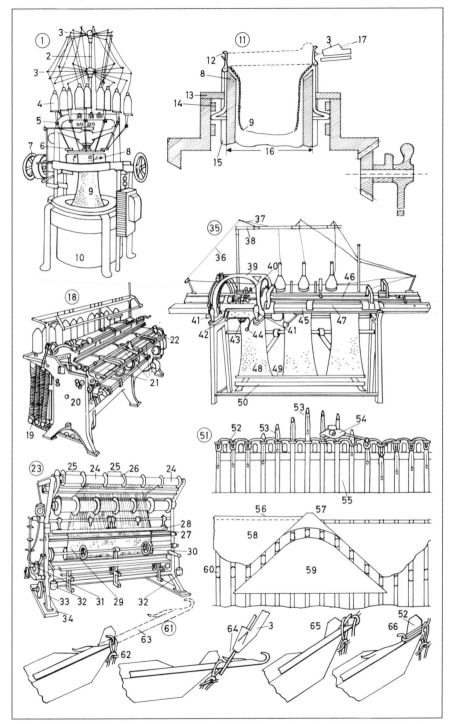

1-65 el procedimiento de acabado *m* de los tejidos
– *finishing*
1 el batán de cilindros *m*, para el enfurtido de los géneros de lana *f* (de los tejidos de lana *f*)
– *rotary milling (fulling) machine for felting the woollen (Am. woolen) fabric*
2 la carga de pesos *m*
– *pressure weights*
3 el cilindro de arrastre *m* superior
– *top milling roller (top fulling roller)*
4 la polea de impulsión *f* del cilindro de arrastre *m* inferior
– *drive wheel of bottom milling roller (bottom fulling roller)*
5 el rodillo guía del tejido
– *fabric guide roller*
6 el cilindro de arrastre *m* inferior
– *bottom milling roller (bottom fulling roller)*
7 la tabla de tracción *f* (el seleccionador)
– *draft board*
8 la máquina de lavar al ancho, para tejidos *m* delicados
– *open-width scouring machine for finer fabrics*
9 la entrada del tejido
– *fabric being drawn off the machine*
10 la caja de mecanismos *m* (la caja de engranajes *m*)
– *drive gearbox*
11 la tubería del agua *f*
– *water inlet pipe*
12 el rodillo guía *f*
– *drawing-in roller*
13 el travesaño tensor
– *scroll-opening roller*
14 la centrífuga pendular, para el secado (el escurrido) de los tejidos
– *pendulum-type hydro-extractor (centrifuge), for extracting liquors from the fabric*
15 el bastidor base
– *machine base*
16 la columna
– *casing over suspension*
17 la caja, con el tambor interior giratorio
– *outer casing containing rotating cage (rotating basket)*
18 la tapa de la centrífuga
– *hydro-extractor (centrifuge) lid*
19 el dispositivo de paro *m* de seguridad *f*
– *stop-motion device (stopping device)*
20 el dispositivo de arranque *m* y de freno *m* automático
– *automatic starting and braking device*

21 la máquina de secar tejidos *m*
– for cotton: *stenter;* for wool: *tenter*
22 el tejido húmedo
– *air-dry fabric*
23 la plataforma de servicio *m*
– *operator's (operative's) platform*
24 la fijación del tejido, mediante cadenas *f* de agujas *f* o de pinzas *f*
– *feeding of fabric by guides onto stenter (tenter) pins or clips*
25 la caja del control eléctrico (la caja de los electroconmutadores)
– *electric control panel*
26 la entrada en pliegues *m* del tejido, para facilitar el proceso de contracción *f* longitudinal en el secado
– *initial overfeed to produce shrink-resistant fabric when dried*
27 el termómetro
– *thermometer*
28 la cámara de secado *m*
– *drying section*
29 la tubería de salida *f* del aire
– *air outlet*
30 la salida del secador
– *plaiter (fabric-plaiting device)*
31 la máquina perchadora para cardar el derecho del tejido con cardas *f* para afelpar
– *wire-roller fabric-raising machine for producing raised or nap surface*
32 la caja de engranajes *m*
– *drive gearbox*
33 el tejido sin cardar
– *unraised cloth*
34 los cilindros rugosos
– *wire-covered rollers*
35 el dispositivo plegador del tejido (el abanico)
– *plaiter (cutting device)*
36 el tejido cardado
– *raised fabric*
37 el banco para el género
– *plaiting-down platform*
38 la prensa continua, para el planchado del tejido
– *rotary press (calendering machine), for press finishing*
39 el paño
– *fabric*
40 los pulsadores y el volante de control *m*
– *control buttons and control wheels*
41 el cilindro de presión *f* calentado
– *heated press bowl*
42 la máquina tundidora del tejido
– *rotary cloth-shearing machine*
43 el aspirador del tamo
– *suction slot, for removing loose fibres (Am. fibers)*
44 la cuchilla de tundir (el cilindro tundidor)
– *doctor blade (cutting cylinder)*

45 la rejilla de protección *f*
– *protective guard*
46 el cepillo giratorio
– *rotating brush*
47 el deslizamiento del tejido
– *curved scray entry*
48 el pedal de mando *m*
– *treadle control*
49 la máquina decatizadora, para la obtención de tejidos *m* inencogibles
– *[non-shrinking] decatizing (decating) fabric-finishing machine*
50 el cilindro decatizador
– *perforated decatizing (decating) cylinder*
51 la pieza de tejido *m*
– *piece of fabric*
52 la manivela
– *cranked control handle*
53 la máquina de rodillos *m* para estampar diez colores *m* (la máquina de estampar tejidos *m*)
– *ten-colour (Am. ten-color) roller printing machine*
54 el bastidor base de la máquina
– *base of the machine*
55 el motor
– *drive motor*
56 la almohadilla (la blanqueta)
– *blanket [of rubber or felt]*
57 el género estampado
– *fabric after printing (printed fabric)*
58 el dispositivo electroconmutador
– *electric control panel (control unit)*
59 la estampación del tejido a la lionesa
– *screen printing*
60 el carro móvil para plantillas *f*
– *mobile screen frame*
61 la raedera (el limpiador)
– *squeegee*
62 la plantilla estampadora
– *pattern stencil*
63 la mesa de estampación *f*
– *screen table*
64 el tejido fijado con goma *f* para ser estampado
– *fabric gummed down on table ready for printing*
65 el estampador textil (el operario estampador)
– *screen printing operator (operative)*

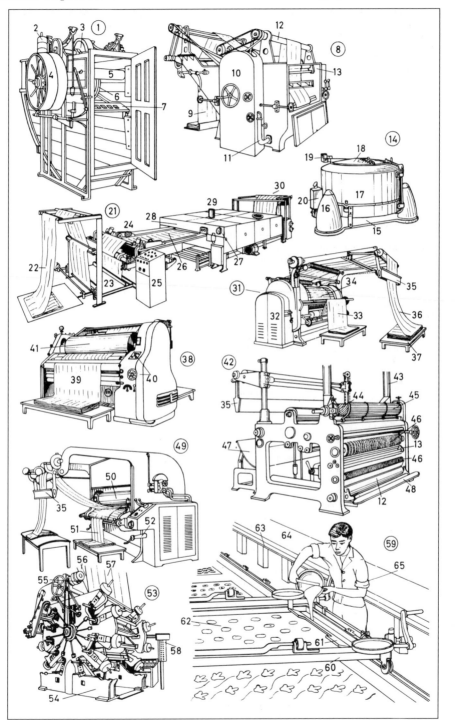

169 Fibras artificiales y sintéticas I   Synthetic (Man-made) Fibres (Am. Fibers) I

1-34 la fabricación del **rayón** (de seda artificial) y de fibras textiles por elaboración *f* de la viscosa
- *manufacture of continuous fila-ment and staple fibre* (Am. *fiber*) *viscose rayon yarns by means of the viscose process*

1-12 de la materia prima a la viscosa
- *from raw material to viscose rayon*

1 la materia base [hojas *f* de celulosa *f* de haya *f* y de pino *m*, láminas *f* de celulosa *f*]
- *basic material [beech and spruce cellulose in form of sheets]*

2 la mezcla de las láminas de celulosa *f*
- *mixing cellulose sheets*

3 la sosa cáustica
- *caustic soda*

4 la impregnación de las láminas de celulosa *f* en sosa *f* cáustica
- *steeping cellulose sheets in caustic soda*

5 el prensado para (el escurrido de) la sosa cáustica sobrante
- *pressing out excess caustic soda*

6 el desfibrado de las láminas de celulosa *f*
- *shredding the cellulose sheets*

7 la maduración de la álcalicelulosa
- *maturing (controlled oxidation) of the alkali-cellulose crumbs*

8 el sulfuro de carbón *m*
- *carbon disulphide* (Am. *carbon disulfide*)

9 la sulfuración (transformación *f* de la álcalicelulosa en xantogenato *m* de celulosa *f*)
- *conversion of alkali-cellulose into cellulose xanthate*

10 la disolución del xantogenato en sosa *f* cáustica, para la obtención de la solución hilable de viscosa *f*
- *dissolving the xanthate in caustic soda for the preparation of the viscose spinning solution*

11 la caldera-depósito al vacío
- *vacuum ripening tanks*

12 el filtro-prensa
- *filter presses*

13-27 de la viscosa al hilo de rayón *m*
- *from viscose to viscose rayon thread*

13 la bomba de hilatura *f*
- *metering pump*

14 la hilera (tobera *f* de hilar)
- *multi-holed spinneret (spinning jet)*

15 el baño de coagulación *f*, para la transformación de la viscosa viscosa (pegajosa) en hilos *m* de celulosa *f* coagulada
- *coagulating (spinning) bath for converting (coagulating) viscose (viscous solution) into solid filaments*

16 el cristalero, una polea de cristal *m*
- *Godet wheel, a glass pulley*

17 la centrífuga de hilar, para la unión de los filamentos
- *Topham centrifugal pot (box) for twisting the filaments into yarn*

18 la corona de rayón *m*
- *viscose rayon cake*

19-27 el tratamiento de la corona de rayón *m*
- *processing of the cake*

19 la desacidificación
- *washing*

20 la desulfuración
- *desulphurizing (desulphurization, Am. desulfurizing, desulfuriza-tion)*

21 el blanqueo
- *bleaching*

22 el acabado de la corona (para dar blancura *f* y ductilidad *f* a la mate-ria)
- *treating of cake to give filaments softness and suppleness*

23 la centrifugación, para la sepa-ración del exceso de líquido *m*
- *hydro-extraction to remove sur-plus moisture*

24 el secado, en la cámara de secado
- *drying in heated room*

25 el bobinado
- *winding yarn from cake into cone form*

26 ia máquina de bobinar
- *cone-winding machine*

27 el hilo de rayón *m* sobre bobina *f* cónica de plegado *m* para la manipulación textil
- *viscose rayon yarn on cone ready for use*

28-34 de la solución hilable de vis-cosa *f* a la fibra textil
- *from viscose spinning solution to viscose rayon staple fibre* (Am. *fiber*)

28 el cable (la cuerda de hilos *m*)
- *filament tow*

29 la instalación de lavado *m* por aspersión *f*
- *overhead spray washing plant*

30 el dispositivo cortador, para cor-tar los hilos a una longitud deter-minada
- *cutting machine for cutting fila-ment tow to desired length*

31 la máquina secadora múltiple para las fibras
- *multiple drying machine for cut-up staple fibre* (Am. *fiber*) *layer (lap)*

32 la correa transportadora
- *conveyor belt (conveyor)*

33 la prensa de balas *f*
- *baling press*

34 las balas de fibras *f* de viscosa *f* listas para el envío
- *bale of viscose rayon ready for dispatch (despatch)*

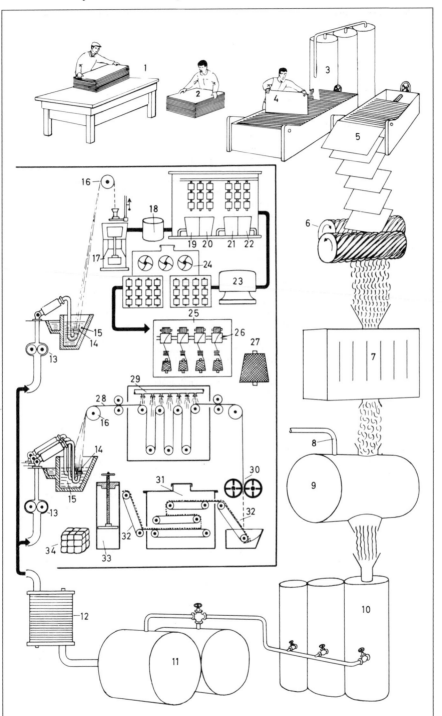

170 Fibras artificiales y sintéticas II   *Synthetic (Man-made) Fibres (Am. Fibers) II*

1-62 la fabricación del perlón
– *manufacture of polyamide (nylon 6, perlon) fibres (Am. fibers)*
1 la hulla [la materia prima para la producción del perlón]
– *coal [raw material for manufacture of polyamide (nylon 6, perlon) fibres (Am. fibers)]*
2 la coquería, para la destilación seca de la hulla
– *coking plant for dry coal distillation*
3 la extracción del alquitrán y del fenol
– *extraction of coal tar and phenol*
4 la destilación gradual del alquitrán
– *gradual distillation of tar*
5 el condensador
– *condenser*
6 la extracción y el transporte del benzol
– *benzene extraction and dispatch (despatch)*
7 el cloro
– *chlorine*
8 la cloración del benzol
– *benzene chlorination*
9 el clorobenzol
– *monochlorobenzene (chlorobenzene)*
10 la sosa cáustica
– *caustic soda solution*
11 la evaporación del clorobenzol y de la sosa cáustica
– *evaporation of chlorobenzene and caustic soda*
12 el depósito de reacción *f* (el autoclave)
– *autoclave*
13 el cloruro de sodio *m* (la sal común), un subproducto
– *sodium chloride (common salt), a by-product*
14 el fenol
– *phenol (carbolic acid)*
15 la alimentación de hidrógeno *m*
– *hydrogen inlet*
16 la hidrogenación del fenol, para la obtención del ciclohexano bruto
– *hydrogenation of phenol to produce raw cyclohexanol*
17 la destilación
– *distillation*
18 el ciclohexano puro
– *pure cyclohexanol*
19 la deshidrogenación
– *oxidation (dehydrogenation)*
20 la formación de la ciclohexanona
– *formation of cyclohexanone (pimehinketone)*
21 la tubería de la hidroxilamina
– *hydroxylamine inlet*

22 la formación de la ciclohexa-nonaoxima
– *formation of cyclohexanoxime*
23 la adición del ácido sulfúrico, para la poliadición molecular
– *addition of sulphuric acid (Am. sulfuric acid) to effect molecular rearrangement*
24 el amoníaco, para la neutralización del ácido sulfúrico
– *ammonia to neutralize sulphuric acid (Am. sulfuric acid)*
25 la formación de la lactama
– *formation of caprolactam oil*
26 la solución de sulfato *m* de amonio *m*
– *ammonium sulphate (Am. ammonium sulfate) solution*
27 el cilindro refrigerador
– *cooling cylinder*
28 la caprolactama
– *caprolactam*
29 la báscula
– *weighing apparatus*
30 la caldera de fusión *f*
– *melting pot*
31 la bomba
– *pump*
32 el filtro
– *filter*
33 la polimerización en el autoclave (recipiente *m* a presión *f*)
– *polymerization in the autoclave*
34 la refrigeración de la poliamida
– *cooling of the polyamide*
35 la fusión de la poliamida
– *solidification of the polyamide*
36 el elevador de rosario *m*
– *vertical lift (Am. elevator)*
37 el extractor, para separar de la poliamida la lactama restante
– *extractor for separating the polyamide from the remaining lactam oil*
38 el secador
– *drier*
39 la escama seca de la poliamida
– *dry polyamide chips*
40 el depósito de escamas *f*
– *chip container*
41 la cámara de hilatura *f* para la fusión de la poliamida y para el prensado a través de las hileras
– *top of spinneret for melting the polyamide and forcing it through spinneret holes (spinning jets)*
42 las hileras
– *spinneret holes (spinning jets)*
43 la solidificación de los hilos de poliamida *f* (de perlón *m*) en la columna refrigerante
– *solidification of polyamide filaments in the cooling tower*

44 el enrollado del hilo
– *collection of extruded filaments into thread form*
45 la torsión preliminar
– *preliminary stretching (preliminary drawing)*
46 el estiraje, para la obtención de gran resistencia *f* y flexibilidad *f* del hilo de poliamida *f*
– *stretching (cold-drawing) of the polyamide thread to achieve high tensile strength*
47 la torsión final
– *final stretching (final drawing)*
48 el lavado de las bobinas
– *washing of yarn packages*
49 la cámara de secado *m*
– *drying chamber*
50 el rebobinado
– *rewinding*
51 la bobina de arrollado *m* cruzado
– *polyamide cone*
52 la bobina de arrollado *m* cruzado lista para enviar
– *polyamide cone ready for dispatch (despatch)*
53 la caldera de mezcla *f*
– *mixer*
54 la polimerización, en la caldera de vacío *m*
– *polymerization under vacua*
55 el estiraje
– *stretching (drawing)*
56 el lavado
– *washing*
57 la preparación, para dejar el hilo en condiciones de ser hilado
– *finishing of tow for spinning*
58 el secado del cable (el secado del hilo)
– *drying of tow*
59 el ondulado del hilo
– *crimping of tow*
60 el cortado del hilo con la longitud de fibra *f* normal
– *cutting of tow into normal staple lengths*
61 la fibra de poliamida *f* (de perlón *m*)
– *polyamide staple*
62 la bala de fibra *f* de poliamida *f* (de perlón *m*)
– *bale of polyamide staple*

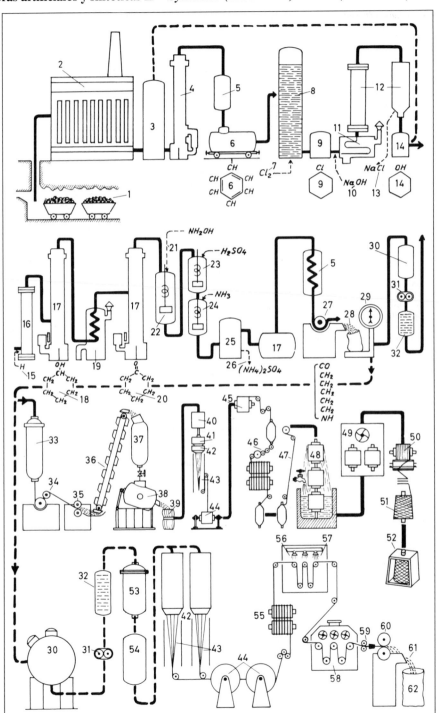

1-29 ligamentos *m* **de tejidos** *m*
[cuadros negros: hilo *m* de urdimbre *f* por encima, hilo de trama *f* por debajo; cuadros blancos: hilo de trama por encima, hilo de urdimbre por debajo]
– **weaves** *[black squares: warp thread raised, weft thread lowered; white squares: weft thread raised, warp thread lowered]*
1 el ligamento tafetán (el ligamento a la plana) [la vista superior del tejido]
– *plain weave (tabby weave) [weave viewed from above]*
2 el hilo de urdimbre *f*
– *warp thread*
3 el hilo de trama *f*
– *weft thread*
4 la carta del ligamento para el tafetán [el proyecto para el tejedor]
– *draft (point paper design) for plain weave*
5 el remetido en los lizos
– *threading draft*
6 el remetido del peine
– *denting draft (reed-threading draft)*
7 el hilo de urdimbre *f* por encima
– *raised warp thread*
8 el hilo de urdimbre *f* por debajo
– *lowered warp thread*
9 la armadura
– *tie-up of shafts in pairs*
10 el picado (el dibujo)
– *treadling diagram*
11 la carta (el patrón) para el ligamento panameño (el ligamento regular, el ligamento inglés)
– *draft for basket weave (hopsack weave, matt weave)*
12 el curso (la parte del ligamento que continúa y se repite)
– *pattern repeat*
13 el patrón (la carta) para el reps por trama *f*
– *draft for warp rib weave*
14 corte *m* de tejido *m* del reps por trama *f*, un corte de urdimbre *f*
– *section of warp rib fabric, a section through the warp*
15 el hilo de *f* trama por debajo
– *lowered weft thread*
16 el hilo de trama *f* por encima
– *raised weft thread*
17 el primer hilo y el segundo hilo de urdimbre *f* [levantados]
– *first and second warp threads [raised]*
18 el tercer hilo y el cuarto hilo de urdimbre *f* [bajados]
– *third and fourth warp threads [lowered]*

19 el patrón del reps acanalado irregular
– *draft for combined rib weave*
20 el remetido de los hilos en los licetes (los lizos adicionales para el orillo del tejido)
– *selvedge (selvage) thread draft (additional shafts for the selvedge)*
21 el remetido de los hilos en los lizos del tejido
– *draft for the fabric shafts*
22 la armadura de los licetes
– *tie-up of selvedge (selvage) shafts*
23 la armadura de los lizos del tejido
– *tie-up of fabric shafts*
24 el orillo en ligamento *m* de tela *f*
– *selvedge (selvage) in plain weave*
25 el corte de tejido *m* del reps acanalado irregular
– *section through combination rib weave*
26 el ligamento del tejido de punto *m* longitudinal
– *thread interlacing of reversible warp-faced cord*
27 el patrón para el ligamento del tejido de punto *m* longitudinal
– *draft (point paper design) for reversible warp-faced cord*
28 los puntos de ligadura *f*
– *interlacing points*
29 el ligamento de barquillo *m* para el patrón de barquillo *m* en el tejido (el ligamento "nido *m* de abeja *f*" o "punto *m* de tripa *f*")
– *weaving draft for honeycomb weave in the fabric*
30-48 ligamentos *m* **fundamentales de tejidos** *m* **y cuerdas** *f*
– *basic knits*
30 la malla, una malla abierta
– *loop, an open loop*
31 la cabeza
– *head*
32 la rama (el lado)
– *side*
33 el pie
– *neck*
34 el punto de ligamento *m* de cabeza *f*
– *head interlocking point*
35 el punto de ligamento *m* de pie *m*
– *neck interlocking point*
36 la malla cerrada
– *closed loop*
37 la red
– *mesh [with inlaid yarn]*
38 la trayectoria diagonal del hilo
– *diagonal floating yarn (diagonal floating thread)*
39 el nudo con ligamento *m* de cabeza *f*
– *loop interlocking at the head*

40 el flotador
– *float*
41 la trayectoria libre (vertical) del hilo
– *loose floating yarn (loose floating thread)*
42 la vuelta de malla *f*
– *course*
43 la trama
– *inlaid yarn*
44 la puntada izquierda-derecha
– *tuck and miss stitch*
45 el cruzado izquierda-derecha
– *pulled-up tuck stitch*
46 la puntada cruzada izquierda-derecha (la puntada al sesgo)
– *staggered tuck stitch*
47 la puntada doble izquierda-derecha
– *2 ×2 tuck and miss stitch*
48 el cruzado doble izquierda-derecha
– *double pulled-up tuck stitch*

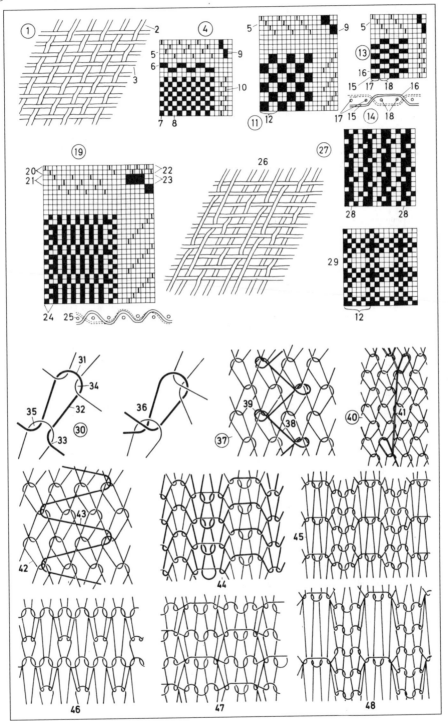

1-52 la fábrica de celulosa *f* al sulfato [esquema]
– *sulphate (Am. sulfate) pulp mill (kraft pulp mill) [in diagram form]*
1 la máquina cortadora con separador *m* de polvo *m*
– *chippers with dust extractor*
2 el tamiz giratorio
– *rotary screen (riffler)*
3 el aparato distribuidor de la celulosa (de la pasta)
– *chip packer (chip distributor)*
4 el soplante
– *blower*
5 el molino centrífugo
– *disintegrator (crusher, chip crusher)*
6 la cámara colectora del polvo
– *dust-settling chamber*
7 el digestor de celulosa *f*
– *digester*
8 el precalentador de lejía *f*
– *liquor preheater*
9 el grifo de control *m*
– *control tap*
10 el tubo giratorio
– *swing pipe*
11 el difusor
– *blow tank (diffuser)*
12 la válvula de pulverización *f*
– *blow valve*
13 la caja del difusor
– *blow pit (diffuser)*
14 el separador de la trementina
– *turpentine separator*
15 el separador central
– *centralized separator*
16 el condensador de inyección *f*
– *jet condenser (injection condenser)*
17 el depósito de condensado *m*
– *storage tank for condensate*
18 el depósito de agua *f* caliente
– *hot water tank*
19 el intercambiador de calor *m*
– *heat exchanger*
20 el filtro
– *filter*
21 el preclasificador
– *presorter*
22 la centrífuga depuradora
– *centrifugal screen*
23 la máquina clasificadora rotativa
– *rotary sorter (rotary strainer)*
24 el cilindro de drenaje *m*
– *concentrator (thickener, decker)*
25 la cuba
– *vat (chest)*
26 el depósito colector, para el agua *f* de vuelta *f*
– *collecting tank for backwater (low box)*
27 el refinador cónico
– *conical refiner (cone refiner, Jordan, Jordan refiner)*
28 el filtro para lejía *f* negra
– *black liquor filter*
29 el depósito de lejía *f* negra
– *black liquor storage tank*
30 el condensador
– *condenser*
31 los separadores
– *separators*
32 el calorífero (el aparato de calefacción *f*)
– *heaters (heating elements)*
33 la bomba de la lejía
– *liquor pump*
34 la bomba de la lejía espesa
– *heavy liquor pump*

35 el depósito de mezcla *f*
– *mixing tank*
36 el depósito de sulfato *m*
– *salt cake storage tank (sodium sulphate storage tank)*
37 el tanque para disolver (el disolvedor)
– *dissolving tank (dissolver)*
38 la caldera de vapor *m*
– *steam heater*
39 el electrofiltro
– *electrostatic precipitator*
40 la bomba de aire *m*
– *air pump*
41 el depósito para la lejía verde poco clara
– *storage tank for the uncleared green liquor*
42 el condensador
– *concentrator (thickener, decker)*
43 el precalentador de lejía *f* verde
– *green liquor preheater*
44 el condensador (el espesador) de lavado *m*
– *concentrator (thickener, decker) for the weak wash liquor (wash water)*
45 el depósito parta la lejía floja
– *storage tank for the weak liquor*
46 el depósito de lejía *f* de cocción *f*
– *storage tank for the cooking liquor*
47 el agitador
– *agitator (stirrer)*
48 el condensador (el espesador)
– *concentrator (thickener, decker)*
49 los agitadores caustificadores
– *causticizing agitators (causticizing stirrers)*
50 el clasificador
– *classifier*
51 el tambor para apagar la cal
– *lime slaker*
52 la cal cocida (calcinada)
– *reconverted lime*
53-65 la instalación para refinar la madera [esquema]
– *groundwood mill (mechanical pulp mill) [diagram]*
53 la trituradora continua
– *continuous grinder (continuous chain grinder)*
54 el colador para las astillas (para los nudos de la madera)
– *strainer (knotter)*
55 la bomba para el agua *f* de la pasta
– *pulp water pump*
56 la centrífuga depuradora
– *centrifugal screen*
57 el clasificador
– *screen (sorter)*
58 el segundo clasificador
– *secondary screen (secondary sorter)*
59 la cuba para la pasta gruesa
– *rejects chest*
60 el refinador cónico
– *conical refiner (cone refiner, Jordan, Jordan refiner)*
61 la máquina de drenaje *m*
– *pulp-drying machine (pulp machine)*
62 la cuba de espesar
– *concentrator (thickener, decker)*
63 la bomba de las aguas residuales
– *waste water pump (white water pump, pulp water pump)*
64 la tubería de vapores *m*
– *steam pipe*
65 la tubería de agua *f*
– *water pipe*

66 la trituradora continua
– *continuous grinder (continuous chain grinder)*
67 la cadena de avance *m*
– *feed chain*
68 la madera molida
– *groundwood*
69 la reducción para la impulsión de la cadena de avance *m*
– *reduction gear for the feed chain drive*
70 el dispositivo cortante de la piedra (de la muela)
– *stone-dressing device*
71 la piedra moledora (la muela)
– *grinding stone (grindstone, pulpstone)*
72 el tubo pulverizador
– *spray pipe*
73 el refinador cónico
– *conical refiner (cone refiner, Jordan, Jordan refiner)*
74 el volante para regular la distancia de las cuchillas
– *handwheel for adjusting the clearance between the knives (blades)*
75 el cono giratorio de las cuchillas
– *rotating bladed cone (rotating bladed plug)*
76 el cono fijo de las cuchillas
– *stationary bladed shell*
77 la entrada para la celulosa (*también:* pasta *f* de madera *f* no refinada)
– *inlet for unrefined cellulose (chemical wood pulp, chemical pulp) or groundwood pulp (mechanical pulp)*
78 la salida para la celulosa (*también:* pasta *f* de madera *f* refinada)
– *outlet for refined cellulose (chemical wood pulp, chemical pulp) or groundwood pulp (mechanical pulp)*
79-86 la instalación para preparar (tratar) la pasta
– *stuff (stock) preparation plant [diagram]*
79 la cinta transportadora para levantar la celulosa o pasta de madera
– *conveyor belt (conveyor) for loading cellulose (chemical wood pulp, chemical pulp) or groundwood pulp (mechanical pulp)*
80 el disociador de celulosa *f*
– *pulper*
81 la cuba de vaciado *m*
– *dump chest*
82 el desintegrador cónico
– *cone breaker*
83 el molino cónico
– *conical refiner (cone refiner, Jordan, Jordan refiner)*
84 el refinador
– *refiner*
85 la cuba de pasta acabada
– *stuff chest (stock chest)*
86 la cuba de máquina *f*
– *machine chest (stuff chest)*

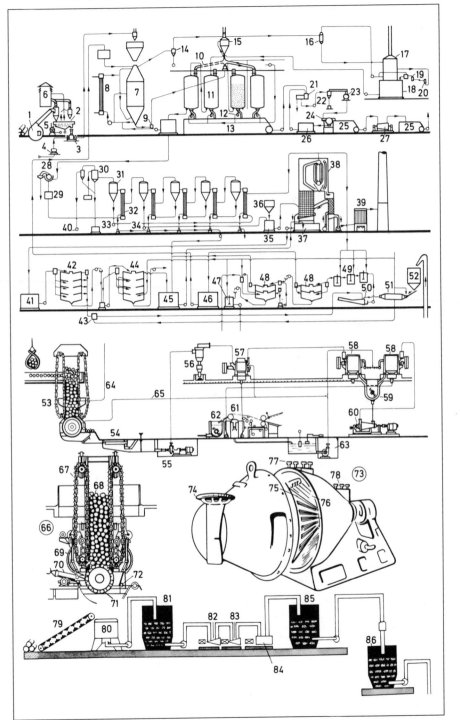

1 la cubeta agitadora, una cubeta mezcladora de la pasta de papel *m*
– *stuff chest (stock chest, machine chest), a mixing chest for stuff (stock)*
2-10 los instrumentos de laboratorio *m* para la pasta de papel *m* y para el examen del papel
– *laboratory apparatus (laboratory equipment) for analysing stuff (stock) and paper*
2 el frasco (de) Erlenmeyer
– *Erlenmeyer flask*
3 el matraz de mezcla *f*
– *volumetric flask*
4 la probeta de medida *f*
– *measuring cylinder*
5 el quemador Bunsen
– *Bunsen burner*
6 las trébedes
– *tripod*
7 el plato de laboratorio *m*
– *petri dish*
8 el soporte de los tubos de ensayo *m*
– *test tube rack*
9 la balanza para el peso bruto
– *balance for measuring basis weight*
10 el micrómetro de espesores *m*
– *micrometer*
11 los depuradores centrífugos delante de la caja de entrada *f* de una máquina de papel *m*
– *centrifugal cleaners ahead of the breastbox (headbox, stuff box) of a paper machine*
12 el tubo vertical
– *standpipe*
13-28 la máquina de papel *m* [esquema]
– *paper machine (production line) [diagram]*
13 la tubería de alimentación *f* para la cubeta de la máquina con purgador de nudos *m* y arena *f*
– *feed-in from the machine chest (stuff chest) with sand table (sand trap, riffler) and knotter*
14 el tamiz (la tela metálica)
– *wire (machine wire)*
15 el aspirador del tamiz
– *vacuum box (suction box)*
16 el rodillo aspirador del tamiz
– *suction roll*
17 el primer fieltro húmedo
– *first wet felt*
18 el segundo fieltro húmedo
– *second wet felt*
19 la primera prensa húmeda
– *first press*
20 la segunda prensa húmeda
– *second press*
21 la prensa offset
– *offset press*
22 el cilindro secador
– *drying cylinder (drier)*

23 el fieltro secador (*también:* el tamiz secador)
– *dry felt (drier felt)*
24 la prensa encoladora
– *size press*
25 el cilindro refrigerador
– *cooling roll*
26 los rodillos de calandrar
– *calender rolls*
27 el casco secador
– *machine hood*
28 la enrolladora
– *delivery reel*
29-35 la máquina de recubrir por extensión *f* de rasqueta *f*
– *blade coating machine (blade coater)*
29 el papel bruto
– *raw paper (body paper)*
30 el rollo continuo de papel *m*
– *web*
31 la instalación para extender la parte delantera
– *coater for the top side*
32 la estufa infrarroja
– *infrared drier*
33 el tambor secador calentado
– *heated drying cylinder*
34 el dispositivo para extender la parte trasera
– *coater for the underside (wire side)*
35 el rollo de papel *m* acabado de extender
– *reel of coated paper*
36 la calandria
– *calender (super-calender)*
37 el sistema de comprimir hidráulico
– *hydraulic system for the press rolls*
38 el rodillo de la calandria
– *calender roll*
39 el mecanismo de desenrollar
– *unwind station*
40 la plataforma de elevación *f*
– *lift platform*
41 el mecanismo de enrollar
– *rewind station (rewinder, re-reeler, reeling machine, re-reeling machine)*
42 el cortador de rollos *m*
– *roll cutter*
43 el tablero de mandos *m*
– *control panel*
44 el aparato de corte (la cuchilla)
– *cutter*
45 el rollo continuo de papel *m*
- *web*
46-51 la fabricación del papel a mano *f*
– *papermaking by hand*
46 el laurente
– *vatman*
47 la tina
– *vat*
48 la forma de mano *f*
– *mould (Am. mold)*

49 el lavador
– *coucher (couchman)*
50 la pila de papel *m* preparado para la prensa *f*
– *post ready for pressing*
51 el fieltro
– *felt*

1 **la composición a mano** _f_ (la sección de cajas _f_ a mano _f_)
– _hand-setting room (hand-composing room)_
2 el chibalete
– _composing frame_
3 la caja tipográfica
– _case (typecase)_
4 la caja colocada en el chibalete
– _case cabinet (case rack)_
5 el cajista (el tipógrafo)
– _hand compositor (compositor, typesetter, maker-up)_
6 el manuscrito (el original)
– _manuscript (typescript)_
7 los caracteres (los tipos)
– _sorts (types, type characters, characters)_
8 la estantería, para lingotes _m_ y blancos _m_ (material _m_ de relleno _m_)
– _rack (case) for furniture (spacing material)_
9 el estante de composición _f_
– _standing type rack (standing matter rack)_
10 el tablero de los moldes
– _storage shelf (shelf for storing formes, Am. forms)_
11 la composición conservada
– _standing type (standing matter)_
12 la galera
– _galley_
13 el componedor
– _composing stick (setting stick)_
14 la regleta (el filete sacalíneas)
– _composing rule (setting rule)_
15 la composición
– _type (type matter, matter)_
16 el cordel para la columna
– _page cord_
17 la punta (el punzón)
– _bodkin_
18 las pinzas
– _tweezers_
19 **la linotipia, una máquina de almacén _m_ múltiple**
– _Linotype line-composing (line-casting, slug-composing, slug-casting) machine, a multi-magazine machine_
20 el mecanismo de distribución _f_
– _distributing mechanism (distributor)_
21 el almacén con las matrices
– _type magazines with matrices (matrixes)_
22 el elevador, para transportar las matrices al distribuidor
– _elevator carrier for distributing the matrices (matrixes)_
23 el componedor
– _assembler_
24 los espacios cuneiformes (espacios _m_ de cuñas _f_)
– _spacebands_

25 el crisol (el dispositivo fundidor)
– _casting mechanism_
26 el alimentador automático de metal _m_
– _metal feeder_
27 la composición mecánica (las líneas fundidas)
– _machine-set matter (cast lines, slugs)_
28 las matrices de mano _f_
– _matrices (matrixes) for hand-setting (sorts)_
29 la matriz de linotipia _f_
– _Linotype matrix_
30 el dentado, para el mecanismo de distribución _f_
– _teeth for the distributing mechanism (distributor)_
31 el ojo de caracteres _m_ (la matriz)
– _face (type face, matrix)_
32-45 **la monotipo, una máquina para componer y fundir en tipo _m_ suelto** (tipo _m_ individual)
– _monotype single-unit composing (typesetting) and casting machine (monotype single-unit composition caster)_
32 la máquina componedora monotipo normal (el teclado)
– _monotype standard composing (typesetting) machine (keyboard)_
33 el carrete (la torre) de papel _m_
– _paper tower_
34 la tira de papel _m_ de composición _f_
– _paper ribbon_
35 el tambor
– _justifying scale_
36 el indicador de unidades _f_
– _unit indicator_
37 el teclado
– _keyboard_
38 el tubo de aire _m_ a presión _f_
– _compressed-air hose_
39 la máquina fundidora monotipo
– _monotype casting machine (monotype caster)_
40 el alimentador automático de metal _m_
– _automatic metal feeder_
41 el muelle de compresión _f_ de la bomba
– _pump compression spring (pump pressure spring)_
42 el bastidor portamatrices
– _matrix case (die case)_
43 el carrete de papel _m_
– _paper tower_
44 la galera, con el tipo suelto (tipo _m_ individual)
– _galley with types (letters, characters, cast single types, cast single letters)_
45 la calefacción eléctrica
– _electric heater (electric heating unit)_

46 el bastidor portamatrices
– _matrix case (die case)_
47 las matrices de los tipos
– _type matrices (matrixes) (letter matrices)_
48 la entalla, para encajar en la guía de corredera _f_ cruzada
– _guide block for engaging with the cross-slide guide_

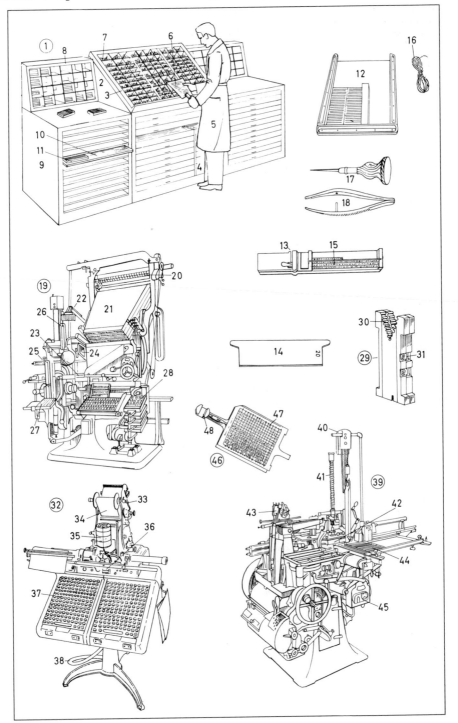

1-17 la composición
- *composition (type matter, type)*
1 la letra inicial
- *initial (initial letter)*
2 la letra seminegra
- *bold type (bold, boldfaced type, heavy type, boldface)*
3 la letra negrita
- *semibold type (semibold)*
4 la línea
- *line*
5 el espacio entre dos renglones *m* (el interlineado)
- *space*
6 la ligadura
- *ligature (double letter)*
7 la letra cursiva (la letra itálica)
- *italic type (italics)*
8 la letra fina
- *light face type (light face)*
9 la letra gruesa (la letra supernegra)
- *extra bold type (extra bold)*
10 la letra negra estrecha
- *bold condensed type (bold condensed)*
11 la letra mayúscula (la letra versal, la letra capital)
- *majuscule (capital letter, capital, upper case letter)*
12 la letra minúscula
- *minuscule (small letter, lower case letter)*
13 la separación (la palabra espaciada)
- *letter spacing (interspacing)*
14 la letra versalita
- *small capitals*
15 el punto y aparte
- *break*
16 la sangría (el principio de párrafo *m*)
- *indention*
17 scher Punkt *m* = 0,376 mm]
- *space*
18 el espacio
- *type sizes [one typographic point = 0.376 mm (Didot system), 0.351 mm (Pica system). The German size-names refer to exact multiples of the Didot (Continental) system. The English names are now obsolete: current English type-sizes are exact multiples of the Pica]*
19 el non plus ultra (2 puntos *m*)
- *six-to-pica (2 points)*
20 el brillante (3 puntos *m*)
- *half nonpareil (four-to-pica) (3 points)*
21 el diamante (4 puntos *m*)
- *brilliant (4 points); sim.: diamond (4 ¹/₂ points)*

22 la perla (5 puntos *m*)
- *pearl (5 points); sim.: ruby (Am. agate) (5 ¹/₂ points)*
23 el nomparell (6 puntos *m*)
- *nonpareil (6 points); sim.: minionette (6 ¹/₂ points)*
24 la miñona (7 puntos *m*)
- *minion (7 points)*
25 la gallarda (8 puntos *m*)
- *brevier (8 points)*
26 el breviario (9 puntos *m*)
- *bourgeois (9 points)*
27 el garamón (10 puntos *m*)
- *long primer (10 points)*
28 la lectura (12 puntos *m*)
- *pica (12 points)*
29 el texto (14 puntos *m*)
- *English (14 points)*
30 la atanasia (16 puntos *m*)
- *great primer (two-line brevier, Am. Columbian) (16 points)*
31 el pequeño parangón (20 puntos *m*)
- *paragon (two-line primer) (20 points)*
32-37 la fabricación de caracteres (tipos *m*, letras *f*)
- *typefounding (type casting)*
32 el grabador de punzones *m*
- *punch cutter*
33 el buril de acero *m*
- *graver (burin, cutter)*
34 la lupa
- *magnifying glass (magnifier)*
35 el cuño (el punzón)
- *punch blank (die blank)*
36 el punzón de acero *m* acabado
- *finished steel punch (finished steel die)*
37 la matriz punzonada
- *punched matrix (stamped matrix, strike, drive)*
38 la letra (el tipo)
- *type (type character, character)*
39 la cabeza
- *head*
40 el hombro
- *shoulder*
41 el punzón
- *counter*
42 el ojo
- *face (type face)*
43 la línea de la letra
- *type line (bodyline)*
44 la altura del tipo
- *height to paper (type height)*
45 la altura del hombro
- *height of shank (height of shoulder)*
46 el cuerpo
- *body size (type size, point size)*

47 el cran
- *nick*
48 el grueso
- *set (width)*
49 la taladradora de matrices *f,* una taladradora especial
- *matrix-boring machine (matrix-engraving machine), a special-purpose boring machine*
50 el soporte
- *stand*
51 la fresa
- *cutter (cutting head)*
52 la mesa de fresar
- *cutting table*
53 el soporte del pantógrafo
- *pantograph carriage*
54 la guía prismática
- *V-way*
55 la plantilla
- *pattern*
56 la mesa portaplantillas
- *pattern table*
57 el punzón copiador
- *follower*
58 el pantógrafo
- *pantograph*
59 el portamatrices
- *matrix clamp*
60 el portafresas
- *cutter spindle*
61 el motor de impulsión *f*
- *drive motor*

Meyer, **Joseph,** Verlagsbuchhändler, Schriftstel-4
ler und Industrieller, *9. 5. 1796 Gotha, †27. 6. 1856
Hildburghausen, erwies sich nach mißglückten Börsen-5
(1816-20 in London) und industriellen Unterneh-6
mungen (1820-23 in Thüringen) als origineller Shake-
speare- und Scott-Übersetzer und fand mit seinem
„Korrespondenzblatt für Kaufleute" 1825 Anklang.
1826 gründete er den Verlag *„Bibliographisches In-*7
stitut" in Gotha (1828 nach Hildburghausen verlegt),-8
den er durch die Vielseitigkeit seiner eigenen Werke
(„Universum", „Das Große Konversations-9
lexikon für die gebildeten Stände", „Meyers-10
Universal-Atlas" 1830-37) sowie durch die Wohlfeil-11
heit und die gediegene Ausstattung seiner volkstüm-
lichen Verlagswerke („Klassikerausgaben", „Meyers-12
Familien- und Groschenbibliothek", „Volksbibliothek
für Naturkunde", „Geschichtsbibliothek", „Meyers
Pfennig-Atlas" u. a.) sowie durch die Entwicklung
neuer Absatzwege (lieferungsweises Erscheinen auf
Subskription und Vertrieb durch Reisebuch--13
handel) zum Welthaus machte. Besonders durch
das **„Universum",** ein historisch-geographisches
Bilderwerk, das in 80000 AUFLAGE und in 12 SPRACHEN-14
erschien, wirkte er auf breiteste Kreise. —15 17
16— Seit Ende der 1830er Jahre trat er unter
großen Opfern für ein einheitliches deutsches Eisen-
bahnnetz ein, doch scheiterten seine Pläne und seine

■ 19
■ 20 (18)
■ 21 N n
■ 22 N n
■ 23 N n
■ 24 N n
■ 25 N n
■ 26 N n
■ 27 N n
■ 28 N n
■ 29 N n
■ 30 N n
■ 31 N n

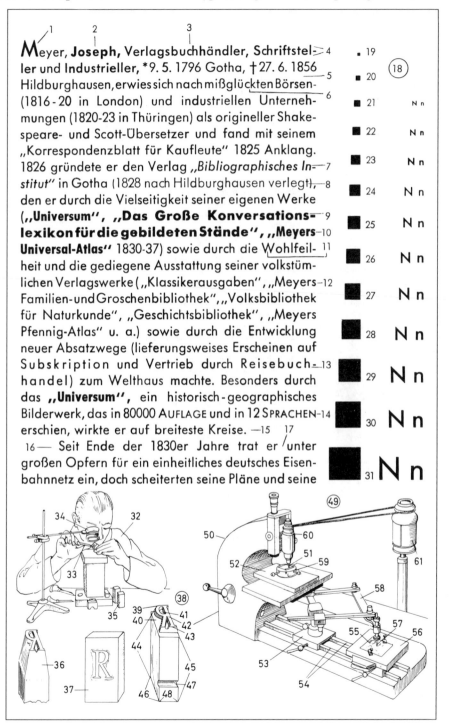

176 Taller de composición III (Fotocomposición)

1-21 los sistemas unificados para la fotocomposición
– *phototypesetting configurations*
1 el sistema unificado off-line (fuera de línea)
– *off-line configuration*
2 *u.* **3** el inventario de composición *f*
– *data capture*
2 el lugar del inventario final
– *terminal for keying unformatted text*
3 el lugar de inventario *m* de corrección *f*
– *text capture and correction terminal*
4 la pantalla de formato *m*
– *layout terminal (page-layout terminal)*
5 el soporte de datos *m*, un disquete
– *data carrier, a diskette (floppy disk)*
6 la unidad de exposición *f*
– *(photo)typesetting unit (photo-typesetter)*
7 el sistema unificado on-line
– *on-line configuration*
8 la terminal de compaginación *f*
– *make-up terminal (page make-up terminal)*
9 la calculadora central (calculadora *f* de composición *f*, computadora *f* de composición
– *central processing unit (typesetting computer)*
10 la estación de cinta *f* magnética (la unidad de memoria *f* de cinta *f* magnética)
– *magnetic tape unit (magnetic tape drive)*
11 los discos de memoria *f*
– *disk store*
12 la impresora (el printer), una impresora láser (el laser printer)
– *printer, a laser printer*
13 la instalación de la exposición
– *phototypesetting machine (photo-typesetter)*
14 la composición del texto (lugar de la composición del texto)
– *text capture (text-capture terminal)*
15 el tipógrafo, el cajista
– *typesetter (keyboarder or typographer)*
16 la pantalla (el monitor)
– *screen (monitor)*
17 la disquetera
– *floppy disk drive*
18 la unidad de cálculo *m* y de memoria *f* con la unidad central y con el disco duro (la memoria de disco *m* duro)
– *computer and memory unit with central processing unit and hard disk*
19 el ratón (un aparato de entrada *f*)
– *mouse, an input device*

20 la bandeja del ratón
– *mouse mat*
21 el teclado (un aparato de entrada *f*)
– *keyboard, an input device*
22 la instalación de fotocomposición *f*
– *direct-entry phototypesetter*
23-33 preimpresión *f* (el desktop publishing, DTP)
– *desktop publishing (DTP)*
23 el disquete con procesadores *m* de texto *m*, diseño *m* y de gráfico *m*
– *diskette (floppy disk) with text, layout, and graphics programs*
24 el escáner (el escáner extraplano), un aparato de exploración *f*
– *scanner (flat-bed scanner)*
25 el ordenador personal (PC) o estación *f* de trabajo *m*
– *personal computer (PC) or work-station*
26 la impresión (la impresión por ordenador *m*)
– *printout (computer printout)*
27 la calculadora de la imagen del retículo (el Raster Image Processor, RIP)
– *raster image processor (RIP)*
28 la impresora láser
– *laser phototypesetter*
29 la prueba (la tirada de prueba *f*)
– *proof*
30 la pantalla de gráficos *m* de alta resolución *f*, un monitor de color *m* de gran formato *m*
– *high-resolution graphics screen, a large-format colour monitor*
31 una parte de la exposición
– *display window*
32 los parámetros tipográficos
– *typographic parameters*
33 la zona de órdenes (la pantalla de órdenes)
– *(typographic) command window*
34 la copiadora automática de películas *f* (la copiadora de películas *f*)
– *film copier*
35-46 la impresora de rayos catódicos
– *cathode ray tube (CRT) typesetter*
35 el sistema de exploración
– *scanning system*
36 el tubo del rayo catódico y scan
– *scan-generating (scanning) cathode ray tube (CRT)*
37 la lente
– *lens*
38 el bastidor de caracteres *f* (el bastidor portamatrices)
– *character grid (matrix case)*
39 la lente del condensador
– *condenser lens*
40 el multiplicador de fotos
– *photomultiplier*
41 el sistema de reproducción
– *output system*

42 el amplificador de vídeo
– *video amplifier*
43 el tubo de escritura
– *character-generating tube (CRT character generator)*
44 el espacio de insolación
– *exposure plane*
45 el bastidor portamatrices
– *matrix case*
46 la ranura de guía *f*
– *guide claw*

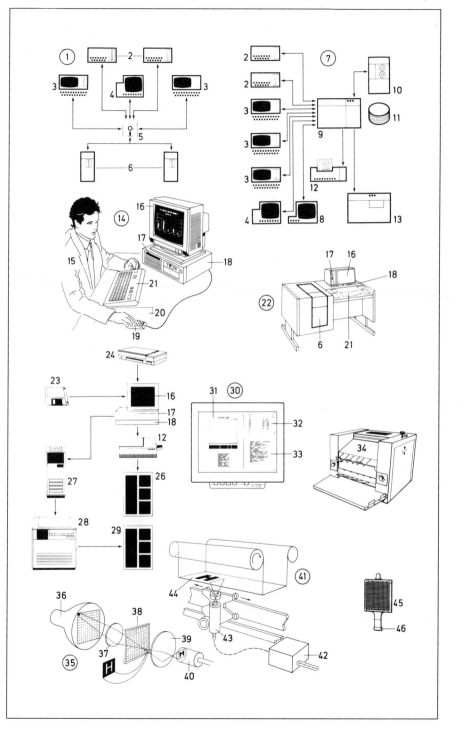

1 la cámara de reproducción f construida a manera f de puente m
– *overhead process camera (overhead copying camera)*
2 el cristal esmerilado
– *focusing screen (ground glass screen)*
3 el marco orientable del cristal esmerilado
– *hinged screen holder*
4 la cruz del eje (el retículo)
– *graticule*
5 el puesto de manejo m (de control m)
– *control console*
6 el pupitre de maniobra f suspendido y orientable
– *hinged bracket-mounted control panel*
7 las escalas de porcentajes m
– *percentage focusing charts*
8 el portapelículas vacío
– *vacuum film holder*
9 el depósito (el almacén) del retículo
– *screen magazine*
10 el fuelle
– *bellows*
11 el estandarte (el bastidor portaobjetivos)
– *standard*
12 el dispositivo indicador
– *register device*
13 el soporte (el caballete) del puente
– *overhead gantry*
14 el portaoriginales
– *copyboard*
15 el bastidor del portaoriginales
– *copyholder*
16 el brazo articulado portalámparas f
– *lamp bracket*
17 la lámpara de xenón m
– *xenon lamp*
18 el original
– *copy (original)*
19 la mesa de retoque m y montaje m
– *retouching and stripping desk*
20 la superficie luminosa
– *illuminated screen*
21 la regulación de la altura y de la inclinación
– *height and angle adjustment*
22 el portamodelos
– *copyboard*
23 el cuentahílos plegable, una lupa (un cristal de aumento m)
– *linen tester, a magnifying glass*
24 la cámara de reproducción f universal
– *universal process and reproduction camera*
25 la caja de la cámara
– *camera body*
26 el fuelle
– *bellows*

27 el portalentes
– *lens carrier*
28 el espejo de ángulo m
– *angled mirror*
29 el soporte en forma f de T
– *stand*
30 el portamodelos
– *copyboard*
31 la lámpara de halógeno m
– *halogen lamp*
32 la cámara de reproducción f vertical, una cámara compacta
– *vertical process camera, a compact camera*
33 la caja de la cámara
– *camera body*
34 el cristal esmerilado
– *focusing screen (ground glass screen)*
35 la tapa de vacío m
– *vacuum back*
36 el panel de mandos m
– *control panel*
37 la lámpara de exposición f (la lámpara del flash)
– *flash lamp*
38 el espejo para la entrada correcta de las imágenes
– *mirror for right-reading images*
39 el scanner (el aparato corrector del color)
– *scanner (colour, Am. color, correction unit)*
40 la armazón inferior
– *base frame*
41 el compartimiento de la lámpara
– *lamp compartment*
42 la caja de la lámpara de xenón m
– *xenon lamp housing*
43 los motores de avance m
– *feed motors*
44 el brazo portadiapositivas
– *transparency arm*
45 el cilindro de exploración f
– *scanning drum*
46 la cabeza de exploración f
– *scanning head*
47 la cabeza de exploración f de máscara f
– *mask-scanning head*
48 el cilindro de máscara f
– *mask drum*
49 el espacio de registro m
– *recording space*
50 el estuche (la cassette) para la luz de día m
– *daylight cassette*
51 el calculador de color m con unidad f de mando m y corrector m selectivo de color m
– *colour (Am. color) computer with control unit and selective colour correction*
52 el aparato de clisar
– *engraving machine*

53 la regulación (el regulador) de grabado m continuo
– *seamless engraving adjustment*
54 el embrague de impulsión f
– *drive clutch*
55 la brida del embrague
– *clutch flange*
56 la torre de impulsión f (la unidad motriz)
– *drive unit*
57 el banco de la máquina
– *machine bed*
58 el portaherramientas
– *equipment carrier*
59 el carro de la bancada
– *bed slide*
60 el panel de control m
– *control panel*
61 el soporte del cojinete
– *bearing block*
62 el cabezal móvil
– *tailstock*
63 la cabeza de exploración f
– *scanning head*
64 el cilindro del modelo
– *copy cylinder*
65 el cojinete central
– *centre (Am. center) bearing*
66 el sistema de grabado m
– *engraving system*
67 el cilindro impresor
– *printing cylinder*
68 el brazo del cilindro
– *cylinder arm*
69 el armario adosado
– *electronics (electronic) cabinet*
70 las unidades de cálculo m
– *computers*
71 la entrada (el empuje) del programa
– *program input*
72 el revelador de películas f automático para las películas de scanner m
– *automatic film processor for scanner films*

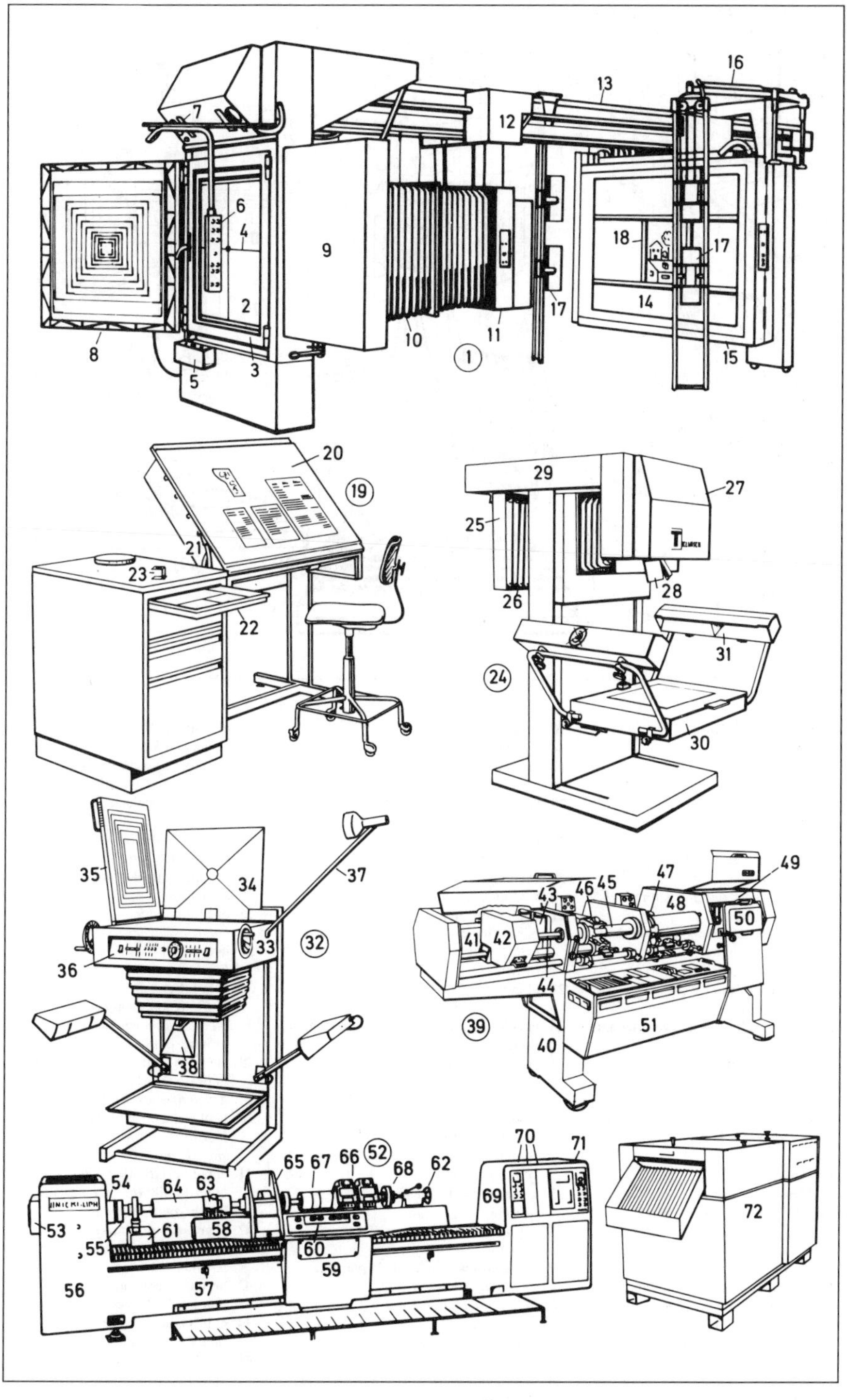
1
2
3
4
5
6
7
8
9
10
11
12
13
14
15
16
17
18
19
20
21
22
23
24
25
26
27
28
29
30
31
32
33
34
35
36
37
38
39
40
41
42
43
44
45
46
47
48
49
50
51
52
53
54
55
56
57
58
59
60
61
62
63
64
65
66
67
68
69
70
71
72

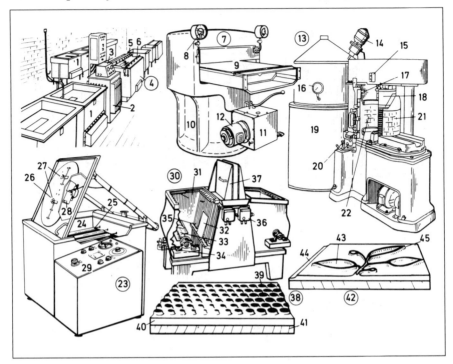

1-6 la instalación galvánica
- *electrotyping plant*
1 la cubeta de lavado *m*
- *cleaning tank*
2 el rectificador de corriente *f*
- *rectifier*
3 el aparato de medida *f* y de regulación *f*
- *measuring and control unit*
4 la pila de galvanizar
- *electroplating tank (electroplating bath, electroplating vat)*
5 la barra del ánodo (con ánodos *m* de cobre *m*)
- *anode rod (with copper anodes)*
6 la barra de moldes *m* (el cátodo)
- *plate rod (cathode)*
7 **la prensa hidráulica para hacer (acuñar) matrices *f***
- *hydraulic moulding* (Am. *molding*) *press*
8 el manómetro
- *pressure gauge* (Am. *gage*) (*manometer*)
9 la mesa para hacer las matrices
- *apron*
10 el pie cilíndrico
- *round base*
11 la bomba hidráulica de presión *f*
- *hydraulic pressure pump*
12 el motor de impulsión *f*
- *drive motor*
13 **la fundidora de plancha *f* curvada**
- *curved plate casting machine (curved electrotype casting machine)*
14 el motor
- *motor*
15 los botones (los pulsadores) de control *m*
- *control knobs*

16 el pirómetro
- *pyrometer*
17 la boca de inyección *f* del metal
- *mouth piece*
18 la cámara de fundición *f*
- *core*
19 el horno de fusión *f*
- *melting furnace*
20 el conmutador
- *starting lever*
21 la plancha curvada fundida (la teja), para la impresión rotativa
- *cast curved plate (cast curved electrotype) for rotary printing*
22 el molde fijo de fundición *f*
- *fixed mould* (Am. *mold*)
23 **la máquina de grabar clisés *m* al agua *f* fuerte**
- *etching machine*
24 la cubeta de grabado *m* con el líquido corrosivo y el producto para la protección de los lados
- *etching tank with etching solution (etchant, mordant) and filming agent (film former)*
25 los cilindros de paleta *f*
- *paddles*
26 el plato rotor
- *turntable*
27 el dispositivo fijador de la plancha
- *plate clamp*
28 el motor de impulsión *f*
- *drive motor*
29 el grupo (la unidad) de control *m*
- *control unit*
30 **la máquina gemela de grabados *m* al agua *f* fuerte**
- *twin etching machine*

31 el baño para el agua *f* fuerte [sección]
- *etching tank (etching bath) [in section]*
32 la plancha de cinc *m* para copiar
- *photoprinted zinc plate*
33 la rueda de paletas *f*
- *paddle*
34 el grifo de desagüe *m*
- *outlet cock (drain cock,* Am. *faucet)*
35 el soporte de la plancha
- *plate rack*
36 el conmutador
- *control switches*
37 la tapa del baño
- *lid*
38 **la autotipia,** un clisé
- *halftone photoengraving (halftone block, halftone plate), a block (plate, printing plate)*
39 el punto de trama *f*, un elemento impreso
- *dot (halftone dot), a printing element*
40 la plancha de cinc *m* grabada al agua *f* fuerte
- *etched zinc plate*
41 el pie del clisé (la madera del clisé)
- *block mount (block mounting, plate mount, plate mounting)*
42 **el grabado de trazo *m***
- *line block (line engraving, line etching, line plate, line cut)*
43 las partes corroídas no impresoras
- *non-printing, deep-etched areas*
44 el biselado del clisé
- *flange (bevel edge)*
45 el costado (el borde) del grabado al agua *f* fuerte
- *sidewall*

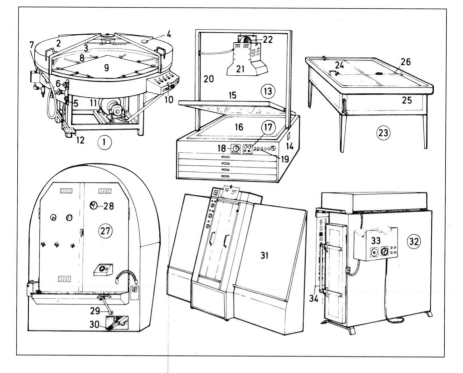

1 la centrífuga de planchas *f*, para emulsionar las planchas de offset *m*
– *plate whirler (whirler, plate-coating machine) for coating offset plates*
2 la tapa deslizante
– *sliding lid*
3 la calefacción eléctrica
– *electric heater*
4 el termómetro
– *temperature gauge* (Am. *gage*)
5 la conexión del agua *f* de aclarado *m*
– *water connection for the spray unit*
6 el lavado por circulación *f*
– *spray unit*
7 la ducha de mano *f*
– *hand spray*
8 las barras de fijación *f* de la plancha
– *plate clamps*
9 la plancha de cinc *m* (*también:* plancha de magnesio *m*, plancha de cobre *m*)
– *zinc plate (also: magnesium plate, copper plate)*
10 el pupitre de control *m*
– *control panel*
11 el motor de impulsión *f*
– *drive motor*
12 el pedal de freno *m*
– *brake pedal*
13 el marco neumático para copiar
– *vacuum printing frame (vacuum frame, printing-down frame)*

14 la armazón inferior del marco para copiar
– *base of the vacuum printing frame (vacuum frame, printing-down frame)*
15 la parte superior del marco con cristal *m* de espejo *m*
– *plate glass frame*
16 la plancha de offset *m* recubierta
– *coated offset plate*
17 el tablero de mando *m*
– *control panel*
18 el regulador del tiempo de exposición *f*
– *exposure timer*
19 el interruptor para la producción del vacío
– *vacuum pump switches*
20 las varillas-guía (el soporte)
– *support*
21 la lámpara para copiar con luz *f* de punto *m*, una lámpara de halógeno *m* de metal *m*
– *point light exposure lamp, a quartz-halogen lamp*
22 el soplante de la lámpara
– *fan blower*
23 la mesa de montaje *m*, para el montaje de películas *f*
– *stripping table (make-up table) for stripping films*
24 la pantalla de vidrio *m* de cristal *m*
– *crystal glass screen*

25 la caja de la luz
– *light box*
26 el dispositivo deslizable de trazado *m*
– *straightedge rules*
27 la secadora centrífuga vertical
– *vertical plate-drying cabinet*
28 el higrómetro
– *hygrometer*
29 la regulación de la velocidad
– *speed control*
30 el pedal del freno
– *brake pedal*
31 la máquina de tratamiento *m* para las planchas presensibilizadas
– *processing machine for presensitized plates*
32 el horno de calcinación *f* para las planchas de esmalte *m* caliente (planchas *f* diazo)
– *burning-in oven for glue-enamel plates (diazo plates)*
33 la caja de mandos *m*
– *control box (control unit)*
34 la plancha diazo
– *diazo plate*

1 la máquina offset *m* de bobinas *f* de
   cuatro colores *m*
– *four-colour* (Am. *four-color*) *rotary offset press (rotary offset machine, web-
   offset press)*
2 la bobina de papel *m* no impreso
– *roll of unprinted paper (blank paper)*
3 el portabobinas (dispositivo *m* para
   colocar la bobina de papel *m* no impreso)
– *reel stand (carrier for the roll of unprinted paper)*
4 los rodillos transportadores del papel
– *forwarding rolls*
5 el regulador lateral de la bobina
– *side margin control (margin control,
   side control, side lay control)*
6-13 los mecanismos entintadores
– *inking units (inker units)*
6 *u.* 7 el mecanismo de retiración *f* del
   amarillo
– *perfecting unit (double unit) for yellow*
6, 8, 10, 12 los mecanismos entintadores
   del mecanismo impresor superior
– *inking units (inker units) in the upper
   printing unit*
7, 9, 11, 13 los mecanismos entintadores
   del mecanismo impresor inferior
– *inking units (inker units) in the lower
   printing unit*
8 *u.* 9 el mecanismo de retiración *f* del
   cyan (azul-verde)
– *perfecting unit (double unit) for cyan*
10 *u.* 11 el mecanismo de retiración *f* del
   magenta
– *perfecting unit (double unit) for magenta*
12 *u.* 13 el mecanismo de retiración *f* del
   negro
– *perfecting unit (double unit) for black*
14 el horno secador
– *drier*
15 la plegadora
– *folder (folder unit)*
16 el pupitre de mando *m*
– *control desk*
17 el pliego impreso
– *sheet*
18 la máquina offset *m* de bobinas *f* de
   cuatro colores *m* [esquema]
– *four-colour* (Am. *four-color*) *rotary offset press (rotary offset machine, web-
   offset press) [diagram]*
19 el portabobinas
– *reel stand*
20 el regulador lateral de la banda de
   papel
– *side margin control (margin control,
   side control, side lay control)*
21 el rodillo entintador
– *inking rollers (ink rollers, inkers)*
22 el tintero
– *ink duct (ink fountain)*
23 los rodillos mojadores
– *damping rollers (dampening rollers,
   dampers, dampeners)*
24 el cilindro de caucho *m*
– *blanket cylinder*
25 el cilindro de plancha *f*
– *plate cylinder*
26 la tira de papel *m*
– *route of the paper (of the web)*
27 el horno secador
– *drier*
28 los cilindros de refrigeración *f*
– *chilling rolls (cooling rollers, chill
   rollers)*

29 la plegadora
– *folder (folder unit)*
30 la máquina offset *m* de hojas *f* de cuatro colores *m* [esquema]
– *four-colour* (Am. *four-colour*) *sheet-fed
   offset machine (offset press) [diagram]*
31 el alimentador de hojas *f*
– *sheet feeder (feeder)*
32 la mesa de alimentación *f*
– *feed table (feed board)*
33 el balancín transmitiendo la hoja al
   tambor alimentador
– *route of the sheets through swing-grip-
   pers to the feed drum*
34 el tambor alimentador
– *feed drum*
35 el cilindro impresor
– *impression cylinder*
36 los tambores de transmisión *f*
– *transfer drums (transfer cylinders)*
37 el cilindro de caucho *m*
– *blanket cylinder*
38 el cilindro de plancha *f*
– *plate cylinder*
39 el mecanismo humedecedor
– *damping unit (dampening unit)*
40 el mecanismo entintador
– *inking unit (inker unit)*
41 el mecanismo impresor
– *printing unit*
42 el tambor expositor (tambor *m* de salida *f*)
– *delivery cylinder*
43 la salida de cadenas *f*
– *chain delivery*
44 la pila de hojas *f*
– *delivery pile*
45 el expositor (la salida) de hojas *f*
– *delivery unit (delivery mechanism)*
46 la máquina offset *m* de un color
– *single-colour* (Am. *single-color*) *offset
   press (offset machine)*
47 la pila de hojas *f* de papel *m* (el papel
   para imprimir)
– *pile of paper (sheets, printing paper)*
48 el alimentador de hojas *f* (un alimentador automático)
– *sheet feeder (feeder), an automatic pile
   feeder*
49 la mesa de alimentación *f*
– *feed table (feed board)*
50 los rodillos entintadores
– *inking rollers (ink rollers, inkers)*
51 el mecanismo entintador
– *inking unit (inker unit)*
52 los rodillos mojadores
– *damping rollers (dampening rollers,
   dampers, dampeners)*
53 el cilindro de la plancha, una plancha
   de zinc *m*
– *plate cylinder, a zinc plate*
54 el cilindro de caucho *m*, un cilindro de
   acero *m* recubierto de caucho *m*
– *blanket cylinder, a steel cylinder with
   rubber blanket*
55 la plataforma de salida *f* de las hojas
   impresas
– *pile delivery unit for the printed sheets*
56 las pinzas prensoras, un dispositivo
   prensor de cadenas *f*
– *gripper bar, a chain gripper*
57 la pila de papel *m* (impreso)
– *pile of printed paper (printed sheets)*

58 la chapa de protección *f* de la correa de
   transmisión *f*
– *guard for the V-belt (vee-belt) drive*
59 la máquina offset *m* de un color [esquema]
– *single-colour* (Am. *single-color*) *offset
   press (offset machine) [diagram]*
60 el mecanismo entintador con los rodillos entintadores
– *inking unit (inker unit) with inking
   rollers (ink rollers, inkers)*
61 el mecanismo mojador con los rodillos
   mojadores
– *damping unit (dampening unit) with
   damping rollers (dampening rollers,
   dampers, dampeners)*
62 el cilindro de la plancha
– *plate cylinder*
63 el cilindro de caucho *m*
– *blanket cylinder*
64 el cilindro impresor
– *impression cylinder*
65 el tambor de salida *f*, con el sistema de
   agarre *m*
– *delivery cylinders with grippers*
66 el piñón de impulsión *f*
– *drive wheel*
67 la mesa de alimentación *f* de hojas *f*
– *feed table (feed board)*
68 el alimentador de hojas *f*
– *sheet feeder (feeder)*
69 la pila de papel *m* (con papel *m* para
   imprimir)
– *pile of unprinted paper (blank paper,
   unprinted sheets, blank sheets)*
70 la máquina de imprimir en offset *m*
   tamaño *m* pequeño
– *small sheet-fed offset press*
71 el mecanismo entintador
– *inking unit (inker unit)*
72 el alimentador por succión *f*
– *suction feeder*
73 la pila de alimentación *f*
– *pile feeder*
74 el cuadro de mandos *m* con contador
   m, manómetro *m*, regulador *m* de aire
   m y conmutador *m* para la alimentación
   de papel *m*
– *instrument panel (control panel) with
   counter, pressure gauge* (Am. *gage*), *air
   regulator, and control switch for the
   sheet feeder (feeder)*
75 la máquina offset *m* plana (prensa *f*
   para sacar pruebas *f* Mailänder)
– *flat-bed offset press (offset machine)
   ('Mailänder' proofing press, proof
   press)*
76 el mecanismo entintador
– *inking unit (inker unit)*
77 los rodillos entintadores
– *inking rollers (ink rollers, inkers)*
78 el lecho (el carro) de impresión *f*
– *bed (press bed, type bed, forme bed,*
   Am. *form bed)*
79 el cilindro de caucho *m*
– *cylinder with rubber blanket*
80 la palanca de arranque *m* y parada *f* de
   los mecanismos de impresión *f*
– *starting and stopping lever for the printing unit*
81 el volante para regular la presión
– *impression-setting wheel (impression-
   adjusting wheel)*

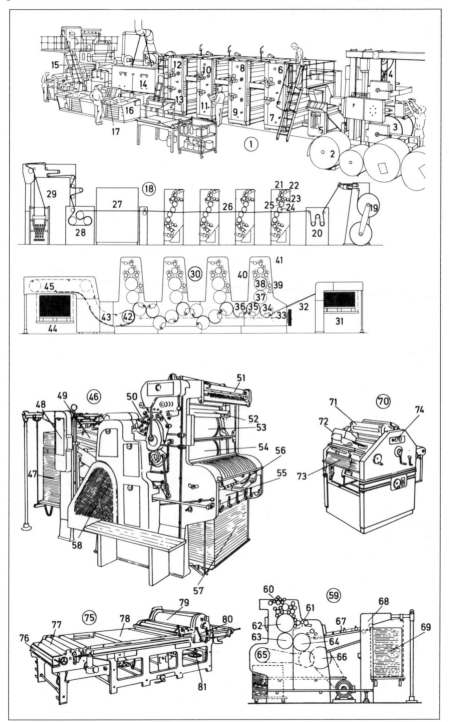

1-65 máquinas *f* tipográficas
– *presses (machines) for letterpress printing (letterpress printing machines)*
1 la rotativa de doble revolución *f*
– *two-revolution flat-bed cylinder press*
2 el cilindro impresor
– *impression cylinder*
3 la palanca de elevación *f* y descenso *m* del cilindro
– *lever for raising or lowering the cylinder*
4 la mesa de alimentación *f*
– *feed table (feed board)*
5 el alimentador automático de hojas *f* [accionado por succión *f* y aire *m* comprimido]
– *automatic sheet feeder (feeder) [operated by vacuum and air blasts]*
6 la bomba de aire *m*, para el mecanismo de alimentación *f* y expulsión *f* de hojas *f*
– *air pump for the feeder and delivery*
7 el mecanismo entintador cilíndrico, con rodillos *m* extendedores y rodillos *m* dadores
– *inking unit (inker unit) with distributing rollers (distributor rollers, distributors) and forme rollers (Am. form rollers)*
8 el mecanismo entintador de mesa *f*
– *ink slab (ink plate) inking unit (inker unit)*
9 la pila de papel *m*, papel *m* para imprimir
– *delivery pile for printed paper*
10 el aparato pulverizador antimácula
– *sprayer (anti set-off apparatus, anti set-off spray) for dusting the printed sheets*
11 el dispositivo de intercalar
– *interleaving device*
12 el pedal, para interrumpir la presión
– *foot pedal for starting and stopping the press*
13 la minerva [corte]
– *platen press (platen machine, platen) [in section]*
14 la alimentación y suelta *f* del papel
– *paper feed and delivery (paper feeding and delivery unit)*
15 la platina de impresión *f*
– *platen*
16 la impulsión de la palanca acodada
– *toggle action (toggle-joint action)*
17 el plato de impresión *f*
– *bed (type bed, press bed, forme bed, Am. form bed)*
18 los rodillos entintadores
– *forme rollers (Am. form rollers) (forme-inking, Am. form-inking, rollers)*
19 el mecanismo entintador, para distribuir la tinta de imprenta *f*
– *inking unit (inker unit) for distributing the ink (printing ink)*

20 la prensa de parada *f* de cilindro *m*
– *stop-cylinder press (stop-cylinder machine)*
21 la mesa de alimentación *f*
– *feed table (feed board)*
22 el alimentador mecánico
– *feeder mechanism (feeding apparatus, feeder)*
23 la pila de papel *m* (con papel *m* para ser impreso)
– *pile of unprinted paper (blank paper, unprinted sheets, blank sheets)*
24 la rejilla de protección *f* del extractor del papel
– *guard for the sheet feeder (feeder)*
25 la pila de papel *m* (con papel impreso)
– *pile of printed paper (printed sheets)*
26 el mecanismo de mando *m*
– *control mechanism*
27 los rodillos entintadores
– *forme rollers (Am. form rollers) (forme-inking, Am. form-inking, rollers)*
28 el mecanismo entintador
– *inking unit (inker unit)*
29 la minerva (la gato) [Heidelberg]
– *[Heidelberg] platen press (platen machine, platen)*
30 la mesa de alimentación *f* con la pila de papel *m* para ser impreso
– *feed table (feed board) with pile of unprinted paper (blank paper, unprinted sheets, blank sheets)*
31 la mesa de distribución *f*
– *delivery table*
32 la palanca de arranque *m* y parada *f*
– *starting and stopping lever*
33 el pulverizador automático
– *delivery blower*
34 la pistola pulverizadora
– *spray gun (sprayer)*
35 la bomba de aire *m*, para succión *f* y soplado *m*
– *air pump for vacuum and air blasts*
36 la forma cerrada (forma *f* de composición *f*)
– *locked-up forme (Am. form)*
37 la composición
– *type (type matter, matter)*
38 el bastidor de cierre *f*
– *chase*
39 la cuña de fijación *f*
– *quoin*
40 la regleta
– *length of furniture*
41 la rotativa tipográfica para periódicos *m*, de hasta 16 páginas *f*
– *rotary letterpress press (rotary letterpress machine, web-fed letterpress machine) for newspapers of up to 16 pages*

42 los cilindros cortadores, para cortar longitudinalmente la banda de papel *m*
– *slitters for dividing the width of the web*
43 la banda de papel *m*
– *web*
44 el cilindro de impresión *f*
– *impression cylinder*
45 el rodillo bailador (el cilindro compensador)
– *jockey roller (compensating roller, compensator, tension roller)*
46 la bobina de papel *m*
– *roll of paper*
47 el freno automático de la bobina de papel *m*
– *automatic brake*
48 el elemento para la impresión de blanco
– *first printing unit*
49 el elemento para la impresión de la segunda cara (retiración *f*)
– *perfecting unit*
50 el mecanismo entintador
– *inking unit (inker unit)*
51 el cilindro portaplanchas (cilindro *m* estereotipo)
– *plate cylinder*
52 el mecanismo de impresión *f* en colores *m*
– *second printing unit*
53 el enderezador del plegado
– *former*
54 el tacómetro, con cuentapliegos *m*
– *tachometer with sheet counter*
55 la plegadora
– *folder (folder unit)*
56 el periódico plegado
– *folded newspaper*
57 el mecanismo entintador, de la máquina rotativa [corte]
– *inking unit (inker unit) for the rotary press (web-fed press) [in section]*
58 la banda de papel *m*
– *web*
59 el cilindro impresor
– *impression cylinder*
60 el cilindro portaplanchas (el cilindro estereotipo)
– *plate cylinder*
61 los rodillos entintadores
– *forme rollers (Am. form rollers) (forme-inking, Am. form-inking, rollers)*
62 el cilindro distribuidor de la tinta
– *distributing rollers (distributor rollers, distributors)*
63 el cilindro tomador de la tinta
– *lifter roller (ductor, ductor roller)*
64 el cilindro del tintero
– *duct roller (fountain roller, ink fountain roller)*
65 la caja de tinta *f* (el tintero)
– *ink duct (ink fountain)*

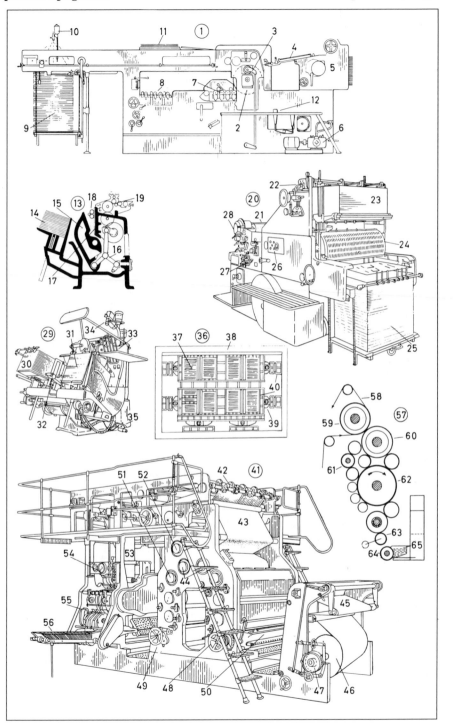

1 la insolación del papel carbón *m*
- *exposure of the carbon tissue (pigment paper)*
2 el chasis neumático
- *vacuum frame*
3 la lámpara de insolación *f*, una hilera de lámparas *f* halógenas
- *exposing lamp, a bank of quartz-halogen lamps*
4 la lámpara con la luz concentrada en un punto
- *point source lamp*
5 la campana de evacuación *f* del calor
- *heat extractor*
6 la máquina de reporte *m* del papel carbón *m*
- *carbon tissue transfer machine (laydown machine, laying machine)*
7 el cilindro de cobre *m* pulido
- *polished copper cylinder*
8 el rodillo de caucho *m* para comprimir el papel carbón *m* insolado
- *rubber roller for pressing on the printed carbon tissue (pigment paper)*
9 la máquina de revelado *m* del rodillo
- *cylinder-processing machine*
10 el rodillo huecograbado recubierto de papel *m* carbón *m*
- *gravure cylinder coated with carbon tissue (pigment paper)*
11 la cuba de revelado *m*
- *developing tank*
12 el retoque del rodillo
- *staging*
13 el rodillo revelado
- *developed cylinder*
14 el retocador efectuando un recubrimiento
- *retoucher painting out (stopping out)*
15 la máquina de grabar al agua *f* fuerte
- *etching machine*
16 la cuba de grabar con el líquido corrosivo
- *etching tank with etching solution (etchant, mordant)*
17 el rodillo de huecograbado *m* copiado
- *printed gravure cylinder*
18 el huecograbador
- *gravure etcher*
19 el disco de cálculo *m*
- *calculator dial*
20 el reloj de control *m*
- *timer*
21 la corrección del grabado
- *revising (correcting) the cylinder*
22 el cilindro huecograbado
- *etched gravure cylinder*

23 el pupitre de corrección *f*
- *ledge*
24 la rotativa de huecograbado *m* multicolor
- *multicolour (Am. multicolor) rotogravure press*
25 la canalización de evacuación *f* de vapores *m* del disolvente
- *exhaust pipe for solvent fumes*
26 el cuerpo de impresión reversible
- *reversible printing unit*
27 la plegadora
- *folder (folder unit)*
28 el pupitre de control *m* y manejo *m*
- *control desk*
29 el mecanismo de salida *f* de periódicos *m*
- *newspaper delivery unit*
30 la cinta transportadora
- *conveyor belt (conveyor)*
31 la pila de periódicos *m* empaquetados
- *bundled stack of newspapers*

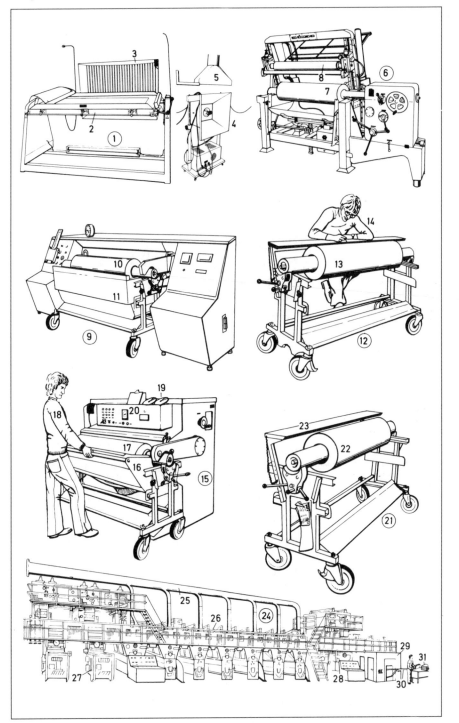

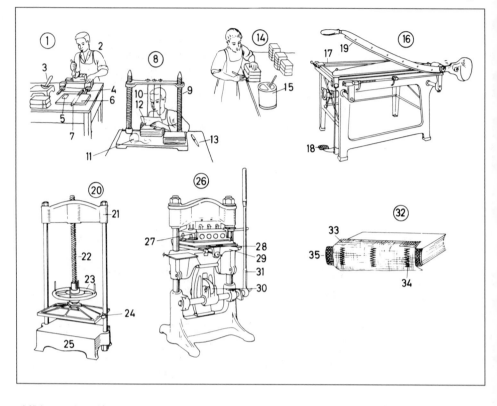

1-35 la encuadernación a mano *f*
– **hand bookbindery** *(hand bindery)*
1 el dorado del lomo de un libro
– *gilding the spine of the book*
2 el dorador, un encuadernador
– *gold finisher (gilder), a bookbinder*
3 el cajetín (el hierro de dorar)
– *fillet*
4 el bastidor (la prensa de encuadernar)
– *holding press (finishing press)*
5 el pan de oro *m*
– *gold leaf*
6 el cojín para el oro
– *gold cushion*
7 el cuchillo para el oro
– *gold knife*
8 la encuadernación en rústica *f*
– *sewing (stitching)*
9 el bastidor de coser
– *sewing frame*
10 la cuerda para el cosido
– *sewing cord*
11 el ovillo de hilo *m*
– *ball of thread (sewing thread)*
12 la colocación del cuadernillo
– *section (signature)*
13 el cuchillo de encuadernador *m*
– *bookbinder's knife*
14 el encolado del lomo
– *gluing the spine*

15 el bote de cola *f*
– *glue pot*
16 la cizalla (la guillotina) de papel *m*
– *board cutter (guillotine)*
17 el dispositivo para enmarcar (la guía)
– *back gauge* (Am. *gage*)
18 el dispositivo de prensado *m*, con pedal *m*
– *clamp with foot pedal*
19 la cuchilla móvil
– *cutting blade*
20 la prensa de tornillo *m*, una prensa de satinar y empaquetar
– *standing press, a nipping press*
21 la cabeza
– *head piece (head beam)*
22 el husillo
– *spindle*
23 el volante
– *handwheel*
24 el plato presionador
– *platen*
25 el pie
– *bed (base)*
26 la prensa doradora y troqueladora, una prensa manual; *anál.:* una prensa de palanca *f* acodada
– *gilding (gold blocking) and embossing press, a hand-lever press;* sim.: *toggle-joint press (toggle-lever press)*

27 la caja para la calefacción
– *heating box*
28 el plato superior colgante (el plato deslizante de guías *f*)
– *sliding plate*
29 la platina de gofrar
– *embossing platen*
30 el sistema de palanca *f* acodada (el sistema de leva *f*)
– *toggle action (toggle-joint action)*
31 la palanca de mano *f*
– *hand lever*
32 el libro encuadernado con gasa *f* (el bloque de páginas *f*)
– *book sewn on gauze (mull, scrim) (book block)*
33 la gasa
– *gauze (mull, scrim)*
34 el cosido
– *sewing (stitching)*
35 la cabezada
– *headband*

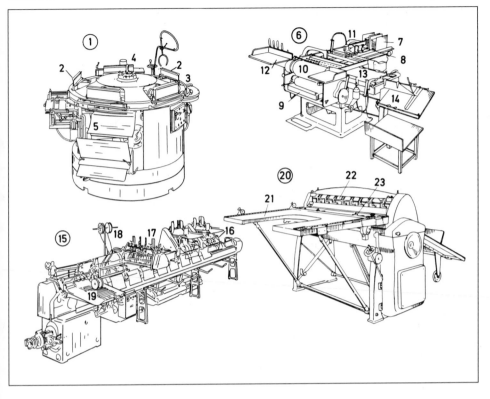

1-23 máquinas *f* de encuadernación *f*
- *bookbinding machines*
1 la encuadernadora sin costura *f*
(la máquina de pegar) para
tiradas *f* pequeñas
- *adhesive binder (perfect binder)*
for short runs
2 el dispositivo para la introducción
manual
- *manual feed station*
3 el dispositivo de refilado *m* y raspado *m*
- *cutoff knife and roughing station*
4 el mecanismo de encolado *m*
- *gluing mechanism*
5 la salida de libros *m*
- *delivery (book delivery)*
6 la máquina de hacer tapas *f*
- *case maker (case-making*
machine)
7 el almacén para las tapas de
cartón *m*
- *board feed hoppers*
8 los sacadores del cartón
- *pick-up suckers*
9 el depósito (la caja) de cola *f*
- *glue tank*

10 el rodillo para empastar
- *cover cylinder*
11 el brazo succionador
- *picker head*
12 la bandeja depósito *m* de los
materiales [tela *f*, papel *m*, piel *f*]
- *feed table for covering materials*
[linen, paper, leather]
13 el mecanismo de prensa
- *pressing mechanism*
14 la mesa de distribución *f*
- *delivery table*
15 la máquina de coser con alambre *m*
- *gang stitcher (gathering and wire-*
stitching machine, gatherer and
wire stitcher)
16 el alimentador de hojas *f*
- *sheet feeder (sheet-feeding station)*
17 el plegador
- *folder-feeding station*
18 el mecanismo para desbobinar el
alambre de coser
- *stitching wire feed mechanism*
19 el mecanismo (la mesa) de entrega *f*
- *delivery table*

20 la cizalla circular para cartón *m*
- *rotary board cutter (rotary board-*
cutting machine)
21 el tablero de introducción del
material, con entalladura *f*
- *feed table with cut-out section*
22 la cuchilla circular
- *rotary cutter*
23 la regla de entrada *f* (la regla
guía)
- *feed guide*

1-35 máquinas *f* de encuadernación *f*
– *bookbinding machines*
1 la guillotina, una máquina automática para cortar papel *m*
– *guillotine (guillotine cutter, automatic guillotine cutter)*
2 el pupitre de mando *m*
– *control panel*
3 el travesaño de presión *f*
– *clamp*
4 el travesaño de avance *m*
– *back gauge* (Am. *gage)*
5 la escala de presión *f* de la prensa
– *calibrated pressure adjustment [to clamp]*
6 el indicador óptico de medida *f*
– *illuminated cutting scale*
7 el mando manual para el travesaño
– *single-hand control for the back gauge* (Am. *gage)*
8 la máquina de plegar con cuchillas *f* y bolsas *f*
– *combined buckle and knife folding machine (combined buckle and knife folder)*
9 la mesa de alimentación *f* de papel *m*
– *feed table (feed board)*
10 las bolsas del plegado
– *fold plates*
11 la escala reguladora de medida *f* del primer pliego
– *stop for making the buckle fold*
12 las cuchillas dobladoras del segundo pliego
– *cross fold knives*
13 la salida de la cinta, para el pliego paralelo
– *belt delivery for parallel-folded signatures*
14 el mecanismo del tercer doblez
– *third cross fold unit*
15 la salida después del tercer doblez
– *delivery tray for cross-folded signatures*
16 la máquina encuadernadora de hilo *m*
– *sewing machine (book-sewing machine)*
17 el portabobinas
– *spool holder*
18 la bobina de hilo *m*
– *thread cop (thread spool)*
19 el portarollo (el tambor) de gasa *f* (de tarlatana *f*)
– *gauze roll holder (mull roll holder, scrim roll holder)*
20 la gasa (la tarlatana)
– *gauze (mull, scrim)*
21 el cuerpo con las agujas de encuadernar
– *needle cylinders with sewing needles*
22 el libro cosido
– *sewn book*

23 la salida
– *delivery*
24 el carro portaagujas
– *reciprocating saddle*
25 el alimentador de hojas *f*
– *sheet feeder (feeder)*
26 el depósito de alimentación *f*
– *feed hopper*
27 la máquina de encartonar libros *m*
– *casing-in machine*
28 la encoladora de pliegue *m*
– *joint and side pasting attachment*
29 la cuchilla
– *blade*
30 el precalentamiento
– *preheater unit*
31 la máquina engomadora, para el encolado a pleno, de lomo *m*, de canto *m* y en tiras *f*
– *gluing machine for whole-surface, stencil, edge, and strip gluing*
32 el depósito para la cola
– *glue tank*
33 el rodillo engomador
– *glue roller*
34 la mesa de alimentación *f*
– *feed table*
35 el depósito de evacuación *f*
– *delivery*
36 el libro
– *book*
37 la sobrecubierta (la camisa), una cubierta publicitaria
– *dust jacket (dust cover, book jacket, wrapper), a publisher's wrapper*
38 la solapa de la sobrecubierta
– *jacket flap*
39 el texto de la solapa
– *blurb*
40-42 la encuadernación del libro
– *binding*
40 la tapa
– *cover (book cover, case)*
41 el lomo
– *spine (backbone, back)*
42 la cabezada
– *tailband (footband)*
43-47 las hojas del título (la portada y la portadilla)
– *preliminary matter (prelims, front matter)*
43 la portadilla (la anteportada o falsa portada *m*)
– *half-title*
44 el título de la obra
– *half-title (bastard title, fly title)*
45 la portada (Amér.: la carátula)
– *title page*
46 autor *m* y título *m* de la obra
– *full title (main title)*
47 el subtítulo
– *subtitle*
48 el pie editorial
– *publisher's imprint (imprint)*

49 las guardas
– *fly leaf (endpaper, endleaf)*
50 la dedicatoria manuscrita
– *handwritten dedication*
51 el ex libris
– *bookplate (ex libris)*
52 el libro abierto
– *open book*
53 la página del libro
– *page*
54 el pliegue
– *fold*
55-58 los márgenes
– *margin*
55 el margen del lomo
– *back margin (inside margin, gutter)*
56 el margen superior (el margen de la cabeza)
– *head margin (upper margin)*
57 el margen exterior (el margen de delante)
– *fore edge margin (outside margin, fore edge)*
58 el margen inferior (el margen del pie)
– *tail margin (foot margin, tail, foot)*
59 la justificación (la caja de impresión *f*)
– *type area*
60 el título del capítulo
– *chapter heading*
61 el asterisco
– *asterisk*
62 la nota a pie *m* de página *f*, una anotación
– *footnote, a note*
63 el número de la página
– *page number*
64 el texto a dos columnas *f*
– *double-column page*
65 la columna
– *column*
66 el titulillo
– *running title (running head)*
67 el subtítulo del capítulo
– *caption*
68 la nota marginal (el registro lateral)
– *marginal note (side note)*
69 la signatura
– *signature (signature code)*
70 el registro fijo (la señal fija)
– *attached bookmark (attached bookmarker)*
71 el registro suelto (la señal suelta)
– *loose bookmark (loose bookmarker)*

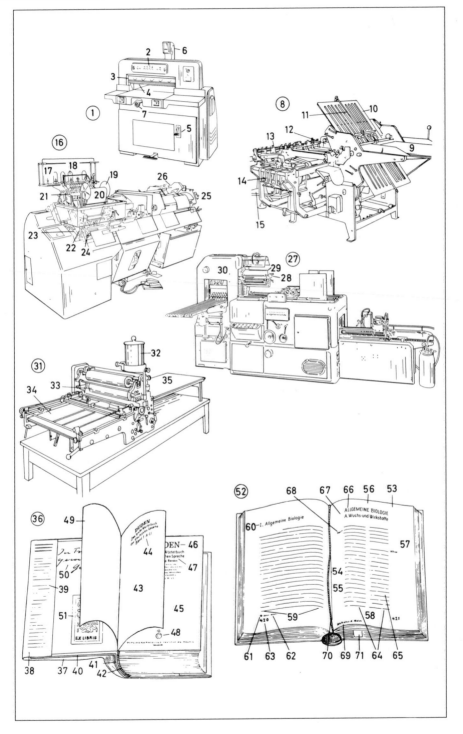

1-54 coches *m* (vehículos *m*)
– *carriages (horse-drawn vehicles)*
1-3, 26-39, 45, 51-54 coches *m* (carruajes *m*)
– *carriages and coaches (coach wagons)*
1 la berlina
– *berlin*
2 el break
– *wagonette;* larger: *brake (break)*
3 el cupé
– *coupé;* sim.: *brougham*
4 la rueda delantera
– *front wheel*
5 la caja
– *coach body*
6 el guardabarros
– *dashboard (splashboard)*
7 el apoyo para los pies
– *footboard*
8 el pescante (el asiento del conductor)
– *coach box (box, coachman's seat, driver's seat)*
9 el farol
– *lamp (lantern)*
10 la ventanilla
– *window*
11 la portezuela (la puerta del coche)
– *door (coach door)*
12 el tirador
– *door handle (handle)*
13 el estribo
– *footboard (carriage step, coach step, step, footpiece)*
14 la capota fija
– *fixed top*
15 la ballesta
– *spring*
16 el freno (la almohadilla–la zapata–del freno)
– *brake (brake block)*
17 la rueda trasera
– *back wheel (rear wheel)*
18 el dogcart, un vehículo de un caballo
– *dogcart, a one-horse carriage*
19 la lanza
– *shafts (thills, poles)*
20 el lacayo (*Chile:* el librea)
– *lackey (lacquey, footman)*
21 la librea, el uniforme del lacayo
– *livery*
22 el cuello galoneado
– *braided (gallooned) collar*
23 la chaqueta galoneada
– *braided (gallooned) coat*
24 la manga galoneada
– *braided (gallooned) sleeve*
25 el sombrero de copa *f*
– *top hat*

26 el coche de alquiler *m* (el coche de punto *m*, el simón, el fiacre; *Chile:* el postino)
– *hackney carriage (hackney coach, cab, growler,* Am. *hack)*
27 el mozo de establo *m* (el mozo de caballos *m*, el mozo de cuadras *f*)
– *stableman (groom)*
28 el caballo (el caballo de tiro *m*)
– *coach horse (carriage horse, cab horse, thill horse, thiller)*
29 el cabriolé con pescante *m* elevado por detrás, un coche de un caballo
– *hansom cab (hansom), a cabriolet, a one-horse chaise (one-horse carriage)*
30 las varas
– *shafts (thills, poles)*
31 las riendas
– *reins (rein,* Am. *line)*
32 el cochero, con macferlán *m*
– *coachman (driver) with inverness*
33 el carabán cubierto (la jardinera), un coche de excursión *f*
– *covered char-a-banc (brake, break), a pleasure vehicle*
34 el cabriolé
– *gig (chaise)*
35 la calesa
– *barouche*
36 el landó, un coche de dos caballos *m; anál.:* el landó pequeño
– *landau, a two-horse carriage;* sim.: *landaulet, landaulette*
37 el ómnibus (el ómnibus con imperial *m*)
– *omnibus (horse-drawn omnibus)*
38 el faetón
– *phaeton*
39 la diligencia (*Chile:* la carretela); *al mismo tiempo:* el coche de viaje *m*
– *Continental stagecoach (mailcoach, diligence);* also: *road coach*
40 el mayoral (el postillón, el cochero de la diligencia)
– *mailcoach driver*
41 la corneta del postillón
– *posthorn*
42 la capota del coche
– *hood*
43 los caballos de posta *f* (los caballos de relevo *m*)
– *post horses (relay horses, relays)*
44 el tílburi
– *tilbury*
45 la troica (el coche ruso de tres caballos *m*)
– *troika (Russian three-horse carriage)*
46 el caballo de varas *f* (el central)
– *leader*

47 el caballo lateral
– *wheeler (wheelhorse, pole horse)*
48 el buggy inglés
– *English buggy*
49 el buggy americano
– *American buggy*
50 el tiro en tándem *m*
– *tandem*
51 la victoria
– *vis-à-vis*
52 la capota plegable
– *collapsible hood (collapsible top)*
53 el mail-coach (la berlina inglesa)
– *mailcoach (English stagecoach)*
54 la silla de posta *f* (el calesín)
– *covered (closed) chaise*

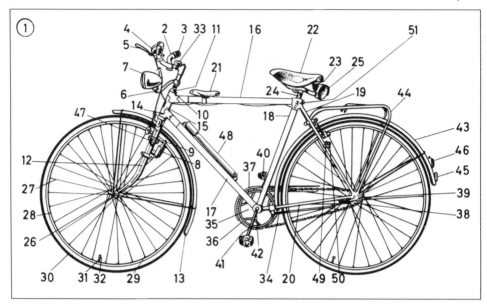

1 la bicicleta (el velocípedo; *pop.:* la bici), una bicicleta de hombre *m*, una bicicleta de paseo *m*
– *bicycle (cycle,* coll. *bike,* Am. *wheel), a gent's bicycle, a touring bicycle (touring cycle, roadster)*
2 el manillar (*Amér.:* el manubrio), un manillar de paseo *m*
– *handlebar (handlebars), a touring cycle handlebar*
3 el puño
– *handlebar grip (handgrip, grip)*
4 el timbre de la bicicleta
– *bicycle bell*
5 el freno de mano *f* (el freno delantero, un freno sobre la llanta)
– *hand brake (front brake, a rim brake)*
6 el soporte del faro
– *lamp bracket*
7 el faro
– *headlamp (bicycle lamp)*
8 la dinamo
– *dynamo*
9 el rodillo de transmisión *f*
– *pulley*
10-12 la horquilla de la rueda delantera
– *front forks*
10 la tija de la horquilla
– *handlebar stem*
11 la cabeza de la horquilla
– *steering head*
12 los tirantes de la horquilla
– *fork blades (fork ends)*
13 el guardabarros delantero (*Ec., Guat., Perú:* el guardafango)
– *front mudguard (Am. front fender)*

14-20 el cuadro de la bicicleta
– *bicycle frame*
14 la barra de dirección *f* (la cabeza de la barra de dirección *f*)
– *steering tube (fork column)*
15 el escudo de la marca
– *head badge*
16 el tubo superior del cuadro (el tubo superior)
– *crossbar (top tube)*
17 el tubo inferior del cuadro (el tubo inferior)
– *down tube*
18 el tubo soporte del sillín (el tubo del sillín)
– *seat tube*
19 la horquilla superior de la rueda trasera
– *seat stays*
20 la horquilla inferior de la rueda trasera
– *chain stays*
21 el sillín para niños *m*
– *child's seat (child carrier seat)*
22 el sillín (el sillín de muelles *m*) de la bicicleta
– *bicycle saddle*
23 el muelle del sillín
– *saddle springs*
24 el soporte (la tija) del sillín
– *seat pillar*
25 la cartera de las herramientas
– *tool bag*
26-32 la rueda (la rueda delantera)
– *wheel (front wheel)*
26 el cubo (el buje)
– *hub*

27 el radio
– *spoke*
28 la llanta
– *rim (wheel rim)*
29 el tensor de radios *m*
– *spoke nipple (spoke flange, spoke end)*
30 el neumático (el neumático de alta presión *f*); *dentro:* la cámara de aire *m; fuera:* la cubierta
– *tyre (Am. tire) (pneumatic tyre, high-pressure tyre);* inside: *tube (inner tube);* outside: *tyre (outer case, cover)*
31 la válvula, una válvula de neumático *m* con tubo *m*, o un obturador a presión *f* con bola *f*
– *valve, a tube valve with valve tube or a patent valve with ball*
32 el capuchón de la válvula
– *valve sealing cap*
33 el tacómetro de bicicleta *f*, con cuentakilómetros *m*
– *bicycle speedometer with milometer*
34 la patilla de apoyo de la bicicleta
– *kick stand (prop stand)*
35-39 la propulsión por cadena *f*
– *chain transmission*
35-42 la transmisión de la bicicleta (la transmisión de cadena *f*)
– *bicycle drive (chain drive)*
35 el plato (la rueda dentada delantera de la cadena)
– *chain wheel*
36 la cadena, una cadena de rodillos *m*
– *chain, a roller chain*
37 el cubrecadena
– *chain guard*

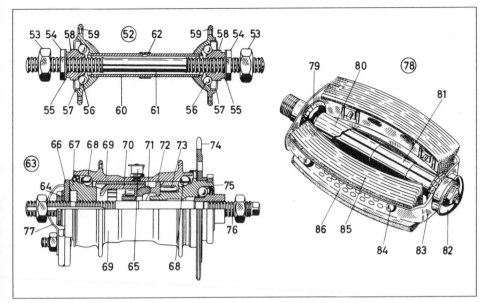

38 el piñón (la rueda dentada trasera de la cadena)
– *sprocket wheel (sprocket)*
39 la tuerca de palometa *f*
– *wing nut (fly nut, butterfly nut)*
40 el pedal
– *pedal*
41 la biela (la manivela de pedal *m*)
– *crank*
42 el eje "pedalier" (el eje de los pedales)
– *bottom bracket bearing*
43 el guardabarros trasero
– *rear mudguard* (Am. *rear fender*)
44 el portaequipajes
– *luggage carrier (carrier)*
45 el catafaro (el reflectante)
– *reflector*
46 la luz trasera (el piloto)
– *rear light (rear lamp)*
47 el descansapiés
– *footrest*
48 la bomba de bicicleta *f* (la bomba de aire *m; Amér.:* el inflador)
– *bicycle pump*
49 la cerradura de la bicicleta, una cerradura de radios *m*
– *bicycle lock, a wheel lock*
50 la llave antirrobo
– *patent key*
51 el número de la bicicleta (el número de fabricación *f*)
– *cycle serial number (factory number, frame number)*
52 el cubo de la rueda delantera
– *front hub (front hub assembly)*
53 la tuerca
– *wheel nut*

54 la contratuerca estrellada
– *locknut (locking nut)*
55 las arandelas suplementarias
– *washer (slotted cone adjusting washer)*
56 la bola
– *ball bearing*
57 la tapa guardapolvo
– *dust cap*
58 el cono
– *cone (adjusting cone)*
59 las cazoletas
– *centre* (Am. *center*) *hub*
60 el caño (el tubo)
– *spindle*
61 el eje
– *axle*
62 el engrasador
– *clip covering lubrication hole (lubricator)*
63 el piñón libre, con freno *m* contrapedal [inexistente en las bicicletas españolas]
– *free-wheel hub with back-pedal brake (with coaster brake)*
64 la tuerca de seguridad *f*
– *safety nut*
65 el orificio de engrase *m* (el lubrificador)
– *lubricator*
66 la palanca del freno
– *brake arm*
67 el cono de la palanca del freno
– *brake arm cone*
68 el anillo interior de bolas *f*, con bolas en el cojinete
– *bearing cup with ball bearings in ball race*

69 la caja del piñón
– *hub shell (hub body, hub barrel)*
70 la cubierta del freno
– *brake casing*
71 el cono del freno
– *brake cone*
72 el tambor de enrollamiento *m*
– *driver*
73 el rodillo de impulsión *f*
– *driving barrel*
74 la corona dentada
– *sprocket*
75 la cabeza de rosca *f*
– *thread head*
76 el eje
– *axle*
77 el bandaje
– *bracket*
78 el pedal de bicicleta *f* (el pedal, un pedal de bloque *m*)
– *bicycle pedal (pedal, reflector pedal)*
79 la arandela
– *cup*
80 la caña del pedal
– *spindle*
81 el eje del pedal
– *axle*
82 la tapa guardapolvo
– *dust cap*
83 el bastidor del pedal
– *pedal frame*
84 el tornillo de sujeción *f* del taco de goma *f*
– *rubber stud*
85 el taco de goma *f*
– *rubber block (rubber tread)*
86 el cristal reflectante
– *glass reflector*

1 la bicicleta plegable
– *folding bicycle*
2 la articulación *f* de bisagra *f (también:* la palanca de ajuste *m)*
– *hinge (also: locking lever)*
3 el manillar regulable
– *adjustable handlebar (handlebars)*
4 el sillín regulable
– *adjustable saddle*
5 las ruedas de apoyo *m* para aprender (las ruedas auxiliares)
– *stabilizers*
6 el ciclomotor
– *motor-assisted bicycle*
7 el motor de dos tiempos *m* refrigerado por aire *m*
– *air-cooled two-stroke engine*
8 la horquilla telehidráulica
– *telescopic forks*
9 el cuadro tubular
– *tubular frame*
10 el depósito de combustible *m*
– *fuel tank (petrol tank,* Am. *gasoline tank)*
11 el manillar elevado
– *semi-rise handlebars*
12 la palanca de embrague *m* de dos velocidades *f*
– *two-speed gear-change (gearshift)*
13 el sillín moldeado
– *high-back polo saddle*
14 el brazo oscilante de la rueda trasera
– *swinging-arm rear fork*
15 el tubo de escape elevado
– *upswept exhaust*
16 la rejilla de protección *f* contra el calor
– *heat shield*
17 la cadena de transmisión *f*
– *drive chain*
18 el arco de protección *f*
– *crash bar (roll bar)*
19 el tacómetro (el cuentakilómetros)
– *speedometer (coll. speedo)*
20 la bicicleta de acumuladores *m* (la bicicleta eléctrica, la city-bike)
– *battery-powered moped, an electrically-powered vehicle*
21 el sillín móvil
– *swivel saddle*
22 el compartimiento de los acumuladores
– *battery compartment*
23 el cesto de alambre *m* (el portaequipajes)
– *wire basket*
24 el ciclomotor
– *touring moped (moped)*
25 el pedal
– *pedal crank (pedal drive, starter pedal)*

26 el motor monocilíndrico de dos tiempos *m*
– *single-cylinder two-stroke engine*
27 la clavija de la bujía
– *spark-plug cap*
28 el depósito de combustible *m* (el depósito de mezcla *f*)
– *fuel tank (petrol tank,* Am. *gasoline tank)*
29 el faro del ciclomotor
– *moped headlamp (front lamp)*
30-35 los accesorios del manillar
– *handlebar fittings*
30 el puño giratorio del gas
– *twist grip throttle control (throttle twist grip)*
31 el puño giratorio para el cambio de velocidades *f*
– *twist grip (gear-change, gearshift)*
32 la palanca de embrague *m*
– *clutch lever*
33 el freno de mano *f*
– *hand brake lever*
34 el velocímetro (el tacómetro, el cuentakilómetros)
– *speedometer (coll. speedo)*
35 el espejo retrovisor
– *rear-view mirror (mirror)*
36 el freno de tambor *m* delantero
– *front wheel drum brake (drum brake)*
37 los cables Bowden
– *Bowden cables (brake cables)*
38 la luz trasera, la luz de freno *m*
– *stop and tail light unit*
39 el velomotor
– *light motorcycle with kickstarter*
40 el tablero de mando *m* con cuentakilómetros *m* y cuentarrevoluciones *m* electrónico
– *housing for instruments with speedometer and electronic rev counter (revolution counter)*
41 la horquilla telehidráulica con goma *f* de protección *f*
– *telescopic shock absorber*
42 el sillín biplaza (de dos asientos *m*)
– *twin seat*
43 el pedal de arranque *m*
– *kickstarter*
44 el descansapiés del pasajero
– *pillion footrest, a footrest*
45 el manillar deportivo
– *handlebar (handlebars)*
46 el guardacadena cerrado herméticamente
– *chain guard*
47 el scooter, el escúter
– *motor scooter (scooter)*
48 el panel lateral fijo
– *removable side panel*
49 el cuadro tubular
– *tubular frame*

50 el revestimiento de chapa *f*
– *metal fairings*
51 el patín de apoyo *m* (la patilla)
– *prop stand (stand)*
52 el pedal de freno *m*
– *foot brake*
53 la bocina (el claxon)
– *horn (hooter)*
54 el gancho para el maletín o la cartera
– *hook for handbag or briefcase*
55 el pedal selector de velocidades *f*
– *foot gear-change control (foot gearshift control)*
56 la motoreta; con una rueda mayor que otra: el chopper
– *high-riser;* sim.: *Chopper*
57 el manillar bifurcado
– *high-rise handlebar (handlebars)*
58 la horquilla imitando a la de la moto
– *imitation motorcycle fork*
59 el sillín
– *banana saddle*
60 el arco cromado
– *chrome bracket*

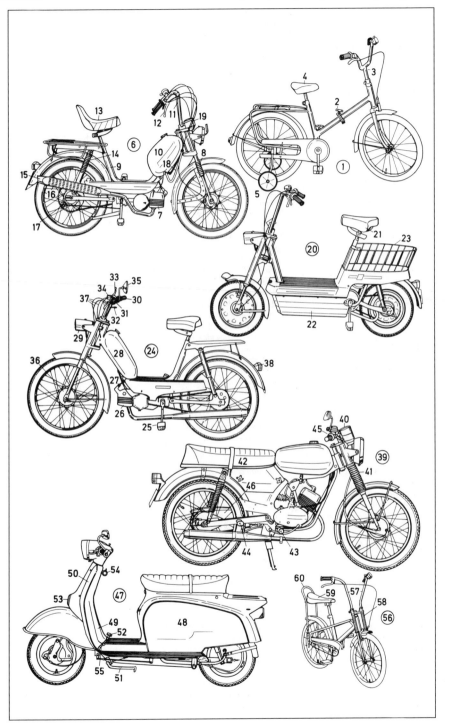

1 el velomotor (la motocicleta) [50 cm³]
 – *lightweight motorcycle (light motorcycle) [50 cc]*
2 el depósito de combustible *m*
 – *fuel tank (petrol tank, Am. gasoline tank)*
3 el motor monocilíndrico de cuatro tiempos *m* refrigerado por aire *m*
 – *air-cooled single-cylinder four-stroke engine (with overhead camshaft)*
4 el carburador
 – *carburettor (Am. carburetor)*
5 el tubo de admisión *f*
 – *intake pipe*
6 el cambio de cinco marchas *f*
 – *five-speed gearbox*
7 la biela oscilante de la rueda trasera
 – *swinging-arm rear fork*
8 la placa de la matrícula
 – *number plate (Am. license plate)*
9 la luz trasera (el piloto)
 – *stop and tail light (rear light)*
10 el faro
 – *headlight (headlamp)*
11 el tambor del freno delantero
 – *front drum brake*
12 el cable del freno, una transmisión Bowden
 – *brake cable (brake line), a Bowden cable*
13 el tambor del freno trasero
 – *rear drum brake*
14 el sillín
 – *racing-style twin seat*
15 el tubo de escape *m* elevado
 – *upswept exhaust*
16 la motocicleta todo terreno *m* [125 cm³] (una moto campera)
 – *scrambling motorcycle (cross-country motorcycle) [125 cc], a light motorcycle*
17 el cuadro de doble soporte *m*
 – *lightweight cradle frame*
18 la placa para el número de competición *f*
 – *number disc (disk)*
19 el sillín monoplaza (de un solo asiento)
 – *solo seat*
20 las aletas de refrigeración *f*
 – *cooling ribs*
21 el soporte (la patilla) de la motocicleta
 – *motorcycle stand*
22 la cadena de la motocicleta
 – *motorcycle chain*
23 la horquilla telehidráulica
 – *telescopic shock absorber*
24 los radios (los rayos)
 – *spokes*
25 la llanta
 – *rim (wheel rim)*

26 el neumático de la motocicleta
 – *motorcycle tyre (Am. tire)*
27 el perfil del neumático
 – *tyre (Am. tire) tread*
28 la palanca del embrague
 – *gear-change lever (gearshift lever)*
29 el puño giratorio del gas
 – *twist grip throttle control (throttle twist grip)*
30 el retrovisor
 – *rear-view mirror (mirror)*
31-58 motocicletas *f* de gran cilindrada *f*
 – *heavy (heavyweight, large-capacity) motorcycles*
31 una moto grande (una moto de carretera *f*) con motor refrigerado por agua *f*
 – *heavyweight motorcycle with water-cooled engine*
32 el freno de disco *m* delantero
 – *front disc (disk) brake*
33 la pinza del freno de disco *m*
 – *disc (disk) brake calliper (caliper)*
34 el eje delantero
 – *floating axle*
35 el radiador del agua *f*
 – *water cooler*
36 el tanque de gasolina *f*
 – *fuel tank (petrol tank, Am. gasoline tank)*
37 el intermitente (el indicador de cambio *m* de dirección *f*)
 – *indicator (indicator light, turn indicator light)*
38 el pedal de arranque
 – *kickstarter*
39 el motor refrigerado por agua *f*
 – *water-cooled engine*
40 el tacómetro (el cuentakilómetros)
 – *speedometer*
41 el cuentarrevoluciones
 – *rev counter (revolution counter)*
42 el intermitente trasero
 – *rear indicator (indicator light)*
43 la moto pesada con carenado *m* integral [1000 cm³]
 – *heavy (heavyweight, high-performance) machine with fairing [1000 cc]*
44 el carenado integral
 – *integrated streamlining, an integrated fairing*
45 la luz intermitente (el intermitente)
 – *indicator (indicator light, turn indicator light)*
46 el cristal transparente
 – *anti-mist windscreen (Am. windshield)*
47 el motor de dos cilindros *m* con transmisión *f* cardán
 – *horizontally-opposed twin engine with cardan transmission*

48 la rueda de aleación *f* de metal ligero
 – *light alloy wheel*
49 la moto de cuatro cilindros *m* [400 cm³]
 – *four-cylinder machine [400 cc]*
50 el motor de cuatro tiempos *m* con cuatro cilindros *m* refrigerado por aire *m*
 – *air-cooled four-cylinder four-stroke engine*
51 el tubo de escape *m* cuatro en uno
 – *four-pipe megaphone exhaust pipe*
52 el dispositivo de arranque *m* (el arrancador) eléctrico
 – *electric starter button*
53 la motocicleta con sidecar *m*
 – *sidecar machine*
54 el sidecar
 – *sidecar body*
55 el parachoques del sidecar
 – *sidecar crash bar*
56 la luz (el piloto) de posición *f*
 – *sidelight (Am. sidemarker lamp)*
57 la rueda del sidecar
 – *sidecar wheel*
58 el parabrisas del sidecar
 – *sidecar windscreen (Am. windshield)*

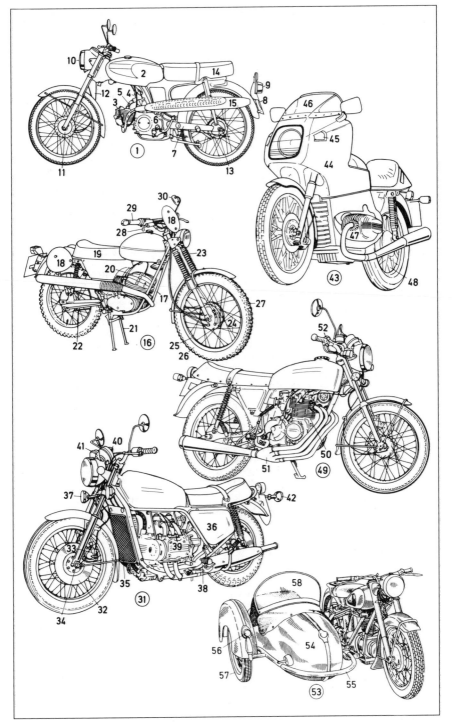

1 el motor de explosión f (Otto) de ocho cilindros m en V con inyección f de gasolina f [corte longitudinal]
– eight-cylinder V (vee) fuel-injection spark-ignition engine (Otto-cycle engine)
2 el motor de explosión f (Otto) [corte transversal]
– cross-section of spark-ignition engine (Otto-cycle internal combustion engine)
3 el motor Diesel de cinco cilindros m en línea f [corte longitudinal]
– sectional view of five-cylinder in-line diesel engine
4 el motor Diesel [corte transversal]
– cross-section of diesel engine
5 el motor rotativo de dos rotores m (el motor Wankel)
– two-rotor Wankel engine (rotary engine)
6 el motor de explosión f (Otto) monocilíndrico de dos tiempos m
– single-cylinder two-stroke internal combustion engine
7 el ventilador
– fan
8 el embrague del ventilador
– fan clutch for viscous drive
9 el distribuidor de encendido m con avance al encendido por depresión f
– ignition distributor (distributor) with vacuum timing control
10 la cadena doble de rodillos m
– double roller chain
11 el árbol de levas f (de camones m)
– camshaft bearing
12 el conducto de ventilación f
– air-bleed duct
13 el engrase del árbol de levas f
– oil pipe for camshaft lubrication
14 el árbol de levas f, un árbol de levas f en cabeza f
– camshaft, an overhead camshaft
15 el colector de admisión f con mariposa f
– venturi throat
16 el filtro de aire m
– intake silencer (absorption silencer, Am. absorption muffler)
17 el regulador de la presión del combustible
– fuel pressure regulator
18 el conducto (el tubo) de admisión f
– inlet manifold
19 el bloque del motor
– cylinder crankcase
20 el volante
– flywheel
21 la biela
– connecting rod (piston rod)
22 el sombrerete del apoyo del cigüeñal
– cover of crankshaft bearing
23 el cigüeñal
– crankshaft
24 el tapón de vaciado m del aceite
– oil bleeder screw (oil drain plug)
25 la cadena de rodillos m de mando m de la bomba de aceite m
– roller chain of oil pump drive

26 el amortiguador de oscilaciones f
– vibration damper
27 el árbol de mando m del distribuidor de encendido m
– distributor shaft for the ignition distributor (distributor)
28 el orificio para echar el aceite
– oil filler neck
29 el cartucho del filtro de aire m
– diaphragm spring
30 las varillas reguladoras
– control linkage
31 los tubos de alimentación f del combustible
– fuel supply pipe (Am. fuel line)
32 el inyector
– fuel injector (injection nozzle)
33 el balancín
– rocker arm
34 el asiento del balancín
– rocker arm mounting
35 la bujía con capuchón m antiparasitario
– spark plug (sparking plug) with suppressor
36 el colector de escape m
– exhaust manifold
37 el pistón con segmentos m de comprensión f y segmento m rascador de aceite m
– piston with piston rings and oil scraper ring
38 el soporte-motor
– engine mounting
39 la brida intermediaria
– dog flange (dog)
40 el cárter superior del aceite
– crankcase
41 el cárter inferior del aceite
– oil sump (sump)
42 la bomba de aceite m
– oil pump
43 el filtro de aceite m
– oil filter
44 el motor de arranque m
– starter motor (starting motor)
45 la culata
– cylinder head
46 la válvula de escape m
– exhaust valve
47 la varilla del nivel de aceite m
– dipstick
48 la tapa de balancines m
– cylinder head cover
49 la cadena remachada doble
– double bushing chain
50 la sonda de temperatura f
– warm-up regulator
51 el cable para el ajuste del ralentí
– tapered needle for idling adjustment
52 la canalización de gas-oil m a presión f
– fuel pressure pipe (fuel pressure line)
53 la canalización para fugas f de gas-oil m
– fuel leak line (drip fuel line)
54 el inyector
– injection nozzle (spray nozzle)
55 la fijación de la bujía de precalentamiento m
– heater plug

56 el disco de equilibrado m
– thrust washer
57 el árbol de piñón m intermediario para el accionamiento de la bomba de inyección f
– intermediate gear shaft for the injection pump drive
58 el mecanismo de avance de la inyección
– injection timer unit
59 la bomba de vacío m
– vacuum pump (low-pressure regulator)
60 el disco de leva f para el accionamiento de la bomba de vacío m
– cam for vacuum pump
61 la bomba de agua f
– water pump (coolant pump)
62 el termostato del agua f de refrigeración f
– cooling water thermostat
63 el termocontacto
– thermo time switch
64 la bomba manual para el gas-oil
– fuel hand pump
65 la bomba de inyección f
– injection pump
66 la bujía de precalentamiento m
– glow plug
67 la válvula de descarga f del aceite
– oil pressure limiting valve
68 el rotor del motor rotativo (el émbolo del motor Wankel)
– rotor
69 la lámina de estanquidad f
– seal
70 el convertidor de par m
– torque converter
71 el embrague monodisco
– single-plate clutch
72 la caja de cambio m
– multi-speed gearing (multi-step gearing)
73 los filtros para purificar los gases del colector de escape m
– port liners in the exhaust manifold for emission control
74 el freno de disco m
– disc (disk) brake
75 el diferencial
– differential gear (differential)
76 el generador de corriente f (la dinamo, el alternador)
– generator
77 el pedal de cambio m de velocidades f
– foot gear-change control (foot gearshift control)
78 el embrague de disco m en seco
– dry multi-plate clutch
79 el carburador horizontal
– cross-draught (Am. cross-draft) carburettor (Am. carburetor)
80 las aletas de refrigeración f
– cooling ribs
81 la correa de distribución f
– V-belt (fan belt)

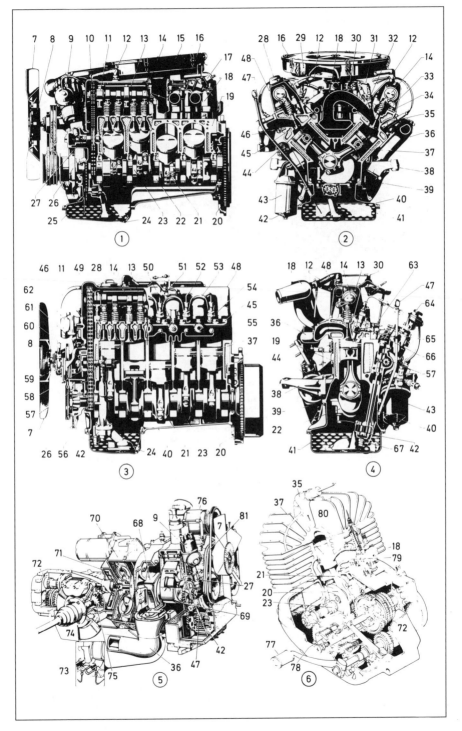

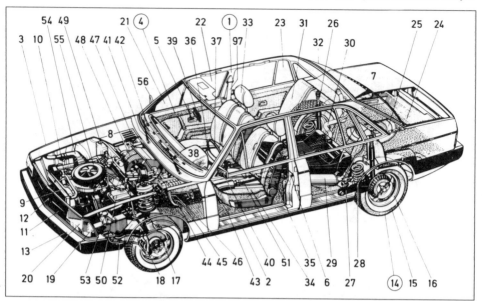

1-56 el coche (el automóvil, el auto; *Amér.:* el carro), un turismo
– *motor car (car, Am. automobile, auto), a passenger vehicle*
1 la carrocería autoportante
– *monocoque body (unitary body)*
2 el chasis (*Amér.:* el chasís; la carrocería)
– *chassis, the understructure of the body*
3 la aleta delantera
– *front wing (Am. front fender)*
4 la puerta del coche
– *car door*
5 el tirador de la puerta
– *door handle*
6 la cerradura de la puerta
– *door lock*
7 la puerta del maletero
– *boot lid (Am. trunk lid)*
8 el capó (*Col., C. Rica, Chile y Mé.:* la tapa del motor)
– *bonnet (Am. hood)*
9 el radiador
– *radiator*
10 la canalización del agua *f* de refrigeración *f*
– *cooling water pipe*
11 la calandra (la rejilla del radiador; *Amér.:* la parrilla)
– *radiator grill*
12 el emblema (la marca del auto)
– *badging*
13 el parachoques delantero con escudo *m* de caucho *m* (*C. Rica, Guat. y S. Dgo.:* el bomper)
– *rubber-covered front bumper (Am. front fender)*
14 la rueda de automóvil *m*, una rueda de disco *m*
– *car wheel, a disc (disk) wheel*
15 el neumático
– *car tyre (Am. automobile tire)*
16 la llanta
– *rim (wheel rim)*
17-18 el freno de disco *m*
– *disc (disk) brake*

17 el disco del freno
– *brake disc (disk) (braking disc)*
18 la pinza del freno
– *calliper (caliper)*
19 el intermitente delantero (*Amér.:* la luz direccional)
– *front indicator light (front turn indicator light)*
20 el faro (*Chile y Pan.:* el foco; *Guat., Mé. y. P. Rico:* la luz) con luz *f* larga (luz *f* de carretera; *Amér.:* luz *f* alta), luz *f* de cruce *m* (luz *f* corta; *Amér.:* luz *f* baja) y luz *f* de posición *f* (*Chile:* luz *f* de estacionamiento *m*)
– *headlight (headlamp) with main beam (high beam), dipped beam (low beam), sidelight (side lamp, Am. sidemarker lamp)*
21 el parabrisas (*Pan. y P. Rico:* el guinchil), un parabrisas panorámico
– *windscreen (Am. windshield), a panoramic windscreen*
22 la ventanilla de la puerta, con manivela *f*
– *crank-operated car window*
23 la ventanilla trasera giratoria (la ventanilla oscilante)
– *quarter light (quarter vent)*
24 el maletero (*Amér.:* el baúl)
– *boot (Am. trunk)*
25 la rueda de repuesto *m*
– *spare wheel*
26 el amortiguador
– *damper (shock absorber)*
27 el brazo oscilante longitudinal
– *trailing arm*
28 el muelle helicoidal
– *coil spring*
29 el silencioso (el silenciador)
– *silencer (Am. muffler)*
30 la ventilación por circulación *f* forzada
– *automatic ventilation system*
31 el asiento trasero
– *rear seats*
32 el cristal trasero
– *rear window*

33 el cabezal (el reposacabezas) regulable
– *adjustable headrest (head restraint)*
34 el asiento del conductor, un asiento reclinable
– *driver's seat, a reclining seat*
35 el respaldo reclinable
– *reclining backrest*
36 el asiento del acompañante; *pop.:* el asiento de la muerte
– *passenger seat*
37 el volante (*Amér.:* el timón; *Col. y P. Rico:* la volanta)
– *steering wheel*
38 el tablero de mandos *m* (el salpicadero) con tacómetro *m*, el cuentarrevoluciones, el reloj, el indicador del nivel de gasolina *f*, el indicador de la temperatura de refrigeración *f* (el termómetro del agua *f*) y el reloj de la presión del aceite
– *centre (Am. center) console containing speedometer (coll. speedo), revolution counter (rev counter, tachometer), clock, fuel gauge (Am. gage), water temperature gauge, oil temperature gauge*
39 el espejo retrovisor interior
– *inside rear-view mirror*
40 el espejo retrovisor exterior del lado izquierdo
– *left-hand wing mirror*
41 el limpiaparabrisas
– *windscreen wiper (Am. windshield wiper)*
42 la abertura de ventilación *f*
– *defroster vents*
43 la moqueta del suelo; *encima:* la alfombrilla
– *carpeting*
44 el pedal del embrague (el embrague)
– *clutch pedal (coll. clutch)*
45 el pedal del freno (el freno)
– *brake pedal (coll. brake)*
46 el pedal del acelerador (el acelerador, el pedal del gas)
– *accelerator pedal (coll. accelerator)*

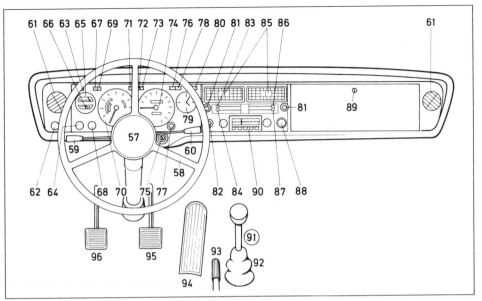

48 el ventilador para la aireación
– *blower fan*
49 el depósito del líquido *m* de freno *m*
– *brake fluid reservoir*
50 la batería
– *battery*
51 el tubo de escape *m*
– *exhaust pipe*
52 el tren delantero con tracción *f* delantera
– *front running gear with front wheel drive*
53 el soporte del motor
– *engine mounting*
54 el silencioso de admisión *f*
– *intake silencer* (Am. *intake muffler*)
55 el filtro del aire
– *air filter* (*air cleaner*)
56 el espejo retrovisor exterior del lado derecho
– *right-hand wing mirror*
57-90 el tablero de mandos *m* (el salpicadero)
– *dashboard* (*fascia panel*)
57 el centro del volante con protector *m* antichoque
– *controlled-collapse steering column*
58 el radio del volante
– *steering wheel spoke*
59 el conmutador de luces *f* y del intermitente
– *indicator and dimming switch*
60 el conmutador del limpiaparabrisas con avisador *m* sonoro
– *wiper/washer switch and horn*
61 la aireación lateral
– *side window blower*
62 el interruptor de la luz de posición *f*
– *sidelight, headlight, and parking light switch*
63 el indicador de la luz antiniebla
– *fog lamp warning light*

64 el interruptor de las luces antiniebla delantera y trasera
– *fog headlamp and rear lamp switch*
65 el indicador del nivel de la gasolina
– *fuel gauge* (Am. *gage*)
66 el termómetro del agua *f* de refrigeración *f*
– *water temperature gauge* (Am. *gage*)
67 el indicador de la luz antiniebla trasera
– *warning light for rear fog lamp*
68 el interruptor del warning
– *hazard flasher switch*
69 el indicador de la luz larga
– *main beam warning light*
70 el cuentarrevoluciones eléctrico
– *electric rev counter* (*revolution counter*)
71 el chivato del nivel de la gasolina
– *fuel warning light*
72 el chivato del freno de mano *f* y del sistema de frenado *m* de los dos circuitos independientes
– *warning light for the hand brake and dual-circuit brake system*
73 el chivato de la presión del aceite
– *oil pressure warning light*
74 el tacómetro (el velocímetro) con cuentakilómetros *m*
– *speedometer* (coll. *speedo*) *with trip mileage recorder*
75 la cerradura antirrobo y de contacto *m*
– *starter and steering lock*
76 el chivato de las luces intermitentes y del warning
– *warning lights for turn indicators and hazard flashers*
77 el potenciómetro de la iluminación interior con puesta *f* a cero del cuentakilómetros parcial
– *switch for the courtesy light and reset button for the trip mileage recorder*
78 el chivato de carga *f*
– *ammeter*
79 el reloj eléctrico
– *electric clock*

80 el chivato de desempañado *m* de la luneta trasera
– *warning light for heated rear window*
81 el interruptor para la ventilación de la parte baja
– *switch for the leg space ventilation*
82 el interruptor para desempañar la luneta trasera
– *rear window heating switch*
83 la palanca para graduar la ventilación
– *ventilation switch*
84 la palanca para regular la temperatura
– *temperature regulator*
85 la aireación regulable
– *fresh-air inlet and control*
86 la palanca para distribuir el aire frío
– *fresh-air regulator*
87 la palanca para distribuir el aire caliente
– *warm-air regulator*
88 el encendedor
– *cigar lighter*
89 el cerradura de la guantera
– *glove compartment* (*glove box*) *lock*
90 la radio
– *car radio*
91 la palanca de cambio *m* de velocidades *f*
– *gear lever* (*gearshift lever*), *a floor-type gear-change*
92 la guarnición (el manguito) de piel *f*
– *leather gaiter*
93 la palanca del freno de mano *f* (*C. Rica y Pan.*: el freno de emergencia *f*)
– *hand brake lever*
94 el pedal del acelerador (el acelerador, el pedal del gas)
– *accelerator pedal*
95 el pedal del freno (el freno)
– *brake pedal*
96 el pedal del embrague (el embrague)
– *clutch pedal*
97 el cinturón de seguridad *f*
– *seat belt* (*safety belt*)

1-15 el carburador, un carburador descendente
- *carburettor* (Am. *carburetor), a downdraught* (Am. *down-draft) carburettor*
1 el chiclé del ralentí
- *idling jet (slow-running jet)*
2 el chiclé del aire del ralentí
- *idling air jet (idle air bleed)*
3 el chiclé de corrección *f* de aire *m*
- *air correction jet*
4 el aire de compensación *f*
- *compensating airstream*
5 el aire principal
- *main airstream*
6 la palomilla de arranque *m* en frío (el starter)
- *choke flap*
7 el pico de salida *f*
- *plunger*
8 el difusor (el venturi)
- *venturi*
9 la palomilla de gases *m*
- *throttle valve (butterfly valve)*
10 el tubo emulsionante
- *emulsion tube*
11 el tornillo de reglaje de la velocidad del ralentí
- *idle mixture adjustment screw*
12 el surtidor principal (*sin.:* el calibre, el chiclé)
- *main jet*
13 la llegada de gasolina *f*
- *fuel inlet* (Am. *gasoline inlet) (inlet manifold)*
14 la cuba de nivel *m* constante
- *float chamber*
15 el flotador
- *float*
16-27 el engrase bajo presión *f*
- *pressure-feed lubricating system*
16 la bomba de aceite *m*
- *oil pump*
17 el cárter del aceite
- *oil sump*
18 la alcachofa de aspiración *f*
- *sump filter*
19 el refrigerador de aceite *m* (el radiador de aceite *m*)
- *oil cooler*
20 el filtro del aceite
- *oil filter*
21 el canal principal de engrase *m*
- *main oil gallery (drilled gallery)*
22 el canal secundario
- *crankshaft drilling (crankshaft tributary, crankshaft bleed)*
23 el cigüeñal
- *crankshaft bearing (main bearing)*
24 el árbol de levas *f* (camones *m*)
- *camshaft bearing*
25 la muñequilla del cigüeñal
- *connecting-rod bearing*
26 el calibre para el eje del pistón
- *gudgeon pin (piston pin)*
27 la canalización superior
- *bleed*
28-47 la caja de cambios *m* sincronizada de cuatro velocidades *f*
- *four-speed synchromesh gearbox*
28 el pedal de embrague *m*
- *clutch pedal*
29 el cigüeñal
- *crankshaft*

30 el árbol motor
- *drive shaft (propeller shaft)*
31 la corona de arranque *m*
- *starting gear ring*
32 el anillo sincronizador para la 3ᵃ y 4ᵃ velocidades
- *sliding sleeve for 3rd and 4th gear*
33 el cono de sincronización *f*
- *synchronizing cone*
34 el piñón helicoidal para la 3ᵃ velocidad
- *helical gear wheel for 3rd gear*
35 el anillo sincronizador de la 1ᵃ y la 2ᵃ velocidad
- *sliding sleeve for 1st and 2nd gear*
36 el piñón helicoidal de la 1ᵃ velocidad
- *helical gear wheel for 1st gear*
37 el árbol intermediario (de reenvío *m*)
- *lay shaft*
38 el accionamiento del tacómetro (del marcador de velocidad)
- *speedometer drive*
39 el piñón para el accionamiento del tacómetro
- *helical gear wheel for speedometer drive*
40 el árbol primario
- *main shaft*
41 los ejes de mando de la horquilla
- *gearshift rods*
42 la horquilla de la 1ᵃ y la 2ᵃ velocidad
- *selector fork for 1st and 2nd gear*
43 el piñón helicoidal de la 2ᵃ velocidad
- *helical gear wheel for 2nd gear*
44 la horquilla de marcha *f* atrás
- *selector head with reverse gear*
45 la horquilla para la 3ᵃ y la 4ᵃ velocidad
- *selector fork for 3rd and 4th gear*
46 la palanca de cambio *m*
- *gear lever (gearshift lever)*
47 el esquema de las marchas
- *gear-change pattern (gearshift pattern, shift pattern)*
48-55 el freno de disco *m*
- *disc (disk) brake [assembly]*
48 el disco del freno
- *brake disc (disk) (braking disc)*
49 la pinza del freno, una pinza fija con las pastillas del freno
- *calliper (caliper), a fixed calliper with friction pads*
50 el tambor del freno de mano *f*
- *servo cylinder (servo unit)*
51 las zapatas del freno
- *brake shoes*
52 el forro del freno
- *brake lining*
53 el racor de la canalización del freno
- *outlet to brake line*
54 el bombín del freno
- *wheel cylinder*
55 el muelle recuperador
- *return spring*
56-59 el mecanismo de dirección *f* (la dirección de tornillo *m* sin fin *m* globoide)
- *steering gear (worm-and-nut steering gear)*
56 el árbol de dirección *f* (la columna de dirección *f*)
- *steering column*
57 el soporte de rodillo *m*
- *worm gear sector*
58 la palanca de mando *m* de dirección *f*
- *steering drop arm*

59 el tornillo sin fin *m* (la espiral)
- *worm*
60-64 el sistema de calefacción *f* regulado por agua *f*
- *water-controlled heater*
60 la entrada de aire *m* frío
- *air intake*
61 el transformador de calor *m*
- *heat exchanger (heater box)*
62 el ventilador de calefacción *f*
- *blower fan*
63 la válvula reguladora
- *flap valve*
64 la abertura para el deshielo
- *defroster vent*
65-71 el eje rígido
- *live axle (rigid axle)*
65 el tubo de reacción *f* (el árbol de transmisión *f*)
- *propeller shaft*
66 el brazo oscilante longitudinal
- *trailing arm*
67 el cojinete de caucho *m*
- *rubber bush*
68 el muelle helicoidal
- *coil spring*
69 el amortiguador
- *damper (shock absorber)*
70 la barra de torsión *f*
- *Panhard rod*
71 la barra estabilizadora
- *stabilizer bar*
72-84 la suspensión McPherson
- *MacPherson strut unit*
72 la placa de fijación *f* en la carrocería
- *body-fixing plate*
73 el soporte de fijación *f* superior
- *upper bearing*
74 el muelle helicoidal
- *suspension spring*
75 el eje (caña *f*) del pistón
- *piston rod*
76 el amortiguador (*P. Rico:* el shockabsorver)
- *suspension damper*
77 la llanta
- *rim (wheel rim)*
78 el gorrón (el muñón, la mangueta)
- *stub axle*
79 el pivote de mangueta *f*
- *steering arm*
80 la rótula del pivote de mangueta *f*
- *track-rod ball-joint*
81 el brazo trasero de triángulo *m* (la horquilla trasera)
- *trailing link arm*
82 el cojinete de caucho *m*
- *bump rubber (rubber bonding)*
83 la caja del eje (el cubo de rueda *f*)
- *lower bearing*
84 el travesaño principal
- *lower suspension arm*

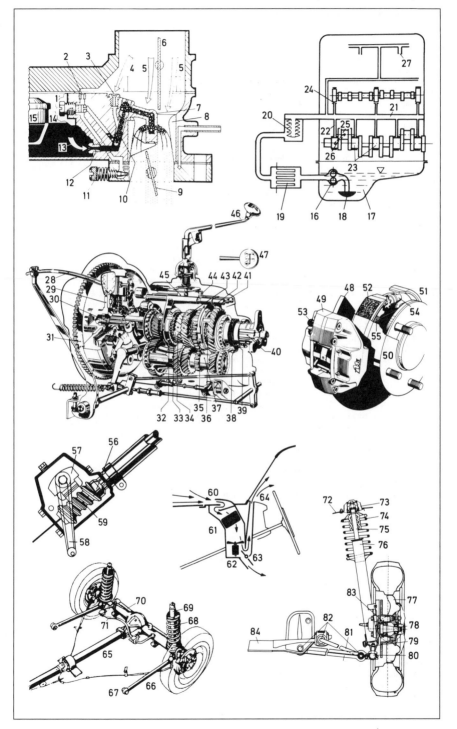

1-36 tipos m **de coches** m (coches m
de turismo m)
– *car models* (Am. *automobile
models)*
1 el cuatro puertas f (la limusina)
de clase f alta
– *four-door touring saloon* (Am.
*four-door sedan) in the upper-
middle range*
2 la puerta del conductor
– *driver's door*
3 la puerta trasera
– *rear door*
4-10 el cuatro puertas f (limusina f)
de clase f media (coche m de clase
f media)
– *four-door saloon* (Am. *four-door
sedan) and four-door hatchback
in the middle range*
4 el coche de tracción f trasera
– *saloon* (Am. *sedan)*
5 el reposacabezas
– *headrests (head restraints)*
6 el asiento delantero
– *front seat*
7 el asiento trasero (el asiento de
atrás)
– *rear seat (back seat)*
8 el coche modelo m deportivo
– *fastback saloon* (Am. *fastback
sedan) (stubback saloon,* Am.
stubback sedan)
9 la puerta trasera
– *tailgate*
10 la parte trasera aerodinámica
– *fastback (stubback)*
11 el todo terreno (con tracción f a las
cuatro ruedas f (vehiculo m 4 × 4)
– *cross-country vehicle with all-
wheel drive (four-wheel drive)*
12 la rueda de repuesto m
– *spare wheel*
13 el arco de tubo m
– *roll bar*
14 el deportivo descapotable
– *cabriolet sports coupé (cabriolet
sports car)*
15 el asiento integral
– *integral seat*
16 la capota automática
– *automatic hood* (Am. *top)
(power-operated hood,* Am. *top)*
17 el coche familiar (vehiculo m
familiar, berlina f)
– *estate car (estate, shooting brake,*
Am. *station wagon)*
18 el maletero
– *boot space (luggage compartment)*
19 el coche pequeño de tres puertas f
– *small three-door car*
20 la puerta trasera
– *back (tailgate)*

21 el faldón trasero
– *sill*
22 el asiento trasero abatible
– *folding back seat*
23 el portaequipajes (el maletero;
Amér.: el baúl)
– *boot (luggage compartment,* Am.
trunk)
24 el techo corredizo (el techo
corredizo de acero m)
– *(sliding) sunroof (steel sliding sunroof)*
25 el turismo de tres puertas f
– *three-door hatchback*
26 el coche de dos plazas f (el cabriolé sport, el deportivo, el cupé)
– *roadster (sports cabrio, sports
cabriolet), a two-seater*
27 el techo duro (la capota
desmontable dura)
– *hard top*
28 el coche deportivo de cuatro
asientos m (con dos asientos m de
transportines m)
– *sports coupé, a two-plus-two (two-
seater with occasional seats)*
29 la parte trasera aerodinámica
– *fastback*
30 el transportín
– *occasional seat*
31 la rueda de ancho m especial
– *low-profile tyre* (Am. *tire) (wide
wheel)*
32 el coche deportivo GT (el coche
deportivo de gran turismo m)
– *gran turismo car* (GT *car)*
33 el parachoques incorporado
– *integral bumper* (Am. *integral
fender)*
34 el spoiler trasero
– *rear spoiler*
35 la parte trasera
– *back*
36 el spoiler delantero
– *front spoiler*

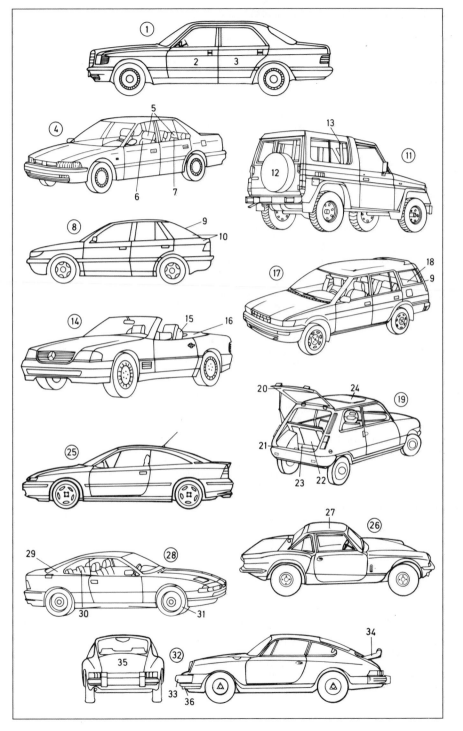

1 el pequeño camión todo terreno *m* con cuatro ruedas *f* motrices
– *light cross-country lorry (light truck, pick-up truck) with all-wheel drive (four-wheel drive)*
2 la cabina
– *cab (driver's cab)*
3 la plataforma de carga *f* (la caja)
– *loading platform (body)*
4 el neumático de recambio *m* (la rueda de repuesto), un neumático todo terreno *m*
– *spare tyre (Am. spare tire), a cross-country tyre*
5 la camioneta (*C. Rica, Guat. y Pan.:* el pick up; *Amér. Central:* la cazadora)
– *light lorry (light truck, pick-up truck)*
6 la camioneta con plataforma *f* (con caja *f*)
– *platform truck*
7 el furgón (la camioneta cerrada)
– *medium van*
8 la puerta lateral corredera (la puerta de carga *f*)
– *sliding side door [for loading and unloading]*
9 el microbús (*Arg.:* el colectivo; *Ec. y Par.:* el micro; *Pan.:* el busito; *S. Dgo.:* el minibús)
– *minibus*
10 la capota (el techo plegable)
– *folding top (sliding roof)*
11 la puerta posterior
– *rear door*
12 la puerta lateral pivotante
– *hinged side door*
13 el maletero (el portaequipajes)
– *luggage compartment*
14 el asiento del viajero
– *passenger seat*
15 la cabina
– *cab (driver's cab)*
16 la rejilla de aireación *f* (la ranura del aire)
– *air inlet*
17 el autobús (el autocar; *Canarias, Cuba y P. Rico:* la guagua)
– *motor coach (coach, bus)*
18 la bodega del autobús (el compartimiento del equipaje)
– *luggage locker*
19 el equipaje de mano *f* (una maleta)
– *hand luggage (suitcase, case)*
20 el camión pesado (el camión de gran tonelaje *m*, el convoy)
– *heavy lorry (heavy truck, heavy motor truck)*
21 el tractor (el vehículo de tiro *m*)
– *tractive unit (tractor, towing vehicle)*
22 el remolque (el trailer)
– *trailer (drawbar trailer)*

23 la plataforma fija (la caja)
– *swop platform (body)*
24 el camión basculante de tres bandas *m*
– *three-way tipper (three-way dump truck)*
25 la plataforma basculante
– *tipping body (dump body)*
26 el gato hidráulico
– *hydraulic cylinder*
27 el container descargado
– *supported container platform*
28 el camión articulado, un camión cisterna *f* (*Col.:* el carrotanque; *Par. y P. Rico:* el camión tanque; *Venez.:* la gandola)
– *articulated vehicle, a vehicle tanker*
29 el tractor del semirremolque
– *tractive unit (tractor, towing vehicle)*
30-33 la cisterna remolcada
– *semi-trailer (skeletal)*
30 la cisterna (el depósito)
– *tank*
31 la articulación giratoria
– *turntable*
32 los patines de ruedas *f*
– *undercarriage*
33 la rueda ode repuesto *m*
– *spare wheel*
34 el autobús pequeño en versión *f* urbana (*Col.:* el bus intermunicipal)
– *midi bus [for short-route town operations]*
35 la puerta exterior basculante
– *outward-opening doors*
36 el autobús de dos pisos *m*
– *double-deck bus (double-decker bus)*
37 el primer piso (el piso bajo)
– *lower deck (lower saloon)*
38 el piso superior
– *upper deck (upper saloon)*
39 la subida
– *boarding platform*
40 el trolebús
– *trolley bus*
41 la pértiga del trole
– *current collector*
42 el trole de contacto *m*
– *trolley (trolley shoe)*
43 el tendido aéreo con dos cables *m* para el doble contacto
– *overhead wires*
44 el remolque del trolebús
– *trolley bus trailer*
45 el acoplamiento con fuelles de caucho *m*
– *pneumatically sprung rubber connection*

1-55 el taller especializado
- *agent's garage (distributor's garage, Am. specialty shop)*
1-23 la sección de diagnóstico *m*
- *diagnostic test bay*
1 el aparato de diagnóstico *m*
- *computer*
2 la clavija de diagnóstico *m*
- *main computer socket*
3 el cable de diagnóstico *m*
- *computer harness (computer cable)*
4 el inversor para la medida automática o manual
- *switch from automatic to manual*
5 la ranura para introducir las fichas del programa
- *slot for program cards*
6 la impresora
- *printout machine (printer)*
7 el informe del diagnóstico (el diagnóstico)
- *condition report, a data printout*
8 el mando manual
- *master selector (hand control)*
9 las lámparas de valoración *f* [verde: bueno; rojo: malo]
- *light read-out [green: OK; red: not OK]*

10 el fichero para las fichas del programa
- *rack for program cards*
11 el interruptor de red *f*
- *mains button*
12 la tecla de programa *m* rápido
- *switch for fast readout*
13 el distribuidor de secuencia *f* de encendido *m*
- *firing sequence insert*
14 la caja de almacenamiento *m* (el archivador)
- *shelf for used cards*
15 la horca portacables
- *cable boom*
16 el cable para medir la temperatura del aceite
- *oil temperature sensor*
17 el comprobador de la convergencia y la inclinación de la rueda hacia la derecha (el alineador de dirección *f*)
- *test equipment for wheel and steering alignment*
18 la placa óptica derecha
- *right-hand optic plate*
19 los transistores de disparo *m*
- *actuating transistors*

20 el conmutador del proyector *m*
- *projector switch*
21 la línea fotorreceptora para medir el ángulo de inclinación *f*
- *check light for wheel alignment, a row of photocells*
22 la línea fotorreceptora para medir la convergencia
- *check light for steering alignment, a row of photocells*
23 el destornillador eléctrico
- *power screwdriver*
24 el comprobador de reglaje *m* de los faros
- *beam setter*
25 la plataforma de elevación *f* hidráulica
- *hydraulic lift*
26 el brazo ajustable de la plataforma de elevación *f*
- *adjustable arm of hydraulic lift*
27 la almohadilla de la plataforma de elevación *f*
- *hydraulic lift pad*
28 la cavidad de la rueda
- *excavation*
29 el manómetro (para medir la presión del aire)
- *pressure gauge (Am. gage)*

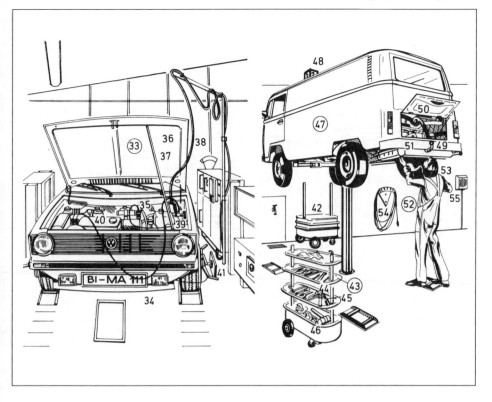

30 el engrasador a presión *f*
– grease gun
31 la caja de las piezas pequeñas
– storage box for small parts
32 el catálogo de las piezas de recambio *m*
– wall chart [of spare parts]
33 el diagnóstico automático
– automatic computer test
34 el automóvil (el auto, el coche), un turismo
– motor car (car, Am. automobile, auto), a passenger vehicle
35 el compartimiento motor
– engine compartment
36 el capó
– bonnet (Am. hood)
37 la varilla del capó
– bonnet support (Am. hood support)
38 el cable de diagnosis *f*
– computer harness (computer cable)
39 el conector hembra (el manguito) de diagnosis *f*
– main computer socket
40 el cable de sonda *f* de la temperatura del aceite
– oil temperature sensor

41 el espejo de rueda *f* para medir ópticamente la convergencia y la inclinación
– wheel mirror for visual wheel and steering alignment
42 el carrito de las herramientas
– tool trolley
43 la herramientas
– tools
44 la llave para tuercas *f*
– impact wrench
45 la llave dinamométrica
– torque wrench
46 el martillo de alisar (aplanar)
– body hammer (roughing-out hammer)
47 el vehículo en reparación, un microbús
– vehicle under repair, a minibus
48 el número de reparación *f*
– car location number
49 el motor trasero
– rear engine
50 la tapa del motor trasero
– tailgate
51 el escape
– exhaust system
52 la reparación del escape
– exhaust repair

53 el mecánico de automóviles *m*
– motor car mechanic (motor vehicle mechanic, Am. automotive mechanic)
54 la goma del aire comprimido
– air hose
55 el interfono
– intercom

1-29 la estación de servicio *m* (la gasolinera; *Mé. y P. Rico:* la gasolinería; *S. Dgo.:* el puesto de gasolina *f*), una estación de autoservicio *m*
– *service station (petrol station, filling station,* Am. *gasoline station, gas station), a self-service station*
1 el distribuidor (el surtidor) de gasolina *f* sin plomo, súper o normal (*anál.:* gasóleo *m*); la bomba de gasolina *f*
– *petrol (*Am. *gasoline) pump (blending pump) for lead-free premium grade and regular petrol (*Am. *gasoline) (sim.: for derv)*
2 la goma del surtidor
– *hose (petrol pump,* Am. *gasoline pump, hose)*
3 la pistola del surtidor
– *nozzle*
4 la suma (la cantidad) de dinero *m* a pagar
– *cash readout*
5 el volumen suministrado
– *volume readout*
6 el precio del litro
– *price display*
7 la señal luminosa
– *indicator light*

8 el automovilista utilizando el surtidor de autoservicio *m*
– *driver using self-service petrol pump (*Am. *gasoline pump)*
9 el extintor
– *fire extinguisher*
10 el distribuidor de servilletas *f* de papel *m*
– *paper-towel dispenser*
11 la servilleta de papel *m*
– *paper towel*
12 el cubo de la basura
– *litter receptacle*
13 el depósito de mezcla *f* de dos tiempos *m*
– *two-stroke blending pump*
14 el cristal (el tubo) de medida *f*
– *meter*
15 el aceite para motores *m*
– *engine oil*
16 la aceitera de motores *m*
– *oil can*
17 el comprobador de la presión de inflado *m*
– *tyre pressure gauge (*Am. *tire pressure gage)*
18 la tubería del aire comprimido
– *air hose*
19 el depósito de aire *m*
– *static air tank*

20 el manómetro (el comprobador de inflado *m*)
– *pressure gauge (*Am. *gage) (manometer)*
21 la tubuladura de inflado *m*
– *air filler neck*
22 el hangar (el box) de reparación *f*
– *repair bay (repair shop)*
23 la manguera de lavado *m*, una manguera de agua *f*
– *car-wash hose, a hose (hosepipe)*
24 la tienda de la estación de servicio *m*
– *accessory shop*
25 el bidón de gasolina *f*
– *petrol can (*Am. *gasoline can)*
26 el capote para la lluvia (el impermeable)
– *rain cape*
27 los neumáticos
– *car tyres (*Am. *automobile tires)*
28 los accesorios para automóviles *m*
– *car accessories*
29 la caja
– *cash desk (console)*

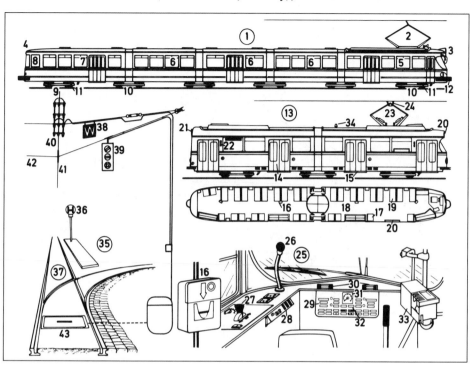

1 el ferrobús articulado de doce ejes *m* para la red interurbana
– *twelve-axle articulated railcar for interurban rail service*
2 el pantógrafo (colector *m* de corriente *f*)
– *current collector*
3 la cabeza (la delantera) del tren
– *head of the railcar*
4 la cola (la trasera) del tren
– *rear of the railcar*
5 el vagón A con motor *m* de tracción *f*
– *carriage A containing the motor*
6 el vagón B (igual: vagón C o D)
– *carriage B (also: carriages C and D)*
7 el vagón E con motor *m* de tracción *f*
– *carriage E containing the motor*
8 el despacho de billetes *m* trasero (*Amér.:* la boletería)
– *rear controller*
9 el bogie de impulsión *f*
– *driving bogie*
10 el bogie portador
– *carrying bogie*
11 el protector de rueda *f* (el quitapiedras)
– *wheel guard*
12 el tope
– *bumper (Am. fender)*
13 el ferrobús articulado *m* urbano e interurbano de seis ejes *m* tipo "Mannheim"
– *six-axle articulated railcar (`Mannheim' type) for tram (Am. streetcar, trolley) and urban rail services*
14 la puerta de entrada *f* y salida *f,* una puerta plegable
– *entrance and exit door, a double folding door*
15 el estribo
– *step*

16 el fechador de billetes *m* (el cancelador de billetes *m*)
– *ticket-cancelling machine*
17 el asiento individual
– *single seat*
18 la plaza sin asiento (el sitio para estar de pie *m,* el pasillo)
– *standing room portion*
19 el asiento doble
– *double seat*
20 la placa indicadora de la línea y del destino
– *route (number) and destination sign*
21 la placa indicadora de la línea
– *route sign (number sign)*
22 el indicador de dirección *f* (el intermitente)
– *indicator (indicator light)*
23 el pantógrafo
– *pantograph (current collector)*
24 las zapatas de arco *m* del pantógrafo de carbono *m* o de aleación *f* de aluminio *m*
– *carbon or aluminium (Am. aluminum) alloy trolley shoes*
25 la cabina del conductor
– *driver's position*
26 el micrófono
– *microphone*
27 el despacho de billetes *m* (*Amér.:* la boletería; el indicador del valor teórico)
– *controller*
28 el aparato de radio *f*
– *radio equipment (radio communication set)*
29 el cuadro (el tablero) de mandos *m*
– *dashboard*
30 la iluminación del cuadro de mandos *m*
– *dashboard lighting*

31 el indicador de velocidad *f* (el velocímetro)
– *speedometer*
32 los botones de mando *m* para abrir las puertas, para los limpiaparabrisas y para la luz interior y exterior
– *buttons controlling doors, windscreen wipers, internal and external lighting*
33 el distribuidor de billetes *m* con cambiador *m* de moneda *f*
– *ticket counter with change machine*
34 la antena radio *f*
– *radio antenna*
35 la estación (la parada)
– *tram stop (Am. streetcar stop, trolley stop)*
36 la placa del punto de parada *f*
– *tram stop sign (Am. streetcar stop sign, trolley stop sign)*
37 la posición de las agujas eléctricas
– *electric change points*
38 la señal de cambio de vía *f*
– *points signal (switch signal)*
39 el transmisor de la señal de cambio *m* de vía *f* (el indicador de dirección *f*)
– *points change indicator*
40 el contacto de catenaria *f*
– *trolley wire contact point*
41 la catenaria
– *trolley wire (overhead contact wire)*
42 el arriostramiento transversal de la línea de toma *f*
– *overhead cross wire*
43 el mecanismo de mando *m* de agujas *f* electromagnético (*también:* electromotor)
– *electric (also: electrohydraulic, electromechanical) points mechanism*

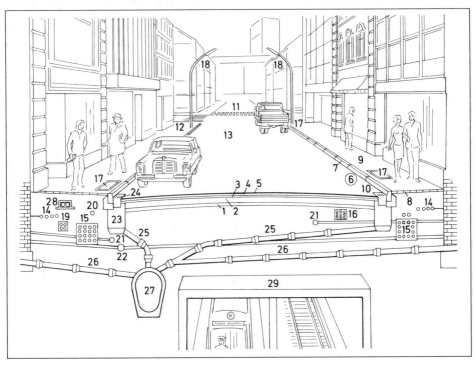

1-5 las capas de la calzada
– *road layers*
1 la capa de protección *f* contra las heladas
– *anti-frost layer*
2 la capa de base *f* bituminosa
– *bituminous sub-base course*
3 la capa adhesiva inferior
– *base course*
4 la capa adhesiva superior
– *binder course*
5 la capa bituminosa de circulación *f* (el revestimiento de la calzada)
– *bituminous surface*
6 el borde de la acera (el bordillo; *Chile:* la solera; *P. Rico:* el cintillo)
– *kerb (curb)*
7 el encintado (la piedra del bordillo)
– *kerbstone (curbstone)*
8 el empedrado de la acera
– *paving (pavement)*
9 la acera (*Guat. y Mé.:* la banqueta; *Amér. Merid.:* la vereda)
– *pavement (Am. sidewalk, walkway)*
10 el arroyo (la reguera)
– *gutter*
11 el paso de peatones *m* (el paso de cebra *f*)
– *pedestrian crossing (zebra crossing, Am. crosswalk)*

12 la esquina de la calle
– *street corner*
13 la calzada
– *street*
14 los cables de suministro *m* de corriente *f*
– *electricity cables*
15 los cables telefónicos
– *telephone cables*
16 la línea telefónica de tránsito *m*
– *telephone cable pipeline*
17 el pozo de cables *m* con recubrimiento *m*
– *cable manhole with cover (with manhole cover)*
18 la farola con luz *f*
– *lamp post with lamp*
19 los cables eléctricos para instalaciones *f* técr.
– *electricity cables for technical installations*
20 la línea telefónica para el empalme de las casas
– *subscribers' (Am. customers') telephone lines*
21 la canalización de gas *m*
– *gas main*
22 la canalización de agua *f* potable
– *water main*
23 la alcantarilla con colector *m* de cieno *m* (*Amér.:* el resumidero)
– *drain*

24 la rejilla del sumidero
– *drain cover*
25 la acometida de la alcantarilla
– *drain pipe*
26 la acometida de las casas para las aguas fecales
– *waste pipe*
27 la cloaca mixta (para las aguas fecales y llovedizas; *Mé.:* la coladera)
– *combined sewer*
28 el conducto de calefacción *f* urbana
– *district heating main*
29 el túnel del metro
– *underground tunnel*

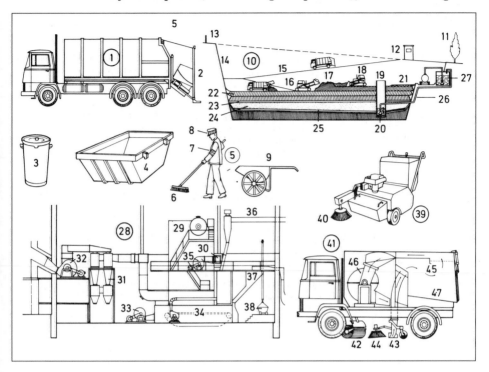

1 el camión de recogida *f* de basuras *f*,
un vehículo que prensa la basura
– *refuse collection vehicle* (Am. *garbage truck*)
2 el dispositivo basculante para los cubos
de la basura, un sistema de vaciado *m*
estanco
– *dustbin-tipping device* (Am. *garbage can dumping device*), a dust-free empty-ing system
3 el cubo de la basura
– *dustbin* (Am. *garbage can, trash can*)
4 el contenedor de basura *f*
– *refuse container* (Am. *garbage container*)
5 el barrendero
– *road sweeper* (Am. *street sweeper*)
6 la escoba
– *broom*
7 el brazalete (con franjas *f* reflectantes)
– *fluorescent armband*
8 la gorra (con franjas *f* reflectantes)
– *cap with fluorescent band*
9 la carretilla del barrendero
– *road sweeper's* (Am. *street sweeper's*) barrow
10 la descarga controlada (el depósito de
basuras *f*; un basurero)
– *controlled tip* (Am. *sanitary landfill, sanitary fill*)
11 la línea de árboles *m* (para que no se
vea el depósito de basuras *f*)
– *screen*
12 el control de entrada *f*
– *weigh office*
13 el vallado para los animales salvajes
– *fence*
14 la pared del foso
– *embankment*

15 la rampa de acceso *m*
– *access ramp*
16 el bulldozer
– *bulldozer*
17 la basura reciente
– *refuse* (Am. *garbage*)
18 el compresor para depositar (la basura)
– *bulldozer for dumping and compacting*
19 el pozo de bomba *f*
– *pump shaft*
20 la bomba para las aguas residuales
– *waste water pump*
21 el recubrimiento poroso
– *porous cover*
22 la basura comprimida y en descomposi-
ción *f*
– *compacted and decomposed refuse*
23 la capa filtrante de grava *f*
– *gravel filter layer*
24 la capa filtrante de morena *f*
– *morainic filter layer*
25 la capa de drenaje *m*
– *drainage layer*
26 la tubería para las aguas residuales
– *drain pipe*
27 el depósito colector de las aguas residuales
– *water tank*
28 la fábrica de incineración *f* de basura *f*
– *refuse* (Am. *garbage*) *incineration unit*
29 la caldera
– *furnace*
30 el hogar de fuel-oil *m*
– *oil-firing system*
31 el separador de polvo *m*
– *separation plant*
32 el ventilador de tracción *f* por
aspiración *f*
– *extraction fan*

33 el ventilador de aire *m* bajo para la
rejilla
– *low-pressure fan for the grate*
34 la rejilla móvil
– *continuous feed grate*
35 el soplante del hogar de fuel-oil *m*
– *fan for the oil-firing system*
36 el transportador de desechos *m* incine-
rados por separado
– *conveyor for separately incinerated material*
37 la instalación de alimentación *f* (carga
f) de carbón *m*
– *coal feed conveyor*
38 el carrito transportador de tierra *f* de
batán *m*
– *truck for carrying fuller's earth*
39 la barredera
– *mechanical sweeper*
40 el cepillo circular
– *circular broom*
41 el vehículo barredor
– *road-sweeping lorry (street-cleaning lorry, street cleaner)*
42 el cilindro escoba
– *cylinder broom*
43 la boca (el tubo) de aspiración *f*
– *suction port*
44 la escoba de alimentación *f*
– *feeder broom*
45 la circulación de aire *m*
– *air flow*
46 el ventilador
– *fan*
47 el depósito (el colector) de barro *m*
– *dust collector*

200 Construcción de carreteras I

1-54 máquinas *f* **para la construcción de carreteras** *f*
- *road-building machinery*

1 la excavadora de pala *f* alta
- *shovel (power shovel, excavator)*

2 la caja de la maquinaria
- *machine housing*

3 la oruga
- *caterpillar mounting* (Am. *caterpillar tractor*)

4 el brazo de la excavadora
- *digging bucket arm (dipper stick)*

5 la pala (el cucharón) de la excavadora
- *digging bucket (bucket)*

6 los dientes de la pala (los dientes rompedores)
- *digging bucket (bucket) teeth*

7 el volquete, un camión de carga *f*
- *tipper (dump truck), a heavy lorry* (Am. *truck*)

8 la caja basculante de chapa *f* de acero *m*
- *tipping body* (Am. *dump body*)

9 el nervado de refuerzo *m*
- *reinforcing rib*

10 el salvacabina
- *extended front*

11 la cabina del conductor
- *cab (driver's cab)*

12 los escombros
- *bulk material*

13 el mecanismo de traílla *f*
- *concrete scraper, an aggregate scraper*

14 la caja montacargas
- *skip hoist*

15 la hormigonera
- *mixing drum (mixer drum), a mixing machine*

16 la oruga excavadora con cubeta *f* de arrastre *m*
- *caterpillar hauling scraper*

17 la cubeta de arrastre *m*
- *scraper blade*

18 la hoja niveladora
- *levelling* (Am. *leveling*) *blade (smoothing blade)*

19 la escarificadora (la niveladora)
- *grader (motor grader)*

20 el escarificador (los arrancadores)
- *scarifier (ripper, road ripper, rooter)*

21 la reja niveladora
- *grader levelling* (Am. *leveling*) *blade (grader ploughshare*, Am. *plowshare)*

22 la corona giratoria de la reja
- *blade-slewing gear (slew turntable)*

23 el ferrocarril de vía *f* estrecha (un ferrocarril de obras *f*)
- *light railway (narrow-gauge*, Am. *narrow-gage), railway)*

24 la locomotora Diesel ligera, una locomotora de vía *f* estrecha
- *light railway (narrow-gauge*, Am. *narrow-gage) diesel locomotive*

25 la vagoneta de remolque *m*
- *trailer wagon (wagon truck, skip)*

26 el pisón de explosión *f* (el pisón de combustión *f* interna), una apisonadora; *más pesado:* el pisón de explosión *f* tipo rana *f*
- *tamper (rammer) [with internal combustion engine]; heavier: frog (frog-type jumping rammer)*

27 las varillas de guía *f* y de control *m*
- *guide rods*

28 la oruga aplanadora (bulldozer *m*)
- *bulldozer*

29 la aplanadera
- *bulldozer blade*

30 el bastidor de empuje *m*
- *pushing frame*

31 la máquina distribuidora de grava *f*
- *road-metal spreading machine (macadam spreader, stone spreader)*

32 la viga apisonadora
- *tamping beam*

33 los patines
- *sole-plate*

34 la chapa de limitación *f* lateral
- *side stop*

35 la pared lateral del depósito de almacenamiento *m*
- *side of storage bin*

36 la apisonadora a motor *m* de tres rulos *m* (cilindros *m*), una apisonadora para obras *f* viales
- *three-wheeled roller, a road roller*

37 el rulo (el cilindro)
- *roller*

38 el tejadillo para todo tiempo *m*
- *all-weather roof*

39 el tractor compresor Diesel
- *mobile diesel-powered air compressor*

40 la botella de oxígeno *m*
- *oxygen cylinder*

41 la esparcidora automotriz de gravilla *f*
- *self-propelled gritter*

42 la aleta esparcidora
- *spreading flap*

43 la acabadora para el recubrimiento de negro (la bituminadora)
- *surface finisher*

44 la chapa de limitación *f* lateral
- *side stop*

45 el depósito de material *m*
- *bin*

46 la bituminadora alquitranadora, con caldera *f* para el alquitrán y el betún
- *tar-spraying machine (bituminous distributor) with tar and bitumen heater*

47 la caldera de alquitrán *m*
- *tar storage tank*

48 la instalación para la mezcla, secado *m* y apisonado *m* del asfalto
- *fully automatic asphalt drying and mixing plant*

49 el elevador de cangilones *m*
- *bucket elevator (elevating conveyor)*

50 el tambor para la mezcla del asfalto
- *asphalt-mixing drum (asphalt mixer drum)*

51 el montacargas llenador
- *filler hoist*

52 la abertura de alimentación *f*
- *filler opening*

53 el inyector de sustancia *f* aglutinante
- *binder injector*

54 la salida del asfalto mezclado
- *mixed asphalt outlet*

55 la sección transversal normal de una carretera
- *typical cross-section of a bituminous road*

56 el arcén de hierba *f*
- *grass verge*

57 la inclinación transversal
- *crossfall*

58 la capa de asfalto *m*
- *asphalt surface (bituminous layer, bituminous coating)*

59 la infraestructura
- *base (base course)*

60 el firme o la capa de grava *f*, una capa de protección *f* contra las heladas
- *hardcore sub-base course (Telford base) or gravel sub-base course, an anti-frost layer*

61 el drenaje del subsuelo
- *sub-drainage*

62 el tubo de drenaje *m* de cemento *m*
- *perforated cement pipe*

63 el canal de drenaje *m*
- *drainage ditch*

64 la cubierta de humus *m* (la capa de mantillo *m*)
- *soil covering*

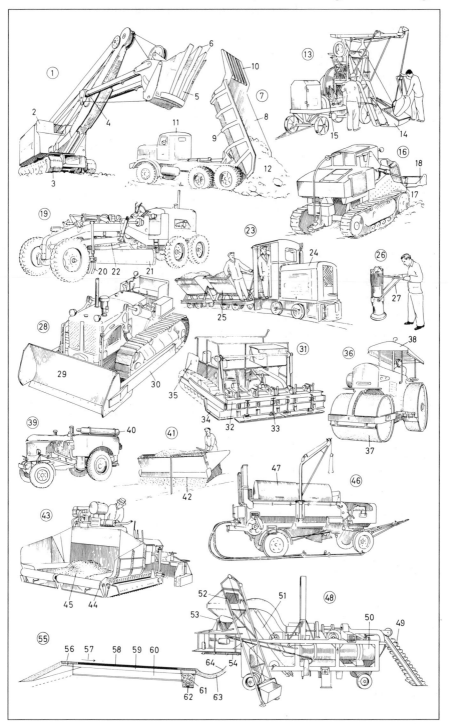

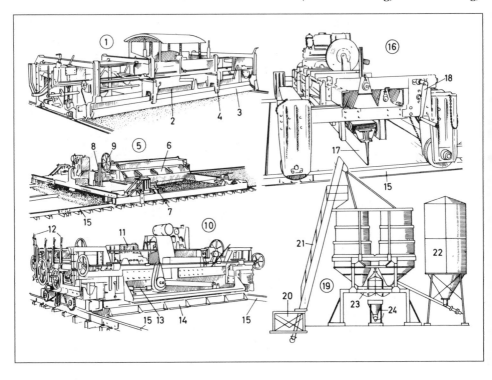

1-24 construcción *f* de carreteras *f* de hormigón *m* (construcción *f* de autopistas *f*)
– *concrete road construction (highway construction)*
1 la niveladora del subsuelo, una máquina para la construcción de carreteras *f*
– *subgrade grader, a road-building machine*
2 la viga apisonadora
– *tamping beam (consolidating beam)*
3 la viga niveladora
– *levelling* (Am. *leveling) beam*
4 los rodillos guía *f* para la viga niveladora
– *roller guides for the levelling* (Am. *leveling) beam*
5 la distribuidora de hormigón *m*
– *concrete spreader*
6 la cubeta distribuidora de hormigón *m*
– *concrete spreader box*
7 la guía de cables *m*
– *cable guides*
8 la palanca de mando *m*
– *control levers*
9 el volante (la rueda de mano *f*) para el vaciado de las cubetas
– *handwheel for emptying the boxes*

10 el vibrador de superficie *f*
– *concrete-vibrating compactor*
11 el engranaje
– *gearing (gears)*
12 las palancas de maniobra *f*
– *control levers (operating levers)*
13 el árbol de impulsión *f* para los vibradores de la viga vibradora
– *axle drive shaft to vibrators (tampers) of vibrating beam*
14 la viga alisadora
– *screeding board (screeding beam)*
15 el soporte de los carriles guía *f*
– *road form*
16 la máquina de cortar juntas *f* (el cortador de juntas *f*)
– *joint cutter*
17 la cuchilla cortadora de juntas *f*
– *joint-cutting blade*
18 la manivela de avance *m*
– *crank for propelling machine*
19 la instalación para la mezcla de hormigón *m*, una estación central de mezcla *f*, una instalación de peso *m* y mezcla *f* automáticos
– *concrete-mixing plant, a stationary central mixing plant, an automatic batching and mixing plant*
20 la artesa colectora
– *collecting bin*

21 el elevador de cangilones *m*
– *bucket elevator*
22 el silo del cemento
– *cement store*
23 la hormigonera de mezcla *f* forzada
– *concrete mixer*
24 la cuba del hormigón
– *concrete pump hopper*

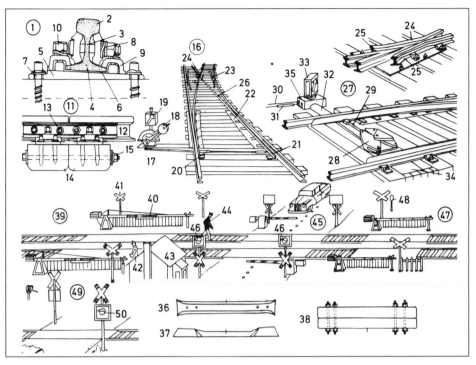

1-38 la vía
– **line** *(track)*
1 el carril (el raíl)
– *rail*
2 la cabeza del raíl
– *rail head*
3 el alma *f* del raíl
– *web (rail web)*
4 el patín del raíl
– *rail foot (rail bottom)*
5 la placa de asiento *m*
– *sole-plate (base plate)*
6 la plantilla
– *cushion*
7 el tirafondo
– *coach screw (coach bolt)*
8 las arandelas de muelle *m* (las arandelas elásticas)
– *lock washers (spring washers)*
9 la placa de sujeción *f*
– *rail clip (clip)*
10 el tornillo de sujeción *f*
– *T-head bolt*
11 la junta de los raíles
– *rail joint (joint)*
12 la eclisa (la mordaza del carril)
– *fishplate*
13 el tornillo de eclisa *f*
– *fishbolt*
14 la traviesa de junta *f* acoplada
– *coupled sleeper (Am. coupled tie, coupled crosstie)*
15 el tornillo de acoplamiento *m*
– *coupling bolt*
16 las agujas movidas a mano *f*
– *manually-operated points (manually-operated switch)*
17 el aparato de maniobra *f* de las agujas movidas a mano *f*
– *switch stand*
18 el contrapeso
– *weight*

19 la señal de agujas *f* (el farol indicando la posición de las agujas)
– *points signal (switch signal, points signal lamp, switch signal lamp)*
20 el tirante de ajuste *m*
– *pull rod*
21 la lengüeta de la aguja
– *switch blade (switch tongue)*
22 el patín de deslizamiento *m*
– *slide chair*
23 el contracarril
– *check rail (guard rail)*
24 el cruzamiento (la punta de corazón *m* de las agujas)
– *frog*
25 la pata de liebre *f*
– *wing rail*
26 el raíl del cambio
– *closure rail*
27 el cambio de agujas *f* a distancia *f*
– *remote-controlled points (remote-controlled switch)*
28 el cerrojo del aparato de cambio *m*
– *point lock (switch lock)*
29 el tirante de unión *f* (del cerrojo con las agujas)
– *stretcher bar*
30 el alambre de transmisión *f*
– *point wire*
31 el tensor
– *turnbuckle*
32 el canal
– *channel*
33 la señal de cambio *m* con alumbrado *m* eléctrico
– *electrically illuminated points signal (switch signal)*
34 el foso del cambio
– *trough*
35 la caja protectora de la transmisión del cambio
– *points motor with protective casing*

36 la traviesa de acero *m*
– *steel sleeper (Am. steel tie, steel crosstie)*
37 la traviesa de hormigón *m*
– *concrete sleeper (Am. concrete tie, concrete crosstie)*
38 la traviesa de junta *f* acoplada
– *coupled sleeper (Am. coupled tie, coupled crosstie)*
39-50 pasos *m* a nivel *m*
– *level crossings (Am. grade crossings)*
39 el paso a nivel *m*, con barrera *f* (P. Rico: el paso-nivel)
– *protected level crossing (Am. protected grade crossing)*
40 la barrera
– *barrier (gate)*
41 la cruz de aviso *m* (la cruz de San Andrés)
– *warning cross (Am. crossbuck)*
42 el guardabarrera
– *crossing keeper (Am. gateman)*
43 la caseta del guardabarrera
– *crossing keeper's box (Am. gateman's box)*
44 el vigilante de la vía
– *linesman (Am. trackwalker)*
45 el paso de media barrera *f*
– *half-barrier crossing*
46 la luz intermitente
– *warning light*
47 la barrera accionada por micrófono *m*
– *intercom-controlled crossing; sim.: telephone-controlled crossing*
48 el interfono
– *intercom system*
49 el paso a nivel *m* sin guarda *f*
– *unprotected level crossing (Am. unprotected grade crossing)*
50 la luz intermitente
– *warning light*

203 Via férrea II (señalización)

1-6 los semáforos
- *stop signals (main signals)*
1 el semáforo, una señal en posición *f* de "parada" *f*
- *stop signal (main signal), a semaphore signal in 'stop' position*
2 el brazo de la señal
- *signal arm (semaphore arm)*
3 el semáforo eléctrico (la señal eléctrica) en posición *f* de "parada" *f*
- *electric stop signal (colour light,* Am. *color light, signal) at 'stop'*
4 la posición de la señal de "disminución *f* de velocidad *f* "
- *signal position: 'proceed at low speed'*
5 la posición de la señal de "vía *f* libre"
- *signal position: 'proceed'*
6 la señal de sustitución *f*
- *substitute signal*
7-24 señales de aviso *m*
- *distant signals*
7 la señal en posición *f* de "parada *f* próxima"
- *semaphore signal at 'be prepared to stop at next signal'*
8 el brazo adicional
- *supplementary semaphore arm*
9 la señal luminosa de aviso *m* de "parada *f* próxima"
- *colour light (Am. color light) distant signal at 'be prepared to stop at next signal'*
10 la posición de la señal de "disminución *f* de velocidad *f* próxima"
- *signal position: 'be prepared to proceed at low speed'*
11 la posición de la señal de "vía *f* libre próxima"
- *signal position: 'proceed main signal ahead'*
12 la señal de aviso *m* con panel *m* adicional para reducción *f* de la distancia de frenado *m* de más del 5%
- *semaphore signal with indicator plate showing a reduction in braking distance of more than 5%*
13 el panel triangular
- *triangle (triangle sign)*
14 la señal luminosa de aviso *m* con luz *f* adicional para reducción *f* de la distancia de frenado *m*
- *colour light (Am. color light) distant signal with indicator light for showing reduced braking distance*
15 la luz blanca adicional
- *supplementary white light*
16 la señal de aviso *m* de "parada *f* próxima" (luz *f* amarilla)
- *distant signal indicating 'be prepared to stop at next signal' (yellow light)*
17 la señal de aviso *m* repetida (la señal de aviso *m* con luz *f* adicional, sin panel *m*)
- *second distant signal (distant signal with supplementary light, without indicator plate)*
18 la señal de aviso *m* con indicación *f* de velocidad *f*
- *distant signal with speed indicator*
19 el indicador de la velocidad (la pancarta de limitación *f* de velocidad *f*)
- *distant speed indicator*

20 la señal de aviso *m* con indicador *m* de dirección *f*
- *distant signal with route indicator*
21 el indicador de dirección *f* (*Cuba y P. Rico:* el abanico)
- *route indicator*
22 la señal de aviso *m* sin brazo *m* adicional en posición *f* de "parada próxima"
- *distant signal without supplementary arm in position: 'be prepared to stop at next signal'*
23 la señal de aviso *m* sin brazo *m* adicional en posición *f* de "vía *f* libre próxima"
- *distant signal without supplementary arm in 'be prepared to proceed' position*
24 el panel de la señal de aviso *m*
- *distant signal identification plate*
25-44 señales *f* **suplementarias**
- *supplementary signals*
25 la placa trapezoidal para marcar el punto de parada *f* en la estación
- *stop board for indicating the stopping point at a control point*
26-29 las señales de aviso *m* **de balizas** *f*
- *approach signs*
26 la señal de aviso *m* de baliza *f* a 100 m de distancia *f* de la señal
- *approach sign 100 m from distant signal*
27 la señal de aviso *m* de baliza *f* a 175 m de distancia *f*
- *approach sign 175 m from distant signal*
28 la señal de aviso *m* de baliza *f* a 250 m de distancia *f*
- *approach sign 250 m from distant signal*
29 la señal de aviso *m* de baliza *f* a menos de un 5% de distancia *f* de la vía de parada *f* de la sección
- *approach sign at a distance of 5% less than the braking distance on the section*
30 la señal a cuadros *m* indicando señales *f* de parada *f* no situadas inmediatamente a la derecha o sobre el raíl de parada *f*
- *chequered sign indicating stop signals (main signals) not positioned immediately to the right of or over the line (track)*
31 u. 32 las placas de parada *f* para indicar el punto de parada *f* frente al tren
- *stop boards to indicate the stopping point of the front of the train*
33 la placa del punto de parada *f* (prepararse para parar)
- *stop board indicating 'be prepared to stop'*
34 u. 35 las placas de quitanieves *m*
- *snow plough (Am. snowplow) signs*
34 la placa quitanieves *m* levantada
- *'raise snow plough (Am. snowplow)' sign*
35 la placa quitanieves *m* bajada
- *'lower snow plough (Am. snowplow)' sign*
36-44 señales *f* **de limitación** *f* **de velocidad** *f*
- *speed restriction signs*

36-38 disco *m* **de limitación** *f* **de velocidad** *f* [velocidad máxima 3 × 10 = 30km/h]
- *speed restriction sign [maximum speed 3 × 10 = 30 kph]*
36 la señal diurna
- *sign for day running*
37 el número de velocidad *f*
- *speed code number*
38 la señal nocturna
- *illuminated sign for night running*
39 el comienzo de la limitación de velocidad *f* provisional
- *commencement of temporary speed restriction*
40 el final de la limitación de velocidad *f* provisional
- *termination of temporary speed restriction*
41 la señal de limitación *f* de velocidad *f* para una sección con limitación *f* de velocidad *f* permanente [velocidad máxima 5 × 10 = 50 km/h]
- *speed restriction sign for a section with a permanent speed restriction [maximum speed 5 × 10 = 50 kph]*
42 el comienzo de la limitación de velocidad *f* permanente
- *commencement of permanent speed restriction*
43 la placa de advertencia de limitación *f* de velocidad *f* [sólo en vías *f* principales]
- *speed restriction warning sign [only on main lines]*
44 la señal de limitación *f* de velocidad *f* [sólo en vías *f* principales]
- *speed restriction sign [only on main lines]*
45-52 señales *f* **de cambio** *m* **de vía** *f*
- *point signals (switch signals)*
45-48 agujas *f* **simples**
- *single points (single switches)*
45 la ramificación recta
- *route straight ahead (main line)*
46 la ramificación doblada [a derecha]
- *[right] branch*
47 la ramificación doblada [a izquierda]
- *[left] branch*
48 la ramificación curva [vista desde el cruce (punta *f* de corazón *m*)]
- *branch [seen from the frog]*
49-52 cruces *m* **de vías** *f* **dobles**
- *double crossover*
49 el cruce rectilíneo de izquierda a derecha
- *route straight ahead from left to right*
50 el cruce rectilíneo de derecha a izquierda
- *route straight ahead from right to left*
51 la curva a la izquierda
- *turnout to the left from the left*
52 la curva a la derecha
- *turnout to the right from the right*
53 el puesto de agujas *f* (*Amér.:* el chucho) **mecánico**
- *manually-operated signal box (Am. signal tower, switch tower)*
54 el juego de palancas *f*
- *lever mechanism*

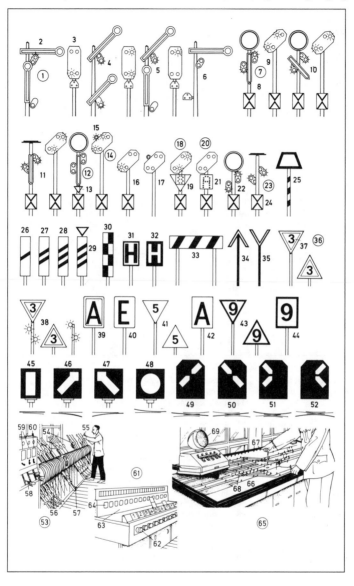

55 la palanca de cambio *m* [azul], una
palanca de cerrojo *m*
– *points lever (switch lever) [blue], a*
lock lever
56 la palanca de señales *f* [rojo]
– *signal lever [red]*
57 el gatillo (el pestillo) de mano *f*
– *catch*
58 la palanca de vía *f* libre
– *route lever*
59 el bloqueo de tramos *m* (de secciones *f*)
– *block instruments*
60 el tablero del bloque
– *block section panel*

61 el cuadro de agujas *f* eléctrico
– *electrically-operated signal box*
  (Am. signal tower, switch tower)
62 la palanca de agujas *f* y de señales *f*
– *points (switch) and signal knobs*
63 el registro de cierre *m*
– *lock indicator panel*
64 el tablero de control *m*
– *track and signal indicator*
65 el cuadro luminoso de agújas *f*
– ***track diagram control layout***
66 el pupitre del diagrama de vías *f*
– *track diagram control panel (domino*
  panel)

67 los pulsadores
– *push buttons*
68 los itinerarios (las vías)
– *routes*
69 el interfono
– *intercom system*

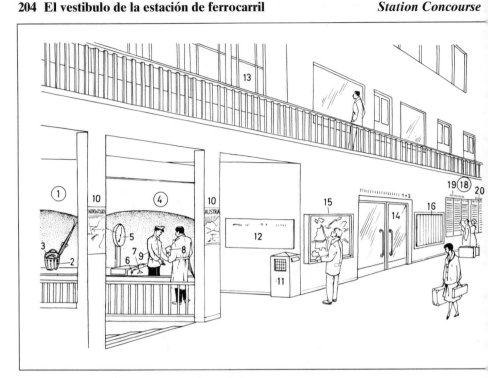

1 el despacho de expedición *f* y recepción *f* de paquetes *m* por expreso *m*
– *parcels office*
2 la carga por expreso *m* (el paquete por expreso *m*)
– *parcels*
3 la canasta con candado *m*
– *basket [with lock]*
4 el despacho de facturación *f* y recepción *f* de equipaje *m*
– *luggage counter*
5 la báscula automática
– *platform scale with dial*
6 la maleta (*Amér.:* la valija)
– *suitcase (case)*
7 la etiqueta (con la dirección) del equipaje
– *luggage sticker*
8 el resguardo de consigna *f*
– *luggage receipt*
9 el empleado del despacho
– *luggage clerk*
10 el cartel publicitario
– *poster (advertisement)*
11 el buzón de la estación
– *station post box (Am. station mailbox)*
12 el cartel informativo
– *station guide*

13 el restaurante de la estación
– *station restaurant*
14 la sala de espera *f*
– *waiting room*
15 el plano de la ciudad
– *map of the town (street map)*
16 el panel guía de ferrocarriles *m*
– *timetable (Am. schedule)*
17 la máquina automática de abonos *m* (la máquina automática de tiques *m*)
– *ticket machine*
18 el horario de trenes *m* de pared *f* (el indicador mural)
– *arrivals and departures board (timetable)*
19 el tablero de las horas de llegada *f*
– *arrival timetable (Am. arrival schedule)*
20 el tablero de las horas de salida *f*
– *departure timetable (Am. departure schedule)*

El vestíbulo de la estación de ferrocarril

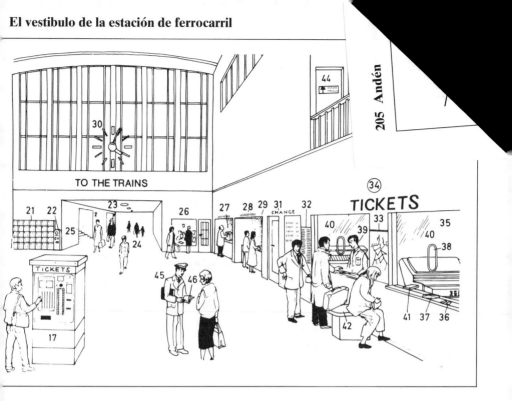

21 la consigna automática
– *left luggage lockers*
22 la máquina automática para cambiar monedas *f*
– *change machine*
23 el túnel de acceso *m* al andén
– *tunnel to the platforms*
24 los pasajeros (viajeros *m*)
– *passengers*
25 la escalera del andén
– *steps to the platforms*
26 la librería de la estación (el quiosco, el puesto, de revistas *f*)
– *station bookstall (Am. station bookstand) (also: magazine kiosk)*
27 la consigna para las maletas (*Amér.*: las valijas)
– *left luggage office (left luggage)*
28 la agencia de viajes *m; también:* la oficina de información *f* de hoteles *m,* la oficina de turismo *m*
– *travel centre (Am. center); also: accommodation bureau*
29 información *f*
– *information office (Am. information bureau)*
30 el reloj de la estación
– *station clock*

31 la sucursal bancaria, con oficina *f* de cambio *m*
– *bank branch with foreign exchange counter*
32 la lista de cambio *m*
– *indicator board showing exchange rates*
33 el plano de la red ferroviaria
– *railway map (Am. railroad map)*
34 el despacho de billetes *m*
– *ticket office*
35 la taquilla de venta *f* de billetes *m*
– *ticket counter*
36 el billete
– *ticket*
37 el platillo giratorio
– *revolving tray*
38 el higiáfono
– *grill*
39 el taquillero (expendedor *m* de billetes *m*)
– *ticket clerk (Am. ticket agent)*
40 el vidrio
– *pane of glass (window)*
41 la guía de bolsillo *m*
– *pocket timetable (Am. pocket train schedule)*

42 el banco para el equipaje
– *luggage rest*
43 el puesto de socorro *m*
– *first aid station*
44 la misión de la estación
– *Travellers' (Am. Travelers') Aid*
45 el agente de información *f* (el empleado de ferrocarril *m; aquí:* el revisor)
– *railway (Am. railroad) information clerk (railway [Am. railroad] employee; here: the guard, conductor)*
46 la guía oficial de ferrocarriles *m*
– *official timetable (official railway guide, Am. train schedule)*

357

1 el andén
– platform
2 la escalera del andén
– steps to the platform
3 el paso superior del andén
– bridge
4 el número de andén m
– platform number
5 el techo del andén
– platform roofing
6 los viajeros
– passengers
7-12 el equipaje
– luggage
7 la maleta (Amér.: la valija)
– suitcase (case)
8 la etiqueta de la maleta
– luggage label
9 la etiqueta del hotel
– hotel sticker
10 el saco de mano f (el bolso de viaje m; Amér.: el carriel; Mé.: el veliz)
– travelling (Am. traveling) bag
11 la sombrerera
– hat box
12 el paraguas, un bastón paraguas m
– umbrella, a walking-stick umbrella
13 el edificio de recepción f
– main building (offices)
14 el andén número 1
– platform

15 el paso a nivel m
– crossing
16 el quiosco rodante de periódicos m
– news trolley
17 el vendedor de periódicos m
– news vendor (Am. news dealer)
18 la lectura para el viaje
– reading matter for the journey
19 el bordillo del andén
– edge of the platform
20 la policía de ferrocarriles m
– railway policeman (Am. railroad policeman)
21 el indicador de dirección f
– destination board
22 la casilla para anunciar la estación f de destino m
– destination indicator
23 la casilla para anunciar la hora de salida f
– departure time indicator
24 la casilla para anunciar el retraso del tren
– delay indicator
25 el tren de ferrocarril m interurbano, un tren automotor
– suburban train, a railcar
26 el compartimiento reservado
– special compartment
27 el altavoz (Amér.: el altoparlante) del andén
– platform loudspeaker

28 el letrero de la estación
– station sign
29 el carro eléctrico
– electric trolley (electric truck)
30 el encargado del equipaje
– loading foreman
31 el mozo de estación f (el mozo de cuerda f; Arg.: el changador; Col.: el altozanero)
– porter (Am. redcap)
32 el carrito del equipaje
– barrow
33 la fuente de agua f potable
– drinking fountain
34 el tren Eurocity eléctrico (el E.C.); también: el trén rápido interurbano
– electric Eurocity express; also: IC express (Intercity express)
35 la locomotora eléctrica, una locomotora exprés eléctrica
– electric locomotive, an express locomotive
36 el arco de toma f de corriente f (el pantógrafo)
– collector bow (sliding bow)
37 el compartimiento secretaría f
– secretarial compartment
38 la placa de ruta f y destino m
– destination board

39 el inspector del material rodante y vagones *m*
– *wheel tapper*
40 el martillo comprobador de ruedas *f*
– *wheel-tapping hammer*
41 el inspector
– *station foreman*
42 el bastón de mando *m* (el bastón de señales *f*)
– *signal*
43 la gorra roja
– *red cap*
44 el agente de información *f*
– *inspector*
45 el horario de bolsillo *m*
– *pocket timetable* (Am. *pocket train schedule)*
46 el reloj del andén
– *platform clock*
47 la señal de partida *f*
– *starting signal*
48 el alumbrado del andén
– *platform lighting*
49 el quiosco (del andén) de refres-cos *m* y comidas *f* para el viaje
– *refreshment kiosk*
50 la botella de cerveza *f*
– *beer bottle*
51 el periódico
– *newspaper*

52 el beso de despedida *f* (*Guat.:* el pico)
– *parting kiss*
53 el abrazo
– *embrace*
54 el banco del andén
– *platform seat*
55 la papelera para los desperdicios
– *litter bin* (Am. *litter basket)*
56 el buzón del andén
– *platform post box* (Am. *platform mailbox)*
57 la cabina telefónica del andén
– *platform telephone*
58 el hilo de contacto *m* (el cable de contacto *m*)
– *trolley wire (overhead contact wire)*
59-61 la vía
– *track*
59 el raíl
– *rail*
60 la traviesa (*Amér.:* el durmiente)
– *sleeper* (Am. *tie, crosstie)*
61 los cascajos (el lecho de cascajos *m*, los balastos)
– *ballast (bed)*

1 la rampa de acceso *m* (la rampa
de vehículos *m*); *anál.:* la rampa
del ganado
– *ramp (vehicle ramp); sim.: livestock ramp*
2 el tractor eléctrico
– *electric truck*
3 la vagoneta (el remolque transportador)
– *trailer*
4 los bultos (los bultos sueltos, fardos *m*, la mercancía en fardos *m*);
en transportes colectivos: carga *f*
colectiva
– *part loads (Am. package freight,
less-than-carload freight); in general traffic: general goods in general consignments (in mixed consignments)*
5 el cajón (la caja)
– *crate*
6 el vagón para la mercancía en fardos *m*
– *goods van (Am. freight car)*
7 el cobertizo de mercancías *f* (el
almacén de mercancías *f*)
– *goods shed (Am. freight house)*
8 la calle de carga *f*
– *loading strip*
9 la rampa del cobertizo (la rampa
de carga *f*)
– *loading dock*
10 la bala de turba *f*
– *bale of peat*
11 la bala de lienzo *m*
– *bale of linen (of linen cloth)*
12 la atadura
– *fastening (cord)*
13 la damajuana (la botella, la garrafa) forrada de paja *f*
– *wicker bottle (wickered bottle,
demijohn)*
14 la carretilla para los sacos
– *trolley*
15 el camión para la mercancía en
fardos *m*
– *goods lorry (Am. freight truck)*
16 la carretilla elevadora de horquilla *f*
– *forklift truck (fork truck, forklift)*
17 la vía de carga *f*
– *loading siding*
18 las mercancías voluminosas
– *bulky goods*
19 el contenedor pequeño propiedad
del ferrocarril
– *small railway-owned (Am. rail-
road-owned) container*
20 el vagón de feriantes *m* (*anál.:* el
vagón de circo *m*)
– *showman's caravan (sim. circus
caravan)*

21 el vagón plano (la batea)
– *flat wagon (Am. flat freight car)*
22 el gálibo
– *loading gauge (Am. gage)*
23 la bala de paja *f*
– *bale of straw*
24 el vagón plataforma con teleros *m*
(la batea con teleros *m*)
– *flat wagon (Am. flatcar) with side
stakes*
25 el parque de coches *m* y de
vagones *m*
– *fleet of lorries (Am. trucks)*
26–39 **el tinglado (el cobertizo) de las
mercancías**
– *goods shed (Am. freight house)*
26 la recepción de mercancías *f* (el
despacho de mercancías *f*)
– *goods office (forwarding office,
Am. freight office)*
27 las mercancías
– *part-load goods (Am. package
freight)*
28 el contratista de mercancías *f*
– *forwarding agent (Am. freight
agent, shipper)*
29 el jefe de carga *f*
– *loading foreman*
30 la carta de porte *m* (el talón de
expedición *f; Amér.:* la boleta de
expedición *f*)
– *consignment note (waybill)*
31 la báscula de los bultos sueltos
– *weighing machine*
32 la paleta
– *pallet*
33 el obrero del cobertizo de mercancías *f*
– *porter*
34 la carretilla eléctrica
– *electric cart (electric truck)*
35 el remolque de la carretilla
– *trailer*
36 el empleado de la oficina de
consignación *f* (la inspección de
carga *f*)
– *loading supervisor*
37 la puerta del cobertizo
– *goods shed door (Am. freight
house door)*
38 el riel guía *f*
– *rail (slide rail)*
39 la polea (la rueda de corredera *f*)
– *roller*
40 la caseta para pesar
– *weighbridge office*
41 la báscula para vagones *m*
– *weighbridge*
42 la estación de maniobras *f*
– *marshalling yard (Am. classification yard, switch yard)*

43 la locomotora de maniobras *f*
– *shunting engine (shunting locomotive, shunter, Am. switch engine,
switcher)*
44 el puesto de control de maniobras *f*
– *marshalling yard signal box (Am.
classification yard switch tower)*
45 el jefe de maniobras *f*
– *yardmaster*
46 la albardilla
– *hump*
47 la vía de maniobras *f*
– *sorting siding (classification siding, classification track)*
48 el freno de vía *f* (el freno de raíl *m*)
– *rail brake (retarder)*
49 la calza (la zapata de freno *m*)
– *slipper brake (slipper)*
50 la vía de maniobras *f* (el
apartadero)
– *storage siding (siding)*
51 el tope fijo (el tope hidráulico)
– *buffer (buffers, Am. bumper)*
52 el vagón completo (*Amér.:* el
carro completo)
– *wagon load (Am. carload)*
53 el almacén
– *warehouse*
54 la estación de contendores *m*
– *container station*
55 la grúa de pórtico *m*
– *gantry crane*
56 el mecanismo de elevación *f*
– *lifting gear (hoisting gear)*
57 el contenedor
– *container*
58 el vagón portacontenedores *m*
– *container wagon (Am. container
car)*
59 el semirremolque
– *semi-trailer*

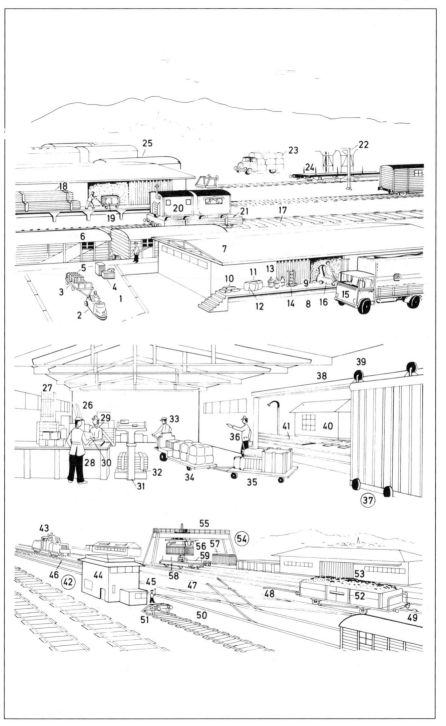

1-21 el vagón de tren *m* **expreso,** un vagón (*Amér.:* un carro)
- *express train coach (express train carriage, express train car, corridor compartment coach), a passenger coach*
1 la vista lateral (el perfil)
- *side elevation (side view)*
2 la caja del vagón
- *coach body*
3 el chasis
- *underframe (frame)*
4 el bogie (el carretón) con suspensión *f* de muelles *m* de acero *m* y amortiguadores *m*
- *bogie (truck) with steel and rubber suspension and shock absorbers*
5 el compartimiento de las baterías
- *battery containers (battery boxes)*
6 el intercambiador de calor *m* para la calefacción a vapor *m* o eléctrica
- *steam and electric heat exchanger for the heating system*
7 la ventanilla de corredera *f*
- *sliding window*
8 la junta con almohadilla *f* de caucho *m*
- *rubber connecting seal*
9 el ventilador estático
- *ventilator*
10-21 el plano
- *plan*
10 el compartimiento de 2ª clase
- *second-class section*
11 el pasillo lateral
- *corridor*
12 el asiento plegable (el traspuntín, el trasportín)
- *folding seat (tip-up seat)*
13 el compartimiento de los pasajeros
- *passenger compartment (compartment)*
14 la puerta del compartimiento
- *compartment door*
15 el lavabo (*Amér.:* el lavatorio)
- *washroom*
16 el retrete (el excusado, el water-closet, el W.C.)
- *toilet (lavatory, WC)*
17 el compartimiento de 1ª clase
- *first-class section*
18 la puerta de vaivén *m*
- *swing door*
19 la puerta corrediza de la pared frontal
- *sliding connecting door*
20 la puerta de entrada *f*
- *door*
21 el vestíbulo
- *vestibule*
22-32 el coche-restaurante (*Amér.:* el vagón-restaurante)
- *dining car (restaurant car, diner)*
22-25 la vista lateral (el perfil)
- *side elevation (side view)*
22 la puerta de entrada *f*
- *door*
23 la puerta de carga *f*
- *loading door*
24 la toma de corriente *f* para el abastecimiento de energía *f* durante la parada
- *current collector for supplying power during stops*
25 los compartimientos de las baterías
- *battery boxes (battery containers)*

26-32 el plano
- *plan*
26 el lavabo del personal
- *staff washroom*
27 el armario de las provisiones
- *storage cupboard*
28 el fregadero
- *washing-up area*
29 la cocina
- *kitchen*
30 la cocina eléctrica con 8 placas *f*
- *electric oven with eight hotplates*
31 la barra (el bar)
- *counter*
32 el comedor
- *dining compartment*
33 la cocina del coche-restaurante
- *dining car kitchen*
34 el jefe de cocina *f*
- *chef (head cook)*
35 la despensa (la alacena)
- *kitchen cabinet*
36 el coche-cama
- *sleeping car (sleeper)*
37 la vista lateral (el perfil)
- *side elevation (side view)*
38-42 el plano
- *plan*
38 el compartimiento de dos camas *f*
- *two-seat twin-berth compartment (two-seat two-berth compartment, Am. bedroom)*
39 la puerta plegable y giratoria
- *folding doors*
40 el lavabo (*Amér.:* el lavatorio)
- *washstand*
41 la habitación de servicio *m*
- *office*
42 el retrete (el excusado, el water-closet, el W.C.)
- *toilet (lavatory, WC)*
43 el compartimiento del tren expreso
- *express train compartment*
44 el asiento acolchado reclinable
- *upholstered reclining seat*
45 el brazo del asiento
- *armrest*
46 el cenicero del brazo del asiento
- *ashtray in the armrest*
47 el reposacabezas ajustable
- *adjustable headrest*
48 la funda de tela *f*
- *antimacassar*
49 el espejo
- *mirror*
50 la percha (el cuelgacapas)
- *coat hook*
51 el portaequipajes
- *luggage rack*
52 la ventanilla del compartimiento
- *compartment window*
53 la mesita plegable
- *fold-away table (pull-down table)*
54 el botón para regular la calefacción
- *heating regulator*
55 la papelera
- *litter receptacle*
56 la cortina de cordón *m*
- *curtain*
57 el reposapiés (el apoyapiés)
- *footrest*

58 el asiento de ventanilla *f*
- *corner seat*
59 el coche de gran capacidad *f*
- *open car*
60 la vista lateral (el perfil)
- *side elevation (side view)*
61-72 el plano
- *plan*
61 el compartimiento de gran capacidad *f*
- *open carriage*
62 la fila de asientos *m* individuales
- *row of single seats*
63 la fila de asientos *m* dobles
- *row of double seats*
64 el asiento reclinable
- *reclining seat*
65 el cojín
- *seat upholstery*
66 el respaldo
- *backrest*
67 la cabecera
- *headrest*
68 la almohadilla de plumas *f* con funda *f* de nylón *m*
- *down-filled headrest cushion with nylon cover*
69 el brazo del asiento con cenicero *m*
- *armrest with ashtray*
70 el guardarropa
- *cloakroom*
71 el guardamaletas
- *luggage compartment*
72 los lavabos
- *toilet (lavatory, WC)*
73 el coche-bar, un coche-restaurante de autoservicio *m*
- *buffet car (quick-service buffet car), a self-service restaurant car*
74 la vista lateral (el perfil)
- *side elevation (side view)*
75 la toma de corriente *f* para el abastecimiento eléctrico durante la parada
- *current collector for supplying power during stops*
76 el plano
- *plan*
77 el comedor
- *dining compartment*
78-79 la barra (el bar)
- *buffet (buffet compartment)*
78 el lado de los clientes
- *customer area*
79 el lado del personal del servicio
- *serving area*
80 la cocina
- *kitchen*
81 el compartimiento del personal
- *staff compartment*
82 los lavabos (los retretes, los W.C.) del personal
- *staff toilet (staff lavatory, staff WC)*
83 los casilleros de comidas *f*
- *food compartments*
84 los platos
- *plates*
85 el cubierto
- *cutlery*
86 la caja
- *till (cash register)*

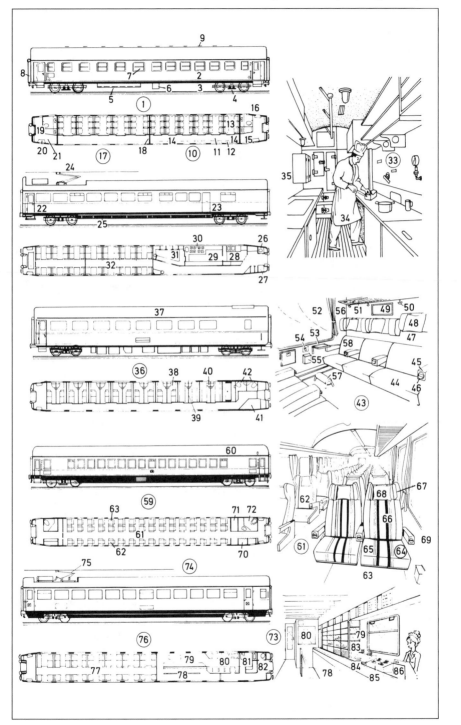

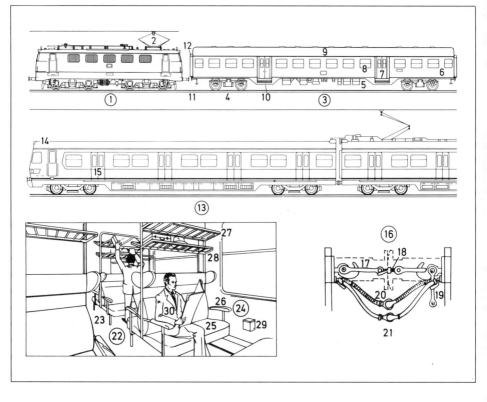

1-30 el servicio local
- *local train service*

1-12 el tren de cercanías *f*
- *local train (short-distance train)*

1 la locomotora eléctrica
- *electric locomotive*

2 el pantógrafo
- *current collector*

3 el vagón del servicio local de cuatro ejes *m*, un vagón de viajeros *m*
- *four-axled coach (four-axled car) for short-distance routes, a passenger coach (passenger car)*

4 el bogie (el carretón) [con freno *m* de discos *m*]
- *bogie (truck) [with disc (disk) brakes]*

5 el chasis
- *underframe (frame)*

6 la caja del vagón con paneles *m* de chapa *f*
- *coach body with metal panelling (Am. paneling)*

7 la puerta doble plegable y giratoria
- *double folding doors*

8 la ventanilla del compartimiento
- *compartment window*

9 el compartimiento de gran capacidad *f*
- *open carriage*

10 la puerta de entrada *f*
- *entrance*

11 el paso [de un vagón a otro]
- *connecting corridor*

12 la junta con almohadilla *f* de caucho *m*
- *rubber connecting seal*

13 el automotor ligero, un automotor de servicio *m* local, un automotor Diesel
- *light railcar, a short-distance railcar*

14 la cabina del maquinista del automotor
- *cab (driver's cab, Am. engineer's cab)*

15 el compartimiento del equipaje
- *carriage door*

16 la conexión de tubos *m* y enganche *m* de vagones *m*
- *connecting hoses and coupling*

17 el eslabón de enganche *m*
- *coupling link*

18 el tensor (el tornillo de acoplamiento *m* con palanca *f* tensora)
- *tensioning device (coupling screw with tensioning lever)*

19 el acoplamiento suelto
- *unlinked coupling*

20 la manga de acoplamiento *m* del conducto de calefacción *f*
- *heating coupling hose (steam coupling hose)*

21 la manga de acoplamiento *m* de la conducción del freno
- *coupling hose (connecting hose) for the compressed-air braking system*

22 el compartimiento de 2ª clase
- *second-class section*

23 el pasillo central
- *central gangway*

24 el compartimiento
- *compartment*

25 el banco (el asiento) acolchado
- *upholstered seat*

26 el brazo del asiento
- *armrest*

27 el portaequipajes (la rejilla para el equipaje)
- *luggage rack*

28 la rejilla para sombreros *m* y para el equipaje pequeño
- *hat and light luggage rack*

29 el cenicero giratorio
- *ashtray*

30 el viajero
- *passenger*

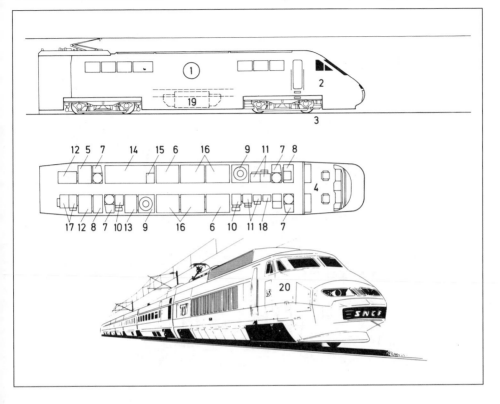

1-19 el tren ICE (Intercity Exprés,
   antes: Intercity Experimental)
 – *Intercity Express (*formerly:
   Intercity Experimental)
1 el tren automotor (el tren de
   coche automotor) de los ferrocarriles alemanes
 – *German Federal Railway trainset*
2 la cabeza motriz (el coche motriz)
 – *driving unit (power car)*
3 el eje de ruedas *f* provisto de
   motores *m* de tracción *f*
 – *driving bogie with traction motors*
4 la cabina del maquinista
 – *cab (driver's cab,* Am. *engineer's
   cab)*
5 la alimentación (el filtro de la
   red)
 – *power supply (traction current filter)*
6 el interruptor automático (el
   transformador, válvula *f*)
 – *contactors (converters, inductance)*
7 la ventilación del motor
 – *traction motor blower*
8 el interruptor automático de
   válvula *f* (el transformador)
 – *inductance protection (converter)*

9 la instalación de la refrigeración
   del aceite *m*
 – *oil-cooling plant*
10 el transformador auxiliar
 – *converter for the auxiliaries*
11 la electrónica
 – *electronics*
12 el mecanismo de mando *m* eléctrico
 – *control current equipment*
13 los mecanismos auxiliares (los
   conmutadores)
 – *auxiliaries (switchgear)*
14 la instalación de aire *m* comprimido
 – *pneumatic equipment*
15 la instalación de aire *m* acondicionado
 – *air-conditioning plant*
16 el transformador de la corriente
   principal
 – *main current converters*
17 la técnica de medición *f* (diagnóstico *m*)
 – *measuring equipment (diagnosis)*
18 el sistema de control de la marcha
   del tren de linea *f*
 – *continuous automatic train-run-
   ning control*

19 el transformador
 – *transformer*
20 el TGV (el Tren de Alta
   Velocidad de los ferrocarriles
   franceses; en España: AVE, Alta
   Velocidad Española)
 – *TGV (Train à Grande Vitesse) of
   the Société Nationale des Chemins
   de Fer Français (SNCF)*

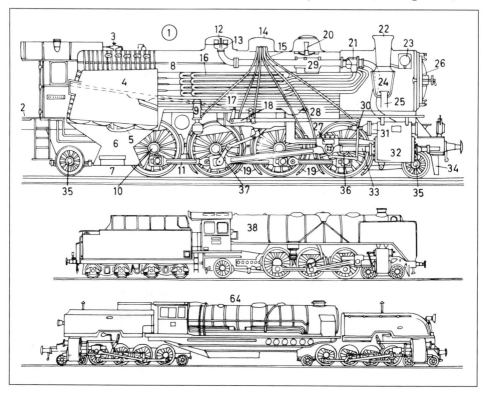

1-69 la locomotora de vapor *m*
– *steam locomotives*
2-37 la caldera de la locomotora y el mecanismo de propulsión *f* **de la locomotora**
– *locomotive boiler and driving gear*
2 la chapa de ténder *m*, con enganche *m*
– *tender platform with coupling*
3 la válvula de seguridad *f*, para la sobrepresión de vapor *m*
– *safety valve for excess boiler pressure*
4 la caja de fuego *m* (el hogar)
– *firebox*
5 el emparrillado basculante
– *drop grate*
6 el cenicero, con ventilación *f*
– *ashpan with damper doors*
7 la compuerta de fondo *m* (la trampilla) del cenicero
– *bottom door of the ashpan*
8 los tubos del humo
– *smoke tubes (flue tubes)*
9 la bomba de alimentación *f* de agua *f*
– *feed pump*
10 el cojinete del eje
– *axle bearing*
11 la biela de acoplamiento *m*
– *connecting rod*

12 la cúpula de caldera *f* (el domo de vapor *m*)
– *steam dome*
13 la válvula reguladora (del vapor)
– *regulator valve (regulator main valve)*
14 el domo de arena *f* (el depósito de arena *f*)
– *sand dome*
15 los tubos de bajada *f* de la arena
– *sand pipes (sand tubes)*
16 la caldera horizontal
– *boiler (boiler barrel)*
17 los tubos del recalentador
– *fire tubes or steam tubes*
18 el cambio de marcha *f*
– *reversing gear (steam reversing gear)*
19 los tubos para echar la arena
– *sand pipes*
20 la válvula de alimentación *f*
– *feed valve*
21 la caja colectora del vapor (el colector de vapor *m*)
– *steam collector*
22 la chimenea (salida *f* de humo *m* y de vapor *m* de escape *m*)
– *chimney (smokestack, smoke outlet and waste steam exhaust)*
23 el precalentador del agua *f* de alimentación *f* (el precalentador de superficie *f*)
– *feedwater preheater (feedwater heater, economizer)*

24 la rejilla parachispas
– *spark arrester*
25 el tubo de escape *m*
– *blast pipe*
26 la puerta de la caja de humos *m*
– *smokebox door*
27 la cruceta
– *cross head*
28 el colector de lodos *m*
– *mud drum*
29 la rejilla separadora de lodos *m* del alimentador del agua *f*
– *top feedwater tray*
30 la vara (el vástago) del distribuidor
– *combination lever*
31 la caja del distribuidor
– *steam chest*
32 el cilindro de vapor *m*
– *cylinder*
33 el vástago del pistón (la biela) con prensaestopa *m*
– *piston rod with stuffing box (packing box)*
34 el quitapiedras (*Arg.:* el miriñaque; *Chile:* la trompa; *P. Rico:* el botavaca)
– *guard iron (rail guard,* Am. *pilot, cowcatcher)*
35 el eje portante
– *carrying axle (running axle, dead axle)*
36 el eje acoplado
– *coupled axle*

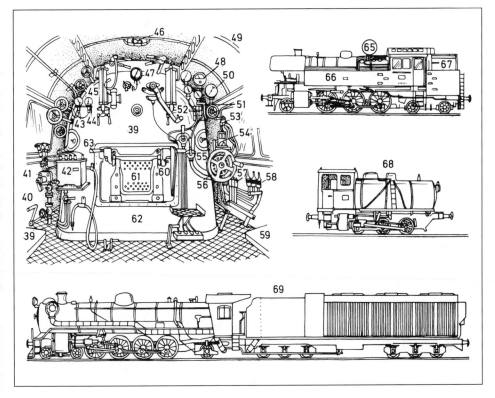

37 el eje motor
– *driving axle*
38 la locomotora con ténder *m* para
tren *m* expreso
– *express locomotive with tender*
**39-63 la cabina del maquinista de la
locomotora de vapor *m***
– *cab (driver's cab,* Am. *engineer's
cab)*
39 el puesto del fogonero
– *fireman's seat*
40 la manivela del emparrillado
móvil (de la parrilla basculante)
– *drop grate lever*
41 la bomba inyectora
– *line steam injector*
42 la bomba de engrase *m* automático
– *automatic lubricant pump (automatic lubricator)*
43 el manómetro del precalentador
– *preheater pressure gauge* (Am.
gage)
44 el manómetro de la calefacción
– *carriage heating pressure gauge*
(Am. *gage)*
45 el indicador del nivel de agua *f*
– *water gauge* (Am. *gage)*
46 el alumbrado
– *light*
47 el manómetro de la caldera
– *boiler pressure gauge* (Am. *gage)*

48 el teletermómetro
– *distant-reading temperature gauge*
(Am. *gage)*
49 la cabina del maquinista
– *cab (driver's cab,* Am. *engineer's
cab)*
50 el manómetro de freno *m*
– *brake pressure gauge* (Am. *gage)*
51 la palanca del silbato de vapor *m*
– *whistle valve handle*
52 el libro horario (la guía de ferrocarriles *m*)
– *driver's timetable* (Am. *engineer's
schedule)*
53 la válvula de freno *m* del maquinista
– *driver's brake valve* (Am. *engineer's brake valve)*
54 el tacógrafo (el indicador de
velocidad *f*, el tacómetro)
– *speed recorder (tachograph)*
55 la palanca del arenero
– *sanding valve*
56 el volante del cambio de marcha *f*
– *reversing wheel*
57 la válvula del freno de emergencia *f*
– *emergency brake valve*
58 la válvula de descarga *f*
– *release valve*

59 el asiento para el maquinista de la
locomotora
– *driver's seat* (Am. *engineer's seat)*
60 la pantalla antideslumbrante
– *firehole shield*
61 la puerta del hogar
– *firehole door*
62 la caldera vertical
– *vertical boiler*
63 la empuñadura para abrir la puerta del hogar
– *firedoor handle handgrip*
64 la locomotra articulada (la locomotora Garrat)
– *articulated locomotive (Garratt
locomotive)*
65 la locomotora ténder *m*
– *tank locomotive*
66 el tanque de agua *f*
– *water tank*
67 el ténder para combustible *m*
– *fuel tender*
68 la locomotora accionada por acumulador *m* de vapor *m* (la locomotora sin hogar *m*)
– *steam storage locomotive (fireless
locomotive)*
69 la locomotora de condensación *f*
– *condensing locomotive (locomotive with condensing tender)*

1 la locomotora eléctrica
– *electric locomotive*
2 el pantógrafo de toma *f* de corriente *f*
– *current collector*
3 el interruptor principal
– *main switch*
4 el transformador de alta tensión *f*
– *high-tension transformer*
5 el cable del techo
– *roof cable*
6 el motor de tracción *f*
– *traction motor*
7 el sistema inductivo de control *m* de la marcha del tren
– *inductive train control system*
8 el depósito principal de aire *m*
– *main air reservoir*
9 el silbato
– *whistle*
10-18 el plano de la locomotora
– *plan of locomotive*
10 el transformador con cambio *m* de conexión *f*
– *transformer with tap changer*
11 el refrigerador de aceite *m* con ventilador *m*
– *oil cooler with blower*
12 la bomba de circulación *f* del aceite
– *oil-circulating pump*
13 el mecanismo del cambio de conexión *f*
– *tap changer driving mechanism*
14 el compresor del aire
– *air compressor*
15 el ventilador del motor de tracción *f*
– *traction motor blower*
16 la caja de bornes *m*
– *terminal box*
17 los condensadores para los motores auxiliares
– *capacitors for auxiliary motors*
18 la tapa del conmutador
– *commutator cover*
19 la cabina del maquinista
– *cab (driver's cab,* Am. *engineer's cab)*
20 el volante del conductor
– *controller handwheel*
21 el interruptor de seguridad *f* del conductor
– *dead man's handle*
22 la válvula de freno del maquinista
– *driver's brake valve (*Am. *engineer's brake valve)*
23 la válvula del freno suplementario
– *ancillary brake valve (auxiliary brake valve)*
24 el manómetro del aire comprimido
– *pressure gauge (*Am. *gage)*

25 el interruptor de sobrepresión *f* del dispositivo de seguridad *f*
– *bypass switch for the dead man's handle*
26 el indicador de la tracción (el amperímetro de los motores de tracción *f*)
– *tractive effort indicator*
27 el voltímetro para la tensión de la calefacción
– *train heating voltage indicator*
28 el voltímetro de tensión *f* del hilo de contacto *m*
– *contact wire voltage indicator (overhead wire voltage indicator)*
29 el voltímetro de alta tensión *f*
– *high-tension voltage indicator*
30 el interruptor de mando *m* del pantógrafo
– *on/off switch for the current collector*
31 el interruptor principal
– *main switch*
32 el interruptor del arenero
– *sander switch (sander control)*
33 el interruptor para el freno de centrífuga *f*
– *anti-skid brake switch*
34 el indicador óptico de funcionamiento *m* de los motores auxiliares
– *visual display for the ancillary systems*
35 el velocímetro (el indicador de la velocidad)
– *speedometer*
36 el indicador del grado *m* de marcha *f*
– *running step indicator*
37 el reloj
– *clock*
38 los botones de mando *m* del sistema inductivo
– *controls for the inductive train control system*
39 el interruptor para la calefacción de la cabina del maquinista
– *cab heating switch*
40 la palanca para el silbato
– *whistle lever*
41 **el coche automotor de mantenimiento de catenarias *f*** (el coche automotor de plataforma *f* regulable), un coche automotor Diesel
– *contact wire maintenance vehicle (overhead wire maintenance vehicle), a diesel railcar*
42 la plataforma de trabajo *m*
– *work platform (working platform)*
43 la escala
– *ladder*

44-54 la instalación de maquinaria *f* del automotor de mantenimiento *m* de catenarias *f*
– *mechanical equipment of the contact wire maintenance vehicle*
44 el compresor de aire *m*
– *air compressor*
45 la bomba de aceite *m* del ventilador
– *blower oil pump*
46 la dinamo
– *generator*
47 el motor Diesel
– *diesel engine*
48 la bomba de inyección *f*
– *injection pump*
49 el silencioso
– *silencer (*Am. *muffler)*
50 el cambio de velocidades *f*
– *change-speed gear*
51 el árbol de transmisión *f* (el árbol de cardán *m*)
– *cardan shaft*
52 el engrase de la pestaña
– *wheel flange lubricator*
53 el engranaje de inversión *f* de marcha *f*
– *reversing gear*
54 el soporte del momento de torsión *f*
– *torque converter bearing*
55 **el automotor de acumuladores *m***
– *accumulator railcar (battery railcar)*
56 la caja de la batería
– *battery box (battery container)*
57 la cabina del maquinista
– *cab (driver's cab,* Am. *engineer's cab)*
58 la disposición de los asientos de 2ª clase *f*
– *second-class seating arrangement*
59 el retrete (el excusado, el watercloset, el W. C.)
– *toilet (lavatory, WC)*
60 **el automotor eléctrico rápido**
– *fast electric multiple-unit train*
61 el coche automotor final
– *front railcar*
62 el coche automotor intermedio
– *driving trailer car*

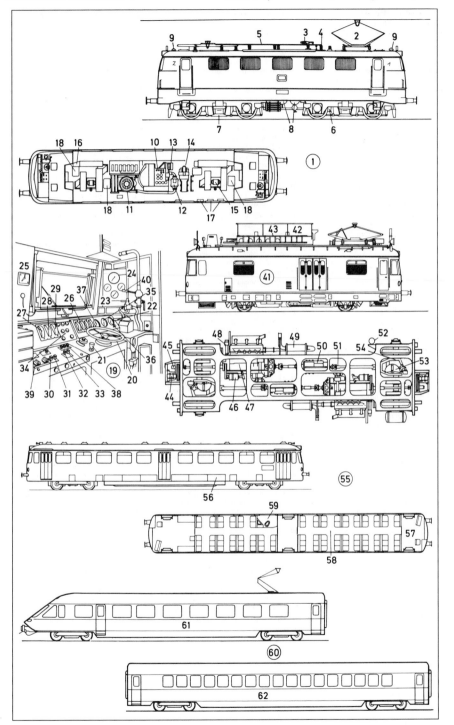

1-84 la locomotora Diesel
- *diesel locomotives*
1 **la locomotora Diesel hidráulica,** una locomotora Diesel de línea *f* para trenes *m* semipesados de viajeros *m* y mercancías *f*
- *diesel-hydraulic locomotive, a mainline locomotive (diesel locomotive) for medium passenger and goods service (freight service)*
2 el bogie (el carretón)
- *bogie (truck)*
3 el juego de ruedas *f*
- *wheel and axle set*
4 el depósito principal de combustible *m*
- *main fuel tank*
5 la cabina del maquinista de una locomotora Diesel
- *cab (driver's cab, Am. engineer's cab) of a diesel locomotive*
6 el manómetro del conducto de aire *m* principal
- *main air pressure gauge (Am. gage)*
7 el manómetro del cilindro de freno *m*
- *brake cylinder pressure gauge (Am. gage)*
8 el manómetro del depósito de aire *m* principal
- *main air reservoir pressure gauge (Am. gage)*
9 el tacómetro (el velocímetro, el indicador de la velocidad *f*)
- *speedometer*
10 el freno de emergencia *f*
- *auxiliary brake*
11 la válvula de freno *m* del maquinista
- *driver's brake valve (Am. engineer's brake valve)*
12 el volante del combinador
- *controller handwheel*
13 el dispositivo de seguridad *f* (de hombre *m* muerto)
- *dead man's handle*
14 el sistema inductivo de control *m* de la marcha del tren
- *inductive train control system*
15 el avisador luminoso
- *signal lights*
16 el reloj
- *clock*
17 el voltímetro de la calefacción
- *voltage meter for the train heating system*
18 el amperímetro de la calefacción
- *current meter for the train heating system*
19 el termómetro del aceite del motor
- *engine oil temperature gauge (Am. gage)*
20 el termómetro del aceite de la transmisión
- *transmission oil temperature gauge (Am. gage)*
21 el termómetro del agua *f* de refrigeración *f*
- *cooling water temperature gauge (Am. gage)*
22 el cuentarrevoluciones del motor
- *revolution counter (rev counter, tachometer)*
23 el aparato de radio *f* del tren
- *radio telephone*
24 la locomotora Diesel hidráulica [en alzado y en plano]
- *diesel-hydraulic locomotive [plan and elevation]*
25 el motor Diesel
- *diesel engine*

26 la instalación de refrigeración *f*
- *cooling unit*
27 la transmisión hidráulica
- *fluid transmission*
28 la transmisión del juego de ruedas *f*
- *wheel and axle drive*
29 el árbol de transmisión *f* (el árbol cardán *m*)
- *cardan shaft*
30 el motor de arranque *m* eléctrico
- *starter motor*
31 la mesa de los instrumentos
- *instrument panel*
32 el pupitre del maquinista
- *driver's control desk (Am. engineer's control desk)*
33 el freno de mano *f*
- *hand brake*
34 el compresor de aire *m* con motor *m* eléctrico (electromotor *m*)
- *air compressor with electric motor*
35 el armario de los aparatos
- *equipment locker*
36 el intercambiador de calor *m* para el aceite de transmisión *f*
- *heat exchanger for transmission oil*
37 el ventilador del recinto de la máquina
- *engine room ventilator*
38 el electroimán inductivo del vehículo
- *magnet for the inductive train control system*
39 el generador de calefacción *f*
- *train heating generator*
40 el armario convertidor de calefacción *f*
- *casing of the train heating system transformer*
41 el precalentador
- *preheater*
42 el silencioso de escape *m*
- *exhaust silencer (Am. exhaust muffler)*
43 el intercambiador de calor *m* auxiliar para el aceite de transmisión *f*
- *auxiliary heat exchanger for the transmission oil*
44 el freno hidráulico
- *hydraulic brake*
45 la caja de las herramientas
- *tool box*
46 la batería de arranque *m*
- *starter battery*
47 **la locomotora Diesel hidráulica** para el servicio de maniobras *f* ligero o medio
- *diesel-hydraulic locomotive for light and medium shunting service*
48 el silencioso de escape *m*
- *exhaust silencer (Am. exhaust muffler)*
49 la campana y el silbato
- *bell and whistle*
50 la radio de maniobras *f*
- *yard radio*
51-67 el alzado de la locomotora
- *elevation of locomotive*
51 el motor Diesel con turbocompresor *m*
- *diesel engine with supercharged turbine*
52 la transmisión hidráulica
- *fluid transmission*
53 la transmisión secundaria
- *output gear box*
54 el radiador
- *radiator*
55 el intercambiador de calor *m* para el aceite de engrase *m* del motor
- *heat exchanger for the engine lubricating oil*
56 el depósito del combustible
- *fuel tank*

57 el depósito de aire *m* principal
- *main air reservoir*
58 el compresor de aire *m*
- *air compressor*
59 las cajas de arena *f*
- *sand boxes*
60 el depósito de reserva de combustible *m*
- *reserve fuel tank*
61 el depósito de combustible *m* auxiliar
- *auxiliary air reservoir*
62 la impulsión del ventilador hidrostático
- *hydrostatic fan drive*
63 el asiento con cofre *m* guardarropa
- *seat with clothes compartment*
64 el volante del freno de mano *f*
- *hand brake wheel*
65 el depósito de igualación *f* (de compensación *f*) del agua *f* de refrigeración *f*
- *cooling water*
66 el balasto de compensación *f*
- *ballast*
67 el volante de mando *m* del motor y de la transmisión
- *engine and transmission control wheel*
68 **la locomotora Diesel pequeña** para el servicio de maniobras *f*
- *small diesel locomotive for shunting service*
69 el silencioso
- *exhaust casing*
70 la bocina
- *horn*
71 el depósito de aire *m* principal
- *main air reservoir*
72 el compresor de aire *m*
- *air compressor*
73 el motor Diesel de ocho cilindros *m*
- *eight-cylinder diesel engine*
74 la transmisión Voith con mecanismo de inversión *f* de marcha *f*
- *Voith transmission with reversing gear*
75 el depósito de fuel-oil *m*
- *heating oil tank (fuel oil tank)*
76 la caja de arena *f*
- *sand box*
77 la instalación de refrigeración *f*
- *cooling unit*
78 el depósito de igualación *f* (de compensación *f*) del agua *f* de refrigeración *f*
- *header tank for the cooling water*
79 el filtro de aire *m* con baño *m* de aceite *m*
- *oil bath air cleaner (oil bath air filter)*
80 el volante del freno de mano *f*
- *hand brake wheel*
81 el volante de mando *m*
- *control wheel*
82 el embrague
- *coupling*
83 el árbol de transmisión *f* (el árbol cardán *m*)
- *cardan shaft*
84 la persiana
- *louvred shutter*

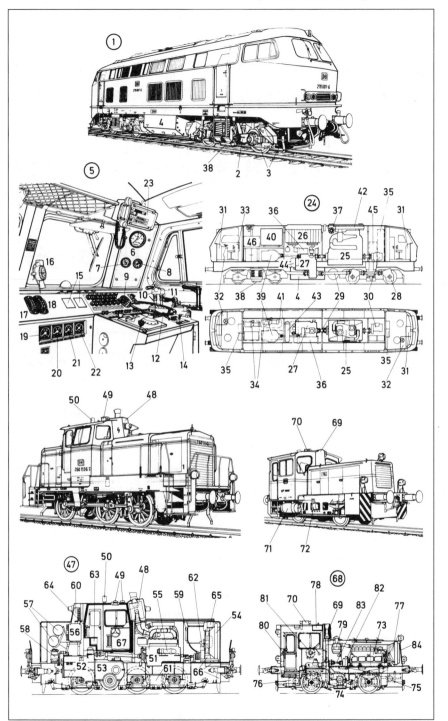

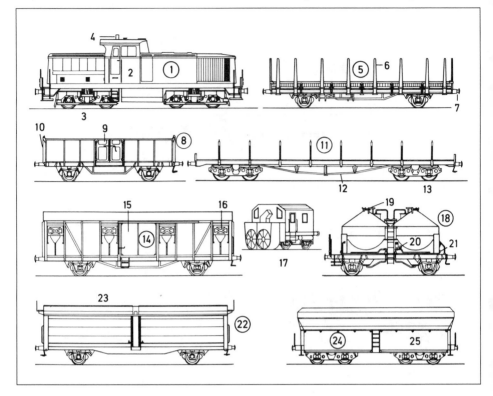

1 la locomotora Diesel hidráulica
– *diesel-hydraulic locomotive*
2 la cabina del maquinista
– *cab (driver's cab,* Am. *engineer's cab)*
3 el juego de ruedas *f*
– *wheel and axle set*
4 la antena para la radio de las maniobras
– *aerial for the yard radio*
5 el vagón plataforma normal
– *standard flat wagon (Am. standard flatcar)*
6 el telero articulado de acero *m*
– *hinged steel stanchion (stanchion)*
7 el tope
– *buffers*
8 el vagón de mercancías *f* abierto normal (la batea; *Amér.:* la zorra)
– *standard open goods wagon (Am. standard open freight car)*
9 las puertas giratorias de la pared lateral
– *revolving side doors*
10 la pared frontal articulada
– *hinged front*
11 el vagón plataforma de bogies *m* normal
– *standard flat wagon (Am. standard flatcar) with bogies*

12 el tirante de refuerzo *m* de bastidor *m*
– *sole bar reinforcement*
13 el bogie (el carretón)
– *bogie (truck)*
14 el vagón de mercancías *f* cubierto
– *covered goods van (covered goods wagon,* Am. *boxcar)*
15 la puerta de corredera *f*
– *sliding door*
16 la ventana de aireación *f*
– *ventilation flap*
17 el quitanieves rotativo, una máquina limpiavías
– *snow blower (rotary snow plough,* Am. *snowplow), a track-clearing vehicle*
18 el vagón para descarga *f* neumática
– *wagon (Am. car) with pneumatic discharge*
19 la boca de carga *f* (la abertura de relleno *m*)
– *filler hole*
20 el empalme de aire *m* comprimido
– *compressed-air supply*
21 el empalme de descarga *f*
– *discharge connection valve*
22 el vagón de techo *m* de corredera *f*
– *goods van (Am. boxcar) with sliding roof*

23 la abertura del techo
– *roof opening*
24 el vagón abierto de bogies *m* de descarga *f* automática
– *bogie open self-discharge wagon (Am. bogie open self-discharge freight car)*
25 el lateral de descarga *f*
– *discharge flap (discharge door)*

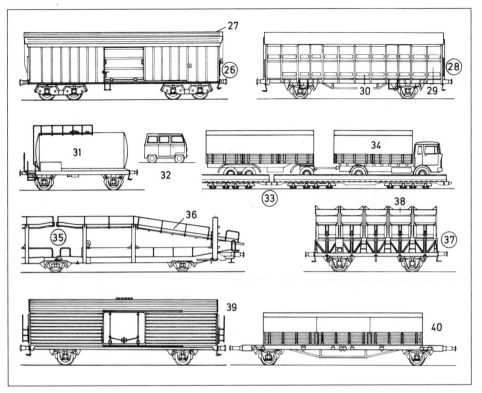

26 el vagón de bogies de techo *m*
pivotante
– *bogie wagon with swivelling (Am.
swiveling) roof*
27 el techo pivotante
– *swivelling (Am. swiveling) roof*
28 el vagón de enrejado *m* de listones *m* de gran capacidad *f* para
el transporte de animales *m*
pequeños
– *large-capacity wagon (Am. large-
capacity car) for small livestock*
29 la pared lateral permeable al aire
– *sidewall with ventilation flaps
(slatted wall)*
30 la ventana de aireación *f*
– *ventilation flap*
31 el vagón cisterna *f*
– *tank wagon (Am. tank car)*
32 el automóvil de raíl *m* (la vagoneta automóvil)
– *track inspection railcar*
33 los vagones de plataforma *f* especial
– *open special wagons (Am. open
special freight cars)*
34 el camión con remolque *m*
– *lorry (Am. truck) with trailer*

35 el vagón de dos pisos *m* para el
transporte de automóviles *m*
– *two-tier car carrier (double-deck
car carrier)*
36 la rampa de acceso *m*
– *hinged upper deck*
37 el vagón con vagonetas *f* basculantes
– *tipper wagon (Am. dump car)
with skips*
38 la vagoneta basculante
– *skip*
39 el vagón frigorífico universal
– *general-purpose refrigerator
wagon (refrigerator van, Am.
refrigerator car)*
40 la estructura superior intercambiable para el vagón plataforma
– *interchangeable bodies for flat
wagons (Am. flatcars)*

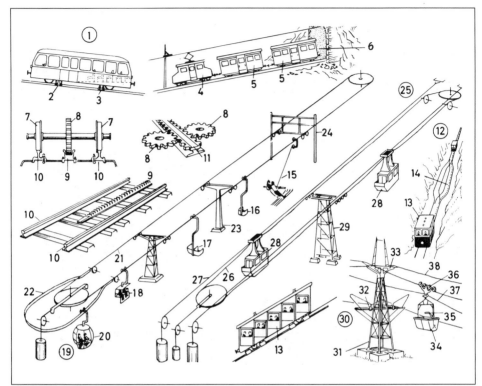

1-14 ferrocarriles *m* **de montaña** *f* **de raíl** *m*
– *mountain railways (Am. mountain rail-roads)*
1 el automotor, con adherencia *f* forzada
– *adhesion railcar*
2 la tracción
– *drive*
3 el freno de emergencia *f*
– *emergency brake*
4 *u.* **5** el ferrocarril de montaña *f* de cremallera *f*
– *rack mountain railway (rack-and-pinion railway, cog railway, Am. cog railroad, rack railroad)*
4 la locomotora eléctrica de cremallera *f*
– *electric rack railway locomotive (Am. electric rack railroad locomotive)*
5 el coche (el vagón) del ferrocarril de cremallera *f*
– *rack railway coach (rack railway trailer, Am. rack railroad car)*
6 el túnel
– *tunnel*
7-11 ferrocarriles *m* de cremallera *f* [sistemas *m*]
– *rack railways (rack-and-pinion railways, Am. rack railroads) [systems]*
7 la rueda de adherencia *f*
– *running wheel (carrying wheel)*
8 la rueda dentada de tracción *f* (el piñón de tracción *f*)
– *driving pinion*
9 la cremallera
– *rack [with teeth machined on top edge]*

10 el raíl
– *rail*
11 la cremallera horizontal doble
– *rack [with teeth on both outer edges]*
12 el funicular
– *funicular railway (funicular, cable railway)*
13 el coche del funicular
– *funicular railway car*
14 el cable de tracción *f*
– *haulage cable*
15-38 funiculares *m* **aéreos de viajeros** *m* (teleféricos *m*)
– *cableways (ropeways, cable suspension lines)*
15-24 teleféricos *m* monocables, teleférico *m* de cable *m* sin fin *m*
– *single-cable ropeways (single-cable suspension lines), endless cableways, endless ropeways*
15 el telesquí
– *drag lift*
16-18 el telesilla
– *chair lift*
16 la telesilla ligera, una telesilla individual
– *lift chair, a single chair*
17 la telesilla doble, una telesilla de dos plazas *f*
– *double lift chair, a two-seater chair*
18 la telesilla doble cubierta
– *double chair (two-seater chair) with coupling*
19 el telecabina, un teleférico de cable *m* sin fin *m*
– *gondola cableway, an endless cableway*

20 la cabina
– *gondola (cabin)*
21 el cable sin fin *m*, un cable portante y de tracción *f*
– *endless cable, a suspension (supporting) and haulage cable*
22 el raíl de maniobra *f* (el raíl de rodeo *m*)
– *U-rail*
23 el pilón soporte *m*
– *single-pylon support*
24 el castillete soporte *m*
– *gantry support*
25 el teleférico bicable, un teleférico de lanzadera *f*
– *double-cable ropeway (double-cable suspension line), a suspension line with balancing cabins*
26 el cable de tracción *f*
– *haulage cable*
27 el cable portante
– *suspension cable (supporting cable)*
28 la cabina para viajeros *m*
– *cabin*
29 el pilón intermedio
– *intermediate support*
30 el teleférico, un teleférico bicable
– *cableway (ropeway, suspension line), a double-cable ropeway (double-cable suspension line)*
31 el castillete con estructura *f* de celosía *f*
– *pylon*
32 la polea del cable de tracción *f*
– *haulage cable roller*

33 el soporte del cable portante
– *cable guide rail (suspension cable bearing)*
34 la caja de la vagoneta, una caja basculante
– *skip, a tipping bucket* (Am. *dumping bucket)*
35 la palanca para descargar el volquete
– *stop*
36 el tren de poleas *f* de rodadura *f*
– *pulley cradle*
37 el cable de tracción *f*
– *haulage cable*
38 el cable portante
– *suspension cable (supporting cable)*
39 **la estación del valle**
– *valley station (lower station)*
40 el foso para el tensor (para el contrapeso)
– *tension weight shaft*
41 el tensor (el contrapeso) del cable portante
– *tension weight for the suspension cable (supporting cable)*
42 el tensor del cable tractor
– *tension weight for the haulage cable*
43 la polea del cable de tensión *f*
– *tension cable pulley*
44 el cable portante
– *suspension cable (supporting cable)*
45 el cable tractor (el cable de tracción *f*)
– *haulage cable*
46 el contracable (el cable inferior)
– *balance cable (lower cable)*
47 el cable auxiliar
– *auxiliary cable (emergency cable)*
48 el dispositivo de tensión *f* del cable auxiliar
– *auxiliary-cable tensioning mechanism (emergency-cable tensioning mechanism)*
49 los rodillos de apoyo *m* del cable tractor
– *haulage cable rollers*
50 el amortiguador de muelle *m*
– *spring buffer* (Am. *spring bumper)*
51 el andén de la estación del valle
– *valley station platform (lower station platform)*
52 la cabina de viajeros *m* (la góndola del teleférico), una cabina de gran capacidad *f*
– *cabin (cableway gondola, ropeway gondola, suspension line gondola), a large-capacity cabin*
53 el tren de poleas *f* de rodadura *f*
– *pulley cradle*
54 el sistema de suspensión *f*
– *suspension gear*
55 el amortiguador del balanceo
– *stabilizer*
56 el tope (la viga de tope *m*)
– *guide rail*
57 **la estación de montaña** *f*
– *top station (upper station)*
58 el soporte del cable portante
– *suspension cable guide (supporting cable guide)*
59 el anclaje del cable portante
– *suspension cable anchorage (supporting cable anchorage)*
60 la batería de rodillos *m* del cable tractor
– *haulage cable rollers*
61 la polea de vuelta *f* del cable tractor
– *haulage cable guide wheel*
62 la polea motriz del cable tractor
– *haulage cable driving pulley*

63 la propulsión (el motor) principal
– *main drive*
64 la propulsión (el motor) de reserva *f*
– *standby drive*
65 la cabina del maquinista
– *control room*
66 **el tren de poleas *f* de rodadura *f* de la cabina**
– **cabin pulley cradle*
67 el travesaño (la viga principal) del tren de poleas *f*
– *main pulley cradle*
68 la cuna doble
– *double cradle*
69 la cuna de dos ruedas *f*
– *two-wheel cradle*
70 los rodillos del tren de poleas *f*
– *running wheels*
71 el freno del cable portante, un freno de emergencia *f* en caso *m* de rotura *f* del cable tractor
– *suspension cable brake (supporting cable brake), an emergency brake in case of haulage cable failure*
72 la articulación (el eje, el bulón) de la suspensión
– *suspension gear bolt*
73 el manguito del cable tractor
– *haulage cable sleeve*
74 el manguito del contracable
– *balance cable sleeve (lower cable sleeve)*
75 la protección para evitar los descarrilamientos
– *derailment guard*
76 **pilones *m* de teleférico *m* (pilones *m* intermedios)**
– **cable supports (ropeway supports, suspension line supports, intermediate supports)*
77 el castillete de acero *m* con estructura *f* de celosía *f*, un castillete armado
– *pylon, a framework support*
78 el castillete (el pilón) de tubos *m* de acero *m*, un apoyo tubular de acero *m*
– *tubular steel pylon, a tubular steel support*
79 el soporte del cable portante (el soporte de apoyo *m*)
– *suspension cable guide rail (supporting cable guide rail, support guide rail)*
80 el andamio (las horcas) del pilón, un montaje para los trabajos en los cables
– *support truss, a frame for work on the cable*
81 los cimientos del pilón
– *base of the support*

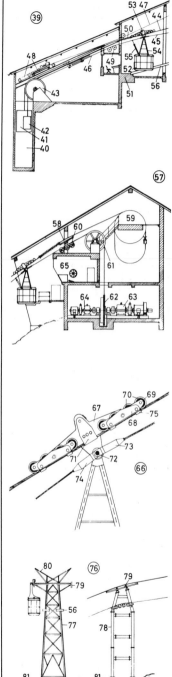

1 el corte transversal de un puente
– *cross-section of a bridge*
2 la plataforma del tablero ortogonal anisótropo
– *orthotropic roadway (orthotropic deck)*
3 la armadura sobre puntales *m*
– *truss (bracing)*
4 el apuntalamiento (el arriostramiento)
– *diagonal brace (diagonal strut)*
5 el cajón hueco
– *hollow tubular section*
6 la chapa del tablero
– *deck slab*
7 el puente de vigas *f*
– *solid-web girder bridge (beam bridge)*
8 el borde superior del tablero
– *road surface*
9 el larguero (arco *m*) superior
– *top flange*
10 el larguero (arco *m*) inferior
– *bottom flange*
11 el soporte (el apoyo) fijo
– *fixed bearing*
12 el soporte (el apoyo) móvil
– *movable bearing*
13 el tramo de puente *m*
– *clear span*
14 la abertura (la luz)
– *span*
15 el puente de cuerdas *f* (el puente colgante primitivo)
– *rope bridge (primitive suspension bridge)*
16 el cable portador
– *carrying rope*
17 el cable colgante
– *suspension rope*
18 la pasarela trenzada
– *woven deck (woven decking)*
19 el puente de acros *m* de piedra *f* (un puente de piedra *f*), un puente macizo
– *stone arch bridge, a solid bridge*
20 el arco del puente
– *arch*
21 el pilar del puente
– *pier*
22 la figura (la estatua) del puente
– *statue of saint on bridge*
23 el puente de arco *m* de entramado *m*
– *trussed arch bridge*
24 el elemento de entramado *m*
– *truss element*
25 el arco de entramado *m*
– *trussed arch*
26 al abertura del arco
– *arch span*
27 el pilar de tierra *f*
– *abutment (end pier)*

28 el puente de arco *m* sobre pilares *m*
– *spandrel-braced arch bridge*
29 el arranque del arco (el espolón)
– *abutment (abutment pier)*
30 el pilar del puente
– *bridge strut*
31 el vértice del arco
– *crown*
32 el puente de casas *f* medieval (el Puente Vecchio de Florencia)
– *covered bridge of the Middle Ages (the Ponte Vecchio in Florence)*
33 el comercio de orfebre *m*
– *goldsmiths' shops*
34 el puente de entramado *m* metálico
– *steel lattice bridge*
35 la diagonal (puntal *m*)
– *counterbrace (crossbrace, diagonal member)*
36 el pilar del puente (la vertical)
– *vertical member*
37 el nudo del entramado
– *truss joint*
38 el pórtico del extremo
– *portal frame*
39 el puente colgante
– *suspension bridge*
40 el cable portador
– *suspension cable*
41 el colgante
– *suspender (hanger)*
42 el pilón (pórtico *m* de puente *m*)
– *tower*
43 el amarre del cable portador
– *suspension cable anchorage*
44 el tirante
– *tied beam [with roadway]*
45 el espolón
– *abutment*
46 el puente de cables *m* oblicuos
– *cable-stayed bridge*
47 el cable de enganche *m* (el cable oblicuo)
– *inclined tension cable*
48 el amarre del cable oblicuo
– *inclined cable anchorage*
49 el puente de hormigón *m* armado
– *reinforced concrete bridge*
50 el arco de hormigón *m* armado
– *reinforced concrete arch*
51 el sistema de cables *m* oblicuos
– *inclined cable system (multiple cable system)*
52 el puente llano, un puente sin pared *f*
– *flat bridge, a plate girder bridge*
53 el tensor transversal
– *stiffener*
54 el pilar
– *pier*
55 el apoyo (apoyo *m* de puente *m*)
– *bridge bearing*

56 el rompehielos
– *cutwater*
57 el puente de elementos *m* prefabricados
– *straits bridge, a bridge built of precast elements*
58 el elemento prefabricado
– *precast construction unit*
59 el viaducto
– *viaduct*
60 la vaguada
– *valley bottom*
61 el pilar de hormigón *m* armado
– *reinforced concrete pier*
62 el andamiaje
– *scaffolding*
63 el puente metálico de celosía *f* giratorio
– *lattice swing bridge*
64 la corona de rotación *f* (la corona giratoria)
– *turntable*
65 el pilar de rotación *f* (el pilar giratorio)
– *pivot pier*
66 la mitad giratoria del puente (el medio puente)
– *pivoting half (pivoting section, pivoting span, movable half) of bridge*
67 el puente giratorio llano
– *flat swing bridge*
68 la pared central
– *middle section*
69 la espiga de giro *m*
– *pivot*
70 el parapeto (la barandilla del puente)
– *parapet (handrailing)*

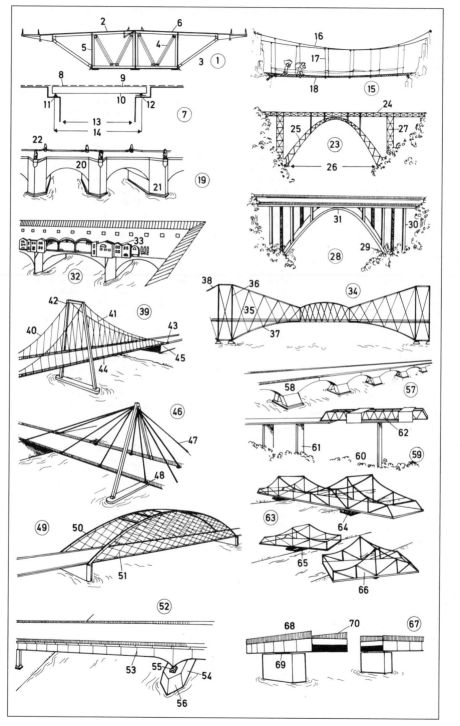

1 la **balsa de cuerda** *f (con propul-sión f propia:* balsa *f* con motor *m; también:* balsa *f* de cadena *f; Cuba:* el andarivel); una balsa para pasajeros *m*
– *cable ferry (also: chain ferry), a passenger ferry*
2 el cable (la cuerda) de la balsa
– *ferry rope (ferry cable)*
3 el brazo de río *m*
– *river branch (river arm)*
4 el islote fluvial
– *river island (river islet)*
5 la parte desplomada de la orilla del río, efecto *m* de una inun-dación
– *collapsed section of riverbank, flood damage*
6 **el transbordador con motor** *m*
– *motor ferry*
7 el embarcadero de los barcos de motor *m*
– *ferry landing stage (motorboat landing stage)*
8 la cimentación sobre pilotes *m*
– *pile foundations*
9 la corriente (el curso del río)
– *current (flow, course)*
10 la balsa volante (el puente volante, la balsa de río *m*), un transbordador de coches *m*
– *flying ferry (river ferry), a car ferry*
11 el transbordador
– *ferry boat*
12 el flotador
– *buoy (float)*
13 el anclaje
– *anchorage*
14 el lugar de anclaje *m* (el puerto de protección *f,* el puerto de invierno *m*)
– *harbour (Am. harbor) for laying up river craft*
15 **la barca de botador** *m,* una barca de pértiga *f (Bol. y Ec.:* la mon-tería)
– *ferry boat (punt)*
16 la pértiga (*Ec.:* el guare; *Perú:* la tangona)
– *pole (punt pole, quant pole)*
17 el barquero (*Col.:* el pasero)
– *ferryman*
18 el brazo muerto del río
– *blind river branch (blind river arm)*
19 el malecón (*Amér. Central y Chile:* el tajamar)
– *groyne (Am. groin)*
20 el espigón (la cabeza del malecón)
– *groyne (Am. groin) head*
21 el canal de navegación *f* (parte *m* del cauce)
– *fairway (navigable part of river)*

22 **la flotilla de remolque** *m*
– *train of barges*
23 el remolcador fluvial de vapor *m*
– *river tug*
24 el cable de remolque *m*
– *tow rope (tow line, towing hawser)*
25 la lancha de remolque *m* (la lan-cha de carga *f,* la gabarra)
– *barge (freight barge, cargo barge, lighter)*
26 el gabarrero
– *bargeman (bargee, lighterman)*
27 **la navegación al la sirga**
– *towing (hauling, haulage)*
28 el mástil de sirga *f*
– *towing mast*
29 el motor de sirga *f*
– *towing engine*
30 la vía de sirga *f*
– *towing track;* form.: *tow path (towing path)*
31 el río, después de la regulación del río
– *river after river training*
32 **el dique contra la inundación** (el dique de invierno *m*)
– *dike (dyke, main dike, flood wall, winter dike)*
33 el canal de desagüe *m*
– *drainage ditch*
34 la esclusa del dique (*Col., Chile, Guat. y Perú:* la toma)
– *dike (dyke) drainage sluice*
35 el muro de ala *f*
– *wing wall*
36 el desagüe, una zanja de drenaje *m*
– *outfall*
37 la zanja lateral (la evacuación del agua *f* de infiltración *f*)
– *drain (infiltration drain)*
38 la berma del dique
– *berm (berme)*
39 la coronación del dique
– *top of dike (dyke)*
40 el declive (la escarpa) del dique
– *dike (dyke) batter (dike slope)*
41 el lecho de inundación *f*
– *flood bed (inundation area)*
42 la zona de inundación *f*
– *flood containment area*
43 el indicador de la corriente
– *current meter*
44 el tablero kilométrico
– *kilometre (Am. kilometer) sign*
45 la casa del guarda del dique; *tam-bién:* la casa del balsero
– *dikereeve's (dykereeve's) house (dikereeve's cottage); also: ferry-man's house (cottage)*
46 el guarda del dique
– *dikereeve (dykereeve)*
47 la rampa del dique
– *dike (dyke) ramp*

48 el dique de verano *m*
– *summer dike (summer dyke)*
49 la presa (el dique) de río *m* (*Col.:* la tupia)
– *levee (embankment)*
50 los sacos de arena *f*
– *sandbags*
51-55 **la consolidación de la orilla**
– *bank protection (bank stabiliza-tion, revetment)*
51 la capa (el relleno) de piedras *f*
– *riprap*
52 el depósito aluvial (el depósito de arena *f*)
– *alluvial deposit (sand deposit)*
53 la fajina (el haz de ramas *f*)
– *fascine (bundle of wooden sticks)*
54 las cercas trenzadas
– *wicker fences*
55 el revestimiento de piedras *f* (el muro de contención *f*)
– *stone pitching*
56 **la draga flotante,** una draga con cadena *f* de cangilones *m*
– *floating dredging machine (dredger), a multi-bucket ladder dredge*
57 la cadena de cangilones *m*
– *bucket elevator chain*
58 el cangilón de extracción *f*
– *dredging bucket*
59 **la draga de succión** *f,* con tubo *m* descendente de aspiración *f* o aspirador *m* de gabarras *f*
– *suction dredger (hydraulic dredger) with trailing suction pipe or barge sucker*
60 la bomba de agua *f* a presión *f*
– *centrifugal pump*
61 la válvula de limpiado *m* de retroacción *f*
– *back scouring valve*
62 la bomba de succión *f,* una bomba de manga *f* con boquillas *f*
– *suction pump, a jet pump with scouring nozzles*

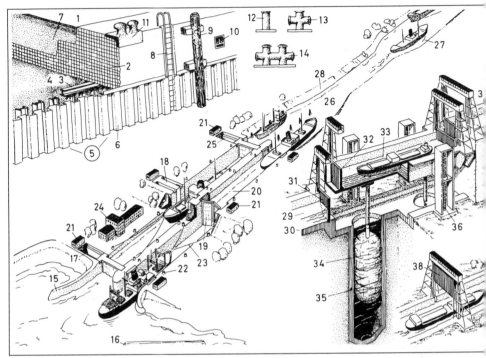

1-14 el muro de muelle *m*
– *quay wall*
1 el pavimento
– *road surface*
2 el cuerpo del muro
– *body of wall*
3 la viga de acero *m*
– *steel sleeper*
4 el pilote de acero *m*
– *steel pile*
5 la hilera de estacas *f* (el tablestacado)
– *sheet pile wall (sheet pile bulkhead, sheet piling)*
6 la tablestaca (la chapa de hierro *m*)
– *box pile*
7 el terraplén (el relleno)
– *backfilling (filling)*
8 la escala
– *ladder*
9 la defensa (pilote *m* de defensa *f*)
– *fender (fender pile)*
10 el nicho bolardo (la cruz de amarre *m*)
– *recessed bollard*
11 el noray (el bolardo) doble
– *double bollard*
12 el noray (el bolardo)
– *bollard*
13 el noray en forma *f* de cruz *f*
– *cross-shaped bollard (cross-shaped mooring bitt)*
14 el noray de doble cruz *f*
– *double cross-shaped bollard (double cross-shaped mooring bitt)*
15-28 el canal
– *canal*

15 *u.* 16 la entrada del canal
– *canal entrance*
15 el malecón (*Amér. Central y Chile:* el tajamar)
– *mole*
16 el rompeolas
– *breakwater*
17-25 la escalera de esclusas *f*
– *staircase of locks*
17 la testa de abajo (el morro inferior)
– *lower level*
18 la compuerta de esclusa *f*, una puerta de corredera *f*
– *lock gate, a sliding gate*
19 la puerta de esclusa *f*
– *mitre (Am. miter) gate*
20 la esclusa (la cámara de la esclusa; *Col., Chile, Guat., y Perú:* la toma)
– *lock (lock chamber)*
21 la sala de máquina *f*
– *power house*
22 el cabrestante de arrastre *m*, un cabrestante
– *warping capstan (hauling capstan), a capstan*
23 el cable de arrastre *m*, un cable (un cabo)
– *warp*
24 el edificio de administración *f* (*ejemplo:* la administración del canal, el servicio de protección *f* de las aguas, la aduana)
– *offices (e.g. canal administration, river police, customs)*
25 la testa de arriba (el morro superior)
– *upper level (head)*

26 el antepuerto de la esclusa, un antepuerto
– *lock approach*
27 el flanco del canal (el apartadero)
– *lay-by*
28 el talud de orilla *f*
– *bank slope*
29-38 el elevador de barcos *m*
– *boat lift (Am. boat elevator)*
29 el tramo inferior del canal
– *lower pound (lower reach)*
30 el fondo del canal
– *canal bed*
31 la puerta del tramo final, una puerta elevadora
– *pound lock gate, a vertical gate*
32 la puerta de cierre *m* de la cámara
– *lock gate*
33 el depósito del barco
– *boat tank (caisson)*
34 el flotador, un cuerpo ascensional
– *float*
35 el pozo del flotador
– *float shaft*
36 el husillo (el tornillo) de elevación *f*
– *lifting spindle*
37 el tramo superior del canal
– *upper pound (upper reach)*
38 la puerta levadiza
– *vertical gate*
39-46 la central hidráulica de bombeo *m*
– *pumping plant and reservoir*
39 el embalse artificial
– *forebay*

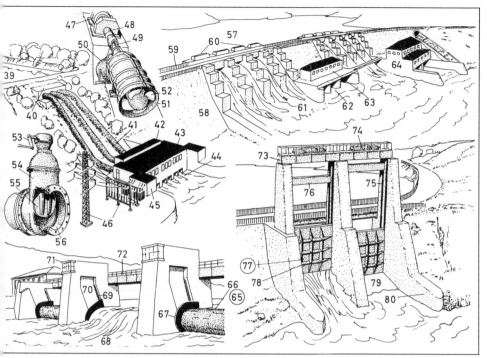

40 el depósito de distribución *f* (la cámara de carga *f*)
– *surge tank*
41 la tubería bajo presión *f*
– *pressure pipeline*
42 la sala de válvulas *f* de compuertas *f*
– *valve house (valve control house)*
43 la sala de turbinas *f* (la sala de bombeo *m*)
– *turbine house (pumping station)*
44 la construcción de salida *f*
– *discharge structure (outlet structure)*
45 la sala de mandos *m*
– *control station*
46 la instalación del transformador
– *transformer station*
47-52 la bomba de rueda *f* de paletas *f* (la bomba de hélice *f*)
– *axial-flow pump (propeller pump)*
47 el motor de impulsión *f*
– *drive motor*
48 la transmisión
– *gear*
49 el árbol motor
– *drive shaft*
50 el tubo de presión *f*
– *pressure pipe*
51 el embudo de aspiración *f*
– *suction head*
52 la rueda de paletas *f* (la hélice)
– *impeller wheel*
53-56 la corredera (la válvula compuerta *f* de paso *m* o de cierre *m*)
– *sluice valve (sluice gate)*
53 la impulsión (el mando) de manivela *f*
– *crank drive*

54 el cuerpo de la válvula
– *valve housing*
55 la válvula
– *sliding valve (sliding gate)*
56 la abertura de descarga *f*
– *discharge opening*
57-64 la presa (*Col.:* la tupia)
– *dam (barrage)*
57 el pantano (*Col.:* el pantanero)
– *reservoir (storage reservoir, impounding reservoir, impounded reservoir)*
58 el muro de contención *f*
– *masonry dam*
59 la coronación del muro
– *crest of dam*
60 el rebosadero (aliviadero *m*)
– *spillway (overflow spillway)*
61 la zona de caída *f*
– *stilling basin (stilling box, stilling pool)*
62 la descarga del fondo
– *scouring tunnel (outlet tunnel, waste water outlet)*
63 la sala de válvulas *f* de compuertas *f*
– *valve house (valve control house)*
64 la sala de turbinas *f*
– *power station*
65-72 el dique de cilindros *m* (la presa cilíndrica), una represa; *otro sistema:* el dique basculante
– *rolling dam (weir), a barrage; other system: shutter weir*
65 el cilindro, el cuerpo de contención *f*
– *roller, a barrier*

66 el coronamiento del cilindro
– *roller top*
67 la chapa lateral
– *flange*
68 el cilindro sumergible
– *submersible roller*
69 la cremallera
– *rack track*
70 el nicho
– *recess*
71 la cabina del mecanismo de elevación *f*
– *hoisting gear cabin*
72 la pasarela de servicio *m*
– *service bridge (walkway)*
73-80 la presa de compuertas *f*
– *sluice dam*
73 el puente del mecanismo de elevación *f* por enrollamiento *m*
– *hoisting gear bridge*
74 el mecanismo de enrollamiento *m*
– *hoisting gear (winding gear)*
75 el canal guía *f*
– *guide groove*
76 el contrapeso
– *counterweight (counterpoise)*
77 la compuerta
– *sluice gate (floodgate)*
78 el nervio de refuerzo *m*
– *reinforcing rib*
79 el fondo de la presa
– *dam sill (weir sill)*
80 el muro de la parte lateral (el contrafuerte)
– *wing wall*

1-6 el barco de remos *m* **germánico** [aproximadamente 400 d. J. C.]; el barco Nydam
– *Germanic rowing boat [ca. AD 400]; the Nydam boat*
1 el codaste
– *stern post*
2 el timonel
– *steersman*
3 los remeros
– *oarsman*
4 la roda
– *stem post (stem)*
5 el remo para bogar
– *oar, for rowing*
6 el timo (el remo timón), un timón lateral para gobernar
– *rudder (steering oar), a side rudder, for steering*
7 **la canoa** (*Col.:* el bote; *Ec.:* el guampo), un tronco de árbol *m* vaciado
– *dugout, a hollowed-out tree trunk*
8 la pagaya
– *paddle*
9-12 la trirreme, un barco de guerra *f* griego o romano
– *trireme, a Greek or Roman warship*
9 el espolón
– *ram*
10 el castillo
– *forecastle (fo'c'sle)*
11 el garabato, un gancho para sujetar el barco enemigo
– *grapple (grapnel, grappling iron), for fastening the enemy ship alongside*
12 las tres líneas de remos *m*
– *three banks (tiers) of oars*
13-17 el barco vikingo (dragón *m* vikingo, barco *m* dragón, el dragón marino, el caballo del mar) [nórdico antiguo]
– *Viking ship (longship, dragon ship) [Norse]*
13 la caña del timón (la barra)
– *helm (tiller)*
14 la horquilla del toldo, con cabezas *f* de caballos *m* esculpidas
– *awning crutch with carved horses' heads*
15 el toldo
– *awning*
16 la cabeza de dragón *m*
– *dragon figurehead*
17 el escudo de protección *f*
– *shield*
18-26 la kogge (la kogge anseática)
– *cog (Hansa cog, Hansa ship)*
18 el cable del ancla *f* (la marona del ancla *f*)
– *anchor cable (anchor rope, anchor hawser)*

19 el castillo de proa *f* (el castillo delantero)
– *forecastle (fo'c'sle)*
20 el bauprés
– *bowsprit*
21 la vela cuadrada aferrada
– *furled (brailed-up) square sail*
22 el pendón de la ciudad
– *town banner (city banner)*
23 el castillo de popa *f* (el castillo trasero)
– *aftercastle (sterncastle)*
24 el timón, un timón de codaste *m*
– *rudder, a stem rudder*
25 la popa redonda
– *elliptical stern (round stern)*
26 la defensa de madera *f*
– *wooden fender*
27-43 la carabela [Santa María, 1492]
– *caravel (carvel) ['Santa María' 1492]*
27 el camarote del almirante
– *admiral's cabin*
28 la verga de popa *f*
– *spanker boom*
29 la mesana, una vela latina
– *mizzen (mizen, mutton spanker, lateen spanker), a lateen sail*
30 la verga de mesana *f* (la verga latina)
– *lateen yard*
31 el palo de mesana *f*
– *mizzen (mizen) mast*
32 la ligada
– *lashing*
33 la vela mayor, una vela cuadrada
– *mainsail (main course), a square sail*
34 la boneta, una vela desmontable
– *bonnet, a removable strip of canvas*
35 la bolina
– *bowline*
36 el briol
– *bunt line (martinet)*
37 la verga mayor
– *main yard*
38 la gavia mayor
– *main topsail*
39 la verga de la gavia mayor
– *main topsail yard*
40 el palo mayor
– *mainmast*
41 la vela de trinquete *m*
– *foresail (fore course)*
42 el palo de trinquete *m*
– *foremast*
43 la cebadera
– *spritsail*
44-50 la galera [siglos XV a XVIII], una galera de esclavos *m*
– *galley [15th to 18th century], a slave galley*
44 el fanal (el farol de popa *f*)
– *lantern*

45 el camarote
– *cabin*
46 la crujía
– *central gangway*
47 el vigilante de los esclavos (el cómitre), con látigo *m*
– *slave driver with whip*
48 los esclavos de la galera (los esclavos remeros, los galeotes)
– *galley slaves*
49 la "rambata", una plataforma cubierta de proa *f*
– *covered platform in the forepart of the ship*
50 el cañón
– *gun*
51-60 el barco de línea *f* [siglos XVIII–XIX], un navío de tres puentes *m*
– *ship of the line (line-of-battle ship) [18th to 19th century], a three-decker*
51 el botalón de foque *m*
– *jib boom*
52 la vela de juanete *m* de proa *f*
– *fore topgallant sail*
53 la vela de juanete *m* del palo mayor
– *main topgallant sail*
54 la vela de juanete *m* de mesana *f*
– *mizzen (mizen) topgallant sail*
55-57 la popa ornamentada
– *gilded stern*
55 el espejo de popa *f*
– *upper stern*
56 la galería (el corredor) de popa *f*
– *stern gallery*
57 el mirador, una estructura con ventanas *f* laterales ornamentadas
– *quarter gallery, a projecting balcony with ornamental portholes*
58 la bovedilla
– *lower stern*
59 las troneras (las portas), para el fuego de andanada *f*
– *gunports for broadside fire*
60 el cierre de la porta
– *gunport shutter*

219 Barco de vela I

Sailing Ship I

1-72 el aparejo y el velamen de una corbeta de tres palos *m*
- *rigging (rig, tackle) and sails of a bark (barque)*
1-9 los palos
- *masts*
1 el bauprés con botalón *m*
- *bowsprit with jib boom*
2-4 el palo de trinquete *m*
- *foremast*
2 el macho del trinquete
- *lower foremast*
3 el mastelero de velacho *m*
- *fore topmast*
4 el mastelero del juanete de proa *f*
- *fore topgallant mast*
5-7 el palo mayor
- *mainmast*
5 el macho del palo mayor
- *lower mainmast*
6 el mastelero de gavia *f*
- *main topmast*
7 el mastelero de juanete *m* mayor
- *main topgallant mast*
8 *u.* **9** el palo de mesana *f*
- *mizzen (mizen) mast*
8 el macho de mesana *f*
- *lower mizzen (lower mizen)*
9 el mastelero de mesana *f*
- *mizzen (mizen) topmast*
10-19 la jarcia muerta
- *standing rigging*
10 el estay
- *forestay, mizzen (mizen) stay, mainstay*
11 el estay del mastelero de trinquete *m*
- *fore topmast stay, main topmast stay, mizzen (mizen) topmast stay*
12 el estay mastelerillo de trinquete *m*
- *fore topgallant stay, mizzen (mizen) topgallant stay, main topgallant stay*
13 el estay mastelerillo sobrejuanete
- *fore royal stay (main royal stay)*
14 el estay de foque *m*
- *jib stay*
15 el barbiquejo
- *bobstay*
16 los obenques
- *shrouds*
17 los obenques de mastelero *m*
- *fore topmast rigging (main topmast rigging, mizzen (mizen) topmast rigging)*
18 los obenques de mastelerillo *m* de trinquete *m*
- *fore topgallant rigging (main topgallant rigging)*
19 los brandales
- *backstays*
20-31 las velas de cuchillo *m*
- *fore-and-aft sails*
20 el contrafoque
- *fore topmast staysail*

21 el fofoque (el foque de dentro)
- *inner jib*
22 el foque
- *outer jib*
23 el petifoque
- *flying jib*
24 la vela del estay de gavia *f*
- *main topmast staysail*
25 la vela del estay de juanete *m*
- *main topgallant staysail*
26 la vela del estay de sobrejuanete *m*
- *main royal staysail*
27 la vela del estay de mesana *f*
- *mizzen (mizen) staysail*
28 la vela del estay de sobremesana *f*
- *mizzen (mizen) topmast staysail*
29 la vela del estay de perico *m*
- *mizzen (mizen) topgallant staysail*
30 la vela cangreja (la mesana)
- *mizzen (mizen, spanker, driver)*
31 la escandalosa
- *gaff topsail*
32-45 las vergas
- *spars*
32 la verga de trinquete *m*
- *foreyard*
33 la verga de velacho *m* bajo
- *lower fore topsail yard*
34 la verga de velacho *m* alto
- *upper fore topsail yard*
35 la verga de juanete *m* bajo de proa *f*
- *lower fore topgallant yard*
36 la verga de juanete *m* alto de proa *f*
- *upper fore topgallant yard*
37 la verga de sobrejuanete *m* de proa *f*
- *fore royal yard*
38 la verga mayor
- *main yard*
39 la verga de gavia *f* baja
- *lower main topsail yard*
40 la verga de gavia *f* alta
- *upper main topsail yard*
41 la verga de juanete *m* mayor bajo
- *lower main topgallant yard*
42 la verga de juanete *m* mayor alto
- *upper main topgallant yard*
43 la verga de sobrejuanete *m* mayor
- *main royal yard*
44 la botavara
- *spanker boom*
45 el pico de la cangreja
- *spanker gaff*
46 el marchapié y estribos *m*
- *footrope*
47 los amantillos
- *lifts*
48 el amantillo de la botavara
- *spanker boom topping lift*
49 el amantillo del pico de la cangreja
- *spanker peak halyard*
50 la cofa de trinquete *m*
- *foretop*

51 la cruceta del mastelero de trinquete *m*
- *fore topmast crosstrees*
52 la cofa mayor (la cofa de gavia *f*)
- *maintop*
53 la cruceta del mastelero mayor (del mastelero de gavia *f*)
- *main topmast crosstrees*
54 la cofa de mesana *f*
- *mizzen (mizen) top*
55-66 las velas cuadradas
- *square sails*
55 la vela de trinquete *m*
- *foresail (fore course)*
56 el velacho bajo
- *lower fore topsail*
57 el velacho alto
- *upper fore topsail*
58 el juanete bajo
- *lower fore topgallant sail*
59 el juanete alto
- *upper fore topgallant sail*
60 el sobrejuanete
- *fore royal*
61 la vela mayor (la mayor)
- *mainsail (main course)*
62 la gavia baja
- *lower main topsail*
63 la gavia alta
- *upper main topsail*
64 el juanete mayor bajo
- *lower main topgallant sail*
65 el juanete mayor alto
- *upper main topgallant sail*
66 el sobrejuanete mayor
- *main royal sail*
67-71 las jarcias de labor *f*
- *running rigging*
67 las brazas
- *braces*
68 las escotas
- *sheets*
69 la escota de botavara *f*
- *spanker sheet*
70 la osta de la cangreja
- *spanker vangs*
71 los brioles
- *bunt line*
72 el rizo
- *reef*

Sf

1-5 formas *f* de velas *f*
– *sail shapes*
1 la vela cangreja
– *gaffsail (small: trysail, spencer)*
2 el foque (la vela de estay *m*)
– *jib*
3 la vela latina
– *lateen sail*
4 la vela al tercio
– *lugsail*
5 la vela de abanico *m*
– *spritsail*
6-8 veleros *m* de un solo palo
– *single-masted sailing boats (Am. sailboats)*
6 la balandra holandesa
– *tjalk*
7 la orza de deriva *f*
– *leeboard*
8 el cúter
– *cutter*
9 u. 10 veleros *m* con un palo de mesana *f*
– *mizzen (mizen) masted sailing boats (Am. sailboats)*
9 el queche
– *ketch-rigged sailing barge*
10 el quechemarín
– *yawl*
11-17 veleros *m* de dos palos *m*
– *two-masted sailing boats (Am. sailboats)*
11-13 la goleta de gavias *f*
– *topsail schooner*
11 la vela mayor
– *mainsail*
12 la cangreja del trinquete
– *boom foresail*
13 la redonda del trinquete (la cuadra)
– *square foresail*
14 el bergantín-goleta *f*
– *brigantine*
15 el palo de goleta *f* (el palo mayor) con velas *f* de cuchillo *m*
– *half-rigged mast with fore-and-aft sails*
16 el trinquete con velas *f* cuadras (redondas)
– *full-rigged mast with square sails*
17 el bergantín redondo
– *brig*
18-27 veleros *m* de tres palos *m*
– *three-masted sailing vessels (three-masters)*
18 la goleta de tres palos *m* con velas *f* cangrejas
– *three-masted schooner*
19 la goleta de tres palos *m* con gavias *f* en el trinquete
– *three-masted topsail schooner*
20 la goleta de gavias *f* de tres palos *m*
– *bark (barque) schooner*

21-23 el bricbarca (la corbeta) de tres palos *m* [compárese aparejo y velamen con la lámina 219]
– *bark (barque) [cf. illustration of rigging and sails in plate 219]*
21 el trinquete
– *foremast*
22 el palo mayor
– *mainmast*
23 el palo de mesana *f*
– *mizzen (mizen) mast*
24-27 el barco completamente aparejado
– *full-rigged ship*
24 el palo de mesana *f*
– *mizzen (mizen) mast*
25 la verga de cruz *f*
– *crossjack yard (crojack yard)*
26 la vela de cruz *f* (la vela redonda)
– *crossjack (crojack)*
27 la fila de portas *f*
– *ports*
28-31 veleros *m* de cuatro palos *m*
– *four-masted sailing ships (four-masters)*
28 la goleta de cuatro palos *m*
– *four-masted schooner*
29 la corbeta (el bricbarca) de cuatro palos *m*
– *four-masted bark (barque)*
30 el palo mayor popel
– *mizzen (mizen) mast*
31 el barco de cuatro palos *m* completamente aparejado
– *four-masted full-rigged ship*
32-34 la corbeta (el bricbarca) de cinco palos *m*
– *five-masted bark (barque)*
32 el sosobre
– *skysail*
33 el palo mayor
– *middle mast*
34 el palo mayor popel
– *mizzen (mizen) mast*
35-37 evolución *f* de los barcos de vela *f* en 400 años *m*
– *development of sailing ships over 400 years*
35 el barco de cinco palos *m* completamente aparejado "Preussen", 1902–1910
– *five-masted full-rigged ship 'Preussen' 1902-10*
36 el clíper inglés "Spindrift", 1867
– *English clipper ship 'Spindrift' 1867*
37 la carabela "Santa María", 1492
– *caravel (carvel) 'Santa Maria' 1492*

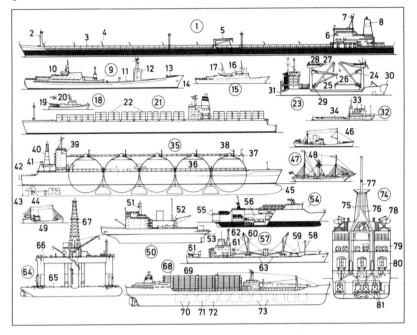

1 **el superpetrolero** (ULCC, ultra large crudeoil carrier) del tipo de puente *m* de mando *m* en la popa
- *ULCC (ultra-large crude carrier) of the 'all-aft' type*
2 el trinquete
- *foremast*
3 la pasarela con las tuberías
- *catwalk with the pipes*
4 la boca de incendio *m*
- *fire gun (fire nozzle)*
5 la grúa del puente
- *deck crane*
6 el castillo de popa *f* con el puente de mando *m*
- *deckhouse with the bridge*
7 el mástil de señales *f* y la antena del radar
- *aft signal (signalling) and radar mast*
8 la chimenea
- *funnel*
9 **un buque experimental a propulsión** *f* **nuclear,** el carguero a granel *m* "Otto Hahn"
- *nuclear research ship 'Otto Hahn', a bulk carrier*
10 las superestructuras de popa *f* (la sala de máquinas *f*)
- *aft superstructure (engine room)*
11 la escotilla de carga *f*
- *cargo hatchway for bulk goods (bulk cargoes)*
12 el puente de mando *m*
- *bridge*
13 el castillo de proa *f*
- *forecastle (fo'c'sle)*
14 la roda
- *stem*
15 **el barco de recreo** *m*
- *seaside pleasure boat*
16 la chimenea falsa
- *dummy funnel*
17 el conducto para el escape de gases *m*
- *exhaust mast*
18 **el buque de salvamento** *m*
- *rescue cruiser*
19 la plataforma de aterrizaje *m* para los helicópteros (el puente de maniobras *f*)
- *helicopter platform (working deck)*
20 el helicóptero de salvamento *m*
- *rescue helicopter*
21 **el buque portacontenedores**
- *all-container ship*

22 los contenedores estibados en la cubierta
- *containers stowed on deck*
23 **el carguero**
- *cargo ship*
24-29 la instalación para la manipulación de las mercancías
- *cargo gear (cargo-handling gear)*
24 el mástil bípodo
- *bipod mast*
25 el mástil de carga *f* de gran capacidad *f*
- *jumbo derrick boom (heavy-lift derrick boom)*
26 la botavara (la flecha)
- *derrick boom (cargo boom)*
27 la candaliza (sistema *m* de poleas *f*; polispasto *m*)
- *tackle*
28 la polea
- *block*
29 el cojinete de aguante *m*
- *thrust bearing*
30 la porta de la roda
- *bow doors*
31 la porta de carga *f* de popa *f*
- *stern loading door*
32 **el reavituallador de las perforaciones off-shore** (perforación *f* en el mar)
- *offshore drilling rig supply vessel*
33 las superestructuras
- *compact superstructure*
34 el puente de carga *f* (el puente de maniobras *f*)
- *loading deck (working deck)*
35 **el buque cisterna** *f* **para gas** *m* **líquido**
- *liquefied-gas tanker*
36 el tanque esférico
- *spherical tank*
37 el mástil (la antena) de televisión *f* para la navegación
- *navigational television receiver mast*
38 el conducto para la salida del gas
- *vent mast*
39 el puente de mando *m*
- *deckhouse*
40 la chimenea
- *funnel*
41 el ventilador
- *ventilator*
42 el espejo de popa *f*
- *transom stern (transom)*
43 la pala del timón
- *rudder blade (rudder)*

44 la hélice
- *ship's propeller (ship's screw)*
45 el bulbo de la roda
- *bulbous bow*
46 el buque de pesca *f* de arrastre *m*
- *steam trawler*
47 **el buque faro** *m* (faro *m* flotante)
- *lightship (light vessel)*
48 el farol (el fanal)
- *lantern (characteristic light)*
49 el barco de pesca *f*
- *smack*
50 **el buque rompehielos**
- *ice breaker*
51 la luz de navegación *f*
- *steaming light mast*
52 el hangar de los helicópteros
- *helicopter hangar*
53 el punto de fijación *f* a la popa para remolcar a un barco por la proa
- *stern towing point, for gripping the bow of ships in tow*
54 **el transbordador de mercancías** *f* (el barco de carga *f* horizontal)
- *roll-on-roll-off (ro-ro) trailer ferry*
55 la porta de carga *f* con rampa *f* de acceso *m*
- *stern port (stern opening) with ramp*
56 el montacargas para vehículos *m* pesados
- *heavy vehicle lifts (Am. heavy vehicle elevators)*
57 **el carguero multifuncional**
- *multi-purpose freighter*
58 el mástil de carga *f* y ventilador *m*
- *ventilator-type samson (sampson) post (ventilator-type king post)*
59 la botavara (la flecha)
- *derrick boom (cargo boom, cargo gear, cargo-handling gear)*
60 el mástil de carga *f*
- *derrick mast*
61 la grúa del puente
- *deck crane*
62 el mástil de carga *f* de gran capacidad *f*
- *jumbo derrick boom (heavy-lift derrick boom)*
63 la escotilla de carga *f*
- *cargo hatchway*
64 **la plataforma de perforación** *f* **semisumergible**
- *semisubmersible drilling vessel*
65 el flotador con la maquinaria
- *floating vessel with machinery*

66 la plataforma de perforación *f*
– *drilling platform*
67 la torre de perforación *f* (de extracción *f*)
– *derrick*
68 el buque de transporte *m* de ganado *m*
– *cattleship (cattle vessel)*
69 las superestructuras para el transporte de ganado *m*
– *superstructure for transporting livestock*
70 los tanques de agua *f* dulce
– *fresh water tanks*
71 el tanque de combustible *m*
– *fuel tank*
72 el tanque del estiércol
– *dung tank*
73 los tanques de forraje *m*
– *fodder tanks*
74 **el transbordador de trenes** *m* (el buque portatrenes, el ferry) [sección transversal]
– *train ferry [cross section]*
75 la chimenea
– *funnel*
76 las tuberías para el escape de gases *m*
– *exhaust pipes*
77 el mástil
– *mast*
78 el bote salvavidas (*Amér. Central y Pan.*: la panga) en su pescante *m* (en la serviola)
– *ship's lifeboat hanging at the davit*
79 la cubierta para automóviles *m*
– *car deck*
80 la cubierta para trenes *m*
– *main deck (train deck)*
81 las máquinas principales
– *main engines*
82 **el transatlántico** (buque *m* de pasajeros *m*; un barco de línea *f*)
– *passenger liner (liner, ocean liner)*
83 la roda
– *stem*
84 la chimenea con revestimiento *m* de rejilla *f*
– *funnel with lattice casing*
85 el empavesado (conjunto *m* de banderas *f* izadas de proa *f* a popa *f* para las fiestas o el primer viaje)
– *flag dressing (rainbow dressing, string of flags extending over mastheads, e.g., on the maiden voyage)*
86 **el pesquero de arrastre** *m*, un buque fac- toría *f*
– *trawler, a factory ship*

87 la horca
– *gallows*
88 la rampa de popa *f*
– *stern ramp*
89 **el carguero portacontenedores**
– *container ship*
90 la carga sobre la cubierta
– *loading bridge (loading platform)*
91 la escala de gato *m*
– *sea ladder (jacob's ladder, rope ladder)*
92 **el remolcador de empuje** *m* **y la gabarra** (chalana *f*; barcaza *f*), dos embarcaciones *f* de interior
– *barge and push tug assembly*
93 el remolcador de empuje *m* (*Amér. Central y Ven.*: el bombote; *Bol., Col., Ec. y Perú*: el batelón)
– *push tug*
94 la gabarra (la chalana) sin motor *m* (*Amér.*: el bongo)
– *tug-pushed dumb barge (tug-pushed lighter)*
95 el barco del práctico
– *pilot boat*
96 **el buque mixto de carga** *f* **y pasajeros** *m*
– *combined cargo and passenger liner*
97 el desembarco de pasajeros *m* por medio de botes *m*
– *passengers disembarking by boat*
98 la escala real
– *accommodation ladder*
99 el buque de cabotaje *m*
– *coaster (coasting vessel)*
100 la lancha aduanera
– *customs or police launch*
101-128 **el vapor de recreo** *m* (el vapor para hacer cruceros *m*)
– *excursion steamer (pleasure steamer)*
101-106 la instalación para la botadura del bote salvavidas
– *lifeboat launching gear*
101 el pescante (la serviola)
– *davit*
102 el brazalete intermedio
– *wire rope span*
103 el guardamancebo
– *lifeline*
104 el aparejo
– *tackle*
105 el motón
– *block*

106 la beta del aparejo
– *fall*
107 el bote salvavidas con su lona *f* impermeable
– *ship's lifeboat (ship's boat) covered with tarpaulin*
108 la roda
– *stem*
109 el pasajero
– *passenger*
110 el camarero (de buque *m*)
– *steward*
111 la tumbona de cubierta *f*
– *deck-chair*
112 el grumete
– *deck hand*
113 el balde
– *deck bucket*
114 el contramaestre
– *boatswain (bo's'n, bo'sun, bosun)*
115 la marinera
– *tunic*
116 el toldo
– *awning*
117 el puntal del toldo
– *stanchion*
118 el listón del toldo
– *ridge rope (jackstay)*
119 la trinca
– *lashing*
120 la amurada
– *bulwark*
121 la barandilla
– *guard rail*
122 el pasamano
– *handrail (top rail)*
123 la escalera de cámara *f*
– *companion ladder (companionway)*
124 la guindola
– *lifebelt (lifebuoy)*
125 el farol de la guindola
– *lifebuoy light (lifebelt light, signal light)*
126 el oficial de guardia *f*
– *officer of the watch (watchkeeper)*
127 la guerrera de marinero *m*
– *reefer (Am. pea jacket)*
128 los gemelos (los anteojos, los prismáticos)
– *binoculars*

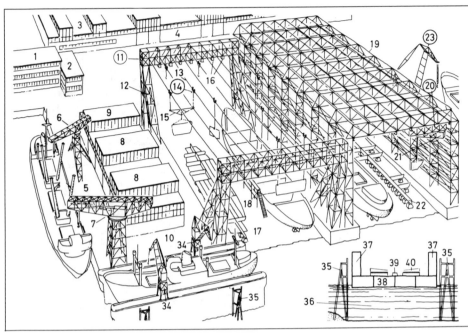

1-43 el astillero (el arsenal; la atarazana)
- *shipyard (shipbuilding yard, dock-yard,* Am. *navy yard)*
1 el edificio de la administración
- *administrative offices*
2 la oficina de dibujo *m* y proyectos *m* de barcos *m*
- *ship-drawing office*
3 *u.* **4** los cobertizos de construcción *f*
- *shipbuilding sheds*
3 la sala de trazado *m* y gálibos *m*
- *mould* (Am. *mold*) *loft*
4 el taller de montaje *m*
- *erection shop*
5-9 el muelle de armamento *m*
- *fitting-out quay*
5 el muelle
- *quay*
6 la grúa de trípode *m*
- *tripod crane*
7 la grúa de cabeza *f* de martillo *m*
- *hammer-headed crane*
8 el taller de maquinaria *f*
- *engineering workshop*
9 el taller de calderería *f*
- *boiler shop*
10 el muelle de reparaciones *f*
- *repair quay*
11-26 las instalaciones de la grada de construcción *f*
- *slipways (slips, building berths, building slips, stocks)*
11-18 la grada de grúa *f* de cable *m* (la grada de pórtico *m*), una grada de construcción *f*
- *cable crane berth, a slipway (build-ing berth)*
11 el pórtico de la grada
- *slipway portal*

12 el pilar del pórtico
- *bridge support*
13 el cable de la grúa
- *crane cable*
14 el carro corredizo
- *crab (jenny)*
15 el travesaño
- *cross piece*
16 la cabina del conductor de la grúa
- *crane driver's cabin (crane driver's cage)*
17 el suelo de la grada
- *slipway floor*
18 el andamiaje, un andamio
- *staging, a scaffold*
19-21 la grada de andamiaje *m*
- *frame slipway*
19 el andamiaje de la grada
- *slipway frame*
20 la grúa móvil de techo *m* (la grúa de caballete *m*)
- *overhead travelling* (Am. *traveling) crane (gantry crane)*
21 el carro corredizo giratorio
- *slewing crab*
22 la quilla en su posición *f*
- *keel in position*
23 la grúa giratoria de brazo *m* oscilante
- *luffing jib crane, a slipway crane*
24 el carril (la vía) de la grúa
- *crane rails (crane track)*
25 la grúa de pórtico *m* móvil (la grúa-puente)
- *gantry crane*
26 la grúa puente
- *gantry (bridge)*
27 las vigas (los pilares) del puente
- *trestles (supports)*

28 el carro corredizo (la grúa móvil)
- *crab (jenny)*
29 las cuadernas del buque en su posición *f*
- *hull frames in position*
30 el buque en construcción *f*
- *ship under construction*
31-33 el dique seco (la dársena de carenaje *m*)
- *dry dock*
31 el suelo del dique (el fondo del dique)
- *dock floor (dock bottom)*
32 la puerta del dique
- *dock gates (caisson)*
33 la casa de bombas *f* (el puesto de máquinas *f*)
- *pumping station (power house)*
34-43 el dique flotante
- *floating dock (pontoon dock)*
34 la grúa del dique, una grúa de brazo *m* oscilante
- *dock crane (dockside crane), a jib crane*
35 los pilotes de defensa *f* (los duques de alba)
- *fender pile*
36-43 la disposición del dique
- *working of docks*
36 la fosa del dique
- *dock basin*
37 *u.* **38** la estructura del dique
- *dock structure*
37 el tanque lateral (el cajón vertical)
- *side tank (side wall)*
38 el tanque del fondo (el cajón horizontal)
- *bottom tank (bottom pontoon)*
39 los picaderos de la quilla
- *keel block*

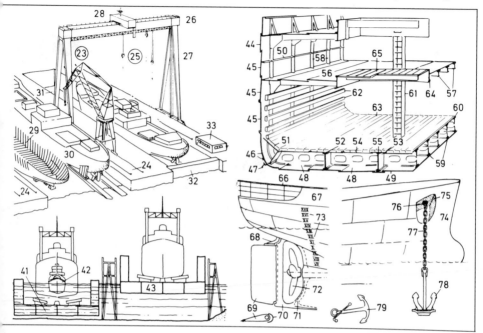

40 los picaderos del pantoque
– *bilge block (bilge shore, side support)*
41-43 la entrada de un buque en el dique
– *docking a ship*
41 el dique flotante inundado
– *flooded floating dock*
42 el remolcador atoando (llevando a remolque *m;* espiando) el buque
– *tug towing the ship*
43 el dique vaciado, después del bombeo del agua *f*
– *emptied (pumped-out) dock*
44-61 los elementos estructurales del buque
– *structural parts of the ship*
44-56 los refuerzos longitudinales
– *longitudinal structure*
44-49 el forro exterior
– *shell (shell plating, skin)*
44 la traca (la hilada) de cinta *f*
– *sheer strake*
45 la traca lateral
– *side strake*
46 la traca de pantoque *m*
– *bilge strake*
47 la quilla de balance *m* (la quilla de pantoque *m*)
– *bilge keel*
48 la traca de fondo *m* (la aparadura)
– *bottom plating*
49 la quilla plana
– *flat plate keel (keel plate)*
50 el trancanil
– *stringer (side stringer)*
51 la plancha marginal del tanque
– *tank margin plate*
52 la sobrequilla lateral
– *longitudinal side girder*

53 la sobrequilla
– *centre (Am. center) plate girder (centre girder, kelson, keelson, vertical keel)*
54 la cubierta del tanque
– *tank top plating (tank top, inner bottom plating)*
55 la traca central
– *centre (Am. center) strake*
56 las planchas de cubierta *f*
– *deck plating*
57 los baos
– *deck beam*
58 la cuaderna
– *frame (rib)*
59 la varenga
– *floor plate*
60 el doble fondo
– *cellular double bottom*
61 el puntal de la bodega
– *hold pillar (pillar)*
62 *u.* **63** las tablas de estiba *f*
– *dunnage*
62 el forro lateral interior de la bodega (las serretas)
– *side battens (side ceiling, spar ceiling)*
63 el forro interior del suelo de la bodega
– *ceiling (floor ceiling)*
64 *u.* **65** la escotilla
– *hatchway*
64 la brazola de la escotilla
– *hatch coaming*
65 el cuartel (la tapa) de la escotilla
– *hatch cover (hatchboard)*
66-72 la popa
– *stern*
66 la barandilla (la batayola)
– *guard rail*

67 la amurada
– *bulwark*
68 la caña del timón
– *rudder stock*
69 *u.* **70** el timón Oertz
– *Oertz rudder*
69 la pala del timón (el azafrán)
– *rudder blade (rudder)*
70 *u.* **71** el codaste
– *stern frame*
70 el codaste del timón
– *rudder post*
71 el codaste de la hélice
– *propeller post (screw post)*
72 la hélice del buque
– *ship's propeller (ship's screw)*
73 las marcas de calado *m*
– *draught (draft) marks*
74-79 la proa
– *bow*
74 la roda, una roda de bulbo *m* (la proa bulbosa)
– *stem, a bulbous stem (bulbous bow)*
75 el escobén del ancla
– *hawse*
76 el tubo del escobén
– *hawse pipe*
77 la cadena del ancla *f*
– *anchor cable (chain cable)*
78 el ancla *f* de patente *f* (el ancla *f* sin cepo *m*)
– *stockless anchor (patent anchor)*
79 el ancla *f* con cepo *m*
– *stocked anchor*

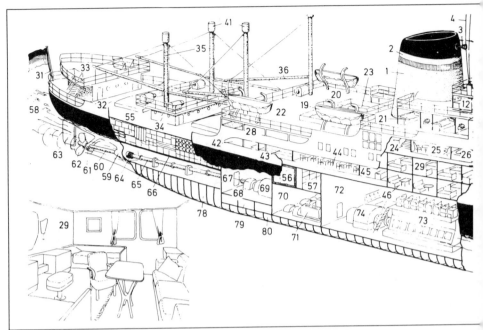

1-71 el barco mixto de carga *f* y pasaje *m* [de tipo antiguo]
- *combined cargo and passenger ship [of the older type]*
1 la chimenea
- *funnel*
2 la contraseña de la chimenea
- *funnel marking*
3 la sirena (la señal usada cuando hay niebla *f*)
- *siren (fog horn)*
4-11 la cubierta de marcación *f* (cubierta *f* goniométrica)
- *compass platform (compass bridge, compass flat, monkey bridge)*
4 las antenas
- *antenna lead-in (antenna down-lead)*
5 la antena de cuadro *m* radiogoniométrica
- *radio direction finder (RDF) antenna (direction finder antenna, rotatable loop antenna, aural null loop antenna)*
6 el compás magnético (la brújula)
- *magnetic compass (mariner's compass)*
7 la lámpara morse *m*
- *morse lamp (signalling, Am. signaling, lamp)*
8 la antena de radar *m*
- *radar antenna (radar scanner)*
9 las banderas de señales *f*
- *code flag signal*
10 la driza de las banderas de señales *f*
- *code flag halyards*

11 el estay de señales *f*
- *triatic stay (signal stay)*
12-18 el puente de mando *m* (el puente)
- *bridge deck (bridge)*
12 la cabina de radio *f*
- *radio room*
13 el camarote del capitán
- *captain's cabin*
14 el cuarto de derrota *f* (la cámara de los instrumentos)
- *navigating bridge*
15 la luz de navegación *f* de estribor *m* [verde; la luz de navegación *f* de babor *m* es roja]
- *starboard sidelight [green; port sidelight red]*
16 el ala *f* del puente de mando *m*
- *wing of bridge*
17 la cenefa (la tira de lona *f* que resguarda del viento)
- *shelter (weather cloth, dodger)*
18 la caseta del timón
- *wheelhouse*
19-21 la cubierta de botes *m*
- *boat deck*
19 el bote salvavidas
- *ship's lifeboat*
20 el pescante (la serviola)
- *davit*
21 el camarote de oficial *m*
- *officer's cabin*
22-27 la cubierta de paseo *m*
- *promenade deck*
22 la cubierta de sol *m*
- *sun deck (lido deck)*

23 la piscina
- *swimming pool*
24 la escalera de cámara *f*
- *companion ladder (companionway)*
25 la biblioteca
- *library (ship's library)*
26 el salón de tertulia *f*
- *lounge*
27 la galería de paseo *m*
- *promenade*
28-30 la cubierta A (la cubierta superior)
- *A-deck*
28 la cubierta semicerrada
- *semi-enclosed deck space*
29 el camarote doble (el camarote de dos camas *f*), un camarote (*Bol. y Río de la Plata:* una cucheta)
- *double-berth cabin, a cabin*
30 el camarote de lujo *m*
- *de luxe cabin*
31 el asta *f* de la bandera
- *ensign staff*
32-47 la cubierta B (la cubierta principal)
- *B-deck (main deck)*
32 la cubierta de popa *f*
- *after deck*
33 la toldilla
- *poop*
34 la chupeta (camareta *f* junto al coronamiento de popa *f*; la cámara alta)
- *deckhouse*

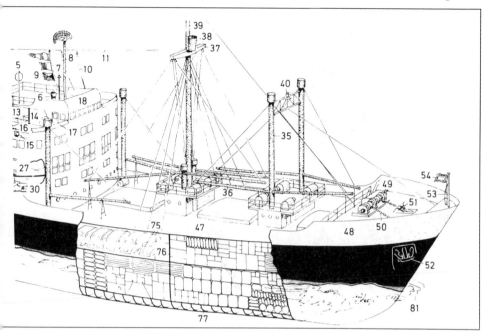

35 el poste de carga *f*
– *samson (sampson) post (king post)*
36 el botalón (la botavara)
– *derrick boom (cargo boom)*
37 la cruceta
– *crosstrees (spreader)*
38 la cofa
– *crow's nest*
39 el mastelero
– *topmast*
40 la luz de navegación *f* de proa *f*
– *forward steaming light*
41 la cabeza del ventilador
– *ventilator lead*
42 la cocina
– *galley (caboose, cookroom, ship's kitchen)*
43 la despensa
– *ship's pantry*
44 el comedor
– *dining room*
45 la oficina del sobrecargo
– *purser's office*
46 el camarote individual
– *single-berth cabin*
47 la cubierta de proa *f*
– *foredeck*
48 el castillo de proa *f*
– *forecastle (fo'c'sle)*
49-51 **el mecanismo de anclaje** *m*
– **ground tackle**
49 la maquinilla (el chigre del ancla *f; Arg.:* el guinche)
– *windlass*
50 la cadena del ancla *f*
– *anchor cable (chain cable)*

51 el estopor
– *compressor (chain compressor)*
52 el ancla *f*
– *anchor*
53 el asta *f* (el mástil) de la bandera de proa *f*
– *jackstaff*
54 la bandera de proa *f*
– *jack*
55 las bodegas de popa *f*
– *after holds*
56 la cámara frigorífica
– *cold storage room (insulated hold)*
57 el pañol
– *store room*
58 la estela
– *wake*
59 la chumacera de la hélice
– *shell bossing (shaft bossing)*
60 la cola del árbol (la parte de atrás del eje)
– *tail shaft (tail end shaft)*
61 el soporte del árbol
– *shaft strut (strut, spectacle frame, propeller strut, propeller bracket)*
62 la hélice de tres paletas *f*
– *three-blade ship's propeller (ship's screw)*
63 la pala del timón
– *rudder blade (rudder)*
64 el prensaestopas (la caja de estopas *f*)
– *stuffing box*
65 el árbol de la hélice (el eje de la hélice)
– *propeller shaft*

66 el túnel de árbol de la hélice
– *shaft alley (shaft tunnel)*
67 el tope de empuje *m*
– *thrust block*
68-74 **la propulsión Diesel eléctrica**
– **diesel-electric drive**
68 la sala de máquinas *f* eléctricas
– *electric engine room*
69 el motor eléctrico
– *electric motor*
70 la sala de máquinas *f* auxiliares
– *auxiliary engine room*
71 las máquinas auxiliares
– *auxiliary engines*
72 la sala de máquinas *f* principales
– *main engine room*
73 el motor principal, un motor Diesel
– *main engine, a diesel engine*
74 el generador
– *generator*
75 las bodegas de proa *f*
– *forward holds*
76 el entrepuente
– *tween deck*
77 la carga
– *cargo*
78 los tanques de lastre *m* de agua *f* (depósitos *m* de doble fondo *m*)
– *ballast tank (deep tank) for water ballast*
79 el tanque de agua *f* dulce
– *fresh water tank*
80 el tanque de combustible *m*
– *fuel tank*
81 la ola levantada por la proa
– *bow wave*

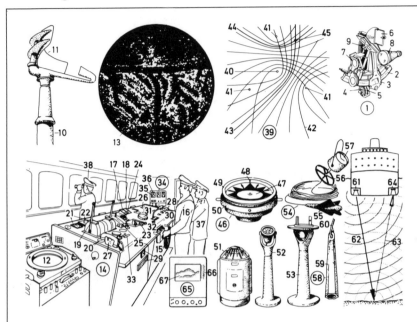

1 **el sextante**
- *sextant*
2 el arco graduado (el limbo)
- *graduated arc*
3 la alidada
- *index bar (index arm)*
4 el tambor micrométrico
- *decimal micrometer*
5 el nonio
- *vernier*
6 el espejo grande
- *index mirror*
7 el espejo pequeño
- *horizon glass (horizon mirror)*
8 el telescopio
- *telescope*
9 la empuñadura
- *grip (handgrip)*
10-13 **el aparato de radar** *m*
- *radar equipment (radar apparatus)*
10 el mástil del radar
- *radar pedestal*
11 la antena reflectora giratoria
- *revolving radar reflector*
12 la pantalla de radar *m*
- *radar display unit (radar screen)*
13 la imagen del radar
- *radar image (radar picture)*
14-38 **la caseta del timón**
- *wheelhouse*
14 el puesto de mando *m* y navegación *f*
- *steering and control position*
15 la rueda del timón
- *ship's wheel for controlling the rudder mechanism*
16 el timonel
- *helmsman (Am. wheelsman)*
17 el indicador del ángulo del timón
- *rudder angle indicator*
18 el piloto automático
- *automatic pilot (autopilot)*
19 el alzaprima de activación *f* de la hélice de paso *m* variable
- *control lever for the variable-pitch propeller (reversible propeller, feathering propeller, feathering screw)*
20 el indicador de paso *m* de la hélice
- *propeller pitch indicator*

21 el indicador de revoluciones *f* del motor principal
- *main engine revolution indicator*
22 el indicador de la velocidad del barco
- *ship's speedometer (log)*
23 el conmutador del timón de proa *f*
- *control switch for bow thruster (bow-manoeuvring, Am. maneuvering, propeller)*
24 el ecógrafo
- *echo recorder (depth recorder, echograph)*
25 el telégrafo transmisor de órdenes *f* a las máquinas
- *engine telegraph (engine order telegraph)*
26 el aparato de control *m* de los amortiguadores del balanceo
- *controls for the anti-rolling system (for the stabilizers)*
27 el teléfono interior a batería *f*
- *local-battery telephone*
28 el aparato de radiotelefonía *f* entre barcos *m*
- *shipping traffic radio telephone*
29 el panel indicador de las luces de navegación *f*
- *navigation light indicator panel (running light indicator panel)*
30 el micrófono del sistema de difusión *f* general (para órdenes *f* y llamadas *f*)
- *microphone for ship's address system*
31 el girocompás (la brújula giroscópica), un compás repetidor
- *gyro compass (gyroscopic compass), a compass repeater*
32 el botón de activación *f* de la sirena del barco
- *control button for the ship's siren (ship's fog horn)*
33 el control de la sobrecarga de los motores principales
- *main engine overload indicator*
34 el aparato Decca para la determinación de la posición del barco
- *Decca position-finder (Decca Navigator)*
35 el indicador de sintonización *f* aproximada
- *rough focusing indicator*
36 el indicador de sintonización *f* nítida
- *fine focusing indicator*

37 el oficial de navegación *f*
- *navigating officer*
38 el capitán
- *captain*
39 **el sistema de navegación** *f* **Decca**
- *Decca navigation system*
40 la estación principal
- *master station*
41 la estación secundaria
- *slave station*
42 la hipérbola cero
- *null hyperbola*
43 la hipérbola de posición *f* 1
- *hyperbolic position line 1*
44 la hipérbola de posición *f* 2
- *hyperbolic position line 2*
45 la posición [del barco]
- *position (fix, ship fix)*
46-53 **compases** *m*
- *compasses*
46 el compás líquido, una brújula magnética
- *liquid compass (fluid compass, spirit compass, wet compass), a magnetic compass*
47 la rosa náutica (la rosa de los vientos)
- *compass card*
48 la línea de fe *f*
- *lubber's line (lubber's mark, lubber's point)*
49 la caja de compás *m*
- *compass bowl*
50 la suspensión cardán
- *gimbal ring*
51-53 la brújula giroscópica (la instalación del girocompás)
- *gyro compass (gyroscopic compass, gyro compass unit)*
51 la brújula maestra (el compás matriz)
- *master compass (master gyro compass)*
52 el compás repetidor
- *compass repeater (gyro repeater)*
53 el compás repetidor con alidada *f*
- *compass repeater with pelorus*
54 **la corredera perfeccionada,** una corredera
- *patent log (screw log, mechanical log, towing log, taffrail log, speedometer), a log*
55 la hélice de la corredera
- *rotator*
56 el regulador de volante *m*
- *governor*

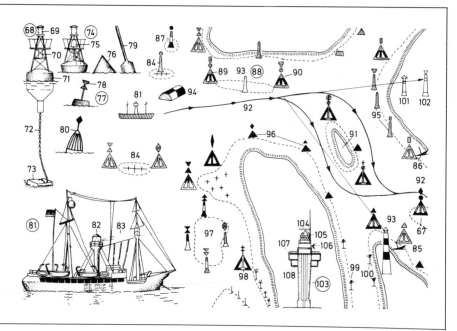

57 el contador de la corredera
- *log clock*
58-67 **sondas** *f*
- *leads*
58 la sonda de mano *m*
- *hand lead*
59 el escandallo
- *lead (lead sinker)*
60 la sondaleza
- *leadline*
61-67 la sonda acústica (la ecosonda)
- *echo sounder (echo sounding machine)*
61 el emisor de sonido *m*
- *sound transmitter*
62 el impulso de la onda sonora
- *sound wave (sound impulse)*
63 el eco
- *echo (sound echo, echo signal)*
64 el receptor del eco
- *echo receiver (hydrophone)*
65 el ecógrafo
- *echograph (echo sounding machine recorder)*
66 la escala de profundidad *f*
- *depth scale*
67 la imagen del eco
- *echogram (depth recording, depth reading)*
68-83 señales *f* en aguas *f* navegables
- *fairway marks (channel marks)*
68-108 **señales** *f* **marítimas**, de balizaje *m* y alumbrado *m*
- **sea marks** *(floating navigational marks) for buoyage and lighting systems*
68 la boya luminosa con silbato *m*
- *light and whistle buoy*
69 el fanal
- *light (warning light)*
70 el silbato
- *whistle*
71 el flotador
- *buoy*
72 la cadena del ancla
- *mooring chain*
73 la piedra de la boya (el ancla *f* de piedra *f*)
- *sinker (mooring sinker)*
74 la boya luminosa de campana *f*
- *light and bell buoy*
75 la campana
- *bell*

76 la boya cónica (de punta *f*)
- *conical buoy*
77 la boya achaflanada
- *can buoy*
78 la señal de tope *m*
- *topmark*
79 la boya con asta *f* (con punta *f*; la boya de espegue *m*)
- *spar buoy*
80 la boya baliza
- *topmark buoy*
81 el barco faro
- *lightship (light vessel)*
82 el mástil de señales
- *lantern mast (lantern tower)*
83 el haz de luz *f*
- *beam of light*
84-102 las señales de un canal navegable
- *fairway markings (channel markings) [German type]*
84 la boya [baliza *f* verde]
- *wreck [green buoys]*
85 naufragio *m* a estribor *m* del canal de navegación *f*
- *wreck to starboard*
86 naufragio *m* a babor del canal
- *wreck to port*
87 bajo *m*
- *shoals (shallows, shallow water, Am. flats)*
88 bajo *m* a babor *m* del canal de navegación *f* principal
- *middle ground to port*
89 bifurcación *f* [el comienzo del bajo; señales *f* de tope *m*: cilindro *m* rojo sobre globo *m* rojo]
- *division (bifurcation) [beginning of the middle ground; topmark: red cylinder above red ball]*
90 confluencia *f* [el final del bajo; señales *f* de tope *m*: cruz *f* de San Antonio roja sobre globo *m* rojo]
- *convergence (confluence) [end of the middle ground; topmark: red St. Antony's cross above red ball]*
91 bajo *m*
- *middle ground*
92 el canal principal
- *main fairway (main navigable channel)*

93 el canal secundario
- *secondary fairway (secondary navigable channel)*
94 la boya de barril *m*
- *can buoy*
95 boyas *f* de babor *m* [rojas]
- *port hand buoys (port hand marks) [red]*
96 boyas *f* de estribor *m* [negras]
- *starboard hand buoys (starboard hand marks) [black]*
97 bajo *m* fuera del canal de navegación *f*
- *shoals (shallows, shallow water, Am. flats) outside the fairway*
98 el centro del canal [señales *f* de tope *m*: cruz *f* doble]
- *middle of the fairway (mid-channel)*
99 postes *m* de estribor *m* [escobas *f* invertidas]
- *starboard markers [inverted broom]*
100 postes *m* de babor *m* [escobas *f* hacia arriba]
- *port markers [upward-pointing broom]*
101 *u.* **102** alineación *f* luminosa (dirección *f* de luces *f*)
- *range lights (leading lights)*
101 la luz de dirección *f* inferior
- *lower range light (lower leading light)*
102 la luz de dirección *f* superior
- *higher range light (higher leading light)*
103 el faro
- *lighthouse*
104 la antena de radar *m*
- *radar antenna (radar scanner)*
105 el fanal
- *lantern (characteristic light)*
106 la antena direccional de radio *f* (la antena radiogoniométrica)
- *radio direction finder (RDF) antenna*
107 el puente (la plataforma) de observación *f* y de máquinas *f*
- *machinery and observation platform (machinery and observation deck)*
108 la vivienda del guardián
- *living quarters*

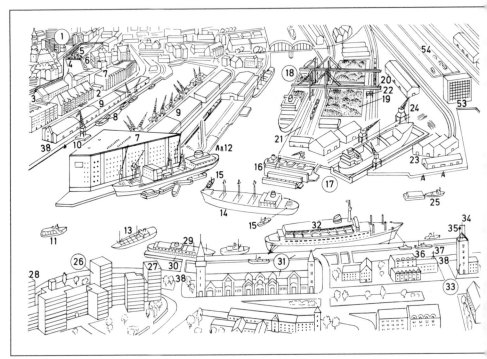

1 el barrio del puerto
- *dock area*
2 el puerto franco
- *free port (foreign trade zone)*
3 la frontera de la zona franca (la verja aduanera)
- *free zone frontier (free zone enclosure)*
4 la barrera aduanera
- *customs barrier*
5 el paso de aduanas f
- *customs entrance*
6 el edificio de aduanas f del puerto
- *port custom house*
7 el almacén
- *entrepôt*
8 la gabarra (la chalana)
- *barge (dumb barge, lighter)*
9 el almacén de tránsito m de mercancías f sueltas
- *break-bulk cargo transit shed (general cargo transit shed, package cargo transit shed)*
10 la grúa flotante
- *floating crane*
11 el transbordador del puerto
- *harbour (Am. harbor) ferry (ferryboat)*
12 los duques de alba
- *fender (dolphin)*
13 la lancha carbonera
- *bunkering boat*

14 el carguero de mercancías f sueltas
- *break-bulk carrier (general cargo ship)*
15 el remolcador
- *tug*
16 el dique flotante
- *floating dock (pontoon dock)*
17 el dique seco
- *dry dock*
18 el muelle de carbón m
- *coal wharf*
19 el depósito de carbón m
- *coal bunker*
20 el puente grúa f de carga f
- *transporter loading bridge*
21 la vía del puerto
- *quayside railway*
22 la tolva del carbón
- *weighing bunker*
23 el cobertizo del astillero (del arsenal)
- *warehouse*
24 la grúa del arsenal
- *quayside crane*
25 la barcaza con la gabarra
- *launch and lighter*
26 el hospital del puerto
- *port hospital*
27 el lazareto (el pabellón de cuarentena f)
- *quarantine wing*

28 el instituto para enfermedades f tropicales (para medicina f tropical)
- *Institute of Tropical Medicine*
29 el vapor de recreo m (el vapor de excursión f)
- *excursion steamer (pleasure steamer)*
30 el embarcadero
- *jetty*
31 el muelle de pasajeros m
- *passenger terminal*
32 el transatlántico (un buque de línea f)
- *liner (passenger liner, ocean liner)*
33 la oficina meteorológica, un observatorio del tiempo
- *meteorological office, a weather station*
34 el mástil de señales f
- *signal mast (signalling mast)*
35 la bola (la señal) de tempestad f (de temporal m; de tormenta f)
- *storm signal*
36 la oficina del puerto
- *port administration offices*
37 el indicador del nivel del agua f
- *tide level indicator*
38 la carretera del muelle
- *quayside road (quayside roadway)*

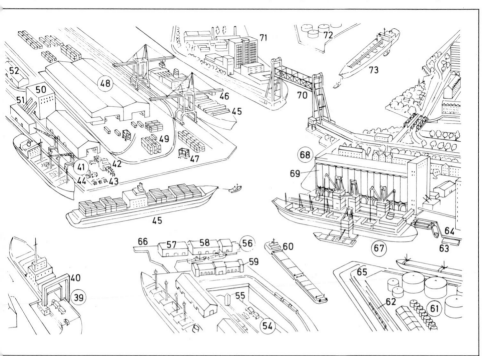

39 el sistema de carga *f* rodante (un transbordador de vehículos *m*, en el que estos entran por sí mismos mediante una rampa o un puente)
– *roll-on roll-off (ro-ro) system (roll-on roll-off operation)*
40 el puente elevador
– *gantry*
41 el sistema de carga *f* por medio de carretillas *f*
– *truck-to-truck system (truck-to-truck operation)*
42 el lote de la carga embalada con chapas *f* de metal *m*
– *foil-wrapped unit loads*
43 las paletas
– *pallets*
44 la carretilla elevadora
– *forklift truck (fork truck, forklift)*
45 el carguero portacontenedores
– *container ship*
46 la grúa de puente *m* rodante sobre dos vías *f* para la carga de contenedores *m*
– *transporter container-loading bridge*
47 el camión portacontenedores
– *container carrier truck*
48 el almacén portacontenedores (terminal *m* de contenedores *m*)
– *container terminal (container berth)*

49 el lote de carga *f*
– *unit load*
50 la cámara frigorífica
– *cold store*
51 la cinta transportadora
– *conveyor belt (conveyor)*
52 el cobertizo de la fruta
– *fruit storage shed (fruit warehouse)*
53 el edificio de oficinas *f*
– *office building*
54 la autopista urbana
– *urban motorway (Am. freeway)*
55 los túneles por debajo del puerto
– *harbour (Am. harbor) tunnels*
56 el puerto pesquero
– *fish dock*
57 el mercado de pescado *m*
– *fish market*
58 la lonja de pescado *m*
– *auction room*
59 la fábrica de conservas *f* de pescado *m*
– *fish-canning factory*
60 el remolcador de empuje *m*
– *push tow*
61 el depósito de tanques *m* de petróleo *m* (el puerto petrolero)
– *tank farm*
62 el ramal ferroviario
– *railway siding*

63 el pontón de abordaje *m* (de atraque *m*)
– *landing pontoon (landing stage)*
64 el muelle rompeolas
– *quay*
65 el rompeolas
– *breakwater (mole)*
66 el embarcadero, una prolongación del muelle
– *pier (jetty), a quay extension*
67 el carguero a granel *m*
– *bulk carrier*
68 el silo
– *silo*
69 la cuba del silo
– *silo cylinder*
70 el puente elevador
– *lift bridge*
71 la zona industrial del puerto
– *industrial plant*
72 los tanques de almacenamiento *m*
– *storage tanks*
73 el petrolero
– *tanker*

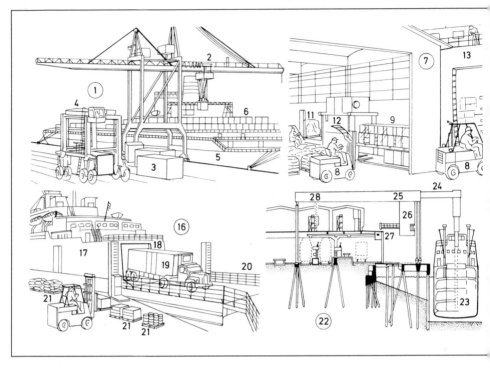

1 la terminal de contenedores *m*, una instalación moderna para el transbordo de mercancías *f*
– *container terminal (container berth), a modern cargo-handling berth*
2 el puente de contenedores *m* (el puente de transbordo *m*)
– *transporter container-loading bridge (loading bridge); sim.: transtainer crane (transtainer)*
3 el contenedor
– *container*
4 el carro transportador
– *truck (carrier)*
5 el buque portacontenedores
– *all-container ship*
6 los contenedores cargados en cubierta *f*
– *containers stowed on deck*
7 el transbordo horizontal de los contenedores por carretilla *f* elevadora de horquilla *f*
– *truck-to-truck handling (horizontal cargo handling with pallets)*
8 la carretilla elevadora de horquilla *f*
– *forklift truck (fork truck, forklift)*
9 la carga unitaria embalada en hojas *f* de plástico *m*
– *unitized foil-wrapped load (unit load)*

10 la paleta plana, una paleta normal
– *flat pallet, a standard pallet*
11 la mercancía en fardos *m* unitarios
– *unitized break-bulk cargo*
12 la máquina para embalar en hojas *f* de plástico *m*
– *heat sealing machine*
13 el carguero de mercancía *f* en fardos *m*
– *break-bulk carrier (general cargo ship)*
14 la abertura de carga *f*
– *cargo hatchway*
15 la carretilla a bordo *m* del buque
– *receiving truck on board ship*
16 la terminal de usos *m* múltiples
– *multi-purpose terminal*
17 el buque de transporte roll-on roll-off (el buque de transbordo *m* horizontal)
– *roll-on roll-off ship (ro-ro-ship)*
18 la puerta trasera
– *stern port (stern opening)*
19 la carga automotriz, un camión de carga *f*
– *driven load, a lorry (Am. truck)*
20 la instalación de expedición *f* de mercancías *f* Ro-ro (la instalación especial Ro-ro)
– *ro-ro depot*
21 la carga unitaria
– *unitized load (unitized package)*

22 la terminal bananera [corte *m*]
– *banana-handling terminal [section]*
23 el elevador de cala *f*
– *seaward tumbler*
24 el brazo saledizo
– *jib*
25 el puente elevador
– *elevator bridge*
26 la eslinga de cadena *f*
– *chain sling*
27 el puesto de claridad *f*
– *lighting station*
28 el sistema de carga *f* de camiones *m* y vagones *m*
– *shore-side tumbler [for loading trains and lorries (Am. trucks)]*
29 el puesto de carga *f* a granel *m*
– *bulk cargo handling*
30 el carguero de mercancía *f* a granel *m*
– *bulk carrier*

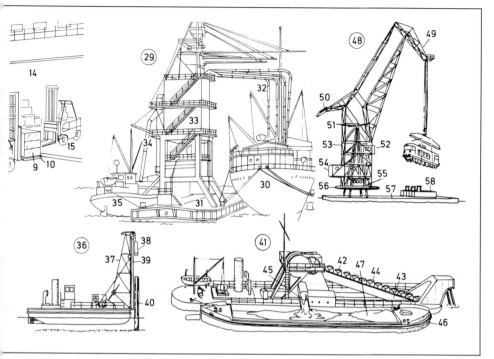

31 el puente grúa *f* de carga *f*
 – *floating bulk-cargo elevator*
32 los tubos de aspiración *f*
 – *suction pipes*
33 el receptor
 – *receiver*
34 el tubo de embarque *m*
 – *delivery pipe*
35 la barcaza de transporte *m* a
 granel *m*
 – *bulk transporter barge*
36 el martinete
 – *floating pile driver*
37 la armazón del martinete
 – *pile driver frame*
38 el mazo
 – *pile hammer*
39 la guía
 – *driving guide rail*
40 el apoyo del martinete basculante
 – *pile*
41 la draga de cangilones *m*, una
 draga
 – *bucket dredger, a dredger*
42 la cadena de cangilones *m*
 – *bucket chain*
43 el transportador de cangilones *m*
 – *bucket ladder*
44 el cangilón de la draga
 – *dredger bucket*
45 el vertedor
 – *chute*

46 el lanchón de la draga
 – *hopper barge*
47 el material dragado
 – *spoil*
48 la grúa flotante
 – *floating crane*
49 el pescante (el brazo de la grúa)
 – *jib (boom)*
50 el contrapeso
 – *counterweight (counterpoise)*
51 el eje ajustable
 – *adjusting spindle*
52 la cabina del conductor
 – *crane driver's cabin (crane driver's
 cage)*
53 la armazón (el chasis) de la grúa
 – *crane framework*
54 la cabina del torno
 – *winch house*
55 el puente de mando *m*
 – *control platform*
56 la plataforma giratoria
 – *turntable*
57 el pontón, una gabarra (*Amér.:*
 chata *f*)
 – *pontoon, a pram*
58 la superestructura de los motores
 – *engine superstructure (engine
 mounting)*

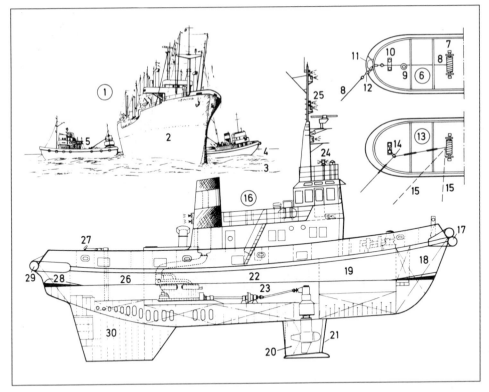

1 el salvamento de un buque
encallado
– *salvaging (salving) of a ship run
aground*
2 el buque encallado
– *ship run aground (damaged vessel)*
3 el banco de arena *f*
– *sandbank; also: quicksand*
4 el alta mar
– *open sea*
5 el remolcador
– *tug (salvage tug)*
6-15 la instalación de remolque *m*
– *towing gear*
6 el material para el remolque
marítimo
– *towing gear for towing at sea*
7 el torno de remolque *m*
– *towing winch (towing machine,
towing engine)*
8 el cable de remolque *m*
– *tow rope (tow line, towing hawser)*
9 la guía de remolque *m*
– *tow rope guide*
10 la pasteca
– *cross-shaped bollard*
11 el escobén
– *hawse hole*

12 la cadena del ancla *f*
– *anchor cable (chain cable)*
13 el material para el remolque en el
puerto
– *towing gear for work in harbours*
(Am. *harbors*)
14 la retenida
– *guest rope*
15 la dirección del cable en ausencia
f de retenida *f*
– *position of the tow rope (tow line,
towing hawser)*
16 el remolcador [proyección vertical]
– *tug (salvage tug) [vertical elevation]*
17 la defensa de estrave *m*
– *bow fender (pudding fender)*
18 el parapeto delantero
– *forepeak*
19 las habitaciones
– *living quarters*
20 la hélice carenada
– *Schottel propeller*
21 la tobera de la hélice
– *Kort vent*
22 la sala de máquinas *f*
– *engine and propeller room*

23 el sistema de acoplamiento (el
embrague)
– *clutch coupling*
24 la cubierta radiogoniométrica
– *compass platform (compass
bridge, compass flat, monkey
bridge)*
25 la instalación para la extinción de
incendios *m*
– *fire-fighting equipment*
26 el pañol (la bodega)
– *stowage*
27 el gancho de remolque *m*
– *tow hook*
28 el parapeto trasero
– *afterpeak*
29 la defensa de popa *f*
– *stern fender*
30 la quilla de maniobras *f*
– *main manoeuvring (Am. maneuvering) keel*

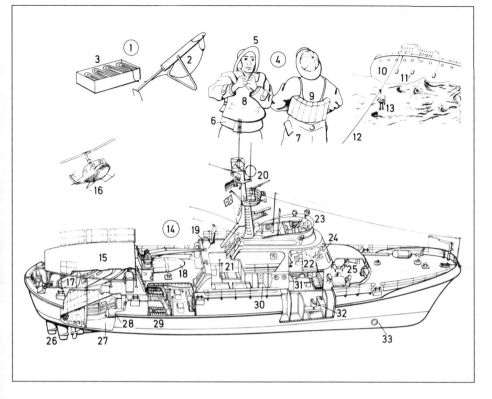

1 el cohete lanzacabos (el lanzacabos)
– *rocket apparatus (rocket gun, line-
throwing gun)*
2 el cohete
– *life rocket (rocket)*
3 el cabo de salvamento *m*
– *rocket line (whip line)*
4 el traje de encerado *m* [traje *m* de
hule *m*; un traje impermeabilizado]
– *oilskins*
5 el sueste (el sombrero de hule *m*)
– *sou'wester (southwester)*
6 la chaqueta de encerado *m*
– *oilskin jacket*
7 el abrigo de encerado *m*
– *oilskin coat*
8 el chaleco salvavidas hinchable
– *inflatable life jacket*
9 el chaleco salvavidas de corcho *m*
– *cork life jacket (cork life preserver)*
10 el buque encallado (averiado)
– *stranded ship (damaged vessel)*
11 los sacos de aceite *m*, para dejar
caer gota a gota el aceite en la
superficie del agua *f*
– *oil bag, for trickling oil on the
water surface*
12 la cuerda de salvamento *m*
– *lifeline*

13 la boya pantalón *m* (el pantalón
de salvamento *m*)
– *breeches buoy*
14 la lancha de salvamento *m*
– *rescue cruiser*
15 la cubierta de aterrizaje *m* para
helicópteros *m*
– *helicopter landing deck*
16 el helicóptero de salvamento *m*
– *rescue helicopter*
17 el bote anejo (*Amér. Central y
Panamá:* la panga)
– *daughter boat*
18 la lancha de goma *f*
– *inflatable boat (inflatable dinghy)*
19 el refugio (la balsa de salvamento *m*)
– *life raft*
20 la instalación de extinción *f* de
incendios *m*
– *fire-fighting equipment for fires at
sea*
21 la enfermería con camarote *m*
(sala *f*) de operaciones *f* y unidad
f de reanimación *f*
– *hospital unit with operating cabin
and exposure bath*
22 el cuarto de los instrumentos
– *navigating bridge*
23 el puente de mando *m* superior
– *upper tier of navigating bridge*

24 el puente de mando *m* inferior
– *lower tier of navigating bridge*
25 el cámara (mesa *f* de oficiales *m*)
– *messroom*
26 la hélice y el timón
– *rudders and propeller (screw)*
27 el pañol (la bodega)
– *stowage*
28 el depósito de espuma *f* para la
extinción de incendios *m*
– *foam can*
29 los motores laterales
– *side engines*
30 las duchas
– *shower*
31 la cabina del patrón
– *coxswain's cabin*
32 la cabina de un miembro de la
tripulación
– *crew member's single-berth cabin*
33 la hélice de estrave *m*
– *bow propeller*

1-14 la disposición de las alas
- *wing configurations*
1 el monoplano de ala *f* alta
- *high-wing monoplane (high-wing plane)*
2 la envergadura
- *span (wing span)*
3 el avión de ala *f* alta
- *shoulder-wing monoplane (shoulder-wing plane)*
4 el avión de ala *f* semialzada
- *midwing monoplane (midwing plane)*
5 el avión de ala *f* baja
- *low-wing monoplane (low-wing plane)*
6 el triplano
- *triplane*
7 el ala *f* alta
- *upper wing*
8 el ala *f* central
- *middle wing (central wing)*
9 el ala *f* baja
- *lower wing*
10 el biplano
- *biplane*
11 el montante, un refuerzo
- *strut*
12 el arriostramiento
- *cross bracing wires*
13 el sesquiplano
- *sesquiplane*
14 el avión de ala *f* baja con ala *f* de pliegue *m*
- *low-wing monoplane (low-wing plane) with cranked wings (inverted gull wings)*
15-22 las formas de las alas
- *wing shapes*
15 el ala *f* elíptica
- *elliptical wing*
16 el ala *f* rectangular
- *rectangular wing*
17 el ala *f* trapezoidal
- *tapered wing*
18 el ala *f* en media luna *f*
- *crescent wing*
19 el ala *f* delta
- *delta wing*
20 el ala *f* en flecha *f* positiva débil
- *swept-back wing with semi-positive sweepback*
21 el ala *f* en flecha *f* positiva fuerte
- *swept-back wing with positive sweepback*
22 el ala *f* ojival
- *ogival wing (ogee wing)*
23-36 las formas de las alas guías
- *tail shapes (tail unit shapes, empennage shapes)*
23 el ala *f* guía normal
- *normal tail (normal tail unit)*

24 *u.* 25 el timón de dirección *f*
- *vertical tail (vertical stabilizer and rudder)*
24 la aleta de dirección *f*
- *vertical stabilizer (vertical fin, tail fin)*
25 el timón de mando *m*
- *rudder*
26 *u.* 27 el estabilizador de elevación *f*
- *horizontal tail*
26 el plano fijo horizontal
- *tailplane (horizontal stabilizer)*
27 el timón de profundidad
- *elevator*
28 las alas guías cruciformes
- *cruciform tail (cruciform tail unit)*
29 las alas guías en T
- *T-tail (T-tail unit)*
30 el cuerpo expulsor
- *lobe*
31 las alas guías en V
- *V-tail (vee-tail, butterfly tail)*
32 las alas guías dobles
- *double tail unit (twin tail unit)*
33 el disco lateral
- *end plate*
34 las alas guías dobles de un avión de doble fuselaje *m*
- *double tail unit (twin tail unit) of a twin-boom aircraft*
35 el fuselaje doble con alas *f* guías horizontales elevadas
- *raised horizontal tail with double booms*
36 el ala *f* guía triple
- *triple tail unit*
37 el sistema de alerones *m*
- *system of flaps*
38 el pico de seguridad *f* móvil
- *extensible slat*
39 el spoiler
- *spoiler*
40 el alerón de doble curvatura *f*
- *double-slotted Fowler flap*
41 el alerón exterior
- *outer aileron (low-speed aileron)*
42 los aerofrenos internos
- *inner spoiler (landing flap, lift dump)*
43 el alerón interior
- *inner aileron (all-speed aileron)*
44 los aerofrenos externos
- *brake flap (air brake)*
45 el perfil de base *f*
- *basic profile*
46-48 los alerones de curvatura *f*
- *plain flaps (simple flaps)*
46 el alerón normal
- *normal flap*
47 el alerón de hendidura *f*
- *slotted flap*

48 el alerón de hendidura *f* doble
- *double-slotted flap*
49 *u.* 50 los alerones de intradós *m*
- *split flaps*
49 el alerón de intradós *m* sencillo
- *plain split flap (simple split flap)*
50 el alerón Zap
- *zap flap*
51 el ala *f* doble
- *extending flap*
52 el alerón Fowler
- *Fowler flap*
53 el pico de seguridad *f*
- *slat*
54 el alerón de pico *m* perfilado
- *profiled leading-edge flap (droop flap)*
55 el alerón Krüger
- *Krüger flap*

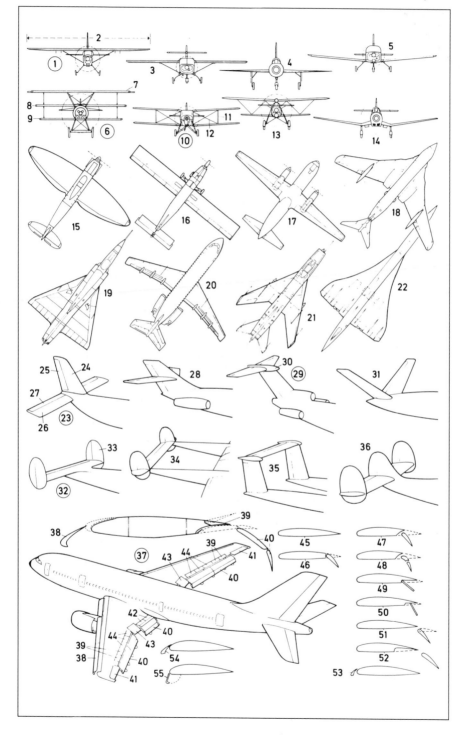

1-31 la cabina de pilotaje *m* de un
monomotor de viaje *m* y de turismo *m*
– *cockpit of a single-engine (single-
engined) racing and passenger aircraft (racing and passenger plane)*
1 el tablero de instrumentos *m* (el
tablero de a bordo *m*)
– *instrument panel*
2 el velocímetro (el tacómetro)
– *air-speed (Am. airspeed) indicator*
3 el horizonte artificial
– *artificial horizon (gyro horizon)*
4 el altímetro
– *altimeter*
5 el radiocompás (la brújula
automática)
– *radio compass (automatic direction finder)*
6 el compás magnético
– *magnetic compass*
7 el manómetro de presión *f* de
admisión *f*
– *boost gauge (Am. gage)*
8 el contador del número de revoluciones *f* (el cuentarrevoluciones)
– *tachometer (rev counter, revolution counter)*
9 el indicador de la temperatura de
los cilindros
– *cylinder temperature gauge (Am.
gage)*
10 el acelerómetro
– *accelerometer*
11 el reloj de a bordo *m*
– *chronometer*
12 el indicador de viraje *m* con
nivelación *f* de bola *f*
– *turn indicator with ball*
13 el giroscopio del rumbo
– *directional gyro*
14 el variómetro
– *vertical speed indicator (rate-of-
climb indicator, variometer)*
15 el indicador VOR [VOR: Very
high frequency omnidirectional
range]
– *VOR radio direction finder
[VOR: very high frequency omnidirectional range]*
16 el indicador de combustible *m* del
depósito izquierdo
– *left tank fuel gauge (Am. gage)*
17 el indicador de combustible *m* del
depósito derecho
– *right tank fuel gauge (Am. gage)*
18 el amperímetro
– *ammeter*
19 el indicador de presión *f* (el
manómetro) del combustible
– *fuel pressure gauge (Am. gage)*
20 el indicador de presión *f* (el
manómetro) del aceite
– *oil pressure gauge (Am. gage)*
21 el indicador de temperatura *f* del
aceite
– *oil temperature gauge (Am. gage)*

22 el aparato de radiotelefonía *f* y de
radionavegación *f*
– *radio and radio navigation equipment*
23 la lámpara para iluminar la carta
– *map light*
24 el volante (la palanca de mando
m) para el accionamiento del
alerón y del timón de profundidad *f*
– *wheel (control column, control
stick) for operating the ailerons
and elevators*
25 el volante para el copiloto
– *co-pilot's wheel*
26 los interruptores
– *switches*
27 los pedales del timón de mando *m*
– *rudder pedals*
28 los pedales del timón de mando *m*
del copiloto
– *co-pilot's rudder pedals*
29 el micrófono para el servicio de
radiofonía *f*
– *microphone for the radio*
30 la palanca del gas
– *throttle lever (throttle control)*
31 el regulador de mezcla *f* (la palanca de mezcla *f*)
– *mixture control*
32-66 la avioneta de viaje *m* y de
deporte *m* **(el monomotor)**
– *single-engine (single-engined)
racing and passenger aircraft
(racing and passenger plane)*
32 la hélice
– *propeller (airscrew)*
33 el casquete de la hélice
– *spinner*
34 el motor de cuatro cilindros *m*
– *flat four engine*
35 la cabina del piloto (la cabina de
pilotaje *m*, la carlinga)
– *cockpit*
36 el asiento del piloto
– *pilot's seat*
37 el asiento del copiloto
– *co-pilot's seat*
38 los asientos de los pasajeros
– *passenger seats*
39 la cubierta
– *hood (canopy, cockpit hood,
cockpit canopy)*
40 la rueda de morro *m* dirigible
– *steerable nose wheel*
41 el tren de aterrizaje *m* principal
– *main undercarriage unit (main
landing gear unit)*
42 el escalón de subida *f*
– *step*
43 el plano de sustentación *f* (el ala *f*)
– *wing*
44 la luz de posición *f* derecha
– *right navigation light (right position light)*
45 el larguero
– *spar*

46 la nervadura
– *rib*
47 el puntal longitudinal
– *stringer (longitudinal reinforcing
member)*
48 el depósito de combustible *m*
– *fuel tank*
49 el faro de aterrizaje *m*
– *landing light*
50 la luz de posición *f* izquierda
– *left navigation light (left position
light)*
51 el pararrayos estático
– *electrostatic conductor*
52 el alerón
– *aileron*
53 la aleta de aterrizaje *m*
– *landing flap*
54 el fuselaje
– *fuselage (body)*
55 la costilla
– *frame (former)*
56 la correa
– *chord*
57 el puntal longitudinal
– *stringer (longitudinal reinforcing
member)*
58 el timón de dirección *f*
– *vertical tail (vertical stabilizer and
rudder)*
59 el estabilizador de dirección *f*
– *vertical stabilizer (vertical fin, tail
fin)*
60 el timón de mando *m*
– *rudder*
61 el estabilizador de elevación *f*
– *horizontal tail*
62 el plano fijo horizontal
– *tailplane (horizontal stabilizer)*
63 el timón de profundidad *f*
– *elevator*
64 la luz intermitente
– *warning light (anticollision light)*
65 la antena dipolo
– *dipole antenna*
66 la antena de alambre *m* largo
– *long-wire antenna (long-conduc-
tor antenna)*
67-72 los movimientos principales del
avión
– *principal manoeuvres (Am.
maneuvers) of the aircraft (aeroplane, plane, Am. airplane)*
67 la inclinación de cabeza *f*
– *pitching*
68 el eje transversal
– *lateral axis*
69 el tambaleo
– *yawing*
70 el eje vertical
– *vertical axis (normal axis)*
71 la rotación (el movimiento giratorio)
– *rolling*
72 el eje longitudinal
– *longitudinal axis*

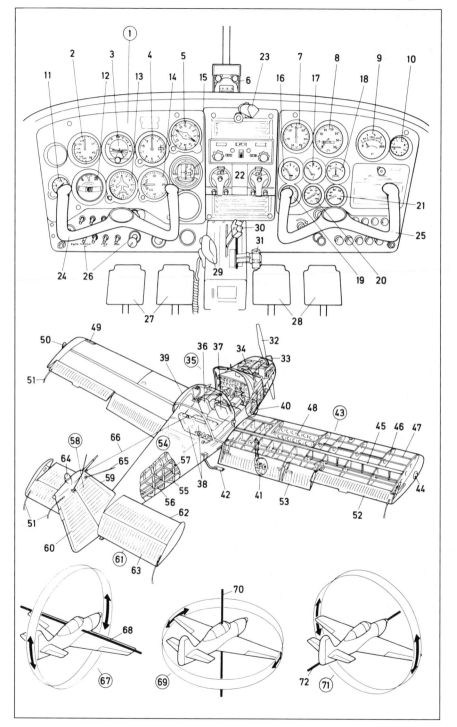

1-33 tipos *m* **de aviones** *m*
– *types of aircraft (aeroplanes, planes,* Am. *airplanes)*
1-6 aviones *m* **de hélice** *f*
– *propeller-driven aircraft (aeroplanes, planes,* Am. *airplanes)*
1 el (avión) monomotor de viaje *m* y de deporte *m* de ala *f* baja
– *single-engine (single-engined) racing and passenger aircraft (racing and passenger plane), a low-wing monoplane (low-wing plane)*
2 el (avión) monomotor de viaje *m* de ala *f* alta
– *single-engine (single-engined) passenger aircraft, a high-wing monoplane (high-wing plane)*
3 el (avión) bimotor comercial y de viaje *m*
– *twin-engine (twin-engined) business and passenger aircraft (business and passenger plane)*
4 el avión de pasajeros *m* para trayectos cortos y medios, un avión turbopropulsado
– *short/medium haul airliner, a turboprop plane (turbopropeller plane, propeller-turbine plane)*
5 el turbopropulsor
– *turboprop engine (turbopropeller engine)*
6 el estabilizador de dirección *f*
– *vertical stabilizer (vertical fin, tail fin)*
7-33 aviones *m* **a reacción** *f*
– *jet planes (jet aeroplanes, jets,* Am. *jet airplanes)*
7 el (avión) birreactor comercial y de turismo *m*
– *twin-jet business and passenger aircraft (business and passenger plane)*
8 el control para la capa límite
– *fence*
9 el depósito del extremo del ala *f*
– *wing-tip tank (tip tank)*
10 el mecanismo propulsor trasero
– *rear engine*
11 el (avión) birreactor de pasajeros *m* para trayectos cortos y medios
– *twin-jet short/medium haul airliner*
12 el (avión) trirreactor para trayectos *m* medios
– *tri-jet medium haul airliner*
13 el (avión) cuatrirreactor para trayectos *m* largos
– *four-jet long haul airliner*
14 el avión de gran capacidad *f* para trayectos *m* largos (el Jumbo)
– *wide-body long haul airliner (jumbo jet)*
15 el avión de pasajeros *m* supersónico [tipo Concorde]
– *supersonic airliner* [Concorde]

16 el pico del fuselaje basculante
– *droop nose*
17 el avión birreactor de gran capacidad *f* para trayectos cortos y medios (el Aerobús)
– *twin-jet wide-body airliner for short/medium haul routes (airbus)*
18 el morro radar, con la antena del radar meteorológico
– *radar nose (radome, radar dome) with weather radar antenna*
19 la cabina de pilotaje *m*
– *cockpit*
20 la cocina de a bordo *m*
– *galley*
21 el espacio de carga *f* (la bodega)
– *cargo hold (hold, underfloor hold)*
22 la cabina de los pasajeros con asientos *m* para los pasajeros
– *passenger cabin with passenger seats*
23 el tren de aterrizaje *m* escamotable del morro
– *retractable nose undercarriage unit (retractable nose landing gear unit)*
24 la puerta del tren de aterrizaje *m*
– *nose undercarriage flap (nose gear flap)*
25 la puerta de pasajeros *m* central
– *centre* (Am. *center*) *passenger door*
26 la góndola con el reactor
– *engine pod with engine (turbojet engine, jet turbine engine, jet engine, jet turbine)*
27 el pararrayos estático
– *electrostatic conductors*
28 el tren de aterrizaje *m* principal escamotable
– *retractable main undercarriage unit (retractable main landing gear unit)*
29 la ventana lateral (la ventanilla lateral)
– *side window*
30 la puerta de pasajeros *m* trasera
– *rear passenger door*
31 los servicios
– *toilet (lavatory, WC)*
32 el mamparo estanco de presión *f*
– *pressure bulkhead*
33 el mecanismo propulsor auxiliar (la turbina de gas *m* auxiliar) para la alimentación de corriente *f*
– *auxiliary engine (auxiliary gas turbine) for the generator unit*

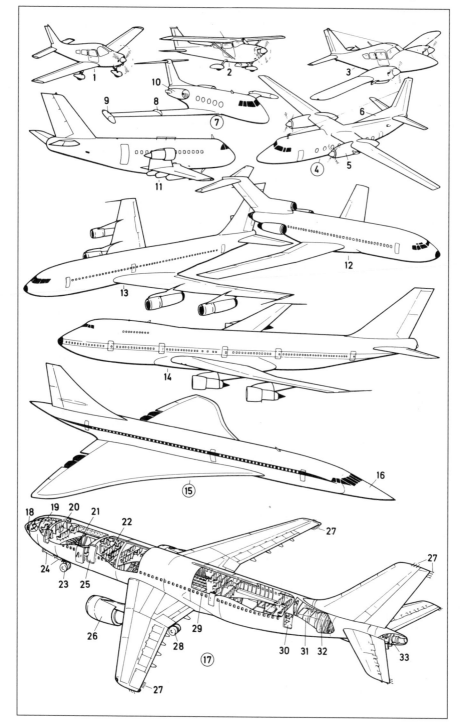

1 **el hidroavión**
– *flying boat, a seaplane*
2 el casco (el fuselaje) del hidroavión
– *hull*
3 el flotador de ala *f* de estabilización *f*
– *stub wing (sea wing)*
4 el arriostramiento del timón y
estabilizador *m* de cola *f*
– *tail bracing wires*
5 el avión flotador, un hidroavión
– *floatplane (float seaplane), a seaplane*
6 el flotador (*Mé.*: la llanta)
– *float*
7 el estabilizador de cola *f*
– *vertical stabilizer (vertical fin, tail
fin)*
8 **el avión anfibio**
– **amphibian** *(amphibian flying
boat)*
9 el casco (el fuselaje) del avión
– *hull*
10 el tren de aterrizaje *m* escamoteable
– *retractable undercarriage
(retractable landing gear)*
11-25 el helicóptero
– **helicopters**
11 el helicóptero universal ligero
– *light multirole helicopter*
12 u. 13 el rotor principal
– *main rotor*
12 el ala *f* giratoria
– *rotary wing (rotor blade)*
13 la cabeza del rotor
– *rotor head*
14 el rotor de cola *f*
– *tail rotor (anti-torque rotor)*
15 los patines de aterrizaje *m*
– *landing skids*
16 el helicóptero grúa *f*
– *flying crane*
17 las turbinas del mecanismo
propulsor (el turborreactor)
– *turbine engines*
18 el tren de aterrizaje *m* de pórtico *m*
– *lifting undercarriage*
19 la plataforma de carga *f* (la
plataforma elevadora)
– *lifting platform*
20 el depósito auxiliar
– *reserve tank*
21 el helicóptero de transporte *m*
– *transport helicopter*
22 los rotores en tándem *m*
– *rotors in tandem*
23 el pilón del rotor
– *rotor pylon*
24 el turborreactor
– *turbine engine*
25 la puerta de carga *f* de la cola
– *tail loading gate*

**26-32 los aviones de despegue *m* y
aterrizaje *m* verticales cortos**
– *V/STOL aircraft (vertical/short
take-off and landing aircraft)*
26 el avión de ala *f* pivotante, un
avión de despegue *m* y aterrizaje
m verticales
– *tilt-wing aircraft, a VTOL aircraft
(vertical take-off and landing aircraft)*
27 el ala *f* pivotante en posición *f*
vertical
– *tilt wing in vertical position*
28 la hélice de contrarrotación *f* de
cola *f*
– *contrarotating tail propellers*
29 el girodino
– *gyrodyne*
30 el turbopropulsor
– *turboprop engine (turbopropeller
engine)*
31 el avión de rotor *m* pivotante
– *convertiplane*
32 el rotor pivotante en posición *f*
vertical
– *tilting rotor in vertical position*
**33-60 los mecanismos propulsores de
avión *m***
– **aircraft engines** *(aero engines)*
**33-50 los estatorreactores (los turbor-
reactores)**
– *jet engines (turbojet engines, jet
turbine engines, jet turbines)*
33 el reactor soplante delantero
– *front fan-jet*
34 el soplante
– *fan*
35 el compresor de baja presión *f*
– *low-pressure compressor*
36 el compresor de alta presión *f*
– *high-pressure compressor*
37 la cámara de combustión *f*
– *combustion chamber*
38 la turbina motor soplante
– *fan-jet turbine*
39 la tobera (la tobera de empuje *m*)
– *nozzle (propelling nozzle, propulsion nozzle)*
40 las turbinas
– *turbines*
41 el canal de la corriente secundaria
– *bypass duct*
42 el reactor soplante trasero (el
reactor soplante de cola *f*)
– *aft fan-jet*
43 el soplante
– *fan*
44 el canal de la corriente secundaria
– *bypass duct*
45 la tobera (la tobera de empuje *m*)
– *nozzle (propelling nozzle, propulsion nozzle)*

46 el reactor de doble flujo *m*
– *bypass engine*
47 las turbinas
– *turbines*
48 el mezclador
– *mixer*
49 la tobera (la tobera de empuje *m*)
– *nozzle (propelling nozzle, propulsion nozzle)*
50 la corriente (el flujo) secundaria
(-o)
– *secondary air flow (bypass air
flow)*
51 el turbopropulsor, un propulsor
de dos árboles *m*
– *turboprop engine (turbopropeller
engine), a twin-shaft engine*
52 la entrada de aire *m* en forma *f* de
anillo *m*
– *annular air intake*
53 la turbina de alta presión *f*
– *high-pressure turbine*
54 la turbina de baja presión *f*
– *low-pressure turbine*
55 la tobera (la tobera de empuje *m*)
– *nozzle (propelling nozzle, propulsion nozzle)*
56 el árbol del embrague
– *shaft*
57 el árbol intermedio
– *intermediate shaft*
58 el árbol de entrada *f* de la transmisión
– *gear shaft*
59 el reductor
– *reduction gear*
60 el árbol de la hélice
– *propeller shaft*

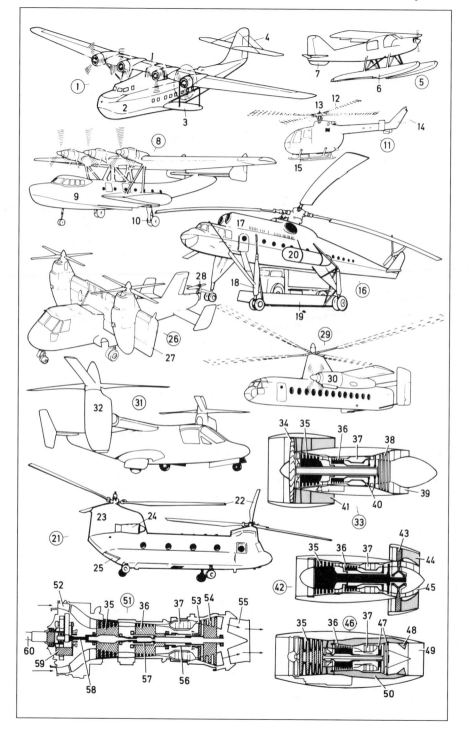

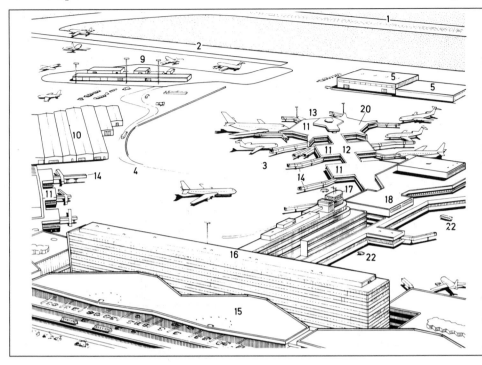

1 la pista *f* de aterrizaje *m* y despegue *m*
– *runway*
2 la pista *f* de rodaje *m*
– *taxiway*
3 la pista *f* de estacionamiento *m*
– *apron*
4 la pista *f* de maniobras *f*
– *apron taxiway*
5 la terminal *f* de equipajes *m*
– *baggage terminal*
6 el túnel *m* de entrada a la terminal de equipajes *m*
– *tunnel entrance to the baggage terminal*
7 el servicio de bomberos *m* del aeropuerto *m*
– *airport fire service*
8 el edificio *m* de los enseres *m* de bomberos *m*
– *fire appliance building*
9 la terminal *f* postal y de carga *f*
– *mail and cargo terminal*
10 el depósito *m* de mercancías *f*
– *cargo warehouse*
11 el punto de encuentros *m*
– *assembly point*
12 el muelle de embarque *m*
– *pier*
13 la cabecera *f* del muelle
– *pierhead*
14 la pasarela *f* (el puente aéreo, el dique) de embarque *m*
– *airbridge*
15 el edificio *m* terminal de viajeros *m* (la terminal de salida *f*)
– *departure building (terminal)*
16 el edificio *m* de administración *f*
– *administration building*
17 la torre de control *m*
– *control tower (tower)*
18 la sala de espera *f*
– *waiting room (lounge)*
19 el restaurante *m* del aeropuerto *m*
– *airport restaurant*

20 la terraza *f* de visitantes *m* (del público)
– *spectators' terrace*
21 el avión *m* en posición *f* de carga *f*
– *aircraft in loading position (nosed in)*
22 los vehículos *m* de servicio *m; p. e.:* el remolque de equipajes *m*, el tanque *m* (la cisterna) de agua *f*, el remolque de provisiones *f*, el vehículo de limpieza *f* de los aseos, el generador de energía *f* de tierra *f*, el camión cisterna *f*
– *service vehicles, e.g. baggage loaders, water tankers, galley loaders, toilet-cleaning vehicles, ground power units, tankers*
23 el tractor (el remolcador) de aviones *m*
– *aircraft tractor (aircraft tug)*
24-53 las señales de información *f* del aeropuerto
– *airport information symbols (pictographs)*
24 aeropuerto *m*
– *'airport'*
25 salidas *f*
– *'departures'*
26 llegadas *f*
– *'arrivals'*
27 pasajeros *m* en tránsito *m*
– *'transit passengers'*
28 sala de espera *f*
– *'waiting room' ('lounge')*
29 punto de encuentros *m*
– *'assembly point' ('meeting point', 'rendezvous point')*
30 terraza *f* de visitantes *m*
– *'spectators' terrace'*
31 información *f*
– *'information'*
32 taxis *m*
– *'taxis'*
33 coches *m* de alquiler *m* (autos *m* de alquiler *m*)
– *'car hire'*
34 tren *m*
– *'trains'*

35 autobús *m*
– *'buses'*
36 entrada *f*
– *'entrance'*
37 salida *f*
– *'exit'*
38 entrega *f* de equipajes *m* (recogida *f* de equipajes *m*)
– *'baggage reclaim'*
39 consigna *f* de equipajes *m*
– *'luggage lockers'*
40 teléfono *m* de urgencias *f*
– *'telephone – emergency calls only'*
41 salida *f* de urgencia *f*
– *'emergency exit'*
42 control *m* de pasaportes *m*
– *'passport check'*
43 sala *f* de prensa *f*
– *'press facilities'*
44 médico *m* (*Amér.:* doctor *m*)
– *'doctor'*
45 farmacia *f*
– *'chemist'* (Am. *'druggist'*)
46 ducha *f*
– *'showers'*
47 servicios *m* de caballeros *m*
– *'gentlemen's toilet' ('gentlemen')*
48 servicios *m* de señoras *f*
– *'ladies toilet' ('ladies')*
49 capilla *f*
– *'chapel'*
50 restaurante *m* (*Amér.:* restaurant *m*)
– *'restaurant'*
51 cambio *m*
– *'change'*
52 tienda *f* libre de impuestos *m*
– *'duty free shop'*
53 peluquería *f*
– *'hairdresser'*

410

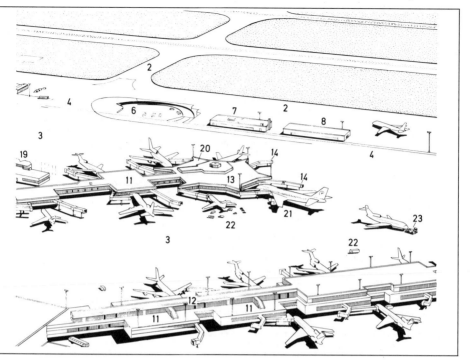

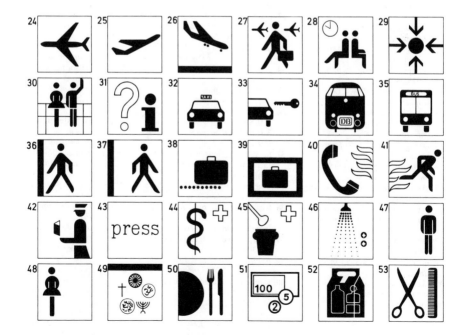

1 el cohete portador Saturno V del "Apolo" [vista *f* de conjunto *m*]
– *Saturn V 'Apolo' booster (booster rocket) [overall view]*
2 el cohete portador Saturno V del "Apolo" [corte *m* general]
– *Saturn V 'Apollo' booster (booster rocket) [overall sectional view]*
3 la primera etapa del cohete S-IC (la etapa de despegue *m*)
– *first rocket stage (S-IC)*
4 los propulsores F-1
– *F-1 engines*
5 el escudo antitérmico (el protector del calor)
– *heat shield (thermal protection shield)*
6 el revestimiento aerodinámico del propulsor
– *aerodynamic engine fairings*
7 la aleta aerodinámica de estabilización *f*
– *aerodynamic stabilizing fins*
8 los retrocohetes separados por etapas *f*, 8 cohetes *m* para 4 pares *m*
– *stage separation retro-rockets, 8 rockets arranged in 4 pairs*
9 el depósito de queroseno *m* (*Amér.:* querosén) (RP-1) [811 000 l]
– *kerosene (RP-1) tank [capacity: 811,000 litres]*
10 los conductos de alimentación *f* del oxígeno líquido
– *liquid oxygen (LOX, LO₂) supply lines, total of 5*
11 el sistema antivortex (dispositivo *m* permanente para evitar la formación de torbellinos *m* en el carburante)
– *anti-vortex system (device for preventing the formation of vortices in the fuel)*
12 el depósito de oxígeno *m* líquido [1 315 000 l]
– *liquid oxygen (LOX, LO₂) tank [capacity: 1,315,000 litres]*
13 la amortiguación (la estabilización) del traqueteo
– *anti-slosh baffles*
14 las botellas de presión *f* para el helio
– *compressed-helium bottles (helium pressure bottles)*
15 el difusor para el oxígeno gaseoso
– *diffuser for gaseous oxygen*
16 la pieza intermedia del depósito
– *inter-tank connector (inter-tank section)*
17 los instrumentos y el control del sistema
– *instruments and system-monitoring devices*
18 la segunda etapa S-II
– *second rocket stage (S-II)*
19 los propulsores J-2
– *J-2 engines*

20 el escudo antitérmico (el protector del calor)
– *heat shield (thermal protection shield)*
21 el soporte del propulsor y la armazón del empuje
– *engine mounts and thrust structure*
22 los cohetes de aceleración *f* para la acumulación del carburante
– *acceleration rockets for fuel acquisition*
23 el conducto de admisión *f* de hidrógeno *m* líquido
– *liquid hydrogen (LH₂) suction line*
24 el depósito de oxígeno *m* líquido [1 315 000 l]
– *liquid oxygen (LOX, LO₂) tank [capacity: 1,315,000 litres]*
25 el tubo vertical
– *standpipe*
26 el depósito de hidrógeno *m* líquido [1 020 000 l]
– *liquid hydrogen (LH₂) tank [capacity: 1,020,000 litres]*
27 el sensor vertical del nivel del combustible
– *fuel level sensor*
28 la plataforma de trabajo *m*
– *work platform (working platform)*
29 la canalización de cables *m*
– *cable duct*
30 el orificio de acceso *m*
– *manhole*
31 el compartimiento intermedio S-IC/S-II
– *S-IC/S-II inter-stage connector (inter-stage section)*
32 el depósito de gas *m* comprimido
– *compressed-gas container (gas pressure vessel)*
33 la tercera etapa del cohete S-IV B
– *third rocket stage (S-IVB)*
34 el propulsor J-2
– *J-2 engine*
35 el cono de empuje *m*
– *nozzle (thrust nozzle)*
36 el compartimiento intermedio S-II/S-IV B
– *S-II/S-IVB inter-stage connector (inter-stage section)*
37 los retrocohetes para la separación por etapas *f* para S-II, 4 cohetes *m*
– *four second-stage (S-II) separation retro-rockets*
38 los cohetes para regular la posición
– *attitude control rockets*
39 el depósito de oxígeno *m* líquido [77 200 l]
– *liquid oxygen (LOX, LO₂) tank [capacity: 77,200 litres]*
40 la tubería (el entramado de tubos *m*)
– *fuel line duct*
41 el depósito de hidrógeno *m* líquido [253 000 l]
– *liquid hydrogen (LH₂) tank [capacity: 253,000 litres]*

42 las sondas de medida *f*
– *measuring probes*
43 los depósitos de gas *m* de helio *m* comprimido
– *compressed-helium tanks (helium pressure vessels)*
44 la ventilación del depósito
– *tank vent*
45 el anillo de la cabina delantera
– *forward frame section*
46 la plataforma de trabajo *m*
– *work platform (working platform)*
47 la canalización de cables *m*
– *cable duct*
48 los cohetes de aceleración *f* para la acumulación del carburante
– *acceleration rockets for fuel acquisition*
49 el anillo de la cabina trasera
– *aft frame section*
50 el depósito de gas *m* comprimido y de helio *m*
– *compressed-helium tanks (helium pressure vessels)*
51 el conducto del hidrógeno líquido
– *liquid hydrogen (LH₂) line*
52 el conducto de oxígeno *m* líquido
– *liquid oxygen (LOX, LO₂) line*
53 el conjunto de instrumentos *m* con 24 paneles *m* solares
– *24-panel instrument unit*
54 el hangar LM
– *LM hangar (lunar module hangar)*
55 el LM (Lunar Module, el módulo lunar)
– *LM (lunar module)*
56 el módulo de servicio Apolo (el SM, Service Module), un compartimiento para abastecimiento *m* y herramientas *f*
– *Apollo SM (service module), containing supplies and equipment*
57 el propulsor principal del módulo de servicio *m*
– *SM (service module) main engine*
58 el depósito de carburante *m*
– *fuel tank*
59 el depósito de tetraóxido *m* de nitrógeno *m*
– *nitrogen tetroxide tank*
60 el sistema de alimentación *f* de gas *m* comprimido
– *pressurized gas delivery system*
61 los depósitos de oxígeno *m*
– *oxygen tanks*
62 las cabinas de combustible *m*
– *fuel cells*
63 los grupos de cohetes *m* de control *m*
– *manoeuvring (Am. maneuvering) rocket assembly*
64 el grupo de antenas *f* dirigidas
– *directional antenna assembly*
65 la cápsula espacial (el módulo de mando *m*)
– *space capsule (command section)*
66 la torre de salvamento *m* para la fase de despegue *m*
– *launch phase escape tower*

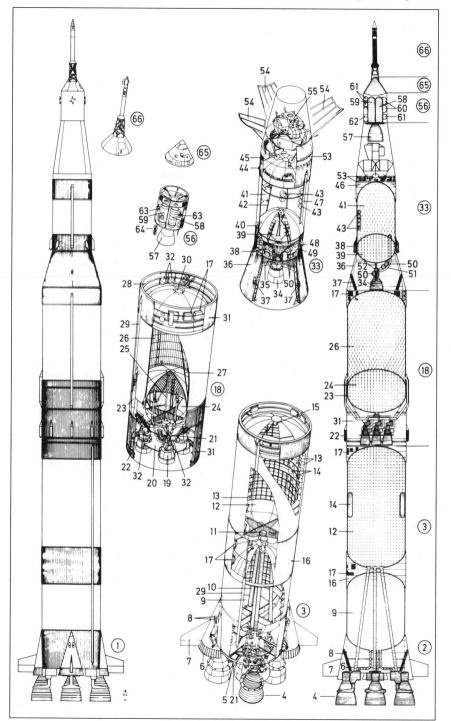

1-45 la nave espacial Orbiter
- *Space Shuttle-Orbiter*
1 la aleta vertical de dos largueros *m*
- *twin-spar (two-spar, double-spar) vertical fin*
2 la estructura del propulsor
- *engine compartment structure*
3 el larguero lateral
- *fin post*
4 la chapa de unión *f* del fuselaje
- *fuselage attachment [of payload bay doors]*
5 la armazón soporte del empuje superior
- *upper thrust mount*
6 la armazón soporte del empuje inferior
- *lower thrust mount*
7 el soporte de la quilla
- *keel*
8 el escudo protector del calor
- *heat shield*
9 el larguero central del fuselaje
- *waist longeron*
10 la cuaderna maestra (la cuaderna principal) fresada integralmente
- *integrally machined (integrally milled) main rib*
11 el borde (el revestimiento) de aleación *f* ligera enteramente reforzado
- *integrally stiffened light alloy skin*
12 el soporte de reja *f*
- *lattice girder*
13 el revestimiento para el aislamiento del compartimiento de carga *f* útil
- *payload bay insulation*
14 la escotilla del compartimiento de carga *f* útil
- *payload bay door*
15 el revestimiento protector del frío
- *low-temperature surface insulation*
16 el compartimiento de la tripulación (la cabina de pilotaje *m*)
- *flight deck (crew compartment)*
17 el asiento (el puesto) del comandante
- *captain's seat (commander's seat)*
18 el asiento del piloto
- *pilot's seat (co-pilot's seat)*
19 la cuaderna de compresión *f* delantera
- *forward pressure bulkhead*
20 la punta (el pico) del fuselaje, una carena curva armada de fibras *f* de carbono *m*
- *nose-section fairings, carbon fibre reinforced nose cone*
21 los depósitos delanteros de carburante *m*
- *forward fuel tanks*
22 las consolas del equipo electrónico de la nave
- *avionics consoles*
23 el tablero de mando *m* para el pilotaje automático
- *automatic flight control panel*
24 la ventanilla de observación *f* superior
- *upward observation windows*
25 la ventanilla de observación *f* delantera
- *forward observation windows*

26 la escotilla de acceso *m* al compartimiento *m* de carga *f* útil
- *entry hatch to payload bay*
27 la esclusa de aire *m*
- *air lock*
28 la escala de acceso *m* al primer puente *m*
- *ladder to lower deck*
29 el brazo manipulador controlado a distancia *f*
- *payload manipulator arm*
30 el tren de aterrizaje *m* delantero con accionamiento *m* hidráulico
- *hydraulically steerable nose wheel*
31 el tren de aterrizaje *m* principal con accionamiento *m* hidráulico
- *hydraulically operated main landing gear*
32 el revestimiento de ataque *m* móvil, armado de fibras *f* de carbono *m*
- *removable (reusable) carbon fibre reinforced leading edge [of wing]*
33 las partes móviles del elevón (alerón)
- *movable elevon sections*
34 la estructura resistente al calor *m* del elevón (alerón)
- *heat-resistant elevon structure*
35 el conducto (la llegada) principal de hidrógeno *m*
- *main liquid hydrogen (LH$_2$) supply*
36 el motor principal de combustibles *m* líquidos
- *main liquid-fuelled rocket engine*
37 la tobera de empuje *m*
- *nozzle (thrust nozzle)*
38 el conducto de refrigeración *f*
- *coolant feed line*
39 las herramientas de mando *m* del motor
- *engine control system*
40 el escudo protector del calor *m*
- *heat shield*
41 la bomba de hidrógeno *m* a alta presión *f*
- *high-pressure liquid hydrogen (LH$_2$) pump*
42 la bomba de oxígeno *m* a alta presión *f*
- *high-pressure liquid oxygen (LOX, LO$_2$) pump*
43 el sistema de mando *m* del empuje
- *thrust vector control system*
44 el propulsor principal de maniobra *f* espacial de mando *m* electromecánico
- *electromechanically controlled orbital manoeuvring (Am. maneuvering) main engine*
45 los depósitos de carburante *m* de las toberas de empuje *m*
- *nozzle fuel tanks (thrust nozzle fuel tanks)*
46 **los depósitos de hidrógeno *m* y de oxígeno *m* eyectables**
- *jettisonable liquid hydrogen and liquid oxygen tank (fuel tank)*
47 la cuaderna circular reforzada integralmente
- *integrally stiffened annular rib (annular frame)*

48 la cuaderna de extremidad *f* hemisférica
- *hemispherical end rib (end frame)*
49 la pasarela trasera de acceso *m* al Orbiter
- *aft attachment to Orbiter*
50 la tubería del hidrógeno
- *liquid hydrogen (LH$_2$) line*
51 la tubería del oxígeno
- *liquid oxygen (LOX, LO$_2$) line*
52 el orificio de acceso *m*
- *manhole*
53 el sistema de amortiguación *f*
- *surge-baffle system (slosh baffle system)*
54 la tubería bajo presión *f* para el depósito de hidrógeno *m*
- *pressure line to liquid hydrogen tank*
55 la canalización principal de electricidad *f*
- *electrical system bus*
56 la tubería de distribución *f* del oxígeno
- *liquid oxygen (LOX, LO$_2$) line*
57 la tubería bajo presión *f* para el depósito de oxígeno *m*
- *pressure line to liquid oxygen tank*
58 **el propulsor de combustible *m* sólido recuperable**
- *recoverable solid-fuel rocket (solid rocket booster)*
59 el compartimiento de los paracaídas auxiliares
- *auxiliary parachute bay*
60 el compartimiento de los paracaídas de salvamento *m* y de los motorescohetes de separación *f* delanteros
- *compartment housing the recovery parachutes and the forward separation rocket motors*
61 la caja (el compartimiento) de cables *m*
- *cable duct*
62 los motores-cohetes de separación *f* traseros
- *aft separation rocket motors*
63 el cono de revestimiento *m* traseros
- *aft skirt*
64 la tobera de empuje *m* (eyección *f*) orientable
- *swivel nozzle (swivelling, Am. swiveling, nozzle)*
65 **el Spacelab (el laboratorio espacial, la estación espacial)**
- *Spacelab (space laboratory, space station)*
66 el laboratorio de uso *m* múltiple
- *multi-purpose laboratory (orbital workshop)*
67 el astronauta
- *astronaut*
68 el telescopio de suspensión *f* cardán
- *gimbal-mounted telescope*
69 la plataforma de los instrumentos de medida *f*
- *measuring instrument platform*
70 el módulo espacial
- *spaceflight module*
71 el túnel de esclusas *f* (la esclusa de comunicación *f*)
- *crew entry tunnel*

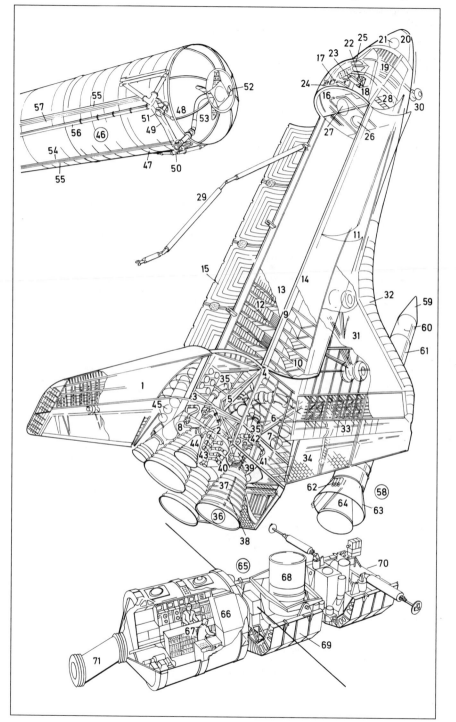

1-30 la sala de ventanillas *f*
- *main hall*
1 la ventanilla de los paquetes
- *parcels counter*
2 la balanza para los paquetes
- *parcels scales*
3 el paquete (el paquete postal;
Arg., Col., Chile y Perú: la
encomienda; Col. y Mé.: el
recomendado)
- *parcel*
4 la dirección pegada, con la etiqueta
del número del paquete
- *stick-on address label with parcel
registration slip*
5 el bote de engrudo *m*
- *glue pot*
6 el pequeño paquete
- *small parcel*
7 la máquina de franquear (*Amér.:*
la máquina de estampillar) de los
boletines de expedición *f*
- *franking machine (Am. postage
meter) for parcel registration cards*
8 la cabina telefónica
- *telephone box (telephone booth,
telephone kiosk, call box)*
9 el teléfono automático de monedas *f*
- *coin-box telephone (pay phone,
public telephone)*
10 el soporte de las guías telefónicas
- *telephone directory rack*
11 el portaguías basculante
- *directory holder*
12 la guía telefónica
- *telephone directory (telephone
book)*
13 los apartados de correos (*Chile y
Perú:* las casillas)
- *post office boxes*
14 la caja del apartado de correos (la
caja postal, la casilla postal)
- *post office box*
15 la ventanilla de venta *f* de los sellos de correos (*Amér.:* de
estampillas *f*)
- *stamp counter*
16 el empleado de ventanilla *f*
- *counter clerk (counter officer)*
17 el recadero (el muchacho de los
recados)
- *company messenger*
18 el registro del correo (el registro
de envíos *m*)
- *record of posting book*
19 el distribuidor de sellos *m* (*Amér.:*
estampillas *f*)
- *counter stamp machine*
20 la carpeta de sellos *m* (*Amér.:*
estampillas *f*)
- *stamp book*
21 la hoja de sellos *m*
- *sheet of stamps*

22 el cajón de valores *m*
- *security drawer*
23 la caja de cambio *m*
- *change rack*
24 el pesacartas
- *letter scales*
25 la ventanilla de las operaciones
financieras (la ventanilla de los
giros y la caja postal)
- *paying-in (Am. deposit), post
office savings, and pensions
counter*
26 la máquina de contabilidad *f*
- *accounting machine*
27 la máquina de timbrar para los
giros postales
- *franking machine for money
orders and paying-in slips (Am.
deposit slips)*
28 el distribuidor de monedas *f*
- *change machine (Am. change-
maker)*
29 el sello de recibo *m*
- *receipt stamp*
30 la ventanilla
- *hatch*
31-44 la instalación de clasificación *f*
de la correspondencia (*fam.:* la
sala de batalla *f*)
- *letter-sorting installation*
31 la introducción de la correspondencia
- *letter feed*
32 las cestas de la correspondencia
amontonada
- *stacked letter containers*
33 el transportador mecánico de alimentación *f*
- *feed conveyor*
34 la máquina ordenadora
- *intermediate stacker*
35 la sección de codificación *f*
- *coding station*
36 la máquina de primera clasificación *f*
- *pre-distributor channel*
37 la calculadora de procesos *m*
- *process control computer*
38 la máquina de clasificación de
cartas *f*
- *distributing machine*
39 la sección de videocodificación *f*
- *video coding station*
40 la pantalla
- *screen*
41 la imagen de la dirección
- *address display*
42 la dirección
- *address*
43 el código postal
- *post code (postal code, Am. zip
code)*
44 el teclado
- *keyboard*

45 el matasellos de puño *m*
- *handstamp*
46 el matasellos de rodillo *m*
- *roller stamp*
47 la máquina de timbrar (la máquina
de matasellar)
- *franking machine*
48 el dispositivo de introducción *f*
- *feed mechanism*
49 el dispositivo de distribución *f*
- *delivery mechanism*
**50-55 la recogida de la corresponden-
cia y el reparto de la correspondencia**
- *postal collection and delivery*
50 el buzón
- *postbox (Am. mailbox)*
51 la bolsa colectora de la correspondencia
- *collection bag*
52 el coche de correos *m*
- *post office van (mail van)*
53 el repartidor (el cartero)
- *postman (Am. mail carrier, letter
carrier, mailman)*
54 la bolsa del cartero
- *delivery pouch (postman's bag,
mailbag)*
55 la remesa de correspondencia *f*
- *letter-rate item*
56-60 los sellados
- *postmarks*
56 el matasellos publicitario
- *postmark advertisement*
57 el matasellos con la fecha
- *date stamp postmark*
58 el sello de franqueo *m*
- *charge postmark*
59 el matasellos especial
- *special postmark*
60 el matasellos de rodillo *m* manual
- *roller postmark*
61 el sello postal (*Amér.:* la estampilla)
- *stamp (postage stamp)*
62 el dentado del sello
- *perforations*

1-41 el teléfono (el aparato telefónico)
– telephone
1 el teléfono de disco *m* selector
– dial telephone
2 el microteléfono (el auricular)
– handset (telephone receiver)
3 el cable del auricular
– receiver cord (handset cord)
4 el cable del aparato telefónico
– telephone cable (telephone cord)
5 la caja del aparato telefónico
– telephone casing (telephone cover)
6 los números telefónicos de urgencia *f*
– emergency numbers
7 el número del aparato
– line number
8 el disco selector
– dial
9 el teléfono compacto
– compact telephone (slimline telephone), an added-feature telephone
10 el auricular
– earpiece (receiver)
11 el teclado con las teclas de función *f*
– keypad with number and function keys (feature keys)
12 la tecla de repetición *f* del número marcado
– last number redial button
13 la tecla de marcación *f* abreviada
– abbreviated dialling key
14 la tecla del altavoz
– speaker key (loudspeaker key)
15 el micrófono
– mouthpiece
16 la tecla para conectar a la red
– line reset button
17 el altavoz
– speaker (loudspeaker)
18 la señal óptica de llamada *f*
– call indicator
19 el teléfono de teclas *f*, un teléfono komfort
– push-button telephone, an added-feature telephone
20 el visualizador de mandos *m*
– display
21 la cerradura de bloqueo *m*
– lock
22 el teléfono de diseño *m*, un teléfono komfort
– novelty telephone, an added-feature telephone
23 la horquilla del teléfono
– (telephone) cradle
24 la manivela (aquí sólo imitación)
– dummy crank
25 la consola abatible con el teclado
– detachable keypad
26 el teléfono inalámbrico (teléfono radio *m*, teléfono *m* móvil)
– cordless (tele)phone (radiophone, mobile phone)
27 la antena
– aerial
28 el piloto de control *m* de batería *f*
– battery strength light
29 el piloto de advertencia *f* para la extralimitación del radio de acción *f*
– out of signal-range indicator
30 el interruptor principal
– power switch
31 el teléfono de tarjeta *f*
– cardphone

32 el visualizador de dos líneas de texto *m* para las tasas telefónicas
– split display showing call charges
33 el botón de selección *f* de idioma *m* para el visualizador
– language select button for the display
34 el botón para conversaciones *f* sucesivas
– follow-on call button
35 la ranura para la tarjeta telefónica
– phonecard slot
36 la tarjeta telefónica (la teletarjeta)
– phonecard (here: telephone credit card)
37 el simbolo telefónico de tarjeta *f*
– phonecard symbol
38 el nombre del usuario
– cardholder's name
39 el número de la tarjeta
– card number
40 la dirección de la inserción
– arrow indicating direction of insertion
41 los platinos del chip
– chips
42-62 el ISDN (la red telefónica digital integradora de servicios)
– ISDN (Integrated Services Digital Network)
42 la terminal multifuncional de telecomunicación *f* (el puesto de trabajo *m* del ISDN)
– multifunction telecommunications terminal (ISDN workstation)
43 la pantalla (el monitor) para el texto de pantalla *f* (Btx), teléfono *m* de imagen *f* y teletexto *m*
– screen (monitor) for viewdata, video telephone, and Teletex
44 la unidad de cálculo *m* y de memoria *f*
– central processing and memory unit
45 la unidad de telefax *m* (el telefax, el telecopiador)
– fax unit (fax)
46 el dispositivo de entrada *f* de datos *m* (el teclado)
– input device (keyboard)
47 el auricular (la conexión con la red de larga distancia *f*)
– telephone receiver (link to the telephone network)
48 el acoplador acústico (también el Modem)
– acoustic coupler (modem)
49 la red a larga distancia *f* (la red TEMEX)
– telecontrol network (TEMEX network)
50 la red telefónica automática
– public telephone network (switched telephone network)
51 los terminales conductores a distancia *f*
– telecontrol centres
52 la central TEMEX
– TEMEX main control centre
53 la instalación de retransmisión *f* TEMEX
– TEMEX transmission equipment
54 el cable telefónico
– telecommunications line (telephone line)
55 la terminal de la red TEMEX
– TEMEX network termination
56 la subestación
– slave station
57 los aparatos de accionamiento *m* a distancia *f*
– telecontrol terminal equipment

58 las instalaciones de acción *f* a larga distancia *f* (los sensores)
– telecontrol terminal equipment (detector, sensor, or control equipment)
59 el aparato de alarma *f* de vidrio *m* roto
– glass-break detector
60 el regulador de temperatura *f*
– temperature controller
61 el teléfono de urgencia *f*
– emergency call
62 el contador (el contador de electricidad *f*)
– meter (electricity meter)
63 el satélite de comunicaciones *f* (el satélite de noticias *f*)
– communications satellite
64 las placas solares (placas de células *f* solares, generador *m* solar)
– solar panel (solar paddle, solar array, solar generator)
65 el módulo de antena *f*
– antenna module
66 la antena de recepción *f* teledirigida
– receiving antenna for control commands
67 las antenas parabólicas
– parabolic antennas
68 el módulo de noticias *f*
– communications module
69 el módulo de accionamiento *m*
– propulsion module
70 el satélite para la radio (el satélite para la televisión)
– broadcasting satellite (television satellite)
71 el módulo de alimentación *f*
– service module
72 los tanques de carburante *m*
– fuel tanks
73 los inyectores teledirigidos
– control jets
74 la estación radiotelegráfica de tierra *f*
– earth station
75 la antena parabólica
– parabolic antenna
76 el reflector principal
– main reflector
77 el reflector de recepción *f*
– feed antenna
78 los rayos radiofónicos
– radio beams
79 la radio por satélite *m*, televisión *f* por satélite *m* y televisión *f* por cable *m*
– satellite broadcasting, satellite television, and cable television
80 el satélite de radio *f*
– broadcasting satellite
81 el estudio de televisión *f*
– television studio
82 la torre de televisión *f*
– television tower
83 la estación terminal
– cablehead station
84 la radio
– terrestrial broadcasting
85 la radio por satélite *m*
– satellite broadcasting
86 la radio direccional
– line-of-sight link (microwave link)
87 la red de cable *m*
– cable network
88 las conexiones por cable *m*
– cable connections

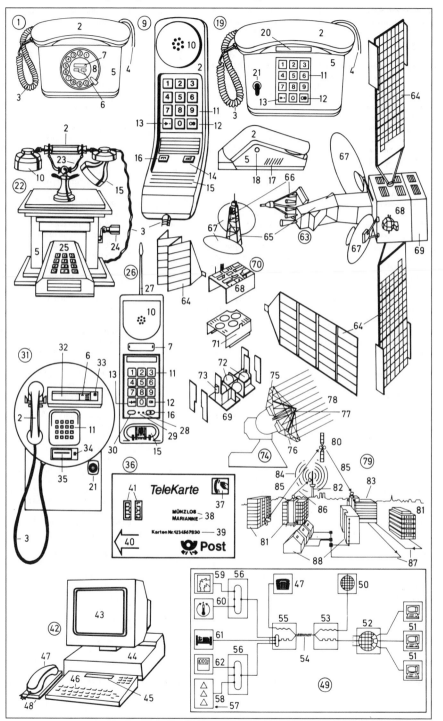

1-6 la cabina central de la toma del sonido de la radio (el estudio de grabación *f* radiofónica)
– *central recording channel of a radio station*
1 la mesa de control *m* y de mando *m*
– *monitoring and control panel*
2 la consola de visualización *f* del programa de radio *f* informatizado (el monitor vídeo)
– *data display terminal (video data terminal, video monitor) for visual display of computer-controlled programmes* (Am. *programs)*
3 el soporte del aparato de amplificación *f* y de alimentación *f*
– *amplifier and mains power unit*
4 el magnetófono de grabación *f* y reproducción *f* de cintas *f* magnéticas de un cuarto de pulgada *f* o 6,35 mm de anchura
– *magnetic sound recording and playback deck for 1/4" magnetic tape*
5 la cinta magnética, la cinta de un cuarto de pulgada
– *magnetic tape, a 1/4" tape*
6 el estuche de bobina de la película
– *film spool holder*
7-15 el estudio de explotación *f* del centro nacional de radio *f*
– *radio switching centre (Am. center) control room*
7 la mesa de control *m* y mando *m*
– *monitoring and control panel*
8 el altavoz de órdenes *f*
– *talkback speaker*
9 el teléfono de batería *f* local
– *local-battery telephone*
10 el micrófono de órdenes *f*
– *talkback microphone*
11 el aparato de visualización *f* de los datos
– *data display terminal (video data terminal)*
12 el teleimpresor
– *teleprinter*
13 el teclado para introducir los datos en la computadora
– *input keyboard for computer data*
14 el teclado para la instalación telefónica de servicio *m*
– *telephone switchboard panel*
15 el altavoz de escucha *f*
– *monitoring speaker (control speaker)*
16-26 el complejo de emisión *f* radiofónica
– *broadcasting centre* (Am. *center)*
16 el estudio de emisión *f* radiofónica
– *recording room*
17 la cabina de control *m* (la cabina de mezcla *f* de sonidos *m*)
– *production control room (control room)*
18 la cabina del locutor
– *studio*
19 el ingeniero de sonido *m*
– *sound engineer (sound control engineer)*

20 el pupitre de mezcla *f* (de control *m*) de sonido *m*
– *sound control desk (sound control console)*
21 el locutor (*Amér.*: el espíquer)
– *newsreader (newscaster)*
22 el director de la emisión
– *duty presentation officer*
23 el teléfono de reportaje *m*
– *telephone for phoned reports*
24 el tocadiscos (*Col., Venez. y Pan.*: el picá)
– *record turntable*
25 el pupitre de mezcla *f* de la cabina de grabación *f* radiofónica
– *recording room mixing console (mixing desk, mixer)*
26 el técnico de sonido *m*
– *sound technician (sound mixer, sound recordist)*
27-53 el estudio de postsincronización *f* de televisión *f*
– *television post-sync studio*
27 la cabina de mezcla *f* (de control *m*) del sonido
– *sound production control room (sound control room)*
28 el estudio de sincronización *f*
– *dubbing studio (dubbing theatre, Am. theater)*
29 la mesa del presentador
– *studio table*
30 la señal de indicación *f* óptica (la señal luminosa)
– *visual signal*
31 el cronómetro electrónico
– *electronic stopclock*
32 la pantalla de proyección *f*
– *projection screen*
33 el monitor de la imagen
– *monitor*
34 el micrófono del presentador
– *studio microphone*
35 el organillo de efectos *m* sonoros
– *sound effects box*
36 el panel de conexión *f* del micrófono
– *microphone socket panel*
37 el altavoz de sonorización *f*
– *recording speaker (recording loudspeaker)*
38 la ventana de control *m*
– *control room window (studio window)*
39 el micrófono de órdenes *f* para los productores
– *producer's talkback microphone*
40 el teléfono de batería *f* local
– *local-battery telephone*
41 el pupitre de mezcla *f* (de control *m*) del sonido
– *sound control desk (sound control console)*
42 el conmutador de grupos *m*
– *group selector switch*
43 el indicador luminoso
– *visual display*
44 el limitador
– *limiter display (clipper display)*

45 las cajitas (los módulos) de ajuste *m* de conexión *f*
– *control modules*
46 las teclas de preescucha *f* (las teclas de la escucha de prueba *f*)
– *pre-listening buttons*
47 el regulador de corredera *f* plano
– *slide control*
48 el corrector universal
– *universal equalizer (universal corrector)*
49 el selector de entrada *f*
– *input selector switches*
50 el altavoz de preescucha *f* (de audición *f* de prueba *f*)
– *pre-listening speaker*
51 el generador del sonido de referencia *f*
– *tone generator*
52 el altavoz de órdenes *f*
– *talkback speaker*
53 el micrófono de órdenes *f*
– *talkback microphone*
54-59 el estudio de premezcla *f* para el doblado y la mezcla de cintas *f* magnéticas perforadas de 16 mm, 17,5 mm, 35 mm
– *pre-mixing room for transferring and mixing 16 mm, 17,5 mm, 35 mm perforated magnetic film*
54 el pupitre de control *m* (de mezcla *f*) del sonido
– *sound control desk (sound control console)*
55 el bloque compacto de grabación *f* y de reproducción *f* magnéticas
– *compact magnetic tape recording and playback equipment*
56 el desenrollador unicelular para la transmisión
– *single playback deck*
57 el aparato central de impulsión *f*
– *central drive unit*
58 el desenrollador unicelular para la grabación y la transmisión
– *single recording and playback deck*
59 la mesa de rebobinado *m*
– *rewind bench*
60-65 la cabina de control *m* de las imágenes
– *final picture quality checking room*
60 el monitor de previsión *f*
– *preview monitor*
61 el monitor de programa *m*
– *programme* (Am. *program) monitor*
62 el cronómetro
– *stopclock*
63 el pupitre de mezcla *f* (de control *m*) de la imagen
– *vision mixer (vision-mixing console, vision-mixing desk)*
64 la instalación de órdenes *f*
– *talkback system (talkback equipment)*
65 el monitor de cámara *f*
– *camera monitor (picture monitor)*

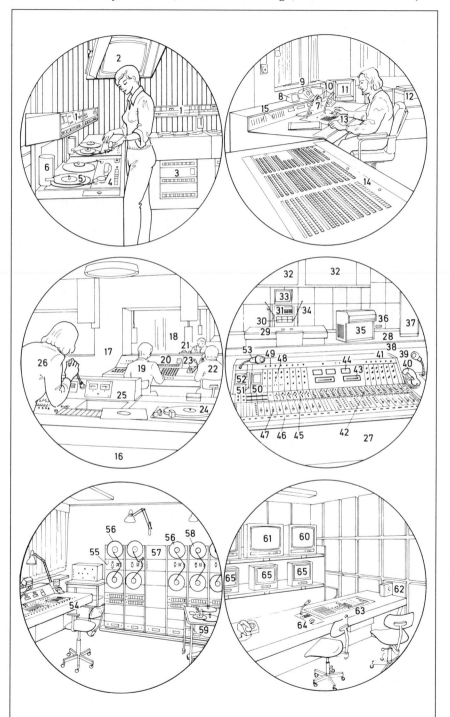

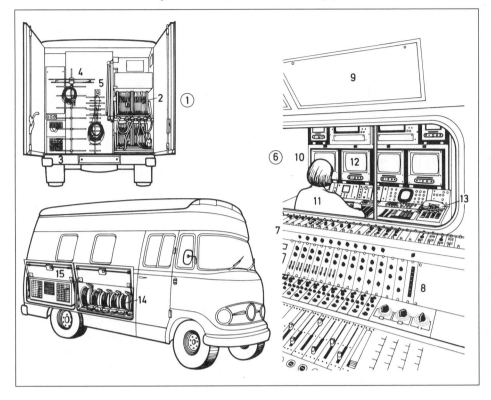

1-15 el coche de reportaje *m* (la
unidad móvil)
– *outside broadcast (OB) vehicle*
 (television OB van; also: sound
 OB van, radio OB van)
1-4 el equipo trasero del coche de
 reportaje *m*
– *rear equipment section of the OB*
 vehicle
2 el cable de cámara *f*
– *camera cable*
3 el panel de conexión *f* de los
 cables
– *cable connection panel*
4 la antena de televisión *f* portátil
 para la primera cadena
– *television (TV) reception aerial*
 (receiving aerial) for Channel I
5 la antena de televisión para la
 segunda cadena
– *television (TV) reception aerial*
 (receiving aerial) for Channel II
6 el equipo interior del coche de
 reportaje *m*
– *interior equipment (on-board*
 equipment) of the OB vehicle
7 la cabina de control *m* del sonido
– *sound production control room*
 (sound control room)

8 el pupitre de control *m* del sonido
– *sound control desk (sound control*
 console)
9 el altavoz de control *m*
– *monitoring loudspeaker*
10 la cabina de control *m* de la imagen
– *vision control room (video control*
 room)
11 el técnico de vídeo *m*
– *video controller (vision controller)*
12 el monitor de cámara *f*
– *camera monitor (picture monitor)*
13 el teléfono de a bordo *m*
– *on-board telephone (intercommu-*
 nication telephone)
14 el cable del micrófono
– *microphone cables*
15 la instalación de climatización *f*
– *air-conditioning plant*

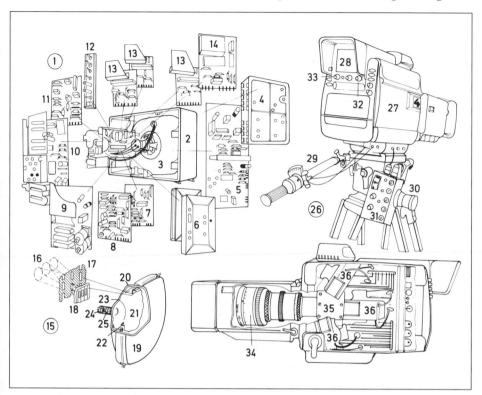

1 el receptor de televisión *f* en color *m* (televisión *f* en color *m;* el aparato de televisión *f* en color *m*) en un diseño por módulos *m*
– *colour* (Am. *color*) *television (TV) receiver (colour television set) of modular design*
2 la caja de la televisión (del televisor)
– *television cabinet*
3 el tubo de televisión *f* (el tubo de imágenes *f*)
– *television tube (picture tube)*
4 el módulo amplificador de frecuencia *f* intermedia (F. I.)
– *IF (intermediate frequency) amplifier module*
5 el módulo de descodificación *f* del color
– *colour* (Am. *color*) *decoder module*
6 el selector VHF y UHF
– *VHF and UHF tuner*
7 el módulo de sincronización *f* horizontal
– *horizontal synchronizing module*
8 el módulo de deflexión *f* vertical
– *vertical deflection module*
9 el módulo de encuadre *m*
– *horizontal linearity control module*
10 el módulo de deflexión *f* horizontal
– *horizontal deflection module*
11 el módulo de regulación *f*
– *control module*

12 el módulo de convergencia *f*
– *convergence module*
13 el módulo de la fase final de color *m*
– *colour* (Am. *color*) *output stage module*
14 el módulo de sonido *m*
– *sound module*
15 el filtro cromático blindado
– *colour* (Am. *color*) *picture tube*
16 los haces de electrones *m*
– *electron beams*
17 la máscara perforada con ranuras *f*
– *shadow mask with elongated holes*
18 las tiras de material *m* fluorescente (luminiscente)
– *strip of fluorescent (luminescent, phosphorescent) material*
19 el revestimiento de material *m* fluorescente
– *coating (film) of fluorescent material*
20 el blindaje interior magnético
– *inner magnetic screen (screening)*
21 el vacío
– *vacuum*
22 la suspensión de la máscara compensada térmicamente
– *temperature-compensated shadow mask mount*
23 el anillo de centrado *m* del sistema de deflexión *f*
– *centring* (Am. *centering*) *ring for the deflection system*

24 el sistema de cañones *m* de electrones *m*
– *electron gun assembly*
25 el cátodo de calentamiento *m* rápido
– *rapid heat-up cathode*
26 **la cámara de televisión** *f*
– *television (TV) camera*
27 la cabeza de la cámara
– *camera head*
28 el monitor de la cámara
– *camera monitor*
29 la palanca para dirigir la cámara
– *control arm (control lever)*
30 el ajuste del enfoque
– *focusing adjustment*
31 el panel de manejo *m* de la cámara
– *control panel*
32 la regulación del contraste
– *contrast control*
33 la regulación de luminosidad *f*
– *brightness control*
34 el zoom
– *zoom lens*
35 el prisma de división *f* de rayos *m* (el separador de rayos *m*)
– *beam-splitting prism (beam splitter)*
36 el módulo de recepción *f* (el tubo de color *m*)
– *pick-up unit (colour,* Am. *color, pick-up tube)*

1-17 el equipo estereofónico (el equipo de alta fidelidad *f*, Hifi), un equipo estándar
– *stereo system (hi-fi system), a midi system*
1 la cadena de alta fidelidad *f* (Hifi)
– *hi-fi stack*
2 la tapa
– *rack lid (rack dust cover, [housing] lid)*
3 el mueble con la puerta delantera de cristal *m*
– *rack (housing) with glass door*
4 el tocadiscos (el tocadiscos analógico, el giradiscos)
– *record player (record deck, analogue [Am. analog] record player)*
5 el sintonizador (receptor *m*, radiorreceptor *m*)
– *tuner (receiver, radio tuner)*
6 el amplificador (amplificador de potencia *f*)
– *amplifier (power amplifier)*
7 la tapa del casete de doble pletina *f*
– *double cassette deck (double cassette recorder)*
8 el reproductor de discos *m* compactos
– *CD player (compact disc player)*
9 el compartimiento para las cintas del casete
– *cassette rack*
10 el compartimiento para discos *m* analógicos y compactos
– *record and compact disc rack*
11 la rueda para el transporte
– *castor*
12 la columna (un bafle de tres altavoces *m*)
– *speaker (loudspeaker), a three-way bass reflex speaker*
13 el altavoz de sonidos *m* agudos
– *tweeter, a dome tweeter or piezo tweeter*
14 el altavoz de sonidos *m* medios
– *mid-range speaker (squawker)*
15 el altavoz de sonidos *m* graves (de tonos *m* bajos)
– *bass speaker (woofer)*
16 el orificio del resonador
– *port*
17 el mando a distancia *f* por infrarrojos *m*
– *infrared remote control [unit] (IR remote control [unit])*
18 el tocadiscos (el tocadiscos analógico)
– *record player (record deck, analogue [Am. analog] record player)*
19 el plato para disco *m* con arranque *m* directo o transmisión *f* correa *f*
– *turntable with direct drive or belt drive*
20 el estroboscopio
– *strobe light (strobe speed control)*
21 el regulador del tono ("Pitch")
– *pitch control*
22 el indicador de la velocidad
– *rpm display*
23 la tecla de parada *f*
– *stop button*

24 la tecla de funcionamiento del arranque automático
– *auto-return button*
25 el selector para la velocidad del plato
– *rpm selector (speed selector)*
26 la tecla de bajada del brazo
– *cue button (down)*
27 la tecla para levantar el brazo
– *cue button (up)*
28 la aguja
– *stylus (needle)*
29 el sistema del brazo acústico
– *pick-up*
30 el selector del diámetro del disco
– *size selector (record size selector)*
31 el brazo
– *tone arm (pick-up arm)*
32 el apoya-brazo
– *tone arm support (pick-up arm support)*
33 el reglaje de la presión de la cabeza del brazo
– *stylus pressure control*
34 el dispositivo anti-skating
– *anti-skate control*
35 el contrapeso del brazo
– *tone arm counterweight (pick-up arm counterweight)*
36 la tapa
– *lid (dust cover)*
37 el sintonizador (receptor *m*, radiorreceptor *m*)
– *tuner (receiver, radio tuner)*
38 el interruptor ("Power")
– *power switch*
39 la tecla de sintonización *f* de emisora *f*
– *tuning button (tuning control)*
40 la tecla para sintonización *f* manual y búsqueda *f* automática silenciosa
– *manual and automatic tuning selection button with muting*
41 la tecla para recepción *f* estéreo/mono
– *stereo/mono selection button*
42 la tecla indicadora de potencia *f*
– *strength-of-signal display button*
43 la tecla de la memoria
– *memory button*
44 las teclas de las emisoras
– *station selection buttons*
45 los selectores de las frecuencias
– *frequency selection buttons ([wave] band selection buttons)*
46 la señal luminosa de emisora *f*
– *station select display*
47 la señal digital fluorescente (el visualizador) de la banda de frecuencia *f*, frecuencia y potencia *f*
– *fluorescent digital display indicating wave band, frequency, and strength of signal*
48 la señal con diodos *m* luminosos (señal *f* LED) para emisión *f* estéreo, mono y para sintonización *f* automática
– *LED indicator for stereo and mono mode and automatic tuning*
49 el amplificador
– *amplifier (power amplifier)*

50 los selectores para el funcionamiento del tocadiscos, CD, radiorreceptor *m*, pletinas *f*, monitor *m*
– *function select buttons for the turntable, tuner, cassette deck (tape deck), CD player, and monitor (tape monitor)*
51 las teclas de filtros *m* (tecla *f* de filtro *m* de agudos *m* o de bajos *m*)
– *filter buttons (high and low filter buttons)*
52 el regulador de graves *m*
– *bass control*
53 el regulador de agudos *m*
– *treble control*
54 el regulador del equilibrado (el balance)
– *balance control*
55 el interruptor de corrección *f* fisiológica (loudness)
– *loudness button*
56 el volumen
– *volume control*
57 la conexión de los auriculares
– *headphone socket*
58 los selectores de altavoces *m*
– *speaker select buttons*
59 la señal con diodos *m* luminosos (LED) para el volumen
– *LED display, a multifunction display*
60 el pictograma de las funciones
– *function display*
61 el receptor, combinación *f* de receptor *m* y amplificador *m*
– *receiver, a combined tuner-amp[lifier]*
62 la tecla selectora del visualizador
– *display select button*
63 el visualizador de cristal *m* líquido (señal *f* LCD), visualizador *m* multifuncional
– *liquid crystal display (LCD), a multifunction display*
64 el ecualizador, corrector *m* de frecuencia *f* para cinta *f* de 2 × 7
– *[graphic] equalizer, a 2 × 7 band [graphic] equalizer*
65 el regulador movible de la cinta de frecuencia *f*
– *equalizer slide controls*
66 la señal de diodos *m* luminosos (señal *f* LED) para la potencia de la señal de la frecuencia de la cinta
– *LED-display spectrum analyser*
67 los auriculares (auriculares *m* estéreo)
– *headphones (stereo headphones)*
68 los cascos acolchados
– *ear pads (ear cushions)*
69 *u.* **70** los micrófonos
– *microphones*
69 el micrófono (el micrófono estéreo direccional)
– *directional microphone (stereo directional microphone)*
70 el micrófono redondeado de condensador *m* eléctrico
– *electret condenser microphone with omnidirectional pick-up characteristic*

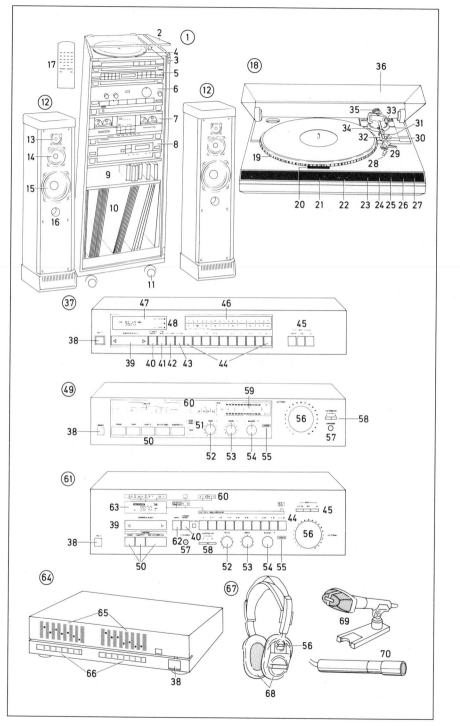

1 la pletina (la grabadora de casetes *f*, la platina)
- *cassette deck (cassette recorder)*
2 el interruptor de la alimentación
- *power switch*
3 la tecla de parada *f* automática de las funciones en la extracción de la casete
- *[stop and] eject button*
4 el compartimiento de la casete (el mecanismo de la casete)
- *cassette holder (cassette drive, cassette transport)*
5 la tapa para protección *f* del polvo
- *dust cover*
6 el contador
- *counter (tape counter)*
7-12 las teclas de funcionamiento *m*
- *transport buttons*
7 la tecla de parada *f* ("Stop")
- *stop button*
8 la tecla de rebobinado *f* ("Review")
- *rewind button*
9 la tecla de reproducción *f* ("Play") para ambas direcciones *f*
- *play buttons for both directions (bidirectional play buttons)*
10 la tecla de avance *m* rápido (FF)
- *fast forward button*
11 la tecla de grabación ("Record")
- *record button*
12 la tecla de pausa *f* ("Pause")
- *pause button*
13 la tecla de puesta *f* a cero *m* ("Reset")
- *counter reset button*
14 las teclas reductoras de ruido *m* (teclas *f* "dolby")
- *noise reduction buttons (Dolby select buttons)*
15 las teclas para la vuelta automática de larga duración *f* ("long play")
- *auto-reverse buttons*
16 el regulador del nivel de grabación *f* (grado *m* de grabación *f*, "Record level")
- *recording level control*
17 las tomas para micrófono *m*
- *microphone sockets*
18 la toma para los auriculares
- *headphone socket*
19 el indicador del nivel, visualizador *m* de diodos *m* luminosos (señal *f* LED)
- *level indicator display (VU meter), an LED display*
20 el indicador del selector de cinta *f*, visualizador *m* de diodos *m* luminosos (señal *f* LED)
- *tape type indicator (tape-bias indicator), an LED display*
21 la doble pletina (la grabadora de doble casete *f*)
- *double cassette deck (double cassette recorder)*
22 la tecla de reproducción *f* ("Play")
- *play button*
23 la tecla de parada *f* ("Stop") y de expulsión *f* ("Eject")
- *[stop and] eject button*
24 la tecla de grabación *f* rápida ("High Speed Dubbing")
- *high-speed dubbing button*
25 los selectores
- *function select button*

26 la señal luminosa de grabación *f*
- *recording indicator light*
27 la señal luminosa de funcionamiento *m*
- *on-off light (power indicator light)*
28 el tocadiscos CD (tocadiscos compact disc, reproductor *m* de CD, tocadiscos digital)
- *CD player (compact disc player, digital compact disc player)*
29 el compartimiento del CD
- *CD drawer*
30 la tecla de función *f* para la apertura y el cierre del compartimiento del CD
- *open/close button for the CD drawer*
31 las teclas de búsqueda *f* de pistas *f*
- *search button and index search button*
32 las teclas de búsqueda *f* manual
- *skip buttons (skip-track buttons)*
33 el regulador del volumen para los auriculares
- *headphone volume control*
34 las teclas de función *f*
- *function select buttons*
35 las señales luminosas de función *f* para la programación, repetición f, reproducción f y pausa *f*
- *programming, track and disc repeat, and pause indicators*
36 las señales de diodos *m* luminosos (señal *f* LED, Display)
- *LED display*
37 las señales luminosas de función *f* para indicar el título y el tiempo
- *remaining time and track-index indicators*
38 el radiocasete portátil con CD incorporado
- *portable radio recorder with integral CD player*
39 el asa
- *handle*
40 el receptor (receptor *m* y amplificador *m* compartido)
- *[radio] receiver (receiver and amplifier)*
41 el tocadiscs CD
- *CD player*
42 el reloj de cuarzo *m* con señal *f* digital y Timer (temporizador *m*)
- *quartz clock with digital display and timer*
43 la doble pletina
- *double cassette recorder*
44 el altavoz
- *loudspeaker*
45-49 la casete
- *audio-cassette (cassette)*
45-47 los tipos de cintas *f*
- *types of tape*
45 la casete de óxido de hierro *m* (casete normal)
- *ferric cassette (iron oxide cassette, normal cassette)*
46 la casete de dióxido *m* de cromo *m*
- *chrome dioxide cassette (chrome cassette)*
47 la casete de metal *m* (casete de dióxido *m* metálico)
- *metal cassette (metal oxide cassette)*
48 la marca del tipo de casete *f*
- *tape type indication (indicating hole)*
49 casetes *f* protegidas contra copia *f*
- *record-protected cassettes*

50 el receptor universal (World Receiver) para la recepción de onda *f* ultracorta (UKW), media (MW), larga (LW) y corta (KW)
- *world receiver for receiving ultra-short wave (USW), medium wave (MW), long wave (LW), and short wave (SW)*
51 la antena, la antena telescópica
- *aerial (rod aerial), a telescopic aerial*
52 las teclas de función *f*
- *function buttons*
53 las teclas de selección *f* de emisora *f*
- *station select buttons*
54 el mando giratorio para sintonizar manualmente emisoras *f*
- *manual tuning knob*
55 el visualizador de cristales *m* líquidos (señal *f* LCD, display) para la frecuencia, alcance *m* de la frecuencia y posición *f* de la memoria
- *liquid crystal display (LCD) showing waveband, frequency, and memory number*
56 el regulador del volumen
- *(sliding) volume control*
57 el radiocasete portátil (Walkman®)
- *cassette player (Walkman® with radio)*
58 los auriculares
- *headphones*
59 el ecualizador, un ecualizador de tres bandas *f*
- *equalizer, a 3-band equalizer*
60 el tocadiscos portátil de CD (Discman®)
- *portable CD player (Discman®)*
61 el disco compacto (CD)
- *compact disc (CD)*
62 la tapa
- *lid*
63 la caja con el mecanismo, amplificador *m*, visualizador *m* y teclas *f* de función *f*
- *casing with transport, amplifier, display, and function buttons*
64 el equipo compacto de alta fidelidad *f* (equipo *m* compacto estéreo)
- *compact hi-fi system (compact stereo system)*
65 el amplificador
- *amplifier section*
66 la pletina digital
- *DAT recorder (digital cassette recorder) (DAT = Digital Audio Tape)*
67 el sensor con rayos *m* infrarrojos para uso *m* a distancia *f*
- *infrared sensor (IR sensor) for the remote control*
68 los selectores de entrada *f* para funcionamiento *m* mono, analógico y digital
- *input selection buttons for mono, analogue (Am. analog), and digital signals*
69 las teclas de memoria *f* para títulos *m* y programas *m*
- *index and program selection buttons*
70 la señal del número del título
- *index number display*
71 la tecla escáner (puesta *f* en marcha *f* automática)
- *auto-scan button*
72 la tecla de búsqueda *f*
- *end-record search button*

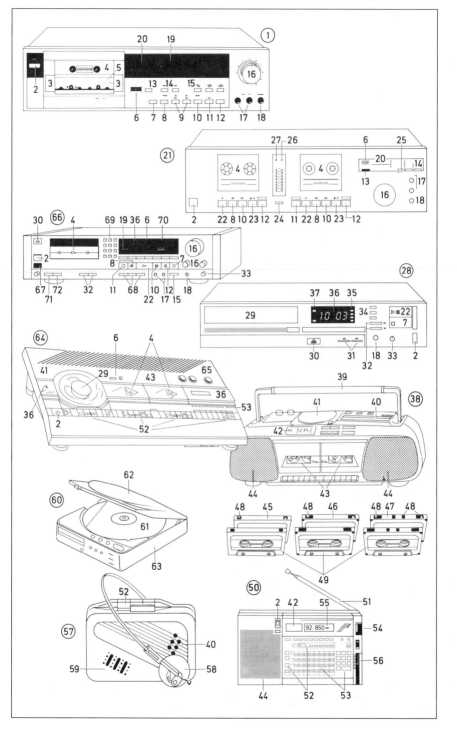

1 la cámara de vídeo *m, antes:* los dos componentes (cámara *f* y grabadora *f* separadas)
– *camcorder (camera recorder),* form: *two-component system (separate camera and recorder)*
2 la cámara de vídeo *m* de bolsillo *m,* un vídeo de 8 mm
– *pocket camcorder, a video-8 camcorder*
3 el objetivo, un objetivo con zoom *m* séxtuple (11–66 mm)
– *lens, a x6 zoom lens (11–66 mm)*
4 el ocular
– *viewfinder (ocular)*
5 el transformador de imagen *f* CCD y obturador *m* de alta velocidad *f,* un chip de 1/2 pulgada *f* con función *f* de cierre *m*
– *CCD image converter (image sensor) and high-speed shutter, a half-inch chip with shutter functions*
6 la casete de vídeo *m*
– *video cassette*
7 la cinta de vídeo *m*
– *videotape*
8 el cabezal
– *head drum*
9 el motor de autofoco
– *autofocus motor*
10 el micrófono integrado
– *built-in microphone (integral microphone)*
11 el cabezal VHS (VHS: Video Home System)
– *VHS head drum (VHS: Video Home System)*
12 la cabeza de borrado *m*
– *erase head*
13 la clavija guía
– *guide pin*
14 la guía de la cinta
– *tape guide*
15 el cilindro de sonido *m*
– *capstan*
16 la cabeza de audiosincronización *f*
– *audio sync head*
17 el rodillo de presión *f*
– *pinch roller*
18 la cabeza vídeo *m*
– *video head*
19 las ranuras de la pared del tambor para la formación del cojín de aire *m*
– *grooves in the wall of the head drum to promote air cushion formation*
20 el esquema de pistas *f* de la grabación de videocasetes *f* (de VCR)
– *VHS track format*
21 la dirección del avance de la cinta
– *direction of tape movement*
22 la dirección de la película
– *direction of recording*

23 la pista de vídeo *m,* una pista en diagonal *f* (sólo pocas pistas *f* dibujadas)
– *video track, a slant track (only a few tracks shown)*
24 la pista sonora
– *sound track (audio track)*
25 la pista de sincronización *f*
– *sync track*
26 la cabeza de sincronización *f*
– *sync head*
27 la cabeza de sonido *m*
– *sound head (audio head)*
28 la cabeza vídeo *m*
– *video head*
29 el videomagnetófono
– *video recorder*
30 el mando a distancia *f* (unidad *f* de control *m* remoto) por infrarrojos *m*
– *infrared remote control*
31 el cuadro de programación *f,* multivisualizador *m*
– *program scale (program dial), a multidisplay*
32 la ranura de introducción de la casete
– *cassette compartment*
33 el mando para adelantar o retrasar la película
– *jog shuttle knob for forward or reverse movement of the [video] picture*
34 el tocadiscos multidisco
– *multidisc player*
35 el mando a distancia *f* por infrarrojos *m*
– *infrared remote control*
36 la bandeja del disco
– *disc drawer*
37-41 los formatos de discos *m*
– *disc formats*
37 el compact disc sencillo (el CD sencillo)
– *single compact disc (single CD)*
38 el audio-CD
– *audio CD*
39 el vídeo-CD
– *video CD*
40 el disco láser pequeño (el disco láser: 20 cm Ø)
– *small laser disc (20 cm)*
41 el disco láser grande (el disco láser: 30 cm Ø)
– *large laser disc (30 cm)*
42 el sistema de exploración *f* láser *m*
– *laser scanning system*
43 el eje del disco
– *[disc] spindle*
44 el eje de avance *m* para la cabeza láser
– *laser-head tracing spindle*
45 la cabeza láser (el grupo láser)
– *laser head (laser unit)*

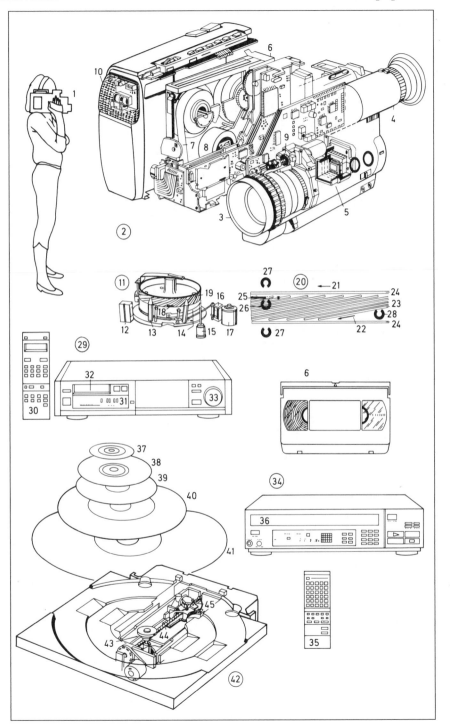

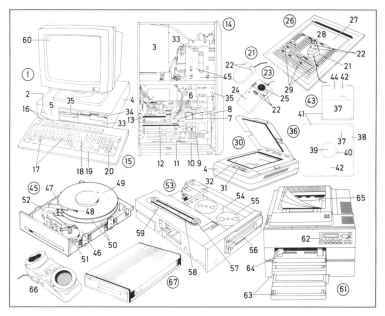

1 el ordenador personal (PC; *semejante:* el laptop)
– *personal computer* (PC; sim.: *laptop*)
2 el interruptor
– *power switch*
3 la alimentación a la red
– *power supply (power pack)*
4 la caja
– *housing*
5 el piloto del disco duro
– *fixed-disk access light*
6 la memoria central
– *main memory*
7 el coprocesador
– *coprocessor socket*
8 la unidad central (CPU, Central Processing Unit), un microprocesador
– *central processing unit (CPU), a micro-processor*
9 la memoria caché (Caché-Controller)
– *cache memory (cache controller)*
10 la ranura (Slot) para la tarjeta de extensión *f* de memoria *f*
– *expansion memory slot*
11 la ranura para la tarjeta gráfica
– *graphics card slot*
12 la controladora combinada de la disquetera y discos duros
– *combined fixed and floppy disk controller*
13 la tarjeta para puertos *m* en serie *f* y paralelo *m*
– *serial and parallel communication card*
14 la torre del PC (Tower) (por dentro)
– *PC tower interior view*
15-67 los periféricos
– *peripherals*
15-32 los dispositivos de entrada *f*
– *built-in devices*
15 el teclado
– *keyboard*
16 las teclas de función *f*
– *function keys*

17 las teclas de las letras y de los números
– *letter keys and number keys (numeric keys)*
18 la tecla de retorno *m* (la tecla *return*)
– *enter key (return key)*
19 las teclas de posición *f* del cursor
– *cursor keys*
20 el bloque numérico
– *number [key]pad (numeric [key]pad)*
21 el ratón
– *mouse*
22 las teclas del ratón
– *mouse buttons*
23 el trackball
– *trackerball (trackball)*
24 el soporte de apoyo *m*
– *handrest*
25 la bola rodante
– *roller ball*
26 la bandeja digitalizadora (el digitalizador, *también* bandeja gráfica)
– *digitizing tablet (digitizer,* also: *graphics tablet)*
27 el campo gráfico
– *graphics area*
28 el retículo
– *cross hairs*
29 los campos de función *f*
– *receiving grids*
30 el escáner
– *scanner*
31 el panel de control *m* con las teclas de función *f*
– *control panel with function keys*
32 el panel de colocación *f* del original *m*
– *scanning surface*
33-59 los dispositivos de memoria *f* masiva (memoria *f* magnética)
– *mass storage devices (magnetic stores, magnetic memories)*
33-44 las disqueteras de los disquetes (disquetera, Floppys)
– *disk drives (drives, floppy disk drives)*

33 la disquetera de disco *m* flexible (disquetera de 5 ¹/₄ pulgadas *f*)
– *minifloppy disk drive (5 ¹/₄ inch [floppy] disk drive)*
34 la tapa de cierre *m*
– *latch*
35 la disquetera de disco *m* flexible (disquetera de 3 ¹/₂ pulgadas *f*)
– *microfloppy disk drive (3 ¹/₂ inch [floppy] disk drive)*
36-44 los disquetes (discos *m* floppy, floppies, *singular:* floppy *f*)
– *diskettes (disks, floppy disks, floppies)*
36 el disco flexible de 5 ¹/₄ pulgadas *f*
– *minifloppy (minifloppy disk, 5 ¹/₄ inch disk, flexible disk)*
37 el sector de grabación *f*
– *label*
38 la muesca para protección *f* de escritura *f*
– *write-protect notch*
39 el orificio para conectar el arranque
– *hole for engaging the drive hub*
40 la ventana de control *m*
– *registration hole*
41 la funda del disquete
– *disk cover (envelope)*
42 la ventana de lectura *f* y escritura *f*
– *access slot for the read-write head*
43 el disco flexible de 3 ¹/₂ pulgadas *f*
– *microfloppy (3 ¹/₂ inch [floppy] disk)*
44 la protección removible del disco
– *sliding shutter*
45 los discos duros (Hard disk)
– *fixed-disk drive (fixed disk, hard disk)*
46 el soporte del disco
– *base plate*
47 el brazo de acceso *m* ("Actuator")
– *access arm (actuator)*
48 la cabeza de lectura *f* y escritura *f*
– *read-write head*

49–67 → S. 431

49 el motor de impulsión *f* para el disco de aluminio *m*, un motor de eje *m*
– *drive motor for the aluminium (Am. aluminum) platters, a spindle drive motor*
50 los discos recubiertos de aluminio *m* magnético
– *magnetic-coated aluminium (Am. aluminum) platters*
51 el motor de impulsión *f* para la cabeza de escritura *f* y lectura *f* (un motor lineal o de secuencia *f*)
– *read-write head drive motor, a linear motor or stepping motor (stepper motor)*
52 el bus de datos *m* e información *f* (cable *m* de mando *m*)
– *data, address, and control bus*
53 la memoria de cinta *f* magnética ("Streamer")
– ***magnetic tape unit** (magnetic tape drive, streamer)*
54 la cinta magnética
– *magnetic tape*
55 la bobina de la cinta magnética
– *magnetic tape reel*
56 la casete de la cinta magnética
– *magnetic tape cassette (magnetic tape cartridge)*
57 la impulsión de la cinta
– *drive post*
58 la transmisión
– *drive band*
59 el motor de impulsión *f*
– *drive motor*
60-65 los dispositivos de salida *f*
– ***output devices***
60 la pantalla (el monitor, display), un monitor de alta resolución *f*
– ***screen** (monitor, display) a high-resolution colour (Am. color) monitor*
61 la impresora (Printer), impresora matricial (*aquí*: impresora láser, laserprinter; *también* impresora por chorro *m* de tinta *f*, impresora de agujas *f*)
– ***printer**, a dot-matrix printer (here: laser printer; also: inkjet printer, needle printer)*
62 el panel de mandos *m* con las teclas de función *f* y visualizador *m*
– *control panel with function keys and display*
63 la bandeja para el papel
– *paper tray (paper cassette)*
64 la bandeja de entrada *f* del papel
– *paper feed path*
65 la salida del papel
– *paper output tray*
66 *u.* **67** los dispositivos para la transmisión de datos *m* (DTD)
– ***devices for long-distance data transmission***
66 el acoplador acústico
– *acoustic coupler*
67 el módem
– *modem*

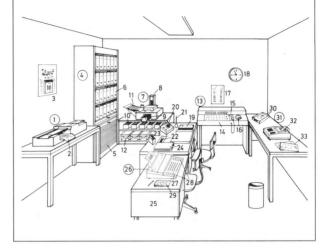

1-33 la oficina de recepción *f* (la oficina de las secretarias)
– ***receptionists office** (secretary's office)*
1 el sistema telecopiador (el emisorreceptor de facsímiles *m*)
– *fax machine*
2 la telecopia (la copia recibida)
– *transmitted or received copy*
3 el calendario (el almanaque) de pared *f*
– *wall calendar*
4 el archivo
– *filing cabinet*
5 la puerta de persiana *f* a corredera *f*
– *tambour door (roll-up door)*
6 el archivador
– *file (document file)*
7 la máquina de imprimir direcciones *f*
– *transfer-type addressing machine*
8 el depósito vertical de recepción *f* de estarcidos *m*
– *vertical stencil magazine*
9 el depósito de estarcidos *m*
– *stencil ejection*
10 la gaveta de almacenaje *m* de estarcidos *m*
– *stencil storage drawer*
11 el dispositivo de alimentación *f* de papel *m*
– *paper feed*
12 las existencias de papel *m* de cartas *f*
– *stock of notepaper*
13 la centralita telefónica interior
– *switchboard (internal telephone exchange)*
14 el teclado de pulsadores *m* para las comunicaciones interiores
– *push-button keyboard for internal connections*
15 el auricular
– *handset*
16 el dial
– *dial*

17 el listín del teléfono interior
– *internal telephone list*
18 el reloj de control *m*
– *master clock (main clock)*
19 el portafirmas
– *folder containing documents, correspondence, etc. for signing (to be signed)*
20 el interfono
– *intercom (office intercom)*
21 el lápiz
– *pen*
22 la bandeja portaplumas (*Amér.*: el canutero)
– *pen and pencil tray*
23 el fichero
– *card index*
24 la pila de formularios *m*
– *stack (set) of forms*
25 la mesa de la máquina de escribir
– *typing desk*
26 la máquina de escribir electrónica con memoria *f*
– *electronic memory typewriter*
27 el teclado de la máquina de escribir, el teclado
– *keyboard*
28 las teclas de función *f*
– *function keys*
29 el bloc de taquigrafía *f*
– *shorthand pad (Am. steno pad)*
30 la bandeja de la correspondencia
– *letter tray*
31 la calculadora de oficina *f*
– *office calculator*
32 la impresora
– *printer*
33 la carta comercial
– *business letter*

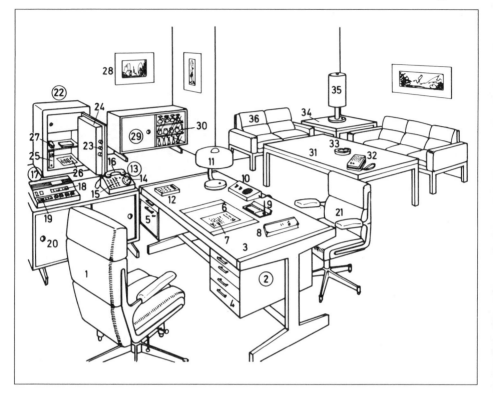

1-36 la oficina (el despacho) del jefe
- *executive's office*
1 el sillón de la mesa de despacho *m* (del escritorio)
- *swivel chair*
2 la mesa de despacho *m* (el escritorio; *Perú:* la carpeta)
- *desk*
3 el tablero de la mesa de despacho *m*
- *desk top*
4 el cajón de la mesa de despacho *m*
- *desk drawer*
5 el armario de puerta *f* abatible
- *cupboard (storage area) with door*
6 el cartapacio (el vade)
- *desk mat (blotter)*
7 la carta comercial
- *business letter*
8 la agenda
- *appointments diary*
9 la bandeja portaplumas (*Amér.:* el canutero)
- *desk set*
10 el interfono
- *intercom (office intercom)*
11 la lámpara de escritorio *m* (de mesa *f* de despacho *m*)
- *desk lamp*
12 la calculadora de bolsillo *m* (la calculadora electrónica)
- *pocket calculator (electronic calculator)*

13 el teléfono, un dispositivo secretaria-jefe
- *telephone, an executive-secretary system*
14 el dial, *también:* el teclado de pulsadores *m*
- *dial; also: push-button keyboard*
15 las teclas de llamada *f*
- *call buttons*
16 el auricular (el auricular de teléfono *m*, el microteléfono)
- *receiver (telephone receiver)*
17 el dictáfono
- *dictating machine*
18 el indicador de la longitud del dictado
- *position indicator*
19 las teclas de manejo *m*
- *control buttons (operating keys)*
20 el armario
- *cabinet*
21 el sillón de la visita
- *visitor's chair*
22 la caja fuerte (la caja de caudales *m*)
- *safe*
23 el pasador de la cerradura
- *bolts*
24 el alojamiento blindado de la cerradura
- *armour-plated (Am. armor-plated) lock area*
25 los documentos confidenciales
- *confidential documents*

26 la patente
- *patent*
27 el dinero en metálico *m* (el dinero efectivo; *P. Rico y S. Dgo.:* el cascajo; *Amér. Central:* el pisto; *Arg., Col., Cuba, Guat. y P. Rico:* el moni; *C. Rica:* el zacatillo)
- *petty cash*
28 el cuadro
- *picture*
29 el mueble bar
- *bar (drinks cabinet)*
30 el servicio del bar
- *bar set*
31-36 el conjunto para las reuniones
- *conference grouping*
31 la mesa de reuniones *f*
- *conference table*
32 el dictáfono de bolsillo *m*
- *pocket-sized dictating machine, a micro-cassette recorder*
33 el cenicero
- *ashtray*
34 la rinconera (la mesa auxiliar; *Amér.:* la esquinera)
- *corner table*
35 la lámpara de mesa *f*
- *table lamp*
36 el sofá de reuniones *f*
- *two-seater sofa [part of the conference grouping]*

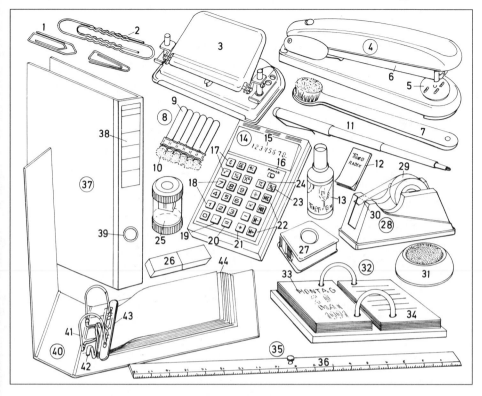

1-44 el material de oficina *f*
- *office equipment (office supplies, office materials)*
1 el clip (*Chile:* el broche) pequeño (*Amér. Central y P. Rico:* el atache)
- *[small] paper clip*
2 el clip grande
- *[large] paper clip*
3 la taladradora
- *punch*
4 la grapadora (*Amér.:* el abrochador)
- *stapler (stapling machine)*
5 la matriz
- *anvil*
6 el tirador de carga *f*
- *spring-loaded magazine*
7 el cepillo de limpieza *f* de los tipos de la máquina de escribir
- *type-cleaning brush*
8 el limpiador de los tipos
- *type cleaner (type-cleaning kit)*
9 el recipiente de líquido *m* disolvente
- *fluid container (fluid reservoir)*
10 la escobilla de limpieza *f*
- *cleaning brush*
11 el rotulador
- *felt tip pen*
12 la hoja de papel *m* correctora de los errores de máquina *f*
- *correcting paper [for typing errors]*
13 el líquido corrector de los errores de máquina *f*
- *correcting fluid [for typing errors]*
14 la calculadora electrónica de bolsillo *m*
- *electronic pocket calculator*

15 la información luminosa de ocho dígitos *m*
- *eight-digit fluorescent display*
16 el interruptor de encendido *m*/apagado *m*
- *on/off switch*
17 las teclas de función *f*
- *function keys*
18 las teclas de cifras *f*
- *number keys*
19 la tecla de coma *f*
- *decimal key*
20 la tecla de resultado *m* (de totalización *m*)
- *'equals' key*
21 las teclas de operaciones *f* aritméticas
- *instruction keys (command keys)*
22 las teclas de la memoria
- *memory keys*
23 la tecla de cálculo *m* del porcentaje
- *percent key (percentage key)*
24 la tecla de π para el cálculo de las longitudes de las circunferencias
- *π-key (pi-key) for mensuration of circles*
25 el sacapuntas
- *pencil sharpener*
26 la goma de borrar de máquina *f* de escribir
- *typewriter rubber*
27 el aparato distribuidor de cinta *f* adhesiva
- *adhesive tape dispenser*
28 el soporte de mesa *f* de la cinta adhesiva
- *adhesive tape holder (roller-type adhesive tape dispenser)*
29 el rollo de cinta *f* adhesiva
- *roll of adhesive tape*

30 la arista (el borde) cortante
- *tear-off edge*
31 la esponjilla humedecedora
- *moistener*
32 la agenda de mesa *f*
- *desk diary*
33 la hoja con la fecha (la hoja de calendario *m*)
- *date sheet (calendar sheet)*
34 la hoja de anotaciones *f* (de notas *f*)
- *memo sheet*
35 la regla
- *ruler*
36 la graduación en centímetros *m* y milímetros *m*
- *centimetre and millimetre (Am. centimeter and millimeter) graduations*
37 el archivador
- *file (document file)*
38 el rótulo del lomo
- *spine label (spine tag)*
39 el orificio para la manipulación
- *finger hole*
40 el clasificador
- *arch board file*
41 el mecanismo del clasificador
- *arch unit*
42 la palanca de abrir o cerrar
- *release lever (locking lever, release/lock lever)*
43 la abrazadera
- *compressor*
44 la relación del estado de cuentas *f*
- *bank statement (statement of account)*

1-48 la oficina colectiva
- *open plan office*
1 el tabique (la mampara de separación *f*)
- *partition wall (partition screen)*
2 el cajón clasificador con un sistema de suspensión *f* de los archivadores
- *filing drawer with suspension file system*
3 el archivador (el clasificador) suspendido
- *suspension file*
4 la lengüeta guía
- *file tab*
5 el archivador
- *file (document file)*
6 la archivera
- *filing clerk*
7 el empleado de oficina *f* (el oficinista)
- *clerical assistant*
8 las apuntes para el archivador
- *note for the files*
9 el teléfono
- *telephone*
10 la estantería de los archivadores
- *filing shelves*
11 la mesa del empleado
- *clerical assistant's desk*
12 el armario de oficina *f*
- *office cupboard*

13 la jardinera con plantas *f*
- *plant stand (planter)*
14 la planta de interior *m*
- *indoor plants (houseplants)*
15 la programadora
- *programmer*
16 la pantalla terminal de datos *m*
- *data display terminal (visual display unit)*
17 el empleado del servicio al cliente
- *customer service representative*
18 el cliente
- *customer*
19 el dibujo realizado por computadora *f*
- *computer-generated design*
20 el tabique de absorción *f* del sonido (de insonorización *f*)
- *sound-absorbing partition*
21 la mecanógrafa
- *typist*
22 la máquina de escribir
- *typewriter*
23 el cajón fichero
- *filing drawer*
24 el fichero de los clientes
- *customer card index*
25 la silla de oficina *f*, una silla giratoria
- *office chair, a swivel chair*
26 la mesa de la máquina de escribir
- *typing desk*

27 el fichero
- *card index box*
28 la estantería de múltiples usos *m*
- *multi-purpose shelving*
29 el jefe
- *proprietor*
30 la carta comercial
- *business letter*
31 la secretaria del jefe (la secretaria de dirección *f*)
- *proprietor's secretary*
32 el bloc de taquigrafía *f*
- *shorthand pad (Am. steno pad)*
33 la audiomecanógrafa
- *audio typist*
34 el dictáfono
- *dictating machine*
35 el auricular en el pabellón de la oreja
- *earphone*
36 la gráfica (el diagrama) estadística (la estadística)
- *statistics chart*
37 el armario de debajo de la mesa de despacho *m*
- *pedestal containing a cupboard or drawers*
38 el armario de puertas *f* de corredera *f*
- *sliding-door cupboard*

39 los elementos dispuestos en forma
f de ángulo *m*
– *office furniture arranged in an*
angular configuration
40 la estantería colgante (suspendida)
– *wall-mounted shelf*
41 la bandeja de correspondencia *f*
– *letter tray*
42 el calendario (el almanaque) de
pared *f*
– *wall calendar*
43 la central de datos *m* (la central
de transmisión *f* de datos *m*, el
banco de datos *m*)
– *data centre (Am. center)*
44 la petición de información *f*
inscrita en la pantalla terminal de
datos *m*
– *calling up information on the data*
display terminal (visual display
unit)
45 la papelera
– *waste paper basket*
46 la estadística de ventas *f*
– *sales statistics*

47 el listado de ordenador *m* (de
tratamiento *m* electrónico de la
información), un impreso plegado
en acordeón *m*
– *EDP print-out, a continuous fan-*
fold sheet
48 el elemento de ensamblaje *m*
– *connecting element*

1 la máquina de escribir eléctrica, una máquina de escribir de cabeza *f* esférica
– *electric typewriter, a golf ball typewriter*
2-6 el teclado
– *keyboard*
2 la barra espaciadora
– *space bar*
3 la tecla de las mayúsculas
– *shift key*
4 la tecla de interlineado *m*
– *line space and carrier return key*
5 la tecla fijamayúsculas
– *shift lock*
6 la tecla de margen *m* (el liberador del margen)
– *margin release key*
7 la tecla del tabulador
– *tabulator key*
8 la tecla de anulación *f* del tabulador
– *tabulator clear key*
9 el interruptor de encendido *m*/apagado *m*
– *on/off switch*
10 la palanca selectora de la intensidad de la impresión
– *striking force control (impression control)*
11 el selector de la cinta
– *ribbon selector*
12 la escala del margen (la escala de marginales *m*)
– *margin scale*
13 el margen izquierdo
– *left margin stop*
14 el margen derecho
– *right margin stop*
15 la cabeza esférica (la cabeza de imprimir, de escribir) con los tipos
– *golf ball (spherical typing element) bearing the types*
16 la cajita de la cinta
– *ribbon cassette*
17 la barra pisapapeles con los rodillos guía
– *paper bail with rollers*
18 el rodillo
– *platen*
19 el tarjetero
– *typing opening (typing window)*
20 la palanca de introducción *f* del papel
– *paper release lever*
21 la palanca de retorno *m* (de marcha *f* atrás) del carro
– *carrier return lever*
22 el botón giratorio del rodillo
– *platen knob*
23 el selector de interlineado *m*
– *line space adjuster*
24 la palanca liberadora del rodillo
– *variable platen action lever*
25 el botón de embrague *m* del rodillo
– *push-in platen variable*
26 la tablilla de apoyo *m* para borrar
– *erasing table*
27 la tapa transparente
– *transparent cover*

28 la cabeza esférica de repuesto *m*
– *exchange golf ball (exchange typing element)*
29 el tipo
– *type*
30 el casquete (la tapa) de la cabeza de imprimir
– *golf ball cap (cap of typing element)*
31 los segmentos dentados
– *teeth*
32 **la fotocopiadora**
– *photocopier (copier, photocopying machine)*
33 la cubierta del original para copias *f* de una en una *f*
– *copyboard cover with single-copy (single-sheet) delivery tray*
34 las bandejas para papel *m* universal
– *universal paper cassette*
35 las bandejas supletorias para el papel
– *adjustable paper cassettes*
36 la tapa delantera
– *front door*
37 la unidad duplex para el transporte vertical
– *dual vertical transport unit*
38 el clasificador
– *sorter*
39 las bandejas para las copias
– *copy delivery bins*
40-43 los mandos
– *control panel displays and control keys*
40 las taclas para ampliación *f*, reducción *f* y programas *f*
– *enlargement, reduction, and program selection keys*
41 las teclas para clasificación *f* y para copias *f* por ambos lados *m*
– *sort mode and two-sided copy keys*
42 el cumador de mandos con teclas para el color, la claridad, tamaño *m* de papel *m* (formato *m*) y número *m* de copias *f* (elección *f* de copias *f*)
– *display with colour, exposure, format, and copy number selection keys*
43 la tecla para copiar
– *start key (copy start key)*
44 **la máquina de plegar cartas *f***
– *letter-folding machine*
45 el dispositivo de alimentación *f* de papel *m*
– *paper feed*
46 el mecanismo de plegado *m*
– *folding mechanism*
47 la bandeja recogedora
– *receiving tray*
48 **la máquina de imprimir (la prensa) en offset de tamaño *m* pequeño**
– *small offset press*
49 el dispositivo de alimentación *f* de papel *m*
– *paper feed*
50 la palanca de tintaje *m* de las placas de imprimir
– *lever for inking the plate cylinder*
51 *u.* 52 la batería de tintaje *m*
– *inking unit (inker unit)*
51 el rodillo distribuidor
– *distributing roller (distributor)*

52 el rodillo entintador
– *ink roller (inking roller, fountain roller)*
53 el botón de regulación *f* de la presión
– *pressure adjustment*
54 la salida del papel impreso
– *sheet delivery (receiving table)*
55 el botón de regulación *f* de la velocidad de impresión *f*
– *printing speed adjustment*
56 el vibrador para alinear los papeles impresos en pilas *f*
– *jogger for aligning the piles of sheets*
57 la pila de papel *m* impreso
– *pile of paper (pile of sheets)*
58 la máquina de plegar (la plegadora)
– *folding machine*
59 la máquina de alzado *m* para tiradas *f* cortas
– *gathering machine (collating machine, assembling machine) for short runs*
60 la estación de alzado *m*
– *gathering station (collating station, assembling station)*
61 la encuadernadora automática para la encuadernación térmica sin cosido *m*
– *adhesive binder (perfect binder) for hot adhesives*
62 **el dictáfono de cinta *f* magnética**
– *magnetic tape dictating machine*
63 los auriculares de casco *m* (el casco auricular, el juego de auriculares *m* con casco *m*)
– *headphones (headset, earphones)*
64 el interruptor de encendido *m*/apagado *m*
– *on/off switch*
65 el mango del micrófono
– *microphone cradle*
66 el enchufe para el interruptor a pedal *m* de la mecanógrafa
– *foot control socket*
67 el enchufe para el teléfono
– *telephone adapter socket*
68 el enchufe para los auriculares de casco *m*
– *headphone socket (earphone socket, headset socket)*
69 el enchufe para el micrófono
– *microphone socket*
70 el altavoz incorporado
– *built-in loudspeaker*
71 la lámpara indicadora (la luz de control *m*)
– *indicator lamp (indicator light)*
72 el compartimiento de la casete
– *cassette compartment*
73 las teclas de marcha *f* adelante, de marcha *f* atrás y de parada *f*
– *forward wind, rewind, and stop buttons*
74 la escala de tiempo *m* (el contador horario) con rayas *f* indicadoras
– *time scale with indexing marks*
75 el cursor de parada *f* de la escala de tiempo *m*
– *time scale stop*

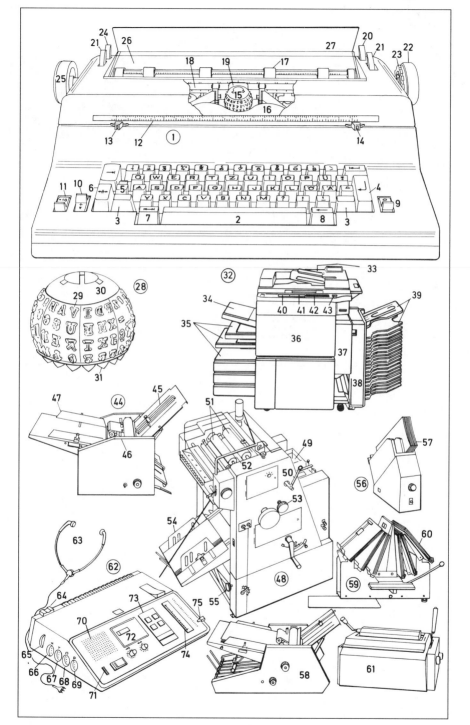

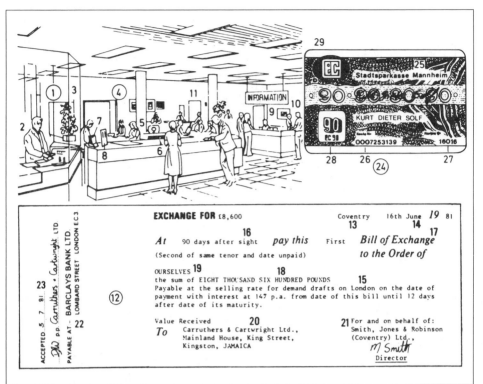

en España:

1-11 el vestíbulo de servicio *m* a los clientes
- *main hall*
1 la caja
- *cashier's desk (cashier's counter)*
2 el cajero
- *teller (cashier)*
3 el cristal antibalas
- *bullet-proof glass*
4 el grupo de empleados *m* de servicio *m*
(asistencia *f* y consejos *m* para cuentas *f*
de ahorro *m*, cuentas *f* privadas y de
empresas *f*, créditos *m* personales)
- *service counters (for service and advice
on savings accounts, private and company accounts, personal loans)*
5 la empleada de banco *m*
- *bank clerk*
6 la clienta del banco
- *customer*
7 los folletos publicitarios
- *brochures*
8 el cartel con las cotizaciones
- *stock list (price list, list of quotations)*
9 el mostrador de información *f*
- *information counter*
10 la ventanilla de cambio *m* de moneda *f*
- *foreign exchange counter*
11 la entrada a la cámara acorazada
- *entrance to strong room*
12 **la letra de cambio** *m; en este caso:* una
letra girada (giro *m*), una letra aceptada
- **bill of exchange** *(bill); here: a draft, an
acceptance (bank acceptance)*
13 el lugar de libramiento *m* (la localidad de
expedición *f*)

- *place of issue*
14 la fecha de libramiento *m* (de expedición
f)
- *date of issue*
15 el lugar de pago *m*
- *place of payment*
16 el día del vencimiento
- *date of maturity (due date)*
17 la cláusula de "letra *f* de cambio *m*" (la
designación del documento como letra *f*
de cambio *m*)
- *bill clause (draft clause)*
18 la cuantía de la letra (el importe de la
letra)
- *value*
19 la orden (el tomador)
- *payee (remittee)*
20 el librado (el girado)
- *drawee (payer)*

21 el librador (el girador)
- *drawer*
22 la domiciliación (el lugar de pago *m*)
- *domicilation (paying agent)*
23 la aceptación
- *acceptance*
24 la tarjeta del eurocheque
- *Eurocheque card*
25 el banco emisor
- *issuing bank (drawee bank)*
26 el número de cuenta *f*
- *account number*
27 el número de tarjeta *f*
- *card number*
28 el holograma (holograma en arco iris *m*)
- *hologram, a white light hologram (rainbow hologram)*
29 al revés: tira magnética
- *(on the back:) magnetic strip*

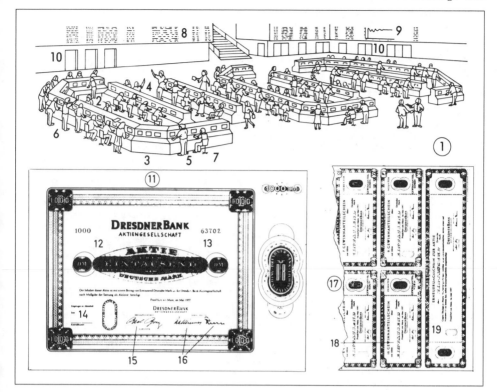

1-10 la Bolsa (la Bolsa de valores *m* y fondos *m* públicos)
– *stock exchange*
1 la sala de la Bolsa
– *exchange hall (exchange floor)*
2 el mercado de valores *m*
– *market for securities*
3 el mostrador para los corredores
– *broker's post*
4 el agente de cambio *m* colegiado, un corredor de comercio *m*
– *sworn stockbroker (exchange broker, stockbroker, Am. specialist), an inside broker*
5 el corredor de comercio *m* (el agente de cambio *m*) libre, para las transacciones del mercado libre
– *kerbstone broker (kerbstoner, curbstone broker, curbstoner, outside broker), a commercial broker dealing in unlisted securities*
6 el miembro de la Bolsa, un particular admitido para las transacciones de Bolsa *f*
– *member of the stock exchange (stock-jobber, Am. floor trader, room trader)*
7 el agente de Bolsa *f*, un empleado de banco *m*
– *stock exchange agent (boardman), a bank employee*
8 el tablón con las cotizaciones bursátiles
– *quotation board*
9 la gráfica
– *index curve*
10 la cabina telefónica

– *telephone box (telephone booth, telephone kiosk, call box)*
11-19 valores *m* (efectos *m*): *clases:* acción *f*, valor *m* de renta *f* fija, título *m* de la deuda, cédula *f* (título *m*) hipotecaria (-o), obligación *f* municipal, obligación *f* industrial, obligación *f* convertible
– *securities;* kinds: *share* (Am. *stock*), *fixed-income security, annuity, bond, debenture bond, municipal bond (corporation stock), industrial bond, convertible bond*
11 la acción (el título); *en este caso:* la acción al portador
– *share certificate* (Am. *stock certificate*); here: *bearer share (share warrant)*
12 el valor nominal de la acción
– *par (par value, nominal par, face par) of the share*
13 el número de orden *m*
– *serial number*
14 el número de folio *m* del libro de registro *m* de acciones *f* del banco
– *page number of entry in bank's share register (bank's stock ledger)*
15 la firma del presidente del Consejo de Inspección *f*
– *signature of the chairman of the board of governors*
16 la firma del presidente del Consejo de Dirección *f*
– *signature of the chairman of the board of directors*
17 la hoja de cupones *m*
– *sheet of coupons (coupon sheet,*

dividend coupon sheet)
18 el cupón de dividendos *m*
– *dividend warrant (dividend coupon)*
19 el talón de renovación *f*
– *talon*

252 Dinero (monedas y billetes)   *Money (Coins and Notes,* Am. *Coins and Bills)*

1-29 monedas *f (clases:* monedas de
oro *m,* de plata *f,* de níquel *m,* de
cobre *m* o de aluminio *m)*
- *coins (coin, coinage, metal money,
specie,* Am. *hard money);* kinds:
*gold, silver, nickel, copper, or alu-
minium,* Am. *aluminum, coins*
1 Atenas: tetradracma *m* en forma *f*
de pepita *f*
- *Athens: tetradrachm (tetradrach-
mon, tetradrachma)*
2 el búho (el ave *f* cívica de Atenas)
- *the owl, emblem of the city of
Athens*
3 áureo *m* (aureus) de Constantino
el Grande
- *aureus of Constantine the Great*
4 bracteata *f* del emperador
Federico I Barbarroja
- *bracteate of Emperor Frederick I
Barbarossa*
5 Francia: luis *m* de oro *m* de Luis
XIV
- *Louis XIV louis-d'or*
6 Prusia: 1 tálero *m* de Federico el
Grande
- *Prussia: I reichstaler (speciestaler)
of Frederick the Great*
7 República Federal Alemana:
moneda *f* de 5 marcos *m* alemanes (DM); 1 DM = 100 pfennigs *m*
- *Federal Republic of Germany: 5
Deutschmarks (DM); 1 DM = 100
pfennigs*
8 el anverso (la cara)
- *obverse*
9 el reverso (la cruz)
- *reverse (subordinate side)*
10 la marca de la ceca
- *mint mark (mintage, exergue)*
11 el cordoncillo
- *legend (inscription on the edge of
a coin)*
12 el dibujo de la moneda, un escudo
de armas *f* nacional
- *device (type), a provincial coat of
arms*
13 Austria: moneda *f* de 25 chelines
m (schilling); 1 sch. = 100
groschen *m*
- *Austria: 25 schillings; 1 sch = 100
groschen*
14 los escudos de armas *f* de las
provincias (de los estados)
- *provincial coats of arms*
15 Suiza: moneda *f* de 5 francos *m;* 1
franco = 100 rappen *m* (céntimos *m)*
- *Switzerland: 5 francs; 1 franc =
100 centimes*
16 Francia: moneda *f* de 1 franco *m*
= 100 céntimos *m*
- *France: 1 franc = 100 centimes*
17 Bélgica: moneda *f* de 100 francos *m*
- *Belgium: 100 francs*

18 Luxemburgo: moneda *f* de 1 franco *m*
- *Luxembourg (Luxemburg): 1
franc*
19 Holanda: moneda *f* de 2 ¹/₂
florines *m;* 1 florín (gulden *m)* =
100 centavos *m*
- *Netherlands: 2 ¹/₂ guilders; 1
guilder (florin, gulden) = 100 cents*
20 Italia: moneda *f* de 200 liras *f;* 1
lira = 100 centésimos *m*
- *Italy: 200 lire (sg. lira)*
21 Estado del Vaticano: moneda *f* de
100 liras *f*
- *Vatican City: 100 lire (sg. lira)*
22 España: moneda *f* de 1 peseta *f* =
100 céntimos *m*
- *Spain: 1 peseta = 100 céntimos*
23 Portugal: moneda *f* de 1 escudo *m*
= 100 centavos *m*
- *Portugal: 1 escudo = 100 centavos*
24 Dinamarca: moneda *f* de 1 corona
f = 100 ores *m*
- *Denmark: 1 krone = 100 öre*
25 Suecia: moneda *f* de 1 corona *f* =
100 ores *m*
- *Sweden: 1 krona = 100 öre*
26 Noruega: moneda *f* de 1 corona *f*
= 100 ores *m*
- *Norway: 1 krone = 100 öre*
27 Checoslovaquia: moneda *f* de 1
corona *f* = 100 halèru *m*
- *Czechoslovakia: 1 koruna = 100
heller*
28 Yugoslavia: moneda *f* de 1 dinar
m = 100 paras *m*
- *Yugoslavia: 1 dinar = 100 paras*
29 Gran Bretaña e Irlanda del Norte:
1 libra *f* esterlina (£) = 100
peniques *m* nuevos
- *United Kingdom of Great Britain
and Northern Ireland: 1 pound
sterling (£1) = 100 new pence (100
p) (sg. new penny, new p)*
30-39 billetes *m* **de banco** *m* (papel *m*
moneda, billetes *m,* moneda *f*
fiduciaria)
- *banknotes* (Am. *bills) (paper
money, notes, treasury notes)*
30 República Federal Alemana: billete *m* de 100 marcos *m* alemanes
(DM)
- *Federal Republic of Germany: 100
DM*
31 el banco emisor
- *bank of issue (bank of circulation)*
32 la filigrana (un retrato)
- *watermark [a portrait]*
33 el valor nominal
- *denomination*
34 Estados Unidos de América: billete *m* de 1 dólar *m* = 100 centavos *m* (*P. Rico: y S. Dgo.:* 1
pavo *m,* 1 tranca *f)*
- *USA: 1 dollar ($1) = 100 cents*

35 las firmas facsímiles
- *facsimile signatures*
36 el sello de control *m*
- *impressed stamp*
37 la designación de la serie (el
número de serie *f*)
- *serial number*
38 Grecia: billete *m* de 1 000 drac-
mas *m;* 1 dracma = 100 leptas *m*
- *Greece: 1,000 drachmas (drach-
mae); 1 drachma = 100 lepta (sg.
lepton)*
39 el retrato
- *portrait*
40-44 la acuñación de moneda *f*
- *striking of coins (coinage,
mintage)*
40 u. **41** los troqueles (los cuños)
- *coining dies (minting dies)*
40 el cuño superior
- *upper die*
41 el cuño inferior
- *lower die*
42 el anillo de acuñación *f*
- *collar*
43 el cospel (la plancha, el flan, el
tejo)
- *coin disc (flan, planchet, blank)*
44 la prensa de acuñación *f*
- *coining press (minting press)*

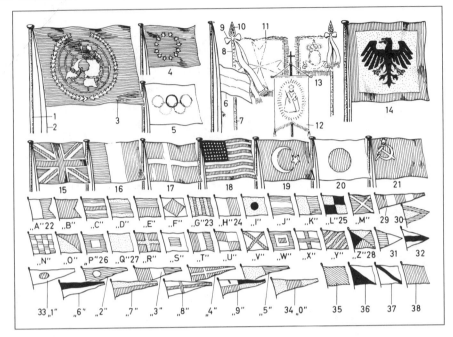

1-3 la bandera de las Naciones Unidas (de la ONU)
- *flag of the United Nations*
1 el asta *f* de la bandera rematada por un sombrerete
- *flagpole (flagstaff) with truck*
2 la driza
- *halyard (halliard, haulyard)*
3 la lanilla
- *hunting*
4 la bandera del Consejo de Europa (la bandera de Europa)
- *flag of the Council of Europe*
5 la bandera olímpica
- *Olympic flag*
6 la bandera a media asta *f* [en señal *f* de duelo *m*]
- *flag at half-mast (Am. at half-staff) [as a token of mourning]*
7-11 el estandarte
- *flag*
7 el asta *f* (el mastil)
- *flagpole (flagstaff)*
8 el bollón (el tachón) de la bandera
- *ornamental stud*
9 la corbata
- *streamer*
10 la moharra
- *pointed tip of the flagpole*
11 la lanilla
- *hunting*
12 el pendón
- *banner (gonfalon)*
13 el estandarte de caballería *f* (el banderín de la caballería)
- *cavalry standard (flag of the cavalry)*
14 el estandarte del Presidente de la República Federal Alemana [la insignia de Jefe *m* del Estado]
- *standard of the German Federal President [ensign of head of state]*

15-21 banderas *f* nacionales (pabellones *m*)
- *national flags*
15 la Unión Jack (Gran Bretaña)
- *the Union Jack (Great Britain)*
16 la bandera tricolor (Francia)
- *the Tricolour (Am. Tricolor) (France)*
17 la Danebrog (Dinamarca)
- *the Danebrog (Dannebrog) (Denmark)*
18 la bandera estrellada (Estados Unidos de América, EEUU)
- *the Stars and Stripes (Star-Spangled Banner) (USA)*
19 la Media Luna (Turquía)
- *the Crescent (Turkey)*
20 la bandera del sol naciente (Japón)
- *the Rising Sun (Japan)*
21 la hoz y el martillo (Unión de Repúblicas Socialistas Soviéticas, URSS)
- *the Hammer and Sickle (USSR)*
22-34 banderas *f* de señales *f*, un juego de banderas
- *signal flags, a hoist*
22-28 banderas *f* de letras *f*
- *letter flags*
22 letra *f* A, una corneta (bandera *f* de dos puntas *f*, de dos farpas *f*)
- *letter A, a burgee (swallow-tailed flag)*
23 letra *f* G, la señal de llamada *f* del práctico
- *G, pilot flag*
24 H ("práctico *m* a bordo *m*")
- *H ('pilot on board')*
25 L ("señal *f* de parada *f* para comunicación *f* importante")
- *L ('you should stop, I have something important to communicate')*
26 P, "a punto *m* de zarpar", una señal de salida *f*
- *P, the Blue Peter ('about to set sail')*

27 W ("requerimiento *m* de aistencia *f* médica")
- *W ('I require medical assistance')*
28 Z, una cuadra (bandera *f* rectangular)
- *Z, an oblong pennant (oblong pendant)*
29 el gallardete del código de señales *f*, un gallardete del Código internacional de señales
- *code pennant (code pendant), used in the International Signals Code*
30-32 gallardetes *m* auxiliares, banderas *f* triangulares
- *substitute flags (repeaters), triangular flags (pennants, pendants)*
33 u. 34 gallardetes *m* de números *m*
- *numeral pennants (numeral pendants)*
33 el número 1
- *number 1*
34 el número 0
- *number 0*
35-38 banderas *f* de Aduana *f*
- *customs flags*
35 la bandera de Aduana *f* de las lanchas aduaneras
- *customs boat pennant (customs boat pendant)*
36 "barco *m* despachado por Aduanas *f* "
- *'ship cleared through customs'*
37 la señal pidiendo despacho *m* de Aduanas *f*
- *customs signal flag*
38 la bandera de pólvora *f* ["carga *f* inflamable"]
- *powder flag ['inflammable (flammable) cargo']*

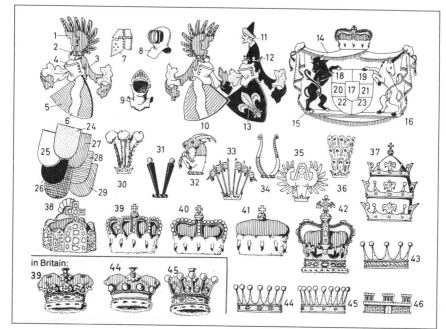

1-36 heráldica *f* (blasón *m*)
- *heraldry (blazonry)*

1, 11, 30-36 cimeras *f*
- *crests*

1-6 el escudo de armas *f* (el blasón)
- *coat-of-arms (achievement of arms, hatchment, achievement)*

2 el tortillo
- *wreath of the colours (Am. colors)*

3 el lambrequín
- *mantle (mantling)*

4, 7-9 yelmos *m* (celadas *f*)
- *helmets (helms)*

4 la celada (el yelmo)
- *tilting helmet (jousting helmet)*

5 el escudo
- *shield*

6 la banda ondeada siniestra
- *bend sinister wavy*

7 el yelmo en forma *f* de cubo *m* (el yelmo cerrado)
- *pot-helmet (pot-helm, heaume)*

8 la celada (el yelmo) de grilleta *f*
- *barred helmet (grilled helmet)*

9 el yelmo abierto (el yelmo con la visera levantada)
- *helmet affronty with visor open*

10-13 el escudo de armas *f* matrimonial (el escudo de alianza *f*, el escudo doble)
- *marital achievement (marshalled, Am. marshaled, coat-of-arms)*

10 el escudo de armas *f* del hombre (del marido)
- *arms of the baron (of the husband)*

11-13 el escudo de armas *f* de la mujer (de la esposa)
- *arms of the family of the femme (of the wife)*

11 el busto humano
- *demi-man; also: demi-woman*

12 la corona de hojas *f*
- *crest coronet*

13 la flor de lis *f*
- *fleur-de-lis*

14 el pabellón heráldico
- *heraldic tent (mantling)*

15 u. **16** tenantes *m*, animales *m* heráldicos
- *supporters (heraldic beasts)*

15 el toro
- *bull*

16 el unicornio
- *unicorn*

17-23 la descripción del escudo de armas *f* (blasón *m*; arte *amb.* de explicar los escudos de armas; la ordenación de los cuarteles [campos] del escudo)
- *blazon*

17 el centro del escudo (el corazón)
- *inescutcheon (heart-shield)*

18-23 los seis cuarteles del escudo
- *quarterings one to six*

18 u. **19** el jefe
- *chief*

18, 20, 22 el flanco *m* diestro
- *dexter (right)*

19, 21, 23 el flanco *m* siniestro
- *sinister (left)*

22 u. **23** la punta
- *base*

24-29 los esmaltes
- *tinctures*

24 u. **25** los metales
- *metals*

24 oro *m* [amarillo]
- *or (gold) [yellow]*

25 plata *f* [blanco]
- *argent (silver) [white]*

26 sable *m* (negro)
- *sable*

27 gules *m* (rojo)
- *gules*

28 azur *m* (azul)
- *azure*

29 sinople *m* (sinoble; verde)
- *vert*

30 las plumas de avestruz *f*
- *ostrich feathers (treble plume)*

31 los garrotes de torneo *m*
- *truncheon*

32 la cabra naciente
- *demi-goat*

33 los pendoncillos de torneo *m*
- *tournament pennons*

34 los cuernos de búfalo *m*
- *buffalo horns*

35 la arpía
- *harpy*

36 el penacho de pavo *m* real
- *plume of peacock's feathers*

37, 38, 42-46 coronas *f*
- *crowns and coronets [continental type]*

37 la tiara papal
- *tiara (papal tiara)*

38 la corona imperial [alemana, hasta 1806]
- *Imperial Crown [German, until 1806]*

39 la corona ducal
- *ducal coronet (duke's coronet)*

40 la corona de príncipe *m*
- *prince's coronet*

41 la corona de príncipe *m* elector (de elector *m*)
- *elector's coronet*

42 la corona real inglesa
- *English Royal Crown*

43-45 coronas *f* de títulos *m* nobiliarios
- *coronets of rank*

43 la corona nobiliaria [de Alemania]
- *baronet's coronet*

44 la corona de barón *m*
- *baron's coronet (baronial coronet)*

45 la corona de conde *m*
- *count's coronet*

46 la corona mural del escudo de armas *f* de una ciudad
- *mauerkrone (mural crown) of a city crest*

1-96 el armamento del ejército de tierra f
– *army armament (army weaponry)*
1-28 armas f **de fuego** m **portátiles**
– *hand weapons*
1 la pistola P 1
– *P1 pistol*
2 el cañón
– *barrel*
3 la mira (el punto de mira f **)**
– *front sight (foresight)*
4 el percutor
– *hammer*
5 el gatillo (el disparador)
– *trigger*
6 la culata
– *pistol grip*
7 la empuñadura y depósito m **del cargador**
– *magazine holder*
8 la metralleta MP 2 **(el subfusil)**
– *MP2 submachine gun*
9 la culata de apoyo m **en el hombro**
– *shoulder rest (butt)*
10 la caja
– *casing (mechanism casing)*
11 la boquilla (la abrazadera)
– *barrel clamp (barrel-clamping nut)*
12 la palanca para cargar el arma f
– *cocking lever (cocking handle)*
13 la caña
– *palm rest*
14 el seguro
– *safety catch*
15 el cargador
– *magazine*
16 el fusil ametrallador G3-A3
– *G3-A3 self-loading rifle*
17 el apagallamas
– *flash hider (flash eliminator)*
18 el dispositivo de disparo m **(el gatillo y el guardamonte)**
– *trigger mechanism*
19 el alza f **(el punto de mira** f **)**
– *notch (sighting notch, rear sight)*
20 el soporte (la montura) de la mira
– *front sight block (foresight block) with front sight (foresight)*
21 la culata del fusil
– *rifle butt (butt)*
22 el lanzagranadas ligero 44 2 A 1
– *44 2A1 light anti-tank rocket launcher*
23 la granada
– *rocket (projectile)*
24 el alza f **telescópica**
– *telescopic sight (telescope sight)*
25 la pieza protectora de la mejilla
– *cheek rest*
26 la ametralladora MG 3
– *MG3 machine gun (Spandau)*
27 el amortiguador del retroceso (del culatazo)
– *recoil booster*
28 la pestaña para el cambio de cañón m
– *belt-changing flap*
29-61 piezas f **de artillería** f **autopropulsada**
– *artillery weapons mounted on self-propelled gun carriages*
29 el obús SF M 110 A 2
– *SFM 110 A2 self-propelled howitzer*
30-32 el chasis
– *gun carriage*
30 la rueda motriz
– *drive wheel*
31 la cadena
– *track*
32 la rueda de corredera f
– *road wheel*

33 la cuba
– *hull*
34 el espolón
– *spade*
35 el cilindro del espolón
– *spade piston*
36 el sistema hidráulico
– *hydraulic system*
37 el cilindro elevador
– *elevating piston*
38 la culata
– *breech ring*
39 el cañón
– *barrel*
40 el freno de la boca de fuego m
– *muzzle*
41 el freno del cañón
– *buffer (buffer recuperator)*
42 el obús autopropulsado blindado M 109 A 3 G
– *M 109 A3 G self-propelled howitzer*
43 la torre blindada
– *armoured (Am. armored) turret*
44 la zona de combate m
– *fighting compartment*
45 la abrazadera soporte m **del cañón**
– *barrel clamp*
46 el extractor de humo m
– *fume extractor*
47 el recuperador
– *barrel recuperator*
48 la defensa antiaérea, ametralladora f
– *light anti-aircraft (AA) machine gun*
49 el sistema lanzamisiles m **(el lanzamisiles)** SF Lance
– *SF Lance missile launch system (missile launcher)*
50 el blindaje de la cadena
– *skirt*
51 el vehículo de cadenas f
– *tracked vehicle*
52 el misil (el misil dirigido)
– *missile (guided missile)*
53 el mecanismo de elevación f
– *elevating gear*
54 la rampa de lanzamiento m
– *launching ramp*
55 el lanzacohetes 110 SF 2
– *110 SF 2 rocket launcher*
56 el sistema regulador del tiro
– *fire control system*
57 el cañón del cohete
– *launching tubes*
58 el blindaje del cañón
– *tube bins*
59 la cureña giratoria
– *turntable*
60 el soporte del vehículo
– *jack*
61 la cabina del conductor
– *driver's cab*
62-87 blindados m
– *armoured (Am. armored) vehicles*
62 el carro de combate m Leopard 2
– *Leopard 2 tank*
63 el cañón de tubo m **liso**
– *smooth-barrelled gun*
64 la escotilla del conductor
– *driver's hatch*
65 el periscopio del comandante
– *commander's periscope*
66 los botes de humo m
– *smoke canister (smoke dispenser)*
67 el blindado espía Lince, **un vehículo anfibio**
– *Luchs armoured (Am. armored) reconnaissance vehicle, an amphibious vehicle*

68 el cañón automático
– *cannon*
69 la escotilla
– *hatch*
70 la antena
– *antenna*
71 la hélice (para ir por el agua f **)**
– *propeller (for propulsion in water)*
72 el blindado de caza f Jaguar 1 (HOT)
– *Jagdpanzer Jaguar 1 ATGW vehicle (HOT)*
73 la instalación para la conducción (parte f **superior) con cabeza** f **direccional**
– *guidance system (upper part) with guidance unit*
74 el tubo de lanzamiento m **para proyectiles** m HOT **guiados**
– *HOT guided-missile launcher*
75 el dispositivo de fuego m **(parte** f **superior)**
– *firing mechanism (upper part)*
76 la cúpula del comandante
– *commander's cupola*
77 el vehículo blindado Marder
– *Marder armoured (Am. armored) personnel carrier*
78 el reflector
– *searchlight*
79 la defensa del blindado, sistema m **de armas** f **dirigidas** MILAN
– *MILAN anti-tank guided-missile system*
80 el blindado de transporte m Zorro m,
un vehículo anfibio
– *Fuchs armoured (Am. armored) personnel and load carrier, an amphibious vehicle*
81 la puerta trasera
– *rear door*
82 el blindado con cañones m **de defensa** f **antiaérea** Gepard
– *Gepard anti-aircraft tank*
83 el radar circular
– *surveillance radar*
84 el radar que sigue la trayectoria para el fuego teledirigido
– *tracking radar for fire control*
85 los cañones automáticos gemelos
– *twin 35 mm cannon*
86 el vehículo de transporte m **de equipos** m M 113 A 1 G
– *M113 A1 G armoured (Am. armored) personnel carrier*
87 la ametralladora sobre la cureña giratoria
– *machine gun on a traversing mount*
88-96 helicópteros m
– *helicopters*
88 el helicóptero de transporte m CH-53 G
– *CH-53 G transport helicopter*
89 el rotor único
– *single rotor*
90 la turbina
– *turbine*
91 el rotor trasero
– *stabilizing tail rotor*
92 el fuselaje
– *fuselage*
93 la cabina
– *cockpit*
94 el helicóptero blindado de defensa f BO-105 P
– *BO-105P anti-tank helicopter*
95 el patín
– *skid*
96 el cañón para el misil dirigido de defensa f **antitanque** HOT
– *HOT anti-tank guided-missile launcher*

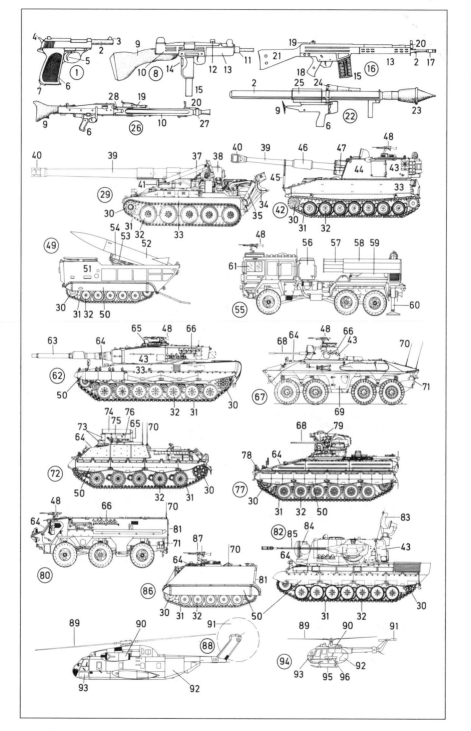

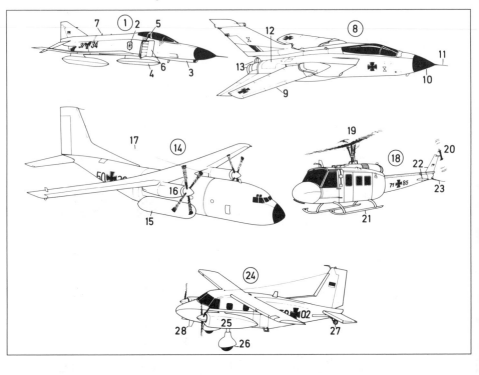

1 **el cazabombardero e interceptor**
   McDonnell-Douglas F-4F
   Phantom II
– McDonnell-Douglas F-4F
   Phantom II *interceptor and fighter-bomber*
2 la insignia del escuadrón
– *squadron marking*
3 el cañón de 20 mm
– *aircraft cannon*
4 el tanque del ala *f* (debajo del ala *f*)
– *wing tank (underwing tank)*
5 la toma de aire *m*
– *air intake*
6 la trampilla de control *m* para la
   capa límite
– *boundary layer control flap*
7 la sonda para el reabastecimiento
   de combustible *m* en vuelo *m*
– *in-flight refuelling (Am. refueling)
   probe (flight refuelling probe, air
   refuelling probe)*
8 **el avión de combate *m* polivalente**
   (MRCA, Multirole Combat
   Aircraft) Panavia 200 Tornado
– Panavia 2000 Tornado *multirole
   combat aircraft (MRCA)*
9 el plano de sustentación *f* giratorio (el ala *f* de geometría *f* variable)
– *swing wing*

10 el radomo (la cúpula del radar)
–   *radar nose (radome, radar dome)*
11 la percha anemométrica (el tubo
    de Pitot)
–   *pitot-static tube (pitot tube)*
12 la trampilla del freno (el freno
    aerodinámico)
–   *brake flap (air brake)*
13 las toberas de postcombustión *f*
    de los reactores
–   *afterburner exhaust nozzles of the
    engines*
14 **el avión de transporte *m* de
    alcance *m* medio** C 160 Transall
–   C160 Transall *medium-range
    transport aircraft*
15 la góndola del tren de aterrizaje *m*
–   *undercarriage housing (landing
    gear housing)*
16 el turbopropulsor (la turbohélice)
–   *propeller-turbine engine (turbo-
    prop engine)*
17 la antena
–   *antenna*
18 **el helicóptero ligero de transporte
    m y rescate *m*** Bell UH-1D
    Iroquois
–   Bell UH-ID Iroquois *light trans-
    port and rescue helicopter*
19 el rotor principal (la hélice de
    propulsión *f*)
–   *main rotor*

20 el rotor antipar trasero (la hélice
    de dirección *f*)
–   *tail rotor*
21 los patines de aterrizaje *m* (los
    esquíes de aterrizaje *m*)
–   *landing skids*
22 los planos fijos de estabilización *f*
–   *stabilizing fins (stabilizing sur-
    faces, stabilizers)*
23 el patín de cola *f*
–   *tail skid*
24 **el avión de transporte *m* y de
    enlace *m*** (de despegue *m* y ate-
    rrizaje *m* corto) Dornier DO 28
    D-2 Skyservant
–   Dornier DO 28 D-2 Skyservant
    *transport and communications
    aircraft*
25 la góndola del motor
–   *engine pod*
26 el tren de aterrizaje *m* principal
–   *main undercarriage unit (main
    landing gear unit)*
27 la rueda de cola *f*
–   *tail wheel*
28 la antena ensiforme (xifoide)
–   *sword antenna*

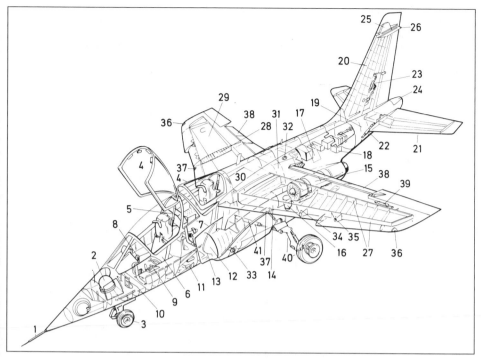

1-41 el avión a reacción *f* franco-alemán de adiestramiento *m* Dornier-Dassault-Breguet Alpha Jet
– Dornier-Dassault-Breguet Alpha Jet Franco-German jet trainer
1 la percha anemométrica (el tubo de Pitot)
– *pitot-static tube (pitot tube)*
2 el depósito de oxígeno *m*
– *oxygen tank*
3 el tren de aterrizaje *m* delantero replegable hacia delante
– *forward-retracting nose wheel*
4 la cúpula de la cabina (de la carlinga)
– *cockpit canopy (cockpit hood)*
5 el gato de la cúpula
– *canopy jack*
6 el asiento del piloto (el asiento del piloto alumno), un asiento de eyección *f*
– *pilot's seat (student pilot's seat), an ejector seat (ejection seat)*
7 el asiento del observador (el asiento del instructor de vuelo *m*), un asiento de eyección *f*
– *observer's seat (instructor's seat), an ejector seat (ejection seat)*
8 la palanca de mando *m*
– *control column (control stick)*
9 la palanca de potencia *f* (el mando de gases *m*)
– *thrust lever*
10 los pedales del timón de dirección *f* con frenos *m*
– *rudder pedals with brakes*
11 el compartimiento de proa *f* del equipo electrónico
– *front avionics bay*
12 la entrada de aire *m* (la toma de aire *m*) del reactor
– *air intake to the engine*

13 el tabique de control *m* para la capa límite
– *boundary layer control flap*
14 el conducto de entrada *f* del aire
– *air intake duct*
15 el turborreactor
– *turbine engine*
16 el depósito de alimentación *f* del sistema hidráulico
– *reservoir for the hydraulic system*
17 el compartimiento de las baterías
– *battery housing*
18 el compartimiento de cola *f* del equipo electrónico
– *rear avionics bay*
19 el compartimiento de equipajes *m*
– *baggage compartment*
20 el plano fijo de deriva *f* de triple larguero *m*
– *triple-spar tail construction*
21 el timón de profundidad *f*
– *horizontal tail*
22 el servomando del timón de profundidad *f*
– *servo-actuating mechanism for the elevator*
23 el servomando del timón de dirección *f*
– *servo-actuating mechanism for the rudder*
24 la caja del paracaídas de frenado *m*
– *brake chute housing (drag chute housing)*
25 la antena perfilada VHF [VHF: Very high frequency]
– *VHF (very high frequency) antenna (UHF antenna)*
26 la antena de altísima frecuencia *f* multidireccional [VOR: Very high frequency omnidirectional range]
– *VOR (very high frequency omnidirectional range) antenna*

27 la superficie de sustentación *f* de doble larguero *m*
– *twin-spar wing construction*
28 la armazón formada por largueros *m*
– *former with integral spars*
29 el tanque integrado en el ala *f*
– *integral wing tanks*
30 el tanque central del fuselaje
– *centre-section (Am. center-section) fuel tank*
31 los tanques del fuselaje
– *fuselage tanks*
32 la sonda de llenado *m* de combustible *m* por gravedad *f*
– *gravity fuelling (Am. fueling) point*
33 la toma de combustible *m* bajo presión *f*
– *pressure fuelling (Am. fueling) point*
34 la suspensión interior del ala *f*
– *inner wing suspension*
35 la suspensión exterior del ala *f*
– *outer wing suspension*
36 las luces de navegación *f* (de posición *f*)
– *navigation lights (position lights)*
37 los faros de aterrizaje *m*
– *landing lights*
38 los alerones de profundidad *f*
– *landing flap*
39 el servomando del alerón
– *aileron actuator*
40 el tren de aterrizaje *m* principal replegable hacia delante
– *forward-retracting main undercarriage unit (main landing gear unit)*
41 el gato hidráulico de levantamiento *m* (el dispositivo retráctil hidromecánico) del tren de aterrizaje *m*
– *undercarriage hydraulic cylinder (landing gear hydraulic cylinder)*

1 **el destructor lanzamisiles** de la clase Hamburg
- *Hamburg class* **guided-missile destroyer**
2 el casco de cubierta *f* corrida
- *hull of flush-deck vessel*
3 la proa (la roda)
- *bow (stem)*
4 el asta *f* (el mástil) de la bandera
- *flagstaff (jackstaff)*
5 el ancla *f*, una ancla de patente *f* (sin cepo *m*)
- *anchor, a stockless anchor (patent anchor)*
6 el cabrestante del ancla *f*
- *anchor capstan (windlass)*
7 el rompeolas
- *breakwater (Am. manger board)*
8 la cuaderna de curvatura *f*
- *chine strake*
9 la cubierta principal
- *main deck*
10-28 superestructuras *f*
- *superstructures*
10 la cubierta superior
- *superstructure deck*
11 la balsa salvavidas
- *life rafts*
12 el esquife (la lancha de a bordo *m*)
- *cutter (ship's boat)*
13 la serviola (el pescante)
- *davit (boat-launching crane)*
14 el puente de mando *m* (el puente)
- *bridge (bridge superstructure)*
15 la luz lateral de posición *f* (de situación *f*)
- *side navigation light (side running light)*
16 la antena
- *antenna*
17 el cuadro radiogoniométrico (el radiogoniómetro)
- *radio direction finder (RDF) frame*
18 el palo de celosía *f* (la torre metálica)
- *lattice mast*
19 la chimenea de proa *f*
- *forward funnel*
20 la chimenea de popa *f*
- *aft funnel*
21 la caperuza de la chimenea (el sombrerete de la chimenea)
- *cowl*
22 la toldilla (el castillo de popa *f*)
- *aft superstructure (poop)*
23 el cabrestante
- *capstan*
24 la escalera de cámara *f* (la escotilla de cámara *f*)
- *companion ladder (companionway, companion hatch)*
25 el asta *f* de la bandera de popa *f*
- *ensign staff*
26 la popa, una popa cuadra (popa *f* de espejo *m*)
- *stern, a transom stern*
27 la línea de flotación *f*
- *waterline*
28 el reflector
- *searchlight*
29-37 el armamento
- *armament*
29 la torreta con un cañón de 100 mm
- *100 mm gun turret*
30 el lanzamisiles de defensa *f* antisubmarina, un lanzamisiles cuádruple
- *four-barrel anti-submarine rocket launcher (missile launcher)*
31 el afuste de dos cañones *m* antiaéreos de 40 mm
- *40 mm twin anti-aircraft (AA) gun*
32 el lanzamisiles de defensa *f* antiaérea MM 38, en su contenedor *m* de lanzamiento *m*
- *MM 38 anti-aircraft (AA) rocket launcher (missile launcher) in launching container*

33 el tubo lanzatorpedos de defensa *f* antisubmarina
- *anti-submarine torpedo tube*
34 la plataforma de lanzamiento *m* de cargas *f* de profundidad *f*
- *depth-charge thrower*
35 el radar de telepuntería *f*
- *weapon system radar*
36 la antena de radar *m*
- *radar antenna (radar scanner)*
37 el telémetro óptico
- *optical rangefinder*
38 **el destructor lanzamisiles** de la clase Lütjens
- *Lütjens class* **guided-missile destroyer**
39 el ancla *f* de proa *f*
- *bower anchor*
40 el guardahélice (la protección de la hélice)
- *propeller guard*
41 el palo trípode de celosía *f*
- *tripod lattice mast*
42 el palo de una sola pieza
- *pole mast*
43 los orificios de ventilación *f* (la rejilla de ventilación *f*)
- *ventilator openings (ventilator grill)*
44 el conducto de salida *f* del humo
- *exhaust pipe*
45 el esquife (la lancha de a bordo *m*)
- *ship's boat*
46 la antena
- *antenna*
47 el cañón multiusos de 127 mm dirigido por radar *m* en su torreta *f*
- *radar-controlled 127 mm all-purpose gun in turret*
48 el cañón multiusos de 127 mm
- *127 mm all-purpose gun*
49 la rampa de lanzamiento *m* de misiles *m* Tartar
- *launcher for Tartar missiles*
50 el lanzamisiles de defensa *f* antisubmarina
- *anti-submarine rocket (ASROC) launcher (missile launcher)*
51 las antenas de radar *m* para el control del tiro
- *fire control radar antennas*
52 el radomo
- *radome (radar dome)*
53 **la fragata** de la clase Bremen
- *Bremen class* **frigate**
54 el cañón de fuego *m* rápido de 76 mm dirigido por radar *m*
- *radar-controlled 76 mm rapid-fire gun*
55 los misiles superficie-aire "Sea Sparrow"
- *Sea Sparrow surface-to-air missiles*
56 la instalación de radar *m* y de telepuntería *f*
- *radar and fire control system*
57 los misiles superficie-superficie "Harpoon"
- *Harpoon surface-to-surface missiles*
58 la chimenea
- *funnel*
59 la caperuza de la chimenea (el sombrerete de la chimenea)
- *cowl*
60 el radar circular del espacio aéreo
- *air/surface search radar*
61 el esquife (la lancha de a bordo *m*)
- *cutter*
62 los misiles superficie-aire de corto alcance *m*
- *close-range surface-to-air missiles*
63 la plataforma para helicópteros *m*
- *helicopter deck*
64 **el submarino** de la clase 206
- *type 206* **submarine**
65 el castillo de proa *f* que se puede inundar
- *flooded foredeck*

66 el casco de presión *f*
- *pressure hull*
67 la torreta
- *turret*
68 los instrumentos retráctiles (escamoteables)
- *retractable instruments*
69 **la lancha rápida lanzamisiles** de la clase 148
- *type 148* **missile-firing fast attack craft**
70 el cañón *f* multiusos de 76 mm con torreta *f*
- *76 mm all-purpose gun with turret*
71 el contenedor de lanzamiento *m* de misiles *m*
- *missile-launching housing*
72 la chupeta (camareta *f* junto al coronamiento de popa *f*, cámara *f* alta)
- *deckhouse*
73 el cañón antiaéreo (DCA) de 40 mm
- *40 mm anti-aircraft (AA) gun*
74 el listón guardahélice (el protector de la hélice)
- *propeller guard moulding (Am. molding)*
75 **la lancha rápida lanzamisiles** de la clase 143
- *type 143* **missile-firing fast attack craft**
76 el rompeolas
- *breakwater (Am. manger board)*
77 el radomo
- *radome (radar dome)*
78 el tubo lanzatorpedos
- *torpedo tube*
79 el conducto de salida *f* de los gases de escape *m*
- *exhaust escape flue*
80 **el cazador de minas** *f* de la clase 331
- *type 331* **mine hunter**
81 el cintón reforzado
- *reinforced rubbing strake*
82 el bote neumático
- *inflatable boat (inflatable dinghy)*
83 la serviola (el pescante) del bote
- *davit*
84 **el dragaminas** (el buque barreminas, el buque buscaminas) de la clase 341
- *type 341* **minesweeper**
85 el torno de tambor *m* para el cable
- *cable winch*
86 el torno de remolque *m*
- *towing winch (towing machine, towing engine)*
87 la draga (el mecanismo para barrer minas *f*)
- *mine-sweeping gear (paravanes)*
88 la grúa
- *crane (davit)*
89 **el buque de desembarco** *m* de la clase Barbe
- *Barbe class* **landing craft**
90 la rampa de proa *f*
- *bow ramp*
91 la rampa de popa *f*
- *stern ramp*
92 **el ténder** (el barco avituallador) de la clase Rhein
- *Rhein class* **tender**
93 **el buque de mantenimiento** *m*, versión *f* taller *m* de reparación *f*, de la clase Lüneburg
- *Lüneburg class* **support ship**
94 **el buque fondeador de minas** *f* (el buque minador, el buque portaminas) de la clase Sachsenwald
- *Sachsenwald class* **mine transport**
95 **el remolcador de salvamento** *m* **en alta mar** *f* de la clase Helgoland
- *Helgoland class* **salvage tug**
96 **el buque cisterna** (el petrolero de reabastecimiento *m* de combustible *m*) de la clase Eifel
- *replenishment tanker 'Eifel'*

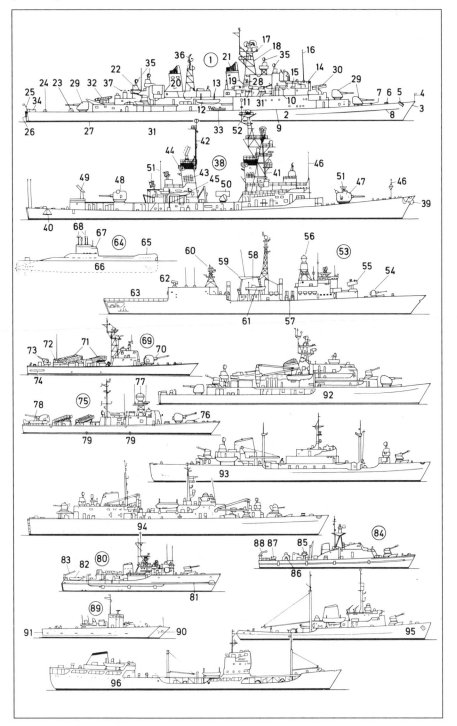

259 Buques de guerra II (buques de guerra modernos)

1 el portaaviones a propulsión *f* nuclear "Nimitz ICVN 68" (EEUU)
– *nuclear-powered aircraft carrier* Nimitz ICVN68 *(USA)*
2-11 el plano lateral
– *body plan*
2 la cubierta de vuelo *m*
– *flight deck*
3 la superestructura (el puente de mando *m*)
– *island (bridge)*
4 el ascensor de aviones *m*
– *aircraft lift (Am. aircraft elevator)*
5 el lanzamisiles óctuplo de defensa *f* antiaérea
– *eight-barrel anti-aircraft (AA) rocket launcher (missile launcher)*
6 el palo de una sola pieza (el poste de antenas *f*)
– *pole mast (antenna mast)*
7 la antena
– *antenna*
8 la antena de radar *m*
– *radar antenna (radar scanner)*
9 la proa blindada
– *fully enclosed bow*
10 la grúa a bordo *m*
– *deck crane*
11 la popa cuadra (la popa de espejo *m*)
– *transom stern*
12-20 el plano de cubierta *f*
– *deck plan*
12 la cubierta de vuelo *m* (la cubierta en ángulo *m*)
– *angle deck (flight deck)*
13 el ascensor de aviones *m*
– *aircraft lift (Am. aircraft elevator)*
14 la catapulta de lanzamiento *m* doble
– *twin launching catapult*
15 la pantalla plegable (móvil) protectora contra las llamaradas
– *hinged (movable) baffle board*
16 el cable de retención *f* (el cable de freno *m*)
– *arrester wire*
17 la red (la barrera) de emergencia *f* para amortiguar el choque
– *emergency crash barrier*
18 el andarivel
– *safety net*
19 el camello
– *caisson (cofferdam)*
20 el lanzamisiles óctuplo de defensa *f* antiaérea
– *eight-barrel anti-aircraft (AA) rocket launcher (missile launcher)*
21 el crucero lanzamisiles "Kara" (URSS)
– Kara class *rocket cruiser (missile cruiser) (USSR)*
22 el casco de cubierta *f* corrida
– *hull of flush-deck vessel*
23 la arrufadura (el arrufo)
– *sheer*
24 el lanzamisiles de doce tubos *m* de defensa *f* antisubmarina
– *twelve-barrel underwater salvo rocket launcher (missile launcher)*
25 el lanzamisiles doble de defensa *f* antiaérea
– *twin anti-aircraft (AA) rocket launcher (missile launcher)*
26 la batería de lanzamiento *m* de 4 misiles *m* de corto recorrido *m*
– *launching housing for 4 short-range rockets (missiles)*
27 la pantalla protectora contra las llamaradas
– *baffle board*
28 el puente de mando *m* (el puente)
– *bridge*
29 la antena de radar *m*
– *radar antenna (radar scanner)*

30 la torreta con dos cañones *m* antiaéreos de 76 mm
– *twin 76 mm anti-aircraft (AA) gun turret*
31 la torre de combate *m*
– *turret*
32 la chimenea
– *funnel*
33 el lanzamisiles doble de defensa *f* antiaérea
– *twin anti-aircraft (AA) rocket launcher (missile launcher)*
34 el cañón automático antiaéreo (de defensa antiaérea, DCA)
– *automatic anti-aircraft (AA) gun*
35 el esquife (la lancha de a bordo *m*)
– *ship's boat*
36 la batería de cinco tubos *m* lanzatorpedos de defensa *f* antisubmarina
– *underwater 5-torpedo housing*
37 el lanzamisiles séxtuplo de defensa *f* antisubmarina
– *underwater 6-salvo rocket launcher (missile launcher)*
38 el hangar de helicópteros *m*
– *helicopter hangar*
39 la plataforma de aterrizaje *m* de los helicópteros
– *helicopter landing platform*
40 el sonar de profundidad *f* variable
– *variable depth sonar (VDS)*
41 el crucero lanzamisiles a propulsión *f* nuclear "California" (EEUU)
– California class *rocket cruiser (missile cruiser) (USA)*
42 el casco
– *hull*
43 la torre de combate *m* de proa *f*
– *forward turret*
44 la torre de combate *m* de popa *f*
– *aft turret*
45 la superestructura de proa *f*
– *forward superstructure*
46 las lanchas de desembarco *m*
– *landing craft*
47 la antena
– *antenna*
48 la antena de radar *m*
– *radar antenna (radar scanner)*
49 el radomo
– *radome (radar dome)*
50 el lanzamisiles contra objetivos *m* aéreos
– *surface-to-air rocket launcher (missile launcher)*
51 el lanzatorpedos de defensa *f* antisubmarina
– *underwater rocket launcher (missile launcher)*
52 el cañón de 127 mm con torreta *f*
– *127 mm gun with turret*
53 la plataforma de aterrizaje *m* de los helicópteros
– *helicopter landing platform*
54 el submarino atómico antisubmarino
– *nuclear-powered fleet submarine*
55-74 la sección central del submarino [esquema]
– *middle section [diagram]*
55 el casco de presión *f*
– *pressure hull*
56 la sala de máquinas *f* auxiliares
– *auxiliary engine room*
57 la bomba de la turbina centrífuga
– *rotary turbine pump*
58 el generador de la turbina a vapor *m* (el turboalternador)
– *steam turbine generator*
59 el árbol (el eje) de la hélice
– *propeller shaft*
60 el cojinete de empuje *m*
– *thrust block*
61 el reductor (el demultiplicador)
– *reduction gear*
62 la turbina de alta o baja presión *f*
– *high and low pressure turbine*

63 el conducto de vapor *m* de alta presión *f* del circuito secundario
– *high-pressure steam pipe for the secondary water circuit (auxiliary water circuit)*
64 el condensador
– *condenser*
65 el circuito primario
– *primary water circuit*
66 el cambiador de calor *m*
– *heat exchanger*
67 la cuba del reactor nuclear
– *nuclear reactor casing (atomic pile casing)*
68 el núcleo del reactor
– *reactor core*
69 los elementos de control *m*
– *control rods*
70 la pantalla de plomo *m* (el blindaje aislante contra las radiaciones)
– *lead screen*
71 la torreta
– *turret*
72 el tubo snorkel
– *snorkel (schnorkel)*
73 el inyector de aire *m* fresco
– *air inlet*
74 los instrumentos retráctiles (escamoteables)
– *retractable instruments*
75 el submarino monocasco de propulsión *f* convencional (Diesel-eléctrica)
– *patrol submarine with conventional (diesel-electric) drive*
76 el casco de presión *f*
– *pressure hull*
77 el castillo de proa *f* que se puede inundar
– *flooded foredeck*
78 la trampilla exterior [del tubo lanzatorpedos]
– *outer flap (outer doors) [for torpedoes]*
79 el tubo lanzatorpedos
– *torpedo tube*
80 la sentina (el pantoque) de proa *f*
– *bow bilge*
81 el ancla *f*
– *anchor*
82 el cabrestante (el torno) del ancla *f*
– *anchor winch*
83 la batería de acumuladores *m*
– *battery*
84 los camarotes con literas *f* plegables
– *living quarters with folding bunks*
85 el camarote del comandante
– *commanding officer's cabin*
86 la escotilla principal
– *main hatchway*
87 el asta *f* (el mástil) de la bandera
– *flagstaff*
88-91 los instrumentos retráctiles (escamoteables)
– *retractable instruments*
88 el periscopio de ataque *m*
– *attack periscope*
89 la antena
– *antenna*
90 el tubo snorkel
– *snorkel (schnorkel)*
91 la antena de radar *m*
– *radar antenna (radar scanner)*
92 la válvula de evacuación *f* de gases *m* de escape *m*
– *exhaust outlet*
93 el compartimiento del tubo de calefacción *f*
– *heat space (hot-pipe space)*
94 el grupo Diesel
– *diesel generators*
95 el timón de profundidad *f* y el timón de dirección *f* de popa *f*
– *aft diving plane and vertical rudder*
96 el timón de profundidad *f* de proa *f*
– *forward vertical rudder*

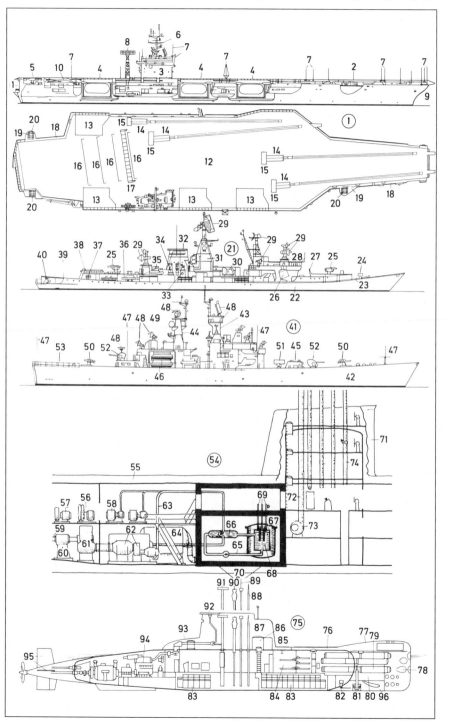

1-85 el colegio de preescolar y enseñan-za f primaria
- *primary school*
1-45 la clase (el aula f)
- *classroom*
1 los pupitres puestos en forma f de herradura f
- *arrangement of desks in a horseshoe*
2 el pupitre doble (*Perú:* la carpeta)
- *double desk*
3 los alumnos (los escolares; *Perú:* los escoleros; *Col., Mé. y Venez.:* los escuelantes; *Bol.:* los escolinos) sen-tados en grupos m
- *pupils (children) in a group (sitting in a group)*
4 el cuaderno de ejercicios m
- *exercise book*
5 el lápiz (el lapicero)
- *pencil*
6 la barrita de cera f
- *wax crayon*
7 la cartera (para llevar en la mano; *Amér.:* el bulto)
- *school bag*
8 el asa f
- *handle*
9 la cartera (para llevar a la espalda)
- *school satchel (satchel)*
10 el bolsillo delantero
- *front pocket*
11 la correa del hombro
- *strap (shoulder strap)*
12 el plumier (el estuche de lápices; m; *Arg. y Chile:* la lapicera)
- *pen and pencil case*
13 el cierre de cremallera f
- *zip* (Am. *zipper*)
14 la pluma estilográfica
- *fountain pen (pen)*
15 la carpeta de anillas f (el archivador)
- *loose-leaf file (ring file)*
16 el libro de lectura f
- *reader*
17 el libro de ortografía f
- *spelling book*
18 el cuaderno de escritura f
- *exercise book (notebook)*
19 el rotulador
- *felt tip pen*
20 el dedo levantado
- *raising the hand*
21 el profesor (*Amér. Central, Chile, Mé., Perú, Urug. y Venez.:* el escuelero)
- *teacher*
22 la mesa del profesor
- *teacher's desk*
23 el libro de clase f
- *register*
24 la bandeja portaplumas
- *pen and pencil tray*
25 el cartapacio
- *desk mat (blotter)*
26 el cristal de la ventana pintado a mano f
- *window painting with finger paints (finger painting)*
27 las acuarelas pintadas por los alumnos
- *pupils' (children's) paintings (water-colours, Am. watercolors*

28 la cruz (el crucifijo)
- *cross*
29 la pizarra de tres paneles m (*Antillas y Río de la Plata:* el pizarrón)
- *three-part blackboard*
30 la pinza para sostener los mapas
- *bracket for holding charts*
31 la ranura para las tizas
- *chalk ledge*
32 la tiza (blanca; *Amér. Central y Mé.:* el tizate)
- *chalk*
33 el dibujo de la pizarra
- *blackboard drawing*
34 el diagrama (el esquema)
- *diagram*
35 el panel lateral reversible
- *reversible side blackboard*
36 el plano de proyección f (la pantalla de proyección f)
- *projection screen*
37 la escuadra
- *triangle*
38 el transportador
- *protractor*
39 la división en grados m
- *divisions*
40 el compás de pizarra f (el compás de tiza f)
- *blackboard compass*
41 la bandeja de la esponja
- *sponge tray*
42 la esponja
- *blackboard sponge (sponge)*
43 el armario de la clase
- *classroom cupboard*
44 el mapa (el mapa mural)
- *map (wall map)*
45 el muro (la pared) de ladrillos m
- *brick wall*
46-85 la clase de trabajos m manuales (el taller)
- ***craft room***
46 el banco de carpintero m
- *workbench*
47 el tornillo de banco m (la mordaza)
- *vice (Am. vise)*
48 la manivela de sujeción f
- *vice (Am. vise) bar*
49 las tijeras
- *scissors*
50-52 el trabajo con pegamento m
- *working with glue (sticking paper, cardboard, etc.)*
50 la superficie para pegar
- *surface to be glued*
51 el tubo de pegamento m
- *tube of glue*
52 el tapón del tubo
- *tube cap*
53 la sierra de marquetería f (la serreta)
- *fretsaw*
54 la cuchilla de la serreta
- *fretsaw blade (saw blade)*
55 la escofina de madera f
- *wood rasp (rasp)*
56 el trozo de madera f aserrado asido por el tornillo de banco m
- *piece of wood held in the vice (Am. vise)*

57 el bote de cola f
- *glue pot*
58 el taburete
- *stool*
59 la escobilla
- *brush*
60 el recogedor
- *pan (dustpan)*
61 las virutas
- *broken china*
62 el esmalte (el trabajo de esmaltado m)
- *enamelling (Am. enameling)*
63 el horno eléctrico para esmaltar
- *electric enamelling (Am. enameling) stove*
64 el cobre en bruto
- *unworked copper*
65 el polvo para esmaltar
- *enamel powder*
66 el colador de hilos m finos de alam-bre m
- *hair sieve*
67-80 los trabajos escolares
- *pupils' (children's) work*
67 las esculturas de arcilla f (los trabajos de modelado m)
- *clay models (models)*
68 la decoración de la ventana en vidrio m coloreado
- *window decoration of coloured (Am. colored) glass*
69 el mosaico de vidrio m
- *glass mosaic picture (glass mosaic)*
70 el móvil
- *mobile*
71 la cometa (la birlocha, la milocha, la pandorga, el pájaro bitango, la pájara, el pandero; *Amér.:* el volan-tín)
- *paper kite (kite)*
72 la construcción de madera f
- *wooden construction*
73 el poliedro
- *polyhedron*
74 las marionetas
- *hand puppets*
75 las máscaras de arcilla f
- *clay masks*
76 las velas de cera f
- *cast candles (wax candles)*
77 la talla de madera f
- *wood carving*
78 el jarro de arcilla f (de barro m)
- *clay jug*
79 las formas geométricas de arcilla f (de barro m)
- *geometrical shapes made of clay*
80 el juguete de madera f
- *wooden toys*
81 los materiales de trabajo m
- *materials*
82 la provisión de madera f
- *stock of wood*
83 las tintas de imprenta f para el grabado en madera f (para la xilografía f)
- *inks for wood cuts*
84 los pinceles
- *paintbrushes*
85 el saco de yeso m
- *bag of plaster of Paris*

261 Colegio II (enseñanza media; enseñanza secundaria)

1-45 el instituto; *anál.:* el colegio de enseñanza *f* media
- *grammar school;* also: *upper band of a comprehensive school* (Am. *alternative school*)

1-13 la clase de química *f*
- *chemistry*
1 el laboratorio de química *f* con los bancos dispuestos en gradas *f*
- *chemistry lab (chemistry laboratory) with tiered rows of seats*
2 el profesor de química *f*
- *chemistry teacher*
3 la mesa de experimentación *f*
- *demonstration bench (teacher's bench)*
4 la toma de agua *f*
- *water pipe*
5 la superficie de la mesa de trabajo *m* embaldosada (alicatada)
- *tiled working surface*
6 el fregadero (la pila)
- *sink*
7 el monitor de vídeo *m*, una pantalla para la difusión de programas *m* pedagógicos
- *television monitor, a screen for educational programmes* (Am. *programs*)
8 el retroproyector
- *overhead projector*
9 el plano de proyección *f* para el papel transparente
- *projector top for skins*
10 la lente de proyección *f* con el espejo inclinado
- *projection lens with right-angle mirror*
11 la mesa de los alumnos equipada para los experimentos
- *pupils' (Am. students') bench with experimental apparatus*
12 el enchufe hembra *f* (la toma de corriente *f*)
- *electrical point (socket)*
13 la mesa de proyección *f*
- *projection table*
14-34 el laboratorio de biología *f*
- *biology preparation room (biology prep room)*
14 el esqueleto
- *skeleton*
15 la colección de cráneos *m*, las reproducciones de cráneos *m*
- *collection of skulls, models (casts) of skulls*
16 la bóveda craneal del Pithecantropus erectus
- *calvarium of Pithecanthropus erectus*
17 el cráneo del Homo steinheimensis
- *skull of Steinheim man*

18 la bóveda craneal del hombre de Pekín (del Sinanthropus)
- *calvarium of Peking man (of Sinanthropus)*
19 el cráneo del hombre de Neanderthal, un cráneo de homínido *m*
- *skull of Neanderthal man, a skull of primitive man*
20 el cráneo del Australopithecus
- *Australopithecine skull (skull of Australopithecus)*
21 el cráneo del Homo sapiens (del hombre actual)
- *skull of present-day man*
22 la mesa de disección *f*
- *dissecting bench*
23 los frascos de productos *m* químicos
- *chemical bottles*
24 la espita del gas
- *gas tap*
25 la cápsula de Petri
- *petri dish*
26 la probeta graduada
- *measuring cylinder*
27 las fichas de trabajo *m* (el material didáctico)
- *work folder containing teaching material*
28 el libro de texto *m* (el manual)
- *textbook*
29 los cultivos bacteriológicos
- *bacteriological cultures*
30 la estufa de incubación *f* microbiana (la estufa de cultivos *m;* la estufa bacteriológica)
- *incubator*
31 el escurridor de probetas *f*
- *test tube rack*
32 el frasco lavador de gases *m*
- *washing bottle*
33 la cubeta
- *water tank*
34 el fregadero
- *sink*
35 el laboratorio de idiomas *m*
- *language laboratory*
36 la pizarra (*Antillas y Río de la Plata:* el pizarrón)
- *blackboard*
37 la consola central
- *console*
38 el casco auricular
- *headphones (headset)*
39 el micrófono
- *microphone*
40 el auricular
- *earcup*
41 el muelle acolchado del casco
- *padded headband (padded headpiece)*

42 la grabadora de programas *m* pedagógicos (la grabadora de cintas *f* magnetofónicas, de casetes *f;* un magnetófono)
- *programme* (Am. *program) recorder, a cassette recorder*
43 el control de volumen *m* de la voz de los alumnos
- *pupil's (Am. student's) volume control*
44 el control de volumen *m* del programa
- *master volume control*
45 el teclado de mandos *m*
- *control buttons (operating keys)*

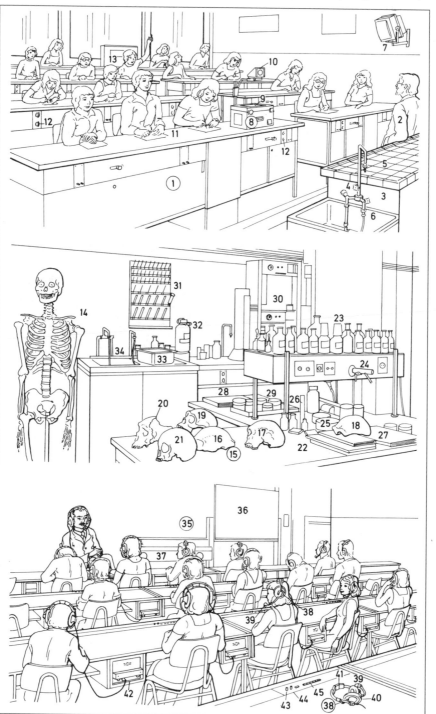

1-28 la Universidad
– *university (college)*
1 la clase (la lección)
– *lecture*
2 el anfiteatro (el aula *f;* el auditorio)
– *lecture room (lecture theatre, Am. theater)*
3 el catedrático de Universidad *f,* un profesor de Universidad *f* o un lector
– *lecturer (university lecturer, college lecturer, Am. assistant professor), a university professor or assistant lecturer*
4 la cátedra
– *lectern*
5 el micrófono
– *microphone*
6 la pizarra con mando *m* automático
– *remote-controlled blackboard*
7 el retroproyector
– *overhead projector*
8 la pantalla para la proyección de películas *f* o diapositivas *f* o a través de un epidiascopio (episcopio, proyector *m* de opacos *m)*
– *projection screen for projecting pictures by means of a film projector, slide projector, or an epidiascope*
9 el estudiante
– *student*

10 la estudiante
– *student*
**11-28 la biblioteca universitaria (*anál.:* biblioteca nacional, biblioteca municipal, biblioteca de Academia)
– *university library;* sim.: *national library, regional or municipal scientific library*
11 el depósito de los libros
– *stack (book stack) with the stock of books*
12 la librería, una estantería de acero *m*
– *bookshelf, a steel shelf*
13 la sala de lectura *f*
– *reading room*
14 la celadora, una bibliotecaria
– *member of the reading room staff, a librarian*
15 la estantería de las revistas, con revistas *f*
– *periodicals rack with periodicals*
16 la estantería de los periódicos (de los diarios)
– *newspaper shelf*
17 la biblioteca de los libros de consulta *f* (manuales *m;* diccionarios *m;* enciclopedias *f*)
– *reference library with reference books (handbooks, encyclopedias, dictionaries)*

18 el servicio de préstamo *m* (la sala de préstamo *m)* y la sala de ficheros *m*
– *lending library and catalogue (Am. catalog) room*
19 el bibliotecario
– *librarian*
20 la mesa de préstamo *m*
– *issue desk*
21 el fichero principal
– *main catalogue (Am. catalog)*
22 la estantería de ficheros *m*
– *card catalogue (Am. catalog)*
23 el cajón de fichas *f* (el fichero, la gaveta de fichas *f*)
– *card catalogue (Am. catalog) drawer*
24 el lector (el usuario de la biblioteca)
– *library user*
25 la ficha de préstamo *m*
– *borrower's ticket (library ticket)*
26 el terminal para préstamo
– *issue terminal*
27 la microficha
– *microfiche (fiche)*
28 el lector de microfichas
– *microfiche reader*

1-15 el mitin electoral
- *election meeting, a public meeting*
1 *u.* **2** la presidencia
- *committee*
1 el presidente
- *chairman*
2 el vocal
- *committee member*
3 la mesa presidencial
- *committee table*
4 la octavilla
- *pamphlet*
5 el orador
- *election speaker (speaker)*
6 la tribuna
- *rostrum*
7 el micrófono
- *microphone*
8 el público (los asistentes)
- *meeting (audience)*
9 el distribuidor de octavillas *f* de propaganda *f* (de folletos *m* de propaganda *f*)
- *man distributing leaflets*
10 el servicio de orden *m*
- *stewards*
11 el brazalete
- *armband (armlet)*

12 el cartelón electoral
- *banner*
13 la pancarta electoral
- *placard*
14 el cartel con la consigna electoral
- *proclamation*
15 el interpelador (*si es intencionadamente:* el reventador)
- *heckler*
16-29 la elección
- *election*
16 el colegio electoral
- *polling station* (polling place)
17 el funcionario del censo
- *polling officers*
18 la lista de votantes
- *electoral list*
19 la tarjeta de elector *m*, con el número de registro *m*
- *polling card with registration number (polling number)*
20 la papeleta de voto *m*, con los nombres de los partidos y de los candidatos
- *ballot paper with the names of the parties and candidates*
21 el sobre para la papeleta de voto *m*
- *ballot envelope*

22 la electora
- *voter*
23 la cabina electoral
- *polling booth*
24 el elector con derecho *m* a voto *m*
- *elector (qualified voter)*
25 el reglamento electoral
- *election regulations*
26 el censo electoral
- *electoral register*
27 el presidente de la mesa electoral
- *election supervisor*
28 la urna (*Mé.:* ánfora *f*)
- *ballot box*
29 la ranura de la urna
- *slot*

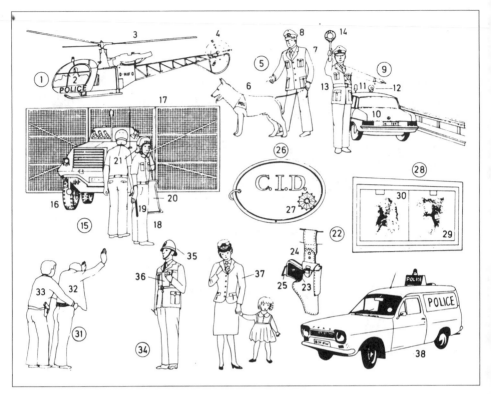

1-33 **el servicio de intervención** *f* **de la**
policía
– *police duties*
1 **el helicóptero de policía** *f* (el
helicóptero de tráfico *m*) para el control del tráfico desde el aire
– *police helicopter (traffic helicopter)*
for controlling traffic from the air
2 la cabina del piloto
– *cockpit*
3 el rotor (el rotor principal)
– *rotor (main rotor)*
4 el rotor de cola *f*
– *tail rotor*
5 **el servicio de los perros policías**
– *use of police dogs*
6 el perro policía
– *police dog*
7 el uniforme
– *uniform*
8 la gorra de servicio *m*, una gorra de visera *f* con escarapela *f* (con cucarda *f*)
– *uniform cap, a peaked cap with cockade*
9 **el control de la circulación** por una
patrulla motorizada de tráfico *m*
– *traffic control by a mobile traffic*
patrol
10 el coche patrulla
– *patrol car*
11 la luz azul (el faro giratorio, la luz
con destellos *m*)
– *blue light*

12 el altavoz
– *loud hailer (loudspeaker)*
13 el policía (el agente) de patrulla *f*
(*Amér. Central, Col., Chile, Ec., Pan.*
y Venez.: el policial; *Arg.:* el poli-
ciano; *Ec. y Col.:* el chapa)
– *patrolman (police patrolman)*
14 el disco de señalización *f* de la policía
– *police signalling (Am. signaling) disc*
(disk)
15 **la policía antidisturbios**
– *riot duty*
16 el coche especial blindado
– *special armoured (Am. armored) car*
17 la barricada
– *barricade*
18 el agente de policía *f* con el equipo
antidisturbios
– *policeman (police officer) in riot gear*
19 la porra de goma *f*
– *truncheon (baton)*
20 el escudo de protección *f*
– *riot shield*
21 el casco de protección *f*
– *protective helmet (helmet)*
22 **la pistola reglamentaria**
– *service pistol*
23 la empuñadura (el puño) de la pistola
– *pistol grip*
24 la pistolera (la funda de la pistola)
– *quick-draw holster*

25 el cargador de la pistola
– *magazine*
26 **la insignia** de la policía judicial
– *police identification disc (disk)*
27 la estrella de la policía
– *police badge*
28 **la dactiloscopia** (la identificación por
comparación *f* de las huellas digi-
tales)
– *fingerprint identification (dacty-*
loscopy)
29 la huella digital
– *fingerprint*
30 el panel luminoso
– *illuminated screen*
31 **el cacheo**
– *search*
32 el sospechoso
– *suspect*
33 el agente de policía *f* judicial de
paisano *m*
– *detective (plainclothes policeman)*
34 el policía inglés (el bobby)
– *English policeman*
35 el casco
– *helmet*
36 el cuaderno de notas *f*
– *pocket book*
37 la mujer policía
– *policewoman*
38 el coche celular (el furgón celular)
– *police van*

1-31 el café (la cafetería); *anál.:* el salón de té *m,* la heladería
– *café, serving cakes and pastries;* sim.: *espresso bar, tea room, ice-cream parlour* (Am. *parlor)*
1 el mostrador (la barra)
– *counter (cake counter)*
2 la cafetera (la máquina de hacer café *m*) a presión *f,* la máquina de café *m*
– *coffee urn, coffee machine*
3 el platillo del dinero
– *tray for the money*
4 la tarta
– *gateau*
5 el merengue (*Hond. y Guat.:* la espumilla) con nata *f* batida
– *meringue with whipped cream*
6 el aprendiz de repostero *m*
– *trainee pastry cook*
7 la señorita del mostrador
– *girl (lady) at the counter*
8 el estante de los periódicos (el revistero)
– *newspaper shelves (newspaper rack)*
9 el aplique
– *wall lamp*
10 el sofá de rinconera *f*
– *corner seat, an upholstered seat*

11 la mesa del café (*Amér.:* la zofra)
– *café table*
12 el tablero de mármol *m*
– *marble top*
13 la camarera (*Col.:* la prendedera)
– *waitress*
14 la bandeja (*Amér.:* la charola)
– *tray*
15 la botella de limonada *f*
– *bottle of lemonade*
16 el vaso de limonada *f*
– *lemonade glass*
17 los jugadores de ajedrez *m* durante una partida
– *chess players playing a game of chess*
18 el servicio de café *m*
– *coffee set*
19 la taza de café *m*
– *cup of coffee*
20 el platillo con azúcar *amb.*
– *small sugar bowl*
21 el jarrito de crema *f*
– *cream jug* (Am. *creamer)*
22-24 los clientes del café
– *café customers*
22 el señor (el caballero; *Amér. Central:* el jalón)
– *gentleman*

23 la señora (la señorita, la dama)
– *lady*
24 el lector de periódicos *m*
– *man reading a newspaper*
25 el periódico
– *newspaper*
26 el portaperiódicos
– *newspaper holder*
27 el café exprés
– *espresso*
28 el helado variado
– *ice cream in assorted flavours* (Am. *flavors)*
29 la tarrina, la copa de helado
– *ice-cream dish (sundae dish)*
30 el café helado
– *iced coffee*
31 la pajita
– *(drinking) straw*

1-27 el restaurante (*menos lujoso:* la casa de comidas *f,* el bar, el local)
– *restaurant*
1-11 la barra
– *bar (counter)*
1 el grifo de la cerveza (el aparato para sevir la cerveza a presión *f*)
– *beer pump (beerpull)*
2 la bandeja escurridora
– *drip tray*
3 el vaso de cerveza *f,* un bock
– *beer glass, a tumbler*
4 la espuma de la cerveza
– *froth (head)*
5 el cenicero esférico con soporte *m*
– *spherical ashtray for cigarette and cigar ash*
6 la jarra de cerveza *f*
– *beer glass (beer mug)*
7 el calentador (el calientacerveza)
– *beer warmer*
8 el barman (el camarero)
– *bartender (barman,* Am. *barkeeper, barkeep)*
9 el estante de los vasos
– *shelf for glasses*
10 el estante de las botellas
– *shelf for bottles*
11 la pila de platos *m* (el montón de loza *f*)
– *stack of plates*
12 el perchero (la percha de pie *m*; el cuelgacapas)
– *coat stand*

13 el gancho para colgar sombreros *m*
– *hat peg*
14 el gancho para colgar abrigos *m* u otras prendas *f*
– *coat hook*
15 el ventilador de pared *f*
– *wall ventilator*
16 la botella
– *bottle*
17 el plato combinado *f*
– *complete meal*
18 la camarera (*Col.:* la prendedera)
– *waitress*
19 la bandeja (*Amér.:* la charola)
– *tray*
20 el postre
– *dessert, a slice of cake*
21 la carta (el menú del día)
– *menu (menu card)*
22 las vinagreras (las angarillas; el convoy; el taller)
– *cruet stand*
23 el palillero
– *toothpick holder*
24 la cerillera (la fosforera; *Amér.:* el cerillero)
– *matchbox holder*
25 el cliente, la clienta
– *customer*
26 el posavasos
– *beer mat*
27 el cubierto
– *meal of the day*

28-44 el bar
– *wine restaurant (wine bar)*
28 el mantel
– *tablecloth*
29 el vaso de agua
– *glass of water*
30 el camarero, un jefe de camareros *m*
– *wine waiter, a head waiter*
31 la carta (la lista) de vinos *m*
– *wine list*
32 la jarra de vino *m*
– *wine carafe*
33 la copa de vino *m*
– *wineglass*
34 la estufa de azulejos *m* (de loza *f*)
– *tiled stove*
35 el azulejo de estufa *f*
– *stove tile*
36 el banco de la estufa
– *stove bench*
37 el panel de madera *f*
– *wooden panelling* (Am. *paneling)*
38 el sofá de rinconera *f*
– *corner seat*
39 la mesa de la tertulia (la mesa reservada a los clientes habituales)
– *table reserved for regular customers*

40 el tertuliano (el contertulio; el
cliente habitual)
– *regular customer*
41 el aparador (*Col., P. Rico, S. Dgo.
y Venez.:* el seibó)
– *cutlery chest*
42 el cubo de hielo *m* para refrescar
el vino
– *wine cooler*
43 la botella de vino *m*
– *bottle of wine*
44 los cubitos de hielo *m*
– *ice cubes (ice, lumps of ice)*
45-78 el restaurante autoservicio *m*
(el self-service)
– *self-service restaurant (cafeteria)*
45 la pila (el montón) de bandejas *f*
– *stack of trays*
46 las pajitas para beber
– *drinking straws (straws)*
47 las servilletas
– *serviettes (napkins)*
48 las casillas de los cubiertos
– *cutlery holders*
49 la vitrina refrigeradora para
platos *m* fríos
– *cool shelf*
50 la raja de melón *m* dulce
– *slice of honeydew melon*
51 el plato de ensalada *f*
– *plate of salad*
52 el plato de queso *m*
– *plate of cheeses*

53 el plato de pescado *m*
– *fish dish*
54 el emparedado (el sandwich)
– *filled roll*
55 el plato de carne *f* con guarnición *f*
– *meat dish with trimmings*
56 el medio pollo
– *half chicken*
57 la cesta de frutas *f*
– *basket of fruit*
58 el zumo de fruta *f*
– *fruit juice*
59 el anaquel de las bebidas
– *drinks shelf*
60 la botella de leche *f*
– *bottle of milk*
61 la botella de agua *f* mineral
– *bottle of mineral water*
62 el menú de dieta *f* cruda (el menú
dietético)
– *vegetarian meal (diet meal)*
63 la bandeja (*Amér.:* la charola)
– *tray*
64 el deslizadero para las bandejas
– *tray counter*
65 los carteles anunciadores de los
platos
– *food price list*
66 la ventana de la cocina para servir
los platos
– *serving hatch*
67 el plato caliente
– *hot meal*

68 el aparato para servir la cerveza
– *beer pump (beerpull)*
69 la caja
– *cash desk*
70 la cajera
– *cashier*
71 el propietario (el jefe)
– *proprietor*
72 la barrera
– *rail*
73 el comedor
– *dining area*
74 la mesa del comedor (*Chile, Ec. y
Mé.:* el trinche)
– *table*
75 el sandwich de queso *m*
– *open sandwich*
76 la copa de helado *m*
– *ice-cream sundae*
77 el salero y el pimentero
– *salt cellar and pepper pot*
78 la decoración de la mesa (el
adorno floral)
– *table decoration (flower arrangement)*

1-26 la recepción (el vestíbulo)
– *vestibule (foyer, reception hall)*
1 el portero
– *doorman (commissionaire)*
2 el casillero del correo, con los
cajetines para las cartas
– *letter rack with pigeon holes*
3 el tablero de las llaves
– *key rack*
4 el globo de luz *f*, un globo de
cristal *m* blanco
– *globe lamp, a frosted glass globe*
5 el tablero de los números (el indicador de llamadas *f*)
– *indicator board*
6 la señal luminosa de llamada *f*
– *indicator light*
7 el recepcionista
– *chief receptionist*
8 el libro de registro *m*
– *register (hotel register)*
9 la llave de la habitación
– *room key*
10 la chapa numerada, con el
número de la habitación
– *number tag (number tab) showing
room number*
11 la factura del hotel
– *hotel bill*
12 el bloque de formularios *m* de
inscripción *f*
– *block of registration forms*

13 el pasaporte
– *passport*
14 el huésped del hotel
– *hotel guest*
15 la maleta de avión *m*, una maleta
ligera *(Amér. Central, Col. Ec. y
Venez.:* el carriel; *Col. y Venez.:* la
maletera) para viajes en avión *m*
– *lightweight suitcase [for air travel]*
16 el pupitre de pared *f*
– *wall desk*
17 el mozo del hotel
– *porter (Am. baggage man)*
18-26 el vestíbulo (el hall)
– *lobby (hotel lobby)*
18 el botones
– *page (pageboy, Am. bell boy)*
19 el gerente (el director) del hotel
– *hotel manager*
20 el comedor (el restaurante del
hotel)
– *dining room (hotel restaurant)*
21 la araña, una lámpara de varios
brazos *m*
– *chandelier*
22 el rincón de la chimenea
– *fireside*
23 la chimenea
– *fireplace*
24 la repisa de la chimenea
– *mantelpiece (mantelshelf)*

25 la lumbre (el fuego encendido)
– *fire*
26 el sillón
– *armchair*
27-38 la habitación del hotel, una
habitación doble con baño *m*
– *hotel room, a double room with
bath*
27 la puerta doble
– *double door*
28 el tablero de timbres *m*
– *service bell panel*
29 el armario
– *wardrobe* (Am. *clothes closet*)
30 el departamento de los trajes
– *clothes compartment*
31 el departamento de la ropa blanca
– *linen compartment*
32 el lavabo doble
– *double washbasin*
33 el camarero de habitación *f*
– *room waiter*
34 el teléfono de habitación *f*
– *room telephone*
35 la alfombra de terciopelo *m*
(*Chile y Perú:* el piso)
– *velour (velours) carpet*

36 la mesita de las flores
- flower stand
37 el ramo de flores f (el ramillete
   artísticamente dispuesto)
- flower arrangement
38 la cama doble
- double bed
39 **el salón de banquetes** m (el salón
   de fiestas f)
- **function room** (banqueting hall)
40-43 los convidados de un banquete
   privado
- party (private party) at table (at a
   banquet)
40 el orador proponiendo un brindis
- speaker proposing a toast
41 el vecino de mesa f del 42
- 42's neighbour (Am. neighbor)
42 el caballero compañero de mesa f
   de la convidada 43
- 43's partner
43 la señora compañera de mesa f
   del 42
- 42's partner
44 el trío del bar
- bar trio
45 el violinista de pie m
- violinist
46 la pareja bailando
- couple dancing (dancing couple)
47 el camarero
- waiter

48 la servilleta
- napkin
49 el cigarillo
- cigarette
50 el cenicero
- ashtray
51 **el bar del hotel**
- **hotel bar**
52 la barra para apoyar los pies
- foot rail
53 el taburete de bar m
- bar stool
54 la barra (el mostrador) del bar
- bar
55 el cliente del bar
- bar customer
56 la copa de cóctel m
- cocktail glass (Am. highball glass)
57 el vaso de whisky m (de güisqui m)
- whisky (whiskey) glass
58 el corcho de la botella de champaña m
- champagne cork
59 el cubo del champaña (el cubo de
   hielo m para refrescar el champaña)
- champagne bucket (champagne
   cooler)
60 el vaso de medidas f
- measuring beaker (measure)
61 la coctelera
- cocktail shaker

62 el barman
- bartender (barman, Am. barkeeper, barkeep)
63 la camarera del bar (Col.: la
   prendedera)
- barmaid
64 el anaquel de las botellas
- shelf for bottles
65 el anaquel de las copas
- shelf for glasses
66 el revestimiento de espejos m
- mirrored panel
67 el recipiente de hielo m
- ice bucket
68 el salón de té
- hotel foyer

1 el parquímetro
- *parking meter*
2 el plano de la ciudad
- *map of the town (street map)*
3 el tablero luminoso
- *illuminated board*
4 la leyenda
- *key*
5 la papelera
- *litter bin (Am. litter basket)*
6 la farola
- *street lamp (street light)*
7 la placa con el nombre de la calle
- *street sign showing the name of the street*
8 el sumidero
- *drain*
9 la tienda de ropa *f* (la tienda de modas *f*; la boutique)
- *clothes shop (fashion house)*
10 el escaparate (*Amér.*: la vidriera)
- *shop window*
11 la exhibición de los géneros en el escaparate
- *window display (shop window display)*
12 la decoración del escaparate
- *window decoration (shop window decoration)*
13 la entrada
- *entrance*
14 la ventana
- *window*

15 la jardinera
- *window box*
16 el anuncio luminoso
- *neon sign*
17 el taller de sastre (la sastrería)
- *tailor's workroom*
18 el transeúnte (*Bol., Chile, Perú y Río de la Plata*: el chasque)
- *pedestrian*
19 la bolsa de la compra
- *shopping bag*
20 el barrendero
- *road sweeper (Am. street sweeper)*
21 la escoba (el escobón)
- *broom*
22 la basura de las calles
- *rubbish (litter)*
23 los raíles del tranvía
- *tramlines (Am. streetcar tracks)*
24 el paso de peatones *m* (el paso de cebra *f*)
- *pedestrian crossing (zebra crossing, Am. crosswalk)*
25 la parada del tranvía
- *tram stop (Am. streetcar stop, trolley stop)*
26 la señal de la parada
- *tram stop sign (Am. streetcar stop sign, trolley stop sign)*
27 el horario del tranvía
- *tram timetable (Am. streetcar schedule, trolley schedule)*

28 el distribuidor automático de billetes *m* (la máquina de tiques *m*)
- *ticket machine*
29 la señal de advertencia *f* de "paso *m* de peatones" *m*
- *'pedestrian crossing' sign*
30 el policía urbano, dirigiendo la circulación (el guardia de la circulación)
- *traffic policeman on traffic duty (point duty)*
31 la manopla reflectante
- *traffic control cuff*
32 la gorra reflectante
- *white cap*
33 la señal de la mano
- *hand signal*
34 el motorista (motociclista *m*)
- *motorcyclist*
35 la motocicleta (moto *f*)
- *motorcycle*
36 la pasajera de la moto (el paquete)
- *pillion passenger (pillion rider)*
37 la librería
- *bookshop*
38 la sombrerería
- *hat shop (hatter's shop); for ladies' hats: milliner's shop*
39 el cartel anunciador del comercio (el rótulo de la tienda)
- *shop sign*
40 la oficina de seguros *m* (de la compañía aseguradora)
- *insurance company office*

41 los grandes almacenes
– *department store*
42 el frente del escaparate
– *shop front*
43 el panel de anuncios *m*
– *advertisement*
44 las banderas
– *flags*
45 el anuncio del tejado en letras *f* luminosas (el luminoso)
– *illuminated letters*
46 el tranvía (*P. Rico:* el trole)
– *tram (Am. streetcar, trolley)*
47 el camión de mudanzas *f*
– *furniture lorry (Am. furniture truck)*
48 el paso elevado (el viaducto)
– *flyover*
49 la iluminación de la calle, un farol suspendido en el centro de la calle
– *suspended street lamp*
50 la raya de parada *f*
– *stop line*
51 la señalización del paso de peatones *m*
– *pedestrian crossing (Am. crosswalk)*
52 el semáforo
– *traffic lights*
53 el poste del semáforo
– *traffic light post*
54 el dispositivo de señales *f* luminosas (el juego de luces *f*)
– *set of lights*

55 las señales luminosas para los peatones
– *pedestrian lights*
56 la cabina telefónica
– *telephone box (telephone booth, telephone kiosk, call box)*
57 la cartelera de cine *m* (el cartel anunciador de la película)
– *cinema (Am. movie) advertisement (film poster, Am. movie poster)*
58 la zona peatonal
– *pedestrian precinct (paved zone)*
59 el café con terraza *f*
– *street café*
60 un grupo de gente *f* sentado en la terraza del café
– *group seated (sitting) at a table*
61 la sombrilla (el parasol)
– *sunshade*
62 la escalera de descenso *m* a los servicios públicos
– *steps to the public lavatories (public conveniences)*
63 la parada de taxis *m*
– *taxi rank (taxi stand)*
64 el taxi (*S. Dgo.:* el concho)
– *taxi (taxicab, cab)*
65 el distintivo del taxi
– *taxi sign*
66 la señal de tráfico *m* "parada *f* de taxis" *m*
– *'taxi rank' ('taxi stand') sign*

67 el teléfono de taxis *m*
– *taxi telephone*
68 la oficina de correos *m*
– *post office*
69 la máquina de cigarrillos *m*
– *cigarette machine*
70 la columna anunciadora
– *advertising pillar*
71 el cartel de publicidad *f*
– *poster (advertisement)*
72 la raya blanca
– *white line*
73 la flecha obligatoria de giro *m* a la izquierda
– *lane arrow for turning left*
74 la flecha obligatoria de seguir en línea *f* recta
– *lane arrow for going straight ahead*
75 el vendedor de periódicos *m* (*Col. y Ec.:* el voceador; *Arg., Perú y Urug.:* el canillita; *Mé.:* el papelero; *Chile:* el suplementero)
– *news vendor (Am. news dealer)*

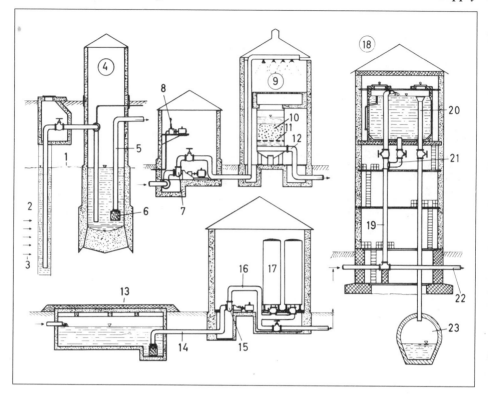

1-66 el abastecimiento de agua *f* potable
- *drinking water supply*
1 el nivel de agua *f* freática (de agua *f* subterránea)
– *water table (groundwater level)*
2 la capa conductora del agua *f* freática
– *water-bearing stratum (aquifer, aquafer)*
3 la corriente de agua *f* subterránea (de agua *f* freática)
– *groundwater stream (underground stream)*
4 el pozo colector del agua *f* natural
– *collector well for raw water*
5 el tubo de aspiración *f*
– *suction pipe*
6 la alcachofa con válvula *f* de fondo *m*
– *pump strainer with foot valve*
7 la bomba aspirante con motor *m*
– *bucket pump with motor*
8 la bomba de vacío *m* con motor *m*
– *vacuum pump with motor*
9 la instalación de filtraje *m* rápido
– *rapid-filter plant*
10 la grava (el guijo) filtrador(-a)
– *filter gravel (filter bed)*
11 el fondo del filtro, una rejilla
– *filter bottom, a grid*

12 el tubo de desagüe *m* del agua *f* filtrada
– *filtered water outlet*
13 el depósito de agua *f* limpia
– *purified water tank*
14 el tubo de aspiración *f* con alcachofa *f* y válvula *f* de fondo *m*
– *suction pipe with pump strainer and foot valve*
15 la bomba principal con motor *m*
– *main pump with motor*
16 la tubería a presión *f*
– *delivery pipe*
17 la caldera de aire *m*
– *compressed-air vessel (air vessel, air receiver)*
18 el depósito elevado de agua *f*
– *water tower*
19 la tubería de subida *f* del agua *f*
– *riser pipe (riser)*
20 el tubo de desagüe *m* del agua *f* sobrante (el rebosadero)
– *overflow pipe*
21 la tubería de bajada *f* del agua *f*
– *outlet*
22 la tubería de la red de distribución *f*
– *distribution main*
23 la alcantarilla del agua *f* residual (el canal para el exceso de agua *f*)
– *excess water conduit*

24-39 el alumbramiento de una fuente
– *tapping a spring*
24 la cámara de la fuente
– *chamber*
25 el muro de arena *f*
– *chamber wall*
26 el pozo de acceso *m*
– *manhole*
27 la chimenea de aireación *f*
– *ventilator*
28 los peldaños de hierro *m*
– *step irons*
29 el terraplén
– *filling (backing)*
30 la válvula de cierre *m* (la llave de paso *m*)
– *outlet control valve*
31 la válvula de vaciado *m*
– *outlet valve*
32 el colador (el filtro)
– *strainer*
33 el tubo de desagüe *m* del agua *f* sobrante (el rebosadero)
– *overflow pipe (overflow)*
34 el desagüe subterráneo
– *bottom outlet*
35 los tubos de terracota *f*
– *earthenware pipes*
36 la capa impermeable
– *impervious stratum (impermeable stratum)*

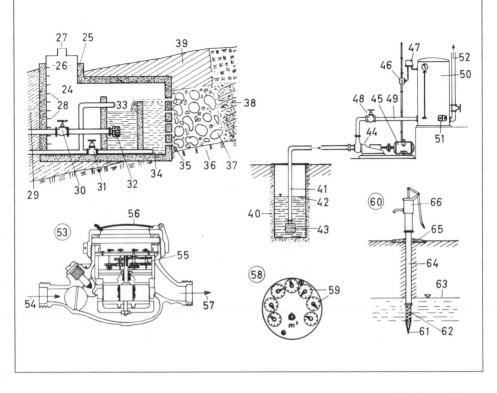

37 la capa de guijarros *m*
– *rough rubble*
38 la capa conductora de agua *f*
– *water-bearing stratum (aquifer, aquafer)*
39 la capa de arcilla *f* apisonada
– *loam seal (clay seal)*
40-52 el abastecimiento individual de agua *f*
– *individual water supply*
40 el pozo
– *well*
41 el tubo de aspiración *f*
– *suction pipe*
42 el nivel de agua *f* subterránea
– *water table (groundwater level)*
43 la alcachofa con válvula *f* de fondo *m*
– *pump strainer with foot valve*
44 la bomba centrífuga
– *centrifugal pump*
45 el motor
– *motor*
46 el interruptor de protección *f* del motor
– *motor safety switch*
47 el controlador de la presión, un conmutador
– *manostat, a switching device*
48 la válvula de cierre *m* (la llave de paso *m*)
– *stop valve*

49 la tubería a presión *f*
– *delivery pipe*
50 la caldera de aire *m*
– *compressed-air vessel (air vessel, air receiver)*
51 el agujero de hombre *m* (el orificio de limpieza *f*)
– *manhole*
52 la tubería de distribución *f* al consumidor
– *delivery pipe*
53 el contador de agua *f (Amér.:* el medidor de agua *f*), un contador de turbina *f*
– *water meter, a rotary meter*
54 la entrada del agua *f*
– *water inlet*
55 el mecanismo contador
– *counter gear assembly*
56 la tapa de cristal *m*
– *cover with glass lid*
57 la salida del agua *f*
– *water outlet*
58 la esfera (el cuadrante) del contador de agua *f*
– *water-meter dial*
59 el mecanismo contador
– *counters*
60 el pozo alumbrado por un pisón
– *driven well (tube well, drive well)*

61 la punta del pisón (la punta de penetración *f*)
– *pile shoe*
62 el filtro
– *filter*
63 el nivel del agua *f* subterránea
– *water table (groundwater level)*
64 el tubo envolvente
– *well casing*
65 los bordes del pozo
– *well head*
66 la bomba de mano *f*
– *hand pump*

1-46 los ejercicios del servicio de incendios *m* (los ejercicios de los bomberos; los ejercicios de extinción *f*, trepa *f*, escalera *f*, salvamento *m*)
- *fire service drill (extinguishing, climbing, ladder, and rescue work)*

1-3 el cuartel de bomberos *m*
- *fire station*

1 la cochera (el garaje) y el cuarto de herramientas *f*
- *engine and appliance room*

2 el alojamiento del personal
- *firemen's (Am. firefighters') quarters*

3 la torre de prácticas *f*
- *drill tower*

4 la sirena de incendios *m* (la sirena de alarma *f*)
- *fire alarm (fire alarm siren, fire siren)*

5 el camión de bomberos *m*
- *fire engine*

6 la luz azul [*en España:* la luz roja] (la luz de advertencia *f*), una luz intermitente (una luz con destellos *m*)
- *blue light (warning light), a flashing light (Am. flashlight)*

7 la sirena
- *horn (hooter)*

8 la bomba a motor *m* (la motobomba), una bomba centrífuga
- *motor pump, a centrifugal pump*

9 la escalera giratoria a motor *m*
- *motor turntable ladder (Am. aerial ladder)*

10 la escalera extensible, una escalera de acero *m* (una escalera mecánica)
- *ladder, a steel ladder (automatic extending ladder)*

11 el mecanismo de la escalera
- *ladder mechanism*

12 el puntal
- *jack*

13 el maquinista
- *ladder operator*

14 la escala de corredera *f*
- *extension ladder*

15 el gancho de derribo *m*
- *ceiling hook (Am. preventer)*

16 la escala de ganchos *m*
- *hook ladder (Am. pompier ladder)*

17 el personal de bomberos *m* sujetando la lona de salvamento *m*
- *holding squad*

18 la lona de bomberos *m* (de salto *m*)
- *jumping sheet (sheet)*

19 la ambulancia (el coche ambulancia *f*)
- *ambulance car (ambulance)*

20 el aparato de reanimación *f*, un aparato de inhalación *f* de oxígeno *m*
- *resuscitator (resuscitation equipment), oxygen apparatus*

21 el sanitario
- *ambulance attendant (ambulance man)*

22 el brazalete
- *armband (armlet, brassard)*

23 las parihuelas (la camilla)
- *stretcher*

24 el hombre inconsciente
- *unconscious man*

25 la boca de riego *m* subterránea
- *pit hydrant*

26 el tubo vertical
- *standpipe (riser, vertical pipe)*

27 la llave de la boca de riego *m*
- *hydrant key*

28 el carrete móvil para la manguera (para la manga)
- *hose reel (Am. hose cart, hose wagon, hose truck, hose carriage)*

29 el acoplamiento de la manguera
- *hose coupling*

30 el conducto de aspiración *f*, una manga (un tubo flexible)
- *soft suction hose*

31 el conducto a presión *f*
- *delivery hose*

32 la pieza de distribución *f*
– *dividing breeching*
33 la boquilla de la manga
– *branch*
34 el equipo de extinción *f*
– *branchmen*
35 la boca de riego *m* de superficie *f*
– *surface hydrant (fire plug)*
36 el jefe de bomberos *m*
– *officer in charge*
37 el bombero
– *fireman (Am. firefighter)*
38 el casco protector contra incendios
m, con el cubrenuca
– *helmet (fireman's helmet, Am. fire
hat) with neck guard (neck flap)*
39 el aparato de oxígeno *m* (de respiración *f*)
– *breathing apparatus*
40 la máscara antigás (la careta contra
gases *m*)
– *face mask*
41 el aparato de radio *f* portátil (el
transmisor-receptor portátil)
– *walkie-talkie set*
42 el reflector portátil (de mano *f*)
– *hand lamp*
43 el hacha *f* de bombero *m*
– *small axe (Am. ax, pompier hatchet)*
44 el cinturón de ganchos *m*
– *hook belt*

45 la cuerda (la cuerda de salvamento *m*)
– *beltline*
46 el traje protector contra el calor de
amianto *m* o de tejido *m* metálico
– *protective clothing of asbestos
(asbestos suit) or of metallic fabric*
47 el camión grúa *f*
– *breakdown lorry (Am. crane truck,
wrecking crane)*
48 la grúa de salvamento *m*
– *lifting crane*
49 el gancho de tracción *f*
– *load hook (draw hook, Am. drag
hook)*
50 la roldana de apoyo *m*
– *support roll*
51 el camión cisterna (el camión-
tanque de extinción *f*), gran
vehículo *m* de extinción *f*
– *water tender, a large fire engine*
52 la bomba a motor *m* portátil
– *portable pump*
53 el camión de las mangueras y herramientas *f*
– *hose layer*
54 los rollos de las mangueras
– *flaked lengths of hose*
55 el tambor del cable
– *cable drum*
56 el cabrestante
– *winch*

57 el filtro de la máscara antigás
– *face mask filter*
58 el carbón activo
– *active carbon (activated carbon,
activated charcoal)*
59 el filtro del polvo
– *dust filter*
60 la abertura de entrada *f* del aire
– *air inlet*
61 el extintor de mano *f*
– *portable fire extinguisher*
62 la válvula de accionamiento *m*
– *operating valve*
63 la manguera de bombeo *m*
– *hose with spray nozzle*
64 el proyector de agua *f* y espuma *f*
– *foam-making branch (Am. foam
gun)*
65 el barco de extinción *f* de incendios *m*
– *fireboat*
66 el cañón de agua *f*
– *monitor (water cannon)*
67 la manga de aspiración *f*
– *suction hose*

1 la cajera
– *cashier*
2 la caja registradora eléctrónica (la caja registradora, caja con escáner *m*)
– *electronic cash register (till) (scanner till)*
3 las teclas de números *m*
– *number keys*
4 el escáner (lápiz *m* de lectura *f* óptica)
– *scanner (light pen)*
5 el cajón del dinero
– *cash drawer (till)*
6 los departamentos del cajón, para monedas *f* de metal *m* y billetes *m* de banco *m*
– *compartments (money compartments) for coins and notes (Am. bills)*
7 el tique de caja *f*
– *receipt (sales check)*
8 el total a pagar
– *amount [to be paid]*
9 las teclas de función *f*
– *function keys*
10 la mercancía
– *goods*
11 el patio de luz *f* (techado con una claraboya)
– *glass-roofed well*
12 el departamento de artículos *m* de caballero *m*
– *men's wear department*

13 la vitrina de exposición *f* (el escaparate interior)
– *showcase (display case, indoor display window)*
14 el mostrador de entrega *f* de los artículos
– *wrapping counter*
15 la canastilla con los artículos a empaquetar
– *tray for purchases*
16 la clienta (la compradora)
– *customer*
17 el departamento de medias *f* (la sección de mercería *f*)
– *hosiery department*
18 la dependienta (la vendedora)
– *shop assistant (Am. salesgirl, saleslady)*
19 el cartel con los precios
– *price card*
20 el soporte para probarse los guantes
– *glove stand*
21 el abrigo tres cuartos
– *duffle coat, a three-quarter length coat*
22 la escalera mecánica
– *escalator*
23 el tubo de luz *f* fluorescente (el tubo de neón *m*)
– *fluorescent light (fluorescent lamp)*

24 la oficina (*por ej.:* la oficina de ventas *f* a crédito *m;* la agencia de viajes *m;* la oficina de la dirección)
– *office (e.g. customer accounts office, travel agency, manager's office)*
25 el cartel publicitario (el anuncio publicitario)
– *poster (advertisement)*
26 el despacho de localidades *f* para teatro *m* y conciertos *m* (el despacho de venta *f* por adelantado)
– *theatre (Am. theater) and concert booking office (advance booking office)*
27 la estantería (*Amér.:* el armazón)
– *shelves*
28 el departamento (la sección) de vestidos *m* de señora *f*
– *ladies' wear department*
29 el vestido confeccionado
– *ready-made dress (ready-to-wear dress,* coll. *off-the-peg dress)*
30 el guardapolvo
– *dust cover*
31 la percha de los vestidos *m*
– *clothes rack*
32 el probador
– *changing booth (fitting booth)*
33 el espejo
– *mirror*

34 el maniquí
– *dummy*
35 la butaca
– *seat (chair)*
36 la revista de modas *f*
– *fashion journal (fashion magazine)*
37 el modista tomando medidas *f*
– *tailor marking a hemline*
38 la cinta métrica
– *measuring tape (tape measure)*
39 el jaboncillo de sastre *m*
– *tailor's chalk (French chalk)*
40 el medidor del largo de falda *f*
– *hemline marker*
41 el abrigo suelto
– *loose-fitting coat*
42 el mostrador de venta *f*
– *sales counter*
43 la cortina de aire *m* caliente
– *warm-air curtain*
44 la escalera
– *stairs*
45 el ascensor
– *lift (Am. elevator)*
46 la caja del ascensor
– *lift cage (lift car, Am. elevator car)*
47 la flecha indicadora de la dirección
– *direction indicators*
48 los botones de mando *m*
– *controls (lift controls, Am. elevator controls)*

49 el indicador del piso (de la planta)
– *floor indicator*
50 la puerta de corredera *f*
– *sliding door*
51 el hueco del ascensor
– *lift shaft (Am. elevator shaft)*
52 el cable de tracción *f*
– *bearer cable*
53 el cable de control *m*
– *control cable*
54 los raíles de deslizamiento *m*
– *guide rail*
55 el cliente (el comprador)
– *customer*
56 los géneros de punto *m*
– *hosiery*
57 los artículos de lencería *f* (mantelerías *f* y ropas *f* de cama *f*)
– *linen goods (table linen and bed linen)*
58 el departamento (la sección) de telas *f*
– *fabric department*
59 la pieza de tela *f* (de paño *m*)
– *roll of fabric (roll of material, roll of cloth)*
60 el encargado del departamento (el jefe de sección *f*)
– *head of department (department manager)*
61 el mostrador de venta *f*
– *sales counter*

62 el departamento de bisutería *f*
– *jewellery (Am. jewelry) department*
63 la señorita de información *f* al cliente *m*
– *customer assistant*
64 la mesa de las ofertas especiales (las gangas)
– *special counter (extra counter)*
65 el cartel con los precios de las ofertas especiales (las gangas)
– *placard advertising special offers*
66 el departamento (la sección) de cortinas *f*
– *curtain department*
67 la decoración de los techos de las estanterías
– *display on top of the shelves*

1-40 el parque francés (parque *m* barroco), un parque palaciego
- *formal garden (French Baroque garden), palace gardens*
1 la gruta
- *grotto (cavern)*
2 la estatua de piedra *f*, una ninfa
- *stone statue, a river nymph*
3 el invernadero de naranjos *m*
- *orangery (orangerie)*
4 el bosquecillo
- *boscage (boskage)*
5 el laberinto de setos *m*
- *maze (labyrinth of paths and hedges)*
6 el teatro al aire libre
- *open-air theatre (Am. theater)*
7 el palacio barroco (un palacio de estilo *m* Luis XIV)
- *Baroque palace*
8 los juegos de agua *f*
- *fountains*
9 la cascada artificial
- *cascade (broken artificial water-fall, artificial falls)*
10 la estatua, un monumento
- *statue, a monument*
11 el pedestal
- *pedestal*

12 el árbol modelado en forma *f* esférica
- *globe-shaped tree*
13 el árbol modelado en forma *f* cónica
- *conical tree*
14 el arbusto ornamental
- *ornamental shrub*
15 la fuente mural
- *wall fountain*
16 el banco del parque
- *park bench*
17 la pérgola
- *pergola (bower, arbour, Am. arbor)*
18 el sendero cubierto de grava *f*
- *gravel path (gravel walk)*
19 el árbol modelado en forma *f* piramidal
- *pyramid tree (pyramidal tree)*
20 el amorcillo
- *cupid (cherub, amoretto, amorino)*
21 la fuente (*Amér.:* el puquio)
- *fountain*
22 el surtidor
- *fountain (jet of water)*
23 la taza (pilón *m*) superior de la fuente
- *overflow basin*

24 la taza inferior de la fuente
- *basin*
25 el borde de la fuente
- *kerb (curb)*
26 el paseante
- *man out for a walk*
27 la guía turística
- *tourist guide*
28 el grupo de turistas *m*
- *group of tourists*
29 el reglamento del parque
- *park by-laws (bye-laws)*
30 el guarda del parque
- *park keeper*
31 la puerta del parque (la verja), una verja de hierro *m* forjado
- *garden gates made of wrought iron*
32 la entrada del parque
- *park entrance*
33 la verja del parque (el enrejado que sirve de muro *m*)
- *park railings*
34 el barrote de la verja
- *railing (bar)*
35 el jarrón de piedra *f*
- *stone vase*
36 el césped
- *lawn*

37 el borde del sendero, un seto vivo recortado
– *border, a trimmed (clipped) hedge*
38 el sendero del parque
– *park path*
39 el parterre
– *parterre*
40 el abedul
– *birch (birch tree)*
41-72 el parque inglés (el jardín inglés)
– *landscaped park (jardin anglais)*
41 el arriate .
– *flower bed*
42 el banco del parque
– *park bench (garden seat)*
43 la papelera
– *litter bin* (Am. *litter basket*)
44 el césped de juegos *m*
– *play area*
45 el río
– *stream*
46 el embarcadero
– *jetty*
47 el puente
– *bridge*
48 la silla del parque
– *park chair*
49 el cercado de los animales
– *animal enclosure*

50 el estanque
– *pond*
51-54 las aves acuáticas
– *waterfowl*
51 el pato salvaje con sus patitos *m*
– *wild duck with young*
52 la oca salvaje
– *goose*
53 el flamenco
– *flamingo*
54 el cisne
– *swan*
55 la isla
– *island*
56 el nenúfar
– *water lily*
57 el café con terraza *f*
– *open-air café*
58 la sombrilla
– *sunshade*
59 el árbol
– *park tree (tree)*
60 la copa del árbol
– *treetop (crown)*
61 el bosquecillo
– *group of trees*
62 el surtidor
– *fountain*
63 el sauce llorón
– *weeping willow*

64 la escultura moderna
– *modern sculpture*
65 el invernadero
– *hothouse*
66 el jardinero
– *park gardener*
67 el escobón para barrer la hojarasca
– *broom*
68 el campo de minigolf *m*
– *minigolf course*
69 el jugador de minigolf *m*
– *minigolf player*
70 el recorrido del minigolf
– *minigolf hole*
71 la madre con el cochecito de niño *m*
– *mother with pram (baby carriage)*
72 la pareja de novios *m*
– *courting couple (young couple)*

1 el tenis de mesa *f* (el ping-pong)
– *table tennis game*
2 la mesa de ping-pong *m*
– *table*
3 la red de ping-pong *m*
– *table tennis net*
4 la raqueta de ping-pong *m*
– *table tennis racket (raquet) (table tennis bat)*
5 la pelota de ping-pong *m*
– *table tennis ball*
6 el volante (el bádminton)
– *badminton game (shuttlecock game)*
7 el volante (el rehilete)
– *shuttlecock*
8 los pasos de gigantes *m*
– *maypole swing*
9 la bicicleta de niño *m*
– *child's bicycle*
10 el fútbol
– *football game (soccer game)*
11 la portería (la meta)
– *goal (goalposts)*
12 el balón de fútbol *m*
– *football*
13 el delantero (el ariete)
– *goal scorer*
14 el portero (el guardameta)
– *goalkeeper*

15 el juego de la comba (*Amér. Central y Cuba:* la suiza; *Chile:* el cordel)
– *skipping (Am. jumping rope)*
16 la cuerda (la comba)
– *skipping rope (Am. skip rope, jump rope, jumping rope)*
17 la torre para escalar
– *climbing tower*
18 el columpio de neumático *m*
– *rubber tyre (Am. tire) swing*
19 el neumático de camión *m*
– *lorry tyre (Am. truck tire)*
20 el balón de rebotes *m*
– *bouncing ball*
21 la construcción para juegos *m* de aventura *f*
– *adventure playground*
22 la escalera de palos *m*
– *log ladder*
23 la vigía (el miradero, la atalaya)
– *lookout platform*
24 el tobogán
– *slide*
25 la papelera
– *litter bin (Am. litter basket)*
26 el oso de peluche *m*
– *teddy bear*
27 el tren de madera *f* de juguete *m*
– *wooden train set*

28 el estanque para chapotear los niños
– *paddling pool*
29 el velero de juguete *m*
– *sailing boat (yacht, Am. sailboat)*
30 el pato de juguete *m*
– *toy duck*
31 el cochecito de niño *m*
– *pram (baby carriage)*
32 la barra fija
– *high bar (bar)*
33 el coche de carreras *f* de niño *m* (el kart)
– *go-cart (soap box)*
34 la bandera de salida *f*
– *starter's flag*
35 el subibaja (*Mé.:* el bimbalete)
– *seesaw*
36 el robot (el autómata)
– *robot*
37 el aeromodelismo
– *flying model aeroplanes (Am. airplanes)*
38 el avión de aeromodelismo *m*
– *model aeroplane (Am. airplane)*
39 el columpio doble
– *double swing*
40 la tabla (el asiento) del columpio
– *swing seat*

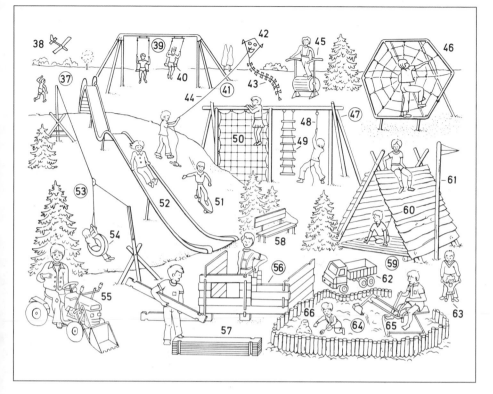

41 el remonte de la cometa
– *flying kites*
42 la cometa (la birlocha, la milocha, la pandorga, el pájaro bitango, la pájara, el pandero; *Amér.:* el volantín)
– *kite*
43 la cola de la cometa
– *tail of the kite*
44 la cuerda (el bramante) de la cometa
– *kite string*
45 el cilindro rotativo
– *revolving drum*
46 la telaraña
– *spider's web*
47 el pórtico de escalada *f*
– *climbing frame*
48 la cuerda
– *climbing rope*
49 la escala de cuerda *f*
– *rope ladder*
50 la red para trepar
– *climbing net*
51 el monopatín
– *skateboard*
52 el tobogán de montaña *f* rusa
– *up-and-down slide*
53 el funicular de neumático *m*
– *rubber tyre* (Am. *tire*) *cable car*

54 el neumático (que sirve de asiento *m*)
– *rubber tyre* (Am. *tire*)
55 el tractor, un vehículo de pedales *m*
– *tractor, a pedal car*
56 la casa de miniatura *f* de elementos *m* de construcción *f* intercambiables
– *den*
57 la plancha de ensamblaje *m*
– *presawn boards*
58 el banco
– *seat (bench)*
59 la tienda (la cabaña) india
– *Indian hut*
60 el tejado para escalar
– *climbing roof*
61 el asta de la bandera
– *flagpole (flagstaff)*
62 el camión de juguete *m*
– *toy lorry* (Am. *toy truck*)
63 la muñeca que anda
– *walking doll*
64 el cajón de arena *f*
– *sandpit* (Am. *sandbox*)
65 la excavadora de juguete *m*
– *toy excavator (toy digger)*
66 el montón de arena *f*
– *sandhill*

1-21 el parque del balneario
– *spa gardens*
1-7 la salina
– *salina (salt works)*
1 la torre de graduación *f* salinera
– *thorn house (graduation house)*
2 las brozas de zarzas *f*
– *thorns (brushwood)*
3 el canal de distribución *f* del agua *f* salobre
– *brine channels*
4 el tubo de agua *f* salobre de la estación de bombeo *m*
– *brine pipe from the pumping station*
5 el guardián de la torre de graduación *f* salinera
– *salt works attendant*
6 *u.* **7** la cura (la terapia) por inhalación *f*
– *inhalational therapy*
6 el inhalatorio al aire libre
– *open-air inhalatorium (outdoor inhalatorium)*
7 el enfermo, durante la inhalación
– *patient inhaling (taking an inhalation)*

8 el pabellón de hidroterapia *f,* con el casino
– *hydropathic (pump room) with kursaal (casino)*
9 el pórtico (los soportales; la arcada)
– *colonnade*
10 el paseo del balneario
– *spa promenade*
11 la avenida de fuentes *f*
– *avenue leading to the mineral spring*
12-14 la cura de reposo *m*
– *rest cure*
12 el césped para el reposo *m*
– *sunbathing area (lawn)*
13 la tumbona
– *deck-chair*
14 el toldo
– *sun canopy*
15 el pabellón de la fuente
– *pump room*
16 la estantería de los vasos
– *rack for glasses*
17 el grifo
– *tap*
18 el paciente del balneario
– *patient taking the waters*

19 el quiosco de música *f*
– *bandstand*
20 la orquesta del balneario, dando un concierto
– *spa orchestra giving a concert*
21 el director de orquesta *f*
– *conductor*

1-33 la ruleta (*P. Rico:* la pica; *Amér.:* la rolata), un juego de suerte *f* (un juego de azar *m*)
– **roulette,** *a game of chance (gambling game)*
1 la sala de la ruleta (la sala de juego *m*) en el casino
– *gaming room in the casino (in the gambling casino)*
2 la caja
– *cash desk*
3 el director del juego
– *tourneur (dealer)*
4 el crupié (el auxiliar del banquero; *Perú, P.Rico y S. Dgo.:* el gurupié)
– *croupier*
5 la raqueta
– *rake*
6 el crupié de cabecera *f*
– *head croupier*
7 el jefe de la sala
– *hall manager*
8 la mesa de la ruleta (la mesa de juego *m*)
– *roulette table (gaming table, gambling table)*
9 el tapete de juego *m* (el tapete verde)
– *roulette layout*

10 la ruleta
– *roulette wheel*
11 la caja de la mesa (la banca)
– *bank*
12 la ficha
– *chip (check, plaque)*
13 la apuesta (la postura)
– *stake*
14 el carné de socio *m* del casino
– *membership card*
15 el jugador de ruleta *f*
– *roulette player*
16 el detective privado (el detective de la casa)
– *private detective (house detective)*
17 el tapete del juego de la ruleta (el tapete verde)
– *roulette layout*
18 el cero
– *zero (nought, 0)*
19 paso *m* (números *m* altos) [números del 19 al 36]
– *passe (high) [numbers 19 to 36]*
20 par [números *m* pares]
– *pair (even numbers)*
21 negro
– *noir (black)*
22 falta *f* (números *m* bajos) [números del 1 al 18]
– *manque (low) [numbers 1 to 18]*

23 impar [números *m* impares]
– *impair [odd numbers]*
24 rojo
– *rouge (red)*
25 primera docena *f* [números *m* del 1 al 12]
– *douze premier (first dozen) [numbers 1 to 12]*
26 segunda docena *f* (docena intermedia) [números *m* del 13 al 24]
– *douze milieu (second dozen) [numbers 13 to 24]*
27 última docena *f* [números *m* del 25 al 36]
– *douze dernier (third dozen) [numbers 25 to 36]*
28 la ruleta
– *roulette wheel (roulette)*
29 el canal de la ruleta
– *roulette bowl*
30 el obstáculo
– *fret (separator)*
31 el disco giratorio, con los números del 0 al 36
– *revolving disc (disk) showing numbers 0 to 36*
32 el aspa *f* giratoria
– *spin*
33 la bola de la ruleta
– *roulette ball*

1-16 el juego del ajedrez (el ajedrez, el juego real), un juego de combinación *f* de movimientos *m* o posiciones *f*
– **chess,** *a game involving combinations of moves, a positional game*
1 el tablero de ajedrez *m*, con las figuras en posición *f* de salida *f*
– *chessboard (board) with the men (chessmen) in position*
2 el escaque blanco (la casilla del tablero de ajedrez *m*)
– *white square (chessboard square)*
3 el escaque negro
– *black square*
4 las figuras blancas (los trebejos blancos, las blancas) en forma *f* simbólica [blancas = B]
– *white chessmen (white pieces) [white = W]*
5 las figuras negras (los trebejos negros, las negras) en forma *f* simbólica [negras = N]
– *black chessmen (black pieces) [black = B]*
6 las letras y los números para designar los escaques en las transcripciones de partidas *f* (jugadas *f*) de ajedrez *m* y problemas *m* de ajedrez
– *letters and numbers for designating chess squares in the notation of chess moves and chess problems*
7 las diferentes figuras del ajedrez
– *individual chessmen (individual pieces)*
8 el rey
– *king*
9 la reina (la dama)
– *queen*
10 el alfil
– *bishop*
11 el caballo
– *knight*
12 la torre
– *rook (castle)*
13 el peón
– *pawn*
14 los movimientos (jugadas *f*) de cada una de las figuras (trebejos *m*)
– *moves of the individual pieces*
15 el mate (el jaque mate), un mate de caballo *m*
– *mate (checkmate), a mate by knight [kt f3 ≠]*
16 el reloj de ajedrez *m*, un reloj doble para los torneos (campeonatos) de ajedrez *m*
– *chess clock, a double clock for chess matches (chess championships)*

17-19 el juego de damas *f* (las damas)
– *draughts (Am. checkers)*
17 el damero (el tablero de las damas)
– *draughtboard (Am. checkerboard)*
18 la dama blanca (la ficha de damas blanca); *también:* la ficha para el juego del chaquete y del tres en raya *f*
– *white draughtsman (Am. checker, checkerman); also: piece for backgammon and nine men's morris*
19 la dama negra (la ficha de damas negra)
– *black draughtsman (Am. checker, checkerman)*
20 el juego de salta *m* (el salta)
– *salta*
21 la ficha del salta
– *salta piece*
22 el damero (el tablero) para el juego del chaquete
– *backgammon board*
23-25 el juego de tres en raya *f* (*Arg.*: el tatetí)
– *nine men's morris*
23 el tablero de tres en raya *f*
– *nine men's morris board*
24 el tres en raya *f*
– *mill*
25 el tres en raya *f* doble
– *double mill*
26-28 el juego del halma
– *halma*
26 el damero (el tablero) para el juego del halma
– *halma board*
27 el corral
– *yard (camp, corner)*
28 las figuras (las fichas) del halma en diferentes colores *m*
– *halma pieces (halma men) of various colours (Am. colors)*
29 el juego de los dados (los dados)
– *dice (dicing)*
30 el cubilete (*Bol., Col., Chile, Ec.* y *Perú:* el cacho; *Venez.:* el tacuro; *Amér. Central:* el churuco)
– *dice cup*
31 los dados
– *dice*
32 los puntos
– *spots (pips)*
33 el juego de dominó *m* (el dominó)
– *dominoes*
34 la ficha de dominó *m*
– *domino (tile)*
35 el doble (*Chile:* el chancho)
– *double*

36 los naipes (las cartas)
– *playing cards*
37 el naipe (la carta) francés (de póquer)
– *French playing card (card)*
38-45 los palos
– *suits*
38 trébol *m*
– *clubs*
39 pica *f*
– *spades*
40 corazón *m*
– *hearts*
41 diamante *m*
– *diamonds*
42-45 los palos alemanes
– *German suits*
42 la bellota [*en las cartas españolas:* bastos *m*]
– *acorns*
43 el verde (la hoja) [*en las cartas españolas:* espadas *f*]
– *leaves*
44 el rojo (el corazón) [*en las cartas españolas:* copas *f*]
– *hearts*
45 el cascabel [*en las cartas españolas:* oros *m*]
– *bells (hawkbells)*

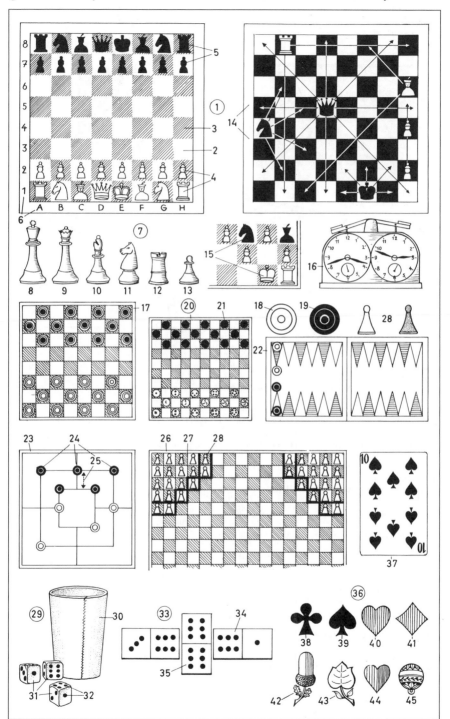

1-19 el billar (el juego del billar)
– billiards
1 la bola de billar *m*, una bola de marfil *m* o de materia *f* plástica
– billiard ball, an ivory or plastic ball
2-6 tacadas *f* de billar *m*
– billiard strokes
2 la tacada en el centro (la tacada horizontal)
– plain stroke (hitting the cue ball dead centre, Am. center)
3 la tacada alta [consigue una carambola]
– top stroke [promotes extra forward rotation]
4 la tacada baja [consigue un retroceso]
– screw-back [imparts a direct recoil or backward motion]
5 la tacada con efecto *m*
– side (running side, Am. English)
6 la tacada con efecto *m* contrario
– check side
7-19 la sala de billar *m*
– billiard room (Am. billiard parlor, billiard saloon, poolroom)
7 el billar francés (el billar de carambolas *f*); *anál.*: el billar alemán o inglés (el billar de troneras *f*)
– French billiards (carom billiards, carrom billiards); sim.: German or English billiards (pocket billiards, Am. pool billiards)

8 el jugador de billar *m*
– billiard player
9 el taco
– cue (billiard cue, billiard stick)
10 la suela, una arandela de cuero *m*
– leather cue tip
11 la bola blanca (de impacto)
– white cue ball
12 la bola roja (de juego, el mingo)
– red object ball
13 la bola blanca del tanto (para anotarse puntos *m*)
– white spot ball (white dot ball)
14 la mesa de billar *m*
– billiard table
15 la superficie de juego *m* cubierta con un paño verde
– table bed with green cloth (billiard cloth, green baize covering)
16 la banda (la banda de goma *f*)
– cushions (rubber cushions, cushioned ledge)
17 el contador del billar, un reloj controlador
– billiard clock, a timer
18 la pizarra de anotaciones *f*
– billiard marker
19 el portatacos (estante de los tacos)
– cue rack

Camping

1-59 el camping (el emplazamiento del camping)
- *camp site (camping site, Am. campground)*
1 la recepción (la oficina)
- *reception (office)*
2 el guardián del camping
- *site warden*
3 el remolque plegable (la roulotte, la caravana plegable)
- *folding trailer (collapsible caravan, collapsible trailer)*
4 la hamaca (*Venez.:* la campechana)
- *hammock*
5 u. 6 las instalaciones sanitarias
- *washing and toilet facilities*
5 los aseos y lavaderos *m*
- *toilets and washrooms (Am. lavatories)*
6 los lavabos y fregaderos *m*
- *washbasins and sinks*
7 el bungalow (el chalé)
- *bungalow (chalet)*
8-11 el campamento de los exploradores (de los boys-scouts, el jamboree)
- *scout camp*
8 la tienda de campaña *f* redonda
- *bell tent*
9 el gallardete (la banderola)
- *pennon*
10 el fuego de campamento *m* (*Pan.:* la fogatada; *Amér. Central, Arg. y Chile:* el fogón)
- *camp fire*
11 el explorador (el boy-scout)
- *boy scout (scout)*
12 el barco de vela *f* (el velero; *Col. y Venez.:* la curiana)
- *sailing boat (yacht, Am. sailboat)*
13 el embarcadero (el desembarcadero, el muelle)
- *landing stage (jetty)*
14 el bote neumático
- *inflatable boat (inflatable dinghy)*
15 el motor fuera borda *f*
- *outboard motor (outboard)*
16 el trimarán
- *trimaran*
17 la bancada (el banco de los remeros)
- *thwart (oarsman's bench)*

18 la chumacera
- *rowlock (oarlock)*
19 el remo (*Perú:* la tangana)
- *oar*
20 el remolque del barco
- *boat trailer (boat carriage)*
21 **la tienda de campaña *f* de caballete *m*** (*Amér.:* la carpa; *Amér. Central y Mé.:* el manteado)
- *ridge tent*
22 el tejado doble
- *flysheet*
23 el viento (una cuerda tensora)
- *guy line (guy)*
24 la estaquilla de la tienda (la estaquilla)
- *tent peg (peg)*
25 el mazo
- *mallet*
26 la arandela para sujetar el suelo de la tienda
- *groundsheet ring*
27 el ábside
- *bell end*
28 la marquesina levantada
- *erected awning*
29 la lámpara de camping *m*
- *storm lantern, a paraffin lamp*
30 el saco de dormir
- *sleeping bag*
31 el colchón hinchable (el colchón neumático)
- *air mattress (inflatable air-bed)*
32 el saco de agua *f* para beber
- *water carrier (drinking water carrier)*
33 la hornilla (la cocina) de dos fuegos *m* de gas *m* propano *m* o de butano *m*
- *double-burner gas cooker for propane gas or butane gas*
34 la botella de gas *m* propano *m* (de butano *m*)
- *propane or butane gas bottle*
35 la olla a presión *f* (la olla exprés)
- *pressure cooker*
36 **la tienda bungalow** (una tienda de paredes *f* verticales)
- *frame tent*
37 la marquesina
- *awning*
38 el palo de la tienda
- *tent pole*
39 la entrada en arco *m*
- *wheelarch doorway*

40 la ventana de ventilación *f*
- *mesh ventilator*
41 la ventana transparente
- *transparent window*
42 el número del emplazamiento de la tienda
- *pitch number*
43 la silla de camping *m*, una silla de tijera *f* (extensible, plegable)
- *folding camp chair*
44 la mesa de camping *m*, una mesa de tijera *f* (extensible, plegable)
- *folding camp table*
45 la vajilla de camping *m*
- *camping eating utensils*
46 el acampador
- *camper*
47 la barbacoa (las parrillas de carbón *m* de leña *f*)
- *charcoal grill (barbecue)*
48 el carbón de leña *f*
- *charcoal*
49 el fuelle
- *bellows*
50 la baca
- *roof rack*
51 los pulpos
- *roof lashing*
52 **el remolque de camping** *m* (la caravana, la roulotte)
- *caravan (Am. trailer)*
53 el cajón para las botellas de gas *m*
- *box for gas bottle*
54 la rueda delantera de guía *f* (de timón *m*)
- *jockey wheel*
55 el acoplamiento (el enganche) del remolque
- *drawbar coupling*
56 la trampilla de ventilación *f* del techo
- *roof ventilator*
57 la marquesina de la caravana
- *caravan awning*
58 la tienda iglú *m* hinchable
- *inflatable igloo tent*
59 la tumbona
- *camp bed (Am. camp cot)*

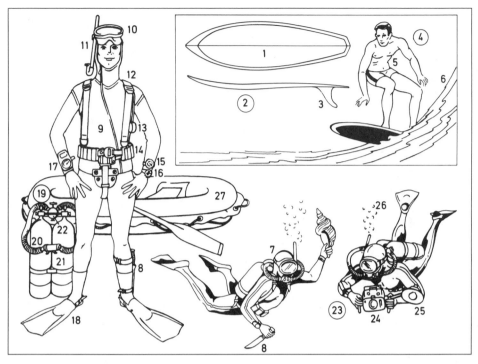

1-6 el surf
– *surf riding (surfing)*
1 la tabla de surf *m* vista por abajo
– *plan view of surfboard*
2 la tabla de surf *m*, una sección
– *section of surfboard*
3 la orza (la aleta estabilizadora)
– *skeg (stabilizing fin)*
4 el deslizamiento al punto de rompimiento *m* de la ola
– *big wave riding*
5 el surfista
– *surfboarder (surfer)*
6 la ola que rompe (el chachón)
– *breaker*
7-27 el buceo (el submarinismo)
– *skin diving (underwater swimming)*
7 el buzo (el hombre rana, el submarinista)
– *skin diver (underwater swimmer)*
8-22 el equipo de buceo *m*
– *underwater swimming set*
8 el cuchillo de buzo *m*
– *knife*
9 el traje de buzo *m* de neopreno *m*, un traje protector contra el frío
– *neoprene wetsuit*
10 las gafas de buceo *m*, unas gafas de presión *f* equilibrada
– *diving mask (face mask, mask), a pressure-equalizing mask*

11 el tubo respiratorio
– *snorkel (schnorkel)*
12 las correas de los aparatos de buceo *m* de aire *m* comprimido
– *harness of diving apparatus*
13 el manómetro para control *m* del contenido (del volumen de aire *m*) de las botellas
– *compressed-air pressure gauge (Am. gage)*
14 el cinturón de plomo *m*
– *weight belt*
15 el batímetro (el batómetro)
– *depth gauge (Am. gage)*
16 el reloj impermeable para el control del tiempo de permanencia *f* bajo el agua
– *waterproof watch for checking duration of dive*
17 el descompresímetro para el control de las etapas de ascensión *f* (las etapas de descompresión *f*)
– *decometer for measuring stages of ascent*
18 la aleta de buceo *m*
– *fin (flipper)*
19 el aparato para la respiración debajo de agua *f* (el pulmón acuático), un aparato de dos botellas *f*
– *diving apparatus (aqualung, scuba) with two cylinders (bottles)*

20 los dos tubos flexibles de la máquina pulmonar
– *two-tube demand regulator*
21 la botella de aire *m* comprimido
– *compressed-air cylinder (compressed-air bottle)*
22 la válvula de las botellas
– *on/off valve*
23 la fotografía submarina
– *underwater photography*
24 la máquina fotográfica submarina (*anál.:* la cámara submarina)
– *underwater camera housing (underwater camera case); sim.: underwater camera*
25 el flash submarino (la antorcha)
– *underwater flashlight*
26 las burbujas de aire *m* espirado
– *exhaust bubbles*
27 el bote neumático
– *inflatable boat (inflatable dinghy)*

1 el socorrista
– *lifesaver (lifeguard)*
2 la cuerda de salvamento *m*
– *lifeline*
3 el salvavidas
– *lifebelt (lifebuoy)*
4 el globo de tempestad *f* (la señal de tempestad *f*)
– *storm signal*
5 el globo horario (la señal indicadora de las horas de baño *m*)
– *time ball*
6 el cartel de advertencias *f*
– *warning sign*
7 el cartel de las mareas, un cartel indicador de las horas de flujo *m* y reflujo *m* (de la marea alta y la marea baja)
– *tide table, a notice board showing times of low tide and high tide*
8 el cartel, con los datos de temperatura *f* del agua y del aire
– *board showing water and air temperature*
9 el embarcadero (el desembarcadero, el muelle)
– *bathing platform*
10 el mástil de los gallardetes
– *pennon staff*
11 el gallardete (la banderola)
– *pennon*
12 el hidropedal
– *paddle boat (pedal boat)*
13 el acuaplano, tirado por una motora (el surf con motora)
– *surf riding (surfing) behind motorboat*
14 el surfista
– *surfboarder (surfer)*

15 la plancha de acuaplano *m* (de surf *m*)
– *surfboard*
16 el esquí acuático
– *water ski*
17 el colchón neumático (el colchón hinchable para la playa)
– *inflatable beach mattress*
18 el balón de playa *f* (para jugar en el agua)
– *beach ball*
19-23 la indumentaria de playa *f*
– *beachwear*
19 el traje playero (el conjunto playero)
– *beach suit*
20 el sombrero playero
– *beach hat*
21 la chaqueta playera
– *beach jacket*
22 los pantalones playeros
– *beach trousers*
23 las playeras
– *beach shoe (bathing shoe)*
24 la bolsa playera
– *beach bag*
25 el albornoz
– *bathing gown (bathing wrap)*
26 el biquini (el bañador de señora *f* de dos piezas *f*)
– *bikini (ladies' two-piece bathing suit)*
27 la braguita (la parte inferior del biquini)
– *bikini bottom*
28 el sujetador (la parte superior del biquini)
– *bikini top*
29 el gorro de baño *m*
– *bathing cap (swimming cap)*
30 el bañista
– *bather*

31 el tenis de anillas *f*
– *deck tennis (quoits)*
32 la anilla de goma *f*
– *rubber ring (quoit)*
33 el flotador de figura *f* de animal *m* inflable
– *inflatable rubber animal*
34 el vigilante de la playa
– *beach attendant*
35 el castillo de arena *f*
– *sand den [built as a wind-break]*
36 el sillón de playa *f* de mimbre *m*
– *roofed wicker beach chair*
37 el pescador subacuático (el buceador de pesca *f* submarina)
– *underwater swimmer*
38 las gafas de buceo *m*
– *diving goggles*
39 el tubo respiratorio
– *snorkel (schnorkel)*
40 el arpón de mano *f* (el dardo para pescar)
– *hand harpoon (fish spear, fish lance)*
41 la aleta de buceo *m*, para la práctica del submarinismo
– *fin (flipper) for diving (for underwater swimming)*
42 la indumentaria de baño *m*
– *bathing suit (swimsuit)*
43 el bañador
– *bathing trunks (swimming trunks)*
44 el gorro de baño *m*
– *bathing cap (swimming cap)*
45 la tienda de campaña *f* de playa *f*, una tienda de campaña *f* de caballete *m*
– *beach tent, a ridge tent*
46 el puesto de socorro *m*
– *lifeguard station*

281 El establecimiento de baños (centro para el ocio, para el tiempo libre)

1-9 la piscina de olas *f* artificiales, una piscina cubierta
- *wave pool, an indoor pool*
1 el oleaje artificial
- *artificial waves*
2 la playa
- *beach area*
3 el borde de la piscina
- *edge of the pool*
4 el vigilante de piscina *f*
- *swimming pool attendant (pool attendant, swimming bath attendant)*
5 la tumbona (*Venez.:* la campechana)
- *sun bed*
6 el flotador
- *lifebelt*
7 los manguitos de natación *f* (los flotadores)
- *water wings*
8 el gorro de baño
- *bathing cap*
9 el canal de acceso *m* a los baños de aguas *f* minerales al aire libre
- *channel to outdoor mineral bath*
10 el solario (baño *m* de sol *m* artificial)
- *solarium*
11 la zona para tenderse a tomar el sol
- *sunbathing area*
12 la bañista tomando un baño de sol *m*
- *sunbather*
13 el sol artificial (las lámparas de rayos *m* ultravioletas)
- *sun ray lamp*
14 la toalla de baño *m*
- *bathing towel*
15 el área *f* nudista (el terreno naturista, desnudista)
- *nudist sunbathing area*
16 el nudista (el adepto al nudismo, a la vida al aire libre en estado *m* de desnudez *f* total)
- *nudist (naturist)*
17 el recinto protegido de las miradas por un muro
- *screen (fence)*
18 la sauna (la sauna finlandesa, el baño de *m* vapor finlandés)
- *mixed sauna*
19 el revestimiento de las paredes en madera *f*
- *wood panelling* (Am. *paneling)*
20 las gradas para sentarse o tenderse
- *tiered benches*
21 la estufa de la sauna
- *sauna stove*
22 los guijarros
- *stones*
23 el higrómetro
- *hygrometer*

24 el termómetro
- *thermometer*
25 la toalla
- *towel*
26 la herrada de agua *f* para la humidificación de los guijarros de la estufa
- *water tub for moistening the stones in the stove*
27 las ramas de abedul *m* para azotar la piel
- *birch rods (birches) for beating the skin*
28 el recinto de enfriamiento *m*, para refrescarse después de la sauna
- *cooling room for cooling off (cooling down) after the sauna*
29 la ducha tibia (templada)
- *lukewarm shower*
30 la piscina de agua *f* fría
- *cold bath*
31 la bañera de remolinos *m* de agua *f* caliente (el baño de masaje *m* subacuático)
- *hot whirlpool (underwater massage bath)*
32 el escalón de acceso *m*
- *step into the bath*
33 el baño de masaje *m*
- *massage bath*
34 el ventilador de inyección *f*
- *jet blower*
35 la bañera de remolinos *m* de agua *f* caliente [esquema]
- *hot whirlpool [diagram]*
36 la sección transversal de la bañera
- *section of the bath*
37 la entrada (el escalón de acceso *m*)
- *step*
38 el banco circular
- *circular seat*
39 el extractor de agua *f*
- *water extractor*
40 el tubo (la cañería) de inyección *f* de agua *f*
- *water jet pipe*
41 el tubo (la cañería) de inyección *f* de aire *m*
- *air jet pipe*

1-32 la piscina (las instalaciones para el deporte de la natación), una piscina al aire libre
– *swimming pool, an open-air swimming pool*
1 la caseta de baño *m*
– *changing cubicle*
2 la ducha
– *shower (shower bath)*
3 el vestuario (*Ec.:* el vestidero)
– *changing room*
4 el área *f* para los baños de sol *m* o tomar el aire
– *sunbathing area*
5-10 la instalación para saltos *m* (el trampolín)
– *diving boards (diving apparatus)*
5 el saltador de la torre
– *diver (highboard diver)*
6 la torre de saltos *m*
– *diving platform*
7 la palanca de diez metros *m*
– *ten-metre (Am. ten-meter) plat-form*
8 la palanca de cinco metros *m*
– *five-metre (Am. five-meter) plat-form*
9 el trampolín de tres metros *m*
– *three-metre (Am. three-meter) springboard (diving board)*
10 el trampolín de un metro
– *one-metre (Am. one-meter) springboard*
11 la piscina para saltos *m*
– *diving pool*
12 el salto de cabeza *f* con el cuerpo extendido (el salto del ángel)
– *straight header*
13 el salto de pie *m*
– *feet-first jump*
14 el salto con el cuerpo encogido (la bomba)
– *tuck jump (haunch jump)*
15 el vigilante de piscina *f*
– *swimming pool attendant (pool attendant, swimming bath atten-dant)*
16-20 la enseñanza de la natación
– *swimming instruction*
16 el profesor de natación *f* (el moni-tor de natación *f*)
– *swimming instructor (swimming teacher)*
17 el alumno de natación *f*, nadando
– *learner-swimmer*
18 la almohadilla flotadora para principiantes *m*
– *float; sim.: water wings*
19 el cinturón de corcho *m*
– *swimming belt (cork jacket)*
20 el aprendizaje en seco
– *land drill*

21 la piscina de los no nadadores
– *non-swimmers' pool*
22 el reguero
– *footbath*
23 la piscina de los nadadores
– *swimmers' pool*
24-32 la competición de natación *f* **en estilo** *m* **libre** de relevos *m*
– *freestyle relay race*
24 el cronometrador
– *timekeeper (lane timekeeper)*
25 el juez de llegada *f*
– *placing judge*
26 el juez de viraje *m*
– *turning judge*
27 el podio de salida *f*
– *starting block (starting place)*
28 el toque en la línea de llegada *f* de un nadador de competición *f*
– *competitor touching the finishing line*
29 el salto de salida *f*
– *starting dive (racing dive)*
30 el juez de salida *f*
– *starter*
31 la calle
– *swimming lane*
32 la corchera
– *rope with cork floats*
33-39 los estilos de natación *f*
– *swimming strokes*
33 la natación a braza *f* (la braza)
– *breaststroke*
34 el estilo mariposa (la mariposa)
– *butterfly stroke*
35 el estilo delfín
– *dolphin butterfly stroke*
36 la marinera (el over)
– *side stroke*
37 el crol
– *crawl stroke (crawl); sim.: trudgen stroke (trudgen, double overarm stroke)*
38 el buceo (la natación bajo el agua)
– *diving (underwater swimming)*
39 la bicicleta (la sustentación en el agua)
– *treading water*
40-45 los saltos (saltos de torre *f*, saltos de trampolín *m*)
– *diving (acrobatic diving, fancy diving, competitive diving, high-board diving)*
40 el salto de la carpa
– *standing take-off pike dive*
41 el salto hacia delante con media vuelta *f* inversa [la patada a la luna]
– *one-half twist isander (reverse dive)*

42 el salto mortal hacia atrás (el doble salto mortal)
– *backward somersault (double backward somersault)*
43 el tirabuzón con impulso *m*
– *running take-off twist dive*
44 la barrena
– *screw dive*
45 el salto en equilibrio *m* sobre las manos
– *armstand dive (handstand dive)*
46-50 el juego de waterpolo *m*
– *water polo*
46 la portería de waterpolo *m*
– *goal*
47 el portero
– *goalkeeper*
48 el balón de waterpolo *m*
– *water polo ball*
49 el defensa
– *back*
50 el delantero
– *forward*

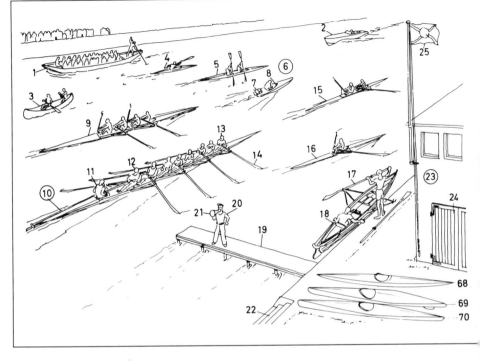

1-18 la toma de posiciones *f* para la regata
(para la regata de remos *m*)
- *taking up positions for the regatta*
1 la batea impulsada a percha *f,* una
barca de recreo *m*
- *punt, a pleasure boat*
2 la motora (la lancha de motor *m*)
- *motorboat*
3 la canoa canadiense
- *Canadian canoe*
4 el kayak (el kayak groenlandés; *Col.:* el
jámparo), una canoa
- *kayak (Alaskan canoe, slalom canoe), a
canoe*
5 el kayak biplaza
- *tandem kayak*
6 el fuera borda (la canoa automóvil con
motor *m* fuera borda *f*)
- *outboard motorboat (outboard speed-
boat, outboard)*
7 el motor fuera borda *f*
- *outboard motor (outboard)*
8 la cabina del piloto
- *cockpit*
9-16 botes *m* de carreras *f* (botes
deportivos, outriggers, botes de regatas
f; Amér. Central y Pan.: la panga)
- *racing boats (sportsboats, outriggers)*
9-15 botes *m* de remos *m* (*Bol. y Ec.:* la
montería)
- *shells (rowing boats, Am. rowboats)*
9 el bote de a cuatro sin timonel *m,* un
bote de obra *f* cerrada (de construcción
f lisa)
- *coxless four, a carvel-built boat*
10 el bote de a ocho (el ocho de carrera *f*)
- *eight (eight-oared racing shell)*

11 el timonel
- *cox*
12 el cabo, un remero
- *stroke, an oarsman*
13 el proel (el "número uno")
- *bow ('number one')*
14 el remo
- *oar*
15 el dos (el bote de remos *m* de a dos)
- *coxless pair*
16 el bote de carreras *f* unipersonal (el skif)
- *single sculler (single skuller, racing
sculler, racing skuller, skiff)*
17 la espadilla
- *scull (skull)*
18 el bote de un remero con timonel *m,* un
bote de tingladillo *m*
- *coxed single, a clinker-built single*
19 el embarcadero (el desembarcadero)
- *jetty (landing stage)*
20 el entrenador de remo *m*
- *rowing coach*
21 el megáfono (la bocina)
- *megaphone*
22 la escalera del muelle
- *quayside steps*
23 el edificio del club (el club)
- *clubhouse (club)*
24 el cobertizo de los botes
- *boathouse*
25 la bandera del club
- *club's flag*
26-33 la yola de a cuatro, una yola (bote *m*
de chumaceras *f,* bote de recreo *m*)
- *four-oared gig, a touring boat*
26 el timón
- *oar*

27 el asiento del timonel
- *cox's seat*
28 la bancada (el banco del remero)
- *thwart (seat)*
29 la chumacera
- *rowlock (oarlock)*
30 la regala
- *gunwale (gunnel)*
31 el durmiente de las bancadas
- *rising*
32 la quilla (la quilla exterior)
- *keel*
33 el forro exterior [en tingladillo *m*]
- *skin (shell, outer skin) [clinker-built]*
34 el canalete de una sola pala (*Filip.:* la
pagaya; *Venez.:* el jarete)
- *single-bladed paddle (paddle)*
35-38 el remo (la espadilla)
- *oar (scull, skull)*
35 el guión
- *grip*
36 el luchadero
- *leather sheath*
37 el cuello del remo
- *shaft (neck)*
38 la pala (la pala del remo)
- *blade*
39 el canalete doble
- *double-bladed paddle (double-ended
paddle)*
40 el anillo engrasador
- *drip ring*
41-50 el asiento de corredera *f*
- *sliding seat*
41 la chumacera (la chumacera giratoria)
- *rowlock (oarlock)*

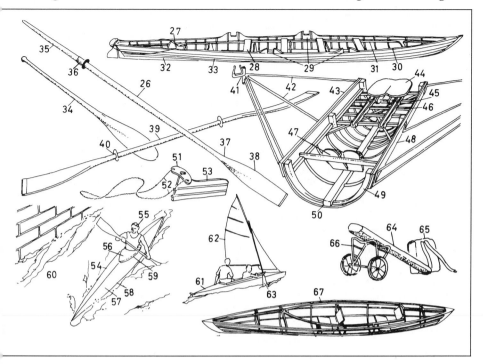

42 el arbotante
- *outrigger*
43 la falca
- *saxboard*
44 el asiento de corredera *f*
- *sliding seat*
45 la corredera (el raíl de deslizamiento *m*)
- *runner*
46 el refuerzo
- *strut*
47 el apoyo
- *stretcher*
48 el forro exterior
- *skin (shell, outer skin)*
49 la cuaderna
- *frame (rib)*
50 la sobrequilla
- *kelson (keelson)*
51-53 el timón (el gobernalle)
- *rudder (steering rudder)*
51 la caña del timón
- *yoke*
52 el guardín
- *lines (steering lines)*
53 la pala (la pala del timón)
- *blade (rudder blade, rudder)*
54-66 canoas *f* plegables
- *folding boats (foldboats, canoes)*
54 la canoa plegable monoplaza, un bote deportivo individual
- *one-man kayak*
55 el canoero (el piragüista)
- *canoeist*

56 la cubierta protectora contra las salpicaduras
- *spraydeck*
57 la cubierta
- *deck*
58 el forro de lona *f* impermeabilizada (el forro exterior)
- *rubber-covered canvas hull*
59 la brazola
- *cockpit coaming (coaming)*
60 el canal construido a lo largo de una presa
- *channel for rafts alongside weir*
61 la canoa plegable biplaza, un bote de recreo *m* con dos asientos *m*
- *two-seater folding kayak, a touring kayak*
62 la vela de una canoa plegable
- *sail of folding kayak*
63 la orza de deriva *f*
- *leeboard*
64 el saco para la armazón
- *bag for the rods*
65 la mochila para el casco (para el forro)
- *rucksack*
66 el remolque para transportar el bote
- *boat trailer (boat carriage)*
67 la armazón (el costillaje) de la canoa plegable
- *frame of folding kayak*
68-70 kayaks *m* (canoas *f*)
- *kayaks*

68 el kayak (la canoa) esquimal
- *Eskimo kayak*
69 el kayak (la canoa) de regatas *f* en aguas *f* turbulentas (*Col. y Venez.*: la curiana)
- *wild-water racing kayak*
70 el kayak (la canoa) de recreo *m*
- *touring kayak*

1-9 el windsurfing (la tabla a vela *f*)
– *windsurfing*
1 el windsurfista (el deportista de windsurfing *m*)
– *windsurfer*
2 la vela
– *sail*
3 la ventana transparente
– *transparent window (window)*
4 el mástil
– *mast*
5 la tabla de surf *m*
– *surfboard*
6 el cojinete móvil para la inclinación del mástil y el gobierno de la tabla
– *universal joint (movable bearing) for adjusting the angle of the mast and for steering*
7 el botalón (la botavara)
– *wishbone*
8 la orza de quilla *f* (desmontable)
– *retractable centreboard (Am. centerboard)*
9 la orza auxiliar
– *rudder*
10-48 el velero (el barco de vela *f*)
– *yacht (sailing boat, Am. sailboat)*
10 la cubierta de proa *f*
– *foredeck*
11 el mástil
– *mast*
12 el trapecio
– *trapeze*
13 la cruceta
– *crosstrees (spreader)*
14 la encapilladura
– *hound*
15 el estay de proa *f*
– *forestay*
16 el foque (el foque genovés, Génova)
– *jib (Genoa jib)*
17 el aparejo para reclamar (el foque)
– *jib downhaul*
18 el obenque
– *side stay (shroud)*
19 el acollador
– *lanyard (also: turnbuckle)*
20 el pie del mástil (la carlinga)
– *foot of the mast*
21 la trapa
– *kicking strap (vang)*
22 la escotera
– *jam cleat*
23 la escota del foque
– *foresheet (jib sheet)*
24 la caja de la orza de quilla *f*
– *centreboard (Am. centerboard) case*
25 el perno de la orza de quilla *f*
– *bitt*

26 la orza de quilla *f*
– *centreboard (Am. centerboard)*
27 el escotero
– *traveller (Am. traveler)*
28 la escota mayor
– *mainsheet*
29 la guía (el pasacabo) de la escota de foque *m*
– *foresheet fairlead (jib fairlead)*
30 la trapa
– *toestraps (hiking straps)*
31 el brazo de la caña del timón
– *tiller extension (hiking stick)*
32 la caña del timón (la barra)
– *tiller*
33 la cabeza del timón
– *rudderhead (rudder stock)*
34 la pala del timón
– *rudder blade (rudder)*
35 el espejo (la popa de espejo *m*, la popa cuadra)
– *transom*
36 el espiche del orificio de desagüe *m*
– *drain plug*
37 el puño de amura *f* de la vela mayor
– *gooseneck*
38 la ventana de la vela
– *window*
39 la botavara
– *boom*
40 el pujamen
– *foot*
41 el puño de escota *f*
– *clew*
42 el caída de proa *f* (el grátil)
– *luff (leading edge)*
43 la funda del sable
– *leech pocket (batten cleat, batten pocket)*
44 el sable
– *batten*
45 la caída de popa *f* (la baluma)
– *leech (trailing edge)*
46 la vela mayor
– *mainsail*
47 la tabla de grátil *m*
– *headboard*
48 la veleta (la grímpola)
– *racing flag (burgee)*
49-65 clases *f* de yates *m* (clases de monotipos *m*)
– *yacht classes*
49 el Flying Dutchman
– *Flying Dutchman*
50 la yola O
– *O-Joller*
51 el dingui Finn
– *Finn dinghy (Finn)*
52 el Pirata
– *pirate*
53 el Sharpie de 12 m²
– *12.00 m² sharpie*

54 el Tempest
– *tempest*
55 el Star
– *star*
56 el Soling
– *soling*
57 el Dragón
– *dragon*
58 el monotipo clase *f* 5,5 m
– *5.5-metre (Am. 5.5-meter) class*
59 el monotipo clase *f* R de 6 m
– *6-metre (Am. 6-meter) R-class*
60 el yate de crucero *m* de 30 m²
– *30.00 m² cruising yacht (coastal cruiser)*
61 la yola de 30 m², un velero de crucero *m*
– *30.00 m² dinghy cruiser*
62 el monotipo de 25 m² con quilla *f*
– *25.00 m² one-design keelboat*
63 el monotipo clase *f* KR
– *KR-class*
64 el catamarán
– *catamaran*
65 el doble casco
– *twin hull*

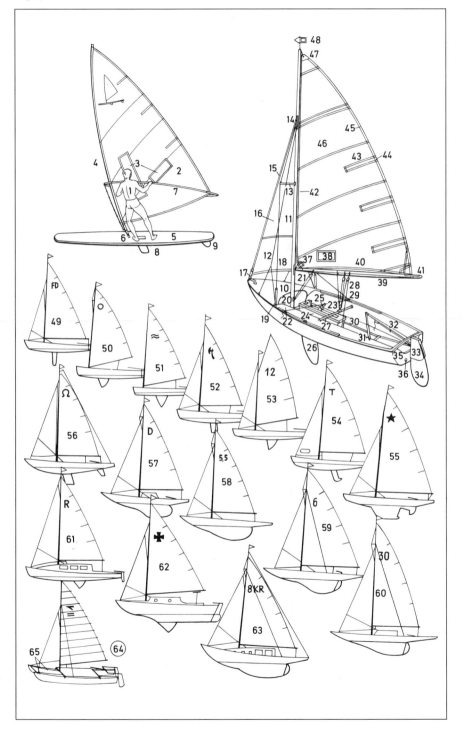

1-13 **disposiciones** *f* **de las velas y direcciones** *f* **del viento**
- *points of sailing and wind directions*
1 la navegación a vela *f* viento *m* en popa *f*
- *sailing downwind (running)*
2 la vela mayor
- *mainsail*
3 el foque
- *jib*
4 la disposición de las velas en forma *f* de tijeras *f*
- *sails set goose-winged*
5 el eje del barco
- *centre (Am. center) line*
6 la dirección del viento
- *wind direction*
7 el barco con el viento contrario (sin viento favorable)
- *yacht stopped head to wind*
8 la vela flameante
- *sail, shivering*
9 la orza (la orzada)
- *luffing*
10 la bolina
- *sailing close-hauled*
11 la navegación con viento *m* a la cuadra (con viento de través)
- *sailing with wind abeam*
12 la navegación con viento *m* a un largo
- *sailing with free wind*
13 la brisa en los estayes de proa *f*
- *quartering wind (quarter wind)*
14-24 **el recorrido de la regata**
- *regatta course*
14 la boya de salida *f* y de llegada *f*
- *starting and finishing buoy*
15 el barco del jurado
- *committee boat*
16 el recorrido triangular (el recorrido de la regata)
- *triangular course (regatta course)*
17 la boya de virada *f* (la baliza de virada)
- *buoy (mark) to be rounded*
18 la boya de señalización *f* del recorrido
- *buoy to be passed*
19 la primera bordada
- *first leg*
20 la segunda bordada
- *second leg*
21 la tercera bordada
- *third leg*
22 la bordada ciñendo el viento
- *windward leg*
23 la bordada con viento *m* en popa *f*
- *downwind leg*
24 la bordada con viento *m* a un largo
- *reaching leg*

25-28 **la virada de bordo** *m*
- *tacking*
25 la bordada ciñendo el viento
- *tack*
26 el trasluche (la virada por redondo)
- *gybing (jibing)*
27 la virada (cambiada *f* del rumbo)
- *going about*
28 la pérdida de altura *f* durante el trasluche
- *loss of distance during the gybe (jibe)*
29-41 **formas** *f* **del casco de las embarcaciones de vela** *f*
- *types of yacht hull*
29-34 el yate de crucero *m* con quilla *f*
- *cruiser keelboat*
29 la popa
- *stern*
30 la proa lanzada (la proa de cuchara *f*)
- *spoon bow*
31 la línea de flotación *f*
- *waterline*
32 la quilla (la quilla con lastre *m*)
- *keel (ballast keel)*
33 el lastre
- *ballast*
34 el timón
- *rudder*
35 el yate de regatas *f* con quilla *f*
- *racing keelboat*
36 la quilla de plomo *m*
- *lead keel*
37-41 el velero
- *keel-centreboard (Am. centerboard) yawl*
37 el timón izable
- *retractable rudder*
38 la bañera
- *cockpit*
39 la superestructura de la caseta
- *cabin superstructure (cabin)*
40 la roda recta (la roda vertical)
- *straight stem*
41 la orza de quilla *f* desmontable
- *retractable centreboard (Am. centerboard)*
42-49 **formas** *f* **de popas** *f* **de las embarcaciones de vela** *f*
- *types of yacht stern*
42 la popa de yate *m* (la popa de bovedilla *f*)
- *yacht stern*
43 la popa cuadra de yate *m* (la popa de espejo *m*)
- *square stern*
44 la popa de canoa *f*
- *canoe stern*
45 la popa de crucero *m*
- *cruiser stern*
46 la placa con el nombre
- *name plate*

47 el dormido
- *deadwood*
48 la popa cuadra (la popa de espejo *m*)
- *transom stern*
49 el espejo
- *transom*
50-57 **el forro de las embarcaciones de madera** *f*
- *timber planking*
50-52 el forro en tingladillo *m*
- *clinker planking (clench planking)*
50 la traca (la hilada) exterior
- *outside strake*
51 la cuaderna, una cuaderna transversal
- *frame (rib)*
52 el roblón
- *clenched nail (riveted nail)*
53 el forro a tope *m*
- *carvel planking*
54 la construcción de cuadernas *f* de costura *f*
- *ribband-carvel construction*
55 la cuaderna de costura *f*, una cuaderna longitudinal
- *ribband, a stringer*
56 el forro a tope *m* en diagonal *f*
- *diagonal carvel planking*
57 el forro interior
- *inner planking*

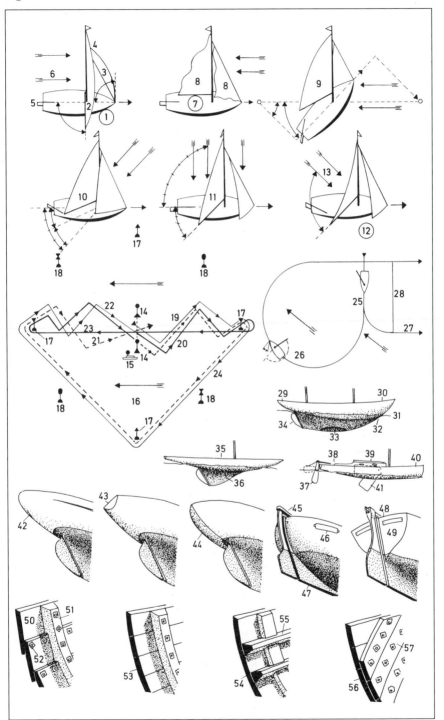

1-5 barcos *m* a motor *m* (barcos *m* deportivos)
– *motorboats (powerboats, sportsboats)*
1 el bote neumático deportivo con motor *m* fuera borda *f* (el fuera borda *f* neumático)
– *inflatable sportsboat with outboard motor (outboard inflatable)*
2 el bote de motor *m* interior con transmisión *f* en Z
– *Z-drive motorboat (outdrive motorboat)*
3 la lancha motora con camarotes *m*
– *cabin cruiser*
4 el yate de crucero *m* a motor *m*
– *motor cruiser*
5 el yate de crucero *m* en alta mar *amb.*, de 30 m de eslora *f*
– *30-metre (Am. 30-meter) oceangoing cruiser*
6 la bandera del club
– *association flag*
7 el nombre del barco (*o:* el número de matrícula *f*)
– *name of craft (or: registration number)*
8 el nombre del club y del puerto de matrícula *f*
– *club membership and port of registry (Am. home port)*
9 la bandera del club en la cruceta de estribor *m*
– *association flag on the starboard crosstrees*
10-14 el régimen de luces *f* de los barcos deportivos en aguas *f* costeras y de lagos *m* (las luces de situación *f*)
– *navigation lights of sportsboats in coastal and inshore waters*
10 la luz de tope *m* blanca
– *white top light*
11 la luz de estribor *m* verde
– *green starboard sidelight*
12 la luz de babor *m* roja
– *red port sidelight*
13 la luz de proa *f* roja y verde
– *green and red bow light (combined lantern)*
14 la luz de popa *f* blanca
– *white stern light*
15-18 anclas *f*
– *anchors*
15 el ancla *f* con cepo *m* (el ancla *f* almirantazgo), una ancla pesada
– *stocked anchor (Admiralty anchor), a bower anchor*
16-18 anclas *f* ligeras
– *lightweight anchor*
16 el ancla *f* de reja *f* de arado *m*
– *CQR anchor (plough, Am. plow, anchor)*
17 el ancla *f* de patente *m* (el ancla *f* sin cepo *m*)
– *stockless anchor (patent anchor)*
18 el ancla *f* Danforth (el ancla *f* para embarcaciones *f* pequeñas de recreo *m*)
– *Danforth anchor*

19 la balsa de salvamento *m*
– *life raft*
20 el chaleco salvavidas
– *life jacket*
21-44 la carrera de motoras *f*
– *powerboat racing*
21 el catamarán con motor *m* fuera borda *f*
– *catamaran with outboard motor*
22 el hidroplano
– *hydroplane*
23 el motor fuera borda *f* de carreras *f*
– *racing outboard motor*
24 la caña del timón
– *tiller*
25 el conducto de la gasolina
– *fuel pipe*
26 el espejo de popa *f*
– *transom*
27 el flotador (*Mé., Col.:* la llanta)
– *buoyancy tube*
28 salida *f* y llegada *f*
– *start and finish*
29 la zona de salida *f*
– *start*
30 la línea de salida *f* y de llegada *f*
– *starting and finishing line*
31 la boya de viraje *m*
– *buoy to be rounded*
32-37 botes *m* con menor desplazamiento *m*
– *displacement boats*
32-34 el bote de cuaderna *f* redonda
– *round-bilge boat*
32 la vista del fondo del casco
– *view of hull bottom*
33 la sección transversal de la proa
– *section of fore ship*
34 la sección transversal de la popa
– *section of aft ship*
35-37 el bote con el fondo del casco en V
– *V-bottom boat (vee-bottom boat)*
35 la vista del fondo del casco
– *view of hull bottom*
36 la sección transversal de la proa
– *section of fore ship*
37 la sección transversal de la popa
– *section of aft ship*
38-44 hidroplanos *m*
– *planing boats (surface skimmers, skimmers)*
38-41 el hidroplano con redientes *m*
– *stepped hydroplane (stepped skimmer)*
38 el perfil
– *side view*
39 la vista del fondo del casco
– *view of hull bottom*
40 la sección transversal de la proa
– *section of fore ship*
41 la sección transversal de la popa
– *section of aft ship*
42 el hidroplano de tres puntos *m* de apoyo *m*
– *three-point hydroplane*
43 la aleta
– *fin*
44 el flotador (*Mé. y Col.:* la llanta)
– *float*

45-62 esquí *m* acuático
– *water skiing*
45 la esquiadora
– *water skier*
46 la salida en aguas *f* profundas
– *deep-water start*
47 el cable (el cable de arrastre *m*)
– *tow line (towing line)*
48 la empuñadura
– *handle*
49-55 el lenguaje de los esquiadores (el código de los esquiadores de señales *f* con la mano)
– *water-ski signalling (code of hand signals from skier to boat driver)*
49 la señal de "más deprisa"
– *signal for 'faster'*
50 la señal de "ralentizar" (de aminorar la velocidad)
– *signal for 'slower' ('slow down')*
51 la señal de "velocidad *f* en orden *m*" (velocidad, de acuerdo)
– *signal for 'speed OK'*
52 la señal de "viraje *m*"
– *signal for 'turn'*
53 la señal de "alto *m*"
– *signal for 'stop'*
54 la señal de "parar el motor"
– *signal for 'cut motor'*
55 la señal de "regreso al embarcadero"
– *signal for 'return to jetty' ('back to dock')*
56-62 tipos *m* de esquíes *m* acuáticos
– *types of water ski*
56 el esquí de figuras, un monoesquí
– *trick ski (figure ski), a monoski*
57 *u.* **58** la fijación de goma *f*
– *rubber binding*
57 la pieza de goma *f* del pie delantero
– *front foot binding*
58 la goma de sujeción *f* del talón
– *heel flap*
59 el estribo del segundo pie
– *strap support for second foot*
60 el esquí de slálom *m*
– *slalom ski*
61 la quilla (la aleta)
– *skeg (fixed fin, fin)*
62 el esquí de saltos *m*
– *jump ski*
63 el hovercraft (el barco sobre un cojín neumático)
– *hovercraft (air-cushion vehicle)*
64 la hélice
– *propeller*
65 el timón
– *rudder*
66 el cojín neumático (el cojín de aire *m*)
– *skirt enclosing air cushion*

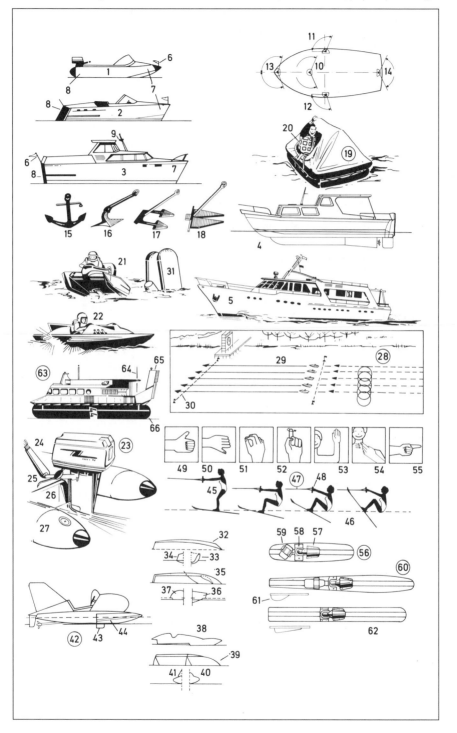

1 el despegue a remolque *m* de un avión
– *aeroplane* (Am. *airplane*) *tow launch (aerotowing)*
2 el avión remolcador, un avión a motor *m*
– *tug (towing plane)*
3 el velero (el planeador) remolcado
– *towed glider (towed sailplane)*
4 el cable de remolque *m*
– *tow rope*
5 el despegue por torno *m*
– *winched launch*
6 el torno de motor *m*
– *motor winch*
7 el paracaídas del cable
– *cable parachute*
8 el motovelero, un planeador con motor *m* auxiliar
– *motorized glider (powered glider)*
9 el planeador (el velero) de altas prestaciones *f*
– *high-performance glider (high-performance sailplane)*
10 el grupo de cola *f* (los estabilizadores) en T
– *T-tail (T-tail unit)*
11 la manga veleta
– *wind sock (wind cone)*
12 la torre de control *m*
– *control tower (tower)*
13 el aeródromo de vuelo *m* sin motor *m*
– *glider field*
14 el hangar
– *hangar*
15 la pista de despegue *m* y aterrizaje *m* para los aviones
– *runway for aeroplanes* (Am. *airplanes*)
16 el vuelo en ondas *f*
– *wave soaring*
17 las ondas a sotavento *m* (las ondas del viento cálido del Sur)
– *lee waves (waves, wave system)*
18 el rotor
– *rotor*
19 las nubes de forma *f* lenticular
– *lenticular clouds (lenticulars)*
20 el vuelo en la térmica
– *thermal soaring*
21 la manga de aire *m* ascendente (la manga térmica, la corriente de aire *m* ascendente)
– *thermal*
22 el cúmulo
– *cumulus cloud (heap cloud, cumulus, woolpack cloud)*
23 el vuelo en frente *m* tormentoso
– *storm-front soaring*
24 el frente tormentoso
– *storm front*
25 la corriente ascendente del frente
– *frontal upcurrent*

26 el cúmulo-nimbo
– *cumulonimbus cloud (cumulonimbus)*
27 el vuelo por la ladera
– *slope soaring*
28 el viento ascendente de la ladera
– *hill upcurrent (orographic lift)*
29 el ala *f* de largueros *m*, un plano de sustentación *f*
– *multispar wing, a wing*
30 el larguero principal, un larguero cajón
– *main spar, a box spar*
31 el herraje de conexión *f*
– *connector fitting*
32 la costilla de sujeción *f*
– *anchor rib*
33 el larguero oblicuo
– *diagonal spar*
34 el borde de ataque *m*
– *leading edge*
35 la costilla principal
– *main rib*
36 la costilla auxiliar (la falsa costilla)
– *nose rib (false rib)*
37 el borde de salida *f*
– *trailing edge*
38 la trampilla del freno (el freno para vuelo *m* en picado, el aerofreno)
– *brake flap (spoiler)*
39 el alerón de curvatura *f* (el flap estabilizador)
– *torsional clamp*
40 el revestimiento
– *covering (skin)*
41 el alerón
– *aileron*
42 los bordes marginales
– *wing tip*
43 el vuelo con ala *f* delta
– *hang gliding*
44 el ala *f* delta
– *hang glider*
45 el piloto de ala *f* delta
– *hang glider pilot*
46 la barra de apoyo *m*
– *control frame*

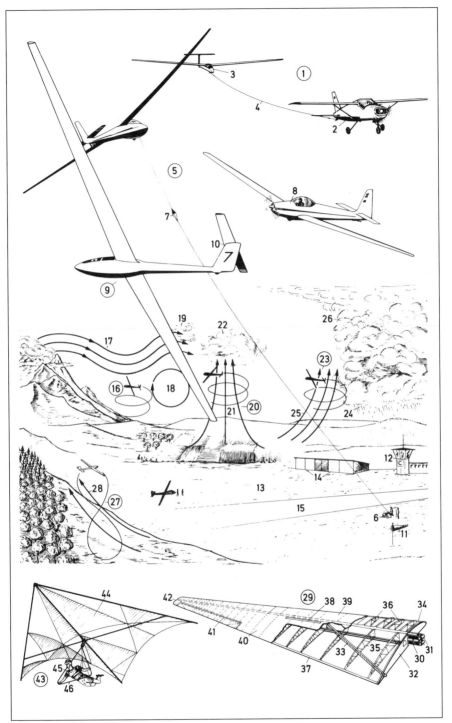

1-9 el vuelo acrobático (las figuras del vuelo acrobático)
– **aerobatics** *(aerobatic manoeuvres,* Am. *maneuvers)*
1 el rizo (el looping)
– *loop*
2 el ocho horizontal
– *horizontal eight*
3 la rueda con cuatro toneles *m* sucesivos
– *rolling circle*
4 la torre
– *stall turn (hammer head)*
5 la campana (el deslizamiento de cola *f*)
– *tail slide (whip stall)*
6 la barrena vertical
– *vertical flick spin*
7 el picado en barrena *f*
– *spin*
8 la barrena horizontal
– *horizontal slow roll*
9 el vuelo invertido
– *inverted flight (negative flight)*
10 **la cabina del piloto** (la carlinga)
– *cockpit*
11 el tablero (el cuadro) de instrumentos *m*
– *instrument panel*
12 el compás
– *compass*
13 el aparato de radionavegación *f*
– *radio and navigation equipment*
14 la palanca de mando *m*
– *control column (control stick)*
15 la manija de los gases
– *throttle lever (throttle control)*
16 la palanca reguladora de la mezcla
– *mixture control*
17 el radioteléfono
– *radio equipment*
18 **el avión biplaza acrobático y deportivo**
– **two-seater plane for racing and aerobatics**
19 la cabina del piloto (la carlinga)
– *cabin*
20 la antena
– *antenna*
21 el plano fijo de deriva *f*
– *vertical stabilizer (vertical fin, tail fin)*
22 el timón de dirección *f*
– *rudder*
23 el plano de profundidad *f* (el plano de cola *f*, el estabilizador horizontal)
– *tailplane (horizontal stabilizer)*
24 el timón de profundidad *f*
– *elevator*
25 el flap estabilizador (el compensador del balanceo)
– *trim tab (trimming tab)*
26 el fuselaje
– *fuselage (body)*
27 el ala *f* (el plano de sustentación *f*)
– *wing*
28 el alerón
– *aileron*
29 el flap (el alerón) de aterrizaje *m* (para reducir la velocidad de aterrizaje *m*)
– *landing flap*
30 el flap estabilizador (el compensador del balanceo)
– *trim tab (trimming tab)*
31 la luz de situación *f* (la luz de posición *f*) [roja]
– *navigation light (position light) [red]*
32 el faro de aterrizaje *m*
– *landing light*
33 el tren de aterrizaje *m* principal
– *main undercarriage unit (main landing gear unit)*
34 la rueda del morro
– *nose wheel*

35 el motor (el propulsor)
– *engine*
36 la hélice
– *propeller (airscrew)*
37-62 el paracaidismo
– **parachuting** *(sport parachuting)*
37 el paracaídas
– *parachute*
38 el casquete
– *canopy*
39 el paracaídas auxiliar
– *pilot chute*
40 las cuerdas de suspensión *f*
– *suspension lines*
41 la cuerda de mando *m*
– *steering line*
42 la correa principal de sustentación *f*
– *riser*
43 el arnés
– *harness*
44 el saco envoltura del paracaídas
– *pack*
45 el sistema de aberturas *f* del paracaídas deportivo
– *system of slots of the sports parachute*
46 las aberturas de dirección *f*
– *turn slots*
47 la chimenea
– *apex*
48 el borde de ataque *m* del casquete
– *skirt*
49 el alerón estabilizador
– *stabilizing panel*
50 u. **51** el salto de estilo *m* (las figuras acrobáticas)
– *style jump*
50 el salto hacia atrás
– *back loop*
51 la espiral (el giro)
– *spiral*
52-54 las señales visuales trazadas en el suelo
– *ground signals*
52 la señal de "autorización *f* de salto" *m* (la cruz del blanco)
– *signal for 'permission to jump' (`conditions are safe') (target cross)*
53 la señal de "prohibición *f* de salto *m* – reemprender el vuelo"
– *signal for 'parachuting suspended – repeat flight'* .
54 la señal de "prohibición *f* de salto *m* – aterrizar inmediatamente"
– *signal for 'parachuting suspended – aircraft must land'*
55 el salto de precisión *f*
– *accuracy jump*
56 la cruz del blanco (el centro del blanco)
– *target cross*
57 el círculo interior del blanco [radio *m* 25 m]
– *inner circle [radius 25 m]*
58 el círculo medio del blanco [radio *m* 50 m]
– *middle circle [radius 50 m]*
59 el círculo exterior del blanco [radio *m* 100 m]
– *outer circle [radius 100 m]*
60-62 posiciones *f* en caída *f* libre
– *free-fall positions*
60 la posición en X, piernas *f* y brazos *m* separados
– *full spread position*
61 la posición de la rana, piernas *f* ligeramente separadas y brazos *m* plegados
– *frog position*
62 la posición en T, piernas *f* unidas y brazos *m* en cruz *f*
– *T position*

63-84 el vuelo en globo *m* **libre** (la aeroestación)
– **ballooning**
63 el globo de gas *m*
– *gas balloon*
64 la barquilla (la cestilla)
– *gondola (balloon basket)*
65 el lastre (los sacos de arena *f*)
– *ballast (sandbags)*
66 la cuerda de amarre *m*
– *mooring line*
67 el anillo de la barquilla
– *hoop*
68 los instrumentos de vuelo *m* (los instrumentos de a bordo *m*)
– *flight instruments (instruments)*
69 la cuerda de arrastre *m* (la cuerda guía)
– *trail rope*
70 el manguito de llenado *m* (el apéndice de llenado)
– *mouth (neck)*
71 las cuerdas del manguito de llenado *m*
– *neck line*
72 la banda de desgarre *m* de emergencia *f*
– *emergency rip panel*
73 la cuerda de desgarre *m* de emergencia *f*
– *emergency ripping line*
74 las patas de ganso *m*
– *network (net)*
75 la banda de desgarre *m*
– *rip panel*
76 la cuerda de desgarre *m* (la cuerda de apertura *f* de la banda de desgarre *m*)
– *ripping line*
77 la válvula
– *valve*
78 la cuerda de la válvula
– *valve line*
79 el globo de aìre *m* caliente (la montgolfiera, el montgolfier)
– *hot-air balloon*
80 la plataforma del quemador
– *burner platform*
81 el manguito de llenado *m* (el apéndice de llenado *m*)
– *mouth*
82 la válvula
– *vent*
83 la banda de desgarre *m*
– *rip panel*
84 la ascensión del globo (la salida del globo)
– *balloon take-off*
85-91 el deporte del aeromodelismo
– **flying model aeroplanes** *(Am. airplanes)*
85 el vuelo teledirigido por radio *m* de un aeromodelo
– *radio-controlled model flight*
86 el aeromodelo en vuelo *m* libre teledirigido
– *remote-controlled free flight model*
87 la teledirección por radio *f* (el aparato de radio *f* de telecontrol), la radio de control *m* a distancia *f*)
– *remote control radio*
88 la antena (la antena emisora)
– *antenna (transmitting antenna)*
89 el aeromodelo dirigido por cable *m*
– *control line model*
90 el sistema de control *m* por un único cable
– *mono-line control system*
91 la perrera volante, un aeromodelo estrafalario
– *flying kennel, a K9-class model*

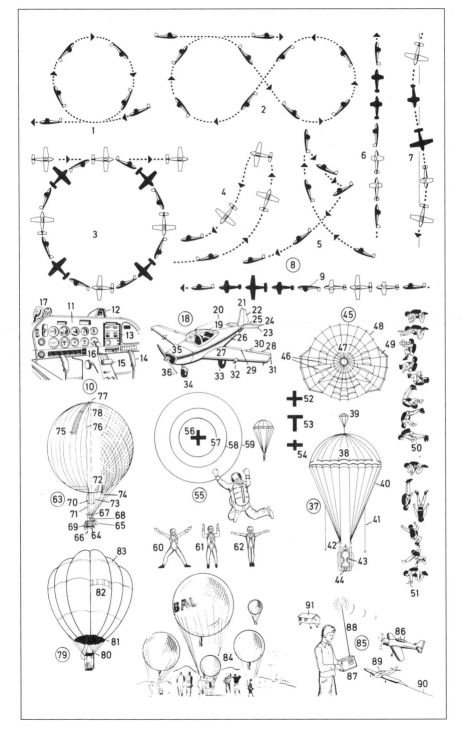

289 Hípica (equitación)   *Horsemanship, Equestrian Sport*

1-7 la doma de caballos *m*
– *dressage*
1 el picadero
– *arena (dressage arena)*
2 la barrera
– *rail*
3 el caballo de doma *f*
– *school horse*
4 la chaqueta de montar negra
– *dark coat (black coat)*
5 los pantalones de montar blancos
– *white breeches*
6 la chistera (el sombrero de copa *f* alta)
– *top hat*
7 el paso (la figura de escuela *f*)
– *gait (also: school figure)*
8-14 el concurso de saltos *m* **de obstáculos** *m* (el concurso hípico)
– *show jumping*
8 el obstáculo (la barrera), un obstáculo semifijo; *anál.:* la empalizada, la doble valla con seto *m* (el oxer), la valla, el muro, el foso, el seto
– *obstacle (fence), an almost-fixed obstacle; sim.: gate, gate and rails, palisade, oxer, mound, wall*
9 el caballo de saltos *m*
– *jumper*
10 la silla de saltos *m*
– *jumping saddle*
11 la barriguera
– *girth*
12 el bridón
– *snaffle*
13 la chaqueta de montar roja
– *red coat (hunting pink, pink; also: dark coat)*
14 la gorra de montar
– *hunting cap (riding cap)*
15 el vendaje
– *bandage*
16-19 el concurso completo de equitación *f*
– *three-day event*
16 la prueba de fondo *m*
– *endurance competition*
17 el recorrido de campo *m* a través (el recorrido de cross *m*, de cross-country *m*)
– *cross-country*
18 el casco protector contra caídas *f*
– *helmet (also: hard hat, hard hunting cap)*
19 la señalización del recorrido
– *course markings*
20-22 la carrera de obstáculos *m* (la carrera de vallas *f*)
– *steeplechase*
20 la ría (precedida de un seto), un obstáculo fijo
– *water jump, a fixed obstacle*

21 el salto
– *jump*
22 la fusta
– *riding switch*
23-40 la carrera al trote
– *harness racing (harness horse racing)*
23 la pista de carreras *f* al trote
– *harness racing track (track)*
24 el sulky
– *sulky*
25 la rueda de rayos *m* con disco *m* protector de plástico *m*
– *spoke wheel (spoked wheel) with plastic wheel disc (disk)*
26 el conductor, con traje *m* de carreras *f* al trote
– *driver in trotting silks*
27 la rienda
– *rein*
28 el caballo trotador (el trotador)
– *trotter*
29 el caballo pío (el caballo picazo)
– *piebald horse*
30 la pantalla para impedir la vista del suelo
– *shadow roll*
31 la rodillera
– *elbow boot*
32 la polaina de goma *f* (la protección de goma)
– *rubber boot*
33 el número de salida *f*
– *number*
34 la tribuna acristalada con ventanillas *f* (taquillas *f*) de apuestas *f*
– *glass-covered grandstand with totalizator windows (tote windows) inside*
35 el marcador
– *totalizator (tote)*
36 el número de salida *f*
– *number [of each runner]*
37 la cotización
– *odds (price, starting price, price offered)*
38 el ganador
– *winners' table*
39 la cotización del ganador
– *winner's price*
40 el tiempo invertido en la carrera
– *time indicator*
41-49 la caza a caballo *m* (la montería), **una caza de rastreo** *m;* *anál.:* la caza del zorro, la caza con papelillos *m*
– *hunt, a drag hunt; sim.: fox hunt, paper chase (paper hunt, hare-and-hounds)*
41 el grupo de cazadores *m*
– *field*
42 la chaqueta de caza *f* roja
– *hunting pink*

43 el perrero de caza *f* (el criado encargado de los perros)
– *whipper-in (whip)*
44 la trompa de caza *f*
– *hunting horn*
45 el cazador mayor
– *Master (Master of foxhounds, MFH)*
46 la jauría
– *pack of hounds (pack)*
47 el perro de caza *f*
– *staghound*
48 el "zorro"
– *drag*
49 el rastro (las huellas artificiales)
– *scented trail (artificial scent)*
50 la carrera al galope (la carrera de velocidad *f*)
– *horse racing (racing)*
51 el grupo en carrera *f* (los caballos de carreras *f; Arg., Bol., Col.* y *Urug.:* los fletes)
– *field (racehorses)*
52 el favorito
– *favourite* (Am. *favorite)*
53 el caballo no favorito (el outsider)
– *outsider*

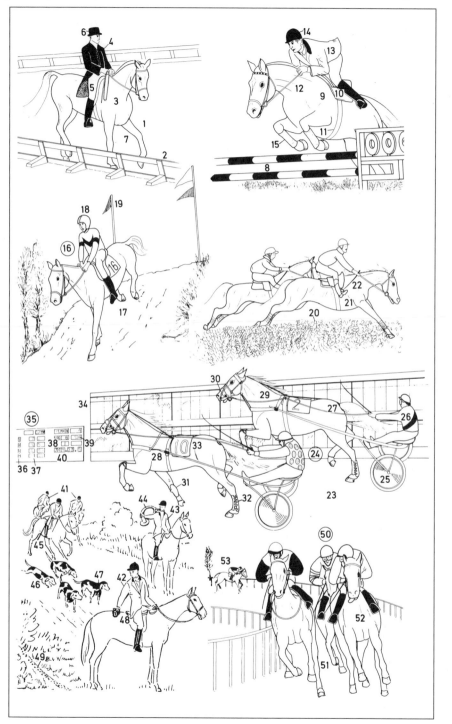

1-23 ciclismo
– *cycle racing*
1 el velódromo (la pista de carreras
f); *en este caso:* el velódromo
cubierto
– *cycling track (cycle track); here:*
indoor track
2-7 la carrera de los seis días
– *six-day race*
2 el corredor de los seis días, un
corredor sobre pista *f* en equipo *m*
– *six-day racer, a track racer (track*
rider) on the track
3 el casco protector
– *crash hat*
4 la dirección de la carrera
– *stewards*
5 el juez de meta *f* (el juez de llegada *f*)
– *judge*
6 el juez contador de las vueltas
– *lap scorer*
7 el vestuario de los corredores
– *rider's box (racer's box)*
8-10 la carrera por carretera *f*
– *road race*
8 el corredor por carretera *f* (el
rutista), un corredor ciclista
– *road racer, a racing cyclist*
9 la camiseta (el maillot) de ciclista *m*
– *racing jersey*
10 la botella para beber
– *water bottle*
11-15 la carrera de persecución *f* tras
moto *f* (la carrera de resistencia *f*)
– *motor-paced racing (long-distance*
racing)
11 el guía, un motorista
– *pacer, a motorcyclist*
12 la moto (la motocicleta) del guía
– *pacer's motorcycle*
13 el rodillo, un dispositivo de protección *f*
– *roller, a safety device*
14 el corredor de fondo *m*, un corredor ciclista tras moto *f*
– *stayer (motor-paced track rider)*
15 la bicicleta de carreras *f* tras moto
f, una bicicleta de carreras *f*
– *motor-paced cycle, a racing cycle*
16 la bicicleta de carreras *f* por carretera *f*
– *racing cycle (racing bicycle) for*
road racing (road race bicycle)
17 el sillín de carreras *f*, un sillín sin
muelles *m*
– *racing saddle, an unsprung saddle*
18 el manillar de carreras *f*
– *racing handlebars (racing handle-*
bar)
19 el neumático (el neumático de
carreras *f*)
– *tubular tyre* (Am. *tire) (racing*
tyre)

20 la cadena con cambio *m* de velocidades *f*
– *chain*
21 el calzapié (el calzapié de carreras *f*)
– *toe clip (racing toe clip)*
22 la correa
– *strap*
23 el neumático de repuesto *m*
– *spare tubular tyre* (Am. *tire)*
24-38 el motorismo
– *motorsports*
24-28 la carrera de motos *f* (motocicletas *f*); *disciplinas:* carreras
sobre hierba *f*, por carretera *f*,
sobre pista *f* de arena *f*, sobre
pista de cemento *m*, sobre pista de
ceniza *f*, carrera en cuesta *f*, carrera sobre hielo *m*, trial *m*, carrera
campo *m* a través, motocross *m*
– *motorcycle racing; disciplines:*
grasstrack racing, road racing, sand
track racing, cement track racing,
speedway [on ash or shale tracks],
mountain racing, ice racing (ice
speedway), scramble racing, trial,
moto cross
24 la pista de arena *f*
– *sand track*
25 el corredor de motos *f*
– *racing motorcyclist (rider)*
26 el traje (el mono) protector de
cuero *m*
– *leather overalls (leathers)*
27 la motocicleta de carreras *f*, una
máquina individual
– *racing motorcycle, a solo machine*
28 el número de salida *f*
– *number (number plate)*
29 la moto con sidecar *m*, en un viraje
– *sidecar combination on the bend*
30 el sidecar
– *sidecar*
31 la moto de carreras *f* de línea *f*
aerodinámica [500 cm³]
– *streamlined racing motorcycle*
[500 cc.]
32 el gymkhana, una competición de
habilidad *f*; *en este caso:* el
motorista caminando en zigzag *m*
– *gymkhana, a competition of skill;*
here: motorcyclist performing a
jump
33 la carrera de campo *m* a través (el
cross), una prueba de resistencia *f*
– *cross-country race, a test in perfor-*
mance
34-38 coches *m* de carreras *f* (bólidos *m*)
– *racing cars*
34 el coche de carreras *f* de Fórmula
1 (un monoplaza)
– *Formula One racing car (a mono*
posto)
35 el spoiler
– *rear spoiler (aerofoil,* Am. *airfoil)*

36 el coche de carreras *f* de Fórmula 2
– *Formula Two racing car (a racing*
car)
37 el coche de carreras *f* super-V
– *Super-Vee racing car*
38 el prototipo, un coche de carreras *f*
– *prototype, a racing car*

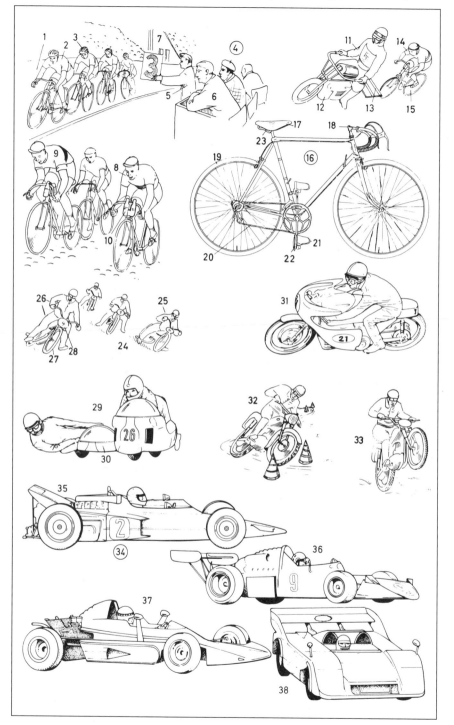

291 Juegos de pelota I (fútbol)

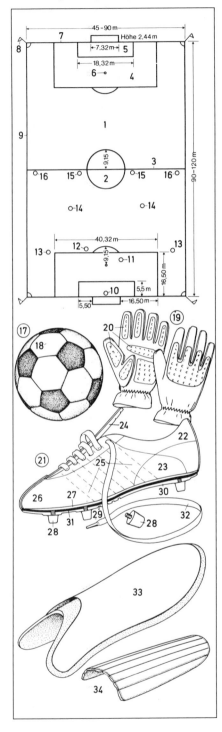

1-16 el campo de fútbol *m* (*Arg. y Urug.:* la cancha)
- *football pitch*
1 el terreno de juego *m*
- *field (park)*
2 el círculo central
- *centre* (Am. *center*) *circle*
3 la línea de medio campo *m*
- *half-way line*
4 el área *f* de penalty *m* (el área *f* de castigo *m*, de dieciséis metros *m*)
- *penalty area*
5 el área *f* de meta *f*
- *goal area*
6 el punto de ejecución *f* del penalty (el punto de penalty *m*)
- *penalty spot*
7 la línea de meta *f*
- *goal line (by-line)*
8 la bandera de esquina *f* (de córner *m*)
- *corner flag*
9 la línea de banda *f*
- *touch line*
10 el guardameta (el portero; *Amér.:* el arquero)
- *goalkeeper*
11 el líbero (el jugador libre)
- *sweeper (libero)*
12 el defensa central
- *inside defender*
13 el defensa lateral (lateral *m* izquierdo, lateral *m* derecho)
- *outside defender*
14 el medio (el centrocampista)
- *midfield players*
15 el interior
- *inside forward (striker)*
16 el extremo (el ala)
- *outside forward (winger)*
17 el balón de fútbol *m*
- *football*
18 la válvula
- *valve*
19 los guantes del portero (del guardameta)
- *goalkeeper's gloves*
20 el acolchado de goma espuma *f*
- *foam rubber padding*
21 la bota de fútbol *m*
- *football boot*
22 el revestimiento de cuero *m*
- *leather lining*
23 el contrafuerte
- *counter*
24 la lengüeta enguatada
- *foam rubber tongue*
25 las franjas laterales
- *bands*
26 la pala (la empella)
- *shaft*
27 la plantilla
- *insole*
28 el taco de rosca *f*
- *screw-in stud*

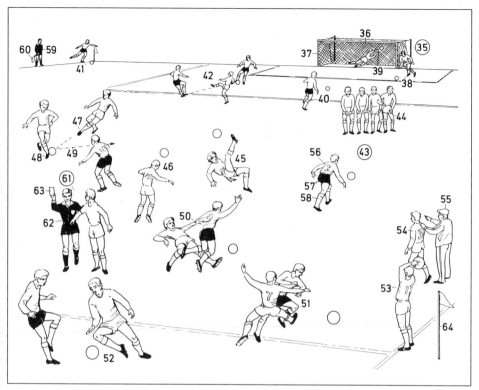

29 la ranura
 – *groove*
30 la suela de nailon *m*
 – *nylon sole*
31 la palmilla
 – *inner sole*
32 el cordón
 – *lace (bootlace)*
33 la espinillera (la canillera) con
 tobillera *f*
 – *football pad with ankle guard*
34 la espinillera
 – *shin guard*
35 la portería (la meta; *Amér.:* el
 arco)
 – *goal*
36 el larguero
 – *crossbar*
37 el poste
 – *post (goalpost)*
38 el saque (el saque de puerta *f*)
 – *goal kick*
39 el despeje de puños *m*
 – *save with the fists*
40 el penalty
 – *penalty (penalty kick)*
41 el saque de esquina *f* (el córner)
 – *corner (corner kick)*

42 el fuera de juego *m*
 – *offside*
43 el tiro libre
 – *free kick*
44 la barrera
 – *wall*
45 el tiro hacia atrás (la contra)
 – *bicycle kick (overhead bicycle
 kick)*
46 el tiro de cabeza *f*
 – *header*
47 el pase
 – *pass (passing the ball)*
48 la recogida del balón
 – *receiving the ball (taking a pass)*
49 el pase corto (la pared)
 – *short pass (one-two)*
50 la falta (la jugada antirreglamen-
 taria)
 – *foul (infringement)*
51 la obstrucción
 – *obstruction*
52 el regate (el dribling)
 – *dribble*
53 el saque de banda *f*
 – *throw-in*
54 el reserva (el jugador suplente)
 – *substitute*

55 el entrenador
 – *coach*
56 la camiseta
 – *shirt (jersey)*
57 el pantalón de deporte *m* (el pantalón corto)
 – *shorts*
58 la media (la media de fútbol *m*)
 – *sock (football sock)*
59 el juez de línea *f* (el linier)
 – *linesman*
60 la bandera del juez de línea *f*
 – *linesman's flag*
61 la expulsión
 – *sending-off*
62 el árbitro
 – *referee*
63 la tarjeta de expulsión *f* (tarjeta
 roja; *como amonestación:* la tarjeta
 amarilla)
 – *red card; as a caution also: yellow
 card*
64 la bandera de la raya de medio
 campo *m*
 – *centre* (Am. *center*) *flag*

1 **el balonmano** (el balonmano sala; el balonmano reducido)
– **handball** *(indoor handball)*
2 el jugador de balonmano *m,* un jugador de equipo *m*
– *handball player, a field player*
3 el delantero, efectuando un lanzamiento con salto *m*
– *attacker, making a jump throw*
4 la defensa
– *defender*
5 la línea de golpe *m* franco (de tiro *m* libre)
– *penalty line*
6 **el hockey**
– *hockey*
7 la portería de hockey *m*
– *goal*
8 el portero (el guardameta; *Amér.:* el arquero)
– *goalkeeper*
9 la protección de la pierna (la espinillera, la rodillera)
– *pad (shin pad, knee pad)*
10 la bota de hockey *m*
– *kicker*
11 la máscara protectora de la cara
– *face guard*
12 el guante
– *glove*
13 el palo de hockey *m* (el stick)
– *hockey stick*
14 la pelota de hockey *m*
– *hockey ball*
15 el jugador de hockey *m*
– *hockey player*
16 el círculo de tiro *m*
– *striking circle*
17 la línea de banda *f*
– *sideline*
18 la esquina
– *corner*
19 **el rugby** (el rugby europeo)
– *rugby (rugby football)*
20 la melée
– *scrum (scrummage)*
21 el balón de rugby *m*
– *rugby ball*
22 **el rugby americano** (el fútbol americano)
– *American football (Am. football)*
23 el jugador llevando el balón, un jugador de rugby *m* americano
– *player carrying the ball, a football player*
24 el casco
– *helmet*
25 la protección de la cara
– *face guard*
26 la camiseta con hombreras *f*
– *padded jersey*
27 el balón
– *ball (pigskin)*
28 **el baloncesto** (el basket-ball)
– *basketball*

29 el balón de baloncesto *m*
– *basketball*
30 el tablero de la canasta
– *backboard*
31 el poste de la canasta
– *backboard support*
32 la canasta (el cesto)
– *basket*
33 el aro de la canasta (del cesto)
– *basket ring*
34 el rectángulo de encuadre *m*
– *target rectangle*
35 el encestador, un jugador de baloncesto *m*
– *basketball player shooting*
36 la línea de fondo *m*
– *end line*
37 el área de tiro *m* libre
– *restricted area*
38 la línea de tiro *m* libre
– *free-throw line*
39 el jugador suplente
– *substitute*
40-69 el béisbol (la pelota base, el base-ball)
– *baseball*
40-58 el campo de juego *m*
– *field (park)*
40 la barrera para los espectadores
– *spectator barrier*
41 el exterior
– *outfielder*
42 el medio (el short-stop)
– *short stop*
43 la segunda base *m*
– *second base*
44 el jugador de base *m*
– *baseman*
45 el corredor
– *runner*
46 la primera base *m*
– *first base*
47 la tercera base *m*
– *third base*
48 la línea de penalización *f* (de falta *f*)
– *foul line (base line)*
49 la plataforma (la base) de lanzamiento *m*
– *pitcher's mound*
50 el pitcher (el lanzador)
– *pitcher*
51 la base meta (la base del cuadro)
– *batter's position*
52 el bateador
– *batter*
53 la base del bateador
– *home base (home plate)*
54 el catcher (el receptor)
– *catcher*
55 el árbitro
– *umpire*
56 el puesto del preparador (del entrenador)
– *coach's box*

57 el preparador (el entrenador)
– *coach*
58 los bateadores suplentes
– *batting order*
59 *u.* **60** los guantes de béisbol *m*
– *baseball gloves (baseball mitts)*
59 el guante del "fielder" (jugador *m* que para la pelota)
– *fielder's glove (fielder's mitt)*
60 el guante del catcher (del receptor)
– *catcher's glove (catcher's mitt)*
61 la pelota de béisbol *m*
– *baseball*
62 el bate
– *bat*
63 el bateador intentando un batazo
– *batter at bat*
64 el catcher (el receptor)
– *catcher*
65 el árbitro
– *umpire*
66 el corredor
– *runner*
67 la almohadilla de la base
– *base plate*
68 el pitcher (el lanzador)
– *pitcher*
69 la plataforma del pitcher (del lanzador)
– *pitcher's mound*
70-76 el criquet
– *cricket*
70 el rastrillo con el travesaño
– *wicket with bails*
71 la línea de tiro *m*
– *bowling crease*
72 la línea del bateador
– *popping crease*
73 el guardián del rastrillo del equipo receptor (del equipo atacante)
– *wicket keeper of the fielding side*
74 el bateador (del equipo defensor)
– *batsman*
75 el bate
– *bat (cricket bat)*
76 el lanzador
– *fielder (bowler)*
77-82 el croquet
– *croquet*
77 el poste de llegada *f*
– *winning peg*
78 el arco de croquet *m*
– *hoop*
79 el poste de viraje *m*
– *corner peg*
80 el jugador de croquet *m*
– *croquet player*
81 el mazo de croquet *m*
– *croquet mallet*
82 la bola (la pelota) de croquet *m*
– *croquet ball*

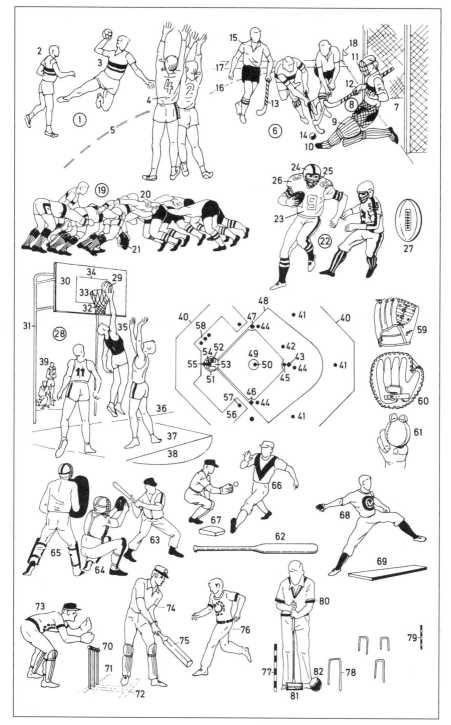

1-42 el tenis
- *tennis*
1 la pista de tenis *m*
- *tennis court*
2 *bis* **3** la línea de banda *f* para el juego de dobles *m* (doble; doble de caballeros *m*, doble de damas *f*, doble mixto)
- *sideline for doubles match (doubles; men's doubles, women's doubles, mixed doubles) (doubles sideline)*
3 *bis* **10** la línea de fondo *m*
- *base line*
4 *bis* **5** la línea de banda *f* para el juego individual (individual *m*; individual de caballeros *m*, individual de damas *f*)
- *sideline for singles match (singles; men's singles, women's singles) (singles sideline)*
6 *bis* **7** la línea de saque *m*
- *service line*
8 *bis* **9** la línea central de saque *m*
- *centre* (Am. *center*) *line*
11 la marca central
- *centre* (Am. *center*) *mark*
12 el cuadro de saque *m*
- *service court*
13 la red (la red de tenis *m*)
- *net (tennis net)*
14 la cinta de la red
- *net strap*
15 el poste de la red
- *net post*
16 el jugador de tenis *m* (el tenista)
- *tennis player*
17 el smash
- *smash*
18 el contrario (el adversario)
- *opponent*
19 el árbitro (el juez de silla)
- *umpire*
20 la silla del árbitro
- *umpire's chair*
21 el micrófono del árbitro
- *umpire's microphone*
22 el recogepelotas
- *ball boy*
23 el juez de red *f*
- *net-cord judge*
24 el juez de línea *f* de banda *f*
- *foot-fault judge*
25 el juez de línea *f* central de saque *m*
- *centre* (Am. *center*) *line judge*
26 el juez de línea *f* de fondo *m*
- *base line judge*
27 el juez de línea *f* de saque *m*
- *service line judge*
28 la pelota de tenis *m*
- *tennis ball*
29 la raqueta de tenis *m*
- *tennis racket (tennis racquet, racket, racquet)*
30 el mango de la raqueta
- *racket handle (racquet handle)*
31 el cordaje de la raqueta (la superficie para golpear la pelota)
- *strings (striking surface)*
32 el tensor
- *press (racket press, racquet press)*
33 la clavija tensora
- *tightening screw*
34 el marcador
- *scoreboard*
35 los resultados de los sets
- *results of sets*

36 el nombre del jugador
- *player's name*
37 el número de sets *m* [ganados por un jugador]
- *number of sets*
38 el número de juegos *m* [ganados por un jugador]
- *state of play*
39 el revés
- *backhand stroke*
40 el derecho
- *forehand stroke*
41 la volea (la volea con golpe *m* derecho a altura *f* normal)
- *volley (forehand volley at normal height)*
42 el saque (el servicio)
- *service*
43 *u.* **44 el juego de volante** *m* (el bádminton)
- *badminton*
43 la raqueta del juego de volante *m* (del bádminton)
- *badminton racket (badminton racquet)*
44 el volante
- *shuttle (shuttlecock)*
45-55 el tenis de mesa *f* (el ping-pong)
- *table tennis*
45 la paleta del tenis de mesa *f* (de ping-pong *m*)
- *table tennis racket (racquet) (table tennis bat)*
46 el mango de la paleta
- *racket (racquet) handle (bat handle)*
47 el revestimiento de la paleta
- *blade covering*
48 la pelota del tenis de mesa *f* (de ping-pong *m*)
- *table tennis ball*
49 los jugadores de tenis *m* de mesa *f* (jugadores de ping-pong *m*); *en este caso: dobles* *m* *mixtos*
- *table tennis players; here: mixed doubles*
50 el resto
- *receiver*
51 el sacador (el saque)
- *server*
52 la mesa de ping-pong *m*
- *table tennis table*
53 la red del tenis de mesa *f* (de ping-pong *m*)
- *table tennis net*
54 la línea de centro *m*
- *centre* (Am. *center*) *line*
55 la línea de banda *f*
- *sideline*
56-71 el balonvolea (el voleibol)
- *volleyball*
56 *u.* **57** la colocación correcta de las manos
- *correct placing of the hands*
58 el balón (la pelota) de balonvolea *m*
- *volleyball*
59 el servicio de balonvolea *m*
- *serving the volleyball*
60 el defensa (el zaguero)
- *blocker*
61 la zona de servicio *m* (de saque *m*)
- *service area*
62 el sacador (el saque)
- *server*
63 el delantero (el jugador de la red)
- *front-line player*
64 la zona de ataque *m*
- *attack area*
65 la línea de ataque *m*

36 *attack line*
66 la zona de defensa *f*
- *defence* (Am. *defense*) *area*
67 el primer árbitro
- *referee*
68 el segundo árbitro
- *umpire*
69 el juez de línea *f*
- *linesman*
70 el marcador
- *scoreboard*
71 el tanteador
- *scorer*
72-78 el juego de balón *m* **a puños** *m*
- *faustball*
72 la línea de fondo *m*
- *base line*
73 la cuerda
- *tape*
74 el balón (la pelota) del juego de balón a puños *m*
- *faustball*
75 el delantero
- *forward*
76 el medio (el jugador de centro *m*)
- *centre* (Am. *center*)
77 el zaguero
- *back*
78 el golpe de martillo *m* (el remate)
- *hammer blow*
79-93 el golf
- *golf*
79-82 el campo de golf *m* (los hoyos)
- *course (holes)*
79 la salida (el sitio de salida, el "tee")
- *teeing ground*
80 el obstáculo natural (el rough, el terreno escabroso)
- *rough*
81 el búnker (el hoyo de arena *f*)
- *bunker* (Am. *sand trap*)
82 el green (el putting green, el terreno nivelado y cubierto de césped *m* alrededor del hoyo)
- *green (putting green)*
83 el jugador de golf *m* (el golfista), en el golpe de salida *f* (en el drive)
- *golfer, driving*
84 el impulso
- *follow-through*
85 el carrito de golf *m*
- *golf trolley*
86 el tiro al hoyo (el put), con un putter
- *putting (holing out)*
87 el hoyo
- *hole*
88 la banderola
- *pin (flagstick)*
89 la pelota de golf *m*
- *golf ball*
90 el tee (la pieza para colocar la pelota)
- *tee*
91 el bastón (el club) de madera *f* (relleno de plomo *m*) un driver; *anál.:* el brassy
- *wood, a driver; sim.: brassie (brassy, brassey)*
92 el bastón (el club) de hierro *m*; el iron
- *iron*
93 el putter
- *putter*

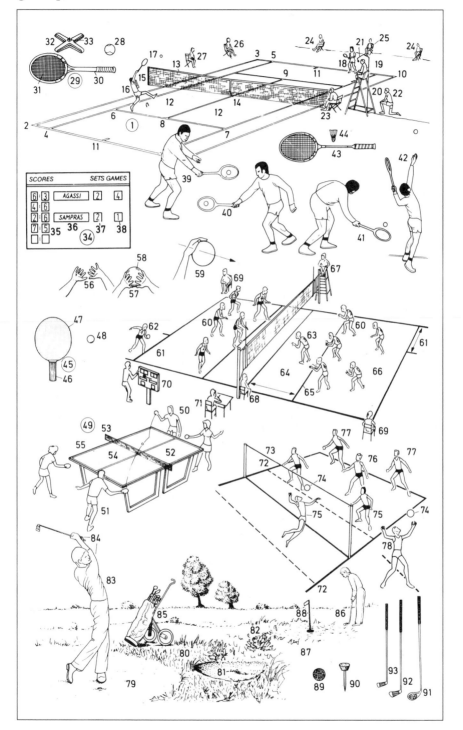

1-33 la esgrima deportiva
- *fencing (modern fencing)*
1-18 la esgrima de florete *m* (el florete)
- *foil*
1 el maestro de esgrima *f* (el maestro de armas *f*)
- *fencing master (fencing instructor)*
2 la pista de esgrima *f*
- *piste*
3 la línea de puesta *f* en guardia *f* (la línea de salida *f*)
- *on guard line*
4 la línea del centro
- *centre (Am. center) line*
5 *u.* **6** los esgrimidores (*Amér.:* los esgrimistas; los floretistas, tiradores *m* de florete *m*) en un asalto
- *fencers (foil fencers, foilsmen, foilists) in a bout*
5 el atacante en una entrada a fondo *m*
- *attacker (attacking fencer) in lunging position (lunging)*
6 el atacado en una parada
- *defender (defending fencer), parrying*
7 el golpe recto (el coup droit), una acción de esgrima *f*
- *straight thrust, a fencing movement*
8 la parada en tercera *f* o en sexta *f*
- *parry of the tierce*
9 la línea de esgrima *f*
- *line of fencing*
10 las tres distancias entre los adversarios en esgrima *f* (larga, media, corta distancia)
- *the three fencing measures (short, medium, and long measure)*
11 el florete, una arma de estocada *f*
- *foil, a thrust weapon*
12 el guante de esgrima *f*
- *fencing glove*
13 la careta de esgrima *f*
- *fencing mask (foil mask)*
14 el peto (la protección del cuello) de la careta de esgrima *f*
- *neck flap (neck guard) on the fencing mask*
15 el chaleco metálico
- *metallic jacket*
16 la chaquetilla de esgrima *f*
- *fencing jacket*
17 las zapatillas de esgrima *f* sin tacón *m*
- *heelless fencing shoes*
18 la posición inicial para el saludo antes del asalto
- *first position for fencer's salute (initial position, on guard position)*

19-24 la esgrima de sable *m*
- *sabre (Am. saber) fencing*
19 el tirador de sable *m*
- *sabreurs (sabre fencers, Am. saber fencers)*
20 el sable ligero (*Bol., Col. y Mé.:* el latón)
- *(light) sabre (Am. saber)*
21 el guante de sable *m*
- *sabre (Am. saber) glove (sabre gauntlet)*
22 la careta de sable *m*
- *sabre (Am. saber) mask*
23 el ataque a la cabeza (el tajo a la cabeza)
- *cut at head*
24 la parada en quinta *f*
- *parry of the fifth (quinte)*
25-33 la esgrima de espada *f* con un marcador de tocados *m* eléctrico
- *épée, with electrical scoring equipment*
25 el tirador de espada *f*
- *épéeist*
26 la espada eléctrica; *anál.:* el florete eléctrico
- *electric épée; also: electric foil*
27 la punta de la espada
- *épée point*
28 el marcador luminoso de tocados *m*
- *scoring lights*
29 la roldana (el carrete del cable)
- *spring-loaded wire spool*
30 la lámpara indicadora de tocado *m*
- *indicator light*
31 el cable
- *wire*
32 el equipo marcador eléctronico
- *electronic scoring equipment*
33 la posición de guardia *f*
- *on guard position*
34-45 las armas de esgrima *f*
- *fencing weapons*
34 el sable ligero (el sable de deporte *m*), una arma de tajos *m* y estocadas *f* (una arma de filo *m* y de punta *f*)
- *light sabre (Am. saber), a cut and thrust weapon*
35 la guarnición (el guardamano)
- *guard*
36 la espada, una arma de estocada *f*
- *épée, a thrust weapon*
37 el florete francés, una arma de estocada *f*
- *French foil, a thrust weapon*
38 la guarnición (la cazoleta)
- *guard (coquille)*
39 el florete italiano
- *Italian foil*
40 el pomo del florete
- *foil pommel*

41 el puño
- *handle*
42 el gavilán
- *cross piece (quillons)*
43 la guarnición (la cazoleta)
- *guard (coquille)*
44 la hoja
- *blade*
45 el botón
- *button*
46 los envolvimientos (las ligaduras)
- *engagements*
47 el envolvimiento en cuarta *f*
- *quarte (carte) engagement*
48 el envolvimiento en tercera *f* (o en sexta *f*)
- *tierce engagement (also: sixte engagement)*
49 el envolvimiento en círculo *m*
- *circling engagement*
50 el envolvimiento en segunda *f* (o en octava *f*)
- *seconde engagement (also: octave engagement)*
51-53 las áreas válidas de tocado *m*
- *target areas*
51 todo el cuerpo en la esgrima de espada *f*
- *the whole body in épée fencing (men)*
52 la cabeza y la parte del cuerpo situada por encima de las ingles en la esgrima de sable *m* (caballeros *m*)
- *head and upper body down to the groin in sabre (Am. saber) fencing (men)*
53 el tronco desde el cuello hasta las ingles en la esgrima de florete *m* (damas *f* y caballeros *m*)
- *trunk from the neck to the groin in foil fencing (ladies and men)*

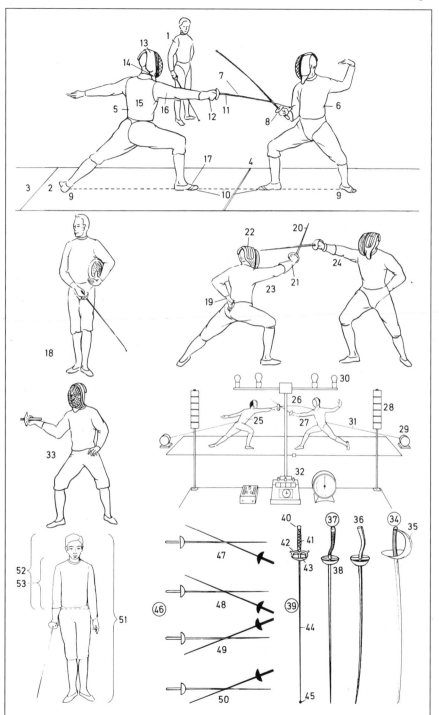

1 la posición de frente *f*
– *basic position (starting position)*
2 la iniciación de carrera *f*
– *running posture*
3 la iniciación de marcha *f*
– *side straddle*
4 la posición de piernas *f* abiertas
– *straddle (forward straddle)*
5 la elevación de talones *m* (la elevación de puntillas *f*)
– *toe stand*
6 la flexión completa de piernas *f*
– *crouch*
7 la posición de rodillas *f*
– *upright kneeling position*
8 la posición sentada sobre los talones, brazos *m* apoyados en la rodilla
– *kneeling position, seat on heels*
9 la posición sentada con flexión *f* completa de piernas *f* y brazos *m* atrás
– *squat*
10 la posición sentada en escuadra *f*
– *L seat (long sitting)*
11 la posición yoga *m*
– *tailor seat (sitting tailor-style)*
12 la flexión *f* pierna *f* izquierda y extensión *f* derecha
– *hurdle (hurdle position)*
13 la V
– *V-seat*
14 el spagat de perfil *m*
– *side split*
15 el spagat de frente *f*
– *forward split*
16 la escuadra *f,* elevación *f* del cuerpo
– *L-support*
17 la V, elevación *f* del cuerpo
– *V-support*
18 la escuadra *f* con piernas *f* separadas, elevación *f* del cuerpo con apoyo *m* sobre las manos
– *straddle seat*
19 el puente
– *bridge*
20 la posición de rodillas *f* con apoyo *m* frontal
– *kneeling front support*
21 el tendido supino con extensión *f* de brazos *m* y flexión *f*
– *front support*
22 el tendido prono, extensión *f* y flexión *f* de brazos *m*
– *back support*
23 la posición en cuclillas *f* con apoyo *m* frontal
– *crouch with front support*
24 la elevación de caderas *f* y extensión *f* de piernas *f,* con apoyo *m* frontal
– *arched front support*

25 el tendido lateral, extensión *f* de brazos *m* y equilibrio *m*
– *side support*
26 el pino con flexión *f* de brazos *m*
– *forearm stand (forearm balance)*
27 el pino
– *handstand*
28 el puntal
– *headstand*
29 el clavo (la vela)
– *shoulder stand (shoulder balance)*
30 la balanza frontal
– *forward horizontal stand (arabesque)*
31 la balanza lateral
– *rearward horizontal stand*
32 la flexión lateral del tronco
– *trunk-bending sideways*
33 la flexión del tronco hacia delante
– *trunk-bending forwards*
34 la flexión del tronco hacia atrás
– *arch*
35 el salto en extensión *f*
– *astride jump (butterfly)*
36 el salto en cuclillas *f*
– *tuck jump*
37 el salto esparrancado (con las piernas abiertas)
– *astride jump*
38 el salto de la carpa
– *pike*
39 el salto de tijera *f* (iniciación *f* de salto *m* de barra *f* de altura *f*)
– *scissor jump*
40 el salto de corzo *m*
– *stag jump (stag leap)*
41 el paso gimnástico (el paso de carrera *f*)
– *running step*
42 el paso con entrada *f* a fondo *m*
– *lunge*
43 la marcha
– *forward pace*
44 el tendido cúbito prono
– *lying on back*
45 el tendido cúbito supino
– *prone position*
46 el tendido lateral
– *lying on side*
47 la posición de brazos *m* hacia abajo
– *holding arms downwards*
48 los brazos en cruz *f*
– *holding (extending) arms sideways*
49 los brazos arriba
– *holding arms raised upward*
50 los brazos al frente
– *holding (extending) arms forward*
51 los brazos oblicuos atrás
– *arms held (extended) backward*
52 las manos en la nuca
– *hands clasped behind the head*

1-11 los aparatos gimnásticos en
gimnasia *f* olímpica masculina
- *gymnastics apparatus in men's*
  Olympic gymnastics
1 el caballo sin arco *m* (el caballo
de saltos *m*)
- *long horse (horse, vaulting horse)*
2 las paralelas
- *parallel bars*
3 la barra
- *bar*
4 las anillas
- *rings (stationary rings)*
5 el caballo con arcos *m*
- *pommel horse (side horse)*
6 el arco
- *pommel*
7 la barra fija
- *horizontal bar (high bar)*
8 la barra
- *bar*
9 el poste (el soporte) de la barra
fija
- *upright*
10 el viento (el tirante) de fijación *f*
- *stay wires*
11 la pista para la gimnasia en el
suelo (la gimnasia de manos *m*
libres, una superficie de 12 x 12 m)
- *floor (12 m × 12 m floor area)*
12-21 aparatos *m* auxiliares y
aparatos *m* de gimnasia *f* escolar y
de club *m*
- *auxiliary apparatus and appara-*
  tus for school and club gymnas-
  tics
12 el trampolín
- *springboard (Reuther board)*
13 la colchoneta dura
- *landing mat*
14 la barra de equilibrio *m* (la barra
sueca)
- *bench*
15 el plinton (*Amér.:* el cajón)
- *box*
16 el elemento del plinton
- *small box*
17 el potro
- *buck*
18 la colchoneta blanda
- *mattress*
19 la cuerda fija
- *climbing rope (rope)*
20 el espaldar sueco (la espaldera)
- *wall bars*
21 la escalera de pared *f*
- *window ladder*
22-39 la posición en relación *f* al
aparato
- *positions in relation to the appa-*
  ratus
22 la posición facial lateral
- *side, facing*

23 la posición dorsal lateral
- *side, facing away*
24 la posición facial transversal
- *end, facing*
25 la posición dorsal transversal
- *end, facing away*
26 la posición facial lateral fuera del
aparato
- *outside, facing*
27 la posición transversal dentro del
aparato (en el extremo de las barras)
- *inside, facing*
28 el apoyo facial
- *front support*
29 el apoyo dorsal
- *back support*
30 la posición sentada a horcajadas *f*
- *straddle position*
31 la posición sentada lateral fuera
del aparato
- *seated position outside*
32 la posición sentada transversal
fuera del aparato
- *riding seat outside*
33 la suspensión facial
- *hang*
34 la suspensión dorsal
- *reverse hang*
35 la suspensión con los brazos flexionados
- *hang with elbows bent*
36 la suspensión invertida
- *piked reverse hang*
37 la suspensión invertida con el
cuerpo en extensión *f* (estirado)
- *straight inverted hang*
38 el apoyo con el cuerpo en extensión *f* (estirado)
- *straight hang*
39 el apoyo flexionado (con los brazos flexionados)
- *bent hang*
40-46 las presas
- *grasps (kinds of grasp)*
40 la presa por encima de la barra
fija (la presa facial)
- *overgrasp on the horizontal bar*
41 la presa por debajo de la barra
fija (la presa dorsal)
- *undergrasp on the horizontal bar*
42 la presa mixta en la barra fija
- *combined grasp on the horizontal bar*
43 la presa en cruz *f* en la barra fija
- *cross grasp on the horizontal bar*
44 la presa cubital en la barra fija
- *rotated grasp on the horizontal bar*
45 la presa radial en las paralelas
- *outside grip on the parallel bars*
46 la presa cubital en las paralelas
- *rotated grasp on the parallel bars*

47 la correa de cuero *m* para la sujeción a la barra
- *leather handstrap*
48-60 ejercicios *m* con los aparatos
- *(apparatus) exercises*
48 el salto en plancha en el caballo
de saltos *m*
- *long-fly on the horse*
49 la elevación con las piernas abiertas en las paralelas
- *rise to straddle on the parallel bars*
50 el cristo en las anillas
- *crucifix on the rings*
51 las tijeras en el caballo con arcos *m*
- *scissors (scissors movement) on*
  the pommel horse
52 la elevación de las piernas en el
pino sobre el suelo
- *legs raising into a handstand on*
  the floor
53 el salto en cuclillas *f* en el caballo
de saltos *m*
- *squat vault on the horse*
54 el círculo por los flancos en el
caballo de arcos *m*
- *double leg circle on the pommel*
  horse
55 el lanzamiento (la caída de pie *m*
hàcia atrás en las anillas)
- *hip circle backwards on the rings*
56 la báscula facial en las anillas
- *lever hang on the rings*
57 el giro hacia atrás en las paralelas
- *rearward swing on the parallel*
  bars
58 la báscula con suspensión *f* del
brazo
- *forward kip into upper arm hang*
  on the parallel bars
59 el giro por debajo de la barra fija
- *backward underswing on the hori-*
  zontal bar
60 el gran molinete
- *backward grand circle on the hori-*
  zontal bar
61-63 el equipo (la indumentaria) **de**
gimnasia *f*
- *gymnastics kit*
61 la camiseta de gimnasia *f*
- *singlet (vest, Am. undershirt)*
62 el pantalón de gimnasia *f*
- *gym trousers*
63 las zapatillas de gimnasia *f*
- *gym shoes*
64 la muñequera
- *wristband*

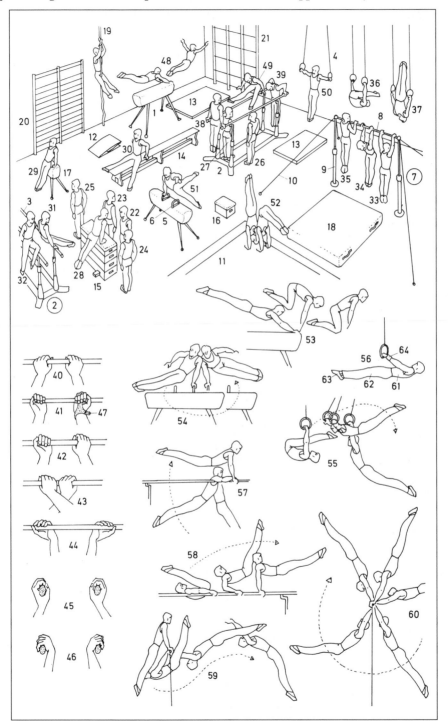

1-6 los aparatos gimnásticos en gimnasia *f* olímpica femenina
– *gymnastics apparatus in women's Olympic gymnastics*
1 el caballo sin arcos (el caballo de saltos *m*)
– *horse (vaulting horse)*
2 la barra de equilibrio *m* (la barra sueca)
– *beam*
3 las paralelas asimétricas
– *asymmetric bars (uneven bars)*
4 la barra inferior
– *bar*
5 el tirante (el viento) de fijación *f*
– *stay wires*
6 el suelo (la superficie del suelo de 12 × 12 m)
– *floor (12 m × 12 m floor area)*
7-14 aparatos *m* auxiliares y aparatos de gimnasia *f* escolar y de club *m*
– *auxiliary apparatus and apparatus for school and club gymnastics*
7 la colchoneta dura
– *landing mat*
8 el trampolín
– *springboard (Reuther board)*
9 el elemento del plinton
– *small box*
10 la cama elástica
– *trampoline*
11 la lona de saltos *m*
– *sheet (web)*
12 el bastidor (el marco)
– *frame*
13 los tensores de goma *f*
– *rubber springs*
14 la minicama elástica para tomar impulso *m*
– *springboard trampoline*
15-32 ejercicios *m* en los aparatos
– *apparatus exercises*
15 el salto mortal hacia atrás con el cuerpo encogido
– *backward somersault*
16 la posición de ayuda *f* (de una gimnasta)
– *spotting position (standing-in position)*
17 el salto mortal hacia atrás con el cuerpo en extensión *f* en la cama elástica
– *vertical backward somersault on the trampoline*
18 el salto mortal hacia delante con el cuerpo encogido en la minicama elástica
– *forward somersault on the springboard trampoline*
19 la voltereta hacia delante en el suelo
– *forward roll on the floor*

20 la voltereta con salto *m* de carpa *f* en el suelo
– *long-fly to forward roll on the floor*
21 la rueda en la barra de equilibrio *m*
– *cartwheel on the beam*
22 la voltereta sobre las manos hacia delante en el caballo de saltos *m*
– *handspring on the horse*
23 el arco hacia atrás en el suelo
– *backward walkover*
24 la voltereta sobre las manos hacia atrás en el suelo
– *back flip (flik-flak) on the floor*
25 la mariposa (la voltereta libre hacia delante) en el suelo
– *free walkover forward on the floor*
26 la voltereta con paso *m* hacia delante en el suelo
– *forward walkover on the floor*
27 la voltereta de cabeza *f* en el suelo
– *headspring on the floor*
28 el balanceo de elevación *f* en las paralelas asimétricas
– *upstart on the asymmetric bars*
29 el molinete libre en las paralelas asimétricas
– *free backward circle on the asymmetric bars*
30 la vuelta en el caballo de saltos *m*
– *face vault over the horse*
31 el volteo en el caballo de saltos *m*
– *flank vault over the horse*
32 la tuerca (el salto y vuelta *f*)
– *back vault (rear vault) over the horse*
33-50 gimnasia *f* con aparatos *m* de mano *f* (gimnasia *f* rítmica)
– *gymnastics with hand apparatus*
33 el lanzamiento en arco *m*
– *hand-to-hand throw*
34 la pelota de gimnasia *f*
– *gymnastic ball*
35 el lanzamiento hacia arriba
– *high toss*
36 el rebote
– *bounce*
37 los círculos con dos mazas *f*
– *hand circling with two clubs*
38 la maza de gimnasia *f*
– *gymnastic club*
39 la oscilación
– *swing*
40 el salto final con el cuerpo encogido
– *tuck jump*
41 el bastón gimnástico
– *bar*
42 el salto
– *skip*
43 la cuerda de saltar
– *rope (skipping rope)*
44 el salto cruzado
– *criss-cross skip*

45 el salto a través del aro
– *skip through the hoop*
46 el aro gimnástico
– *gymnastic hoop*
47 el círculo frontal
– *hand circle*
48 la serpiente
– *serpent*
49 la cinta gimnástica
– *gymnastic ribbon*
50 la espiral
– *spiral*
51 *u*. 52 el equipo de gimnasia *f*
– *gymnastics kit*
51 las mallas (la ropa de gimnasia *f*)
– *leotard*
52 las zapatillas de gimnasia *f*
– *gym shoes*

1-8 la carrera
- *running*
1-6 la salida
- *start*
1 el bloque de salida *f*
- *starting block*
2 el soporte del pie
- *adjustable block (pedal)*
3 la posición de salida *f*
- *start*
4 la salida en cuclillas *f*
- *crouch start*
5 el corredor, un sprinter (un velocista); *también:* el corredor de medio fondo *m*, el corredor de fondo *m*
- *runner, a sprinter; also: middle-distance runner, long-distance runner*
6 la pista de carreras *f*, una pista de ceniza *f* o de material *m* sintético
- *running track (track), a cinder track or synthetic track*
7 *u.* **8** la carrera de vallas *f; anál.:* la carrera de obstáculos *m* variados (el steeplechase)
- *hurdles (hurdle racing); sim.: steeplechase*
7 el salto de la valla
- *clearing the hurdle*
8 la valla
- *hurdle*
9-41 los saltos
- *jumping and vaulting*
9-27 el salto de altura *f*
- *high jump*
9 el salto Fosbury
- *Fosbury flop (Fosbury, flop)*
10 el saltador de altura *f*
- *high jumper*
11 la rotación alrededor del eje longitudinal y transversal del cuerpo
- *body rotation (rotation on the body's longitudinal and latitudinal axes)*
12 la caída de espaldas *f*
- *shoulder landing*
13 el saltómetro
- *upright*
14 el listón (la barra)
- *bar (crossbar)*
15 el Barrel Roll
- *Eastern roll*
16 el Western Roll (el rodillo californiano)
- *Western roll*
17 el rodillo
- *roll*
18 la técnica de rodillo *m*
- *rotation*
19 la caída
- *landing*
20 la escala de altura *f*
- *height scale*

21 la técnica de salto *m* de tijera *f* con giro *m*
- *Eastern cut-off*
22 el salto de tijera *f*
- *scissors (scissor jump)*
23 el salto de rodillo *m*
- *straddle (straddle jump)*
24 la técnica de rodillo *m*
- *turn*
25 la posición de las seis en el reloj (la pierna libre en posición *f* vertical)
- *vertical free leg*
26 el salto
- *take-off*
27 la pierna en extensión *f*
- *free leg*
28-36 el salto con pértiga *f*
- *pole vault*
28 la pértiga
- *pole (vaulting pole)*
29 el saltador de pértiga *f* en la fase de elevación *f*
- *pole vaulter (vaulter) in the pull-up phase*
30 la técnica del impulso
- *swing*
31 el franqueamiento de la barra (el saltador salvando el listón)
- *crossing the bar*
32 el aparato de salto *m* de altura *f*
- *high jump apparatus (high jump equipment)*
33 el saltómetro
- *upright*
34 el listón (la barra)
- *bar (crossbar)*
35 el cajón de batir
- *box*
36 la colchoneta para la caída
- *landing area (landing pad)*
37-41 el salto de longitud *f*
- *long jump*
37 el salto
- *take-off*
38 la tabla de batir (la tabla de salto *m*)
- *take-off board*
39 el foso
- *landing area*
40 el salto con golpe *m* de tijera *f*
- *hitch-kick*
41 la proyección del cuerpo hacia delante
- *hang*
42-47 el lanzamiento de martillo *m*
- *hammer throw*
42 el martillo
- *hammer*
43 la cabeza del martillo
- *hammer head*
44 el cable de acero *m*
- *handle*

45 el puño del martillo
- *grip*
46 la presa del martillo
- *holding the grip*
47 el guante
- *glove*
48 el lanzamiento de peso *m*
- *shot put*
49 el peso
- *shot (weight)*
50 la técnica O'Brien
- *O'Brien technique*
51-53 el lanzamiento de jabalina *f*
- *javelin throw*
51 la presa con el dedo índice y el pulgar *m*
- *grip with thumb and index finger*
52 la presa con el pulgar y el dedo medio (dedo corazón)
- *grip with thumb and middle finger*
53 la presa en forma *f* de tenazas *f*
- *horseshoe grip*
54 la ligadura
- *binding*

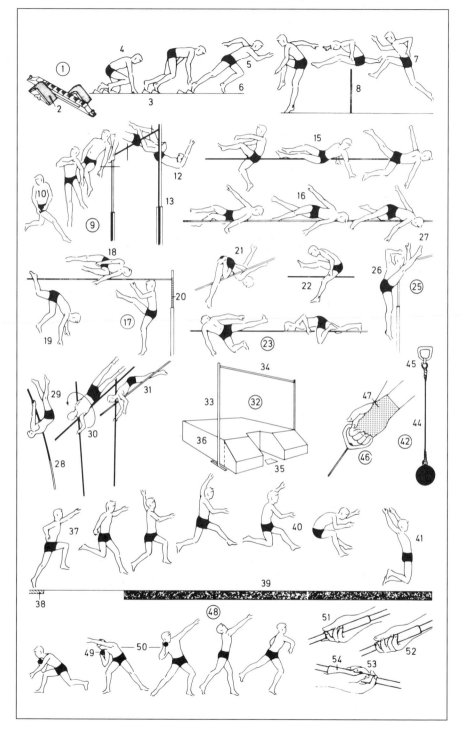

1-5 la halterofilia (el lavantamiento de pesos *m*)
– *weightlifting*
1 el levantamiento con arranque *m*
– *squat-style snatch*
2 el levantador de pesos *m*
– *weightlifter*
3 la barra de discos *m*
– *disc (disk) barbell*
4 el levantamiento con impulso *m* (el impulso con paso *m* al frente)
– *jerk with split*
5 el peso inmovilizado
– *maintained lift*
6-12 la lucha
– *wrestling*
6-9 la lucha grecorromana
– *Greco-Roman wrestling*
6 la lucha de pie *m*
– *standing wrestling (wrestling in standing position)*
7 el luchador
– *wrestler*
8 la lucha en el suelo (*en este caso:* el inicio de un movimiento de desasimiento *m*)
– *on-the-ground wrestling (*here: the *referee's position)*
9 el puente
– *bridge*
10-12 la lucha libre
– *freestyle wrestling*
10 la llave de brazo *m* lateral con presa *f* de pierna *f*
– *bar arm (arm bar) with grapevine*
11 la doble llave de pierna *f*
– *double leg lock*
12 la colchoneta de lucha *f*
– *wrestling mat (mat)*
13-17 el judo (*anál.:* el jiu-jitsu)
– *judo* (sim.: ju-jitsu, jiu-jitsu, ju-jutsu)
13 el derribo del oponente adelante y hacia la derecha
– *drawing the opponent off balance to the right and forward*
14 el judoka
– *judoka (judoist)*
15 el cinturón de colores *m* indicando el grado
– *coloured (*Am. *colored) belt, as a symbol of Dan grade*
16 el judoka neutral
– *referee*
17 el lanzamiento de judo *m*
– *judo throw*
18 *u.* **19 el karate**
– *karate*
18 el karateka
– *karateka*
19 la patada lateral, una técnica de pierna *f*
– *side thrust kick, a kicking technique*

20-50 el boxeo (el pugilato, el combate de boxeo)
– *boxing (boxing match)*
20-24 los aparatos de entrenamiento *m*
– *training apparatus (training equipment)*
20 la pelota suspendida por los dos extremos (el boxing-ball)
– *[spring-supported] punch ball*
21 el saco de arena *f*
– *punch bag (*Am. *punching bag)*
22 la pelota suspendida en un solo punto (el point-ball)
– *speed ball*
23 la pera de maíz *m* (la pera de boxeo *m*)
– *[suspended] punch ball*
24 el balón con plataforma *f* (el balón piriforme, el balón para pegar puñetazos *m*)
– *punch ball*
25 el boxeador (el púgil), un boxeador amateur (el combate con camiseta *f*), o un boxeador profesional (el combate sin camiseta)
– *boxer, an amateur boxer (boxes in a singlet, vest,* Am. *undershirt) or a professional boxer (boxes without singlet)*
26 el guante de boxeo *m*
– *boxing glove*
27 el compañero de entrenamiento *m* (el sparring)
– *sparring partner*
28 el directo
– *straight punch (straight blow)*
29 la flexión y la esquiva lateral
– *ducking and sidestepping*
30 la protección de la cabeza
– *headguard*
31 el cuerpo a cuerpo; *en este caso:* el clinch
– *infighting;* here: *clinch*
32 el gancho hacia arriba (el uppercut)
– *uppercut*
33 el gancho a la cabeza (el gancho hacia un lado)
– *hook to the head (hook, left hook or right hook)*
34 el golpe bajo, un golpe prohibido
– *punch below the belt, a foul punch (illegal punch, foul)*
35-50 el combate de boxeo *m*, un campeonato
– *boxing match (boxing contest), a title fight (title bout)*
35 el ring (el cuadrilátero de boxeo *m*)
– *boxing ring (ring)*
36 las cuerdas
– *ropes*
37 los tirantes de fijación *f* del ring
– *stay wire (stay rope)*

38 el rincón neutral
– *neutral corner*
39 el vencedor
– *winner*
40 el boxeador vencido por fuera de combate *m* (por knock-out, por K.O.)
– *loser by a knockout*
41 el árbitro
– *referee*
42 la cuenta de los segundos
– *counting out*
43 el juez que adjudica los puntos
– *judge*
44 el segundo (el asistente)
– *second*
45 el representante (el mánager, el organizador)
– *manager*
46 el gong (la campana)
– *gong*
47 el cronometrador
– *timekeeper*
48 el levantador del acta *f*
– *record keeper*
49 el fotógrafo de prensa *f*
– *press photographer*
50 el reportero de deportes *m*
– *sports reporter (reporter)*

1-57 el alpinismo (el montañismo, la ascensión a las altas montañas)
– *mountaineering (mountain climbing, Alpinism)*
1 el refugio (el albergue alpino, la cabaña de montaña *f*)
– *hut (Alpine Club hut, mountain hut, base)*
2-13 la escalada (la escalada en roca *f*) [técnicas *f* de escalada *f* en roca]
– *climbing (rock climbing) [rock climbing technique]*
2 la pared rocosa (la roca, la pared cortada a pico *m*)
– *rock face (rock wall)*
3 la quiebra (la quiebra longitudinal, transversal u oblicua)
– *fissure, (vertical, horizontal, or diagonal fissure)*
4 la cornisa (la cornisa rocosa, de hierba *f*, pedregosa, cornisa de nieve *f* o de hielo *m*)
– *ledge (rock ledge, grass ledge, scree ledge, snow ledge, ice ledge)*
5 el alpinista (el escalador)
– *mountaineer (climber, mountain climber, Alpinist)*
6 el anorak (la chaqueta enguatada para la nieve)
– *anorak (high-altitude anorak, snowshirt, padded jacket)*
7 los pantalones de escalada *f*
– *breeches (climbing breeches)*
8 la chimenea
– *chimney*
9 el pitón de roca *f* (la punta rocosa)
– *belay (spike, rock spike)*
10 el amarre de seguridad *f*
– *belay*
11 el nudo corredizo
– *rope sling (sling)*
12 la cuerda de escalada *f*
– *rope*
13 la cornisa
– *spur*
14-21 la escalada en hielo *m* [técnica *f* de escalada en hielo]
– *snow and ice climbing [snow and ice climbing technique]*
14 la pared de hielo *m* (la ladera de nieve *f* helada)
– *ice slope (firn slope)*
15 el escalador de hielo *m*
– *snow and ice climber*
16 el piolet (la piqueta)
– *ice axe (Am. ax)*
17 el escalón (el escalón tallado en el hielo)
– *step (ice step)*

18 las gafas de nieve *f*
– *snow goggles*
19 la capucha (la capucha del anorak)
– *hood (anorak hood)*
20 la cornisa (la cornisa de nieve *f*, de nieve *f* helada)
– *cornice (snow cornice)*
21 el picacho (el picacho de hielo *m*, de nieve *f* helada)
– *ridge (ice ridge)*
22-27 la cordada [la marcha en cordada]
– *rope (roped party) [roped trek]*
22 el glaciar
– *glacier*
23 la grieta del glaciar
– *crevasse*
24 el puente de nieve *f* (el puente de nieve helada)
– *snow bridge*
25 el primero de la cordada (el jefe de la cordada)
– *leader*
26 el segundo de la cordada
– *second man (belayer)*
27 el tercero de la cordada (el último hombre)
– *third man (non-belayer)*
28-30 el descenso en rapel *m*
– *roping down (abseiling, rapelling)*
28 el nudo corredizo del descenso en rapel *m*
– *abseil sling*
29 el descenso con mosquetón *m*
– *sling seat*
30 el descenso "Dülfer"
– *Dülfer seat*
31-57 el equipo de alpinismo *m* (el equipo de montañismo *m*, el equipo de escalada *f* en roca *f* o hielo *m*)
– *mountaineering equipment (climbing equipment, snow and ice climbing equipment)*
31 el piolet (la piqueta)
– *ice axe (Am. ax)*
32 la correa de la muñeca
– *wrist sling*
33 el pico
– *pick*
34 la pala
– *adze (Am. adz)*
35 el ojo del piolet
– *karabiner hole*
36 el piolet para el hielo
– *short-shafted ice axe (Am. ax)*
37 el martillo para el hielo (el martillo mixto para hielo *m* y roca *f*)
– *hammer axe (Am. ax)*

38 el pitón universal (el pitón para usos *m* múltiples)
– *general-purpose piton*
39 el pitón para el descenso en rapel *m* (el pitón de anillo *m*)
– *abseil piton (ringed piton)*
40 el pitón de rosca *f* para hielo *m* (el pitón en forma *f* de sacacorchos *m*)
– *ice piton (semi-tubular screw ice piton, corkscrew piton)*
41 el pitón de muescas *f* para hielo *m*
– *drive-in ice piton*
42 la bota de alpinismo *m*
– *mountaineering boot*
43 la suela estriada (la suela con muescas *f*, perfilada)
– *corrugated sole*
44 la bota de escalada *f*
– *climbing boot*
45 el borde rugoso de ebonita *f*
– *roughened stiff rubber upper*
46 el mosquetón
– *karabiner*
47 el cierre de rosca *f*
– *screwgate*
48 el crampón (el crampón ligero, el crampón de doce o diez puntas *f*)
– *crampons (lightweight crampons, twelve-point crampons, ten-point crampons)*
49 las puntas delanteras
– *front points*
50 la protección de la punta
– *point guards*
51 la correa del crampón
– *crampon strap*
52 la fijación del crampón por cable *m*
– *crampon cable fastener*
53 el casco protector contra los golpes de las piedras
– *safety helmet (protective helmet)*
54 la lámpara del casco
– *helmet lamp*
55 las polainas para la nieve
– *snow gaiters*
56 el cinturón de escalada *f*
– *climbing harness*
57 el cinturón de asiento *m*
– *sit harness*

1-72 el esquí
– *skiing*
1 el esquí compacto
– *compact ski*
2 la fijación de seguridad *f* del esquí
– *safety binding (release binding)*
3 la correa de sujeción *f*
– *strap*
4 el canto de acero *m*
– *steel edge*
5 el bastón de esquí *m*
– *ski stick (ski pole)*
6 el puño del bastón
– *grip*
7 la correa para la mano
– *loop*
8 la arandela
– *basket*
9 el traje de esquí de una sola pieza (el mono) para mujeres *f*
– *ladies' one-piece ski suit*
10 el gorro de esquí *m*
– *skiing cap (ski cap)*
11 las gafas de esquí *m*
– *skiing goggles*
12 la bota de esquí de suela *f* reforzada
– *cemented sole skiing boot*
13 el casco de esquí *m*
– *crash helmet*
14-20 el equipo de esquí *m* de fondo *m*
– *cross-country equipment*
14 el esquí de fondo *m*
– *cross-country ski*
15 la fijación de ratonera *f* para esquí *m* de fondo *m*
– *cross-country rat trap binding*
16 la bota de esquí *m* de fondo *m*
– *cross-country boot*
17 el traje de esquí *m* de fondo *m*
– *cross-country gear*
18 la gorra de visera *f*
– *peaked cap*
19 las gafas de sol *m*
– *sunglasses*
20 los bastones de esquí *m* de fondo *m*, de bambú *m*
– *cross-country poles made of bamboo*
21-24 utensilios *m* de encerar los esquíes
– *ski-waxing equipment*
21 la cera para esquí *m*
– *ski wax*
22 la plancha de encerar (la lámpara de soldar)
– *waxing iron (blowlamp, blowtorch)*
23 el aplicador de cera *f* de corcho *m*
– *waxing cork*
24 el rascador (el raspador de cera *f*)
– *wax scraper*
25 el bastón de carrera *f*
– *downhill racing pole*

26 el paso en forma *f* de espina *f* de pescado *m*, para escalar una pendiente
– *herringbone, for climbing a slope*
27 el paso en escalera *f*, para escalar una pendiente
– *sidestep, for climbing a slope*
28 la bolsa de cadera *f*
– *ski bag*
29 el slálom
– *slalom*
30 el poste de la puerta
– *gate pole*
31 el traje de carrera *f*
– *racing suit*
32 la carrera de descenso *m* (el descenso)
– *downhill racing*
33 el "huevo", la posición ideal en el descenso
– *'egg' position, the ideal downhill racing position*
34 el esquí de descenso *m*
– *downhill ski*
35 el salto con esquíes *m*
– *ski jumping*
36 el "pez", la posición en vuelo *m*
– *lean forward*
37 el dorsal (el número de salida *f*)
– *number*
38 el esquí de salto *m*
– *ski jumping ski*
39 las ranuras guías (3 a 5 ranuras)
– *grooves (3 to 5 grooves)*
40 la fijación de cable *m*
– *cable binding*
41 la bota de salto *m*
– *ski jumping boots*
42 la carrera de fondo *m*
– *cross-country*
43 el mono de carrera *f*
– *cross-country stretch-suit*
44 el recorrido
– *course*
45 las banderolas de señalización *f* (la señalización del recorrido)
– *course-marking flag*
46 las diferentes capas de un esquí moderno
– *layers of a modern ski*
47 el núcleo especial
– *special core*
48 las láminas
– *laminates*
49 la lámina de amortiguación *f*
– *stabilizing layer (stabilizer)*
50 el canto de acero *m*
– *steel edge*
51 el canto superior de aluminio *m*
– *aluminium (Am. aluminum) upper edge*

52 la superficie de deslizamiento *m* de material *m* sintético
– *synthetic bottom (artificial bottom)*
53 el estribo de suguridad *f*
– *safety jet*
54-56 los elementos de fijación *f*
– *parts of the binding*
54 la pieza automática del talón
– *automatic heel unit*
55 la pieza de sujeción *f* de la punta del pie
– *toe unit*
56 el freno del esquí
– *ski stop*
57-63 los remontes de esquí *m*
– *ski lift*
57 el telesilla biplaza
– *double chair lift*
58 la barra de seguridad *f*, con reposapiés *m*
– *safety bar with footrest*
59 el telesquí
– *ski lift*
60 el rastro
– *track*
61 el gancho de suspensión *f*
– *hook*
62 la garrucha automática para el cable
– *automatic cable pulley*
63 el cable de tracción *f*
– *haulage cable*
64 el slálom
– *slalom*
65 la puerta abierta
– *open gate*
66 la puerta vertical ciega (cerrada)
– *closed vertical gate*
67 la puerta vertical abierta
– *open vertical gate*
68 la doble puerta en diagonal *m*
– *transversal chicane*
69 la horquilla
– *hairpin*
70 la doble puerta vertical desplazada
– *elbow*
71 el corredor
– *corridor*
72 la chicana Allais (el paso en zigzag *m* Allais)
– *Allais chicane*

1-26 **el patinaje sobre hielo** *m*
- *ice skating*
1 la patinadora sobre hielo *m* (una patinadora individual)
- *ice skater, a solo skater*
2 la pierna de apoyo *m*
- *tracing leg*
3 la pierna libre
- *free leg*
4 los patinadores por parejas *f*
- *pair skaters*
5 la espiral de la muerte
- *death spiral*
6 el paso del arco
- *pivot*
7 el salto de corzo *m*
- *stag jump (stag leap)*
8 la pirueta sentada con salto *m*
- *jump-sit-spin*
9 la pirueta de pie *m*
- *upright spin*
10 el pie asido
- *holding the foot*
11-19 las figuras obligatorias del patinaje sobre hielo *m*
- *compulsory figures*
11 el ocho
- *curve eight*
12 la serpiente
- *change*
13 el tres
- *three*
14 el tres doble
- *double-three*
15 el lazo
- *loop*
16 el lazo de serpiente *m*
- *change loop*
17 el contratrés
- *bracket*
18 la contravuelta
- *counter*
19 la vuelta
- *rocker*
20-25 patines *m* (patines para el patinaje sobre hielo *m*)
- *ice skates*
20 el patín para patinaje *m* de velocidad *f*
- *speed skating set (speed skate)*
21 el canto
- *edge*
22 la hoja (la cuchilla) cóncava
- *hollow grinding (hollow ridge, concave ridge)*
23 el patín de hockey *m* sobre hielo *m*
- *ice hockey set (ice hockey skate)*
24 la bota para patinaje *m* sobre hielo *m*
- *ice skating boot*
25 la funda protectora
- *skate guard*

26 el patinador de volocidad *f*
- *speed skater*
27 *u.* **28 el patinaje a vela** *f*
- *skate sailing*
27 el patinador a vela *f*
- *skate sailor*
28 la vela de mano *f*
- *hand sail*
29-37 el hockey sobre hielo *m*
- *ice hockey*
29 el jugador de hockey *m* sobre hielo *m*
- *ice hockey player*
30 el stick de hockey *m* sobre hielo *m*
- *ice hockey stick*
31 el mango del stick
- *stick handle*
32 la pala del stick
- *stick blade*
33 la espinillera
- *shin pad*
34 el casco protector
- *headgear (protective helmet)*
35 el puck (un disco de ebonita *f*)
- *puck, a vulcanized rubber disc (disk)*
36 el portero (el guardameta)
- *goalkeeper*
37 la portería (la meta)
- *goal*
38-40 el curling alemán (el tiro del palo sobre hielo *m*)
- *ice-stick shooting (Bavarian curling)*
38 el jugador de curling *m* alemán (el tirador del palo sobre hielo *m*)
- *ice-stick shooter (Bavarian curler)*
39 el palo
- *ice stick*
40 el cubo de madera *f* (la meta)
- *block*
41-43 el curling
- *curling*
41 el jugador de curling *m*
- *curler*
42 la piedra del curling
- *curling stone (granite)*
43 la escoba del curling
- *curling brush (curling broom, besom)*
44-46 la navegación a vela *f* **sobre hielo** *m*
- *ice yachting (iceboating, ice sailing)*
44 el velero sobre hielo *m*
- *ice yacht (iceboat)*
45 el patín
- *steering runner*
46 el balancín (la batanga)
- *outrigged runner*

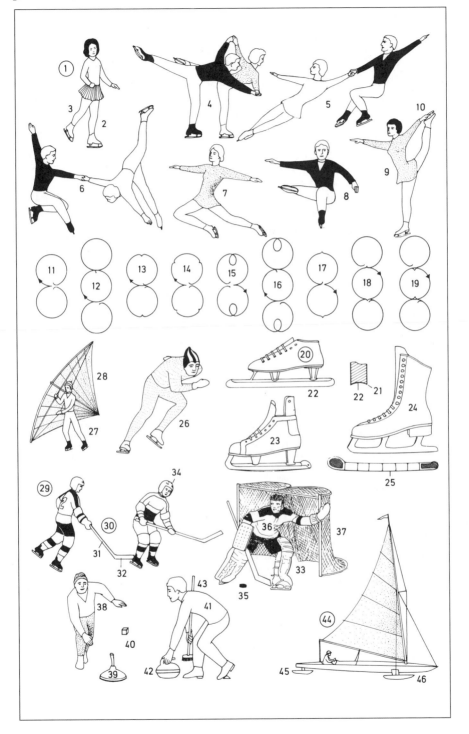

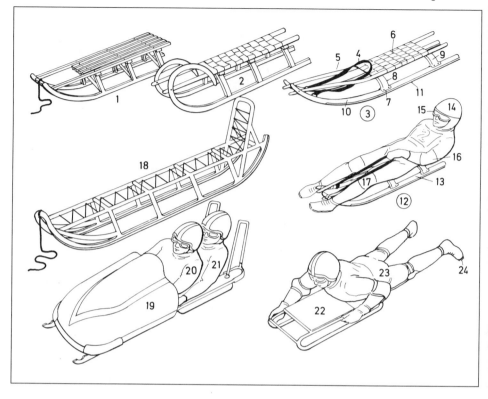

1 el trineo rígido (el luge)
– *toboggan (sledge,* Am. *sled)*
2 el luge con asiento *m* de correas *f*
trenzadas
– *toboggan (sledge,* Am. *sled) with
seat of plaid straps*
3 el luge modelo *m* júnior
– *junior luge toboggan (junior luge,
junior toboggan)*
4 los tirantes de conducción *f*
– *rein*
5 el larguero
– *bar (strut)*
6 el asiento
– *seat*
7 la plancha de ensamblaje *m* del
patín
– *bracket*
8 el puntal delantero
– *front prop*
9 el puntal trasero
– *rear prop*
10 el patín móvil
– *movable runner*
11 el carril
– *metal face*
12 el corredor de luge *m*
– *luge tobogganer*

13 el luge de carreras *f* (el luge de
competición *f*)
– *luge toboggan (luge, toboggan)*
14 el casco protector
– *crash helmet*
15 las gafas de carreras *f*
– *goggles*
16 el protector del codo
– *elbow pad*
17 la rodillera
– *knee pad*
18 el trineo Nansen, un trineo polar
– *Nansen sledge, a polar sledge*
19-21 el bobsleigh
– *bobsleigh (bobsledding)*
19 el bob (el bobsleigh), un bob de
dos
– *bobsleigh (bobsled), a two-man
bobsleigh (a boblet)*
20 el capitán (el conductor del bob)
– *steersman*
21 el encargado del freno
– *brakeman*
22-24 el deslizamiento en skeleton *m*
– *skeleton tobogganing (Cresta
tobogganing)*
22 el skeleton
– *skeleton (skeleton toboggan)*

23 el conductor de skeleton *m*
– *skeleton rider*
24 las garras de hierro *m* (el crampón), para conducir y frenar
– *rake, for braking and steering*

1 el alud (la avalancha); *clases:* alud de nieve *f* en polvo *m*, alud de témpanos *m*
– *avalanche (snow avalanche, Am. snowslide);* kinds: *wind avalanche, ground avalanche*
2 el rompealudes, un muro de desviación *f*; *anál.:* la cuña de aludes *m*
– *avalanche wall, a deflecting wall (diverting wall);* sim.: *avalanche wedge*
3 la galería de protección *f* contra aludes *m*
– *avalanche gallery*
4 la nevada
– *snowfall*
5 el ventisquero (la nieve amontonada)
– *snowdrift*
6 la empalizada contra la nieve
– *snow fence*
7 el bosque de protección *f* contra aludes *m*
– *avalanche forest [planted as protection against avalanches]*
8 el camión del servicio municipal de limpieza *f*
– *street-cleaning lorry (street cleaner)*

9 la pala quitanieves
– *snow plough (Am. snowplow) attachment*
10 la cadena antideslizante
– *snow chain (skid chain, tyre chain, Am. tire chain)*
11 el capó (la cubierta) del radiador
– *radiator bonnet (Am. radiator hood)*
12 la ventana del radiador y el enrejado (la pantalla) de la ventana
– *radiator shutter and shutter opening (louvre shutter)*
13 el muñeco de nieve *f*
– *snowman*
14 la batalla con bolas *f* de nieve *f*
– *snowball fight*
15 la bola de nieve *f*
– *snowball*
16 el skibob
– *ski bob*
17 el resbaladero
– *slide*
18 el joven resbalando sobre el hielo
– *boy, sliding*
19 el hielo resbaladizo
– *icy surface (icy ground)*
20 la capa de nieve *f* sobre el tejado
– *covering of snow, on the roof*

21 el carámbano
– *icicle*
22 el paleador, paleando nieve *f*
– *man clearing snow*
23 la pala para la nieve
– *snow push (snow shovel)*
24 el montón de nieve *f*
– *heap of snow*
25 el trineo de caballos *m*
– *horse-drawn sleigh (horse sleigh)*
26 los cascabeles (las campanillas) del trineo
– *sleigh bells (bells, set of bells)*
27 el folgo
– *foot muff (Am. foot bag)*
28 las orejeras
– *earmuff*
29 el trineo de silla *f* (el trineo impulsado por el pie; *anál.:* el trineo de empuje *m*)
– *handsledge (tread sledge);* sim.: *push sledge*
30 la nieve fangosa (la nieve fundida, el lodo)
– *slush*

1-11 la disposición de los bolos (el cuadro de los bolos)
– *skittle frame*
1-13 el juego de los bolos (el boliche; *Amér.:* el balero)
– *skittles*
1 el bolo de la esquina anterior (el primero)
– *front pin (front)*
2 el bolo de la calle anterior izquierda, una dama
– *left front second pin (left front second)*
3 la calle anterior izquierda
– *running three [left]*
4 el bolo de la calle anterior derecha, una dama
– *right front second pin (right front second)*
5 la calle anterior derecha
– *running three [right]*
6 el bolo de la esquina izquierda, un peón
– *left corner pin (left corner), a corner (copper)*
7 el rey (el birlón)
– *landlord*
8 el bolo de la esquina derecha, un peón
– *right corner pin (right corner), a corner (copper)*
9 el bolo de la calle posterior izquierda, una dama
– *back left second pin (back left second)*
10 el bolo de la calle posterior derecha, una dama
– *back right second pin (back right second)*
11 el bolo de la esquina posterior (el último)
– *back pin (back)*
12 el bolo
– *pin*
13 el rey (el birlón)
– *landlord*
14-20 la bolera
– **tenpin bowling**
14 la disposición de los bolos
– *frame*
15 la bola con agujeros *m* para los dedos
– *bowling ball (with finger holes)*
16 el agujero para asir la bola
– *finger hole*
17-20 las clases de lanzamientos *m*
– *deliveries*
17 el lanzamiento en línea *f* recta
– *straight ball*
18 el lanzamiento en gancho *m*
– *hook ball (hook)*
19 el lanzamiento en arco *m*
– *curve*
20 el lanzamiento en arco *m* inverso al de arriba
– *back-up ball (back-up)*
21 **las bochas** (el juego de bochas, la petanca); *anál.:* el juego italiano de boccia, el juego inglés de bolos
– *boules; sim.: Italian game of boccie, green bowls (bowls)*
22 el jugador de bochas *f*
– *boules player*
23 el boliche (el bolín)
– *jack (target jack)*
24 la bocha (la bola de lanzamiento *m*) estriada
– *grooved boule*
25 el grupo de jugadores *m*
– *group of players*
26 el tiro con fusil *m*
– **rifle shooting**
27-29 posiciones *f* de tiro *m*
– *shooting positions*
27 la posición de pie *m*
– *standing position*
28 la posición de rodillas *f*
– *kneeling position*
29 la posición tendida
– *prone position*

30-33 blancos *m*
– *targets*
30 el blanco para el tiro con fusil *m* a 50 m de distancia *f*
– *target for 50 m events (50 m target)*
31 el círculo
– *circle*
32 el blanco para el tiro con fusil *m* a 100 m de distancia *f*
– *target for 100 m events (100 m target)*
33 el blanco móvil (el jabalí corriendo)
– *bobbing target (turning target, running-boar target)*
34-39 las municiones deportivas
– *ammunition*
34 el balín (el diábolo) para escopeta *f* de aire *m* comprimido
– *air rifle cartridge*
35 el cartucho con fulminante *m* en la base para carabina *f* de pequeño calibre *m*
– *rimfire cartridge for zimmerstutzen (indoor target rifle), a smallbore German single-shot rifle*
36 la cápsula
– *case head*
37 la bala en el extremo
– *caseless round*
38 el cartucho calibre *m* 22 de rifle *m* largo
– *.22 long rifle cartridge*
39 el cartucho calibre *m* 222 del Remington
– *.222 Remington cartridge*
40-49 fusiles *m* deportivos
– *sporting rifles*
40 el fusil de aire *m* comprimido
– *air rifle*
41 la dioptra (la pínula)
– *optical sight*
42 la mira
– *front sight (foresight)*
43 el fusil estándar de pequeño calibre *m*
– *smallbore standard rifle*
44 el arma *f* de pequeño calibre *m* para tiro *m* libre internacional
– *international smallbore free rifle*
45 la pieza de apoyo *m* en la mano para la posición de pie *m*
– *palm rest for standing position*
46 la cantonera con gancho *m*
– *butt plate with hook*
47 la culata con orificio *m* para el pulgar
– *butt with thumb hole*
48 el fusil de pequeño calibre *m* para el blanco móvil (para el jabalí corriendo)
– *smallbore rifle for bobbing target (turning target)*
49 la mira telescópica
– *telescopic sight (riflescope, telescope sight)*
50 la dioptra de puntería *f* con mira *f* redonda
– *optical ring sight*
51 la dioptra de puntería *f* con mira *f* de lámina *f*
– *optical ring and bead sight*
52-66 el tiro con arco *m*
– **archery** *(target archery)*
52 el tiro
– *shot*
53 el arquero
– *archer*
54 el arco de competición *f*
– *competition bow*
55 el brazo elástico
– *riser*
56 el alza
– *point-of-aim mark*
57 la empuñadura
– *grip (handle)*
58 el estabilizador
– *stabilizer*
59 la cuerda del arco
– *bow string (string)*

60 la flecha
– *arrow*
61 la punta de la flecha
– *pile (point) of the arrow*
62 las plumas de dirección *f* (las plumas de pavo *m*)
– *fletching*
63 la muesca
– *nock*
64 el astil de la flecha
– *shaft*
65 las marcas del tirador
– *cresting*
66 el blanco
– *target*
67 el juego de pelota *f* vasca (*vasco:* jai alai)
– *Basque game of pelota (jai alai)*
68 el pelotari
– *pelota player*
69 la cesta (la chistera)
– *wicker basket (cesta)*
70-78 el skeet, una clase de tiro *m* al plato
– **skeet** *(skeet shooting), a kind of clay pigeon shooting*
70 la escopeta de dos cañones *m* de skeet *m* (de tiro *m* al plato)
– *skeet over-and-under shotgun*
71 la boca del cañón con calibre *m* especial para tiro *m* al plato
– *muzzle with skeet choke*
72 la posición de "listo" reclamando plato *m*
– *ready position on call*
73 la posición de disparo *m* (de fuego *m*)
– *firing position*
74 el campo de tiro *m* al plato (el campo de skeet *m*)
– *shooting range*
75 la cabina alta
– *high house*
76 la cabina baja
– *low house*
77 la trayectoria del plato
– *target's path*
78 el puesto de tiro *m*
– *shooting station (shooting box)*
79 la rueda gigante
– **aero wheel**
80 el asidero
– *handle*
81 el reposapiés
– *footrest*
82 el karting (la carrera de karts *m*)
– **go-karting** *(karting)*
83 el kart
– *go-kart (kart)*
84 el número de salida *f*
– *number plate (number)*
85 los pedales
– *pedals*
86 el neumático sin perfil *m*
– *pneumatic tyre (Am. tire)*
87 el tanque (el depósito) de gasolina *f*
– *petrol tank (Am. gasoline tank)*
88 el chasis
– *frame*
89 el volante
– *steering wheel*
90 el asiento en forma *f* de concha *f*
– *bucket seat*
91 el tabique protector contra el fuego
– *protective bulkhead*
92 el motor de dos tiempos *m*
– *two-stroke engine*
93 el silenciador
– *silencer (Am. muffler)*

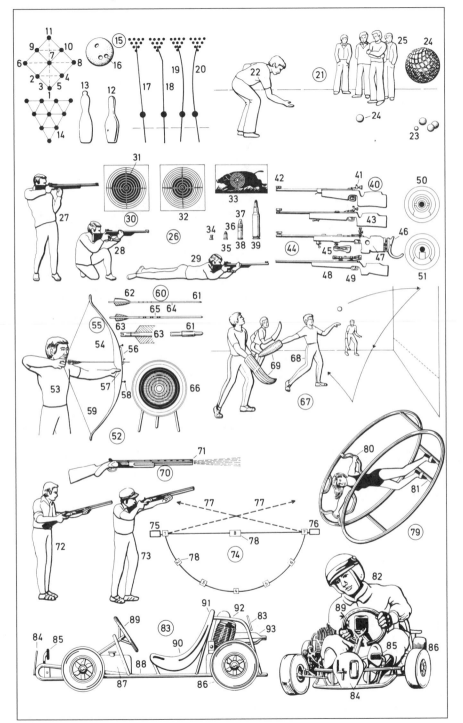

1-48 el baile de máscaras *f* (el baile
de disfraces *m*, la mascarada)
– **masked ball** *(masquerade, fancy-
dress ball)*
1 la sala de baile *m*
– *ballroom*
2 la orquesta de música *f* pop (la
banda de música *f* pop), una
orquesta de baile *m*
– *pop group, a dance band*
3 el músico pop
– *pop musician*
4 el farolillo veneciano
– *paper lantern*
5 la cadeneta de papel *m*
– *festoon (string of decorations)*
6-48 los disfraces de la mascarada
– *disguise (fancy dress) at the masquerade*
6 la bruja
– *witch*
7 la máscara (la careta)
– *mask*
8 el trampero (el cazador de pieles *f*)
– *fur trapper (trapper)*
9 la muchacha apache
– *Apache girl*
10 la media de malla *f*
– *net stocking*
11 el primer premio de la tómbola,
una cesta surtida
– *first prize in the tombola (raffle), a
hamper*

12 la pierrette
– *pierrette*
13 el antifaz
– *half mask (domino)*
14 el demonio (el diablo)
– *devil*
15 el dominó
– *domino*
16 la hawaiana
– *hula-hula girl (Hawaii girl)*
17 la guirnalda (el collar de flores *f*)
– *garland*
18 la falda de rafia *f*
– *grass skirt (hula skirt)*
19 el pierrot
– *pierrot*
20 la gola
– *ruff*
21 la midinette
– *midinette*
22 el vestido a lo Biedermeier (el
vestido Luis Felipe)
– *Biedermeier dress*
23 la papalina
– *poke bonnet*
24 el escote con los lunares
– *décolletage with beauty spot*
25 la bayadera (la danzarina hindú)
– *bayadère (Hindu dancing girl)*
26 el Grande de España
– *grandee*
27 la colombina
– *Columbine*

28 el maharajá
– *maharaja (maharajah)*
29 el mandarín, un dignatario chino
– *mandarin, a Chinese dignitary*
30 la mujer exótica
– *exotic girl (exotic)*
31 el vaquero (el cowboy)
– *cowboy; sim.: gaucho (vaquero)*
32 la vampiresa, con vestido *m* de
fantasía *f*
– *vamp, in fancy dress*
33 el petimetre (el dandi, el
pisaverde, el lechuguino, el
gomoso, el niño gótico; *Mé.*: el
catrín), un disfraz de carácter *m*
– *dandy (fop, beau), a disguise*
34 la escarapela (el distintivo del
baile de máscaras *f*)
– *rosette*
35 el arlequín
– *harlequin*
36 la zíngara (la gitana)
– *gipsy (gypsy) girl*
37 la cocote (la mujer de costumbres
f ligeras, la cortesana, la dama
galante)
– *cocotte (demi-monde, demi-
mondaine, demi-rep)*
38 el bufón
– *owl-glass, a fool (jester, buffoon)*
39 el gorro del bufón (el gorro de
cascabeles *m*)
– *foolscap (jester's cap and bells)*

40 el cascabelero (el sonajero)
 – *rattle*
41 la odalisca, una esclava oriental del harén
 – *odalisque, Eastern female slave in Sultan's seraglio*
42 el pantalón bombacho
 – *chalwar (pantaloons)*
43 el pirata (el corsario)
 – *pirate (buccaneer)*
44 el tatuaje
 – *tattoo*
45 el gorro de papel *m*
 – *paper hat*
46 la nariz de cartón *m*
 – *false nose*
47 la matraca (la carraca)
 – *clapper (rattle)*
48 la palmeta de bufón *m*
 – *slapstick*
49-54 artificios *m* pirotécnicos
 – *fireworks*
49 el fulminante (el pistón)
 – *percussion cap*
50 el bombón explosivo
 – *cracker*
51 la bombita fulminante
 – *banger*
52 el buscapiés (*C. Rica:* el cachiflín)
 – *jumping jack*

53 el petardo
 – *cannon cracker (maroon, maroon)*
54 el cohete (el volador; *Ec.:* el volatero)
 – *rocket*
55 la bola de confeti *m*
 – *paper ball*
56 la caja de sorpresa *f*
 – *jack-in-the-box, a joke*
57-70 el desfile (la cabalgata) de carnaval *m*
 – *carnival procession*
57 la carroza de carnaval *m*
 – *carnival float (carnival truck)*
58 el príncipe Carnaval
 – *King Carnival*
59 el cascabelero (la insignia del bufón; de la locura, el cetro de bufón *m*)
 – *bauble (fool's sceptre,* Am. *scepter)*
60 la orden de bufón *m* (la orden de carnaval *m*)
 – *fool's badge*
61 la princesa Carnaval
 – *Queen Carnival*
62 el confeti (*Guat.:* los retacitos *pl.*)
 – *confetti*

63 el gigantón, una figura burlesca
 – *giant figure, a satirical figure*
64 la reina de la belleza
 – *beauty queen*
65 la figura de cuento *m* de hadas *f*
 – *fairy-tale figure*
66 la serpentina
 – *paper streamer*
67 la cantinera de la guardia del príncipe
 – *majorette*
68 la guardia del príncipe
 – *king's guard*
69 el polichinela, un payaso
 – *buffoon, a clown*
70 el tambor de lansquenete *m*
 – *lansquenet's drum*

1-63 el circo ambulante
- *travelling (Am. traveling) circus*
1 la carpa del circo (la tienda del circo), una carpa de cuatro mástiles
- *circus tent (big top), a four-pole tent*
2 el mástil de la carpa
- *tent pole*
3 el reflector
- *spotlight*
4 el técnico de iluminación *f*
- *lighting technician*
5 la plataforma para el artista
- *trapeze platform*
6 el trapecio
- *trapeze*
7 el trapecista
- *trapeze artist*
8 la escalera de cuerda *f*
- *rope ladder*
9 la tribuna de la banda de música *f*
- *bandstand*
10 la banda del circo
- *circus band*
11 la entrada a la pista
- *ring entrance (arena entrance)*
12 el túnel de espera *f* de los artistas
- *wings*
13 el puntal de la tienda
- *tent prop (prop)*

14 la red de protección *f* (la red de seguridad *f*)
- *safety net*
15 la gradería de los espectadores
- *seats for the spectators*
16 el palco del circo
- *circus box*
17 el director del circo
- *circus manager*
18 el representante (el agente) de los artistas
- *artiste agent (agent)*
19 la entrada y salida *f*
- *entrance and exit*
20 el pasillo de acceso *m* a la gradería
- *steps*
21 la pista
- *ring (arena)*
22 la barrera
- *ring fence*
23 el payaso músico (*Pan.*: el parrampán; *Chile*: el catimbao)
- *musical clown (clown)*
24 el payaso (el payaso "cara *f* blanca"; el clown; *Chile*: el catimbao)
- *clown*
25 el "número cómico", un número de circo *m*
- *comic turn (clown act), a circus act*

26 los caballistas (los artistas ecuestres)
- *circus riders (bareback riders)*
27 el mozo de pista *f*, un mozo de circo *m*
- *ring attendant, a circus attendant*
28 la torre humana (el castillo)
- *pyramid*
29 el hombre base
- *support*
30 *u.* **31** la doma libre
- *performance by liberty horses*
30 el caballo de circo *m*, en una levade (encabritado)
- *circus horse, performing the levade (pesade)*
31 el domador, un caballista (*Amér.*: el chalán, el amansador)
- *ringmaster, a trainer*
32 el volteador a caballo *m*
- *vaulter*
33 la salida de emergencia *f*
- *emergency exit*
34 la caravana (el remolque, la rulotte)
- *caravan (circus caravan, Am. trailer)*
35 el acróbata de trampolín *m* (*Amér.*: el maromero)
- *springboard acrobat (springboard artist)*

36 el trampolín
 – *springboard*
37 el lanzador de cuchillos *m*
 – *knife thrower*
38 el tirador de pistola *f*
 – *circus marksman*
39 la ayudante
 – *assistant*
40 la volatinera (la funámbula; *Cuba:*
 la caballitera)
 – *tightrope dancer*
41 el alambre
 – *tightrope*
42 el balancín (*Amér.:* la balanza)
 – *balancing pole*
43 el número de lanzamiento *m*
 – *throwing act*
44 el número de equilibrio *m*
 – *balancing act*
45 el hombre base
 – *support*
46 la pértiga (la vara de bambú *m*)
 – *pole (bamboo pole)*
47 el acróbata
 – *acrobat*
48 el equilibrista
 – *equilibrist (balancer)*
49 la jaula de fieras *f*, una jaula circular
 – *wild animal cage, a round cage*
50 el enrejado de la jaula
 – *bars of the cage*

51 el túnel de la jaula de fieras *f* (el
 pasillo enrejado para las fieras)
 – *passage (barred passage, passage
 for the wild animals)*
52 el domador (el domador de fieras *f*)
 – *tamer (wild animal tamer)*
53 el látigo (el fuete; *Amér.:* el enero,
 el chicote, el chirrión, el rejo;
 Amér. Central y Ec.: el acial, la
 coyunda)
 – *whip*
54 la horquilla protectora
 – *fork (protective fork)*
55 el pedestal
 – *pedestal*
56 la fiera (el tigre, el león)
 – *wild animal (tiger, lion)*
57 el taburete para los animales
 – *stand*
58 el aro para saltar
 – *hoop (jumping hoop)*
59 el subibaja
 – *seesaw*
60 la pelota
 – *ball*
61 el campamento de tiendas *f*
 – *camp*
62 el remolque (la caravana) jaula *f*
 – *cage caravan*
63 la exhibición de animales *m*
 – *menagerie*

1-69 la feria (la feria anual, la fiesta
mayor, la fiesta del pueblo)
– *fair (annual fair)*
1 el real de la feria
– *fairground*
2 el tiovivo (los caballitos, el carru-
sel; *P. Rico:* la machina)
– *children's merry-go-round,
(whirligig), a roundabout (*Am.
carousel)*
3 el puesto de refrescos *m* y bebidas
f (*Chile:* la venta)
– *refreshment stall (drinks stall)*
4 las voladoras
– *chairoplane*
5 el tren del infierno
– *up-and-down roundabout*
6 la barraca de feria *f*
– *show booth (booth)*
7 la caja (el despacho de billetes *m*)
– *box (box office)*
8 el pregonero
– *barker*
9 la medium
– *medium*
10 el feriante
– *showman*
11 la máquina de medir la fuerza (el
dinamómetro)
– *try-your-strength machine*
12 el vendedor ambulante
– *hawker*

13 el globo (*Bol.:* el tucucho)
– *balloon*
14 el matasuegras
– *paper serpent*
15 el molinete (la voladera)
– *windmill*
16 el carterista (el ladrón, el ratero;
Chile: el arpista)
– *pickpocket (thief)*
17 el vendedor
– *vendor*
18 la miel turca
– *nougat*
19 el túnel de los horrores (la cámara
de los horrores)
– *ghost train*
20 el monstruo
– *monster*
21 el dragón
– *dragon*
22 el monstruo
– *monster*
23 la cervecería de feria *f*
– *beer marquee*
24 el barracón de las atracciones
– *sideshow*
25-28 los artistas ambulantes
– *travelling (*Am. *traveling) artistes
(travelling show people)*
25 el tragafuegos (el pirófago)
– *fire eater*

26 el tragasables
– *sword swallower*
27 el forzudo (el hércules)
– *strong man*
28 el especialista en desatarse
– *escapologist*
29 los espectadores
– *spectators*
30 el vendedor de helados *m*
– *ice-cream vendor (ice-cream man)*
31 el cucurucho de helado *m*
– *ice-cream cornet, with ice cream*
32 el puesto de salchichas *f* asadas
– *sausage stand*
33 la parrilla
– *grill (*Am. *broiler)*
34 la salchicha asada
– *bratwurst (grilled sausage,* Am.
broiled sausage)
35 las tenacillas para coger las
salchichas
– *sausage tongs*
36 la echadora de cartas *f,* una adivina
– *fortune teller*
37 la noria gigante
– *big wheel (Ferris wheel)*
38 el orquestión (el órgano
automático), un instrumento de
música *f*
– *orchestrion (automatic organ), an
automatic musical instrument*

39 la montaña rusa
– *scenic railway (switchback)*
40 el tobogán
– *toboggan slide (chute)*
41 el columpio de barcos *m*
– *swing boats*
42 el columpio volteador
– *swing boat, turning full circle*
43 el volteo (la voltereta)
– *full circle*
44 la tómbola (*Amér. Central:* el turno)
– *lottery booth (tombola booth)*
45 la rueda de la fortuna
– *wheel of fortune*
46 la rueda del diablo (la rueda del tifón)
– *devil's wheel (typhoon wheel)*
47 la anilla para lanzar
– *throwing ring (quoit)*
48 los premios
– *prizes*
49 el hombre anuncio (el hombre "sandwich") con zancos *m*
– *sandwich man on stilts*
50 el cartel de anuncio *m*
– *sandwich board (placard)*
51 el vendedor de cigarrillos *m*, un vendedor ambulante
– *cigarette seller, an itinerant trader (a hawker)*

52 la batea
– *tray*
53 el puesto de frutas *f*
– *fruit stall*
54 el motorista del muro de la muerte
– *wall-of-death rider*
55 el barracón de la risa (el barracón de espejos *m*)
– *hall of mirrors*
56 el espejo cóncavo
– *concave mirror*
57 el espejo convexo
– *convex mirror*
58 la barraca de tiro *m* al blanco
– *shooting gallery*
59 la barca
– *giant swing boat*
60 el rastro (el mercado de viejo)
– *junk stalls (second-hand stalls)*
61 el puesto de socorro *m*
– *first aid tent (first aid post)*
62 la pista de los coches de choque *m*
– *dodgems (bumper cars)*
63 el coche de choque *m*
– *dodgem (bumper car)*
64-66 la cacharrería
– *pottery stand*
64 el pregonero
– *barker*
65 la vendedora
– *market woman*

66 los cacharros de loza *f*
– *pottery*
67 los visitantes de la feria
– *visitors to the fair*
68 la barraca de figuras *f* de cera *f*
– *waxworks*
69 la figura de cera *f*
– *wax figure*

1 la máquina de coser de pedal *m*
– *treadle sewing machine*
2 el florero
– *flower vase*
3 el espejo de pared *f*
– *wall mirror*
4 la estufa
– *cylindrical stove*
5 el tubo de la estufa
– *stovepipe*
6 el codo del tubo de la estufa
– *stovepipe elbow*
7 la puerta de la estufa
– *stove door*
8 la pantalla de la estufa
– *stove screen*
9 el cubo del carbón
– *coal scuttle*
10 la cesta para las astillas
– *firewood basket*
11 la muñeca
– *doll*
12 el oso de peluche *m*
– *teddy bear*
13 el organillo (*Mé.*: el cilindro)
– *barrel organ*
14 el orquestrión (un instrumento de música *f* automático)
– *orchestrion*
15 el disco metálico perforado (el disco de las notas)
– *metal disc (disk)*
16 el receptor de radio *f* (el aparato de radio *f*, la radio, el receptor)
– *radio (radio set, joc.: 'steam radio'), a superheterodyne (superhet)*

17 la pantalla acústica (el baffle)
– *baffle board*
18 el ojo mágico, un tubo indicador de la sintonización
– *'magic eye', a tuning indicator valve*
19 la abertura del altavoz
– *loudspeaker aperture*
20 los pulsadores para la selección de las emisoras
– *station selector buttons (station preset buttons)*
21 el botón de sintonización *f*
– *tuning knob*
22 las escalas de campos *m* de frecuencia *f*
– *frequency bands*
23 el detector (el receptor de galena *f*)
– *crystal detector (crystal set)*
24 los auriculares de casco *m*
– *headphones (headset)*
25 la cámara plegable (la cámara de fuelle *m*)
– *folding camera*
26 el fuelle
– *bellows*
27 la chapa base de la corredera
– *hinged cover*
28 los extensores
– *spring extension*
29 el vendedor
– *salesman*
30 la cámara de cajón *m*
– *box camera*
31 el gramófono (un fonógrafo)
– *gramophone*
32 el disco de gramófono *m*
– *record (gramophone record)*

33 el pick-up (el brazo de toma *f* de sonido *m*, el portaagujas) con la aguja del gramófono
– *needle head with gramophone needle*
34 el altavoz
– *horn*
35 la caja del gramófono
– *gramophone box*
36 el portadiscos
– *record rack*
37 el magnetófono
– *tape recorder, a portable tape recorder*
38 el flash
– *flashgun*
39 la bombilla de flash *m*
– *flash bulb*
40 u. 41 el flash electrónico
– *electronic flash (electronic flashgun)*
40 la antorcha
– *flash head*
41 el acumulador
– *accumulator*
42 el proyector de diapositivas *f*
– *slide projector*
43 el portadiapositivas
– *slide holder*
44 la caja de la lámpara
– *lamphouse*
45 el candelero
– *candlestick*
46 la concha de Santiago (la concha de peregrino *m*)
– *scallop shell*
47 los cubiertos
– *cutlery*

48 el plato de recuerdo *m*
 - *souvenir plate*
49 el caballete para el secado de las placas
fotográficas
 - *drying rack for photographic plates*
50 la placa fotográfica
 - *photographic plate*
51 el disparador automático
 - *delayed-action release*
52 los soldaditos de plomo *m* (*anál.:* los
soldaditos de estaño *m*)
 - *tin soldiers (*sim.:* lead soldiers)*
53 el jarro de cerveza *f*
 - *beer mug (stein)*
54 la trompeta
 - *bugle*
55 los libros de segunda mano *m*
 - *second-hand books*
56 el reloj de pesas *f*
 - *grandfather clock*
57 el mueble del reloj
 - *clock case*
58 la péndola (el péndulo del reloj)
 - *pendulum*
59 la pesa de la marcha
 - *time weight*
60 la pesa de los toques
 - *striking weight*
61 la mecedora
 - *rocking chair*
62 el traje de marinero *m*
 - *sailor suit*
63 la gorra de marinero *m*
 - *sailor's hat*
64 el palanganero
 - *washing set*

65 la palangana
 - *washing basin*
66 el jarro de agua *f*
 - *water jug*
67 el soporte de la palangana
 - *washstand*
68 el removedor de la ropa
 - *dolly*
69 la tina de lavar
 - *washtub*
70 la tabla de lavar
 - *washboard*
71 el trompo de música *f* (*Col.:* el zambilo-
co; *Venez.:* la zaranda)
 - *humming top*
72 la pizarra (*Antillas y Río de la Plata:* el
pizarrón)
 - *slate*
73 el plumier (el plumero, la cajita de
plumas *f* o lápices *m; Arg. y Chile:* la
lapicera)
 - *pencil box*
74 la máquina sumadora-calculadora, una
máquina para sumar, restar y multi-
plicar
 - *adding and subtracting machine*
75 el rollo de papel *m*
 - *paper roll*
76 las teclas de números *m*
 - *number keys*
77 el ábaco
 - *abacus*
78 el tintero, un tintero con tapadera *f*
 - *inkwell, with lid*
79 la máquina de escribir
 - *typewriter*

80 la máquina calculadora
 - *[hand-operated] calculating machine
(calculator)*
81 la manivela de accionamiento *m*
 - *operating handle*
82 el registro de resultado *m*
 - *result register (product register)*
83 el mecanismo contador rotativo
 - *rotary counting mechanism (rotary
counter)*
84 la balanza de cocina *f* (el peso de cocina *f*)
 - *kitchen scales*
85 las enaguas (*Col.:* las hormadoras)
 - *waist slip (underskirt)*
86 el carro de adrales *m*
 - *wooden handcart*
87 el reloj de pared *f*
 - *wall clock*
88 la botella metálica de agua *f* caliente
 - *bed warmer*
89 la lechera (la vasija para leche *f*)
 - *milk churn*

1-13 los estudios cinematográficos
- *film studios (studio complex,* Am.
  movie studios)
1 el escenario exterior (el terreno
para el rodaje de exteriores *m*)
- *lot (studio lot)*
2 los laboratorios de copia *f*
- *processing laboratories (film laboratories, motion picture laboratories)*
3 las salas de montaje *m* (de corte *m*)
- *cutting rooms*
4 el edificio de la administración
- *administration building (office
building, offices)*
5 el depósito de películas *f* (el archivo de películas, la cinemateca)
- *film (motion picture) storage vault
(film library, motion picture
library)*
6 los talleres
- *workshop*
7 el decorado (el escenario de exteriores *m*)
- *film set (Am. movie set)*
8 la estación eléctrica
- *power house*
9 los laboratorios técnicos y de
investigación *f*
- *technical and research laboratories*
10 el grupo de estudios *m*
- *groups of stages*

11 el estanque de hormigón *m* para
escenas *f* acuáticas
- *concrete tank for marine
sequences*
12 el ciclorama
- *cyclorama*
13 la colina del ciclorama
- *hill*
14-60 filmaciones *f*
- *shooting (filming)*
14 el estudio de música *f* (el auditorio)
- *music recording studio (music
recording theatre,* Am. *theater)*
15 el revestimiento "acústico" de la
pared
- *'acoustic' wall lining*
16 la pantalla
- *screen (projection screen)*
17 la orquesta cinematográfica
- *film orchestra*
18 el rodaje en exteriores *m*
- *exterior shooting (outdoor shooting, exterior filming, outdoor filming)*
19 la cámara sincrónica controlada
por cristal *m* de cuarzo *m*
- *camera with crystal-controlled
drive*
20 el operador (el cameraman)
- *cameraman*
21 la ayudante de dirección *f*
- *assistant director*

22 el ayudante del micrófono
- *boom operator (boom swinger)*
23 el jefe (el operador) de sonido *m*
- *recording engineer (sound
recordist)*
24 el magnetófono portátil controlado por cristal *m* de cuarzo *m*
- *portable sound recorder with crystal-controlled drive*
25 la jirafa del micrófono
- *microphone boom*
26-60 la filmación de interiores *m* en
el plató (en el escenario sonoro)
- *shooting (filming) in the studio
(on the sound stage, on the stage,
in the filming hall)*
26 el jefe de producción *f*
- *production manager*
27 la estrella principal (la actriz de
cine *m*)
- *leading lady (film actress, film
star, star)*
28 el actor principal
- *leading man (film actor, film star,
star)*
29 el extra (el comparsa, el actor
secundario)
- *film extra (extra)*
30 el dispositivo de micrófonos *m*
para la grabación estereofónica y
los efectos sonoros
- *arrangement of microphones for
stereo and sound effects*

31 el micrófono de estudio *m*
 – *studio microphone*
32 el cable del micrófono
 – *microphone cable*
33 el bastidor y el telón de fondo *m*
 – *side flats and background*
34 el claquista
 – *clapper boy*
35 la claqueta sincrónica, con tabilla *f* con el título de la película, el número de la escena y el número de la toma
 – *clapper board (clapper) with slates (boards) for the film title, shot number (scene number), and take number*
36 el maquillador (el peluquero cinematógrafo)
 – *make-up artist (hairstylist)*
37 el electricista
 – *lighting electrician (studio electrician, lighting man,* Am. *gaffer)*
38 el reflector
 – *diffusing screen*
39 la script-girl (la secretaria del estudio)
 – *continuity girl (script girl)*
40 el director cinematográfico
 – *film director (director)*
41 el operador (el cameraman)
 – *cameraman (first cameraman)*
42 el ayudante del operador
 – *camera operator, an assistant cameraman (camera assistant)*

43 el arquitecto cinematográfico
 – *set designer (art director)*
44 el director de fotografía *f* y de sonido *m* (el director general)
 – *director of photography*
45 el guión cinematográfico
 – *filmscript (script, shooting script,* Am. *movie script)*
46 el ayudante de dirección *f*
 – *assistant director*
47 la cámara cinematográfica insonorizada (la cámara de televisión), una cámara de imagen *f* ancha (una cámara *f* Cinemascope)
 – *soundproof film camera (soundproof motion picture camera), a wide screen camera (cinemascope camera)*
48 la cubierta de la cámara a prueba *f* de sonidos *m*
 – *soundproof housing (soundproof cover, blimp)*
49 la grúa de la cámara
 – *camera crane (dolly)*
50 el trípode ajustable
 – *hydraulic stand*
51 la pantalla negra (la pantalla absorbente), para eliminar los reflejos
 – *mask (screen) for protection from spill light (gobo, nigger)*

52 el foco supletorio sobre trípode *m*
 – *tripod spotlight (fill-in light, filler light, fill light, filler)*
53 la pasarela de focos *m*
 – *spotlight catwalk*
54 la cabina de toma *f* de sonido *m*
 – *recording room*
55 el ingeniero de sonido *m*
 – *recording engineer (sound recordist)*
56 el pupitre de mezcla *f*
 – *mixing console (mixing desk)*
57 el ayudante del ingeniero de sonido *m*
 – *sound assistant (assistant sound engineer)*
58 el equipo de registro *m* magnético del sonido
 – *magnetic sound recording equipment (magnetic sound recorder)*
59 el equipo de amplificación *f* y trucaje *m*, para la reverberación y los efectos sonoros
 – *amplifier and special effects equipment, e.g. for echo and sound effects*
60 la cámara sonora (la cámara de fotosonido *m*)
 – *sound recording camera (optical sound recorder)*

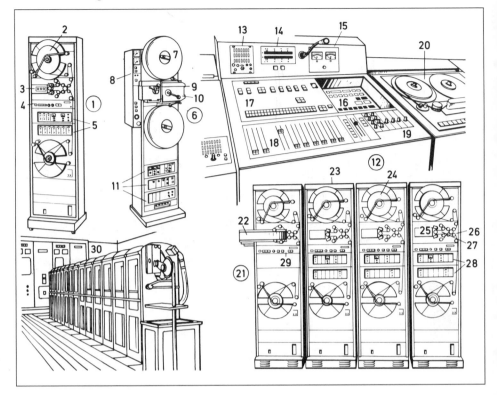

1-46 grabación f y copia f del sonido
- **sound recording and re-recording (dubbing)**
1 el equipo de grabación f magnética del sonido
- magnetic sound recording equipment (magnetic sound recorder)
2 la bobina de la película magnética
- magnetic film spool
3 el portacabezas magnético
- magnetic head support assembly
4 el tablero de mando m
- control panel
5 el amplificador de registro m y de lectura f del sonido magnético
- magnetic sound recording and playback amplifier
6 la cámara de fotosonido m (la cámara de sonido m, la cámara cinematográfica de fotosonido m)
- optical sound recorder (sound recording camera, optical sound recording equipment)
7 la cassette de película f de luz f diurna
- daylight film magazine
8 el panel de mando m y de control m
- control and monitoring panel

9 el ocular para el control m óptico del registro de fotosonido m
- eyepiece for visual control of optical sound recording
10 el desenrollador
- deck
11 el amplificador de registro m y la alimentación de la red
- recording amplifier and mains power unit
12 el pupitre de mando m
- control desk (control console)
13 el altavoz de control m
- monitoring loudspeaker (control loudspeaker)
14 los indicadores del nivel de registro m
- recording level indicators
15 los dispositivos de control m
- monitoring instruments
16 el panel de conjuntores m
- jack panel
17 el panel de mando m
- control panel
18 el regulador de corredera f
- sliding control
19 el corrector
- equalizer

20 el plato de sonido m magnético
- magnetic sound deck
21 el equipo de mezcla f para películas f magnéticas
- mixer for magnetic film
22 el proyector de película f
- film projector
23 el equipo de registro m y de lectura f
- recording and playback equipment
24 la bobina de película f
- film reel (film spool)
25 el portacabezas con la cabeza de registro m, la cabeza de lectura f y la cabeza supresora
- head support assembly for the recording head, playback head, and erase head
26 el mecanismo de impulsión de la película
- film transport mechanism
27 el filtro de sincronización f
- synchronizing filter
28 el amplificador del sonido magnético
- magnetic sound amplifier

29 el panel de mando *m*
– *control panel*
30 las máquinas para revelar películas *f* en el laboratorio de copiado *m*
– *film-processing machines (film-developing machines) in the processing laboratory (film laboratory, motion picture laboratory)*
31 el estudio de resonancia *f*
– *echo chamber*
32 el altavoz del estudio de resonancia *f*
– *echo chamber loudspeaker*
33 el micrófono del estudio de resonancia *f*
– *echo chamber microphone*
34-36 la mezcla de sonido *m* (la mezcla de varias bandas de sonido *m*)
– *sound mixing (sound dubbing, mixing of several sound tracks)*
34 el estudio de mezcla *f*
– *mixing room (dubbing room)*
35 el pupitre de mezcla *f*, para el sonido monocanal o estereofónico
– *mixing console (mixing desk) for mono or stereo sound*

36 los ingenieros de mezcla *f* de sonido *m*, en el trabajo de mezcla *f*
– *dubbing mixers (recording engineers, sound recordists) dubbing (mixing)*
37-41 la sincronización (la postsincronización, el doblaje)
– *synchronization (syncing, dubbing, post-synchronization, post-syncing)*
37 el estudio de sincronización *f* (de doblaje *m*)
– *dubbing studio (dubbing theatre, Am. theater)*
38 el director de doblaje *m*
– *dubbing director*
39 la locutora de doblaje *m*
– *dubbing speaker (dubbing actress)*
40 el micrófono de jirafa *f*
– *boom microphone*
41 el cable del sonido
– *microphone cable*
42-46 el montaje
– *cutting (editing)*

42 la mesa de montaje *m*
– *cutting table (editing table, cutting bench)*
43 el jefe de montaje *m*
– *film editor (cutter)*
44 los platos para las bandas de imágenes *f* y sonidos *m*
– *film turntables for picture and sound tracks*
45 la proyección de imágenes *f*
– *projection of the picture*
46 el altavoz
– *loudspeaker*

1-23 la proyección cinematográfica
- *film projection (motion picture projection)*
1 el cinema (el cine, la sala de cine)
- *cinema (picture house, Am. movie theater, movie house)*
2 la taquilla del cine (*Amér.:* la boletería)
- *cinema box office (Am. movie theater box office)*
3 la entrada de cine *m* (*Amér.:* el boleto)
- *cinema ticket (Am. movie theater ticket)*
4 la acomodadora
- *usherette*
5 los espectadores del cine (el público del cine)
- *cinemagoers (filmgoers, cinema audience, Am. moviegoers, movie audience)*
6 el alumbrado de seguridad *f* (el alumbrado de emergencia *f*)
- *safety lighting (emergency lighting)*
7 la salida de urgencia *f* (de emergencia *f*)
- *emergency exit*
8 el escenario
- *stage*
9 las filas de butacas *f*
- *rows of seats (rows)*
10 el telón (la cortina de la pantalla)
- *stage curtain (screen curtain)*

11 la pantalla (la pantalla de proyección *f*)
- *screen (projection screen)*
12 la cabina de proyección *f*
- *projection room (projection booth)*
13 el proyector (la máquina) de la izquierda
- *lefthand projector*
14 el proyector de la derecha
- *righthand projector*
15 la ventanilla de la cabina, con aberturas para la proyección y la observación
- *projection room window with projection window and observation port*
16 el tambor de película *f*
- *reel drum (spool box)*
17 el panel de interruptores *m* para la iluminación de la sala
- *house light dimmers (auditorium lighting control)*
18 el rectificador de corriente *f*, un rectificador de selenio *m* o de vapor de mercurio *m* para las lámparas de proyección *f*
- *rectifier, a selenium or mercury vapour rectifier for the projection lamps*
19 el amplificador
- *amplifier*
20 el operador de proyección *f*
- *projectionist*

21 la mesa rebobinadora, para el rebobinado de la película
- *rewind bench for rewinding the film*
22 la cola para película *f*
- *film cement (splicing cement)*
23 el proyector de diapositivas *f*, para diapositivas *f* de publicidad *f*
- *slide projector for advertisements*
24-52 proyectores *m* de películas *f*
- *film projectors*
24 el proyector de películas *f* sonoras
- *sound projector (film projector, cinema projector, theatre projector, Am. movie projector)*
25-38 el mecanismo para el paso de la película
- *projector mechanism*
25 los tambores protegidos contra incendios *m*, con refrigeración *f* por una corriente de aceite *m*
- *fireproof reel drums (spool boxes) with circulating oil cooling system*
26 el tambor dentado para desenrollar la película
- *feed sprocket (supply sprocket)*
27 el tambor dentado para enrollar la película
- *take-up sprocket*
28 el lector del sonido magnético
- *magnetic head cluster*

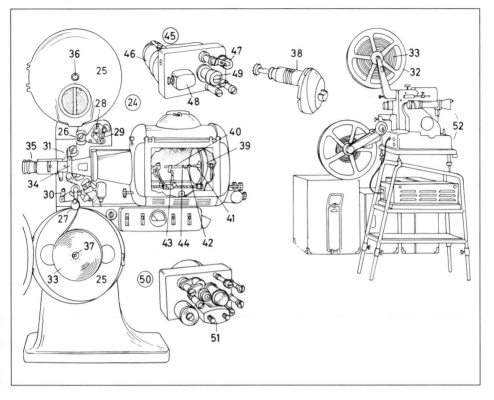

29 el rodillo de cambio *m*, con dispositivo *m* de encuadre *m*
– *guide roller (guiding roller) with framing control*
30 la rueda tensora, para la preestabilización de la película; *también:* el contacto de rotura *f* de la película
– *loop former for smoothing out the intermittent movement; also: film break detector*
31 el deslizador de la película
– *film path*
32 la bobina de la película (el carrete)
– *film reel (film spool)*
33 el rollo de la película
– *reel of film*
34 la ventanilla de proyección *f*, con turbosoplador *f* refrigerador de la película
– *film gate (picture gate, projector gate) with cooling fan*
35 el objetivo de proyección *f*
– *projection lens (projector lens)*
36 el eje de desbobinado *m*
– *feed spindle*
37 el eje de fricción *f* del bobinado
– *take-up spindle with friction drive*
38 el mecanismo Cruz de Malta
– *maltese cross mechanism (maltese cross movement, Geneva movement)*
39-44 la cámara de lámparas *f*
– *lamphouse*

39 la lámpara reflectora de arco *m*, con espejo *m* hueco no esférico y magneto *f* sopladora para la estabilización del arco voltaico (*también:* la lámpara de xenón *m* de alta presión *f*)
– *mirror arc lamp, with aspherical (non-spherical) concave mirror and blowout magnet for stabilizing the arc (also: high-pressure xenon arc lamp)*
40 el carbón positivo
– *positive carbon (positive carbon rod)*
41 el carbón negativo
– *negative carbon (negative carbon rod)*
42 el arco luminoso (el arco voltaico, el arco eléctrico)
– *arc*
43 el portacarbón
– *carbon rod holder*
44 el cráter del carbón
– *crater (carbon crater)*
45 el grupo fotoeléctrico de producción *f* del sonido [previsto también para la reproducción estereofónica por varios canales *m* de tonos *m* de luz *f* y para el sistema de contrafase *f*]
– *optical sound unit [also designed for multi-channel optical stereophonic sound and for push-pull sound tracks]*

46 la óptica de lectura del sonido
– *sound optics*
47 la cabeza sonora (la cabeza de lectura del sonido)
– *sound head*
48 la lámpara de sonido *m*, en su alojamiento *m*
– *exciter lamp in housing*
49 la célula fotoeléctrica (en el eje hueco)
– *photocell in hollow drum*
50 el aparato accesorio del sonido magnético de cuatro canales *m*
– *attachable four-track magnetic sound unit (penthouse head, magnetic sound head)*
51 la cabeza magnética de cuatro pistas *f*
– *four-track magnetic head*
52 el proyector de películas *f* estrechas, para cine *m* ambulante
– *narrow-gauge* (Am. *narrow-gage) cinema projector for mobile cinema*

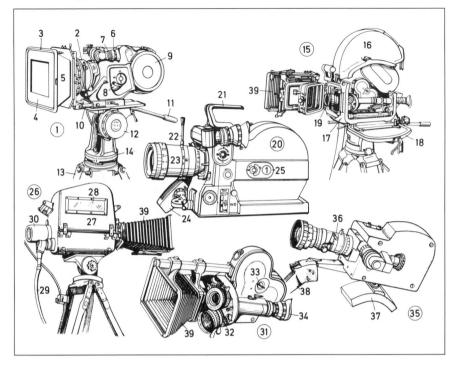

1-6 las cinco posiciones
- *the five positions (ballet positions)*
1 la primera posición
- *first position*
2 la segunda posición
- *second position*
3 la tercera posición
- *third position*
4 la cuarta posición [avanzada]
- *fourth position [open]*
5 la cuarta posición [cruzada; la quinta posición abierta]
- *fourth position [crossed; extended fifth position]*
6 la quinta posición
- *fifth position*
7-10 les ports de bras (las posiciones de los brazos)
- *ports de bras (arm positions)*
7 le port de bras à côté (la posición de brazo *m* al lado)
- *port de bras à coté*
8 le port de bras en bas (la posición de brazo *m* en bajo)
- *port de bras en bas*
9 le port de bras en avant (la posición de brazo *m* adelante)
- *port de bras en avant*
10 le port de bras en haut (la posición de brazo *m* en alto)
- *port de bras en haut*

11 le degagé à la quatrième devant (la salida de la cuarta por delante)
- *dégagé à la quatrième devant*
12 le degagé à la quatrième derrière (la salida de la cuarta por detrás)
- *dégagé à la quatrième derrière*
13 el effacé
- *effacé*
14 el sur le cou-de-pied
- *sur le cou-de-pied*
15 el écarté
- *écarté*
16 el croisé (el cruzado)
- *croisé*
17 la attitude (la posición)
- *attitude*
18 el arabesco
- *arabesque*
19 la punta
- *à pointe (on full point)*
20 el spagat (la caída con piernas *f* abiertas)
- *splits*
21 la cabriole (la cabriola, el salto en el aire)
- *cabriole (capriole)*
22 el entrechat (el entrechat quatre, el cruce con cuatro cambios *m*)
- *entrechat (entrechat quatre)*

23 la preparación [para la pirueta, por ejemplo]
- *préparation [e.g. for a pirouette]*
24 la pirouette (la pirueta, la vuelta)
- *pirouette*
25 le corps de ballet (el cuerpo de ballet *m*)
- *corps de ballet*
26 la bailarina de ballet *m*
- *ballet dancer (ballerina)*
27 u. 28 le pas de trois (el paso de tres)
- *pas de trois*
27 la primera bailarina
- *prima ballerina*
28 el primer bailarín
- *principal male dancer (leading soloist)*
29 el tutú (la falda corta de bailarina *f*)
- *tutu*
30 la zapatilla de punta *f*, una zapatilla de ballet *m*
- *point shoe, a ballet shoe (ballet slipper)*
31 el vestido de bailarina *f*
- *ballet skirt*

1-4 las aberturas de telón
- *types of curtain operation*
1 la abertura a la griega
- *draw curtain (side parting)*
2 la abertura a la italiana
- *tableau curtain (bunching up sideways)*
3 la abertura a la alemana
- *fly curtain (vertical ascent)*
4 la abertura combinada a la griega-alemana
- *combined fly and draw curtain*
5-11 el vestíbulo del guardarropa
- *cloakroom hall (Am. checkroom hall)*
5 el guardarropa
- *cloakroom (Am. checkroom)*
6 la encargada del guardarropa
- *cloakroom attendant (Am. checkroom attendant)*
7 la contraseña del guardarropa (el número del guardarropa)
- *cloakroom ticket (Am. check)*
8 el espectador
- *playgoer (theatregoer, Am. theatergoer)*
9 los gemelos de teatro *m*
- *opera glass (opera glasses)*
10 el revisor
- *commissionaire*
11 la entrada de teatro *m* (*Amér.:* el boleto), un billete de admisión *f*
- *theatre (Am. theater) ticket, an admission ticket*
12 *u.* **13 el foyer** (la sala *f* de descanso *m*)
- *foyer (lobby, crush room)*
12 el acomodador
- *usher;* form.: *box attendant*
13 el programa
- *programme (Am. program)*
14-27 la sala de teatro *m*
- *auditorium and stage*
14 el escenario
- *stage*
15 el proscenio
- *proscenium*
16-20 la sala de espectadores *m* (la sala del auditorio)
- *auditorium*
16 la galería (el gallinero, el paraíso; *Mé.:* la chilla)
- *gallery (balcony)*
17 el segundo palco (el anfiteatro)
- *upper circle*
18 el primer palco (el principal)
- *dress circle (Am. balcony, mezzanine)*
19 el patio de butacas *f* (la platea; *Mé.:* el mosquete)
- *front stalls*

20 la butaca (la butaca de espectador *m*, la butaca de teatro *m*)
- *seat (theatre seat, Am. theater seat)*
21-27 el ensayo
- *rehearsal (stage rehearsal)*
21 el coro del teatro
- *chorus*
22 el cantante
- *singer*
23 la cantante
- *singer*
24 el foso de la orquesta
- *orchestra pit*
25 la orquesta
- *orchestra*
26 el director
- *conductor*
27 la batuta (el director de orquesta *f*)
- *baton (conductor's baton)*
28-42 la sala de pintura *f*, un taller de teatro *m*
- *paint room, a workshop*
28 el tramoyista
- *stagehand (scene shifter)*
29 el puente de trabajo *m*
- *catwalk (bridge)*
30 la pieza de quitaipón (las decoraciones *f* movibles)
- *set piece*
31 el refuerzo
- *reinforcing struts*
32 el aplique (el forrado)
- *built piece (built unit)*
33 el telón de fondo *m*
- *backcloth (backdrop)*
34 la caja de pinturas *f* portátil
- *portable box for paint containers*
35 el pintor de escenarios *m*, un pintor de decorados *m*
- *scene painter, a scenic artist*
36 la paleta móvil
- *paint trolley*
37 el escenógrafo
- *stage designer (set designer)*
38 el encargado del vestuario
- *costume designer*
39 el diseño de un traje
- *design for a costume*
40 el figurín
- *sketch for a costume*
41 la maqueta de escenario *m*
- *model stage*
42 la maqueta de decoración *f*
- *model of the set*
43-52 el vestuario de los artistas
- *dressing room*
43 el espejo para el maquillaje
- *dressing room mirror*
44 el peinador de maquillaje *m*
- *make-up gown*

45 la mesa de maquillaje *m*
- *make-up table*
46 la barrita (el lápiz de maquillaje *m*)
- *greasepaint stick*
47 el maestro maquillador
- *chief make-up artist (chief make-up man)*
48 el maquillador (el peluquero de teatro *m*)
- *make-up artist (hairstylist)*
49 la peluca
- *wig*
50 los accesorios
- *props (properties)*
51 el vestido teatral
- *theatrical costume*
52 la lámpara de llamada *f* a escena *f*
- *call light*

1-60 la caja de escena con la maquinaria (la maquinaria superior – bambalina *f* – y la maquinaria inferior – fosos *m* –)
- *stagehouse with machinery (machinery in the flies and below stage)*
1 el puesto de control *m*
- *control room*
2 el pupitre de control *m* con dispositivos *m* de memoria *f* para los efectos luminosos
- *control console (lighting console, lighting control console) with preset control for presetting lighting effects*
3 el plano del puesto de control *m*
- *lighting plot (light plot)*
4 el telar
- *grid (gridiron)*
5 la galería de trabajo *m*
- *fly floor (fly gallery)*
6 el sistema de rociadura *f*, para la protección de incendios *m*
- *sprinkler system for fire prevention (for fire protection)*
7 el maestro (el encargado) del telar
- *fly man*
8 las cuerdas (del telón) del foro
- *fly lines (lines)*
9 el horizonte redondo (el ciclorama)
- *cyclorama*
10 el telón de fondo *m*
- *backcloth (backdrop, background)*
11 el arco, una pieza colgada intermedia
- *arch, a drop cloth*
12 la bambalina
- *border*
13 la caja del alumbrado superior
- *compartment (compartment-type, compartmentalized) batten (Am. border light)*
14 los cuerpos de alumbrado *m* de escena *f*
- *stage lighting units (stage lights)*
15 el alumbrado horizontal (el alumbrado (del telón) de fondo *m*)
- *horizon lights (backdrop lights)*
16 los reflectores de escena *f* móviles
- *adjustable acting area lights (acting area spotlights)*
17 los aparatos proyectores de imágenes *f*
- *scenery projectors (projectors)*
18 el cañón de agua *f* (un dispositivo de seguridad *f*)
- *monitor (water cannon) (piece of safety equipment)*

19 el puente de iluminación *f* móvil
- *travelling (Am. traveling) lighting bridge (travelling lighting gallery)*
20 el electricista
- *lighting operator (lighting man)*
21 el reflector de proscenio *m*
- *portal spotlight (tower spotlight)*
22 el telón de boca *f*
- *adjustable proscenium*
23 la cortina de escena *f*
- *curtain (theatrical curtain)*
24 el telón de hierro *m* (el telón metálico)
- *iron curtain (safety curtain, fire curtain)*
25 el proscenio
- *forestage (apron)*
26 las candilejas
- *footlight (footlights, floats)*
27 la concha del apuntador
- *prompt box*
28 el apuntador (*Ec. y Guat.*: el soplador; *Amér. Central*: el soplón)
- *prompter*
29 el pupitre de transpunte *m*
- *stage manager's desk*
30 el transpunte (el registrador de escena *f*)
- *stage director (stage manager)*
31 el escenario giratorio
- *revolving stage*
32 el escotillón
- *trap opening*
33 la tapa del escotillón
- *lift (Am. elevator)*
34 el tablado del escotillón, un tablado escalonado
- *bridge (Am. elevator), a rostrum*
35 los elementos de decoración *f*
- *pieces of scenery*
36 la escena
- *scene*
37 el actor (el comediante)
- *actor*
38 la actriz (la comediante)
- *actress*
39 los figurantes (los comparsas)
- *extras (supers, supernumeraries)*
40 el director artístico (el director de escena *f*)
- *director (producer)*
41 el guión (el texto)
- *prompt book (prompt script)*
42 la mesa del director de escena *f*
- *director's table (producer's table)*
43 el ayudante del director de escena *f*
- *assistant director (assistant producer)*
44 el libro de escena *f*
- *director's script (producer's script)*

45 el jefe de escenografía *f*
- *stage carpenter*
46 el tramoyista
- *stagehand (scene shifter)*
47 la pieza de quitaipón *m*
- *set piece*
48 el reflector de lente *f* de espejo *m*
- *mirror spot (mirror spotlight)*
49 el panel giratorio de filtros *m* coloreados (con disco *m* de color *m*)
- *automatic filter change (with colour filters, colour mediums, gelatines)*
50 la instalación de prensa *f* hidráulica
- *hydraulic plant room*
51 el depósito de agua *f*
- *water tank*
52 el tubo de succión *f*
- *suction pipe*
53 la bomba de presión *f* hidráulica
- *hydraulic pump*
54 la tubería bajo presión *f*
- *pressure pipe*
55 la cámara de presión *f* (el acumulador)
- *pressure tank (accumulator)*
56 el manómetro de contacto *m*
- *pressure gauge (Am. gage)*
57 el indicador del nivel del agua *f*
- *level indicator (liquid level indicator)*
58 la palanca de control *m*
- *control lever*
59 el maquinista (el mecánico, el jefe de máquinas)
- *operator*
60 los pistones hidráulicos (los émbolos)
- *rams*

1 el bar	**14** la iluminación de la pista de baile *m*	**25** el discjockey
– *bar*	– *dance floor lighting*	– *disc jockey*
2 la camarera del bar (*Col.:* la prendedera)	**15** la caja del altavoz	**26** el pupitre de mezcla *f*
	– *speaker (loudspeaker)*	– *mixing console (mixing desk, mixer)*
– *barmaid*	**16** la pista de baile *m*	**27** la pandereta
3 el taburete de bar *m*	– *dance floor*	– *tambourine*
– *bar stool*	**17** *u.* **18** la pareja	**28** la pared de cristal *m*
4 el estante de botellas *f*	– *dancing couple*	– *mirrored wall*
– *shelf for bottles*	**17** la chica (la joven) que baila	**29** el revestimiento del techo
5 el estante de vasos *m*	– *dancer*	– *ceiling tiles*
– *shelf for glasses*	**18** el chico (el joven) que baila	**30** el sistema de aireación *f*
6 el vaso para cerveza *f*	– *dancer*	– *ventilators*
– *beer glass*	**19** el tocadiscos (*Amér.:* el pick-up)	**31** los servicios
7 los vasos para vino *m* y para licor *m*	– *record player*	– *toilets (lavatories, WC)*
– *wine and liqueur glasses*	**20** el micrófono (*fam.:* el micro)	**32** la bebida larga (la copa larga, el long drink)
8 el grifo distribuidor de cerveza *f*	– *microphone*	
– *beer tap (tap)*	**21** el magnetófono	– *long drink*
9 el mostrador del bar (la barra)	– *tape recorder*	**33** el cóctel
– *bar*	**22** *u.* **23** el equipo de esterofonía *f* (la cadena hi-fi)	– *cocktail* (Am. *highball*)
10 el frigorífico		
– *refrigerator (fridge,* Am. *icebox)*	– *stereo system (stereo equipment)*	
11 las lámparas del bar	**22** el tuner (el sintonizador)	
– *bar lamps*	– *tuner*	
12 la iluminación indirecta	**23** el amplificador	
– *indirect lighting*	– *amplifier*	
13 la batería de proyectores *m*	**24** los discos	
– *colour* (Am. *color*) *organ (clavilux)*	– *records (discs)*	

1-33 el cabaret (el nightclub)
- *nightclub (night spot)*
1 el guardarropa
- *cloakroom (Am. checkroom)*
2 la señorita del guardarropa
- *cloakroom attendant (Am. checkroom attendant)*
3 la orquesta de baile *m*
- *band*
4 el clarinete
- *clarinet*
5 el clarinetista
- *clarinettist (Am. clarinetist)*
6 la trompeta
- *trumpet*
7 el trompetista
- *trumpeter*
8 la guitarra
- *guitar*
9 el guitarrista
- *guitarist (guitar player)*
10 la batería
- *drums*
11 el batería
- *drummer*
12 la caja del altavoz (el altavoz)
- *speaker (loudspeaker)*
13 el bar
- *bar*

14 la camarera del bar (*Col.:* la prendedera)
- *barmaid*
15 el mostrador del bar (la barra)
- *bar*
16 el taburete de bar *m*
- *bar stool*
17 el magnetófono
- *tape recorder*
18 el receptor (de radio *f*, el aparato de radio *f*, la radio)
- *receiver*
19 las bebidas alcohólicas
- *spirits*
20 el proyector de películas *f* estrechas para películas *f* pornográficas (películas *f* eróticas)
- *cine projector for porno films (sex films, blue movies)*
21 la caja de la pantalla con la pantalla
- *box containing screen*
22 la escena
- *stage*
23 la iluminación de la escena
- *stage lighting*
24 el reflector de escena *f*
- *spotlight*

25 la iluminación de la bambalina
- *festoon lighting*
26 la bombilla de la bambalina
- *festoon lamp (lamp, light bulb)*
27-32 el striptease (el número del desnudo)
- *striptease act (striptease number)*
27 la artista de striptease *m*
- *striptease artist (stripper)*
28 la liga
- *suspender (Am. garter)*
29 el sostén (el sujetador)
- *brassière (bra)*
30 la estola de piel *f* (el cuello de piel *f*)
- *fur stole*
31 los guantes
- *gloves*
32 la media
- *stocking*
33 la animadora
- *hostess*

1-33 la corrida de toros
- *bullfight (corrida, corrida de toros)*
1 el quiebro
- *mock bullfight*
2 el novillero (el torero principiante)
- *novice (aspirant matador, novillero)*
3 la imitación de toro (un carro en forma f de toro m)
- *mock bull (dummy bull)*
4 el banderillero principiante
- *novice banderillero (apprentice banderillero)*
5 la plaza de toros (la arena, el ruedo) [esquema]
- *bullring (plaza de toros) [diagram]*
6 la entrada principal
- *main entrance*
7 los palcos
- *boxes*
8 los tendidos (*si son cubiertos, en la parte superior:* las andanadas)
- *stands*
9 la arena (el ruedo)
- *arena (ring)*
10 la puerta de los toreros
- *bullfighters' entrance*
11 la puerta del toril (la puerta de los corrales)
- *torril door*
12 la puerta de salida f para los toros muertos
- *exit gate for killed bulls*
13 el desolladero
- *slaughterhouse*
14 el toril (el corral, el chiquero)
- *bull pens (corrals)*
15 el patio de los caballos
- *paddock*
16 el picador
- *lancer on horseback (picador)*
17 la pica (la vara, la garrocha)
- *lance (pike pole, javelin)*
18 el caballo encaparazonado
- *armoured (Am. armored) horse*
19 la coraza de hierro m de la pierna (la mona)
- *leg armour (Am. armor)*
20 el sombrero redondo del picador (el sombrero castoreño)
- *picador's round hat*
21 el banderillero, un torero, un peón
- *banderillero, a torero*
22 las banderillas
- *banderillas (barbed darts)*
23 la faja
- *shirtwaist*
24 el pase
- *bullfight*

25 el matador (el espada), un torero
- *matador (swordsman), a torero*
26 la coleta (la moña)
- *queue, a distinguishing mark of the matador*
27 la muleta (el trapo; *anál.:* la capa, el capote)
- *red cloak (capa)*
28 el toro de lidia f (el toro bravo)
- *fighting bull*
29 la montera
- *montera [hat made of tiny black silk chenille balls]*
30 la estocada
- *killing the bull (kill, estocada)*
31 el matador de corridas f benéficas [sin traje m de luces f]
- *matador in charity performances [without professional uniform]*
32 la espada (el estoque)
- *estoque (sword)*
33 la muleta (el trapo; *anál.:* la capa, el capote)
- *muleta*
34 el rodeo
- *rodeo*
35 el toro joven (el novillo)
- *young bull*
36 el vaquero
- *cowboy*
37 el sombrero del vaquero (el sombrero tejano)
- *stetson (stetson hat)*
38 el pañuelo de cuello m
- *scarf (necktie)*
39 el jinete de rodeo m
- *rodeo rider*
40 el lazo
- *lasso*

1 *u.* **2 notación** *f* **medieval**
– *medieval (mediaeval) notes*
1 la notación coral (la notación cuadrada)
– *plainsong notation (neumes, neums, pneumes, square notation)*
2 la notación mensural
– *mensural notation*
3-7 las notas
– *musical note (note)*
3 la cabeza (el punto, el neuma)
– *note head*
4 la vírgula (el tallo, el vástago)
– *note stem (note tail)*
5 el corchete
– *hook*
6 la barra
– *stroke*
7 el punto de alargamiento *m* (el puntillo)
– *dot indicating augmentation of note's value*
8-11 las claves
– *clefs*
8 la clave de sol *m*
– *treble clef (G-clef, violin clef)*
9 la clave de fa *m*
– *bass clef (F-clef)*
10 la clave de do *m*, para viola *f*
– *alto clef (C-clef)*
11 la clave de do *m*, para violencelo *m*
– *tenor clef*
12-19 los valores de las notas
– *note values*
12 la breve (la cuadrada)
– *breve (brevis,* Am. *double-whole note)*
13 la semibreve (la redonda)
– *semibreve (Am. whole note)*
14 la mínima (la blanca)
– *minim (Am. half note)*
15 la negra
– *crotchet (Am. quarter note)*
16 la corchea
– *quaver (Am. eighth note)*
17 la semicorchea
– *semiquaver (Am. sixteenth note)*
18 la fusa
– *demisemiquaver (Am. thirty-second note)*
19 la semifusa
– *hemidemisemiquaver (Am. sixty-fourth note)*
20-27 los silencios (las pausas)
– *rests*
20 el silencio de cuadrada *f*
– *breve rest*
21 el silencio de redonda *f*
– *semibreve rest (Am. whole rest)*
22 el silencio de blanca *f*
– *minim rest (Am. half rest)*
23 el silencio de negra *f*
– *crotchet rest (Am. quarter rest)*
24 el silencio de corchea *f*
– *quaver rest (Am. eighth rest)*
25 el silencio de semicorchea *f*
– *semiquaver rest (Am. sixteenth rest)*

26 el silencio de fusa *f*
– *demisemiquaver rest (Am. thirty-second rest)*
27 el silencio de semifusa *f*
– *hemidemisemiquaver rest (Am. sixty-fourth rest)*
28-42 el compás (el tiempo)
– *time (time signatures, measure,* Am. *meter)*
28 el dos por ocho
– *two-eight time*
29 el dos por cuatro
– *two-four time*
30 el dos por dos
– *two-two time*
31 el cuatro por ocho
– *four-eight time*
32 el cuatro por cuatro
– *four-four time (common time)*
33 el cuatro por dos
– *four-two time*
34 el seis por ocho
– *six-eight time*
35 el seis por cuatro
– *six-four time*
36 el tres por ocho
– *three-eight time*
37 el tres por cuatro
– *three-four time*
38 el tres por dos
– *three-two time*
39 el nueve por ocho
– *nine-eight time*
40 el nueve por cuatro
– *nine-four time*
41 el cinco por cuatro
– *five-four time*
42 la barra de compás *m*
– *bar (bar line, measure line)*
43 *u.* 44 el pentagrama
– *staff (stave)*
43 la línea
– *line of the staff*
44 el espacio (la línea y espacio *m*)
– *space*
45-49 las escalas (las gamas)
– *scales*
45 la escala de do *m* mayor (la escala diatónica mayor); sonidos *m* fundamentales: do, re, mi, fa, sol, la, si, do
– *C major scale naturals: c, d, e, f, g, a, b, c*
46 la escala de la *m* menor [natural]; notas fundamentales: la, si, do, re, mi, fa, sol, la
– *A minor scale [natural] naturals: a, b, c, d, e, f, g, a*
47 la escala de la *m* menor [armónica]
– *A minor scale [harmonic]*
48 la escala de la *m* menor [melódica] (la escala diatónica menor)
– *A minor scale [melodic]*
49 la escala cromática
– *chromatic scale*
50-54 las alteraciones (los accidentales)
– *accidentals (inflections, key signatures)*

50 *u.* **51 los signos de elevación** *f*
– *signs indicating the raising of a note*
50 el sostenido (la elevación de un semitono)
– *sharp (raising the note a semitone or half-step)*
51 el doble sostenido (la elevación de dos semitonos *m*)
– *double sharp (raising the note a tone or full-step)*
52 *u.* **53 los signos que bajan la nota**
– *signs indicating the lowering of a note*
52 el bemol (la bajada de un semitono)
– *flat (lowering the note a semitone or half-step)*
53 el doble bemol (la bajada de dos semitonos *m*)
– *double flat (lowering the note a tone or full-step)*
54 el becuadro
– *natural*
55-68 las tonalidades (tonalidades *f* mayores y sus relativas tonalidades *f* menores; con las mismas alteraciones)
– *keys (major keys and the related minor keys having the same signature)*
55 do *m* mayor (la *m* menor)
– *C major (A minor)*
56 sol *m* mayor (mi *m* menor)
– *G major (E minor)*
57 re *m* mayor (si *m* menor)
– *D major (B minor)*
58 la *m* mayor (fa *m* sostenido menor)
– *A major (F sharp minor)*
59 mi *m* mayor (do *m* sostenido menor)
– *E major (C sharp minor)*
60 si *m* mayor (sol *m* sostenido menor)
– *B major (G sharp minor)*
61 fa *m* sostenido mayor (re *m* sostenido menor)
– *F sharp major (D sharp minor)*
62 do *m* mayor (la *m* menor)
– *C major (A minor)*
63 fa *m* mayor (re *m* menor)
– *F major (D minor)*
64 si *m* bemol mayor (sol *m* menor)
– *B flat major (G minor)*
65 mi *m* bemol mayor (do *m* menor)
– *E flat major (C minor)*
66 la *m* bemol mayor (fa *m* menor)
– *A flat major (F minor)*
67 re *m* bemol mayor (si *m* bemol menor)
– *D flat major (B flat minor)*
68 sol *m* bemol mayor (mi *m* bemol menor)
– *G flat major (E flat minor)*

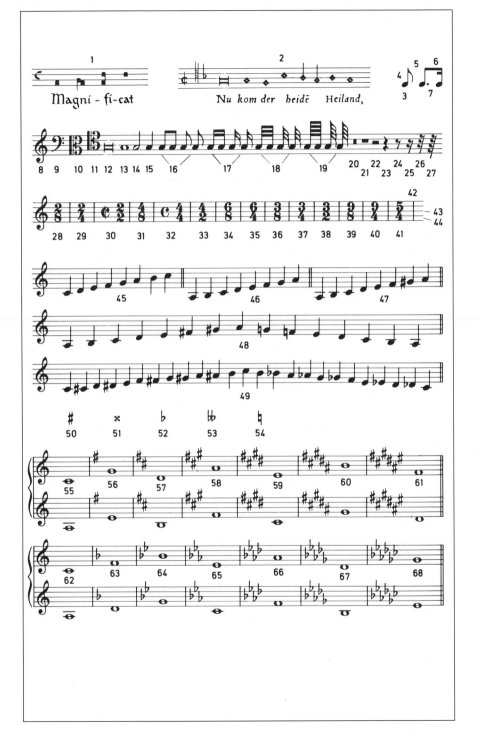

321 Notación musical II   *Musical Notation II*

1-5 el acorde
- *chord*

1-4 los acordes perfectos (acordes *m* de quinta *f*, tríadas *f*)
- *triad*

1 el acorde perfecto mayor
- *major triad*

2 el acorde perfecto menor
- *minor triad*

3 el acorde de quinta *f* disminuida
- *diminished triad*

4 el acorde de quinta *f* aumentada
- *augmented triad*

5 el acorde de séptima *f*
- *chord of four notes, a chord of the seventh (seventh chord, dominant seventh chord)*

6-13 los intervalos
- *intervals*

6 el unísono
- *unison (unison interval)*

7 la segunda mayor
- *major second*

8 la tercera mayor
- *major third*

9 la cuarta
- *perfect fourth*

10 la quinta
- *perfect fifth*

11 la sexta mayor
- *major sixth*

12 la séptima mayor
- *major seventh*

13 la octava
- *perfect octave*

14-22 los adornos
- *ornaments (graces, grace notes)*

14 la apoyatura larga
- *long appoggiatura*

15 la apoyatura breve
- *acciaccatura (short appoggiatura)*

16 la apoyatura doble
- *slide*

17 el trino sin mordente *m*
- *trill (shake) without turn*

18 el trino con mordente *m*
- *trill (shake) with turn*

19 el mordente superior (el semimordente, el mordente imperfecto)
- *upper mordent (inverted mordent, pralltriller)*

20 el mordente inferior
- *lower mordent (mordent)*

21 el gruppetto
- *turn*

22 el arpegio
- *arpeggio*

23-26 otros signos *m* de notación *f*
- *other signs in musical notation*

23 el tresillo, *por analogía:* el dosillo (el bisillo), el cuatrillo, el cinquillo (el quintillo), el seisillo y el septillo
- *triplet; corresponding groupings: duplet (couplet), quadruplet, quintuplet, sextolet (sextuplet), septolet (septuplet, septimole)*

24 la ligadura
- *tie (bind)*

25 el calderón (la fermata), un signo de duración *f*
- *pause (pause sign)*

26 la doble barra *f* de repetición *f*
- *repeat mark*

27-41 las indicaciones de movimiento *m* (de velocidad *f*)
- *expression marks (signs of relative intensity)*

27 el acento
- *marcato (marcando, markiert, attack, strong accent)*

28 presto (rápido)
- *presto (quick, fast)*

29 portato
- *portato (lourer, mezzo staccato, carried)*

30 tenuto (manteniendo el movimiento sin acelerar)
- *tenuto (held)*

31 crescendo (aumentando)
- *crescendo (increasing gradually in power)*

32 decrescendo (disminuyendo)
- *decrescendo (diminuendo, decreasing or diminishing gradually in power)*

33 legato (ligado)
- *legato (bound)*

34 staccato (punteado)
- *staccato (detached)*

35 piano (suave)
- *piano (soft)*

36 pianísimo (muy suave)
- *pianissimo (very soft)*

37 pianísimo piano (con la máxima suavidad posible)
- *pianissimo piano (as soft as possible)*

38 forte (fuerte)
- *forte (loud)*

39 fortísimo (muy fuerte)
- *fortissimo (very loud)*

40 forte fortísimo (con la máxima fuerza posible)
- *forte fortissimo (double fortissimo, as loud as possible)*

41 fortepiano (se ataca fuerte y se continúa suave)
- *forte piano (loud and immediately soft again)*

42-50 la escala musical
- *divisions of the compass*

42 la subcontraoctava
- *subcontra octave (double contra octave)*

43 la contraoctava
- *contra octave*

44 la primera octava
- *great octave*

45 la segunda octava
- *small octave*

46 la tercera octava
- *one-line octave*

47 la cuarta octava
- *two-line octave*

48 la quinta octava
- *three-line octave*

49 la sexta octava
- *four-line octave*

50 la séptima octava
- *five-line octave*

322 Instrumentos de música I

Musical Instruments I

1 la lur, una trompeta de bronce *m*
 – *lur, a bronze trumpet*
2 la flauta de Pan (la siringa)
 – *panpipes (Pandean pipes, syrinx)*
3 la diaula, una flauta doble
 – *aulos, a double shawm*
4 el aulos
 – *aulos pipe*
5 la phorbeia (sujetador *m* de los labios)
 – *phorbeia (peristomion, capistrum, mouth band)*
6 el cromorno
 – *crumhorn (crummhorn, cromorne, krumbhorn, krummhorn)*
7 la flauta de pico *m* (la flauta dulce; *Perú:* la chaina; *Ec.:* el pijuano; *Chile:* la pivilca)
 – *recorder (fipple flute)*
8 la cornamusa; *anál.:* la gaita, la musette
 – *bagpipe;* sim.: *musette*
9 el saco del aire
 – *bag*
10 el caramillo melódico
 – *chanter (melody pipe)*
11 los bordones (para el acompañamiento)
 – *drone (drone pipe)*
12 la corneta curvada
 – *curved cornett (zink)*
13 la serpiente
 – *serpent*
14 la chirimía; *más grande:* la bombarda (la dulzaina)
 – *shawm (schalmeyes);* larger: *bombard (bombarde, pommer)*
15 la cítara; *anál. y más pequeña:* la lira
 – *cythara (cithara);* sim. and smaller: *lyre*
16 el brazo de la caja
 – *arm*
17 el puente
 – *bridge*
18 la caja de resonancia *f*
 – *sound box (resonating chamber, resonator)*
19 el plectro, una púa (*Chile:* la uñeta)
 – *plectrum, a plucking device*
20 la pochette (el violín de bolsillo *m*, el violín de pequeño formato *m*)
 – *kit (pochette), a miniature violin*
21 la cítara, un instrumento de cuerdas *f* punteadas; *anál.:* la pandora
 – *cittern (cithern, cither, cister, citole), a plucked instrument;* sim.: *pandora (bandora, bandore)*
22 la rosa (la boca, la tarraja)
 – *sound hole*

23 la viola, una viola de gamba *f; más grande:* el violón (el contrabajo; *Mé.:* el tololoche)
 – *viol (descant viol, treble viol, a viola da gamba);* larger: *tenor viol, bass viol (viola da gamba, gamba), violone (double bass viol)*
24 el arco de viola *f*
 – *viol bow*
25 la zanfonía (la viella, la symphonia, la rotata, la chifonía, el organistrum)
 – *hurdy-gurdy (vielle à roue, symphonia, armonie, organistrum)*
26 la rueda de fricción *f*
 – *friction wheel*
27 la cubierta
 – *wheel cover (wheel guard)*
28 el teclado
 – *keyboard (keys)*
29 la caja de resonancia *f*
 – *resonating body (resonator, sound box)*
30 las cuerdas melódicas
 – *melody strings*
31 las cuerdas del bordón
 – *drone strings (drones, bourdons)*
32 el cémbalo (el tímpano, el salterio, el dulcemele)
 – *dulcimer*
33 el bastidor
 – *rib (resonator wall)*
34 el macillo para el cémbalo de Valais
 – *beater for the Valasian dulcimer*
35 el martillo para el cémbalo de Appenzell
 – *hammer (stick) for the Appenzell dulcimer*
36 el clavicordio; *clases:* el clavicordio ligado y el clavicordio independiente
 – *clavichord;* kinds: *fretted or unfretted clavichord*
37 el mecanismo del clavicordio
 – *clavichord mechanism*
38 la tecla
 – *key (key lever)*
39 la palanca de balanza *f* (el soporte de la tecla)
 – *balance rail*
40 la espiga guía *f*
 – *guiding blade*
41 la ranura guía *f*
 – *guiding slot*
42 el soporte (el apoyo)
 – *resting rail*
43 la tangente (el martinete de latón *m*)
 – *tangent*

44 la cuerda
 – *string*
45 el clavicémbalo, un clavecín; *anál.:* la espineta (el virginal)
 – *harpsichord (clavicembalo, cembalo), a wing-shaped stringed keyboard instrument;* sim.: *spinet (virginal)*
46 el teclado (manual) superior
 – *upper keyboard (upper manual)*
47 el teclado (manual) inferior
 – *lower keyboard (lower manual)*
48 el mecanismo del clavicémbalo
 – *harpsichord mechanism*
49 la tecla
 – *key (key lever)*
50 el saltador (el martinete)
 – *jack*
51 la parrilla guía *f* de los martinetes
 – *slide (register)*
52 la lengüeta
 – *tongue*
53 el plectro (el cañón de pluma *f*)
 – *quill plectrum*
54 el apagador del sonido
 – *damper*
55 la cuerda
 – *string*
56 el órgano portátil (el órgano real); *más grande:* el órgano positivo
 – *portative organ, a portable organ;* larger: *positive organ (positive)*
57 el tubo
 – *pipe (flue pipe)*
58 el fuelle
 – *bellows*

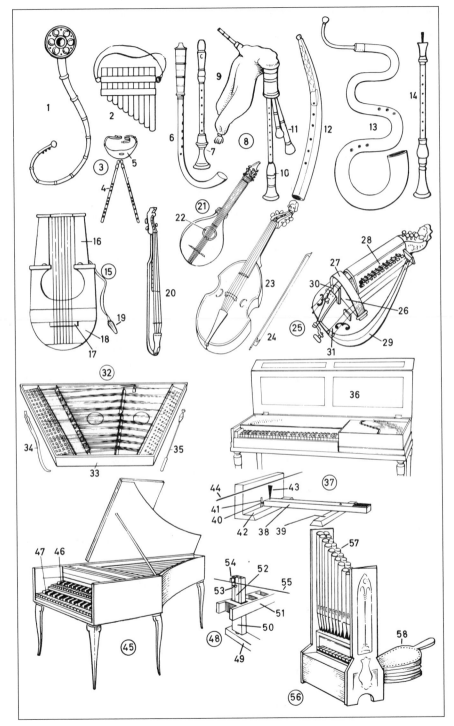

323 Instrumentos de música II   *Musical Instruments II*

1-62 los instrumentos de orquesta *f*
- *orchestral instruments*

1-27 los instrumentos de cuerda *f,*
los instrumentos de arco *m*
- *stringed instruments, bowed instruments*

1 el violín
- *violin*

2 el mástil (el mango) del violín
- *neck of the violin*

3 la caja de resonancia *f* (la caja del violín, el "barco")
- *resonating body (violin body, sound box of the violin)*

4 el costado
- *rib (side wall)*

5 el puente del violín
- *violin bridge*

6 la ranura en forma *f* de efe, una abertura acústica
- *F-hole, a sound hole*

7 el cordal (el ceja)
- *tailpiece*

8 el mentonero
- *chin rest*

9 las cuerdas (las cuerdas de violín *m*): la cuerda de sol, la cuerda de re, la cuerda de la, la cuerda de mi
- *strings (violin strings, fiddle strings): G-string, D-string, A-string, E-string*

10 la sordina
- *mute (sordino)*

11 la colofonia
- *resin (rosin, colophony)*

12 el arco de violín *m*
- *violin bow (bow)*

13 la nuez
- *nut (frog)*

14 la baqueta (la varilla; *Amér.:* el bolillo)
- *stick (bow stick)*

15 la mecha del arco de violín *m*, una mecha de cerdas *f* de caballo *m*
- *hair of the violin bow (horsehair)*

16 el violoncelo
- *violoncello (cello), a member of the da gamba violin family*

17 la voluta
- *scroll*

18 la clavija
- *tuning peg (peg)*

19 el clavijero
- *pegbox*

20 la ceja
- *nut*

21 el mástil (el mango)
- *fingerboard*

22 la púa (*Chile:* la uñeta)
- *spike (tailpin)*

23 el contrabajo (el violón; *Mé.:* el tololoche)
- *double bass (contrabass, violone, double bass viol,* Am. *bass)*

24 la tapa armónica
- *belly (top, soundboard)*

25 el costado
- *rib (side wall)*

26 el borde
- *purfling (inlay)*

27 la viola
- *viola*

28-38 los instrumentos de viento-madera
- *woodwind instruments (woodwinds)*

28 el fagote; *más grande:* el contrafagote
- *bassoon;* larger: *double bassoon (contrabassoon)*

29 la boquilla, con la lengüeta doble
- *tube with double reed*

30 el flautín (el piccolo)
- *piccolo (small flute, piccolo flute, flauto piccolo)*

31 la flauta mayor, una flauta travesera
- *flute (German flute), a cross flute (transverse flute, side-blown flute)*

32 la llave de la flauta
- *key*

33 el agujero
- *fingerhole*

34 el clarinete; *mayor:* el clarinete bajo (*Amér.:* la chirimía)
- *clarinet;* larger: *bass clarinet*

35 la llave
- *key (brille)*

36 la boquilla
- *mouthpiece*

37 el pabellón
- *bell*

38 el oboe; *variedades:* el oboe de amor *m,* los oboes tenor: el oboe de caccia, el corno inglés; el oboe barítono
- *oboe (hautboy);* kinds: *oboe d'amore; tenor oboes: oboe da caccia, cor anglais; heckelphone (baritone oboe)*

39-48 los instrumentos de viento-metal
- *brass instruments (brass)*

39 el corno tenor (el fiscorno), un cornetín
- *tenor horn*

40 el pistón (la válvula)
- *valve*

41 el corno de caza *f,* una trompa de pistones *m*
- *French horn (horn, waldhorn), a valve horn*

42 el pabellón
- *bell*

43 la trompeta; *mayor:* trompeta baja; *más pequeña:* la corneta (de pistones *m*)
- *trumpet;* larger: *Bb cornet;* smaller: *cornet*

44 la tuba (el bombardón); *anál.:* el helicón, la tuba de contrabajo *m*
- *bass tuba (tuba, bombardon);* sim.: *helicon (pellitone), contrabass tuba*

45 el pulsador
- *thumb hold*

46 el trombón de varas *f; variedades:* el trombón alto, el trombón tenor, el trombón bajo
- *trombone;* kinds: *alto trombone, tenor trombone, bass trombone*

47 la vara corredera
- *trombone slide (slide)*

48 el pabellón
- *bell*

49-59 los instrumentos de percusión *f*
- *percussion instruments*

49 el triángulo
- *triangle*

50 los platillos
- *cymbals*

51-59 los instrumentos de membrana *f*
- *membranophones*

51 el tambor pequeño (*Pan.:* el repicador; *Perú:* la tinya)
- *side drum (snare drum)*

52 la membrana (la piel, el parche)
- *drum head (head, upper head, batter head, vellum)*

53 el tornillo tensor
- *tensioning screw*

54 la baqueta (el palillo de tambor *m; Amér.:* el bolillo)
- *drumstick*

55 el tambor mayor (el bombo)
- *bass drum (Turkish drum)*

56 la baqueta (el mazo)
- *stick (padded stick)*

57 el timbal, un timbal de tornillos *m; anál.:* el timbal mecánico
- *kettledrum (timpano), a screw-tensioned drum;* sim.: *machine drum (mechanically tuned drum)*

58 la membrana (la piel del timbal)
- *kettledrum skin (kettledrum vellum)*

59 el tornillo tensor para afinar
- *tuning screw*

60 el arpa *f,* una arpa de pedales *m*
- *harp, a pedal harp*

61 las cuerdas
- *strings*

62 el pedal
- *pedal*

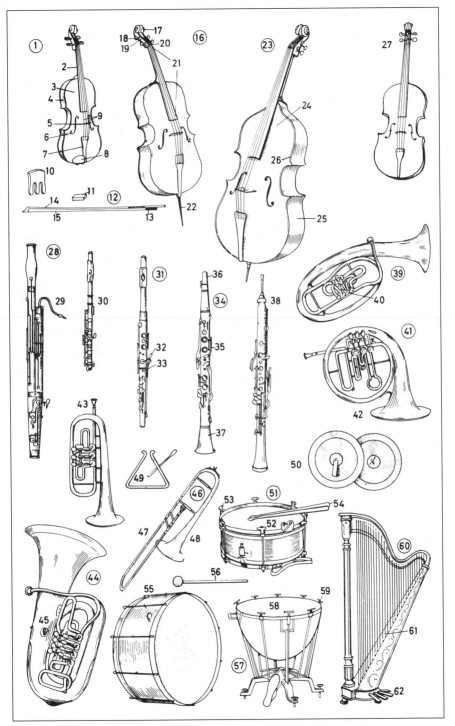

1-46 instrumentos *m* de música *f* popular
– *popular musical instruments (folk instruments)*
1-31 instrumentos de cuerda *f*
– *stringed instruments*
1 el laúd; *mayores:* la tiorba, el chitarrone
– *lute; larger: theorbo, chitarrone*
2 la caja de resonancia *f*
– *resonating body (resonator)*
3 la tabla armónica
– *soundboard (belly, table)*
4 el cordal (la ceja inferior)
– *string fastener (string holder)*
5 la rosa (la tarraja)
– *sound hole (rose)*
6 la cuerda, una cuerda de tripa *f*
– *string, a gut (catgut) string*
7 el cuello
– *neck*
8 el mástil (el mango)
– *fingerboard*
9 el traste
– *fret*
10 el clavijero
– *head (bent-back pegbox, swan-head pegbox, pegbox)*
11 la clavija
– *tuning peg (peg, lute pin)*
12 la guitarra
– *guitar*
13 el cordal
– *string holder*
14 la cuerda, una cuerda de tripa *f* o de perlón *m*
– *string, a gut (catgut) or nylon string*
15 la caja de resonancia *f*
– *resonating body (resonating chamber, resonator, sound box)*
16 la mandolina (*Amér. Central, Chile y Perú:* la bandolina)
– *mandolin (mandoline)*
17 el cubrecuerdas
– *sleeve protector (cuff protector)*
18 el cuello
– *neck*
19 el clavijero
– *pegdisc*
20 el plectro (la púa; *Chile:* la uñeta)
– *plectrum*
21 la cítara
– *zither (plucked zither)*
22 la tablilla de afinar
– *pin block (wrest pin block, wrest plank)*
23 la clavija de afinamiento *m*
– *tuning pin (wrest pin)*
24 las cuerdas de acompañamiento *m* (las cuerdas bajas, las cuerdas de bordón *m; Arg. y Urug.:* las bordonas)
– *accompaniment strings (bass strings, unfretted strings, open strings)*
25 las cuerdas melódicas (las cuerdas de tocar)
– *melody strings (fretted strings, stopped strings)*

26 la encorvadura de la caja de resonancia *f*
– *semicircular projection of the resonating sound box (resonating body)*
27 el plectro de sortija *f*
– *ring plectrum*
28 la balalaica
– *balalaika*
29 el banjo
– *banjo*
30 la caja-tambor
– *tambourine-like body*
31 la piel (la membrana)
– *parchment membrane*
32 la ocarina, una flauta ovoide
– *ocarina, a globular flute*
33 la embocadura (la boquilla)
– *mouthpiece*
34 el agujero
– *fingerhole*
35 la armónica de boca *f*
– *mouth organ (harmonica)*
36 el acordeón; *anál.:* la concertina, el bandoneón
– *accordion; sim.: piano accordion, concertina, bandoneon*
37 el fuelle
– *bellows*
38 el cierre del fuelle
– *bellows strap*
39 el teclado-piano melódico
– *melody side (keyboard side, melody keys)*
40 el teclado
– *keyboard (keys)*
41 el registro de tiple *m*
– *treble stop (treble coupler, treble register)*
42 la tecla del registro
– *stop lever*
43 los botones de los bajos (la parte del acompañamiento)
– *bass side (accompaniment side, bass studs, bass press-studs, bass buttons)*
44 el registro de los bajos
– *bass stop (bass coupler, bass register)*
45 la pandereta; *anál.:* el pandero
– *tambourine*
46 las castañuelas (las castañetas)
– *castanets*
47-78 instrumentos de jazz *m*
– *jazz band instruments (dance band instruments)*
47-58 instrumentos de percusión *f*
– *percussion instruments*
47-54 la batería de jazz *m*
– *drum kit (drum set, drums)*
47 el bombo (el tambor gordo; *Pan.:* el pujador)
– *bass drum*
48 la caja clara (el tambor)
– *small tom-tom*
49 el tom-tom
– *large tom-tom*

50 el doble platillo agudo
– *high-hat cymbals (choke cymbals, Charleston cymbals, cup cymbals)*
51 el platillo grave
– *cymbal*
52 el soporte del platillo
– *cymbal stand (cymbal holder)*
53 la escobilla de jazz *m*, una escobilla de metal *m*
– *wire brush*
54 el mecanismo del pedal
– *pedal mechanism*
55 la conga
– *conga drum (conga)*
56 el círculo tensor
– *tension hoop*
57 los timbales
– *timbales*
58 los bongoes
– *bongo drums (bongos)*
59 las maracas (*Bol.:* los maracos); *anál.:* los sonajeros de rumba *f*
– *maracas; sim.: shakers*
60 el guiro
– *guiro*
61 el xilófono; *anál.:* la marimba, el balafo
– *xylophone; form.: straw fiddle; sim.: marimbaphone (steel marimba), tubaphone*
62 la lámina de madera *f*
– *wooden slab*
63 la caja de resonancia *f*
– *resonating chamber (sound box)*
64 el mazo (el percusor)
– *beater*
65 la trompeta de jazz *m*
– *jazz trumpet*
66 el pistón (la válvula)
– *valve*
67 el gancho de apoyo *m* del dedo
– *finger hook*
68 la sordina
– *mute (sordino)*
69 el saxófono
– *saxophone*
70 el pabellón
– *bell*
71 el tubo de embocadura *f*
– *crook*
72 la boquilla
– *mouthpiece*
73 la guitarra de jazz *m*
– *struck guitar (jazz guitar)*
74 la escotadura (para facilitar la digitación)
– *hollow to facilitate fingering*
75 el vibráfono
– *vibraphone (Am. vibraharp)*
76 el bastidor metálico
– *metal frame*
77 la lámina de metal *m*
– *metal bar*
78 el tubo metálico
– *tubular metal resonator*

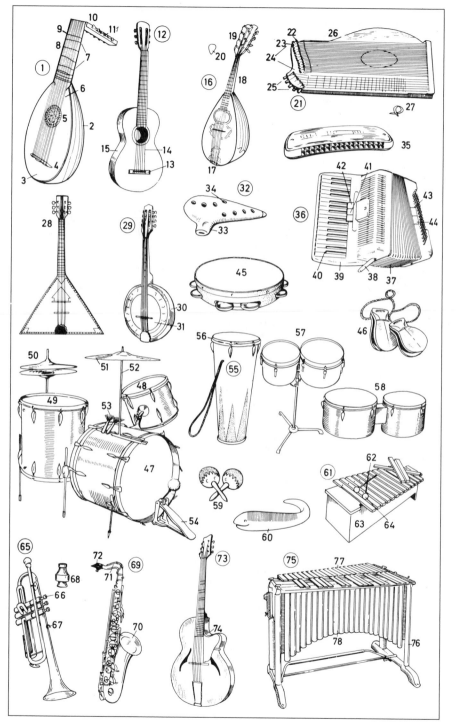

1 el piano (el piano recto, el piano vertical), un instrumento de teclado *m; forma pequeña:* el pianino; *formas antecesoras:* el pantaleón, el clavicordio; la celesta que tiene lengüetas *f* en lugar de cuerdas *f*
– *piano (pianoforte, upright piano, upright, vertical piano, spinet piano, console piano), a keyboard instrument (keyed instrument); smaller form: cottage piano (pianino); earlier forms: pantaleon; celesta, with steel bars instead of strings*
2-18 la mecánica del piano
– *piano action (piano mechanism)*
2 el cuadro de hierro *m*
– *iron frame*
3 el martillo; *en conjunto:* el mecanismo de percusión *f*
– *hammer; collectively: striking mechanism*
4 *u.* **5** el teclado (las teclas del piano)
– *keyboard (piano keys)*
4 la tecla blanca (la tecla de marfil *m*)
– *white key (ivory key)*
5 la tecla negra (la tecla de ébano *m*)
– *black key (ebony key)*
6 la caja del piano
– *piano case*
7 las cuerdas del piano
– *strings (piano strings)*
8 *u.* **9** los pedales del piano
– *piano pedals*
8 el pedal derecho (el pedal fuerte), para reforzar la vibración
– *right pedal (sustaining pedal, damper pedal; loosely: forte pedal, loud pedal) for raising the dampers*
9 el pedal izquierdo (el pedal piano, el pedal suave, el pedal dulce) para amortiguar el sonido
– *left pedal (soft pedal; loosely: piano pedal) for reducing the striking distance of the hammers on the strings*
10 las cuerdas de tiples *m* (las cuerdas agudas)
– *treble strings*
11 el puente de las cuerdas tiples *m*
– *treble bridge (treble belly bridge)*
12 las cuerdas bajas (las cuerdas graves, los bordones)
– *bass strings*
13 el puente de las cuerdas bajas
– *bass bridge (bass belly bridge)*
14 la clavija de sujeción *f*
– *hitch pin*
15 la barra soporte de los martillos
– *hammer rail*
16 el soporte del mecanismo
– *brace*

17 la clavija de afinamiento *m*
– *tuning pin (wrest pin, tuning peg)*
18 la tabla-clavijero
– *pin block (wrest pin block, wrest plank)*
19 el metrónomo
– *metronome*
20 la llave de afinar
– *tuning hammer (tuning key, wrest)*
21 la cuña para afinar
– *tuning wedge*
22-39 la mecánica de las teclas
– *key action (key mechanism)*
22 el travesaño del mecanismo
– *beam*
23 la palanca que acciona los apagadores
– *damper-lifting lever*
24 la cabeza de macillo (el fieltro del macillo)
– *felt-covered hammer head*
25 el mango del macillo
– *hammer shank*
26 el listón de apoyo *m* de los macillos
– *hammer rail*
27 el apresador
– *check (back check)*
28 el fieltro del apresador
– *check felt (back check felt)*
29 el alambre del apresador
– *wire stem of the check (wire stem of the back check)*
30 el cric (el gato)
– *sticker (hopper, hammer jack, hammer lever)*
31 el contraapresador
– *button*
32 la palanca levadora
– *action lever*
33 el piloto
– *pilot*
34 el alambre del piloto
– *pilot wire*
35 el astil de la brida
– *tape wire*
36 la brida (una brida de cuero *m*)
– *tape*
37 el apagador
– *damper (damper block)*
38 el brazo del apagador
– *damper lifter*
39 el listón de apoyo *m* de los apagadores
– *damper rest rail*
40 el piano de cola *f* (el piano de concierto *m; más pequeño:* el piano de media cola *f;* el piano de cuarto de cola *f; otra forma:* el piano cuadrado)
– *grand piano (horizontal piano, grand, concert grand, for the concert hall; smaller: baby grand piano, boudoir piano; other form: square piano, table piano)*

41 los pedales del piano de cola *f;* el pedal derecho para reforzar la vibración; el pedal izquierdo para disminuir la resonancia (por deslizamiento lateral del teclado; es golpeada una sola cuerda "una corda")
– *grand piano pedals; right pedal for raising the dampers; left pedal for softening the tone (shifting the keyboard so that only one string is struck 'una corda')*
42 el soporte del pedal
– *pedal bracket*
43 el armonio (el órgano)
– *harmonium (reed organ, melodium)*
44 el registro
– *draw stop (stop, stop knob)*
45 las rodilleras
– *knee lever (knee swell, swell)*
46 los pedales que accionan el fuelle (los pedales neumáticos)
– *pedal (bellows pedal)*
47 la caja del armonio
– *harmonium case*
48 el teclado (manual)
– *harmonium keyboard (manual)*

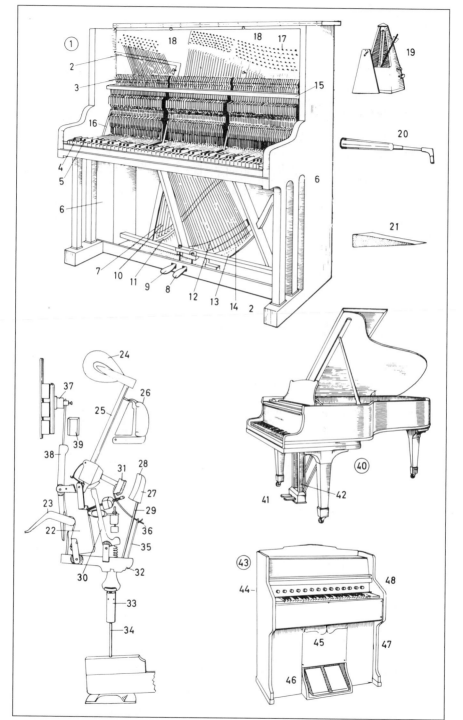

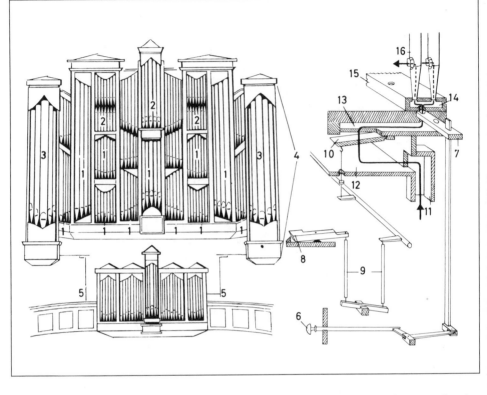

1-52 el órgano (el órgano de iglesia *f*)
– *organ (church organ)*
1-5 los cañones postizos (la tubería
postiza; la fachada de órgano *m*)
– *front view of organ (organ case)*
[built according to classical princi-
ples]
1-3 los tubos de la fachada del
órgano
– *display pipes (face pipes)*
1 la caja principal
– *Hauptwerk (approx. English equiv-*
alent: great organ)
2 la caja superior
– *Oberwerk (approx. English equiva-*
lent: swell organ)
3 los tubos de pedal *m*
– *pedal pipes*
4 la torre de pedal *m*
– *pedal tower*
5 el positivo dorsal
– *Rückpositiv (approx. English*
equivalent: choir organ)
6-16 la transmisión mecánica; *otros*
sistemas: la transmisión neumática,
la transmisión eléctrica
– *tracker action (mechanical action);*
other systems: pneumatic action,
electric action
6 el registro
– *draw stop (stop, stop knob)*

7 el registro de corredera *f*
– *slider (slide)*
8 la tecla
– *key (key lever)*
9 las varillas transmisoras
– *sticker*
10 la válvula
– *pallet*
11 el canal de viento *m* (el conducto
de aire *m*)
– *wind trunk*
12-14 el secreto (el distribuidor de aire
m), un secreto de corredera *f; otros*
tipos: el cono resonante, la membrana resonadora
– *wind chest, a slider wind chest;*
other types: sliderless wind chest
(unit wind chest), spring chest,
kegellade chest (cone chest),
diaphragm chest
12 la cámara de aire *m*
– *wind chest (wind chest box)*
13 el canal de la caja de resonancia *f*
– *groove*
14 el canal de la caja superior
– *upper board groove*
15 el soporte (el zócalo) de los tubos
– *upper board*
16 el tubo de un registro
– *pipe of a particular stop*

17-35 los tubos de órgano *m* (los tubos
acústicos)
– *organ pipes (pipes)*
17-22 el tubo de lengüeta *f* de metal
m, un trombón de varas *f*
– *metal reed pipe (set of pipes: reed*
stop), a posaune stop
17 el pie (la punta)
– *boot*
18 la garganta
– *shallot*
19 la lengüeta
– *tongue*
20 la cabeza (el núcleo) de plomo *m*
– *block*
21 el alambre afinador
– *tuning wire (tuning crook)*
22 el pabellón
– *tube*
23-30 el tubo abierto labial de metal
m, un salicional
– *open metal flue pipe, a salicional*
23 el pie
– *foot*
24 el paso del aire
– *flue pipe windway (flue pipe duct)*
25 la boca
– *mouth (cutup)*
26 el labio inferior
– *lower lip*

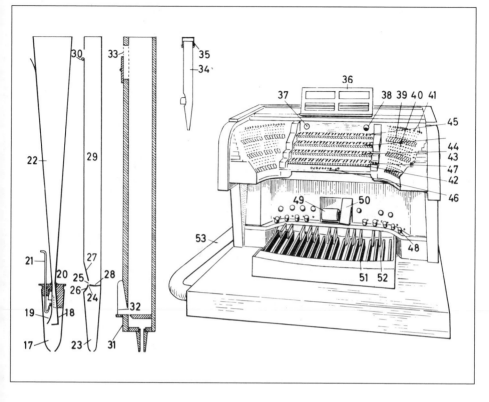

27 el labio superior
 – *upper lip*
28 el obturador
 – *languid*
29 el cuerpo (el cañón) del tubo
 – *body of the pipe (pipe)*
30 la entalla, un dispositivo para afinar
 – *tuning flap (tuning tongue), a tuning device*
31-33 el tubo labial abierto de madera f, un principal
 – *open wooden flue pipe (open wood), principal (diapason)*
31 la cápsula (el secreto)
 – *cap*
32 el oído
 – *ear*
33 la entella de afinar, con corredera f
 – *tuning hole (tuning slot), with slide*
34 el tubo labial tapado
 – *stopped flue pipe*
35 el sombrero metálico (el casquete metálico)
 – *stopper*
36-52 la consola de un órgano de transmisión f eléctrica
 – *organ console (console) of an electric action organ*
36 el atril
 – *music rest (music stand)*

37 el indicador de posición f de los rodillos
 – *crescendo roller indicator*
38 el voltímetro
 – *voltmeter*
39 la tecla de registro m
 – *stop tab (rocker)*
40 la tecla para juegos m libres
 – *free combination stud (free combination knob)*
41 el anulador de los juegos de lengüetería f, acoplamientos m, etc.
 – *cancel buttons for reeds, couplers etc.*
42 el manual I, para el positivo dorsal (el órgano de coro m)
 – *manual I, for the Rückpositiv (choir organ)*
43 el manual II, para la caja principal
 – *manual II, for the Hauptwerk (great organ)*
44 el manual III, para la caja superior
 – *manual III, for the Oberwerk (swell organ)*
45 el manual IV, para el solo de órgano m
 – *manual IV, for the Schwellwerk (solo organ)*

46 los botones pulsadores y los botones de combinación f, para el registro manual, las combinaciones libres o fijas y combinaciones f mixtas
 – *thumb pistons controlling the manual stops (free or fixed combinations) and buttons for setting the combinations*
47 los interruptores de aire m y de corriente f
 – *switches for current to blower and action*
48 el pistón a pedal m, para el acoplamiento
 – *toe piston, for the coupler*
49 el rodillo de crescendo m
 – *crescendo roller (general crescendo roller)*
50 el pedal de expresión f
 – *balanced swell pedal*
51 el pedal de notas f naturales
 – *pedal key [natural]*
52 el pedal de notas f alteradas
 – *pedal key [sharp or flat]*
53 el cable
 – *cable (transmission cable)*

1-61 seres *m* **de fábula** *f* (animales *m* fabulosos), animales *m* y figuras *f* mitológicas
– *fabulous creatures (fabulous animals), mythical creatures*
1 el dragón
– *dragon*
2 el cuerpo de serpiente *f*
– *serpent's body*
3 la garra
– *claws (claw)*
4 el ala *f* de murciélago *m*
– *bat's wing*
5 la boca de lengua *f* bífida
– *fork-tongued mouth*
6 la lengua bífida
– *forked tongue*
7 el unicornio (el monoceronte) [símbolo *m* de la virginidad]
– *unicorn [symbol of virginity]*
8 el cuerno retorcido en espiral *f*
– *spirally twisted horn*
9 el ave fénix
– *Phoenix*
10 las llamas o cenizas *f* de la resurrección
– *flames or ashes of resurrection*
11 el grifo
– *griffin (griffon, gryphon)*
12 la cabeza de águila *f*
– *eagle's head*
13 la garra de grifo *m*
– *griffin's claws*
14 el cuerpo de león *m*
– *lion's body*
15 el ala *f*
– *wing*
16 la quimera, un monstruo
– *chimera (chimaera), a monster*
17 la cabeza de león *m*
– *lion's head*
18 la cabeza de cabra *f*
– *goat's head*
19 el cuerpo de dragón *m* [y la cola de culebra *f*]
– *dragon's body*
20 la esfinge, una figura simbólica
– *sphinx, a symbolic figure*
21 la cabeza humana
– *human head*
22 el cuerpo de león *m*
– *lion's body*
23 la sirena, la sirena de cola *f* de pez *m* (la ondina, la náyade, la ninfa); *anál.*: la nereida, la oceánida (divinidades *f* marinas; diosas *f* del mar); *varón*: el tritón
– *mermaid (nix, nixie, water nixie, sea maid, sea maiden, naiad, water nymph, water elf, ocean nymph, sea nymph, river nymph); sim.: Nereids, Oceanids (sea divinities, sea deities, sea goddesses); male: nix (merman, seaman)*

24 el cuerpo de mujer *f*
– *woman's trunk*
25 la cola de pez *m* (la cola de delfín *m*)
– *fish's tail (dolphin's tail)*
26 Pegaso (el corcel de los poetas, el corcel de las musas, el caballo alado)
– *Pegasus (favourite, Am. favorite, steed of the Muses, winged horse); sim.: hippogryph*
27 el cuerpo de caballo *m*
– *horse's body*
28 las alas
– *wings*
29 el cancerbero (el perro del infierno)
– *Cerberus (hellhound)*
30 el cuerpo de perro *m* con tres cabezas *f*
– *three-headed dog's body*
31 la cola de serpiente *f*
– *serpent's tail*
32 la hidra de Lerna
– *Lernaean (Lernean) Hydra*
33 el cuerpo de serpiente *f* con nueve cabezas *f*
– *nine-headed serpent's body*
34 el basilisco
– *basilisk (cockatrice) [in English legend usually with two legs]*
35 la cabeza de gallo *m*
– *cock's head*
36 el cuerpo de dragón *m*
– *dragon's body*
37 el titán, un gigante
– *giant (titan)*
38 la roca
– *rock*
39 el pie de serpiente *f*
– *serpent's foot*
40 el tritón, una divinidad del mar
– *triton, a merman (demigod of the sea)*
41 el cuerno de concha *f*
– *conch shell trumpet*
42 el pie de caballo *m*
– *horse's hoof*
43 la cola de pez *m*
– *fish's tail*
44 el hipocampo (el caballo marino, el caballo de Neptuno)
– *hippocampus*
45 el tronco de caballo *m*
– *horse's trunk*
46 la cola de pez *m*
– *fish's tail*
47 el toro marino, un monstruo marino
– *sea ox, a sea monster*
48 el cuerpo de toro *m*
– *monster's body*
49 la cola de pez *m*
– *fish's tail*

50 el dragón de las siete cabezas de la revelación (la bestia del Apocalipsis)
– *seven-headed dragon of St. John's Revelation (Revelations, Apocalypse)*
51 el ala *f*
– *wing*
52 el centauro, un ser mitad *f* hombre *m* y mitad *f* caballo *m* (el hipocentauro)
– *centaur (hippocentaur), half man and half beast*
53 el torso de hombre *m* con arco *m* y flecha *f*
– *man's body with bow and arrow*
54 el cuerpo de caballo *m*
– *horse's body*
55 la arpía, un espíritu del aire (un espíritu de la tempestad)
– *harpy, a winged monster*
56 la cabeza de mujer *f*
– *woman's head*
57 el cuerpo de ave *f*
– *bird's body*
58 la sirena, mitad *f* mujer *f* y mitad *f* ave *f*, una divinidad infernal
– *siren, a daemon*
59 el cuerpo de mujer *f*
– *woman's body*
60 el ala *f*
– *wing*
61 la garra de ave *f*
– *bird's claw*

1-40 hallazgos *m* prehistóricos
– *prehistoric finds*
1-9 el período paleolítico y el período mesolítico
– *Old Stone Age (Palaeolithic, Paleolithic, period) and Mesolithic period*
1 el hacha *f* de sílex *m*, de pedernal *m*
– *hand axe (Am. ax) (fist hatchet), a stone tool*
2 la punta de flecha *f* arrojadiza, de hueso *m*
– *head of throwing spear, made of bone*
3 el arpón, de hueso *m*
– *bone harpoon*
4 la punta
– *head*
5 el dardo arrojadizo, de la cornamenta del reno
– *harpoon thrower, made of reindeer antler*
6 el guijarro pintado
– *painted pebble*
7 la cabeza de caballo *m* salvaje, una talla
– *head of a wild horse, a carving*
8 el ídolo de la Edad de Piedra, una estatuilla de marfil *m*
– *Stone Age idol, an ivory statuette*
9 el bisonte, una pintura rupestre [pintura *f* de las cavernas]
– *bison, a cave painting (rock painting) [cave art, cave painting]*
10-20 el período neolítico
– *New Stone Age (Neolithic period)*
10 el ánfora *f* [cerámica *f* acordelada, cerámica *f* de cordel *m*]
– *amphora [corded ware]*
11 la olla abombada [civilización *f* megalítica]
– *bowl [menhir group]*
12 la botella de cuello *m* [cultura *f* de los vasos de embudo *m*]
– *collared flask [Funnel-Beaker culture]*
13 la vasija adornada con espirales *f* [cerámica de cintas *f*]
– *vessel with spiral pattern [spiral design pottery]*
14 el vaso campaniforme [cultura *f* de los vasos campaniformes]
– *bell beaker [bell beaker culture]*
15 el palafito, una vivienda lacustre
– *pile dwelling (lake dwelling, lacustrine dwelling)*
16 el dolmen, una tumba megalítica; *otras clases:* el pasillo mortuorio, la galería mortuoria; *cubierto de tierra f, guijas f, piedras f:* el túmulo
– *dolmen (cromlech), a megalithic tomb (coll.: giant's tomb); other kinds: passage grave, gallery grave (long cist); when covered with earth: tumulus (barrow, mound)*

17 el cofre sepulcral de piedra *f* con inhumación *f* en posición *f* encogida
– *stone cist, a contracted burial*
18 el menhir (*anál.:* el Hinkelstein alemán, un monolito)
– *menhir (standing stone), a monolith*
19 el hacha *f* en forma *f* de barco *m*, una hacha de combate *m* de piedra *f*
– *boat axe (Am. ax), a stone battle axe*
20 la figurita humana de terracota *f* (un ídolo)
– *clay figurine, an idol*
21-40 la Edad de Bronce *m* y **la Edad de Hierro** *m; épocas:* el período de Hallstatt, el período de La Tène
– *Bronze Age and Iron Age; epochs: Hallstatt period, La Tène period*
21 la punta de lanza *f* de bronce *m*
– *bronze spear head*
22 el puñal de bronce *m* con empuñadura *f*
– *hafted bronze dagger*
23 el hacha *f* de cubo *m*, una hacha de bronce *m* con el mango sujetado por medio de arandelas *f*
– *socketed axe (Am. ax), a bronze axe with haft fastened to rings*
24 el disco (el broche) del cinturón
– *girdle clasp*
25 la gargantilla
– *necklace (lunula)*
26 el collar de oro *m*
– *gold neck ring*
27 la fíbula de arco *m* de violín *m*, una fíbula (imperdible *m*)
– *violin-bow fibula (safety pin)*
28 la fíbula serpentiforme; *otras clases:* la fíbula de barca *f;* la fíbula de ballesta *f*
– *serpentine fibula; other kinds: boat fibula, arc fibula*
29 la aguja de cabeza *f* esférica
– *bulb-head pin, a bronze pin*
30 la fíbula de doble espiral *f; anál.:* la fíbula de discos *m*
– *two-piece spiral fibula; sim.: disc (disk) fibula*
31 el cuchillo de bronce *m* con mango *m*
– *hafted bronze knife*
32 la llave de hierro *m*
– *iron key*
33 la reja de arado *m*
– *ploughshare (Am. plowshare)*
34 la sítula de chapa *f* de bronce *m*, una ofrenda funeraria
– *sheet-bronze situla, a funerary vessel*

35 el cántaro de asa *f* [cerámica *f* de incisiones *f* de muescas *f*]
– *pitcher [chip-carved pottery]*
36 el carro para el culto en miniatura *f* (carro *m* para el culto)
– *miniature ritual cart (miniature ritual chariot)*
37 la moneda celta de plata *f*
– *Celtic silver coin*
38 la urna en forma *f* de cara *f*, una urna cineraria; *otras formas:* la urna en forma *f* de casa *f*; la urna abollonada
– *face urn, a cinerary urn; other kinds: domestic urn, embossed urn*
39 la tumba-urna en una cámara hecha con piedras *f*
– *urn grave in stone chamber*
40 la urna de cuello *m* cilíndrico
– *urn with cylindrical neck*

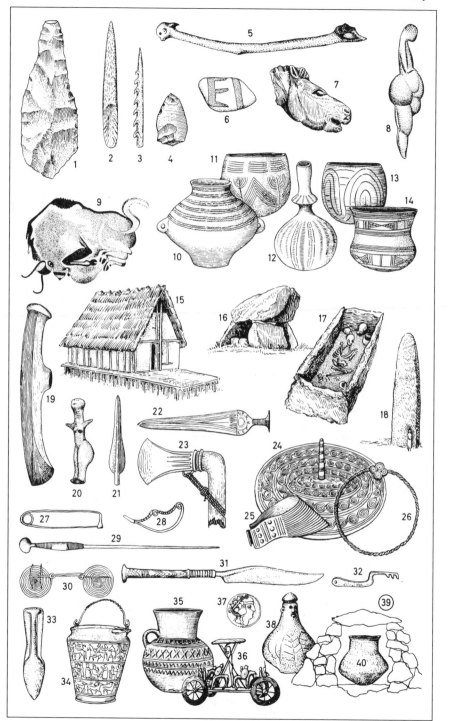

1 **el castillo** (el alcázar, la fortaleza)
– *knight's castle (castle)*
2 el patio del castillo
– *inner ward (inner bailey)*
3 el pozo
– *draw well*
4 la torre del homenaje (la torre principal)
– *keep (donjon)*
5 las mazmorras
– *dungeon*
6 la galería de almenas *f*
– *battlements (crenellation)*
7 la almena
– *merlon*
8 la plataforma de defensa *f*
– *tower platform*
9 el vigía
– *watchman*
10 los aposentos de las damas
– *ladies' apartments (bowers)*
11 la buharda (la lumbrera)
– *dormer window (dormer)*
12 la logia (el balcón)
– *balcony*
13 el almacén (la despensa)
– *storehouse (magazine)*
14 la torre de ángulo *m*
– *angle tower*
15 la muralla
– *curtain wall (curtains, enclosure wall)*
16 el bastión
– *bastion*
17 la torre del cuerpo de guardia *f*
– *angle tower*
18 la barbacana (la tronera, la saetera)
– *crenel (embrasure)*
19 la cortina
– *inner wall*
20 el adarve (el camino de ronda *f*)
– *battlemented parapet*
21 el parapeto
– *parapet (breastwork)*
22 la torre de entrada *f*
– *gatehouse*
23 el matacán [una abertura para dejar caer piedras *f*, pez *f*, aceite *m* y agua *f* hirviendo sobre los asaltantes]
– *machicolation (machicoulis)*
24 el rastrillo
– *portcullis*
25 el puente levadizo
– *drawbridge*
26 el contrafuerte
– *buttress*
27 las dependencias del servicio del castillo
– *offices and service rooms*
28 la garita de vigía *f*
– *turret*
29 la capilla del castillo
– *chapel*
30 la gran sala
– *great hall*
31 el palenque (la liza, la esplanada del castillo) [el campo de batalla *f* en los torneos]
– *outer ward (outer bailey)*

32 la barbacana
– *castle gate*
33 el foso de entrada *f*
– *moat (ditch)*
34 el camino de acceso *m*
– *approach*
35 la atalaya (la torre de vigía *f*)
– *watchtower (turret)*
36 la empalizada (la estacada)
– *palisade (pallisade, palisading)*
37 el foso
– *moat (ditch, fosse)*
38-65 **la armadura del caballero**
– *knight's armour* (Am. *armor*)
38 el arnés (la armadura)
– *suit of armour* (Am. *armor*)
39-42 el yelmo (la celada)
– *helmet*
39 la cimera (la campana)
– *skull*
40 la visera (la ventana)
– *visor (vizor)*
41 la babera
– *beaver*
42 la gola
– *throat piece*
43 la gorguera
– *gorget*
44 la espaldera
– *épaulière*
45 la hombrera
– *pallette (pauldron, besageur)*
46 el peto
– *breastplate (cuirass)*
47 el guardabrazo
– *brassard (rear brace and vambrace)*
48 el codal
– *cubitière (coudière, couter)*
49 la escarcela (el faldar)
– *tasse (tasset)*
50 el guantelete (la manopla)
– *gauntlet*
51 la cota de mallas *f*
– *habergeon (haubergeon)*
52 el quijote
– *cuisse (cuish, cuissard, cuissart)*
53 la rodillera
– *knee cap (knee piece, genouillère, poleyn)*
54 la greba
– *jambeau (greave)*
55 el escarpe
– *solleret (sabaton, sabbaton)*
56 la tarja (el escudo largo)
– *pavis (pavise, pavais)*
57 la rodela (el escudo redondo)
– *buckler (round shield)*
58 la bloca
– *boss (umbo)*
59 el capiello de fierro *m*
– *iron hat*
60 el morrión
– *morion*
61 la barbuta
– *light casque*
62 tipos *m* de cotas *f* de malla *f* (de loriga *f*)
– *types of mail and armour* (Am. *armor*)

63 la malla de anillos *m* (la loriga de anillos *m*)
– *mail (chain mail, chain armour,* Am. *armor)*
64 la cota de escamas *f* (una malla clavada)
– *scale armour* (Am. *armor*)
65 la cota de placas *f* (una malla clavada)
– *plate armour* (Am. *armor*)
66 **la investidura de caballero** *m*
– *accolade (dubbing, knighting)*
67 el señor feudal
– *liege lord, a knight*
68 el caballero novel
– *esquire*
69 el copero
– *cup bearer*
70 el trovador (el ministril, el juglar)
– *minstrel (minnesinger, troubadour)*
71 **el torneo (la justa)**
– *tournament (tourney, joust, just, tilt)*
72 el cruzado
– *crusader*
73 el templario
– *Knight Templar*
74 la gualdrapa
– *caparison (trappings)*
75 el heraldo (el rey de armas *f*)
– *herald (marshal at tournament)*
76 los pertrechos (los arneses, las armas) para el torneo
– *tilting armour* (Am. *armor*)
77 el yelmo de torneo *m* (de parada *f*)
– *tilting helmet (jousting helmet)*
78 el penacho (el airón)
– *panache (plume of feathers)*
79 la adarga de torneo *m* (de parada *f*)
– *tilting target (tilting shield)*
80 el ristre
– *lance rest*
81 la lanza de torneo *m*
– *tilting lance (lance)*
82 el guardamano de la lanza
– *vamplate*
83-88 **la armadura del caballo (las bardas)**
– *horse armour* (Am. *armor*)
83 la capizana
– *neck guard (neck piece)*
84 la testera
– *chamfron (chaffron, chafron, chamfrain, chanfron)*
85 la barda del pecho del caballo
– *poitrel*
86 la flanqueza
– *flanchard (flancard)*
87 la silla de torneo *m*
– *tournament saddle*
88 la barda de la grupa
– *rump piece (quarter piece)*

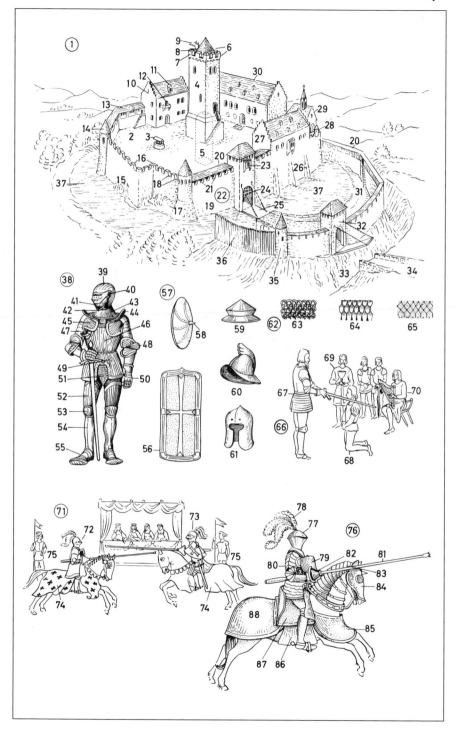

1-30 la iglesia (el templo) **protes-tante (iglesia** *f* **evangélica)**
- *Protestant church*
1 el presbiterio
- *chancel*
2 el facistol con paramento *m*
- *lectern*
3 la alfombra del altar
- *altar carpet*
4 el altar (la mesa eucarística)
- *altar (communion table, Lord's table, holy table)*
5 las gradas del altar
- *altar steps*
6 el paño del altar
- *altar cloth*
7 el cirio del altar (*Mé.:* la veladora)
- *altar candle*
8 la píxide (la caja del pan ácimo)
- *pyx (pix)*
9 la patena
- *paten (patin, patine)*
10 el cáliz
- *chalice (communion cup)*
11 la Biblia (las Sagradas Escrituras)
- *Bible (Holy Bible, Scriptures, Holy Scripture)*
12 el crucifijo del altar
- *altar crucifix*
13 el cuadro del altar
- *altarpiece*
14 la vidriera
- *church window*
15 la pintura de vidrio *m* (la pintura sobre cristal *m*)
- *stained glass*
16 el candelabro de pared *f*
- *wall candelabrum*
17 la puerta de la sacristía
- *vestry door (sacristy door)*
18 la escalera del púlpito
- *pulpit steps*
19 el púlpito
- *pulpit*
20 el antipendio
- *antependium*
21 el sombrero del púlpito (el tor-navoz)
- *canopy, a soundboard (sounding board)*
22 el predicador (el pastor) con las vestiduras sacerdotales (con el sobrepelliz)
- *preacher (pastor, vicar, clergyman, rector) in his robes (vestments, canonicals)*
23 la balaustrada del púlpito
- *pulpit balustrade*
24 el tablón indicador de los números de los himnos
- *hymn board showing hymn numbers*
25 la tribuna del templo (la galería)
- *gallery*

26 el sacristán
- *verger (sexton, sacristan)*
27 el pasillo central
- *aisle*
28 el banco de la iglesia; *en conjunto:* la sillería
- *pew;* collectively: *pews (seating)*
29 el fiel; *en conjunto:* la congre-gación de los fieles
- *churchgoer (worshipper);* collec-tively: *congregation*
30 el himnario (el libro de himnos *m*)
- *hymn book*
31-62 la iglesia (el templo) **católica(-o)**
- *Roman Catholic church*
31 las gradas del altar
- *altar steps*
32 el presbiterio (el coro)
- *presbytery (choir, chancel, sacrari-um, sanctuary)*
33 el altar (el ara)
- *altar*
34 los cirios del altar
- *altar candles*
35 el crucifijo del altar
- *altar cross*
36 el paño del altar
- *altar cloth*
37 el ambón (atril *m* para la predi-cación)
- *lectern*
38 el misal
- *missal (mass book)*
39 el sacerdote (el cura)
- *priest*
40 el acólito (el monaguillo; *S. Dgo.:* el clérigo)
- *server*
41 los asientos para los sacerdotes [*asientos m* unidos: sillería *f; sepa-rados, móviles:* no tiene un nom-bre particular]
- *sedilia*
42 el tabernáculo
- *tabernacle*
43 el soporte del tabernáculo
- *stele (stela)*
44 el cirio pascual (*Chile y Perú:* el velón)
- *paschal candle (Easter candle)*
45 el candelero del cirio pascual
- *paschal candlestick (Easter can-dlestick)*
46 la campanilla de la sacristía
- *sanctus bell*
47 la cruz de las procesiones
- *processional cross*
48 la decoración del altar
- *altar decoration (foliage, flower arrangement)*
49 la lámpara del Santísimo (la lám-para del sagrario) [una lámpara de aceite *m* siempre encendida]
- *sanctuary lamp*

50 el cuadro del altar, un cuadro de Cristo
- *altarpiece, a picture of Christ*
51 la imagen de la Virgen
- *Madonna (statue of the Virgin Mary)*
52 la mesa de los cirios votivos
- *pricket*
53 los cirios votivos
- *votive candles*
54 el vía crucis (la estación del vía crucis)
- *station of the Cross*
55 el cepillo de las limosnas (*Chile, Guat., Hond.:* la alcancía)
- *offertory box*
56 la estantería de las publicaciones
- *literature stand*
57 las publicaciones
- *literature (pamphlets, tracts)*
58 el sacristán (*pop.:* rapavelas *m*)
- *verger (sexton, sacristan)*
59 la limosnera (la bolsa de las limosnas)
- *offertory bag*
60 la limosna
- *offering*
61 el fiel (el creyente)
- *Christian (man praying)*
62 el devocionario
- *prayer book*

1 **la iglesia**
– *church*
2 el campanario (*anál.*: la espadaña,
la torre de la iglesia)
– *steeple*
3 el gallo de la veleta
– *weathercock*
4 la veleta (la giralda, la giraldilla)
– *weather vane (wind vane)*
5 el botón del chapitel
– *spire ball*
6 la aguja (el chapitel) de la torre
– *church spire (spire)*
7 el reloj de la torre
– *church clock (tower clock)*
8 la lumbrera del campanario
– *belfry window*
9 la campana eléctrica
– *electrically operated bell*
10 la cruz del caballete (de la cumbrera)
– *ridge cross*
11 el tejado de la iglesia
– *church roof*
12 la capilla conmemorativa (votiva)
– *memorial chapel*
13 la sacristía, un edificio anejo
– *vestry (sacristy), an annexe
(annex)*
14 la placa (la lápida) conmemorativa, el epitafio
– *memorial tablet (memorial plate,
wall memorial, wall stone)*
15 la entrada lateral
– *side entrance*
16 el portal (la puerta) de la iglesia
– *church door (main door, portal)*
17 el feligrés
– *churchgoer*
18 el muro del cementerio (del camposanto)
– *graveyard wall (churchyard wall)*
19 la puerta del cementerio (del
camposanto)
– *graveyard gate (churchyard gate,
lichgate, lychgate)*
20 la casa del párroco
– *vicarage (parsonage, rectory)*
21-41 el cementerio (camposanto *m*)
– *graveyard (churchyard, God's
acre,* Am. *burying ground)*
21 la capilla mortuoria (el depósito
de cadáveres *m*)
– *mortuary*
22 el sepulturero (el enterrador;
Amér. Central y Perú: el pan-
teonero)
– *grave digger*
23 la tumba (el sepulcro)
– *grave (tomb)*
24 el montículo de la tumba
– *grave mound*
25 la cruz de la tumba
– *cross*

26 la lápida sepulcral
– *gravestone (headstone, tombstone)*
27 la tumba familiar
– *family grave (family tomb)*
28 la capilla del cementerio
– *graveyard chapel*
29 la tumba de niño *m*
– *child's grave*
30 la tumba de urna *f*
– *urn grave*
31 la urna
– *urn*
32 la tumba de soldado *m*
– *soldier's grave*
33-41 el entierro (la inhumación, el
sepelio; *Chile:* la sepultación)
– *funeral (burial)*
33 el acompañamiento (las personas
que asisten al entierro)
– *mourners*
34 la fosa (la sepultura)
– *grave*
35 el ataúd (el féretro)
– *coffin (Am. casket)*
36 la pala
– *spade*
37 el clérigo
– *clergyman*
38 los dolientes
– *the bereaved*
39 el velo de viuda *f*, un velo de luto *m*
– *widow's veil, a mourning veil*
40 los empleados de pompas *f* fúne-
bres
– *pallbearers*
41 las parihuelas (las andas)
– *bier*
42-50 la procesión (la procesión religiosa)
– *procession (religious procession)*
42 la cruz de la procesión, un guión
– *processional crucifix*
43 el crucero (el cruciferario)
– *cross bearer (crucifer)*
44 el estandarte de la procesión, un
estandarte de la iglesia
– *processional banner, a church
banner*
45 el acólito (el monaguillo; *S. Dgo.:*
el clérigo)
– *acolyte*
46 el portador del palio
– *canopy bearer*
47 el sacerdote
– *priest*
48 la custodia con el Santísimo
– *monstrance with the Blessed
Sacrament (consecrated Host)*
49 el palio (*si es de tela f* de seda *f*:
baldaquín *m*, baldaquino *m*)
– *canopy (baldachin, baldaquin)*
50 las monjas (las religiosas)
– *nuns*

51 los participantes en la procesión
– *participants in the procession*
52-58 el monasterio (el convento)
– *monastery*
52 el claustro
– *cloister*
53 el patio conventual
– *monastery garden*
54 el monje (el fraile), un benedictino
– *monk, a Benedictine monk*
55 la cogulla
– *habit (monk's habit)*
56 la capilla (la capucha)
– *cowl (hood)*
57 la tonsura
– *tonsure*
58 el breviario
– *breviary*
59 **la catacumba,** un cementerio subterráneo de los primeros tiempos
del cristianismo
– *catacomb, an early Christian
underground burial place*
60 el nicho sepulcral (el arcosolio)
– *niche (tomb recess, arcosolium)*
61 la losa (la lápida)
– *stone slab*

1 el bautizo cristiano (*el sacramento:* el bautismo)
– *Christian baptism (christening)*
2 el baptisterio
– *baptistery (baptistry)*
3 el clérigo (el pastor) protestante (clérigo *m* evangélico)
– *Protestant clergyman*
4 la ropa talar (el sobrepelliz)
– *robes (vestments, canonicals)*
5 el alzacuello
– *bands*
6 el cuello
– *collar*
7 el bautizado
– *child to be baptized (christened)*
8 la ropa de cristianar
– *christening robe (christening dress)*
9 el velo de cristianar
– *christening shawl*
10 la pila bautismal
– *font*
11 la taza de la pila bautismal
– *font basin*
12 el agua *f* bautismal (el agua *f* bendita)
– *baptismal water*
13 los padrinos
– *godparents*
14 el matrimonio canónico (la boda religiosa)
– *church wedding (wedding ceremony, marriage ceremony)*
15 u. 16 los novios (los contrayentes)
– *bridal couple*
15 la novia
– *bride*
16 el novio
– *bridegroom (groom)*
17 el anillo de boda *f* (el anillo, la alianza; *Col.:* la argolla)
– *ring (wedding ring)*
18 el ramo de novia *f* (*Cuba y P. Rico:* la pucha)
– *bride's bouquet (bridal bouquet)*
19 la corona de novia *f* [*en España:* de azahar *m*]
– *bridal wreath*
20 el velo de novia *f*
– *veil (bridal veil)*
21 el ramito de mirto *m* [*en España:* un clavel o una gardenia]
– *[myrtle] buttonhole*
22 el clérigo (el sacerdote, el cura)
– *clergyman*
23 los testigos
– *witnesses [to the marriage]*
24 la dama de honor *m*
– *bridesmaid*
25 el reclinatorio
– *kneeler*
26 la comunión
– *Holy Communion*

27 los comulgantes
– *communicants*
28 la hostia (la sagrada forma, el pan eucarístico)
– *Host (wafer)*
29 el cáliz de la comunión (el cáliz del vino eucarístico)
– *communion cup*
30 el rosario
– *rosary*
31 la cuenta de los misterios (la cuenta de los padrenuestros, el diez; *Col.:* el pasador)
– *paternoster*
32 la avemaría (la cuenta del avemaría; *cada diez cuentas:* un misterio)
– *Ave Maria;* set of 10: *decade*
33 el crucifijo
– *crucifix*
34-54 objetos *m* litúrgicos (objetos *m* sagrados, objetos *m* de culto *m*)
– *liturgical vessels (ecclesiastical vessels)*
34 la custodia (el ostensorio)
– *monstrance*
35 la hostia (la hostia grande, el Santísimo)
– *Host (consecrated Host, Blessed Sacrament)*
36 el viril
– *lunula (lunule)*
37 la corona de rayos *m*
– *rays*
38 el incensario (el turíbulo) para incensaciones *f* litúrgicas
– *censer (thurible), for offering incense (for incensing)*
39 la cadenilla del incensario
– *thurible chain*
40 la tapa del braserillo del incensario
– *thurible cover*
41 el braserillo del incensario
– *thurible bowl*
42 la naveta del incienso
– *incense boat*
43 la cucharilla para coger el incienso
– *incense spoon*
44 las vinajeras
– *cruet set*
45 la vinajera del agua
– *water cruet*
46 la vinajera del vino
– *wine cruet*
47 el acetre
– *holy water basin*
48 el copón con las hostias pequeñas para la comunión de los fieles
– *ciborium containing the sacred wafers*
49 el cáliz
– *chalice*

50 la copa para la comunión de los fieles
– *dish for communion wafers*
51 la patena
– *paten (patin, patine)*
52 la campanilla del altar (la campanilla del Sanctus)
– *altar bells*
53 la píxide
– *pyx (pix)*
54 el hisopo
– *aspergillum*
55-72 formas *f* de cruces *f* cristianas
– *forms of Christian crosses*
55 la cruz latina (la cruz de la Pasión)
– *Latin cross (cross of the Passion)*
56 la cruz griega
– *Greek cross*
57 la cruz rusa
– *Russian cross*
58 la cruz de San Pedro
– *St. Peter's cross*
59 la cruz de San Antonio (la cruz de Tau; la cruz en T)
– *St. Anthony's cross (tau cross)*
60 la cruz de San Andrés (la cruz decusada, la cruz de Borgoña)
– *St. Andrew's cross (saltire cross)*
61 la cruz bifurcada (la cruz de infamia, la cruz de los ladrones del Calvario)
– *Y-cross*
62 la cruz de Lorena
– *cross of Lorraine*
63 la cruz egipcia (la cruz de asa *f*)
– *ansate cross*
64 la cruz patriarcal
– *patriarchal cross*
65 la cruz cardenalicia
– *cardinal's cross*
66 la cruz papal
– *papal cross*
67 la cruz de Constantino, un monograma de Cristo
– *Constantinian cross, a monogram of Christ (CHR)*
68 la cruz recrucetada
– *crosslet*
69 la cruz anclada
– *cross moline*
70 la cruz potenzada
– *cross of Jerusalem*
71 la cruz trebolada (la cruz de San Lázaro, la cruz de Brabante)
– *cross botonnée (cross treflée)*
72 la cruz de Jerusalén (la cruz del Santo Sepulcro)
– *fivefold cross (quintuple cross)*
73 la cruz celta
– *Celtic cross*

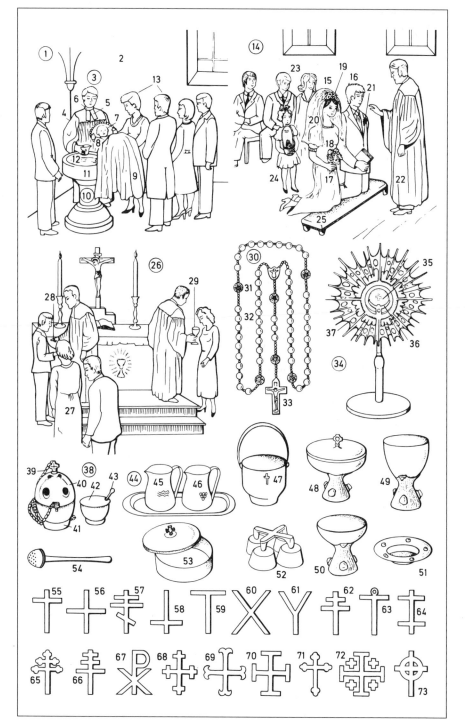

1-18 arte *m* **egipcio**
– *Egyptian art*
1 la pirámide, una pirámide cuadrangular, una tumba real
– *pyramid, a royal tomb*
2 la cámara del rey
– *king's chamber*
3 la cámara de la reina
– *queen's chamber*
4 el canal de aireación *f*
– *air passage*
5 la cámara mortuoria
– *coffin chamber*
6 el complejo funerario (la
pirámide con sus templos *m*)
– *pyramid site*
7 el templo funerario
– *funerary temple*
8 el templo del valle
– *valley temple*
9 el pilono (la portada)
– *pylon, a monumental gateway*
10 los obeliscos
– *obelisks*
11 la esfinge egipcia
– *Egyptian sphinx*
12 el disco solar alado
– *winged sun disc (sun disk)*
13 la columna lotiforme
– *lotus column*
14 el capitel en capullo *m* (el capitel
cerrado)
– *knob-leaf capital (bud-shaped
capital)*
15 la columna papiriforme
– *papyrus column*
16 el capitel campaniforme (el capitel abierto)
– *bell-shaped capital*
17 la columna de capitel *m* palmiforme
– *palm column*
18 el pilar hathórico
– *ornamented column*
19 *u*. 20 arte *m* **babilónico**
– *Babylonian art*
19 el friso babilónico
– *Babylonian frieze*
20 el bajorrelieve de ladrillo *m* vidriado
– *glazed relief tile*
21-28 arte *m* **de los persas** [aque-
ménides]
– *art of the Persians*
21 la torre sepulcral (la torre mortuoria)
– *tower tomb*
22 la pirámide escalonada
– *stepped pyramid*
23 la columna persa aqueménide
– *double bull column*
24 el follaje invertido
– *projecting leaves*
25 el capitel palmiforme
– *palm capital*

26 la voluta
– *volute (scroll)*
27 el fuste estriado
– *shaft*
28 el capitel de toros *m* adosados por
el dorso
– *double bull capital*
29-36 arte *m* **de los asirios**
– *art of the Assyrians*
29 el palacio de Sargón, una planta
de un palacio
– *Sargon's Palace, palace buildings*
30 la muralla de la ciudad
– *city wall*
31 la muralla del palacio
– *castle wall*
32 la torre del templo (el zigurat),
una pirámide escalonada
– *temple tower (ziggurat), a stepped
(terraced) tower*
33 la escalinata
– *outside staircase*
34 la puerta principal
– *main portal*
35 la placa decorativa de la puerta
– *portal relief*
36 la figura de la puerta (un toro
alado)
– *portal figure*
37 arte *m* **de Asia Menor**
– *art of Asia Minor*
38 la tumba excavada en la roca (un
hipogeo)
– *rock tomb*

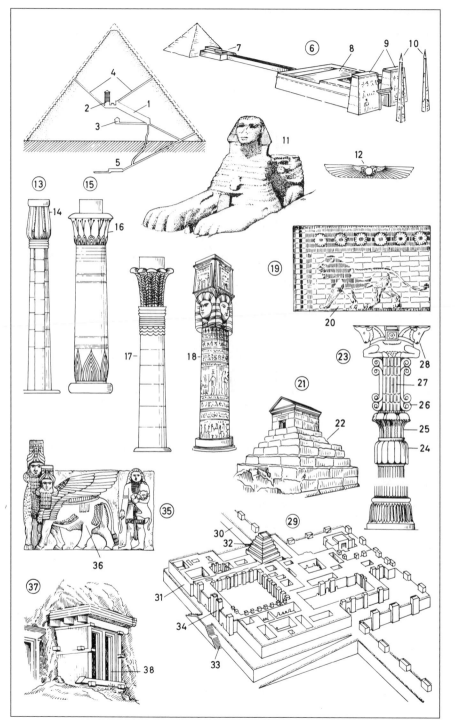

1-48 arte *m* griego
– **Greek art**
1-7 la Acrópolis
– *the Acropolis*
1 el Partenón, un templo dórico
– *the Parthenon, a Doric temple*
2 el peristilo (la galería de columnas *f*)
– *peristyle*
3 el frontón (el frontispicio)
– *pediment*
4 el estereóbato (el basamento)
– *crepidoma (stereobate)*
5 la estatua
– *statue*
6 la muralla del templo
– *temple wall*
7 los propileos
– *propylaea*
8 la columna dórica
– *Doric column*
9 la columna jónica
– *Ionic column*
10 la columna corintia
– *Corinthian column*
11-14 la cornisa
– *cornice*
11 la sima
– *cyma*
12 el geison
– *corona*
13 el mútulo
– *mutule*
14 el dentículo
– *dentils*
15 el triglifo
– *triglyph*
16 la metopa, un adorno del friso
– *metope, a frieze decoration*
17 el sofito (la cara interior del goterón, la régula)
– *regula*
18 el arquitrabe (el epistilo)
– *epistyle (architrave)*
19 la tenia (el cimacio)
– *cyma (cymatium, kymation)*
20-25 el capitel
– *capital*
20 el ábaco
– *abacus*
21 el equino
– *echinus*
22 el collarino
– *hypotrachelium (gorgerin)*
23 la voluta [en el capitel corintio: el caulículo]
– *volute (scroll)*
24 el cojinete
– *volute cushion*
25 la corona de hojas *f*
– *acanthus*
26 el fuste de la columna
– *column shaft*

27 las estrías (la canaladura)
– *flutes (grooves, channels)*
28-31 la basa
– *base*
28 el toro (el bocel)
– *[upper] torus*
29 la escocia (el troquilo)
– *trochilus (concave moulding,* Am. *molding)*
30 el toro (el bocel) inferior
– *[lower] torus*
31 el plinto
– *plinth*
32 el estilóbato
– *stylobate*
33 la estela
– *stele (stela)*
34 la acrótera del frontispicio
– *acroterion (acroterium, acroter)*
35 el hermes (el estípite con busto *m*)
– *herm (herma, hermes)*
36 la cariátide; *masculino:* el atlante
– *caryatid;* male: *Atlas*
37 el vaso griego
– *Greek vase*
38-43 ornamentos *m* griegos
– *Greek ornamentation (Greek decoration, Greek decorative designs)*
38 el cordón de perlas *f*, una cinta ornamental
– *bead-and-dart moulding (*Am. *molding), an ornamental band*
39 la cinta de ondas *f*
– *running dog (Vitruvian scroll)*
40 el adorno de hojas *f*
– *leaf ornament*
41 las palmetas
– *palmette*
42 la tenia (el filete, el listel) de ovas *f* (de ovos *m*, de óvolos *m*)
– *egg and dart (egg and tongue, egg and anchor) cyma*
43 el meandro (la greca)
– *meander*
44 el teatro griego (el anfiteatro griego)
– *Greek theatre (*Am. *theater)*
45 la escena (el edificio de la escena)
– *scene*
46 el proscenio
– *proscenium*
47 la orquesta
– *orchestra*
48 el altar de los sacrificios
– *thymele (altar)*
49-52 arte *m* etrusco
– **Etruscan art**
49 el templo etrusco
– *Etruscan temple*
50 el pórtico (el atrio)
– *portico*
51 la cella (la sala principal)
– *cella*

52 la viguería (las vigas)
– *entablature*
53-60 arte *m* romano
– **Roman art**
53 el acueducto
– *aqueduct*
54 el canal de agua *f*
– *conduit (water channel)*
55 el edificio de planta *f* central
– *centrally-planned building (centralized building)*
56 el pórtico
– *portico*
57 el listel (el filete, la tenia)
– *reglet*
58 la cúpula
– *cupola*
59 el arco de triunfo *m* (el arco triunfal)
– *triumphal arch*
60 el ático
– *attic*
61-71 arte *m* paleocristiano
– **Early Christian art**
61 la basílica
– *basilica*
62 la nave central
– *nave*
63 la nave lateral
– *aisle*
64 el ábside
– *apse*
65 el campanario
– *campanile*
66 el atrio
– *atrium*
67 el pórtico de columnas *f* (la galería porticada)
– *colonnade*
68 la fuente de las abluciones
– *fountain*
69 el altar
– *altar*
70 la claraboya lateral (el claristorio)
– *clerestory (clearstory)*
71 el arco triunfal
– *triumphal arch*
72-75 arte *m* bizantino
– **Byzantine art**
72 *u.* **73** el sistema de cúpulas *f*
– *dome system*
72 la cúpula central (la media esfera, la bóveda semiesférica)
– *main dome*
73 la media cúpula (el cuarto de esfera *f*)
– *semidome*
74 la pechina
– *pendentive*
75 el ojo, una claraboya
– *eye, a lighting aperture*

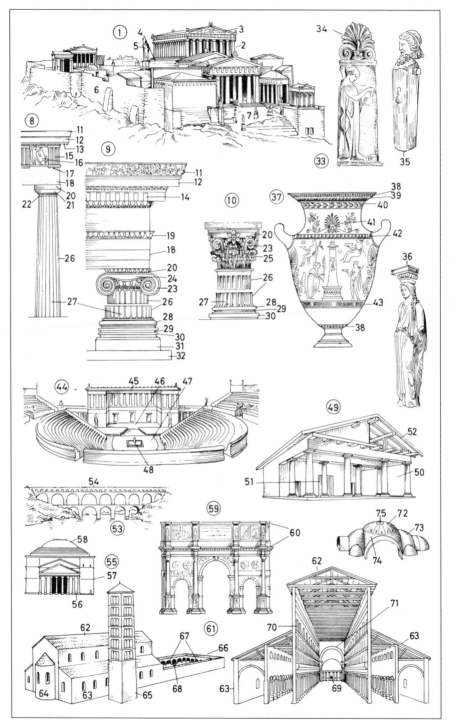

1-21 arte *m* románico
- *Romanesque art*
1-13 la iglesia románica, una catedral
- *Romanesque church, a cathedral*
1 la nave central
- *nave*
2 la nave lateral
- *aisle*
3 el crucero (la nave transversal, el transepto)
- *transept*
4 el coro (el presbiterio)
- *choir (chancel)*
5 el ábside
- *apse*
6 la torre del crucero (el cimborrio)
- *central tower* (Am. *center tower*)
7 el tejado piramidal de la torre (el tejado a cuatro vertientes *f*, a cuatro aguas *f*)
- *pyramidal tower roof*
8 la arcada
- *arcading*
9 el friso de arquillos *m* ciegos (de arquillos *m* lombardos)
- *frieze of round arcading*
10 la arcada ciega (la arcada mural)
- *blind arcade (blind arcading)*
11 la lesena, una banda lombarda
- *lesene, a pilaster strip*
12 el óculo
- *circular window*
13 la portada lateral (la puerta del crucero)
- *side entrance*
14-16 ornamentos *m* románicos
- *Romanesque ornamentation (Romanesque decoration, Romanesque decorative designs)*
14 la moldura escaqueada (el ajedrezado)
- *chequered* (Am. *checkered*) *pattern (chequered design)*
15 el adorno imbricado (el adorno en escamas *f*)
- *imbrication (imbricated design)*
16 el adorno en zigzag *m* (el adorno dentado)
- *chevron design*
17 el sistema románico de bóvedas *f*
- *Romanesque system of vaulting*
18 el arco fajón (el arco perpiaño)
- *transverse arch*
19 el formero
- *barrel vault (tunnel vault)*
20 el pilar
- *pillar*
21 el capitel cúbico (el capitel bloque *m*, el capitel cojín *m*)
- *cushion capital*
22-41 arte *m* gótico
- *Gothic art*

22 la iglesia gótica [fachada *f* occidental], una catedral
- *Gothic church [westwork, west end, west façade], a cathedral*
23 el rosetón
- *rose window*
24 la portada de la iglesia, una puerta abocinada
- *church door (main door, portal), a recessed portal*
25 la arquivolta
- *archivolt*
26 el tímpano
- *tympanum*
27 *u*. 28 el sistema de soportes *m* exteriores
- *Gothic structural system*
27-35 la arquitectura gótica (el sistema de construcción *f* gótico)
- *buttresses*
27 el contrafuerte (el estribo)
- *buttress*
28 el arbotante (el botarel)
- *flying buttress*
29 el pináculo, un remate del contrafuerte
- *pinnacle*
30 la gárgola
- *gargoyle*
31 *u*. 32 la bóveda de crucería *f* (la bóveda ojival, la bóveda de nervios *m*)
- *cross vault (groin vault)*
31 las nervaduras (la crucería, los cruceros, los nervios, las costillas)
- *ribs (cross ribs)*
32 la clave de bóveda *f*
- *boss (pendant)*
33 el triforio (la galería interior de una iglesia por encima de la nave lateral)
- *triforium*
34 el pilar fasciculado (el pilar en haz *m* de baquetones *m*)
- *clustered pier (compound pier)*
35 la columna embebida (la columna entregada)
- *respond (engaged pillar)*
36 el gablete
- *pediment*
37 el florón
- *finial*
38 el gancho
- *crocket*
39 *u*. 40 la tracería
- *tracery*
39 *u*. 41 la ventana de tracería *f*, una ventana lanceolada
- *tracery window, a lancet window*
39 el rosetón cuadrifolio
- *quatrefoil*

40 el rosetón de cinco lóbulos *m* (el pentafolio)
- *cinquefoil*
41 los montantes (los maineles, los parteluces)
- *mullions*
42-54 arte *m* del Renacimiento
- *Renaissance art*
42 la iglesia renacentista
- *Renaissance church*
43 el resalte, una parte saliente del edificio
- *projection, a projecting part of the building*
44 el tambor
- *drum*
45 la linterna
- *lantern*
46 la pilastra (el pilar entregado)
- *pilaster (engaged pillar)*
47 el palacio renacentista
- *Renaissance palace*
48 la cornisa
- *cornice*
49 la ventana con frontón *m* (la ventana de hastial *m*)
- *pedimental window*
50 la ventana con frontón *m* curvo
- *pedimental window [with round gable]*
51 el almohadillado (la obra rústica, una cadena almohadillada)
- *rustication (rustic work)*
52 el listel (el filete, la cinta)
- *string course*
53 el sarcófago (la tumba con figura *f* yacente)
- *sarcophagus*
54 el festón (la guirnalda)
- *festoon (garland)*

1-8 arte *m* **barroco**
- *Baroque art*
1 la iglesia barroca
- *Baroque church*
2 el ojo de buey *m* (la lumbrera, la lucarna, el óculo)
- *bull's eye*
3 la linterna (el lucernario)
- *bulbous cupola*
4 la buharda
- *dormer window (dormer)*
5 el frontón rebajado (el frontón curvo)
- *curved gable*
6 las columnas geminadas
- *twin columns*
7 la tarja (la tarjeta, la cartela, el cartucho, el escusón)
- *cartouche*
8 la voluta
- *scrollwork*
9-13 el arte rococó
- *Rococo art*
9 la pared rococó
- *Rococo wall*
10 la corona, una mediacaña (una moldura cóncava)
- *coving, a hollow moulding (Am. molding)*
11 el marco ornamental
- *framing*
12 la sobrepuerta
- *ornamental moulding (Am. molding)*
13 la rocalla, un ornamento del rococó
- *rocaille, a Rococo ornament*
14 la mesa de estilo *m* Luis XVI
- *table in Louis Seize style (Louis Seize table)*
15 el edificio neoclásico (el edificio de estilo *m* neoclásico), una fachada (una entrada *f*)
- *neoclassical building (building in neoclassical style), a gateway*
16 la mesa de estilo *m* Imperio
- *Empire table (table in the Empire style)*
17 el sofá Biedermeier (el sofá de estilo *m* Biedermeier)
- *Biedermeier sofa (sofa in the Biedermeier style)*
18 el sillón de estilo *m* Art Nouveau
- *Art Nouveau easy chair (easy chair in the Art Nouveau style)*
19-37 los arcos
- *types of arch*
19 el arco (el arco mural)
- *arch*
20 la jamba
- *abutment*
21 la imposta
- *impost*
22 el salmer, una dovela
- *springer, a voussoir (wedge stone)*
23 la clave
- *keystone*

24 la cara frontal de la jamba
- *face*
25 el intradós
- *intrados*
26 el extradós (el trasdós)
- *extrados*
27 el arco de medio punto *m*
- *round arch*
28 el arco rebajado (el arco escarzano)
- *segmental arch (basket handle)*
29 el arco elíptico
- *parabolic arch*
30 el arco de herradura *f* (el arco árabe)
- *horseshoe arch*
31 el arco ojival (el arco apuntado)
- *lancet arch*
32 el arco trebolado
- *trefoil arch*
33 el arco adintelado (el arco a nivel *m*)
- *shouldered arch*
34 el arco convexo (el arco en gola *f*)
- *convex arch*
35 el arco de cortina *f* (el arco festoneado)
- *tented arch*
36 el arco conopial (el arco aquillado)
- *ogee arch (keel arch)*
37 el arco Tudor
- *Tudor arch*
38-50 bóvedas *f*
- *types of vault*
38 la bóveda de cañón *m* (la bóveda de medio cañón *m*)
- *barrel vault (tunnel vault)*
39 la corona
- *crown*
40 el riñón de la bóveda
- *side*
41 la bóveda claustral (la bóveda de rincón *m* de claustro *m*, la bóveda de aljibe, la bóveda esquifada)
- *cloister vault (cloistered vault)*
42 la bóveda de arista *f*
- *groin vault (groined vault)*
43 la bóveda de crucería *f* (la bóveda nervada)
- *rib vault (ribbed vault)*
44 la bóveda estrellada
- *stellar vault*
45 la bóveda reticulada
- *net vault*
46 la bóveda en abanico *m*
- *fan vault*
47 la bóveda en artesa *f*
- *trough vault*
48 el faldón abombado
- *trough*
49 la bóveda de caveto *m* (la bóveda de esgucio *m*)
- *cavetto vault*
50 el caveto (el esgucio)
- *cavetto*

1-6 arte *m* chino
– Chinese art
1 la pagoda (pagoda *f* de varios
pisos *m*), una torre templo *m*
*– pagoda (multi-storey, multistory,
pagoda), a temple tower*
2 el tejado de gradas *f*
– storey (story) roof (roof of storey)
3 el pailu, una puerta de triunfo *m*
*– pailou (pailoo), a memorial arch-
way*
4 el pasaje
– archway
5 el jarrón de porcelana *f*
– porcelain vase
6 la labor de esculpido *m* en laca *f*
– incised lacquered work
7-11 arte *m* japonés
– Japanese art
7 el templo
– temple
8 el campanil (la torre de las cam-
panas)
– bell tower
9 la armazón de soporte *m*
– supporting structure
10 el Bodhisattva, un santo budista
*– bodhisattva (boddhisattva), a
Buddhist saint*
11 el pórtico japonés (el torii)
– torii, a gateway
12-18 arte *m* islámico
– Islamic art
12 la mezquita
– mosque
13 el alminar (el minarete), una torre
de oración *f*
– minaret, a prayer tower
14 el mihrab (el nicho de las ple-
garias)
– mihrab
15 el mimbar (el púlpito)
– minbar (mimbar, pulpit)
16 el mausoleo, una tumba
– mausoleum, a tomb
17 la bóveda de mocárabes *m* (de
mucarnas *f*)
– stalactite vault (stalactitic vault)
18 el capitel árabe (un capitel nazarita)
– Arabian capital
19-28 arte *m* indio
– Indian art
19 el Siva danzante, un dios indio
*– dancing Siva (Shiva), an Indian
god*
20 la estatua de Buda
– statue of Buddha
21 la estupa (la pagoda india), una
construcción en bóveda *f,* un edificio sagrado budista
*– stupa (Indian pagoda), a mound
(dome), a Buddhist shrine*
22 la sombrilla (el quitasol)
– umbrella

23 el vallado de piedra *f*
– stone wall (Am. stone fence)
24 la puerta de entrada *f*
– gate
25 las instalaciones del templo
– temple buildings
26 la sikhara (la torre del templo)
*– shikara (sikar, sikhara, temple
tower)*
27 el interior de la chaitya
– chaitya hall
28 la chaitya, una estupa pequeña
– chaitya, a small stupa

1-43 el estudio (el taller)
- *studio*
1 el ventanal del estudio (una lumbrera, un tragaluz)
- *studio skylight*
2 el pintor, un artista
- *painter, an artist*
3 el caballete de estudio *m*
- *studio easel*
4 el boceto a tiza *f,* con el contorno de la figura
- *chalk sketch, with the composition (rough draft)*
5 el lápiz de tiza *f*
- *crayon (piece of chalk)*
6-19 utensilios *m* (materiales *m*) de pintura *f*
- *painting materials*
6 el pincel plano
- *flat brush*
7 el pincel de pelos *m*
- *camel hair brush*
8 el pincel redondo
- *round brush*
9 el pincel para la primera capa
- *priming brush*
10 la caja de pinturas *f*
- *box of paints (paintbox)*
11 el tubo de pintura *f* al óleo
- *tube of oil paint*
12 el barniz
- *varnish*
13 el aguarrás
- *thinner*
14 el cuchillo paleta *f*
- *palette knife*

15 la espátula para pintar
- *spatula*
16 el carboncillo
- *charcoal pencil (charcoal, piece of charcoal)*
17 el color para pintar al temple (a la aguada)
- *tempera (gouache)*
18 la acuarela (el color al agua *f*)
- *watercolour (Am. watercolor)*
19 el lápiz pastel
- *pastel crayon*
20 el bastidor
- *wedged stretcher (canvas stretcher)*
21 el lienzo (la tela)
- *canvas*
22 el cartón preparado para la pintura, con la superficie de pintar
- *piece of hardboard, with painting surface*
23 el tablero
- *wooden board*
24 el tablero de fibras *f* (el tablero de madera *f* prensada, de conglomerado *m*)
- *fibreboard (Am. fiberboard)*
25 la mesa de pintura *f*
- *painting table*
26 el caballete plegable (portátil)
- *folding easel*
27 la naturaleza muerta, un motivo
- *still life group, a motif*
28 la paleta
- *palette*

29 el soporte del pincel (el tarrito de la paleta)
- *palette dipper*
30 la plataforma
- *platform*
31 el maniquí
- *lay figure (mannequin, manikin)*
32 la modelo de desnudos *m* (la modelo, el desnudo)
- *nude model (model, nude)*
33 el ropaje
- *drapery*
34 el caballete de dibujo *m*
- *drawing easel*
35 el bloc (el cuaderno) de dibujo *m* (el bloque de apuntes *m,* de bocetos *m*)
- *sketch pad*
36 el estudio al óleo
- *study in oils*
37 el mosaico
- *mosaic (tessellation)*
38 la figura del mosaico
- *mosaic figure*
39 las teselas
- *tesserae*
40 el fresco (la pintura mural)
- *fresco (mural)*
41 el esgrafiado (la pintura con grafio *m*)
- *sgraffito*
42 el enlucido
- *plaster*
43 el boceto (el bosquejo, el esbozo)
- *cartoon*

1-38 el taller
- *studio*
1 el escultor
- *sculptor*
2 el compás de proporciones *f*
- *proportional dividers*
3 el compás de espesor *m*
- *calliper (caliper)*
4 el modelo de yeso *m*, un vaciado de yeso *m*
- *plaster model, a plaster cast*
5 el bloque de piedra *f* (la piedra en bruto, sin labrar)
- *block of stone (stone block)*
6 el modelador (el escultor en arcilla *f*)
- *modeller (Am. modeler)*
7 la figura de arcilla *f*, un torso
- *clay figure, a torso*
8 el rollo de arcilla *f*, una masa modelable
- *roll of clay, a modelling (Am. modeling) substance*
9 la tarima para modelar
- *modelling (Am. modeling) stand*
10 la espátula de modelar
- *wooden modelling (Am. modeling) tool*
11 el alambre de modelar (el raspador de escultor *m*)
- *wire modelling (Am. modeling) tool*
12 la espadilla
- *beating wood*

13 el cincel dentado (el estique)
- *claw chisel (toothed chisel, tooth chisel)*
14 el cincel plano (el formón)
- *flat chisel*
15 el puntero
- *point (punch)*
16 el martillo de cabeza *f* de hierro *m*
- *iron-headed hammer*
17 la gubia
- *gouge (hollow chisel)*
18 el cincel cuchara *f* (el cincel curvo)
- *spoon chisel*
19 el escoplo en bisel *m*, un escoplo
- *wood chisel, a bevelled-edge chisel*
20 la gubia triangular
- *V-shaped gouge*
21 el mazo (el martillo de madera *f*)
- *mallet*
22 la armazón (el esqueleto)
- *framework*
23 la base (el tablero que sirve de base *f*)
- *baseboard*
24 el soporte de la armazón (la barra de metal *m*)
- *armature support (metal rod)*
25 la armadura
- *armature*
26 la escultura de cera *f*
- *wax model*
27 el bloque de madera *f*
- *block of wood*

28 el escultor en madera *f* (el tallista)
- *wood carver (wood sculptor)*
29 el saco de polvo *m* de yeso *m* (el yeso)
- *sack of gypsum powder (gypsum)*
30 el cajón de arcilla *f*
- *clay box*
31 la arcilla de modelar (la arcilla)
- *modelling (Am. modeling) clay*
32 la estatua, una escultura
- *statue, a sculpture*
33 el bajo relieve (el bajorrelieve)
- *low relief (bas-relief)*
34 el tablero de modelar
- *modelling (Am. modeling) board*
35 la armazón de alambre *m*, una alambrera
- *wire frame, wire netting*
36 el medallón circular
- *circular medallion (tondo)*
37 la máscara
- *mask*
38 la placa conmemorativa
- *plaque*

1-13 el grabado en madera *f* (la xilografía), un procedimiento de grabado en relieve *m*
- **wood engraving** *(xylography), a relief printing method (a letterpress printing method)*
1 la plancha de madera *f* cortada contra la fibra para el grabado a tinta *f* sobre madera, un bloque de madera
- *end-grain block for wood engravings, a wooden block*
2 la plancha de madera *f* cortada en el sentido de la fibra para la talla en madera *f* (grabado *m* de relieve *m*), un molde de madera *f*
- *wooden plank for woodcutting, a relief image carrier*
3 el grabado en relieve *m* (las partes en relieve, reproducidas después por entintado *m*)
- *positive cut*
4 la talla (el vaciado) en el sentido de la fibra de la madera
- *plank cut*
5 el buril de contornear (el punzón)
- *burin (graver)*
6 la gubia redonda
- *U-shaped gouge*
7 el escoplo
- *scorper (scauper, scalper)*
8 la gubia
- *scoop*
9 el cincel de rincón *m* (el cincel de esquina *f*)
- *V-shaped gouge*
10 el cuchillo de contornear
- *contour knife*
11 la bruza
- *brush*
12 el rodillo de gelatina *f*
- *roller (brayer)*
13 el frotador (la muñeca)
- *pad (wiper)*
14-24 el grabado en cobre *m* (la calcografía, el grabado en talla *f* dulce), un procedimiento de huecograbado *m; clases:* el grabado al agua *f* fuerte, la mediatinta (grabado *m* al humo), el aguatinta, el grabado punteado
- **copperplate engraving** *(chalcography), an intaglio process; kinds: etching, mezzotint, aquatint, crayon engraving*
14 el martillo de moldear (la embutidera)
- *hammer*
15 el punzón
- *burin*
16 la punta seca para el grabado al agua *f* fuerte
- *etching needle (engraver)*
17 el bruñidor, con rascador *m*
- *scraper and burnisher*
18 la ruleta estriada para el grabado punteado (la moleta de graneado *m*)
- *roulette*
19 el graneador para el grabado al humo
- *rocking tool (rocker)*
20 el buril de cabeza *f* redonda, un buril de grabador *m*
- *round-headed graver, a graver (burin)*
21 la piedra de aceite *m*
- *oilstone*
22 el tampón entintador (la bola de entintar)
- *dabber (inking ball, ink ball)*

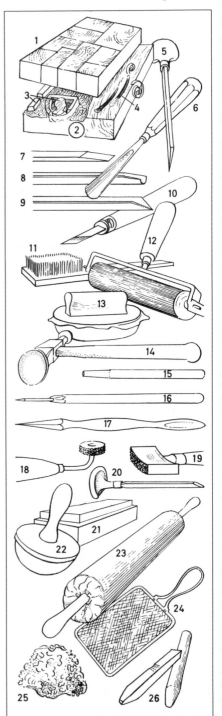

23 el rodillo entintador de cuero *m*
– *leather roller*
24 el tamiz de graneado *m*
– *sieve*
25 *u.* **26 la litografía** (el grabado en piedra *f*), un procedimiento de grabado de superficie *f* (planografía *f*)
– *lithography (stone lithography), a planographic printing method*
25 la esponja para humedecer la piedra litográfica
– *sponge for moistening the lithographic stone*
26 el lápiz (el jaboncillo) litográfico (el lápiz graso), un jaboncillo
– *lithographic crayons (greasy chalk)*
27-64 **el taller gráfico,** una imprenta
– *graphic art studio,* a printing office (Am. *printery*)
27 la hoja volante
– *broadside (broadsheet, single sheet)*
28 la impresión polícroma (la impresión en color *m*, la cromolitografía)
– *full-colour* (Am. *full-color*) *print (colour print, chromolithograph)*
29 la minerva (la prensa de platina *f*), una prensa manual
– *platen press, a hand press*
30 la rótula
– *toggle*
31 la platina, una plataforma de la prensa
– *platen*
32 la forma (el molde de imprenta *f*)
– *type forme* (Am. *form*)
33 la manivela de alimentación *f*
– *feed mechanism*

34 la barra de la prensa
– *bar (devil's tail)*
35 el impresor
– *pressman*
36 la prensa de plancha *f* de cobre *m*
– *copperplate press*
37 la imposición de cartón *m*
– *tympan*
38 el regulador de presión *f*
– *pressure regulator*
39 el volante en estrella *f*
– *star wheel*
40 el cilindro
– *cylinder*
41 el tímpano (la mesa de impresión *f*)
– *bed*
42 la mantilla de fieltro *m*
– *felt cloth*
43 la prueba
– *proof (pull)*
44 el grabador en cobre *m* (el calcógrafo)
– *copperplate engraver*
45 el litógrafo, esmerilando la piedra
– *lithographer (litho artist), grinding the stone*
46 el disco de esmerilar
– *grinding disc (disk)*
47 el graneado
– *grain (granular texture)*
48 la arena de cristal *m*
– *pulverized glass*
49 la solución de goma *f*
– *rubber solution*
50 las pinzas
– *tongs*

51 la cubeta de agua *f* fuerte para el mordido del grabado al agua fuerte
– *etching bath for etching*
52 la placa de zinc *m*
– *zinc plate*
53 la placa pulimentada de cobre *m*
– *polished copperplate*
54 el molde cuadriculado (el grabado de líneas *f* entrecruzadas)
– *cross hatch*
55 la zona atacada por el ácido (la parte de la placa de cobre *m* puesta al desnudo por una punta seca y corroída por el ácido)
– *etching ground*
56 la zona no grabada (cubierta por una capa protectora de barniz *m*)
– *non-printing area*
57 la piedra litográfica
– *lithographic stone*
58 las marcas de alineación *f* (las señales de ajuste *m*)
– *register marks*
59 la superficie de impresión *f*
– *printing surface (printing image carrier)*
60 la prensa litográfica
– *lithographic press*
61 la palanca de impresión *f*
– *lever*
62 el husillo de ajuste *m* del raspador
– *scraper adjustment*
63 el raspador
– *scraper*
64 la cama de piedra *f*
– *bed*

1-20 escrituras *f* de los diferentes pueblos
- *scripts of various peoples*
1 jeroglíficos *m* del antiguo Egipto, una escritura pictográfica
- *ancient Egyptian hieroglyphics, a pictorial system of writing*
2 árabe
- *Arabic*
3 armenia
- *Armenian*
4 georgiana
- *Georgian*
5 china
- *Chinese*
6 japonesa
- *Japanese*
7 hebrea
- *Hebrew (Hebraic)*
8 escritura *f* cuneiforme
- *cuneiform script*
9 devanagari *m* (la escritura del sánscrito)
- *Devanagari, script employed in Sanskrit*
10 siamesa
- *Siamese*
11 tamúlica
- *Tamil*
12 tibetana
- *Tibetan*
13 escritura *f* sinaítica
- *Sinaitic script*
14 fenicia
- *Phoenician*
15 griega
- *Greek*
16 versal *f* latina (mayúscula *f* romana, capital *f* romana)
- *Roman capitals*
17 uncial
- *uncial (uncials, uncial script)*
18 minúscula *f* carolingia
- *Carolingian (Carlovingian, Caroline) minuscule*
19 runas *f* (escritura *f* rúnica)
- *runes*
20 cirílica
- *Cyrillic*
21-26 escribanías *f* antiguas
- *ancient writing implements*
21 estilete *m* de acero *m* indio, un punzón para escribir sobre hojas *f* de palmera *f*
- *Indian steel stylus for writing on palm leaves*
22 punzón *m* para la escritura del antiguo Egipto, una cañucela de junco *m*
- *ancient Egyptian reed pen*
23 pluma *f* de caña *f*
- *writing cane*
24 pincel *m* de escribir
- *brush*
25 pluma *f* romana de metal *m* (estilete *m*)
- *Roman metal pen (stylus)*
26 pluma *f* de ganso *m*
- *quill (quill pen)*

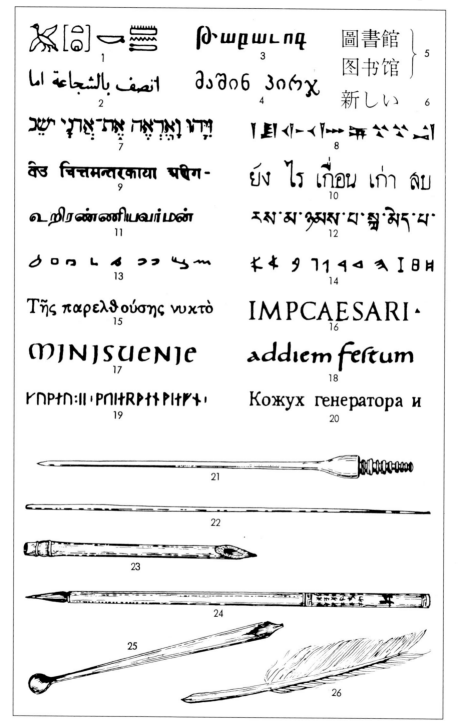

1-15 tipos *m* **de letra** *f* (tipos *m* de caracteres *m*)
– *types (type faces)*
1 el tipo de letra *f* gótica
– *Gothic type (German black-letter type)*
2 la letra gótica (el tipo Schwabacher)
– *Schwabacher type (German black-letter type)*
3 la letra alemana
– *Fraktur (German black-letter type)*
4 la antigua renacentista (medieval)
– *Humanist (Mediaeval)*
5 la antigua preclasicista (antigua barroca)
– *Transitional*
6 la antigua clasicista
– *Didone*
7 la letra grotesca
– *Sanserif (Sanserif type, Grotesque)*
8 la egipcia
– *Egyptian*
9 el tipo de máquina *f* de escribir
– *typescript (typewriting)*
10 la letra inglesa
– *English hand (English handwriting, English writing)*
11 la letra alemana
– *German hand (German handwriting, German writing)*
12 la letra latina
– *Latin script*
13 la taquigrafía (la estenografía)
– *shorthand (shorthand writing, stenography)*
14 la escritura fonética (transcripción *f* fonética)
– *phonetics (phonetic transcription)*
15 el braille
– *Braille*
16-29 signos *m* **de puntuación** *f*
– *punctuation marks (stops)*
16 el punto
– *full stop (period, full point)*
17 los dos puntos
– *colon*
18 la coma
– *comma*
19 el punto y coma
– *semicolon*
20 el signo de interrogación *f* [en español, para abrir: ¿; para cerrar: ?]
– *question mark (interrogation point, interrogation mark)*
21 el signo de admiración *f* [en español, para abrir: ¡; para cerrar: !]
– *exclamation mark* (Am. *exclamation point)*
22 el apóstrofo (la comilla de valor *m*)
– *apostrophe*

23 la raya
– *dash (em rule)*
24 los paréntesis
– *parentheses (round brackets)*
25 los corchetes
– *square brackets*
26 las comillas
– *quotation mark (double quotation marks, paired quotation marks, inverted commas)*
27 las comillas francesas
– *guillemet (French quotation mark)*
28 el guión
– *hyphen*
29 los puntos suspensivos
– *marks of omission (ellipsis)*
30-35 acentos *m* **y signos** *m* **diacríticos**
– *accents and diacritical marks (diacritics)*
30 el acento agudo [en español puede ir sobre cualquier vocal]
– *acute accent (acute)*
31 el acento grave [no existe en español]
– *grave accent (grave)*
32 el acento circunflejo [no existe en español]
– *circumflex accent (circumflex)*
33 la cedilla [debajo de la c]
– *cedilla [under c]*
34 la diéresis (la crema) [sobre la e]
– *diaeresis* (Am. *dieresis) [over e]*
35 la tilde [sobre la n], una eñe
– *tilde [over n]*
36 el signo de párrafo *m*
– *section mark*
37-70 el periódico, un diario nacional
– *newspaper, a national daily newspaper*
37 la página del periódico
– *newspaper page*
38 la primera página
– *front page*
39 la cabecera del periódico
– *newspaper heading*
40 la regla (el filete) de cabecera *f* con el pie de imprenta *f*
– *head rules and imprint*
41 el subtítulo
– *subheading*
42 la fecha de publicación *f*
– *date of publication*
43 el número de registro *m* postal del periódico
– *Post Office registration number*
44 el titular
– *headline*
45 la columna
– *column*
46 el título de la columna
– *column heading*
47 el filete de la columna
– *column rule*

48 el editorial (artículo *m* de fondo *m*)
– *leading article (leader, editorial)*
49 la referencia del artículo
– *reference to related article*
50 la noticia breve
– *brief news item*
51 la sección política
– *political section*
52 el titular de la página interior
– *page heading*
53 la caricatura
– *cartoon*
54 el reportaje del corresponsal
– *report by newspaper's own correspondent*
55 la sigla de la agencia de prensa *f*
– *news agency's sign*
56 el anuncio publicitario (la publicidad)
– *advertisement* (coll. *ad)*
57 la sección deportiva (los deportes)
– *sports section*
58 la foto de prensa *f*
– *press photo*
59 el pie de la foto
– *caption*
60 el reportaje deportivo
– *sports report*
61 la noticia deportiva
– *sports news item*
62 la sección de noticias *f* nacionales e internacionales
– *home and overseas news section*
63 las noticias diversas
– *news in brief (miscellaneous news)*
64 la programación de televisión *f*
– *television programmes* (Am. *programs)*
65 el parte meteorológico (el tiempo)
– *weather report*
66 el mapa meteorológico
– *weather chart (weather map)*
67 el folletín
– *arts section (feuilleton)*
68 la esquela mortuoria
– *death notice*
69 la sección de anuncios *m* [también: los anuncios por palabras *f*]
– *advertisements (classified advertising)*
70 el anuncio de empleo *m*, una oferta de empleo *m*
– *job advertisement, a vacancy (a situation offered)*

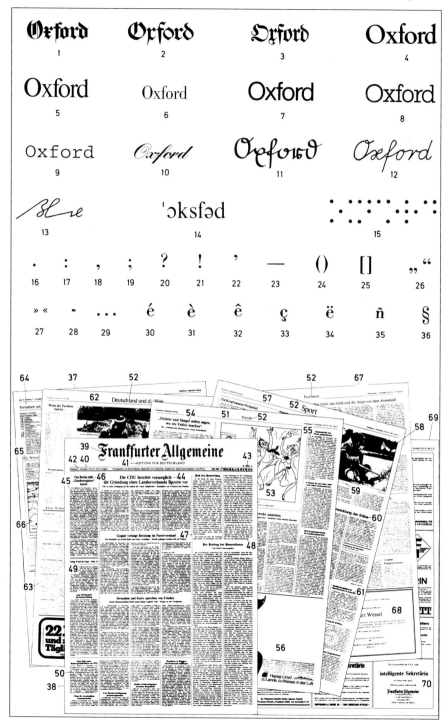

$\mathfrak{Oxford}$
1

$\mathfrak{Oxford}$
2

$\mathfrak{Oxford}$
3

Oxford
4

Oxford
5

Oxford
6

Oxford
7

Oxford
8

Oxford
9

Oxford
10

Oxford
11

Oxford
12

13

'ɔksfəd
14

15

·
16

:
17

,
18

;
19

?
20

!
21

'
22

—
23

()
24

[]
25

,, ''
26

» «
27

-
28

...
29

é
30

è
31

ê
32

ç
33

ë
34

ñ
35

§
36

Frankfurter Allgemeine
—ZEITUNG FÜR DEUTSCHLAND—

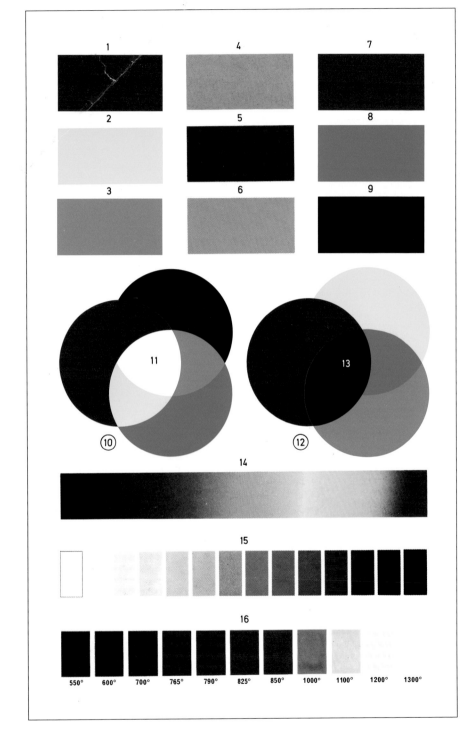

1 rojo
– *red*
2 amarillo
– *yellow*
3 azul (azul marino)
– *blue*
4 rosa
– *pink*
5 marrón
– *brown*
6 azul celeste
– *azure (sky blue)*
7 naranja
– *orange*
8 verde
– *green*
9 violeta (añil)
– *violet*
10 la mezcla aditiva de colores *m*
– *additive mixture of colours* (Am. *colors*)
11 blanco
– *white*
12 la mezcla sustractiva de colores *m*
– *subtractive mixture of colours* (Am. *colors*)
13 negro
– *black*
14 el espectro solar (los colores del arco iris)
– *solar spectrum (colours,* Am. *colors, of the rainbow)*
15 la escala de grises *m*
– *grey* (Am. *gray) scale*
16 los colores de la escala de incandescencia *f*
– *heat colours* (Am. *colors)*

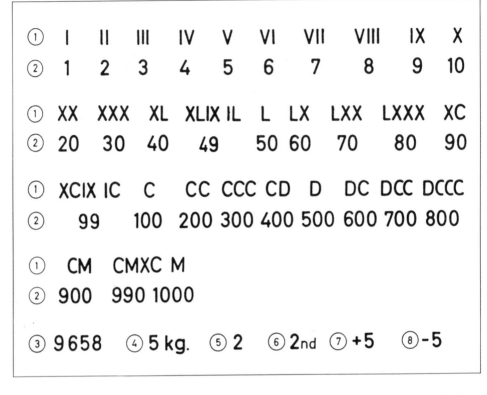

① I II III IV V VI VII VIII IX X
② 1 2 3 4 5 6 7 8 9 10

① XX XXX XL XLIX IL L LX LXX LXXX XC
② 20 30 40 49 50 60 70 80 90

① XCIX IC C CC CCC CD D DC DCC DCCC
② 99 100 200 300 400 500 600 700 800

① CM CMXC M
② 900 990 1000

③ 9658 ④ 5 kg. ⑤ 2 ⑥ 2nd ⑦ +5 ⑧ -5

1-26 aritmética *f*
– *arithmetic*
1-22 el número
– *numbers*
1 las cifras romanas (los números romanos)
– *Roman numerals*
2 las cifras arábigas (los números arábigos)
– *Arabic numerals*
3 el número abstracto, un número de cuatro cifras *f* (de cuatro dígitos *m*, de cuatro guarismos *m*) [8: las unidades; 5: las decenas; 6: las centenas; 9: las unidades de millar *m*]
– *abstract number, a four-figure number [8: units; 5: tens; 6: hundreds; 9: thousands]*
4 el número concreto (tamaño *m* físico, formado por el valor numérico y la unidad o bien el símbolo de unidad *f*)
– *concrete number (physical quantity consisting of the numerical value and the unit or unit symbol)*
5 el número cardinal
– *cardinal number (cardinal)*

6 el número ordinal [en español: 2 º]
– *ordinal number (ordinal)*
7 el número positivo [con el signo positivo]
– *positive number [with plus sign]*
8 el número negativo [con el signo negativo]
– *negative number [with minus sign]*
9 símbolos *m* algebraicos
– *algebraic symbols*
10 el número mixto [3: el número entero; 1/3 la fracción (el número fraccionario, el quebrado)]
– *mixed number [3: whole number (integer); 1/3 : fraction]*
11 números *m* pares
– *even numbers*
12 números *m* impares
– *odd numbers*
13 números *m* primos
– *prime numbers*
14 el número complejo [3: la parte real; 2√–1 la parte imaginaria]
– *complex number [3: real part; 2√–1: imaginary part]*
15 *u.* **16** quebrados *m* comunes
– *vulgar fractions*

15 la fracción propia (el quebrado propio) [2: el numerador; la raya de quebrado *m* (la línea horizontal, el signo de división *f*) 3: el denominador]
– *proper fraction [2: numerator, horizontal line; 3: denominator]*
16 la fracción impropia (el quebrado impropio), *al mismo tiempo* la recíproca (fracción *f* inversa) de la 15
– *improper fraction, also the reciprocal of item 15*
17 la fracción compuesta
– *compound fraction (complex fraction)*
18 la fracción impropia [cuando al reducirla resulta un número entero]
– *improper fraction [when cancelled down produces a whole number]*
19 fracciones *f* de diferente denominador *m* [35: el común denominador]
– *fractions of different denominations [35: common denominator]*

⑨ a, b, c ...   ⑩ $3\frac{1}{3}$ ⑪ 2, 4, 6, 8   ⑫ 1, 3, 5, 7

⑬ 3, 5, 7, 11   ⑭ $3 + 2\sqrt{-1}$ ⑮ $\frac{2}{3}$ ⑯ $\frac{3}{2}$

⑰ $\dfrac{\frac{5}{6}}{\frac{3}{4}}$ ⑱ $\frac{12}{4}$ ⑲ $\frac{4}{5} + \frac{2}{7} = \frac{38}{35}$ ⑳ 0·357

㉑ $0·6666.... = 0·\overline{6}$ ㉒   ㉓ $3 + 2 = 5$

㉔ $3 - 2 = 1$ ㉕ $3 \cdot 2 = 6$ ㉖ $6 \div 2 = 3$
 $3 \times 2 = 6$

20 la fracción decimal propia con la coma de decimales *m* y los lugares de los decimales [3: las décimas; 5: las centésimas; 7: las milésimas]
– *proper decimal fraction with decimal point and decimal places [3: tenths; 5: hundredths; 7: thousandths]*
21 la fracción decimal periódica infinita
– *recurring decimal*
22 el período
– *recurring decimal*
23-26 las operaciones fundamentales de aritmética *f*
– *fundamental arithmetical operations*
23 la adición (suma *f*); [3 y 2: los sumandos (términos *m* de la suma); + : el signo más (el signo de adición *f*); = : el signo de igualdad *f*; 5: la suma (el resultado)]
– *addition (adding) [3 and 2: the terms of the sum; + : plus sign; = : equals sign; 5: the sum]*

24 la sustracción (resta *f*); [3: el minuendo; – : el signo menos (el signo de sustracción *f*); 2: el sustraendo; l: el resto (la diferencia)]
– *subtraction (subtracting); [3: the minuend; – : minus sign; 2: the subtrahend; 1: the remainder (difference)]*
25 la multiplicación; [3: el multiplicando; · *o* × : el signo de multiplicación *f*; 2: el multiplicador; 2 y 3: factores *m*; 6: el producto]
– *multiplication (multiplying); [3: the multiplicand; × : multiplication sign; 2: the multiplier; 2 and 3: factors; 6: the product]*
26 la división; [6: el dividendo; ÷ : el signo de división *f*; 2: el divisor; 3: el cociente]
– *division (dividing); [6: the dividend; ÷ : division sign; 2: the divisor; 3: the quotient]*

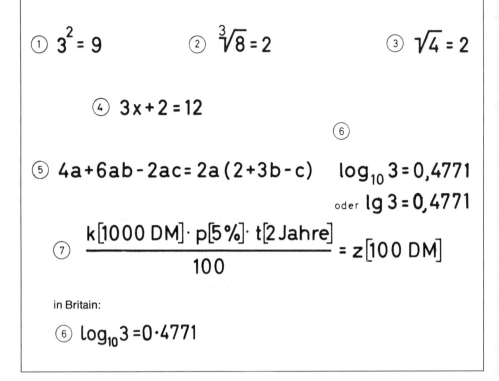

① $3^2 = 9$ ② $\sqrt[3]{8} = 2$ ③ $\sqrt{4} = 2$

④ $3x + 2 = 12$

⑤ $4a + 6ab - 2ac = 2a(2 + 3b - c)$ ⑥ $\log_{10} 3 = 0,4771$

oder $\lg 3 = 0,4771$

⑦ $\dfrac{k[1000\ DM] \cdot p[5\%] \cdot t[2\ Jahre]}{100} = z[100\ DM]$

in Britain:

⑥ $\log_{10} 3 = 0 \cdot 4771$

1-24 aritmética f
– *arithmetic*
1-10 operaciones f **de aritmética** f **superior**
– *advanced arithmetical operations*
1 la elevación a una potencia (la potenciación); [3 al cuadrado: la potencia; 3: la base; 2: el exponente (el índice); 9: el valor de la potencia]
– *raising to a power [three squared (3^2): the power; 3: the base; 2: the exponent (index); 9: value of the power]*
2 la extracción de raíces f (la radicación); [raíz f cúbica de 8: la raíz cúbica; 8: el radicando; 3: el índice de la raíz; √: el radical (el signo de extracción f de raíces f); 2: el valor de la raíz]
– *evolution (extracting a root); [cube root of 8: cube root; 8: the radical; 3: the index (degree) of the root; √: radical sign; 2: value of the root]*
3 la raíz cuadrada
– *square root*
4 u. **5** el álgebra f
– *algebra*

4 la ecuación de primer grado m; [3, 2: los coeficientes, x: la incógnita]
– *simple equation [3, 2: the coefficients; x: the unknown quantity]*
5 la ecuación idéntica (de identidad f) [a, b, c: los símbolos algebraicos]
– *identical equation; [a, b, c: algebraic symbols]*
6 el cálculo logarítmico (la logaritmación); [log: el símbolo de logaritmo m; lg: el símbolo del logaritmo decimal; 3: el número cuyo logaritmo m se busca; 10: la base; 0: la característica; 4 771: la mantisa; 0,4771: el logaritmo]
– *logarithmic calculation (taking the logarithm, log); [log: logarithm sign; 3: number whose logarithm is required; 10: the base; 0: the characteristic; 4771: the mantissa; 0.4771: the logarithm]*
7 la fórmula de interés m simple; [c: el capital inicial; r: el rédito (el tanto por ciento m); t: el tiempo; i: el interés (la ganancia); %: el signo del tanto por ciento m]
– *simple interest formula; [P: the principal; R: rate of interest; T: time; I: interest (profit); %: percentage sign]*

8-10 la regla de tres [≙ : equivalente a]
– *rule of three (rule-of-three sum, simple proportion)*
8 el planteamiento de la ecuación con la incógnita x (con la cantidad desconocida)
– *statement with the unknown quantity x*
9 la ecuación (ecuación f determinada)
– *equation (conditional equation)*
10 la solución
– *solution*
11-14 matemáticas f **superiores**
– *higher mathematics*
11 la progresión aritmética con los términos 2, 4, 6, 8
– *arithmetical series with the elements 2, 4, 6, 8*
12 la progresión geométrica
– *geometrical series*

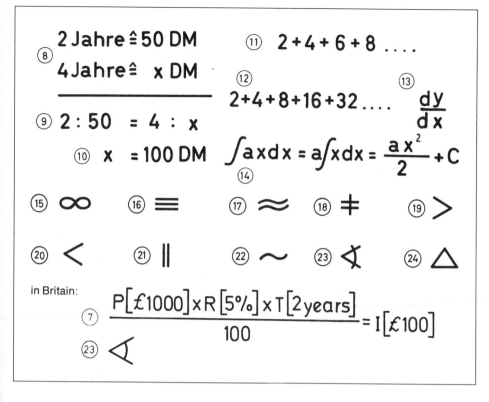

⑧ $\dfrac{2\,\text{Jahre} \triangleq 50\,\text{DM}}{4\,\text{Jahre} \triangleq \ \text{x}\,\text{DM}}$

⑨ $2:50 = 4:\text{x}$

⑩ $\text{x} = 100\,\text{DM}$

⑪ $2+4+6+8\ldots.$

⑫ $2+4+8+16+32\ldots.$ ⑬ $\dfrac{dy}{dx}$

⑭ $\displaystyle\int a\,\text{x}\,d\text{x} = a\!\int\!\text{x}\,d\text{x} = \dfrac{a\,\text{x}^2}{2}+C$

⑮ ∞ ⑯ $\equiv$ ⑰ $\approx$ ⑱ $\doteqdot$ ⑲ $>$

⑳ $<$ ㉑ $\parallel$ ㉒ $\sim$ ㉓ $\sphericalangle$ ㉔ $\triangle$

in Britain:

⑦ $\dfrac{P\,[\text{\pounds}1000] \times R\,[5\%] \times T\,[2\,\text{years}]}{100} = I\,[\text{\pounds}100]$

㉓ $\sphericalangle$

---

13 *u.* **14 el cálculo infinitesimal**
– *infinitesimal calculus*
13 la derivada (el cociente diferencial, la derivación); [dx, dy: las diferenciales; d: el signo de diferencial]
– *derivative [dx, dy: the differentials; d: differential sign]*
14 la integral (el cálculo integral, la integración) [x: la variable de integración f; c: la constante de la integral; ∫ el signo de la integral; dx: la diferencial]
– *integral (integration); [x: the variable; C: constant of integration; ∫: the integral sign; dx: the differential]*
15-24 signos *m* **matemáticos**
– *mathematical symbols*
15 infinito
– *infinity*
16 idéntico (el signo de identidad f)
– *identically equal to (the sign of identity)*
17 casi igual
– *approximately equal to*
18 no idéntico (el signo de la no identidad)
– *unequal to*
19 mayor que
– *greater than*

20 menor que
– *less than*
21-24 signos *m* **geométricos**
– *geometrical symbols*
21 paralelo (el signo de paralelismo *m*)
– *parallel (sign of parallelism)*
22 semejante (el signo de la semejanza)
– *similar to (sign of similarity)*
23 el signo de ángulo *m*
– *angle symbol*
24 el signo de triángulo *m*
– *triangle symbol*

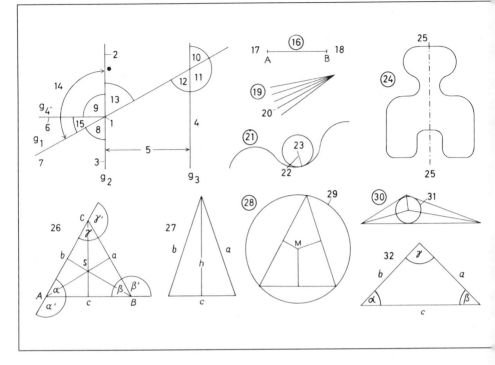

1-58 geometría *f* plana (geometría *f* elemental, geometría *f* euclidiana)
– *plane geometry (elementary geometry, Euclidian geometry)*
1-23 punto *m*, línea *f*, ángulo *m*
– *point, line, angle*
1 el punto [punto *m* de intersección *f* de g₁ y g₂], el vértice de 8
– *point [point of intersection of g₁ and g₂], the angular point of 8*
2 *u.* **3** la línea recta g₂
– *straight line g₂*
4 la paralela a g₂
– *the parallel to g₂*
5 la distancia entre las líneas rectas g₂ y g₃
– *distance between the straight lines g₂ and g₃*
6 la perpendicular (g₄) a g₂
– *perpendicular (g₄) on g₂*
7 *u.* **3** los lados del ángulo 8
– *the arms of 8*
8 *u.* **13** ángulos *m* opuestos por el vértice
– *vertically opposite angles*
8 el ángulo
– *angle*
9 el ángulo recto [90°]
– *right angle [90°]*
10, 11 *u.* **12** el ángulo cóncavo
– *reflex angle*

10 el ángulo agudo, al mismo tiempo ángulo *m* alterno con el 8
– *acute angle, also the alternate angle to 8*
11 el ángulo obtuso
– *obtuse angle*
12 el ángulo correspondiente al 10
– *corresponding angle to 10*
13, 9 *u.* **15** el ángulo llano [180°]
– *straight angle [180°]*
14 el ángulo adyacente; *en este caso:* el ángulo suplementario del 13
– *adjacent angle; here: supplementary angle to 13*
15 el ángulo complementario del 8
– *complementary angle to 8*
16 el segmento rectilíneo AB
– *straight line AB*
17 el extremo A
– *end A*
18 el extremo B
– *end B*
19 el haz de rayos *m*
– *pencil of rays*
20 el rayo
– *ray*
21 la línea curva
– *curved line*
22 un radio de curvatura *f*
– *radius of curvature*
23 un centro de curvatura *f*
– *centre* (Am. *center*) *of curvature*

24-58 las superficies planas
– *plane surfaces*
24 la figura simétrica
– *symmetrical figure*
25 el eje de simetría *f*
– *axis of symmetry*
26-32 triángulos *m*
– *plane triangles*
26 el triángulo equilátero; [A, B, C: los vértices; a, b, c: los lados; α (alfa), β (beta), γ (gamma): los ángulos interiores; α', β', γ': los ángulos exteriores; S: el centro]
– *equilateral triangle; [A, B, C: the vertices; a, b, c: the sides; α (alpha), β (beta), γ (gamma): the interior angles; α', β', γ': the exterior angles; S: the centre* (Am. *center)]*
27 el triángulo isósceles; [a, b: los lados; c: la base; h: la perpendicular, una altura]
– *isosceles triangle [a, b: the sides (legs); c: the base; h: the perpendicular, an altitude]*
28 el triángulo acutángulo con las mediatrices
– *acute-angled triangle with perpendicular bisectors of the sides*
29 el círculo circunscrito
– *circumcircle (circumscribed circle)*

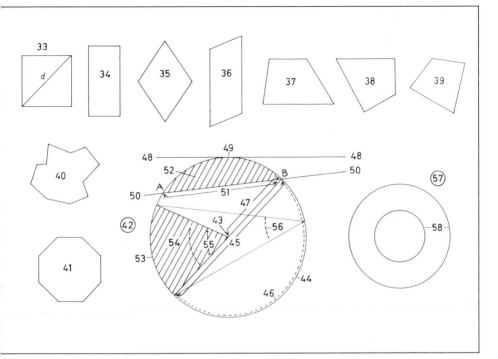

30 el triángulo obtusángulo con las
bisectrices
– *obtuse-angled triangle with bisec-*
tors of the angles
31 el círculo inscrito
– *inscribed circle*
32 el triángulo rectángulo y las funciones trigonométricas de los ángulos; [a, b: los catetos; c: la
hipotenusa; γ : el ángulo recto; a:c
= sen α (seno *m*); b:c = cos α
(coseno *m*); a:b = tg α (tangente *f*);
b:a = cotg α (cotangente *f*)]
– *right-angled triangle and the*
trigonometrical functions of
angles; [a, b: the catheti; c: the
hypotenuse; γ : the right angle; a/c
= sin α (sine); b/c = cos α (cosine);
a/b = tan α (tangent); b/a = cot α
(cotangent)
33-39 cuadriláteros *m*
– *quadrilaterals*
33-36 paralelogramos *m*
– *parallelograms*
33 el cuadrado [d: una diagonal]
– *square [d: a diagonal]*
34 el rectángulo
– *rectangle*
35 el rombo
– *rhombus (rhomb, lozenge)*
36 el romboide
– *rhomboid*

37 el trapecio
– *trapezium*
38 el deltoide (cometa *f*)
– *deltoid (kite)*
39 el cuadrilátero irregular
– *irregular quadrilateral*
40 el polígono
– *polygon*
41 el polígono regular
– *regular polygon*
42 el círculo
– *circle*
43 el centro
– *centre (Am. center)*
44 la circunferencia
– *circumference (periphery)*
45 el diámetro
– *diameter*
46 el semicírculo
– *semicircle*
47 el radio (r)
– *radius (r)*
48 la tangente
– *tangent*
49 el punto de contacto *m* (P)
– *point of contact(P)*
50 la secante
– *secant*
51 la cuerda AB
– *the chord AB*
52 el segmento circular
– *segment*

53 el arco de circunferencia *f*
– *arc*
54 el sector circular
– *sector*
55 el ángulo central
– *angle subtended by the arc at the*
centre (Am. center) (centre, Am.
center, angle)
56 el ángulo inscrito
– *circumferential angle*
57 la corona circular
– *ring (annulus)*
58 círculos *m* concéntricos
– *concentric circles*

1 el sistema de coordenadas *f* ortogonales (rectangulares, carte-
sianas)
- *system of right-angled coordinates*

2 u. **3** los ejes de coordenadas *f*
- *axes of coordinates (coordinate
axes)*

2 el eje de abscisas *f* (eje *m* de las x)
- *axis of abscissae (x-axis)*

3 el eje de ordenadas *f* (eje *m* de las y)
- *axis of ordinates (y-axis)*

4 el origen de coordenadas *f* (punto
m cero)
- *origin of ordinates*

5 el cuadrante [I-IV del 1^0 al 4^0
cuadrante]
- *quadrant [I-IV: 1st to 4th quad-
rant]*

6 la dirección positiva
- *positive direction*

7 la dirección negativa
- *negative direction*

8 los puntos [P_1 y P_2] en el sistema de
coordenadas *f*; x_1 e y_1 [o x_2 e y_2
respectivamente]: sus coordenadas *f*
- *points [P_1 and P_2] in the system of
coordinates; x_1 and y_1 [and x_2 and
y_2 respectively] their coordinates*

9 el valor de la abscisa [x_1 o x_2
respectivamente] (las abscisas)
- *values of the abscissae [x_1 and x_2]
(the abscissae)*

10 el valor de la ordenada [y_1 o y_2
respectivamente] (las ordenadas)
- *values of the ordinates [y_1 and y_2]
(the ordinates)*

11-29 las secciones cónicas
- *conic sections*

11 las curvas en el sistema de coordenadas *f*
- *curves in the system of coordinates*

12 rectas *f* [a: la pendiente de la
recta; b: la intersección de la recta
con la ordenada; c: la raíz de la
recta]
- *plane curves [a: the gradient
(slope) of the curve; b: the ordinates' intersection of the curve; c:
the root of the curve]*

13 las curvas
- *inflected curves*

14 la parábola, una curva de segundo
grado *m*
- *parabola, a curve of the second
degree*

15 las ramas de la parábola
- *branches of the parabola*

16 el vértice de la parábola
- *vertex of the parabola*

17 el eje de la parábola
- *axis of the parabola*

18 una curva de tercer grado *m*
- *a curve of the third degree*

19 el máximo de la curva
- *maximum of the curve*

20 el mínimo de la curva
- *minimum of the curve*

21 el punto de inflexión *f*
- *point of inflexion (of inflection)*

22 la elipse
- *ellipse*

23 el eje mayor
- *transverse axis (major axis)*

24 el eje menor
- *conjugate axis (minor axis)*

25 los focos de la elipse [F_1 y F_2]
- *foci of the ellipse [F_1 and F_2]*

26 la hipérbola
- *hyperbola*

27 los focos [F_1 y F_2]
- *foci [F_1 and F_2]*

28 los vértices [S_1 y S_2]
- *vertices [S_1 and S_2]*

29 las asíntotas [a y b]
- *asymptotes [a and b]*

30-46 cuerpos *m* geométricos
- *solids*

30 el cubo
- *cube*

31 el cuadrado, una cara
- *square, a plane (plane surface)*

32 la arista
- *edge*

33 el vértice
- *corner*

34 el prisma cuadrangular
- *quadratic prism*

35 la base
- *base*

36 el paralelepípedo rectangular
- *parallelepiped*

37 el prisma triangular
- *triangular prism*

38 el cilindro, un cilindro recto
- *cylinder, a right cylinder*

39 la base, una cara circular
- *base, a circular plane*

40 la superficie lateral
- *curved surface*

41 la esfera
- *sphere*

42 el elipsoide de revolución *f*
- *ellipsoid of revolution*

43 el cono
- *cone*

44 la altura del cono
- *height of the cone (cone height)*

45 el cono truncado
- *truncated cone (frustum of a cone)*

46 la pirámide cuadrangular
- *quadrilateral pyramid*

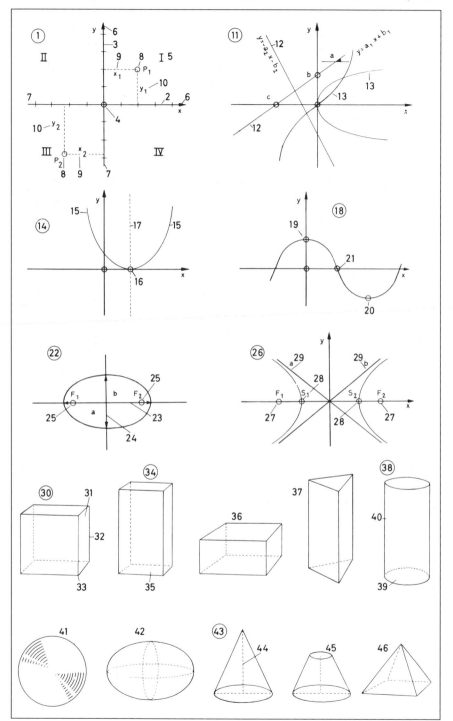

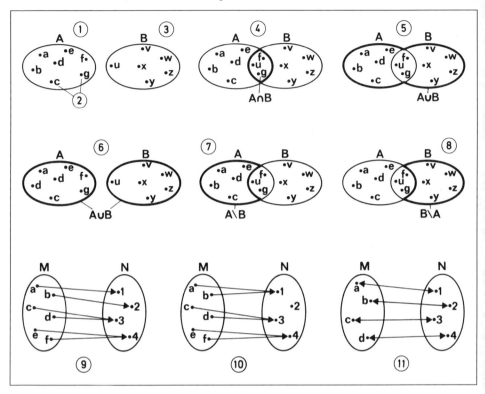

1 el conjunto A, el conjunto {a, b, c, d, e, f, g}
– *the set A, the set {a, b, c, d, e, f, g}*
2 los elementos del conjunto A
– *elements (members) of the set A*
3 el conjunto B, el conjunto {u, v, w, x, y, z}
– *the set B, the set {u, v, w, x, y, z}*
4 la intersección de los conjuntos A y B, A ∩ B = {f, g, u}
– *intersection of the sets A and B , A ∩ B = {f, g, u}*
5 *u.* **6** la unión de los conjuntos A y B, A ∪ B = {a, b, c, d, e, f, g, u, v, w, x, y, z}
– *union of the sets A and B, A ∪ B = {a, b, c, d, e, f, g, u, v, w, x, y, z}*
7 la diferencia de los conjuntos A – B = {a, b, c, d, e}
– *complement of the set B, B′ = {a, b, c, d, e}*
8 la diferencia de los conjuntos B – A = {v, w, x, y, z}
– *complement of the set A, A′ = {v, w, x, y, z}*
9-11 las aplicaciones
– *mappings*

9 la aplicación del conjunto M sobre el conjunto N
– *mapping of the set M on to the set N*
10 la aplicación del conjunto M en el conjunto N
– *mapping of the set M into the set N*
11 la aplicación biunívoca del conjunto M en el conjunto N
– *one-to-one mapping of the set M on to the set N*

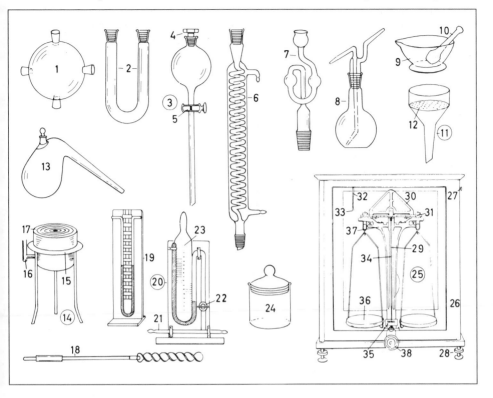

1-38 los aparatos de laboratorio *m*
- *laboratory apparatus (laboratory equipment)*
1 el globo Scheidt
- *Scheidt globe*
2 el tubo en U
- *U-tube*
3 el embudo de separación *f* (el tubo de bromo *m*)
- *separating funnel*
4 el tapón octogonal
- *octagonal ground-glass stopper*
5 la llave
- *tap (Am. faucet)*
6 el refrigerador de serpentín *m*
- *coiled condenser*
7 la válvula de seguridad *f*
- *air lock*
8 el frasco lavador
- *wash-bottle*
9 el mortero
- *mortar*
10 la mano del mortero
- *pestle*
11 el filtro de vacío *m* (el filtro de Büchner)
- *filter funnel (Büchner funnel)*
12 el filtro (tamiz *m*)
- *filter (filter plate)*

13 la retorta
- *retort*
14 el baño María
- *water bath*
15 el trípode
- *tripod*
16 el indicador del nivel del agua *f*
- *water gauge (Am. gage)*
17 las arandelas
- *insertion rings*
18 el agitador
- *stirrer*
19 el medidor de alta y baja presión *f* (el manómetro)
- *manometer for measuring positive and negative pressures*
20 el manómetro (vacuómetro *m*) de espejo *m*, para medir presiones *f* pequeñas
- *mirror manometer for measuring small pressures*
21 el tubo de succión *f*
- *inlet*
22 la llave (la espita)
- *tap (Am. faucet)*
23 la escala de cursor *m*
- *sliding scale*
24 el bote de pesar
- *weighing bottle*

25 la balanza de análisis *m*
- *analytical balance*
26 la caja
- *case*
27 el panel anterior levadizo
- *sliding front panel*
28 el soporte de tres puntos *m* (el tornillo nivelador)
- *three-point support*
29 la columna de la balanza
- *column (balance column)*
30 el astil de la balanza
- *balance beam (beam)*
31 el carril de corredera *f*
- *rider bar*
32 el agarrador de corredera *f*
- *rider holder*
33 la corredera
- *rider*
34 el fiel
- *pointer*
35 la escala
- *scale*
36 el platillo
- *scale pan*
37 el inmovilizador
- *stop*
38 el botón de inmovilización *f*
- *stop knob*

1-63 los aparatos de laboratorio *m*
– **laboratory apparatus** *(laboratory equipment)*
1 el mechero Bunsen
– *Bunsen burner*
2 el tubo de entrada *f* del gas
– *gas inlet (gas inlet pipe)*
3 el regulador del aire
– *air regulator*
4 el mechero Teclu
– *Teclu burner*
5 el tubo de unión *f*
– *pipe union*
6 el regulador del gas
– *gas regulator*
7 el tubo
– *stem*
8 el regulador del aire
– *air regulator*
9 el soplete
– *bench torch*
10 el revestimiento
– *casing*
11 la entrada de oxígeno *m*
– *oxygen inlet*
12 la entrada de hidrógeno *m*
– *hydrogen inlet*
13 la boquilla del oxígeno
– *oxygen jet*
14 el trípode
– *tripod*
15 la anilla
– *ring (retort ring)*
16 el embudo
– *funnel*
17 el triángulo de arcilla *f*
– *pipe clay triangle*
18 la tela metálica
– *wire gauze*
19 la tela metálica con amianto *m*
– *wire gauze with asbestos centre* *(Am. center)*
20 el vaso de precipitados *m*
– *beaker*
21 la bureta, para medir líquidos *m*
– *burette (for measuring the volume of liquids)*
22 el soporte de la bureta
– *burette stand*
23 la abrazadera de la bureta
– *burette clamp*
24 la pipeta graduada
– *graduated pipette*
25 la pipeta ordinaria
– *pipette*
26 la probeta graduada
– *measuring cylinder (measuring glass)*
27 la probeta graduada con tapón *m*
– *measuring flask*
28 el matraz de mezclas *f*
– *volumetric flask*
29 la cápsula, de porcelana *f*
– *evaporating dish (evaporating basin), made of porcelain*

30 la abrazadera de tubos *m*
– *tube clamp (tube clip, pinchcock)*
31 el crisol de arcilla *f*, con tapadera *f*
– *clay crucible with lid*
32 las pinzas del crisol
– *crucible tongs*
33 la agarradera (la grapa)
– *clamp*
34 el tubo de ensayo *m*
– *test tube*
35 el soporte de los tubos de ensayo *m*
– *test tube rack*
36 el matraz de fondo *m* plano
– *flat-bottomed flask*
37 la boca esmerilada
– *ground glass neck*
38 el matraz redondo, de cuello *m* largo
– *long-necked round-bottomed flask*
39 el matraz cónico (el Erlenmeyer)
– *Erlenmeyer flask (conical flask)*
40 el frasco de filtración *f*
– *filter flask*
41 el filtro de papel *m* plegado
– *fluted filter*
42 la llave de un solo paso
– *one-way tap*
43 el tubo de cloruro *m* cálcico (el tubo de secado *m*)
– *calcium chloride tube*
44 el tapón con llave *f*
– *stopper with tap*
45 la probeta
– *cylinder*
46 el alambique (el aparato de destilación *f*)
– *distillation apparatus (distilling apparatus)*
47 el matraz de destilación *f*
– *distillation flask (distilling flask)*
48 el condensador (el refrigerante)
– *condenser*
49 la llave de retorno *m*, una llave de dos pasos *m*
– *return tap, a two-way tap*
50 el matraz de destilación *f*
– *distillation flask (distilling flask, Claisen flask)*
51 el desecador
– *desiccator*
52 la tapa con un tubo ajustado
– *lid with fitted tube*
53 la llave
– *tap*
54 la salvilla del desecador, de porcelana *f*
– *desiccator insert made of porcelain*
55 el matraz de tres bocas *f*
– *three-necked flask*
56 la pieza de conexión *f* (el tubo en Y)
– *connecting piece (Y-tube)*
57 el frasco de tres bocas *f*
– *three-necked bottle*
58 el frasco para limpiar gas *m*
– *gas-washing bottle*

59 el aparato para producir gas *m* (aparato *m* Kipp)
– *gas generator (Kipp's apparatus, Am. Kipp generator)*
60 el recipiente de rebosamiento *m*
– *overflow container*
61 el recipiente de la sustancia
– *container for the solid*
62 el recipiente del ácido
– *acid container*
63 la toma del gas
– *gas outlet*

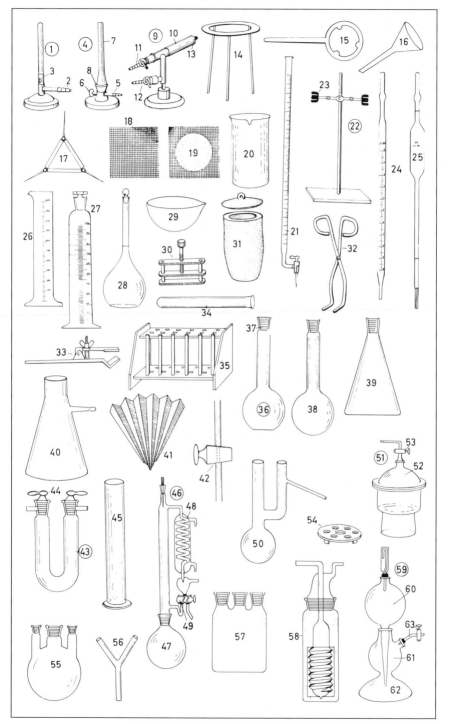

1-26 formas *f* fundamentales de los cristales y combinaciónes *f* de cristales *m* (estructura *f* de los cristales)
– *basic crystal forms and crystal combinations [structure of crystals]*
1-17 el sistema regular de cristalización *f* (cúbico, isométrico)
– *regular (cubic, tesseral, isometric) crystal system*
1 el tetraedro (poliedro *m* de cuatro caras *f*, la tetraedrita) [cobre *m* gris]
– *tetrahedron (four-faced polyhedron) [tetrahedrite, fahlerz, fahl ore]*
2 el hexaedro (cubo *m*, poliedro *m* de seis caras *f*), un holoédrico [sal *f* gema]
– *hexahedron (cube, six-faced polyhedron), a holohedron [rock salt]*
3 el centro de simetría *f* (el centro del cristal)
– *centre (Am. center) of symmetry (crystal centre)*
4 un eje de simetría *f*
– *axis of symmetry (rotation axis)*
5 un plano de simetría *f*
– *plane of symmetry*
6 el octaedro (poliedro *m* de ocho caras *f*) [oro *m*]
– *octahedron (eight-faced polyhedron) [gold]*
7 el dodecaedro romboidal (el rombododecaedro) [granate *m*]
– *rhombic dodecahedron [garnet]*
8 el dodecaedro pentagonal [pirita *f*]
– *pentagonal dodecahedron [pyrite, iron pyrites]*
9 el pentágono (polígono *m* de cinco lados *m*)
– *pentagon (five-sided polygon)*
10 el octaedro piramidado [diamante *m*]
– *triakis-octahedron [diamond]*
11 el icosaedro (poliedro *m* de veinte caras *f*), un poliedro regular
– *icosahedron (twenty-faced polyhedron), a regular polyhedron*
12 el icositetraedro (poliedro *m* de veinticuatro caras *f*) [leucita *f*]
– *icositetrahedron (twenty-four-faced polyhedron) [leucite]*
13 el hexaquioctaedro (poliedro *m* de cuarenta y ocho caras *f*) [diamante *m*]
– *hexakis-octahedron (hexoctahedron, forty-eight-faced polyhedron) [diamond]*
14 el octaedro con cubo *m* [galena *f*]
– *octahedron with cube [galena]*
15 un hexágono (polígono *m* de seis lados *m*)
– *hexagon (six-sided polygon)*

16 el cubo con octaedro *m* [espato *m* flúor *m*]
– *cube with octahedron [fluorite, fluorspar]*
17 un octógono (polígono *m* de ocho lados *m*)
– *octagon (eight-sided polygon)*
18 *u*. 19 el sistema de cristalización *f* tetragonal
– *tetragonal crystal system*
18 la pirámide tetragonal
– *tetragonal dipyramid (tetragonal bipyramid)*
19 el protoprisma con protopirámide *f* [circón *m*]
– *protoprism with protopyramid [zircon]*
20-22 el sistema de cristalización *f* hexagonal
– *hexagonal crystal system*
20 el protoprisma con protopirámide *f* y deutopirámide *f* y base *f* pinacoide [apatito *m*]
– *protoprism with protopyramid, deutero-pyramid and basal pinacoid [apatite]*
21 el prisma hexagonal
– *hexagonal prism*
22 el prisma hexagonal (el prisma ditrigonal) con romboedro *m* [calcita *f* (espato *m* de Islandia)]
– *hexagonal (ditrigonal) biprism with rhombohedron [calcite]*
23 la pirámide ortorrómbica (el sistema rómbico) [azufre *m*]
– *orthorhombic pyramid (rhombic crystal system) [sulphur, Am. sulfur]*
24 *u*. 25 el sistema de cristalización *f* monoclínico (sistema *m* oblicuo, sistema *m* monosimétrico)
– *monoclinic crystal system*
24 el prisma monoclínico con clinopinacoide *m* y hemipirámide *f* (hemiedro *m*) [yeso *m*]
– *monoclinic prism with clinoprinacoid and hemipyramid (hemihedron) [gypsum]*
25 el ortopinacoide (cristal *m* gemelo en cola *f* de golondrina *f*) [yeso *m*]
– *orthopinacoid (swallowtail twin crystal) [gypsum]*
26 el pinacoide triclínico (sistema *m* triclínico) [sulfato *m* de cobre *m*]
– *triclinic pinacoids (triclinic crystal system) [copper sulphate, Am. copper sulfate]*
27-33 aparatos *m* para medir cristales *m* (para la cristalometría)
– *apparatus for measuring crystals for crystallometry)*
27 el goniómetro de contacto *m*
– *contact goniometer*

28 el goniómetro por reflexión *f*
– *reflecting goniometer*
29 el cristal
– *crystal*
30 el colimador
– *collimator*
31 el telescopio de observación *f*
– *observation telescope*
32 el círculo graduado
– *divided circle (graduated circle)*
33 la lupa, para leer el ángulo de rotación *f*
– *lens for reading the angle of rotation*

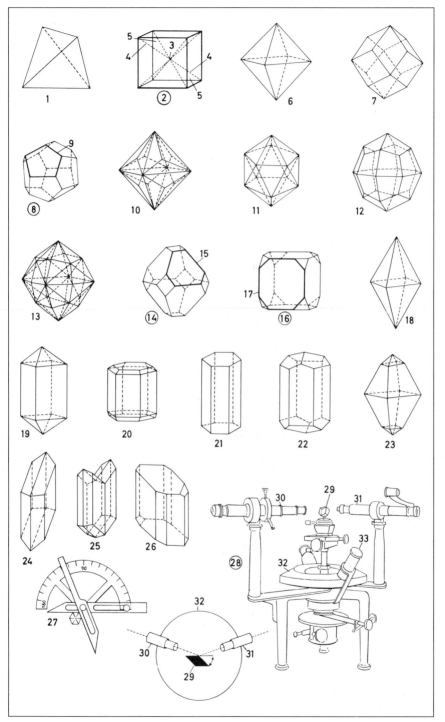

1 el poste totémico (el pilar totémico)
– *totem pole*
2 el totem, una representación esculpida y pintada, figurativa o simbólica
– *totem, a carved and painted pictorial or symbolic representation*
3 el indio de las praderas (*Amér.*: el indio de las sabanas)
– *plains Indian*
4 el mustang, un caballo de las estepas
– *mustang, a prairie horse*
5 el lazo, una larga cuerda arrojadiza con nudo *m* corredizo de fácil cierre *m*
– *lasso, a long throwing-rope with running noose*
6 la pipa de la paz
– *pipe of peace*
7 la tienda india (la tienda de los indios norteamericanos, el tipi)
– *wigwam (tepee, teepee)*
8 el poste de la tienda
– *tent pole*
9 la trampilla para el humo
– *smoke flap*
10 la mujer india norteamericana (la squaw)
– *squaw, an Indian woman*
11 el jefe indio
– *Indian chief*
12 el tocado, un adorno de plumas *f*
– *headdress, an ornamental feather headdress*
13 la pintura de guerra *f*
– *war paint*
14 el collar, de uñas *f* de oso *m*
– *necklace of bear claws*
15 el cuero cabelludo arrancado al enemigo, un trofeo
– *scalp (cut from enemy's head), a trophy*
16 el hacha *f* de guerra *f* de los indios norteamericanos (el tomahawk)
– *tomahawk, a battle axe (Am. ax)*
17 las polainas (polainas *f* de cuero *m* de venado *m*)
– *leggings*
18 el mocasín, un zapato bajo (de cuero *m* y corteza *f* vegetal)
– *moccasin, a shoe of leather and bast*
19 la piragua de los indios de los bosques
– *canoe of the forest Indians*
20 el templo maya, una pirámide escalonada
– *Maya temple, a stepped pyramid*
21 la momia
– *mummy*
22 los quipos (la cuerda con nudos *m*, la escritura de nudos *m* de los incas)
– *quipa (knotted threads, knotted code of the Incas)*

23 el indio (el indio de Centro y Sudamérica); *en este caso:* el indio del altiplano
– *Indio (Indian of Central and South America); here: highland Indian*
24 el poncho, una manta con abertura *f* para el cuello, especie *f* de capote *m* sin mangas *f*
– *poncho, a blanket with a head opening used as an armless cloak-like wrap*
25 el indio de la selva tropical
– *Indian of the tropical forest*
26 la cerbatana (la bodoquera; *Bol.*: la pacuna)
– *blowpipe*
27 el carcaj
– *quiver*
28 la flecha
– *dart*
29 la punta de la flecha
– *dart point*
30 la cabeza reducida, un trofeo
– *shrunken head, a trophy*
31 las boleadoras, una arma arrojadiza y de captura *f*
– *bola (bolas), a throwing and entangling device*
32 la bola de piedra *f* o metal *m* forrada de cuero *m*
– *leather-covered stone or metal ball*
33 el palafito (una choza sobre pilares *m*)
– *pile dwelling*
34 el bailarín Duk-duk, un miembro de una sociedad secreta de hombres *m*
– *duk-duk dancer, a member of a duk-duk (men's secret society)*
35 la canoa con batanga *f* (con balancín *m*)
– *outrigger canoe (canoe with outrigger)*
36 la batanga (el balancín)
– *outrigger*
37 el aborigen (el indígena, el nativo) australiano
– *Australian aborigine*
38 el taparrabo de cabellos *m* humanos
– *loincloth of human hair*
39 el bumerang, una arma arrojadiza de madera *f*
– *boomerang, a wooden missile*
40 el lanzajabalinas con jabalinas *f*
– *throwing stick (spear thrower) with spears*

1 el esquimal
  – Eskimo
2 el perro de trineo m, un perro
   polar (un perro esquimal)
  – sledge dog (sled dog), a husky
3 el trineo de perros m
  – dog sledge (dog sled)
4 el iglú, una choza de nieve f en
   forma f de cúpula f
  – igloo, a dome-shaped snow hut
5 el bloque de nieve f
  – block of snow
6 el túnel de entrada f
  – entrance tunnel
7 la lámpara de aceite m de pescado
   m (de ballena f o foca f)
  – blubber-oil lamp
8 la tablilla arrojadiza
  – wooden missile
9 el espiche
  – lance
10 el arpón de una sola punta
  – harpoon
11 el saco de aire m (el flotador del
   arpón)
  – skin float
12 el kayak, una canoa ligera individual
  – kayak, a light one-man canoe
13 la armazón de madera f o hueso
   m recubierta de piel f
  – skin-covered wooden or bone
   frame
14 el zagual (el canalete)
  – paddle
15 el atalaje de reno m
  – reindeer harness
16 el reno
  – reindeer
17 el ostiaco
  – Ostyak (Ostiak)
18 el trineo con respaldo m (el trineo
   de viajeros m)
  – passenger sledge
19 la yurta, una tienda vivienda f de
   los nómadas de Asia f Central y
   Occidental
  – yurt (yurta), a dwelling tent of the
   western and central Asiatic
   nomads
20 la cubierta de fieltro m
  – felt covering
21 la abertura para el humo
  – smoke outlet
22 el kirghís
  – Kirghiz
23 el gorro de piel f de oveja f
  – sheepskin cap
24 el chamán
  – shaman
25 el adorno de flecos m
  – decorative fringe
26 el tambor de bastidor m
  – frame drum

27 el tibetano
  – Tibetan
28 la escopeta de horquilla f
  – flintlock with bayonets
29 el molino de oraciones f
  – prayer wheel
30 la bota de fieltro m
  – felt boot
31 el barco vivienda (la casa flotante,
   el sampán)
  – houseboat (sampan)
32 el junco
  – junk
33 la vela de estera f
  – mat sail
34 la jinrikisha (la rikisha)
  – rickshaw (ricksha)
35 el culí de la jinrikisha
  – rickshaw coolie (cooly)
36 el lampión [un farolillo chino]
  – Chinese lantern
37 el samurai
  – samurai
38 la armadura enguatada
  – padded armour (Am. armor)
39 la geisha
  – geisha
40 el quimono
  – kimono
41 el obi (faja f de seda f japonesa)
  – obi
42 el abanico
  – fan
43 el culi
  – coolie (cooly)
44 el cris, un puñal malayo
  – kris (creese, crease), a Malayan
   dagger
45 el encantador de serpientes f
  – snake charmer
46 el turbante
  – turban
47 la flauta
  – flute
48 la serpiente danzante
  – dancing snake

1 la caravana de camellos *m*
– *camel caravan*
2 el animal para montar
– *riding animal*
3 el animal de carga *f*
– *pack animal*
4 el oasis
– *oasis*
5 el palmeral
– *grove of palm trees*
6 el beduino
– *bedouin (beduin)*
7 el albornoz
– *burnous*
8 el guerrero masai
– *Masai warrior*
9 el peinado
– *headdress (hairdress)*
10 el escudo
– *shield*
11 el cuero de buey *m* pintado
– *painted ox hide*
12 la lanza de hoja *f* larga
– *long-bladed spear*
13 el negro
– *negro*
14 el tambor de danza *f* (el tam-tam)
– *dance drum*
15 el cuchillo arrojadizo
– *throwing knife*
16 la máscara de madera *f*
– *wooden mask*
17 la figura del antepasado
– *figure of an ancestor*
18 el tambor de señales *f*
– *slit gong*
19 el palillo (la baqueta; *C. Rica:* el bolillo) del tambor
– *drumstick*
20 la canoa, una embarcación hecha vaciando un tronco de árbol *m*
– *dugout, a boat hollowed out of a tree trunk*
21 la choza del negro
– *negro hut*
22 la negra
– *negress*
23 el disco labial
– *lip plug (labret)*
24 la piedra de moler
– *grinding stone*
25 la mujer herera
– *Herero woman*
26 la toca de cuero *m*
– *leather cap*
27 la calabaza (*Amér.:* el porongo) [calabaza *f* vinatera]
– *calabash (gourd)*
28 la choza en forma *f* de colmena *f*
– *beehive-shaped hut*
29 el bosquimano
– *bushman*

30 la estaquilla de la oreja
– *earplug*
31 el taparrabo
– *loincloth*
32 el arco
– *bow*
33 el quirri, una clava (cachiporra *f*) de cabeza *f* redonda y gruesa
– *knobkerry (knobkerrie), a club with round, knobbed end*
34 la mujer bosquimana obteniendo fuego *m* por taladramiento *m*
– *bushman woman making a fire by twirling a stick*
35 el abrigo contra el viento
– *windbreak*
36 el zulú en atuendo *m* de danza *f*
– *Zulu in dance costume*
37 el bastón de danza *f*
– *dancing stick*
38 el anillo de la pierna
– *bangle*
39 el cuerno de guerra *f* de marfil *m*
– *ivory war horn*
40 la cadena de amuletos *m* y dados *m*
– *string of amulets and bones*
41 el pigmeo
– *pigmy*
42 la chifla (el chifle, el silbato) mágico para conjurar los espíritus
– *magic pipe for exorcising evil spirits*
43 el fetiche
– *fetish*

1 mujer *f* griega
– *Greek woman*
2 el peplo
– *peplos*
3 hombre *m* griego
– *Greek*
4 el petaso (sombrero *m* tesalio)
– *petasus (Thessalonian hat)*
5 el chitón, una túnica interior de lino *m*
– *chiton, a linen gown worn as a basic garment*
6 el himatión, un manto de lana *f*
– *himation, woollen* (Am. *woolen*) *cloak*
7 mujer *f* romana
– *Roman woman*
8 el tupé de la frente
– *toupee wig (partial wig)*
9 la estola
– *stola*
10 la palla, un manto de color *m*
– *palla, a coloured* (Am. *colored*) *wrap*
11 hombre *m* romano
– *Roman*
12 la túnica
– *tunica (tunic)*
13 la toga
– *toga*
14 la orla de púrpura *f*
– *purple border (purple band)*
15 emperatriz *f* bizantina
– *Byzantine empress*
16 la diadema de perlas *f*
– *pearl diadem*
17 los pinjantes
– *jewels*

18 el manto de púrpura *f*
– *purple cloak*
19 el vestido
– *long tunic*
20 princesa *f* alemana [siglo *m* XIII]
– *German princess [13th cent.]*
21 la diadema
– *crown (diadem)*
22 el griñón (la impla)
– *chinband*
23 la campanilla
– *tassel*
24 la presilla del manto
– *cloak cord*
25 el vestido ceñido
– *girt-up gown (girt-up surcoat, girt-up tunic)*
26 el manto
– *cloak*
27 alemán *m* en indumentaria *f* española [alrededor de 1575]
– *German dressed in the Spanish style [ca. 1575]*
28 el birrete
– *wide-brimmed cap*
29 la capa corta (capa *f* a la española)
– *short cloak (Spanish cloak, short cape)*
30 el jubón enguatado
– *padded doublet (stuffed doublet, peasecod)*
31 las trusas (los gregüescos acolchados y acuchillados)
– *stuffed trunk-hose*

32 lansquenete *m* [alrededor de 1530]
– *lansquenet (German mercenary soldier) [ca. 1530]*
33 el jubón acuchillado
– *slashed doublet (paned doublet)*
34 los pantalones bombachos
– *Pluderhose (loose breeches, paned trunk-hose, slops)*
35 mujer *f* basiliense [alrededor de 1525]
– *woman of Basle [ca. 1525]*
36 el sobretodo
– *overgown (gown)*
37 la saya
– *undergown (petticoat)*
38 mujer *f* de Nuremberg [alrededor de 1500]
– *woman of Nuremberg [ca. 1500]*
39 la esclavina
– *shoulder cape*
40 hombre *m* borgoñón [siglo *m* XV]
– *Burgundian [15th cent.]*
41 el jubón corto
– *short doublet*
42 los zapatos de punta *f* (zapatos *m* a la polaca)
– *piked shoes (peaked shoes, copped shoes, crackowes, poulaines)*
43 los chanclos (zuecos *m*, galochas *f*)
– *pattens (clogs)*
44 joven *m* noble [alrededor de 1400]
– *young nobleman [ca. 1400]*

45 el sayo corto
– *short, padded doublet (short, quilted doublet, jerkin)*
46 la manga festoneada
– *dagged sleeves (petal-scalloped sleeves)*
47 la calza
– *hose*
48 patricia *f* de Augsburgo [alrededor de 1575]
– *Augsburg patrician lady [ca. 1575]*
49 las mangas de bullones *m*
– *puffed sleeve*
50 el sobretodo
– *overgown (gown, open gown, sleeveless gown)*
51 dama *f* francesa [alrededor de 1600]
– *French lady [ca. 1600]*
52 la gorguera en muela *f* de molino *m*
– *millstone ruff (cartwheel ruff, ruff)*
53 el talle encorsetado (la cintura de avispa *f*)
– *corseted waist (wasp waist)*
54 caballero *m* [alrededor de 1650]
– *gentleman [ca. 1650]*
55 el sombrero blando (flexible) sueco
– *wide-brimmed felt hat (cavalier hat)*
56 el cuello de lino *m*
– *falling collar (wide-falling collar) of linen*
57 el forro de tela *m* blanca
– *white lining*

58 la bota alta (la bota con rodillera *f*)
– *jack boots (bucket-top boots)*
59 dama *f* [alrededor de 1650]
– *lady [ca. 1650]*
60 las mangas de bullones *m*
– *full puffed sleeves (puffed sleeves)*
61 caballero *m* [alrededor de 1700]
– *gentleman [ca. 1700]*
62 el sombrero de tres picos *m* (el tricornio)
– *three-cornered hat*
63 el espadín
– *dress sword*
64 dama *f* [alrededor de 1700]
– *lady [ca. 1700]*
65 el tocado (la toca) de encajes *m*
– *lace fontange (high headdress of lace)*
66 el manto de encajes *m*
– *lace-trimmed loose-hanging gown (loose-fitting housecoat, robe de chambre, negligée, contouche)*
67 la orla recamada
– *band of embroidery*
68 dama *f* [alrededor de 1880]
– *lady [ca. 1880]*
69 el polisón (*Chile:* la potolina)
– *bustle*
70 dama *f* [alrededor de 1858]
– *lady [ca. 1858]*
71 la capota (la papalina)
– *poke bonnet*

72 el miriñaque
– *crinoline*
73 caballero *m* del período Biedermeier
– *gentleman of the Biedermeier period*
74 el cuello alto (la marquesota; *fam.:* el foque)
– *high collar (choker collar)*
75 el chaleco floreado
– *embroidered waistcoat (vest)*
76 la levita
– *frock coat*
77 la peluca de coleta *f*
– *pigtail wig*
78 la cinta de la coleta (el lazo de la coleta)
– *ribbon (bow)*
79 damas *f* en trajes *m* de corte *f* [alrededor de 1780]
– *ladies in court dress [ca. 1780]*
80 la cola
– *train*
81 el peinado rococó
– *upswept Rococo coiffure*
82 el adorno del cabello
– *hair decoration*
83 el tontillo (el guardainfante)
– *panniered overskirt*

1 el recinto (la instalación) al aire libre
– *outdoor enclosure*
2 la roca natural
– *rocks*
3 el foso de separación *f*, un foso lleno
de agua *f*
– *moat*
4 el muro de protección *f*
– *enclosing wall*
5 los animales expuestos; *en este caso:*
una manada de leones *m*
– *animals on show;* here: *a pride of
lions*
6 el visitante del zoo
– *visitor to the zoo*
7 el cartel de advertencia *f*
– *notice*
8 la pajarera (el recinto para los
pájaros)
– *aviary*
9 el recinto de los elefantes
– *elephant enclosure*
10 la casa de los animales (*por ej.:* la casa
de las fieras, la casa de las jirafas, la
casa de los elefantes, la casa de los
monos)
– *animal house (e.g. carnivore house,
giraffe house, elephant house, monkey
house)*
11 la jaula exterior (la jaula de verano *m*)
– *outside cage (summer quarters)*
12 el recinto de los reptiles
– *reptile enclosure*

13 el cocodrilo del Nilo
– *Nile crocodile*
14 el terrario-acuario
– *terrarium and aquarium*
15 la vitrina
– *glass case*
16 la entrada de aire *m* fresco
– *fresh-air inlet*
17 la salida de aire *m* (la ventilación)
– *ventilator*
18 la calefacción del fondo de la vitrina
– *underfloor heating*
19 el acuario
– *aquarium*
20 el cartel explicativo
– *information plate*
21 la flora de una zona climática
– *flora in artificially maintained climate*

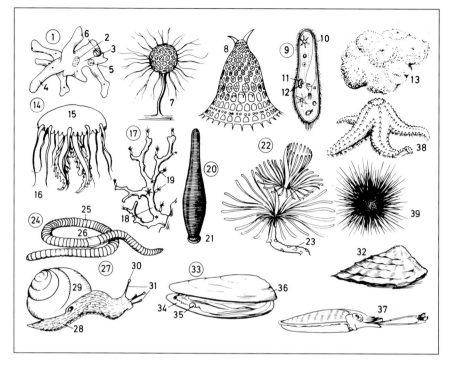

1-12 animales *m* unicelulares (proto-
zoarios *m*, protozoos *m*, infusorios *m*)
– **unicellular** *(one-celled, single-celled)*
  animals *(protozoans)*
1 la ameba, un rizópodo
– *amoeba, a rhizopod*
2 el núcleo de la célula
– *cell nucleus*
3 el protoplasma
– *protoplasm*
4 el seudópodo
– *pseudopod*
5 la vejiguilla excretora (la vacuola pulsátil), un orgánulo
– *excretory vacuole (contractile vacuole,
  an organelle)*
6 la vejiguilla de alimentación *f* (la vacuola alimenticia)
– *food vacuole*
7 el actinomorfo, un heliozoario
– *Actinophrys, a heliozoan*
8 el radiolario; *en este caso:* el esqueleto
silíceo
– *radiolarian; here: siliceous skeleton*
9 el animálculo zapatilla (paramecio
m), un infusorio ciliado
– *slipper animalcule, a Paramecium (ciliate infusorian)*
10 el cilio
– *cilium*
11 el macronúcleo
– *macronucleus (meganucleus)*
12 el micronúcleo
– *micronucleus*
13-39 animales *m* multicelulares (meta-
zoarios *m*)
– **multicellular animals** *(metazoans)*

13 la esponja, un espongiario
– *bath sponge, a porifer (sponge)*
14 la medusa, un acalefo de disco *m*
(medusa *f* de sombrilla *f*, aguamala *f*,
un acalefo), un celentéreo
– *medusa, a discomedusa, a coelenterate*
15 la sombrilla
– *umbrella*
16 el tentáculo
– *tentacle*
17 el coral rojo, un coral (antozoario *m*,
constructor de arrecifes *m*)
– *red coral (precious coral), a coral animal (anthozoan, reef-building animal)*
18 la rama de coral *m*
– *coral colony*
19 el pólipo coralígeno
– *coral polyp*
20-26 gusanos *m* (vermes *m*)
– *worms (Vermes)*
20 la sanguijuela, un anélido (gusano *m*
de anillos *m*)
– *leech, an annelid*
21 la ventosa
– *sucker*
22 el espirógrafo, un gusano con filamentos *m*
– *Spirographis, a bristle worm*
23 el tubo
– *tube*
24 la lombriz de tierra *f*
– *earthworm*
25 el segmento
– *segment*
26 el clitelo [la zona de acoplamiento *m*]
– *clitellum [accessory reproductive
organ]*

27-36 moluscos *m*
– *molluscs* (Am. *mollusks*)
27 el caracol (el caracol de las viñas), un
gasterópodo
– *edible snail, a snail*
28 el pie reptante
– *creeping foot*
29 la concha (la concha de caracol *m*)
– *shell (snail shell)*
30 el ojo peduncular
– *stalked eye*
31 los pares de tentáculos (cuernos *m*)
– *tentacles (feelers)*
32 la ostra
– *oyster*
33 la madreperla de río *m*
– *freshwater pearl mussel*
34 el nácar
– *mother-of-pearl (nacre)*
35 la perla
– *pearl*
36 la valva
– *mussel shell*
37 la jibia (la sepia), un cefalópodo
– *cuttlefish, a cephalopod*
38 u. 39 equinodermos *m*
– *echinoderms*
38 la estrella de mar *amb.* (la estrellamar)
– *starfish (sea star)*
39 el erizo de mar *amb.* (el equino)
– *sea urchin (sea hedgehog)*

1 *u.* 2 **crustáceos** *m*
– **crustaceans**
1 la dromia velluda (el cangrejo faquín), un cangrejo
– *mitten crab, a crab*
2 el asélido común (la cochinilla de agua *f*)
– *water slater*
3-39, 48-56 **insectos** *m*
– **insects**
3 la libélula (el caballito del diablo, el dragón volador), un odonato
– *water nymph (dragonfly), a homopteran (homopterous insect), a dragonfly*
4 el escorpión acuático (la nepa, la chinche acuática, el garapito), un hemíptero
– *water scorpion (water bug), a rhynchophore*
5 el sifón respiratorio
– *raptorial leg*
6 la efémera (la cachipolla, la efímera, la mosca de pesca *f*)
– *mayfly (dayfly, ephemerid)*
7 el ojo compuesto
– *compound eye*
8 la langosta migratoria (el saltamontes verde), un ortóptero
– *green grasshopper (green locust, meadow grasshopper), an orthopteron (orthopterous insect)*
9 la larva
– *larva (grub)*
10 el insecto adulto, el imago, un insecto perfecto
– *adult insect, an imago*
11 la pata saltadora
– *leaping hind leg*
12 la frigánea (el frígano, la mosca de primavera *f*, la polilla de agua *f*), un neuróptero
– *caddis fly (spring fly, water moth), a neuropteran*
13 el pulgón (la mosca verde), un piojo de las plantas
– *aphid (greenfly), a plant louse*
14 el pulgón áptero (la filoxera)
– *wingless aphid*
15 el pulgón alado
– *winged aphid*
16-20 **dípteros** *m*
– **dipterous insects** *(dipterans)*
16 el cénzalo (el mosquito; *Amér.*: el zancudo), un cínife
– *gnat (mosquito, midge), a culicid*
17 la trompa chupadora
– *proboscis (sucking organ)*
18 la mosca (azul) de la carne (la moscarda, el moscón, el moscardón)
– *bluebottle (blowfly), a fly*
19 la cresa
– *maggot (larva)*

20 la crisálida (la ninfa)
– *chrysalis (pupa)*
21 *u.* 22 la hormiga
– *ant*
21-23 **himenópteros** *m*
– **Hymenoptera**
21 la hembra alada (la reina)
– *winged female*
22 la obrera
– *worker*
23 el abejorro (el abejón)
– *bumblebee (humblebee)*
24-39 **escarabajos** *m* (coleópteros *m*)
– **beetles** *(Coleoptera)*
24 el ciervo volante (el lucano ciervo, el escarabajo cornudo), un escarabeoideo
– *stag beetle, a lamellicorn beetle*
25 las mandíbulas (las tenazas)
– *mandibles*
26 los palpos maxilares
– *trophi*
27 la antena
– *antenna (feeler)*
28 la cabeza
– *head*
29 *u.* 30 el tórax
– *thorax*
29 el protórax (el pronoto, el escudo del cuello, el escudo torácico)
– *thoracic shield (prothorax)*
30 el escutelo (el escudete)
– *scutellum*
31 los arcos dorsales de los segmentos
– *tergites*
32 el estigma (el orificio respiratorio)
– *stigma*
33 el ala *f* (el ala *f* posterior)
– *wing (hind wing)*
34 la nervadura del ala *f* (la vena del ala *f*)
– *nervure*
35 el punto por donde se pliega el ala *f*
– *point at which the wing folds*
36 el élitro
– *elytron (forewing)*
37 la mariquita (la vaca de San Antón), un coccinélido
– *ladybird (Am. ladybug), a coccinellid*
38 el ergates carpintero, un cerambícido
– *Ergates faber, a longicorn beetle (longicorn)*
39 el escarabajo pelotero (el escarabajo del estiércol), un escarabeoideo
– *dung beetle, a lamellicorn beetle*
40-47 **arácnidos** *m*
– **arachnids**
40 el escorpión común (el alacrán)
– *Euscorpius flavicandus, a scorpion*

41 el pedipalpo prensil
– *cheliped with chelicer*
42 el palpo maxilar
– *maxillary antenna (maxillary feeler)*
43 el aguijón caudal (*Amér. Central:* el chuzo), una uña venenosa
– *tail sting*
44-46 **arañas** *f*
– **spiders**
44 la garrapata común (el ixodes, la garrapata de los perros), un ácaro
– *wood tick (dog tick)*
45 la araña de jardín *m* (la epeira, la araña de cruz *f*), una araña de telaraña *f* circular
– *cross spider (garden spider), an orb spinner*
46 la hilera
– *spinneret*
47 la telaraña
– *spider's web (web)*
48-56 **mariposas** *f* (lepidópteros *m*)
– **Lepidoptera** *(butterflies and moths)*
48 la mariposa de la seda (el bómbix del moral), un bombícido
– *mulberry-feeding moth (silk moth), a bombycid moth*
49 los huevos
– *eggs*
50 el gusano de la seda (la oruga)
– *silkworm*
51 el capullo
– *cocoon*
52 el macaón, una papiliónida (la cola de golondrina *f*)
– *swallowtail, a butterfly*
53 la antena
– *antenna (feeler)*
54 la mancha en forma *f* de ojo *m*
– *eyespot*
55 la esfinge del aligustre, una mariposa nocturna
– *privet hawkmoth, a hawkmoth (sphinx)*
56 la trompa
– *proboscis*

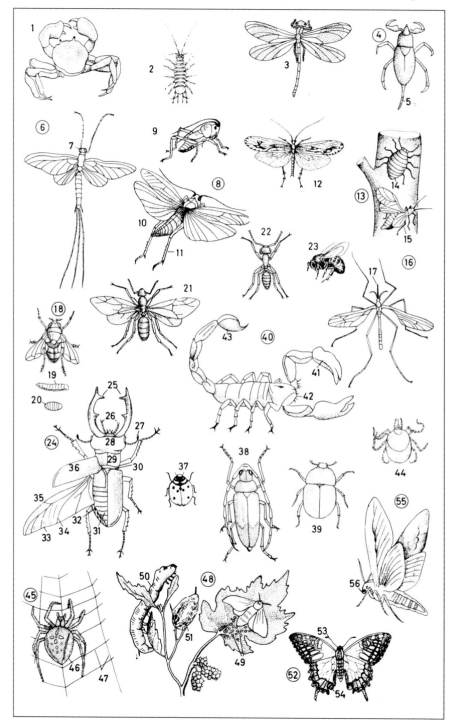

1-3 aves *f* corredoras
- *flightless birds*
1 el casuario de cresta, un casuario; *anál.:* el emú
- *cassowary;* sim.: *emu*
2 el avestruz; *anál.:* el ñandú, el avestruz de América (*Arg. y Bol.:* el suri; *Chile:* el tuyú)
- *ostrich*
3 la nidada de huevos *m* de avestruz *m* [12-14 huevos]
- *clutch of ostrich eggs [12-14 eggs]*
4 el pingüino imperial (el pájaro bobo, el pájaro niño; *Guat.:* el tolobojo), un pingüino (una palmípeda, nadadora, no voladora)
- *king penguin, a penguin, a flightless bird*

5-10 palmípedas *f*
- *web-footed birds*
5 el pelícano común (el pelícano rosa, la platalea; *Amér.:* el alcatraz; *Pan.:* el cuaco; *Venez.:* el buchón, el tocotoco), una pelicánida
- *white pelican (wood stork, ibis, wood ibis, spoonbill, brent goose, Am. brant goose, brant), a pelican*
6 la pata palmípeda
- *webfoot (webbed foot)*
7 la membrana interdigital
- *web (palmations) of webbed foot (palmate foot)*
8 la mandíbula inferior, con la bolsa
- *lower mandible with gular pouch*
9 el alcatraz común (el onocrótalo, el pelícano americano), una súlida
- *northern gannet (gannet, solan goose), a gannet*
10 el cormorán moñudo (el cuervo marino, el corvejón; *Cuba:* la corúa), una falocrocorácida con las alas extendidas "posando"
- *green cormorant (shag), a cormorant displaying with spread wings*

11-14 aves *f* de alas *f* largas (aves marinas)
- *long-winged birds* (seabirds)
11 el charrancito, una golondrina de mar *amb.* (una esterna), zambulléndose en busca *f* de comida *f*
- *common sea swallow, a sea swallow (tern), diving for food*
12 el fulmar, un petrel (una ave de las tempestades; *anál.:* una pardela)
- *fulmar*
13 el arao común, una uría, un álcido
- *guillemot, an auk*
14 la gaviota reidora (la gaviota común, la gaviota de cabeza *f* negra), una gaviota
- *black-headed gull (mire crow), a gull*

15-17 anserinos *m*
- *Anseres*
15 la serreta grande, un mergo
- *goosander (common merganser), a sawbill*
16 el cisne común (el cisne mudo, el cisne negro), un cisne
- *mute swan, a swan*
17 la protuberancia del pico
- *knob on the bill*
18 la garza real (la garza cenicienta), una ardeida, una ave zancuda
- *common heron, a heron*

19-21 limícolas *m*
- *plovers*
19 la cigüeñuela (*Arg.:* el yabirú; *Venez.:* el soldado)
- *stilt (stilt bird, stilt plover)*
20 la foja (la focha, el fallaris, la gallareta), una fúlica, una rálida; *anál.:* el rascón, la polla
- *coot, a rail*
21 el avefría *f*
- *lapwing (green plover, peewit, pewit)*
22 la codorniz, una faisánida; *anál.:* la perdiz
- *quail, a gallinaceous bird*
23 la tórtola (*Mé.:* el mucuy), una paloma torcaz
- *turtle dove, a pigeon*
24 el vencejo (el arrejaco, el arrejaque); *anál.:* el avión, la salangana; una apodida
- *swift*
25 la abubilla común (la upupa), una tenuirrostra, una upúpida
- *hoopoe, a roller*
26 el penacho de plumas *f* eréctiles
- *erectile crest*
27 el pico picapinos (el pájaro carpintero, el picamaderos, el picaposte, el picarrelincho, el pico barreno, el pico carpintero), un pico, una pícida; *anál.:* el torcecuello (*Hond.:* el checo), el pito
- *spotted woodpecker, a woodpecker; related: wryneck*
28 la entrada del nido
- *entrance to the nest*
29 la cavidad nidal (el hueco de la empolladura)
- *nesting cavity*
30 el cuclillo (el cuco), una cucúlida; *anál.:* el críalo
- *cuckoo*

1, 3, 4, 5, 7, 9, 10 aves *f* canoras
- *songbirds*
1 el jilguero (el sirguero, el pintacilgo, el pintadillo, la cardelina, el
colorín, el sietecolores), un
fringílido
- *goldfinch, a finch*
2 el abejaruco (el azulejo)
- *bee eater*
3 el colirrojo de los jardines (el colirrojo real), un túrdido
- *redstart (star finch), a thrush*
4 el herrerillo común, un párido
- *bluetit, a tit (titmouse), a resident
bird (non-migratory bird)*
5 el camachuelo común, una ave
sedentaria
- *bullfinch*
6 la carraca
- *common roller (roller)*
7 la oropéndola (la lútea, el oriol, el
papafigo, el vireo, el virio), una ave
migratoria (una ave de paso *m*)
- *golden oriole, a migratory bird*
8 el martín pescador (el alción, el
guardarrío, el pájaro polilla; *Perú:*
el camaronero)
- *kingfisher*
9 la lavandera blanca (la
aguzanieves, la aguanieves, el
andarríos, la apuranieves, la
nevatilla, la nevereta, la pajarita
de las nieves, la pizpita), una
lavandera (pezpítalo *m,* caudatré-
mula *f,* doradillo *m,* motacila *f,*
motalita *f*)
- *white wagtail, a wagtail*
10 el pinzón vulgar (el pinchón)
- *chaffinch*

1-20 aves *f* canoras
- *songbirds*

1-3 córvidos *m*
- *Corvidae (corvine birds, crows)*

1 el arrendajo común, un gárrulo
- *jay (nutcracker)*

2 la graja (el grajo, el cuervo merendero); *anál.:* la corneja (la chova), el cuervo, la grajilla
- *rook, a crow*

3 la urraca (la picaza, la marica, la cotorra, la gaya, la pega, la picaraza)
- *magpie*

4 el estornino pinto
- *starling (pastor, shepherd bird)*

5 el gorrión común (el pardal, el gurriato; *Mé.:* el burrión)
- *house sparrow*

6-8 fringílidos *m*
- *finches*

6 *u.* **7** emberizas *f* (escribanos *m*)
- *buntings*

6 el escribano cerillo
- *yellowhammer (yellow bunting)*

7 el escribano hortelano
- *ortolan (ortolan bunting)*

8 el lúgano; *anál.:* el verderón (el verdecillo, el verdorol, el verdezuelo, el verdón)
- *siskin (aberdevine)*

9 el carbonero común
- *great titmouse (great tit, ox eye), a titmouse (tit)*

10 el reyezuelo sencillo; *anál.:* el reyezuelo listado; un régulo
- *golden-crested wren (goldcrest); sim.: firecrest, one of the Regulidae*

11 el trepador azul
- *nuthatch*

12 el chochín
- *wren*

13-17 túrdidos *m*
- *thrushes*

13 el mirlo común (la merla, la mirla)
- *blackbird*

14 el ruiseñor común (*poético:* la filomena, la filomela)
- *nightingale (poet.: philomel, philomela)*

15 el petirrojo
- *robin (redbreast, robin redbreast)*

16 el zorzal común, un tordo
- *song thrush (throstle, mavis)*

17 el ruiseñor alemán
- *thrush nightingale*

18 *u.* **19** alondras *f*
- *larks*

18 la totovía (la tova)
- *woodlark*

19 la cogujada común (la cochevís, la copada, la golerita); *anál.:* la alondra (la calandria, la copetuda, la terrera)
- *crested lark (tufted lark)*

20 la golondrina común, una hirundínida
- *common swallow (barn swallow, chimney swallow), a swallow*

1-13 aves *f* rapaces (aves *f* de rapiña *f*) **diurnas**
– *diurnal birds of prey*
1-4 falcónidas *f*
– *falcons*
1 el esmerejón
– *merlin*
2 el halcón común (el halcón peregrino)
– *peregrine falcon*
3 los "calzones" (el plumaje del muslo)
– *leg feathers*
4 el tarso
– *tarsus*
5-9 águilas *f*
– *eagles*
5 el pigargo
– *white-tailed sea eagle (white-tailed eagle, grey sea eagle, erne)*
6 el pico corvo
– *hooked beak*
7 la garra
– *claw (talon)*
8 la cola
– *tail*
9 el ratonero común
– *common buzzard*
10-13 accípitres *m*
– *accipiters*
10 el azor
– *goshawk*

11 el milano rojo (el milano real)
– *common European kite (glede, kite)*
12 el gavilán
– *sparrow hawk (spar-hawk)*
13 el aguilucho lagunero
– *marsh harrier (moor buzzard, moor harrier, moor hawk)*
14-19 aves *f* rapaces nocturnas (estrígidas *f*)
– *owls*
14 el búho chico; *más pequeño:* el autillo
– *long-eared owl (horned owl)*
15 el búho real (*Perú:* el carancho)
– *eagle-owl (great horned owl)*
16 el plumicornio (los mechones de plumas *f* en forma *f* de orejas *f*)
– *plumicorn (feathered ear, ear tuft, ear, horn)*
17 la lechuza (*Arg. y Urug.:* el quitilipi)
– *barn owl (white owl, silver owl, yellow owl, church owl, screech owl)*
18 el "velo" (el cerco facial de plumas *f*)
– *facial disc (disk)*
19 el mochuelo común
– *little owl (sparrow owl)*

1 la cacatúa de cresta *f* amarilla, un
  papagayo
– *sulphur-crested cockatoo, a parrot*
2 el guacamayo (el ara)
– *blue-and-yellow macaw*
3 el ave del Paraíso azul
– *blue bird of paradise*
4 el colibrí sappho, un colibrí (el
  pájaro mosca, el picaflor; *Arg.:* el
  rundún; *Col.:* el rumbo; *Mé. y. P.*
  Rico: el chupamirto)
– *sappho*
5 el cardenal (*Col.:* el titiribí)
– *cardinal (cardinal bird)*
6 el tucán (*Arg. y Venez.:* el
  tucano), una ave trepadora
– *toucan (red-billed toucan), one of*
  the Piciformes

1-18 peces *m*
– *fishes*
1 el jaquetón (el tiburón azul), un tiburón (lamia *f*, marrajo *m*), un escualo
– *man-eater (blue shark, requin), a shark*
2 la nariz (el morro)
– *nose (snout)*
3 las hendiduras branquiales
– *gill slit (gill cleft)*
4 la carpa de laguna *f* (la carpa de río *m*, la carpa de espejo *m*), un ciprínido
– *carp, a mirror carp (carp)*
5 el opérculo
– *gill cover (operculum)*
6 la aleta dorsal
– *dorsal fin*
7 la aleta pectoral
– *pectoral fin*
8 la aleta ventral
– *pelvic fin (abdominal fin, ventral fin)*
9 la aleta anal
– *anal fin*
10 la aleta caudal
– *caudal fin (tail fin)*
11 la escama
– *scale*
12 el siluro (*anál.: Venez.:* el laulao)
– *catfish (sheatfish, sheathfish, wels)*
13 el barbillón
– *barbel*
14 el arenque
– *herring*
15 la trucha de río *m*, una trucha
– *brown trout (German brown trout), a trout*
16 el lucio común
– *pike (northern pike)*
17 la anguila (*Amér.:* la anguilla)
– *freshwater eel (eel)*
18 el caballito de mar *amb.* (el hipocampo, el caballo marino)
– *sea horse (Hippocampus, horse-fish)*
19 el penacho de branquias *f*
– *tufted gills*
20-26 anfibios *m* (batracios *m*)
– **Amphibia** *(amphibians)*
20-22 urodelos *m* (anfibios *m* con cola *f*)
– *salamanders*
20 el tritón crestado, un tritón (salamandra *f* acuática)
– *greater water newt (crested newt), a water newt*
21 la cresta dorsal
– *dorsal crest*
22 la salamandra común, una salamandra
– *fire salamander, a salamander*
23-26 anuros *m* (anfibios *m* sin cola *f*)
– *salientians (anurans, batrachians)*
23 el sapo común, un sapo (escuerzo *m*)
– *European toad, a toad*

24 la rana de San Antonio (la rana de zarzal *m*, la rubeta, la rana bermeja)
– *tree frog (tree toad)*
25 el saco vocal
– *vocal sac (vocal pouch, croaking sac)*
26 el disco adhesivo (el cojinete discoidal adhesivo)
– *adhesive disc (disk)*
27-41 reptiles *m*
– *reptiles*
27 *u.* **30-37 saurios** *m*
– *lizards*
27 la lagartija (la regalterna, la sargantana)
– *sand lizard*
28 la tortuga de carey *m*
– *hawksbill turtle (hawksbill)*
29 el caparazón (la concha, el escudo, el espaldar)
– *carapace (shell)*
30 el basilisco (*Amér.:* la iguana)
– *basilisk*
31 el varano del desierto, un varano; *más pequeño:* el lagarto
– *desert monitor, a monitor lizard (monitor)*
32 la iguana verde, una iguana
– *common iguana, an iguana*
33 el camaleón, un camaleónido
– *chameleon, one of the Chamaeleontidae (Rhiptoglossa)*
34 la pata prensil
– *prehensile foot*
35 la cola prensil
– *prehensile tail*
36 la salamanquesa de pared *f*, una salamanquesa (salamandria *f*)
– *wall gecko, a gecko*
37 el lución (*anál.:* la serpiente de vidrio *m*, la serpiente quebradiza, la serpiente ciega, el lagarto de cristal *m*), un ánguido, un lagarto ápodo
– *slowworm (blindworm), one of the Anguidae*
38-41 ofidios *m* (serpientes *f; Amér. Central:* los mazacotes)
– **snakes**
38 la serpiente de collar *m* (la serpiente acuática), una culebra
– *ringed snake (ring snake, water snake, grass snake), a colubrid*
39 los lunares (el collar)
– *collar*
40 *u.* **41** víboras *f*
– *vipers (adders)*
40 la víbora común, una serpiente venenosa
– *common viper, a poisonous (venomous) snake*
41 el áspid
– *asp (asp viper)*

1-6 mariposas *f* **diurnas** (lepidópteros *m* diurnos)
- *butterflies*
1 la vanesa atalanta, una ninfálida
- *re(admiral*
2 el pavo real, una ninfálida
- *peacock butterfly*
3 la aurora, una piérida
- *orange tip (orange tip butterfly)*
4 la limonera, una piérida
- *brimstone (brimstone butterfly)*
5 la antíope, una ninfálida
- *Camberwell beauty (mourning cloak, mourning cloak butterfly)*
6 la hormiguera de lunares *m*, una licénida
- *blue (lycaenid butterfly, lycaenid)*
7-11 mariposas *f* **nocturnas** (lepidópteros *m* nocturnos)
- *moths (Heterocera)*
7 la quelonia (la gitana)
- *garden tiger*
8 la catocala nupcial
- *red underwing*
9 la mariposa de calavera *f* (la esfinge de calavera *f*), una esfíngida
- *death's-head moth (death's-head hawkmoth), a hawkmoth (sphinx)*
10 la oruga
- *caterpillar*
11 la crisálida (la ninfa)
- *chrysalis (pupa)*

1 el ornitorrinco, un monotrema (un mamífero ovíparo)
– *platypus (duck-bill, duck-mole), a monotreme (oviparous mammal)*
2 u. **3 marsupiales** m (didelfos m)
– **marsupial mammals** *(marsupials)*
2 la zarigüeya norteamericana (*Mé.:* el tlacuache; *Arg.:* la comadreja), un didelfo (un marsupial)
– *New World opossum, a didelphid*
3 el canguro rojo gigante, un canguro
– *red kangaroo (red flyer), a kangaroo*
4-7 insectívoros m
– **insectivores** *(insect-eating mammals)*
4 el topo
– *mole*
5 el erizo
– *hedgehog*
6 la púa
– *spine*
7 la musaraña doméstica (el musgaño doméstico), una musaraña
– *shrew (shrew mouse), one of the Soricidae*
8 el armadillo (*Mé.:* el ayotoste; *Arg., Bol. y Chile:* el tatú)
– *nine-banded armadillo (peba)*
9 el orejudo, un gimnorrino, un mamífero volador (un quiróptero, un murciélago) (*Col.:* el chimbilá; *Amér. Merid.:* el vampiro)
– *long-eared bat (flitter-mouse), a flying mammal (chiropter, chiropteran)*
10 el pangolín, un mamífero con escamas f
– *pangolin (scaly ant-eater), a scaly mammal*
11 el perezoso (*Arg. y Bol.:* el aí; *Venez.:* el pereza; *Amér. Central, Bol., Ec. y Venez.:* el perico ligero; *Guayana:* el unau)
– *two-toed sloth (unau)*
12-19 roedores m
– **rodents**
12 el conejillo de Indias (*Amér.:* el cobayo, la cobaya)
– *guinea pig (cavy)*
13 el puerco espín
– *porcupine*
14 el castor del Plata (*Arg. y Chile:* el coipo, el coipú; *Arg. y Bol.:* el quiyá)
– *beaver*
15 el jerbo
– *jerboa*
16 el hámster (la marmota de Alemania, la rata del trigo)
– *hamster*
17 la rata de agua f, un arvícola
– *water vole*

18 la marmota
– *marmot*
19 la ardilla (*Costa Rica:* el tuche)
– *squirrel*
20 el elefante africano, un proboscidio
– *African elephant, a proboscidean (proboscidian)*
21 la trompa
– *trunk (proboscis)*
22 el colmillo
– *tusk*
23 el manatí (*Amér.:* el peje buey; *Bol.:* el lamantín), un sirénido
– *manatee (manati, lamantin), a sirenian*
24 el damán sudafricano, un lamnunguio
– *South African dassie (das, coney, hyrax), a procaviid*
25-31 ungulados m
– **ungulates**
25-27 perisodáctilos m (ungulados m de dedos m impares)
– **odd-toed ungulates**
25 el rinoceronte africano, un rinoceronte (un nasicornio)
– *African black rhino, a rhinoceros (nasicorn)*
26 el tapir sudamericano (*Río de la Plata, Bol. y Perú:* el anta f; *Arg.:* la gran bestia, el pinchaco; *Perú:* la sachavaca; *Amér. Central, Bol. y Ec.:* el tapiro)
– *Brazilian tapir, a tapir*
27 la cebra
– *zebra*
28-31 artiodáctilos m (ungulados m de dedos m pares)
– **even-toed ungulates**
28-30 rumiantes m
– **ruminants**
28 la llama (*Amér. Merid.:* la oveja, el paco; *Ec.:* el llamingo, la runallama); *anál.:* la alpaca (*Amér. Merid.:* el paco)
– *llama*
29 el camello bactriano (el camello de dos gibas f)
– *Bactrian camel (two-humped camel)*
30 el guanaco (*Arg.:* el teque)
– *guanaco*
31 el hipopótamo
– *hippopotamus*

1-10 ungulados *m,* **rumiantes** *m*
– ***ungulates, ruminants***
1 el alce (el anta *f*)
– *elk (moose)*
2 el uapití
– *wapiti* (Am. *elk)*
3 la gamuza
– *chamois*
4 la jirafa
– *giraffe*
5 la cervicabra, un antílope
– *black buck, an antelope*
6 el muflón
– *mouflon (moufflon)*
7 el íbice (la cabra montés, el hirco)
– *ibex (rock goat, bouquetin, stein-bock)*
8 el búfalo
– *water buffalo (Indian buffalo, water ox)*
9 el bisonte (*Mé.:* el búfalo)
– *bison*
10 el buey almizclero
– *musk ox*
11-22 carnívoros *m* (carniceros *m*)
– ***carnivores** (beasts of prey)*
11-13 cánidos *m*
– ***Camidae***
11 el chacal (*Río de la Plata:* el aguará); *anál.:* el coyote
– *black-backed jackal (jackal)*
12 el zorro común (la zorra, la raposa, la vulpeja)
– *red fox*
13 el lobo
– *wolf*
14-17 mustélidos *m*
– ***martens***
14 la garduña (la fuina)
– *stone marten (beach marten)*
15 la marta cibelina (la marta cebellina)
– *sable*
16 la comadreja (la mustela)
– *weasel*
17 la nutria marina, una nutria
– *sea otter, an otter*
18-22 pinnípedos *m*
– ***seals** (pinnipeds)*
18 el oso marino
– *fur seal (sea bear, ursine seal)*
19 la foca (el lobo marino, el becerro marino, el carnero marino, el vítulo marino)
– *common seal (sea calf, sea dog)*
20 la morsa
– *walrus (morse)*
21 el bigote
– *whiskers*
22 el colmillo
– *tusk*
23-29 cetáceos *m*
– ***whales***

23 la marsopa (el puerco marino)
– *bottle-nosed dolphin (bottle-nose dolphin)*
24 el delfín común (el arroaz, el golfín, la tonina; *Hond., Mé. y Perú:* el bufeo)
– *common dolphin*
25 el cachalote
– *sperm whale (cachalot)*
26 las narices
– *blowhole (spout hole)*
27 la aleta dorsal
– *dorsal fin*
28 la aleta pectoral
– *flipper*
29 la aleta caudal
– *tail flukes (tail)*

1-11 carnívoros *m* (carniceros *m*)
– **carnivores** *(beasts of prey)*
1 la hiena rayada, una hiena
– *striped hyena, a hyena*
2-8 felinos *m*
– **felines** *(cats)*
2 el león
– *lion*
3 la melena
– *mane (lion's mane)*
4 la garra (la zarpa)
– *paw*
5 el tigre
– *tiger*
6 el leopardo (el pardal)
– *leopard*
7 el guepardo (la onza)
– *cheetah (hunting leopard)*
8 el lince (el lobo cerval)
– *lynx*
9-11 úrsidos *m*
– **bears**
9 el mapache (el oso lavador; *Cuba:*
el perro mudo)
– *raccoon (racoon, Am. coon)*
10 el oso común (el oso pardo)
– *brown bear*
11 el oso blanco (el oso polar)
– *polar bear (white bear)*
12 *u.* **13** monos *m*
– *monkeys*
12-16 primates *m*
– **primates**
12 el macaco rheso
– *rhesus monkey (rhesus, rhesus
macaque)*
13 el babuino (el zambo)
– *baboon*
14-16 antropoides *m*
– **anthropoids** *(anthropoid apes,
great apes)*
14 el chimpancé
– *chimpanzee*
15 el orangután (el jocó)
– *orang-utan (orang-outan)*
16 el gorila
– *gorilla*

1 Gigantocypris agassizi (el ostrácodo gigante)
– *Gigantocypris agassizi*
2 Macropharynx longicaudatus (la
anguila pelícano)
– *Eupharynx pelecanoides (pelican
eel, pelican fish)*
3 Metacrinus, un crinoideo (un lirio
de mar *amb.*), un equinodermo
– *Metacrinus (feather star), a sea
lily, an echinoderm*
4 Licoteutis diadema (la lámpara
maravillosa), una sepia [luminis-
cente]
– *Lycoteuthis diadema (jewelled
squid), a cuttlefish [luminescent]*
5 Atolla, una medusa abisal, un
celentéreo
– *Atolla, a deep-sea medusa, a coelenterate*
6 Melanocetes, un pediculado
[luminiscente]
– *Melanocetes, a pediculate [lumi-
nescent]*
7 Lophocalyx philippensis, una
esponja silícea
– *Lophocalyx philippensis, a glass
sponge*
8 Mopsea, un coral córneo [colonia *f*]
– *Mopsea, a sea fan [colony]*
9 Hydrallmania, un pólipo hidroide,
un pólipo, un celentéreo [colonia *f*]
– *Hydrallmania, a hydroid polyp, a
coelenterate [colony]*
10 Malacosteus indicus, un
estomiátido [luminiscente]
– *Malacosteus indicus, a stomiatid
[luminescent]*
11 Brisinga endecacnemos, un ofi-
uroideo, un equinodermo
[luminiscente sólo cuando está
excitado]
– *Brisinga endecacnemos, a sand star
(brittle star), an echinoderm [lumi-
nescent only when stimulated]*
12 Pasiphaea, un camarón, un
crustáceo
– *Pasiphaea, a shrimp, a crustacean*
13 Echiostoma, un estomiátido, un
pez abisal [luminiscente]
– *Echiostoma, a stomiatid, a fish
[luminescent]*
14 Umbellula encrinus, una penna-
túlida, un celentéreo [colonia *f*
luminiscente]
– *Umbellula encrinus, a sea pen (sea
feather), a coelenterate [colony,
luminescent]*
15 Polycheles, un crustáceo
– *Polycheles, a crustacean*
16 Lithodes, un crustáceo, un cangrejo
– *Lithodes, a crustacean, a crab*

17 Archaster, una estrella de mar
amb. (una estrellamar, un aste-
roideo), un equinodermo
– *Archaster, a starfish (sea star), an
echinoderm*
18 Oneirophanta, una holoturia, un
equinodermo
– *Oneirophanta, a sea cucumber, an
echinoderm*
19 Palaeopneustes niasicus, un erizo
de mar *amb.*, un equinodermo
– *Palaeopneustes niasicus, a sea
urchin (sea hedgehog), an echinoderm*
20 Chitonactis, una anémona de mar
amb. (actinia *f*), un celentéreo
– *Chitonactis, a sea anemone
(actinia), a coelenterate*

1 el árbol
– *tree*
2 el tronco
– *bole (tree trunk, trunk, stem)*
3 la copa (*Venez.:* el copo)
– *crown of tree (crown)*
4 la cima
– *top of tree (treetop)*
5 la rama
– *bough (limb, branch)*
6 el ramo
– *twig (branch)*
7 el tronco [corte *m* transversal]
– *bole (tree trunk) [cross section]*
8 la corteza
– *bark (rind)*
9 el líber
– *phloem (bast sieve tissue, inner fibrous bark)*
10 el cambium
– *cambium (cambium ring)*
11 los radios medulares
– *medullary rays (vascular rays, pith rays)*
12 la albura (el alborno)
– *sapwood (sap, alburnum)*
13 el duramen (el corazón)
– *heartwood (duramen)*
14 la médula
– *pith*
15 **la planta**
– ***plant***
16-18 la raíz
– *root*
16 la raíz principal
– *primary root*
17 la raíz secundaria
– *secondary root*
18 el pelo absorbente (el pelo radical)
– *root hair*
19-25 el tallo
– *shoot (sprout)*
19 la hoja
– *leaf*
20 el tallo
– *stalk*
21 el tallo secundario (la rama de primer orden *m*)
– *side shoot (offshoot)*
22 la yema terminal
– *terminal bud*
23 la flor
– *flower*
24 el botón floral (el capullo)
– *flower bud*
25 la axila foliar, con la yema axilar
– *leaf axil with axillary bud*
26 **la hoja**
– ***leaf***
27 el pecíolo
– *leaf stalk (petiole)*
28 el limbo (la lámina foliar)
– *leaf blade (blade, lamina)*
29 la nervadura de la hoja
– *venation (veins, nervures, ribs)*
30 el nervio medial
– *midrib (nerve)*
31-38 formas *f* de las hojas
– *leaf shapes*
31 linear (lineal)
– *linear*
32 lanceolada
– *lanceolate*
33 orbicular
– *orbicular (orbiculate)*
34 acicular
– *acerose (acerous, acerate, acicular, needle-shaped)*
35 acorazonada
– *cordate*

36 oval
– *ovate*
37 sagitada
– *sagittate*
38 arriñonada
– *reniform*
39-42 hojas *f* compuestas
– *compound leaves*
39 digitada (compuesta palmeada)
– *digitate (digitated, palmate, quinquefoliolate)*
40 compuesta pinnada (pinnatífida)
– *pinnatifid*
41 paripinnada
– *abruptly pinnate*
42 imparipinnada
– *odd-pinnate*
43-50 clases *f* de hojas *f* según el borde del limbo
– *leaf margin shapes*
43 entera
– *entire*
44 aserrada
– *serrate (serrulate, saw-toothed)*
45 denticulada
– *doubly toothed*
46 festoneada
– *crenate*
47 dentada
– *dentate*
48 lobulada
– *sinuate*
49 ciliada
– *ciliate (ciliated)*
50 el cilio
– *cilium*
51 **la flor**
– ***flower***
52 el pedúnculo (el pedicelo, el pezón)
– *flower stalk (flower stem, scape)*
53 el receptáculo (el tálamo)
– *receptacle (floral axis, thalamus, torus)*
54 el ovario
– *ovary*
55 el estilo
– *style*
56 el estigma
– *stigma*
57 el estambre
– *stamen*
58 el sépalo
– *sepal*
59 el pétalo
– *petal*
60 ovario *m* y estambre *m* [corte *m*]
– *ovary and stamen [section]*
61 la pared del ovario
– *ovary wall*
62 la cavidad del ovario
– *ovary cavity*
63 el óvulo
– *ovule*
64 el saco embrional
– *embryo sac*
65 el polen
– *pollen*
66 el tubo polínico
– *pollen tube*
67-77 inflorescencias *f*
– *inflorescences*
67 la espiga
– *spike (racemose spike)*
68 el racimo
– *raceme (simple raceme)*
69 la panícula
– *panicle*
70 la cima bípara (discasio *m*)
– *cyme*
71 el espádice
– *spadix (fleshy spike)*

72 la umbela
– *umbel (simple umbel)*
73 la cabezuela (el capítulo)
– *capitulum*
74 el capítulo convexo (la cabezuela discoide)
– *composite head (discoid flower head)*
75 el capítulo cóncavo (la cabezuela globulosa)
– *hollow flower head*
76 la cima unípara escorpioide
– *bostryx (helicoid cyme)*
77 la cima unípara helicoide (el ripidio)
– *cincinnus (scorpioid cyme, curled cyme)*
78-82 raíces *f*
– *roots*
78 las raíces adventicias
– *adventitious roots*
79 la raíz tuberosa
– *tuber (tuberous root, swollen taproot)*
80 las raíces aéreas (las raíces trepadoras, las raíces adventicias)
– *adventitious roots (aerial roots)*
81 las espinas de la raíz
– *root thorns*
82 las raíces respiratorias
– *pneumatophores*
83-85 el tallo de hierba *f*
– *blade of grass*
83 la vaina
– *leaf sheath*
84 la lígula
– *ligule (ligula)*
85 el limbo
– *leaf blade (lamina)*
86 la semilla
– *embryo (seed, germ)*
87 el cotiledón
– *cotyledon (seed leaf, seed lobe)*
88 la radícula
– *radicle*
89 el hipocótilo
– *hypocotyl*
90 la plúmula
– *plumule (leaf bud)*
91-102 frutos *m*
– *fruits*
91-96 frutos *m* dehiscentes
– *dehiscent fruits*
91 el folículo
– *follicle*
92 la legumbre
– *legume (pod)*
93 la silicua
– *siliqua (pod)*
94 la cápsula loculicida
– *schizocarp*
95 el pixidio
– *pyxidium (circumscissile seed vessel)*
96 la cápsula foraminal (la cápsula poricida)
– *poricidal capsule (porose capsule)*
97-102 frutos *m* indehiscentes
– *indehiscent fruits*
97 la baya
– *berry*
98 la nuez
– *nut*
99 la drupa (la cereza)
– *drupe (stone fruit) (cherry)*
100 el fruto compuesto (el escaramujo)
– *aggregate fruit (compound fruit) (rose hip)*
101 la multidrupa (la frambuesa), un fruto compuesto
– *aggregate fruit (compound fruit) (raspberry)*
102 el pomo (la manzana)
– *pome (apple)*

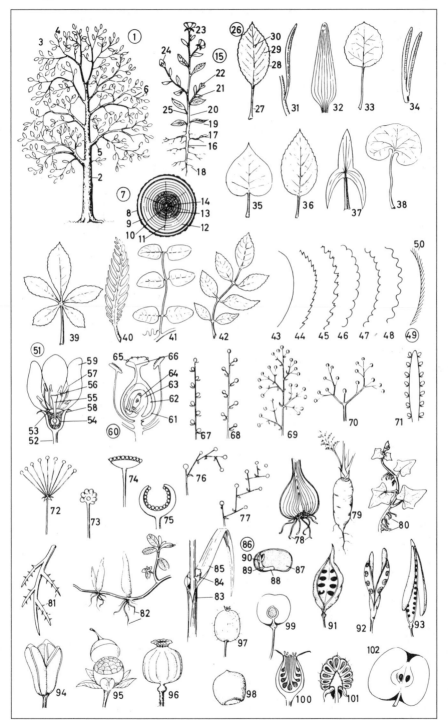

1-73 árboles *m* de hoja *f* caduca
(árboles *m* caducifolios)
– *deciduous trees*
1 el roble
– *oak (oak tree)*
2 la rama florida
– *flowering branch*
3 la rama con frutos *m*
– *fruiting branch*
4 el fruto (la bellota)
– *fruit (acorn)*
5 el cascabillo (la cúpula)
– *cupule (cup)*
6 la flor femenina
– *female flower*
7 la bráctea
– *bract*
8 la inflorescencia masculina
– *male inflorescence*
9 el abedul
– *birch (birch tree)*
10 la rama con amentos *m* (candeli-
llas *f*), una rama florida
– *branch with catkins, a flowering
branch*
11 la rama con frutos *m*
– *fruiting branch*
12 la sámara
– *scale (catkin scale)*
13 la flor femenina
– *female flower*
14 la flor masculina
– *male flower*
15 el álamo; *anál.:* el chopo
– *poplar*
16 la rama florida
– *flowering branch*
17 la flor
– *flower*
18 la rama con frutos *m*
– *fruiting branch*
19 el fruto
– *fruit*
20 la semilla
– *seed*
21 la hoja del álamo temblón
– *leaf of the aspen (trembling
poplar)*
22 la infrutescencia
– *infructescence*
23 la hoja del álamo blanco
– *leaf of the white poplar (silver
poplar, silverleaf)*
24 el sauce cabruno; *anál.:* el
salguero, la salguera, la sarga
– *sallow (goat willow)*
25 la rama con los botones florales
(con los capullos)
– *branch with flower buds*
26 el amento (la candelilla) con
detalle *m* de una flor
– *catkin with single flower*

27 la rama con hojas *f* (*Chile:* el
quimpo)
– *branch with leaves*
28 el fruto
– *fruit*
29 la rama con hojas *f* de la salguera
blanca
– *osier branch with leaves*
30 el aliso (el alno)
– *alder*
31 la rama con frutos *m*
– *fruiting branch*
32 la rama florida con los conos (las
piñas) del año anterior
– *branch with previous year's cone*
33 el haya *f*
– *beech (beech tree)*
34 la rama florida
– *flowering branch*
35 el friz (la flor del haya *f*)
– *flower*
36 la rama con frutos *m*
– *fruiting branch*
37 el hayuco (el fruto del haya *f*)
– *beech nut*
38 el fresno
– *ash (ash tree)*
39 la rama florida
– *flowering branch*
40 la flor
– *flower*
41 la rama con frutos *m*
– *fruiting branch*
42 el serbal (el serbo)
– *mountain ash (rowan, quickbeam)*
43 la inflorescencia
– *inflorescence*
44 la infrutescencia
– *infructescence*
45 el fruto (la serba) [corte *m* longi-
tudinal]
– *fruit [longitudinal section]*
46 el tilo (la tila, la teja)
– *lime (lime tree, linden, linden tree)*
47 la rama con frutos *m*
– *fruiting branch*
48 la inflorescencia
– *inflorescence*
49 el olmo (el negrillo)
– *elm (elm tree)*
50 la rama con frutos *m*
– *fruiting branch*
51 la rama florida
– *flowering branch*
52 la flor
– *flower*
53 el arce (el moscón, el sácere) real
(el arce platanoide)
– *maple (maple tree)*
54 la rama florida
– *flowering branch*

55 la flor
– *flower*
56 la rama con frutos *m*
– *fruiting branch*
57 el fruto en doble sámara *f* (disámara *f*)
– *maple seed with wings (winged
maple seed)*
58 el castaño de Indias
– *horse chestnut (horse chestnut
tree, chestnut, chestnut tree, buck-
eye)*
59 la rama con frutos *m* jóvenes
– *branch with young fruits*
60 la castaña (la semilla del castaño)
– *chestnut (horse chestnut)*
61 el fruto maduro
– *mature (ripe) fruit*
62 la flor [corte *m* longitudinal]
– *flower [longitudinal section]*
63 el carpe
– *hornbeam (yoke elm)*
64 la rama con frutos *m*
– *fruiting branch*
65 el fruto
– *seed*
66 la rama florida
– *flowering branch*
67 el plátano híbrido (*Amér. Merid.:*
el volador)
– *plane (plane tree)*
68 la hoja
– *leaf*
69 la infrutescencia y el fruto
– *infructescence and fruit*
70 la robinia (la falsa acacia)
– *false acacia (locust tree)*
71 la rama florida
– *flowering branch*
72 parte *f* de la infrutescencia
– *part of the infructescence*
73 la base del pecíolo con estípulas *f*
– *base of the leaf stalk with stipules*

1-71 coníferas *f* (árboles *m* de hojas *f* aciculares, árboles *m* de hoja *f* perenne)
- *coniferous trees (conifers)*
1 el abeto común (el abeto blanco, el pinabete)
- *silver fir (European silver fir, common silver fir)*
2 el cono (la piña, el estróbilo), un fruto
- *fir cone, a fruit cone*
3 el eje del cono
- *cone axis*
4 el cono femenino
- *female flower cone*
5 la escama de la bráctea
- *bract scale (bract)*
6 el cono masculino
- *male flower shoot*
7 el estambre
- *stamen*
8 la escama del cono
- *cone scale*
9 la semilla con ala *f*
- *seed with wing (winged seed)*
10 la semilla [corte *m* longitudinal]
- *seed [longitudinal section]*
11 la aguja de abeto *m* (la hoja acicular)
- *fir needle (needle)*
12 la pícea (el abeto falso)
- *spruce (spruce fir)*
13 el cono (la piña) de la pícea
- *spruce cone*
14 la escama del cono
- *cone scale*
15 la semilla
- *seed*
16 el cono femenino
- *female flower cone*
17 el cono masculino (la inflorescencia masculina)
- *male inflorescence*
18 el estambre
- *stamen*
19 la aguja de la pícea (del abeto falso; la hoja acicular)
- *spruce needle*
20 el pino (el pino albar, el pino silvestre, el pino rojo)
- *pine (Scots pine)*
21 el pino enano (el pino de montaña *f*, el pino negro)
- *dwarf pine*
22 el cono femenino
- *female flower cone*
23 el haz de dos agujas *f* de un renuevo joven
- *short shoot with bundle of two leaves*
24 el cono masculino (las inflorescencias masculinas)
- *male inflorescences*
25 el vástago (el renuevo) anual
- *annual growth*

26 la piña del pino
- *pine cone*
27 la escama de la piña
- *cone scale*
28 la semilla
- *seed*
29 el cono del pino cembro, un fruto
- *fruit cone of the arolla pine (Swiss stone pine)*
30 el cono del pino de Weymouth (del pino blanco, del pino canadiense), un fruto
- *fruit cone of the Weymouth pine (white pine)*
31 el vástago joven [corte *m* transversal]
- *short shoot [cross section]*
32 el alerce (el pino alerce, el lárice)
- *larch*
33 la rama florida
- *flowering branch*
34 la escama del cono femenino (la escama ovulífera)
- *scale of the female flower cone*
35 la antera
- *anther*
36 la rama con una piña de alerce *m*
- *branch with larch cones (fruit cones)*
37 la semilla
- *seed*
38 la escama de la piña
- *cone scale*
39 el árbol de la vida (la tuya)
- *arbor vitae (tree of life, thuja)*
40 la rama con frutos *m*
- *fruiting branch*
41 el cono, un fruto
- *fruit cone*
42 la escama
- *scale*
43 la rama con flores *f* masculinas y femeninas
- *branch with male and female flowers*
44 el brote (el vástago) masculino
- *male shoot*
45 la escama, con sacos *m* polínicos
- *scale with pollen sacs*
46 el brote (el vástago) femenino
- *female shoot*
47 el enebro (el junípero, la cada); *anál.:* la sabina
- *juniper (juniper tree)*
48 el brote (el vástago) femenino [corte *m* longitudinal]
- *female shoot [longitudinal section]*
49 el brote (el vástago) masculino
- *male shoot*
50 la escama, con sacos *m* polínicos
- *scale with pollen sacs*
51 la rama con frutos *m*
- *fruiting branch*
52 la enebrina (la baya del junípero, del enebro)
- *juniper berry*

53 el fruto [corte *m* transversal]
- *fruit [cross section]*
54 la semilla
- *seed*
55 el pino piñonero (el pino real, el pino manso, el pino donal)
- *stone pine*
56 el brote (el vástago) masculino
- *male shoot*
57 el cono con semillas *f* [corte *m* longitudinal]
- *fruit cone with seeds [longitudinal section]*
58 el ciprés (*poético:* el ciprasio)
- *cypress*
59 la rama con frutos *m* (con piñuelas *f*)
- *fruiting branch*
60 la semilla
- *seed*
61 el tejo
- *yew (yew tree)*
62 el cono masculino y el cono femenino
- *male flower shoot and female flower cone*
63 la rama con frutos *m*
- *fruiting branch*
64 el fruto
- *fruit*
65 el cedro (*Perú:* el cibui)
- *cedar (cedar tree)*
66 la rama con frutos *m*
- *fruiting branch*
67 la escama del fruto
- *fruit scale*
68 el cono masculino y el cono femenino
- *male flower shoot and female flower cone*
69 la secoya (la secuoya)
- *mammoth tree (Wellingtonia, sequoia)*
70 la rama con frutos *m*
- *fruiting branch*
71 la semilla
- *seed*

1 la forsitia
– *forsythia*
2 el ovario y el estambre
– *ovary and stamen*
3 la hoja
– *leaf*
4 el jazmín amarillo
– *yellow-flowered jasmine (jasmin, jessamine)*
5 la flor [corte *m* longitudinal] con estilo *m*, ovario *m* y estambres *m*
– *flower [longitudinal section] with styles, ovaries, and stamens*
6 el aligustre común (la alheña, el ligustro)
– *privet (common privet)*
7 la flor
– *flower*
8 la infrutescencia
– *infructescence*
9 la jeringuilla (la celinda)
– *mock orange (sweet syringa)*
10 el viburno (la bola de nieve *f*, mundillo *m*, sauquillo *m*) común
– *snowball (snowball bush, guelder rose)*
11 la flor
– *flower*
12 los frutos
– *fruits*
13 la adelfa (el baladre, el laurel rosa)
– *oleander (rosebay, rose laurel)*
14 la flor [corte *m* longitudinal]
– *flower [longitudinal section]*
15 la magnolia roja
– *red magnolia*
16 la hoja
– *leaf*
17 el membrillo (el membrillero) japonés
– *japonica (japanese quince)*
18 el fruto
– *fruit*
19 el boj común
– *common box (box, box tree)*
20 la flor femenina
– *female flower*
21 la flor masculina
– *male flower*
22 el fruto [corte *m* longitudinal]
– *fruit [longitudinal section]*
23 la weigelia
– *weigela (weigelia)*
24 la yuca [parte *f* de la inflorescencia]
– *yucca [part of the inflorescence]*
25 la hoja
– *leaf*
26 el escaramujo (el agavanzo, la mosqueta silvestre, la zarzaperruna)
– *dog rose (briar rose, wild briar)*

27 el fruto
– *fruit*
28 la espirea del Japón (la kerria)
– *kerria*
29 el fruto
– *fruit*
30 el cornejo hembra (el cerezo silvestre)
– *cornelian cherry*
31 la flor
– *flower*
32 el fruto (la cereza silvestre)
– *fruit (cornelian cherry)*
33 el mirto de Brabante (el arrayán brabántico; *Mé.:* el haya *f*)
– *sweet gale (gale)*

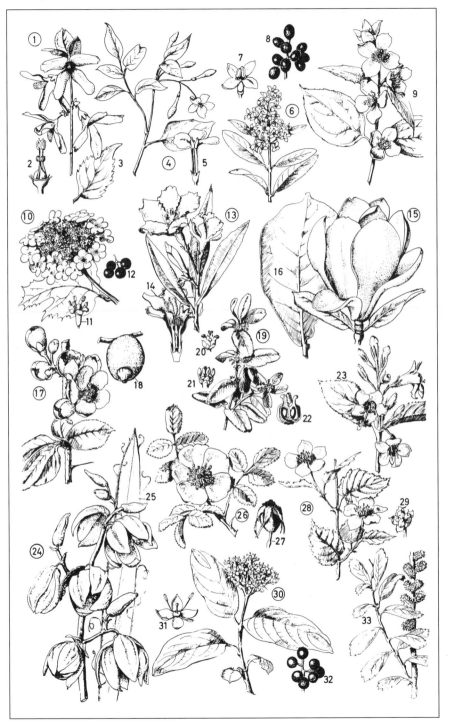

1 el tulipero (el tulipanero) común
– *tulip tree (tulip poplar, saddle tree,*
   whitewood)
2 los carpelos
– *carpels*
3 el estambre
– *stamen*
4 el fruto
– *fruit*
5 el hisopo
– *hyssop*
6 la flor [vista *f* por delante]
– *flower [front view]*
7 la flor
– *flower*
8 el cáliz con fruto *m*
– *calyx with fruit*
9 el acebo (el agrifolio, el aquifolio)
– *holly*
10 la flor hermafrodita (la flor
   andrógina)
– *androgynous (hermaphroditic,*
   hermaphrodite) flower
11 la flor masculina
– *male flower*
12 el fruto con los huesos al descu-
   bierto
– *fruit with stones exposed*
13 la madreselva
– *honeysuckle (woodbine, wood-*
   bind)
14 los botones florales (los capullos)
– *flower buds*
15 la flor [corte *m*]
– *flower [cut open]*
16 la viña loca
– *Virginia creeper (American ivy,*
   woodbine)
17 la flor abierta
– *open flower*
18 la inflorescencia
– *infructescence*
19 el fruto [corte *m* longitudinal]
– *fruit [longitudinal section]*
20 la retama de escobas *f* (la retama
   negra, el escobón)
– *broom*
21 la flor con los pétalos quitados
– *flower with the petals removed*
22 la vaina verde
– *immature (unripe) legume (pod)*
23 la espirea (la ulmaria)
– *spiraea*
24 la flor [corte *m* longitudinal]
– *flower [longitudinal section]*
25 el fruto
– *fruit*
26 el carpelo
– *carpel*
27 el endrino
– *blackthorn (sloe)*
28 las hojas
– *leaves*

29 los frutos
– *fruits*
30 el espino (el espino albar, el
   espino blanco, el majuelo, la exia-
   canta, el níspero silvestre; *Amér.:*
   el espinillo)
– *single-pistilled hawthorn (thorn,*
   may)
31 el fruto
– *fruit*
32 el laburno (el cítiso de los Alpes,
   la lluvia de oro *m*, el ébano falso,
   el codeso, el borne, el piorno)
– *laburnum (golden chain, golden*
   rain)
33 el racimo de flores *f*
– *raceme*
34 los frutos
– *fruits*
35 el saúco negro (el sabuco, el
   canillero)
– *black elder (elder)*
36 las flores del saúco (una cima)
– *elder flowers*
37 las bayas del saúco
– *elderberries*

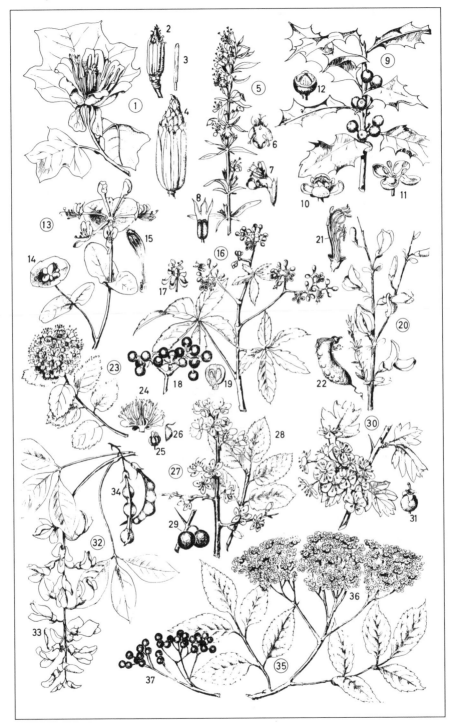

375 Flores de prados y linderos I

1 la saxífraga de hoja *f* redonda (la saxífraga dorada)
– *rotundifoliate (rotundifolious) saxifrage (rotundifoliate break-stone)*
2 la hoja
– *leaf*
3 la flor
– *flower*
4 el fruto
– *fruit*
5 la anémona común (la pulsatilla)
– *anemone (windflower)*
6 la flor [corte *m* longitudinal]
– *flower [longitudinal section]*
7 el fruto
– *fruit*
8 el ranúnculo (la francesilla, la marimoña)
– *buttercup (meadow buttercup, but-terflower, goldcup, king cup, crowfoot)*
9 la hoja de la raíz
– *basal leaf*
10 el fruto
– *fruit*
11 el mastuerzo (la cardamina)
– *lady's smock (ladysmock, cuckoo flower)*
12 la hoja basilar
– *basal leaf*
13 el fruto
– *fruit*
14 la campánula (la campanilla)
– *harebell (hairbell, bluebell)*
15 la hoja de la raíz
– *basal leaf*
16 la flor [corte *m* longitudinal]
– *flower [longitudinal section]*
17 el fruto
– *fruit*
18 la hiedra terrestre
– *ground ivy (ale hoof)*
19 la flor [corte *m* longitudinal]
– *flower [longitudinal section]*
20 la flor [vista *f* de frente]
– *flower [front view]*
21 la uva de gato *m* (el racimillo, la vermicularia)
– *stonecrop*
22 la verónica
– *speedwell*
23 la flor
– *flower*
24 el fruto
– *fruit*
25 la semilla
– *seed*
26 la hierba de la moneda
– *moneywort*
27 la cápsula dehiscente del fruto
– *dehisced fruit*
28 la semilla
– *seed*

29 la escabiosa menor
– *small scabious*
30 la hoja de la raíz
– *basal leaf*
31 la flor radiada (la lígula radiada)
– *ray floret (flower of outer series)*
32 la florecilla del disco
– *disc (disk) floret (flower of inner series)*
33 el periclino (el periforanto, la peri-foriantia) con aristas *f*
– *involucral calyx with pappus bris-tles*
34 el ovario con aristas *f*
– *ovary with pappus*
35 el fruto
– *fruit*
36 la celidonia menor
– *lesser celandine*
37 el fruto
– *fruit*
38 la axila de la hoja con bulbillo *m*
– *leaf axil with bulbil*
39 la espiguilla (la hierba de punta; *Chile:* el piojillo)
– *annual meadow grass*
40 la flor
– *flower*
41 la espiguilla [vista *f* de costado]
– *spikelet [side view]*
42 la espiguilla [vista *f* de frente]
– *spikelet [front view]*
43 la cariópside (fruto *m* indehis-cente)
– *caryopsis, an indehiscent fruit*
44 el manojo de hierba *f*
– *tuft of grass (clump of grass)*
45 la consuelda (el sínfito mayor)
– *comfrey*
46 la flor [corte *m* longitudinal]
– *flower [longitudinal section]*
47 el fruto
– *fruit*

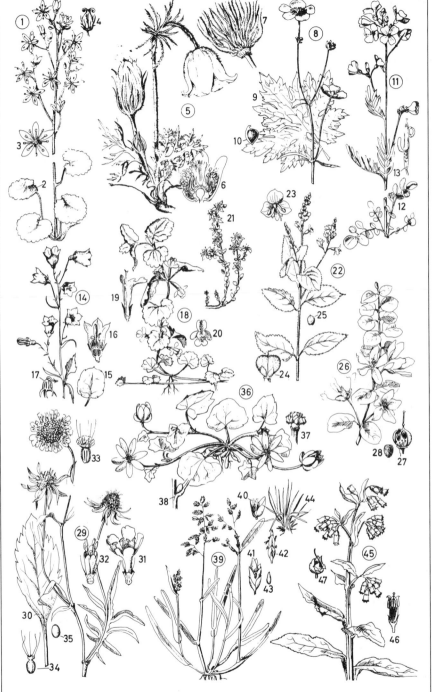

376 Flores de prados y linderos II

1 la margarita menor (*Arg.:* la
coqueta; *Col.:* la pascua)
– *daisy (Am. English daisy)*
2 la flor
– *flower*
3 el fruto
– *fruit*
4 la margarita mayor
– *oxeye daisy (white oxeye daisy,
marguerite)*
5 la flor
– *flower*
6 el fruto
– *fruit*
7 la astrancia
– *masterwort*
8 la vellorita; *anál.:* la primavera
– *cowslip*
9 el gordolobo (el verbasco)
– *great mullein (Aaron's rod, shepherd's club)*
10 la bistorta
– *bistort (snakeweed)*
11 la flor
– *flower*
12 la centaura negra
– *knapweed*
13 la malva común
– *common mallow*
14 el fruto
– *fruit*
15 la aquilea (la milenrama, la alta-
rreina, la artemisa bastarda, la
hierba meona, la milhojas; *Col.:* la
viuda)
– *yarrow*
16 la hierba del carpintero
– *self-heal*
17 el cuernecillo
– *bird's foot trefoil (bird's foot
clover)*
18 el equiseto (la cola de caballo *m*)
[un retoño]
– *horsetail (equisetum) [a shoot]*
19 la flor (el cono)
– *flower (strobile)*
20 la cambronera (el arto)
– *campion (catchfly)*
21 la flor del cuclillo
– *ragged robin (cuckoo flower)*
22 la aristoloquia
– *birthwort*
23 la flor
– *flower*
24 el geranio
– *crane's bill*
25 la achicoria común
– *wild chicory (witloof, succory,
wild endive)*
26 la silene, una cariofilácea
– *common toadflax (butter-and-
eggs)*
27 el zapatito de dama *f*
– *lady's slipper (Venus's slipper,
Am. moccasin flower)*
28 el satirión, una orquídea
– *orchis (wild orchid), an orchid*

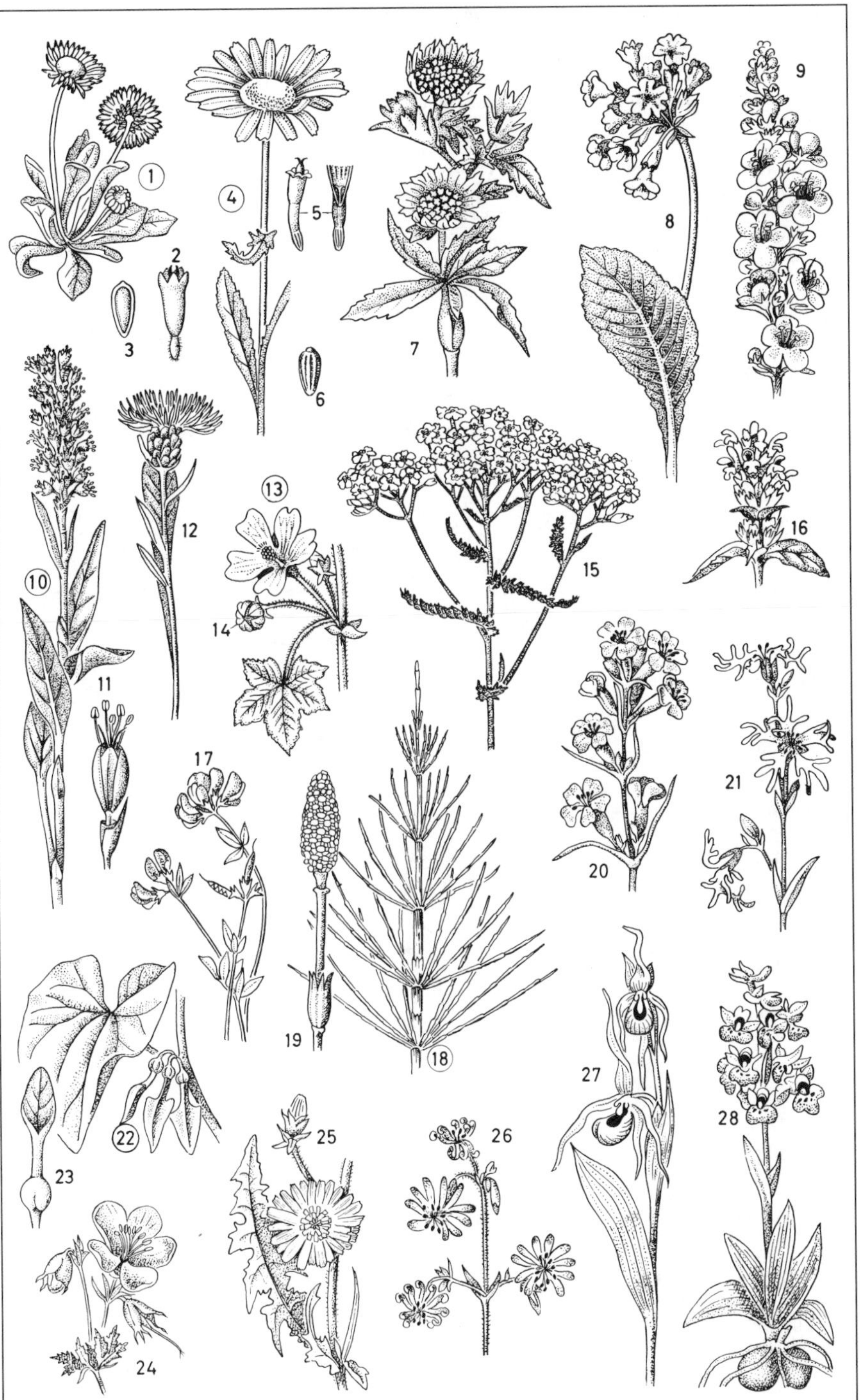
1
2
3
4
5
6
7
8
9
10
11
12
13
14
15
16
17
18
19
20
21
22
23
24
25
26
27
28

377 Plantas de bosque, lagunas y páramos

1 la nemorosa (la anémona de bosque *m*)
- *wood anemone (anemone, windflower)*
2 el lirio de los valles (la convalaria, el muguete)
- *lily of the valley*
3 el pie de gato *m; anál.:* la siempreviva (la perpetua)
- *cat's foot (milkwort);* sim.: *sandflower (everlasting)*
4 el martagón (la azucena silvestre, el lirio silvestre)
- *turk's cap (turk's cap lily)*
5 la barba de cabrón *m* (aruncus sylvestris)
- *goatsbeard (goat's beard)*
6 el ajo de oso *m*
- *ramson*
7 la pulmonaria
- *lungwort*
8 la fumaria
- *corydalis*
9 la hierba callera
- *orpine (livelong)*
10 la lauréola (el torvisco, el mezéreon, la adelfilla)
- *daphne*
11 la nometoques (la balsamina grande, la hierba de Santa Catalina; *Amér.:* la china, la chinarrosa)
- *touch-me-not*
12 el pampajarito, la pimienta de muros *m*
- *staghorn (stag horn moss, stag's horn, stag's horn moss, coral evergreen)*
13 la grasilla (la tiraña), una planta carnívora
- *butterwort, an insectivorous plant*
14 la drósera (la atrapamoscas)
- *sundew;* sim.: *Venus's flytrap*
15 la gayuba (la uvaduz)
- *bearberry*
16 el polipodio, un helecho; *anál.:* el aspidio, el culantrillo, la rueda de muros *m*
- *polypody (polypod), a fern;* sim.: *male fern, brake (bracken, eagle fern), royal fern (royal osmund, king's fern, ditch fern)*
17 el musgo capilar, un musgo
- *haircap moss (hair moss, golden maidenhair), a moss*
18 el erióforo, una ciperácea
- *cotton grass (cotton rush)*
19 el brezo (la brecina, la querihuela, el biércol, el urce); *anál.:* la carroncha (el brezo negro)
- *heather (heath, ling);* sim.: *bell heather (cross-leaved heather)*
20 el heliantemo, una jara
- *rock rose (sun rose)*

21 el ledo de los pantanos
- *marsh tea*
22 el cálamo aromático (el ácoro verdadero)
- *sweet flag (sweet calamus, sweet sedge)*
23 el arándano (el mirtilo, el ráspano, la anavia); *anál.:* el arándano rojo, el arándano negro
- *bilberry (whortleberry, huckleberry, blueberry);* sim.: *cowberry (red whortleberry), bog bilberry (bog whortleberry), crowberry (crakeberry)*

378 Plantas alpinas, acuáticas y de pantano

1-13 plantas *f* alpinas
– *alpine plants*
1 el rododendro
– *alpine rose (alpine rhododendron)*
2 la rama florida
– *flowering shoot*
3 la campanilla de los Alpes (la soldanella alpina)
– *alpine soldanella (soldanella)*
4 la corola desplegada
– *corolla opened out*
5 la cápsula de las semillas *f* con el estilo
– *seed vessel with the style*
6 la escobilla parda
– *alpine wormwood*
7 la inflorescencia
– *inflorescence*
8 la oreja de oso *m*
– *auricula*
9 el leontopodio (la flor de nieve *f*, la edelweiss)
– *edelweiss*
10 las formas de las flores
– *flower shapes*
11 el fruto con el vilano
– *fruit with pappus tuft*
12 el corte de una cabezuela
– *part of flower head (of capitulum)*
13 la genciana de primavera *f*
– *stemless alpine gentian*
14-57 plantas *f* acuáticas y de pantano *m*
– *aquatic plants (water plants) and marsh plants*
14 el nenúfar (el lirio de agua *f*)
– *white water lily*
15 la hoja
– *leaf*
16 la flor
– *flower*
17 la Victoria regia (el lirio gigante del Amazonas)
– *Queen Victoria water lily (Victoria regia water lily, royal water lily, Amazon water lily)*
18 la hoja
– *leaf*
19 el envés de la hoja
– *underside of the leaf*
20 la flor
– *flower*
21 la anea, la espadaña
– *reed mace bulrush (cattail, cat's tail, cattail flag, club rush)*
22 la parte masculina del espádice
– *male part of the spadix*
23 la flor masculina
– *male flower*
24 la parte femenina
– *female part*

25 la flor femenina
– *female flower*
26 el nomeolvides
– *forget-me-not*
27 la rama en flor *f*
– *flowering shoot*
28 la flor [corte *m*]
– *flower [section]*
29 la hidrocara (el mordisco de rana *f*)
– *frog's bit*
30 el berro amargo (el berro de fuente *f*)
– *watercress*
31 el tallo con flores *f* y frutos *m* jóvenes
– *stalk with flowers and immature (unripe) fruits*
32 la flor
– *flower*
33 la vaina con semillas *f*
– *siliqua (pod) with seeds*
34 dos semillas *f*
– *two seeds*
35 la lenteja de agua *f*
– *duckweed (duck's meat)*
36 la planta en flor *f*
– *plant in flower*
37 la flor
– *flower*
38 el fruto
– *fruit*
39 el junco florido
– *flowering rush*
40 la umbela
– *flower umbel*
41 las hojas
– *leaves*
42 el fruto
– *fruit*
43 el alga *f* verde
– *green alga*
44 la alisma (el llantén de agua *f*, el pan de ranas *f*)
– *water plantain*
45 la hoja
– *leaf*
46 la panícula (la inflorescencia)
– *panicle*
47 la flor
– *flower*
48 el golfo (el sargazo azucarado), una laminaria
– *honey wrack, a brown alga*
49 el talo
– *thallus (plant body, frond)*
50 el órgano de fijación *f*
– *holdfast*
51 la sagitaria
– *arrow head*
52 las formas de las hojas
– *leaf shapes*

53 la inflorescencia con flores *f* masculinas [arriba] y flores femeninas [abajo]
– *inflorescence with male flowers [above] and female flowers [below]*
54 la hierba marina (la zostera marina)
– *sea grass*
55 la inflorescencia
– *inflorescence*
56 la elodea
– *Canadian waterweed (Canadian pondweed)*
57 la flor
– *flower*

1 el acónito (el anapelo, el napelo);
anál.: la uva lupina, el matalobos,
el pardal, la verga
- *aconite (monkshood, wolfsbane,
  helmet flower)*
2 el digital (la dedalera, la gual-
daperra, la viluria, la giloria)
- *foxglove (Digitalis)*
3 el cólquico (la quitameriendas, la
flor de otoño *m; Bol., Col. y Perú:*
el cólchico)
- *meadow saffron (naked lady,
  naked boys)*
4 la cicuta (el perejil lobuno; *Perú:*
la montezanahoria)
- *hemlock (Conium)*
5 la hierba mora (el tomatillo del
diablo, el solano negro; *Arg. y
Par.:* el arachichú)
- *black nightshade (common nightshade, petty morel)*
6 el beleño negro
- *henbane*
7 la belladona
- *deadly nightshade (belladonna,
  banewort, dwale), a solanaceous
  herb*
8 el estramonio (la hierba hedionda, la higuera loca, la estramóni-
ca, la manzana espinosa; *Amér.:* el
chamico; *Mé.:* el toloache; *Col.:* el
gigantín)
- *thorn apple (stramonium, stramo-
  ny, Am. jimson weed, jimpson
  weed, Jamestown weed,
  stinkweed)*
9 el aro (el alcatraz, el arón, el jaro,
el jarillo, el jarrillo, la tragontina,
el yaro; *Hond.:* el quiscamote;
Col.: la rascadera)
- *cuckoo pint (lords-and-ladies,
  wild arum, wake-robin)*
10-13 hongos *m* venenosos (setas *f*
venenosas)
- *poisonous fungi (poisonous mush-
  rooms, toadstools)*
10 la amanita de las moscas (el agárico de las moscas, la falsa oronja,
la matamoscas), un agárico
- *fly agaric (fly amanita, fly fungus),
  an agaric*
11 la oronja verde (la seta mortal)
- *amanita*
12 el boleto de Satanás (*Bol., Chile,
Ec. y Perú:* la callampa; *Col.,
Chile y Ec.:* la callamba)
- *Satan's mushroom*
13 el níscalo falso
- *woolly milk cap*

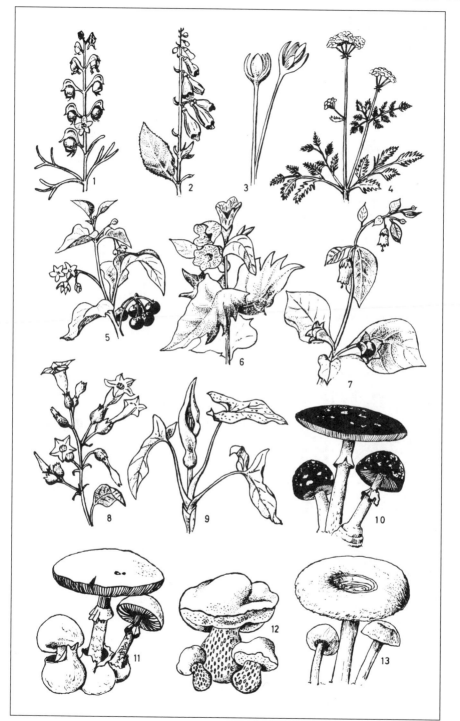

1 la manzanilla (la camamila, la camomila; *Perú:* la sachaman-zanilla)
- *camomile (chamomile, wild camomile)*
2 el árnica *f* (el tabaco de montaña *f,* el tabaco borde, la estornudadera)
- *arnica*
3 la menta (la hierbabuena, la hierba santa)
- *peppermint*
4 el ajenjo (el absintio)
- *wormwood (absinth)*
5 la valeriana (la hierba de los gatos; *Ec.:* la guasilla; *Perú:* el turpu)
- *valerian (allheal)*
6 el hinojo; *anál.:* el eneldo
- *fennel*
7 el espliego (la alhucema, la lavanda)
- *lavender*
8 el tusilago (la fárfara, la uña de caballo *m,* el pie de caballo *m,* la pata de asno *m*)
- *coltsfoot*
9 la atanasia (el tanaceto, la hierba lombriguera, la hierba de Santa María)
- *tansy*
10 la centáurea mayor
- *centaury*
11 el llantén menor (la lancéola, la quinquenervia)
- *ribwort (ribwort plantain, ribgrass)*
12 el malvavisco (la altea)
- *marshmallow*
13 el arraclán (la frángula)
- *alder buckthorn (alder dogwood)*
14 el ricino (la oherva, la querva, la higuera del infierno, la higuereta, la higuerilla, la palmacristi, el rezno; *Venez.:* el tártago)
- *castor-oil plant (Palma Christi)*
15 la adormidera
- *opium poppy*
16 el sen (la casia; *Col.:* la bajagua; *Cuba y S. Dgo.:* la guajaba; *Hond.:* el saragundí, el zambrano; *P. Rico:* la talantala); *las hojas secas:* las hojas de sen *m*
- *senna (cassia);* the dried leaflets: *senna leaves*
17 el quino (el árbol de la quina, el cascarillo)
- *cinchona (chinchona)*
18 el alcanforero
- *camphor tree (camphor laurel)*
19 el betel
- *betel palm (areca, areca palm)*
20 la nuez de betel *m* (la areca)
- *betel nut (areca nut)*

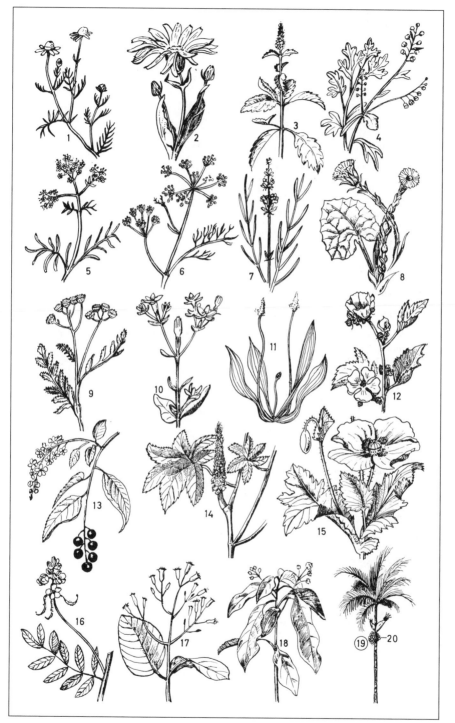

1 el champiñón silvestre (el hongo comestible)
- *meadow mushroom (field mushroom)*
2 el afieltramiento de hifas *f* (el micelio) con cuerpos *m* fructificados (hongos *m*)
- *mycelial threads (hyphae, mycelium) with fruiting bodies*
3 hongo *m* [corte *m* longitudinal]
- *mushroom [longitudinal section]*
4 el sombrerete (el píleo) con laminillas *f* (hojuelas *f*)
- *cap (pileus) with gills*
5 la vola (el velum)
- *veil (velum)*
6 la laminilla [corte *m*]
- *gill [section]*
7 el basidio [en la laminilla con basidioesporas *f*]
- *basidia [on the gill with basidiospores]*
8 las esporas germinales
- *germinating basidiospores (spores)*
9 la trufa (la criadilla de tierra *f*)
- *truffle*
10 el hongo [vista *f* exterior]
- *truffle [external view]*
11 el hongo [corte *m*]
- *truffle [section]*
12 interior *m* con la teca con esporas *f* [corte *m*]
- *interior showing asci [section]*
13 dos tecas *f* con las esporas
- *two asci with the ascospores (spores)*
14 la cantarela
- *chanterelle (chantarelle)*
15 el rebozuelo (la cabrilla)
- *Chestnut Boletus*
16 el boleto comestible (la calabaza)
- *cep (cepe, squirrel's bread, Boletus edulis)*
17 la capa tuberosa
- *layer of tubes (hymenium)*
18 el tallo
- *stem (stipe)*
19 el bejín blando
- *puffball (Bovista nigrescens)*
20 el bejín plomizo
- *devil's tobacco pouch (common puffball)*
21 el boleto anillado
- *Brown Ring Boletus (Boletus luteus)*
22 el boleto áspero
- *Birch Boletus (Boletus scaber)*
23 el mízcalo (el níscalo)
- *Russula vesca*
24 el hidno imbricado
- *scaled prickle fungus*
25 la cabeza de fraile *m* (la platera)
- *slender funnel fungus*

26 la colmenilla redonda
- *morel (Morchella esculenta)*
27 la colmenilla cónica
- *morel (Morchella conica)*
28 la armilaria color *m* de miel *f*
- *honey fungus*
29 el tricoloma ecuestre (la seta de los caballeros)
- *saffron milk cap*
30 el apagador (la galamperna)
- *parasol mushroom*
31 la gamuza (la lengua de gato *m*)
- *hedgehog fungus (yellow prickle fungus)*
32 la ramaria apretada
- *yellow coral fungus (goatsbeard, goat's beard, coral Clavaria)*
33 la foliota cambiante
- *little cluster fungus*

382 Plantas estimulantes y especias tropicales

1 el cafeto (el árbol del café)
 – *coffee tree (coffee plant)*
2 la rama con frutos *m*
 – *fruiting branch*
3 la rama florida
 – *flowering branch*
4 la flor
 – *flower*
5 el fruto con los dos granos [corte *m* longitudinal]
 – *fruit with two beans [longitudinal section]*
6 el grano de café *m; después de preparado:* el café
 – *coffee bean; when processed: coffee*
7 el té
 – *tea plant (tea tree)*
8 la rama florida
 – *flowering branch*
9 la hoja del té: *después de preparada:* el té
 – *tea leaf; when processed: tea*
10 el fruto
 – *fruit*
11 el mate (la hierba mate, el té del Paraguay, el té de los jesuitas, la hierba del Paraguay)
 – *maté shrub (maté, yerba maté, Paraguay tea)*
12 la rama florida con las flores hermafroditas
 – *flowering branch with androgynous (hermaphroditic, hermaphrodite) flowers*
13 la flor masculina
 – *male flower*
14 la flor hermafrodita
 – *androgynous (hermaphroditic, hermaphrodite) flower*
15 el fruto
 – *fruit*
16 el cacao (el teobroma)
 – *cacao tree (cacao)*
17 la rama con flores *f* y frutos *m*
 – *branch with flowers and fruits*
18 la flor [corte *m* longitudinal]
 – *flower [longitudinal section]*
19 el grano de cacao *m; después de preparado:* el cacao, el cacao en polvo *m*
 – *cacao beans (cocoa beans); when processed: cocoa, cocoa powder*
20 la semilla [corte *m* longitudinal]
 – *seed [longitudinal section]*
21 el embrión
 – *embryo*
22 el árbol de la canela (el canelo, el canelero)
 – *cinnamon tree (cinnamon)*
23 la rama florida
 – *flowering branch*
24 el fruto
 – *fruit*

25 la corteza del canelo (la canela en rama *f*); *molida:* la canela en polvo *m*
 – *cinnamon bark; when crushed: cinnamon*
26 el clavero (el árbol del clavo)
 – *clove tree*
27 la rama florida
 – *flowering branch*
28 la yema; *desecada:* el clavo
 – *flower bud; when dried: clove*
29 la flor
 – *flower*
30 la mirística
 – *nutmeg tree*
31 la rama florida
 – *flowering branch*
32 la flor femenina [corte *m* longitudinal]
 – *female flower [longitudinal section]*
33 el fruto maduro
 – *mature (ripe) fruit*
34 la flor de mirística *f*, una semilla rodeada por el arilo (el macis)
 – *nutmeg with mace, a seed with laciniate aril*
35 la semilla [corte *m* transversal]; *seca:* la nuez moscada
 – *seed [cross section]; when dried: nutmeg*
36 el pimentero (el pimiento)
 – *pepper plant*
37 la rama con frutos *m*
 – *fruiting branch*
38 la inflorescencia
 – *inflorescence*
39 el fruto [corte *m* longitudinal] con el grano de pimienta *f* (la pimienta); *molida:* la pimienta molida, la pimienta en polvo *m*
 – *fruit [longitudinal section] with seed (peppercorn); when ground: pepper*
40 la planta de tabaco *m* de Virginia (*Chile:* de pitrén)
 – *Virginia tobacco plant*
41 la rama florida
 – *flowering shoot*
42 la flor
 – *flower*
43 la hoja de tabaco *m; seca:* el tabaco
 – *tobacco leaf; when cured: tobacco*
44 la cápsula de fruto maduro
 – *mature (ripe) fruit capsule*
45 la semilla
 – *seed*
46 la vainilla
 – *vanilla plant*
47 la rama florida
 – *flowering shoot*

48 la vaina de la vainilla; *curada:* el bastoncillo de vainilla
 – *vanilla pod; when cured: stick of vanilla*
49 el pistachero (el alfóncigo)
 – *pistachio tree*
50 la rama florida con las flores femeninas
 – *flowering branch with female flowers*
51 la almendra del alfóncigo (el pistacho)
 – *drupe (pistachio, pistachio nut)*
52 la caña de azúcar *m* (la caña dulce, la caña melar)
 – *sugar cane*
53 la planta en flor *f*
 – *plant (habit) in bloom*
54 la panícula (la inflorescencia)
 – *panicle*
55 la flor
 – *flower*

1 la colza (el nabo; *Col.:* la rabancá)
 – *rape (cole, coleseed)*
2 la hoja basal
 – *basal leaf*
3 la flor [corte *m* longitudinal]
 – *flower [longitudinal section]*
4 la silicua madura
 – *mature (ripe) siliqua (pod)*
5 la semilla oleaginosa
 – *oleiferous seed*
6 el lino
 – *flax*
7 el tallo florido
 – *peduncle (pedicel, flower stalk)*
8 la cápsula del fruto
 – *seed vessel (boll)*
9 el cáñamo
 – *hemp*
10 la planta femenina con frutos *m*
 – *fruiting female (pistillate) plant*
11 la inflorescencia femenina
 – *female inflorescence*
12 la flor
 – *flower*
13 la inflorescencia masculina
 – *male inflorescence*
14 el fruto
 – *fruit*
15 la semilla
 – *seed*
16 el algodonero (*Arg. y Par.:* el mandiyú; *Arg.:* el amandiyú)
 – *cotton*
17 la flor
 – *flower*
18 el fruto
 – *fruit*
19 la borra (la pelusa del algodón, el algodón)
 – *lint [cotton wool]*
20 la ceiba
 – *silk-cotton tree (kapok tree, capoc tree, ceiba tree)*
21 el fruto
 – *fruit*
22 la rama florida
 – *flowering branch*
23 la semilla
 – *seed*
24 la semilla [corte *m* longitudinal]
 – *seed [longitudinal section]*
25 el yute
 – *jute*
26 la rama florida
 – *flowering branch*
27 la flor
 – *flower*
28 el fruto
 – *fruit*

29 el olivo (la oliva, la olivera, el aceituno)
 – *olive tree (olive)*
30 la rama florida
 – *flowering branch*
31 la flor
 – *flower*
32 la aceituna (la oliva)
 – *fruit*
33 el árbol del caucho (la cauchera)
 – *rubber tree (rubber plant)*
34 la rama con frutos *m*
 – *fruiting branch*
35 el higo
 – *fig*
36 la flor
 – *flower*
37 el árbol de la gutapercha
 – *gutta-percha tree*
38 la rama florida
 – *flowering branch*
39 la flor
 – *flower*
40 el fruto
 – *fruit*
41 el cacahuete (el cacahuate, el cacahuey, el cacahué, el maní; *Arg. y Bol.:* el mandubí)
 – *peanut (ground nut, monkey nut)*
42 la rama florida
 – *flowering shoot*
43 la raíz con frutos *m*
 – *root with fruits*
44 el fruto [corte *m* longitudinal]
 – *nut (kernel) [longitudinal section]*
45 el ajonjolí (la alegría, el sésamo)
 – *sesame plant (simsim, benniseed)*
46 la rama con flores y frutas *f*
 – *flowers and fruiting branch*
47 la flor [corte *m* longitudinal]
 – *flower [longitudinal section]*
48 el cocotero (el coco, la palma de coco *m*, la palma indiana)
 – *coconut palm (coconut tree, coco palm, cocoa palm)*
49 la inflorescencia
 – *inflorescence*
50 la flor femenina
 – *female flower*
51 la flor masculina [corte *m* longitudinal]
 – *male flower [longitudinal section]*
52 el fruto [corte *m* longitudinal]
 – *fruit [longitudinal section]*
53 el coco
 – *coconut (cokernut)*
54 la palmera de aceite *m*
 – *oil palm*

55 el espádice masculino con la flor
 – *male spadix*
56 la inflorescencia con el fruto
 – *infructescence with fruit*
57 la semilla con los orificios germinativos
 – *seed with micropyles (foramina) (foraminate seed)*
58 el sagú (*Venez.:* el guapo; *P. Rico:* la maranta; *P. Rico y S. Dgo.:* la yuquilla)
 – *sago palm*
59 el fruto
 – *fruit*
60 el bambú (*Amér.:* la caña brava; *Venez.:* el mavi; *Mé.:* el otate; *Cuba y Venez.:* el pito; *Col., Ec. y Venez.:* la guadua; *Bol. y Río de la Plata:* la tacuara; *Perú:* la zacuara)
 – *bamboo stem (bamboo culm)*
61 la rama con hojas *f*
 – *branch with leaves*
62 la espiga de flores *f*
 – *spike*
63 el trozo de caña *f* con nudos *m*
 – *part of bamboo stem with joints*
64 el papiro
 – *papyrus plant (paper reed, paper rush)*
65 el copete de flores *f*
 – *umbel*
66 la espiga de flores *f*
 – *spike*

384 Frutos meridionales

1 la palmera datilera (la palma, la datilera)
– date palm (date)
2 la palmera con frutos *m*
– fruiting palm
3 la hoja de la palmera (la palma)
– palm frond
4 el espádice masculino
– male spadix
5 la flor masculina
– male flower
6 el espádice femenino
– female spadix
7 la flor femenina
– female flower
8 una rama con frutos *m*
– stand of fruit
9 el dátil
– date
10 el hueso del dátil (la semilla)
– date kernel
11 el higo
– fig
12 la rama con frutas *f* compuestas
– branch with pseudocarps
13 el higo con flores *f* [corte *m* longitudinal]
– fig with flowers [longitudinal section]
14 la flor femenina
– female flower
15 la flor masculina
– male flower
16 el granado
– pomegranate
17 la rama florida
– flowering branch
18 la flor [corte *m* longitudinal, separada la corola]
– flower [longitudinal section, corolla removed]
19 el fruto (la granada)
– fruit
20 la semilla (el grano) [corte *m* longitudinal]
– seed [longitudinal section]
21 la semilla [corte *m* transversal]
– seed [cross section]
22 el embrión
– embryo
23 el limón; *anál.:* la mandarina, la naranja (*Antillas y Venez.:* la china), la toronja (el pomelo; *Filip.:* el luchán)
– lemon; sim.: tangerine (mandarin), orange, grapefruit
24 la rama florida
– flowering branch
25 la flor del naranjo (el azahar) [corte *m* longitudinal]
– orange flower [longitudinal section]
26 el fruto
– fruit

27 la naranja [corte *m* transversal]
– orange [cross section]
28 el banano (el plátano, el platanero; *P. Rico:* el comisario, el fotoco; *Antillas:* el guineo; *Par.:* la pacobá; *Pan.:* el patriota; *anál.: Amér. Central, Antillas, Col., Ec., Pan., Perú y Venez.:* el dominico; *Col., Cuba, Mé., Pan., Perú y P. Rico:* el morado)
– banana plant (banana tree)
29 la corona de hojas *f*
– crown
30 el seudotronco con las hojas envainadas
– herbaceous stalk with overlapping leaf sheaths
31 la florescencia con frutos *m* jóvenes
– inflorescence with young fruits
32 la infrutescencia
– infructescence (bunch of fruit)
33 la banana (el plátano) [los nombres en América son variadísimos y coinciden con los del árbol]
– banana
34 la flor de la banana
– banana flower
35 la hoja de banano *m* [esquema *m*]
– banana leaf [diagram]
36 el almendro
– almond
37 la rama florida
– flowering branch
38 la rama con frutos *m*
– fruiting branch
39 el fruto (la almendra)
– fruit
40 la cáscara con la semilla [de la almendra]
– drupe containing seed [almond]
41 el algarrobo
– carob
42 la rama con flores *f* femeninas
– branch with female flowers
43 la flor femenina
– female flower
44 la flor masculina
– male flower
45 el fruto (la algarroba)
– fruit
46 la vaina-fruto [corte *m* transversal]
– siliqua (pod) [cross section]
47 la semilla
– seed
48 el castaño
– sweet chestnut (Spanish chestnut)
49 la rama florida
– flowering branch
50 la inflorescencia femenina
– female inflorescence
51 la flor masculina
– male flower

52 la cúpula (el erizo) con las semillas (las castañas)
– cupule, containing seeds
53 la nuez del Brasil
– Brazil nut
54 la rama florida
– flowering branch
55 la hoja
– leaf
56 la flor [vista *f* desde arriba]
– flower [from above]
57 la flor [corte *m* longitudinal]
– flower [longitudinal section]
58 el fruto capsular abierto con las semillas
– opened capsule, containing seeds
59 la nuez del Brasil (la castaña del Marañón) [corte *m* transversal]
– Brazil nut [cross section]
60 la nuez [corte *m* longitudinal]
– nut [longitudinal section]
61 el ananás (la piña de América, la piña tropical)
– pineapple plant (pineapple)
62 la fruta compuesta (el seudocarpo) con la corona de hojas *f*
– pseudocarp with crown of leaves
63 la espiga de flores *f*
– syncarp
64 la flor del ananás
– pineapple flower
65 la flor [corte *m* longitudinal]
– flower [longitudinal section]

Índice

Las cifras en negritas que siguen a las entradas corresponden a los números de los cuadros de ilustraciones, y las que están en redondas son las referentes a las ilustraciones de esos cuadros. Los homónimos de significación diferente, así como las palabras que figuran en varios cuadros, se distinguen a través de la indicación en cursiva de los dominios léxicos en que aparecen.

La siguiente lista contiene las abreviaturas que se han empleado para señalar los campos en que se utiliza la voz. No se especifican las abreviaturas que son fácilmente comprensibles.

~ del chapitel **331** 5
~ de los bajos **324** 43
~ de mando **132** 58; **271** 48
~ de mando del sistema inductivo **211** 38
~ de mando para abrir las puertas **197** 32
~ de mando para la luz interior y exterior **197** 32
~ de mando para los limpiaparabrisas **197** 32
~ de palillo **30** 66
~ de parada **110** 22
~ de puesta en cero **2** 7
~ de regulación de la presión **249** 53
~ de regulación de la velocidad de impresión **249** 55
~ de regulación de la ventilación **26** 27
~ de regulación de los tiempos de exposición **115** 19
~ de selección de idioma para el visualizador **237** 33
~ de trucaje **117** 84
botones *Estación* **204** 17
~ *Hotel* **267** 18
botón fino **112** 5
~ floral **370** 24; **371** 25; **374** 14
~ giratorio del rodillo **249** 22
~ grueso **112** 4
~ micrométrico **14** 52
~ para ajustar la distancia **114** 28
~ para conversaciones sucesivas **237** 34
~ para correcciones de luz, motor y de la amplitud del autofoco **115** 2
~ para las funciones de iluminación **115** 3
~ para regular el monitor **25** 29
~ para regular la calefacción **207** 54
~ pulsador **326** 46
boutique **268** 9
bóveda *Bodega* **79** 1
~ *Arte* **335** 32; **336** 38-50
~ claustral **336** 41
~ craneal del hombre de Pekín **261** 18
~ craneal del Pithecantropus erectus **261** 16
~ de aljibe **336** 41
~ de arista **336** 42
~ de cañón **336** 38
~ de caveto **336** 49
~ de crucería **335** 31-32; **336** 43
~ de esgucio **336** 49
~ de medio cañón **336** 38
~ de mocárabes **337** 17
~ de nervios **335** 31-32
~ de rincón de claustro **336** 41
~ en abanico **336** 46
~ en artesa **336** 47
~ esquifada **336** 41
~ estrellada **336** 44
~ nervada **336** 43
~ ojival **335** 31-32
~ reticulada **336** 45
~ semiesférica **334** 72
bovedilla *Cerám.* **159** 24
~ *Barco* **218** 58

box **75** 2
~ de reparación **196** 22
boxeador **299** 25
~ amateur **299** 25
~ profesional **299** 25
~ vencido por fuera de combate **299** 40
boxeo **299** 20-50
boxer **70** 10
boxing-ball **299** 20
boya **15** 10
~ achaflanada **224** 77
~ con asta **224** 79
~ cónica **224** 76
~ de babor **224** 95
~ de barril **224** 94
~ de espegue **224** 79
~ de estribor **224** 96
~ de salida y de llegada **285** 14
~ de señalización del recorrido **285** 18
~ de virada **285** 17
~ de viraje **286** 31
~ luminosa con silbato **224** 68
~ luminosa de campana **224** 74
~ pantalón **228** 13
boyarín **90** 2
Boyero **3** 30
boy-scout **278** 11
bozal **70** 31
bozalillo **71** 7-11
bráctea **371** 7; **372** 5
bracteada del emperador Federico I Barbarroja **252** 4
braga **32** 8
~ pantalón **32** 10
bragañal de plástico **29** 10
braga slip **32** 15
bragueta **29** 35; **32** 24; **33** 48
braguita **280** 27
~ de plástico **28** 22
braille **342** 15
bramante de la cometa **273** 44
brandal **219** 19
branquia **364** 3, 19
braserillo del incensario **332** 41
brassy **293** 91
braza *Barco* **219** 67
~ *Natac.* **282** 33
bracelete *Joya* **36** 3, 17
~ *Reloj.* **110** 5
~ *Elecc.* **263** 11
~ *Bomberos* **270** 22
~ con franjas reflectantes **199** 7
~ de perlas cultivadas **36** 9
~ de piedras finas **36** 25
~ de piedras preciosas **36** 25
~ intermedio **221** 102
brazo *Anat.* **16** 43-48; **17** 12-14
~ *Estar* **42** 22
~ *Perro* **70** 5
~ *Electrón* **241** 31
~ adicional **203** 8
~ ajustable de la plataforma de elevación **195** 26
~ articulado portalámparas **177** 16
~ de acceso **244** 47

~ de batir **166** 17
~ de extensión **132** 63
~ de la caja **322** 16
~ de la caña del timón **284** 31
~ de la desembocadura **13** 2
~ de la excavadora **200** 4
~ de la grúa *Puerto* **226** 49
~ del apagador **325** 38
~ de la señal **203** 2
~ del asiento **207** 45; **208** 26
~ del asiento con cenicero **207** 69
~ del cilindro **177** 68
~ del micrófono telescópico **117** 23
~ del sillón *Apart.* **46** 28
~ del sillón *Peluq.* **106** 18
~ de medida **142** 38
~ de reproducción **115** 64
~ de río **13** 2; **216** 3
~ de soldar **142** 30
~ de sujeción **2** 47
~ de tiro **62** 20
~ de toma de sonido **309** 33
~ de tubo **114** 44
~ elástico **305** 55
~ en cabestrillo **21** 2
~ en forma de tubo *Máq.-herr.* **150** 41
~ fluvial **13** 2
~ giratorio del monitor **27** 24
brazola **283** 59
brazolada **90** 29
brazola de la escotilla **222** 64
brazo manipulador controlado a distancia **235** 29
~ muerto del río **216** 18
~ orientable *Hosp.* **26** 13
~ orientable *Sastre* **104** 27
~ orientable del casco **105** 26
~ oscilante de la rueda trasera **188** 14
~ oscilante longitudinal **191** 27; **192** 66
~ para el arco voltaico **152** 47
~ para las chispas **152** 47
~ portabobinas giratorio **117** 92
~ portadiapositivas **177** 44
~ portaelectrodos **142** 24
~ radial **150** 24
~ registrador **10** 7, 12, 21
~ saledizo **226** 24
brazos al frente **295** 50
~ arriba **295** 49
~ en cruz **295** 48
~ hacia abajo **295** 47
~ oblicuos atrás **295** 51
brazo succionador **184** 11
~ trasero de triángulo **192** 81
brazuelo *Caballo* **72** 21
~ *Matad.* **95** 8, 49
break *Coche* **186** 2
brecina **377** 19
brécol **57** 32
brecha **13** 34
~ de la chimenea **11** 27
breitschwanz **30** 60
breve *Máq.* **320** 12
~ *Escrit.* **342** 50
breviario *Fotocomp.* **175** 26
~ *Igl.* **331** 58
brezo **377** 19

~ negro **377** 19
~ veteado **107** 41
bricbarca de cinco palos **220** 32-34
~ de cuatro palos **220** 29
~ de tres palos **220** 21-23
bricolaje **134**
brida *Caballo* **71** 25, 33
~ *Construc.* **122** 31
~ *Mús.* **325** 36
~ de cuero **325** 36
~ del embrague **177** 55
~ de protección **64** 55
~ intermediaria **190** 39
bridón **289** 12
brik de leche **99** 45
brillante **175** 20
briol **218** 36; **219** 71
briolet con caras **36** 86
brisa en los estayes de proa **285** 13
Brisinga endecacnemos **369** 11
broca *Construc.* **120** 65
~ *Petról.* **145** 21
~ de centrar de tres puntas **135** 11
~ de cuchara **135** 16
~ de fresado horizontal **150** 32
~ de fresado vertical **150** 30
~ de madera **135** 11
~ espiral *Bric.* **134** 49
~ espiral *Cerraj.* **140** 59
brócoli **57** 32
brocha de empapelador **128** 40
~ de encolar **128** 27
~ del engrudo **128** 27
~ de motear **129** 18
~ de pulir **108** 44
~ de recubrir **129** 3
brochal **120** 41; **121** 71
brocha plana **129** 17
broche *Joya* **36** 7, 10
~ alargado con brillante **36** 18
~ del cinturón **328** 24
~ de marfil **36** 30
~ de perlas **36** 7
~ moderno **36** 19
bronquio **20** 5
brote *Planta* **54** 26
~ *Agric.* **68** 16
~ de la hoja **59** 47
~ femenino **372** 46, 48
~ largo **78** 3
~ masculino **372** 44, 49, 56
~ rastrero **58** 20
broza de zarzas **274** 2
bruja **306** 6
brújula **223** 6
~ automática **230** 5
~ giroscópica **224** 31, 51-53
~ maestra **224** 51
~ magnética **224** 46
bruñidor *Orfebre* **108** 48
~ *Art. gráf.* **340** 17
bruza *Apar. hogar* **50** 56
~ *Caballo* **71** 55
~ *Art. gráf.* **340** 11
buceador de pesca submarina **280** 37
buceo **279** 7-27; **282** 38
buche **73** 20
buchón **359** 5
Buda **337** 20
buey *An. dom.* **73** 1
~ *Etnogr.* **354** 11

~ mezcladora del color 116 43-45
~ motriz 209 2
~ niveladora de cine 114 48
~ para cepillar la alfombra 50 79
~ para la peluca 105 39
~ para limpiar en seco la alfombra 50 79
~ para sacudir la alfombra 50 79
~ reducida 352 30
~ sonora 312 47
~ superior 121 74, 80
~ supresora 311 25
~ unificadora del sonido y de la imagen 117 102
~ vídeo 243 26, 36
~ y la parte del cuerpo situada por encima de las ingles en la esgrima de sable 294 52
cabezuela 61 14; 370 73; 378 12
~ discoide 370 74
~ globulosa 370 75
cabina *Autom.* 194 2, 15
~ *FFCC* 214 20
~ *FFAA* 255 93
~ alta 305 75
~ baja 305 76
~ Cassegrain 5 4
~ central de la toma del sonido de la radio 238 1-6
~ con arco de seguridad 85 36
~ de combustible 234 62
~ de control 238 17
~ de control de la imagen 239 10
~ de control de las imágenes 238 60-65
~ de control del sonido 238 27; 239 7
~ de gran capacidad 214 52
~ del conductor *Agric.* 64 36
~ del conductor *Tranv.* 197 25
~ del conductor *Carret.* 200 11
~ del conductor *Puerto* 226 52
~ del conductor 255 61
~ del conductor de la grúa 119 35; 222 16
~ del locutor 238 18
~ del maquinista 209 4; 210 49; 211 19, 57; 213 2; 214 65
~ del maquinista de la locomotora de vapor 210 39-63
~ del maquinista del automotor 208 14
~ del maquinista de una locomotora Diesel 212 5
~ del mecanismo de elevación 217 71
~ de los pasajeros 231 22
~ del patrón 228 31
~ del piloto *Avión* 230 35
~ del piloto *Policía* 264 2
~ del piloto *Remo* 283 8
~ del piloto *Dep. aéreo* 288 10, 19
~ del torno 226 54
~ de mezcla del sonido 238 27

~ de mezcla de sonidos 238 17
~ de pilotaje *Avión* 230 35; 231 19
~ de pilotaje *Astron.* 235 16
~ de pilotaje de un monomotor de viaje y de turismo 230 1-31
~ de proyección *Astron.* 5 27
~ de proyección *Cine* 312 12
~ de radio 223 12
~ de toma de sonido 310 54
~ de un miembro de la tripulación 228 32
~ de viajeros 214 52
~ electoral 263 23
~ inferior 234 49
~ para mirar los huevos al trasluz 74 47
~ para viajeros 214 28
~ superior 234 45
~ telefónica 236 8; 251 10; 268 56
~ telefónica del andén 205 57
cabio 121 76
~ central 121 51
~ de hormigón 119 4
~ de la cresta 121 62
~ del caballete 121 43
~ de lima tesa 121 62
~ inferior 121 44; 122 40
~ lateral 121 39
cable *Central el.* 153 41
~ *Fibra* 169 28
~ *Cons. hidr.* 217 23
~ *Barco a motor, esquí acuát.* 286 47
~ *Esgr.* 294 31
~ *Mús.* 326 53
~ auxiliar 214 47
~ Bowden 188 37
~ colgante 215 17
~ conductor de alta tensión 152 32
~ de acero 298 44
~ de alimentación 94 9
~ de alta tensión 152 33
~ de alta tensión, para corriente trifásica 153 42
~ de apoyo 2 30
~ de arrastre *Cons. hidr.* 217 23
~ de arrastre *Barco a motor, esquí acuát.* 286 47
~ de cámara 239 2
~ de conexión *Soldadura* 142 25
~ de conexión con el paciente 25 43
~ de conexión con la impresora de papel 25 56
~ de conexión con la unidad de control central 25 20
~ de conexión del sonido 117 8
~ de contacto 205 58
~ de control 271 53
~ de diagnosis 195 38
~ de diagnóstico 195 3
~ de enganche 215 47
~ de freno 259 16
~ de impulsos 117 72
~ de la balsa 216 2
~ de la corriente *Cocina* 39 25

~ de la corriente *Jardín* 56 32
~ de la grúa 222 13
~ del ancla 218 18
~ del aparato telefónico 237 4
~ de las sondas de la red 90 14
~ del auricular 237 13
~ del electrodo del estimulador cardíaco temporal 25 25
~ del freno *Tejido* 166 61
~ del freno *Moto* 189 12
~ del micrófono 117 25; 239 14; 310 32
~ del sonido 311 41
~ del sonido piloto 313 29
~ del techo 211 5
~ de mando 244 52
~ de medida 116 38
~ de perforación 145 7
~ de remolque *Río* 216 24
~ de remolque *Salvamento* 227 8
~ de remolque *Vuelo sin motor* 287 4
~ de retención 259 16
~ de sincronización 313 29
~ de soldar 142 19
~ de sonda de la temperatura del aceite 195 40
~ de suministro de corriente 14
~ de tracción *FFCC* 214 14, 26, 37, 45
~ de tracción *Grandes alm.* 271 52
~ de tracción *Dep. inv.* 301 63
~ de tres polos 127 44
~ disparador 114 38
~ eléctrico para instalaciones técnicas 198 19
~ inferior 214 46
~ oblicuo 215 47
~ para cerrar la red 90 26
~ para el ajuste del ralentí 190 51
~ para medir la temperatura del aceite 195 16
~ portador *Construc.* 119 37
~ portador *Puente* 215 16, 40
~ portante *FFCC* 214 27, 38, 44
~ portante y de tracción 214 21
~ sin fin 214 21
~ telefónico 198 15; 237 54
~ termoplástico resistente a la humedad 127 42
~ tractor 214 45
cabo *Cestero* 136 23
~ *Cons. hidr.* 217 23
~ *Remo* 283 12
~ de salvamento 228 3
~ 3 27; 4 62
cabra 73 14
Cabra de Mar 3 36; 4 62
cabra montés 367 7
~ naciente 254 32
cabrestante *Fotogr.* 117 34
~ *Cons. hidr.* 217 23
~ *Buque guerra* 258 23
~ *Bomberos* 270 56
~ de arrastre 217 22
~ del ancla 258 6; 259 82

cabria auxiliar de la grúa 147 61
cabrilla 381 15
cabrio 121 28, 36; 122 19
~ central 121 56
~ de copete 121 61
~ de la lima hoya 121 64
~ del copete 121 63
~ de quiebra 121 31
~ de unión 121 55, 61
cabriola *Caballo* 71 5
~ *Ballet* 314 21
cabriole 314 21
cabriolé 186 34
~ con pescante elevado por detrás 186 29
~ sport 193 26
cabrio principal 121 55
cabrón 73 14
cabuchón 35 4
cabujón 36 78-81
~ octogonal 36 81
~ ovalado 36 80
~ redondo 36 78
cacahuate 383 41
cacahué 383 41
cacahuete 383 41
cacahuetes 45 41
cacahuey 383 41
cacao *Comest.* 98 66
~ *Planta estim., trop.* 382 16, 19
~ en polvo 382 19
cacatúa de cresta amarilla 363 1
cacería, clases 86 1-52
cacillo 40 16
cachalote 367 25
cacharrería 308 64-66
cacharro de loza 308 66
cache-controller 244 9
cacheo 264 31
cachiflín 306 52
cachimba corta 107 33
cachipolla 358 6
cachiporra de cabeza redonda y gruesa 354 33
cacho 276 30
cachón 279 6
cachorro 73 16
cada 372 47
cadena *Ganado* 75 15
~ *Superm.* 99 95
~ *Bicicl.* 187 36
~ *Moto* 189 22
~ *FFAA* 255 31
~ almohadillada 335 51
~ antideslizante 304 10
~ con cambio de velocidades 290 20
~ con monedas 36 36
~ de amuletos y dados 354 40
~ de apoyo 74 14
~ de alta fidelidad 241 1
~ de avance 172 67
~ de cangilones 216 57; 226 42
~ del ancla 222 77; 223 50; 224 72; 227 12
~ de la sierra *Silvic.* 85 14
~ de la sierra *Construc.* 120 16
~ de la vara 71 20
~ de los chapones 163 45
~ de rodillos 187 36
~ de rodillos de mando de la bomba de aceite 190 25
~ de seguridad 126 3
~ de suspensión 65 17

~ fotográfica con adaptador **112** 64
~ fotográfica con objetivos intercambiables **115** 1-24
~ fotográfica de cartuchos **114** 11
~ fotográfica de gran formato **112** 25
~ fotográfica de mano de gran formato **114** 36
~ fotográfica de paso universal **114** 1
~ fotográfica de pequeño formato **112** 26; **114** 1
~ fotográfica para película y para placas **113** 40
~ fotográfica pocket **114** 16
~ fotográfica réflex de doble lente **114** 22
~ fotográfica réflex de pequeño formato con un solo objetivo **115** 1-24
~ frigorífica *Matad.* **94** 21-24
~ frigorífica *Barco* **223** 56
~ frigorífica *Puerto* **225** 50
~ generadora de impulsos **117** 71
~ hecha con piedras **328** 39
~ instamatic **114** 11
~ ligera **313** 20
~ métrica universal para fotogrametría **112** 67
~ miniatura **23** 7
~ mortuoria **333** 5
~ móvil de fumigación **83** 15
~ para calentar el aire **147** 30
~ para calentar el gas **147** 28
~ para fotos de pequeño formato **23** 7
~ para película de 35 mm **313** 1
~ para película normal **313** 1
~ plegable **309** 25
~ secadora **159** 17
~ sincrónica controlada por cristal de cuarzo **310** 19
~ sonora *Fotogr.* **117** 22
~ sonora *Cine* **310** 60; **313** 26
~ sonora de súper 8 **117** 1
~ submarina *Fotogr.* **117** 57
~ submarina *Surf, Buceo* **279** 24
~ topográfica para la producción de series coincidentes de imágenes **14** 63
camarera **265** 13; **266** 18
~ del bar **267** 63; **317** 2; **318** 14
camarero **221** 1 10; **266** 8, 30; **267** 47
~ de habitación **267** 33
camareta junto al coronamiento de popa **223** 34; **258** 72
camarón **369** 12
camaronero **360** 8
camarote **218** 45; **223** 29
~ con literas plegables **259** 84
~ del almirante **218** 27
~ del capitán **223** 13
~ del comandante **259** 85

~ de lujo **223** 30
~ de oficial **223** 21
~ doble **223** 29
~ individual **223** 46
cambiada del rumbo **285** 27
cambiador de calor **259** 66
cambio **233** 51
~ de agujas a distancia **202** 27
~ de cinco marchas **189** 6
~ de marcha **210** 18
~ de moneda **250** 10
~ de velocidad **65** 23
~ de velocidad de la toma de fuerza **65** 40
~ de velocidades *Riego* **67** 21
~ de velocidades *Autom.* **191** 91
~ de velocidades *FFCC* **211** 50
~ de velocidades *Cicl., motor.* **290** 20
cambium **370** 10
cambronera **376** 20
camello *Buque guerra* **259** 19
~ *Etnogr.* **354** 1
~ bactriano **366** 29
~ de dos gibas **366** 29
cameraman *Fotogr.* **117** 67
~ *Cine* **310** 20, 41
camilla **270** 23
~ de emergencia **21** 23
~ de replanteo **118** 69
camino **44** 16
~ abierto en el monte **84** 1
~ de acceso **329** 34
~ de herradura **12** 46
~ del jardín **51** 14
~ de losas **37** 45
~ de ronda **329** 20
Camino de Santiago **3** 35
camino de tablones **118** 79
~ forestal *Mapa* **15** 102
~ forestal *Silvic.* **84** 3
~ transitable regularmente cuidado **15** 99
~ vecinal **63** 18
camión **194**
~ articulado **194** 28
~ basculante de tres bandas **194** 24
~ cisterna *Autom.* **194** 28
~ cisterna *Aerop.* **233** 22
~ cisterna *Bomberos* **270** 51
~ cisterna de leche **76** 2
~ con remolque **213** 34
~ de bomberos **270** 5
~ de carga *Carret.* **200** 7
~ de carga *Puerto* **226** 19
~ de gran tonelaje **194** 20
~ de juguete *Hab. niños* **47** 38
~ de juguete *Parque* **273** 62
~ de las mangueras y herramientas **270** 53
~ del servicio municipal de limpieza **304** 8
~ de mudanzas **268** 47
~ de recogida de basuras **199** 1
camioneta **194** 5
~ cerrada **194** 7
~ con caja **194** 6
~ con plataforma **194** 6
camión grúa **270** 47
~ para la mercancía en fardos **206** 15
~ pesado **194** 20

~ portacontenedores **225** 47
~ tanque **194** 28
camión-tanque de extinción **270** 51
camión todo terreno con cuatro ruedas motrices **194** 1
camisa *Ropa* **29** 61
~ *Encuad.* **185** 37
~ a cuadros **33** 50
~ de caballero **32** 38-47
~ de cama **32** 37
~ de mangas cortas **33** 33
~ de punto **33** 36
~ de smoking **32** 43
~ de sport **32** 38; **33** 37
camiseta **29** 6, 27; **31** 38; **32** 25; **291** 56
~ con hombreras **292** 26
~ de ciclista **290** 9
~ de espaldas desnudas **31** 64
~ de gimnasia **296** 61
~ del pijama **32** 18
~ de malla **32** 22
~ de mangas cortas **29** 7; **32** 28
~ de red **32** 22
~ de señora **32** 7
camisilla **32** 25
camisita **28** 23
~ de bebé **29** 8
camisola **32** 16
camisón **32** 16
cámomila **380** 1
campamento de los boys-scouts **278** 8-11
~ de los exploradores **278** 8-11
~ de tiendas **307** 61
campana *Cocina* **39** 17
~ *FFCC* **212** 49
~ *Naveg.* **224** 75
~ *Dep. aéreo* **288** 5
~ *Halter., pesos* **299** 46
~ *Caball.* **329** 39
~ de evacuación del calor **182** 5
~ de la chimenea **137** 7
~ del tragante **147** 6
~ eléctrica **331** 9
~ extractora de humos **46** 31
campanario *Igl.* **331** 2
~ *Arte* **334** 65
campanil **337** 8
campanilla *Anat.* **19** 22
~ *Flor* **60** 10
~ *Moda* **355** 23
ʼ *Flor* **375** 14
~ de invierno **60** 1
~ del altar **332** 52
~ de la sacristía **330** 46
~ de los Alpes **378** 3
~ del Sanctus **332** 52
~ del trineo **304** 26
campánula **375** 14
campechana *Camping* **278** 4
~ *Baños* **281** 5
campera **30** 38; **33** 39
campesino **62** 6
camping **278** 1-59
campiña **63** 17
campo **63** 4
~ de batalla *Mapa* **15** 93
~ de batalla *Caball.* **329** 31
~ de función **244** 27
~ de fútbol **291** 1-16
~ de golf **293** 79-82

~ de juego **292** 40-58
~ de minigolf **272** 68
~ de skeet **305** 74
~ de tiro al plato **305** 74
~ gráfico **244** 27
camposanto **331** 21-41
canadiense **283** 3
canal *Mapa* **15** 57
~ *Riego* **67** 13
~ *Matad.* **95** 40
~ *FFCC* **202** 32
~ *Cons. hidr.* **217** 15-28
canaladura **334** 27
canal, centro **224** 98
~ construido a lo largo de una presa **283** 60
~ de acceso a los baños de aguas minerales **281** 9
~ de agua **334** 54
~ de aire **155** 35
~ de aireación **333** 4
~ de alimentación *Sider.* **147** 22
~ de alimentación *Aserr.* **157** 55
~ de aspiración **145** 51
~ de desagüe **216** 33
~ de distribución del agua salobre **274** 3
~ de drenaje **200** 63
~ de evacuación del agua **155** 41
~ de la aguja **167** 15
~ de la caja de resonancia **326** 13
~ de la caja superior **326** 14
~ de la colada **148** 3
~ de la corriente secundaria **232** 41, 44
~ de la escoria **148** 12
~ de la laguna **13** 34
~ de la ruleta **275** 29
~ de la turbina al lado de la cuenca **155** 41
~ de la turbina al lado del mar **155** 40
~ del gas **152** 12
~ del hierro **147** 35
~ del tejado **37** 6; **38** 9
~ de navegación **216** 21
~ de polvo **163** 22
~ de tiro del ventilador **144** 22
~ de traída del agua **155** 40
~ de vaporización **50** 14
~ de viento **326** 11
canalete **353** 14
~ de una sola pala **283** 34
~ doble **283** 39
canal guía **217** 75
canalización de agua potable **198** 22
~ de cables **234** 29, 47
~ de evacuación de vapores del disolvente **182** 25
~ de gas **198** 21
~ de gas-oil a presión **190** 52
~ del agua de refrigeración **191** 10
~ del agua salada **145** 33
~ del aire comprimido **138** 5
~ de refrigerante **138** 26
~ de transporte del petróleo refinado **145** 35
~ para fugas de gas-oil **190** 53
~ principal de electricidad **235** 55

~ trifásica **127** 14
~ tripolar **127** 67
clavijero **323** 19; **324** 10, 19
clavillo **106** 36
clavo *Tornill.* **143** 51
~ *Gimn.* **295** 29
~ *Planta estim., trop.* **382** 28
~ de alambre galvanizado **122** 74
~ de cabeza redonda **121** 95
~ de hierro forjado **121** 94
~ de madera **121** 92
~ de techar **143** 55
~ para colocar pizarra **122** 74
~ para el cartón **122** 96
~ para las varillas **128** 30
claxon **188** 53
clema **127** 29
clérigo **330** 40; **331** 37, 45; **332** 22
~ evangélico **332** 3
~ protestante **332** 3
clienta *Restaur.* **266** 25
~ *Grandes alm.* **271** 16
cliente *Comest.* **98** 43
~ *Superm.* **99** 2, 18
~ *Ópt.* **111** 2
~ *Oficina* **248** 18
~ *Restaur.* **266** 25
~ *Grandes alm.* **271** 55
~ del banco **250** 6
~ del bar **267** 55
~ del café **265** 22-24
~ habitual **266** 40
clima boreal **9** 56
~ de la Tierra **9** 53-58
~ de la tundra **9** 57
~ del hielo eterno **9** 58
~ ecuatorial **9** 53
~ polar **9** 57-58
climatología **9**
clinch **299** 31
clineja **34** 29
clínica quirúrgica **26** 1-54
clinopinacoide **351** 24
clip de la pluma **2** 18
~ de los tirantes **32** 31
clíper inglés **220** 36
clip grande **247** 2
~ pequeño **247** 1
clisé **178** 38
clitelo **357** 26
clítoris **20** 88
clivia **53** 8
cloaca mixta **198** 27
cloración del benzol **170** 8
cloro **170** 7
clorobenzol **170** 9
cloruro **1** 10
~ de sodio **1** 9
~ de sodio **170** 13
clown **307** 24
club **283** 23
~ de madera **293** 91, 92
cobaya **366** 12
cobayo **366** 12
cobertizo de aserrado **120** 3
~ de construcción **222** 3-4
~ de la fruta **225** 52
~ de las herramientas **52** 3
~ de las máquinas **62** 15
~ de las mercancías **206** 26-39
~ del astillero **225** 23
~ de los botes **283** 24
~ de los útiles **55** 1
~ de mercancías **206** 7

cobija **122** 58
cobijo **43** 8
cobranza **86** 36
cobre en bruto **260** 64
~ gris **351** 1
coccinélido **358** 37
cocción **92** 42-53
cóccix **17** 5; **20** 60
cociente **344** 26
~ diferencial **345** 13
cocina **39**
~ *FFCC* **207** 29, 80
~ *Barco* **223** 42
~ de a bordo **231** 20
~ de dos fuegos de gas **278** 33
~ de gas **39** 12
~ de la charcutería **96** 31-59
~ del coche-restaurante **207** 33
~ eléctrica *cocina* **39** 12
~ eléctrica *Apart.* **46** 32
~ eléctrica *FFCC* **207** 30
cocker **70** 38
coco **383** 48, 53
cocodrilo *Font.* **126** 61
~ *Elec.* **127** 47
~ *Bric.* **134** 11
~ del Nilo **356** 13
cocoideo **80** 35
cocote **306** 37
cocotero **383** 48
cóctel **317** 33
coctelera **267** 61
cocha **13** 33
coche **186** 1-3, 26-39, 45, 51-54
~ *Autom.* **191** 1-56
~ *Taller* **195** 34
~ ambulancia **270** 19
~ automotor de manteni-
miento de catenarias **211** 41
~ automotor de plataforma
regulable **211** 41
~ automotor Diesel **209** 1; **211** 41
~ automotor final **211** 61
~ automotor intermedio **211** 62
coche-bar **207** 73
coche-cama **207** 36
coche celular **264** 38
cochecito de la muñeca **47** 10; **48** 24, 31
~ de mimbre **48** 24
~ de niño **28** 30; **273** 31
~ de niño con visión
panorámica **28** 34
coche de alquiler **186** 26
~ de caballos **186**
~ de carreras **290** 34-38
~ de carreras de Fórmula 1 **290** 34
~ de carreras de Formula 2 **290** 36
~ de carreras de niño **273** 33
~ de carreras super-V **290** 37
~ de caza **86** 18
~ de clase media **193** 4-10
~ de correos **236** 52
~ de choque **308** 63
~ de dos caballos **186** 36
~ de dos plazas **193** 26
~ de excursión **186** 33
~ de ferrocarril de cremallera **214** 5

~ de gran capacidad **207** 59
~ del funicular **214** 13
~ deportivo de cuatro
asientos **193** 28
~ deportivo de gran
turismo **193** 32
~ deportivo GT **193** 32
~ de punto **186** 26
~ de reportaje **239** 1-15
~ de tracción trasera **193** 4
~ de turismo **193** 1-36
~ de un caballo **186** 29
~ de viaje **186** 39
~ especial blindado **264** 16
~ familiar **193** 17
~ modelo deportivo **193** 8
~ motriz **209** 2
~ patrulla **264** 10
~ pequeño de tres puertas **193** 19
cochera **270** 1
coche-restaurante **207** 22-32
~ de autoservicio **207** 73
cochero **186** 32
Cochero **3** 27
cochero de la diligencia **186** 40
coche ruso de tres caballos **186** 45
coches de alquiler **233** 33
coche, tipos **193** 1-36
cochevís **361** 19
cochinilla de agua **358** 2
~ de humedad **81** 6
~ de San José **80** 35
cochinillo *An. dom.* **73** 9
~ *Ganado* **75** 39
cochino *Granja* **62** 10
~ *An. dom.* **73** 9
cochorro **82** 1
codal **329** 48
codaste **218** 1; **222** 70-71
~ de la hélice **222** 71
~ del timón **222** 70
codeso **374** 32
codificación **236** 35
código de los esquiadores de
señales con la mano **286** 49-55
~ postal **236** 43
codillo *Caballo* **72** 20
~ *Caza* **88** 17, 38
~ *Matad.* **95** 38, 49
~ *Construc.* **121** 41
~ de ángulo **121** 57
~ trasero **95** 54
codo *Anat.* **16** 45
~ *Font.* **126** 52
~ *Máq.-herr.* **150** 40
~ conductor de vapor **153** 28
~ de cardán **67** 6
~ de empalme de la bomba **67** 8
~ de la bajada de aguas **37** 12
~ del tubo de la estufa **309** 6
~ , pliegue del
~ reductor **126** 49
codorniz **359** 22
coeficiente **345** 4
cofa **223** 38
~ de gavia **219** 52
~ de mesana **219** 54
~ de trinquete **219** 50
~ mayor **219** 52
cofre **36** 31
~ sepulcral de piedra **328** 17

cogedor de frutas **56** 22
cogienda **63** 31-41
cogujada común **361** 19
cogulla **331** 55
cohete *Salvamento* **228** 2
~ *Carnaval* **306** 54
~ de aceleración para la
acumulación del carbu-
rante **234** 22, 48
~ de control **234** 63
~ de maniobra **6** 5
~ de maniobra del módulo
lunar **6** 39
~ de pilotaje **6** 5
~ lanzacabos **228** 1
~ para regular la posición **234** 38
~ portador **234** 2
~ portador Saturno V del
„Apolo" **234** 1
~ S-IC **234** 3
cohombro **57** 13
coipo **366** 14
coipú **366** 14
cojín *Estar* **42** 27
~ *FFCC* **207** 65
~ de aire **243** 27; **286** 66
~ del asiento **42** 23
~ del sofá **46** 17
~ de molde **104** 23
cojinete *Arte* **334** 24
~ central **177** 65
~ de aguante **221** 29
~ de bolas **143** 69
~ de caucho **192** 67, 82
~ de empuje **259** 60
~ delantero para estabilizar
la broca horizontal **150** 33
~ del cilindro **148** 60
~ del eje **210** 10
~ de rodillos **164** 47
~ de rosca **140** 61
~ de soporte **91** 10
~ discoidal adhesivo **364** 26
~ guía **113** 14
~ móvil para la inclinación
del mástil y el gobierno
de la tabla **284** 6
cojín neumático **286** 66
~ para el oro **183** 6
col **57** 32
cola *Perro* **70** 12
~ *Caballo* **72** 38
~ *Caza* **88** 19, 47, 49, 62, 67, 75, 80
~ *Molino* **91** 32
~ *Construc.* **122** 89
~ *Encuad.* **183** 15; **184** 9; **185** 32
~ *Colegio* **260** 5
~ *Moda* **355** 80
~ *Ave* **362** 8
~ blanca **134** 36
~ cortada **70** 12
colada *Sider.* **147** 54
~ continua **148** 24-29
cola de caballo **73** 40
~ de caballo *Flor* **376** 18
~ de carpintero *Carp.* **132** 13
~ de carpintero *Bric.* **134** 36
~ de delfín **327** 25
~ de golondrina *Cristal.* **351** 25
~ de golondrina *Articul.* **358** 52
~ de la cometa **273** 43
~ del árbol **223** 60

~ de curvatura **258** 8
~ de extremidad hemisférica **235** 48
~ del buque en su posición **222** 29
~ longitudinal **285** 55
~ maestra fresada integralmente **235** 10
~ transversal **285** 51
cuadernillo **183** 12
cuaderno **47** 24
~ de dibujo **338** 35
~ de ejercicios **260** 4
~ de escritura **260** 18
~ de notas **264** 36
~ de papel de fumar **107** 17
cuadra *Granja* **62** 2
~ *Ganado* **75** 1
~ *Barco* **220** 13
~ *Bandera* **253** 28
cuadrada **320** 12
cuadrado **345** 1; **346** 33; **347** 31
cuadrante *Reloj.* **110** 25
~ *Matem.* **347** 5
~ del contador de agua **269** 58
cuadrilátero **346** 33-39
~ de boxeo **299** 35
~ irregular **346** 39
cuadrilla de vaciadores **148** 13
cuadrirreactor para trayectos largos **231** 13
cuadrito de los caracteres **151** 31
cuadro *Dorm.* **43** 20
~ *Matad.* **95** 39
~ *Oficina* **246** 28
~ de agudeza visual **22** 32
~ de agujas eléctrico **203** 61
~ de Cristo **330** 50
~ de doble soporte **189** 17
~ de hierro **325** 2
~ de instrumentos **288** 11
~ de la bicicleta **187** 14-20
~ del altar **330** 13, 50
~ de los bolos **305** 1-11
~ de mandos *Offset* **180** 74
~ de mandos *Tranv.* **197** 29
~ de mandos *Oficina* **249** 42
~ de programación **243** 31
~ de saque **293** 12
~ de sedimentos de la orina **23** 58
~ luminoso de agujas **203** 65
~ radiogoniométrico **258** 17
~ tubular **188** 9, 49
cuajada **76** 45
cuantía de la letra **250** 18
cuarta **321** 9
~ octava **321** 47
cuartel **254** 18-23
~ de bomberos **270** 1-3
~ de la escotilla **222** 65
cuartito de la ducha **49** 39
cuarto creciente **4** 4
~ de derrota **223** 14
~ dedo **19** 55
~ de esfera **334** 73
~ de estar **42**
~ de herramientas *Casa* **37** 32
~ de herramientas *Bomberos* **270** 1
~ de la caldera **38** 38-43
~ de la calefacción **55** 7

~ delantero **88** 25
~ de los instrumentos **228** 22
~ de vaca **94** 22
~ menguante **4** 6
cuartón **120** 10
cuarto oscuro **116** 21
~ trasero *Caballo* **72** 33-37
~ trasero *Caza* **88** 22
cuarzo **110** 37
~ oscilante **110** 37
cuascle **71** 44
cuatrillo **321** 23
cuatro por cuatro **320** 32
~ por dos **320** 33
~ por ocho **320** 31
~ puertas de clase alta **193** 1
~ puertas de clase media **193** 4-10
cuba *Meteor.* **10** 46
~ *Tonel.* **130** 1
~ *Papel* **172** 25
~ *FFAA* **255** 33
~ con la fusión de vidrio **162** 50
~ de aclarado **165** 49
~ de amasar **96** 40
~ de espesar **172** 62
~ de fermentación **93** 8
~ de grabar con el líquido corrosivo **182** 16
~ de la escoria **147** 10
~ del alto horno **147** 7
~ de la pintura **165** 47
~ de la tolva **147** 5
~ del hormigón **201** 24
~ del reactor nuclear **259** 67
~ del silo **225** 69
~ de maceración **92** 43
~ de máquina **172** 86
~ de nivel constante **192** 14
~ de pasta acabada **172** 85
~ de pintura **130** 15
~ de revelado **182** 11
~ de vaciado **172** 81
~ para la pasta gruesa **172** 59
cubeta *Sombr.* **35** 36
~ *Colegio* **261** 33
~ agitadora **173** 1
~ con vidrio fundido **162** 50
~ de agua fuerte **340** 51
~ de arrastre **200** 17
~ de clarificación **162** 4
~ de coloración **23** 50
~ de forma arriñonada **23** 45
~ de fusión **162** 3, 14
~ de grabado **178** 24
~ delantera del detergente **50** 27
~ de la semilla **54** 2
~ de lavado *Fotogr.* **116** 15
~ de lavado *Clisé* **178** 1
~ de la verdura **39** 4
~ de los instrumentos **26** 39; **27** 5
~ de revelado **116** 25
~ de trabajo **162** 5
~ distribuidora de hormigón **201** 6
~ mezcladora de la pasta de papel **173** 1
~ para la impresión **24** 56
~ para las virutas y para refrigerar el aceite lubricante **149** 44

~ refrigerante **162** 15
~ semiautomática de revelado con termostato **116** 56
cúbico **351** 1-17
cubierta *Bicicl.* **187** 30
~ *Avión* **230** 39
~ *Remo* **283** 57
~ *Mús.* **322** 27
~ A **223** 28-30
~ B **223** 32-34
~ con filtro **2** 14
~ de aterrizaje para helicópteros **228** 15
~ de botes **223** 19-21
~ de cartón asfáltico **122** 90
~ de fibrocemento **122** 90-103
~ de fibrocemento ondulado **122** 97
~ de fieltro **353** 20
~ de hormigón **154** 20
~ de humus **200** 64
~ de la caja **143** 80
~ de la cámara a prueba de sonidos **310** 48
~ de la cumbrera **122** 99
~ de la leva **167** 13
~ de la mesa **141** 16
~ de la tabla de planchar **50** 17
~ del caballete **122** 99
~ del freno *Tornill.* **143** 106
~ del freno *Bicicl.* **187** 70
~ del original para copias de una en una **249** 33
~ del radiador **304** 11
~ del reactor **1** 57
~ del tanque **222** 54
~ del tubo contador **2** 20
~ de madera **55** 9
~ de marcación **223** 4-11
~ de paseo **223** 22-27
~ de popa **223** 32
~ de proa *Barco* **223** 47
~ de proa *Vela* **284** 10
~ de protección *Meteor.* **10** 41
~ de protección *Herr.* **138** 9
~ de puentes con doble apoyo vertical **121** 37
~ de sol **223** 22
~ de tablas **55** 9
~ de tejas **122** 1, 45-60
~ de tela asfáltica **122** 90-103
~ de una sola cámara **121** 42
~ de uralita® **122** 90-103
~ de vuelo **259** 2, 12
~ en ángulo **259** 12
~ exterior blanda **59** 42
~ goniométrica **223** 4-11
~ holandesa con armadura de copete **121** 60
~ inferior **146** 35
~ intermedia **146** 36
~ para automóviles **221** 79
~ para el par de cilindros de aspiración **163** 21
~ para helicópteros **146** 7
~ para trenes **221** 80
~ principal *Barco* **223** 32-34
~ principal *Buque guerra* **258** 9
~ protectora **140** 20
~ protectora contra las salpicaduras **283** 56
~ provisional de la caja de la escalera **118** 22

~ publicitaria **185** 37
~ quebrantada **121** 18
~ radiogoniométrica **227** 24
~ semicerrada **223** 28
~ superior *Petról.* **146** 37
~ superior *Barco* **223** 28-30
~ superior *Buque guerra* **258** 10
cubierto *Meteor.* **9** 23
~ *Comed.* **44** 5
~ *Mesa* **45** 3-12
~ *FFCC* **207** 85
~ *Restaur.* **266** 27
~ *Rastro* **309** 47
~ de la ensalada **45** 24
~ de pescado **45** 8
~ de trinchar **45** 69-70
cubilete *Sombr.* **35** 36
~ *Juego* **276** 30
~ del ordeñador **75** 30
~ de los dados **47** 42
~ de salida para medir la viscosidad **129** 38
cubilote **148** 1
~ para el hormigón **119** 38
cubital posterior **18** 58
cúbito **17** 14
~ de caldo **98** 27
~ de hielo **266** 44
~ de sopa **98** 26
cubo *Apar. hogar* **50** 54
~ *Bicicl.* **187** 26
~ *Matem.* **347** 30
~ *Cristal.* **351** 2
~ con arena de relleno **158** 29
~ con octaedro **351** 16
~ de contar **48** 17
~ de hielo para refrescar el vino **266** 42
~ de la basura *Med.* **22** 70
~ de la basura *Carnic.* **96** 46
~ de la basura *Est. serv.* **196** 12
~ de la basura *Limp. públ.* **199** 3
~ de la escalera **37** 72
~ de la ropa blanca **50** 21
~ de la rueda delantera **187** 52
~ del carbón **309** 9
~ del champaña **267** 59
~ de madera *Molino* **91** 27
~ de madera *Dep. inv.* **302** 40
~ de pintura **129** 10
~ de rueda **192** 83
~ de tejador **122** 22
~ -flash **114** 73
~ de hielo **134** 18
cubrecadena **187** 37
cubrecuerdas **324** 17
cubrejunta **119** 65
cubrenuca **270** 38
cucaracha doméstica **81** 17
cucarda **264** 8
cuclillas **295** 36
cuclillo *Ave* **359** 30
~ *Flor* **376** 21
cuco **359** 30
cucúlida **359** 30
cucurucho **98** 49
cucurucho de helado **308** 31
cuchara *Pesca* **89** 2
~ *Construc.* **118** 56
~ de colada **148** 23
~ de la excavadora **118** 82
~ de madera **40** 3

~ después del trasplante **84** 10

cultura de los vasos campaniformes **328** 14

~ de los vasos de embudo **328** 12

cumbre **12** 40

cumbrera **121** 48; **122** 93

cúmulo *Meteor.* **8** 1

~ *Vuelo sin motor* **287** 22

~ -nimbo **287** 26

cúmulonimbo **8** 17

cumulus **8** 1

~ congestus **8** 2

~ humilis **8** 1

cuna con ruedecillas **28** 1

~ de dos ruedas **214** 69

~ doble **214** 68

cuneiforme **341** 8

cuña *Construc.* **119** 15

~ *Carp.* **132** 19

~ *Herr.* **137** 31

~ *Cantera* **158** 7

~ de aludes **304** 2

~ de fijación *Silvic.* **85** 9

~ de fijación *Tipogr.* **181** 39

~ de la pila **157** 37

~ de madera dura **121** 96

~ de tala **84** 30; **85** 4

~ para afinar **325** 21

cuño *Fotocomp.* **175** 35

~ *Dinero* **252** 40-41

~ inferior **252** 41

~ superior **252** 40

cupé *Coche* **186** 3

~ *Autom.* **193** 26

cupón de dividendos **251** 18

cúpula *Fruta* **59** 50

~ *cúpula* **334** 58, 72-73

~ *Arbol.* **371** 5

~ *Vela* **384** 52

~ central **334** 72

~ de caldera **210** 12

~ de la cabina **257** 4

~ de la caldera **92** 45

~ del comandante **255** 76

~ del observatorio **5** 12

~ del radar **256** 10

~ de proyección **5** 21

~ en forma de bulbo **121** 25

~ giratoria **5** 12

~ movible **5** 14

cura **330** 39; **332** 22

~ de reposo **274** 12-14

~ por inhalación **274** 6-7

curculiónido **80** 49

cureña giratoria **255**

cureta para el curetaje **26** 52

~ para el raspado **26** 52

curiana *Ins.* **81** 17

~ *Camping* **278** 12

~ *Remo* **283** 69

curling *Dep. inv.* **302** 41-43

~ alemán **302** 38-40

cursiva **175** 7

curso **171** 12

~ aparente del Sol **4** 10-21

~ aparente del Sol el 21 de diciembre **4** 18

~ aparente del Sol el 21 de marzo, el 21 de septiembre **4** 19

~ aparente del Sol el 21 de junio **4** 20

~ del polo celeste **4** 24

~ del río **216** 9

cursor **349** 23

~ del diafragma de abertura **112** 16

~ de parada de la escala de tiempo **249** 75

curva **346** 21; **347** 13

~ a la derecha **203** 52

~ a la izquierda **203** 51

~ balística **87** 79

~ del anzuelo **89** 81

~ de las temperaturas **7** 37

~ de nivel **15** 62

~ de nivel submarina **15** 11

~ de segundo grado **347** 14

~ de tercer grado **347** 18

curvador **136** 34

curvadora de tubos **126** 82

curva en el sistema de coordenadas **347** 11

~ hipsométrica de la superficie terrestre **11** 6-12

curvatura *Avión* **229** 46-48

~ *Matem.* **346** 22

cúspide del punto de mira **87** 72

custodia **332** 34

~ con el Santísimo **331** 48

cúter **220** 8

Cygnus **3** 23

chabota **139** 40

chacal **367** 11

chacra **62**

chaflán *Construc.* **121** 11, 17

~ *Tornill.* **143** 62

~ del tejado **122** 10

chaina **322** 7

chaira **94** 16

chaitya **337** 28

chal **31** 71

chala **68** 33

chalán **307** 31

chalana **221** 92; **225** 8

~ sin motor **221** 94

chalaza **74** 63

chalé **276** 7

chaleco **33** 4

~ acolchado **30** 16

~ blanco del frac **33** 15

~ de punto **33** 53

~ enguatado **30** 16

~ floreado **355** 75

~ metálico **294** 15

~ salvavidas **286** 20

~ salvavidas de corcho **228** 9

~ salvavidas hinchable **228** 8

chal triangular **31** 71

chamán **353** 24

chamarra **43** 7

chamarro **43** 8

chamba **13** 23

chamico **379** 8

chamorro **16** 53

champán **98** 63

champiñón silvestre **381** 1

champú **105** 32; **106** 20

chancadora **158** 19

chancho *Granja* **62** 10

~ *An. dom.* **73** 9

~ *Juego* **276** 35

chanclo **355** 43

chanchería **96** 1-30

chandal **33** 27

chaneca **34** 30

changador **205** 31

chapa **264** 13

~ base de la corredera **309** 27

~ de hierro **217** 6

~ de la botella **93** 27

~ del alza **87** 67

~ de limitación lateral **200** 34, 44

~ del objetivo **114** 52

~ del tablero **215** 6

~ de madera **133** 2

~ de protección de la correa de transmisión **180** 58

~ de ténder con enganche **210** 2

~ de unión del fuselaje **235** 4

~ lateral **217** 67

chapalolo **50** 55

chapa numerada **267** 10

~ ondulada **122** 98

chaparrón **8** 19

chape **34** 30

chapitel de la torre **331** 6

chapola **365**

chapón de limpieza **164** 22

chapucero **134** 61

chaqueta **29** 3, 51; **33** 2

~ de ante **30** 58

~ de caza roja **289** 42

~ de cuero **33** 43

~ de encerado **228** 6

~ del chandal con cremallera **33** 28

~ del traje **31** 2

~ de mangas cortas **33** 26

~ de montar negra **289** 4

~ de montar roja **289** 13

~ de popelina **31** 37

~ de punto **31** 50; **33** 30

~ de símil piel **29** 44

~ de sport **33** 39

~ de visón **30** 1

~ galoneada **186** 23

~ ligera **33** 54

~ playera **280** 21

~ vaquera **31** 59; **33** 21

chaquete **276** 18

chaquetilla de esgrima **294** 16

chaquetón **28** 25

chàqueton de paño **33** 63

charca del pantano **13** 23

charola **265** 14; **266** 19, 63

charqueza **89** 29

charrancito **359** 11

chasis *Agric.* **64** 51

~ *Autom.* **191** 2

~ *FFCC* **207** 3; **208** 5

~ *FFAA* **255** 30-32

~ *Dep.* **305** 88

chasis **191** 2

chasis de la bomba **67** 14

~ de la grúa **226** 53

~ de pequeño formato **112** 35

~ de remolque en construcción **138** 28

~ de riego **62** 28

~ neumático **182** 2

chasque **268** 18

chata **226** 57

chaucha **57** 8

chaveta **143** 19, 73-74, 78

~ con talón **143** 74

~ de boquilla roscada **126** 63

~ de resorte **143** 73

~ embutida **143** 73

chayo **118** 85

checo **359** 27

Checoslovaquia **252** 27

chelín **252** 13

chianti **98** 61

chibalete **174** 2

chibuquí **107** 32

chicana Allais **301** 72

chica que baila **317** 17, 18

chiclé **192** 12

~ de corrección de aire **192** 3

~ del aire del ralentí **192** 2

~ del ralentí **192** 1

chicote **307** 53

chiche **16** 28-29

chifla **354** 42

chifle mágico para conjurar los espíritus **354** 42

chifonía **322** 25

chigre del ancla **223** 49

chilapeño **35** 35

chile **57** 42

chilicote **81** 7

chilla **315** 16

chimba **34** 30

chimbilá **366** 9

chimenea de ventilación **92** 14

chimenea *Mapa* **15** 38

~ *Casa* **37** 10; **38** 5

~ *Construc.* **118** 21; **120** 47; **122** 13

~ *Central el.* **152** 15

~ *Energ. mod.* **155** 12

~ *FFCC* **210** 22

~ *Barco* **221** 8, 40, 75; **223** 1

~ *Buque guerra* **258** 58; **259** 32

~ *Hotel* **267** 23

~ *Dep. aéreo* **288** 47

~ *Alpin.* **300** 8

~ con revestimiento de rejilla **221** 84

~ de aireación **269** 27

~ de evacuación **154** 37

~ del aire de escape **155** 25

~ del convertidor **147** 67

~ de popa **258** 20

~ de proa **258** 19

~ de un volcán apagado **11** 28

~ falsa **221** 16

~ para los gases quemados de los generadores **146** 2

~ volcánica **11** 17

chimpancé **368** 14

china *Escrit.* **341** 5

~ *Planta* **377** 11

~ *Fruto merid.* **384** 23

chinarrosa **377** 11

chinche **81** 39

~ acuática **358** 4

~ de las camas **81** 39

chingue **32** 20

chip de 1/2 pulgada con función de cierre **243** 5

chiquero **319** 14

chircal **15** 89

chirimía **322** 14; **323** 84

chirrión **307** 53

chistera *Sombr.* **35** 36

~ *Hípica* **289** 6

~ *Dep.* **305** 69

chitarrone **324** 1

chitón **355** 3

Chitonactis **369** 20

chivato **127** 20

~ de carga **191** 78

~ de desempañado de la luneta trasera **191** 80

~ de la presión del aceite **191** 73

~ de las luces intermitentes y del warning **191** 76

~ *Matem.* 345 13, 14
difusor *Papel* 172 11
~ *Autom.* 192 8
~ para el oxígeno gaseoso 234 15
~ para medir la luz incidente 114 60
digestor de celulosa 172 7
digitada 370 39
digital 379 2
digitalizador 244 26
dígito 344 3
dignatario chino 306 29
dije 36 35
~ de piedras finas 36 14
~ de piedras preciosas 36 14
diligencia 186 39
Dinamarca *Dinero* 252 24
~ *Bandera* 253 17
dinamo *Bicicl.* 187 8
~ *Motor* 190 76
~ *FFCC* 211 46
dinamómetro 308 11
dinar 252 28
dinero 252
~ efectivo 246 27
~ en metálico 246 27
dingui Finn 284 51
dintel de cemento armado 118 13
~ de la ventana *Casa* 37 25
~ de la ventana *Construc.* 118 9; 120 57
dioptra *Fotogr.* 117 58
~ *Dep.* 305 41
~ de puntería 305 50, 51
diosa del mar 327 23
dios indio 337 19
diploma de maestría 106 42
~ de maestro peluquero 106 42
díptero 358 16-20
dique *Aerop.* 233 14
~ basculante 217 65-72
~ contra la inundación 216 32
~ de cilindros 217 65-72
~ de contención 155 38
~ de esclusas 15 58
~ de invierno 216 32
~ de reparaciones 222 10
~ de río 216 49
~ de verano 216 48
~ flotante *Cons. naval.* 222 34-43
~ flotante *Puerto* 225 16
~ flotante inundado 222 41
~ seco *Cons. naval.* 222 31-33
~ seco *Puerto* 225 17
~ vaciado 222 43
dirección 236 42
~ de acodamiento 85 31, 37
~ de corte 151 27
~ de la carrera 290 4
~ de la inserción 237 40
~ de la película 243 22
~ del avance de la cinta 243 21
~ del cable en ausencia de retenida 227 15
~ de los rayos del Sol 4 9
~ de luces 224 101-102
~ del viento 9 9-19
~ del viento 285 1-13
~ de tornillo sin fin globoide 192 56-59
~ hidráulica 65 41
~ negativa 347 7

~ pegada 236 4
~ pivotante 85 31, 37
~ positiva 347 6
directo 299 28
director 315 26
~ artístico 316 40
~ cinematográfico 310 40
~ de doblaje 311 38
~ de escena 316 40
~ de fotografía y de sonido 310 44
~ de la emisión 238 22
~ del circo 307 17
~ del hotel 267 19
~ del juego 275 3
~ de orquesta 274 21
~ general 310 44
disámara 371 57
discjockey 317 25
Discman® 242 60
disco *Apart.* 46 15
~ *Discot.* 317 24
~ abrasivo 133 27; 134 23
~ adhesivo 364 26
~ compacto 242 61
~ de cálculo *Fotogr.* 114 57
~ de cálculo *Huecogr.* 182 19
~ de carborundo 24 35
~ de color 316 49
~ de ebonita 302 35
~ de equilibrado 190 56
~ de esmeril 24 36
~ de esmerilar 340 46
~ de freno 143 98
~ de goma 134 22
~ de gramófono 309 32
~ de las notas 309 15
~ del cinturón 328 24
~ de leva para el accionamiento de la bomba de vacío 190 60
~ del freno 166 60
~ del freno *Tejido* 166 60
~ del freno *Autom.* 191 17; 192 48
~ de limitación de velocidad 203 36-38
~ del plegador 165 30; 166 49
~ dentado 65 85
~ de paño 100 10
~ de piel de cordero 134 21
~ de plata 10 24
~ de pulimentar 100 7
~ de pulir 134 22
~ de señalización de la policía 264 14
~ de soporte del cilindro 130 28
~ duro 244 45
~ floppy 244 36-44
~ frotador 165 21
~ giratorio 275 31
~ graduado 151 51
~ labial 354 23
~ láser grande 243 41
~ láser pequeño 243 40
~ láser: 30 cm ∅ 243 41
~ láser: 20 cm ∅ 243 40
~ lateral 229 33
~ lija 134 25
~ metálico perforado 309 15
~ protector de plástico 289 25
~ recubierto de aluminio magnético 244 50
~ redondo 65 84

~ discos de memoria 176 11
disco selector 237 8
~ solar 4 36
~ solar alado 333 12
discoteca 317
diseño de un traje 315 39
disfraz de carácter 306 33
~ de la mascarada 306 6-48
dislocación 11 50
disminuyendo 321 32
disociador de celulosa 172 80
disolución del xantogenato en sosa cáustica 169 10
disolvedor 172 37
disparador *Méd.* 23 9
~ *Coza* 87 12
~ *Matad.* 94 6
~ *Fotogr.* 114 12, 31
~ *FFAA* 255 5
~ *Cine* 313 38
~ automático 309 51
~ con empalme para el disparador de cable 117 6
~ de cable 115 62
dispensador de algodón 22 36
~ de esparadrapo y de elementos pequeños 22 64
Display 242 36, 55; 244 60
disposición de las alas 229 1-14
~ de las velas 285 1-13
~ de las velas en forma de tijeras 285 4
~ del dique 222 36-43
~ de los asientos de 2ª clase 211 58
~ de los bolos 305 1-11, 14
~ de los discos en forma de X 65 83
dispositivo alimentador 164 59
~ anti-skating 241 34
~ basculante 147 44
~ basculante para los cubos de la basura 199 2
~ cortador 169 30
~ cortante de la piedra 172 70
~ de ajuste 148 61-65
~ de ajuste para armar los cristales de los relojes 109 29
~ de alimentación de papel 245 11; 249 45, 49
~ de arranque eléctrico 189 52
~ de arranque y de freno automático 168 20
~ de aspiración de los gérmenes 92 38
~ de aspiración del polvo de esmerilado 133 28
~ de caída 137 39
~ de carga 62 41
~ de cierre 90 27
~ de circulación del gas 83 16
~ de control 311 15
~ de corte *Estudio* 151 15
~ de corte *Vidrio* 162 19
~ de costura 133 5
~ de descarga 62 42
~ de disparo 255 18
~ de distribución 236 49
~ de elevación de la puerta 139 55
~ de eliminación de piedras 64 9

~ de encuadre 312 29
~ de enfoque primario 5 11
~ de enfoque secundario 5 11
~ de enrollamiento 163 15
~ de entrada 244 15-32
~ de entrada de datos 237 46
~ de esparcimiento 62 22
~ de fijación 150 15
~ de fijación de la madera 132 51
~ de fuego 255 75
~ de hacer marcas con la espuma 83 9
~ de hombre muerto 212 13
~ de infusión 25 14
~ de intercalar 181 11
~ de introducción 236 48
~ de limpieza 92 36
~ de macrofotografía 115 81-98
~ de medida 112 51
~ de memoria masiva 244 33-59
~ de memoria para los efectos luminosos 316 2
~ de micrófonos para la grabación estereofónica 310 30
~ de paro de seguridad 168 19
~ de pegar 133 29
~ de plegado de la cinta 163 62
~ de prensado 183 18
~ de protección 290 13
~ de pulverización 83 58
~ de recogida 62 41
~ de refilado 184 3
~ de regulación de la tensión del elevador de remolachas 64 94
~ de remolque 65 50, 61
~ de salida 244 60-65
~ de sacudida de la cinta transportadora de hierbas 64 77
~ de seguridad *Apar. hogar* 50 18
~ de seguridad *Aserr.* 157 59
~ de seguridad *FFCC* 212 13
~ de seguridad *Teatro* 316 25
~ de señales luminosas 268 54
~ de sincronización *Fotogr.* 117 77
~ de sincronización *Central el.* 153 32
~ deslizable de trazado 179 26
~ de sujeción *Átomo* 2 43
~ de sujeción *Bric.* 134 42
~ de sujeción de cadenas 157 41
~ de tensión del cable auxiliar 214 48
~ de vaciado 89 9
~ electroconmutador 168 58
~ fijador de la hoja de la sierra 157 47
~ fijador de la placa 178 27
~ fijador de los tableros 132 70

~ fijador para las muestras pequeñas **117** 56
~ fundidor **174** 25
~ hidromecánico del tren de aterrizaje **257** 41
~ indicador **177** 12
~ móvil de riego **67** 3
~ Norton **149** 8
~ para afinar **326** 30
~ para colocar la bobina de papel no impreso **180** 3
~ para encanillar **104** 16
~ para enmarcar **183** 17
~ para extender la parte trasera **173** 34
~ para la introducción manual **184** 2
~ para la transmisión de datos (DTD) **244** 66-67
~ para regular el largo **100** 20
~ para regular la anchura **100** 19
~ para regular la profundidad de la mesa de apoyo **133** 21
~ para regular la tensión del hilo **100** 22
~ para separar el gas y el petróleo **146** 9
~ pendular **2** 35
~ permanente para evitar la formación de torbellinos en el carburante **234** 11
~ plegador del tejido **168** 35
~ prensor de cadenas **180** 56
~ tensor **167** 32
~ volcador **147** 59
disquete **244** 8; **176** 5
~ con procesadores de texto, diseño y gráfico **176** 23
disquetera **176** 17; **244** 33-44
~ de 5¼ pulgadas **244** 33
~ de disco flexible **244** 33, 35
~ de disco flexible de 5¼ pulgadas **244** 36
~ de disco flexible de 3½ pulgadas **244** 43
~ de 3½ pulgadas **244** 35
~ de los disquetes **244** 36-44, 33
distanciador *Fotogr.* **117** 59
~ *Construc.* **119** 81
distancia entre las líneas rectas **346** 5
~ entre los adversarios en esgrima **294** 10
~ entre los remaches **143** 60
~ focal continuamente variable **313** 23
distintivo del baile de máscaras **306** 34
~ del taxi **268** 65
distribución del oxígeno **235** 56
distribuidor **62** 42
distribuidora de hormigón **201** 5
distribuidor automático de billetes **228** 28
~ de aceite **109** 4
~ de aire **326** 12-14
~ de billetes con cambiador de moneda **197** 33

~ de cajas **74** 53
~ de encendido con avance al encendido por depresión **190** 9
~ de estiércol **63** 39, 21
~ de gasolina sin plomo **196** 1
~ de monedas **236** 28
~ de octavillas de propaganda **263** 9
~ de papel de cocina **40** 1
~ de secuencia de encendido **195** 13
~ de sellos **236** 19
~ de servilletas de papel **196** 10
~ de tres vías **92** 34
disyuntor *Central el.* **152** 34; **153** 51, 62
diversas clases de deporte **305**
dividendo **344** 26
divinidad marina **327** 23
división *Matem.* **344** 26
~ del cielo **3** 1-8
~ en grados **260** 39
divisor **344** 26
doberman **70** 27
doblado de cintas magnéticas perforadas **238** 54-59
~ de las mechas de carda **164** 5
doblaje **311** 37-41
doble **276** 35
~ barra de repetición **321** 26
~ bemol **320** 53
~ bisel de encaje **121** 91
~ casco **284** 65
~ fondo **222** 60
~ listón **122** 43
~ llave de pierna **299** 11
~ platillo agudo **324** 50
~ pletina **242** 21, 43
~ puerta en diagonal **301** 68
~ puerta vertical desplazada **301** 70
dobles **293** 2 hasta 3
doble salto mortal **282** 42
dobles de caballeros **293** 2 hasta 3
~ de damas **293** 2 hasta 3
~ mixtos **293** 2 hasta 3
doble sostenido **320** 51
docena intermedia **275** 26
~ primera **275** 25
~ segunda **275** 26
~ última **275** 27
doctor **233** 44
documento confidencial **246** 25
dodecaedro pentagonal **351** 8
~ romboidal **351** 7
dogcart **186** 18
dogo alemán **70** 14
dogos **70** 1-14
doguillo **70** 9
doguino **70** 9
dólar **252** 33
doliente **331** 38
dolina **13** 71
dolmen **328** 16
doma de caballos **289** 1-7
domador **307** 31, 52
~ de fieras **307** 52
doma libre **307** 30-31
do mayor **320** 55, 62
do menor **320** 65

domiciliación **250** 22
dominguejo **52** 27
dominico **384** 28
dominó *Juego* **276** 33
~ *Carnaval* **306** 15
domo de arena **210** 14
~ de vapor **210** 12
doradillo **360** 9
dorado **129** 40
~ del lomo de un libro **183** 1
dorador **183** 2
dormido **285** 47
dormitorio **43**
dorsal **301** 37
~ ancho **18** 59
dorso de la mano **19** 83
~ del pie **19** 61
dos **283** 15
dosel *Bebé* **28** 32
~ *Hab. niños* **47** 12
~ *J. infancia* **48** 26
dosificador del endurecedor **130** 33
dosillo **321** 23
dosímetro **2** 8-23
~ anular de película **2** 11
~ de película **2** 8
do sostenido menor **320** 59
dos por cuatro **320** 29
~ por dos **320** 30
~ por ocho **320** 28
~ puntos **342** 17
dovela **336** 22
dracma **252** 39
Draco **3** 32
draga *Puerto* **226** 41
~ *Buque guerra* **258** 87
~ con cadena de cangilones **216** 56
~ de cangilones **226** 41
~ de succión **216** 59
~ flotante **216** 56
dragaminas de la clase **341**, **258** 84
Dragón *Astron.* **3** 32
dragón *Ser fabul.* **327** 1
~ *Vela* **284** 57
~ *Feria* **308** 21
~ de las siete cabezas de la revelación **327** 50
~ marino **218** 13-17
~ vikingo **218** 13-17
~ volador **358** 3
drenaje **145** 32
~ de agua **144** 46
~ del subsuelo **200** 61
dríada **51** 7
dribling **291** 52
drive **293** 83
driver **293** 91
driza **253** 2
~ de las banderas de señales **223** 10
dromia velluda **358** 1
drop **98** 76
drósera **377** 14
drupa *Fruta* **59** 1-36
~ *Botán.* **370** 99
~ dehiscente **59** 41, 43
ducha *Salvamento* **228** 30
~ *Aerop.* **233** 46
~ *Natac.* **282** 30
~ de mano *Baño* **49** 41
~ de mano *Peluq.* **105** 30; **106** 13
~ de mano *Offset* **179** 7
~ de tubo flexible **126** 30
~ regulable **49** 41
~ tibia **281** 29

duela **130** 9
dulce *Panad.* **97** 17-47
~ *Comest.* **98** 75-86
~ americano **97** 39
~ cubierto de azúcar **97** 43
~ de ciruelas **97** 43
~ de molde cubierto con una capa de chocolate **97** 34
~ de pisos **97** 46
~ en trozos **97** 43
~ espolvoreado con recortes de pasta **97** 43
dulcemele **322** 32
dulzaina **322** 14
duna **13** 39
~ en forma de media luna **13** 40
~ movediza **13** 39
duodeno **20** 14, 43
duque de alba *Cons. naval* **222** 35
~ de alba *Puerto* **225** 12
duramen *Construc.* **120** 84
~ *Botán.* **370** 13
durmiente *Construc.* **120** 49
~ *Estación* **205** 60
~ de las bancadas **283** 31

E

ébano falso **374** 32
ebonita **300** 45
E. C.
écarté **314** 15
eclipse lunar **4** 29-35
~ solar **4** 29-35
~ total **4** 33
~ total de Sol **4** 39, 41
eclíptica **3** 2
eclisa *Construc.* **122** 48
~ *FFCC* **202** 12
eco **224** 63
ecógrafo **224** 24, 65
ecosonda **224** 61-67
ecuación **345** 9
~ con la incógnita x **345** 8
~ de identidad **345** 5
~ de primer grado **345** 4
~ determinada **345** 9
ecuador **14** 1
~ celeste **3** 3
ecualizador **241** 64; **242** 59
~ de tres bandas **242** 59
echadora de cartas **308** 36
Echiostoma **369** 13
echona **56** 8
Edad de Bronce **328** 21-40
~ de Hierro **328** 21-40
edelweiss **378** 9
edificio anejo **331** 13
~ colateral **62** 14
~ contiguo **154** 36
~ de administración *Cons. hidr.* **217** 24
~ de administración *Aerop.* **233** 16
~ de aduanas del puerto **225** 6
~ de calderas **152** 1-21
~ de la administración *Mina* **144** 18
~ de la administración *Cons. naval* **222** 1
~ de la administración *Cine* **310** 4
~ de la escena **334** 45

~ de la mina **144** 4
~ del club **283** 23
~ de los enseres de bomberos **233** 8
~ del pozo **144** 4
~ del reactor **154** 20
~ de oficinas **225** 53
~ de planta central **334** 55
~ de recepción **205** 13
~ neoclásico **336** 15
~ público **15** 54
~ sagrado budista **337** 21
~ terminal de viajeros **233** 15
editorial **342** 48
edredón **43** 8
educación preescolar **48** 1-20
EEUU **253** 18
efecto **251** 11-19
~ de los terremotos **11** 45-54
~ de una inundación **216** 5
~ sonoro **310** 30, 59
efémera **358** 6
effacé **314** 13
efímera **358** 6
egipcia **342** 8
eje *Peluq.* **106** 36
~ *Construc.* **123** 78
~ *Tornill* **143** 61
~ *Estudio* **151** 30
~ *Bicicl.* **187** 61, 76
~ acoplado **210** 36
~ ajustable **226** 51
~ celeste **4** 10
~ de abscisas **347** 2
~ de avance para la cabeza láser **243** 44
~ de coordenadas **347** 2-3
~ de declinación **113** 5, 17
~ de desbobinado **312** 36
~ de fricción del bobinado **312** 37
~ de giro **91** 5
~ de la eclíptica **4** 22
~ de la hélice *Barro* **223** 65
~ de la hélice *Buque guerra* **259** 59
~ del ánima **87** 38
~ delantero **189** 34
~ del anticlinal **12** 17
~ de la parábola **347** 17
~ de la suspensión **214** 72
~ de las x **347** 2
~ de las y **347** 3
~ de la Tierra **4** 22-28
~ del barco **285** 5
~ del carrete **114** 8
~ del cono **372** 3
~ del disco **243** 43
~ del molino **91** 12
~ de los pedales **187** 42
~ del pedal **187** 81
~ del pistón **192** 75
~ del sinclinal **12** 19
~ de mando de la horquilla **192** 41
~ de ordenadas **347** 3
~ de ruedas provisto de motores de tracción **209** 3
~ de simetría *Matem.* **346** 25
~ de simetría *Cristal.* **351** 4
~ fijo **65** 33
~ horario *Astron.* **5** 8
~ horario *Opt.* **113** 18
~ hueco **312** 49
~ instantáneo de rotación **4** 25

~ longitudinal **230** 72
~ mayor **347** 23
~ medio de rotación **4** 27
~ menor *Matem.* **347** 24
~ motor *FFCC* **210** 37
~, para el movimiento de las alas batidoras **163** 24
~ „pedalier" **187** 42
~ polar **113** 18
~ portante **210** 35
~ principal **166** 50
ejercicio con los aparatos **296** 48-60
~ de extinción, trepa, escalera salvamento **270** 1-46
~ de los bomberos **270** 1-46
~ del servicio de incendios **270** 1-46
~ en los aparatos **297** 15-32
~ gimnástico con aparatos **296, 297**
~ gimnástico sin aparatos **295**
ejército del aire **256, 257**
~ de tierra **255**
eje rígido **192** 65-71
~ transversal **230** 68
~ vertical **230** 70
~ y soporte para impulsar el banco de anillas **164** 42
ejote **57** 8
elástico del calcetín **32** 33
~ de punto **31** 70
elaténido **80** 37, 38
elección **263** 16-29
~ de gafas **111** 5
~ de montura **111** 5
elecciones **263**
elector **263** 22
elector con derecho a voto **263** 24
electricidad **235** 55
electricista **127** 1
~ *Cine* **310** 37
~ *Teatro* **316** 20
electrocardiógrafo *Med.* **23** 28
~ *Hosp.* **25** 27, 41
~ portátil **23** 28
electrocardiograma **25** 28
electroconmutador **168** 58
electrodo *Hosp.* **25** 35
~ *Matad.* **94** 8
~ *Soldadura* **142** 10
~ *Sider.* **147** 52
~ central **2** 3
~ de correa **23** 30
~ del estimulador cardíaco temporal **25** 25
~ de platino iridiado **24** 44
~ de ventosa **23** 29
~ introducido a través de la vena **25** 38
~ para el tratamiento de un shock **25** 26
~, salida del **25** 34
electrofiltro *Coque* **156** 20
~ *Cemen.* **160** 7
~ *Papel* **172** 39
electroimán del vehículo inductivo **212** 38
electrón **1** 3, 17, 32
electrónica **209** 11
~ de entretenimiento I **241**
~ de entretenimiento II **242**
~ recreativa I **241**
~ recreativa II **242**
electrón libre **1** 25
electrotomo **22** 38
electroválvula **139** 23

elefante *Zoo* **356** 9
~ africano **366** 20
~ de tela **47** 6
elemento *Estar* **42** 1
~ *Oficina* **248** 39
~ de central solar **155** 28
~ de construcción intercambiable **273** 56
~ de control **259** 69
~ de decoración **316** 35
~ de ensamblaje **248** 48
~ de entramado **215** 24
~ de fijación **301** 54-56
~ del conjunto A **348** 2
~ del plinton **296** 16; **279** 9
~ del radiador **38** 77
~ de percepción **10** 22
~ estructural del buque **222** 44-61
~ impreso **178** 39
~ prefabricado **215** 58
elementos dispuestos en forma de ángulo **248** 39
elemento sensitivo **10** 22
elevación a una potencia **345** 1
~ con las piernas abiertas en las paralelas **296** 49
~ de caderas y extensión de piernas **295** 24
~ de dos semitonos **320** 51
~ de las piernas en el pino sobre el suelo **296** 52
~ del cuerpo **295** 16, 17
~ del cuerpo con apoyo sobre las manos **295** 18
~ de puntillas **295** 5
~ de talones **295** 5
~ de un semitono **320** 50
elevador *Deut.* **24** 48
~ *Caza* **87** 18
~ de barcos **217** 29-38
~ de cala **226** 23
~ de cangilones **200** 49; **201** 21
~ de cebada **92** 33
~ de espigas **64** 2
~ de las hojas **64** 90
~ de malta **92** 35
~ de rosario **170** 36
~, para transportar las matrices al distribuidor **174** 22
elevón **235** 33
el gorgojo **80** 49
elimo arenario **15** 7
elipse **347** 22
elipsoide de revolución **347** 42
élitro *Ins.* **81** 8
~ *Plaga* **82** 10
~ *Articul.* **358** 36
elixir dentífrico **49** 36
elodea **378** 56
embalaje de yute **163** 4
embaldosado del zócalo **123** 21
embalse artificial **217** 39
embarcación hecha vaciando un tronco de árbol **354** 20
embarcadero *Mapa* **15** 59
~ *Puerto* **225** 30, 66
~ *Parque* **272** 46
~ *Camping* **278** 13
~ *Playa* **280** 9
~ *Remo* **283** 19
~ de los barcos de motor **216** 7
embarque **233** 12
emberiza **361** 6-7

emblema **191** 12
embocadura *Construc.* **122** 30
~ *Mús.* **324** 33
émbolo *Carp.* **133** 47
~ *Teatro* **316** 60
~ buzo **145** 23
~ del motor Wankel **190** 68
embotellado **93** 22
embotellador circular semiautomático **79** 9
embrague *Agric.* **65** 39
~ *Autom.* **191** 44, 96
~ *FFCC* **212** 82
~ *Salvamento* **227** 23
~ de disco en seco **190** 78
~ de fricción de láminas **139** 21
~ de impulsión **177** 54
~ del ventilador **190** 8
~ de toma de fuerza **65** 40
~ hidráulico **65** 37
~ monodisco **190** 71
~ principal **65** 39
embrión *Planta estim., trop.* **382** 21
~ *Fruto merid.* **384** 22
embudo *Fotogr.* **116** 12
~ *Quím.* **350** 16
~ de aspiración **217** 51
~ de entrada de las mechas **164** 15
~ de separación **349** 3
~ guía de las mechas **164** 15
embutidera **340** 14
embutido *Carnic.* **96** 6-11
~ *Comest.* **98** 4
~ *Superm.* **99** 54
embutidor de mano **96** 49
~ de mesa **96** 49
eminencia frontal **16** 4
emisión radiofónica **238** 16-26
emisor de sonido **224** 61
empacadora de alta presión **63** 35
~ de paja **63** 35
empalizada *Huerto* **52** 10
~ *Hípica* **289** 8
~ *Caball.* **329** 36
~ contra la nieve **304** 6
empalme a presión **67** 9
~ de aire comprimido **213** 20
~ de descarga **213** 21
~ de la toma de fuerza **64** 63
~ de tubo **67** 5
empapelado **128** 18-53
empapelador **128**
empaquetadora automática de huevos **74** 48
emparedado *Mesa* **45** 39
~ *Restaur.* **266** 54
emparrillado basculante **210** 5
empaste **24** 30
empavesado **221** 85
empedrado de la acera **198** 8
empeine **19** 61
empella *Zapat.* **100** 60
~ *Jue. pelota* **291** 26
emperatriz bizantina **355** 15
emplazamiento del almacén de material **144** 17
~ de la madera cortada **157** 32
~ de la tienda **278** 42
~ del camping **278** 1-59

galocha **355** 43
galope a la izquierda **72** 42
~ de carrera **72** 43-44
~ en el momento de la
caída sobre los remos
anteriores **72** 43
~ en el momento en que los
cuatro pies están en el
aire **72** 44
~ tendido **72** 43-44
galpón **62** 15
galvanómetro registrador **11**
44
galvanoplastia **178**
gallarda **175** 25
gallardete *Camping* **278** 9
~ *Playa* **280** 10, 11
~ auxiliar **253** 30-32
~ del código de señales **253**
29
~ de número **253** 33-34
gallardía **60** 19
gallareta **359** 20
gallina *Granja* **62** 36
~ *An. dom.* **73** 19-26
~ americana **74** 56
~ bantam **74** 56
~ cebada *Comest.* **98** 7
~ cebada *Superm.* **99** 58
~ de Guinea **73** 27
~ enana **74** 56
~ para caldo **99** 60
~ ponedora **74** 57
gallinero *Avic.* **74** 11
~ *Teatro* **315** 16
~ de los pollos **74** 5
gallo *Hierba* **62** 37
~ *An. dom.* **73** 19-26
gallocresta **69** 10
gallo de bosque **88** 72
~ de la veleta **331** 3
~ silvestre **86** 11; **88** 66
gama *Caza* **88** 40
~ *Mús.* **320** 45-49
gamarrón **71** 7-11
gamo **88** 40-41
gamuza *Mamif.* **367** 3
~ *Hongo* **381** 31
ganado de pasto **62** 45
~ mayor **73** 1-2
ganador **289** 38
ganado vacuno **73** 1
ganancia **345** 7
gancho *Vestib.* **41** 2
~ *Caballo* **71** 37-49
~ *Apic.* **77** 10
~ *Ins.* **81** 38
~ *Pesca* **89** 77
~ *Matad.* **94** 21
~ *Bomberos* **270** 44
~ *Dep.* **305** 46
~ *Arte* **335** 38
~ a la cabeza **299** 33
~ bífido **77** 8
~ candente **77** 55
~ circular **135** 17
~ de apoyo del dedo **324** 67
~ de conexión **122** 64
~ de cumbrera **122** 65
~ de derribo **270** 15
~ de la cuerda para tender
la ropa **38** 22
~ de la escalera **122** 69
~ de la grúa **139** 45
~ del banco **132** 36
~ del cordón **50** 65
~ del cubo **122** 23
~ del huso **164** 49
~ del tejado **38** 6
~ del tirante **71** 14

~ de palanca **85** 6
~ de remolque **227** 27
~ de suspensión **301** 61
~ de tiro **65** 19
~ de tiro para regular la
altura **64** 60
~ de tracción *Pétrol.* **145** 9
~ de tracción *Bomberos*
270 49
~ hacia arriba **299** 32
~ hacia un lado **299** 33
~ para colgar abrigos **266**
14
~ para colgar sombreros
266 13
~ para dar la vuelta a los
troncos **85** 7
~ para el maletín o la cartera **188** 54
~ para la madera **85** 29
~ para las escalas **122** 15
~ para sujetar el barco enemigo **218** 11
gandola **194** 28
ganglio linfático **19** 10
gansa **73** 34
ganso *An. dom.* **73** 34
~ *Escrit.* **341** 26
garabato *Carnic.* **96** 55
~ *Barco* **218** 11
garaje *Casa* **37** 32, 79
~ *Granja* **62** 15
~ *Bomberos* **270** 1
garamón **175** 27
garañón **72** 2, 3
garapito **358** 4
garbanzo forrajero **69** 19
garceta **88** 6
gardenia **332** 21
garduña **367** 14
garfio **143** 44
garganta *Geogr.* **13** 52
~ *Anat.* **16** 19
~ *Caballo* **72** 16
~ *Mús.* **326** 18
~ de la culata **87** 7
gargantilla **328** 25
gargantón **71** 15
gárgola **335** 30
garita de vigía **329** 28
~ meteorológica **10** 49
garlancha **66** 5
garlopa *Construc.* **120** 64
~ *Carp.* **132** 39
garra *Caza* **88** 50
~ *Máq. herr.* **149** 35, 37
~ *Ser. fabul.* **327** 3
~ *Ave* **362** 7
~ *Mamif.* **368** 4
~ de ave **327** 61
~ de grifo **327** 13
garrafa forrada de paja **206**
13
garrafita para el licor **45** 48
garra orientable **157** 29
garrapata común **358** 44
~ de los perros **358** 44
garras de hierro **303** 24
garrete **16** 51
garrocha **319** 17
garrón **95** 5, 10
garrote de torneo **254** 31
garrotín **35** 15
garrucha automática para el
cable **301** 62
~ con perno de arrastre
135 9
gárrulo **361** 1
garúa **9** 33
garza cenicienta **359** 18

~ real *Caza* **86** 46
~ real *Ave* **359** 18
gas *Avión* **230** 30
~ *Dep. aéreo* **288** 15
~ *Quím.* **350** 2, 6, 58, 59, 63
gasa **183** 33; **185** 20
~ esterilizada *Auxilio* **21** 6
~ esterilizada *Med.* **22** 58
gas butano **278** 33
~ comprimido **234** 32, 43,
50, 60
~ de combustión **145** 52
~ de coquería **156** 16-45
~ inerte **138** 29
~ ligero **145** 38
~ líquido **145** 53
~ natural **12** 30
gasoil **145** 42
gasóleo **38** 50
gasolina **286** 25
~ de aviación **145** 57
~ normal **145** 54
~ para automóvil **145** 54
~ súper **145** 55
gasolinera **196** 1-29
gasómetro **144** 12
gas propano **278** 33
gasterópodo **357** 27
gata **73** 17
gatillo *Parás.* **83** 26
~ *Caza* **87** 12
~ *Matad.* **94** 6
~ *FFAA* **255** 5, 18
~ de mano **203** 57
~ y el guardamonte **255** 18
gato *Granja* **62** 3
~ *An. dom.* **73** 17
~ *Construc.* **120** 66
~ *Tipogr.* **181** 29
~ de angora **73** 17
~ de armar **130** 12
~ de la cúpula **257** 5
~ hidráulico *Silvic.* **84** 25;
85 21
~ hidráulico *Autom.* **194** 26
~ hidráulico de levanta-
miento del tren de aterrizaje **257** 41
gaveta de almacanaje de
estarcidos **245** 10
~ de fichas **262** 23
gavia alta **219** 63
~ baja **219** 62
~ mayor **218** 38
gavilán *Esgr.* **294** 42
~ *Ave* **362** 12
gavilladora de torbellino **64**
40-45
gaviota **359** 14
~ común **359** 14
~ de cabeza negra **359** 14
~ reidora **359** 14
gaya **361** 3
gayuba **377** 15
gazapo *An. dom.* **73** 18
~ *Caza* **88** 65
géiser **11** 21
geiserita **11** 23
geisha **353** 39
geisino **334** 12
gemelo *Anat.* **18** 62
~ *Joya* **36** 17
Gemelos *Astron.* **3** 28; **4** 55
gemelos *Ropa* **32** 46
~ *Opt.* **111** 17
~ *Barco* **221** 128
~ de campo **86** 6
~ de teatro **315** 9
Gemini **3** 28; **4** 55

genciana de primavera **378**
13
generador *Energ. nucl.* **154**
15, 47, 53
~ *Barco* **223** 74
~ de calefacción **212** 39
~ de corriente **190** 76
~ de energía de tierra **233**
22
~ de impulsos programable
25 33
~ de la turbina a vapor **259**
58
~ del sonido de referencia
238 51
~ del sonido piloto **313** 30
~ de orientación **155** 46
~ de rayos X **24** 22
~ de vapor **154** 9, 26, 44
~ eólico **55** 34
~ solar **237** 64
~ trifásico *Central el.* **153**
26
~ trifásico *Energ. nucl.* **154**
34
género de punto **271** 56
~ estampado **168** 57
Génova **284** 16
geodesia **14** 46-62
geografía general **11; 12; 13**
geología **12** 1-33
geómetra **82** 28
geometría **346; 347**
~ elemental **346** 1-58
~ euclidiana **346** 1-58
~ plana **346** 1-58
georgiana **341** 4
geraniácea **53** 1
geranio *Planta* **53** 1
~ *Flor* **376** 24
gerbera **51** 26
gerente del hotel **267** 19
germen de la planta **68** 14
gesneriácea **53** 7
giba **366** 29
gigantín **379** 8
Gigantocypris agassizi **369** 1
gigantón **306** 63
giloria **379** 2
gimnasia con aparatos de
mano **297** 33-50
~ de aparatos **296**
~ de manos libres **296** 11
~ femenina **297**
~ olímpica femenina **297**
1-6
~ olímpica masculina **296**
1-11
~ rítmica **297** 33-50
~ sin aparatos **295**
gimnorrino **366** 9
giradiscos **241** 4
girado **20** 20
girador *Cerv.* **92** 46
~ *Banco* **250** 21
giralda **331** 4
giraldilla **331** 4
giramachos **140** 30
girasol *Jardín* **51** 35
~ *Huerto* **52** 7
~ *Planta* **68** 24
giro *Correo* **236** 25
~ *Dep. aéreo* **288** 51
girocompás **224** 31
giro del electrón **1** 4
girodino **232** 29
giro hacia atrás en las paralelas **296** 57
~ por debajo de la barra
fija **296** 59

~ indicadora de tocado **294** 30
~ maravillosa **369** 4
~ morse **223** 7
~ para copiar con luz de punto **179** 21
~ para iluminar la carta **230** 23
~ para la luz reflejada **112** 59
~ reflectora de arco **312** 39
~ sin sombras **27** 25
lamparilla de alcohol **24** 57
lampión **353** 36
lampista **125** 17
lana **355** 6
lancéola **380** 11
lanceolada **370** 32
lanceta **77** 11
lancha **9** 31
~ aduanera **221** 100
~ carbonera **225** 13
~ de a bordo **258** 12, 45, 61; **259** 35
~ de carga **216** 25
~ de desembarco **259** 46
~ de goma **228** 18
~ de motor **283** 2
~ de remolque **216** 25
~ de salvamento **228** 14
~ motora con camarotes **286** 3
~ rápida lanzamisiles **258** 69, 75
lanchón de la draga **226** 46
landó **186** 36
~ con visión panorámica **28** 34
~ pequeño **186** 36
langosta migratoria **358** 8
lanilla **253** 3, 11
lansquenete Carnaval **306** 70
~ Moda **355** 32
lanza Granja **62** 20
~ Caballo **71** 21
~ Coche **186** 19
lanzacabos **228** 1
lanzacohetes **110** SF 2 **255** 55
lanza de aspersión **83** 29
~ de hoja larga **354** 12
~ del chorro **83** 22
~ de pulverización con boquilla **83** 46
lanzadera Labores **102** 20
~ Tejido **166** 9, 26
~ para malla **102** 26
lanza de remolque **64** 47
~ de tiro **64** 61; **65** 18
~ de torneo **329** 81
lanzador Jue. pelota **292** 50, 68, 76
~ de cuchillos **307** 37
~ ligero 44 2A1 **255** 22
lanzajabalinas **352** 40
lanzamiento **296** 55
~, clases **305** 17-20
~ con salto **292** 3
~ de dos manos con carrete **89** 32
~ de jabalina **298** 51-53
~ de judo **299** 17
~ de martillo **298** 42-47
~ de peso **298** 48
~ en arco Gimn. **297** 33
~ en arco Dep. **305** 19, 20
~ en gancho **305** 18
~ en línea recta **305** 17
~ hacia arriba **297** 35

lanzamisiles contra objetivos aéreos **259** 50
~ cuádruple **258** 30
~ de defensa antiaérea MM 38 **258** 32
~ de defensa antisubmarina **258** 30, 50
~ de doce tubos de defensa antisubmarina **259** 24
~ doble de defensa antiaérea **259** 25, 33
~ óctuplo de defensa antiaérea **259** 5, 20
~ séxtuplo de defensa antisubmarina **259** 37
lanza para oxígeno **147** 49
lanzatorpedos de defensa antisubmarina **259** 51
~ SF Lance **255** 49
lapicera Colegio **260** 12
~ Rastro **309** 73
lapicero **260** 5
~ de presión **151** 45
lápida **331** 61
~ conmemorativa **331** 14
~ sepulcral **331** 26
lápiz Hab. niños **47** 26
~ Colegio **260** 5
~ de albañil **118** 51
~ de borrar **151** 41
~ de carpintero **120** 77
~ de cera **48** 11
~ de color Hab. niños **47** 26
~ de color J. infancia **48** 11
~ de lectura óptica **271** 4
~ de maquillaje **315** 46
~ de tiza **338** 5
~ graso **340** 26
~ litográfico **340** 26
~ pastel **338** 19
larguero Casa **38** 16
~ Avión **230** 45
~ FFAA **257** 28
~ Jue. pelota **291** 36
~ Dep. inv. **303** 5
~ cajón **287** 30
~ central del fuselaje **235** 9
~ de la cama **43** 5
~ inferior **215** 10
~ lateral **235** 3
~ oblicuo **287** 33
~ principal **287** 30
~ superior **215** 9
lárice **372** 32
laringe **20** 2-3
larva Fruta **58** 64
~ Apic. **77** 27
~ Paras. **80** 6, 19, 36, 41, 46
~ Jus. **81** 20
~ Plaga **82** 12, 25
~ Articul. **358** 9
~ adulta **80** 53
~ de agrótido **80** 44
~ de elaténido **80** 38
~ del abejorro sanjuanero **82** 12
~ en la cámara larval **82** 36
~ joven **80** 54
láser printer **176** 12
laserprinter **244** 61
lasioderma serricorne **81** 25
lastra de ajuste **108** 26
~ de medidas **108** 25
lastre Vela **285** 33
~ Dep. aéreo **288** 65
lata con asa **129** 8
~ con mango **129** 7
~ de betún **50** 39
~ de cerveza Cerv. **93** 25
~ de cerveza Superm. **99** 73

~ de conserva **99** 91
~ del cebo **89** 24
~ de los gusanos **89** 24
~ de pintura **129** 7-8
~ de zumo de frutas **99** 75
lateral de descarga **213** 25
~ derecho **291** 13
~ izquierdo **291** 13
látigo **307** 53
latina **342** 12
latitud **14** 6
~ geográfica **14** 6
latón **294** 20
laúd **324** 1
laulao **364** 12
laurel rosa **373** 13
laurente **173** 46
lauréola **377** 10
lavabo Baño **49** 24
~ Peluq. **106** 11
~ Petról. **146** 29
~ FFCC **207** 15, 40
~ Camping **278** 6
~ del personal **207** 26, 82
~ doble **267** 32
~ para los cabellos **105** 29
~ para los esputos **23** 25
lavabos **207** 72
lavadero **278** 5
lavado **170** 56
~ de las bobinas **170** 48
~ de las botellas **93** 18
~ por circulación **179** 6
lavador Baño **49** 24
~ Caza **87** 61
~ Papel **173** 49
lavadora **50** 23
~ automática **50** 23
lavador de ácido sulfhídrico **156** 22
~ de amoníaco **156** 23
~ de benceno **156** 24
~ de gases **261** 32
lavamanos Deut. **24** 15
~ Peluq. **106** 12
lava, meseta de **11** 14
lavanda **380** 7
lavandera **360** 9
~ blanca **360** 9
lavaplatos **39** 33-36
lava, río de **11** 18
lavatorio Baño **49** 24
~ FFCC **207** 15, 40
lavavajillas **39** 40
laya Jardín **56** 2
~ Agric. **66** 22
~ semiautomática **56** 12
lazareto **225** 27
lazo Ropa **30** 46
~ Dep. inv. **302** 15
~ Toros, rodeo **319** 40
~ Etnogr. **352** 5
~ de la coleta Pein. **34** 7
~ de la coleta Moda **355** 78
~ de serpiente **302** 16
~ de smoking **32** 47; **33** 11
lebrato **88** 59
lebreles **70** 23, 24
lebrón **88** 59
lección **262** 1
lector **262** 3, 24
lector del sonido magnético **312** 28
~ de microfichas **262** 28
~ de periódicos **265** 24
lectura **175** 28
~ de los segundos **110** 21
~ del sonido **312** 46
~ digital con cifras giratorias **110** 20

~ para el viaje **205** 18
leche **99** 44
~ condensada **98** 15
~ de larga duración **99** 44
~ descremada **76** 17
~ en lata **98** 15
~ esterilizada **76** 16
~ fresca **76** 15
~ pasteurizada y homogeneizada **99** 44
lechera **309** 89
lechocino **61** 12
lecho de agujas **167** 55
~ de arena **123** 8
~ de cascajos **205** 61
~ de hormigón **123** 13
~ de impresión **180** 78
~ de inundación **216** 41
~ de la prensa **133** 50
~ del río **13** 68
~ de roca **13** 70
lechón An. dom. **73** 9
~ Ganado **75** 42
lechoncillo **75** 42
lechuga **57** 36
~ silvestre **57** 38
lechuguino **306** 33
lechuza **362** 17
ledo de los pantanos **377** 21
legato **321** 33
legumbre Hortal. **57** 1-11
~ Botán. **370** 92
~ en conserva **96** 27
lencería **32** 1-15
lengua Anat. **17** 52; **19** 25
~ Caza **88** 2
~ bífida **327** 6
~ de gato Comest. **98** 84
~ de gato Hongo **381** 31
lenguaje de los esquiadores **286** 49-55
lengüeta Zapat. **100** 65
~ Calz. **101** 32
~ Mús. **322** 52; **326** 19
~ de la aguja **202** 21
~ de la película **114** 9
~ doble **323** 29
~ enguatada **291** 24
~ guía **248** 4
lente **176** 37
~ de aumento **113** 38
~ del condensador **113** 32; **176** 39
~ del objetivo **113** 36
~ de proyección con el espejo inclinado **261** 10
lenteja de agua **378** 35
lente para imágenes lejanas **115** 49
~ suplementaria **117** 55
leñamen **120** 85
Leo **3** 17; **4** 57
león **3** 17; **4** 57
~ Circo **307** 56
~ Zoo **356** 5
~ Mamíf. **368** 2
leontopodio **378** 9
leopardo **368** 6
leotardo **29** 42; **32** 12
~ sin pie **32** 11
lepidóptero Fruta **58** 62
~ Parás. **80** 1
~ Articul. **358** 48-56
~ Lepidóp. **365**
~ diurno **365** 1-6
~ nocturno **365** 7-11
lepisma saccharina **81** 14
lepta **252** 39
lesena **335** 11
letra **175** 32-37, 38

~ sonora *Atmósf.* **7** 14
~ sonora *Naveg.* **224** 62
~ superficial **11** 36
ondina **327** 23
ondulado del hilo **170** 59
Oneirophanta **369** 18
onocrótalo **359** 9
onza **368** 7
operación de aritmética superior **345** 1-10
~ fundamental de aritmética **344** 23-26
operador *Fotogr.* **117** 67
~ *Cine* **310** 20, 42
~ de máquinas **118** 32
~ de proyección **312** 20
~ de sonido **310** 23
operaria mechera **164** 24
operario estampador **168** 65
opérculo *Apic.* **77** 39
~ *Pez., anfib., rept.* **364** 5
óptica de iluminación **112** 7
~ de lectura del sonido **312** 46
~ de toma de vistas **313** 2
óptico **111** 1
oquedal **84** 4
orador **263** 5
~ proponiendo un brindis **267** 40
orangután **368** 15
orbicular **370** 33
~ de los labios, músculo **19** 8
~ de los párpados, músculo **19** 5
órbita aparente anual del sol **3** 2
~ de la Luna **4** 1
~ del electrón **1** 6
~ estacionaria **1** 8
Orbiter **235** 1-45
orden **250** 19
ordenación de los cuarteles del escudo **254** 17-23
ordenada **347** 3, 10
~ ordenador personal **176** 25; **244** 1
orden de bufón **306** 60
~ de carnaval **306** 60
ordeñador **75** 25
ordinal **344** 6
ore **252** 24, 25, 26
oreja *Anat.* **16** 18; **17** 56
~ *Caballo* **72** 1
~ *An. dom.* **73** 11
~ *Caza* **88** 16, 32, 44, 61
~ colgante **70** 2
~ del zapato **100** 65
~ de oso **378** 8
orejera **304** 28
orejona **71** 50-51
orejudo **366** 9
orfebre **108** 17
organillo **309** 13
~ de efectos sonoros **238** 35
organistrum **322** 25
organizador **299** 45
órgano **325** 43; **326** 1-52
~ automático **308** 38
~ de adherencia **81** 36
~ de coro **326** 42
~ de defensa **77** 10-14
~ de fijación **378** 50
~ de iglesia **326** 1-52
~ del equilibrio y del oído **17** 56-65
~ de transmisión eléctrica **326** 36-52

~ hilador **164** 51
~ interno **20** 1-57
~ portátil **322** 56
~ positivo **322** 56
~ real **322** 56
~ sexual femenino **20** 79-88
~ sexual masculino **20** 66-77
orgánulo **357** 5
orientación **12** 2
orificio de acceso **234** 30; **235** 52
~ de acceso al depósito de almacenamiento **93** 13
~ de desagüe **284** 36
~ de engrase **187** 65
~ de introducción del objeto **113** 33
~ de limpieza **269** 51
~ del resonador **241** 16
~ de relleno **50** 12
~ de ventilación **258** 43
~ germinativo **383** 57
~ para conectar el arranque **244** 39
~ para echar el aceite **190** 28
~ para el pulgar **305** 47
~ para la chaveta **143** 25
~ para la manipulación **247** 39
~ respiratorio **358** 32
~ uterino externo **20** 85
origen de coordenadas **347** 4
original **174** 6; **177** 18
orilla **13** 4
~ del río **216** 5
orillo del tejido **166** 11
~ en ligamento de tela **171** 24
orinal **28** 47
oriol **360** 7
Orión **3** 13
orla del área crepuscular **4** 21
~ de púrpura **355** 14
~ recamada **355** 67
ornamento del rococó **336** 13
~ griego **334** 38-43
~ románico **335** 14-16
ornitorrinco **366** 1
oro *Heráld.* **254** 24
~ *Cristal.* **351** 6
~ de aplique **129** 45
~ en hojas **129** 45
orogénesis **12** 4-20
oronja verde **379** 11
oropéndola **360** 7
oros **276** 45
orquesta **315** 25
~ cinematográfica **310** 17
~ de baile *Carnaval* **306** 2
~ de baile *Cabar.* **318** 3
~ del balneario **274** 20
~ de música pop **306** 2
orquesta **334** 47
orquestrión *Feria* **308** 38
~ *Rastro* **309** 14
orquídea **376** 28
ortega **88** 69
ortiga **61** 33
ortopinacoide **351** 25
ortóptero **358** 8
oruga *Parás.* **80** 3, 14, 17, 29, 44
~ *Plaga* **82** 16, 20, 31, 44, 47
~ *Carret.* **200** 3
~ *Articul.* **358** 50
~ *Lepidóp.* **365** 10

~ aplanadora **200** 28
~ comiendo **80** 8
~ de la 1ª generación **80** 24
~ de la 2ª generación **80** 23
~ de la grosella espinosa **58** 5
~ de la mariposa **58** 64
~ de la pequeña mariposa blanca de la col **80** 48
~ de la polilla de los cereales **81** 30
~ excavadora con cubeta de arrastre **200** 16
orugas marchando en procesión **82** 16
orza *Surf, Buceo* **279** 3
~ *Vela* **285** 9
~ auxiliar **284** 9
orzada **285** 9
orza de deriva *Barco* **220** 7
~ de deriva *Remo* **283** 63
~ de quilla **284** 8, 26
~ de quilla desmontable **285** 41
Osa Mayor **3** 29, 34
osamenta **17** 1-29
oscilación **297** 39
oscuridad parcial **4** 34
~ total **4** 35
osito de peluche **28** 46
oso blanco **368** 11
~ común **368** 10
~ de peluche **309** 12
~ de peluche **273** 26
~ de peluche con balancín **48** 30
~ lavador **368** 9
~ marino **367** 18
~ pardo **368** 10
~ polar **368** 11
osta de la cangreja **219** 70
ostensorio **332** 34
ostiaco **353** 17
ostra **357** 32
ostrácodo gigante **369** 1
otate **383** 60
otoscopio **22** 74
outrigger **283** 9-16
outsider **289** 53
ova **334** 42
oval **370** 36
ovario *Anat.* **20** 83
~ *Fruta* **58** 40
~ *Botán.* **370** 54, 60
~ *Arb. ornam.* **373** 2, 5
~ con aristas **375** 34
~ inferior **58** 7
oveja *An. dom.* **73** 13
~ *Ganado* **75** 10
~ *Mamíf.* **366** 28
over **282** 36
ovillo de hilo **183** 11
ovo **334** 42
óvulo *Anat.* **20** 84
~ *Fruta* **58** 39
~ *Botán.* **370** 63
~ en el ovario central **59** 14
oxer **289** 8
oxígeno *Átomo* **1** 13
~ *Soldadura* **141** 3, 21
~ *Astron.* **234** 61; **235** 51, 56
~ *Quím.* **350** 11, 13
~ a alta presión **235** 42
~ gaseoso **234** 15
~ líquido **234** 10, 12, 24, 39, 52
oxímetro **27** 13
ozono **7** 13, 19

P

P **253** 26
pabellón *Bandera* **253** 15-21
~ *Mús.* **323** 37, 42, 48; **324** 70; **326** 22
~ auditivo **17** 56
~ de cuarentena **225** 27
~ de hidroterapia **274** 8
~ de la fuente **274** 15
~ heráldico **254** 14
pabete **28** 42
paca de paja **63** 34
~ de turba **55** 31
paciente *Méd.* **22** 2
~ *Dent.* **24** 2
~ citado **22** 3
~ del balneario **274** 18
paco **366** 28
pacobá **384** 28
pacora **89** 39
pacuna **352** 26
padrino **332** 13
pagaya *Barco* **218** 8
~ *Remo* **283** 34
página **185** 53
~ del periódico **342** 37
~ interior **342** 52
pagoda **337** 1
~ de varios pisos **337** 1
~ india **337** 21
pailón **40** 16
pailu **337** 3
paisaje de invierno **304**
paisano **62** 6
paja *Cocina* **39** 36
~ *Baño* **49** 2
~ *Cestero* **136** 30
~ *Parque* **273** 42
pajarera **356** 8
pajarilla **60** 10
pajarita **32** 47; **33** 11
~ blanca **33** 16
~ de las nieves **360** 9
pájaro *Zoo* **356** 8
~ *Ave* **360; 361**
~ bitango *Colegio* **260** 71
~ bitango *Parque* **273** 42
~ bobo **359** 4
~ carpintero **359** 27
~ mosca **363** 4
~ niño **359** 4
~ polilla **360** 8
~ reclamo **86** 48
pajaza *Avic.* **74** 8
~ *Ganado* **75** 6
pajita para beber **265** 31; **266** 46
pajuela **107** 22
pala *Zapat.* **100** 60
~ *Herr.* **137** 27
~ *Remo* **283** 38, 53
~ *Jue. pelota* **291** 26
~ *Alpin.* **300** 34
~ *Igl.* **331** 37
palabra espaciada **175** 13
palacio barroco **272** 7
~ de estilo Luis XIV **272** 7
~ de Sargón **333** 29
~ renacentista **335** 47
paladar blando **19** 21
~ duro **19** 20
pala de carbón **38** 43
~ de cuero flexible **101** 46
~ de la cuchara **45** 63
~ de la excavadora **200** 5
~ de las patatas **66** 5
~ del remo **283** 38

~ del stick **302** 32
~ del tenis de mesa **293** 45
~ del timón *Barco* **221** 43
~ del timón *Cons. naval* **222** 69
~ del timón *Barco* **223** 63
~ del timón *Remo* **283** 53
~ del timón *Vela* **284** 34
~ de madera **91** 24
~ de pana de canutillo **101** 26
~ de pescado **45** 65
~ de tejido de rizo **101** 23
Palaeopneustes niasicus **369** 19
pala excavadora **118** 81
palafito *Prehist.* **328** 15
~ *Etnogr.* **352** 33
pala matamoscas **83** 32
palanca *Cerraj.* **140** 5
~ *Cantera* **158** 32
~ conmutadora **167** 44
~ cruciforme **149** 43
~ de abrir o cerrar **247** 42
~ de accionamiento **83** 21
~ de accionamiento de la excéntrica **166** 58
~ de agujas y de señales **203** 62
~ de ajuste **188** 2
~ de arranque y parada **181** 32
~ de arranque y parada de los mecanismos de impresión **180** 80
~ de balanza **322** 39
~ de cambio *Carp.* **132** 56
~ del cambio *Autom.* **192** 46
~ del cambio *FFCC* **203** 55
~ de cambio del par motor **65** 34
~ de cambio de velocidad de rotación de la broca de fresado **150** 28
~ de cambio de velocidades **191** 91
~ de cerrojo **203** 55
~ de cierre **87** 25
~ de cinco metros **282** 8
~ de control **316** 58
~ de desbloqueo de la varilla registradora **10** 15
~ de diez metros **282** 7
~ de elevación y descenso del cilindro **181** 3
~ de embrague **188** 32
~ de embrague de dos velocidades **188** 12
~ de embrague y desembrague **166** 8
~ de impresión **340** 61
~ de introducción del papel **249** 20
~ de la bomba **83** 45
~ de la cisterna **49** 17
~ del arenero **210** 55
~ del embrague **189** 28
~ del freno **187** 66
~ del freno **166** 62
~ del freno **56** 38
~ del freno de mano **191** 93
~ del gas **230** 30
~ del mecanismo de avance **149** 10
~ del pie **100** 27
~ del silbato de vapor **210** 51
~ del zoom Fotogr. **117** 54
~ *Cine* **313** 36

~ de mando *Agric.* **64** 59
~ de mando *Fotogr.* **117** 63
~ de mando *Carret.* **201** 8
~ de mando *FFAA* **257** 8
~ de mando *Dep. aéreo* **288** 14
~ de mando de dirección **192** 58
~ de mando del reductor **149** 3
~ de mando para el accionamiento del alerón y del timón de profundidad **230** 24
~ de maniobra **201** 12
~ de maniobra para la marcha a la derecha o a la izquierda del husillo principal **149** 11
~ de mano *Carp.* **132** 55
~ *Cine* **313** 11
~ de mezcla **230** 31
~ de paro de la máquina **164** 6, 32
~ de pedal **163** 28
~ de potencia **257** 9
~ de puesta en marcha **163** 17
~ de rebobinado **114** 6
~ de retorno **249** 21
~ de señales **203** 56
~ de servicio **126** 19
~ de sujeción **132** 67
~ de sujeción de la cinta **133** 16
~ de tintaje de las placas de imprimir **249** 50
~ de velocidad **65** 35
~ de vía libre **203** 58
~ flotante **65** 43
~ levadora **325** 32
~ liberadora del rodillo **249** 24
~ oscilante **67** 34
~ para bajar o subir los valores programados manualmente **115** 16
~ para cargar el arma **255** 12
~ para descargar el volquete **214** 35
~ para dirigir la cámara **240** 29
~ para distribuir el aire caliente **191** 87
~ para distribuir el aire frío **191** 86
~ para el bloqueo del casquillo **149** 28
~ para el mecanismo de viraje del husillo patrón **149** 6
~ para el mecanismo inversor del sentido del avance **149** 14
~ para el movimiento longitudinal y transversal **149** 17
~ para el silbato **211** 40
~ para graduar la ventilación **191** 83
~ para la cabeza de afilado **157** 46
~ para la tuerca partida del husillo principal **149** 19
~ para los cambios de avance y de pasos de rosca **149** 9
~ para agarrar **163** 40

~ para regular el zoom **313** 22
~ para regular la temperatura **191** 84
~ para roscas normales y de paso empinado **149** 4
~ que acciona los apagadores **325** 23
~ reguladora **165** 13
~ reguladora de alimentación **163** 28
~ reguladora de la mezcla **288** 16
~ selectora **192** 47
~ selectora de la intesidad de la impresión **249** 10
palancón **66** 6
palangana *Dent.* **24** 15
~ *Rastro* **309** 65
palanganero **309** 64
palangre **90** 28
pala para el mantillo **55** 14
~ para espárragos **45** 77
~ para la nieve **304** 23
~ para mover el fuego **137** 2
~ para remover la tierra **56** 2
~ quitanieves **304** 9
palastro **140** 36
palco *Teatro* **315** 17, 18
~ *Toros, rodeo* **319** 7
~ del circo **307** 16
paleador **304** 22
palendra **66** 1
palenque **329** 31
paleolitico **328** 1-9
paleta *Hortic.* **55** 36
~ *Caza* **88** 9
~ *Estación* **206** 32
~ *Puerto* **225** 43
~ *Pint., dib.* **338** 28
~ curva **91** 38
~ de albañil **118** 52
~ inferior del espéculo **23** 14
~ móvil **315** 36
~ para cortar el papel de la pared **128** 41
~ para probar el café **98** 72
~ plana **226** 10
~ recta **91** 40
paletilla *Caballo* **72** 18
~ *Matad.* **95** 30
~ con la mano **95** 42
paleto **88** 40
paletón **140** 35
palillero **266** 23
palillo de tambor *Mús.* **323** 54
~ *Etnogr.* **354** 19
palio **331** 49
palma *Caza* **88** 9
~ *Fruto merid.* **384** 1, 3
palmacristi **380** 14
palmada de sincronización **117** 69
palma de coco **383** 48
~ de la mano **19** 71
palmer **149** 62
pálmer **149** 62
palmera **97** 30
~ con frutos **384** 2
~ datilera **384** 1
~ de aceite **383** 54
palmeral **354** 5
palmeta **334** 41
~ de bufón **306** 48
~ *Verrier* **52** 1

palmilla **291** 31
palmípeda **359** 4, 5-10
palo *Barco* **219** 1-9
~ *Juego* **276** 38-45
~ *Dep. inv.* **302** 39
~ alemán **276** 42-45
~ de celosía **258** 18
~ de goleta **220** 15
~ de hockey **292** 13
~ de la tienda **278** 38
~ del cepillo **50** 49
~ de mesana *Barco* **218** 31; **219** 8-9
~ de mesana **220** 23, 24
~ de mimbre **136** 15
~ de trinquete **218** 42; **219** 2-4
~ de una sola pieza **258** 42; **259** 6
~ *An. dom.* **73** 33
paloma torcaz **359** 23
palo mayor *Barco* **218** 40; **219** 5-7; **220** 15, 22
~ mayor popel **220** 30, 34
palometa **187** 39
palomilla de arranque en frío **192** 6
~ de gases **192** 9
palomita **32** 47; **33** 11
palomo **73** 33
palo trípode de celosía **258** 41
palpo maxilar **358** 26, 42
palto **31** 5
palustre **118** 52
palla **355** 10
pamela **35** 21
pampajarito **377** 12
pámpana **78** 4
pámpano **78** 2
pan **97** 2
~ ácimo **330** 8
panadería **97** 1-54
panadora **40** 3
pan alargado **97** 8
panal artificial **77** 42
~ de miel **77** 31-43
~ natural **77** 60
panamá **35** 16
pan blanco **97** 9
~ blanco francés **97** 12
pancarta de limitación de velocidad **203** 19
~ electoral **263** 13
pan casero **99** 14
~ cateto *Panad.* **97** 6
~ cateto *Superm.* **99** 14
panceta **96** 2
pancito **97** 13
pan, clases **97** 6-12
páncreas **20** 44
pan de especias **97** 51
~ de germen de trigo **97** 48
~ de mezcla **97** 8
~ de oro **183** 5
~ de queso **99** 40
~ de ranas **378** 44
pandereta *Discot.* **317** 27
~ *Mús.* **324** 45
pandero *Colegio* **260** 71
~ *Parque* **273** 8
~ *Mús.* **324** 45
pan de trigo y centeno **97** 8
~ de Viena **97** 9
pandora **322** 21
pandorga *Colegio* **260** 71
~ *Parque* **273** 42
panecillo *Mesa* **45** 21

píleo **381** 4
pileta de agua **55** 29
pilón **215** 42
~ de azúcar **99** 64
~ del rotor **232** 23
~ de teleférico **214** 76
~ de tubos de acero **214** 78
~ intermedio **214** 29, 76
pilono **333** 9
pilón soporte **214** 23
~ superior de la fuente **272**
  23
píloro **20** 42
pilotaje automático **235** 23
pilote de acero **217** 4
~ de defensa *Cons. hidr.*
  217 9
~ de defensa *Cons. naval*
  222 35
piloto *Bicicl.* **187** 46
~ *Moto* **189** 9
~ *Avión* **230** 35, 36
~ *Astron.* **235** 18
~ *Mús.* **325** 33
~ de advertencia para la
  extralimitación del radio
  de acción **237** 29
~ automático **224** 18
~ de ala delta **287** 45
~ de control de batería **237**
  28
~ del disco duro **244** 5
~ de posición **189** 56
pimentero *Restaur.* **266** 77
~ *Planta estim., trop.* **382**
  36
pimienta **382** 39
~ de muros **377** 12
~ en polvo **382** 39
~ molida **382** 39
pimiento **382** 36
~ picante **57** 42
pimpinela mayor **69** 28
pimpolo de la flor **59** 28
pinabete **372** 1
pinacoide triclínico **351** 26
pináculo **335** 29
pincel *J. infancia* **48** 7
~ *Colegio* **260** 84
~ de borrar **151** 47
~ de dorador **129** 54
~ de escribir **341** 24
~ de motear **129** 54
~ de pelos **338** 7
~ para el polvo **109** 18
~ para la primera capa
  338 9
~ para las letras **129** 41
~ para los radiadores **129**
  21
~ para resaltar los contornos **129** 20
~ plano **338** 6
~ redondo *Pintor* **129** 19
~ redondo *Pint., dib.* **338** 8
pinchaco **366** 26
pincho **66** 4
pinchón **360** 10
ping-pong *Parque* **273** 1
~ *Jue. pelota* **293** 45-55
pingüino **359** 4
~ imperial **359** 4
pinjante **355** 17
pinnatífida **370** 40
pinnípedo **367** 18-22
pino *Gimn.* **295** 27
~ *Coníf.* **372** 20
~ albar **372** 20
~ alerce **372** 32
~ blanco **372** 30

~ canadiense **372** 30
~ con flexión de brazos **295**
  26
~ de montaña **372** 21
~ de Weymouth **372** 30
~ donal **372** 55
~ enano **372** 21
~ manso **372** 55
~ negro **372** 21
~ piñonero **372** 55
~ real **372** 55
~ rojo **372** 20
~ silvestre **372** 20
pintacilgo **360** 1
pintada **73** 27
pintadillo **360** 1
Pintor *Astron.* 3 47
pintor *Pintor* **129** 2
~ de decorados **315** 35
~ de escenarios **315** 35
~ de porcelana **161** 17
pintura *Pintor* **129** 1
~ *Pint., dib.* **338** 10
~ con grafito **338** 41
~ con pistola **129** 28
~ de dispersión **129** 4
~ de guerra **352** 13
~ de las cavernas **328** 9
~ de vidrio **330** 15
~ mural **338** 40
~ rupestre **328** 9
~ sobre cristal **330** 15
pínula **305** 41
pinza **121** 59
~ *Máq. herr.* **150** 44
~ abdominal **81** 12
~ con las puntas cortadas
  100 52
~ del crisol **350** 32
~ del freno **191** 18; **192**
  49
~ del freno de disco **189** 33
~ del tubo **40** 20
~ de masa **142** 35
~ de revelado **116** 47
~ desmochada **100** 52
~ de sujeción **157** 13
~ doble **121** 50
~ fija con las pastillas del
  freno **192** 49
~ orientable **157** 29
~ para el cabello **105** 11
~ para película **114** 14
~ para rizar el cabello **105**
  14
~ para sostener los mapas
  260 30
~ prensora **180** 56
pinzas *Méd.* **22** 52
~ *Reloj.* **109** 14
~ *Fotocomp.* **174** 18
~ *Art. gráf.* **340** 50
~ cortantes **162** 44
~ de asidero **23** 12
~ de biopsia **23** 17
~ de secuestro **26** 45
pinza sencilla **121** 49
pinzas Kocher **22** 49
~ para arterias **26** 49
~ para ligaduras **26** 44
~ para soldar por puntos
  142 23
pinza suctoria **77** 9
pinzón vulgar **360** 10
piña *Árbol.* **371** 32
~ *Coníf.* **372** 2, 13
~ de América **384** 61
~ del pino **372** 26
~ tropical *Superm.* **99** 85

~ tropical *Fruto merid.* **384**
  61
piñón *Ópt.* **112** 39
~ *Tornill.* **143** 92
~ *Hilat.* **164** 48
~ *Bicicl.* **187** 38
~ de cambio *Hilat.* **164** 40
~ de cambio *Tejido* **166**
  19
~ de impulsión **180** 66
~ del árbol de excéntrica
  166 55
~ del eje cigüeñal **166** 51
~ de regulación frontal **114**
  51
~ de regulación trasera **114**
  55
~ de tracción **214** 8
~ helicoidal de la 1.ª velocidad **192** 36
~ helicoidal de la 2.ª velocidad **192** 43
~ helicoidal para la 3.ª velocidad **192** 34
~ libre **187** 63
~ para el accionamiento
  del tacómetro **192** 39
piñuela **372** 59
pío **289** 29
piocha **34** 17
piojillo **375** 39
piojo de cuerpo **81** 41
~ de las plantas **358** 13
~ de las ropas **81** 41
~ humano **81** 41
piolet **300** 16, 31
~ para el hielo **300** 36
piorno **374** 32
pipa **42** 12
~ ahumadora **77** 59
~ corta **107** 33
~ de agua **107** 42
~ de barro **107** 34
~ de la paz **352** 6
~ del apicultor **77** 59
~ de madera de brezo **107**
  39
~ larga **107** 35
pipario **42** 11
pipeta **22** 72
~ automática **23** 44
~ graduada **350** 24
~ ordinaria **350** 25
pipio **90** 29
pipirigallo **69** 10
piquera *Apic.* **77** 48
~ *Sider.* **148** 21
~ de colada **147** 50
piqueta *Construc.* **118** 53
~ *Alpin.* **300** 16, 31
piragua de los indios de los
  bosques **352** 19
piragüista **283** 55
piral de la vid **80** 22
~ del roble **82** 43
pirámide *Huerto* **52** 16
~ *Arte* **333** 1
~ con sus templos **333** 6
~ cuadrangular *Arte* **333** 1
~ cuadrangular *Matem.*
  347 46
~ de vidrio **5** 19
~ escalonada *Arte* **333** 22,
  32
~ escalonada *Etnogr.* **352**
  2
~ ortorrómbica **351** 23
~ tetragonal **351** 18
Pirata *Vela* **284** 52
pirata *Carnaval* **306** 43

pirheliómetro de disco de
  plata **10** 23
pirita **351** 8
pirófago **308** 25
pirómetro **178** 16
pirouette **314** 24
~ *Ballet* **314** 24
~ de pie **302** 9
~ sentada con salto **302** 8
pisadera **44** 16
pisaverde **306** 33
piscicultura **89** 1-19
piscina *Barco* **223** 23
~ *Natac.* **282** 1-32
~ al aire libre **282** 1-32
~ cubierta **281** 1-9
~ de agua fría **281** 30
~ de los no nadadores **282**
  21, 23
~ de olas artificiales **281**
  1-9
~ para saltos **282** 11
Piscis **4** 64
piso *Casa* **37** 3, 82
~ *Dorm.* **43** 22
~ *Construc.* **123** 41
~ *Hotel* **267** 35
~ bajo **194** 37
~ de bajada **6** 28-36
~ de subida **6** 37-47
pisón *Construc.* **119** 83
~ *Abast. agua* **269** 60
~ de combustión interna
  200 26
~ de explosión **200** 26
piso superior **194** 38
pista **307** 21
pistachero **382** 49
pistacho **382** 51
pista de arena **290** 24
~ de aterrizaje y despegue
  233 1
~ de baile **317** 16
~ de carreras *Cicl., motor*
  290 1
~ de carreras *Atlet.* **298** 6
~ de carreras al trote **289**
  23
~ de ceniza **298** 6
~ de despegue y aterrizaje
  para los aviones **287** 15
~ de esgrima **294** 2
~ de estacionamiento
  233 3
~ de los coches de choque
  308 62
~ de maniobras **233** 4
~ de material sintético
  298 6
~ de rodaje **233** 2
~ de sincronización **243** 33
~ de tenis **293** 1
~ de vídeo **243** 23
~ en diagonal **243** 31
~ para la gimnasia en el
  suelo **296** 11
~ sonora **243** 24
~ vídeo **243** 31
pistilo **68** 34
pisto **246** 27
pistola de aire caliente **130**
  25
~ del surtidor **196** 3
~ de perno percutor **94** 3
~ de pulverización **129** 32
~ de soldar **134** 56
~ P 1 **255** 1
~ pulverizadora *Parás.* **83**
  18

~ *Textil* **168** 61
rafia *Planta* **54** 35
~ *Cestero* **136** 29
raigón **24** 27
raigrás italiano **69** 26
rail *FFCC* **202** 1; **214** 10
~ *Estación* **205** 59
~ de deslizamiento *Grandes alm.* **271** 54
~ de deslizamiento *Remo* **283** 45
~ de la cadena **85** 16
~ del cambio **202** 26
~ del tranvía **268** 23
~ de maniobra **214** 22
~ de recubrimiento sobre las agujas de lengüeta **167** 56
~ de rodeo **214** 22
~ de viraje **164** 17
raíz *Anat.* **19** 36
~ *Planta* **54** 21
~ *Agric.* **68** 17, 45
~ *Matem.* **345** 2
~ *Botán.* **370** 16-18, 78-82
~ adventicia **370** 78, 80
~ aérea **370** 80
~ con frutos **383** 43
~ cuadrada **345** 3
~ cúbica **345** 2
~ de la recta **347** 12
~ principal **370** 16
~ respiratoria **370** 82
~ secundaria **370** 17
~ trepadora **370** 80
~ tuberosa **370** 79
raja de la manga **30** 48
~ del costado **30** 49
~ del culo **16** 41
~ de melón rociada con miel **266** 50
rajadera **96** 35
rajador **136** 35
ralentizar **286** 50
rálida **359** 20
rama *Tejido* **171** 32
~ *Botán.* **370** 5
~ con amentos **371** 10
~ con flores femeninas **384** 42
~ con flores masculinas y femeninas **372** 43
~ con flores y frutas **383** 46
~ con flores y frutos **382** 17
~ con frutas compuestas **384** 12
~ con frutos *Fruta* **59** 30, 48
~ con frutos *Árbol.* **371** 3, 11, 18, 31, 36, 41, 47, 50, 56, 64
~ con frutos *Conif.* **372** 40, 51, 59, 63
~ con frutos *Planta estim., trop.* **382** 2, 37
~ con frutos *Planta ind.* **383** 34
~ con frutos *Fruto merid.* **384** 8, 38
~ con frutos del ciruelo **59** 19
~ con hojas **371** 27
~ con hojas **383** 61
~ con hojas de la salguera blanca **371** 29
~ con los botones florales **371** 25
~ con una piña de alerce **372** 36

~ de abedul para azotar la piel **281** 27
~ de coral **357** 18
~ de la parábola **347** 15
~ de primer orden **370** 21
~ en flor **378** 27
~ en flor del albaricoquero **59** 33
~ en flor del avellano **59** 44
~ en flor del cerezo **59** 1
~ en flor del grosellero **58** 14
~ en flor del manzano **58** 52
~ en flor del nogal **59** 37
~ en flor del peral **58** 32
~ florecida de la grosella espinosa **58** 2
~ florida *Fruta* **59** 26
~ florida *Árbol* **371** 2, 10, 16, 32, 34, 39, 51, 54, 66, 71
~ florida *Conif.* **372** 33
~ florida *Planta* **378** 2
~ florida *Planta estim., trop.* **382** 3, 8, 12, 23, 27, 31, 41, 47, 50
~ florida *Planta ind.* **383** 26, 30, 38, 22, 42
~ florida *Fruto merid.* **384** 17, 24, 37, 49, 54
~ horquillada para la fijación **54** 13
ramal *Mapa* **15** 23
~ *Font.* **126** 8
~ ferroviario **225** 62
ramaria apretada **381** 32
rambata **218** 49
ramificación curva **203** 48
~ doblada a derecha **203** 46
~ doblada a izquierda **203** 47
~ recta **203** 45
ramillete artísticamente dispuesto **267** 37
ramito de mirto **332** 21
ramo **370** 6
~ de flores **267** 37
~ de novia **332** 18
rampa **119** 41; **123** 30
~ de acceso *Mapa* **15** 16
~ de acceso *Limp. públ.* **199** 15
~ de acceso *Estación* **206** 1
~ de acceso *FFCC* **213** 36
~ de carga **206** 9
~ de lanzamiento **255** 54
~ de lanzamiento de misiles *Tartar* **258** 49
~ del cobertizo **206** 9
~ del coque **156** 12
~ del dique **216** 47
~ del ganado **206** 1
~ de popa *Barco* **221** 88
~ de popa *Buque guerra* **258** 91
~ de proa **258** 90
~ de vehículos **206** 1
rana bermeja **364** 24
~ de San Antonio **364** 24
~ de zarzal **364** 24
rancho *Sombr.* **35** 35
~ *Granja* **62**
ranita **29** 22
ranúnculo **375** 8
ranura *Tornill.* **143** 49
~ *Jue. pelota* **291** 29
~ de guía **176** 46
~ de inserción de filtros **117** 38

~ de introducción de la casete **243** 32
~ de la aguja **167** 15
~ del aire **194** 16
~ de la pared del tambor para la formación del cojín de aire **243** 19
~ de la urna **263** 29
~ del chasis **114** 10
~ del tornillo **143** 38
~ de sensibilidad de la película **117** 37
~ en forma de efe **323** 6
~ en zigzag **165** 11
~ guía *Fotogr.* **117** 36
~ guía *Dep. inv.* **301** 39
~ guía *Mús.* **322** 41
~ para el pulsador **166** 32
~ para introducir las fichas del programa **195** 5
~ para la chaveta **143** 66, 85
~ para la tarjeta de extensión de memoria **244** 10
~ para la tarjeta gráfica **244** 11
~ para la tarjeta telefónica **237** 35
~ para las tizas **260** 31
rapavelas **330** 58
rapé **107** 20
rapel **300** 28-30
rápido **321** 28
rapónchigo **57** 38
raposa **367** 12
rappen **252** 15
raqueta **275** 5
~ del juego de volante **293** 43
~ de ping-pong **273** 4
~ de tenis *Vestib.* **41** 13
~ de tenis *Jue. pelota* **293** 29
rascadera **379** 9
rascador *Carnic.* **96** 42
~ *Construc.* **120** 79
~ *Cerraj.* **140** 63
~ *Dep. inv.* **301** 24
~ *Art. gráf.* **340** 17
~ triangular **140** 63
rascamoño **60** 22
rascón **359** 20
rasera **96** 43
raspador *Méd.* **22** 50
~ *Casa* **38** 33
~ *Tabaco* **107** 24, 45
~ *Pintor* **129** 23
~ *Art. gráf.* **340** 63
~ de árboles **56** 14
~ de cera **301** 24
~ de corteza **56** 14
~ de escultor **339** 11
~ de papeles pintados **128** 15
~ de sierra **134** 6
ráspano **377** 23
Raster Image Processor **176** 27
rasqueta **71** 54
rastrillador **163** 42
rastrillo *Jardín* **56** 4
~ *Agric.* **64** 44; **66** 23
~ *Jue. pelota* **292** 70
~ *Caball.* **329** 24
~ del césped **51** 4
~ para el heno **66** 23
rastro *Caza* **86** 8
~ *Hípica* **289** 49
~ *Dep. inv.* **301** 60
~ *Feria* **308** 60

~ *Rastro* **309**
rastrojera **63** 33
rastrojo **63** 36
rastro para el heno **66** 23
~ para las patatas **66** 20
rata de agua **366** 17
~ del trigo **366** 16
ratero **308** 16
ratón **176** 19; **244** 21
ratonera **83** 36
ratonero común **362** 9
raya *Ropa* **33** 6
~ *Caza* **87** 36
~ *Escrit.* **342** 23
~ al lado **34** 14
~ blanca **268** 72
~ del pantalón **33** 6
~ de parada **268** 50
~ de quebrado **344** 15
rayador **125** 9
raya en medio **34** 9
rayo *Tornill.* **143** 88
~ *Moto* **189** 24
~ *Matem.* **346** 20
~ coudé **5** 3
rayón **88** 51
~ sobre bobina cónica de plegado **169** 27
rayos radiofónicos **237** 78
~ X **1** 56
razas de perros **70**
reacción en cadena **1** 41
~ en cadena controlada **1** 48
reactor **154** 3, 41, 50
~ atómico **1** 48
~ de agua a presión **154** 19
~ de doble flujo **232** 46
~ nuclear *Energ. nucl.* **154** 19
~ nuclear *Buque guerra* **259** 67
~ soplante de cola **232** 42
~ soplante delantero **232** 33
~ soplante trasero **232** 42
~ superregenerador rápido **154** 1
real de la feria **308** 1
reanimador eléctrico **21** 27
reavituallador de las perforaciones offshore **221** 32
rebanada de pan **45** 22, 37
rebarbado **148** 38-45, 43
re bemol mayor **320** 67
rebobinado **170** 50
~ de la película **312** 21
rebobinador del hilo **104** 16
reborde de anillos **55** 38
rebosadero *Casa* **38** 69
~ *Baño* **49** 25, 45
~ *Pesca* **89** 5
~ *Cons. hidr.* **217** 60
~ *Abast. agua* **269** 20, 33
rebote **297** 36
rebozuelo **381** 15
recadero **236** 17
recalentador **152** 9
recalentamiento **162** 27, 35
recámara *Dorm.* **43**
~ *Caza* **87** 15
recambio del tiralíneas **151** 58
recorrido del minigolf **272** 70
recepción *Hotel* **267** 1-26
~ *Camping* **278** 1
~ de cebada **92** 41
~ de la leche **76** 1
~ de mercancías **206** 26

~ de apoyo 270 50
roleta 275 1-33
rollito de nata 97 17
rollizo Construc. 119 13; 120 2, 35
~ Aserr. 157 30
rollo 157 30
~ continuo de papel 173 30, 45
~ de arcilla 339 8
~ de cinta adhesiva 247 29
~ de esparadrapo 26 54
~ de hilo 89 21
~ de la manguera 270 54
~ de la película 312 33
~ de madera 157 30
~ de papel Estudio 151 14
~ de papel Oficina 249 33
~ de papel Rastro 309 75
~ de papel acabado de extender 173 35
~ de papel crepé 49 11
~ de papel de desecho 128 5
~ de película de 120 114 19
~ de plano 151 10
~ de tela del batán 163 47
romana 355 7
romano 355 11
rombo 346 35
rombododecaedro 351 7
romboedro 351 22
rombo en talla escalonada 36 59
romboide 346 36
romo 98 56
rompealud 304 2
rompecabezas 48 9
rompehielos Puente 215 56
~ Barco 231 50
rompeolas Cons. hidr. 217 16
~ Puerto 225 65
~ Buque guerra 258 7, 76
rompiente, llano del 13 31
rompimiento de la ola 279 4
ron 98 57
ropa blanca sucia 50 22
~ de caballero 33
~ de cama del moisés 28 31
~ de cristianar 332 8
~ de gimnasia 297 51
~ de invierno 30
~ de jóvenes 29 48-68
~ de niños 29
~ de niños pequeños 29 1-12
~ de noche 32
~ de noche de caballero 32 35-37
~ de señora 30; 31
~ de verano 31
~ interior 32
~ interior de caballero 32 22-29
~ interior de señora 32 1-15
ropaje 338 33
ropa talar 332 4
ropero 43 1
rosa Mús. 322 22; 324 5
~ Color 343 4
~ china 60 15
~ de los vientos 224 47
~ de marfil tallado 36 29
~ de tallo alto Jardín 51 25
~ de tallo alto Huerto 52 21
~ doble 60 17
~ india 60 15
rosal 52 13, 21
~ común 52 13
~ de tallo alto 52 21

~ trepador 52 12
rosa náutica 224 47
rosario 332 30
rosca Apar. hogar 50 50
~ Riego 67 38
~ Panad. 97 38
~ Tornill. 143 16, 68
~ de la bombilla 127 59
~ de madera 143 47
~ golosa 143 47
roseta Hortic. 55 28
~ Caza 88 5, 29
~ de la ducha 49 42
rosetón 335 23
~ cuadrifolio 335 39
~ de cinco lóbulos 335 40
rosquilla 97 44
~ grande 99 16
rota 136 32
rotación 230 71
~ alrededor del eje longitudinal y transversal del cuerpo 298 11
rotata 322 25
rotativa de doble revolución 181 1
~ de huecograbado multicolor 182 24
~ tipográfica 181 41
rotor Reloj. 110 24
~ Energ. mod. 155 45
~ Avión 232 12-13
~ Policía 264 3
~ Vuelo sin motor 287 18
~ antipar trasero 256 20
~ de aletas 64 73
~ de cola Avión 232 14
~ de cola Policía 264 4
~ de cuchillas 85 25
~ del motor rotativo 190 68
~ en tándem 232 22
~ pivotante en posición vertical 232 32
~ principal FFAA 256 19
~ principal Policía 264 3
~ trasero 255 91
~ único 255 89
rótula Átomo 2 41
~ Anat. 17 23
~ Art. gráf. 340 30
~ del pivote de manigueta 192 80
rotulador Hab. niños 47 26
~ J. infancia 48 18
~ Oficina 247 11
~ Colegio 260 19
rótulo 118 47
~ de la tienda 268 39
~ del lomo 247 38
rough 293 80
roulotte 278 3, 52
RP-1 234 9
rubeta 364 24
rubí sintético 110 25
rudecilla 83 61
rueda Agric. 64 41, 56
~ Riego 67 24
~ An. dom. 73 29
~ Bicicl. 187 26-32
~ auxiliar 187 5
~ con cuatro toneles sucesivos 288 3
~ de adherencia 214 7
~ de ajuste 110 15
~ de aletas 35
~ de áncora 110 32
~ de ancho especial 193 31
~ de apoyo Agric. 65 59, 63
~ de apoyo Bicicl. 188 5

~ de apoyo con regulación de profundidad 64 88
~ de automóvil 191 14
~ de camión 138 21
~ de cola 256 27
~ de corona 110 33
~ de corredera Estación 206 39
~ de corredera FFAA 255 32
~ de dientes en ángulo 143 87
~ de disco 191 14
~ de fricción 322 26
~ de fundición de metal ligero 189 48
~ de graduación del diafragma 114 34
~ de la cuerda 110 33
~ de la fortuna 308 45
~ delantera 186 4
~ delantera de guía 278 54
~ del caballón 65 15
~ del diablo 308 46
~ del mecanismo de relojería 10 14
~ del morro 288 34
~ del sidecar 189 57
~ del surco 65 16
~ del tiempo de exposición 114 35
~ del tifón 308 46
~ del timón 224 15
~ de molino de agua 91 35
~ de morro dirigible 230 40
~ de muros 377 16
~ dentada Molino 91 7
~ dentada Tornill. 143 82-96
~ dentada cilíndrica doble helicoidal 143 87
~ dentada cónica 143 91
~ dentada delantera de la cadena 187 35
~ dentada del eje cigüeñal 166 51
~ dentada de tracción 214 8
~ dentada trasera de la cadena 187 38
~ de paletas Hortic. 55 55
~ de paletas Clisé 178 33
~ de paletas Cons. hidr. 217 52
~ de queso 99 40
~ de rayos 289 25
~ de repuesto 191 25; 193 12; 194 4, 33
~ de sujeción 110 27
~ de timón 278 54
~ direccional 64 86
~ direccional trasera 64 39
~ elevadora 64 74
~ en la barra de equilibrio 297 21
~ gigante 305 79
~ hidráulica de corriente alta 91 35
~ hidráulica de corriente baja 91 39
~ hidráulica de corriente media 91 37
~ impulsora y motor 167 31
~ motriz Agric. 65 80
~ motriz Ópt. 112 39
~ motriz FFCC 209 3
~ motriz FFAA 255 30
~ para el transporte 241 11
~ tensora 312 30

~ trasera 186 17
~ volante 104 15
ruedecilla 50 81
ruedo 319 5, 9
rugby 292 19
~ americano 292 22
ruina 15 72
ruiponce 57 38
ruiseñor común 361 14
ruleta 275 1-33, 10, 28
~ estriada para el grabado punteado 340 18
~ para calcar 129 42
rulo Peluq. 105 12
~ Carret. 200 37
rulote 307 34
rumbo Avión 230 13
~ Ave 363 4
~ An. dom. 73 1
~ Mamíf. 366 28-30; 367 1-10
runa 341 19
runallama 366 28
rundún 363 4
rutista 290 8

S

sabana 13 46
sábana 43 9
~ de cama 50 5
~ de lino 43 9
sabina 372 47
sable Heráld. 254 26
~ Vela 284 44
~ de deporte 294 34
~ ligero 294 20, 34
sabuco 374 35
sacabocados Zapat. 100 45
~ Hojal. 125 13
~ de asa 100 46
sacaclavos Zapat. 100 47
~ Bric. 134 32
sacacorchos Cocina 40 18
~ Mesa 45 46
sacador 293 51, 62
~ del cartón 184 8
sacapuntas 247 25
sacarificación 92 44
sacerdote 330 39; 331 47; 332 22
sácere 371 53
saco 29 51; 22 2, 21
~ de aceite 228 11
~ de agua para beber 278 32
~ de aire 353 11
~ de ante 30 58
~ de arena Río 216 50
~ de arena Dep. aéreo 288 65
~ de arena Halter., pesos 299 21
~ de cemento 118 43
~ de desinfección 83 56
~ de dormir 278 30
~ de dormir del bebé 28 17
~ del aire 322 9
~ del polvo 50 62
~ del traje 31 2
~ de mano 205 10
~ de polvo de yeso 339 29
~ de popelina 31 37
~ de punto 31 50
~ de yeso 260 85
~ embrional 370 64

~ para despiezar **94** 20
~ para huesos **96** 56
~ para metales **134** 17
~ pequeña **127** 52
~ rápida **138** 23
~ tronzadora **120** 14
sietecolores **360** 1
Siete Hermanas **3** 26
sifón *Meteor.* **10** 43
~ *Baño* **49** 27
~ inodoro **126** 26
~ respiratorio **358** 5
sigla de la agencia de prensa **342** 55
signatura **185** 69
signo convencional de un mapa **15** 1-114
~ de adición **344** 23
~ de admiración **342** 21
~ de ángulo **345** 23
~ de diferencial **345** 13
~ de división **344** 15, 26
~ de duración **321** 25
~ de elevación **320** 50-51
~ de extracción de raíces **345** 2
~ de identidad **345** 16
~ de igualdad **344** 23
~ de interrogación **342** 20
~ de la integral **345** 14
~ de la no identidad **345** 18
~ de la semejanza **345** 22
~ del tanto por ciento **345** 7
~ de multiplicación **344** 25
~ de notación **321** 23-26
~ de paralelismo **345** 21
~ de párrafo **342** 36
~ de puntuación **342** 16-29
~ de sustracción **344** 24
~ de triángulo **345** 24
~ diacrítico **342** 30-35
~ geométrico **345** 21-24
~ más **344** 23
~ matemático **345** 15-24
~ menos **344** 24
~ negativo **344** 8
~ positivo **344** 7
~ que baja la nota **320** 52-53
signos de los planetas **4** 42-45
~ del Zodiaco **4** 53-64
S II **234** 18, 31, 36, 37
sikhara **337** 26
silbato *FFCC* **211** 9; **212** 49
~ *Naveg.* **224** 70
~ de vapor **40** 11
~ mágico para conjurar los espíritus **354** 42
silenciador *Autom.* **191** 29
~ *Dep.* **305** 93
silencio **320** 20-27
~ de blanca **320** 22
~ de corchea **320** 24
~ de cuadrada **320** 20
~ de fusa **320** 26
~ de negra **320** 23
~ de redonda **320** 21
~ de semicorchea **320** 25
~ de semifdifusa **320** 27
silencioso *Autom.* **191** 29
~ *FFCC* **211** 49; **212** 69
~ de admisión **191** 54
~ de escape **212** 42, 48
silene **376** 26
sílex **328** 1
silicio **1** 14
silicua **370** 93
~ madura **383** 4
silo *Avic.* **74** 24
~ *Puerto* **225** 68

~ de abono líquido **62** 13
~ de cebada **92** 31
~ de harina **97** 74
~ de homogeneización **160** 5
~ del cemento **201** 22
~ de los componentes de carbón de coque **156** 3
~ de malta **92** 37
~ de politileno **62** 43
~ elevado **62** 11
~ para el cemento *Construc.* **119** 30
~ para el cemento *Cemen.* **160** 15
~ para el forraje **62** 11, 43
~ para las materias primas pulverizadas **160** 5
~ -torre **62** 11
silueta cardíaca en rayos X **25** 39
siluro **364** 12
silvicultura **84; 85**
silla **42** 34
~ alta de niño **28** 33
~ con ruedas **28** 37
~ de anilla improvisada **21** 22
~ de camping **278** 43
~ de cocina **39** 43
~ de jardín **37** 49
~ del árbitro **293** 20
~ de la reina **21** 21
~ del comedor **44** 10
~ del parque **272** 48
~ de montar **71** 37-49
~ de oficina **248** 25
~ de paseo **71** 37-44
~ de posta **186** 54
~ de saltos **289** 10
~ de tijera **278** 43
~ de torneo **329** 87
~ extensible **278** 43
~ giratoria **248** 25
~ inglesa **71** 45-49
~ metálica de tubo **41** 21
~ plegable *Bebé* **28** 33
~ plegable *Camping* **278** 43
sillar **158** 30
sillería **330** 28, 41
silleta **42** 34
sillín *Caballo* **71** 17, 31, 37, 45
~ *Bicicl.* **188** 59
~ *Moto* **189** 14
~ biplaza **188** 42
~ de carreras **290** 17
~ de la bicicleta **187** 22
~ de muelles de la bicicleta **187** 22
~ moldeado **188** 13
~ monoplaza **189** 19
~ móvil **188** 21
~ para niños **187** 21
~ regulable **188** 4
~ sin muelles **290** 17
sillón *Estar* **42** 21
~ *Hotel* **267** 26
~ de dentista **24** 3
~ de estilo Art Nouveau **336** 18
~ de la mesa de despacho **246** 1
~ de la visita **246** 21
~ del escritorio **46** 27
~ de mimbre **43** 3
~ de peluquería **105** 17
~ de peluquería regulable **106** 16

~ de playa de mimbre **280** 36
~ para el reconocimiento oftalmológico **111** 43
sima *Geogr.* **11** 4
~ *Arte* **334** 11
si mayor **320** 60
símbolo algebraico **344** 9; **345** 5
~ del logaritmo decimal **345** 6
~ de logaritmo **345** 6
símbolos de los planetas **4** 42-45
~ del Zodiaco **4** 53-64
símbolo telefónico de tarjeta **237** 37
si menor **320** 57
simetría *Matem.* **346** 25
~ *Cristal.* **351** 3, 4, 5
simiente **63** 12
simón **186** 26
sinaítica **341** 13
sinclinal **12** 18
~, eje del **12** 19
sincronización *Fotogr.* **117** 65
~ *Cine* **311** 37-41
sincronizador *Dent.* **24** 52
~ *Central el.* **153** 32
sincrotrón **2** 49
sínfisis del pubis **20** 65
sínfito mayor *Planta* **69** 13
~ mayor *Flor* **375** 45
siningia **53** 7
sin nubes **9** 20
sinople **254** 29
sintonización automática **23** 38
sintonizador *Electrón* **241** 5
~ *Discot.* **317** 22
sirena *Barco* **223** 3
~ *Bomberos* **270** 7
~ *Ser fabul.* **327** 23, 58
~ de alarma **270** 4
~ de cola de pez **327** 23
~ de incendios **270** 4
sirénido **62** 48
sirga *Pesca* **90** 12
~ *Río* **216** 27
sirguero **360** 1
siringa **322** 2
Sirio **3** 14
siripita **81** 7
sismógrafo horizontal **11** 39
sismología **11** 32-38
sismómetro **11** 39
sistama solar **4** 42-45
sistema activo de anclaje **6** 47
~ antivortex **234** 11
~ automático de alimentación y recogida **74** 23-27
~ automático del diafragma **117** 20
~ circulatorio **18** 1-21
~ de aberturas del paracaídas deportivo **288** 45
~ de accionamiento del carro de presa **157** 15
~ de acoplamiento **227** 23
~ de agua a presión **154** 40
~ de agua de refrigeración **154** 55
~ de agua en ebullición **154** 49
~ de aireación **317** 30
~ de alerones **229** 37
~ de alimentación **74** 49-51

~ de alimentación de gas comprimido **234** 60
~ de alunizaje **6** 31
~ de amortiguación **235** 53
~ de armas dirigidas MILAN **255** 79
~ de bomba de calor **155** 1
~ de cables oblicuos **215** 51
~ de calefacción regulado por agua **192** 60-64
~ de cañones de electrones **240** 24
~ de carga de camiones y vagones **226** 28
~ de carga por medio de carretillas **225** 41
~ de carga rodante **225** 39
~ de comprimir hidráulico **173** 37
~ de construcción gótico **335** 27-35
~ de control de la marcha del tren de línea **209** 18
~ de control por un único cable **288** 90
~ de coordenadas ortogonales **347** 1
~ de cristalización hexagonal **351** 20-22
~ de cristalización monoclínico **351** 24-25
~ de cristalización tetragonal **351** 18-19
~ de cúpulas **334** 72-73
~ de dos tuberías **126** 22
~ de energía de la nave espacial **6** 8
~ de exploración **176** 35
~ de exploración láser **243** 45
~ de grabado **177** 66
~ de grutas **13** 76
~ del brazo acústico **241** 29
~ de leva **183** 30
~ de mando del empuje **235** 43
~ de navegación Decca **224** 39
~ de palanca acodada **183** 30
~ de palancas para la regulación de la alimentación **163** 31
~ de poleas **221** 27
~ de producción de la radiación **113** 31
~ de recogida de los huevos **74** 34
~ de refrigeración **154** 48
~ de reproducción **176** 41
~ de retículo **87** 31
~ de rociadura **316** 6
~ de soportes exteriores **335** 27-28
~ de suspensión **214** 54
~ de tala **84** 4-14
~ de vacíado estanco **199** 2
~ de vientos **9** 46-52
~ hidráulico *Forja* **139** 36
~ hidráulico *FFAA* **255** 36
~ hidráulico de elevación **65** 24-29
~ inductivo de control de la marcha del tren **211** 7; **212** 14
~ lanzamisiles SF lance **255** 49
~ monosimétrico **351** 24-25
~ muscular **18** 34-64
~ nervioso **18** 22-33

~ voluble de la judía **57** 10
tambaleo **230** 69
tambor *Meteor.* **10** 5, 16, 20
~ *Fotocomp.* **174** 35
~ *Mús.* **324** 48
~ *Arte* **335** 44
~ alimentador **180** 34
~ con muescas **165** 10
~ con púas de muelle **64** 4
~ de bastidor **353** 26
~ de conducción de la paja
64 13
~ de corte **64** 34
~ de danza **354** 14
~ de enrollamiento **187** 72
~ de gasa **185** 19
~ de lansquenete **306** 70
~ de lavado **50** 24
~ del cable **270** 55
~ del freno **138** 11
~ del freno delantero **189**
11
~ del freno de mano **192** 50
~ del freno trasero **189** 13
~ dentado para desenrollar
la película **312** 26
~ dentado para enrollar la
película **312** 27
~ de película **312** 16
~ de recolección **64** 4
~ de revelado **116** 20
~ de revelado de papel **116**
48
~ de revólver, para el cambio automático de las
canillas **166** 5
~ de salida **180** 42, 65
~ de secado **50** 29
~ de señales **354** 18
~ desgranador **64** 12
~ de transmisión **180** 36
~ expositor **180** 42
~ gordo **324** 47
~ graduado **149** 64
~, gran **163** 43
~ impulsor **165** 32
~ mayor **323** 55
~ mezclador **118** 34
~ micrométrico **224** 4
~ para apagar la cal **172** 51
~ para la mezcla del asfalto
200 50
~ pequeño **323** 51
~ protegido contra incen-
dios **312** 25
~ secador calentador **173** 33
tamiz *Papel* **173** 14
~ *Quím.* **349** 12
~ de graneado **340** 24
~ de la paja **64** 14
~ de la paja corta **64** 17
~ giratorio **172** 2
~ secador **173** 23
tampón de tinta **22** 30
~ entintador **340** 22
tam-tam **354** 14
tamúlica **341** 11
tanaceto **380** 9
tándem **186** 50
tangana **278** 19
tangente *Mús.* **322** 43
~ *Matem.* **346** 32, 48
tangona **216** 16
tanque central del fuselaje
257 30
~ cisterna del mosto **78** 16
~ de afinado de la nata **76**
31
~ de agua *FFCC* **210** 66
~ de agua *Aerop.* **233** 22

~ de agua dulce **221** 70;
223 79
~ de almacenamiento
Petról. **145** 72
~ de almacenamiento
Puerto **225** 72
~ de carburante para helicópteros **146** 18
~ de combustible **221** 80;
223 71
~ de forraje **221** 73
~ de gasóleo **146** 13
~ de gasolina **189** 36; **305**
87
~ del ala **256** 4
~ de la leche agria **76** 42
~ de la leche cruda **76** 5
~ de la leche descremada
76 17
~ de la leche esterilizada **76**
16
~ de lastre de agua **223** 78
~ del cuajo **76** 48
~ de leche fresca **76** 15
~ del estiércol **221** 72
~ del fondo **222** 38
~ del fuselaje **257** 31
~ de materia plástica **79** 4
~ de nata **76** 19
~ de reserva para el agua
salada **146** 17
~ de suero **76** 18
~ esférico *Petról.* **145** 73
~ esférico *Barco* **221** 36
~ integrado en el ala **257** 29
~ lateral **222** 37
~ para disolver **172** 37
~ para el agua potable **146**
16
~ para el almacenamiento
de cemento **146** 15
tanques de carburante **237**
72
~ de oxígeno e hidrógeno
6 6
tanteador **293** 71
tanto por ciento **345** 7
tapa *Encuad.* **95** 13, 37
~ *Encuad.* **185** 40
~ *Electrón.* **241** 2, 36; **242**
62
~ abovedada **38** 48
~ armónica **323** 24
~ con un tubo ajustado **350**
52
~ de balancines **190** 48
~ de cierre **244** 34
~ de cristal **269** 56
~ de la cabeza de imprimir
249 30
~ de la cazoleta **107** 37
~ de la centrífuga **168** 18
~ de la escotilla **222** 65
~ delantera **249** 36
~ de la pantalla de enfoque
114 23
~ del baño **178** 37
~ del batán **166** 6
~ del braserillo del incensario **332** 40
~ del casete de doble pletina **241** 7
~ del conmutador **211** 18
~ del escotillón **316** 33
~ del motor **191** 8
~ del motor trasero **195** 50
~ del registro **38** 46
~ del retrete con una
cubierta de felpa **49** 14
tapadera *Cocina* **40** 13

~ *Orfebre* **108** 9
~ *Quím.* **350** 31
~ de la caldera **92** 45
~ del agujero de entrada
130 19
~ de la pipa **107** 37
tapa de rosca **83** 40
~ deslizante **179** 2
~ de vacío **177** 35
tapado **30** 61
tapadora **76** 27
tapa guardapolvo **187** 57, 82
tapajuntas **123** 64
tápalo **31** 71
tapanca **71** 7-11
tapa para protección del
polvo **242** 5
~ posterior para los datos
115 52
tapa roscada **115** 11
taparrabo **354** 31
~ de cabellos humanos **352**
38
tapa transparente **249** 27
tapegua **86** 20
tapete de juego **275** 9
~ de la mesa **46** 35
~ del juego de la ruleta **275**
17
~ de piel **108** 21
~ verde **275** 17
~ verde **275** 9
tapicería **134** 59
tapioca **98** 39
tapiro **366** 26
tapir sudamericano **366** 26
tapizado de un sillón **134** 59
tapón *Riego* **67** 36
~ *Quím.* **350** 27
~ "bueno" **149** 57
~ con llave **350** 44
~ de aceptación **149** 57
~ de la botella **93** 27
~ del tubo **260** 52
~ de rechazo **149** 58
~ de vaciado del aceite **190**
24
~ "malo" **149** 58
~ octogonal **349** 4
taquigrafía **342** 13
taquilla **134** 10
~ de apuestas **289** 34
~ del cine **312** 2
~ de venta de billetes **204**
35
taquillero **204** 39
tarima **78** 20
~ para modelar **339** 9
tarja *Caball.* **329** 56
~ *Arte* **336** 7
tarjeta **336** 7
~ amarilla **291** 63
~ de elector **263** 19
~ de expulsión **291** 63
~ del chip con programas
especiales de foto **115** 9
~ del eurocheque **250** 24
~ de mesa **45** 13
~ para puertos en serie y
paralelo **244** 13
~ roja **291** 63
~ telefónica **237** 36
tarjetero **249** 19
tarlatana **185** 20
tarraja **322** 22; **324** 5
tarraza **72** 31
tarrina **265** 29
tarrito de la paleta **338** 29
tarro de crema **99** 27
~ de cuajada **76** 45

~ de especia **39** 32
~ de miel **77** 63
tarso *Anat.* **17** 26
~ *Ave* **362** 4
tarta *Panad.* **97** 22-24
~ *Superm.* **99** 15
~ *Café* **265** 4
~ de cerezas **97** 22
~ de cerezas de la Selva
Negra **97** 24
~ de crema **97** 24
~ de crema de mantequilla
97 24
~ de fresas **97** 22
~ de frutas *Panad.* **97** 22
~ de frutas *Superm.* **99** 20
~ de grosellas **97** 22
~ de melocotón **97** 22
~ de nata **97** 24
~ de queso **97** 23
~ de ruibarbo **97** 22
tártago **380** 14
tartita **97** 20
tas **125** 23
~ de banco **140** 14
tatetí **276** 23-25
tatú **366** 8
tatuaje **306** 44
Tauro **4** 54
tauromaquia **319**
Taurus **3** 25
taxi **268** 64
taxis **233** 32
tayacán **63** 10
taza **24** 15
~ de café *Comed.* **44** 29
~ de café *Café* **265** 19
~ de la pila bautismal **332**
11
~ del retrete **49** 13
~ inferior de la fuente **272**
24
~ para niño **28** 27
~ superior de la fuente **272**
23
té *Superm.* **99** 69
~ *Font.* **126** 44
~ *Planta estim., trop.* **382**
7, 9
teatro **315**; **316**
~ al aire libre **272** 67
~ griego **334** 44
teca con esporas **381** 13
~ con esporas **381** 12
teckel **70** 39
~ de pelo corto **70** 39
tecla **322** 38, 49; **326** 8
~ blanca **325** 4
~ de anulación del tabulador **249** 8
~ de avance rápido **242**
10
~ de bajada del brazo **241**
26
~ de búsqueda **242** 72
~ de búsqueda de pistas
242 31
~ de búsqueda manual **242**
32
~ de cálculo del porcentaje
247 23
~ de cifra **247** 18
~ de coma **247** 19
~ de ébano **325** 5
~ de expulsión **242** 23
~ de filtro de agudos o de
bajos **241** 51
~ de filtros **241** 51
~ de función *C. cálc.* **244**
16

V

V 295 13, 17
vaca *An. dom.* 73 1
~ *Matad.* 94 2; 95 14-37
~ de San Antón 358 37
~ lechera *Granja* 62 34
~ lechera *Ganado* 75 17
vaciado 340 4
~ de yeso 339 4
vaciador 148 8
vacío *RTV* 240 21
~ *Quím.* 349 11
vacuola alimenticia 357 6
~ pulsátil 357 5
vacuómetro de espejo 349 20
vade 246 6
vademécum de los medicamentos registrados 22 23
vagina 20 86
vagón 207 1-21
~ abierto de bogies de descarga automática 213 24
~ cisterna 213 31
~ completo 206 52
~ con vagonetas basculantes 213 37
~ de bogies de techo pivotante 213 26
~ de carga *Mina* 144 8
~ de carga *Coque* 156 6
~ de circo 206 20
~ de dos pisos para el transporte de automóviles 213 35
~ de enrejado de listones 213 28
~ de extinción del coque 144 11
~ de feriantes 206 20
~ del ferrocarril de cremallera 214 5
~ del servicio local de cuatro ejes 208 3
~ de mercancías abierto normal 213 8
~ de mercancías cubierto 213 14
~ de plataforma especial 213 33
~ de techo de corredera 213 22
~ de tren expreso 207 1-21
~ de viajeros 208 3
~ E con motor de tracción 197 7
vagoneta 206 3
~ automóvil 213 32
~ basculante 213 38
~ basculante 119 28
~ con chatarra ligera de hierro 147 64
~ de gran capacidad 158 14
~ de remolque 200 25
~ volquete para los lingotes 148 49
vagón frigorífico universal 213 39
~ para descarga neumática 213 18
~ para la mercancía en fardos 206 6
~ plano 206 21
~ plataforma con teleros 206 24
~ plataforma de bogies normal 213 11
~ plataforma normal 213 5

~ portacontenedores 206 58
~ -restaurante 207 22-32
vaguada 215 60
vaina *Hortal.* 57 6
~ *Hierba* 61 20, 23
~ *Planta* 69 8, 16
~ *Botán.* 370 83
~ *Arb. ornam.* 374 22
~ *Planta* 378 33
~ con las semillas 57 11
~ de cartón 87 50
~ de cuchillos 94 12
~ del aguijón 77 12
~ de la hoja 68 9, 21
~ de la vainilla 382 48
~ en forma de bolsa 61 11
~ -fruto 384 46
vainica 102 14
vainilla 382 46
vajilla de camping 278 45
vale 98 44
valeriana 380 5
~ de huerta 57 38
valija 204 6; 205 7
valor 251 11-19
~ de la abscisa 347 9
~ de la ordenada 347 10
~ de la potencia 345 1
~ de la raíz 345 2
~ de las notas 320 12-19
~ de renta fija 251 11-19
~ nominal 252 32
~ nominal de la acción 251 12
valva 357 36
válvula *Casa* 38 73
~ *Bicicl.* 187 31
~ *FFCC* 209 6
~ *Cons. hidr.* 217 55
~ *Dep. aéreo* 288 77, 82
~ *Jue. pelota* 291 18
~ *Mús.* 323 40; 324 66; 326 10
~ aórtica 20 49
~ compuerta 217 53-56
~ de acceso 6 21
~ de accionamiento 270 62
~ de alimentación 210 20
~ de cierre *Soldadura* 141 7
~ de cierre *Abast. agua* 269 30, 48
~ de control 153 52
~ de desagüe 126 16
~ de descarga 210 58
~ de descarga del aceite 190 67
~ de escape *Motor* 190 46
~ de Eustaquio 20 48
~ de evacuación de gases de escape 259 92
~ de fondo 269 6, 14, 43
~ de fondo del depósito 38 49
~ de freno del maquinista 210 53; 211 22; 212 11
~ de las botellas 279 22
~ del freno de emergencia 210 57
~ del freno suplementario 211 23
~ del gas combustible 141 32
~ de limpiado de retroacción 216 61
~ del oxígeno 141 29
~ de neumático con tubo 187 31
~ de pulverización 172 12
~ de regulación 38 75

~ de seguridad *Casa* 38 70
~ de seguridad *Cocina* 40 22
~ de seguridad *FFCC* 210 3
~ de seguridad *Quím.* 349 7
~ de vaciado 269 31
~ hidráulica de baja presión 141 8
~ inyectora 83 34
~ mitral 20 47
~ pulmonar 20 50
~ reductora 155 7
~ reductora de la presión 141 5
~ reguladora *Hosp.* 27 43
~ reguladora *Central el.* 153 29
~ reguladora *Autom.* 192 63
~ reguladora del vapor 210 13
válvulas del corazón 20 46-47
válvula semilunar 20 48
~ tricúspide 20 46
valla *Hípica* 289 8
~ *Atlet.* 298 8
~ con seto 289 8
~ del huerto 52 10
~ de madera *Casa* 37 53
~ de madera *Huerto* 52 10
~ de madera *Construc.* 118 44
~ de protección 118 44
vallado de piedra 337 23
~ para los animales salvajes 199 13
valle de depresión 13 55
~ en forma de U 13 55
~ en forma de V 13 53
~ en forma de V abierta 13 54
~ fluvial 13 57-70
~ , fondo del 13 67
~ , forma de 13 52-56
~ seco 13 75
~ sinclinal 13 56
~ viejo 13 56
vampiresa 306 32
vampiro 366 9
vanesa atalanta 365 1
vapor condensado 154 51
~ de agua 154 51
~ de excursión 225 29
~ de recreo *Barco* 221 101-128
~ de recreo *Puerto* 225 29
~ para hacer cruceros 221 101-128
vaquería 62 7
vaqueriza 75 14
vaquero *Carnaval* 306 31
~ *Toros, rodeo* 319 36
vara *Caballo* 71 21
~ *Pesca* 89 30
~ *Coche* 186 30
~ *Toros, rodeo* 319 17
~ corredera 323 47
~ de bambú 307 46
~ del distribuidor 210 30
varano 364 31
varenga 222 59
variable de integración 345 14
variador de velocidad 163 29
variedad de café 98 67
variedades de pan 99 11
varilla *Pesca* 89 54
~ *Tornill.* 143 15
~ *Mús.* 323 14

~ de aportación 141 12
~ de arrastre 145 14
~ de aspersión 56 25
~ de batir 39 23
~ de colada 148 9
~ de elevación 65 29
~ de empalme 119 10
~ de fusión 141 12
~ de guía de control 200 27
~ de la bomba 145 25
~ de la escoria 148 17
~ de la malla 102 25
~ del capó 195 37
~ del nivel de aceite 190 47
~ de mimbre 136 14
~ de modelar 161 20
~ de perforación 145 19
~ de plomo 124 13
~ de recubrimiento 123 57, 64
~ de soldar 108 38
~ guía 136 24
~ -guía 179 20
varillaje 136 25
~ de pulverización de péndulo 83 27
varilla para papel pintado 128 29
~ pulimentada 145 27
~ registradora 10 7, 12, 21
~ reguladora 190 30
~ tapón 148 10
~ transmisora 326 9
variómetro 230 14
vasija adornada con espirales 328 13
~ de fluoruro 128 7
~ para leche 309 89
vasito de aguardiente 45 90
vaso 317 5
~ campaniforme 328 14
~ de agua *Dent.* 24 13
~ de agua *J. infancia* 48 8
~ de agua *Restaur.* 266 29
~ de cerveza *Mesa* 45 91
~ de cerveza *Cerv.* 93 30
~ de cerveza *Restaur.* 266 3
~ de embudo 328 12
~ de limonada 265 16
~ de medidas 267 60
~ de precipitados 350 20
~ de vino *Comed.* 44 9
~ de vino *Bodega* 79 19
~ de whisky 267 57
~ griego 334 37
~ para cerveza 317 6
~ para los dientes 49 28
~ para vino y para licor 317 7
~ sanguíneo 19 33
vástago *Planta* 54 16, 24
~ *Tornill.* 143 15
~ *Mús.* 320 4
~ anual 372 25
~ del distribuidor 210 30
~ del pistón con prensaestopa 210 33
~ del tope del paro 166 45
~ femenino 372 46, 48
~ joven 372 31
~ masculino 372 44, 49, 56
vasto externo 18 46
~ interno 18 46
vecino de mesa 267 41
Vega *Astron.* 3 22
~ *Geogr.* 13 13, 62
vehículo 186 1-54
~ anfibio 255 67, 80
~ barredor 199 41
~ blindado *Marder* 255 77

Index

Ordering

In this index the entries are ordered as follows:
1. Entries consisting of single words, e.g.: 'hair'.
2. Entries consisting of noun + adjective. Within this category the adjectives are entered alphabetically, e.g. 'hair, bobbed' is followed by 'hair, closely-cropped'.
Where adjective and noun are regarded as elements of a single lexical item, they are not inverted, e.g.: 'blue spruce', not 'spruce, blue'.
3. Entries consisting of other phrases, e.g. 'hair curler', 'ham on the bone', are alphabetized as headwords.
Where a whole phrase makes the meaning or use of a headword highly specific, the whole phrase is entered alphabetically. For example 'ham on the bone' follows 'hammock'.

References

The numbers in bold type refer to the sections in which the word may be found, and those in normal type refer to the items named in the pictures. Homonyms, and in some cases uses of the same word in different fields, are distinguished by section headings (in italics), some of which are abbreviated, to help to identify at a glance the field required. In most cases the full form referred to by the abbreviations will be obvious. Those which are not explained in the following list:

Agr.	Agriculture / Agricultural	*Hydr. Engl.*	Hydraulic Engineering
Alp. Plants	Alpine Plants	*Impl.*	Implements
Art. Studio	Artist's Studio	*Inf. Tech.*	Information Technology
Bldg.	Building	*Intern. Combust. Eng.*	Internal Combustion Engine
Carp.	Carpenter	*Moon L.*	Moon Landing
Cement Wks.	Cement Works	*Music Not.*	Musical Notation
Cost.	Costumes	*Overh. Irrign.*	Overhead Irrigation
Cyc.	Cycle	*Platem.*	Platemaking
Decid.	Deciduous	*Plant. Propagn.*	Propagation of Plants
D.I.Y.	Do-it-yourself	*Rm.*	Room
Dom. Anim.	Domestic Animals	*Serv. Stat.*	Service Station
Equest.	Equestrian Sport	*Sp.*	Sports
Fabul. Creat.	Fabulous Creatures	*Text.*	Textile[s]
Gdn.	Garden	*Veg.*	Vegetable[s]

A

Aaron's rod **376** 9
abacus **309** 77
abacus *Art* **334** 20
abattoir **94**
abbreviated dialling key **237** 13
abdomen *Man* **16** 35-37, 36
abdomen *Bees* **77** 10-19
abdomen *Forest Pests* **82** 9
abdomen, lower ~ **16** 37
abdomen, upper ~ **16** 35
abductor hallucis **18** 49
abductor of the hallux **18** 49
aberdevine **361** 8
aborigine, Australian ~ **352** 37
abrasion platform **13** 31
abrasive wheel combination **111** 28, 35
abscissa **347** 9
abseiling **300** 28-30
abseil piton **300** 39
abseil sling **300** 28
absinth **380** 4
absorber attachment **27** 44
absorption dynamometer **143** 97-107
absorption muffler **190** 16
absorption silencer **190** 16
abutment *Bridges* **215** 27, 29, 45
abutment *Art* **336** 20
abutment pier **215** 29
acanthus **334** 25

acceleration lane **15** 16
acceleration rocket **234** 22, 4
accelerator **191** 46
accelerator lock **85** 17
accelerator pedal **191** 46, 94
accelerometer **230** 10
accent, acute ~ **342** 30
accent, circumflex ~ **342** 32
accent, grave ~ **342** 31
accent, strong ~ **321** 27
accents **342** 30-35
acceptance **250** 12, 23
access arm **244** 47
access balcony **37** 72-76
access flap **62** 1, 25
accessories **115** 54-74
accessory shoe **114** 4; **115** 4
accessory shop **196** 24
access ramp **199** 15
access slot **244** 42
acciaccatura **321** 15
accipiters **362** 10-13
accolade **329** 66
accommodation **146** 33
accommodation bureau **204** 28
accommodation ladder **221** 98
accomodation module **146** 33
accompaniment side **324** 43
accompaniment string **324** 24
accordion **324** 36
account, private ~ **250** 4
accounting machine **236** 26
account number **250** 26
accumulator **309** 41
accumulator *Theatre* **316** 55
accumulator railcar **211** 55

accuracy jump **288** 55
acerate **370** 34
acerose **370** 34
acerous **370** 34
acetylene connection **141** 31
acetylene control **141** 32
acetylene cylinder **141** 2, 22
achene **58** 23
achievement **254** 1-6
achievement, marital ~ **254** 10-13
achievement of arms **254** 1-6
Achilles' tendon **18** 48
acicular **370** 34
acid container **350** 62
Ackermann steering system **85** 31, 37
acolyte **331** 45
aconite **379** 1
acorn **371** 4
acorns **276** 42
acoustic coupler **237** 48; **244** 66
acrobat **307** 47
Acropolis **334** 1-7
acroter **334** 34
acroterion **334** 34
acroterium **334** 34
acting area light **316** 16
acting area spotlight **316** 16
actinia **369** 20
Actinophrys **357** 7
action **326** 6-16
action lever **325** 32
activated blade attachment **84** 33
actor **316** 37

actress **316** 38
actuating transistor **195** 19
actuator **244** 47
acuity projector **111** 47
acute **342** 30
ad **342** 56
Adam's apple **19** 13
adapter **112** 55
adapter, four-socket ~ **127** 8
adapter, four-way ~ **127** 8
adapter ring **115** 55
added-feature telephone **237** 9, 19, 22
adders **364** 40 *u.* 41
adding **344** 23
adding and subtracting machine **309** 74
addition **344** 23
address **236** 42
address bus **244** 52
address display **236** 41
addressing machine, transfer-type ~ **245** 7
address label **236** 4
address system, ship's ~ **224** 30
A-deck **223** 28-30
adhesion railcar **214** 1
adhesive, hot ~ **249** 61
adhesive binder *Bookbind.* **184** 1
adhesive binder *Office* **249** 61
adhesive tape dispenser **247** 27
adhesive tape dispenser, roller-type ~ **247** 28
adhesive tape holder **247** 28
adjusting cone **187** 58

cotton boll, ripe ~ **163** 1
cotton feed **163** 9
cotton-feeding brattice **163** 8
cotton grass **377** 18
cotton reel **104** 9
cotton rush **377** 18
cotton spinning **163; 164**
cotton wool ball **99** 30
cotton wool packet **99** 28
cotyledon **370** 87
couch *Doc.* **22** 43
couch *Weeds* **61** 30
coucher **173** 49
couch grass **61** 30
couch man **173** 49
coudé ray path **5** 3
coudière **329** 48
coulee **13** 45
coulter **65** 10
coulter, disc ~ **64** 66; **65** 69
coulter, drill ~ **65** 76
coulter, rolling ~ **64** 66; **65** 69
coulter, skim ~ **65** 68
counter *Child. Rm.* **47** 28
counter *Shoem.* **100** 59
counter *Shoes* **101** 37
counter *Cotton Spin.* **163** 61
counter *Typesett. Rm.* **175** 41
counter *Offset Print.* **180** 74
counter *Railw.* **207** 31
counter *Audio* **242** 6
counter *Café* **265** 1
counter *Restaurant* **266** 1-11
counter *Water* **269** 59
counter *Ball Games* **291** 23
counter *Winter Sp.* **302** 18
counter *Flea Market* **309** 83
counter, cashier's ~ **250** 1
counter, extra ~ **271** 64
counter, special ~ **271** 64
counterblow hammer **139** 5
counterbrace **215** 35
counter clerk **236** 16
counter gear assembly **269** 55
counter officer **236** 16
counterpoise *Optic. Instr.*
  113 19
counterpoise *Hydr. Eng.*
  217 76
counterpoise *Docks* **226** 50
counter reset button **242** 13
counter stamp machine **236** 19
counter tube **2** 21
counter tube casing **2** 20
counterweight *Overh. Irrign.*
  67 37
counterweight *Optic. Instr.*
  113 19
counterweight *Bldg. Site*
  119 33
counterweight *Forging* **139** 34
counterweight *Hydr. Eng.*
  217 76
counterweight *Docks* **226** 50
counting, automatic ~ **74** 52
counting beads **47** 14
counting blocks **48** 17
counting mechanism **309** 83
counting out **299** 42
country estate **15** 94
countryside in winter **304**
coupé *Carriages* **186** 3
coupé *Car* **193** 14, 28
couple **267** 46; **272** 72; **317** 17
  u. 18
couple, bridal ~ **332** 15 *u.* 16
coupler *Bldg. Site* **119** 53
coupler *Plumb. etc.* **126** 43
coupler *Music. Instr.* **326** 41
couplet **321** 23
coupling *Agr. Mach.* **65** 61
coupling *Bldg. Site* **119** 53

coupling *Railw* **208** 16; **210** 2;
  212 82; **214** 18
coupling, front ~ **65** 50
coupling, unlinked ~ **208** 19
coupling bolt **202** 15
coupling hook **122** 64
coupling hose **208** 21
coupling link **208** 17
coupling screw **208** 18
coupling spindle **148** 58
coupon **251** 17
coupon sheet **251** 17
courbette **71** 6
course *Weaves* **171** 42
course *Ball Games* **293** 79-82
course *Winter Sp.* **301** 44
course, damp-proof ~ **123** 42
course, first ~ **118** 67
course, second ~ **118** 68
course, triangular ~ **285** 16
course counter **167** 43
course-marking flag **301** 45
course markings **289** 19
courser **70** 24
court dress **355** 79
courtesy light **191** 77
court shoe **101** 29
court shoe, fabric ~ **101** 54
court shoe, sling-back ~ **101** 53
couter **329** 48
cove **13** 7
cover *Dining Rm.* **44** 5
cover *Tablew. etc.* **45** 3-12
cover *Optic. Instr.* **113** 13
cover *Bldg. Site* **118** 22
cover *Bookbind.* **185** 40
cover *Bicycle* **118** 30
cover *Water* **269** 56
cover, glass ~ *Kitch. Utensils*
  40 7
cover, glass ~ *Energy Sources*
  155 33
cover, hinged ~ **309** 27
cover, nylon ~ **207** 68
cover, porous ~ **199** 21
cover, screw-on ~ **83** 40
cover, soundproof ~ **310** 48
cover, terry ~ **49** 14
cover, transparent ~ **249** 27
coverall **29** 23
cover cylinder **184** 10
covering **287** 40
covering, felt ~ **353** 20
covering, green baize ~
  277 15
covering material **184** 12
cover with filter **2** 14
coving **336** 10
cow **73** 1
cowberry **377** 23
cowboy **306** 31; **319** 36
cowboy boot **101** 9
cowcatcher **210** 34
cow corn **68** 31
cowl *Blacksm.* **137** 7
cowl *Warships* **258** 21, 59
cowl *Church* **331** 56
cowl collar **30** 3
cowl neck jumper **30** 2
Cowper's gland **20** 75
cowshed *Farm Bldgs.* **62** 7
cowshed *Livestock* **75** 14
cowslip **37** 68
cox **283** 11
coxed single **283** 18
coxless four **283** 9
coxless pair **283** 15
CPU **244** 8
CQR anchor **286** 16
Crab *Astron.* **4** 56
crab *Shipbuild.* **222** 14, 28
crab *Arthropods* **358** 1
crab *Deep Sea Fauna* **369** 16

crab apple tree **58** 51
crab louse **81** 40
cracker **306** 50
cracker, catalytic ~ **145** 48
crackowe **355** 42
cradle **237** 23
cradle, bouncing ~ **28** 2
cradle, double ~ **214** 68
cradle, two-wheel ~ **214** 69
cradle frame, lightweight ~
  189 17
craft room **260** 46-85
crakeberry **377** 23
cramp **119** 58; **120** 66
cramp iron **119** 58; **121** 97
crampon **300** 48
crampon cable fastener **300** 52
crampon strap **300** 51
Crane *Astron.* **3** 42
crane *Warships* **258** 88
crane, floating ~ **225** 10;
  226 48
crane, flying ~ **232** 16
crane, hammer-headed ~
  222 7
crane, overhead ~ **222** 20
crane, polar ~ **154** 38
crane, revolving ~ **146** 3
crane, travelling ~ **147** 41;
  222 20
crane cable **222** 13
crane framework **226** 53
crane hoist, auxiliary ~
  147 61
crane hook **139** 45
crane motor **157** 28
crane's bill **53** 1; **376** 24
crane track **119** 27
crane truck **270** 47
crank *Agr. Mach.* **64** 43
crank *Bicycle* **187** 41
crank *Road Constr.* **201** 18
crankcase **190** 40
crank drive **217** 53
crankshaft **166** 50; **190** 23;
  192 29
crankshaft bearing **190** 22;
  192 23
crankshaft bleed **192** 22
crankshaft drilling **192** 22
crankshaft tributary **192** 22
crankshaft wheel **166** 51
crash bar **188** 18
crash barrier **259** 17
crash hat **290** 3
crash helmet **301** 213; **303** 14
crate **76** 30; **206** 5
crater **312** 44
crater, volcanic ~ **11** 16
cravat **32** 40
craw **73** 20
craw **282** 37
crawl stroke **282** 37
crayon **47** 26; **338** 5
crayon, wax ~ **48** 11; **260** 6
crayon engraving **340** 14-24
cream **99** 27, 46
cream, whipped ~ **97** 28;
  265 5
cream beater **76** 13
cream cake **97** 24
creamer **265** 21
creamery butter machine
  76 33
cream jar **28** 13; **99** 27
cream jug **265** 21
cream maturing vat **76** 31
cream pie **97** 24
cream puff **97** 27
cream roll **97** 17
cream separator **76** 14
cream slice **97** 21
cream supply pump **76** 40

cream tank **76** 19
cream tube **99** 33
crease *Men's Wear* **33** 6
crease *Ethnol.* **353** 44
creatures, fabulous ~
  327 1-61
creatures, mythical ~
  327 1-61
creek *Phys. Geog.* **13** 8
creek *Map* **15** 80
creel *Fish Farm.* **89** 25
creel *Cotton Spin.* **164** 28, 58
creel *Weaving* **165** 25
creel, full ~ **164** 41
creeper **51** 5; **52** 5; **53** 2; **57** 8
creeping foot **357** 28
creese **353** 44
crenate **370** 46
crenel **329** 18
crenellation **329** 6
crepidoma **334** 4
crescendo **321** 31
crescendo roller **326** 49
crescendo roller indicator
  326 37
crescent *Astron.* **4** 3, 7
crescent *Bakery* **97** 32
crescent *Supermkt.* **99** 13
Crescent *Flags* **253** 19
crescent-forming machine
  97 64
crescent moon **4** 3, 7
crescent roll **97** 32; **99** 13
crescent wing **229** 18
crest *Horse* **72** 12, 14
crest *Dom. Anim.* **73** 22
crest *Heraldry* **254** 1
crest, dorsal ~ **364** 21
crest, erectile ~ **359** 26
Cresta tobogganing **303** 22-24
crest coronet **254** 12
crested lark **361** 19
crested newt **364** 20
cresting **305** 65
crest of dam **217** 59
crests **254** 1, 11, 30-36
crevasse **12** 50; **300** 23
crew compartment **6** 41; **235** 16
crew cut **34** 11
crew entry tunnel **235** 71
cricket **292** 70-76
cricket bat **292** 75
crimping **170** 59
crimping iron **106** 26
crimson clover **69** 4
crinoline **355** 72
crispbread **97** 50
criss-cross skip **297** 44
cristobalite **1** 12
croaking sac **364** 25
crocket **335** 38
croisé **314** 16
croissant **97** 32; **99** 13
crojack **220** 26
crojack yard **220** 25
cromlech **328** 16
crook **324** 71
crook of the arm **16** 44
crop **73** 20
crops, arable ~ **68**
croquant **98** 85
croquet **292** 77-82
croquet ball **292** 82
croquet mallet **292** 81
croquet player **292** 80
Cross *Astron.* **3** 44
cross *Plumb. etc.* **126** 50
cross *School* **260** 28
cross *Church* **331** 25
cross, ansate ~ **332** 63
cross, cardinal's ~ **332** 65
cross, Constantinian ~ **332** 67
cross, fivefold ~ **332** 72

toilet-cleaning vehicle 233 22
toilet lid 49 14
toilet pan 49 13
toilet paper 49 11
toiletries 99 27-35
toilet roll holder 49 10
toilets 317 31
toilet seat 49 15
toilet water 105 37; 106 9
tomahawk 352 16
tomato 57 12; 99 82
tomato plant 55 44
tomb 331 23; 337 16
tomb, giant's ~ 328 16
tomb, megalithic ~ 328 16
tomb, royal ~ 333 1
tombola 306 11
tombola booth 308 44
tomb recess 331 60
tombstone 331 26
tom cat 73 17
tom-tom 324 48, 49
tondo 339 36
tone 320 51, 53
tone arm 241 31
tone arm counterweight
    241 35
tone arm support 241 32
tone generator 238 51
tongs Atom 2 44
tongs Glass Prod. 162 44
tongs Graphic Art 340 50
tongs, concreter's ~ 119 85
tongs, flat ~ 137 24
tongs, round ~ 137 25
tongue Man 17 52; 19 25
tongue Tablew. etc. 45 52
tongue Game 88 2
tongue Shoem. 100 65
tongue Shoes 101 32
tongue Music. Instr. 322 52;
    326 19
tongue, foam rubber ~ 291 24
tongue, forked ~ 327 6
tonsil 19 23
tonsil, palatine ~ 19 23
tonsure 331 57
tool 195 43
tool, stone ~ 328 1
tool bag 187 25
tool bit holder 149 45
tool box D.I.Y. 134 35
tool box Mach. Tools 150 13
tool box Railw. 212 45
tool cabinet 134 1-34
tool case 127 49
tool cupboard 134 1-34
tool grinder 137 18
tool-grinding machine 137 18
tool post 149 21
tool rest 135 5; 149 22
tools 119 77-89
tool shank 149 49
tool shed 37 32; 52 3; 55 1
tool slide 149 22
tool trolley 195 42
tooth Man 19 28-37
tooth Mach. Parts etc. 143 83
tooth Typesett. Rm. 174 30
tooth Office 249 31
tooth, bicuspid ~ 19 18
tooth, canine ~ 19 17
tooth, molar ~ 19 18, 35
tooth, porcelain ~ 24 29
tooth, premolar ~ 19 18
toothbrush, electric ~ 49 29
tooth chisel 339 13
toothed 370 45
tooth glass 49 28
toothing, spiral ~ 143 92 u. 93
toothing plane 132 17
tooth mug 49 28
toothpaste box 99 31

toothpick holder 266 23
tooth pulp 19 32
tooth-root elevator 24 48
tooth scaler 24 45
top 12 40; 193 10; 323 24
top, automatic ~ 193 16
top, collapsible ~ 186 52
top, elasticated ~ 32 33
top, fireclay ~ 108 9
top, fixed ~ 186 14
top, folding ~ 194 10
top, humming ~ 309 71
top, leather ~ 35 19
top, marble ~ 265 12
top, power-operated ~ 193 16
top, shirred ~ 29 15
top clearer 164 22
top gases 145 38
top hat 35 36; 186 25; 289 6
top light, white ~ 286 10
top lighting, incident ~
    112 63
topmark 224 78, 90
topmark buoy 224 80
topmast 223 39
topography, fluvial ~ 13 1-13
topper 64 85
topping 266 54
topping knife 64 87
top rail 121 122
top ring 89 52
top roller, light ~ 164 18
tops 145 38
topsail schooner, three masted
    ~ 220 19
top side Meat 95 37
top side Paperm. 173 31
top slide 149 22, 42
top stroke 277 3
top tube 187 16
torch 127 26
torch lighter 141 27
torero 319 21, 25
torii 337 11
torpedo housing, underwater
    ~ 259 36
torpedo tube 258 78; 259 79
torque converter 190 70
torque converter bearing
    211 54
torque converter lever 65 34
torque wrench 195 45
torril door 319 11
torsional clamp 287 39
torso 339 7
Torsteel 119 82
torten 97 22-24
tortrix moth 80 9
torus Art 334 28, 30
torus Bot. 370 53
totalizator 289 35
totalizator window 289 34
tote 289 35
totem 352 2
totem pole 352 1
tote window 289 34
toucan 363 6
touchline 291 9
touch-me-not 377 11
toupee wig 355 8
toupet 34 2
touring bicycle 187 1
touring boat 283 26-33
touring cycle 187 1
touring cycle handlebar 187 2
touring kayak 283 61, 70
touring moped 188 24
touring saloon, four-door ~
    193 1
tourist 272 28
tourist guide 272 27
tournament 329 71
tournament pennon 254 33

tournament saddle 329 87
tourneur 275 3
tourney 329 71
tourniquet, emergency ~
    21 15
tourniquet, surgeon's ~ 26 48
tow First Aid 21 37 u. 38
tow Synth. Fibres 170 57, 58,
    59, 60
towage 227
towel 106 25; 281 25
towel, paper ~ 40 1; 106 5
towel rail 49 8
tower Map 15 53
tower Bldg. Site 119 34
tower Bridges 215 42
tower Airport 233 17
tower Gliding 287 12
tower, central ~ 335 6
tower, lattice steel ~ 152 36
tower, stepped ~ 333 32
tower, terraced ~ 333 32
tower clock 331 7
tower crane 47 39; 119 31
tower platform 329 8
tower roof, pyramidal ~ 335 7
tower slewing crane 119 31
tower spotlight 316 21
tower tomb 333 21
tow hook 227 27
towing First Aid 21 37 u. 38
towing Rivers 216 27
towing engine Rivers 216 29
towing engine Salvage 227 7
towing engine Warships
    258 86
towing gear 227 6-15, 6, 13
towing hawser 216 24; 227 8,
    15
towing line 286 47
towing log 224 54
towing machine 227 7; 258 86
towing mast 216 28
towing path 216 30
towing plane 287 2
towing track 216 30
towing vehicle 194 21, 29
towing winch 227 7; 258 86
tow line 216 24; 227 8, 15;
    286 47
town 15 51; 268
town banner 218 22
town centre 268
tow path 216 30
tow rope Rivers 216 24
tow rope Salvage 227 8, 15
tow rope Gliding 287 4
tow rope guide 227 9
toy, soft ~ 46 13; 47 6, 7, 41
toy, wooden ~ 260 80
toy duck 28 10
toys 48 21-32
toy shop 47 27
T position 288 62
trace 71 22, 24, 35
trace monitor 25 54
tracer 153 45
tracer element 153 45
tracery 335 39 u. 40
tracery window 335 39-41
trachea 17 50; 20 4
tracing head 141 37
tracing leg 302 2
tracing wheel 129 42
track Atom 2 37
track Hunt. 86 8
track Cine Film 117 82
track Railw. 202 1-38
track Station 205 59-61
track Army 255 31
track Equest. 289 23
track Cyc. Racing 290 2
track Winter Sp. 301 60

track, cinder ~ 298 6
track, indoor ~ 290 1
track, sand ~ 290 24
track, synthetic ~ 298 6
track, unfenced ~ 15 102
track and field events 298
track and signal indicator
    203 64
trackball 244 23
track-clearing vehicle 213 17
track diagram control layout
    203 65
track diagram control panel
    203 66
tracker action 326 6-16
tracker ball 244 23
trackhound 70 42, 43
track-index indicator 242 37
track indicator 65 81
tracking radar 255 84
track inspection railcar 213 32
track racer 290 2
track repeat indicator 242 35
track rider 290 2
track rider, motor-paced ~
    290 14
track rod 65 47
track-rod ball-joint 192 80
tracksuit 33 27
tracksuit bottoms 33 29
tracksuit top 33 28
trackwalker 202 44
tract 330 51
traction current converter
    209 5
traction motor 209 3; 211 6
tractive effort indicator 211 26
tractive unit 194 21, 29
tractor 62 38; 64 46; 65 20;
    67 17; 85 43; 194 21, 29;
    273 55
tractor, narrow-track ~ 78 21
tractor driver 62 39
tractor unit 85 43
trader, itinerant ~ 308 51
trades 9 48, 49
tradesman 98 41
trade winds 9 48, 49
traffic control 264 9
traffic control cuff 268 31
traffic helicopter 264 1
traffic light post 268 53
traffic lights 268 52
traffic patrol 264 9
traffic policeman 268 30
trail 86 8
trail, scented ~ 289 49
trailer Farm Bldgs. 62 40
trailer Agr. 63 27, 38
trailer Blacksm. 138 10
trailer Lorries etc. 194 22
trailer Station 206 3, 35
trailer Camping 278 52
trailer, collapsible ~ 278 3
trailer, folding ~ 278 3
trailer, tip-up ~ 56 42
trailer frame 138 28
trailering 278
trailer wagon 200 25
trailing arm 191 27; 192 66
trailing cable hanger 133 39
trailing cable support 133 39
trailing edge Sailing 284 45
trailing edge Gliding 287 37
trailing link arm 192 81
trail rope 288 69
train 355 80
train, electric ~ 197
train, interurban ~ 197
train, local ~ 208 1-12
train, short-distance ~
    208 1-12
train, suburban ~ 205 25